Biographical Dictionary
Of The Left

Volume IV

by

Francis X. Gannon

WESTERN ISLANDS

BOSTON   LOS ANGELES

78 06664

TABLE OF CONTENTS

Foreword By The Publisher v

Introduction vii

Organizations Of The Left 1

Biographical Dictionary Of The Left 215

Index Of Organizations 649

Index Of Biographies 655

FOREWORD BY THE PUBLISHER

It is the hope of the publishers that Volume IV of the *Biographical Dictionary Of The Left* will be a valuable addition to the library of any serious student of collectivism in America. For this volume contains background information on many of the most influential early leaders of the Left — men and women whose whole lives were ruled by a single passion: the desire to achieve a socialist world. None of the men and women studied in this volume are still living, but their influence lives on. It would be difficult indeed to find one person in the United States whose life has not been affected by their philosophies and their activities.

Because of the actions of these men and women and those who have followed them — whether blindly, or mistakenly, or with deliberately evil intent — capitalism and individual freedom are threatened; amorality and open immorality, war, and hatred are all around us.

What will the future bring? Former Communist Whittaker Chambers spelled it out in his autobiography, *Witness*. He said: ". . . in this century . . . will be decided for generations whether all mankind is to become free, or whether, in the struggle, civilization as we know it is to be completely destroyed or completely changed. It is our fate to live upon that turning point in history."

Because we believe that the most effective way to destroy the threat of Communism is to tell the truth about it and its practitioners, we present this Biographical Dictionary. It is our present expectation that it will consist of eight volumes in uniform format, and will contain in all about two thousand names. As an aid to the reader and as an important preface to the biographies included, each volume begins with a section on organizations of the Left — the organizations to which the individuals have belonged and in which they have worked.

Because of the urgent need for keeping such a reference dictionary up to date, we shall continue to bring out each compilation of biographical sketches as it is ready. All the names in any one volume will be alphabetized in one sequence between its covers. To assist the reader in locating a particular entry, each volume since the first has included a cumulative index of the organizations and individuals covered in that and all preceding volumes.

Each volume is prepared by, or under the careful supervision of, Dr. Francis X. Gannon, head of the Research Department of The John Birch Society. Dr. Gannon, who received his Ph.D. in History from Georgetown University, has long been a worthy disciple of his great teacher, the eminent historian Charles Callan Tansill. Sound scholarship in his chosen field, and unimpeachable accuracy in every line he writes, have been imperative considerations for Dr. Gannon, as they were for Dr. Tansill before him.

Believing it better to err a hundred times on the side of restraint and understatement than to err even once, no matter how slightly, on the side of exaggeration or abuse, Dr. Gannon will provide in these volumes as much dependable information concerning leaders of the Liberal-leftist persuasion as space, time, and other practical limitations permit.

— Editorial Staff, Western Islands

INTRODUCTION

There is a Left in America; there has been a Left since at least the middle of the last century. That is a fact of life. To deny it is to deny the existence of a far-flung establishment whose members have been working tirelessly for decades to socialize, or — if you please — Sovietize, the United States. The present volume is the record of early as well as more recent leftists, now dead, who helped to spearhead the movement in its earlier years.

To determine why any particular individual may have become a leftist is not the purpose of the study of which this volume is the fourth report. He may have arrived on the Left motivated by genuine idealism, incurable do-goodism, scholarly curiosity, compassionate brotherhood, or a sentiment no more harmful than desire for adventure. Or his motives may have been of a crasser nature: financial, political, or social opportunism, or dedication to Socialism or Communism or some variant of these alien totalitarian systems.

What does matter for this report is that the individual during his lifetime was on the Left, working for leftist causes. A pattern of the positions he held, his media and affiliations, his causes — domestic and foreign — and his activities can be recognized.

The leftist came then, as he still does today, from Ivy League, state, and sectarian universities and colleges. He received Rhodes and later Fulbright scholarships; Guggenheim and Nieman Fellowships; Carnegie and Ford and 20th Century Fund grants; Pulitzer and Nobel prizes; Sidney Hillman and Freedom House Awards; and sinecures at foundations or university and government research centers. He had his plays or books reviewed favorably in the *New York Times, New Republic, Time*, and *The Nation*. He studied abroad at the London School of Economics at Oxford or graduate schools in New Delhi or Geneva. He joined the NAACP, the Council on

Foreign Relations, the Union for Democratic Action – later Americans for Democratic Action – or one or many Communist fronts.

The leftist has always been in government offices on federal, state, and local levels – by election or appointment, or in consultative or advisory capacities; in radio and television, in commercial and educational films, on newspapers and magazines, on trade organs and scholarly journals – as commentator, editor, producer, director, publisher, writer, cartoonist, reviewer; in religion – all creeds – preaching, writing, and politicking; on university and college campuses – as teacher, administrator, researcher, scholar-in-residence, and student activist; in organized labor; in business and trade associations; in the rather recently developed "think" factories, which are government-financed research projects involving the most critical problems of diplomacy, economics, military strategy, and national security; and in the arts – as illustrator, painter, sculptor, playwright, novelist, poet, and entertainer.

After Franklin Roosevelt inaugurated the New Deal, the leftist was to be found in the higher echelons of Henry Wallace's Department of Agriculture, the Treasury Department of Henry Morgenthau and Harry Dexter White, the National Labor Relations Board, the Office of Education, the State Department, and Frances Perkins' Department of Labor. Some leftists even moved into the White House, and others wormed their way onto Congressional committee staffs.

In the circumstances immediately surrounding World War II, the leftist sought his niche in the Office of Price Administration, the Office of Strategic Services, the Office of War Information, the War Production Board, and the Board of Economic Warfare. Later, he was to be found in the Central Intelligence Agency; on the United Nations staff; in the foreign aid programs (under their ever-changing names); in the Alliance for Progress, the Office of Economic Opportunity, the Peace Corps, and the Department of Health, Education, and Welfare.

Look for the leftist today in the AFL-CIO, on the Supreme

Court, in the Foreign Policy Association, in the American Assembly, in the National Council of Churches, at the New School for Social Research, in the Brookings Institution, in Chambers of Commerce, in gubernatorial mansions, on Wall Street, in Congress, in the Anti-Defamation League, in the Institute for American Democracy, in mental health associations, in American Friends of Vietnam, in the Republican and Democrat parties, and marching side by side with black powerites, trampling upon the civil rights of others and violating law and order.

The causes of the American leftist on the domestic scene have from the beginning been directed toward the exaltation of society and the state by attacks upon individual and family dignity and property rights. The leftist has promoted confiscatory taxation, deficit spending, deliberate inflation, and wilful debauchery of the entire monetary system. Fraudulent and compulsory insurance schemes have been presented as social security; federal control and domination of education as aid; dictatorial ukases as judicial decisions.

The leftist has preached that Joe McCarthy had to go – Alger Hiss was framed – Owen Lattimore was an objective scholar – Jomo Kenyatta is a statesman – Titoism is a gentle kind of Communism – Castro and Sukarno and Ben Bella were George Washington reincarnated – the United Nations is mankind's best and last hope – *extreme* leftists and extreme rightists are equally dangerous – the U.S. Constitution was written for horse-and-buggy days – the Communists have mellowed – loyalty oaths attack academic freedom – better-Red-than-dead – Congressional committees are inquisitorial except when presided over by Fulbright or Celler or Symington – and the Third World War (a nuclear holocaust) is just around the corner unless the military-industrial complex can be ground to bits in a Pentagon computer.

In the State Department and elsewhere, the leftist has not turned his back on Alger Hiss, and the Department's leftward foreign policy has been the work of Dean Acheson's protégés,

George Kennan's disciples, and the Institute of Pacific Relations veterans led by Dean Rusk. Communist aggression and Communist subversion have always been derogated as fantasies. Today, business as usual with Communist enemies is encouraged even in times of hot war (which the leftist calls cold). Red China is brought into the "peace-loving" United Nations and Red Chinese consular missions are invited into the United States, and leftists continue to agitate for full diplomatic recognition of Red China while our faithful ally, Nationalist China, is cast into diplomatic limbo. The leftist wants nuclear treaties and disarmament; dialogue with the Communists; a United Nations "peacekeeping" force; and most of all, peaceful coexistence with the Communist tyrants who are irrevocably bent on world conquest. In all these things today's leftist is a direct descendant of the pioneer leftists discussed in the present volume.

The leftist is not necessarily — though he may be — scribbling the latest party line in the pages of *The Worker* or grinding out revolutionary tracts in a dank cellar or dusty loft. The Left includes — as indeed it has always done — far more than a hard core of disciplined members of the Communist Party. Legions of leftists have gravitated — not merely by coincidence — toward common bases of activity. The leftist here in the United States is present today in greater numbers, is more secure in his influence, and is accelerating his program faster, than ever before. He may deny that he is part of any "establishment," but his denials will be more heated if he is accused of being a "rightist."

In the following biographical sketches and the accounts of leftist organizations that precede them, we present the leftists of an earlier day in their environment as it was then and still remains today.

Francis X. Gannon

NOTE TO THE READER

Phrases contained in quotation marks, characterizing various organizations and publications, are quoted from *Guide to Subversive Organizations and Publications*, prepared and released by the Committee on Un-American Activities of the U.S. House of Representatives, December 1, 1961. Most of the reports in that publication are in turn verbatim quotations from reports of Federal government and Congressional authorities, namely, the committee itself (HCUA), the Senate Judiciary Committee and its Internal Security Subcommittee, and the Subversive Activities Control Board; and from letters to the Loyalty Review Board from United States Attorneys General Francis Biddle, Tom Clark, and J. Howard McGrath; and also from reports of State or (then) territorial investigating committees (California, Hawaii, Massachusetts, New York, Ohio). It should be noted that no revision of the *Guide*, first published in 1951, has been issued since 1961.

In some instances, the quotations are derived from governmental sources which antedated the authorities cited in the *Guide*. In fewer instances, quotations are from contemporary Congressional committee sources.

Organizations Of The Left

ABRAHAM LINCOLN BRIGADE
   AMERICAN COMMITTEE TO SAVE REFUGEES
   AMERICAN FRIENDS OF SPANISH DEMOCRACY
   COORDINATING COMMITTEE TO LIFT THE SPANISH
      EMBARGO
   FRIENDS OF THE ABRAHAM LINCOLN BRIGADE
   JOINT ANTI–FASCIST REFUGEE COMMITTEE
   LAWYERS' COMMITTEE ON AMERICAN RELATIONS WITH
      SPAIN
   MEDICAL BUREAU AND NORTH AMERICAN COMMITEE
      TO AID SPANISH DEMOCRACY
   NEGRO PEOPLE'S COMMITTEE TO AID SPANISH
      DEMOCRACY
   VETERANS OF THE ABRAHAM LINCOLN BRIGADE

During the course of the Spanish Civil War (1936-1939), the Communist International made a desperate attempt to become the dominant force in Spain, so as to bring that nation into the orbit of the Soviet Union. The opportunity for the Comintern's intervention came about because the Spanish Communist Party was aligned with other leftist groups on the Republican or so-called Loyalist side of the war, which were under attack by Francisco Franco's Falange forces. Although the Spanish Communist Party formed only a numerical minority of the Republican forces, the Comintern used its propaganda machine so efficiently that the war was portrayed as an Armageddon between Communists and Fascists, and all other parties and issues were relegated to oblivion.

From the highest levels of the Comintern, the Spanish Civil War was described as "the greatest event in the struggle of the masses of the people in the capitalist countries for their emancipation, second only to the October Socialist Revolution of 1917." The chairman of the Comintern, Georgi Dimitrov, wrote: "If we are briefly to formulate the most important, immediate task which the whole situation today places before the world proletariat, . . . [it] may be reduced to the following: To exert every effort to help the Spanish people to crush the fascist rebels . . . . The most urgent . . . task, the very first at the moment, is that of organizing international aid to the Spanish people for their victory over fascism."

To increase the Communist flavor of the Republican belligerents, the Soviet Union sent money, planes, tanks, arms, munitions, and men to Spain. Moscow's International Labor Defense was assigned the task of helping the Republican war effort. Soldiers and medical personnel were recruited and sent to Spain from Belgium, Canada, Britain, France, Italy, Germany, and Poland. Medical supplies and money were collected through the International Labor Defense's vast network in Europe and America.

On the American scene, the response to the Comintern's directives was immediate. Charles Krumbein, of the Communist Party's Central Committee, and Frank N. Trager, secretary of the Socialist Party in New York, established the United Committee in Support of the Struggle Against Fascism in Spain. A fund-raising drive conducted by leftwing labor unions and Communist fronts was oversubscribed in three-weeks' time because of the generosity of CIO unions, especially the United Mine Workers under John L. Lewis.

The Comintern's plan for success in the Spanish Civil War was to use the strategy of the united front: all elements in battle would be fighting under the banner of Republican unity, but the control of the forces would rest with the Communists, who would assume full credit in the event of victory. The same strategy was employed on the American scene. To support the Republican cause, liberals, Socialists, would-be progressives, innocents, dupes, and Communists would work in a gigantic aid-for-Republicans campaign, which would be under the complete domination and control of the Communists. The cause of Communism was not pushed forward to inspire the campaign: the united front was anti-fascist, a cause that could be sold to non-Communists on the left.

In the United States, General Secretary Earl Browder of the Communist Party promoted the united front strategy. Said Browder: "It is the duty of every American worker and every progressive to help the Spanish people defeat the fascist invasion . . . . We who believe in progress must come out openly in support of the Spanish people . . . . I appeal to the Socialist Party . . . to work out an independent program of action against the Spanish fascists . . . . We must support the action of the Soviet Union in exposing the criminal actions of the fascist dictators . . . . Collect all the money possible in your organizations and among your friends to buy munitions, food and clothing for the defenders of Spanish democracy."

Almost entirely through the efforts of the Communist Party in the United States, about three thousand men and women were recruited for service in Spain. Earl Browder boasted that about 60 per cent of the recruits were previously members of the Communist Party. Most of the Americans who went to Spain were placed in the Fifteenth International Brigade. The first Americans to arrive formed the Abraham Lincoln Battalion and later arrivals formed the George Washington Battalion, but after both groups suffered "severe decimation in combat," the remainder of the two groups merged into the Lincoln-Washington Battalion — which, in Communist legend, became known as the Abraham Lincoln Brigade.

The Subversive Activities Control Board has described the status of the Americans in Spain: "The ALB, as all other International Brigades in Spain, functioned under the domination and control of the Comintern. Its members were subject to, and the recipients of, Communist discipline for political dissidence; a Political Commissar system organized under the leadership of Comintern agents André Marty and Luigi Longo, and dominated by Communists, functioned throughout the International Brigades, including the ALB, for the purpose of maintaining the political reliability of troops from the Communist viewpoint and of dispensing Communist indoctrination; a secret police operated within the International Brigades, including the ALB, to maintain and enforce Communist discipline, and ALB members functioned within this police system; [and] ALB members recruited Americans in Spain to be Soviet agents and were trained by Soviet personnel there and so functioned."

The top command of all the International Brigades was held by émigré officers from the Soviet Union. The training of Americans, most of whom had absolutely no prior military service, was conducted under the supervision of Soviet Union officers. There were Americans, however, in responsible positions. Robert Minor, a sometime acting general secretary of the Communist Party, was the head of the American forces in Spain. He acted within the framework of the Comintern's secretariat which was on the scene in charge of the International Brigades. John Gates, who was a member of the

Communist Party's New York State Committee, held the rank of lieutenant colonel and was a political commissar with the ALB. William Lawrence was political commissar at a military base in Spain; he was the organizational secretary of the Communist Party in New York State. Joe Dallet was a political commissar; he had been a Communist Party organizer in Youngstown, Ohio, and on several occasions had run for political office on the Communist Party ticket. Dave Doran was a political commissar. Doran had been a leader in the Young Communist League. T.H. Wintringham was the *Daily Worker's* military expert; in Spain he was the military instructor for the ALB. Saul Wellman, who was also a commissar, had been a member of the New York State committee of the Young Communist League. Steve Nelson, from the national committee of the Communist Party, was a colonel in the ALB. Milton Wolff, a leader in the Young Communist League, was a major in the ALB. Among the better known Communists who also served in Spain were Archie Brown, actor Leif Erickson, Dr. Leo Eloesser of San Francisco, Homer Chase, Dr. Edward Barsky of New York, Phil Bard, and writer Alvah Bessie. In Spain, the ALB received visits from Earl Browder, Joseph North of the *Daily Worker*, and a host of fellow-travelers and bleeding-heart liberals who regarded a visit to the Republican lines as a status symbol.

The issue of "anti-Fascism" proved to be a bonanza for the Comintern and for the Communist Party of the United States. The strategy of fighting fascism through a united front naturally attracted the dedicated Communists and their inveterate fellow travelers. It also served as a magnet to attract the support of hundreds and even thousands of individuals who had never before joined — or joined with such enthusiasm — in Communist fronts. The Communists did not hide the fact that the fronts were theirs. They appealed to non-Communists to join them in their fronts for a greater cause — anti-fascism — than anything that divided Communists and non-Communists. It was simply the raising of a cry: "Anti-fascists of America unite!" And it was undeniable that non-Communists — liberals, progressives, Socialists — did not form their own anti-fascist groups; they knowingly joined Communist fronts.

One of the largest enterprises formed to support the Republicans was the Medical Bureau and North American Committee To Aid Spanish Democracy. It began as the North American Committee To Aid

Spanish Democracy, with Bishop Francis J. McConnell as chairman and Herman Reissig as national director. Paul H. Douglas (later U.S. Senator) was honorary chairman. Members included Devere Allen, Jerome Davis, Albert Einstein, actress Florence Eldridge, Arnold Gingrich, Joseph Lash, Frank McCulloch, Arthur McDowell, A. Philip Randolph, Paul Robeson, the Reverend Guy Emery Shipler, Upton Sinclair, and the Reverend William Spofford. At the same time, there was in existence the Medical Bureau To Aid Spanish Democracy, under the chairmanship of Walter B. Cannon. Members included Van Wyck Brooks, Kyle Crichton (alias Robert Forsythe), Countee Cullen, Babette Deutsch, Edna Ferber, Lewis Gannett, Martha Gellhorn, Granville Hicks, Langston Hughes, George S. Kaufman, Rockwell Kent, Sinclair Lewis, Archibald MacLeish, Clifford Odets, Dorothy Parker, Elliot Paul, Elmer Rice, Upton Sinclair, Donald Ogden Stewart, and Art Young. A "national medical committee" associated with the front included Dr. Thomas Addis (Communist friend of J. Robert Oppenheimer), Dr. Ernst Boas, and Dr. Haven Emerson. A third group, calling itself the North American Spanish Aid Committee, included Congressman Vito Marcantonio, Dr. Edward Barsky, Millen Brand, Louis Bromfield, Dashiell Hammett, Lillian Hellman, Ernest Hemingway (whose novel, *For Whom the Bell Tolls*, glorified the Spanish Republicans), Elliot Paul, George Seldes, Herman Shumlin, Paul Robeson, Upton Sinclair, Mary E. Woolley, and Max Yergan. Eventually, the umbrella organization was known as the Medical Bureau and North American Committee To Aid Spanish Democracy. It had Bishop McConnell and Walter Cannon as co-chairmen. Its membership included that of the Medical Bureau and the two North American committees. Among its additional members were Bishop Benjamin Brewster, Paul de Kruif, Theodore Dreiser, Frank P. Graham (later U.S. Senator), Helen Hall, Fannie Hurst, Serge Koussevitsky, Felix Frankfurter (later Associate Justice of the Supreme Court), Paul Muni, Bishop G. Bromley Oxnam, Bishop Robert L. Paddock, Bishop Edward L. Parsons, Sylvia Sidney, Rabbi Abba Silver, George Abbott, Marc Connelly, Morris Ernst, George Gershwin, Lorenz Hart, Moss Hart, Arthur Garfield Hays, Sidney Kingsley, Burgess Meredith, Philip Merivale, James Melton, Otto Soglow, Orson Welles, Rabbi Stephen S. Wise, and James Waterman Wise.

The Medical Bureau and North American Committee was also

supported by a host of affiliates including various branches of the Communist Party, the American League for Peace and Democracy, the American Student Union, the Anti-Fascist Literature Society, the Association for the Study of Negro Life and History, the Ben Leider Memorial Fund, the Book and Magazine Guild, the Canadian Committee to Aid Spanish Democracy, the Church League for Industrial Democracy, the Committee To Establish Youth Centers in Harlem, the Confederated Spanish Societies, the Federal Employees' Ambulance Committee, the Finnish Workers' Federation, the Foster Parents' Plan for Children in Spain, the German-American Committee for Spanish Relief, the International Brotherhood of Sleeping Car Porters, International Labor Defense, the International Workers Order, the Italian Committee To Aid Children of Spain, the League for Industrial Democracy, Lettish Workers Unity, the Lithuanian Committee To Aid Spanish Democracy, the Musicians' Committee To Aid Spanish Children, the National Council of Negro Women, the National Maritime Union, the National Negro Congress, the Portuguese Anti-Fascist Group, Progressive Women's Council, the Samuel Levinger Memorial Committee, local branches of the Socialist Party, locals of the Teachers Union of New York, the Theatre Arts Committee, and the Young Communist League.

A remarkable feature of the war period and even the post-war era was the unprecedented proliferation of Communist fronts, all of which had as their basic and common denominator support for the Republican cause, whether the aid was given for the Republican army, the Americans fighting or serving in Spain, or adult and child refugees. It appeared very much as if the Communists believed that if there were enough fronts with different titles then it might be possible to reach every potential "anti-fascist" sympathizer in the United States. In retrospect, the Communists did benefit from the variety of fronts. Many individuals who joined the "anti-fascist" fronts had never before belonged to a front organization, and later, in many cases, they seemed to avoid other fronts; the Spanish Civil War was their parlor-pink period. But some individuals who joined fronts in that era began a lifetime habit of membership in a wide variety of fronts. Still other individuals joined a great number of anti-fascist, Spanish Republican fronts, as if the scatter-gun approach to the "cause" would somehow magnify their energies and effectiveness. A flagrant instance of the scatter-gun approach occurred in 1938, when it was announced in the Communist journal *New Masses* that a Committee To Save Spain and China would hold a meeting in New York City. Bishop Robert L. Paddock and the Reverend Guy Emery Shipler were chairman and treasurer, respectively. The sponsors of the Committee were real Communist front war horses: Bishop Francis J. McConnell, Maxwell Anderson, Robert Morss Lovett, Reverend Henry Smith Leiper, A.T. Whitney, Van Wyck Brooks, Rabbi Stephen S. Wise, Harry F. Ward, Harry Overstreet, and Sherwood Eddy. The entire work of this Committee To Save Spain and China consisted of one two-hour meeting in Carnegie Hall where the members listened to a series of speeches.

There were a number of fronts devoted to the plight of war refugees. The Special Committee on Un-American Activities evaluated this type of front and reported: "Communist committees to save refugees perform a most valuable function for the international Communist movement. In the first place these committees are a fruitful source of revenue from sympathetic individuals. In the second place they serve as rescue agencies for foreign Communist operatives. With outposts throughout the world manned by those enjoying Communist confidence, they also serve as a means of blackjacking refugees in a desperate plight to do the bidding of the international network which the Communists have established in this field, having at its disposal considerable financial, passport, transportation, and other facilities."

One of the major fronts devoted to the refugee problem was the American Committee To Save Refugees, with Walter Rautenstrauch as chairman. The executive board included Ernst and Franz Boas, Helen M. Lynd, the Reverend James H. Robinson, and Robert K. Speer. Its sponsors included Comfort A. Adams, Henry A. Atkinson, George E. Axtelle, Roland H. Bainton, Bishop James Chamberlain Baker, Walter B. Cannon, Anton J. Carlson, Rufus E. Clement, Henry Sloane Coffin, the Reverend Theodore De Luca, Martha Dodd, Dorothy N. Douglas, Henry Pratt Fairchild, Guy Stanton Ford, Christian Gauss, Marion Hathway, John Haynes Holmes, Ellsworth Huntington, Oliver H. Larkin, Kenneth Leslie, Bishop Francis J. McConnell, William A. Neilson, Bishop Edward L. Parsons, Vida Scudder, Guy Emery Shipler, Harold Urey, Charles C. Webber, Carl Wittke, and Mary E. Woolley.

With the end of the Spanish Civil War and the defeat of the Republicans, the American Committee To Save Refugees did not go out of business. The Committee's officers and members belonged to a number of fronts which had faithfully followed the twists and turns of the Communist line in relation to the European scene. They had propagandized for peace and against fascism until the Hitler-Stalin pact of 1939. The anti-fascist tirades quieted down during the two-year life of the pact, but when Hitler invaded the Soviet Union in 1941, the American Committee To Save Refugees was revivified. The same officers and sponsors now turned their wrath against Hitler. In a public statement, Hitlerism was excoriated but the Soviet Union was staunchly defended: "For nearly ten years we have watched the steady destruction of the cultural life of nation after nation. Science and the arts, literature and education have either been wiped out entirely or twisted to barbaric and inhuman ends wherever fascism has laid its hands.

"Today the people of three countries — England, the Soviet Union, and China — are engaged in a struggle which must have but one outcome, the emancipation of all mankind from the curse of Hitlerism. We, men and women whose service to society lies within the cultural spheres, dare not sit back quietly with our books and our test tubes while the fate of our country and of the world hangs in the balance. We hereby pledge our utmost efforts to secure the fullest possible aid to these heroic opponents of Hitlerism which the productive capacity of our land will permit.

"We must speak out all the more firmly now because of the involvement of the Soviet Union in the war. With profound dismay we have seen the emergence into the full light of day of the internal enemies of American democracy, those who have seized upon the new turn of events to raise false issues in order to mislead our people away from the one fundamental threat to our existence as a free nation, Hitlerism. We say to these Quislings, who secretly desire and even work for the victory of fascism: The American people will not be misled. The American people stand unshakably behind the people of England, of the Soviet Union, and of China in their struggle.

"We say further that there can be no victory over Hitlerism abroad if democracy is destroyed at home. The protection of civil liberties and the rights of labor, the maintenance of adequate living standards, the elimination of all forms of racial and religious discrimination from our public and private life — these are an integral part of the worldwide defense of human liberty.

"Never before in history has man had the technical potentialities and resources available to him today. Even outside the fascist countries there is need for much improvement in the functioning of human society. Final victory of the forces of freedom will release men everywhere from their present bondage to war and tyranny so that they may fully exploit their knowledge resources in the service of humanity. That final victory must be won. To that end, we call for a nation-wide popular expression of firm solidarity and for the utmost material assistance by our government to England, the Soviet Union, and China."

In the issuance of the public statement, which was merely a contribution to the Soviet Union's foreign policy ("We must speak out all the more firmly now because of the involvement of the Soviet Union in the war"), the American Committee To Save Refugees was joined by scores of individuals, including writers Ray Stannard Baker, Cedric Belfrage, Herbert Biberman, Louis Bromfield, Van Wyck Brooks, Sherwood Eddy, Lion Feuchtwanger, Albert Guerard, Dashiell Hammett, Otto Harbach, Ben Hecht, Mark A. De Wolfe Howe, Fannie Hurst, Marquis James, John Howard Lawson, Emil Lengyel, Albert Maltz, Thomas Mann, Clifford Odets, Donald Ogden Stewart, Ida Tarbell, Richard Wright, and Lin Yutang; scientists and educators Carl Becker, Ruth Benedict, Haakon Chevalier, Ned Dearborn, Haven Emerson, Alice Hamilton, Robert M. MacIver, Karl Menninger, Samuel Eliot Morrison, Harry Overstreet, Ralph Barton Perry, Edward Alsworth Ross, Bernadotte Schmitt, Preston Slosson, Vilhjalmur Stefansson, Dirk Struik, Harold Vinacke, Leroy Waterman, Goodwin Watson, and Mary E. Woolley; and artists or fine arts experts George Biddle, Adolph Dehn, James Montgomery Flagg, Hugo Gellert, William Gropper, Arthur Upham Pope, and Max Weber.

Under the auspices of the American Committee To Save Refugees, Ernest Hemingway and playwright Lillian Hellman conducted a dinner-forum with guest speakers Edgar Snow (Mao Tse-tung's prolific apologist), Johannes Steel, Emil Lengyel, and Pierre van Paassen. Among the sponsors for the affair were Harry Elmer Barnes, Dr. Edward Barsky, Algernon Black, Congressman Emanuel Celler, Stuart Chase, Mady Christians, Muriel Draper, Dorothy Canfield Fisher, Horace Kallen, Ruth McKenney, Hendrik Van Loon, and Orson Welles.

In the Spanish war and post-war years, the American Committee To

Save Refugees worked closely with the Exiled Writers Committee and the United American Spanish Aid Committee. The Exiled Writers Committee was a wing of the League of American Writers, which was affiliated with Moscow's International Union of Revolutionary Writers and could trace its lineage back to the Communists' John Reed Clubs.

The United American Spanish Aid Committee had for its ostensible purpose the rescue and rehabilitation of Spanish Republican refugees and ex-International Brigade members who had fled to France but who would be resettled in Latin American countries. The United Committee had as co-chairmen Edward K. Barsky, who had fought in Spain with the International Brigade; Dr. Thomas Addis, a Communist; and Martha Dodd, who would one day flee from the United States to escape charges of espionage. Most of the executive board and sponsors were members of other "anti-fascist" committees. Some of the heretofore unfamiliar names included Ralph Gundlach, Carol King, Ferdinand Smith, Josephine Truslow Adams, Edwin Berry Burgum, Fielding Burke, Henry W.L. Dana, John P. Davis, Olin Downes, Lynn Fontanne, Stephen Fritchman, Helen Keller, and Jack McMichael.

The United American Spanish Aid Committee was responsible for administering the American Rescue Ship Mission. The Special Committee on Un-American Activities noted that the Mission "was organized during the period of the Stalin-Hitler pact [August 1939-June 1941]. That was a period when, as a rule, only the most confirmed and conscious fellow travelers of the Communist Party adhered to the Party's front organizations. It may, therefore, be assumed that few, if any, of those who associated themselves with the American Rescue Ship Mission were deluded innocents." The Special Committee then commented on the personnel of the Mission: "We find the following well-known Communist fellow travelers: Helen Bryan, one-time highly placed executive of the American League for Peace and Democracy; William E. Dodd Jr., employee of the Federal Communications Commission, whose salary was cut off by the Congress of the United States; Dorothy W. Douglas, professor at Smith College, who has been a confirmed supporter of the Communist Party's projects through all the twists and turns of the party line; J.A. MacCallum, the Philadelphia preacher whose name appears frequently in support of Communist Party enterprises; Paul Muni, Hollywood motion-picture actor, who appears always ready to endorse a Communist Party project; George

Marshall, one of the outstanding financial and moral backers of the Communist Party; Kirtley F. Mather, Harvard professor, who has done yeoman service for the Communist Party over a period of many years; Paul Robeson, Negro singer, who has publicly declared his preference for the Soviet Union over the United States; Henry E. Sigerist, Johns Hopkins University professor, who has one of the longest records of un-American activity on behalf of Communist Party enterprises to be found during the past 10 years; Herman Shumlin, the theatrical producer whose devotion to the Communist Party has been such that he may well carry a party membership card around with him; Edward K. Barsky, physician, who undoubtedly holds a membership card in the Communist Party; Vilhjalmur Stefansson, the famous explorer, who frequently lends a helping hand to the Communist Party; Annette Ruben-stein, who, like many others on this list of American Rescue Ship Mission sponsors, was active in the seditious American Peace Mobilization; Earl Robinson, composer of the 'Ballad for Americans,' who has been one of the most prominent American Communists of recent years; Marion Hath-way, Pittsburgh social worker whose name is found in many lists of the Communist Party's fellow travelers; Dan Gillmor, publisher of the now defunct and un-American magazine which was called *Friday*; and Mar-garet I. Lamont, who with her husband Corliss has given substantial moral and financial support to communism in the United States.

"In short, the foregoing sponsors of the American Rescue Ship Mission make up one of the most influential American lists of Communist Party supporters in the United States. Many of these persons have achieved national distinction in the fields of music, acting, letters, medicine, religion, exploration, or teaching. To large sections of the American public they may have been known only for their outstanding contributions in these fields, and it may, therefore, come as a profound shock to these Americans to learn that such persons as Paul Muni, the actor, Paul Robeson, the singer, and Vilhjalmur Stefansson the explorer, and the others have been so intimately associated with the Communist Party. There is nothing novel in this phenomenon so far as the American scene is concerned; it has been present in the Communist movements of other countries."

In March 1942, the Exiled Writers Committee, the United American Spanish Aid Committee, and the American Committee To Save Refugees merged to form the Joint Anti-Fascist Refugee Committee.

Communist Edward Barsky was chairman and Walter Rautenstrauch was honorary chairman of the Joint Committee. Among the most prominent members were Louis Bromfield, Joseph Curran, Paul Robeson, and Carl Sandburg. Among the supporters of the Joint Committee were Communists Max Bedacht, Ernest De Maio, William Gropper, Ben Gold, Donald Henderson, and Herbert March. Other sponsors included Faith Baldwin, Margaret Culkin Banning, Elisabeth Bergner, Henry Seidel Canby, J. Edward Bromberg, Ilka Chase, Congressman John M. Coffee, Aaron Copland, Walter Damrosch, Ambassador Joseph E. Davies, Walter Duranty, Albert Einstein, John Erskine, Howard Fast, Mrs. J. Borden Harriman, Sidney Hillman, George Jessel, Alvin Johnson, Ring Lardner, Jr., Eduard Lindeman, Maurice Maeterlinck, André Maurois, Yehudi Menuhin, Governor Culbert Olson, Molly Picon, Jacob Potofsky, Adam Clayton Powell Jr., Michael Quill, Quentin Reynolds, Gale Sondergaard, Bill Stern, Rex Stout, U.S. Senator Elbert Thomas, Dalton Trumbo, Orson Welles, and Mary Woolley. The Joint Anti-Fascist Refugee Committee, with its origins in the earlier "anti-fascist" committees of the Spanish war years, was certainly one of the most notable accomplishments in the Communists' front history. While maintaining complete control of the three committees that merged to form the joint committee, the Communists were still able to attract previously inactive individuals to support their project of rescuing and rehabilitating Communists or those who supported the Communists in the Spanish Civil War. The refugees, of course, were never called Communists, but always "anti-fascists."

During the Spanish Civil War, Communists everywhere were concerned about United States neutrality laws, which prevented war materials from being shipped to Spain. The ban on shipments worked much more of a hardship upon the Red Republican forces than on those of Franco. In the United States, the Communists waged a vigorous pressure campaign for repeal of the Neutrality Act, and the main burden of the campaign was carried by the American Friends of Spanish Democracy. Its chairman was Bishop Robert L. Paddock, the vice chairman was John Dewey, the chairman and vice chairman of the executive committee were Samuel G. Inman and Guy Emery Shipler, respectively. The treasurer was W. W. Norton. On the executive committee were Roger N. Baldwin, the Reverend John Paul Jones, Corliss Lamont, Reinhold Niebuhr, George Soule, Robert K. Speer, the

Reverend William B. Spofford, and Maxwell Stewart. Committee members included Devere Allen, Newton Arvin, Harry Elmer Barnes, Carleton Beals, Stephen Vincent Benét, Alfred Bingham, Algernon Black, Bruce Bliven, Heywood Broun, Malcolm Cowley, John Dos Passos, Paul H. Douglas, Stephen Duggan, Sherwood Eddy, Henry Pratt Fairchild, Denna Fleming, Waldo Frank, Frank Graham, Matthew Josephson, Paul Kellogg, Freda Kirchwey, Max Lerner, Bishop Francis J. McConnell, Archibald MacLeish, John Mackay, Vito Marcantonio, Lewis Mumford, Harry Overstreet, Bishop Edward L. Parsons, Charles Edward Russell, Arthur M. Schlesinger, Leland Stowe, Mary Van Kleeck, Willard Uphaus, Oswald Garrison Villard, Lillian Wald, David Rhys Williams, and Stephen S. Wise.

In 1938, the American Friends of Spanish Democracy released a letter addressed to President Roosevelt and the Foreign Affairs and Foreign Relations Committees of the Congress. The signers of the letter wanted the Neutrality Act repealed so that the Red Republicans in Spain could receive help from the United States. They insisted that a defeat of the Reds in Spain was "fraught with great danger to democratic institutions." Among the signers of the Communist-front-sponsored letter were former Secretary of State Henry L. Stimson and former U.S. Ambassador to Germany William E. Dodd. In addition to regular sponsors of American Friends of Spanish Democracy, the signers included W. Lewis Abbott of the University of Colorado; Fred W. Adams of Boston University's School of Theology; L.L. Bernard of Washington University in St. Louis; Bishop Chauncey Brewster of Connecticut; Crane Brinton of Harvard University; Dan Brummitt, editor of *Christian Advocate*; Ada Mae Coe of Wellesley College; Stuart Cuthbertson of the University of Chicago; Frank Ewart of Colgate University; Dorothy Canfield Fisher; Warner Fite of Princeton University; President Everett Herrick of Andover-Newton Theological Institute; Jesse Holmes of Swarthmore College; Charles Houston of the National Association for the Advancement of Colored People; Alvin Johnson and Horace Kallen of New School for Social Research; Leonard Lawson of Hobart College; Reinhold Niebuhr of Union Theological Seminary; James B. Pratt of Williams College; Herbert Priestley of the University of California; Vida Scudder of Wellesley College; Harry F. Ward of Union Theological Seminary; Colston Warne of Amherst College; and President A. F. Whitney of the Brotherhood of Railway Trainmen.

One of the largest Communist fronts concerned with getting war materials to the Red Republicans was the Coordinating Committee To Lift the Embargo. It was an auxiliary of the North American Committee To Aid Spanish Democracy. On the committee were university and college presidents and deans including Dean Leonard T. Backer (University of North Carolina); Dean Thomas E. Benner (University of Illinois); Samuel Capen (University of Buffalo); Robert Clothier (Rutgers College); Ada Comstock (Radcliffe College); Dean Christian Gauss (Princeton University); Frank Graham (University of North Carolina); Roswell Ham (Mount Holyoke College); Franklin Johnson (Colby College); Robert Leigh (Bennington College); Daniel Marsh (Boston University); Irving Maurer (Beloit College); Paul Moody (Middlebury College); William Neilson (Smith College); George Norlin (University of Colorado); Marion Park (Bryn Mawr College); Dean F. K. Richtmyer (Cornell University's Graduate School); Rufus von Kleinsmid (University of Southern California); and President Emeritus Mary E. Woolley (Mount Holyoke College). They were joined by the presidents of the United Federal Workers; the Federation of Architects, Engineers, Chemists and Technicians; the American Newspaper Guild; the International Brotherhood of Papermakers; the American Federation of Teachers; the International Fur Workers Union; the United Cannery, Agricultural, Packing and Allied Workers Union; the Brotherhood of Blacksmith and Drop Forgers; the United Office and Professional Workers; the United Furniture Workers; the International Woodworkers; the Brotherhood of Sleeping Car Porters; and the Brotherhood of Railway Trainmen. The Committee had thirty-nine lawyers, most of them from the National Lawyers Guild ("foremost legal bulwark of the Communist Party"), and seventy-eight writers, most of them from the League of American Writers ("subversive and Communist"). There were large contingents of musicians, psychologists, clergy, physicians and surgeons, and social workers. Among the organizations which threw their full support to the Coordinating Committee were Sidney Hillman's Amalgamated Clothing Workers of America; the American Artists' Congress ("Communist front"); the Communist-controlled American Communications Association; the American Federation of Teachers; the American League for Peace and Democracy ("subversive and Communist"); the American Relief Committee for the Victims of Italian Fascism; the American Security League; the American Student Union ("Communist front" – "subversive and un-

American"); the American Unitarian Association; the Central Conference of American Rabbis; the Committee on Social Action of the Congregational Church; the Conference on Pan-American Democracy ("Communist front"); the Descendants of the American Revolution ("Communist front"); the International Juridical Association ("Communist front"); International Labor Defense ("legal arm of the Communist Party"); International Workers Order ("subversive and Communist"); the League of American Writers ("subversive and Communist"); the League of Nations Association of Greater New York; the Lithuanian Committee To Aid Spanish Democracy; the Methodist Federation for Social Service ("Communist front"); the National Council of Jewish Women; the National Lawyers Guild ("foremost legal bulwark of the Communist Party"); Nature Friends of America ("subversive and Communist"); New Theatre of Philadelphia ("Communist front"); People's Lobby (dominated by Socialists); the Southern Conference for Human Welfare ("Communist front"); and the Theatre Arts Committee ("Communist front").

In the waning weeks of the Spanish Civil War, the Washington Committee To Lift the Spanish Embargo joined the Coordinating Committee To Lift the Spanish Embargo in sponsorship of a full-page advertisement in the *New York Times* (January 31, 1939). The advertisement was in the form of an "open letter to the government and people of the United States." Excerpts from the "open letter" indicate the pure Communist line as propounded before the Hitler-Stalin pact of August 1939: "While you read this message, a major human tragedy is taking place. A question of the greatest importance to our country and to the entire world is being decided. A brave nation is fighting against terrible odds, not only for its own independence and freedom, but for the very life of democracy everywhere.

"The whole world knows now that the 'Franco Revolt' is in reality an invasion. Hitler and Mussolini are bent on destroying the Spanish Republic, and with its destruction gaining vastly increased power in the campaign against the democracies. They have set out to replace a hopeful young republic with a dictatorship patterned on the Nazi and Fascist models.

"With indescribable brutality and complete disregard for world opinion, they have warred against both the armies and the women and children of Spain. It is clear that they intend to use Spain as a means of crippling French and British democracy, and as a powerful springboard to South and Central America, where their agents have for years been busy spreading propaganda against democracy and for fascism.

"If Franco, Hitler and Mussolini win in Spain, the fascist penetration of the Western Hemisphere will be immensely strengthened. This will mean a greatly increased defense problem for the United States.

"It must not be allowed to happen! Democracy cannot permit unending aggression against it. 'Appeasement' has failed. China, Ethiopia, Austria, Czecho-Slovakia, Spain witness its failure. What can our country do? The American people want peace. They abhor aggression and warring dictatorships. They are committed to the democratic way of life.

"The hard fact is that by our embargo against Spain we are giving aid to Hitler and Mussolini and all they stand for. Our embargo is helping to destroy a republic which stands as a powerful bulwark against the fascist plans. If that republic is destroyed, much of the responsibility will be ours.

"To the plea that the United States must remain neutral we can only reply that an embargo which permits aid to aggressors and denies it to the victim is flagrantly unneutral . . . . A policy which places a friendly, recognized, democratically-elected government on the same plane with the foreign-aided insurrectionist cannot, by any canon of law or tradition, be called neutrality. The embargo, as our most distinguished lawyers and historians have insisted, is a clear violation of international law.

"It is not too late. The Spanish Republic still lives. Its people, who still control Central Spain with Valencia and iron-willed Madrid, have no intention of surrendering. A simple act of justice on the part of The United States of America can still turn the tide in favor of democracy. We who have signed this letter want to hear the cheer of hope and new courage that will go up in every land, including our own, when the word goes out that The United States has lifted the embargo against Spain."

It was an inescapable fact that many — if not most — of those who signed the "open letter" denouncing aggression and warring dictatorships were serving a Communist front established on orders from the Soviet Union, which in a few months would despoil Poland in collusion with the same Hitler who was denounced in the "open letter."

One other group which worked in harmony with the Coordinating

Committee was the Lawyers' Committee on American Relations with Spain, which was organized in January 1938 and from then until the end of the war fought to have the embargo on Spain lifted. The Lawyers' Committee sponsored radio programs, public forums, and public meetings. It provided research and legal arguments for interested anti-embargo groups. It held a widely publicized two-day conference in Washington, and its members made the most of the opportunity to apply personal pressure upon federal government officials to support their anti-embargo appeal. The Lawyers Committee was led by Paul J. Kern as chairman. For honorary vice chairmen, there were Henry T. Hunt, Robert W. Kenny, and Malcolm Sharp. Some of the better known judges, practicing attorneys, and law school administrators and faculty included Louis B. Boudin, Felix S. Cohen, John P. Davis, Osmond K. Fraenkel, Arthur Garfield Hays, Charles H. Houston, Dorothy Kenyon, Vito Marcantonio, Carey McWilliams, Justine Wise Potier, Lee Pressman, Harry Sacher, and Maurice Sugar. Most of the members were also affiliated with the National Lawyers Guild ("the foremost legal bulwark of the Communist Party").

There were many minor fronts established by the Communists and most of them either merged with larger fronts or else passed out of existence after a brief flurry of activity. Some were used for their propaganda value, such as the Julius Rosenthal Memorial Committee for Aid of Basque Children. Communists Robert W. Dunn and Donald Ogden Stewart were members of the Committee, but except for one fund-raising concert, the Memorial Committee amounted to nothing. Of more promise was the Ben Leider Memorial Committee. The *Daily Worker* suggested the founding of this committee in honor of the first American to die while fighting with the Reds in Spain. Said the *Worker*: "Leider died the death of a true American, a true Communist." Heywood Broun of the American Newspaper Guild organized the Memorial Committee, and was joined by some notable Communists and fellow travelers: Franklin P. Adams, Phil Bard, Congressman John T. Bernard, John Dewey, Joseph Freeman, Angelo Herndon, Rex Ingram, Arthur Kober, Max Lerner, and Harrison Smith; but this glittering array did nothing except gain a little publicity for the cause.

One of the smallest fronts was the Washington Friends of Spanish Democracy, an affiliate of the North American Committee To Aid Spanish Democracy. What the Washington front lacked in size, it made up in notoriety. Leon Henderson, a New Deal luminary, was president of the front. Other New Dealers with Henderson were David Saposs and Edwin Smith. Writers Robert S. Allen and Marquis Child were in the group, as well as the Reverend Russell Clinch, Robert Marshall (who would leave a large estate for the benefit of the Communist cause), Leland Stowe, and Mrs. Louis Brandeis, wife of the Associate Justice of the Supreme Court.

One of the first Communist fronts organized in 1936 was the American Society for Technical Aid to Spanish Democracy, with Waldo Frank as chairman and John Howard Lawson as secretary. Rebecca Grecht, from Communist Party headquarters, was executive secretary, and Abraham Unger, a veteran Communist, was treasurer. The members of the executive board were impressive: Michael Blankfort, Van Wyck Brooks, Malcolm Cowley, Kyle Crichton, Joseph Freeman, Ben Gold, Henry Hart, Lewis Mumford, George Sklar, and Alexander Trachtenberg. The organization, however, despite its top-heavy Communist presence, faded away.

The "united front" strategy called for many fronts to attract specialized groups, and some of these proved to be very active in the "anti-fascist" campaign. The Federation of Faculty Committees for Aid to the Spanish People was headed by Lyman R. Bradley. The Social Workers Committee To Aid Spanish Democracy had a heavy complement of women activists: Mildred Fairchild, Mary Van Kleeck, Lillian Wald, Helen Hall, Marion Hathway and Mary Simkhovitch. They were joined by Samuel Gerson, Sheldon Glueck, Paul Kellogg, and John Kingsbury, among others.

The Negro People's Committee To Aid Spanish Democracy was headed by Paul Robeson, who had long been a notorious Soviet apologist. Among those who worked with Robeson were President R. B. Atwood of Kentucky State College; Mary McLeod Bethune; Bishop Shelton Hale of New York; Countee Cullen; Attorney Earl Dickerson of Chicago; Dean W.J. Faulker of Fisk University; E. Franklin Frazier of Howard University; Vice President Arthur Fauset of the National Negro Congress; Communist labor leader Ishmael Flory; President John M. Gandy of Virginia State College; Communist Angelo Herndon; William Pickens of the National Association for the Advancement of Colored People; President James E. Shepard of North Carolina State College; Communist Ferdinand C. Smith of the National Maritime Union;

President L. K. Williams of the National Baptist Convention; Robert C. Weaver of the Department of the Interior; Dean Charles H. Wesley of Howard University; and Louise Thompson of the International Workers Order.

In New York, there was the Writers' and Artists' Committee for Medical Aid to Spain. Most of its members were from the League of American Writers and everyone in this group belonged to one or more other Communist fronts in the "anti-fascist" arena.

There was a Musicians' Committee To Aid Spanish Democracy with Pablo Casals (persona non grata in Spain) as honorary chairman. Its members included Marc Blitzstein, Olin Downes, Albert Einstein, Rudolph Ganz, Alma Gluck, John Hammond, Sol Hurok, Serge Koussevitzky, Wallingford Riegger, and Sigmund Spaeth. In Hollywood, there was a Motion Picture Artists Spanish Aid Committee. Its executive board included Herbert Biberman, Florence Eldridge, Lewis Milestone, Madeline Ruthven, Donald Ogden Stewart, and Franchot Tone. Among its sponsors were Sherwood Anderson, Richard Arlen, Edward Arnold, Melvyn Douglas, Paul H. Douglas, Theodore Dreiser, Martha Graham, Fanny Hurst, Robert Kenny, Sinclair Lewis, Paul Muni, and Sylvia Sidney. This front had an extraordinary list of international sponsors, including George Bernard Shaw; David Lloyd George; André Malraux, Romain Rolland, and Édouard Herriot of France; and Heinrich Mann and Lion Feuchtwanger of Germany.

The two largest Communist fronts that emerged from the Spanish Civil War were the Veterans of the Abraham Lincoln Brigade and Friends of the Abraham Lincoln Brigade. On December 18, 1937, about fifty veterans of the International Brigade convened in New York to form their own organization with membership "open to all Americans who served in Spain in the International Brigade and who left Spain with the permission of the International Brigade." They decided that their group would be a "major force for peace and against fascism in the United States."

In the meantime, Friends of the Abraham Lincoln Brigade was founded under the complete control of the Communist Party. Organized in cities throughout the United States, the FALB raised money to finance the ALB operation and, at the same time, to serve as a propaganda outlet for the Communist Party. The organization actively recruited for the ALB, working within the proliferation of so-called Spanish relief organizations. In addition, it aided the returning veterans of the ALB with money, clothing, medical and dental care, and legal help for those who encountered difficulties with the federal government in the matter of passports and their service with a foreign power. The aid which the FALB gave to the ALB in Spain and to the veterans was not commensurate with the money collected for those purposes. One veteran, John G. Honeycombe, estimated that no more than 20 per cent of the funds ever reached the Americans in Spain. He said that the greater part of the money was spent on propaganda campaigns on behalf of the Communist Party. In fact, the FALB made no attempt to keep an accurate accounting of contributions received or expenditures.

The importance of the organization was attested by the Communist Party's General Secretary, Earl Browder, who called together a group of Communist officials and told them: "The purpose of this meeting tonight is to launch the campaign for 50,000 members of the Friends of the Abraham Lincoln Battalion .... The Friends of the Abraham Lincoln Battalion must be enabled to maintain and increase its supply of the small comforts and necessities to the boys in Spain." On another occasion he instructed the Communists that they had "a political task to perpetuate and popularize the glorious history of the Abraham Lincoln Brigade, and support the organization of its Friends."

The Communists responded to Browder's instructions and the FALB received support from the American Artists' Congress ("Communist front"); the Amkino Corporation ("a Soviet film organization"); the *Daily Worker* ("official organ of the Communist Party"); *Fight* ("the official organ of the American League for Peace and Democracy, subversive and Communist"); Garrison Films ("producers of Communist films"); the International Workers Order ("one of the strongest Communist organizations"); the *Morning Freiheit* ("Jewish Communist newspaper"); Prompt Press ("a Communist printing house"); the Workers School ("established by the Communist Party"); and World Tourists ("Soviet tourist agency").

When the Veterans of the Abraham Lincoln Brigade was organized, it adopted as its program assistance to "the Friends of the Abraham Lincoln Brigade in their work of providing the Americans in Spain with comforts and in their work of rehabilitation; to help to rally the support of the democratic people in America to the democratic people in Spain; to cooperate with any and all organizations working for peace and democracy; to affiliate and cooperate with organizations formed in other countries by veterans of the International Brigade."

The Friends and the Veterans did work together by participating in May Day Parades, in parades and "anti-fascist" demonstrations conducted by the American League for Peace and Democracy, and at Communist Party conventions and meetings. The Spanish Republican Army uniform was much in evidence at these gatherings, and the Veterans brandished their clenched fists in the salute that was used constantly in Spain by the Red soldiers and had been widely publicized in photographs from the Spanish front.

The Friends and the Veterans were especially active on the propaganda front as they pursued the Communist line to promote the best interests of the Soviet Union vis-à-vis American foreign policy. Prior to the Hitler-Stalin Pact of 1939, the two groups promoted an anti-fascist denunciation directed at Hitler's Germany. During the course of the Hitler-Stalin Pact (1939-1941), they promoted neutrality for the United States, while Hitler and Stalin conducted their rapacious conquest of Poland.

The Friends of the Abraham Lincoln Brigade were led at various times by Phil Bard and William Lawrence as executive secretaries, Paul Crosbie and David McK. White as chairmen, William Lieder as treasurer, and Jack R. Miller as national organizer. In their fund-raising and propaganda programs they received major support from such individuals as Francis J. Gorman, president of the United Textile Workers of America, who served as chairman of a Trade Union Rehabilitation Committee to support the FALB. He claimed: "More than 90% of the members of the Lincoln Brigade are trade unionists . . . heroically fighting for the American traditions of democracy." Stanley Isaacs, the Manhattan Borough President, President Heywood Broun of the American Newspaper Guild, and President Harry Sherman of Book-of-the-Month Club were fund-raisers for the FALB. Other supporters came from all walks of life; they included Jay Allen, Congressman Thomas Amlie of Wisconsin, Helen Arthur, Nathan Asch, Ernest S. Bates, Ralph Bates, Clyde Beals, Robert Benchley, Stephen Vincent Benét, William Rose Benét, Congressman John T. Bernard of Minnesota, Ernst Boas, Louis B. Boudin, Asa Bordages, Millen Brand, James L. Brewer, Walter Briehl, Remo Bufano, James Cagney, Abram Chasins, Lester Cohen,

Kyle Crichton, Jerome Davis, Pierre De Lanux, Martha Dodd, Muriel Draper, Albert Einstein, Mordecai Ezekiel, Jacob Fisher, Louis Fisher, Jay Franklin, Leo Gallagher, Lee E. Geyer, J. W. Gillette, Joseph Gollomb, Dashiell Hammett, Henry Hart, Lillian Hellman, Ernest Hemingway, John Housman, Quincy Howe, Langston Hughes, Fannie Hurst, Rosetta Hurwitz, Gardner Jackson, H. V. Kaltenborn, Fred Keating, Robert W. Kenny, Paul Kern, John A. Kingsbury, Arthur Kober, Julia Church Kolar, Alexander Lehrman, Walter Liebman, Archibald MacLeish, Congressman Vito Marcantonio of New York, Kirtley Mather, Carey McWilliams, John E. Middleton, Victor Moore, Congressman Jerry O'Connell of Montana, Clifford Odets, Dorothy Parker, Ursula Parrott, Walter Polakov, Wallingford Reigger, William Rollins Jr., Carl Sandburg, Frank Scully, George Seldes, Vincent Sheean, Guy Emery Shipler, Herman Shumlin, Upton Sinclair, Isabel Walker Soule, Alfred K. Stern, Donald Ogden Stewart, Wilmer T. Stone, Leland Stowe, Paul Strum, Congressman Henry Tiegen of Minnesota, Harold Urey, Orson Welles, William L. White, A. F. Whitney, Paul Willert, James Waterman Wise, Mary E. Woolley, Max Yergan, and Art Young. Through the wide variety of interests represented by their supporters, the Friends of the Abraham Lincoln Brigade were guaranteed a collective friend-at-court in Broadway and Hollywood theatrical circles, in the metropolitan press and religious journals, in literary and mass-circulation magazines, in radio, and in academic circles on campus and elsewhere. Those who supported the FALB ranged from parlor pinks to the radical chic set to knee-jerk liberals to hard-core Communist sympathizers. Many of them held office in Communist fronts; most of them belonged to a number of fronts. Their interlocking membership in the FALB guaranteed that the causes of the ALB were fortified throughout the entire network of the so-called united front.

The Veterans of the Abraham Lincoln Brigade were led at various times by Steve Nelson, Milton Wolff, Aaron Johnson, Irving Fajans, Douglas Roach, Dennis Jordan, Walter Garland, and Bob Klonsky. Because of the inherent secrecy of the Communist Party, there has never been an accurate count of how many Americans actually served in the International Brigade or how many survived. Many used false passports and aliases to reach Spain. The Red leaders in Spain never provided accurate casualty figures. Edwin Rolfe, the "official" historian of the ALB, claimed that 2,800 Americans served in Spain and less than

1,000 were killed. Arthur H. Landis, a veteran of the ALB, in the most recent of several such histories, *The Abraham Lincoln Brigade*, estimated that 1,600 of 3,300 Americans fighting in Spain were killed. The Subversive Activities Control Board stated that about 1,800 of approximately 3,000 returned from Spain to the United States and that, as of 1955, less than 600 survived.

On December 24, 1939, the Friends of the Abraham Lincoln Brigade disbanded and relinquished its administration to the Veterans of the Abraham Lincoln Brigade. The Veterans, in the immediate period thereafter, were concerned with efforts to have their comrades returned to the United States from imprisonment in Spain or in France, where many had fled at the conclusion of the war. There were also some difficulties with the federal government, although the authorities never pursued prosecutions against the ALB with any real vigor. However, in its projects the Veterans of the Abraham Lincoln Brigade did receive considerable support from reliable Communist front veterans, including Thomas Addis, Newton Arvin, Alfred Bingham, Marc Blitzstein, Anita Block, Dorothy Brewster, Walter Briehl, Van Wyck Brooks, Bennett Cerf, Zechariah Chafee Jr., Aaron Copland, Malcolm Cowley, Ephraim Cross, Countee Cullen, Robert W. Dunn, Leo Eloesser, Henry Pratt Fairchild, Frances Grant, William Gropper, Ralph Gundlach, Charles Houston, William Lloyd Imes, Horace Kallen, Helen Keller, Dorothy Kenyon, Alfred Kreymborg, Donald G. Lothrop, Robert S. Lynd, Albert Maltz, George Marshall, F. O. Matthiessen, Clifford McAvoy, Harvey O'Connor, Elliot Paul, Walter Rautenstrauch, Quentin Reynolds, Paul Robeson, Irwin Shaw, Bernhard J. Stern, Anna Louise Strong, C. Fayette Taylor, James Thurber, Louis Untermeyer, Mary Heaton Vorse, Harry F. Ward, and Goodwin Watson.

In 1946, the House Committee on Un-American Activities cited the Veterans as a Communist front. In 1947 and 1948, the Attorney General of the United States cited the group as subversive and Communist. In 1955, the Subversive Activities Control Board concluded that it was "directed, dominated and controlled by the Communist Party of the United States." The SACB ordered the VALB to register with the Department of Justice as a Communist front organization. The Veterans fought the order, with the aid of the Emergency Civil Liberties Committee and its counsel, Leonard Boudin. In 1965, the Attorney General of the United States, Nicholas

Katzenbach, decided to abandon the attempt to get the Veterans to register. He said that the VALB had diminished by attrition through the years and that, because of its requirements for membership, there was no potential for new membership. Since 1965, the relatively few survivors of the VALB have been content to make infrequent tirades against the Franco regime in Spain.

ALL-AMERICA ANTI-IMPERIALIST LEAGUE

At the 1925 national convention of the Communist Party (then called the Workers Party), it was reported: "Under the present Central Executive Committee the Workers Party of America has for the first time made anti-imperialist work one of its basic activities — the most important step in this direction being the successful organization of the All-America Anti-Imperialist League . . . endorsed by the Comintern [Communist International] and Profitern [Red International of Labor Unions]."

The All-America Anti-Imperialist League (AAAIL) was the American section of Moscow's International League Against Imperialism, known also as the League Against Imperialism or the League for National Independence. Willi Muenzenberg, a German Communist, was international secretary of the International League Against Imperialism; Bertrand Russell, British Communist, was head of the English section; and on the international presidium were Japanese Communist Sen Katayama; Communist Diego Rivera, Mexican artist; Jawaharlal Nehru, Indian Communist; and Albert Einstein, the German mathematician who would later come to the United States as an exile and carry on a lifetime of Communist activity.

In the AAAIL's publication, *The Anti-Imperialist Review*, the program of the AAAIL was outlined: "(1) The complete national independence of the colonial and semi-colonial peoples; (2) the full right of self-determination for all oppressed nationalities; (3) the removal of the imperialist armed forces from all colonial and semi-colonial countries; (4) complete freedom of movement for all national-revolutionary organizations, and in particular for all revolutionary working class and peasant organizations; (5) the confiscation without compensation of all undertakings, mines, banks, plantations, and lands at present in the possession of the imperialists and the nationalization of the same . . . the abolition of all debts to the

24

imperialists and the abolition of all reparation payments; and (6) the confiscation without compensation of all lands at present in the possession of rich landowners and the distribution of the same amongst the working peasants."

From 1925 until 1933, when the program of the AAAIL was taken over by the American League Against War and Fascism, the AAAIL served the international Communist movement by agitating against the United States, especially in those sections of Latin America where the Communists either had, or were trying to gain, a strong foothold. There were campaigns against the continuance of the Monroe Doctrine as the basic United States foreign policy for the Western Hemisphere. There were also campaigns against "United States imperialism in the Far East." The organs of the AAAIL, *The Anti-Imperialist Review* and *Upsurge*, were printed by Communist Party publishing houses.

The AAAIL had branches in New York City and eleven other cities in the United States. It had sections in Argentina, Brazil, Colombia, Cuba, Guatemala, Haiti, Mexico, Nicaragua, Peru, Puerto Rico, and Salvador, and also in the Philippines and China. Throughout its entire network, while propagandizing against the United States, the AAAIL attempted to drum up support for the Soviet Union and the Chinese Communists, who were making their big move against Chiang Kai-shek's regime.

To insure recognition by comrades everywhere that the AAAIL was a Communist Party operation, the AAAIL named as honorary presidents Maxim Gorki of the Soviet Union, Madame Sun Yat-sen of China, Henri Barbusse of France, and Upton Sinclair of the United States — all universally known as Communists, except for Sinclair, whose Socialism was undeniable but whose Marxian writings were highly acceptable in Communist countries.

On the American scene, the AAAIL was saturated with well-known Communists. *Upsurge*, one of AAAIL's publications, was strictly Communist-line and had as writers such Communists as Albert G. Gomez, Donald Henderson, John R. Perry, and William Simons. Activists in the AAAIL were personally instructed by General Secretary of the Communist Party Earl Browder; James Allen from the Negro section of the Communist Party; and other Communist Party leaders, including Robert W. Dunn, Harry Gannes, and Louise Thompson.

Two veteran Communists served successively as secretary of the

AAAIL: Manuel Gomez and William Simons. Other prominent Communists on either the AAAIL's national committee or on committees of the AAAIL's regional sections included Bishop William M. Brown, Louis Budenz, Arthur Calhoun, Henry W. L. Dana, William F. Dunne, Elizabeth Gurley Flynn, William Z. Foster, Ben Gold, Carl Haessler, Sam Herman, Paxton Hibben, Langston Hughes, Jay Lovestone, Scott Nearing, Max Schachtman, Harriet Silverman, Lawrence Todd, Albert Weisbord, and Charlotte Whitney.

Very few Communist fronts in the United States have ever been more clearly identified as totally under Communist control and totally subservient to Moscow than the AAAIL. Those individuals affiliated with the AAAIL who were not formal members of the Communist Party could not reasonably claim that they were duped into the AAAIL or that they did not know of its complete Communist nature. Many of them would claim under oath and otherwise that they were not Communists and that the organizations they represented were not in the Communist Party's orbit. These "non-Communists" included attorney Clarence Darrow; writer Waldo Frank; the Reverend John Haynes Holmes; Paul Jones, the associate director of the Fellowship of Reconciliation; Ellen Hayes of Wellesley College; Robert Morss Lovett of the University of Chicago; William Pickens of the National Association for the Advancement of Colored People; the Reverend David Rhys Williams; Lucia Ames Mead of the Women's International League for Peace and Freedom; H.S. Bucklin of Brown University; Justine Wise of Yale University; John F. Markey of the University of Minnesota; Marx Lewis of the Socialist Party; Henry Duel of the League for Industrial Democracy; Lewis Gannett and Freda Kirchwey of *Nation*; Arthur Garfield Hays of the American Civil Liberties Union; Harriot Blatch of the League for Industrial Democracy; Lillian Herstein of the Socialist Party; and William Holly and Roger Baldwin of the American Civil Liberties Union.

AMERICAN FUND FOR PUBLIC SERVICE

In the 1920's and 1930's, Communist, Socialist, and anarchist projects received considerable financial aid in the form of outright gifts or phony loans from the American Fund for Public Service, a tax-exempt foundation, which was generally known as the Garland Fund. The Fund was established by Charles Garland, son of Wall Street broker James A. Garland, who had been so indoctrinated at Harvard University that he became averse to personal property and decided to give away his inheritance. The inheritance, in 1922, amounted to $900,000, largely in conservative securities, including a large block of common stock in the First National Bank of New York. Within a few years, despite persistent spending, the value of the Fund increased more than two-fold because of the bull market conditions on Wall Street.

Throughout the life of the Fund, the officers and directors were a self-perpetuating elite group of Communists and Socialists, or, if they did not have formal Party affiliations, were fellow travelers with an unmistakable devotion to radicalism. The Fund's personnel included Roger Baldwin, Robert W. Dunn, Morris L. Ernst, Elizabeth Gurley Flynn, William Z. Foster, Lewis S. Gannett, Benjamin Gitlow, Clinton S. Golden, Sidney Hillman, James Weldon Johnson, Freda Kirchwey, Robert Morss Lovett, Judah L. Magnes, Mary E. McDowell, Clarina Michelson, Scott Nearing, Walter Nelles, Norman Thomas, and Harry F. Ward. Not only did this group represent the leadership of the Communist Party and the Socialist Party; it also represented the guiding forces of just about every major Communist front, Communist enterprise; and Socialist institution in America.

Among the organizations that received handouts from the Garland Fund were the All-America Anti-Imperialist League ("the [Communist] Party was wholly responsible for the establishment and subsequent control of the league"); the ultra-leftist American Civil Liberties Union; Brookwood Labor College ("Communist"); Camp Tamiment (Socialist establishment); the Committee on Coal and Great Power (Socialist); the Committee on Militarism in Education (a supporting organization of the United States Congress Against War, "completely under the control of the Communist Party"); Commonwealth College ("Communist"); the Emergency Committee for Strikers Relief (Socialist); the House of the Masses (a Communist institution in Detroit); the Industrial Workers of the World [Wobblies] ("subversive and un-American"); the International Committee for Political Prisoners (an ultra-leftist fund-raising enterprise for seditionists); International Labor Defense ("subversive and Communist" — "legal arm of the Communist Party" — "part of an international network of organizations for the defense of Communist lawbreakers"); the Labor Research Association (a Communist subsidiary run by a Communist, Robert W. Dunn); the League for

Industrial Democracy (the most important and influential Socialist proselyting and propaganda group on American university and college campuses); the League for Mutual Aid ("a Communist enterprise"); the Manumit School (operated by Communist Scott Nearing's wife); the ultra-radical National Association for the Advancement of Colored People; the National Consumers League (Socialist); the National Mooney-Billings Committee (dominated by Socialists); Pioneer Camps and Pioneer Youth of America (Socialist); Russian Reconstruction Farms ("Communist enterprise"); the Sacco-Vanzetti Defense Committee (part of a Communist Party propaganda campaign); the Trade Union Educational League ("formed pursuant to instructions from the Communist International" and directed by William Z. Foster, Communist Party leader); the Women's International League for Peace and Freedom (ultra-leftist-pacifist); Workers International Relief ("Communist front"); Workers School of New York City ("part of a system of Communist Party schools"); and the Young Workers League [Young Communist League, American Youth for Democracy] ("subversive and Communist" – "formed . . . for the purpose of exploiting to the advantage of a foreign power the idealism, inexperience and craving to join which is characteristic of American college youth" – "part of Soviet psychological warfare against the United States"). In dispensing Garland Fund largesse to these various fronts and enterprises, the Fund's officers and directors were feathering their own nests, since they had either a direct or a strong indirect connection with all of these institutions.

The Fund was strong in its support of the printed word. It contributed money to such Communist publishing houses as International Publishers and Workers Library Publishers and such Communist or Socialist publications as the *Daily Worker, Il Nuovo Mondo, Labor Age, New Leader, Novy Mir,* and *World Tomorrow. The New Masses* ("weekly journal of the Communist Party") was established by and published by the Garland Fund. The Federated Press ("Communist-controlled news syndicate" – "organized for the purpose of promulgating Communist ideas and misinformation into the bloodstream of public opinion") and the ultra-radical "intellectual" *New Republic* received the Fund's largesse.

The Fund established and operated the Vanguard Press for the express purpose of printing Communist and Socialist authors' works, which were distributed through the Rand Book Store of the Rand School of Social Science. The Rand School, which was particularly favored by the Fund, was a Marxian-Socialist training school for labor agitators. In connection with the Rand School and its Labor Research Department, the Garland Fund financed the publishing of the *American Labor Year Book.*

Labor was of particular interest to the Communists and Socialists who directed the Garland Fund's disbursements. Fund money was poured into Communist-led strike activities, especially in the notorious strikes at Passaic, New Jersey; Gastonia, North Carolina; and Centralia, Washington. Among the Communist and Socialist-controlled unions and labor organizations which received the Fund's support were the Agricultural Workers Industrial Union, the Amalgamated Textile Workers Union, the American Federation of Teachers, the Central Trades and Labor Council, the Cooperative Central Exchange, the Cooperative League of America, the International Ladies' Garment Workers Union, the Marine Workers League, the National Textile Workers, the Northern States Cooperative League, the Teachers Union of New York City, and the Women's Trade Union League. Legal fees and bail funds were provided for individuals who ran afoul of the law in the course of strikes.

The Fund financed a variety of research and study projects which were designed to produce anti-capitalist, pro-Communist, pro-Socialist propaganda. Some of the individuals who received subsidies, salaries, or expenses for such projects included Paul Blanshard, William E.B. DuBois, Robert W. Dunn, Max Eastman, Stephen Raushenbush, and Mary Heaton Vorse. Campus activists promoting pacifism received financial help to produce student publications and to attend pacifist conventions and congresses. The National Urban League and lesser urban leagues received monies, as did the American Birth Control League.

One of the Fund's major enterprises was the organization of studies of American imperialism, a favorite target of Communist-line preachments. The Garland Fund Committee on American Imperialism was directed by old-time radical Harry Elmer Barnes, who was assisted by a glittering array of leftist academicians, politicians, and publicists including Roger N. Baldwin, Edwin M. Borchard, Emanuel Celler, Paul H. Douglas, Robert W. Dunn, Kenneth Durant, Edward M. Earle, Morris

L. Ernst, Lewis Gannett, Ernest Gruening, Manly O. Hudson, Samuel Guy Inman, James Weldon Johnson, Basil M. Manly, Charles Clayton Morrison, Scott Nearing, Kirby Page, Otto Schoenrich, Henrik Shipstead, John F. Sinclair, Edgar Speyer, Moorfield Story, Oswald Garrison Villard, and Arthur Warner. In its anti-American imperialism activities, the Garland Fund financed the writing and publishing of *American Foreign Investments*, by Robert W. Dunn, and *Dollar Diplomacy*, by Joseph Freeman and Scott Nearing — all three authors were Communists.

AMERICAN LEAGUE AGAINST WAR AND FASCISM
AMERICAN COMMITTEE FOR STRUGGLE AGAINST WAR
AMERICAN LEAGUE FOR PEACE AND DEMOCRACY
AMERICAN PEACE MOBILIZATION
AMERICAN PEOPLE'S MEETING
CONGRESS OF INDUSTRIAL ORGANIZATIONS POLITICAL
    ACTION COMMITTEE
EMERGENCY PEACE MOBILIZATION
FIRST UNITED STATES CONGRESS AGAINST WAR
INTERNATIONAL ASSOCIATION OF WAR VETERANS
INTERNATIONAL COMMITTEE FOR STRUGGLE AGAINST
    WAR
NATIONAL CITIZENS POLITICAL ACTION COMMITTEE
UNITED STATES VETERANS COUNCIL
WORKERS EX-SERVICEMEN'S LEAGUE
WORLD CONGRESS AGAINST WAR

On May Day, 1920, the Communist International established the *Internationale des Anciens Combattants* (the International Association of War Veterans) and appointed as chairman Henri Barbusse, a French Communist. The Barbusse-led organization was the Comintern's answer to the *Fédération Internationale des Anciens Combattants,* to which the American Legion belonged.

In the United States, the Communist Party had been negligent in forming a national group to join Barbusse's International Association. It was not until 1930 that the American Communists formed the Workers Ex-Servicemen's League, and not until 1932 did the group ally itself with the International Association of War Veterans. In July 1932, the Communists' *Party Organizer* outlined the role the Workers Ex-Servicemen's League was expected to fill: "Our task in the struggle against imperialist war: We seem to take it for granted that a civil war will break out at the outbreak of war. But miracles do not happen . . . . We must penetrate the armed forces and establish an organization inside . . . . Work among ex-soldiers is of tremendous importance because they will be the nucleus of the army not tomorrow but today . . . . We must organize the ex-servicemen on the basis of their demands; bonus, relief, etc." Rasmus Borgen, a former Communist involved in veterans' affairs, later testified before the Special House Committee on Un-American Activities. He said that the Workers Ex-Servicemen's League was designed "to spread Communistic propaganda among the war veterans and to disrupt such organizations as the American Legion, Veterans of Foreign Wars, and the Disabled Americans, but this did not meet with success." In 1934, Moscow's International Association of War Veterans ordered the Workers Ex-Servicemen's League to change its name to the American League of Ex-Servicemen. Borgen testified that under the new name "a more friendly attitude was taken toward the other veterans' organizations. The League was not to be known to have any connection with the Communist Party, but individuals were to preach the doctrine of Communism to all new members, or, in other words, to use the league as a stepping stone toward the Communist Party . . . . In July 1936 the American League of Ex-Servicemen was disbanded and its members ordered by the national leaders to join other veterans' organizations . . . . Early in 1936 the Communist Party organized the United States Veterans Council. This organization was to act as an advisory council for Communists working in the American Legion, Veterans of Foreign Wars, and the Disabled American Veterans . . . . In addition . . . a veterans' commission was established in the various districts of the Communist Party, consisting of [a] district organizer of the Communist Party, and veterans who, as members of the Communist Party, were active in veterans' organizations."

Behind Barbusse's Association was the Comintern's International Committee for Struggle against War. Among the American members of the International Committee were writers Sherwood Anderson, Malcolm Cowley, Theodore Dreiser, John Dos Passos, and Upton Sinclair, and two well-known Communists: Ella Reeve Bloor, "mother" of the Communist Party USA, and Henry Wadsworth Longfellow Dana, grandson of the poet. The foreign contingent included Barbusse and

Romain Rolland of France; Albert Einstein and Heinrich Mann of Germany; Havelock Ellis and Bertrand Russell of England; Maxim Gorki of the Soviet Union; Madame Sun Yat-sen of China; Sen Katayama of Japan; and Michael Karolyi of Hungary.

In August 1932, Moscow's International Committee for Struggle Against War (ICSW), through Barbusse and the International Association of War Veterans, issued a call for a World Congress Against War to be held in Amsterdam. The American branch of the ICSW responded by sending delegates, as did the American Communists' Workers Ex-Servicemen's League. At Amsterdam the American delegation joined in a Communist-drafted resolution to "organize to fight against the production of war munitions, prevent the transportation of troops, munitions and all kinds of war materials [and] apply all methods and means however difficult in order to carry on with success the fight against imperialist war." They also pledged "to dedicate ourselves with all our resources to our immediate and pressing tasks, taking our stand: against armaments, against war preparations and for that reason against the imperialist powers that rule us; against the campaign of propaganda and slander aimed at the Soviet Union, the country of Socialist construction which we will not allow to be touched; for the effective support of the Japanese workers who have raised the standard of struggle against their own imperialist government."

When the Amsterdam Congress ended, the American delegates of the ICSW established the American Committee for Struggle Against War (ACSW). Big names from the academic and literary fields were all over the roster: Newton Arvin, Harry Elmer Barnes, Franz Boas, Edwin M. Borchard, W.E.B. DuBois, Sidney Hook, Corliss Lamont, Eduard Lindeman, Robert Morss Lovett, Scott Nearing, Lincoln Steffens, Bernhard J. Stern, and Thornton Wilder. Well-known Communists were also very much in evidence: besides "Mother" Bloor, there were Joseph Brodsky, Joseph Freeman, Donald Henderson, James H. Sheldon, and Maurice Sugar. Other recruits to the ACSW included Oakley Johnson, A.A. Heller, Roger Baldwin, Leopold Stokowski, Lillian Wald, and Ella Winter.

The newly-formed American Committee for Struggle Against War issued a call for the first United States Congress Against War. Among those whose names were joined to this chain of Moscow-directed activities on an "arrangements committee" for the U.S. Congress

Against War were Communists James W. Ford, William Z. Foster, Gilbert Green, Clarence Hathaway, Robert Minor, and Jack Stachel. They were joined by Socialist leaders Harry Laidler, Mary Fox, Julius Gerber, Edward Levinson, Charles Solomon, Norman Thomas, Gus Tyler, and Louise Thompson. Other radicals with them included Abraham J. Muste, Robert Morss Lovett, and Powers Hapgood.

By September 29, 1933, when the First U.S. Congress Against War was held in New York City, there could be no question about the entire operation being completely inspired, dominated, and controlled by the Communist Party. Yet notwithstanding this unmistakable fact, the Congress received the support of organizations whose leaders were constantly denying that they personally were Communists or that their organizations were Communist or pro-Communist. Some of the "supporting organizations" were obviously Communist in nature, such as the Young Communist League, but others included the Committee on Militarism in Education; the Conference for Progressive Labor Action; the Farmers Union Cooperative Marketing Association; the Fellowship of Reconciliation; the League for Industrial Democracy; John Dewey's People's Lobby; the Socialist Party of America; the War Resisters League; Jane Addams' Women's International League for Peace and Freedom; World Peaceways, Inc.; the Women's Peace Society; and the Industrial Workers of the World.

The First U.S. Congress Against War was held from September 29 until October 2, 1933. Henri Barbusse came from France to address the gathering. Others who spoke at the Congress included Devere Allen of the War Resisters League, General Secretary Earl Browder of the Communist Party USA, Field Secretary William Pickens of the National Association for the Advancement of Colored People, and the Reverend Reinhold Niebuhr, professor at Union Theological Seminary. Barbusse set the tone for the Congress when he called upon "all American workers of hand and brain . . . to join as one man in a movement to which the revolutionaries of all European countries have already pledged their adherence – the struggle to the death against Fascism and imperialist war."

The Moscow-called U.S. Congress Against War met at a time when the Soviet Union was just emerging from one of Stalin's idiotic and absolutely hopeless five-year plans for industrial and agricultural betterment. Millions of Russian people were dead or dying from a government-created famine. From a military and diplomatic perspective the Soviet Union was a have-not power. The collectivism taught by Marx-Engels-Lenin had proved unworkable and catastrophic for the people and the economy of the Soviet Union. From a public relations viewpoint, the Soviet Union was a pariah in most of the world community of powers. Information had circulated about the ruthless suppression by the Stalinist regime of religion and all civil freedoms.

A "manifesto" issued by the American Communists and their fellow travelers at the U.S. Congress Against War revealed the desperate lengths to which the Soviet government and its apologists would go to becloud the true status of the Soviet Union and its peoples by trying to focus attention upon Fascism rather than Communism, and upon wars everywhere, with no mention of the war waged by the Stalinist regime against its subject peoples. Mixing pebbles of truth with boulders of lies, the "manifesto," offered as an "appeal to the working men and women of America" and "to all victims of war," said: "The black cloud of imperialist war hangs over the world. The peoples must arouse themselves and take immediate action against the wars now going on in the Far East and Latin America, against intervention in Cuba, against the increasing preparations for war, and against the growing danger of a new world war.

"After ten years of futility, the World Disarmament Conference [in London] is meeting to perform once more the grim comedy of promises, to screen the actions of the imperialist governments which are preparing, more intensively than ever before in history, for a new war. The Four Power Pact [United States, Great Britain, France, Japan] is already exposed as nothing but a new manoeuver for position in the coming war between the imperialist rivals, and an attempt to establish a united imperialist front against the Soviet Union. The rise of Fascism in Europe and especially in Germany, and the sharpened aggressive policy of Japanese militarism, have brought all the imperialist antagonisms to the breaking point and greatly increased the danger of a war of intervention against the Soviet Union. The greatest naval race in history is now on among the United States, England and Japan. The British-American antagonism is being fought out in Latin-America already by open war – the so-called local wars being in reality struggles between these imperialist powers. The presence of thirty American warships in Cuban waters is itself an act of war against the Cuban revolution. The collapse of the World Economic Conference revealed only too clearly that the great powers are unable and unwilling to solve the basic international problems by peaceful means and that they will resort to a new imperialist war in an attempt to divert the attention of the masses from their misery and as the only capitalist way out of the crisis.

"The rapid rise of Fascism is closely related to the increasing war danger. Fascism means forced labor, militarization, lower standards of living, and the accentuation of national hatreds and chauvinist incitements as instruments for the 'moral' preparation for war. It sets the people of one country against the people of another, and exploits the internal racial and national groups within each country in order to prevent them from uniting in joint action to solve their common problems.

"The war danger arises inevitably out of the very nature of monopolistic capitalism – the ownership of the means of production by a small capitalist class and the complete domination of government by this class. The imminent war danger is only another expression of the fundamental crisis of the capitalist system, which continues its existence only at the cost of intensificiation of exploitation and oppression of the masses at home and in the colonies, and of struggle among the imperialist powers for a redivision of markets and sources of raw materials.

"Only in the Soviet Union has this basic cause of war been removed. There are no classes or groups which can benefit from war or war preparations. Therefore the Soviet Union pursues a positive and vigorous peace policy and alone among the governments proposes total disarmament. Serious struggle against war involves rallying all forces around this peace policy and opposing all attempts to weaken or destroy the Soviet Union.

"The government of the United States in spite of peaceful professions is more aggressively than ever following policies whose only logical result is war. The whole program of the Roosevelt administration is permeated by preparedness for war, expressed in the extraordinary military and naval budget, mobilization of industry and manpower, naval concentration in the Pacific Ocean, intervention in Cuba, the continued maintenance of armed forces in China, the loans to

Chiang Kai-shek, the initiation of currency and tariff wars – all of which gave the lie to the peaceful declarations of the United States government.

"Under the guise of public works, the N.R.A. has diverted immense funds from the care of starving millions to the building of a vastly larger navy and to mechanization of the army. The widespread unemployment has been utilized to concentrate young men in so-called reforestation camps, which the War Department is using for trial military mobilizations. The military training of youth in the schools and colleges is being further developed. More and more, national holidays and specially prepared demonstrations are being used to glorify the armed forces and to stimulate the war spirit among the masses. Hundreds of factories are working overtime to produce munitions and basic war materials for shipment to the warring countries in South Africa and the Far East. A centralized war control of industry, along the lines of the War Industries Board of 1917, is being established. As in 1917, it is drawing the upper leadership of many trade unions into active collaboration in the war machine.

"This Congress Against War warns the masses against reliance upon the League of Nations and the Kellogg Pacts as effective instruments of peace. The Congress declares that this illusion becomes particularly dangerous at the present moment, especially when it is put forth as in the recent Congress of the Labor and Socialist International and the International Federation of Trade Unions as a method of combatting the war danger.

"We can effectively combat war only by arousing and organizing the masses within each country for active struggle against the war policies of their own imperialist governments, whether these governments are working individually or through the League of Nations. The Congress declares that the basic force in the imperialist countries for struggle against the war danger is the working class, organizing around it in close alliance all of the exploited sections of the population, working farmers, intellectuals, the oppressed Negro people and all toiling masses and all organizations and groups which are generally opposed to war on any basis. The anti-war movement allies itself with the masses in the colonial and semi-colonial countries against imperialist domination, and gives full support to their immediate and unconditional dependence."

The "manifesto" so eagerly agreed to by the Soviet Union's

American puppets was, of course, only the Communist-line of the moment. Those who drafted the "manifesto" knew only too well that three of the great powers had virtually ruined their own navies, as would be proven a few years later at the outbreak of World War II. The United States was reeling economically from a frightful depression that was being counter-attacked by a President whose advisers were recommending to him panaceas straight from the teachings of Marx. At the very time the "manifesto" was issued, the Soviet Union was feverishly seeking diplomatic recognition from the United States — which became an accomplished fact forty-six *days* after the U.S. Congress Against War adjourned.

The 2,600 Americans in attendance at the U.S. Congress Against War pledged "to effect a nation-wide agitation and organization against war preparations and war." To these ends they adopted a ten-point program: "(1) To work towards the stopping of the manufacture and transport of munitions and all other materials essential to the conduct of war, through mass demonstrations, picketing and strikes; (2) to expose everywhere the extensive preparations for war being carried on under the guise of aiding National Recovery; (3) to demand the transfer of all war funds to relief of the unemployed, and the replacement of all such devices as the Civilian Conservation Camps by a federal system of social insurance paid for by the government and employers; (4) to oppose the policies of American Imperialism in the Far East, in Latin America, especially now in Cuba, and throughout the world; to support the struggles of all colonial peoples against the imperialist policies of exploitation and armed suppression; (5) to support the peace policies of the Soviet Union, for total and universal disarmament which today with the support of masses in all countries constitute the clearest and most effective opposition to war throughout the world; to oppose all attempts to weaken the Soviet Union, whether these take the form of misrepresentation and false propaganda, diplomatic maneuvering or intervention by imperialist governments; (6) to oppose all developments leading to Fascism in this country and abroad, and especially in Germany; to oppose the increasingly widespread use of the armed forces against the workers, farmers, and the special terrorizing and suppression of Negroes in their attempts to maintain a decent standard of living; to oppose the growing encroachments upon the civil liberties of these groups as a growing fascization of our so-called 'democratic' government; (7) to win the armed forces to the support of this program; (8) to enlist for our program the women in industry and in the home; and to enlist the youth, especially those who, by the crisis, have been deprived of training in the industries and are therefore more susceptible to fascist and war propaganda; (9) to give effective international support to all workers and anti-war fighters against their own imperialist governments; and (10) to form committees of action against war and fascism in every important center and industry, particularly in the basic war industries; to secure the support for this program of all organizations seeking to prevent war, paying special attention to labor, veteran, unemployed and farmer organizations."

Out of the First U.S. Congress Against War there emerged a new organizational name, the American League Against War and Fascism (ALWF). The usual personalities were very much in evidence. J.B. Matthews, a veteran fellow traveler, was the first chairman. Before the ALWF held its first national congress under the new name, the Reverend Harry F. Ward assumed the chairmanship. Ward had been for many years the Red genius of the Union Theological Seminary, which sent a steady procession of its graduates into Communist fronts, projects, and enterprises. Ward's vice-chairmen in the ALWF were Robert Morss Lovett of the University of Chicago; Lincoln Steffens, a Communist and one of America's earliest and most persistent Soviet sympathizers; and Earl Browder, General Secretary of the CPUSA. On the ALWF's national bureau were Communists Clarence Hathaway and Donald Henderson, and Roger Baldwin, the perennial leader of the American Civil Liberties Union. There was a sizable representation of notorious Communists on the national executive committee, including "Mother" Bloor, Harry Bridges, Ben Gold, Gil Green, Langston Hughes, Manning Johnson, and Louis Weinstock. They were joined by academicians George S. Counts, Eduard Lindeman, and Colston Warne, along with such well-known radicals as Louis Adamic, Elmer Benson, Bruce Bliven, Joseph Curran, A. A. Heller, Freda Kirchwey, Waldo McNutt, Bishop Francis J. McConnell, Adam Clayton Powell Jr., Frederick L. Schuman, Maxwell Stewart, Mary Van Kleeck, James Wechsler, A. F. Whitney and James Waterman Wise. Under Ward's chairmanship, the ALWF published a monthly journal, *Fight* (known later as *Fight Against War and Fascism* and then as *Fight for Peace and Democracy*).

When the ALWF met in Chicago during September 1934, the leaders claimed that 3,332 delegates, representing 1,807,210 people, were in attendance. When the second ALWF congress was held in Cleveland sixteen months later, the claims were that 2,070 delegates from 1,840 organizations, comprising 3,292,624 members, were in attendance. By 1936, the ALWF was considered by the Communist Party as the best possible "main instrument for the defense of the Soviet Union." At the 9th annual convention of the Communist Party in 1936, it was resolved that the Party would work untiringly to help widen the basis of the League, especially among the trade unions and farm organizations. The Party's General Secretary Earl Browder described the ALWF as a "transmission belt . . . by which the Communists attempt to reach the masses of the people."

By 1936, under Ward's leadership, the ALWF had expanded the ten-point program adopted in 1933 with language that certainly was subversive enough so that anyone adhering to the program was indulging in more than a mild flirtation with subversion. The ALWF was no place for innocents or dupes. It was an organization for dedicated Communists and hard-core fellow travelers, since "the only condition of membership" was "willingness to support its concrete program." The ten points, as expanded, read: "(1) To work toward the stopping of the manufacture and transport of munitions in time of peace or war, and in time of war, the transport of all other materials essential to the conduct of war, through mass demonstrations, picketing and strikes; and to enlist the professional classes in educational propaganda against war and for participation with workers and farmers in anti-war actions. (2) To expose at every point the extensive preparations for war being carried on by the government of the United States, (a) under the guise of 'national defense' and (b) by diversion to war preparations of funds for relief projects and public works; to demand that relief funds be spent only in constructive work or for adequate relief, and that the huge additional budgets now being spent in preparation for war be transferred to the extension of health and education. (3) To resist the increasing militarization of youth in schools, CCC and CMTC camps and the use of their dependence upon relief to get them into the armed forces.

"(4) To demand total and universal disarmament, as proposed by the Soviet Union to the League of Nations, and to support all measures that move clearly toward that goal. (5) To demand that neutrality legislation effectively cover all war supplies, loans and credits, and permit no discretion to the President; more particularly, to promote and support refusal of workers to handle all materials of war; to organize and support public condemnation of those who seek profit from the sale of war materials and war loans; to organize mass support for every effort, national or international, which in our judgment, as occasion arises, is directed toward postponing, restricting, or shortening war. (6) To oppose the policies of American imperialism in Latin America, the Far East and throughout the world; to give the support of our protests and demands to all peoples who are resisting exploitation, aggression and suppression by imperialist powers; to those in all lands who struggle against the war measures and fascist policies of their own governments, and to all who suffer under the fascist state.

"(7) To demonstrate constantly the relationship between war and fascism; to expose and counteract fascist propaganda, both foreign and native; to prevent the formation of fascist forces in this country. (8) To oppose all developments leading to Fascism, particularly the increasingly widespread use of armed forces and vigilante terrorism against workers, unemployed, farmers, Negroes, and other racial minorities, who are exercising their constitutional rights to protest against unbearable conditions and to organize for their own advancement. (9) To resist the attempts of our American fascists to destroy — by legislation, executive order, judicial decree, or lawless action — or guaranteed civil rights of free speech, free press, free assembly, the right to organize, picket and demonstrate; and further to resist all forms of discrimination against foreign born based on their political or labor activities. (10) To oppose all legislation or orders denying citizens in the armed forces their constitutional right to receive printed matter or personal appeals in behalf of this or any other program, designed to secure peace, freedom and justice; and to defend their right to join organizations on the same basis as other citizens."

In November 1937, the ALWF held its third congress at Pittsburgh, and another name change took place. The ALWF became the American League for Peace and Democracy. Harry Ward remained as national chairman and Robert Morss Lovett as national vice chairman. The new name evidently had a special attraction for scores of fellow travelers who had not appeared in the literature of the ALWF. Out of the Red woodwork came Mary McLeod Bethune, Franz Boas, James B. Carey, Paul de Kruif, Melvyn Douglas, Dorothy Canfield Fisher, Abram Flaxer, William Lloyd Imes, E. Stanley Jones, Robert W. Kenny, Rockwell Kent, Oliver Larkin, Max Lerner, Kirtley Mather, Harvey O'Connor, Paul Robeson, Robert K. Speer, William B. Spofford, Guy Emery Shipler, Donald Ogden Stewart, Channing Tobias, Goodwin Watson, and Congressmen Vito Marcantonio, Usher Burdick, John M. Coffee, and Henry Teigan. Behind the change of name there was apparently a change in tactics. The better-known Communists such as Browder, "Mother" Bloor, and Gil Green were no longer mentioned in the literature of the organization. Inflammatory language was less evident. The Soviet Union was rarely mentioned. Instead the new face of the old front was demonstrating concern for labor unions, for Negroes, for the foreign born. The Communists were there in the ALPD, but they were behind the scenes, and they promulgated the Communist line through what was easily identifiable as one of the most effective and powerful front organizations ever to serve the Communist Party.

Much of the ALPD's success was due in great part to the organization of branches in major cities throughout the country. The ALPD also created minor fronts to make itself even more attractive to individuals who for one reason or another did not join the old ALWF with its blatant pro-Soviet bias. The ALWF created the China Aid to urge an embargo on Japan and a boycott of Japanese goods; and a "National Labor Committee" to fight against repeal of the Wagner Labor Relations Act. The National Peoples Committee Against Hearst was directed against "the un-American activities of William Randolph Hearst, chief exponent of war and Fascism."

On August 24, 1939, the ALPD suffered a crushing blow with the signing of the Hitler-Stalin pact of nonaggression. Communists and fellow travelers were bewildered by the turn of events. For years they had been directed to propagandize against Hitler's fascism, his bestial chauvinism. The Nazi regime had been described as "a government system of political gangsterism, a system of provocation and torture practiced upon the working class and the revolutionary elements of the peasantry, the petty bourgeoisie and the intelligentsia." Many Communist Party members, fellow travelers, dupes, and innocents who had worked for the ALPD and its predecessor organizations were shocked, for the Soviet Union and Nazi Germany were now in the same tent, ostensibly at peace with one another. There were defections from the Communist Party and from Communist fronts. Leftwing liberals who had been willing to overlook the barbaric conduct of the Stalin regime within the Soviet Union simply could not countenance an alliance between Stalin and Hitler. For at least seven years, they had been pounded with anti-Hitler propaganda — the Communist machine had done its job too well.

Within a week of the signing of the Hilter-Stalin pact, a rationalization was offered by Vyacheslav Molotov, Stalin's foreign minister and the negotiator of the pact. He explained: "It must be confessed that there were some short-sighted people even in our own country, who, carried away by over-simplified anti-Fascist propaganda, forgot about this provocative work of our enemies. Mindful of this, Stalin even then suggested the possibility of other, unhostile, good neighborly relations between Germany and the U.S.S.R. It can now be seen that on the whole Germany correctly understood these statements of Stalin and drew practical conclusions from them." In simple terms, the Communists were being told from Moscow to throw away their history books and start again on a new venture.

From the Comintern's spokesman Georgi Dimitrov, the Communists in the United States now learned that Hitler and his Germany were no longer the villains. The new targets for Communist abuse were the "British and French war incendiaries" — "America that is feverishly preparing for war" — "an imperialist revolutionary war against the people's interest."

At the 1940 national convention of the Communist Party USA, Earl Browder told the gathering that the Party had to follow "the course for building the anti-imperialist front of struggle for peace, economic security, prosperity, and civil rights, and for leading the American people further on the road to the achievement of socialism." The convention wasted no time in following the Moscow-dictated line, and the Party pledged to "rally the American people against the economic royalists — the enslavers of our day — the warmongers who would trample upon the Americanism which is the conquest of generations of American toilers." The convention adopted a resolution stating that "the Communist Party, knowing that it voices the deepest desire of the overwhelming majority of the American people, calls for closed ranks to oppose the deadly drive, under pretext of defense, to engulf the people of the United States and the two American continents in this imperial war of plunder on the side of Anglo-French imperialism."

Once the Hitler-Stalin pact was signed, the leaders of the American League for Peace and Democracy was searching for a way to recover from what had been a major setback for front activity on the American scene. It was especially necessary to counterattack those forces which were determined upon a course of intervention by the United States on the side of Britain and France in the European conflict. Hitler waited only a week after the signing of the pact with Stalin to invade Poland, and two days later Britain and France declared war upon Germany — Stalin's ally.

On February 1, 1940, the Communists disbanded the American League for Peace and Democracy — the occasion was a testimonial dinner for the League's chairman Harry F. Ward. The dissolution of the League was explained in a release: "The coming of the war which the American League for Peace and Democracy has some years endeavored to prevent, bringing with it the increased attack on democratic rights for which we sought to prepare the American people, has created a situation in which a different program and type of organization are needed to preserve democratic rights in wartime and thereby help keep the United States out of war; therefore the National Board of the American League for Peace and Democracy resolves to cease activities as of this date, February 1, 1940."

On May Day 1940, the Communist leaders announced the new tack to be followed by Party members and their fellow travelers. No longer was there any mention of fascism. Now the Party would rally under banners "for jobs, security, civil liberty, peace." The British and French would be told that "the Yanks are not coming." The American people would be led to "support the peace policy of the Soviet Union," and the major slogan would be: "Stop the Imperialist War" (that is, stop Britain and France from fighting Germany, which had already conquered Poland and shared Polish territory as spoils of war with the "peace-loving" Soviet Union).

The Communists and their fellow travelers wasted no time in setting out on a new course for front activity. The first major move was a call for an Emergency Peace Mobilization. The slogan was: "Mobilize for Peace To Defend Democratic America!" One of the major fronts used to prepare the run-of-the-mill activists for the "call" was the Committee To Defend America by Keeping Out of War. Its basic purpose was to propagandize against a national defense program, the lend-lease program, conscription, and anything else in the United States that appeared as a possible aid to Britain and France vis-à-vis the Nazi-Soviet alliance. In its propaganda, the Committee To Defend America said: "Each day the danger of America's involvement in war becomes more immediate. Yet we all know that the American people do not want war . . . . The American people will insist that the best defense is to keep out of war. They will express their determination to protect labor standards, social welfare, civil liberties, and their opposition to any attempt at regimentation through conscription." The Committee To Defend did not flaunt well-known Communist names in its roll of sponsors. It relied upon the fellow-traveling leaders of "respectable" organizations to bamboozle Americans into support of the new line: union leaders, heads and high officials of Negro organizations, editors of "liberal" publications, and religious leaders. Many of the old stand-bys were in evidence: Harry Elmer Barnes, Franz Boas of Columbia University, Joseph Curran of the National Maritime Union, Henry W.L. Dana, Theodore Dreiser, Rockwell Kent, Oliver Larkin of Smith College, John Howland Lathrop, Kenneth Leslie of *Protestant Digest*, Robert Morss Lovett, Congressman Vito Marcantonio, George Murphy of the National Association for the Advancement of Colored People, Mike Quill of the Transport Workers Union, Walter Rautenstrauch of Columbia University, Paul Robeson, George Seldes, William B. Spofford of the Church League for Industrial Democracy, Dirk Struik, and Oswald Garrison Villard. These individuals and those they were able to bring to the cause, having weathered the storm of the Hitler-Stalin pact, earned their niches in the fellow-travelers' hall of fame.

Those who issued the call for an Emergency Peace Mobilization in 1940 knew that it was futile to try and sell Hitler as a peace-loving ally of the Soviet Union. He was still an excellent bogey for the Communists in the United States to raise as a warning that "a Hitler could happen here." As for the Soviet Union, the best strategy was to ignore mention of it. Thus when the call for an Emergency Peace Mobilization came, it said: "The lengthening shadow of war creeps over our land. Powerful voices — spreading confusion and hysteria — demand that our youth shed their blood on foreign soil. Powerful voices suggest in the name of security that we Nazify America and come to terms with Hitler. They would exploit youth's desire to defend our country, our people, and our free institutions in order to conscript, gag, and regiment them in labor camps. They would exploit labor's desire to defend our country, our people, and our free institutions by the stealthy application of M[obilization]-Day plans in order to shackle labor and subvert our democratic rights. Are we to permit — by silence or inaction — this destruction of everything we have struggled to build up for generations? The few who cry for war are as nothing compared to the 93% of the people who want peace — if the people speak."

From August 31 until September 2, 1940, the Emergency Peace Mobilization met in Chicago, and the estimated 6,000 delegates produced the American Peace Mobilization, which would later be cited by the Special House Committee on Un-American Activities as "one of the most seditious organizations which ever operated in the United States." At Chicago, the American Peace Mobilization was launched with a five-plank program: Keep out of war; defeat militarism and regimentation; restore the bill of rights; stop war profiteering; and guarantee a decent living standard for all.

The officers of the American Peace Mobilization included Chairman John B. Thompson, a Presbyterian minister from Oklahoma; Vice Chairman Theodore Dreiser, the author; Frederick Vanderbilt Field, a millionaire Communist and executive secretary of the Communists' Institute of Pacific Relations; Congressman Vito Marcantonio of New York City; President Reid Robinson of the Mine, Mill and Smelter Workers Union; President Max Yergan of the National Negro Congress; national chairman Jack McMichael of the subversive and Communist American Youth Congress; Vice President Morris Watson of the American Newspaper Guild; Katherine Terrill, literature secretary for the Congregational Christian Churches; and Paul Robeson, the noted baritone. The theatrical and literary fields were well represented on the national council of the American Peace Mobilization by Herbert Biberman, Marc Blitzstein, Millen Brand, Langston Hughes, Carey McWilliams, Carl Sandburg, George Seldes, Donald Ogden Stewart, and Richard Wright.

The most important group of American Peace Mobilization sponsors came from union leaders in the Congress of Industrial Organizations (CIO). They included the presidents of the Transport Workers Union

(Michael J. Quill), the National Association of Die Casters (George C. Peacock), the Federation of Architects, Engineers, Chemists and Technicians (Lewis A. Berne), the State, County and Municipal Workers of America (Abram Flaxer), International Fur and Leather Workers Union (Ben Gold), United Cannery, Agricultural, Packing, and Allied Workers of America (Donald Henderson), International Union of Fishermen and Allied Workers of America (J.F. Jurich), National Maritime Union (Joseph Curran), United Office and Professional Workers of America (Lewis Merrill), International Woodworkers of America (O.M. Horton), American Communications Association (Joseph Selly), Fur Dressers and Dyers (Anthony Baratta), and United Gas, Coke, and Chemical Workers of America (N.H. Annis). Other unions were represented with the American Peace Mobilization by their vice presidents, executive secretaries, general managers, or other high officials. Large union locals and regional and state councils were sponsored with the result that the American Peace Mobilization and the CIO were literally co-partners in a major Communist front. The CIO leaders made a major contribution to the American Peace Mobilization in late 1940 and early 1941 by conducting strikes of aircraft workers, transport workers, miners, and other industrial groups.

On January 27, 1941, at a meeting of the American Peace Mobilization in Washington, D.C., a call for a national convention was issued: "We are in danger. The tragic days of 1917 and an AEF are almost here again. Our trade unions are under attack. The right to strike is being taken away. Our farmers are being driven from their land; their products are selling below cost. We are paying more for food. Our rents are being increased. Our wages are being held down. Unemployment continues and our relief is being cut.

"Discrimination against our Negro people is increasing. Attacks against the Jewish people are being intensified. Our non-citizens have been fingerprinted. There are virtually no jobs for youth. Four million people are being placed under military law. Congress continues to deny the vote to ten million American citizens. Minority parties are being rapidly suppressed. We are being intimidated and spied upon. Our persons and our papers are being seized without warrant. Our Constitutional rights are being taken from us.

"This is how democracy was blacked out in Germany and in France, how it is being blacked out in England, and how it will be blacked out here unless labor and the people unite and act. These things have happened to us because our statesmen and economic royalists are violating the will of the people. Men in high places are dragging us into a war three thousand miles away. This is not a war to wipe out the evils of Hitlerism and tyranny. It is not a war to liberate the peoples of Germany or France, India or Ireland, Africa or Asia. It is not a war to defend democracy. It is a war to line the pockets of corporate interests at the expense of the peoples of the World.

"The Tory bill 1776 would enable these corporate interests to drag America more deeply into this war. It would give the President of the United States the power: To get us into total war against the will of the people. To substitute government by decree for constitutional government. To disregard any law on the books. To give away our ships, our planes, our guns, our vital resources to any foreign country. 'All out' aid to the British Empire or any other such warring empire means total war for the American people.

"There Is a Way Out. The drive toward fascist rule in America and total war can be stopped. Sovereignty belongs to the people. A united people's anti-war movement can save America from the horrors of war and the barbarity of fascism. In order to: Get out and stay out of World War II, fight every step to war. Regain and strengthen our democracy. Defend the rights of labor. Work for a people's peace.

"We call upon workers from mill and mine and factory, from office and railroad and ship; upon the farmers; upon the unemployed; upon the churches; upon the Negro people, the women, the youth, the aged and all, to meet in their unions and organizations and shops and mass meetings and churches to elect and send their representatives to an American People's Meeting in the City of New York on April 5 and 6, 1941, to take the steps to mobilize the people for Peace, Liberty and the Common Welfare."

On April 5 and 6, 1941, the American People's Meeting took place as scheduled in New York City. The significance of what proved to be the first and last national convention of the American Peace Mobilization was discussed in the weekly journal of the Communist Party, *New Masses* (May 6, 1941), by Joseph Starobin: "The five thousand and fifty-eight delegates who came from 385 cities in forty states, the 1,700 or more representatives of labor unions, the thousands of people from peace clubs, organizations of every kind and character need no one to explain the significance of the American People's Meeting in New York last month. Hundreds of thousands, perhaps millions of people, are already being told as delegates report back to their union meetings and community rallies, about the turbulent drama, the excitement, the power of that great mobilization against war.

" . . . The main fact is that the mobilization of the American people against this war is under way. There is in existence, and there is growing, a coalition of progressive forces, of every type and character, bringing forward new leaders from the heart of the masses – that great mobilization which alone holds out the hope of saving our country from the social and moral catastrophe which the misrulers of this nation are preparing.

"True enough, there was an important anti-war movement before the war broke out. Millions of men and women who remembered keenly what the last war had done to their lives, were resolved it must never happen again. Millions of the younger generation, who experienced the post-war disillusion in their most impressionable years, who came of age at the depth of the crisis, were resolved that the only fight worth fighting was the fight against war.

" . . . At the beginning of the thirties, when the Versailles peace was obviously falling apart, new movements came forward, like the American League Against War and Fascism. They arose out of the upheaval in the educational world. Men and women from the working class took a major share in their leadership. They emphasized the principle of solidarity among all peoples. They gave a wide currency to the peace policies of the Soviet Union. They raised the first voice for Spain, for the boycott against Japanese silk. They led the sympathy movement for Czechoslovakia – and as we look back upon it now, these were all efforts to prevent this war from breaking out.

"When the war finally overtook us, the anti-war movement suffered a serious confusion, and with the exception of a few brave folk, an abdication of leadership. The situation demanded clarity on one main problem: what kind of war could this be, if the men who declared it were the ones who had defied the will of their own peoples for peace, had betrayed half of Europe, had collaborated with fascism? The situation demanded precisely the action which this leadership had promised for years: it demanded that the fight against war be carried forward under the conditions of the war itself. In this crisis, the primarily middle class leadership of the anti-war forces revealed its colossal impotence. . . .

"In their fright at the changes in world affairs countless writers, actors, educators, ministers abdicated every pretense to leadership of the people. While they proceeded to confuse everybody else, they insisted that the Communists were confusing them, although it was the Communist Party which first cut through the confusion. Having cut themselves off from the source of whatever clarity they formerly possessed, they concealed their own unwillingness to think the new problem through by heaping ridicule and slander on those who were trying to think the problem through. It was the liberals' last stand. From then on, they could hope to gain a mass hearing only as marionettes of a most brutal, decadent imperialism. They became, as they are becoming, the architects of American fascism.

"The new problem — how to continue the fight for progess and peace — was complicated by two main facts. The first was that the leadership of the forces making for war rested in the hands of the President. It was not easy for people to recognize the vast deception in which Mr. Roosevelt became engaged: the deception of getting the nation reconciled to war by promising to defend its peace. It was doubly difficult because the President's chief influence lay among the workers, the Negro people, the youth and urban middle classes on whose shoulders fell the task of challenging his program. He was able to conceal his intentions by trading on achievements of the past.

"The second complication was different. The instinctive feeling against war happened to be dispersed among hundreds of thousands of families of the agricultural midwest, the seat of the isolationist tradition. There were the least organized, the most difficult groups to organize effectively.

"It took most of the following year to cut through these problems. A beginning was made by the American Youth Congress Institute on Lincoln's birthday, 1940. But it was not until Labor Day of last year that the Emergency Peace Mobilization took form — a movement which had broken with Roosevelt and yet carried the most advanced sections of the trade unions, and other progressive bodies with it; a movement which could tap the instinctive anti-war feeling among the people independently of the reactionary isolationists. EPM was a brave beginning. It came forward at the most difficult time, when France had fallen, when Britain's future course was uncertain, when extraordinary arms appropriations, the unprecedented peacetime draft, the exchange

49

of destroyers for bases were pushed through on the wave of a hysteria that the country would be invaded before the next sunrise.

"By contrast with EPM, the American People's Meeting last month has made remarkable strides. New leaders have come forward, old ones have gained a new stature. Men like Frederick V. Field personify intellectuals who know that the future of all scientific endeavor depends upon organizing the people against this war. That great tribune, Dr. Harry F. Ward, has come out of a temporary retirement to renew on a higher level his great work of the past. Ministers like John V. Thompson, of Norman, Oklahoma, are inspiring a whole generation of young men in and out of the churches to a new sense of personal dedication. John P. Davis, Max Yergan, Paul Robeson — younger men like James Jackson — are contributing the voice of the Negro people. They are champions of a real national unity which terrifies Southern reactionaries, Northern New Dealers. Trade unionists like Reid Robinson, of the Mine, Mill and Smelter Workers, or Joseph Curran, of the National Maritime Union, indicate by their actions that the backbone of this anti-war movement must be the working class, the fact which distinguishes it from predecessors. A man like Vito Marcantonio has given meaning to Andrew Jackson's maxim: 'One man with courage is a majority.'

"But the big thing about the American People's Meeting was its mass representation. Double the number of states, forty in all, were represented, twice as many as last September, most of them from the Alleghenies and beyond. Although the labor delegation, some 1,717, was only a few hundred more than at the EPM, the important thing is that the number of local unions participating, both CIO and AFL, rose from sixty to 500. In other words, the labor delegation this time came from unions where a real discussion about APM took place: they were really elected delegates.

"Some 728 people came as observers from organizations which weren't quite sure they could affiliate with APM but wanted time to decide. This very uncertainty is important — it means that the issue of APM was being debated and mulled over by hundreds of thousands more than were actually represented thus far.

"Whole delegations came from the picket lines of some of labor's historic struggles, from Allis-Chalmers, from Ford, from International Harvester. Key industries like electrical and machine tool, like auto, transport, and communications, were represented. For the first time, coal miners and steel workers made their appearance in numbers.

"One of the most significant facts was the Negro delegation, some 354, a large share from the South.... Some 300 or more delegates represented national groups — the Bulgarians, Slovaks, Poles, Italians, Czechs, Irish, who make up the industrial east. They are a particularly important section of the people. The war in Europe makes a very strong impact on them. Britain has been exploiting their sympathies cleverly, setting up phantom governments in London, shipping men like General Sikorski across to whoop it up for the war. Nobody realizes better than the President how important these Americans of foreign origin can be. Nobody, that is, except APM.

"The unique merit of APM is that it has recognized we face a total war. The rulers of this country are not taking us into just a military conflict, a continuation of the last war. It won't be just a series of battles, on land, sea, and air — which having won, we shall return to life as it was. What they are undertaking is actually a permanent transformation of American life. They are trying to make us into a militarized, semi-fascist state; the needs and aspirations of the working class will be forcibly suppressed; the resentment of the middle classes will be diverted into anti-Negro and anti-Semitic channels; the grip of the monopolies on our economic life will be strengthened; a section of the youth will be indefinitely engaged trying to maintain access to the constantly shrinking markets of a constantly shrinking imperialist world. This isn't just a war; it is a convulsion. It is the paroxysm of a social system in its death throes.

"APM has recognized this fact. Its program, therefore, is a total program. War and peace today involve the preservation of civil liberties, the rights of the foreign-born, the demand of the Negro people for full equality, the maintenance of free education, the right of workers to build their unions, raise their wages, the needs of the little business man.

"But APM is even more. It cannot help but become the embryo of a new political configuration in American life — the answer to the unprecedented crisis in our political system revealed in last November's election. Earl Browder called it the most peculiar election campaign in our history. But what gave it that peculiar character? It was not simply the fact that the executive insisted upon retaining office for the third consecutive term. It was not simply that the nation stood at the crossroads in foreign and domestic policies. It was peculiar because it revealed that the problems of the American people can no longer be solved within the framework of the two-party system. The major issue was the war, but when the people tried to solve that problem within the two-party system, the ruling class resorted to a desperate and dangerous strategem. They picked a candidate on the Republican ticket who they knew in advance would support the President's foreign policy irrespective of his 'campaign oratory.' . . .

"When the people get wise to the full magnitude of the deception, when they figure out the real authors and its implications, there must be a profound upheaval with repercussions that break out of the two existing parties. There will be a revulsion against this war and everything it is doing to American life. That revulsion will seek new political channels. . . .

"The men who rule this country cannot gain the allegiance of the people to preserve the status quo. To millions of people, the status quo — our way of life — means unemployment. It means disease, discrimination, disappointment. It has meant a decade of moral dissolution, culminating in a war which every man and woman dreads. In the last few months, therefore, more and more emphasis is being placed on the 'new social order' that will come when the war is won — the President's 'four freedoms everywhere in the world.'

"But that 'new social order' is even less realizable during and after this war than it was the last time. American capitalism made some fundamental miscalculations, unavoidable but also irreversible. After the last war, it permitted British imperialism to run the world while it cleaned up on the profits. It clung to this policy even when British imperialism was running the world to the ground, when the war against the Soviet Union misfired. The result was that Germany gained a powerful headstart. To defeat Germany, it should certainly be clear by now, involves a long, drawn-out struggle over many years, a struggle in which only the continued fascization of American life — in the face of enormous internal resistance — can bring victory. And what can victory possibly mean?

" . . . Victory is a will o' the wisp. Victory is likely to find American imperialism with even more disorganized world markets, fewer colonial areas to exploit, and perhaps all of Europe gone for the capitalist system. Victory will find us a highly militarized, semi-fascist state — subject to the same dynamic which gnaws away at Hitler. . . .

"The plain fact of the matter is that only a People's Government in this country today — and in the shortest space of time — can save us from the long drawn out paroxysm of this war. . . . Only a People's Government can gain the support of the hemisphere, of the peoples of Asia, of the Soviet Union, of the oppressed men and women of Europe. Only a People's Movement has the vitality, the *élan*, the organizing power to realize those 'four freedoms' with which Roosevelt now deceives us."

Even while the American People's Meeting was being held in New York City, the American Peace Mobilization was supervising a picket-line of placard-carrying demonstrators at the White House. Roosevelt was denounced as a war monger and a tool of Wall Street; the war was an imperialist conflict; lend-lease was a tool to perpetuate imperialism. In March 1941, the official line had been laid down by the American Peace Mobilization's hierarchy: "But even if we don't approve of England's war, isn't her side still preferable to Hitler's; and isn't it better to fight and beat Hitler with England than without her? No. An English victory will result in the same sort of imperialist, anti-democratic peace as will a Nazi victory."

On June 22, 1941, less than six weeks after the American Peace Mobilization's first national convention, and while its pickets were still parading in front of the White House, the American Peace Mobilization was bombed out of existence — Hitler had invaded the Soviet Union; the Hitler-Stalin pact of nonaggression was just a memory. Same faces — new name: the American Peace Mobilization was dead; the American People's Mobilization was alive. Lend-lease was good and should be poured into the Soviet Union. Britain and France were the gallant fighting allies of the Soviet Union in a war to save four freedoms or whatever else the gallant warrior Franklin Roosevelt invented. He was no longer a would-be Hitler or a tool of Wall Street. There was no more ranting and raving about imperialism or colonialism or a fascist America. The Communists and their fronts and the liberals, dupes, and innocents who supported the fronts were now enthusiastic supporters of an all-out war effort. The Soviet Union was now endangered and it behooved Americans to support any and all powers fighting against Germany and its axis allies, Japan and Italy. Where the cry had been

"The Yanks are not coming," now the cry was to get into the war as speedily as possible. And, for the most part, labor strikes and slow-downs became a thing of the past.

After June 22, 1941, the paramount objective of the Communists in the United States was to do all in their power to avert defeat for the Soviet Union. The Communists realized that their objective could not be attained unless the entire industrial and military might of the United States was marshaled against the axis powers. The Communists also realized, especially after the Japanese attacked Pearl Harbor, that Franklin Roosevelt was ideally situated to prosecute the war, and the Communists did not want to see Roosevelt out of the White House until the Soviet Union was safe from Nazi Germany's onslaughts.

In July 1943, two of the Communist Party leaders, Earl Browder and Eugene Dennis, set down the Communist line as to how the industrial and military resources of the United States could best be mobilized. They implied that a Communist-backed political front in support of Roosevelt would guarantee the Soviet Union's cause a friend in the White House.

Writing in the official monthly magazine of the Communist Party, *The Communist*, Browder wrote: "We must unite the C.I.O. behind the leadership of Phil Murray and his clear and correct program for the labor movement, and we must work with every honest leading element who goes along with Murray in the fullest collaboration, giving them our confidence and support without any regard to possible past or present ideological differences . . . . We must build the unit of all anti-Axis elements for the war now, and for the 1944 elections, which are already a practical issue today in the course of the conduct of the war."

In the same issue of *The Communist*, Dennis wrote: "In analyzing the political situation and alignments within the country, special consideration should be given to the approaching 1944 elections. To begin with, we must understand that next year's national elections are not a post-war problem and not a problem to be resolved solely in 1944 . . . . Recent experience has proved that one of the most important channels for developing labor's united action and influencing political developments is in the formation and activity of joint labor legislative committees."

The same message, urging united political action through the power of organized labor, was carried throughout the range of Communist Party publications. On July 7, 1943, shortly after the message was broadcast throughout the Communist Party's press media, the executive board of the Congress of Industrial Organizations (CIO) established the CIO-Political Action Committee (CIO-PAC). Of the forty-nine members of the executive committee, at least eighteen were Communists.

President Philip Murray of the CIO appointed Sidney Hillman as chairman of the CIO-PAC, with R.J. Thomas as secretary, and Sherman H. Dalrymple, David J. McDonald, and Albert J. Fitzgerald as members of the executive committee. Hillman, the head of the Amalgamated Clothing Workers Union, with John L. Lewis of the United Mine Workers, had founded the CIO in 1937, and from the beginning the CIO had been heavily weighted with Communists who were leaders of international unions and who, as such, had led the crippling strikes against American industries before the Soviet Union was invaded by Nazi Germany's armies.

It was Hillman's sole purpose to use the CIO-PAC as a major campaign force to ensure victory for Roosevelt and the Democratic Party in 1944. He wasted no time in putting his CIO-PAC to work. Some CIO-affiliated unions made compulsory assessments for the CIO-PAC's political fund. Union leaders and CIO officials stumped the country making political speeches. Some unions compelled their members to register to vote.

In the early spring of 1944, the Special House Committee on Un-American Activities branded the CIO-PAC as representing "in its main outlines a subversive Communist campaign to subvert the Congress of the United States to its totalitarian program." The SHCUA also found that "the political views and philosophy of the Communist Party and of the C.I.O. Political Action Committee coincide in every detail." The SHCUA also took notice of thirty-four leaders working in the CIO-PAC and offered "a mass of detailed evidence in order that there may be no doubt in any quarter of the fact that these individuals are properly and fairly labeled 'Communist.' " The thirty-four were: John T. Bernard, Lewis A. Berne, Neil Brant, Harry Bridges, Philip M. Connelly, Joseph Curran, Julius Emspak, Abram Flaxer, Eleanor Fowler, Ben Gold, Donald Henderson, Sidney Hillman, Helen Kay, Herbert March, Frank R. McGrath, Lewis Merrill, Lew H. Michener, Saul Mills, Wyndham Mortimer, Morris Muster, Frederick N. Myers, Eleanor

Nelson, Grant Oakes, Jerry J. O'Connell, Lee Pressman, Michael J. Quill, Mervyn Rathbone, Reid Robinson, Harry Sacher, Joseph P. Selly, William Sentner, Seymour Siporin, Ferdinand C. Smith, Louise Thompson, and Ruth Young.

On May 30, 1943, the Moscow-based Communist International announced that it was dissolving itself. It had always been the instrumentality through which the Soviet Union dominated and controlled the Communist Parties throughout the world. To non-Communists, the Comintern was a symbol of subversion. The dissolution of the Comintern was, of course, merely a hoax. The Soviet Union leaders were hopeful that the gesture would be regarded by non-Communists as evidence of goodwill toward the Soviet Union's wartime allies.

On the American scene, the Communist Party perpetrated a similar hoax. In January 1944, the national committee of the Communist Party decided to change the Party's name to Communist Political Association. In the background behind this change was the Teheran Conference, where, from November 28 until December 1, 1943, British Prime Minister Winston Churchill and President Roosevelt had met with the Soviet Union's Premier Stalin. In January 1944, Earl Browder, speaking at a Communist Party rally, expounded on what the Teheran line was — the new line for the Communist Party USA, soon to be the Communist Political Association. Said Browder: "Before Teheran, the world faced two central questions: Was it possible for Great Britain, the Soviet Union, and the United States to bring their full combined power to bear against the main enemy, Nazi Germany, in full coalition warfare, and thus ensure the quickest and least costly victory in the war? Would this coalition, after the destruction of its common enemy, break up into its component parts, each going its own way, and thus open up immediately a new period of revolutionary upheavals and international war that would inevitably culminate in World War III?

"Churchill, Stalin, and Roosevelt in Teheran expressed the determination to 'work together in the war and in the peace that will follow.' This single sentence reflected the insuperable difficulties in waging a joint war without having a joint perspective for the peace to follow, the impossibility of any perspective for a long peace unless the war is jointly fought and jointly won. Both phases of this declaration must be taken with equal seriousness. We cannot accept one and reject the other.

"When Churchill, Stalin, and Roosevelt can say they 'have surveyed the problems of the future,' and that they 'are sure that our concord will make it an enduring peace'; when they hold out a perspective of a future which will 'banish the scourge and terror of war for many generations' – then we may be sure that these three men have found a path to which, as realists, they expect to win not only the great majority of their own people, but the 'overwhelming masses of the peoples of the world.' They were not playing with diplomatic phrases. They were projecting a practical policy.

"The difficulties which stand in the way of such agreement are known. Not so widely understood is the fact that the motive for agreement for the post-war period is equally as forceful as the motive for agreement on the joint war. There is the equally strong motive that without a coalition peace the alternative is the spread of civil wars over vast areas, culminating finally and inevitably in a new World War between nations.

"Those who have said, light-heartedly, that it was the pressure of Hitler that forged the Anglo-Soviet-American coalition, and that as soon as Hitler is gone the coalition will fly apart overnight, were but shallow thinkers who underestimated the depth of the world crisis through which we live. Likewise they underestimate the amount of effective intelligence that has been achieved by mankind. Roosevelt, Stalin, and Churchill at Teheran were the representatives of the collective intelligence of mankind facing the threatening supreme catastrophe of history and determined to avert it.

"Clearly, when Roosevelt, Stalin, and Churchill registered such basic agreement in Teheran, they were registering not alone their own personal convictions, but spoke for a growing majority in their own countries, as well as the rest of the world. Capitalism and socialism have begun to find the way to peaceful coexistence and collaboration in the same world.

"National unity in the United States cannot be built upon preconceived plans, because it must be a compromise between classes, groups, and tendencies which have not agreed on the shape of a plan, and which can only agree as their unity in action takes shape step by step. It is my considered judgment that the American people are so ill-prepared, subjectively, for any deep-going change in the direction of socialism that post-war plans with such an aim would not unite the

57

nation, but would further divide it. And they would divide and weaken precisely the democratic and progressive camp, while they would unite and strengthen the most reactionary forces in the country. In their practical effect, they would help the anti-Teheran forces to come to power in the United States.

"If the national unity of the war period is to be extended and even strengthened in the post-war period, then we must recognize that in the United States this requires from the Marxists the reaffirmation of our wartime policy that we will not raise the issue of socialism in such a form and manner as to endanger or weaken that national unity.

"The most reactionary and pro-Fascist circles in the United States have taken up the banner of 'Free Enterprise' in their bid for power in the 1944 elections. They hope thereby to throw confusion into the democratic-progressive camp, most of which is also committed to 'free enterprise' as a synonym for capitalism. Marxists will not help the reactionaries by opposing the slogan of 'Free Enterprise' with any form of counterslogan. If anyone wishes to describe the existing system of capitalism in the United States as 'free enterprise,' that is all right with us, and we frankly declare that we are ready to cooperate in making this capitalism work effectively in the post-war period with the least possible burdens upon the people. We do not in any degree draw political lines of division for the 1944 elections on any form of the issue of 'Free Enterprise.'

"Even such elementary measures as nationalization of the banks, railroads, coal and steel, although they would obviously make American capitalist economy much stronger and more capable of solving its problems, would be resisted desperately by powerful circles in America. Such measures would not now have even the united support of the labor movement. Therefore they cannot be the program for national unity. The issue of 'Free Enterprise' is not in any way an issue in the Congressional and Presidential elections. The policy of supporters of Teheran must be to seek and facilitate support from all classes and groups, with the working people as the main base, from the big bourgeoisie to the Communists.

"On the whole, labor, and especially the C.I.O. under Philip Murray's leadership, has a magnificent record of support of the war, of all-out production, of patience in the face of provocation, and of firm adherence to the no-strike policy . . . .

"All of labor's present organized efforts looking toward effective political action must be deepened, strengthened, and made broader and more inclusive. All this must culminate in a great united effort in the 1944 elections, to guarantee the continuation of Roosevelt's policies, and to change the political complexion of Congress to make it a help instead of a hindrance in winning the war and establishing a stable peace.

"Obviously, to realize the promise of Teheran the broadest democratic-progressive united front must be maintained in the United States. Equally obviously, the Communists will be a part, and a small minority part, of that united front. The Communist organization will be in a long-term alliance with forces much larger than itself. It follows from this fact, that in the peculiar American sense of the word, the Communists will not be operating as a 'Party,' that is, with their own separate candidates in elections, except under special circumstances when they may be forced to act through 'independent candidates.' That is already our practical situation; and we are now extending the perspective of national unity for many years into the future. It is no longer an 'emergency' situation but is merging into a 'normal' situation.

"All these considerations point to the expediency of a decision that the Communist organization in the United States should adjust its name to correspond more exactly to the American political tradition and its own practical political role. What is called the two-party system in the United States is an old tradition which dominates most American minds. It recognizes as a 'Party' only that particular combination which is in power, and the combination of the opposition which is an immediate alternative to take power. All lesser political groupings are contained within the 'two major parties,' which are in fact coalitions of many groups which in most countries would be separate parties; or if the lesser group takes the name of 'Party,' and becomes one of the so-called minor parties, it is regarded as a sect which has withdrawn itself from the practical political life of the nation.

"We are not in our new course entering any other party. The Communists are not joining the Democratic Party; the Communists are not joining the Republican Party; we are not endorsing either of the major parties, and we are not condemning either of the major parties. We are taking the line of issues and not of parties, and of choosing men as they stand for or against issues without regard to party labels. I don't mean we have any objections to our individual members registering in one or other of the parties when their local community life calls for it and their associates and fellows are following that course. But I mean that the Communist movement and our organization is not committed to any party label or any party organization.

"The two major parties are essentially institutionalized channels, semigovernmental in their nature, through which the citizenry groups and regroups itself from election to election according to the leadership that is thrown up and the issues that are thereby developed. If we are identifying ourselves with any general big political grouping in the country, then it is with the democratic-progressive movement within all parties, and we can say we are joining ourselves with the great body of independent voters."

At the 1944 national convention of the Communist Party, the name change took place, but the Communist Political Association had the same leadership and the same members and, as usual, it slavishly followed the line laid down from Moscow. But the maneuver was a successful political ruse. The Party's faithful — members and fellow travelers and sympathizers — read Browder's message clearly: support the CIO in its campaign to elect Roosevelt and a Democratic Congress.

By the time the 1944 presidential campaign got under way, Sidney Hillman's CIO-PAC had evolved into a much more inclusive group under the name of National Citizens Political Action Committee (NCPAC). The officers of the NCPAC included Hillman as chairman, President James G. Patton of the National Farmers Union and Freda Kirchwey, publisher of *Nation*, as co-vice-chairmen. The treasurer was R. J. Thomas, president of the United Automobile, Aircraft, Agricultural Implement Workers of America; the comptroller was James H. McGill of McGill Manufacturing Company; and the secretary was Clark Foreman, president of the Southern Conference for Human Welfare. The executive committee included Verda White Barnes of the CIO; former Governor Elmer Benson of Minnesota; Van Bittner of the United Steelworkers; James Loeb, executive secretary of the Union for Democratic Action; Lucy R. Mason of the CIO; Philip Murray, president of the CIO; Gifford Pinchot of Pennsylvania; Robert C. Weaver of Chicago; and A.F. Whitney, president of the Brotherhood of Railroad Trainmen.

Members of the NCPAC from unions included C.B. Baldwin (CIO);

James B. Carey (CIO); Joseph Curran (National Maritime Union); Sherman Dalrymple (United Rubber Workers); Albert J. Fitzgerald (United Electrical, Radio and Machine Workers of America); John Green (Marine and Shipbuilding Workers); Allan Haywood (Federal Workers of America); Alfred Baker Lewis (Trade Union Accident and Health Association); Emil Rieve (Textile Workers Union); Reid Robinson (Mine, Mill and Smelter Workers); Frank Rosenblum (Amalgamated Clothing Workers); Willard Townsend (United Transport Service Employees); J. Raymond Walsh (CIO); and Aubrey Williams (National Farmers Union). Foundations were represented by Will Alexander and Edwin Embree (Julius Rosenwald Fund) and Mary Van Kleeck (Russell Sage Foundation). Academicians and religious leaders included Mary McLeod Bethune, Ernst Boas, W. Russell Bowie, Albert Sprague Coolidge, E. Franklin Frazier, William Hastie, Oscar Lange, W.J. Luyten, Wesley Maurer, Francis J. McConnell, Francis McMahon, William A. Neilson, Reinhold Niebuhr, Liston Pope, Arthur Schlesinger, Frederick L. Schuman, Alan Sweeney, and Richard R. Wright Jr.

Writers, editors, publishers, and journalists included Louis Adamic, Catherine Bauer, William Rose Benét, Bruce Bliven, Michael M. Davis, Roscoe Dunjee, Ethel DuPont, John Kenneth Galbraith, Ben Hecht, Langston Hughes, Frank Kingdon, Adam Kulikowski, Max Lerner, Metz Lochard, Carey McWilliams, Hiram Motherwell, Jennings Perry, Katherine Anne Porter, Nelson Poynter, A.W. Ricker, H. Frank Ryan, Sheldon Sackett, Lillian Smith, George Soule, Carter Wesley, James Waterman Wise, and P.B. Young. The theatrical field was represented by Marc Connelly, E.Y. Harburg, Canada Lee, Paul Robeson, Edward G. Robinson, and Orson Welles.

Organizational leaders included Zlatko Balokovic (United Committee of South Slavic Americans); Zarko Bunzick (Serbian Vidovdas Congress); James A. Dombrowski (Southern Conference for Human Welfare); Leo Kryzycki (American Slav Congress); Frank McCulloch (Mullenbach Institute); W.T. Osowski (American Slav Congress); V.X. Platek (National Slovak Society); Martin Popper (National Lawyers Guild); Ira Reid (Southern Regional Council); Mercedes Speir (Richmond Consumers Cooperative); and Julian Steele (National Association for the Advancement of Colored People). There was also an assortment of lawyers, politicians, clubwomen, and a sprinkling of businessmen.

The officers and members of Hillman's NCPAC did not make an

imposing numerical group. However, the individuals — almost without exception — had careers and contacts in Communist fronts, projects, and enterprises which in many cases spanned a decade or two or even longer. The entire group served as a rallying point for those who recognized their names on a national, regional, or local basis. The collective character of the group made the NCPAC an ideal Communist front: the objective of the Communists was accomplished in a highly successful manner, yet the presence of Communists in control was not in obvious evidence. The Communists had learned their lessons well since the days when they flaunted their presence in the American Committee for Struggle Against War and the American League Against War and Fascism.

CIVIL RIGHTS CONGRESS

AFRICAN BLOOD BROTHERHOOD
AMERICAN NEGRO LABOR CONGRESS
LEAGUE OF STRUGGLE FOR NEGRO RIGHTS
NATIONAL FEDERATION FOR CONSTITUTIONAL
  LIBERTIES
NATIONAL NEGRO CONGRESS
WASHINGTON COMMITTEE FOR DEMOCRATIC ACTION

In April 1946, the Civil Rights Congress was formed by a merger of International Labor Defense, the legal arm of the Communist Party, the National Federation for Constitutional Liberties, and the National Negro Congress.

The first Communist front established in the United States for the purpose of agitating among Negroes was the African Blood Brotherhood. It came into being in 1921, simultaneously with the Workers (Communist) Party. The Brotherhood was described in Communist Party literature as "a working class, revolutionary, anti-capitalist, anti-imperialist organization." It was headed by Cyril Briggs, a Negro Communist.

In the Communist Party organ, *The Toiler* (December 10, 1921), the place of the African Blood Brotherhood in the Negro "liberation" movement was described as follows:

"That the Negro people are at last waking to a realization of their rights and, accordingly, to participation in the universal liberation struggle of the exploited masses of the world, must be, of necessity, a source of constant and intense gratification to all workers who are genuinely class-conscious.

"The efforts of the Negroes to throw off the yoke of the white capitalist-imperialists cannot fail to react favorably on our fight against the same enemy. In spite of the folly and blindness of most of their present leaders, the Negroes, to attain any measure of success in their struggle against the imperialist governments of Europe and North America, must come eventually to a full realization of the identity of their interests with those of other oppressed people and of the class-conscious white workers. They are beginning to realize that not all white people are their enemies, and that the same group which oppresses and exploits them also exploits and oppresses the working masses of the white race.

"Every blow struck for Negro liberation will be a blow struck for the world Proletariat, since whether the Negroes consciously will it or not the effects will be the weakening of the capitalist foe of both the 'subject peoples' and the exploited white workers. In like manner, every blow struck for the liberation of the Proletariat will be a blow struck for the Negroes, both as Negroes and as workers. The difficulties which will face the proletarian struggle in Europe and America will be increased so long as the enemy is able to draw on the colonies for material resources and fighting men with which to war upon the workers in the home-lands. This is a truth that, while fully recognized by the Communist International and its millions of followers in all countries, is generally blinked at by the leaders of the British Labor Party and other traitors to the Workers' Cause. It is largely on account of these traitors that the Negroes have not yet been brought to a realization of the primacy of their workers' interests over their merely racial interests. For this reason a short survey has to be made from a racial angle.

"At present there are two great outstanding sections or phases of the Negro Liberation Movement with headquarters in the United States. These are the Universal Negro Improvement Association, better known as the Garvey Movement, and the African Blood Brotherhood . . . . Of the two great sections of the Liberation Movement emanating in the United States and now encircling the globe and demanding full Negro liberation, the African Blood Brotherhood, or A.B.B., headed by Cyril Briggs, appears to have the better tactical direction, which, together with a clear realization of the underlying causes and intensity of the struggle, makes it the most effective Negro organization in the field. It is the only Negro organization that the capitalists view with any degree of alarm . . . . The A.B.B. recognizes the capitalist-imperialist system as the cause of the economic slavery of the Negro people and loses no opportunity to drive home to the Negro masses this most important point. Moreover, A.B.B. tactics are based upon the idea expressed by the Indian proverb that 'the enemy of my enemy is my friend,' and the organization openly seeks the co-operation of all other forces genuinely opposed to the capitalist-imperialist system.

"While placing a free Africa as the chief of its ultimate aims, the A.B.B. has no intention of surrendering any rights that the Negro has won in other parts of the world, or of letting up on the fight for liberty — 'political, economic, social' — in the United States. It is at present carrying on a most uncompromising fight for the rights of the Negro workers in this country to organize for the betterment of their condition, the raising of their standard of living, and for shorter hours and higher wages. At the same time it seeks to imbue the Negro workers with a sense of the necessity of working-class solidarity to the success of the struggle against the capitalist-imperialist system which it asks Negroes to wage both as Negroes and as workers. The A.B.B. is a genuine working-class organization, composed of Negro workers, and with Negro workers at the helm.

"The A.B.B. is fighting the battles of the Negro workers in the political, economic and social field; educating and organizing them to take their place in the class struggle as workers as well as oppressed peoples. So that the Negroes will not rid Africa or any country from white exploiters in order to turn it over to imperialists of their own race but that a Workers' Republic may be established, since only under a Workers' Republic can the oppressed masses of any race hope to throw off the chains of economic slavery."

In 1925, the African Blood Brotherhood was supplanted by the American Negro Labor Congress, also headed by Briggs. The Congress was established under the direction of the Communist International, but the Comintern was not satisfied with the Congress as a viable organization. In 1928, the Comintern resolved: "Every effort should be made to strengthen this organization as a medium through which we can extend the work of the Party among the Negro masses and mobilize the Negro workers under our leadership." John Pepper, the Comintern's agent in the United States, said in 1928: "The American Negro Labor Congress, which is still very weak, must be reorganized and activized. The Communists working within this organization should try to make it serve as an intermediary mass organization, as a medium through which the Party can extend its work among the Negro masses and mobilize the Negro workers under its leadership." Pepper was quite critical of International Labor Defense because it "so far has almost completely neglected work amongst the Negro masses." In order to help the American Negro Labor Congress, Pepper directed the ILD to "put in the forefront of its propaganda, agitation and activities, energetic campaigns against lynching and juridical oppression of the Negroes."

It is customary among Communists that when a front proves to be unsuccessful, one remedy used is a change of name. In 1930, the American Negro Labor Congress became the League of Struggle for Negro Rights. The League was not exclusively for Negroes, although the Negro writer Langston Hughes, a Communist, was the president. His vice presidents included James W. Ford, William L. Patterson, Robert Minor, and Benjamin Davis Jr. – all Communists. His executive board included Louise Thompson and Leonard Patterson – both Communists. The League's national council included such well-known Communist Party leaders as Earl Browder, William Z. Foster, Gil Green, Clarence Hathaway, Joseph Brodsky, Robert W. Dunn, Israel Amter, William F. Dunne, Angelo Herndon, Ann Burlak, Manning Johnson, Claude Lightfoot, and Herbert Newton. This group not only included the most prominent white Party leaders but also the most important Negroes in the Party, all of whom were veteran organizers and some of whom had received their training in the Soviet Union.

In Communist literature, the aims of the League were presented as being to obtain for Negroes "complete economic, social and political equality; the right of self-determination in the Black Belt [more than one hundred counties, extending from Virginia to the Mississippi delta, in which Negroes were a majority of the population and were regarded by the Communists as a 'national' group]; confiscation for distribution among Negroes and small white farmers and share-croppers of the land now held by big southern landlords and capitalists," and to cooperate with International Labor Defense "to fight Jim Crowism, terror and persecution of Negroes generally."

In 1935, the national committee of the Communist Party was unhappy with the lack of progress by the League of Struggle for Negro Rights. After discussions on the highest levels of the Party, it was decided that the Communist Party should form a broad and all-inclusive organization to deal with the American Negro and his problems. James W. Ford and the Negro Commission of the Communist Party were given the direct responsibility for setting up the National Negro Congress. Ford and the Negro Commission went outside the Party for the new organization's president — A. Philip Randolph, the founder and head of the Brotherhood of Sleeping Car Porters.

The "call" for a National Negro Congress was issued "to all Negroes, native and foreign born; to all Negro organizations, churches, labor unions, farm and share-croppers' organizations; to all fraternal, civic, professional and political groups; and to all organizations and persons of whatever race, who are willing to fight for economic and social justice for Negroes." A statement accompanying the "call" included the following:

"Today the whole of the United States faces the crisis of mass unemployment, lower standards of living, hunger and misery. For Negroes this crisis shakes the foundation of their social and economic existence in the nation. For them six terrible years of depression have meant an intolerable double exploitation both as Negroes and as workers.

"Negro workers on farms, in factories and in households as servants see their wages fall while prices increase. Discrimination against them has increased on the job. They can no longer be certain that tomorrow will find them employed. Negro miners are attacked and railroad workers are intimidated by white gangs inspired by bosses into quitting work; and an increasing number of barriers are erected against Negroes getting jobs by unions, which, following anti-working class policies, deny Negroes union privileges and union membership. Negro women are being literally driven out of industrial employment. Negro youth find less and less opportunity to earn a living. This growing futility stunts the growth of a whole generation of Negro people. On government building projects discrimination against employment of Negro artisans continues. Even so-called 'Negro' jobs are no longer available. Unemployment spreads, and in every section of the nation the Negro is fast becoming a jobless race.

"The Negro farm population in the South is fast becoming landless. We face the fact that within the past fifteen years not only have Negroes not gained in land ownership but they have lost possession of more than four million acres of farm land; and, furthermore, there is a steady decline in the already pitiable farm wage. Negro youth is deprived of adequate educational opportunities. A striking manifestation of this appears in the professional and technical fields. Moreover, the present marked retrenchment in education affects Negro students in the South especially, since their separate schools, inadequate at best, are always curtailed first and disproportionately.

"Not hunger and poverty alone plague the existence of Black America. The denial of citizenship rights creates a double burden. The ballot, the most elemental right of a citizen, is effectively denied two-thirds of the entire Negro population. In the courts of the land, the Negro is denied justice. He is illegally kept from jury service, and made to face daily unfair trials and inhuman sentences. Negroes are mobbed and lynched while Congress cynically refuses to enact a federal anti-lynching law. They are excluded from public places, even from restaurants in the nation's Capital. All of these manifestations of injustice have become more severe.

"We believe that this Congress will furnish the opportunity for considering the problems that face the Negro people and that a plan of action – the collective wisdom of all freedom-loving sections of our population – can be intelligently worked out for the solution of these problems. By unity of action we can create a nation-wide public opinion which will force real consideration from public officials, such as no single organization can hope to muster. The sincerity of purpose of all organizations to whom this call is addressed assures harmonious cooperation in the common cause for justice."

The National Negro Congress, at the outset, concentrated on seven issues: "(1) The right of Negroes to jobs at decent living wages and for the right to join all trade unions. For the right to equal wages and equal labor conditions with other workers. For the organization of Negro workers with their fellow white workers into democratically controlled trade unions. (2) Relief and security for every needy Negro family; and for genuine social and unemployment insurance without discrimination. (3) Aid to the Negro farm population, to ease the burden of debts and taxation; for the right of farmers, tenants and sharecroppers to organize and bargain collectively. (4) A fight against lynching, mob violence and police brutality; for enactment of a federal anti-lynching law; for the right to vote, serve on juries and enjoy complete civil liberty. (5) The right of Negro youth to equal opportunity in education and in the economic life of the community. (6) For complete equality for Negro women; for their right, along with all women, to equal pay for equal work; for their right to a suitable environment for themselves and their children — an environment which demands adequate housing, good schools, and recreational facilities; for their right to organize as consumers. (7) To oppose war and fascism, the attempted subjugation of Negro people in Ethiopia, the oppression of colonial nations throughout the world; for the independence of Ethiopia."

The first National Negro Congress was held on February 14, 1936. At that meeting James W. Ford, a perennial vice presidential candidate on the Communist Party ticket, was a main speaker. Others who were active at the Congress included Benjamin Davis Jr. and Louise Thompson of the Communist Party's Central Committee, and Edward E. Strong, a leader of the Young Communist League and chairman of the presiding committee of the Youth Section of the National Negro Congress.

A. Philip Randolph delivered the keynote address, in which he condemned the "hard deceptive and brutal capitalist order" and stated that "the maneuvering and disposing of the forces of Negro peoples and their sympathetic allies against their enemies can only be effectively worked out through the tactics and strategy of the united front." He denied that the Congress was dominated by Communists. He denied that either he or John P. Davis, the secretary of the Congress, was a Communist. Davis was, in fact, an organizer of fronts for the Communist Party. Randolph also said that he was "willing to go down fighting for the rights of any Negro to exercise his constitutional right as a free man to join the Communist Party or any other party he may choose to join."

Four months after the first National Negro Congress had met, the Communist Party's General Secretary Earl Browder reported to the national convention of the Communist Party that the National Negro Congress had "found the correct road to a broad unity of the varied progressive forces among the Negro people and their friends . . . [and] Communists and all progressives can well continue to give it their energetic and steadfast support . . . [and that] Communists have earned an unchallenged place in it."

In October 1937, the second National Negro Congress was held. Major addresses were delivered by James W. Ford; Clarence Hathaway, a long-time leader of the Communist Party; and Louise Thompson of the Communist Party's Central Committee and her husband, William L. Patterson, vice president of the Communists' International Labor Defense and also a top leader of the Communist Party. Other speakers were Max Yergan, a writer for the Communists' *Sunday Worker*, and a veteran fellow traveler; Philip Murray, a top official of the Red-ridden Congress of Industrial Organizations (CIO), and a fellow traveler; Henry Winston from the executive committee of the Young Communist League; Harry F. Ward from Union Theological Seminary, one of the most experienced of the fellow travelers in America; Herbert Benjamin, a Communist and a top official of the Workers' Alliance of America; B.D. Amis from the Central Committee of the Communist Party; Abner W. Berry, an official of the Communist Party; Angelo Herndon, a former national chairman of the Young Communist League; and Richard Wright, a Communist.

The second Congress received greetings from Communists, Communist groups, and fellow travelers, including Walter Reuther of the United Automobile Workers; Ben Gold, president of the International Fur Workers' Union; Negro Communists fighting in the Spanish Civil War; John L. Lewis of the United Mine Workers; Donald Henderson of the United Cannery, Agricultural, Packing, and Allied Workers; and the Communist-organized Southern Tenant Farmers' Union.

The National Negro Congress maintained a very close relationship with major Communist fronts such as the American League Against War and Fascism, the International Labor Defense, and a host of national and regional fronts which were active among Negroes.

In April 1940, the third National Negro Congress met and A. Philip Randolph refused to be a candidate for a third term as president. He alleged that he had discovered the organization to be "deliberately packed with Communists and C.I.O. members who were either Communists or sympathizers with Communists." This was a most surprising discovery for Randolph, who had been hand-picked by the Communists to be president. He had been surrounded by publicly avowed Communists in the Congress for more than four years. He had led the Congress in Communist Party demonstrations. He had cooperated fully with well-known and easily recognizable Communist fronts. The Communist press had served as a highly favorable outlet for the Congress' publicity. And, most important, the Congress during his tenure had adhered strictly to the Communist line in domestic and foreign policy matters. It continued to do so under his successor, Max Yergan.

In 1942, Attorney General Francis Biddle reported: "The National Negro Congress, throughout its existence, has closely followed the Communist Party line, espousing causes and adopting issues sponsored by the Party, and with regard thereto, has sought to affiliate itself and form 'united fronts' with other organizations. It has characterized all legislation deemed a threat to the civil liberties of Communists or any alien or minority group as 'repressive and fascist' and has endorsed the defense of the Scottsboro Boys, Angelo Herndon and Tom Mooney. It is also actively engaged in the current campaigns to free Earl Browder and for the discontinuance of the Dies Committee. In the field of American foreign policy it called for united action on the part of the Democracies (including the Soviet Union) against fascism prior to the Russo-German pact of non-aggression, but after the signing of the pact assailed the 'imperialist conflict' as having 'nothing to do with saving and extending democracy.' When the Nazis attacked Russia, however, the leaders of the Congress advocated all-out aid to the Soviet Union and urged immediate entrance of the United States into the war on the side of Britain and the Allies.

"In the fields of activity normally attractive to Negro organizations, the National Negro Congress has been an agitational force against lynching and all forms of so-called negro discrimination, lobbying for or against legislation on such questions through mass demonstrations, picket lines, telegrams, letters and petitions. In the field of organized labor it has assisted the unions in their strikes and organizational work, and advocates union membership for all negroes. Presently it is in the forefront of the struggle, along with numerous other penetrated or Communist-led negro organizations, for increased employment of colored persons in war industries, greater opportunities for the Negro in the Army and Navy, and for additional civil rights.

"Throughout its existence, the Congress has worked closely with other Communist front organizations, all of which has been faithfully reported in the Communist press. Leaders of these groups are guests or speakers at functions of the Congress or send their greetings and pledges of support, which, in turn, are reciprocated by officers of the Negro Congress. It frequently joins such organizations in sponsoring meetings and demonstrations and is affiliated with some of them, such as the American Council on Soviet Relations.

"From the record of its activities and the composition of its governing bodies, there can be little doubt that it has served as what James W. Ford, elected to the Executive Committee in 1937, predicted: 'an important sector of the Democratic Front,' sponsored and supported by the Communist Party."

In 1946, after being unmistakably branded as Communist, the National Negro Congress was ready to merge with International Labor Defense and the National Federation for Constitutional Liberties to form the Civil Rights Congress.

The National Federation for Constitutional Liberties (NFCL) had its origin in June 1939, when a "call" was issued for a conference on constitutional liberties in America by a provisional committee which included Franz Boas, Elmer Benson, Carey McWilliams, Max Yergan, Ned Dearborn, Tom Mooney, Jack McMichael, and Robert K. Speer — all well-known fellow travelers. The "call" was sponsored by an impressive group of Communists, academicians, theatrical personalities, writers, and clergy. They included Josephine Truslow Adams (liaison between President Franklin Roosevelt and Communist Party General Secretary Earl Browder); George Axtelle; Marc Blitzstein; the Reverend Dwight Bradley; Congressman John M. Coffee; Communist Party officials John P. Davis, Bella Dodd, Robert W. Dunn, and William L. Patterson; Arthur J. Goldberg (future Associate Justice of the Supreme Court); Dashiell Hammett; Attorney Carol King; Oliver Larkin; Alain Locke; Robert Morss Lovett; Halford E. Luccock; Robert S. Lynd; Congressman Vito Marcantonio; F.O. Matthiessen; U.S. Senator James E. Murray; writers Elliot Paul and I.F. Stone; union official Michael Quill; Walter Rautenstrauch; Donald Ogden Stewart; Channing Tobias; Colston E. Warne; Leroy Waterman; Doxey Wilkerson; Ella Winter; and Richard Wright.

The conference met for three days in June 1939 in Washington, D.C. The theme of the conference was set in its "call," which stated: "The long dreadful nightmare of total war has become the terrible reality of

Europe today. Its shadow falls across our own peaceful land. Its horror arouses among our people the fears that too easily become panic, mutual suspicion and persecution. To all the enemies of American freedom, war offers the excuse for its destruction.

"The rights of labor, the rights of political and national minorities, the rights of citizens are under attack. The attack is gathering momentum. With alarming speed it moves toward abrogation of the Bill of Rights and the annulment of all our Constitutional guarantees of liberty.

"Each day's events show more clearly the trend and the pattern. Unless the words and the acts of thinking people call a halt, our democracy will be annihilated. The time is short. Action now is imperative. Responding to the challenge of this crisis, a group of people from the ranks of labor and the adherents of American democracy is meeting in Washington to plan and put in motion a program to preserve our traditional way of life."

The conferees were addressed by Pearl Hart of the National Lawyers Guild ("the foremost legal bulwark of the Communist Party"); James Dombrowski, representing the Southern Conference for Human Welfare ("Communist front"); Max Yergan, representing the National Negro Congress; Elizabeth Gurley Flynn, from the national committee of the Communist Party; Carey McWilliams, chairman of the American Committee for Protection of Foreign Born ("subversive and Communist"); Alfred K. Stern, chairman of the National Emergency Conference for Democratic Rights ("Communist front" — "subversive and un-American"); Josephine Truslow Adams, representing the Descendants of the American Revolution ("Communist front"); Morris Watson, vice president of the American Newspaper Guild; Congressman Frank M. Fries of Illinois; Joseph Curran, president of the National Maritime Union; Frances Williams, executive secretary of the American Youth Congress ("subversive and Communist"); and Edwin S. Smith, a Communist and a member of the National Labor Relations Board.

In April 1940, many of the same crowd, who had met in June 1939 at the conference on constitutional liberties, attended a "national action conference for civil rights" in Washington, D.C. The "call" for the conference said: "Everywhere throughout America the people have swung into action in defense of their civil rights. There is deep and mounting indignation at the attacks on Constitutional liberties.

"These attacks are directed at the people – in homes, in factories, on farms, in organizations. They are directed against freedom of speech, press and assembly; the right to organize and bargain collectively; the right to privacy of membership lists; the right to vote as you please; the right to freedom of worship and opinion. They are carried on with police violence and vigilante intimidation.

"These attacks are initiated or supported, in many instances, by agencies of federal, state and local government. Other assaults, less direct but more subversive of the people's sovereignty, are governmental proposals for mediation, arbitration, super-labor tribunals on a 'voluntary' basis.

"In Congress, now ready for enactment are bills on wire tapping; universal fingerprinting; repeal and drastic amendment of the National Labor Relations Act; outlawing closed shops; prohibiting strikes; deportation or concentration camps for aliens; outlawing minority parties; life imprisonment for 'treachery'; death sentence for 'sabotage'; and life imprisonment for advocating changes in government.

"In 43 state legislatures, similar bills, or worse, are under consideration. In the face of these attacks, the people have refused to give ground. They have moved forward, strong and unyielding, in defense of our American liberties which the forces of reaction, under the cloak of war hysteria, would destroy. From coast to coast come reports of successful action: New organizations to defend civil liberties are springing up. State-wide conferences to defend civil rights are being organized. From thousands of people come mass protests.

"Everywhere the fight for civil rights, though different in detail, in essence is the same. The time has now come to pool our experiences and ideas. Systematic strategy is required on a national scale to defend Constitutional liberties."

The April 1940 "call" was issued by the National Federation for Constitutional Liberties – a new front – and was printed in the *New Masses*, the weekly journal of the Communist Party. In effect, the April 1940 conference was the founding meeting of the National Federation for Constitutional Liberties. The agenda for the first NFCL was a varied one. Panel discussions were held on rights of franchise; labor's rights; discrimination against racial, national and religious minorities; and freedom of speech, press and assembly. The issues under consideration covered the hysterical spectrum and included poll taxes, political intimidation, police terrorization of voters, vigilante attacks upon minority political parties, economic persecution of minority political parties, legislation against minority political parties, federal and state anti-labor legislation, compulsory strike mediation, persecution of labor leaders and unions, attacks on labor by federal and state legislative investigating committees and the FBI, persecution of aliens, American concentration camps, anti-Semitism, Jim Crowism in defense industries and the armed services, intimidation-by-fear techniques such as smear tactics, blacklists, and character investigations used by the FBI, the House Committee on Un-American Activities, and the U.S. Civil Service Commission, and the Gestapo technique of wire-tapping.

The original officers of the NFCL were simply self-appointed and they included the Reverend Owen A. Knox of Detroit as chairman and Josephine Truslow Adams, Vito Marcantonio, Carey McWilliams, Alfred K. Stern, and Max Yergan as vice chairmen. The executive committee included Alice Barrows, Dashiell Hammett, Joseph Curran, Michael Quill, the Reverend William B. Spofford, Robert K. Speer, and Nathan Witt. The Communist Party was well represented among the sponsors of the initial NFCL conference: Thomas Addis, John P. Davis, Bella Dodd, Robert W. Dunn, Ishmael Flory, Albert Maltz, Harvey O'Connor, and Elizabeth Gurley Flynn. The usual complement from the campuses was present: Franz and Ernst Boas, Harold Chapman Brown, Marion Hathway, Oliver Larkin, Walter Rautenstrauch, and Doxey Wilkerson. The faithful fellow travelers' fraternity-sorority was represented by Elmer Benson, Rockwell Kent, Carol King, Robert Morss Lovett, and Donald Ogden Stewart.

At the first meeting of the NFCL, Communist Party official Elizabeth Gurley Flynn, in a major address, told the gathering: "The acid test of democracy in 1940 is the right of the Communist Party to exist as a lawful legal party." Edwin S. Smith, from the National Labor Relations Board, presented the then-current Communist Party line: "The fact that Hitler with the cooperation of a powerful section of German industry made aggression the cornerstone of national effort is closely related to the fact that the fascist government proceeded to suppress parliamentary democracy, progressive groups, the rights of labor, and freedom of expression generally . . . .

"Under such circumstances, the engineering of propaganda to unite the people behind the war effort so succeeds in stifling individual expression of opinion and in thwarting minority thought and action that the struggle to regain lost liberties becomes exceedingly arduous . . . . The first and primary task is to see that America keeps out of the European war. The second is to make sure that the national defense program itself does not become an instrument by which, short of war, the forces of reaction can succeed in striking vital blows at democracy.

"Already the spirit of mass fear leading to attacks on civil rights is rising. Sometimes this has been fomented by hasty and ill-considered acts of agencies of government . . . . So far little enough has been done by government, state or national, to counteract such fears or to discourage such manifestations."

After only two years of existence, the NFCL was the subject of a citation by Attorney General Francis Biddle, who reported: "The National Federation for Constitutional Liberties, with headquarters in Washington, D.C., and affiliates throughout the United States, is part of what Lenin called 'the solar system of organizations,' ostensibly having no connection with the Communist Party, by which Communists attempt to create sympathizers and supporters of their program among those who would never affiliate themselves openly with the Party. Membership in the National Federation, or its affiliates, likewise consists of those sympathetic to the stated aims of the organization, who may or may not be aware of its Communist control, as well as Party members and fellow travellers.

"The program of the Federation parallels closely the Communist Party line of 1940. This adherence to the Party line is illustrated by the opposition, contained in much of the Federation's pamphlet literature, to compulsory military training, which 'would introduce dangerous major steps in the direction of fascist control over the entire life of the community and especially over the labor movement.' It was at this time that Communists were opposing conscription and the entire national defense program. One of the tactics which they used to attack the program was the emphasis on the threat to civil liberties and the rights of labor and of minority groups. Thus the National Federation for Constitutional Liberties served a useful function to Communists as it declared that 'Ours is the task of true national defense.'

"The National Federation represents the principle of interlocking leadership common to Communist 'front' and penetrated organizations.

Owen A. Knox, the national chairman (resigned September 30, 1941), for example, is treasurer of the Michigan Civil Rights Federation and a member of the national committee of International Labor Defense and of the Citizens Committee To Free Earl Browder. Most of the national sponsors and most of the national executive committee and many of the local heads of the Federation are leaders of Communist organizations or are prominently identified with Communist activities.

"The activities of the National Federation have been manifest chiefly in the various committees specially created for the defense of certain individuals . . . . Through pamphlet literature and by appearances of members before legislative committees, the Federation has also been active in behalf of or in opposition to legislation. It has led the recent fight against the continuance of the Dies Committtee, taken up by all Communist 'front' organizations throughout the country. In both these aspects it has operated in close affiliation with the International Labor Defense. The latter has now become clearly identified as a Communist organization and has thus lost much of its usefulness in attracting adherents. The National Federation for Constitutional Liberties is one of the equivalent organizations set up to attract those who would not openly affiliate themselves with Communist groups if apprised of the facts."

One of the major projects of the NFCL was a petition, bearing about one thousand signatures, directed toward the House of Representatives and urging the abolition of the Special Committee [Dies Committee] on Un-American Activities. In little more than four years, the Dies Committee had exposed a large part of the Communist conspiracy in the United States. The exposure included hundreds of Communists and crypto-Communists as well as hundreds of big and little Communist fronts. The Communist Party had not suffered severe damage because of the Dies Committee, but the threat was ever present, and the NFCL was specifically organized "to protect Communist subversion from any penalties under the law."

In its petition to abolish the Dies Committee the NFCL said: "We have observed the divisive workings of the Dies Committee and its chairman, Martin Dies. It is our belief that, on the basis of its record, the Committee must be terminated, because: (1) The Dies Committee, by allowing itself to become a forum for the proponents of intolerance and hatred, has undermined the very foundations of national unity, and has violated our pledge that all loyal Americans, irrespective of their racial, religious or political beliefs shall be united in common struggle against the enemy. (2) The Dies Committee, by continued and repeated attacks on our great ally, the Soviet Union, has utilized its resources to obstruct the cooperation of the United Nations which is a prerequisite for victory. (3) The Dies Committee has attempted, by its unprincipled and unfounded attacks on trade unions and their officials, to destroy the American labor movement which is a vital and decisive factor in the war effort, and which has made the war record of our free workers the pride of the nation. (4) The Dies Committee not only has deliberately suppressed information concerning the activities of Nazi cohorts in this country but has gone out of its way to shield such Axis propagandists as Pelley, Winrod, Viereck, Hudson, Kullgren, Sanctuary, Edmondson, True, and many others now convicted or under indictment for sedition by the Government of the United States. (5) The Dies Committee, to hide its flagrant fraternizing with fascists, has utilized its Congressional prestige to continue an undemocratic, un-American and openly obstructionist campaign of vilification against thousands of the staunchest supporters of the war and of the democratic way of life, and has campaigned equally viciously against government officials and government employees who have been vigorous protectors of our national interest.

"The actions of the Dies Committee are too dangerous to be allowed to go unheeded by the House of Representatives. The American people who are fighting this war for freedom will no longer countenance the shame of the Dies Committee.

"Continuation of the Dies Committee would interfere seriously with the prosecution of the war. The Dies Committee must be discontinued. All obstacles must be swept aside, that in 1943 a united people may fight on to victory. This is a call for unity. We call upon the American people, their organizations, their public officials, and particularly their elected representatives, to join with us and to demand that the House of Representatives — Abolish the Dies Committee as a Step Toward Victory in 1943."

The drive against the Dies Committee had been one of the first projects undertaken by the NFCL's Washington, D.C. affiliate, the Washington Committee for Democratic Action. On May 27, 1940, the Washington Committee held a mock trial of the Dies Committee with

Rockwell Kent as judge. Witnesses were Muriel Draper — a citizen; Leo Huberman — representing the press; the Reverend William B. Spofford — the church; Frances Williams of the American Youth Congress — youth; Frederick Myers of the National Maritime Union — labor; Henrietta Buckmaster — writers; Jules Yanover — books; Doxey Wilkerson of Howard University — education; Morris Watson of the Communists' American Peace Mobilization — peace; John B. Davis of the National Negro Congress — Negroes; and Hugh B. Miller, chairman of the Washington Committee for Democratic Action — government workers.

In 1946, Eugene Dennis and other top officials of the Communist Party decided that the National Federation for Constitutional Liberties should be merged with the National Negro Congress and the International Labor Defense to form the Civil Rights Congress. The three organizations going out of business had been so badly discredited by repeated exposure that their effectiveness and usefulness were at an end. Consequently, the Communists followed their usual procedure — inaugurate another front with a new name but with substantially the same personnel and the same objectives.

The first public indication that there was to be a new front came in March 1946, when an "initiating committee for a congress on civil rights was announced." It included Elmer Benson, chairman of the executive council of Sidney Hillman's National Citizens' Political Action Committee; labor leaders Julius Emspak and Jess Fletcher; publicists Norman Corwin, Carey McWilliams, and Johannes Steel; clergymen Edwin Poteat, president of Colgate-Rochester Divinity College and Bishop Edward L. Parsons of San Francisco; entertainers Paul Robeson and Edward G. Robinson; Benjamin Mays, president of Morehouse College; Charlotte Hawkins, president of Palmer Institute; Evans Carlson; and George Marshall, chairman of the National Federation for Constitutional Liberties.

In April 1946, still another initiating committee issued a call to a conference "to safeguard civil, labor, and minority rights in New York." The "call" stated: "The war against fascism is not ended. An enemy offensive is now being waged against the common people of the United States — labor, Negroes, Jewish people, the foreign-born, progressives and all their organizations — in a relentless drive to establish fascism in our own country." Conspicuous in this initiating committee were Max Yergan, president of the National Negro Congress; Vito Marcantonio, president of International Labor Defense; and Milton Kemnitz, executive secretary of the National Federation for Constitutional Liberties. This initiating committee met on April 13, 1946, in New York City, and constituted itself as the New York Conference on Civil Rights.

On April 27 and 28, 1946, the New York Conference on Civil Rights met in Detroit, where the merger of International Labor Defense, the National Negro Congress, and the National Federation for Constitutional Liberties resulted in the formation of the Civil Rights Congress.

In 1957, the Subversive Activities Control Board said that the merger "was created and established by the Communist Party as an organization which would utilize defense of civil rights for Party purposes and raise and maintain mass defense and bail funds for Party use . . . . [The Civil Rights Congress] succeeded to the role of the International Labor Defense as the Party's legal defense arm. With increasing congressional and executive action in 1948, designed to meet the threat of Communist subversion, *e.g.,* the indictment of the Party's national board under the Smith Act, the Party immediately directed . . . [the Civil Rights Congress] to fulfill its primary function to defend against the threat to the Party . . . . [The Civil Rights Congress'] major activity became the defense of Party leaders, and the Party continued to assign functionaries and members as officers of or to work in the Civil Rights Congress to insure that the CRC would operate in accordance with the Party program . . . . In addition, it is found that such Party representatives constitute an important medium through which the Party exercises continuous domination and control over the operation of CRC."

The Civil Rights Congress did not affect much of a disguise to hide its Communist-front character. Its two honorary chairmen, Harry F. Ward of Union Theological Seminary and Benjamin E. Mays of Morehouse College, were well-known fellow-travelers. Its executive director, Milton Kaufman of the American Newspaper Guild, was a familiar figure in Communist fronts. Its field director, Milton Kemnitz, had been the executive secretary of the National Federation for Constitutional Liberties. The vice chairmen, with the exception of Mary McLeod Bethune, were second-rate fellow travelers; George Addes, the

Reverend Charles A. Hill, Ira Latimer, Stanley Nowak, Lawrence Rivkin, and Vincent Sheean. The real power in the Civil Rights Congress rested with the top level Communist Party officials and influential Communist Party members who ran the operation behind the window-dressing of fellow-travelers. They included Joseph Brodsky, Thelma Dale, Julius Emspak, Elizabeth Gurley Flynn, Leo Gallagher, Donald Henderson, Langston Hughes, Albert E. Kahn, Irving Potash, Michael J. Quill, Ferdinand C. Smith, and Louis Weinstock.

The chairman of the board of the Civil Rights Congress was George Marshall. He had considerable experience in Communist fronts and enterprises as an officer or member in the American Committee for Democracy and Intellectual Freedom, the American Committee To Save Refugees, the American League for Peace and Democracy, the American Peace Mobilization, the American Rescue Ship Mission, the Citizens' Committee for Harry Bridges, the Council on African Affairs, the Council for Pan American Democracy, the National Emergency Conference for Democratic Rights, the Open Letter to American Liberals, the Open Letter for Closer Cooperation with the Soviet Union, the Provisional Committee To Rebuild the American Labor Party, *Soviet Russia Today*, the United American Spanish Aid Committee, Friends of the Soviet Union, and Friends of the Abraham Lincoln Brigade. He had been chairman of the National Federation for Constitutional Liberties. But most important, he was trustee of the Robert Marshall Foundation, established with his wealthy brother's legacy. Robert Marshall had left one-half of his estate, valued at more than one and a half million dollars, for "the promotion and advancement of an economic system in the United States based upon the theory of production for use and not for profit." As the administrator of his brother's estate, George Marshall poured funds into a long series of Communist fronts, including the Civil Rights Congress. He eventually landed in a federal prison, convicted of contempt of Congress.

The preamble to the Constitution of the Civil Rights Congress was a fairly clever exercise of the Communist line. Without a single reference either to Communism or to Communists, it presented the objectives, strategy, and tactics of the Communist Party in its struggle to evade punishment for its subversive activities. The preamble read: "The Civil Rights Congress declares that now more than ever the united action of all democratic forces is needed to achieve maximum effectiveness in the realization of a common program and coordination action in the defense of civil rights vital to the growth of a democratic American democracy.

"All social, economic and political aspects of American life are affected today by the infringements upon American liberties and the determined offensive being waged against the use of the Constitution and the Bill of Rights. The enemies of our democracy hope to achieve their objectives of silencing all those who differ with present governmental policy through dividing, demoralizing, or terrorizing the people.

"Daily, they grow more arrogant in their attacks on labor, more vicious in their assaults upon the Negro and Jewish people and racial, political, and religious minorities. Their objective is total repression of free speech and free thought in America, to destroy our trade unions and peoples' organizations, and to lead our Nation down the road to fascism and war.

"To meet this challenge to the American heritage of freedom and democracy, it is necessary that the people's fight for their democratic heritage and their freedom be coordinated and unified on a Nation-wide basis. Therefore, the objective of the Civil Rights Congress will be: To strive constantly to safeguard and extend all democratic rights, especially the rights of labor, the Negro people and the Jewish people, and of racial, political, religious, and national minorities; to combat all forms of discrimination against these groups or their leaders; to defend and aid victims of the fight for civil rights; to fight against the fascist-minded, their program of jimcrow and segregation, anti-Semitism, red-baiting, and discrimination against the foreign-born. To these ends the Civil Rights Congress dedicates itself — To educate and mobilize the democratic forces of America in the defense and advancement of their civil rights and democratic rights and to assist in coordination of all efforts in that direction. To promote the unity of all groups and individuals dedicated to the defeat of fascism in all its forms. To work together wherever possible and in all solidarity action with all men and women of good will who seek the achievement of these aims. To fight against the creation or establishment of any legislative committees or activities of any agency of Government which seeks to prevent the use of constitutional guarantees by the people or the extension of their civil rights or which victimizes leaders of the people through loyalty tests, un-American committees, subversive lists, and to abolish these."

To implement its constitution, the Civil Rights Congress waged an extensive battle on behalf of Soviet agents Leon Josephson and Gerhart Eisler. It fought against alleged anti-Negro terror and alleged police brutality in New York City. It opposed anti-Communist legislation, loyalty investigations of federal employees, anti-strike injunction laws, and the Taft-Hartley labor act. It agitated on the usual issues that Communists raised to gain sympathy among various groups: poll taxes; lynchings; segregation in the armed services, in public places, and among government employees; housing; fair employment practices; and the high cost of living. It joined in the perennial and widespread campaign to abolish the House Committee on Un-American Activities. It went to the defense of Communist Party leaders and other Communists who were on trial for violations of the Smith Act or other anti-subversion statutes.

The Subversive Activities Control Board summarized the work of the Civil Rights Congress: "The CRC conducted picket lines, issued literature, distributed petitions, sponsored mass rallies and demonstrations, and propagandized ... civil rights cases, principally those involving Negroes, in order to arouse and gain mass support for the Party and its various programs and to raise funds for the defense of the Party. In so functioning, the CRC has, pursuant to the Party's united front technique, associated the Party's struggle with the defense of civil liberties, Negro rights and protection of the foreign born. It has, also, pursuant to Party strategy, recruited persons to join the CRC, for eventual recruitment into the Party. The CRC has raised and utilized in excess of one million dollars for legal defense and bail for Party leaders and members ... [and] has through mass campaigns aroused support for the Party and its policies. It is reasonable to conclude that this support would not have been realized in the same degree without the efforts of ... [the CRC] in its ostensible role as other than a Communist organization."

Perhaps no Communist front ever had more cooperation from other fronts than did the Civil Rights Congress. In the course of its work, the CRC was supported by the American Labor Party, American Youth for Democracy, the International Workers Order, the United Negro and Allied Veterans of America, the Worker's Bookshop, the American

Committee for Protection of Foreign Born, People's Songs, Friends of the German-American, and the German-American Labor Council. In one drive to abolish the House Committee on Un-American Activities, more than five hundred union officials from the CIO and the AFL supported the CRC. They represented the American Communications Association; the United Automobile Workers; the Cleaners and Dyers; the United Electric, Radio, and Machine Workers; the United Farm Equipment and Metal Workers; the Food, Tobacco, Agricultural and Allied Workers; the International Union of Fishermen and Allied Workers; the Fur and Leather Workers; the United Furniture Workers; the United Gas, Coke and Chemical Workers; the Federation of Glass, Ceramic and Silica Sand Workers; the International Longshoremen's Workers Union; the National Maritime Cooks and Stewards Association; the National Maritime Union; the National Marine Engineers; the Industrial Union of Marine and Shipbuilding Workers; the Mine, Mill and Smelter Workers; the American Newspaper Guild; the United Office and Professional Workers; the United Packinghouse Workers; the United Paperworkers; the United Rubber Workers; the United Shoe Workers; the United Steel Workers; the United Retail, Wholesale Department Store Employees; the Transport Workers Union; the Stone and Allied Quarry Workers; the Textile Workers Union; the International Woodworkers of America; the Utility Workers of America; and scores of state and local labor councils.

More than forty members of the CRC had been active in the American Peace Mobilization and more than eighty had been associated with the National Federation for Constitutional Liberties. It meant that the CRC had a hard-core of fellow-traveling activists from major Communist fronts. The membership of the CRC included a large representation of clergy, of university and college administrators and faculty, Broadway and Hollywood personalities, social workers, attorneys, editors, and writers. Among the organizations whose top leadership was represented in the CRC were the National Association for the Advancement of Colored People, the American Slav Congress, Progressive Citizens of America, the Associated Negro Press, the Methodist Federation for Social Service, the *Protestant*, the National Bar Association, the National Baptist Convention, the People's Institute of Applied Religion, the Southern Negro Youth Congress, the *Christian Register*, the National Committee To Combat Anti-Semitism, the Central Conference of American Rabbis, the Congress of American Women, the Federation of Architects, Engineers, Chemists and Technicians, the National Farmers Union, the Southern Conference for Human Welfare, the National Federation for Social Service, and various intra-church organizations.

In 1950, a House Select Committee on Lobbying Activities investigated the Civil Rights Congress and held hearings at which William L. Patterson was the chief witness. Patterson succeeded Milton Kaufman as national executive secretary of the CRC in 1948. Patterson proved to be an uncooperative witness. He pleaded the Fifth Amendment when asked about his Communist Party membership, although it was public knowledge that he had served on the central committee of the Communist Party. He refused to make a full disclosure of the records of the CRC, and he was eventually charged with contempt of Congress. In his prepared statement addressed to the Select Committee, Patterson proved to be in complete control of the Communist line as he described conditions in America with such terms as "legal and illegal terror" — "American fascism" — "terrible menace of racism" — "thought control" — "police state regulation." And he stressed that "the defense of the rights of the Communist Party . . . is the most vital sector" of the historic struggle engaged in by the Civil Rights Congress.

COMINFORM'S MID-CENTURY PEACE CAMPAIGN
AMERICAN CONTINENTAL CONGRESS FOR PEACE
AMERICAN PEACE CRUSADE
COMMITTEE FOR PEACEFUL ALTERNATIVES TO THE
    ATLANTIC PACT
CONGRESS OF AMERICAN WOMEN
LABOR YOUTH LEAGUE
MID-CENTURY CONFERENCE FOR PEACE
NATIONAL LABOR CONFERENCE FOR PEACE
PEACE INFORMATION CENTER
SCIENTIFIC AND CULTURAL CONFERENCE FOR
    WORLD PEACE
STOCKHOLM PEACE APPEAL
WOMEN'S INTERNATIONAL DEMOCRATIC FEDERATION
WORLD CONGRESS OF INTELLECTUALS
WORLD PEACE CONGRESS (PARIS)

*WORLD PEACE CONGRESS (SHEFFIELD, ENGLAND –
WARSAW, POLAND)
WORLD PEACE COUNCIL*

In 1919, the Communist Party of Russia under the leadership of Nikolai Lenin convened the First Congress of the Third (or Communist) International in Moscow. For five years the international Communist movement had been without a centralized disciplinary control center. The Second International, which had endured from 1889 until 1914, had been a rather loosely organized federation of national Socialist parties. The Communists had hoped that, when world revolution erupted, the Socialist parties throughout the world would be incorporated into Communist parties and the result would be a single international Communist organization.

When world revolution did not break out, Lenin became impatient and decided on a new strategy to hasten the event. He explained: "The First International [1864-1876] laid the foundations of the proletarian, international struggle for Socialism. The Second International [1889-1914] marked the epoch in which the soil was prepared for a broad, mass, widespread movement in a number of countries. The Third (Communist) International gathered the fruits of the work of the Second International, purged it of its opportunistic, social-chauvinist, bourgeois and petty-bourgeois dross, and has begun to effect the dictatorship of the proletariat." To effect the "purge" of the Second International, Lenin invited only left-wing Socialists to the First Congress of the Third International.

Lenin laid down strict rules for the Third International, which would be known as the Comintern. He was creating a world-wide, highly disciplined army. He said: "The parties affiliated to the Communist International must be built on the principle of democratic centralism. In the present epoch of acute civil war the Communist Party will be able to perform its duty only if it is organised in the most centralised manner, only if iron discipline bordering on military discipline prevails in it, and if its party centre is a powerful organ of authority, enjoying wide powers and the general confidence of the members of the Party."

Lenin emerged from the First Congress of the Comintern in control of his own Russian Communist Party and the Communist Parties of Bulgaria, Finland, France, Italy, the Netherlands, Norway, Slovakia, Sweden, Switzerland, and the United States. Other Communist Parties throughout the world soon fell in line and joined the Comintern.

At the Second Congress of the Comintern in 1920, Lenin spoke in plain terms of his ambitions for world conquest by Communism: ".... Everywhere we have a proletarian army, although sometimes badly organised, needing reorganisation; and if our international comrades now help us to organise a united army, no shortcomings will hinder us in the pursuit of our cause. And this cause is the world proletarian revolution, the cause of creating a worldwide Soviet Republic."

At the same time Lenin boasted: "The Congress created a solidarity and discipline of Communist Parties the world over such as has never existed before, and which will enable the vanguard of the workers' revolution to march forward to its great goal, the overthrow of the yoke of capital, with seven-league strides."

The members of the Comintern were told explicitly that their major task was to subvert non-Communist governments: "Communism rejects parliamentarism as the form of the future; it rejects it as a form of the class dictatorship of the proletariat; it rejects the possibility of winning over the parliaments permanently; its fixed aim is to destroy parliamentarism. Therefore there can be a question only of utilizing bourgeois state institutions with the object of destroying them. – It is necessary, immediately, for all legal Communist Parties to form illegal organizations for the purpose of systematically carrying on illegal work, and of fully preparing for the moment when the bourgeoisie resorts to persecution. Illegal work is particularly necessary in the army, the navy and police . . . ."

From 1919 until 1943, the Comintern operated out of Moscow and was in the hands of Communist leaders of the Soviet Union. Communist Parties throughout the world were dominated and controlled by the Comintern, which used its affiliates as a major instrumentality of the Soviet Union's foreign policy. This policy included the subversion of non-Communist governments by the instigation of class warfare and social revolution.

In 1943, the Comintern's hierarchy under the leadership of Stalin accomplished a major propaganda coup by announcing the dissolution of the Comintern. In effect, the Soviet Union told its gullible wartime allies that subversion of non-Communist governments was no longer the keystone of Soviet foreign policy and world revolution, for the realization of a "worldwide Soviet republic" was no longer a goal. The announced dissolution of the Comintern could not have been phonier. From the Kremlin to Communists everywhere, the real instructions were to carry on business as usual. The ritual of formal dissolution was carried on for the benefit of gullible national leaders who were desperately eager to believe that Stalin was a trustworthy ally and a man of good will. The Presidium of the Executive Committee of the Comintern proposed in 1943: "The Communist International, as the directing center of the international working class movement, is to be dissolved, thus freeing the sections of the Communist International from their obligations arising from the statutes and resolutions of the Congresses of the Communist International." Not a single affiliate disagreed with the proposal and for worldwide public consumption the Comintern was out of business. However, the Comintern never interrupted its work for a moment — only the name was gone. A Spanish Communist, Enrique Castro Delgado, who worked in Moscow for the Comintern, described just what transpired after the "dissolution" of 1943: "There was no doubt whatsoever that the dissolution was nothing but a formality. [Georgi] Dimitrov [Secretary General of the Communist International] no longer has his office in the building situated to the right of the Agricultural Exposition where the Comintern was housed before its dissolution; he has it now on the third floor of one of the buildings of the Central Committee of the Russian Communist Party. The other secretaries likewise have their offices in different places. The offices of Dolores Ibarruri, [Mathias] Rakosi and Ana Pauker are on the Place of the Soviet, in front of the building of the Moscow Soviet, in a small house with a garden and a fountain . . . .

"The rest of us, members of the editorial boards of the clandestine broadcasting, no longer have to submit to the censorship of Togliatti, but to that of Friedrich, who turns over our copy to Togliatti, who turns it over to Dimitrov. Everything is just as it used to be. The heads of the foreign parties' delegations, as the ex-secretaries, continue to consult Dimitrov, either meeting him personally or getting instructions from him through Stepanov. Everything is just as it used to be. The cadre's section keeps its offices and its files, which grow with every change in the direction of the parties. Everything is just as it used to be. The foreign press correspondents of the Comintern continue to send information periodically on everything that is going on in the world to the Section of Information and Propaganda of the 'dissolved' Comintern. Everything is just as it used to be.

"The secret apparatus of the 'dissolved' Comintern keeps its offices on the main floor of the former Comintern building. And it continues to receive the secret reports of the parties, one copy of which is sent to Dimitrov and another copy to the Foreign Section of the Russian Communist Party, headed by [Andrei] Zhdanov. It continues to send out Dimitrov's instructions to different Communist parties abroad, to organize trips of persons summoned to the Soviet Union or to arrange their departure. Everything is just as it used to be."

To ensure that Communist Parties throughout the world did not waver in their allegiance to the "dissolved" Comintern, foreign leaders of the Comintern returned to their native countries to assume personal control of their respective Communist Parties: Dimitrov to Bulgaria, Rakosi to Hungary, Otto Kuusinen to Finland, Klement Gottwald to Czecho-Slovakia, Palmiro Togliatti to Italy, Maurice Thorez to France, Sanzo Nozaka to Japan, Boleslaw Bierut to Poland, Wilhelm Pieck to Germany, and Li Li-san to Manchuria.

In the United States, the Communist Party not only agreed to the "dissolution" of the Comintern but even dissolved itself in a phony move. In May 1944, at a national convention, the CPUSA voted dissolution, and the Communists immediately re-grouped as the Communist Political Association. Party leader Earl Browder explained for the benefit of gullible Americans: "In the interest of national unity and to enable the Communists to function most effectively in the changed political conditions and to make still greater contributions towards winning the war and securing a durable peace, . . . the American Communists should renounce the aim of partisan advancement and the Party form of organization." Party members, however, could read in their own magazine, *The Communist*, that the change of name was really as meaningless as the "dissolution" of the Comintern and CPUSA. Eugene Dennis, a Communist leader, wrote: "We Communists will be called upon to multiply our mass work, including during the elections, in collaboration with the other sectors of national unity, with all win-the-war forces, especially with the trade unions. This will not only require the most active participation of the Communists in labor's political organizations and campaigns, it will also necessitate a great strengthening and expansion of our independent, Communist political activity. It will especially require that we vastly improve and multiply our mass agitation and propaganda, our Communist political-education mass work, nationally and on a local scale. It will further require that we bring about a radical improvement in the Marxist-Leninist training and development of all party personnel and members, particularly of our trade union cadres, so that we will be better equipped, theoretically and practically, to meet our great responsibilities, to solve the complex strategic and tactical problems of the new historical period we are entering.

"Finally, it is clear that whatever changes we may make in our party's name and electoral status, the fundamental objective and characteristics of our party will remain. For, irrespective of name, we are and shall continue to be an American working class political organization, guided by the science of Marxism-Leninism. And because of this, now and on the morrow, we shall be in the vanguard, defending and promoting, at all times, the vital interests and welfare of the working class and of our nation and people."

The Communist Political Association, as a name, lasted only until June 1945, when the Communists, after working for the reelection of President Franklin D. Roosevelt, reverted to their old name of Communist Party, U.S.A.

In September 1945, the Communist leaders in the Soviet Union decided that the time was opportune to bring the Comintern up from its four-year underground position. At a secret meeting in Poland, Communist Party leaders from the Soviet Union, Bulgaria, Czecho-Slovakia, France, Hungary, Italy, Poland, Rumania, and Yugoslavia instituted the Information Bureau of the Communist and Workers Parties, known as the Cominform. The ostensible excuse for the secret meeting was "to arrange for closer integration of policies which had begun to be overshadowed by nationalist sentiment" and to counteract the "disunity of Communist Parties."

The leading figure at the founding meeting of the Cominform was Andrei Zhdanov of the Soviet Union, formerly the major spokesman for the Comintern. He told the Cominform delegates: "The fundamental changes caused by the war on the international scene and in the position of individual countries has entirely changed the political landscape of the world. A new alignment of political forces has arisen. The more the war recedes into the past, the more distinct become two major trends in post-war international policy, corresponding to the division of the political forces operating on the international arena into two major camps; the imperialist and anti-democratic camp, on the one hand, and the anti-imperialist and democratic camp, on the other. The principal driving force of the imperialist camp is the USA. Allied with it are Great Britain and France .... The anti-fascist forces comprise the second camp. This camp is based on the USSR and the new democracies. It also includes countries that have broken with imperialism and have firmly set foot on the path of democratic development, such as Rumania, Hungary, and Finland .... The anti-imperialist camp is backed by the labor and democratic movement and by the fraternal Communist Parties in all countries, by the fighters for national liberation in the colonies and dependencies, by all progressive and democratic forces in every country. The purpose of this camp is to resist the threat of new wars and imperialist expansion, to strengthen democracy and to extirpate the vestiges of fascism .... The change in the general alignment of forces between the capitalist world and the Socialist world brought about by the war has still further enhanced the significance of the foreign policy of the Soviet state and enlarged the scope of its activity on the international arena."

William Z. Foster, chairman of the CPUSA, played his role as Zhdanov's puppet to perfection when he issued a pamphlet ("The Meaning of the Nine-Party Conference") in which he interpreted the significance of the Cominform for his comrades: "The simple reality is that the nine-party Communist conference, and the Information Bureau which it set up, have as their purpose to put the peoples of Europe on guard against the attempt of Wall Street imperialism to conquer and enslave them .... The nine Communist Parties, in their joint conference, were also correct in warning their nations and all humanity of the Fascist danger involved in the offensive of Wall Street imperialism against the peoples of Europe and the rest of the world .... The statement of the nine Communist Parties also does a major service in awakening the peoples of Europe and the world to the growing danger of a new world war, as a consequence of the ruthless expansionist drive of American big business."

A manifesto that emanated from the first meeting of the Cominform was an all-out attack upon the United States, which was portrayed as the archenemy of the anti-fascist forces – the Communists. The United

States was described as having fought in World War II for the "elimination of competition on the world market and the consolidation of their dominant position," while the Soviet Union and its satellites were portrayed as having fought for democracy and against fascism. In the postwar period, the United States was charged with being an aggressor in military, strategic, economic, and ideological areas, while the Communists were simply seeking "peace and friendship."

Although only nine European Communist parties were represented at the Cominform meeting, Communists throughout the world were reminded that the Comintern was back in business under a new name: "Certain comrades considered the disbandment of the Comintern as a liquidation of all ties and contacts between them and their Communist brother parties. But experience demonstrates that such a separation of the Communist parties is . . . harmful and unnatural . . . . Even Communists of countries connected by an alliance feel impaired in their efforts to establish relations of friendship . . . . The continuation of such a dispersal of forces could lead to a weakening of mutual understanding and even to serious mistakes."

No matter the appearance of the Cominform as an "information bureau" exclusively supported by nine European Communist parties, it was the major vehicle of communication between the Communist Party of the Soviet Union and its affiliated branches throughout the world, including the United States. The chief propaganda gimmick in the Cominform's work was the representation of the Soviet Union as being in search of peace and the United States, in search of imperialism. The Cominform reached Communists everywhere with its propaganda message through its publication, *For a Lasting Peace, For a People's Democracy*, which was required instructional reading for every Communist in the United States.

One of the first moves made under the auspices of the Cominform was the publication of an open letter, signed by twelve well-known Soviet writers and addressed to "writers and men of culture in the United States of America." The theme of the letter was that Soviet intellectuals wished to find their counterparts in America who were willing to join in a "peace" campaign to offset the imperialistic and fascistic elements in the United States. The letter read, in part: "The ideas of fascism . . . have of late been constantly finding champions and proponents among prominent statesmen, diplomats, military men, industrialists, journalists, and even scientists in your country . . . . Men of letters, men of art and culture, are people whose lips are not to be sealed so easily by police truncheons, by gags, or banknotes. The peoples of the world want to hear their voices from the pages of newspapers, magazines, and books, from the boards of theaters, from canvases and screens . . . . We call upon you, masters of American culture, to raise your voice against the new threat of fascism, against the instigators of war . . . ."

The response to the Soviet writers' open letter was given in the United States in the pages of the Communist monthly, *Masses and Mainstream*, by fifteen Communists: James S. Allen, Herbert Aptheker, Alvah Bessie, Richard O. Boyer, Howard Fast, Ben Field, Barbara Giles, V.J. Jerome, Meridel LeSueur, A.B. Magil, Joseph North, Isidor Schneider, Howard Selsam, Samuel Sillen, and Doxey Wilkerson. The American Communists, presuming to speak for the American intellectual community, willingly joined in the condemnation of the United States as hell-bent on militaristic imperialism throughout the world.

With the response from America, the way was paved for the Cominform to convoke a World Congress of Intellectuals from August 25 to August 28, 1948, at Wroclaw, Poland. Americans who went to Wroclaw included writers George Abbe, Saul Carson, Norman Corwin, Albert E. Kahn, Edita Morris, J.V. Morris, Donald Ogden Stewart, Juri Suhl, and Ella Winter; sculptor Jo Davidson; attorneys Clifford Durr and O. John Rogge; Dr. and Mrs. Jack Paradise; artist William Gropper; publisher Freda Kirchwey; actress Catherine Corwin; academicians Leta Cromwell, G.S. Delatour, Bryn J. Hovde, and Colston E. Warne; social worker J.H. Smith; businessman Nathan D. Sachs; psychologist E.T. Prothro; painter Florence Davidson; journalist Yaroslaw Chyz; Virginia Durr; James Sheldon; Jacques Ferrand; and astronomer Harlow Shapley.

The tone of the World Congress of Intellectuals was set by Alexander Fadayev, the general secretary of the Union of Soviet Writers, who said: "American monopolists find beasts indispensable for the realization of their plans for world domination. Reactionary writers, scientists, philosophers, and artists are ready to serve their masters. They place on a pedestal schizophrenics and drug addicts, sadists and pimps, provocateurs and monsters, spies and gangsters. These beast-like creatures fill the pages of novels, volumes of poetry, casts of moving pictures.

"The imperialists of that country, whose façade by the irony of fate is adorned by the Statue of Liberty, have taken upon themselves in great haste the role of conspirators and organizers of a new war. After the Second World War, the entire world was divided into two camps: the democratic, antifascist, anti-imperialist camp led by the Soviet Union, and the antidemocratic, reactionary, imperialist camp led by the ruling circles of the United States of America."

The main American speaker at Wroclaw was Albert E. Kahn, whose remarks were the subject of a commentary in the *New Times* of Moscow: "Albert E. Kahn, member of the American Progressive Party and a well-known publicist, agreed with those delegates who compared modern American policy to the policy of Hitlerite Germany, which had unleashed the Second World War. The Hitlerites started off in the same way as America's ruling circles are now proceeding. In a vivid speech, replete with factual material, Albert E. Kahn stressed that power in America had been seized by a small but extremely powerful group of financiers and industrialists. The Truman doctrine and Marshall plan, he said, were not the brain child of the American people, but the monstrosity of Washington and Wall Street."

Through its journal, *For A Lasting Peace, For A People's Democracy*, the Cominform described the World Congress of Intellectuals as "proof of the great progress made by the intellectuals after World War II" and "the strivings of the intellectuals to unite in the struggle for peace." In the same item, the Cominform said: "The [Wroclaw] Congress' decisions confront the Communist Parties and especially the Communist intellectuals with the important and honorable task of being in the forefront – in bringing together and organizing the intellectuals of their countries for the defense of peace and culture."

The Cominform's "peace" drive was in full gear after Wroclaw and the Cominform issued directives on strategy and tactics to be employed in furtherance of the drive: "Particular attention should be devoted to drawing into the peace movement trade-unions, women's, youth, cooperative, sport, cultural, education, religious, and other organizations, and also scientists, writers, journalists, cultural workers, parliamentary, and other political and public leaders." Communists were instructed to infiltrate "all mass public associations" and to spread the Soviet peace propaganda by "mass demonstrations, meetings, rallies, drawing up of petitions and protests, questionnaires, formation of peace committees in towns and in the countryside." They were further told that "it is necessary to proceed from the concrete conditions in each country, skillfully combining various forms and methods of the movement with the general tasks."

Out of the World Congress of Intellectuals at Wroclaw there developed a permanent International Committee of Intellectuals in Defense of Peace, with a program calling for national branches and national meetings similar to the Wroclaw congress.

In the United States, the response to the Wroclaw program was the Scientific and Cultural Conference for World Peace, held in New York City on March 25, 26, and 27, 1949. It was a "peace" congress inaugurated by the National Council of the Arts, Sciences and Professions. The National Council was an offshoot of the Independent Citizens Committee of the Arts, Sciences, and Professions.

The Independent Citizens Committee was organized by Lionel Berman, a Communist. Former Communist Party official Louis Budenz testified under oath: "The Independent Citizens Committee of the Arts, Sciences, and Professions was worked out originally in my office in the *Daily Worker*. It was worked out by the cultural commission of the *Daily Worker*, of which Lionel Berman, the cultural section organizer of the Party, was a member, and he was entrusted not only by that meeting but by the political committee, as the result of these discussions, with the task of forming the Independent Citizens Committee of the Arts, Sciences, and Professions."

Among the sponsors of the Scientific and Cultural Conference who belonged to the Berman-organized Independent Citizens Committee were Louis Adamic, Gregory Ain, Samuel L.M. Barlow, Leonard Bernstein, Henry Blankfort, Kermit Bloomgarden, Ernst P. Boas, Theodore Brameld, Millen Brand, Henrietta Buckmaster, Rufus F. Clement, Aaron Copland, Norman Corwin, Leo Davidoff, Jo Davidson, Olin Downes, Paul Draper, Albert Einstein, Philip Evergood, Henry Pratt Fairchild, Howard Fast, Jose Ferrer, E.Y. Harburg, Lillian Hellman, Ira Hirschmann, Langston Hughes, Crockett Johnson, Robert W. Kenny, I.M. Kolthoff, Leon Kroll, John Howard Lawson, Ring Lardner, Thomas Mann, John McManus, Linus Pauling, John P. Peters, Walter Rautenstrauch, Paul Robeson, Harold Rome, Artur Schnabel, Artie Shaw, Harlow Shapley, Herman Shumlin, John Sloan, Donald Ogden Stewart, Dalton Trumbo, and Max Weber.

The Scientific and Cultural Conference had what proved to be a five point program: "(1) To provide a propagandist forum against the Marshall plan, the North Atlantic defense pact, and American foreign policy in general. (2) To promote support for the foreign policy of the Soviet Union. (3) To mobilize American intellectuals in the field of arts, science, and letters behind this program, even to the point of civil disobedience against the American Government. (4) To prepare the way for a subsequent world peace congress in Paris on April 20 to 24, 1949, with similar aims on a world scale and under similar Communist auspices. (5) To discredit American culture and to extol the virtues of Soviet culture."

Members of the Communist Party were very much in evidence at the Scientific and Cultural Conference. They included Alexander Trachtenberg, the head of the Party's International Publishers; John Gates of the Party's national board; Claudia Jones of the Party's national committee; Thomas Addis, Herbert Aptheker, James Aronson, Edward K. Barsky, Howard Fast, William Gropper, Kyle Crichton, and Richard Boyer. Also present were Communists from the Soviet Union and its satellites. Among the American fellow travelers who took a very active part in the proceedings of the Conference were Dorothy Brewster, Donovan J. McCune, Theodor Rosebury, and Gene Weltfish of Columbia University; clergymen Shelton Hale Bishop, John Howland Lathrop, S. Harrington Littell, Arthur W. Moulton, Louis Newman, and Guy Emery Shipler; Allan M. Butler, F.O. Matthiessen, Harlow Shapley, and Walter Orr Roberts of Harvard University; Herbert John Davis of Smith College; John J. DeBoer of the University of Illinois; Marshall E. Dimock of Northwestern University; Henry Pratt Fairchild of New York University; John Gillen of the University of North Carolina; W.A. Higinbotham of Brookhaven National Laboratory; Hayward Keniston of the University of Michigan; Ira De A. Reid of Haverford College; Rose Russell of the United Public Workers; Henry T. Shotwell of the American Institute of Architects; Colston W. Warne of Amherst College; newsmen Olin Downes of the *New York Times* and T.O. Thackrey of the *New York Post*; Negro leader W.E.B. DuBois and his wife Shirley Graham; screenwriter John Howard Lawson; Bert James Loewenberg of Sarah Lawrence College; attorneys Clifford Durr and O. John Rogge; novelist Norman Mailer; poet Louis Untermeyer; radio commentator Arthur Gaeth; Victor Bernstein; Aaron Copland; Phillip

Evergood; Howard Fast; Morton Gould; Jacob Lawrence; Ray Lev; David M. Lubbock; Charles A. Madison; Grace E. Marcus; Albert Mayer; Philip Morrison; Clifford Odets; Anton Refregier; Julius Schreiber; Agnes Smedley; Isidor F. Stone; Paul Sweezy; Helen Tamiris; Allan A. Twichell; Henry Agard Wallace; Sam Wanamaker; Theodore Ward; Henry Willcox; Ira Wolfert; and Edward Young.

One of the largest groups among the sponsors was the clergy, including Charles B. Ackley, Stacy Adams, Wade Crawford Barclay, Thoburn T. Brumbaugh, Jonah E. Caplan, D.A. Jessurun Cardozo, Mark A. Chamberlain, Karl M. Chworowsky, John W. Darr Jr., Joseph Fletcher, Louis C. Gerstein, Herbert S. Goldstein, Charles A. Hill, Chester E. Hodgson, Kenneth de P. Hughes, Felix A. Levy, Donald G. Lothrop, Jack R. McMichael, J. Edward Moseley, F. Hastings Smythe, Elias L. Solomon, Carl D. Soule, Sidney S. Tedesche, T.K. Thompson, W.J. Walls, Harry F. Ward, Owen Whitfield, and Evans A. Worthley. The entertainment business was heavily represented by George Antheil, Stella Adler, Leonard Bernstein, Herbert J. Biberman, Marc Blitzstein, Marlon Brando, J. Edward Bromberg, Charlie Chaplin, Edward Chodorov, Lee J. Cobb, Lester Cole, Howard da Silva, Jules Dassin, Edward Dmytryk, Paul Draper, Jose Ferrer, Will Geer, Jack Guilford, Uta Hagen, E.Y. Harburg, Judy Holliday, Libby Holman, Kim Hunter, Garson Kanin, Millard Lampell, Ring Lardner Jr., Albert Maltz, Arthur Miller, Mitch Miller, Eugene Ormandy, Wallingford Riegger, Paul Robeson, Harold Rome, Budd Schulberg, Artie Shaw, Herman Shumlin, Gale Sondergaard, Isaac Stern, Donald Ogden Stewart, Dalton Trumbo, and William Wyler.

It was only natural that the Scientific and Cultural Conference, since it was a hate-America-love-the-Soviet-Union feast, would attract the support of the inveterate Communist front members. The old stand-bys — crypto-Communists, Socialists, Soviet apologists, Fifth Amendment pleaders, campus radicals — made the Conference extra-conspicuous by their sponsorship. They included Louis Adamic, Alice Prentice Barrows, Algernon Black, Michael Blankfort, Ernst Boas, Kay Boyle, Theodore Brameld, Millen Brand, Edwin Berry Burgum, Angus Cameron, Rufus E. Clement, Jo Davidson, Hallie Flanagan Davis, Jerome Davis, Adolf Dehn, Earl B. Dickerson, Martha Dodd and husband Alfred K. Stern, Harl R. Douglass, Muriel Draper, Albert Einstein, Haven Emerson, Thomas I. Emerson, Guy Endore, Lion Feuchtwanger, Margaret Halsey,

Dashiell Hammett, Pearl Hart, Georgia Harkness, Marion Hathway, Lillian Hellman, Langston Hughes, Matthew Josephson, Albert E. Kahn, Robert W. Kenny, Rockwell Kent, Corliss Lamont, Oliver Larkin, Emil Lengyel, Kenneth Leslie, Oliver S. Loud, Robert Morss Lovett, Helen M. and Robert S. Lynd, Carey McWilliams, Curtis D. MacDougall, Erika and Thomas Mann, Clyde R. Miller, Scott Nearing, Frank Oppenheimer, Dorothy Parker, Linus Pauling, Arthur Upham Pope, Walter Rautenstrauch, Muriel Rukeyser, Robert St. John, Ben Shahn, Johannes Steel, Bernhard J. Stern, Dirk Struik, Studs Terkel, Mary Van Kleeck, Oswald Veblen, Nym Wales, Max Weber, Ella Winter, and James Waterman Wise.

The Scientific and Cultural Conference was unquestionably one of the most successful pro-Soviet events of all time. The "peace" campaign initiated by the Cominform had attracted Americans who in their various vocations and professions reached an impressive share of the American populace through the various communications media, books, plays, films, and through their responsible positions on campuses, in churches, in art and scientific circles, in service clubs and organizations, and in the publishing and editorial areas. The Conference received world-wide publicity that dwelled upon the spectacle of Americans and foreigners from the Soviet Union and its satellites engaging in virulent denunciation of the United States and receiving the plaudits of the conferees.

From New York the Cominform's "peace" campaign moved to Paris and Prague, where from April 20 until April 24, 1949, there was held the World Congress of Partisans for Peace, generally known as the World Peace Congress. Two international Communist fronts, the Women's International Democratic Federation and the International Committee of Intellectuals in Defense of Peace, went through the ritual of issuing the call for the Congress. All the delegates were to meet in Paris, but when the French government barred almost four hundred delegates from entering France, the excluded group met in Prague simultaneously with the Paris Congress. The chairman of the Congress was French Communist Frédéric Joliot-Curie, who was head of the French atomic energy commission and the chief representative at the Congress of the World Federation of Scientific Workers. The theme of the Congress did not differ substantially from that of the New York Conference of the previous month. Stalin and the Soviet Union were portrayed as peace-loving. The United States was excoriated in typical Communist jargon, wherein imperialism-fascism-colonialism-militarism are standard synonyms for Americanism. The headline speakers were Soviet luminaries Alexander Fadeyev and Ilya Ehrenburg and Americans Howard Fast, Leo Krzycki (president of the American Slav Congress), O. John Rogge, and Paul Robeson. The Congress applauded wildly when Robeson said: "It is certainly unthinkable for myself and the Negro people to go to war in the interests of those who have oppressed us [in America] for generations . . . [against the Soviet Union] which in one generation has raised our people [Negroes] to the full dignity of mankind."

At the Paris-Prague congress, the Communists were insistent that pacifists were not in control of the Communists' "peace" movement. In the Cominform's journal (*For a Lasting Peace, For a People's Democracy*), it was stated: "The peace movement is gaining momentum among the civil population, and will spread to the personnel of armies, navies, and air forces of the capitalist countries." Which simply meant that the Cominform's agents and stooges would work to subvert the "capitalists" by proselyting them for peace and setting them up for an easy conquest by militant Communists. The Soviet government, through its controlled press, described the tenor of the World Peace Congress as: "We shall not ask for peace of the warmongers but impose peace on them."

The American delegation to the World Peace Congress was led by co-chairmen W.E.B. DuBois, O. John Rogge, and Bishop Arthur W. Moulton. The American sponsors of the Congress – more than two hundred of them – were almost without exception veterans of the Scientific and Cultural Conference. Their message to the Congress was: "As American citizens deeply concerned with the welfare of our land and the maintenance of world peace, we send our warmest greetings to the World Peace Congress, unprecedented in its proportion and so deeply meaningful at this crucial instant in the history of mankind. We join with millions of men and women of other lands in voicing the heartfelt and inflexible resolve that there must not be another war. We stand firmly united in the common determination that peace must prevail in the world."

At the conclusion of the World Peace Congress, a Permanent Committee of the World Peace Congress was established. It included such world-famous Communists as Frédéric and Irène Joliot-Curie and

Pablo Picasso of France; Hewlett Johnson, the "Red Dean" of Canterbury; Alexander Fadeyev, Ilya Ehrenburg, and Metropolitan Nikolai of the Soviet Union; Pablo Neruda of Chile; and Lazaro Cardenas and Lombardo Toledano of Mexico. On the Permanent Committee were eight Americans: W.E.B. DuBois, Howard Fast, Paul Robeson, Bishop Arthur W. Moulton, Albert E. Kahn, O. John Rogge, Gene Weltfish, and Donald Henderson.

The American Continental Congress for Peace, held from September 5 until September 10, 1949, at Mexico City, was another step in the Cominform's "peace" campaign. The American women who issued the call to the Congress included a number of officers from the Congress of American Women, a Communist front. They were Muriel Draper, Susan B. Anthony MacAvoy, Vivian Carter Mason, Eslanda G. Robeson, Rose Russell, Maude Slye, Jeanette Stern Turner, and Charlotte Stern. Other "callers" included Charlotta Bass, Charlotte Hawkins Brown, Viola M. Brown, Mineola V. Ingersol, Ada B. Jackson, Frances Leber, Helen S. Mangold, Elizabeth Sasuly, Marion Ulmer, Daisy Kendall Ward, Ella Winter, and Margaret Zorach. Among the more prominent sponsors of the Congress were Edward K. Barsky, Martha Dodd, Olin Downes, Waldo Frank, Dashiell Hammett, Rockwell Kent, Clifford Odets, Albert Maltz, Thomas Mann, Vito Marcantonio, Bishop Arthur W. Moulton, Harlow Shapley, Agnes Smedley, Donald Ogden Stewart, Henry Agard Wallace, Colston E. Warne, and James Waterman Wise. Actively recruiting for delegates to attend the Congress were Charlie Chaplin, John Clark, W.E.B. DuBois, Uta Hagen, Charles Houston, Robert W. Kenny, Linus Pauling, Paul Robeson, O. John Rogge, Ben Shahn, Reverend John B. Thompson, and Gene Weltfish. Pauling and DuBois were vice presidents of the Continental Congress but the real directors of the meeting were the French Communists Roger Garaudy and Paul Eluard. The honorary presidents of the Congress were such world famous Communists as Luis Carlos Prestes of Brazil, Giuseppi di Vittorio of Italy, Alexander Fadeyev of the Soviet Union, Frédéric Joliot-Curie of France, Dolores Ibarruri of Spain, and Paul Robeson of the United States. Activists at the Congress included such Communists as Pablo O'Higgins, Esther Chapas, Lombardo Toledano, Diego Rivera, Narciso Bassols, Fernando Bamboa, and Alfaro Siquieros of Mexico; Lazaro Pena and Juan Mariello of Cuba; and Salvador Ocampo and Pablo Neruda of Chile.

At the American Continental Congress for World Peace, held in neighboring Mexico, the usual Communist line about United States exploitation of Latin America was the keynote, while at the same time the Soviet Union was extolled as the world's greatest force for peace. The Permanent Committee of the World Peace Congress, which had been established in April 1949 at the Paris-Prague Congress, met between March 15 and March 19, 1950 in Stockholm, Sweden. Americans Albert Kahn, Rockwell Kent, Johannes Steel, and O. John Rogge attended and participated in the usual anti-American tirades. But the most important development at Stockholm was the launching of a massive peace-petition campaign. The petition was known variously as the World Peace Appeal, the Stockholm Peace Petition, and the Stockholm Peace Appeal. The petition said: "Throughout the world — in China, Italy, Israel, in England and Brazil, in France and Mexico, in Finland and Poland, Sweden and the Soviet Union, in Africa and India and in the United States — tens of millions of people of all faiths and creeds, all races are signing this appeal. If we, the people, say no to war there will be peace. We demand the outlawing of the atomic weapons as instruments of aggression and mass murder of peoples. We demand strict international control to enforce this measure. We believe that any government which first uses atomic weapons against any other country whatsoever will be committing a crime against humanity and should be dealt with as a war criminal. We call on all men and women of good will throughout the world to sign this appeal."

The Subversive Activities Control Board characterized the Stockholm Peace Appeal as being used "for the purpose of combatting the foreign policies of the United States, specifically at a time when the United States had the atomic bomb and other countries did not have it; that the circulation of the peace petition was a tactic of the [Communist] Party in the program to achieve world Communism."

The House Committee on Un-American Activities offered a rather incisive analysis of the "peace" petition. "It is the boldest and most extensive piece of psychological warfare ever conducted by any organization on a world scale. Moreoever, it was shrewdly contrived and carefully timed. The World Peace Appeal was launched 3 months before the outbreak of Communist armed aggression against South Korea. Obviously the appeal was intended as a smoke screen for such aggression. And even though the Korean conflict completely exposed the falsity of the Communists' 'peace' movement, the petition appeal is brazenly continuing today . . . .

"Here is what is behind these demands, however. Well aware that the United States, for its own protection against Soviet aggression, has established superiority in the development of atomic weapons, the Communists hope to weaken American defenses by demanding the outlawing of atomic weapons. The second misleading demand in the petition is for 'strict international control' of atomic weapons. Authorized representatives of the American Government in the field of atomic energy have pointed out that international control is impossible without provision for international inspection of plants within each country by an international authority. Under these conditions, the United States generously offered before the United Nations to turn over to the international authority all the materials, facilities, and know-how in our possession, as well as to dispose of all atom bombs and other atomic weapons. Every nation in the world except Soviet Russia and her satellites accepted the American plan as fair and workable. Thus, it is Soviet Russia which has prevented international controls over the atom bomb.

"The petition demand that 'any government which first uses atomic weapons against any other country . . . should be dealt with as a war criminal' is intended to tie our hands in the case of aggressive wars instigated by Communists. The petition is cleverly directed to 'all men and women of good will throughout the world.' The petition fails to mention that the signer would be supporting the cruelest and most ruthless dictatorship known to recorded history, which has just launched an unprovoked and brutal attack on the South Korean Republic. It is as if Adolph Hitler were appealing to 'men of good will.' Regrettably, to a number of intellectuals in our country and elsewhere the paradox is not apparent.

"By soliciting names and addresses from 'peace' petition signers, the Communists are in a position to establish a huge Red mailing list which can be used for the circulation of Communist propaganda. In Switzerland, a cross mark is made against the name of anyone who refuses to sign the petitions and the individual is threatened with reprisals in the event of Communist control of the Swiss Government. In iron-curtain countries, those who have refused to sign have been thrown into jail. In Moscow, the Communist Party organ, *Pravda*, announced that anyone in any country who refused to sign the petition automatically became 'an accomplice and henchman of the war-mongers' in the eyes of the Communists.

"Also illustrative of the pressure exerted in Communist-dominated countries to get signers to 'peace petitions' is the following incident: The Polish delegates to an International Congress of Architects, held in Paris, stated that they could not participate in the congress unless that body approved the Stockholm peace petition. Lacking such approval, the Polish delegation renounced the congress. The same type of pressure has been applied to the churches in Communist Poland. Instructors in church schools in a given locality are called in to sign the Stockholm pledge. If they refuse, they are told the Government will forbid them to teach the young. Thus, the Warsaw regime has coerced a few priests into signing the petition . . . . The conclusion is obvious that the 'peace' petition campaign provides another example of Communist willingness to use any trickery or deceit to achieve their ends."

While the "petition" campaign was in full swing, a second World Peace Congress was scheduled to be held in Sheffield, England, from November 13 until November 19, 1950. The Reverend Joseph Fletcher of the Episcopal Theological Seminary of Cambridge, Massachusetts, was chosen as the acting head of the sponsoring committee in the United States. The acting secretary of the same committee was the Reverend Robert M. Muir. The members of the sponsoring committee included Episcopal Bishops W. Appleton Lawrence of Massachusetts, Arthur W. Moulton of Utah, and John Moore Walker of Georgia; Charlotta Bass, publisher of the *California Eagle*; Dr. Allan Butler of Harvard University's Medical School; Anton Carlson of the University of Chicago; W.E.B. DuBois; E. Franklin Frazier of Howard University; Reverend John Paul Jones of New York; John A. Kingsbury of New York; Robert Morss Lovett; Philip Morrison of Cornell University; Theodor Rosebury of Columbia University; Vida Scudder of Wellesley College; Fred Stover, president of the Ohio Farmers Union; Artur Schnabel, concert pianist; Bishop W.J. Walls of Illinois; and Fleming James of Yale University's Divinity School.

The actual American delegation included Jones, Kingsbury, Walls, and Muir, the head of the delegation. They were joined by Theresa Robinson of Washington, D.C.; Reverend Linwood Fauntleroy of Oakland, California; Dorothy Cole of Chicago; Angeline Mensik of the

Czech-American Peace Committee; Reverend Warren McKenna of Boston; Reverend Willard Uphaus of World Fellowship; O. John Rogge; and Charles F. Howard of Des Moines.

The plans for the second World Peace Congress were upset when the British government refused to allow many of the delegates to enter England. From an expected congress of two thousand, only five hundred delegates were present in Sheffield on the scheduled opening day. Those present heard the customary anti-United States, pro-Soviet Union "peace" talks from Hewlett Johnson, the "Red Dean" of Canterbury; Pablo Picasso, the Spanish Communist; and the Americans O. John Rogge and Reverend John Paul Jones.

After one day at Sheffield, the World Peace Congress was transferred to Warsaw, Poland, and on November 16 more than seventeen hundred delegates were on hand for the second opening session. French Communist Frédéric Joliot-Curie was the presiding officer.

On the first day at Warsaw, a presidium of the Congress was elected. It included delegates from North Korea and Red China, as well as United States delegates W.E.B. DuBois, Paul Robeson, Thomas Mann, Howard Fast, and Reverend Joseph Fletcher.

The anti-American, pro-Soviet speeches of the Americans Willard Uphaus and Charles F. Howard contributed to the success of the Congress, which signified, according to the Soviet government, that there was invincible power in the "movement for the warding off of a new war being prepared by the bosses of the imperialist camp and first of all by those of the United States."

Before the second World Peace Congress adjourned, a World Peace Council was formed with a presidium of 208 members from all over the world. The American members of the presidium included Reverend John W. Darr Jr., Ernest De Maio, W.E.B. DuBois, Howard Fast, Reverend Joseph F. Fletcher, Charles F. Howard, Bishop Arthur Moulton, Reverend Robert Muir, Dr. Clementina Paolone, Paul Robeson, Theresa Robinson, Fred Stover, and Willard Uphaus.

In the meantime, the Cominform-directed Stockholm Peace Appeal campaign was being pushed very hard by the Communist Party and its stooges in the United States. Joseph Starobin, the foreign news editor of the Party's *Daily Worker*, was appointed as executive secretary of the Party's Peace Committee. Starobin announced plans to get five million American signatures on the Stockholm petition. He opened a Peace

Information Center in New York City, with Elizabeth Moos as executive director of the Center. The executive secretary of the Center was Abbott Simon and the chairman was W.E.B. DuBois. The octogenarian DuBois had been involved in every step along the way of the Cominform's "peace" campaign. Simon was a longtime workhorse for the Communist Party, which he had served in various capacities, in front projects including the Youth Industrial Branch of the Communist Party, the American Youth Congress, the Committee to Defend America by Keeping Out of War, the National Win-the-Peace Committee, and the National Council of American-Soviet Friendship.

The Peace Information Center remained in operation only about eight months. In February 1951, five of its officers, including Moos, DuBois, and Simon, were indicted by a federal grand jury for failure to register under the Foreign Agents Registration Act. (They were all acquitted at a later date.)

Long before the Peace Information Center closed down, the Communist Party's petition campaign had run into some strong opposition — from both expected and unexpected quarters. From the office of its National Commander, the American Legion issued a statement: "The Communist fifth column is behind the so-called 'peace petitions' now being circulated in the United States. This is a coldly calculated, Kremlin-directed plot to soften up the minds, morale, and will power of the American people to resist aggression. The circulation of these petitions, whether they call for outlawing of atomic weapons or for peace at any cost, is a desperate bid to swerve the American people from resolute action to wishful thinking. It is a masterful psychological stroke designed to accomplish two Communist objectives.

"In the United States the purpose of these petitions is to embarrass our Government and to disrupt our national unity. Abroad, the aim of such petitions is to show up America as the enemy of peace on the basis of worthless papers addressed to no one and bearing the names of millions of Red slaves and dupes in other areas of the world .... The petitions are being circulated in the United States through numerous Communist-front organizations which masquerade under civic, economic, social, racial, religious, or humanitarian labels. Anyone having even the slightest doubt about a group that is trying to get his signature should contact the National Americanism Commission of the American Legion in Indianapolis for advice."

In its *Weekly News Service,* the American Federation of Labor said of the Stockholm Peace Appeal: "The American Federation of Labor vigorously condemns the so-called Stockholm Peace Appeal as a rank fraud. We urge every workingman and workingwoman to spurn the peddlers of this spurious petition. We call upon every loyal American, every true lover of peace, to refuse to sign or circulate it. We cannot urge too strongly every self-respecting American to treat those who are the organizers of this 'Stockholm movement' and the purveyors of its petitions as enemies of the American people operating under false colors.

"Not only in far-off Korea do enemies of the American people disguise themselves as Americans. In our own country, in our factories, shops, offices, churches, schools, and on our streets, enemies of America also disguise themselves and pose as Americans.

"Camouflage is a Communist weapon of war which can be just as deadly against our sons and brothers in the U.S. as in Korea. The so-called Stockholm Petition is precisely such a weapon. The fake peace petition does not oppose all aggression with all weapons. It singles out only one weapon – the one in which our country still holds the lead and which provides our country and the other democracies with a measure of military security against the gigantic Russian war machine . . . . Were these fake peace maneuvers to succeed, were the U.S. to fall into the Russian bear trap of banning atomic weapons – while Russia rejects America's plan for their effective international inspection, control and elimination – the possibility for Communist world domination by the Soviets would be enormously enhanced. That is just what the petition promoters and the sinister signature seekers want . . . .

"Cruel confirmation of this strategy of the Stockholm petitioners is at hand in Korea; that is why the Communist drive for signatures coincides with the Moscow-directed invasion of South Korea. It was carefully planned to hide and help the brutal aggression of the Soviet dictators against the people of Korea, the American people, and the United Nations as an effective agency of world peace . . . .

"The Communists are not waging a peace offensive. The Communists are waging an offensive against peace, liberty, and social progress. The American Federation of Labor is confident that organized labor will lead the Nation in unmasking and upbraiding those enemies within our country with the same determination that our armed forces are fighting against the Communist enemy from without."

The Congress of Industrial Organizations (CIO), which certainly did not have a history of anti-Communist activism, opposed the petition campaign through its executive board, which issued a belated release (more than two months after the *Daily Worker* announced the Communist Party's campaign to secure five million signatures in the United States) condemning the program: "Despite the fact that the Communists and their dupes in this country are presently condoning, defending, and supporting the present aggressive sneak attack by Communists on the South Korean Republic, they continue nevertheless to offer this specious document as an appeal to 'men of good will.' Behind the document stands the usual Communist fog of misrepresentation, deceit, and treachery.

"An analysis of the timing and wording of this 'Petition' should alone establish its origin as a piece of Communist propaganda. The date of the Petition should be especially noted. It was drafted simultaneously with the plot against South Korea, and it was timed to tie the hands of the United States and other peace-loving nations with propaganda ropes before the vicious assault was made without warning on the Republic of South Korea.

"The content of the document itself deals with atomic energy as a weapon of war. It presumably calls for the outlawing of atomic war. Coupled with this demand is a wholly misleading and lying appeal for international control of atomic energy. Every American knows that our government and every other government, with the exception of the Soviet Union and her satellites, supports the United Nations' formula for such control. The UN formula has been stymied by the veto of the U.S.S.R., because it would require that government to open its atomic energy operation to international inspection.

"This alleged peace petition says nothing about general disarmament because that, of course, would involve the tremendous Red Armies that are being kept under arms, and it would also involve the disarmament by the Soviet Union of its North Korean satellite. This Executive Board denounces the Stockholm Peace Petition and its communist-directed variations as a vicious fraud intended to mislead the American people and particularly union members."

Even later than the CIO, the International Confederation of Free

Trade Unions opposed the petition campaign, using the device of an "open letter" addressed to those who had already signed the "peace" petitions.

A joint statement from the Federal Council of Churches, the National Catholic Welfare Conference, and the Synagogue Council of America described the Stockholm Appeal as a "spurious peace petition, which has already deceived many well-meaning people here and abroad, [and] is a camouflage designed to confuse the free societies and to conceal the aggressive policies revealed in the invasion of Korea."

Despite the widespread opposition and pointed warnings against the Stockholm Peace Appeal, many Americans — far from "well-meaning people" — affixed their signatures to the Cominform-designed petition. They included clergymen Lee H. Ball, Raymond Calkins, Albert B. Cleage Jr., A.R. Clippinger, J. Raymond Cope, Benjamin D. Dagwell, John Darr Jr., Joseph Fletcher, William A. Fountain, George M. Gibson, Charles A. Hill, Kenneth de P. Hughes, Arthur W. Moulton, Paul Roberts, W.J. Walls, Harry F. Ward, and David Rhys Williams; academicians E. Franklin Frazier (Howard University), Irwin R. Beiler (University of Miami), Anton Carlson and Rudolf Carnap (University of Chicago), Allan M. Butler and Pitirim Sorokin (Harvard University), Dorothy Douglas and S. Ralph Harlow (Smith College), Louise Pettibone Smith and Vida Scudder (Wellesley College), Walter Rautenstrauch, Dorothy Brewster, Bernhard J. Stern, and Gene Weltfish (Columbia University), Edwin Berry Bergum and Henry Pratt Fairchild (New York University), Ephraim Cross (City College of New York), Frank S. Freeman (Cornell University), Oliver S. Loud (Antioch College), C. DeWitt Eldridge (George Washington University), Ronald Levy (Roosevelt College), Ralph H. Turner (Oberlin College), Barrows Dunham (Temple University), and Kurt Anderson (Bennington College); authors Lion Feuchtwanger, John Howard Lawson, Millen Brand, Thomas Mann, Martha Dodd, Shirley Graham, Dashiell Hammett, Florence Converse, and Cedric Belfrage; William Patterson of the Civil Rights Congress; Aubrey Williams, editor of the *Southern Farmer*; radio commentator Johannes Steel; poets Muriel Rukeyser and Alfred Kreymborg; Ben Margolis of the National Lawyers Guild; artists Anton Refregier and Rockwell Kent; Holland Roberts; Helen M. Lynd; musicians Ray Lev, Duke Ellington, and Wallingford Riegger; attorneys Charles F. Howard and O. John Rogge; James A. Dombrowski; singer

Paul Robeson; Emily Greene Balch of Women's International League for Peace and Freedom; former Minnesota Governor Elmer Benson; Albert E. Kahn; James Imbrie; union leaders Donald Henderson and Rose Russell; Communist author Herbert Aptheker; Communist union leader Ferdinand C. Smith; artist Marc Chagall; playwright Jerome Chodorov; Ralph Gundlach; Ewart Guinier; Milton Galamison; Russ Nixon; Muriel Draper of the Congress of American Women; and W.E.B. DuBois.

When the Communist Party found its Peace Information Center closed down by the federal grand jury, it turned the Stockholm Peace Appeal program over to a new front, the American Peace Crusade. DuBois, who had been indicted because of his position as chairman of the Peace Information Center, stayed loyal to the Cominform's program and was a charter sponsor of the American Peace Crusade. He was joined by such Communist stalwarts as Herbert Biberman, Harry Bridges, Maurice Travis, Ben Gold, Paul Robeson, Albert E. Kahn, Alex Sirota, and Howard Fast. Abbott Simon, who had been executive secretary of the Peace Information Center, was the publicity director for the American Peace Crusade. The Crusade's original sponsors included: Bishop Cameron C. Alleyne, Charlotta Bass, Elmer Benson, Edward Biberman, Herbert J. Biberman, Rabbi Abraham J. Bick, Dorothy Brewster, Harry Bridges, Charlotte Hawkins Brown, Hugh Bryson, Rev. Dudley H. Burr, Allan Butler, Alvin Christman, George A. Coe, Dorothy B. Cole, Abraham Cronbach, Bishop Benjamin D. Dagwell, Jerome Davis, Mark A. Dawber, Ernest De Maio, Earl B. Dickerson, James Dombrowski, W.E.B. DuBois, Henry Pratt Fairchild, Howard Fast, Rev. G. Linwood Fauntleroy, Abram Flaxer, Royal Wilbur France, Rev. Stephen Fritchman, Ben Gold, Carlton B. Goodlett, Uta Hagen, Alice Hamilton, Talbot Hamlin, Rev. Charles A. Hill, Charles P. Howard, Rev. Kenneth DeB. Hughes, James Imbrie, Albert Kahn, Rev. Massie Kennard, Rockwell Kent, John A. Kingsbury, Oliver S. Loud, Robert Morss Lovett, Bishop Walter A. Mitchell, Philip Morrison, Bishop Arthur M. Moulton, Clementina J. Paolone, Linus Pauling, Eslanda Goode and Paul Robeson, Fred W. Stover, Dr. Theodor A. Rosebury, Alex Sirota, Louise Pettebone Smith, Pitirim Sorokin, Mary Church Terrell, Maurice Travis, and James N. Wolfe.

The first major project of the American Peace Crusade was a "Peace Pilgrimage" to Washington, D.C. The event took place on March 15,

1951, and the highlights of the agenda were demands directed toward government officials that the United States summarily withdraw from the Korean War and support a move to seat Red China in the United Nations. Also on the agenda were protests against universal military training, against extension of the draft, against the dispatch to Europe of American troops, and against the re-armament of Germany. On the Washington scene, the "pilgrims" sent delegations to visit individual Senators, Representatives, and executive officers in an effort to gain support for their program. When the visits were concluded, the "pilgrims" met in a convention atmosphere where they heard the Communist-line "peace" pep talks and diatribes from veteran agitators including Paul Robeson, Philip Morrison, Clementina J. Paolone, Robert Morss Lovett, and Douglas Glasgow.

On the same day that the "Peace Pilgrimage" took place, the *Daily Worker* announced that 166 Americans, including 40 rabbis and Protestant ministers, had joined the American Peace Crusade. The newcomers included Reverend Rolland E. Wolfe (Western Reserve University), Reverend J. Clyde Keegan (Casper, Wyoming), Rabbi Robert E. Goldberg (Hamden, Connecticut), George S. McGovern, later U.S. Senator (Dakota Wesleyan University), William Wells Denton (University of Arizona), Harvey Roberts (Virginia State College), C. Sheldon Hart (Carleton College), Anatol Rapoport (University of Chicago), actress Karen Morley, John M. Marsalka (president of the American Slav Congress), Florence Luscomb (Cambridge, Massachusetts), David Poindexter (Salem, Oregon), G. Murray Branch (Morehouse College), Curtis D. MacDougall (Northwestern University), John T. Bernard (United Electrical Workers), Holland Roberts (San Francisco), and Dashiell Hammett (writer).

Before the American Peace Crusade adjourned its "peace pilgrimage" in Washington, it was announced that its next venture would be a "nation-wide congress" to be held in Chicago in June 1951. The Cominform's "peace" program was now in full swing. The Stockholm Peace Appeal had more or less faded into obscurity but the "peace" campaign, in true Communist fashion, was simply adopting new names and guises.

In 1957, the Subversive Activities Control Board evaluated the American Peace Crusade as "operated under the management, direction, and supervision of persons who are predominantly members and functionaries of the Communist Party . . . and acting as representatives of the Party . . . although this relationship is not made known to the public. The APC attempts to achieve its goals by means of sponsoring and promoting mass meetings and rallies, sending speakers on tours throughout the country, and issuing and distributing leaflets, petitions, and other literature. While ostensibly promoting and advancing various positions and programs as necessary in order to have peace throughout the world . . . the APC in fact promotes and advances the positions and programs of the Communist Party. The entire resources and efforts of the . . . APC are thus devoted to promoting and advancing the 'peace' line of the Communist Party, including, as it does, attempting to align people behind a so-called 'camp of peace' led by the Soviet Union, and against a so-called 'camp of imperialism' said by the Communists to be led by the United States." The Senate Internal Security Subcommittee in its analysis of the American Peace Crusade said: "As part of Soviet psychological warfare against the United States, Communist fronts seek to paralyze America's will to resist Communist aggression by idealizing Russia's aims and methods, discrediting the United States, spreading defeatism and demoralization . . . specializing in this field . . . have been such organizations as the American Peace Crusade."

The Cominform and its agents and stooges in the United States, throughout its "peace" campaign of the late 1940's and early 1950's, never relied exclusively on one front or one gimmick or one target. The "peace" campaign was waged as war would be waged. There were strategic and tactical maneuvers, shifting of battle-lines, retreats and advances, changes of personnel in secondary command positions, and — most important — constant efforts to gain new recruits for the "peace" army.

On April 14, 1949, the United States and Canada joined with ten Western European nations in the North Atlantic Treaty Organization. The pact which brought these nations together was a simple defensive treaty stating that "an armed attack against one or more of them in Europe and North America shall be considered an attack against all." The Cominform and its agents in the United States immediately applied a Communist-line interpretation to NATO: the pact was aggressive, imperialist, colonialist, a threat to world peace, and a warmongering gesture directed against the "peace-loving" Soviet Union. It all added up to another excuse for the Comintern and the Communist Party, USA, to create another front in the "peace" campaign. Credit for getting the new front in motion was given to Albert Einstein, Thomas Mann, Reverend Edwin Dahlberg, Bishop W.J. Waldo, and Emily Greene Balch — all aged stalwarts of the Communist movement. In July 1949, a call was issued for a Conference on Peaceful Alternatives to the Atlantic Pact. Following the Conference, there was formed a Continuations Committee of the Conference for Peaceful Alternatives to the Atlantic Pact and then finally the definitive name of the front was adopted: Committee for Peaceful Alternatives to the Atlantic Pact. The new organization had as honorary chairmen Thomas Mann and Bishop W.J. Walls; chairman of the board Robert J. Havighurst; co-chairmen Rabbi Abraham Cronbach, Kermit Eby, W.H. Jernagin, and Reverend John B. Thompson; and vice chairmen Charlotte Hawkins Brown, Mark A. Dawber, Mrs. Welthy H. Fisher, D.V. Jemison, Halford Luccock, Albert Palmer, Franklin L. Sheeder, and Linus Pauling. The executive board included Reverend J. Burt Bouwman, Rabbi Stanley Brav, Rabbi Jonah E. Caplan, Reverend M.E. Dorr, Harl Douglas, Clifford Durr, Rabbi Alvin Fine, Rabbi Oscar Fleishaker, George Fowler, Reverend Edgar Jackson, Reverend Massie Kennard, Hugo Leaming, Reverend Donald Matthews, George Mecklenberg, Renée Shapiro, Reverend Robert Stone, Mrs. M.E. Tilly, Reverend Willard Uphaus, Reverend Edgar M. Wahlberg, Lorell Weiss, Reverend Wayne White, and Aubrey Williams. There was also formed a Chicago Committee for Peaceful Alternatives to the Atlantic Pact, with Reverend John B. Thompson, from the University of Chicago, as chairman. His executive committee included Robert J. Havighurst of the University of Chicago; Truman Kirkpatrick of the American Friends Service Committee; Bishop W.J. Walls; Russell Ballard, director of the Hull House in Chicago; Curtis D. MacDougall of Northwestern University; Rabbi Samuel Teitelbaum of the Hillell Foundation in Evanston, Illinois; Maud Slye of the University of Chicago; Reverend Wilfred Wakefield of Brookfield, Illinois; and R. Citron and Albert G. Watson of the Fellowship of Reconciliation.

In August and December 1949, the Committee of Peaceful Alternatives to the Atlantic Pact issued open letters directed to the attention of United States Senators and President Harry Truman. The signers of the Communist-line letters were drawn mostly from the ranks of the clergy. There was also in evidence the usual battalion of front regulars, including Lee H. Ball, Edward K. Barsky, Elmer A. Benson, John T. Bernard, Lyman R. Bradley, Hugh Bryson, Anton J. Carlson, Charles Collins, John W. Darr, Jerome Davis, Hugh DeLacy, Martha Dodd, James A. Dombrowski, Dorothy W. Douglas, Muriel Draper, W.E.B. DuBois, Bertram Edises, Thomas I. Emerson, Philip Evergood, Clark Foreman, Stephen H. Fritchman, Elinor Gimbel, Josiah W. Gitt, B.Z. Goldberg, Harry Gottlieb, Nora K. Harris, Leo Huberman, Langston Hughes, W.A. Hunton, Oakley C. Johnson, Millard Lampell, Kenneth Leslie, Rockwell Kent, Thomas Mann, Clifford T. McAvoy, Bernard V. McGroarty, Jack R. McMichael, William Howard Melish, Clyde R. Miller, Richard Morford, Philip D. Morrison, Linus Pauling, Martin Popper, Holland Roberts, O. John Rogge, Rose Russell, Margaret Schlauch, Frederick L. Schuman, I.F. Stone, Fred W. Stover, Leon Straus, Mary Church Terrell, John B. Thompson, Jeannett S. Turner, Sam Wanamaker, Harry F. Ward, Colston E. Warne, and Gene Weltfish.

A number of known Communist Party members joined in the "open letter" campaign. They included Louise Berman, Howard Fast, Ben Gold, Max Perlow, Reverend Eliot White, Abram Flaxer, Elizabeth Sasuly, Arthur Osman, Albert Maltz, Dalton Trumbo, Donald Henderson, Abraham Lederman, Ralph H. Gundlach, Albert E. Kahn, Elizabeth Moos, Dirk Struik, and Agnes Smedley.

In 1950, the Committee for Peaceful Alternatives to the Atlantic Pact sponsored the Mid-Century Conference for Peace, held May 29 and 30 in Chicago. The "call" for the Conference was issued by David Baker, president of the Associated Church Press; Emily Greene Balch of the Women's International League for Peace and Freedom; Wade Crawford Barclay of the Methodist Board of Missions; Charlotte Hawkins Brown, president of the Palmer Institute; Rabbi Jonah E. Caplan of Astoria, New York; Reverend Donald Cloward of the Northern Baptist Convention; Mrs. Howard G. Colwell, president of the Northern Baptist Convention; Abraham Cronbach of Hebrew Union College; Mark Dawber of Long Beach, New York; Kermit Eby of the University of Chicago; Rabbi Alvin Fine of San Francisco; Mrs. Welthy H. Fisher of the United Council of Church Women; E. Franklin Frazier of Howard University; Rabbi Robert Gordis of the Jewish Theological Seminary; Bishop S.L. Greene of the African Methodist Church; Georgia Harkness of the Garrett Biblical Institute; Robert J. Havighurst of the University of Chicago; Charles W. Iglehart, chairman of the board of directors of the Fellowship of Reconciliation; D.V. Jemison, president of the National Baptist Convention; W.H. Jernagin, of the Fraternal Council of Negro Churches; Jameson Jones, president of the National Conference of Methodist Youth; Rabbi Leo Jung of the Rabbinical Council of America; Reverend William E. Lampe of the Evangelical and Reformed Church in Philadelphia; Halford E. Luccock of Yale University's Divinity School; Lester G. McAllister of Berkeley, California; author Thomas Mann; Donald L. Mathews of Union Theological Seminary; Benjamin E. Mays, president of Morehouse College; Walter G. Muelder, dean at Boston University; John S. Nolle, president emeritus of Grinnell College; Albert W. Palmer of Altadena, California; Episcopal Bishop Edward L. Parsons of California; Linus Pauling of the California Institute of Technology; George V. Schick, secretary of the Evangelical Lutheran Synodical Conference; Reverend Franklin I. Sheeder of the Evangelical and Reformed Church in Philadelphia; author Odell Shepard; Pitirim Sorokin of Harvard University; Charles Turck, president of Macalester College; Oswald Veblen of the Institute for Advanced Study; Bishop W.J. Walls of the African Methodist Episcopal Zion Church in Chicago; Goodwin Watson of Columbia University's Teachers' College; and Bishop Richard R. Wright Jr. of the African Methodist Episcopal Church in Atlanta.

The Mid-Century Conference for Peace was held as scheduled. Over the two-day period the conferees heard speeches, and participated in work seminars and discussions on such topics as the cold war; the requirements of peace; the effects of fear on family and community; the effects of the A-bomb and H-bomb; economics, trade, and foreign policy; civil liberties; and — of course — peace and peaceful alternatives to the cold war. From the expressed viewpoint of the Communists, in Moscow and in the United States, the Conference was a huge success. They appreciated the scathing indictments of the United States and the worshipful praises heaped upon the Soviet Union. The House Committee on Un-American Activities regarded the Conference as "aimed at assembling as many gullible persons as possible under Communist direction and turning them into a vast sounding board for Communist propaganda."

The number of gullible and not-so-gullible persons who sponsored the Mid-Century Conference for Peace must have exceeded the most optimistic expectations of the Communists who directed the entire affair. Not only were the old reliable front supporters in their usual element, but there were a remarkable number of clergymen in what was so obviously a Communist-dominated gathering. The sponsors included Edith Abbott and Russell W. Ballard of Hull House, Bishops A.J. Allen and C.C. Alleyne of the African Methodist Episcopal Church, Rabbi Michael Alper of the Jewish Institute of Religion, Reverend Karl Baehr of the American Christian Palestine Committee, De Witt C. Baldwin of the University of Michigan, Albert E. Barnett of the Garrett Biblical Institute, Cyrus P. Barnum Jr. of the University of Minnesota, Irwin R. Beiler of the University of Miami, former Governor of Minnesota Elmer Benson, Frederick K. Beutel of the University of Nebraska's Law School, Algernon L. Black of the New York Society for Ethical Culture, Reverend Charles F. Boss of the Methodist Church's Commission on World Peace, editor Reverend J.W. Bradbury of the *Watchman Examiner*, Theodore Brameld of New York University, G. Murray Branch of Morehouse College, Dorothy Brewster of Columbia University, editor Reverend J.S. Brookens of the *African Methodist Episcopal Review*, Robert W. Browning of Northwestern University, T.T. Brumbaugh of the Methodist Board of Missions, David Bryn-Jones of Carleton College, Edwin A. Burt of Cornell University, Allan M. Butler of Harvard University's Medical School, Kenneth Neill Cameron of the University of Indiana, Rabbi Jessurun D. Cardozo of New York, Anton J. Carlson and Rudolph Carnap, Reverend and Mrs. Mark A. Chamberlain of Oregon, president Bernhard Christensen of Augsburg College, president Reverend Albert Buckner Coe of the Massachusetts Conference of Congregational Churches, Reverend George A. Coe of the Union Theological Seminary, Edwin Grant Conklin of Princeton University, author Florence Converse, Reverend Henry Hitt Crane of Detroit, Episcopal Bishop Benjamin D. Dagwell of Oregon, George Dahl of Yale University's Divinity School, Phyllis Ann Davies of Keuka College, Jerome Davis, Reverend Warren J. Day of Union Theological Seminary, John J. DeBoer of the University of Illinois, Reverend Purd E. Deitz of Eden Theological Seminary, W.W. Denton of the University of Arizona, W. Marshon De Poister of Grinnell College, Charlotte D'Evelyn of Mount Holyoke College, Harold De Wolfe of Boston University, attorney Earl B. Dickerson, Frank Dobie of the University of Texas, Witherspoon Dodge of the National Religion and Labor Foundation, Hedley S. Dimmock of George Williams College, Dorothy

W. Douglas of Smith College, Mary E. Dreier of the Women's Trade Union League, W.E.B. DuBois, David Dunn and H. Stanley Dunn of the Evangelical and Reformed Seminary, L.C. Dunn of Columbia University, Clifford Durr, playwright Armand d'Usseau, Thomas I. Emerson of Yale University's Law School, president John Scott Everton of Kalamazoo College, writer Lion Feuchtwanger, editor Harold E. Fey of *Christian Century*, Reverend Joseph Fletcher of the Episcopal Theological School, president Reverend George A. Fowler of the Church Federation of Greater Chicago, Frank S. Freeman of Cornell University, Reverend Stephen H. Fritchman of Los Angeles, Bishop Carey A. Gibbs of the African Methodist Episcopal Church, Reverend George Miles Gibson of McCormick Theological Seminary, publisher Josiah W. Gitt of the *York* (Pa.) *Gazette*, Rabbi Roland B. Gittelsohn of New York, Carlton B. Goodlett of San Francisco, writer Shirley Graham, David Haber of Yale University's Law School, Bishop J. Arthur Hamlett of the Colored Methodist Episcopal Church, C.H. Hamlin of the Atlantic Christian College, Harrison L. Harley of Simmons College, C. Sheldon Hart of Carleton College, conference superintendent Reverend William C.F. Hayes of the Evangelical United Brethren, labor leader Donald Henderson, president emeritus Everett C. Herack of Newton Theological School, Reverend Charles A. Hill of Detroit, Leslie Pickney of Cheyney State Teachers College, former president Cecil E. Hinshaw of William Penn College, Reverend John Haynes Holmes of New York, Walter M. Horton of Oberlin's Graduate School of Theology, Reverend E. Stanley Jones of New York, Reverend John Paul Jones of Brooklyn, Mordecai M. Kaplan of the Jewish Theological Seminary of America, A.C. Keller of the University of Washington, Carl Kepner of Dickinson College, Methodist Bishop Paul B. Kern of New York, Velma Ruth King of Southwestern (Kansas) College, I.M. Kolthof of the University of Minnesota, president Leo Krzycki of the American Slav Congress, writer Corliss Lamont, Reverend Donald G. Lathrop of Boston, Reverend John Howland Lathrop of Brooklyn, Robert L. Lindsey of Union Theological Seminary, Rayford W. Logan of Howard University, Reverend Herman H. Long of Fisk University, Oliver S. Loud of Antioch College, Curtis D. MacDougall of Northwestern University, F.L. Marcuse of Cornell University, vice chairman Mary Bacon Mason of the War Resisters League, Kirtley Mather of Harvard University, retired Protestant Episcopal Bishop Walter Mitchell of Arizona, F.M.

Ashley of Rutgers University, Reverend Robert W. Moon of San Francisco, Philip Morrison of Cornell University, retired Protestant Episcopal Bishop Arthur W. Moulton of Utah, Stuart Mudd of the University of Pennsylvania's School of Medicine, Reverend Robert Muir of Boston, Skillman E. Myers of Goddard College, Seth Neddermeyer of the University of Washington, playwright Clifford Odets, Protestant Episcopal Bishop C. Ashton Oldham of Albany, Reverend Edward L. Peet of California, president E.C. Peters of Paine College, Seymour M. Pitcher of the State University of Iowa, Rabbi David De Sola Pool of New York, Bishop Frank M. Reid of Allen University, director Holland Roberts of the California Labor School, Bishop Paul Roberts of Denver, Theodor Rosebury of New York University, Ernest W. Saunders of Morningside College, J. Nevin Sayre of the International Fellowship of Reconciliation, Alfred G. Scattergood and J. Henry Scattergood of the Religious Society of Friends, T.C. Schneirla of the American Museum of Natural History, Harlow Shapley of Harvard University, John F. Shepard of the University of Michigan, editor Guy Emery Shipler of *The Churchman*, author John Somerville, Reverend Alexander Stewart of Union Theological Seminary, Isidor F. Stone, president Fred W. Stover of the Iowa Farmers Union, Stanley I. Stuber of Church World Service Inc., president Glen Talbot of the North Dakota Farmers Union, honorary president Mary Church Terrell of the National Association for the Advancement of Colored People, poet Louis Untermeyer of New York, executive secretary Willard Uphaus of the National Religion and Labor Foundation, writer Mark Van Doren, writer Pierre Van Paassen, Maurice Visscher of the University of Minnesota, Bishop Paris A. Wallace of the African Methodist Episcopal Zion Church, F.W. Went of the California Institute of Technology, Henry Nelson Wieman of the University of Oregon, vice chairman Howell O. Wilkins of the World Christian Youth Commission, editor Aubrey Williams of the *Southern Farmer*, Justice James A. Wolfe of the Utah Supreme Court, Rolland E. Wolfe of Western Reserve University, Thomas Woody of the University of Pennsylvania, and W.A. Young of Baker University.

While clergymen and academicians were attracted into the Cominform's "peace" campaign through the creation of such fronts as the American Peace Crusade, the Committee for a Peaceful Alternative to the Atlantic Pact, and the Mid-Century Conference for Peace, the

Communists in the United States also concentrated on other groups — labor, youth, and women.

In the April 13, 1949 issue of the *New York Times*, a group of minor union officials and a few union executives placed a signed advertisement. Under a totally presumptuous headline (Labor Wants Peace Talks Not A Pact For War — A Statement On The North Atlantic Pact), the advertisement read: "The United States Senate, which recently filibustered the civil rights bills to death, has been called upon to push through the North Atlantic Pact at top legislative speed.

"It is argued that the North Atlantic Pact is urgently needed to secure world peace. Yet many, here and abroad, are alarmed over the pact and fear that, far from promoting peace, it may lead to war. This is our fear. We, the undersigned, see neither hope nor promise in a world divided into hostile blocs.

"It makes no sense to say, as the Secretary of State has said, that the North Atlantic Pact is in the spirit of the United Nations Charter and conforms to its provisions. The North Atlantic Pact is the opposite of the United Nations. It is the final climax in a series of events which have disunited the original United Nations. It is clearly a pact for war based on the assumption that peace is either impossible or undesirable.

"We fervently believe that peace — which the overwhelming majority in all countries earnestly want — is possible. We are convinced that the controversy between the United States and the U.S.S.R. can be resolved in negotiations for a peaceful settlement. The pact closes the door on negotiation.

"Millions of dollars of American taxpayers' money are to go to the pact's signatories for arms and armies. Less than four years after the conclusion of the last war, the United States evidently is ready to promote a full-fledged international armaments race. This is the road to war — not peace.

"As trade-unionists, we are especially alarmed over policies which put American economy on a war footing, give our industries a stake in the continuance of the armaments race, and fill Americans with a fear of peace as bad for business and harmful to national prosperity. We are convinced that the true road to prosperity lies in the development of peacetime industry, designed to meet the mounting needs of consumers. The dread of a depression should be met by forthright action to protect the living standards of Americans, employed and unemployed.

"The North Atlantic Pact is a very serious departure from traditional American policy. It should not be rushed through to meet a fictitious deadline. We urge all Americans, regardless of their political differences, to call upon the President, the Secretary of State, and the Congress to arrange for free and unrestricted public hearings before, as a Nation, we are committed to a course which many of us feel is fraught with peril to America and the world."

The signers of the paid advertisement were for the most part officers of locals belonging to the United Wholesale and Warehouse Workers, the United Shoe Workers, the International Fur and Leather Workers, the United Office and Professional Workers, the Hotel and Club Employees, the United Public Workers, the International Jewelry Workers, the Brotherhood of Painters and Paperhangers, and the Building Service International. The great majority of the 267 signers were in locals affiliated with the CIO. Some of the signers were either known Communist Party members or else their ties with the Communist Party were a matter of public record. They included Ben Gold, Max Perlow, Arthur Osman, John Steuben, William Michelson, Isidore Rosenberg, Frank Dutto, and Joseph P. Selly.

In the Communist press, over a period of several months, there were frequent reports that the labor "leaders" who had signed the *New York Times* advertisement were making preparations for a front that would work for "peace." In June 1949, it was announced that an arrangements committee was formed for the purpose of calling a National Labor Conference for Peace. The committee consisted of honorary chairman Bernard McGroarty of the Stereotypers Union (AFL), chairman Sam Curry, president of Local 347 of the United Packinghouse Workers in Chicago, secretary Sven Anderson, vice president of Local 453 of the United Auto Workers, and executive secretary James Wishart, educational director of the Progressive Citizens of America and the Communist-controlled Fur Workers District Council.

In July 1949, the arrangements committee issued its formal call for a National Labor Conference for Peace to be held on October 1 and 2, 1949, in Chicago. The "call" received favorable attention in the Communist Party press and the arrangements committee invited Communists affiliated with the World Federation of Trade Unions to attend the October meeting.

When the National Labor Conference for Peace did meet as

scheduled, the conferees were treated to the same Communist line that was delivered at the meetings of the American Continental Congress for Peace, the American Peace Crusade, the Committee for Peaceful Alternatives to the Atlantic Pact, and the Mid-Century Conference for Peace. Speakers at the Conference included Paul Robeson; Henry Agard Wallace, who had been the unsuccessful presidential candidate of the Progressive Party in 1948; Fred Stover, president of the Iowa Farmers Union; Merton Scott, national peace board secretary of the Five Years Meeting of Friends (Quakers); New York Congressman Vito Marcantonio; Ewart Guinier, international secretary-treasurer of the United Public Workers; Tom Fitzpatrick of the United Electrical, Radio and Machine Workers, who had been a Fifth Amendment pleader when asked about his Communist Party membership; and Halois Moorehead, business agent for the Building Service Employees in New York, whose pro-Communist Party ties were undeniable. The Conference received the fullest support of Communist labor organizations, including the Soviet Trade Union Council, the World Federation of Trade Unions, the Latin-American Federation of Labor, the Polish Central Trade Union Council, the All-China Federation of Labor, and the Philippine Congress of Labor Organizations.

The officials of the National Labor Conference for Peace cooperated with the Cominform's various projects and fronts, but the effectiveness of the Conference was nullified because the national leaders of organized labor did not endorse the Conference. The same lack of effectiveness characterized an affiliate of the National Labor Conference for Peace, the Labor Youth League.

The Labor Youth League was organized in May 1949 by Leon Wofsy, a Communist Party official active in the various Party youth organizations. Besides supporting the National Labor Conference for Peace, Wofsy's group was active in gathering signatures for the Stockholm Peace Appeal and in supporting the Mid-Century Conference for Peace.

The most important women's group in the Cominform's "peace" campaign in the United States was the Congress of American Women. Its members were present at the World Peace Congresses, the Scientific and Cultural Conference for World Peace, and in the other fronts and projects engineered by the Communist Party, USA. The Congress of American Women began and continued as a subsidiary of the Women's International Democratic Federation (WIDF).

The WIDF was organized in 1945 during the International Women's Anti-Fascist Congress, held in Paris. The Paris Congress was called together by the Communist-controlled *Union des Femmes Françaises*, and the call was answered by Communist and pro-Communist delegates from Belgium, Britain, China, Czecho-Slovakia, Italy, Spain, and the Soviet Union. During the Congress, a French Communist, Eugénie Cotton, proposed the establishment of an initiative committee to work for the formation of an International Women's Congress. The initiative committee was formed, with Eugénie Cotton as chairman, and invitations to attend a plenary session of the International Women's Congress were sent to Communist-controlled organizations, especially women's organizations. In September 1945, the original group of delegates in the "initiative committee" was assured of support by women from Algiers, Bulgaria, Denmark, Finland, Greece, Mexico, Norway, Poland, Portugal, Rumania, Sweden, Switzerland, and the United States.

From the United States, the "initiative committee" received the complete support of the Communist and subversive National Council of American-Soviet Friendship. The educational director of the Women's Committee of the National Council was Jessica Smith, the editor of the Communist-controlled *Soviet Russia Today*. Smith wrote: "When the program and aims of the International Women's Congress become widely known, American women may be counted on to play an important role in this organization. On behalf of the Women's Committee of the National Council of American-Soviet Friendship, which I have the honor to represent, I assure you that we shall do everything in our power to obtain and stimulate the widest support for the great aims of the congress."

The International Women's Congress which met in Paris from November 26 until December 1, 1945, became, in fact, the founding meeting of the Women's International Democratic Federation. The largest delegation — forty members — came from the Soviet Union, dressed in military uniforms bedecked with medals. Thirteen American women were there: Gene Weltfish, Beryl Parker, Ann Bradford, Charlotte Hawkins Brown, Henrietta Buckmaster, Thelma Dale, Muriel Draper, Elizabeth Gurley Flynn, Mrs. Frederic March (Florence Eldridge), Vivian Carter Mason, Mrs. Gifford Pinchot, Jeannette Stern Turner, and Eleanor T. Vaughan. Thelma Dale was a member of the

New York State Committee of the Communist Party. Thyra Edwards was a member of the Young Communist League. Elizabeth Gurley Flynn, the commissar of the delegation, was a member of the National Committee and chairman of the Women's Commission of the Communist Party. Ruth Young was a member of the Young Communist League. All of the women had long Communist front records.

There was never any doubt that the WIDF was completely dominated by the Soviet Union. Although Eugénie Cotton of France was the WIDF's first president, the entire operation was run by Nina Popova of the Soviet Union in her position as executive vice president. Not long after the first meeting of the WIDF, Popova wrote of her experiences in Paris: "We Soviet delegates felt like elder sisters . . . the congress delegates treated the representatives of our great people with tenderness, admiration, and high esteem . . . . Even far away from our borders, the greatness of our country, the heroism of its people, the fame of its army, and the wisdom of our leaders, accompanied us."

It was only natural that the first meeting for the WIDF should be nothing less than an anti-United States, pro-Soviet Union festival. The American delegates were rubbing elbows with some of the world's most important women Communists, including Albania's Nadjimie Hoxha, wife of that nation's Communist Prime Minister; Alice Sportisse, a central committee member of Algeria's Communist Party; Tsola Dragoicheva, general secretary of Bulgaria's Communist Party; Tsai Chang, central executive committee member of China's Communist Party; Anezka Hodinova-Spurna, Communist vice president of Czecho-Slovakia; Marie-Claude Vaillant-Couturier and Jeannette Vermeersch, members of the central committee of France's Communist Party (Vermeersch was the wife of Maurice Thorez, general secretary of France's Communist Party); Chryssa Hadjivassiliou, member of the Politburo of Greece's Communist Party; Magda Joboru, central committee member of Hungary's Communist Party; Ana Pauker, the Communist ruler of Rumania; and Dolores Ibarruri, secretary-general of Spain's Communist Party.

The announced program of the WIDF was to solve a multitude of economic, juridical, and social problems that agitate women, except in the Soviet Union, where all the problems had already been solved. There were discussions on the inequality of pay between men and women, on the status of women with regard to civil and property rights, on child care and mothers' health, and on women's suffrage. In the midst of this Soviet propaganda ploy, the thirteen American delegates at Paris "pledged themselves to return home and organize American women to carry out the program outlined at Paris." The American delegates kept their word.

On March 8, 1946, the Congress of American Women (CAW) was organized. Significantly, the organizers were celebrating International Women's Day, an international Communist holiday, and they had attended a celebration at the Soviet Union's consulate in New York City. Those present at the first meeting of CAW heard reports on the first congress of the Women's International Democratic Federation from Gene Weltfish, Muriel Draper, Vivian Carter Mason, and Henrietta Buckmaster.

Elizabeth Gurley Flynn, who along with another prominent Communist, Margaret Cowl, kept tight control over CAW, announced: "We feel the urgency of organizing this anti-Fascist women's congress to keep the peace."

On May 25, 1946, CAW held its first "working" conference. An election of officers was held with Gene Weltfish chosen as president, Muriel Draper as executive vice president, Helen Phillips as treasurer, Josephine Timms as secretary, and Thyra Edwards as recording secretary. The vice chairmen were Susan B. Anthony II, Charlotte Hawkins Brown, Elinor Gimbel, Vivian Carter Mason, Mrs. Frederic March, Beryl Parker, Mrs. Gifford Pinchot, Jeannette Turner, and Ruth Young. Other women who were prominent in the early activities of CAW included Grace Allen Bangs, Clara Bodian, Dorothy Dunbar Bromley, Frances Damon, Bella V. Dodd, Katherine Earnshaw, Dorothy Gottlieb, Sidonie M. Gruenberg, Anna Center Schneiderman, Mary Van Kleeck, and Mrs. Stephen S. Wise. The Communist and/or pro-Communist flavor of the group was unmistakable.

At this "working" conference, the main speaker was Ella Reeve Bloor, celebrated as the "mother" of the Communist Party, USA. The conference also received a message from General Secretary Vaillant-Couturier of the Women's International Democratic Federation, who expressed the hope that the American women would "act as a check to all reactionary forces who are trying, everywhere, ways of dividing and ways of preventing the democratic forces from strengthening their hand." The message was clearly a call for anti-United States, pro-Soviet action by CAW.

The House Committee on Un-American Activities later reported on CAW: "The purpose of these organizations [CAW and the Women's International Democratic Federation] is not to deal primarily with women's problems, as such, but rather to serve as a specialized arm of Soviet political warfare in the current 'peace' campaign to disarm and demobilize the United States and democratic nations generally, in order to render them helpless in the face of the Communist drive for world conquest. While professedly American in name, the Congress of American Women has been anti-American and pro-Soviet since its inception. In fact, the Congress of American Women, as well as its parent body, the Women's International Democratic Federation, has consistently denounced and opposed all recognized non-Communist women's organizations both here and abroad . . . .

"The Congress of American Women is a part of a solar system of international Communist-front organizations which have been established in recent years, consisting of the Women's International Democratic Federation, the World Federation of Democratic Youth (American affiliates: the American Youth for Democracy, the Labor Youth League, and the American Youth for a Free World), the World Peace Congress (American affiliate: the Scientific and Cultural Conference for World Peace), the All-Slav Congress (American affiliate: the American Slav Congress), and the World Federation of Trade-Unions (American supporters including the left-wing unions within the Congress of Industrial Organizaions). While operating against the democratic nations under close Soviet direction and control, these international Communist-front organizations have not yet been the subject of any coordinated action by the various democracies under attack . . . .

"In its international 'peace' offensive, the Soviet propaganda machine seeks to utilize the World Federation of Democratic Women and its American affiliate, the Congress of American Women, to promulgate the following anti-American propaganda: (1) That America is preparing to initiate a 'new war.' (2) That the Atlantic Defense Pact is really 'aggressive' in character. (3) That the Soviet Union, with its huge standing army, expansionist program, aggressive 'cold war,' and active fifth column, is the only country which really desires to maintain world peace. (4) Support of the Red Army in the event of war, in accordance with the declarations of leading Communists: Maurice Thorez of France, Palmiro Togliatti of Italy, Harry Pollitt of England,

and William Z. Foster of the United States. (5) To utilize women's groups to 'strike a blow at the rear' of the non-Soviet armies in the event of a conflict. (6) To carry on propaganda to the effect that conditions in the United States are so bad that this country is not worth defending, and that on the other hand conditions in the Soviet Union are so vastly superior that it is the only country worth defending. (7) To attack the Marshall plan despite the fact that housewives throughout the world are its chief beneficiaries.

"The Congress of American Women has received open cooperation and support from the Soviet Embassy in this country, while its parent body and foreign affiliates have received similar aid from Communist governments abroad . . . . Proclaimed originally as the 'first women's political-action organization since the suffrage movement,' the Congress of American Women is just another Communist hoax specifically designed to ensnare idealistically minded but politically gullible women . . . .

"The chief purpose of the Congress of American Women is to act as part of a world-wide pressure mechanism among women, in support of Soviet foreign and domestic policy. From its inception this group has displayed a marked anti-American bias. Its real aims are discreetly hidden behind a smoke screen of such attractive idealistic bait as equal rights for women 'in all aspects of political, economic, legal, cultural, and social life,' the extension of educational and health benefits, child care, 'defeat of the maneuvers of the Fascists,' and unity for world peace. The Congress of American Women and its international parent body assume that these purposes have reached their fruition in the Soviet Union and that the United States is chiefly derelict along these lines."

For all practical purposes, membership in the Congress of American Women and the Women's International Democratic Federation was one and the same thing. There was absolutely no distinction between the policies of the two groups. The programs of CAW and other national affiliates of the WIDF varied according to local circumstances but they were guided by the same ideology at all times. Whether at home or abroad, the American women joined in the clamorous denunciation of the United States and the hysterical glorification of the Soviet Union.

The statements which emanated from CAW or WIDF meetings indicated that the Cominform's basic "peace" campaign was clearly understood by the well-disciplined women: "We did not experience the moral and physical sufferings that were inflicted by the Nazis on our allies . . . . What a stirring experience to meet and shake hands at this congress . . . with women who fought so splendidly during the years of war and political struggle. Particularly warm and full of sympathy is the mutual understanding between American and Soviet women." (Muriel Draper of the United States) — "We should use this example of the country of socialism [the Soviet Union] to demonstrate to American women that Communists actively champion the rights of women . . . which bourgeois democracies grant them only piecemeal after tremendous struggles." (Elizabeth Gurley Flynn of the United States) — "My greetings to the Soviet women, who are tirelessly working for peace." (Gene Weltfish of the United States) — "The struggle between these two opposite camps is becoming more and more evident. The first, headed by the U.S.A., is pursuing a policy that is directed toward strengthening imperialism, toward establishing the world domination of the American monopolies, toward the strangulation of democracy, and toward universal support for the reactionary and antidemocratic pro-Fascist regimes and movements. The anti-imperialistic and anti-Fascist forces constitute the other camp, the base of which is formed by the U.S.S.R. and the other countries of the new democracies . . . . The imperialist and reactionary policy of the U.S.A. is encountering the firm resistance of the U.S.S.R., of the countries of the new democracy, who have thrown off Anglo-American imperialist tutelage . . . . In this grave situation the WIDF has shown that it stands firmly in the camp of the active champions of democracy." — "[American imperialists are] directing the Fascist detachments in Greece which are shooting the peaceful population; bribing sheiks and emirs in Arab countries; seizing foreign territory in Greenland and proclaiming it as their own and building military bases on it; striving to place [in Latin America] representatives of the American stock exchange and the general staff in leading positions which enable them to direct the life of those countries." — "The imperialists are once again at work — overtly and covertly — preparing a new war. They are howling in a hundred and one different strains about its inevitability, artificially fanning a war psychosis, mustering all the forces of world reaction for new military adventures, trying to intimidate the peoples and to enslave them by using the threat of war as a means of blackmail. All the means of psychological pressure — the daily and periodical press, radio, the cinema — are being employed by the reactionaries to stir up public opinion and to slander the democratic countries. Who are they that are provoking a new war? ... The American and British reactionaries are urged on by an insatiable thirst for new billions of dollars and insane aspirations for world domination. They are the chief instigators of war. Sisters! Do not believe the lies of the reactionaries! ... The Soviet Union is the basic force engaged in the struggle for peace the world over. Women of all countries! We appeal to you to intensify the struggle for peace, to repulse with vigour the instigators of a new war!" (Nina Popova of the Soviet Union) — "A sinister role has been played by the Government of the United States, which, in violation of all international agreements, is pursuing a policy of expansion and of fomenting war. But this policy comes into collision with the powerful will of that staunch champion of peace, the Soviet Union. The United States Government is waging a campaign of slander against the Soviet Union, whose prestige among the peoples of the whole world has risen still higher since the war. Ninety percent of the losses sustained by Hitler's forces were inflicted by the Soviet Army . . . . The Soviet Union brought liberation . . . . The Soviet Union is the land where the great dream of Socialism that lies in the hearts of all men and women has come true." (Eugénie Cotton of France) — "The reactionaries of the U.S.A. use all possible means to give simple people the monstrous idea that there is danger of aggression on the part of the Soviet Union . . . . [This is] degrading expansionist propaganda. The instigators of a new war must be exposed . . . . The warmongers must be surrounded by the hate and contempt of all people. We must see to it that the hundreds of millions of women, in whatever corner of the globe they may live, know that the aggressive circles in the United States and England are the most dangerous enemies of peace and security." (Nina Popova of the Soviet Union) — "The constitutions of the new democracies acknowledge the basic human rights, the equality of women, and this gives them a basis to work enthusiastically for the economic stabilization of their countries. Only the Soviet Union, the nation of victorious socialism, has reached the stage of complete equality in women's rights . . . . Women in the capitalist countries are denied equal rights not only in the political respect but also in the sphere of marital and civil rights . . . . In the people's democracies women's economic equality is assured by law. If there have been such striking changes in the people's democracies, then what can be said of the Soviet Union, where the complete economic equality of women really exists . . . .?" (Helen Phillips of the United States) — "The imperialists are seeking to crush the people's liberation movement by force of arms but are encountering the ever-mounting resistance of the colonial peoples, including the women . . . [who] are aware that the imperialists are seeking to enslave the colonial countries, to seize their wealth and exploit their cheap labor. That is why the women of Asia and Africa are following with alarm the activities of the American imperialists who are setting up military bases in the East, encouraging Japanese imperialism, and preparing a new world shambles. The position of women in the Soviet Union serves as an inspiring example to all colonial peoples . . . that is why women in all countries look with admiration and hope to the Soviet state which . . . is the bulwark of freedom and democracy." (Tsai Chang of China) — "We have gathered at our second international congress in a tense world situation, at a time of fierce struggle between the forces of reaction and the forces of democracy . . . in order to unite . . . for the struggle against the war-mongers . . . . To be able to fight the warmongers successfully, the women of all countries must know who the enemies of peace are. They must know that the inspirers and organizers of aggression, the inspirers and organizers of another war, are the present rulers of the United States and Great Britain . . . . The American imperialists are utilizing the Marshall plan as a means of enslaving the peoples of western Europe, Latin America, and many other countries; they are robbing these countries of their sovereignty and are subordinating them to the military interest of the United States. Reactionary circles in the United States and Great Britain are hatching insane plans of conquest in an endeavor to establish the world domination of the Anglo-American bloc. The Soviet Union is the vanguard of the international camp that stands for peace and democracy. This explains why the spearhead of the aggressive policy of the fomenters of another war is directed primarily against the Soviet Union . . . . The foreign policy of the U.S.S.R. is guided by respect for the independence and sovereignty of all countries, big and small . . . ." (Nina Popova of the Soviet Union) — "The plan of Anglo-American and French imperialism is . . . to make the people pay for the preparation of the next war, while the profits will go to the arms manufacturers . . . . We owe this criminal French policy to American imperialism because, without its power, the French people would have already put an end to French reaction . . . . This interference takes the form of the Marshall plan, the so-called 'European recovery program' . . . . Above all, the Marshall plan means war . . . . The reactionaries are carrying through this policy in the name of 'western civilization' against 'the East,' that is to say, against socialism and the Soviet Union . . . ." (Jeannette Vermeersch of France) – "We, the women of Latin America, solemnly declare: 'Our sons shall never serve American imperialism and shall never take part in a war against the great Soviet Union and the people's democracies.' " (Fanny Edelman of Argentina) – "At the end of the war, millions of people passionately hoped that our country would continue to follow the path of friendship and cooperation with the Soviet Union and the new democracies. But, instead of this, they have seen their hopes . . . fading in face of an imperialist policy which has led to our country's enslavement to the American dollar, a policy leading to a new war . . . . They dread the establishment of United States bombing bases in Britain." (Nora Wooster of England) – "When the resistance of a people becomes an obstacle to the realization of expansionist American plans for domination, then the Wall Street imperialists, assisted by local reactionaries, fall back on fascism . . . . Anglo-American intervention in Greek internal affairs is no different from German occupation. The royalist Fascists and their American bosses are trying to drown in blood the Greek people's desire to be free and independent. With barbaric cruelty they slaughter Greek patriots, sparing neither women nor children. The People's Liberation Army [Communist] of Greece is showing, however, how powerful a force is the people's will to victory." (Chryssa Hadjivassiliou of Greece) – "Attracted by our large oil fields and by our proximity to the Soviet Union American imperialism has forced itself upon us. At one with its English predecessor, it is trying to stifle all popular movement and wants to make Iran into a fortress against the U.S.S.R." (Miriam Firouz of Iran) – "Owing to the interference of the American imperialists, the peaceful reconstruction of the Free Republic of Trieste has not been successful." (Marie Bernetti-Bernetic of Trieste) – "This document condemns the quest for world supremacy, the policy of aggression, of fomenting a new world war, pursued by the rulers of the United States and Britain . . . . It calls upon the women of all lands to expose the warmongers . . . to demand the reduction of armaments and military expenditures, and the prohibition of the atomic bomb; to organize mass meetings and processions calling for a struggle . . . against fascism and aggression." (M. Makarova of the Soviet Union) — "Some of the people I spoke to, who were opposed to the [Hungarian] government, were non-Communists. So, you see they get better treatment than the Communists over here." (Nora Stanton Barney of the United States) — "[Hungary provided me with my] first taste of freedom." (Halois Moorehead of the United States) — "While the Soviet government has a conscious political philosophy and program designed to bring women into equality, ours does not; and it is here that we reach . . . the problem. For it is up to the progressive movement to supply that conscious leadership . . . it means . . . struggle together with such organizations as the Congress of American Women . . . as a way of arresting the drive of the monopolists toward reaction and war." (Betty Millard of the United States) — "Certain reactionary forces in the United States are making every effort to gain control of the sources of our national life and well-being at the expense of the working men and women. These forces are operating through monopoly capital and international cartels, and by means of those members of the United States Congress whose interests are identified with these groups, and who are thereby largely responsible. These reactionary forces are aided in their action by the United States Chamber of Commerce, its subsidiary city chambers of commerce, and the National Association of Manufacturers. [The reactionary propaganda] is insidiously spread throughout the country by the tyranny of the press and the syndicated columnists, as well as by the widely-heard radio commentators." (Report of CAW to WIDF) — "Hostility to the Soviet Union is initiated by reactionary militarist elements in our Government with the help of the monopoly press, radio, film and other propaganda." (Muriel Draper of the United States)

Congress of American Women members who held positions in or attended congresses of the Women's International Democratic Federation included Zelma Corning Brandt; Margaret Cowl, who had been on the central committee of the Communist Party, USA; Anna Devunich; Manya Carrel Finger; Elinor Gimbel; Minnie Golden; Dorothy Hayes; Ada Jackson; Leona Karkov; Pearl Lawes, a member of the New York State Committee of the Communist Party; Betty Millard, a former editor of the Communist publication, *New Masses*; Halois Moorehead; Rheua Pearce; Helen Phillips; Marie Reed; Rose Rose; Anna Louise

Strong, one of the world's most notorious Communists; Rose Thaler; Josephine Timms; Agnes Vukcevich; Rose Weinstock; Ella Winter; and Josephine Zakrajsek. Every one of these women had a hard-core history of affiliations with the Communist Party or its fronts. Officials of the Congress of American Women who did not travel abroad to WIDF meetings included Mrs. Zlatko Balokovic; Sylvia Beitscher; Harriet Black; Clara Bodian, a member of the Women's Commission of the Communist Party, USA; Dorothy Douglas; Virginia W. Epstein; June Gordon; Gertrude Lane; Clara Savage Littledale; Mary Jane Melish; Audley Moore, member of the Women's Commission of the Communist Party, USA; Jean Muir; Estelle Osborne; Mrs. Eugene V. Personnet; Mrs. Louise Pitner; Eslanda Robeson, wife of Paul Robeson, a Communist; Rose Russell; Lillian Rubin; Maude Slye; Faye Stephenson; Charlotte Stern; Rose Tillotson, a Communist Party political candidate; Ann Wharton; Betty Willett; and Olga Zemaitis, wife of a Communist Party organizer. Without exception, every one of these CAW officials had close ties with the Communist Party or its fronts.

On the American scene, the CAW demonstrated against United States aid to Greece and Turkey when those two nations were threatened by Communist takeovers; gave support to Henry A. Wallace and his Progressive Party in the 1948 presidential election; protested against legislation designed to outlaw the Communist Party; urged United States foreign aid to the Soviet Union's satellites; supported Red China vis-à-vis Nationalist China; demonstrated on behalf of convicted Communist Party leaders and other individual Communists, including Soviet spy Gerhart Eisler; sent delegations to the Cominform's World Congresses; protested against the deportation of Communist aliens; demonstrated against the draft; and urged unilateral disarmament for the United States. The CAW extended American hospitality to Communists from all over the world and took part in the celebration of Communist holidays.

In 1949, when the Congress of American Women held its convention, the event was hailed in the Cominform's journal, *For a Lasting Peace, For a People's Democracy*: "The national convention of the American Women's Congress held in New York at the beginning of the month adopted the congress rules and a program in defense of peace and democratic rights embodying the main aims of the World Federation of Democratic Women to which the congress is affiliated.

The convention pointed out that in view of the war danger fomented by the American monopolists, American women bore a special responsibility. It stressed the need to mobilize the broadest sections of women to fight for peace. The convention demanded that the atom bomb should be outlawed . . . and that the Atlantic pact be annulled."

The Congress of American Women was formally affiliated with the American Labor Party ("Communist dissimulation extends into the field of political parties forming political front organizations such as the . . . American Labor Party"); the American Slav Congress ("Moscow-inspired and directed federation of Communist-dominated organizations seeking by methods of propaganda and pressure to subvert the 10,000,000 people in this country of Slavic birth or descent"); the International Workers Order ("from its very inception demonstrated by its pronouncements, its activities, and the authoritative statements of the Communist Party that it is a subservient instrument of the Communist Party of the United States"); and the National Council of American-Soviet Friendship ("subversive and Communist" – "specializing in pro-Soviet propaganda"). Large numbers of CAW's membership were made up of groups from unions with strongly entrenched Communist leadership, including the United Electrical, Radio, and Machine Workers of America (CIO); the American Communications Association (CIO); the United Public Workers (CIO); the Food, Tobacco, and Agricultural and Allied Workers (CIO); the United Office and Professional Workers of America (CIO); the United Shoe Workers of America (CIO); the Joint Board of Fur Dressers and Dyers; and the Painters Union, District Council 9 (AFL).

The CAW supported or cooperated with the National Federation for Constitutional Liberties ("under Communist Party domination and headed by responsible Party functionaries" – "one of the viciously subversive organizations of the Communist Party"); People's Radio Foundation ("subversive and Communist organization"); American Youth for Democracy ("subversive and Communist" – "part of Soviet psychological warfare against the United States"); the American Committee for Greek Democracy ("Communist front"); the Committee for a Democratic Far Eastern Policy ("Communist"); the National Negro Congress ("subversive and Communist" – "characterized as an organization operating in the field of civil rights under Communist Party domination and headed by responsible Party functionaries"); the National Citizens' Political Action Committee ("Communist front");

the Independent Citizens Committee of the Arts, Sciences and Professions ("Communist front"); the Win-the-Peace Conference ("Communist front"); the Jefferson School of Social Science ("a Communist institution modeled along the lines of the new Communist policy which led to the decision to change the Communist Party into some kind of an educational institution"); the National Lawyers Guild ("the foremost legal bulwark of the Communist Party, its front organizations, and controlled unions"); and the American-Russian Institute ("subversive" − "Communist" − "specializing in pro-Soviet propaganda"). The CAW also campaigned actively for Communist Party candidates in state and municipal elections.

JOHN REED CLUBS
LEAGUE OF AMERICAN WRITERS
INTERNATIONAL UNION OF REVOLUTIONARY WRITERS

In the early history of the Communist Party, its most widely publicized charter member was John Reed, a member of the Communist International who was honored by the Soviet Union by being buried in the Kremlin wall in Moscow.

In *New Masses* (January 1930), Michael Gold reported: "The John Reed Club was organized about two months ago here in New York. It is a small group of writers, artists, sculptors, musicians and dancers of revolutionary tendencies . . . . At the next meeting I shall propose the following: That every writer in the group attach himself to one of the industries. That he spend the next few years in and out of this industry, studying it from every angle, making himself an expert in it, so that when he writes of it he will write like an insider, not like a bourgeois intellectual observer. He will help on the publicity in strikes, etc. He will have his roots in something real. The old Fabians used to get together and write essays on the books they had read. We will get close to the realities."

The John Reed Clubs engaged in a variety of activities. They agitated against the arrest of Communists, against governmental investigations of Communism and Communists, and against proposed or existing anti-Communist legislation. They propagandized for Communist projects and enterprises. John Reed Clubs were established in various cities including New York City, Chicago, Philadelphia, Hollywood, Indianapolis, Boston, Detroit, St. Louis, Grand Rapids, Milwaukee, Hartford,

Santa Fe, and Mena, Arkansas. Many of the clubs published periodicals: *New Force* (Detroit); *New Left, Leftward, Blast, Partisan Review* – all in New York City; *Anvil* (St. Louis); *Cauldron* (Grand Rapids); *Left Front* (Chicago); *Left Review* (Philadelphia); and *Partisan Magazine* (Hollywood). There was a John Reed Club of Art in New York City, where members were instructed in revolutionary art, dance, and song. There were similar "Art" centers in Detroit, Chicago, and Boston. In New York City, there was also a John Reed School of Art, and a similar institution was connected with the John Reed Club in Boston. New York had, in addition, a John Reed Club Writers School.

In July 1930, Harry Alan Potamkin – founder and secretary of the John Reed Clubs – wrote in *New Masses*: "The John Reed Club has continued active on the workers' cultural front. The splendid May 1 parade from Rutgers Square to Union Square included not only cartoon-posters designed and made by the artists of the John Reed Club, but also a John Reed Club division. The press committee of the club has done excellent work in support of the International Labor Defense campaign for class war prisoners. The signatures of noted writers, artists, and educators were secured to the club's statement later issued to the press. The International Labor Defense has been further supported by the John Reed Club in an entertainment arranged by the club on May 14, with Gene Schachner as chairman. Emjo Basshe directed and staged one act of Singing Jailbirds, with members and nonmembers participating. Gropper, Klein, Burck, entertained with satirical cartoons. An International Labor Defense benefit at Camp Nitgedaiget was attended by Mike Gold, L. Adohmyan, J. Pass, and Jacob Burck.

"The John Reed Club cooperated with the Proletpen, Jewish Proletarian writers group, in the Freiheit's Moishe Nadir celebration which filled Carnegie Hall to overflow. Gropper's cartoons were well received. Edith Segal led the Red Dancers. Adolph Wolf greeted Nadir for the club. The club joined in hailing the first Chinese Soviet Congress; and in the United Front Conference Against Lynching, called by the New York district of the Communist Party.

"Interest in the club's work is evinced by letters from the revolutionary groups in China and the Soviet Union, and even from remote and esoteric Hollywood. The members' exhibit of paintings, drawings, and sculpture still continues at the clubrooms. Club members continue speaking at workers' clubs. Walt Carman spoke on literature and revolution in America, Joshua Kunitz on Russian literature, both at the Hungarian Workers' Club. The workers' summer camps will have a number of club members in their cultural work. The writers are preparing playlets for the workers vacationing in their camps.

"The cultural work will be furthered in a worker's film movement being organized, which will carry over to the United States of America a force now active in England, Denmark, and Germany. Beginnings are being made by members writing on films — especially for the *New Masses* and the *Daily Worker*; in members' activities in the making and editing of workers' films; in talks to workers' clubs; in cooperation with working class organizations like the Workers' International Relief and the International Labor Defense; and in support of meritorious pictures, such as that given by the club to the Vostokkino's Turksib. The work will be correlated and integrated this coming fall, and a film group will be mobilized for the study of the technique of picture-making and the education of workers in the cinema as an ideological and artistic medium.

"Publishers are adding to their lists the work of club members. Charles Yale Harrison's *Generals Die in Bed* has appeared in England, Canada, and is issued by William Morrow in New York. It will appear soon in Soviet Russia, Germany, and Japan. Michael Gold's children's story, *Charlie Chaplin's Parade*, with illustrations by Otto Soglow, is on Harcourt, Brace's list for the fall. William Gropper's circus story told in drawings, film style, comes out this fall with Coward McCann. Many of the revolutionary writers and artists have emigrated for the summer to work on paintings for fall exhibitions and forthcoming books."

In the Communists' *Daily Worker* (February 21, 1931), it was reported: "The club, in a little over a year of its existence, has done good work in the revolutionary movement, conducting campaigns against the anti-Soviet 'holy' crusade, cooperating in the campaign in defense of political prisoners, helping with posters for demonstrations, arranging pageants, and a portion of its members taking active part in the Communist election campaign.

"It should broaden and enlarge its present work along the lines of the program of the Kharkov conference of revolutionary writers. It should keep closer contact with the life and everyday struggles of the working class, giving more attention to the development of proletarian literature, to the development of new worker writers and artists, as well as to winning over the radicalized intellectuals. It should become a real force in the struggle for racial equality, especially for the Negro masses, and give greater effort to exposing social-fascism and petty bourgeois tendencies and to the fight against imperialist war and the defense of the Soviet Union."

The first major campaign of the John Reed Clubs was an advertisement in the *New York Times* (May 19, 1930) as a protest against anti-Communist propaganda and alleged Red-baiting. Among those signing the protest were: Franz Boas, Hugo Gellert, C. Hartley Grattan, Sherwood Anderson, William Gropper, Malcolm Cowley, Horace Gregory of *Nation* and *New Republic*, Adolph Dehn, Ralph Harlow, Babette Deutsch and her husband Avrahm Yarmolinsky, Carl Van Doren, John Dos Passos, Communist Party leader Robert W. Dunn, Max Eastman, Waldo Frank, Frank Kingdon, Alfred Kreymborg, Joshua Kunitz, Louis Lozowick, Anna Rosenberg, Arthur Garfield Hays of the American Civil Liberties Union, Josephine Herbst, Henry L. Mencken, Scott Nearing, Joseph North, Harvey O'Connor, Upton Sinclair, Otto Soglow, Genevieve Taggard, Carlo Tresca, Jim Tully, Louis Untermeyer, Edmund Wilson, and Art Young. Among the signatories were novelists, cartoonists, poets, union leaders, journalists, academicians, artists, editors, attorneys, and clergy. Their work was to be found throughout the Communist press, liberal publications, Socialist literature, textbooks, and the regular press. Their art works were in major museums.

National officers of the John Reed Clubs included Communist writers Jack Conroy and Joshua Kunitz, Communist Joseph Freeman of the American Civil Liberties Union, and Communists Eugene Gordon and Edward Dahlberg. Other leaders of the John Reed Clubs were Lewis Mumford, Ben Shahn, Henry W.L. Dana, Mary Heaton Vorse, and William Browder, secretary of the International Labor Defense. John Reed Club authors included A. Abramowitz, J.S. Balch, Maxwell Bodenheim, Miriam Clark, Eugene Clay, Clifton Cuthbert, Leon Dennen, John Dos Passos, Ben Field, Sam Gasper, Hugo Gellert, John Gregory, Warren Huddlestone, Thomas Jordan, John Howard Lawson, Tillie Lerner, Melvin Levy, Grace Lumpkin, Helen Moore, Edward Newhouse, Paul Peters, Bob Reed, John C. Rogers, Jacques Roumain, Muriel Rukeyser, John Wexley, and Richard Wright.

In April 1935, a call was issued for a national convention of a League of American Writers that would be affiliated with Moscow's

International Union of Revolutionary Writers – the same sort of affiliation as maintained by the John Reed Clubs. The call for the convention was signed by the General Secretary of the Communist Party and members of the John Reed Clubs, including Nelson Algren, Arnold B. Armstrong, Nathan Asch, Maxwell Bodenheim, Thomas Boyd, Bob Brown, Fielding Burke, Kenneth Burke, Erskine Caldwell, Alan Calmer, Robert Cantwell, Robert Coates, Lester Cohen, Jack Conroy, Malcolm Cowley, Edward Dahlberg, Theodore Dreiser, Guy Endore, James T. Farrell, Kenneth Fearing, Ben Field, Waldo Frank, Joseph Freeman, Michael Gold, Eugene Gordon, Horace Gregory, Henry Hart, Clarence Hathaway, Josephine Herbst, Robert Herrick, Granville Hicks, Langston Hughes, Orrick Johns, Arthur Kallet, Lincoln Kirstein, Herbert Kline, Joshua Kunitz, John Howard Lawson, Tillie Lerner, Meridel LeSueur, Melvin Levy, Robert Morss Lovett, Louis Lozowick, Grace Lumpkin, Lewis Mumford, Edward Newhouse, Joseph North, Moissaye Olgin, Samuel Ornitz, Myra Page, John Dos Passos, Paul Peters, Allen Porter, Harold Preece, William Rollins, Paul Romaine, Isidor Schneider, Edwin Seaver, Claire Sifton, Paul Sifton, George Sklar, John L. Spivak, Lincoln Steffens, Philip Stevenson, Genevieve Taggard, Alexander Trachtenberg, Nathaniel West, Ella Winter, and Richard Wright.

The call expressed the need for a further organization of revolutionary writers to convince the people of the necessity for the struggles against capitalism and for the institution of Marxism and to fight "fascist" tendencies in the United States. The call was for writers "who have clearly indicated their sympathy with the revolutionary cause; who do not need to be convinced of the decay of capitalism, of the inevitability of revolution." In its literature, the League said: "The Communist says frankly: art, an instrument in the class struggle, must be developed by the proletariat as one of its weapons."

The founding congress of the League of American Writers was held on April 26, 1935, in New York City. Waldo Frank was elected Chairman of the League. An honorary presiding committee for the congress consisted of foreign Communists including Henri Barbusse, Romain Rolland, Ludwig Renn, Heinrich Mann, Maxim Gorki, Feodor Gladov, Mikhail Sholokhov, Sergei Tretiakov, Jacques Roumain, Hu Lan-chi, Kirohata Kurahara, Juan de la Cabada, Juan Marinello, Rafael Alberti, and Giovanni Germanetto. The congress received greetings from Communists the world over: the American-born Agnes Smedley from China; Johannes Becher and Anna Sechers from Paris; Boris Pilnyak, Sergei Tretiakov, and Feodor Gladkov from the Soviet Union; Anderson Nexo from Denmark; Madame Sun Yat-Sen from China; the China League of Left Writers; and the Union of Soviet Writers.

The International Union of Revolutionary Writers exhorted the League of American Writers: "Develop the art of revolution! May your Congress be the impetus to a wide front of struggle against fascism, against imperialist war, and for the defense of the Soviet Union, the fatherland of the toilers of the world." Earl Browder addressed the first congress of the League of American Writers, saying: "There is a political party which plays an increasingly influential role, the Communist Party. Yes, the Communist Party is a force, in every phase of life of the masses, even that of poets, dramatists, novelists and critics . . . . We also understand that if you could have found any other political party which had anything significant to say about cultural problems, you would also have invited it to be represented. It is one of the signs of the times that there is no such political party in the United States."

The *Daily Worker's* editor Clarence Hathaway wrote: "We have run all of the advance material on the Congress, and many articles dealing with it . . . . The *Daily Worker* did so because as the organ of the Communist Party in the United States, it was conscious that we must not only win the overwhelming mass of the American workers and farmers for the revolutionary position, but that the writers, the intellectuals generally and the middle class, must be made active allies of the working class in its struggle against capitalism."

Alan Calmer, a member of the League of American Writers, described the link between the John Reed Clubs and the League: "The first revolutionary writers' congress in a capitalist country opened in New York City on the eve of May Day 1935. It marked the beginning of a new period in American left-wing literature . . . . In the first years of the great economic crisis, revolutionary literature was created within the organizational skeleton of the *New Masses* and the John Reed Clubs . . . . The chief shortcoming of the revolutionary cultural movement was characterized at the second national conference of the John Reed Clubs in 1934 as the old malady of sectarianism . . . . While the more enlightened Communist writers and Party leaders sharply attacked this tendency for years . . . . Speaking at the John Reed conference in the name of the Communist Party, Alexander Trachtenberg told the young writers gathered there, that 'our cultural allies are very dear to us . . . .'

"Pointing to these handicaps, the delegates to the conference instructed their executive committee to take the initiative in sponsoring a broad conference of leftwing authors . . . . A new organization committee was formed, which gradually involved more and more sympathetic writers into the leadership of the committee which issued the 'Call for an American Writers Congress' at the beginning of 1935."

The thoroughly Communist character of the League was admitted by its members. Kenneth Burke said that the "Congress [of the League of American Writers] was unquestionably made possible only by the vitality and organizing ability of the Communist Party." Philip Rahv said: "The overwhelming majority of delegates were either Communists or sympathizers of Communism." Archibald MacLeish said that he was one of "those who, not themselves Communists, stand with the Communists in active opposition to the menace of fascism." However, MacLeish could not have been more profound in his sympathy for Communism. To his fellow members of the League at its first congress he described "a very successful experiment toward a better world . . . being conducted in a place which has come to be known as the Union of Soviet Socialist Republics." Evelyn Scott wrote: "The League of American Writers was from its inception bound by its every manifesto and resolution both to support Soviet policies, and to compel American culture to adopt the trend to forcible methods made inevitable in Russia."

The first executive committee of the League of American Writers included Kenneth Burke, Harold Clurman, Malcolm Cowley, Waldo Frank, Joseph Freeman, Michael Gold, Henry Hart, Josephine Herbst, Granville Hicks, Matthew Josephson, Alfred Kreymborg, John Howard Lawson, Albert Maltz, Isidor Schneider, Edwin Seaver, Genevieve Taggard, and Alexander Trachtenberg.

The national council of the League included Nelson Algren, Michael Blankfort, Maxwell Bodenheim, Van Wyck Brooks, Sterling Brown, Fielding Burke, Alan Calmer, Robert Cantwell, Harry Carlisle, Eugene Clay, Merle Colby, Jack Conroy, Edward Dahlberg, Leonard Ehrlich, James T. Farrell, Kenneth Fearing, Angel Flores, Horace Gregory, Robert Herrick, Sidney Howard, Orrick Johns, Joshua Kunitz, Tillie

Lerner, Meridel LeSueur, Robert Morss Lovett, Grace Lumpkin, Lewis Mumford, Moishe Nadir, Clifford Odets, M.J. Olgin, Joseph Opatashu, Paul Peters, Rebecca Pitts, William Rollins, Jr., George Sklar, Agnes Smedley, Lincoln Steffens, James Waterman Wise, and Richard Wright.

Eligibility to the League of American Writers was "open to all writers whose work has been published or used with reasonable frequency in channels of more than local scope, including magazines, newspapers, the radio, the stage, and the screen. Membership in good standing is contingent upon the acceptance and observance of the aims as set forth below, and upon payment of dues."

The announced purposes of the League were: "To enlist writers in all parts of the United States in a national cultural organization for peace and democracy and against fascism and reaction. To defend the political and social institutions that guarantee a healthy atmosphere for the perpetuation of culture; to insist on the democratic rights of education, freedom of thought and expression. To stimulate the interest of other writers in our program, and to offer younger writers in particular our fraternal interest and help. To support progressive trade-union organization, especially among professionals and in the liberal arts. To effect an alliance, in the interest of culture, between American writers and all progressive forces. To support the people's front in all countries. To cooperate with similar organizations of writers in other countries."

The members of the League certainly lived up to the aim of cooperating with similar organizations of writers in other countries. They did this by their contribution (by writing articles or otherwise) to *International Literature*, the official organ of the International Union of Revolutionary Writers, published in Moscow. The members included Nelson Algren, Newton Arvin, Emjo Basshe, Michael Blankfort, Maxwell Bodenheim, Earl Browder, Bob Brown, Sterling Brown, Fielding Burke, Kenneth Burke, Stanley Burshaw, Erskine Caldwell, Walter Carman, Harold Clurman, Merle Colby, Jack Conroy, Malcolm Cowley, Kyle Crichton, Countee Cullen, Edward Dahlberg, Theodore Dreiser, Ed Falkowski, James T. Ferrell, Kenneth Fearing, Ben Field, Louis Fischer, Ford Maddox Ford, Waldo Frank, Joseph Freeman, Michael Gold, Manuel Gomez, Eugene Gordon, Horace Gregory, Albert Halper, Alfred Hayes, Josephine Herbst, Robert Herrick, John Herrman, Granville Hicks, Langston Hughes, Orrick Johns, Josephine

Johnson, Oakley Johnson, William N. Jones, Matthew Josephson, Joseph Kalar, Herbert Kline, Alfred Kreymborg, Joshua Kunitz, Corliss Lamont, John Howard Lawson, Ruth Lechlitner, Tillie Lerner, Meridel LeSueur, Melvin Levy, H.H. Lewis, Robert Morss Lovett, Grace Lumpkin, Norman MacLeod, Albert Maltz, Leonard Mins, Scott Nearing, Edward Newhouse, Clifford Odets, Joseph Opatashu, Samuel Ornitz, Myra Page, John Dos Passos, Paul Peters, Wallace Phelps, Rebecca Pitts, Elmer Rice, William Rollins, Isidor Schneider, Edwin Seaver, George Sklar, Agnes Smedley, John Spivak, Paul Strand, Anna Louise Strong, Earl Sydnor, Genevieve Taggard, Alexander Trachtenberg, Mary Heaton Vorse, Nathaniel West, John Wexley, Edwin Wolfe, Richard Wright, Louis Zara, and Leane Zugsmith.

Almost simultaneously with the founding of the League of American Writers, the Communist International concentrated upon a strategy of infiltration whereby Communists, rather than flaunting their open control of their own front organizations, would move into other organizations and control them from within. In keeping with their plan, Communists removed themselves from visible positions in fronts. This was done in the hope that non-Communist liberals would be enticed into fronts which served Communist purposes behind a facade of idealistic-appearing programs. There was stress on civil liberties, constitutional rights, the rights of labor, protection of aliens, and expansion of the traditional freedoms of speech, assembly, and the press. Under the sugar coating of idealism, there was the practical application of the Communist line. The fronts were basically working to protect the Communists as they attempted to subvert the structure of American government and society, and to promote the best interests of the Soviet Union by supporting a United States foreign policy that would complement that of the Soviet Union on the international scene. No matter how harmless in appearance were the Communist fronts, no matter how laudable seemed their motives, no matter how respectable appeared their ostensible leaders, no matter how high the regard their members commanded in the academic community or press or literary field or the arts or the professions, the day-to-day operation was directed at subversion of the United States through collusion with Moscow and its agents everywhere.

In its beginnings the League of American Writers was so saturated with known Communists and its literature was so obviously Communist propaganda that only the most gullible or ignorant dupes could have been deceived into believing that it was a liberal front. When the Communist International decided to tone down the appearance of its fronts, the League underwent a phony metamorphosis. It made its appeal to those liberals who considered fascism more deadly than Communism, who thought the Soviet Union was a peace-loving state being threatened by imperialist-colonialist war-mongering powers, and who considered anti-Communist activities as a threat to freedom and prelude to totalitarianism in the United States.

The overall strategy of the Communist International worked. Dupes and innocents and would-be liberals flocked into Communist fronts to do the work of the Communists without formally committing themselves to membership in the Communist Party. The new recruits, either for their own individual reasons or because of their individual intellectual deficiencies, were blind to the fact that by adhering to the League and its policies they supported every twist and turn in the zigzag course of the Communist line. They operated from two premises: the Soviet Union represented peace; the Communist Party was concerned about the general welfare; therefore, all who opposed the Soviet Union and/or the Communist Party were warmongering reactionaries, at home and abroad.

In 1939, the League adopted "a domestic program based on support of progressive New Deal measures and opposition to the reactionary and fascist enemies of the New Deal." As for foreign policy: "To safeguard peace, the congress [of the League of American Writers] voted in favor of concerted action by the United States, the Soviet Union, England and France to resist the aggressions of fascism." Heretofore, England and France had been anathema to the Communists and the United States just another warmongering-imperialist-colonialist power. When the League, in 1939, was concentrating its fire upon fascist aggression in Europe and upon the fascist and reactionary enemies of the New Deal in the United States, Donald Ogden Stewart was president of the League. His vice presidents were Van Wyck Brooks, Erskine Caldwell, Malcolm Cowley, Paul de Kruif, Langston Hughes, Meridel Le Sueur, and Upton Sinclair. The most prominent members or collaborators of the League were a combination of charter members and those liberals who were attracted to the League in the few years when its visible hue went from rosy red to pink. They included Margaret Culkin Banning, Ruth Benedict, Stephen Vincent Benét,

William Rose Benét, Algernon D. Black, Louis Bromfield, Earl Browder, Henry Seidel Canby, Walter B. Cannon, James B. Carey, Emanuel Chapman, John M. Coffee, Jerome Davis, Thomas E. Dewey, Martha Dodd, Theodore Dreiser, Harry Emerson Fosdick, Samuel Grafton, William Green, Granville Hicks, John Haynes Holmes, Leo Huberman, Harold Ickes, Robert H. Jackson, Rockwell Kent, Paul de Kruif, Lewis E. Lawes, John Howard Lawson, Eduard C. Lindeman, Albert Maltz, Ruth McKenney, Karl Menninger, Tom Mooney, George Norlin, Samuel Putnam, Kingsley Roberts, Anna Rochester, George Seldes, Bernhard J. Stern, Rex Stout, Genevieve Taggard, Ida M. Tarbell, Dorothy Thompson, Mary Heaton Vorse, Henry A. Wallace, Goodwin Watson, A.F. Whitney, Albert Rhys Williams, Mary E. Woolley, and Leane Zugsmith.

No sooner had the League decided to support positive resistance to fascism than Stalin and Hitler signed a non-aggression pact. Peace-loving Communism was now in the same tent with the arch-fascism of Nazi Germany. The League made a quick reversal; while Europe was reeling from the invasion and rape of Poland by Hitler and Stalin was sharing in the division of Poland, it behooved the Communists in the United States to adopt a new line. In June 1940, the League issued a plea for nonintervention in the European war by the United States, so as not to disturb the rapacious successes of the Nazi-Communist alliance. The plea said, in part: "The greatest danger to our peace at this time lies in the possibility that the profound antifascist sentiments of the American people will be misused to lead them into the war .... We maintain, however, that this war in Europe is not one in which the American people should take part ... ; on the contrary, we maintain that our participation will result only in the prolongation of the war, in the abolition of our own liberties, in the substitution of a tyrannical M-Day control for the rights we cherish, in death lists and purposeless social misery, in cataclysmic depression. We urge all Americans to combine their strength, to unite in boldest opposition to the hysteria of the moment .... "

The Hitler-Stalin pact of 1939 caused a few defections from the League of American Writers, notably those of Archibald MacLeish, Malcolm Cowley, Van Wyck Brooks, Thomas Mann, Oliver La Farge, Louis Bromfield, and Granville Hicks. Torn between their sympathy for Communism and hatred of fascism, they decided to take a vacation from the dilemma. Most of them returned to the pro-Communist fold when Hitler invaded the Soviet Union in 1941.

Two weeks before the German attack upon the Soviet Union, the League of American Writers met in its fourth congress. In its call to the congress, the League said: "We are gathering to reaffirm the aims of our three previous Congresses. In 1935, in 1937, and again in 1939, we declared our indissoluble ties with the American people. We proclaimed our unalterable conviction that reaction and its wars are the greatest enemies of a free and flourishing culture. We resolved to promote an atmosphere in which the literary crafts could be discussed cooperatively without compulsion or fear. We expressed our solidarity with the other progressive writers of this hemisphere and of the world.

"In 1941, the values by which we have lived are facing unprecedented attacks. Half of the world is at war and the other half is endangered by attempts to draw it into war. We had warned of the consequences of 'non-intervention' in Spain, of aid to the aggressor in China, of appeasement at Munich. Today, these consequences are tragically apparent. We have warned that America must be defended not by involvement in this war, or by steps toward dictatorship, or by pursuing a course of imperialist expansion, but by preserving peace and expanding democracy on the economic, political, and cultural levels. Today, we must ask whether the present policy of the administration and the program of big business are not leading us toward war and fascism in the name of resistance to war and fascism.

"Our lives and our work, as craftsmen and as human beings, are at stake. We have special problems to meet: censorship and diversion of art to further a war the people do not want; diminishing outlets for the expression of our honest convictions; disregard for the needs of anti-fascist writers who seek asylum in the Americas. Wherever the right to speak is lost we too are the losers. Wherever civil liberties are abridged, our stories, poems, plays, essays, and books are abrogated. The attacks on trade unions, political minorities, and education are attacks on our basic convictions as writers and as citizens.

"We know that our existence as free writers, spokesmen of a free people, depends on our continued loyalty to the principles which govern the work of the League of American Writers. We therefore call our fellow writers, and our associates in the related cultural crafts, to the Fourth Biennial Congress to consider the following questions: How best as writers can we resist the drive toward war and reaction which threatens our democratic culture? What can we do to extend further help to persecuted writers of other lands? What can we do to restore the WPA cultural projects and to transform them into permanent Peoples Art Projects vital to the nation's strength? What measures can we take to combat and surmount the growing restrictions on our work as honest craftsmen? How can we contribute to a genuine cultural interchange between the peoples of the Americas? How can we enrich America's imperishable democratic literature and extend its audience?"

Those who joined in issuing the call to the League's 1941 congress were truly the hard-core committed pro-Soviet sympathizers. When liberals and even Communists were dismayed at the Hitler-Stalin pact, those who remained with the League were far beyond the pale of dupery or innocence. Among the better known were Alvah Bessie, William Blake, Marc Blitzstein, Millen Brand, Dorothy Brewster, Edwin Berry Burgum, Fielding Burke, Vera Caspary, Haakon Chevalier, Lester Cole, H.W.L. Dana, Martha Dodd, Pietro di Donato, Muriel Draper, Theodore Dreiser, Frederick V. Field, Dashiell Hammett, Lillian Hellman, Langston Hughes, Paul Jarrico, Gordon Kahn, Rockwell Kent, Alfred Kreymborg, Joshua Kunitz, Corliss Lamont, John Howard Lawson, Meridel LeSueur, Robert Morss Lovett, Helen Merrell Lynd, Ruth McKenney, Carey McWilliams, Albert Maltz, Bruce Minton, Walter Rautenstrauch, Harold J. Rome, Robert Rossen, Vida D. Scudder, George Seldes, Bernhard J. Stern, Donald Ogden Stewart, Anna Louise Strong, Genevieve Taggard, Harry F. Ward, Orson Welles, and Richard Wright.

Once the Hitler-Stalin nonaggression pact was broken, the League of American Writers quickly adapted to the new situation. All-out aid for the Soviet Union and its "gallant allies," France and England, was urged in the struggle against Germany. Black became white; water became iron. Intervention on the side of the Soviet Union in the European war was pressed upon the Roosevelt Administration. The i's of the Communist line were dotted and the t's crossed meticulously by the League.

In little more than eleven years, the original band of John Reed Club members had made an enormous contribution to the Communist cause. Their League of American Writers, through the printed word and otherwise, had proved to be one of the most reliable and influential propaganda outlets ever devised by the Communist International. From the John Reed Club and its League of American Writers came the *New Masses, Partisan Review*, the Theatre Union, the New Theatre, the Film and Foto League, the Book Union, the Exiled Writers Committee, Film Audiences for Democracy, Frontier Films, and other fronts, publications, and enterprises which served the Communist Party through some of its most trying years in the United States. There was not a major front that was not heavily manned by Reed or League members, and at the same time bookstalls, newspapers, periodicals, the Broadway stage, book clubs, Hollywood films mirrored the pro-Communist lion's share of the communications media.

NATIONAL COMMITTEE FOR THE DEFENSE OF POLITICAL PRISONERS
EMERGENCY COMMITTEE FOR SOUTHERN POLITICAL PRISONERS
NATIONAL COMMITTEE FOR PEOPLE'S RIGHTS

In 1930, six Communists were arrested in Georgia and charged with sedition. Those arrested, except for Herbert Newton and Ann "Red Flame" Burlak, were not prominent except within Communist Party circles. Nevertheless, since they were apprehended while conducting Party business, their defense was of concern to the Moscow-controlled International Labor Defense and the newly-organized John Reed Clubs, a Communist front.

Theodore Dreiser, the celebrated novelist and fellow-traveler who would die a Communist, headed a special front, the Emergency Committee for Southern Political Prisoners, to raise funds for the defense of the Atlanta six. Dreiser, a member of the John Reed Clubs, was made chairman of the Emergency Committee; John Dos Passos, a Reed member, was treasurer. They were aided by other Reed Club members: Sherwood Anderson, William Rose Benét, Malcolm Cowley, Waldo Frank, Josephine Herbst, Alfred Kreymborg, Scott Nearing, Burton Rascoe, Upton Sinclair, Louis Untermeyer, Carl Van Doren, and Edmund Wilson.

Out of the Emergency Committee, there developed the National Committee for Defense of Political Prisoners (NCDPP), a subsidiary of International Labor Defense. The NCDPP operated out of Communist Party headquarters in New York City. Dreiser and Dos Passos remained as chairman and treasurer, respectively. Lincoln Steffens and Sherwood

Anderson were vice chairmen. Holdover members from the Emergency Committee included Benét, Cowley, Frank, Herbst, Kreymborg, Rascoe, and Sinclair. They were joined by literary lights and others, most of whom were Reed Club members, including Harry Elmer Barnes, Franz Boas, Edward Dahlberg, Adolph Dehn, Hugo Gellert, C. Hartley Grattan, Langston Hughes, Louis Lozowick, Edna St. Vincent Millay, Samuel Ornitz, James Rorty, Bernhard J. Stern, Mary Heaton Vorse, and Ella Winter.

Although the International Labor Defense was responsible for the establishment and direction of the NCDPP, it described the NCDPP as "an independent organization composed mainly of prominent writers, artists and professionals interested in aid to the victims of terror and reaction." The "victims of terror and reaction" were invariably Communists or fellow-travelers arrested in the course of Communist-instigated strikes or demonstrations or illegal political activities. It was not merely a coincidence that those defended by the NCDPP had their causes pleaded in the pages of the *Daily Worker*, publications of International Labor Defense, and other Communist Party organs. One Communist *cause célèbre* after another became the concern of the NCDPP: the Scottsboro Boys; the defense of Communist Angelo Herndon; the defense of Communist Lawrence Simpson; the defense of Luiz Carlos Prestes, the head of Brazil's Communist Party; the defense of Pedro Albizu Campos, Puerto Rican Communist leader; and Communist labor agitators throughout the country.

As the NCDPP increased its activities it attracted the usual array of fellow travelers to swell its membership. They included Louis Adamic, Nathan Asch, Crane Brinton, Erskine Caldwell, Marc Connelly, Aaron Copland, George S. Counts, Kyle Crichton, Henry W.L. Dana, Guy Endore, James T. Farrell, Osmond K. Fraenkel, John H. Hammond Jr., Granville Hicks, Quincy Howe, Matthew Josephson, Joshua Kunitz, Robert Morss Lovett, Lewis Mumford, and Maxwell Stewart. The executive secretary was Joseph Gelders, a well-known Communist.

In 1938, the NCDPP changed its name to the National Committee for People's Rights (NCPR). The change seemed to be a signal for more individuals to sign on as members. Rockwell Kent, Ella Winter, and John Howard Lawson were chairman, vice chairman, and treasurer, respectively. New members included J. Edward Bromberg, Bennett Cerf, Muriel Draper, Lillian Hellman, George S. Kaufman, Bruce

Minton, George Seldes, George Soule, and Donald Ogden Stewart.

The Attorney General of the United States, Francis Biddle, reported that the NCDPP and the NCPR were "substantially equivalent to International Labor Defense, legal arm of the Communist Party. Unlike International Labor Defense, however, which operates principally among the middle and lower classes, the . . . [NCDPP-NCPR] caters to financially and socially prominent liberals to attract the influence of their patronage and their contributions in support of 'civil liberties' cases selected for defense." Biddle also reported that funds were diverted from the NCDPP-NCPR to Communist Party uses.

NATIONAL COMMITTEE TO SECURE JUSTICE IN THE ROSENBERG CASE

NATIONAL COMMITTEE TO SECURE JUSTICE FOR MORTON SOBELL IN THE ROSENBERG CASE

On June 19, 1953, wife and husband Ethel and Julius Rosenberg were executed at Sing Sing Prison in New York. They had been convicted for participation in a conspiracy to commit espionage against the United States.

The Rosenbergs' troubles with the law began on May 23, 1950, when Harry Gold, a co-conspirator of theirs, was arrested. He pleaded guilty on July 20 and was sentenced to thirty years' imprisonment. On June 16, David Greenglass, another co-conspirator, was arrested; he was indicted three weeks later. Greenglass pleaded guilty and received a fifteen-year sentence. On July 17 Julius Rosenberg was arrested, and on August 11, Ethel Rosenberg. They were both indicted on August 17. On January 30, 1951, the Rosenbergs and Greenglass were again indicted, along with Morton Sobell and Anatoli Yakoulev, a Soviet vice-consul. Yakoulev fled from prosecution to the Soviet Union. Gold and Greenglass became government witnesses.

The trial of the Rosenbergs and Sobell was held at the Second District Court in New York City and lasted from March 6 until March 29, when a jury of twelve unanimously agreed to a verdict of guilty for the three defendants. The Rosenbergs were sentenced to death and Sobell received thirty years' imprisonment. In sentencing the Rosenbergs, Judge Irving R. Kaufman said: "I consider your crime worse than murder. Plain deliberate contemplated murder is dwarfed in magnitude by comparison with the crime you have committed. Committing the act of murder, the criminal kills only his victim . . . but in your case I believe your conduct in putting in the hands of the Russians the A-bomb years before our best scientists predicted Russia would perfect the bomb, has already caused, in my opinion, the Communist aggression in Korea with the resulting casualties exceeding 50,000, and who knows but that millions more innocent people may pay the price of your treason. Indeed, by your betrayal, you have undoubtedly altered the course of history to the disadvantage of our country." During the course of the trial, the Rosenbergs testified in direct, cross, re-direct, and re-cross examination. Sobell did not testify.

The three co-defendants were Communists. During their testimony, the Rosenbergs frequently invoked the protection of the Fifth Amendment. Communism and membership in the Communist Party, however, were not at issue during the trial. As a matter of fact, on frequent occasions during the course of the trial, Judge Kaufman reminded the jurors, the prosecution, and the defense that "proof of Communist Party membership or activity does not prove the offense charged in this indictment."

After the Rosenbergs were sentenced, their case underwent twenty-seven months of legal review. The United States Court of Appeals rejected their appeals seven times. The Supreme Court of the United States, on seven occasions, refused to review the decision. Three appeals for executive clemency were rejected by the President of the United States.

At the conclusion of the trial Emanuel H. Bloch, defense counsel, said: "I would like to say to the Court on behalf of all defense counsel that we feel you have treated us with utmost courtesy, that you have extended to us the privileges that we expect as lawyers, and despite any disagreements we have had with the Court on questions of law, we feel that the trial has been conducted, and we hope that we have contributed our share, with the dignity and decorum that befits an American trial . . . . I want to extend my appreciation to the Court for its courtesies, and again I repeat I want to extend my appreciation for the courtesies extended to me and my staff by Mr. Saypol and the members of his staff as well as the members of the FBI, and I would like to say to the jury that a lawyer does not always win a case; all the lawyer expects is a jury to decide a case on the evidence with mature deliberation. I feel satisfied by reason of the length of time that you took with your deliberations that you examined very carefully the evidence and came to a certain conclusion."

At the funeral of the Rosenbergs in 1953, Bloch said: "We must dedicate ourselves to the greatest fight in our country's history, the fight to resist fascism. This was the face of Nazism that killed the Rosenbergs. They have provided an inspiration to millions throughout the world . . . . The people of America should know – just as the rest of the world knows – that America today, by virtue of the execution of the Rosenbergs, is living beneath the heel of a military dictatorship garbed in civilian clothes. I place their murder at the door of President Eisenhower, Attorney General Brownell, and J. Edgar Hoover . . . . They did not pull the switch but they were the ones who directed the one who pulled the switch . . . . Let the records show that the Rosenbergs received no justice. Two very simple, sweet, tender, intelligent and cultured people have been killed . . . . The men who are running our country have no hearts – their hearts are of stone – they have hard minds, hard eyes, they have the souls of murderers, and this was an act of cold and deliberate murder."

During the course of the Rosenberg-Sobell trial, the Communist press ignored the proceedings. Only after the three co-defendants were sentenced was the silence broken. On April 6, 1951, the Communist Party's *Daily Worker* announced: "Rosenbergs Sentenced to Death, Made Scapegoats for Korean War." The *Worker* said: "The judge had tried the case amid an atmosphere of war hysteria never before witnessed in America . . . . The sentencing of the Rosenbergs climaxed the trial into which the commercial press and prosecuting attorneys pumped the fullest measure of war hysteria."

On April 9, 1951, the *Worker* carried a long editorial ("The Meaning of the Rosenberg Death Sentence") on its front page. The editorialist noted that the *Jewish Daily Forward* had described the Rosenbergs' sentence as "horrible and cruel." The *Worker* then commented: "When a paper of that reactionary character finds itself compelled to speak in this manner, even amid the prevailing hysteria, that can only mean that millions of Americans, especially among the Jewish community, must feel the same way . . . . People sense . . . some deep immorality here, some calculated political motive leading to hysteria and vengeance . . . The Court tried to justify this first-time death sentence during peacetime by manufacturing a crude political myth and a fantastic upside-down interpretation of world events . . . ."

"Can there be any doubt as to what has been going on in this astounding case, timed for the eve of the Supreme Court decision on the case of the framed 11 Communist Party leaders for opposing the war in Korea? It is a myth that the Soviet Union 'stole' the 'secret' of atomic science from us . . . . The notion that the Rosenbergs 'turned the A-bomb over to Russia' is based on abysmal ignorance and is aimed at manufacturing a myth.

"Secondly, it is a myth that the Soviet Union plans atomic war upon us. On the contrary, it is Washington which brandishes the A-bomb in the face of mankind, just as it used it against the helpless Japanese city without the slightest military justification . . . . What Judge Kaufman is doing is to use the alleged espionage of 2 Jewish citizens to turn the hatred of the families of 57,000 American casualties away from the warmakers in Washington toward 'Jews and Communists.' Not since the days when the Czar fomented pogroms, and the Nazis explained the sufferings of Germany in the same fashion, has this pogrom tactic been so brazenly used."

In the fall of 1951, the Communists decided to make the case of the Rosenbergs a *cause célèbre* much in the manner of the earlier Sacco-Vanzetti case, the Scottsboro Boys, the Tom Mooney-Warren K. Billings case, and the contemporary Hollywood Ten and Twelve Communist Party Leaders cases.

On August 8, 1951, the Communist publication *National Guardian* announced that it would "expose the 'evidence' on which two beloved and respected American parents had been sentenced to death." On August 15, 1951, the journal began publication of a seven-part series of articles by its special correspondent William A. Reuben. The series was entitled "The Rosenberg Conviction: Is This the Dreyfus Case of Cold War America?" Reuben's thesis was simple: the Rosenbergs were framed and persecuted. He wrote: "The facts of the arrest, trial and conviction, and sentencing of Julius and Ethel Rosenberg indicate that, at the very least, there is grave doubt of their complicity in any alleged atom spy conspiracy whatsoever; and at the very worst, that they, too, have been convicted on trumped-up evidence — not so much to silence their own two small voices of political protest, but rather to implant in the public mind with savage emphasis the belief that all holders of radical views are a menace to the Nation and to silence through mortal fear all who dare to hold views at variance with the administration of our country. Outside of lynch law, there is probably no more appalling example in American memory of yielding to hysteria in the face of judicial tradition and historic and scientific fact than Judge Kaufman's death sentence of Julius and Ethel Rosenberg."

At the conclusion of Reuben's series, the *National Guardian* announced that Reuben would be provisional chairman of a national committee to defend the Rosenbergs. A fact sheet was published alleging that the Rosenbergs were convicted on unsubstantial and incredible evidence, that the prosecution had prejudiced and inflamed the jury by introducing extraneous issues throughout the trial, and that a suspicion of anti-Semitism tainted the entire trial.

On January 16, 1952, the *National Guardian* carried an advertisement of its own created national committee. The text brought the readers up-to-date on the alleged activities of the National Committee To Secure Justice in the Rosenberg Case: "A mother writes from the death house: 'We said, and we say again, that we are victims of the greatest type of political frame-up ever known in America.' For your courage: We thank the editors of *National Guardian* for their articles revealing the gross injustice perpetrated in the Rosenberg case. For your humanity: We thank the many hundreds of *Guardian* readers who responded so magnificently to our appeal for funds and sponsors to help secure justice in the Rosenberg case.

"Your support has made possible: Establishment of a national office at 246 Fifth Avenue, New York City. Publication in pamphlet form of William A. Reuben's *Guardian* articles (25,000 sold and paid for in three weeks; 25,000 more now on the presses). Preparation of a compelling fact sheet for national distribution. Activity from Maine to California. Preparation of a nationwide speakers tour. Preparation for big public meetings in major cities in the next two months. Advertisements in major English and Yiddish newspapers around the country, some of which have already been placed. Payment of certain legal expenses. A happier holiday for the Rosenberg children. Establishment of a national committee whose sponsors include: Honorable Robert Morss Lovett, Dr. Katherine Dodd, Mrs. Bessie Mitchell, B.Z. Goldberg, Captain Hugh N. Mulzac, and the Reverend Spencer Kennard. Joseph Brainin is provisional chairman.

"But we have just begun to act! Write to President Truman,

Attorney General McGrath and your senators – ask that the verdict and sentence be set aside. Contribute funds for the committee. Order pamphlets, ask for speakers."

Two months after the *National Guardian's* announcement that a national committee was being formed, the *Daily Worker* reported: "Joseph Brainin, well-known journalist and author, announced yesterday that 125 American men and women from all over the United States, have joined with him in forming a National Committee to Secure Justice in the Rosenberg Case. The Rosenbergs, Ethel and Julius, were convicted in April 1951 on a charge of 'conspiracy to commit espionage' and sentenced to death. To this day, they continue to assert their innocence. They are now in Sing Sing, awaiting appeal."

The sponsors of the National Committee included known Communists Nelson Algren; Herbert Aptheker; Edward K. Barsky; Gertrude Evans; Leon Straus; and Elizabeth Todd; and veteran Communist fronters Ivan Von Auw; Edwin Berry Burgum, chairman of the National Council of the Arts, Sciences and Professions ("a Communist front used to appeal to special occupational groups"); Alice Hill Byrne; John F. Clewe; Rabbi Abraham Cronbach; Ephraim Cross; Katherine Dodd; W.E.B. DuBois, whose contributions to Communism at home and abroad were legendary; Waldo Frank; Joseph Friedman; John T. Gojack; B.Z. Goldberg, on the board of directors of the National Council of American-Soviet Friendship ("subversive and Communist" – "specializing in pro-Soviet propaganda"); Shirley Graham, wife of W.E.B. DuBois, and a pro-Communist activist in her own right at home and abroad; Louis Harding Horr; James Imbrie; Reverend J. Spencer Kennard Jr.; Robert Morss Lovett, an all-time champion of Communist projects and causes; John Marsalka, president of the American Slav Congress ("Moscow-inspired and directed federation of Communist-dominated organizations seeking by methods of propaganda and pressure to subvert the 10,000,000 people in this country of Slavic birth or descent"); John T. McManus, general manager of the *National Guardian* ("virtual official propaganda arm of Soviet Russia"); Bessie Mitchell; Captain Hugh N. Mulzac, chairman of the New York Committee of the American Committee for Protection of Foreign Born ("founded by the Communist Party in order to exploit racial divisions in the United States for its own revolutionary purposes"); John L. Simon; Lois Timmins; Leonard Tushnet; and Gene Weltfish, president of the Congress of American Women ("subversive and Communist"). Joseph Brainin, the chairman of the National Committee, was a Russian-born naturalized American with a history of close ties with the Communist Party. Emily and David Alman, husband and wife, who were treasurer and executive secretary, respectively, of the National Committee, would plead the Fifth Amendment when asked about their membership in the Communist Party. The organizational director, Aaron Schneider, had a hard-core Communist front record and was an instructor at the Communist Party's Jefferson School of Social Science. Don Rothenberg, the Washington, D.C., representative, and Mrs. Morton Sobell, the busiest lecturer for the National Committee, were Communist Party functionaries.

In 1956, the House Committee on Un-American Activities reviewed the work of the National Committee To Secure Justice for the Rosenbergs (and Morton Sobell). The HUAC found that the National Committee's mammoth propaganda campaign was "designed to obliterate the crime and exploit the Rosenbergs and their codefendant, Morton Sobell, for the purposes of international Communism . . . . Nowhere has the craven hypocrisy of communism been exposed so tellingly as in the monstrous campaign organized in behalf of atomic espionage agents Julius and Ethel Rosenberg, whose treason brought them death in Sing Sing's electric chair and Communist martyrdom.

"Fraud was the hallmark of this Communist undertaking — fraud with sinister purpose and spectacular profit: it sought to blacken the name of America throughout the world, and milked the American people of some half million dollars while it did so . . . .

"Actually, the efforts of the Communists were never designed to benefit the spies. The Rosenbergs, as individuals, were of no concern to them. The purposes of the Communist campaign went far beyond the Rosenbergs, though it squeezed from them the last possible particle of value. A study of the activities and the records of the Rosenberg campaign point clearly to the fact that it was created for these objectives: (1) To vilify the United States and its institutions and spread the lie that its Government is bent on annihilating minority groups and suppressing genuine political dissent; (2) To provide additional funds for the overall Communist program of subversion and propaganda; (3) To recruit new members and sympathizers for the Communist apparatus, crumbling under the impact of the Korean War, official pressure, and the exposure of Communist infiltration in government, education, and labor; (4) To refurbish the badly tarnished reputation of the Communist Party; (5) To create and exploit divisive anti-Semitic propaganda; (6) To bolster the Communist campaign to capture American churches; (7) To divert attention from anti-Semitic pogroms in Russia and Soviet satellite nations; (8) To discredit American courts and judicial procedures, and cast doubt on all investigations and convictions of Communists.

"The campaign was craftily fashioned to offer a diverse choice of appeals to those who were not Communists or deliberate participants in Communist activity. It entrapped many genuinely motivated by ideals of charity and mercy and Christian compassion. It stimulated the almost reflective reaction of those who saw a recrudescence of nazism in any action against any Jew, and frightened gullible members of religious and racial minorities into believing that the sentence of the Rosenbergs was a prelude to their own doom. Gathered in, too, were the misfits who like to believe that they are handicapped by our political and economic system, and those prone to blame their failures on religious and minority prejudice instead of their own inadequacies.

"The campaign attracted, in particular, many sincerely opposed to capital punishment, and it was these who can rightly feel most victimized by the dishonesty of the Rosenberg solicitations.

"The Rosenberg committee raised no objection to capital punishment in principle — particularly behind the Iron Curtain. Two representatives of the committee called on an official of a society dedicated to the abolition of capital punishment to urge that organization to join in opposing the death penalty for the Rosenbergs. The callers were asked whether they were against all capital punishment. It soon became evident that they were against capital punishment only when it applied to the Rosenbergs. The execution of a thousand persons whom they considered 'Fascists' would not have caused them the slightest qualm.

"The propaganda motifs of the campaign, the various assignments given participants, the tenor of the meetings were all calculated to condition newly attracted dupes to the 'atmosphere and ethic of conspiracy,' and to begin the transfer of their loyalty from America to the Soviet Union."

Dr. S. Andhil Fineberg, whose *The Rosenberg Case: Fact and Fiction,* published in 1953, remains the best analysis of the trial and campaign, offered his analysis of what the Communists accomplished in their exploitation of the Rosenbergs: "(1) They have made certain that Julius and Ethel Rosenberg, who were pre-disposed to remain silent anyhow, will never reveal what they know about the Communist spy system. The 'martyrdom' of these traitors is now assured and they will be played up in future Communist propaganda. (2) By focusing attention on a phony case of alleged judicial and political murder in the United States, the Reds have drawn public attention away from the barbaric injustices of the Kremlin at the very time that an open campaign of Communist anti-Semitism was being launched. (3) In their speeches and pamphlets about the Rosenbergs the Commies have injected a tremendous amount of anti-American propaganda, picturing the average American as the exploited victim of a ruling clique that intends to make huge profits out of war. The Rosenbergs were 'peace heroes.' Large sums collected from non-Communists and even anti-Communists were made available for Communist propaganda. (4) The pro-Rosenberg agitators have instilled fear, suspicion and confusion in the hearts of many susceptible individuals here and abroad. Some of those who were drawn into the campaign for the Rosenbergs are now potential Communists. Party workers will now be able to recruit them. (5) The Communist schemers that managed the Committee To Secure Justice for the Rosenbergs have built one of the largest and most successful Communist front organizations ever created in the United States. Those who contributed funds, services, or even signatures for the pro-Rosenberg campaign are now candidates for other jobs requiring the help of non-Communists. Having established contact with these easy marks, the Reds will be able to make further use of them. (6) Persons of relative unimportance have tasted publicity and aggrandizement which puffed their pride. Whatever following they have thus gained within their own circles will be exploited by front organizations which will dangle the lure of further publicity. (7) The hard-core Communists now know by excellent practice how to conduct a propaganda campaign by fraudulently playing upon the compassion and kindness of the unwary. With this self-assurance the faithful followers of the Kremlin will be ready and eager to serve their masters again by staging similar hubbubs in other cases where they can pretend to be the defenders of freedom of speech, of justice for the wronged, or the like."

Although the Communists waited until after the Rosenbergs' trial before getting a campaign under way, once they did, the full propaganda machinery was put in use. They employed public rallies, lecture tours, newspaper advertisements, handbills, press releases, circular mailings, radio and television announcements, and public demonstrations. The entire Communist press and the complete network of Communist fronts worked in the campaign.

The Communist line to be taken in the campaign was set down in the February 28, 1952 issue of the *Daily Worker*: "The Rosenberg Case is a ghastly political frameup. It was arranged to provide blood victims to the witchhunters, to open the door to new violence, anti-Semitism, and court lynchings of peace advocates and Marxists as 'spies.' The war-hungry witchhunters consider all opponents of their war-made policies – of whatever tendency, Marxist or otherwise – as 'spies' and 'potential spies.' The judicial lynching of the Rosenbergs can mean a wave of frameups against citizens of every political belief if they cross the path of the McCarthyites and the McCarrans raving for victims.

"There is not one iota of evidence to show that the Rosenbergs committed the fantastic 'crime' for which they have been made the first victims in the entire history of the United States to face death on these charges . . . . The 'Atomic Secret' is a newspaper headline myth. There never was such a 'secret.' In the second place, Soviet science had mastered atomic energy long before the Hiroshima massacre; it did not need the scribblings of an Army sergeant [Greenglass] on a matchbox to explain the intricate problems of atomic power. Even the science editor of *Life Magazine* showed that this Sergeant's 'atomic drawing' was a weird and unworkable contraption . . . .

". . . The Government has patched up this frameup to sell the fraud that a belief in Marxism, friendship with the Soviet Union, or membership in the working class Communist Party is to make one a 'spy' or a 'potential spy.' This was the meaning of the [Elizabeth] Bentley performance . . . . The Government has no evidence, and could never have any evidence that working class Marxist activity for peace, democracy, and socialism constitutes 'espionage.' The Government is compelled to manufacture this myth; the Rosenbergs are the sacrificial victims for it.

"As is always the case in the advance of this Fascist-style brutality, the Rosenbergs will not be the last victims if it is not halted by the country now. The blood of the Rosenbergs is intended to pave the way

156

for McCarran's concentration camps, for the roundup and murder of political leaders of all views, and for the arrest and judicial murder of any political opponents of the McCarthys, McCarrans, and the war plotters. The Rosenberg defense committee should unite citizens of all views in halting this revolting injustice. President Truman should get demands from the whole country for a halt to this judicial lynching."

In March 1952, the National Committee held its first well-attended rally for the Rosenbergs at New York City's Pythian Hall. An audience of about one thousand heard speakers including William Reuben, who had written the *National Guardian's* series of articles to launch the pro-Rosenberg campaign; Rabbi Louis D. Gross, editor of the *Jewish Examiner*; Joseph Brainin, chairman of the National Committee; Mary Van Kleeck, a stalwart of Communist fronts; and Albert E. Kahn, a Communist writer. Kahn read what he purported to be a "message from the death house," written by the Rosenbergs, in which they said: "We cannot believe that we are simply victims of some nightmarish miscarriage of justice, that we are victims of a case of mistaken identity. It seems to us that it was inevitable that five years of oppressive laws, of a wave of persecutions, of heresy hunting, should lead to a barbaric sentence of death against two innocent persons. We are an ordinary man and wife, and it was inevitable that ordinary people would be grievously persecuted by the history of these past few years.

"Like others we spoke for peace, because we did not want our two little sons to live in the shadow of war and death. Like others we spoke for the liberties of our fellow citizens, because we believe, and want our children to believe, in the fine democratic traditions of our country. That is why we are in the death house today, as warning to all ordinary men and women, like you yourselves, that there are forces today which hope to silence by death those who speak for peace and democracy.

"But, you see, we are not silent today, even though we are behind bars. And we say to you that no matter what happens to us, you must not be silent. We are not martyrs or heroes, nor do we wish to be. We want to live, we want to be reunited with each other, we want to be with our children again. But we will not pay the price that is asked of us to betray our hopes for the peaceful, neighborly, democratic world which our children and all children need if they are to carry on the human race."

The rally at Pythian Hall set the tone for most of the National

Committee's activities throughout 1952. The procedure was also followed by the numerous local committees that were established around the country. In the New York City area there were about a dozen separate committees. Full-time and part-time salaries for organizational workers in Chicago, Boston, Washington, and Philadelphia were paid by the National Committee. Reuben, David Alman, Mrs. Morton Sobell, and Joseph Brainin traveled from city to city speaking before rallies and helping to raise funds for the cause.

In Boston, the Rosenberg campaign was inaugurated and controlled by the Communist Party in the person of a local functionary, Herman Tamsky. Tamsky, whose wife, Florence, was also a Communist, worked along with another husband and wife team, Philip and Sue Koritz, and ran the Boston branch of the National Committee. Active on the scene were Herbert Zimmerman, the Communist Party's local educational director, and Communists Edith Abber and Sid Ravden. Dirk Struik, who was suspended from the faculty of Massachusetts Institute of Technology, after being indicted for subversive activities, was a member of the Boston Committee. James W. Glatis, who worked for the FBI in Boston as an undercover man in the Communist Party, was assigned to the Boston Rosenberg group by Ann ("Red Flame") Burlak, the leader of the Communist Party in New England. Glatis learned that the specific purposes of the Boston group were: "First, the securing of financial assistance, or securing funds for the Communist Party, and secondly, there was the necessity of using this particular issue on a basis of propagandizing the fact that one of the reasons why the Rosenbergs were being executed was because they were Jewish. In other words, giving them a foundational basis for preaching there was anti-Semitism in the United States; and, third, and most important to the Communist Party, was the fact that there were anti-Semitic programs taking place within the Soviet Union."

The Washington, D.C. branch of the National Committee expended most of its energies in vigils and picket lines at the White House. The local leaders were Ethel Weichrod and John B. Stone. Weichrod would plead the Fifth Amendment when asked her Communist Party affiliations. Stone was a correspondent for the Communist Party's Federated Press news service. Others in the Washington group included William Glazier, Edward Fischer, John Martinez, Gertrude Evans, Mary Church Terrell, and Joseph Forer. Forer, an attorney, was a familiar figure in congressional investigative committee hearing rooms, where he served as counsel for many Communists and Fifth Amendment pleaders.

In California, the Rosenberg campaign was widespread and active due to the cooperation the National Committee received from established Communist fronts, including the California Civil Rights Congress, the Independent Progressive Party, and the California Council of the Arts, Sciences and Professions. Activists in the Los Angeles area included Sophie Davidson; William Esterman, chairman of the National Lawyers Guild of Southern California ("the foremost legal bulwark of the Communist Party, its front organizations, and controlled unions"); John Howard Lawson, one of the "Hollywood Ten" who went to prison for contempt of Congress; Communist writer Samuel Ornitz; Horace Alexander, congressional candidate on the ticket of the Independent Progressive Party (part of "one of the largest and most successful fronts ever created by the Communists"); Dr. Murray Abowitz; Jack Berman; Helen Blair; Reuben W. Borough; Madeline Borough; John F. Clewe; Belle Parsons Clewe; Rabbi Franklin Cohn; Nat P. Corner, the Reverend Carl Crain, Jack Flier, Reverend Stephen H. Fritchman; Dr. Sanford Goldner; Martin Hall, a long-time Communist in Germany and the United States; Hugh Hardyman; Sarajo Lord; Sylvia Major; Paul Major; the Reverend Howard G. Matson; John McTernan; Wyndham Mortimer; Pauline Schindler, and Olive Thompson.

As an auxiliary to the organization led by Sophie Davidson, there was established the Non-Partisan Committee for Clemency for the Rosenbergs. It was composed of Dr. and Mrs. Murray Abowitz, Milnor Alexander, Sam Houston Allen, C.A. Berry, Reuben W. Borough, Madeline Borough, Dr. and Mrs. Walter Briehl, Cleophus Brown, the Reverend Ernest Caldecott, Belle Parsons Clewe, John F. Clewe, Nat P. Corner, Anne Corner, the Reverend Carl Crain, Mrs. Terry Duxler, Guy Endore, William B. Esterman, Hazel E. Field, Dr. T. Perceval Gerson, Dr. Sanford Goldner, attorney Grover Johnson, Robert W. Kenny, Daniel G. Marshall, Mrs. Dorothy N. Marshall, the Reverend Howard G. Matson, Judge Stanley Moffatt, Elsa Peters Morse, Reid Robinson, Goldie Radoff, the Reverend Edwin P. Ryland, Victor Shapiro, Chaim Shapiro, Laurence P. Sperber, Fred H. Steinmetz, Dr. Harold Koppleman, Dr. George A. Warmer, the Reverend Hugh Weston, and John Wexley.

Along the way the Rosenberg campaign picked up other supporters in Los Angeles and Southern California, including actress Ann Revere;

the Reverend G. Randolph; attorney Daniel G. Marshall; Janet Stevenson; George Bradow, leader in the Communist-dominated Fur and Leather Workers Union; attorney Ben Margolis, a veteran of Communist front enterprises; Oda Alvarez, congressional candidate on the ticket of the Independent Progressive Party (part of "one of the largest and most successful fronts ever created by the Communists"); Cleophus Brown, president of the Los Angeles Negro Labor Council; P. Price Cobbs; George M. Cowell; Gregory Duboff; Frances Fritchman; N.R. Herzberg; Peter W. Hill; Ruthven L. Johnson; Ignacio Lopez; Robert S. Morris Jr.; Katherine McTernan; Emarald Olson; Linus Pauling; Thomas L. Perry; Matt Richman; Ruth Richman; Vernon C. Robinson; Elf Scharlin; Eleanor Smith; Ruth Speigel; Sidney Spiegel; Gerald Tannen; Lois Tannen; Benny Carter; the Reverend John Gabrielson; the Reverend E.W. Rakestraw; the Reverend Frederick Strathdee; and Margit Markowitz.

In San Francisco, two old friends of the Rosenbergs, Sylvia and Harry Steingart, ran the Bay Area Committee To Save the Rosenbergs. Harry Steingart and Julius Rosenberg had been fellow members and fellow officials of the Federation of Architects, Engineers, Chemists and Technicians, which had been organized by the Communists as an espionage auxiliary in scientific fields. Among the activists in the Steingarts' group were Alvah Bessie, a Communist screen writer; the Reverend Nolan Mills; Sidney Roger, a leftist radio commentator; Vivian Hallinan; and Phil Mezey.

The Chicago Roseberg Committee was one of the busiest auxiliaries in the country. Its honorary chairman was Nelson Algren and the executive secretary was Josephine Granat. The treasurer was Ann Markin and the chairman was Gertrude Noyes, wife of Henry H. Noyes, head of the Illinois chapter of the American Peace Crusade ("Communist front"). Josephine Granat would plead the Fifth Amendment when asked if she were a member of the Communist Party and if Nelson Algren had been connected with the Chicago Committee.

In December 1952, the Granat-led Chicagoans sent a request to President Harry Truman to extend executive clemency to the Rosenbergs. The signers of the request included James Luther Adams of the Meadville Theological Seminary; Professor Samuel K. Allison; Margaret Bauer of the Parkway Community Center; aviatrix Janet H. Braggs; Anton J. Carlson of the University of Chicago; Harmon Craig of the University of Chicago's Institute of Nuclear Studies; attorney Earl B.

Dickerson, a perennial supporter of Communist projects; Kermit Eby of the University of Chicago; Peter Gaberman of the Chicago Medical School; Rabbi David Graubert; Robert G. Havighurst of the University of Chicago and a myriad of Communist fronts; A. Eustace Hayden of the Chicago Ethical Society; the Reverend Reynolds N. Hoover; attorney Sidney Jones; Harry Kalven of the University of Chicago's Law School; Alex Kaplan; the Reverend Bernard Loomer, dean of the University of Chicago's Divinity School; the Reverend George Nishimoto of the Ellis Community Center; the Reverend Victor Obenhaus; Professor Robert Redfield; Curtis W. Reese, dean of the Abraham Lincoln Center; Boris Rubenstein; Rabbi Melvin H. Rush; Malcolm Sharp of the University of Chicago's Law School; Waitstill H. Sharp; Rabbi Ralph Simon; Mrs. Max Targ; George H. Watson of Roosevelt College; Katherine Winslow; Helen Wright, dean of the University of Chicago's School of Social Service Administration; William Card; Lyle Cooper, research director for the United Packinghouse Workers of America; attorney Eugene Cotton; W.E. Cunningham, M.D.; Norman Dolnick, publicity director for the United Public Workers of America; Evelyn Mills Duvall; Dorothy Saterquest; the Reverend Joseph Evans of the Metropolitan Communist Church; attorney Joseph P. Antonow; Roland Bailey; the Reverend William T. Baird of Essex Community Church and a host of Communist fronts, enterprises, and projects; architect Arthur Bassin; Margaret Goss Burroughs of the South Side Art Center; the Reverend Royall D. Caldwell; Charles Fischer of the United Public Workers of America; Rabbi G. George Fox; attorney Edward Fruchtman; Mr. and Mrs. Ben Greenspan; the Reverend J.C. Hayes Sr.; Hyman J. Hirshfield, M.D.; Bert F. Hoselitz; Mr. and Mrs. Eli Hulbert; attorney Leonard Karlin; Mrs. Kenesaw Landis II; Mrs. Fern Gayden; Mrs. Bernard Loomer; Jerome J. Lubin, M.D.; Joseph E. Mayer; attorney Irving Meyers; the Reverend Leslie T. Pennington; Robert Pickus; Dr. and Mrs. J.D. Podore; Dale Pontius; Darrel D. Randell; Anatol Rapoport; attorney Raymond L. Richman; Harry N. Richter, M.D.; Lila Rose; attorney Philip Rubin; Morrison Sharp; attorney Ira Silber; Sara Simonsgaard; Albert Soglin of the Illinois Institute of Technology; Jeremiah Stamler, M.D.; John B. Thompson, dean of the Rockefeller Chapel at the University of Chicago and a veteran Communist fronter; James Toman, M.D.; Charlotte Towle; Alex S. Tulsky, M.D.; Idell Umbles; Frank Wagner Jr.; Harold H. Was, M.D.; the

Reverend Harry Walden; attorney Richard P. Watt; attorney Bernard Weissbourd; Helen L. Williams of the Women's International League for Peace and Freedom; and Quentin Young, M.D., noted for his pro-Communist activities.

Many of those who petitioned President Truman in December also petitioned President Eisenhower in February 1953. In their petition to Eisenhower they said: "The unprecedented death sentence given the Rosenbergs is both a product of and a contributing factor to the current hysteria and fear. Our society today is fraught with tensions and conflicts. Hence, we cannot look at this case in terms of the Rosenbergs alone. Are we so far removed from our faith and our heritage as to equate mercy with weakness and strength with reprisal? We need to symbolize to ourselves and to others that in a period of severe testing we have the courage to endure even the hard threat of conspiracy. It is the strong who are able to grant clemency. In safeguarding our Democracy, we must not adopt the harsh, totalitarian methods which we have always abhorred in other countries. The sentence of death does not rest easily upon the conscience of an America rich in the tradition of mercy. We appeal to you to act at once and grant clemency to Julius and Ethel Rosenberg."

The original petitioners were joined by Richard C. Blakeslee of Northwestern University; attorney Landon L. Chapman; Mabel L. Cohen; the Reverend Ralph Hall Collis; Thomas E. Colgan; the Reverend David Cole; the Reverend James S. Cackey; the Reverend Wallace F. Ault; the Reverend Alexander A. Balden; Mrs. Jacob Bednow; Professor Daniel Zelinsky; Rabbi S. Burr Yampol; attorney Charles Wolff; Helen Joy Weinberg of the Artist Equity Association; the Reverend J.W. Ward; Birgit Vennesland of the University of Chicago; Stephen Varro; Margit Varro; William M. Trumbull of Northwestern University; Charlotte Towle of the University of Chicago; the Reverend F.C. Tourvin; the Reverend Alva Tomkins; attorney Joseph J. Ticktin; the Reverend G.W. Thomas; Mandel A. Terman; Rabbi Samuel Teitelbaum; Samuel F. Strong; Rabbi Joseph M. Strauss; the Reverend Stanley Stevens; Professor William T. Starr; Harry Stark; B. Julian Smith, general secretary of the General Board of Christian Education for the Colored Methodist Episcopal Church; Thomas L. Slater; attorney Everett Simpson; Rabbi Ralph Simon, president of the Chicago Rabbinical Association; attorney Samuel S. Siegel; attorney Morris J.

Sherman; attorney A.E. Sharrow; Peter and Thalia Selz; J. Herzl Segal; the Reverend P. Scalone; P.M. Santos; Ernest Samuels of Northwestern University; Rabbi Nathan I. Sachs; Ralph R. Sackley; attorney Bernard H. Sachar; J. Coert Rylaarsdam; attorney David B. Rothstein; attorney Ned Rosin; attorney Joseph Rosenstein; Alex Rosenberg; attorney Richard Rittman; Professor Daniel Resch; Jesse Reicher of the Illinois Institute of Technology; Robert Redfield; the Reverend Louis Rawls; attorney Harry S. Posner; George W. Platzman of the University of Chicago; John E. Pixton Jr. of Northwestern University; attorney Louis L. Perlman; the Reverend P. Burton Nelson; the Reverend Jacob Moscowitz; Helen Rand Miller; attorney D. Rex McBride; Alba Mazzitelli of Roosevelt College; Joseph E. Mayer of the University of Chicago; the Reverend H. Allen Maxwell; attorney Harvey Malawsky; Robert Morss Lovett; attorney Wenzel J. Love; attorney Stephen Love; Dr. and Mrs. Maurice Lorber; the Reverend Byron C. Lambert; the Reverend Ludwig C. Kutz; attorney Warren Krinsky; the Reverend William Koshewa; the Reverend Edward L. Kohlmann; architect Leonard Klarich; attorney Philip A. Klapman; the Reverend M.B. Kenner; the Reverend Julian J. Keiser; artists Joshua Kaganove and Alfonso Iannelli; Roger H. Hildebrand of the University of Chicago; William L. Hawley, dean of students at the University of Chicago's Divinity School; the Reverend Leland Harder; the Reverend Henry A. Gustafson Jr.; attorney Homer C. Griffin; attorney Howard Greene; Eugene Goldwasser of the University of Chicago; the Reverend Paul W. Caton; George Barr Carson Jr. of the University of Chicago; Carl W. Coudit of Northwestern University; and the Reverend Joseph M. Evans.

In Detroit, the Rosenberg group was led by and saturated by Communists, including Pat Rush; Anne Shore, director of the Michigan Civil Rights Congress ("created and established by the Communist Party"); Arthur McPhaul, executive secretary of the Michigan Civil Rights Congress; Phil Halper; Sol Grossman; Nelson Davis; Eve Neidelman; Lydia Mates; Gert Schatz; Ethel Jacobowitz; Helen Travis; and Tom Crow. Also active in the Detroit group were the Reverend Percy Fullman and the Reverend Henry Hitt Crane.

The Milwaukee group was led by John Gilman, a Communist Party functionary. At one point in his publicity releases on behalf of the Rosenbergs, he wrote: "We have stated before that the Rosenberg case was McCarthyism in its most extreme form . . . . This plot, based primarily on hysteria and fear and not on evidence, was needed in 1950 to create support for the unpopular Korean war. The McCarthys are trying to work up a war fever again . . . . Why have they hidden the fact that the Rosenbergs never did have their day in court?"

Gilman was also responsible for an "open letter" addressed to President Harry Truman which followed the Communist line but, at the same time, lied about Gilman's bachelor's degree and his year of graduate studies at the University of Wisconsin. The letter read: "Tonight two young people sit, or pace the floor of their cells, in the death house of Sing Sing Prison. One is Julius Rosenberg, an obscure graduate engineer. The other is his wife, Ethel. They have been sentenced to death in the electric chair. Their two children, Robbie, 5, and Michael, 9, are still waiting for their mother and father to come home.

"The Supreme Court has refused their request for a hearing. Only you, Mr. President, can halt their execution. Our laws have given you authority and obligation to grant executive clemency when clemency is just. You recently exercised this authority by granting clemency to the man who killed a White House guard in an attempt on your life.

"The Rosenbergs were accused of conspiracy to commit espionage. A jury upheld the charge. A judge, breaking every precedent in American history of such cases, sentenced them to die in the electric chair. (As you know, Mr. President, no civilian court has ever – either in peace or war – pronounced a death sentence on this charge. Axis Sally and Tokyo Rose were found guilty of treason in working for the enemy and 10 years imprisonment was deemed sufficient punishment.)

"Julius and Ethel Rosenberg have steadfastly denied any guilt. Many prominent attornies [sic], scholars, pastors, priests and rabbis have studied the evidence and expressed serious doubts as to whether they are guilty. Typical among opinions of these people is this statement of the eminent scholar, Rabbi Dr. Meyer Sharff: 'I have studied and pondered long over the facts in the Rosenberg case . . . . I came to the firm conviction that something had to be done to save these persons from an undeserved fate.'

"More than 50,000 Americans have signed a legal brief urging a new trial. Many who are noncommittal regarding guilt or innocence, believe the Rosenbergs should not be killed and have joined the request for clemency. The fear is expressed that we are facing a repetition of the shameful episode in American history — the frameup and execution of Sacco and Vanzetti.

"Others have been executed — only to have history prove them innocent. So long as one single doubt of their guilt remains, the Rosenbergs must not die. If punishment for wrongdoing is the objective, this mother and father have suffered the tortures of the damned as they faced death during two years of imprisonment. Only the merciful spirit of the American people and their fervent desire to guard our traditions of justice, plus action by yourself, can save these two from the horror of death in the electric chair."

At the time that Gilman caused this letter to be circulated, Julius and Ethel Rosenberg were age 36 and 38, respectively. They had been engaged in Communist Party activities throughout their adult lives. They broke every precedent by being the first spies in the United States caught stealing atomic secrets and giving those secrets to a hostile Soviet Union. They not only "steadfastly denied any guilt" but repeatedly refused to answer questions when on the witness stand. There was no plausible relationship between the Rosenbergs' crime of espionage and the murder committed during an armed robbery by Sacco and Vanzetti three decades earlier.

In Pennsylvania, the Rosenberg operation was under the complete direction of Communists, who included Jean D. Frantjis, Sylvia Freedland, Ted Norton, Billie Jane Lipsett, Adelaide and Irving Riskin, Maude and Scott Nicol, and Harriet Karol.

In June 1952, the National Committee circulated an "amicus curiae" brief in an effort to obtain 100,000 signatures for presentation to the Supreme Court of the United States. The brief totally ignored the fact that the defendants' social beliefs were not an issue in the trial, nor did the casualties and reversals in Korea have any relation to the Rosenbergs' guilt of espionage committed years before the outbreak of the Korean War. The brief said: "We believe that the trial of Julius and Ethel Rosenberg and Morton Sobell on a charge of conspiring to commit espionage, which resulted in death sentences for the Rosenbergs and a 30 year sentence for their co-defendant, lacked guarantees of fairness which all Americans have a right to expect under the Constitution.

"We believe that the Prosecutor and Trial Judge permitted fear and prejudice to dominate the trial by (1) attributing to the defendants social beliefs which are today the target of virtually every public tribunal, and (2) attributing to them reversals and casualties suffered in Korea.

"We believe that transient political and social passions have no place in our courts, that to deprive even one American of the right to a fair trial is to injure the rights of all Americans.

"We therefore authorize the inclusion of our names in an Amicus Brief to the Supreme Court of the United States, petitioning that the verdicts and sentences be set aside, and that a new trial be ordered based on Constitutional guarantees of impartiality and fairness in accordance with the best traditions of American justice."

On the New York scene, rallies were popular among the pro-Rosenberg crowd. Among those who spoke at these rallies were such veteran Communist front stalwarts as Ephraim Cross, Abraham Cronbach, and Meyer Sharff. In November 1952, at the New York Palm Garden, a Theatre Rally To Secure Clemency for the Rosenbergs was held. Actor Peter Lawrence, a Fifth Amendment pleader, sent out announcements for the rally and said: "The Rosenbergs face death. We cannot allow this savage sentence, unprecedented in all of American history, to be carried out. We cannot allow the Rosenbergs to die while grave doubts persist and multiply as to the fairness of their trial." Sponsors of the Threatre Rally included Nelson Algren, Dorothy Brewster, David Burliuk, Morris Carnovsky, Howard da Silva, Ossie Davis and his wife Ruby Dee, Shirley Graham, Edward Eliscu, Waldo Frank, Robert Gwathmey, Dashiell Hammett, Mervin Jules, Rockwell Kent, Frank Kleinholz, Ray Lev, Anton Refregier, Arthur Pollock, Paul Robeson, Martin Wolfson, Philip Evergood, Howard Fast, Max Goberman, Jack Levine, and Sam Moore. Among those who actively participated in the rally were Robeson, da Silva, Carnovsky, Lou Gilbert, Ken Harvey, Milroy Ingram, John T. McManus, Al Moss, Martha Schlamme, Phoebe Brand, Mrs. Morton Sobell, Virginia Downing, De Witt Drury, Marjorie Nelson, Ring Lardner Jr., John Howard Lawson, Miles Malleson, Waldo Salt, Anna Seghars, and David Alfaro Siqueiros.

In December 1952, New York members of the Civil Rights Congress — about 200 of them — went to the Sing Sing Prison where they demonstrated outside the gates of the prison on behalf of the Rosenbergs. Among those who made the trip were actress Karen Morley, William Patterson, Bessie Mitchell, Aubrey Grossman, and Elaine Ross.

NATIONAL COMMITTEE TO SECURE JUSTICE IN ROSENBERG CASE

In January 1953, the National Committee received its greatest boost from Harold Urey, a professor of chemistry at the University of Chicago's Institute for Nuclear Studies. Urey could make no pretensions to knowledge of law and he never appeared at the trial of the Rosenbergs, but that did not prevent him from making dogmatic judgments about the trial, the validity of evidence, and other matters surrounding the entire Rosenberg situation. In a letter to the *New York Times*, Urey wrote: "After reading the testimony of the Rosenberg case I find that I cannot put to rest my doubts about the verdict and wish to cite the following points: (1) Max Elitcher's testimony is of doubtful value. He says that he and Julius talked about espionage but never transferred any information for some five years. This doesn't seem probable to me. (2) No certain conspiracy between Sobell and Rosenberg is established. (3) The connections to others than Ruth and David Greenglass are not established. Miss Bentley was unable to identify the telephone voice that said, 'This is Julius' with the voice of Julius Rosenberg. If 'Julius' did not refer to him in this case, it probably did not when Harry Gold said, 'I came from Julius,' when he met Greenglass in New Mexico. From Gold's testimony it seems that he knew nothing of Rosenberg at all. It seems unbelievable to me that the name of an arch conspirator would be used in such identification phrases. (4) No contact between the Rosenbergs and Anatoli A. Yakovlev is established. (5) The Government's case rests on the testimony of Ruth and David Greenglass. He had pleaded guilty, but had not been sentenced and hoped for clemency. She has never been charged and tried, obviously it seems a reward for her testimony. A family feud between the Greenglasses and Rosenbergs existed because of a business altercation. The Rosenbergs' testimony flatly contradicted that of the Greenglasses.

"I found the Rosenbergs' testimony more believable than that of the Greenglasses, although I realize that I have not had the jurors' advantage of hearing and seeing the witnesses. Is it customary for spies to be paid in wrist watches and console tables? Greenglass and Fuchs were paid in cash. The Rosenbergs appear to have been as poor as church mice and the statement that Julius was spending $50 or $75 a night in night clubs seems to me to be a very doubtful one. Had he done this, he would have been obviously and unaccountably rich to all his associates.

"However, even if the verdict is correct, I am amazed at the unequal punishment for the same crime. For the very same conspiracy Ruth Greenglass was never brought to trial, though she admitted her guilt on the witness stand; David Greenglass got fifteen years; Morton Sobell and Harry Gold got thirty years, and Ethel and Julius Rosenberg got death. Only the last two took the witness stand and maintained their innocence. If capital punishment is to be given in the future for espionage I should like to have it introduced in a case for which the evidence rests on the testimony of witnesses who did not stand to profit from their testimony. I do not regard self-confessed criminals as reliable witnesses.

"We are engaged in a cold war with the tyrannical Government of the U.S.S.R. We wish to win the approval and loyalty of the good people of the world. Would it not be embarrassing if, after the execution of the Rosenbergs, it could be shown that the United States had executed two innocent people and let a guilty one go completely free? And, remember, somewhere there is a representative of the U.S.S.R. who knows what the facts are."

Urey's strange and unscientific letter on behalf of the Rosenbergs can be best appreciated in light of his previous history. In 1946, when Urey was interviewed about the disclosures of atomic espionage in Canada, the Communists' *Daily Worker* reported: "Even if there were an atomic bomb secret, which he denied, Urey said that the Soviet Union could not be blamed for obtaining technical information in Canada." In 1949, the *Washington Times-Herald* quoted Urey as saying: "I would fire every security officer in every atomic plant and laboratory in the United States with the exception of Los Alamos." (Ironically enough, it was from Los Alamos that the Greenglass-Gold-Sobell-Rosenberg-Yakovlev conspiracy stole the atomic secrets.)

On January 13, 1953, shortly after Urey's letter appeared in the *New York Times*, the same journal carried a letter from one of Urey's scientific colleagues, Albert Einstein, who wrote to President Truman: "My conscience compels me to urge you to commute the death sentence of Julius and Ethel Rosenberg. This appeal to you is prompted by the same reasons which were set forth so convincingly by my distinguished colleague, Harold C. Urey, in his letter of January 5, 1953 to *The New York Times.*"

On April 26, 1953, Urey did an unexpected partial flip-flop in his thinking when he addressed a letter to a New York City Rosenberg rally. At that time, he wrote: "(1) There has been much discussion of the importance of the secret data which Greenglass states he gave to the 'Russians.' I believe this data was important and that it was not publicly known at the time that it was disclosed, and I have been assured of the correctness of this conclusion by competent scientific men who were at Los Alamos at the time. Scientists who have made contrary statements are uninformed on the subject . . . . (2) It seems probable to me that a mechanic such as Greenglass, capable of making metal parts from drawings, should be able to reproduce those drawings in rough form after a lapse of some years. No great scientific knowledge is required to understand the approximate shape, arrangement and size of the mechanical object and considerable information of this kind could have been acquired and transmitted by Greenglass. This does not mean that he could be expected to understand the theoretical or scientific reasons for the construction of the atom bomb . . . ."

Urey, however, reversed whatever flip-flop he made when he sent a telegram to President Eisenhower on June 12, 1953: "The case against the Rosenbergs outrages logic and justice. It depends on the testimony of Greenglass and his wife, both confessed spies and alleged accomplices of the Rosenbergs. Greenglass is supposed to have revealed to the Russians the 'secret' of the atomic bomb. Though the information supposed to have been transmitted could have been important, a man of Greenglass' capacity is wholly incapable of transmitting the physics, chemistry and mathematics of the atomic bomb to anyone. He and his wife were the only ones who pretended to connect the Rosenbergs with atomic espionage. New evidence makes even more plain what was plain enough before, that the prosecution's case has no logic in it, and that it depends upon the blowing up of patently perjured testimony. I tried to see the Attorney General this past week but was unable to secure an appointment. On behalf of all those interested in the defense, I ask to be allowed to present my understanding of the case to you, Mr. President."

At about the same time that Urey and Einstein were adding to their careers of pro-Communist activities, the National Committee proudly boasted that fifteen hundred American clergymen had petitioned the President to extend clemency to the Rosenbergs. In the petition, they said: "We are not partisans. Our plea does not hang on the decision of the Rosenbergs' guilt or innocence, nor the degree of their wrongdoing. We ask you in the spirit of love which casts out fear to mitigate a punishment of such terrible finality, which, for the offense, is unique in our history." The petitioners nowhere indicated that they had any realization of the circumstances of the trial wherein the Rosenbergs with their hostile, intransigent, and arrogant attitude literally disdained to offer any mitigating reasons for the jury and judge to show any mercy toward them for their part in the heinous crime of espionage on behalf of the Soviet Union.

The emphasis upon the Rosenbergs as parents deserving of clemency was a recurring theme in the National Committee's propaganda. In one of the pleas directed to the White House, an appeal read: "As citizens, we address our plea to you for mercy for Ethel and Julius Rosenberg now under sentence of death. Thousands of religious leaders of all denominations, newspapers, periodicals, hundreds of trade union leaders and labor organizations, and tens of thousands of other Americans, representing every section of community life, have asked that the lives of these two young parents be spared. Without reference to the question of guilt or innocence we join thousands upon thousands of Americans, in this plea that you grant clemency to Ethel and Julius Rosenberg."

Among those seeking mercy for the "young parents" who were also young spies were academicians James Luther Adams, Samuel K. Allison, Roland Bainton, Rudolf Carnap, John Codington, Edward U. Condon, W.E.B. DuBois, Thomas I. Emerson, Peter Gaberman, David Haber, Alexander Kaplan, Bernard Loomer, Robert Morss Lovett, Walter G. Muelder, Linus Pauling, Harlow Shapley, G. Murray Branch, Anton J. Carlson, Zechariah Chafee Jr., Ephraim Cross, Katherine Dodd, Kermit Eby, Albert Einstein, A. Eustace Hayden, William G. Houk, E. Winston Jones, Harry Kalvan, Max Lerner, Stephen Love, Philip Morrison, H. Richard Niebuhr, J.H. Randall Jr., Anatol Rapoport, Malcolm Sharp, Harold Urey, and Helen Wright; clergy Rabbi Shepherd Z. Baum, the Reverend T.E. Brown, the Reverend Henry Hitt Crane, Rabbi Abraham Cronbach, the Reverend Rudolph Gilbert, Rabbi David Graubart, the Reverend John Paul Jones, the Reverend Thomas McCandless, the Reverend Frank North, Bishop Paul Roberts, the Reverend John Nevin Sayer, Rabbi Meyer Sharff, Rabbi Abba Hillel Silver, the Reverend Jesse W. Stitt, Rabbi Franklin Cohen, the Reverend Joseph Evans, Rabbi Louis D. Gross, the Reverend Carl A. Hansen, the Reverend Clarence D. Herriott, Rabbi I. Usher Kirshblum, the Reverend John Howland Lathrop, and Rabbi Ralph Simon; and such Communist-front warhorses as Abraham J. Muste, Chief Justice James H. Wolfe of Utah, Paul Robeson, John T. McManus, Rockwell Kent, Ernest De Maio, Nelson Algren, Quentin Young, Norman Thomas, Anton Refregier, Mary Van Kleeck, Freda Kirchwey, Robert W. Kenny, Earl B. Dickerson, Waldo Frank, Ben Gold, and Arthur Garfield Hays.

The emotional pleas for the "obscure engineer," the "housewife," the "young parents," or the victims of a "frameup" or "lynching" or "witch hunt" or "McCarthyism" or "anti-Semitism" or "fascism" were all a part of a cleverly contrived campaign to entice as many gullible people as possible into the propaganda mill. The Communists and their veteran fellow travelers knew that the pejorative language was the most effective façade to obscure the nature of the Rosenbergs and their crime.

As part of the emotional binge surrounding the save-the-Rosenbergs campaign were the purported "Death House Letters of Julius and Ethel Rosenberg." A constant stream of epistles allegedly written by one or the other of the prisoners — or by both of them jointly — flowed to the public press or to the speakers' platforms at pro-Rosenberg rallies. Eventually the "death house letters" were collected and published in book form and translated into several languages.

Excerpts from the writings of the imprisoned Rosenbergs — or their ghost writers — indicate that there was a realization that legal avenues for clemency were blocked because of the open-and-shut case which had convicted the spies. Therefore, the recourse was to inflammatory emotionalism playing upon fears and prejudices and blind sympathies. In some ways the "death house letters" appear to be a deliberately constructed satire on the use of Communist jargon.

From Sing Sing to each other, to their friends, to their lawyers, and to the legal authorities they wrote: "We do not pretend that we are unafraid. But we fear also for those for whom our death sentence is a precedent, for those who like us may find themselves in our place, unless you, who are free today, make us free again." (Ethel and Julius) — "Here, now . . . the [Eisenhower] Administration wants to stain the good name of our country with the blood of the Rosenbergs. We are confident that the people will raise a mighty cry against this new danger which threatens to engulf millions by dooming two innocent Americans first." (Julius) — "If we are executed, it will be the murder of innocent people and the shame will be upon the government of the United States. History will record — whether we live or not — that we were the victims of the most monstrous frame-up in the history of our country." (Julius and Ethel) — "It seems to me that the Federal courts have adopted the abominable medieval practice of the Southern Bourbons, legal lynching of Negroes — and are now attempting, as in our case, to apply this to political prisoners. Mark my words, dearest, the harsh sentence passed on us is part of the atomic hysteria designed to brutalize the minds of the people in order to make it easier for them to accept as a commonplace thing long prison terms and even death sentences for political prisoners. It serves the added nefarious purpose of establishing a fear paralysis among progressive Americans . . . . The most important thing is that the camouflage has to be ripped away, the loud braying of jackals of hate has to be answered with reason and fact, and only positive organizations of free people and their ensuing direct action can successfully save the peace and assure freedom in our country. That is why I am positive growing numbers of people will come to understand our fight and join with us to win so just a cause." (Julius) — "My beloved husband, I feel so discouraged by this unjustifiable attack on a legally constituted American Party [the Communist Party]! The specter of fascism looms enormous and menacing." (Ethel) — "When I was arrested and subsequently when I went to trial I told our lawyers it is very difficult to beat a case like this in an atmosphere fraught with war talk, witch hunts, and frenzied super-patriotic mouthings of 200 per cent 'Americans.' In plain English the facts and law of the land were thrown out the window and prejudice and emotion ruled . . . Practically the entire press has embarked on a jingoistic campaign. Open bellicose statements, editorials, columns intensified among a welter of utterly confusing and contradictory news reports must be having a deleterious effect on the public. For it must be exceedingly difficult for the people to obtain any fair degree of facts which are essential for them to know in order to get any idea of what is taking place and what they are facing. It seems to me that the task facing the outspoken progressives, leaders and honest men and women is not only more difficult, but also most urgent . . . . One thing is certain, I've been reading and listening to so many beautiful words and lovely high sounding principles in lengthy dissertations. All empty words, for they are bred on false premises and are leading to reaction, decay and war — always in the guise of peace and the 'free' world." (Julius)

For the benefit of the National Committee's rally organizers and fund raisers, Julius and Ethel wrote: "Yesterday, we were offered a deal by the Attorney General of the United States. We were told that if we cooperated with the Government, our lives would be spared. By asking us to repudiate the truth of our innocence, the Government admits its own doubts concerning our guilt. We will not help purify the foul record of a fraudulent conviction and a barbaric sentence.

"We solemnly declare, now and forevermore, that we will not be coerced, even under pain of death, to bear false witness and to yield up to tyranny our rights as free Americans. Our respect for truth, conscience, and human dignity is not for sale. Justice is not some bauble to be sold to the highest bidder. If we are executed, it will be murder of innocent people and shame will be on the Government of the United States. History will record, whether we live or not, that we were the victims of the most monstrous frameup in the history of our country."

To the Circuit Court of Appeals, the Rosenbergs wrote: "We are husband and wife. We are firmly united by ties of marriage, the love we bear our two fine sons and one another. As one, we seek relief from sentences that would produce the unutterable tragedy of the destruction of our small family, and set a precedent for the abandonment, in America, of the civilized appreciation of the worth of human life.

"We have suffered deeply for the past 2 years. Torn from our children and in the shadow of death, we have been isolated, like caged animals, from the mainstream of life. We have never known the ease of riches or even comfort. At times we have felt the pangs of want. We come from a humble background and we are humble people. Were it not for the criminal accusations against us, we would have lived out our lives simply, like most people, unknown to the world, except for those few whose lives crossed ours.

"We are conscious that were we to accept this verdict, express guilt, the conventional penitence and remorse, the Court's mind might be more easily swayed to mitigate our sentences. But this course is not open to us. We are innocent, as we have proclaimed and maintained from the time of our arrest. This is the whole truth. To forsake this truth is to pay too high a price even for the priceless gift of life – for life thus purchased we could not live out in dignity and self-respect . . . ."

To the public-at-large, the Rosenbergs – who were given seven opportunities in the Court of Appeals, and seven opportunities to approach the Supreme Court – offered themselves as victims of a conspiracy rather than as convicted conspirators: "Our pleas to the Supreme Court have been restricted by legal protocol, but before the bar of public opinion we cannot reassert often or emphatically enough our complete innocence of the charge.

"One matter should be made unequivocally clear. No matter what the result, we will continue in our determination to expose the political frameup perpetrated against us by those who would silence by death, through spurious espionage accusations, opposition to the conspiracy to impose war abroad and a police state at home.

"We do not want to die. We are young and yearn for a long life of accomplishment. Yet, if the only alternative to death is the purchase of life at the cost of personal dignity and abandonment of the struggle for democracy and ethical standards, there is no future for us or any legacy we can leave our children or those who survive and follow us.

"For what is life without the right to live it? Death holds no horror as great as the horror of a sterile existence devoid of social responsibility and the courage of one's convictions. We believe that our fellow Americans share these sentiments. We believe that they will save us – and themselves – from this conspiracy to put to death innocent Americans."

The original date set for the execution of the Rosenbergs was the week of January 12, 1953. The extension of the date through the legal processes resulted in June 19 as the date of execution. In the six-month period prior to the execution, the National Committee conducted a series of events geared to seeking clemency. From February 23 until February 26, there was a round-the-clock vigil at the White House by 2000 participants. On March 18, 1953, there were 1100 people at a $25-a-plate dinner at New York City's Capitol Hotel. The dinner was held under the auspices of Professionals for Clemency. The chairman was Sarah Lichtenberg, and Stephen Love of Northwestern University presided at the dinner. Sponsors of the affair included the Reverend Walter Bennett, Leon Beverly, Rabbi Abraham Cronbach, Professor Arthur K. Davis, Earl B. Dickerson, Dr. Arnold B. Donawa, Waldo Frank, the Reverend J. Spencer Kennard Jr., Dr. Bernard Loomer, Dr. Philip Morrison, Herbert Paley, the Reverend Antonio Perrota, Leon Quat, and Mary Church Terrell.

On March 29 in Carnegie Hall, the National Council of the Arts, Sciences and Professions ("Communist front") held a fund-raising rally, presided over by Henry Pratt Fairchild, professor emeritus of New York University. Following the rally, a "clemency" dinner was held with Dean Bernard Loomer of the University of Chicago's Divinity School as the featured speaker.

On April 26, at Randall Island Stadium in New York City, ten thousand people assembled for a "clemency" rally. The *Daily Worker* described what the rally-goers could expect: "A cast of 500, including choral groups and professional stage, screen, and radio performers will be featured in the 'Rosenberg Story,' the dramatic spectacle . . . to be in the form of a living newspaper, will dramatize the two years' efforts of people in the United States and throughout the world to save the lives of Ethel and Julius Rosenberg . . . top flight writers have created an original script, portraying, through narrative, drama, and song, the outstanding moments of the dramatic movement that has thus far succeeded in staying the execution of the East Side couple. Reenacted in the living newspaper will be the outstanding trial scenes . . . as well as the clemency and prayer vigils that took place in Washington and all over the world."

The entertainment world, next to the clergy, provided the Communists the most support throughout the Rosenbergs' imprisonment. Letterheads, petitions, and advertisements found actors, actresses, script writers, playwrights, directors, and producers in prominent display. Almost all of the individuals had long histories of Communist associations. Many of them had found succor in the Fifth Amendment when asked about their Communist Party membership, and some would end up in prison, convicted of contempt of Congress. Few suffered any retardation of their successful careers in the theater. They included husband and wife Ossie Davis and Ruby Dee, Paul Robeson, Howard da Silva, Morris Carnosky, Lucy Brown, Ray Lev, Max Goberman, Martin Wolfson, Albert Maltz, Karen Morley, Alvah Bessie, Gale Sondergaard, Lester Cole, John Howard Lawson, and Herbert Biberman. Paul Robeson, the Negro baritone, was especially active on behalf of the Rosenbergs. He attended rallies, helped in fund raising, and he was in the forefront of the Civil Rights Congress's efforts to work with the Rosenberg committees. In one handbill issued by the Civil Rights Congress, Robeson joined W.E.B. DuBois, William L. Patterson, and the Baptist Ministers' Conference to urge, "Stop the legal lynching of Ethel and Julius Rosenberg." The tasteless text of the handbill read: "The 'rape' and 'murder' frame-ups of innocent Negroes are terrorizing the Negro people, and dividing all Americans in their demands for democracy and peace. It is well known how Negroes are framed in the South and given death penalties when white men, for the same offense, are given only short sentences or let off scot-free. Similarly here, the only time the death penalty is used on a peacetime espionage charge the victims are a Jewish couple.

"The same frame-up system which has taken the lives of Willie McGee, the Martinsville Seven and hundreds of other innocent Negro victims — lying witnesses, a rigged jury which excluded Jews, promotion-hungry prosecutors, a biased judge — turned out this death sentence. Every American who fights to save the Rosenbergs aids the fight to save his own human and democratic rights, his right to speak for peace. The Negro people, by acting to win clemency for the innocent Rosenbergs, can deal a tremendous blow against the frame-up system which has taken so many Negro lives, and which now threatens to take the lives of all Americans, Negro and white, who advocate constitutional rights and peace."

The aged DuBois, who held high positions in Communist fronts at home and abroad, gave the Rosenberg campaign its most memorable bit of anti-Americanism: "We are the murderers hurling mud/ We are the witch hunters drinking blood." On another occasion DuBois declared: "America should be asking a pardon from the Rosenbergs and not the Rosenbergs who should be asking for clemency."

The thousands of Americans who worked in the save-the-Rosenbergs campaign never had a scintilla of an excuse to remain in ignorance of the fact that the Rosenbergs were valuable propaganda tools for the Communist Party, USA. The Party's leaders talked of the Rosenbergs in terms that could only mean that they were talking of their own: "Behind bars, they have proven themselves more powerful than guns and lies." (*Daily Worker*) — "The Rosenbergs are responding magnificently." (Party Chairman William Z. Foster)

On June 12, 1953, on the front page of the *Daily Worker*, Foster, Elizabeth Gurley Flynn, and Pettis Perry, speaking as the Party's National Committee, gave instructions to the Party's faithful as to the last-ditch efforts that should be made: " 'Into the Fight to Save the Rosenbergs' — Day and night activity can still save the lives of the Rosenbergs, the National Committee of the Communist Party declared yesterday.

"We earnestly appeal to every progressive, to every member of working class and people's organizations, to view it as his most sacred of all obligations in these hours to plunge fully into the people's fight to save the Rosenbergs. No other duty or task can be higher than this between now and June 18.

"Here is what you can do without delay: (1) Wire or write personally to President Eisenhower urging commutation of the death sentence. (2) Collect signatures for such appeals in your neighborhood, apartment house, shop, office, retail stores, and streets. Phone friends and neighbors and ask them to join the clemency plea. (3) Ask your fellow tradeunion members and union officials to urge Eisenhower to grant commutation of the death penalty. (4) Organize delegations of your neighbors, ministers, union members, and leaders to visit Congressmen, State and city officials asking them to memorialize the President to reverse the death sentence. (5) Support and help organize all demonstrations, picket lines, and committees engaged in fighting for clemency.

"To save the Rosenbergs is to help save our country, America, from injustice, anti-Semitism, and the plots of those who would spread hysteria, repression and fear in the U.S."

On June 18, 1953, when the Supreme Court of the United States was sitting in an extraordinary session to deliberate the merits of a stay of execution, Foster sent a telegram to the President: "Vast multitudes of people in this country and throughout the world are demanding clemency for Ethel and Julius Rosenberg. Obviously this couple have been convicted on the basis of perjured testimony. They did not have a fair trial in courts which worked in an atmosphere of war hysteria and pro-Fascist intimidation. The Rosenbergs are the victims of a frame-up . . . .

"Mr. President, are you going to yield to the aggressive pressure of the anti-Semites, Negro haters, redbaiters and Fascist-like warmongers? . . . . The execution of the Rosenbergs would be a savage political crime . . . . Already untold millions of people, alarmed by the huge military establishment and aggressive foreign policies of the United States Government . . . have come to fear the United States as bearing a sinister threat of fascism and a new world war . . . . Time and again the record of our country has been besmirched by political murders, carried through by the courts and the Government . . . . Now it is proposed to add the Rosenbergs to the long list of frameup victims of political savagery . . . ."

On the same day that Foster was beleaguering the White House, the *Worker's* front-page carried the Rosenberg's last plea to the President: "We appealed to you once before. Our sentences, we declared there, violated truth and the instincts of civilized humanity. We told you the truth. We are innocent. We now again solemnly declare our innocence.

"The guilt in this case, if we die, will be America's. The shame, if we die, will dishonor this generation, and pervade history until future Americans recapture the heritage of truth, justice, and equality before the law. Our case has made new precedents in the law of this land — evil precedents, unjust, inhuman, and with not even that concern for human life shown the protection of the rights of property . . . .

". . . the Supreme Court has just denied us a stay of execution . . . . And yet, unheard of in the annals of our law, four judges — four of the most distinguished members of that bench — had voted to let us live, at least long enough to vindicate our rights before them. Instead, our accusers torture us, in the face of death, with the guaranty of life for the price of a confession of guilt . . . .

"We refuse the iniquitous bargain even as perhaps the last few days of our young lifes [*sic*] are slipping away . . . . We cannot besmirch our name by bearing false witness to save ourselves. Do not dishonor America, Mr. President, by considering, as a condition of our right to survive, the delivery of a confession of guilt of a crime we did not commit . . . . You may not believe us, but the passage of even the few short months since last we appealed to you, is confirming our prediction that, in the inexorable operation of time and conscience, the truth of our innocence would emerge . . . . If you will not hear our voices, hear the voices of the world . . . .

"Hear the great and the humble: from Einstein, whose name is legend, to the tyros in the laboratories of Manchester; from struggling students at Grenoble to Oxford professors; from the world-famous movie directors of Rome to the bit players of London; from the dock workers at Liège to cotton spinners of India; from the peasants of Italy to the philosophers of Israel; from Mauriac, the Nobel *littérateur,* to reporters in Mexico City; from the stenographers of Rotterdam to the transport workers of England; from the auto workers of Detroit to the auto workers of Paris; from Nexo of Denmark to Sequieros of Mexico to Seghers of Germany to Duhamel of France; from Australia to Argentina; from Uruguay to Sweden, from Cuba to Canada to New Zealand.

"Read the tons of petitions, letters, postcards, stacked high in your filing rooms, from the plain and gentle folk of our land. They marched before your door in such numbers as never before, as have their brothers and sisters in London, Paris, Melbourne, Buenos Aires, Ottawa, Rome. They ask you not to orphan our two young boys. They ask brotherhood and peace to spare our lives. Hear the great and humble for the sake of America."

When the Rosenbergs were executed and their funeral rites had been held, the *Worker* offered a parting tribute in an editorial ("Their Nobility Will Triumph"): "The men who killed Ethel and Julius Rosenberg think they are finished with this innocent Jewish couple whom they have cynically blamed for the criminal slaughter in Korea, and on whom Eisenhower now dares to blame the future atomic war which he wants us to think is 'inevitable.'

"But never were frightened and desperate politicians more mistaken! Six years after they murdered John Brown, his executioners heard all America and the world singing his triumphant epitaph: 'John Brown's body lies a-moldering in the grave/ But his soul goes marching on!'

"That is how it is with Ethel and Julius Rosenberg. In murdering the Rosenbergs, against whom there was not a single shred of evidence except the bought perjury of one single FBI-terrorized stoolpigeon, the Eisenhower government not only drags the name of America in the mud, but also kills what few illusions might still remain in the world about its real nature.

"The Rosenbergs were killed in an atmosphere of a Southern lynch town. The legal farce was a cover-up for a prearranged lynching. The

179

jury was terrorized. The witnesses were perjured. The press and prosecution howled for blood. The Supreme Court did not have the decency or the courage to look at the original trial record, or at the new documentary evidence which unmasked the biggest fake in our judicial history. But the world speaks its admiration for this humble and obscure couple whose souls were as pure as their executioners were vile.

"This humble couple aroused the sympathy of the world because, with the rarest of moral courage and purity, they simply would not buy their personal safety by betraying America to a police-dictated lie! They would not buy the 'lie-or-die' proposition with which the Washington police tortured them in the death cell for two whole years – even up to the last minute as they went to their deaths. History will surely vindicate them as the noblest of innocent human beings.

"The fight to establish the innocence of the Rosenbergs is just beginning. 'Their soul goes marching on.' Their martyrdom will spur new people's struggles against political frameups, against police-state thought control, against the McCarthyite brutes who seek to shed the blood of the American people and the blood of all humanity. The truth about this new and more terrible Dreyfus Case must be carried into every home, every union, every church, every American conscience! The Rosenbergs have not died in vain. This is the pledge of every decent human being in America today."

On June 23, 1953, the *Worker* carried a parting salute from Foster, Flynn, and Pettis ("Ethel and Julius Rosenberg Were Heroes in the Battle for Democracy"), in which the martyrdom of the Rosenbergs received the imprimatur of the Communist hierarchy: "Ethel and Julius Rosenberg were brutally murdered in an act of fascist violence by a ruling class that is desperate, in the face of the rising forces of peace and democracy. The murderers of the Rosenbergs hoped they could intimidate the fight for peace and democracy by hurling into its face the murdered bodies of Ethel and Julius Rosenberg. But these rulers, who try to cover with brutality and arrogance their fear of the peoples of America and the world, were never more mistaken.

"The Rosenbergs died innocent – heroes of democracy. They gave to America and to the world an example of heroism and self-sacrificing patriotism which tore the mask off the vile frameup concocted against them personally, and against the American people as a whole.

"What the FBI political police, the Truman administration, and then the Eisenhower-Brownell leadership had demanded of them, and of Morton Sobell whom they buried in jail for thirty years, that they help open the gates to fascism, to anti-labor, anti-Semitic violence in the United States.

"The top officials in Government, especially the department of frameup headed by J. Edgar Hoover, plotted to force the humble Jewish couple to betray democracy by 'fingering' the progressive and Marxist movement as an 'espionage conspiracy.' They had hoped to force this innocent couple to commit this perjury in order that the hatred of the American people for the Korean war, for the entire 'inevitable atomic war' line of the atom bomb maniacs, should be directed in pogrom-fashion against the working class vanguard, the Communists, the Negro and Jewish people, the labor and progressive forces generally.

"In short, the plot to frame the Rosenbergs on the basis of a fantasy created by the FBI in a deal with a frightened and chronic liar was a political plot to assist in advancing the McCarthyite pro-Fascist reign of fear in the United States, to brutalize the population, and get it to accept the further fascination of the United States without resistance.

"The Rosenberg case became the focus of the entire world's hatred of Washington's war policies, of the hatred and resistance to the effort to McCarthyize America in the image of the Swastika. Though foully murdered by the Eisenhower-Brownell-J. Edgar Hoover forces, in an atmosphere of McCarthyism, the Rosenbergs succeeded in unmasking the plot before the eyes of literally the majority of mankind. Though dead, they live on, growing more powerful every minute as the world camp of peace and democracy refuses to let their murderers get away with their conspiracy.

"The task is now for us Americans not to falter in the face of this challenge, but to take inspiration from the courage of these two patriotic Americans who would not give the Jew haters and the war plotters what they wanted. It is up to us now to see the lessons of the Rosenberg case and to act on them! (1) The truth about the 'why and wherefores' of the frameup must be brought to the labor movement which should be shown that behind the Rosenberg frameup stood the worst enemies of all labor; that if the Rosenbergs could be framed 'as spies,' then any labor leader or militant worker can be framed by the same forces on trumped-up charges of any kind. The Rosenberg case —

like the Sacco-Vanzetti and Mooney and later cases – is a labor case. (2) To warn the labor movement and the people as a whole that behind the Rosenberg 'spy hoax' new attacks are being plotted against the rights and living conditions of the people, and to help organize united resistance to stem the tide of fascism. (3) To explain that the Rosenberg fight helped to bring into being a spirit of resistance to McCarthyism which can be built on and expanded; that the Rosenberg's heroism will inspire more and more Americans as the truth becomes known to millions. (4) To show that the Rosenberg fight merges with the people's hatred of the Korean war, of the suicidal foreign policies of Washington, and that the fight to expose the criminals behind the Rosenberg frameup is a vital part of the peace and democracy battles, just as the fight for Dreyfus in France was a fight for French democracy against militarism and war.

"The pro-Fascist forces will try in their hatred of the growing forces of peace and democracy to spread more anti-Semitism, more violence, more frameups. But the road before them is far from a clear one. On the contrary, they have roused new resistance by their barbarous crime."

One of the most vitriolic summations of the Rosenberg saga appeared in the Communist journal *Masses and Mainstream*: "The fiendish murder of Ethel and Julius Rosenberg has lacerated the moral sense of mankind and brought heavy shame to our country. With deep grief and burning anger, the entire world stands aghast at the frenzied lynching of two beautiful human beings whose crime was their passion for peace and truth. Every pretended shred of decency was stripped from the war-mad, fascist-bent executioners as they rushed, in defiance of legal process and with contempt for the common opinion of humanity, to snuff out the lives of the devoted young Jewish parents. And the barbarism of generals and bankers who rule America was all the more grimly illuminated by the nobility of their victims, who to the last moment held their heads high in the knowledge of their innocence and the ultimate triumph of their ideals.

"Beyond the terrible injustice to the Rosenbergs, beyond the dishonor to the American people, is the threat of the Eisenhower Administration to fulfill the larger purpose of this frameup. That purpose is to terrify and insensitize the people still further into submitting to a Nazi program.

"But the battle of the Rosenbergs is not over . . . . The real facts in the case must still be brought to the people, most of whom have not yet been awakened to their peril. The purpose of the frameup must still be exposed to many millions. The most glorious chapter of the Rosenberg story remains to be written by an American people rousing itself against the horrible fate intended by the atomaniacs."

During the last week before the Rosenbergs' execution, the National Committee managed to conduct its greatest demonstrations. For six days, picket lines of as many as 7,000 individuals marched around the White House area. On the evening of the execution, defense attorney Emanuel Bloch, who made a vain attempt to see the President and get a last minute reprieve for his clients, said: "The actions of the Government of the United States in this case reveal to the entire world that the people who are running the Government are much more barbaric than the Nazis when they had power in Germany."

In New York City on the night of the execution, at least 5,000 gathered for a "prayer" meeting where no prayers were heard. Instead, the crowd listened to diatribes from Leon Straus, William Patterson, Albert Kahn, Irving Stern, and Yuri Suhl. Howard Fast told the gathering: "This is the hour of our country's shame." Kahn said: "They are not spies. They are not traitors. It is those who want to kill them who are traitors to America."

Shortly after the funeral of the Rosenbergs, the National Committee To Secure Justice in the Rosenberg Case issued a statement: "Although Ethel and Julius Rosenberg have been pronounced 'legally dead' they shall live to haunt the courts which condemned them and the officials who refused the simple act of mercy which could have kept them alive until they could have vindicated themselves. The very memory of them will one day cause America to look back with shame on the era of hysteria under which they were tortured and put to death. We shall continue this fight until Rosenbergs' names are cleared and their innocence proved . . . . We shall continue to press for a review of the Rosenberg case for reasons which transcend them, and even their children."

The interest of the National Committee was quickly diverted to Morton Sobell, who although sentenced to thirty years' imprisonment had been virtually ignored while the furor over the Rosenbergs held center stage. In July 1953, the National Committee began a new campaign by declaring: "The execution of Ethel and Julius Rosenberg was carried out in the same atmosphere of extreme passion, disregard for due process, and abandonment of humane considerations that marked their trial and sentencing . . . .

"We believe that it would be in the best interests of our country and its judicial process to continue all efforts to ascertain the truth in the Rosenberg case; that the trial and sentencing of the Rosenbergs' codefendant, Morton Sobell, requires steps leading towards a new trial; that efforts be made to secure public support for a transfer of Morton Sobell from imprisonment at Alcatraz . . . To these ends the committee calls upon the many diverse groups throughout the country who concerned themselves with either a new trial or clemency for the Rosenbergs to dedicate themselves anew to justice in the Rosenberg-Sobell case . . . . We urge such groups to begin their public activity by holding Declaration of Justice meetings . . . to begin to familiarize the public with the facts in their codefendant's case."

On July 19, 1953, in Los Angeles, more than a thousand persons gathered "to pledge the widest possible support to the widest possible movement to guarantee Sobell's immediate transfer from Alcatraz [prison] and the ultimate reversal of [his] thirty-year sentence." The National Committee's officers, Joseph Brainin and David Alman, and Mrs. Morton Sobell, were on the scene. Mrs. Sobell told the audience that her husband, Morton, "is innocent and we stand together with the Rosenbergs who chose to die rather than lie."

In August and September 1953, two major meetings of the National Committee were held in New York. More than 1,000 persons were introduced to the slogan: "Free Sobell — Vindicate the Rosenbergs." Copies of the *Death House Letters* and subscriptions to *National Guardian* were sold. The *Guardian's* general manager John T. McManus addressed the crowd as did Emily Alman who said: "By refusing to 'confess' and name names for a crime of which they swore innocence, Ethel and Julius Rosenberg inspired patriotic Americans to stand up against injustice." According to Dr. Fineberg in his *Rosenberg Case*, it was at this meeting that Mrs. Alman revealed what she considered had been the key to success for the National Committee: "We started out with a tiny group of people who were bent on freeing the Rosenbergs. But we showed that we could get all kinds of people — those who believed they were innocent, those who believed they were guilty but the sentence was too severe, those who weren't sure about their guilt and thought they should have a new trial — we could get all these people, many who disagreed with us, to march together! We showed that we could learn to put on a hat in order to get the support of a rabbi and that we could win friends by saying: these are people with two children."

At Randall's Island, Mrs. Sobell and Emily Alman were the featured speakers at a meeting, attended by about 5,000, who paid a dollar or more into the coffers of the National Committee.

In Chicago on October 10 and 11, 1953, at a national conference, the National Committee To Secure Justice in the Rosenberg Case became the National Committee To Secure Justice for Morton Sobell in the Rosenberg Case. Daniel Marshall and Joseph Brainin were chosen as co-chairmen with Emily Alman as national executive secretary. A policy committee was formed, with Joseph Granat, Herman Tamsky, David Alman, Leonard Tushnet, Sylvia Steingart, and Peggy Strauss. The finance committee was composed of Don Rothenberg, Reid Robinson, Yuri Suhl, and Gertrude Soltker. The organizational secretary was Norma Aronson and the publicity director was Ted Jacobs. For all practical purposes, except for a few shifts of personnel and a slight name change, the National Committee was still in business.

The first major move of the Sobell Committee took place in December 1953 when a thirty-five page brief was filed with the Senate Judiciary Committee accompanied by a demand that the Senate investigate the conduct of the Attorney General's office with regard to the Rosenberg-Sobell case. The brief focused on a seven-point Bill of Particulars, alleging that the Attorney General's office: "(1) knowingly engaged in an unlawful campaign of misrepresentations of fact through press releases prior to the trial and thus falsified essential aspects of the case, influencing public opinion to prejudge the defendants; (2) knowingly used and encouraged perjured testimony against the Rosenbergs and against Morton Sobell; (3) promised rewards and in fact did give such rewards to several witnesses in the Rosenberg-Sobell case; (4) attempted and still attempts to keep from the courts documents that reveal the perjuries and the part the Attorney General's Office played in obtaining these perjuries; (5) engaged in the use of mental torture against the Rosenbergs and mental torture, as well as physical violence, against Morton Sobell; (6) by deception and misrepresentation, misled the Supreme Court on the day of the Rosenbergs' execution; (7) by withholding information, by deception, and by outright falsehoods, misled two Presidents of the United States who had before them appeals for clemency."

The brief did nothing for Sobell, but it did garner publicity for the new committee, which had offered no new evidence and had simply repeated the same old charges that had been rejected over a two-year period in the Appeals Courts.

On February 12, 1954, the Sobell Committee held a dinner in Chicago to pay tribute to Harold Urey, whose amateurish excursions into legal matters had proven to be a boon to the efforts of the Rosenberg Committee. Urey was presented a bound volume of scrolls, allegedly signed by 6,000 "prominent persons throughout the world honoring [him] for his achievements as a scientist and contributions as a citizen." The signers included Robert M. Hutchins of the Fund for the Republic, historian Arnold Toynbee, Reverend Henry Hitt Crane, Kirtley Mather, James Franck, Linus Pauling, Henry Steele Commager, Roger Baldwin, Percy Julian, A. Philip Randolph, Robert Strozier, Abraham Cronbach, and Alexander Meiklejohn. Associated with the Urey dinner were Carey McWilliams, Stephen Love, Malcolm Sharp, Gertrude Gunther, Ruth Rothstein, Ruth Belmont, and David Soltker. The dinner served as a prelude to a meeting on the following day of members of the National Sobell Committee and representatives of local chapters from around the country.

At the conclusion of the business meeting, the Sobell Committee agreed on a program of action that was outlined in a report prepared by David Alman: "There are in our country today a number of cases historically related to the one that has been our prime interest since the fall of 1951. The same prosecutors, judges, and witnesses appeared in a number of them. They all led to the Rosenberg-Sobell case, to the ultimate stigma of treason upon the names of non-conformists, to the ultimate sentence of death. Were it not for an extraordinary campaign of enlightenment, involving at its height the participation of several million people, the Rosenberg-Sobell case would have led us into a time of wholesale executions and repeated sentences of living death.

"Today, the Rosenberg-Sobell case haunts the equilibrium [sic] of all who directly or indirectly participated in its frauds and cruelties. No case in our time commanded so much attention, drew so many advocates, created so many doubts, or compelled so much self-justification on the part of the team of executioners. Other verdicts in other related cases may be reversed without laying bare to the American people the lengths to which life and freedom have been subordinated to the demands of transitional policies at home and abroad. Indeed, that has happened in some instances. But were the Rosenberg-Sobell case to obtain a new and honest verdict, no other related case could stand unchanged. No person connected with the Attorney General's conduct of the case could remain in public life, and some would undoubtedly find themselves indicted. No piece of legislation resting on the Rosenberg-Sobell case for its justification could remain unchanged. And all design for further attacks on life and liberty, in the name of saving the nation, would have to be set aside.

"Wherever men and women are in prison today solely for social, economic, or political nonconformity, their hope lies in an exposure of the Rosenberg-Sobell case, for that is a key to all undeserved prison doors. The nationwide justice and clemency campaigns between the fall of 1951 and June of 1953, and the constant — if not yet intense — efforts around Morton Sobell, have been an indispensable background to many new developments in our country. There is today a growing sentiment for the restoration of due process in the courts.

"A new step forward was created by the advocates of Morton Sobell on the night of February 12, when the dinner to Dr. Urey took place. Dr. Urey and the other eminent guests that evening chose to speak directly under the auspices of the Chicago Sobell Committee, and they made it clear that the Sobell case was, to their thinking, of key importance in our times. Some 6,000 Americans, in a scroll to Dr. Urey, made known their belief — at the very least — that they applauded the great scientist's exercise of his right to speak his mind on the case itself. Some of these signers, like Dr. Urey himself, are Nobel prize winners. Others are eminent in science, religion, philosophy, and history.

"Within less than 24 hours following this historic event newspapers throughout the country carrying portions of Dr. Urey's speech, placed at least some of the facts in the case before large numbers of the American people. With this impetus, and within the framework of an improving atmosphere, the various committees, groups, or individuals who have interested themselves in the Sobell case have an extraordinary opportunity to move towards new, more far-reaching steps leading to Morton Sobell's freedom.

"The National Committee, therefore, is now preparing public and legal steps that will carry the case to a new stage. This program will reflect the willingness of large numbers of people to take a second look at the conduct of the Attorney General's office, and their growing apprehension that our standards of justice have been flagrantly abused. This program will be cognizant of the fact that we are entering a time when our fellow citizens can be moved not only by humane and ethical considerations, but by indignation at exposed falsehood.

"This program will be characterized, in the first place, by the placing of the facts in the case before larger numbers of the American people. Dr. Urey's speech and the press coverage that followed it, was the initial step in that direction. Now, new ways must be devised to make public the contradiction in testimony, the perjuries, the tortures, and cruelties involved in the case.

"This program will be characterized, secondly, by activities directed at all three branches of our government. Our attorneys will press in the courts for transfer, for review, for a new trial. Our appeal for an investigation by an appropriate Committee of Congress will be renewed, with the solicitation of public support for such a step. Within the Executive Department, we will press for transfer, for the withdrawal of objection to a court review, and finally, if necessary, an appeal for Presidential pardon or commutation.

"The third characteristic of this program will be its widespread scope. Every section of the population, regardless of its station in public, in private life, will be reached with the facts in the case. The scientist, minister, lawyer, educator, social worker, union leader, the worker, housewife, and student must all find themselves in possession of the facts and encouraged to take whatever steps are appropriate to the moment.

"The fourth characteristic will be a further seeking out of the diversity of levels upon which people can take action on the case. The Sobell Case is replete with inhuman and immoral acts by the Attorney General's Office, as well as with grievous denial of due process and outright fraud. The process of enlightenment for differing persons and sections can begin at any of these points, and must always tend to move towards fuller knowledge. We have seen, heretofore, that many persons, while actually doubting the validity of the verdict and sentences, nevertheless chose to limit the expression of their opinion to humane questions. These opinions are of extreme value to the efforts on Sobell's behalf. To raise those opinions and actions to a more effective level, it is necessary to enlighten people on the key importance of the case for the future of democracy in our courts and country. Those who share our view that Sobell is the victim of a terrible fraud, and yet limit the range of their appeal, can be made to understand that it is in the best interests of our country that they come to grips with the fundamental issues of the case.

"Such a program requires a detailed plan of activities, most carefully thought out, exceedingly flexible, and realistic in purpose and fulfillment. It cannot be entirely blueprinted, but must be created step by step as new developments take place, as our program of education grows and takes hold, and as new situations arise.

"It is essential to keep in mind that, regardless of the step we call for at any particular moment, we must seek to find the broadest and most numerous support. This applies equally to the campaign for transfer now being strengthened and to a possibly not too distant campaign for Presidential commutation of sentence. Just as the former must find the means of embracing all shades of opinion – from the humane to the advocate of Sobell's innocence, so the latter must encompass these as well, so that even persons believing in Sobell's guilt will recognize that his sentence was far too severe and that his freedom would materially aid the growing sentiment against extremism and unprecedented harshness in the courts."

The campaign on behalf of Morton Sobell generally concentrated on demands for a new trial or for an executive pardon or commutation of his sentence. In the course of events, the campaign did nothing for Sobell. It did, however, serve as a propaganda tool for the Communist Party. Sobell was destined to spend eighteen years in federal prisons – Alcatraz; Atlanta, Georgia; Springfield, Missouri; and Lewisburg, Pennsylvania. The efforts on his behalf never approached the extensive and emotional peak that characterized the campaign to save the Rosenbergs from execution. Sobell's cause, however, was standard fare for readers of the Communist press.

In the mid-1950's those who supported Sobell included Murray Abowitz of Los Angeles; Milnor Alexander of the American Friends Service Committee; Roland H. Bainton of Yale University's Divinity School; the Reverend William T. Baird of Chicago; the Reverend Reginold

H. Bass of Brooklyn; Helen Marston Beardsley of Los Angeles; Edward Biberman of Los Angeles; Leo Bigelman of Los Angeles; Jessie F. Binford of Chicago's Hull House; David Blackwell of the University of California; Derk Bodde of the University of Pennsylvania; Reuben W. Borough of Los Angeles; Murray Branch of Morehouse College; Robert L. Brook of Los Angeles; Anton J. Carlson of the University of Chicago; Rabbi Franklin Cohn of Los Angeles; Ephraim Cross of the City College of New York; news commentator Elmer Davis; psychologist Frank Davis; Dorothy Day of the *Catholic Worker*; Rabbi Julian B. Feibelman; attorney John F. Finerty; attorney J. Allan Frankel; the Reverend G. Shubert Frye of Syracuse; Maxwell Geismar; Edwin R. Goodenough of Yale University; Alice Hamilton; William Harrison, publisher of the *Boston Chronicle*; the Reverend John Paul Jones of Brooklyn; Isaac Kolthoff of the University of Minnesota; professor emeritus J. M. Kuehne of the University of Texas; the Reverend John Howland Lathrop of Brooklyn; Norman Lavet of North Hollywood, California; Paul H. Lehmann, director of graduate studies at Princeton Theological Seminary; Milton Lester of Beverly Hills; Milton Z. London of Los Angeles; Bernard M. Loomer of the Univeristy of Chicago's Divinity School; attorney Daniel Marshall of Los Angeles; Leo Mayer of New York; attorney Louis McCabe of Philadelphia; the Reverend Sidney G. Menk of New York; author Lewis Mumford; Gardner Murphy of Topeka; Scott Nearing; Theodora Ninesteel of Los Angeles; Judge Patrick H. O'Brien of Detroit; Victor Paschkis of Columbia University; Linus Pauling; Alexander E. Pennes of Los Angeles; attorney Richard W. Petherbridge of El Centro, California; the Reverend Dreyden L. Phelps of Berkeley, California; the Reverend Irving E. Putnam of Minneapolis; Anatol Rapoport of the University of Michigan; Oscar K. Rice of the University of North Carolina; Malcolm Sharp of the University of Chicago's Law School; Margaret T. Simkin of Los Angeles; Judge Edward P. Totten of Santa Ana, California; Harold Urey; Francis D. Wormuth of the University of Utah; and Frank Weymouth of Los Angeles.

By 1965, Sobell's wife estimated that about $1 million had been spent on efforts to free him. His case was constantly before the United States Court of Appeals or the Supreme Court of the United States. In 1962, he became eligible for parole but his application was rejected annually until 1969. The Sobell Committee tried to capitalize on the

Rosenbergs' history. In its fund-raising efforts, the Sobell group sold the Rosenbergs' *Death House Letters*, sympathetic books by John Wexley and Malcolm Sharp, and an eight-volume set of the Rosenbergs-Sobell trial.

The usual arguments offered on behalf of Sobell to attract sympathetic supporters were much along the lines that marked the pleas for the Rosenbergs. Sobell was portrayed as a victim of perjured testimony, a frame-up contrived by the Federal Bureau of Investigation, and victim of a miscarriage of justice.

Harold Urey, who had done yeoman service for the Rosenbergs with his amateurish pretensions to legal knowledge, was joined by others who allegedly "have studied the trial record of his [Sobell's] case" and who came away "convinced of a miscarriage of justice." In 1960, Sobell's freedom was appealed for by the alleged students of the trial record, including the Reverend Abraham J. Muste, whose name graced practically every Communist front appeal; the Reverend Donald Harrington, an inveterate joiner of Communist fronts; Norman Thomas, the patriarch of the Socialist Party; Professor Victor Paschkis; Rabbi Harry Halpern; Jerome Nathanson; journalist Murray Kempton; writer Maxwell Geismar; Leo Mayer; John F. Finerty, who had been associated with Emanuel Bloch as the Rosenbergs' defense counsel; Max Eastman, whose ideological posture was always unpredictable; Reinhold Niebuhr, who was tireless in protestations of anti-Communism as he joined one Communist front after another; Horace Kallen; Dwight Macdonald; Conrad Lynn; the Reverend Thomas Kilgore; Howard Radest; and the Reverend John Haynes Holmes. Pete Seeger, the Communist Party's favorite folk-singer, joined the Sobell cause, as did the arch-agitator Martin Luther King Jr.

Honorary sponsors of the Sobell committee (membership of the Committee was never publicized) included the Reverend George A. Ackerly, the Reverend Gross W. Alexander, David Andrews, Leo Berman, Rabbi Samuel Bernstein, Warren K. Billings, Rabbi Balfour Brickner, A. Burns Chalmers, Ruth Gage-Colby, Harold A. Cranefield, Dr. Bernard D. Davis, David Dellinger, Lloyd Donnell, the Reverend George H. Dunne, S.J., the Reverend John E. Evans, Jules Feiffer, Rabbi Morris Fishman, Waldo Frank, the Reverend G. Shubert Frye, the Reverend Erwin A. Gaede, Rabbi Robert E. Goldberg, Dr. Luigi Gorini, Rabbi Avery Grossfield, Dr. A. Eustace Haydon, Russell Johnson, the

Reverend Joseph P. King, Professor Charles P. Larrowe, Donald E.J. McNamara, Albert Maltz, Milton Mayer, the Reverend Peter McCormack, Stanley Moffatt, Dr. E.F. Patterson, Professor Dale Pontius, Bertha C. Reynolds, Henry Roth, Reverend Francis S. Tucker, Clara M. Vincent, Leroy Waterman, Rabbi Jacob J. Weinstein, and Professor H.H. Wilson.

In 1965, the biggest push for Sobell's freedom came with the publication of *Invitation to an Inquest*, written by the husband and wife team of Walter and Miriam Schneir. Schneir was a member of the Emergency Civil Liberties Committee, a Communist front. The publication of the book was accompanied by a fresh outbreak of publicity for the Rosenbergs-Sobell case, especially in the *New York Times*. By 1965, Sobell had a new team of lawyers: Arthur Kinoy, William Kunstler, and Marshall Perlin, who petitioned the courts for a new Sobell trial; but their efforts were in vain.

As late as 1968, the Sobell committee was still trying to capitalize on the Schneirs' book when a full-page advertisement was placed in the *New York Times*, as a fund-raising move, through sale of the book by the committee.

The Schneirs' book described Sobell and the Rosenbergs as innocent victims of prejudice, perjury, forgery, and fraud. As a selling point, the advertisement said of the book: "If you've believed for years that Ethel and Julius Rosenberg were executed because they stole the secret of the atomic bomb and gave it to the Russians . . . that Morton Sobell was sentenced to thirty years in jail because he, too, was a spy . . . that the original trial record of the case was gone over by the Supreme Court and approved as fair and just . . . then reading *Invitation to an Inquest*, by Walter and Miriam Schneir (Doubleday, hardcover; Delta, paperback), is going to be an eye-opening experience for you.

"Because this quiet, restrained and factual book doesn't just question these beliefs. It claims they are totally and completely untrue!

"It claims that the Rosenbergs not only didn't steal atom-bomb secrets . . . they weren't even charged in the indictment with stealing them! That the 'atomic-bomb sketch' they allegedly stole (drawn by a prosecution witness and kept secret by the government until recently) was, in the words of scientists who worked on the actual A-bomb, a 'caricature,' 'worthless,' 'false'! That a key government witness later admitted he had lied under oath many, many times! That the wife of another prime witness acknowledged her husband had a 'tendency to hysteria,' and 'would say things were so even if they were not'! That the Supreme Court never once passed on the fairness of the trial! And that agents of the F.B.I. were undoubtedly involved in forging a vital piece of evidence that sealed the defendants' fate! And the book backs up its contentions by going to the record and letting the facts — and the contradictions — speak for themselves."

The Schneirs' book was really nothing but a re-hash of charges that had been raised over the years, some of them as early as 1952 and 1953. The Schneirs, like others before them, created and annihilated straw men.

In the normal course of events, Sobell was paroled from his prison term on January 14, 1969. He placed the major blame for his plight upon his chief trial lawyer, the late Edward Kuntz, who, Sobell claimed, had refused to allow him to testify in his own defense at the 1951 trial. (Why Sobell didn't fire the attorney and testify on his own initiative went unexplained.) Sobell also, in an interview, said that his and the Rosenbergs' convictions were a fraud perpetrated by the corporate establishment, which had determined that a political trial was a necessity during the "early days of McCarthyism." Sobell immediately plunged back into Communist Party circles and the Sobell committee announced that it would re-organize for its "long term, historic task of remembrance and exoneration."

NATIONAL LAWYERS GUILD

*INTERNATIONAL ASSOCIATION OF DEMOCRATIC
   LAWYERS*
INTERNATIONAL JURIDICAL ASSOCIATION
INTERNATIONAL LABOR DEFENSE
INTERNATIONAL RED AID

In February 1937, the National Lawyers Guild was organized during the course of a four-day convention in Washington, D.C. It had as its announced purpose to act as "a professional organization which shall function as an effective social force in the service of the people to the end that human rights shall be regarded as more sacred than property rights." Once the National Lawyers Guild (NLG) made a distinction between property rights and human rights, it landed square in the middle of the Communist-Socialist camp.

The language of adverse citations against the NLG by congressional investigating committees serves as a useful introduction to the entire subversive history of the organization. In 1950, the House Committee on Un-American Activities said: "The National Lawyers Guild is the foremost legal bulwark of the Communist Party, its front organizations, and controlled unions. Since its inception it has never failed to rally to the legal defense of the Communist Party and individual members thereof, including known espionage agents. It has consistently fought against national, State, and local legislation aimed at curbing the Communist conspiracy. It has been most articulate in its attacks upon all agencies of the Government seeking to expose or prosecute the subversive activities of the Communist network, including national, State, and local investigative committees, the Department of Justice, the FBI, and law enforcement agencies generally." In 1956, the Senate Internal Security Subcommittee said: "To defend the cases of Communist lawbreakers, fronts have been devised making special appeals in behalf of civil liberties and reaching out far beyond the confines of the Communist Party itself. Among these organizations are the . . . [and the] National Lawyers Guild. When the Communist Party itself is under fire these offer a bulwark of protection."

Early in its history, the NLG was the object of a self-serving piece in *New Masses,* the weekly journal of the Communist Party. Charles Recht, a member of the NLG, wrote ("Defense for the Counsel — The Need for the National Lawyers Guild"): "With the growth of the American Labor Party in New York, and kindred progressive movements throughout the United States, the lawyers, who in many of the smaller communities are the nerve centers of political activities, will be an invaluable aid in galvanizing the latent liberal elements of the country into a political force. The National Lawyers Guild can and will form one of the most important adjuncts to a progressive movement representing the interests of the workers and farmers." When Recht, an attorney for the Soviet government, spoke of "a progressive movement," he was simply using the Communists' Aesopian language to describe the Communist movement.

The International Labor Defense was delighted to see the NLG instituted: "The emergence of the National Lawyers Guild is regarded by the International Labor Defense as a heartening expression of the devotion of thousands of American attorneys to the American principle of democracy, and a concrete step on their part in the struggle to maintain and enlarge democratic rights."

The NLG was not unique when it was founded in 1937. The defense of the Communist Party and Communists had been of special concern to the Communist International since 1922, when the parent organization, International Labor Defense, was founded. The NLG never became a formal affiliate of either the International Labor Defense or its offshoot, the International Juridical Association, but on the American scene the three groups worked for identical objectives, and the existence of interlocking memberships made the groups — for all practical purposes — a highly cohesive network.

In 1922 at the Fourth Congress of the Comintern in Moscow, the Communist Parties were instructed "to establish an organization to render material and moral aid to the imprisoned victims of capitalism." To coordinate the various organizations' efforts throughout the world, the Comintern established the International Red Aid. In 1927, after being in operation for two years, International Labor Defense became the American section of International Red Aid. At the first conference of the American ILD, an executive committee of thirty-one members was elected. Twenty-two of the thirty-one were Communist Party members, including such well known figures as Robert W. Dunn, James P. Cannon, Robert Minor, William Z. Foster, C.E. Ruthenberg, Benjamin Gitlow, and Max Bedacht. Others on the committee included fellow travelers Alice Stone Blackwell and David Rhys Williams, and Socialist Party leader Eugene V. Debs.

Benjamin Gitlow, a charter member of the Communist Party and a member of the ILD's executive committee for four years, later became a staunch anti-Communist. In testimony before the Special House Committee on Un-American Activities, Gitlow said: "It [the ILD] is the legal defense organization of the Communist Party and of the Communist International in this country, and serves, also, as a highly political and propagandist Communist organization. The International Labor Defense from its very inception has been consciously used by the Communist Party to enable the party to gain a foothold in all kinds of organizations, particularly in trade unions, and it has been one of the most effective recruiting organizations for the Communist Party."

In the ILD's official organ, *Labor Defender* (later known as *Equal Justice*), it was written: "From the ILD structure itself, the organizational policy radiated outward to broaden the base of the movement for labor defense and relief, and for maintaining and enlarging democratic rights . . . . Many new forms of organization have sprung up, widening the network of a still loosely coordinated movement. Among these are trade-union defense committees . . . civil rights groups, committees against lynching, and for Negro rights; anti-Fascist groups and conferences . . . regional bodies embracing various sorts of organizations carrying on work in defense of civil rights . . . . Many of these, the International Labor Defense has initiated, either directly or through the work and influence of its membership. All of them have received the heartiest support of the organization in concrete ways . . . . The International Labor Defense was and continues to be of primary importance also as a coordinating factor in this movement." This was not idle boasting. In the 1930's and 1940's, the ILD as an organization or through its prominent members was directly involved in the creation and/or activities of literally scores of Communist front organizations, including the National Lawyers Guild.

Over the years some of the Communist Party's most famous leaders were officials of the ILD including J. Louis Engdahl, William L. Patterson, Anna Damon, Elizabeth Gurley Flynn, James W. Ford, Norman H. Tallentire, Karl Reeve, Scott Nearing, Ella Reeve "Mother" Bloor, Henry W.L. Dana, Juliet Stuart Poyntz, Max Bedacht, Joseph Brodsky, Earl Browder, Benjamin Davis Jr., Bruce Minton, and Angelo Herndon. Crypto-Communists, less well-known Communists, and reliable veteran fellow-travelers were officers and members or participants in ILD activities. They included Vito Marcantonio, Robert Morss Lovett, Carol King, Winifred Chappell, James Waterman Wise, George Axtelle, Ishmael Flory, Rockwell Kent, and Doxey Wilkerson.

In 1939, the biennial National Conference of the ILD had a large number of participating organizations, including unions such as the American Federation of Teachers; the Federation of Architects, Engineers, Chemists and Technicians; the International Longshoremen's and Warehousemen's Union; the National Maritime Union; the State, County and Municipal Workers; the Mine, Mill and Smelter Workers; and many others. A large number of Communist fronts were represented, as were the American Civil Liberties Union and the National Association for the Advancement of Colored People. The ILD Conference received friendly greetings from the Attorney General of the United States, Frank Murphy; United States Senators Claude Pepper, Lewis B. Schwellenbach, Theodore Green, and Elbert Thomas; and U.S. Representatives Abe Murdock, Adolph Sabath, Thomas F. Ford, Michael J. Bradley, and Sam Massingale.

The ILD's *Labor Defender* had an imposing array of Communists and fellow-travellers on its masthead: Henri Barbusse; Whittaker Chambers, John Dos Passos, Maxim Gorki, Josephine Herbst, Grace Hutchins, Lincoln Steffens, Waldo Frank, John Howard Lawson, Langston Hughes, Robert Minor, and Joseph Freeman.

Involved in ILD's "charitable" drives for the relief of "political" prisoners were Congressmen John T. Bernard, Usher Burdick, Paul Kvale, Jerry O'Connell, Bryson Scott, and Henry Teigan; Stella Adler, Marc Blitzstein, Millen Brand, E.B. Burgum, Malcolm Cowley, Joseph Curran, Jerome Davis, Archibald MacLeish, Kirtley Mather, Vincent Sheean, Mary E. Woolley, and Richard Wright.

Every activity of the ILD was carried on under the direct orders of Moscow's International Red Aid, which simply meant that every individual and organization connected with ILD was — wittingly or not — doing the work of the Comintern, whether that involved the establishment of Communist fronts, propaganda attacks upon "imperialism" and "fascism," proselytizing and propagandizing racial and national groups, or organizing lawyers to defend Communists or their fronts and fellow-travelers.

In an over-simplification of the relationship of the ILD, the National Lawyers Guild, and the International Juridical Association (IJA), it might be said that the ILD organized defenses for Communists and fellow travelers, the IJA provided the legal research for the defense, and the National Lawyers Guild provided the defense attorneys. In actual practice, the functions of the three organizations more often than not intertwined and overlapped, but this situation was consistent with the fact that there was interlocking membership amongst the three organizations, all of which were committed to the same Red objectives.

The IJA, founded in 1931, was an offshoot of the ILD. The preamble to the IJA's constitution stated: "Present America offers the example of a country discarding traditions of liberty and freedom, and substituting legislative, administrative and judicial tyranny. This country [the United States], once known to the world as the haven of refuge of oppressed peoples, now excludes, or deports, those daring to voice unpopular opinions; with a constitution supposed to protect freedom of expression, it now persecutes and imprisons its political dissenters." The IJA announced its purposes: "To combat . . . and resist increasing executive, judicial, legislative and administrative oppression . . . . To support the defense of political prisoners, especially in the courts . . . . To rally to the support of workers and their organizations . . . against the forces of the state whenever and wherever the latter aligns itself on the side of special privilege. To help establish in this country and throughout the world social and legal justice."

Officials of the International Juridical Association included well-known Communists, crypto-Communists, and fellow-travelers, including Harry Elmer Barnes, Paul F. Brissenden, Benjamin J. Davis, Joseph R. Brodsky, John P. Davis, Thomas I. Emerson, Abe Fortas, Lloyd K. Garrison, Walter Gellhorn, Pearl Hart, Henry T. Hunt, Robert W. Kenny, Carol King, Yetta Land, Max Lowenthal, Osmond K. Fraenkel, Thurgood Marshall, Carey McWilliams, David K. Niles, Lee Pressman, Maurice Sugar, Colston E. Warne, Roy Wilkins, and Nathan Witt. Alger Hiss was a prominent member.

Not everyone connected with the IJA was a practicing lawyer. The organization included law teachers, criminologists, writers, government officials, editors and publicists, and organization leaders. In its activities, the IJA participated in cases where Communists ran afoul of the law or cases involving deportation proceedings, lobbied against anti-Communist legislation, and defended leftwing union activists. The official organ of the IJA was the *IJA Monthly Bulletin*. In 1942, the editors of the *Bulletin* announced that they were merging their publication with *Lawyers Guild Review*, the official organ of the National Lawyers Guild. The editors said that the merger with the NLG "would greatly widen the area of our influence," but shortly thereafter the IJA went out of existence. And, in 1946, the ILD ceased to operate as an entity. It merged with another Communist front, the National Federation for Constitutional Liberties, to form a new front, the Civil Rights Congress.

In 1946, the NLG became an affiliate of another international Communist front, the newly-formed International Association of Democratic Lawyers (known also as the International Association of Democratic Jurists). The IADL was as devoted to the Communist cause as the International Labor Defense.

Throughout its history, the lawyers of the NLG have worked to extricate the Communist Party, members of the Party, and Communist spies from all sorts of legal difficulties. The NLG's lawyers have defended their clients in deportation hearings, in criminal suits, against contempt and perjury charges, and against charges of espionage and subversion. They have appeared with their clients at congressional and state legislature investigative hearings. Some of the more prominent clients of the NLG have included Ben Gold and his Fur and Leather Workers Union; Soviet spy Gerhart Eisler; Communist leader Steven Nelson, who achieved fame with the Communist Abraham Lincoln Brigade; Communist lawyer John Abt and three of his colleagues from a Washington spy ring, Nathan Silvermaster, Lee Pressman, and Nathan Witt; the Hollywood Ten, convicted of contempt of Congress; the "Eleven" Communist Party leaders; Frank Oppenheimer, brother of J. Robert Oppenheimer; Richard Morford of the subversive National Council of American-Soviet Friendship; Edward Barsky and other officials of the subversive Joint Anti-Fascist Refugee Committee; Valentin Gubitchev, Soviet spy; and Harry Bridges, the West Coast labor leader.

Of importance in the relationship between NLG lawyers and their clients is the fact that the Communists, except in extremely rare instances, do not employ lawyers unless the lawyers are willing to abide by the Party's directives and propaganda line. With the NLG lawyer present in the investigative committee hearing, the client was invariably an uncooperative and hostile witness. The Fifth and other Amendments were invoked, along with argumentative extraneous matter. Hearings and even court trials became shouting matches, and NLG lawyers seemed to thrive on contempt citations brought against them. The hearing room and court room became battlefields. The House Committee on Un-American Activities said: "The real nature of the [National Lawyers] Guild's philosophy comes into sharp focus during court procedures. Almost without exception, its leading members, despite their oaths as lawyers to uphold the dignity of the court and respect the constitutional mores of jurisprudence, seek to bring the court and its procedures into disrepute. They substitute insult for argument, resort to intimidation of judges by picket lines, parades, and personal abuse."

The conduct to be followed by the NLG lawyers was in keeping with a Communist Party guideline: "A Communist must utilize a political trial to help on the revolutionary struggle. Our tactics in the public proceedings of the law courts are not tactics of defense but of attack. Without clinging to legal formalities, the Communist must use the trial as a means of bringing his indictments against the dominant capitalist regime and of courageously voicing the views of his Party."

The NLG came into being at the very time the Communists were promoting the united front strategy. Under those circumstances the NLG, as an organization, in its literature and pronouncements followed every twist and turn of the Communist line. This held true for purely domestic matters and also for foreign policy affairs. The NLG joined with big and little Communist fronts in a perpetual campaign of abuse against anti-Communist, anti-subversive investigating committees on all levels of government. The same held true for campaigns to repeal existing legislation or to block proposed legislation which was anti-Communist or anti-subversive in character. The NLG opposed loyalty oaths for teachers and public officials. It opposed anti-Communist, anti-subversive security measures of all kinds in government and private industry. It waged a constant campaign of abuse against J. Edgar Hoover and the Federal Bureau of Investigation. It opposed finger-printing and even identification cards for aliens. If the NLG were to be taken literally, the United States was a terrorized police state with freedoms and rights virtually non-existent.

In the matter of foreign affairs, the NLG easily survived as a pro-Soviet entity through the Hitler-Stalin Pact, which had proved to be a critical test for the loyalty of Communists and fellow travelers. To the NLG — no matter the complete about-face vis-à-vis "fascism" whereby the Soviet government's foreign policy, which had been centered upon anti-Hitlerism, was suddenly dominated by a non-aggression treaty with Nazi Germany — the Soviet Union could do no wrong, despite the illogic, hypocrisy, and tergiversation that were evident even to hard-core Communists and starry-eyed liberals. There were a few defections from the NLG by dupes who came to realize that the NLG was not an idealistic group pursuing rectification of civil wrongs and reinforcement of rights and freedoms. When the Soviet Union went to war against Finland, there were a few more defections, but after that the NLG was going to be safe from further internecine difficulties, and its pro-Soviet sympathies and activities unencumbered by debate.

The general tone of the NLG's foreign policy was to condemn

imperialism and colonialism except with reference to the Soviet Union. The NLG opposed the Franco regime in Spain, Chiang Kai-shek's in China, Syngman Rhee's in South Korea – while supporting the Reds in the same countries. It condoned the Soviet rape of Poland, the Baltic States, the Balkan States, and central Europe. It endorsed the Soviet line on nuclear warfare, disarmament, "peace," and "cold war" treaties and alliances.

Many of the NLG's most prominent lawyers were either members of the Communist Party, closely associated with officials of the Party, Communist front leaders, or else fellow-travelers of such obvious commitment to the Party's cause that only a hair-line distinction could be made between them and the Party's regulars. They included David J. Bentall, Louis Boudin, Joseph R. Brodsky, John P. Davis, George Crockett, Bartley Crum, Clifford Durr, Thomas I. Emerson, Stanley Faulkner, Joseph Forer, Osmond K. Fraenkel, Walter Gellhorn, Pearl M. Hart, Henry T. Hunt, Robert W. Kenney, Carol Weiss King, Carey McWilliams, Martin Popper, Lee Pressman, Whitney North Seymour, Maurice Sugar, Abraham Unger, O. John Rogge, Earl B. Dickerson, Leonard Boudin, and Thurgood Marshall.

It cannot be argued that the NLG's lawyers served simply in the role of counsel for the defense. They were pleading a cause – the same cause they served in every major Communist front on the American scene and many international ones as well. They pleaded the cause in their writings and in their teachings. Many had university positions or editorial positions and some were in the employ of the federal government. There were even judges among them. They pursued their cause from one generation of law school graduates to another. They have never ceased their work with leftist unions, "civil rights" agitators, individual Communists, or the Communist Party. No matter the chairman or makeup of an investigating committee, from the days of Martin Dies through Wood-Rankin-McCarran-McCarthy-Jenner-McClellan-Walter-Ichord, the NLG has not changed its tactics.

OPEN LETTER FOR CLOSER COOPERATION WITH THE SOVIET UNION

On August 14, 1939 – ten days before Hitler and Stalin concluded a nonagression pact, four hundred Americans signed an "Open Letter for Closer Cooperation with the Soviet Union." The letter and signatures

OPEN LETTER FOR CLOSE COOPERATION WITH THE SOVIET UNION

appeared in the September issue of *Soviet Russia Today*, a Communist publication. Collectively, the signatories were a representative cross-section of the so-called intellectual community. Individually, some of them were universally recognized as leaders in their respective fields. There could be no doubt that together they exerted tremendous influence upon a large audience through their work on campuses, in publications, in the theater, in the arts, in science, and in organizations where they were either leaders or prominent members.

Only a handful of the signatories could make any claim to expertise gained either through education or through practical experience in political and/or diplomatic affairs. Only a few had ever been in the Soviet Union or had even the slightest pretension to sound knowledge about the Soviet Union. Most of the signatories had been repeatedly associated with the Moscow-directed united front of Communist fronts in the United States that flourished on dupes and innocents recruited from the "intellectual" community. There were some, of course, who were not dupes or innocents but, rather, willing tools — for one reason or another — of the Communists. They belonged to the breed of fellow-travelers, willing to work for and cooperate in one Communist project after another but unwilling to become formal card-carrying, dues-paying members of the Communist Party.

When the "Open Letter" was released, the signatories said: "A number of . . . committees have been formed which gave lip service to democracy and peace while actually attacking the Soviet Union and aiding reaction. Honest persons approached by such committees should scrutinize their aims very carefully and support only those groups genuinely interested in preserving cultures and freedom and refusing to serve as instruments for attacking the Soviet Union or aiding Fascism in any other way . . . . Our object is to point out the real purpose behind all these attempts to bracket the Soviet Union with the Fascist states, and to make it clear that the Soviet and Fascist policies are dramatically opposed."

Ironically, before the "Open Letter" appeared in print, the nonaggression pact was concluded between the Soviet regime and that of Nazi Germany. For their own devious reasons, Hitler and Stalin came to an understanding at a critical juncture in the course of their respective domestic and foreign policies. By the time the "Open Letter" did appear in print, Hitler — encouraged by Stalin — had invaded and conquered Poland, and two weeks after the "Open Letter" appeared in print Poland was divided between Stalin and Hitler.

In their anxiety to demonstrate the virtues of "Soviet socialism" vis-à-vis "totalitarian fascism," the signatories stressed what they alleged were ten basic points of difference between the two isms. It is not enough to say that the points were ludicrous or ridiculous. Each and every point was a deliberately contrived lie, so that the net result was a classic example of thoroughly mendacious tampering with history and reality. Of course, from their Red Olympus, the signatories offered no tiny shred of proof to buttress any one of the "basic" points. The points were: "(1) The Soviet Union continues as always to be a consistent bulwark against war and aggression, and works unceasingly for the goal of a peaceful international order. (2) It has eliminated racial and national prejudice within its borders, freed the minority peoples enslaved under the Tsars, stimulated the development of the culture and economic welfare of these peoples, and made the expression of anti-Semitism or any racial animosity a criminal offense. (3) It has socialized the means of production and distribution through the public ownership of industry and the collectivization of agriculture. (4) It has established nationwide socialist planning, resulting in increasingly higher living standards and the abolition of unemployment and depression. (5) It has built the trade unions, in which almost 24,000,000 workers are organized, into the very fabric of its society. (6) The Soviet Union has emancipated woman and the family, and has developed an advanced system of child care. (7) From the viewpoint of cultural freedom, the difference between the Soviet Union and the Fascist countries is most striking. The Soviet Union has effected one of the most far-reaching cultural and educational advances in all history, and among a population which at the start was almost three-fourths illiterate. Those writers and thinkers whose books have been burned by the Nazis are published in the Soviet Union. The best literature from Homer to Thomas Mann, the best thought from Aristotle to Lenin, is available to the masses of the Soviet people, who themselves actively participate in the creation of culture. (8) It has replaced the myths and superstitions of old Russia with the truths and techniques of experimental science, extending scientific procedures to every field, from economics to public health. And it has made science and scientific study available to the mass of the people. (9) The Soviet Union considers political dictatorship a transitional form and has shown a steadily expanding democracy in every sphere. Its epoch-making new Constitution guarantees Soviet citizens universal suffrage, civil liberties, the right to employment, to leisure, to free education, to free medical care, to material security in sickness and old age, to equality of the sexes in all fields of activity, and to equality of all races and nationalities. (10) In relation to Russia's past, the country has been advancing rapidly along the road of material and cultural progress in ways that the American people can understand and appreciate."

In a brief epilogue to the "basic" points, the signatories said: "The Soviet Union has an economic system different from our own. But Soviet aims and achievements make it clear that there exists a sound and permanent basis in mutual ideals for cooperation between the U.S.A. and the USSR on behalf of world peace and the security and freedom of all nations."

Those responsible for the "Open Letter" included academicians Thomas Addis (Stanford University); Newton Arvin (Smith College); Dorothy Brewster, L.C. Dunn, Willystine Goodsell, Walter Rautenstrauch, and Bernhard Stern (Columbia University); Edwin Berry Burgum, Robert Chambers, Henry Pratt Fairchild, Robert Gessner, and Margaret Schlauch (New York University); Robert A. Brady, Haakon Chevalier, Alexander Kaun, and Paul Radin (University of California); Stanley Dodge (University of Michigan); George B. Cressey (Syracuse University); Mildred Fairchild and Herbert Miller (Bryn Mawr College); Samuel N. Harper (University of Chicago); Norman Himes (Colgate University); Max Lerner and Frederick L. Schuman (Williams College); Halford E. Luccock and John P. Peters (Yale University); F.O. Mathiessen and Ernest J. Simmons (Harvard University); Anita Marburg (Sarah Lawrence College); Clifford T. McAvoy (City College of New York); V.J. McGill (Hunter College); Robert McGregor (Reed College); Alan Porter (Vassar College); Vida Scudder (Wellesley); Dirk Struik and C. Fayette Taylor (Massachusetts Institute of Technology); and Harry F. Ward (Union Theological Seminary).

From the writing fraternity, the theater, and the arts there were Marc Blitzstein, Anita Block, Millen Brand, J. Edward Bromberg, Vera Caspary, Kyle Crichton, Paul de Kruif, Muriel Draper, Waldo Frank, Hugo Gellert, Dashiell Hammett, Ernest Hemingway, Granville Hicks, Langston Hughes, Sam Jaffe, Matthew Josephson, George Kauffman,

Alfred Kreymborg, Corliss Lamont, John Howard Lawson, Aline MacMahon, Ruth McKenney, Clifford Odets, S.J. Perelman, Harold J. Rome, George Seldes, Vincent Sheean, Herman Shumlin, Lionel Stander, Donald Ogden Stewart, James Thurber, Louis Untermeyer, Max Weber, Albert Rhys Williams, William Carlos Williams, Ella Winter, and Richard Wright. There were also Louis Birk, editor of Modern Age Books; Robert Morss Lovett of *New Republic*; Maxwell Stewart of *Nation*; Thomas A. Bisson of the Foreign Policy Association; Mary Van Kleeck of the Russell Sage Foundation; and Mortimer Graves of the American Council of Learned Societies.

RAND SCHOOL OF SOCIAL SCIENCE

In the 1890's, British Fabian Socialists were instrumental in the establishment of the American Fabian Socialist Society, which in 1901 merged with other Socialist groups to form the American Socialist Society. In 1906, the American Socialist Society founded the Rand School of Social Science in New York.

The Rand School was made possible through the generosity of Mrs. Elizabeth Rand and her daughter Carrie Rand Herron. Mrs. Rand had for many years been the patroness of George D. Herron, a former Congregationalist minister and, as of 1902, the first chairman of the Socialist Party of America. Mrs. Rand died in 1905 and in her will left a trust fund of $200,000 to "carry on and further the work to which I have devoted the later years of my life." The "work" had been the promotion of Socialism. Mrs. Rand had named Carrie and George Herron trustees of the fund. With a supplemental gift of money from Carrie Herron, Mrs. Rand's legacy was used to establish "an intellectual center for the Socialist movement in the United States" – the Rand School. Members of the original board of directors for the School were certifiable Socialists who declared themselves to be "in full accord with the principles and tactics of the modern Socialist movement in America." They were Algernon Lee, Job Harriman, Benjamin Hanford, William Mailly, Leonard D. Abbott, and Henry Slobodin. The board was assisted by an advisory committee consisting of Charles A. Beard, P.A. Levine, and Herman Schlueter.

From the very beginning, the Rand School maintained very close ties with the newly formed Intercollegiate Socialist Society (later the League for Industrial Democracy). For a few years the ISS and the

Rand School shared office facilities. Two of Rand's early secretaries, Algernon Lee and W.H. Ghent, served as secretaries for the ISS, and Rose Hanna, the assistant secretary of Rand, worked simultaneously for the ISS. (Hanna later worked in Moscow for the Open Road Travel Bureau, which arranged tours to the Soviet Union for American labor contingents.)

The main link between the Rand School and the ISS in the early years was Morris Hillquit, a labor lawyer, a top Socialist Party official, and a founder of ISS. Carrie and George Herron made Hillquit a co-trustee of the Rand School. (The Herrons left the United States to reside in Italy. Their marriage had created a scandal that attracted nationwide attention. Herron had been recently divorced on grounds of desertion of his wife and children. Two months after the divorce, he married Carrie Rand in a bizarre non-religious "companionable" ceremony that was described in the *International Socialist Review* as "A Socialist Wedding.")

With the Herrons out of the way, the Rand School began its long history as a Marxian-Socialist training school for labor agitators. Hillquit, a lawyer for Sidney Hillman's Amalgamated Clothing Workers Union, added the ACWU to the Rand School as a close affiliate. The same sort of relationship has always existed between the Rand School and the International Ladies' Garment Workers Union.

In its early years, the Rand School, which had no ties with any accredited college or university, attracted working men and women, most of them from the garment industry in New York and almost all of them either immigrants or children of immigrants. They became conspicuous in strikes throughout the garment and textile industries and also in the violent strikes instigated by the Industrial Workers of the World, the Wobblies. Students and "alumni" of Rand School conducted Red Sunday School classes for children, and also helped to establish labor "schools" throughout the country.

The formative years at Rand School were marked by a great deal of attention by Socialists from campuses and public life, who served as officers and faculty members of the school. In its early literature the Rand School said: "The educational work of the Socialist Party has been conducted for the most part in a haphazard way. Definite and systematic courses of study have rarely been persisted in, until the Rand School of Social Science of New York City answered the demand for training and formulated an educational program. The school, while not strictly a party institution, is owned and controlled by the American Socialist Society, an incorporated body, which has always followed the policy of taking in only Party members. The detailed administration is in the hands of an Educational Director and Executive Secretary, chosen by and responsible to a Board of Directors, elected annually by the Society . . . .

"The school had a very definite object — that of providing an auxiliary or specialized agency to serve the Socialist and Trade Union Movement of the United States in an educational capacity — to offer to the outside public an opportunity for studying the principles, purposes, and methods of this movement; and to offer to the adherents of the movement instruction and training along lines calculated to make them more efficient workers for the Cause . . . .

"That object it has pursued with ever increasing success. In spite of many handicaps, it has grown year by year. It began as a purely local institution, with a library and reading room and with evening and Sunday classes and lecture courses for residents of New York City who wished to spend in study such time as they could spare from their daily labor. This, which was at first the whole school, now continues as its Local Department."

In other parts of its literature, the Rand School described itself as "an autonomous auxiliary to the working class movement in the United States, as represented by the Socialist Party on the political field, and by the progressive organizations of labor on the field of industry." *The Case of the Rand School*, published in 1919, contains the following statement: "Rand students, when they finish their training, go out to be lecturers, street speakers, teachers and organizers in the labor movement. They become leading spirits among their fellows, for they have supplemented their toil-worn knowledge of present social and industrial evils with an intelligent, constructive idealism that builds a new and better way where the present system fails and collapses."

After a few years of operation, the Rand School opened a book store, which distributed books and pamphlets that were exclusively Socialist and Communist literature. In 1911, the Rand School inaugurated a full-time course of study, which meant a six-month term. (By 1916, the School's administrators estimated that graduates from the full-time course were approximately 50 percent native-born

Americans; the other half were immigrants from Russia, Germany, Finland, Austria-Hungary, Denmark, Ireland, Poland, Wales, Canada, and China.)

In 1913, the Rand School inaugurated correspondence courses, a program endorsed by the national executive committee of the Socialist Party. Party locals throughout the country were urged to form study classes in conjunction with the correspondence courses.

Also in 1913, the Rand School established an East Side Branch in New York City, located in the offices of the *Jewish Daily Forward*. The Branch was an immediate success, and about one thousand students attended its classes in each of the first several years of operation. At the same time, the Rand School supervised study classes at Socialist Party locals in the Greater New York area.

In 1915, a Department of Labor Research was instituted at Rand School. It served as a clearing-house and distribution center for information "useful to the working-class movement, to make it accessible to students, and especially to put it at the service of the Socialist Party, of the Trade Unions, and of Socialist lawmakers and public officials."

In 1917, largely through a financial gift from A.A. Heller, the Rand School moved to new and larger quarters in a building it purchased from the YWCA. (Heller, a millionaire, bankrolled International Publishers, the Communist Party's printing house. He made a great deal of money in Russia, where he did business on a concession from Lenin with his International Oxygen Company.) In the 1920's and 1930's, the Rand School was the beneficiary of many handouts from the Garland Fund, which supported a host of Communist and Socialist enterprises.

By 1924, the Rand School boasted of a library with more than 6,000 bound volumes, a fairly complete file of current periodicals, and a collection of original sources, reports, and pamphlets on the Socialist and labor movement of the United States and foreign countries. Its Labor Research Department was compiling and issuing the annual *American Labor Year Book*. The School had also helped to found the Labor Education Council in conjunction with the Amalgamated Knit Goods Workers, the Fancy Leather Goods Workers, the Furriers' Union, and the United Cloth Hat and Cap Makers. The Council was one more means by which the Rand School exerted its influence upon the radical-led Socialist unions in the various parts of the clothing industry.

During World War I, the Rand School, in keeping with its Socialist character, was a hotbed of pacifism. Almost all members of the Socialist Party were firmly opposed to American preparedness for or intervention in the European conflict. They also opposed conscription; many of the Socialists were conscientious objectors; and it was the policy of the Socialist Party to encourage resistance to conscription.

In the course of the war, the Rand School published and distributed *The Great Madness*, a pamphlet written by a Socialist luminary, Scott Nearing. The federal government brought suit, under sedition statutes, against Nearing and the Rand School. Nearing was acquitted but the School was found guilty and fined $3,000.

After Nearing's acquittal, the New York legislature – in an anti-Bolshevik move – appointed Senator Clayton R. Lusk as head of a committee to investigate radical activities. One of Lusk's first moves was to obtain a search warrant and to lead his investigators, accompanied by State Police, on a raid of the Rand School's premises. After obtaining the School's records and files, Lusk obtained an injunction to close the school.

Samuel Untermeyer, a New York lawyer whose brother Louis taught at Rand School, had the injunction lifted, and the Lusk Committee was forced to return the materials seized in the raid. These actions were soon followed by passage in the New York legislature of the so-called Lusk Laws, by which all private schools in New York would have had to be licensed by the State.

The Rand School, with its allies in the Socialist Party and the large clothing industry unions, was able to exert so much pressure on the New York Governor, Alfred E. Smith, that he made an opportunistic capitulation and vetoed the Lusk Laws.

In 1921, there was an attempt to re-introduce the Lusk Laws, but it failed, and the Rand School continued to function more busily than ever. In that year, in imitation of the British Fabian Socialists, the Rand School opened a summer school at Camp Tamiment in the beautiful Pennsylvania Pocono Mountain area near the Delaware Water Gap.

The importance of the Rand School to Socialists can be judged by the fact that its officers, directors, and faculty included the most notable names in Socialist circles, recruited from major universities and colleges, the literary and legal fields, organized labor leadership, and the political arena. They included Jack L. Afros, Henry Apotheker, Emily

Greene Balch, Charles A. Beard, S.E. Beardsley, Anna Bercovitz, Allen L. Benson, D.P. Berenberg, Anita Block, William E. Bohn, Louis B. Boudin, Robert W. Bruere, Augustus Claessens, Marc Connelly, Morris Cohen, Henry W.L. Dana, John Dewey, Herman Epstein, Nathan Fine, W.J. Ghent, Franklin H. Giddings, Stetson Gilman, Benjamin Glassberg, Alexander Goldenweiser, Benjamin Gruenberg, Morris Hillquit, Marx Lewis, I.A. Hourwich, Rebecca A. Jarvis, Florence Kelley, George R. Kirkpatrick, Algernon Lee, William N. Leiserson, Louis P. Lochner, Ludwig Lore, Bela Low, Duncan MacDonald, Anna A. Maley, James H. Maurer, David S. Muzzey, Scott Nearing, William Noyes, Leland Olds, Chandler Owen, Charlotte Perkins, Juliet Stuart Poyntz, A. Philip Randolph, Edward Allsworth Ross, George Ross, Lucien Sanial, Theodore Schapiro, Joseph Schlossberg, Max Schonberg, Vida Scudder, George Soule, John Spargo, Helen L. Sumner, Frank Tannenbaum, Norman Thomas, Alexander Trachtenberg, Louis Untermeyer, Hendrik Van Loon, Louis Waldman, James P. Warbasse, Gregory Zilboorg, and Charles F. Zueblin.

Among those who taught sessions at Camp Tamiment's summer school were Mary Austin, Otto Beyer, Arthur W. Calhoun, Stuart Chase, Evans Clark, Taraknath Das, Solon De Leon, Robert Ferrari, Jessie W. Hughan, Joseph Jablonower, William Soskin, George Soule, and Norman Thomas.

Those who helped the Rand School through fund-raising efforts included Heywood Broun, Jerome Davis, Paul H. Douglas, Elizabeth Gilman, John Haynes Holmes, Fanny Hurst, Helen Keller, William H. Kilpatrick, Fiorello La Guardia, Margaret I. Lamont, Broadus Mitchell, William P. Montague, Elmer Rice, Gilbert Seldes, Clarence Senior, Upton Sinclair, Michael Strange, and Oswald Garrison Villard.

Although the Socialists in the United States have undergone periods of failure in the political field and have experienced factional disputes, and lost defectors to the right and left of the ideological spectrum, they have maintained and increased their power and influence in the labor movement. In effect, the Rand School (known since 1935 as the Tamiment Institute and Library) has been the center of the nation's most important Socialist complex, which includes not only the Socialist Party but also the League for Industrial Democracy, the clothing industry and other major unions, the *New Leader*, and the Workmen's Circle. The Rand School officers, faculty, and students have been conspicuously present in every major radical front organization, project, and enterprise for more than half a century. They have attained prominence in state and Federal government positions. Many have served in the Congress of the United States. They have reached high positions in academic institutions, in publishing firms, in the communications media, and — of course — in organized labor. Beyond these individual achievements, the Rand School's personnel have maintained a close relationship with British Fabians and other foreign Socialists. Many of Britain's Fabians have visited Rand, including Norman Angell, Margaret Bondfield, Margaret Cole, Bertrand Russell, Toni Sender, and John Strachey.

In the past couple of decades, the Rand School has not seemed to alarm even conservative anti-Socialist Americans. It has been doing business as usual but it is generally ignored as an innocuous and aged — even out-dated — left-of-center nuisance at worst. In some quarters it has even been regarded as a center of anti-Communism.

One of the rare realistic appraisals of the Rand School to appear in recent years was in the Veritas Foundation's *The Great Deceit*, which presented the following view of 1958 "leftists in respectable garb": "In recent years in New York City, there have been meetings held in a dignified looking building at 7 East 15th Street. Groups of well-dressed men and women gather to discuss 'social' problems generally under the broad designation of the 'social sciences.'

"In one session there were people such as Professor Richard B. Morris of Columbia University, Dr. Lewis Lorwin, and Frances Gates, of the Social Sciences Reference Service of the University of California. This meeting was scheduled under the prosaic heading of 'Studying Labor History.' In another meeting, John Kenneth Galbraith was awarded an annual book award in the Waldorf Astoria Hotel. Presiding at the ceremonies was Dr. George N. Shuster, president of Hunter College, and the presentation was made by United States Senator Paul H. Douglas. Subsequently, Galbraith's acceptance speech was published in the February 2, 1958 issue of *The New Leader*, an old socialist publication. At another meeting, Leo Rosten of *Look* Magazine, William Nichols of *This Week* Magazine, and Frank Stanton, the head of the Columbia Broadcasting System, gathered to discuss the harmless-sounding topic of 'Mass Culture and Mass Media.'

"All this was done under the auspices of a harmless sounding organization called The Tamiment Institute and Library. In brochures we learn that 'The Tamiment Institute and Library is a private nonprofit and non-partisan institution sponsored by the People's Educational Camp Society of Tamiment, Pennsylvania.' However, under the heading of 'Advisory Committee' we read the names of Norman Thomas, socialist leader, Reinhold Niebuhr, socialist theologian, Daniel Bell, socialist leader, Sidney Hook, former communist and now in the socialist camp (Fabian), George N. Shuster, president of Hunter College, New York City, with a record of leftist associations, and J. Robert Oppenheimer (who was dropped by the Atomic Energy Commission because of doubts raised, as a security risk).

"The building which now houses the Tamiment Institute is the same that was purchased many years ago for the Rand School of Social Science. The Rand School of Social Science, founded by the American Socialist Society, eventually ran out of endowed funds and reorganized itself under this new name. The Rand School label had already been thoroughly discredited and hence became unsuitable as a cover.

"In the hot weather the meetings moved to a luxurious socialistic camp in the mountains of Pennsylvania where the proceedings are conducted in cooler surroundings of natural splendor. There we find a hall called the Morris Hillquit Memorial Library of the Tamiment Cultural Center, Tamiment, Pennsylvania. The late Morris Hillquit was the head of the Socialist Party in the 1920's and also a participant in the League for Industrial Democracy and the Rand School of Social Science. He had been a militant defender of the Bolshevik Revolution and a vociferous supporter of the Communist International.

"Thus the Tamiment Institute and Library is a new name for the old Rand School of Social Science and it has replaced the latter as an adjunct of L.I.D. It is the American counterpart of the British Fabian Research Bureau. The Fabian organization and its American twin feed organized packages of information to leftists in all walks of life, to undermine our system of free enterprise and individual freedom.

"Rand School teachers and pupils have always served as conspicuous luminaries in socialist and communist movements of all shades. Today, this ghost of the old Rand School of Social Science even engages in the fashionable game of 'anti-communism,' although its 'anti-communism' is of an innocuous type which merely slaps the reds on the wrist. Any serious attempt to check the Kremlin element is met with a chorus of 'danger to freedom of expression' by these same 'Fabian socialists.' "

In 1963, the Tamiment Library of radical literature became a part of the New York University Libraries system. The Tamiment Institute currently describes itself in far less inflammatory language than in earlier years. Now it is "an adult educational institution devoted to the furthering of a better understanding of the political, social, and economic complexities of contemporary society."

"... *We are aware that since 1949, at least, no Communist has had any vestige of membership* [in the Communist Party], *and even the rank and file members are only associated in units of five or six members. For many years, those in key and delicate positions were obliged under Party discipline not to attend branch meetings and no cards were issued to them* .... *We get a key to the tactic whereby some persons who are asked the question* [as to their Communist Party membership] *refuse to answer and some others with a long pro-Communist record answer in the negative. The former group includes those who attended branches and had cards when they were in an obscure position; the latter group has among it those who were in key or delicate positions when they became Communists. These latter people can easily swear that they are not affiliated, since charges of perjury cannot successfully be placed against them. It is the* records *of pro-Communists in education, government, or other agencies which should be primarily considered, therefore, and not whether technically they can be proved to be Communists. If those records reveal a consistent aid to Soviet Russia, its fifth column here, and its fronts, then these individuals are enemies of the United States and should be recognized as such.*"

Louis Budenz
The Techniques of Communism

Biographical Dictionary Of The Left

LOUIS ADAMIC was born on March 23, 1899 in Blato, Slovenia, son of Ana and Anton Adamic. He came to the United States in 1913 and was naturalized as an American citizen in 1918. He married Stella Sanders. From 1910 until 1913, he attended the Gymnasium of Ljubljana. He attended, for a brief time, the University of California. He was the author of *Dynamite* (1931; revised in 1934 and 1947); *Laughing in the Jungle* (1932); *The Native's Return* (1934); *Grandsons* (1935); *Cradle of Life* (1936); *The House in Antigua* (1937); *My America* (1938); *From Many Lands* (1940); *Two-Way Passage* (1941); *What's Your Name* (1942); *My Native Land* (1943); *A Nation of Nations* (1945); *Dinner at the White House* (1946); and *The Eagle and the Roots* (1952, posthumously). In 1940 and 1941, he was editor of *Common Ground*. From 1945 until 1948, he was publisher and editor of *Trends and Tides* (a Communist-line magazine). From 1943 until 1951, he was general editor of *The Peoples of America* series. In 1932 and 1933, he held a Guggenheim fellowship. He was awarded grants-in-aid by the Rockefeller Foundation (1937) and the Carnegie Foundation (1939, 1940, and 1941).

Adamic's first job in the United States was as a newspaper loader for a Slovenian language newspaper in New York City. During World War I, he served in the United States Army. Later, he worked as a longshoreman in California and as a textile worker in Paterson, New Jersey. In the 1920's, he translated Slovenian, Croation, and Serbian stories into English. Most of them were pub-lished in *Living Age*. His translation of Ivan Cankar's *Yerney's Justice*, a Slovenian language novel, was published in book form in 1926. In 1928, Henry L. Mencken published Adamic's first story in *American Mercury*.

Adamic's first two published books (*Dynamite* and *Laughing in the Jungle*) were bitterly critical of the United States but they did establish him as a writer. In 1932, he was awarded a Guggenheim fellowship on the strength of an outline of a novel he submitted with the proposal that he write it during a visit to his native Slovenia. The novel was not written, but instead he wrote *The Native's Return*, an autobiographical account of his return to Yugoslavia and his disillusionment. (*Laughing in the Jungle, Dinner at the White House*, and *The Eagle and the Roots* were also autobiographical.) Adamic's literary reputation was greatly enhanced when his *The Native's Return* was made a Book-of-the-Month Club selection. He began to have books published at a rate of almost one a year and he produced magazine articles that were published in the large-circulation magazines in America.

Adamic's prolific literary output brought him recognition as one of the foremost experts in America on Yugoslav and Balkan affairs. He was undoubtedly the most influential writer to emerge from Yugoslavia, but one of his former compatriots, Bogdan Raditsa, offered a critical appraisal of his credentials as an expert: "He [Adamic] continued to hate those in his native land who were influential, the Catholic Church and the intelligentsia, neither of which has at any time found him to be an important writer. In America people thought more of him. Here, the fact that he lacked a solid European education, that he never even attended high school, that he possessed an extremely superficial knowledge of European culture, literature, and history, was unimportant. I talked with him often in the Slovenian tongue; his knowledge of it was primitive, surprisingly poor. His knowledge of Yugoslav history was scanty and inaccurate. When he wrote on the subject, he often evinced ignorance of basic facts. His prose was alive and often brilliant, but those of his books dealing with Yugoslavia were never translated into Yugoslav — a fact unknown to almost all Americans — because no one would take them seriously. They were mostly the products of hasty journalism, readable and apparently informative. His knowledge and understanding of Europe, old and new, was confused, limited, and biased. He had an instinctive taste for the worst elements of the Marxist analysis of European developments. Complexities, nuances, subtleties eluded his understanding. He was a typical example of that South Eastern European half-intelligentsia whose only answer to the problems of the modern world was Communism or Fascism. His books on Yugoslavia . . . were enjoyable, but they were rife with inanities, inaccuracies, and distorted 'socialist' judgments." ("My Memories of Louis Adamic," *American Mercury*, December 1951.)

In his first published book, *Dynamite*, Adamic made no secret of the facts that he was far from being Americanized and that he was an ideological leftist. Said he of his work: "The story that I present here is, as I see it, a criticism of your American capitalist-democratic civilization, the most severe criticism, it seems to me, that anyone could write . . . America is at the crossroads . . . Right or Left? . . . But eventually it will be left, for in its very nature . . . it is a left or revolutionary country." When he visited his homeland in 1932 and 1933, he was in close contact with Yugoslav Communists. In his *The Native's Return*, in the Communist publication *New Masses* of September 1933, and in his pamphlet *Struggle*, he wrote reports on underground activities of Yugoslav Communists. His pro-Communist sympathies were starkly evident in *The Native's Return*, in which he wrote: "I see now that the salvation of the Yugoslav people and other small backward nations in that part of the world lies, clearly and inescapably, in the direction of Russia. They will have to overthrow their present racketeer rulers, form a Balkan or East European federation of collective national republics and in some mutually satisfactory way attach themselves to the U.S.S.R. . . . Now I see why the Russian Revolution was necessary, from the standpoint not only of backward, peasant Russia, but of the world at large." In the Communists' *Daily Worker* of September 22, 1934, he wrote: "The ideas, principles, and methods which are the basis of the Soviet Union doubtless are the highest promise and hope that humanity has today." In the same issue of the *Worker*, he wrote: "And, of course, there is the New Deal in the United States, with its imperialism, that will bring on a new world war, which I expect will end in a world revolution, in the sovietization of all the countries."

In the 1930's and 1940's, Adamic became deeply involved in Communist and other leftist activities in the United States.

Adamic's affiliations included the

ultra-radical American Civil Liberties Union; American Committee for Protection of Foreign Born ("founded by the Communist Party in order to exploit racial divisions in the United States for its own revolutionary purposes"); the American Council for a Democratic Greece ("subversive and Communist"); the American Committee for Spanish Freedom ("Communist"); the American Friends of Spanish Democracy ("Communist front"); the American Labor Party ("Communist dissimulation extends into the field of political parties forming political front organizations such as the . . . American Labor Party"); the American League Against War and Fascism ("subversive and Communist" – "established in the United States in an effort to create public sentiment on behalf of a foreign policy adapted to the interests of the Soviet Union"); the American Round Table on India ("Communist front"); the American-Russian Institute ("subversive" – "Communist" – "specializing in pro-Soviet propaganda"); the American Writers Congress ("subversive"); American Youth for Democracy ("subversive and Communist" – "part of Soviet psychological warfare against the United States"); the Association of Young Writers and Artists ("Communist front"); the Celebration of the 25th Anniversary of the Red Army (Communist enterprise); the Civil Rights Congress ("created and established by the Communist Party as an organization which would utilize defense of civil rights for Party purposes and raise and maintain mass defense and bail funds for Party use"); the Committee for a Democratic Far Eastern Policy ("Communist"); the Conference on Pan-American Democracy ("Communist front"); the Coordinating Committee To Lift the [Spanish] Embargo ("one of the numer-

ous Communist-front enterprises which were organized around the Communists' agitation over the Spanish Civil War"); the Council for Democracy (ultra leftist); the Council for the Advancement of the Americas (ultra-leftist); *Daily People's World* ("official Communist Party organ"); *Daily Worker* ("official Communist Party organ"); a Dinner in Honor of Ferdinand Smith, a Communist official; *Fight* ("official organ of the American League Against War and Fascism, subversive and Communist"); Film Audiences for Democracy ("Communist front"); Films for Democracy ("Communist front"); the Foreign Policy Association (a highly influential and highly effective pro-Communist vehicle); the Independent Citizens Committee of the Arts, Sciences, and Professions ("Communist front"); the Japanese-American Committee for Democracy ("Communist-controlled organization"); the Joint Anti-Fascist Refugee Committee ("subversive and Communist"); the League of American Writers ("subversive and Communist" – began openly to follow the Communist Party line as dictated by the foreign policy of the Soviet Union"); *Masses and Mainstream* ("Communist magazine"); the National Citizens Political Action Committee ("Communist front"); the National Committee for Defense of Political Prisoners ("subversive and Communist"); the National Committee for People's Rights ("Communist front"); the National Committee to Combat Anti-Semitism ("Communist front"); the National Conference on American Policy in China and the Far East ("Communist"); the National Conference on American Policy in Greece ("Communist front"); the National Council of American-Soviet Friendship ("subversive and Communist" – "specializing in pro-Soviet propaganda"); the

National Council of the Arts, Sciences, and Professions ("Communist front used to appeal to special occupational groups"); the National Emergency Conference ("Communist front"); the National Emergency Conference for Democratic Rights ("Communist front" – "subversive"); the National Federation for Constitutional Liberties ("under Communist Party domination and headed by responsible Party functionaries" – "one of the viciously subversive organizations of the Communist Party"); the *National Guardian* ("virtual official propaganda arm of Soviet Russia"); National Youth for [Henry A.] Wallace Committee ("Communist-controlled"); *New Masses* ("weekly journal of the Communist Party"); the Non-Partisan Committee for the Re-election of Congressman Vito Marcantonio ("Communist front"); Progressive Citizens of America ("political Communist front" – "subversive"); the Reichstag Fire Trial and Anniversary Committee ("Communist front . . . formed . . . by prominent Communists and Communist sympathizers"); the Scientific and Cultural Conference for World Peace ("a propaganda front for Soviet foreign policy and Soviet culture"); the Southern Negro Youth Congress ("subversive and among the affiliates and committees of the Communist Party, USA, which seeks to alter the form of government of the United States by unconstitutional means"); and *Soviet Russia Today* ("the leading propaganda journal for the Soviet Union in the United States").

Adamic's major contributions to the Communist cause were made through his affiliations with a galaxy of Yugoslavia-oriented organizations and through his pro-Stalinist and pro-Soviet Union pleadings in his writings and public speeches. During World War II, he was one of the most active and influential Communist propagandists on the American scene. When the Germans invaded Yugoslavia, the large American reading audience he had acquired over the years relied upon him for information and guidance in the Yugoslav war situation. In the beginnings of the Yugoslav-German confrontation, he urged all-out support for the forces of the anti-Communist General Mikhailovich. However, when international Communists decided that Josip Broz Tito and his Communist partisan forces had the potential to fight the Germans equally as well as Mikhailovich, Adamic abruptly turned against Mikhailovich and became Tito's leading mouthpiece.

The extent of Adamic's influence on behalf of Tito was probably best demonstrated through the occasion of what became for him a famous White House dinner. The dinner invitation came to Adamic because of Eleanor Roosevelt's admiration for his *Two-Way Passage*, published in 1941. On January 13, 1942, Adamic and his wife were dinner guests of President and Mrs. Roosevelt. To Adamic's surprise, British Prime Minister Winston Churchill was also at the dinner. Adamic urged Roosevelt and Churchill to send help to Mikhailovich as soon as possible. In this Adamic was following the contemporary Communist line on Mikhailovich.

Adamic's meeting with the Roosevelts and Churchill became the subject of his 1946 book, *Dinner at the White House*. In the book, however, Adamic's earlier pro-Mikhailovich stance was not mentioned because, in the meantime, the Communists had followed the directives of the Soviet Union's Premier Stalin and decided that Tito – not Mikhailovich – was to be supported as Yugoslavia's leader. Stalin influenced Churchill and

Roosevelt to sponsor Tito. Adamic faithfully followed the Communist switch and in *Dinner at the White House* he wrote: "The Mikhailovich legend was a hoax perpetrated by the Yugoslav government-in-exile." (The book had at least one interesting sequel. Because of the content of a footnote, Churchill successfully sued Adamic for libel, winning a $20,000 judgment.)

Adamic continued his relationship with President Roosevelt and he continued to exert influence on American policy vis-à-vis Yugoslavia and the Balkans in general. For example, in reply to a letter from Adamic to Roosevelt, the President wrote, on March 3, 1942: "Your letter of February 3 has been very useful in the studies and discussions which are in progress concerning eventual methods of military operations in enemy-occupied countries.

"While the projects which might be worked out would by their nature be unsuitable for discussion in correspondence, I can assure you that the Government departments and agencies interested in work of this kind are giving serious examination to many factors such as those you mention. They are obliged of course to coordinate their discussions, since questions regarding foreign enlistments, finance, selective service classifications, etc., all enter into the matter, as well as considerations of general war strategy.

"The information and suggestions contained in your interesting letter, concerning Yugoslavia and Greece in particular, will be most helpful in this work."

The type of advice Adamic offered Roosevelt can be judged by a passage from his 1943 book, *My Native Land*: "I see now that the salvation of the Yugoslav people and other small backward nations in that part of the world lies, clearly and inescapably, in the direction of Russia. They will have to overthrow their present racketeer rulers, form a Balkan or East European federation of collectivist national republics, and in some mutually satisfactory way, attach themselves to the U.S.S.R. Now I see why the Russian Revolution was necessary, from the standpoint not only of backward, peasant Russia, but of the world at large."

Bogdan Raditsa, who worked closely with Adamic from 1940 until 1944 on behalf of Yugoslavia, described Adamic's status on the American scene: "By the end of 1942 Adamic was the leading force in the organization of the United Committee of South Slav Americans, a front organization — in which the Communist Party, as we discovered later, was in real control. At that time he repeated again and again that Yugoslavia had to become part of the Soviet Union. 'They want to go the Russian way and Russiaward.'

"The American Communists of Yugoslav descent distributed Adamic's books everywhere as their most effective propaganda. His books were sold to immigrants who did not even know how to read them. He addressed meetings at which few understood the language in which he talked. But the fanatic Communists translated Adamic's thinking into such simply-understood slogans as this: 'You are going, you Slavs, to lead the world! Not only in Europe, but even here in this country — thanks to Russia. The American Slavs will become the leading group, the new uppercrust.' At the time Adamic wrote: 'I believe that the Congress [of American Slovenians] should be deeply impressed by the fact that Soviet Russia is the only great power so far which has officially and unequivocally expressed itself in favor of a united Slovenia . . . .' "

For his base of operations, Adamic used the American Committee for Free Yugoslavia ("in line with the policy of the Communist Party and the American Slav Congress, this organization has been active in support of the Communist Yugoslav leader, Marshal Tito, and in condemnation of his rival, Mikhailovich"); the American Association for Reconstruction in Yugoslavia ("headed by a Communist"); the American Committee for Yugoslav Relief ("subversive and Communist"); his own Communist-line publication, *Trends and Tides*; the United Committee of South Slavic Americans ("subversive and Communist" – "Communist-controlled"); and the American Slav Congress ("Moscow-inspired and directed federation of Communist-dominated organizations seeking by methods of propaganda and pressure to subvert the 10,000,000 people of Slavic birth or descent").

In 1949, the House Committee on Un-American Activities, in its "Report on the American Slav Congress and Associated Organizations," reviewed some of Adamic's activities: "Operating through other Slavic-front organizations and not directly as an official of the American Slav Congress, Louis Adamic, as a speaker, sponsor, and writer, has been a tower of strength for that organization. His articles have been featured in the *Slavic American* and he was a leading speaker at meetings of the American Slav Congress on September 20 to 22, 1946, and October 12, 1947, both in New York City. As honorary president of the Slovenian American National Council, honorary president of the American Committee for Free Yugoslavia, honorary president of the United Committee of (South) Slavic Americans and editor of its publications, co-chairman of the American Committee for Yugoslav Relief and honorary president of the American Association for Reconstruction in Yugoslavia, Inc., he has been in a position to exploit powerful social contacts in their behalf. These organizations constitute a supporting and affiliated bloc with the American Slav Congress.

"The extent of Mr. Adamic's influence in Yugoslavia can be measured by the fact that he was welcomed at the Zemun Airport at Belgrade on January 14, 1949, by Boris Kidritch, member of the Yugoslav Politburo and chairman of the State Planning Commission, Dr. Ales Bebler, Assistant Foreign Minister of Yugoslavia, Vladimir Dedijer, director of the Federal Information Department, Ivo Andric, chairman of the Yugoslav Writers' Union, and Dusan Timotijevic, chairman of the Council of Journalists of Yugoslavia. It is thought that his mission may have had for its purpose a reconciliation between Belgrade and Moscow and the healing of the rift with Marshal Tito. The Yugoslav Home Service, in its broadcast of January 17, 1949, paid the following tribute to Adamic's contribution to its present Communist regime: 'Adamic wrote letters to President Roosevelt, Churchill, and to the Soviet Ambassador in Washington. Besides Adamic procured the necessary financial means for publishing a paper of Yugoslav newspapermen in London. Articles written by Adamic on our partisans and leaders of the national liberation movement have been greatly echoed in our own and in the foreign press. For all these reasons, Louis Adamic is a very welcome guest for our peoples.'

"Writing in the *New York Star* of July 11, 1948, 6 months before this visit, he said: 'Never, before or since the rift, have the Yugoslavs made a statement or published so much as a suggestion that they entertain the faintest aspiration to be independent of the U.S.S.R.... Never, before or since the rift, have the Yugoslavs hinted with a single word that they do not, or some day might not, wish to remain in the Soviet orbit.... The rift has brought on no perceptible drop in the Yugoslavs' open resentment of the United States, more precisely of "Wall Street," as the base of world reaction which is spearheading imperialism and the drive toward World War III.'

"*Adamic and the Slovene National Congress*: The Slovene National Congress is affiliated with the American Slav Congress. It held its first sessions in Cleveland on December 5-7, 1942, at Slovene National Home, 6417 St. Clair Avenue NE. It was officially claimed that 550 delegates representing 250,000 Slovenes of birth and descent attended the meeting. The chief ideological spokesman of this meeting was Louis Adamic, who was chairman of Referat No. 1 on 'The War and the American Slovenes.' Mr. Adamic's overweening sympathy for the Soviet Union and what it stands for, is clearly expressed in his statement of acceptance of this post, published in *The Worker* of December 6, 1942, page 8, from which we quote in part: 'I feel honored to have been selected for this function.... There seems to be no doubt that the Osvobodilina Fronte Partisan troops have engaged the Axis in imporant battles.... Nor is there any doubt that the commanders of some of the Partisan troops are Communist or men who are sympathetic to Communism or to Russia or both, while the majority of the rank-and-file is not Communist, but strongly pro-Russian. It is more than probable also that in Slovenia and in the

rest of Yugoslavia there are Soviet commissars or Soviet army officers who are the advisers if not the supreme commanders of the Partisan troops.... There is no doubt that Russia as a government or state is deeply interested in Yugoslavia as a whole and perhaps particularly in Slovenia – both in an immediate military sense and from the long-range view which may take in the post-war period.... I believe that the Congress should be deeply impressed by the fact that Soviet Russia is the only great power so far which has officially and unequivocally expressed itself in favor of a united Slovenia.... It may be important to have in mind that to all appearances, General Mihailovich is no factor in the Slovenian military, ideological or general political situation.'

"It should be noted that Mr. Adamic's attacks on General Mihailovich, representing the Yugoslav Government-in-exile, correspond in their timing and character to similar attacks by the Soviet Government and the Communist press throughout the world after July 1942. It is essential to go more deeply into Adamic's viewpoint and record because he is the spokesman of various Communist-front organizations operating among the Slavic population in America. He has been accused of having the ambition to become America's 'High Comissioner in the Balkans.' Hence the following pro-Soviet, pro-Communist views of Louis Adamic are of more than passing significance: 'I believe that a majority of people forming the Yugoslav Liberation Front and the Bulgarian underground are eager or ready for Sovietization.... If Sovietization – with all it implies – does occur, it may be the simplest process. The Yugoslav federation would become a republic within the Soviet Union, and would most likely be headed by Tito or

Dimitroff.' (The *Bulletin*, Vol. 1, No. 3, October 20, 1943, pp. 1,2, official organ of the United Committee of Slavic Americans, Louis Adamic, editor, quoted from *My Native Land*, by the same author.)

"As against the 'Western imperialist powers,' Mr. Adamic editorially refers to the Russian Revolution as 'the most massive event so far in the twentieth century' and adds that 'in some ways we are farther from democracy than Russia was even before 1941.'

"Mr. Adamic even goes so far as to suggest that Anglo-American officers might meet with death if they do not carry out preconceived ideas as to the settlement of the Balkan problem. We quote Mr. Adamic from his October 20, 1943, *Bulletin*, excerpts from *My Native Land*: 'If the Anglo-American forces come into the country with the wrong approach and protect the Darlan so no one will be able to get at him, someone will be apt to kill the highest British or American officer he can get at.'

"Mr. Adamic sponsored the publication of a pamphlet called *The Truth About Yugoslavia*, published by Mirko Markovich, past editor of the Communist paper *Slobodna Rech*, printed in Serbian. The pamphlet was printed under union label 209 of the Prompt Press, publishers for the Communist Party.

"*Adamic and the United Committee of South Slavic Americans*: At best, the Balkan situation presents a most confused picture to Americans. The multiplication of committees under Communist domination intensified that confusion and tended to encourage Americans to keep clear of the mess, to the evident advantage of the Soviet Union.

"In a special article appearing in the *Worker* of September 5, 1943, Louis Adamic explained to Louis F. Budenz, then editor of this Communist paper, the aims of the United Conference of South-Slavic Americans, formed at Cleveland in August 1943 and previously known as the United Yugoslav Committee. This conference sought to unite Serbians, Croatians, Slovenians, and Bulgarians into one organization . . . .

"Mr. Adamic pointed out that his organization opposed the attitude of 'many of our high officials in Washington.' He particularly deplored the attitude of the mayor of a large city whose population is about 70 percent new-immigrant (Mayor Frank J. Lausche, of Cleveland), who refused to cooperate with the United Committee of South-Slavic Americans on the ground that his city was already the scene of 'serious differences within the immigrant groups as to the adjustments necessary in Europe after the war.' The mayor felt that the committee might make that situation more acute. Adamic mentioned his committee's opposition to the aims of the Yugoslav Government-in-exile and to General Mihailovich. He estimated that his group represented 'over a million people.'

"At Cleveland, a 10-point program was adopted, pledging support to the partisan army of Yugoslavia under Tito and urging the United Nations to cooperate with the so-called National Anti-Fascist Liberation Council in Yugoslavia, allied with Tito.

"Mr. Adamic has pointed out in his bulletin of September 7, 1943, that the August 7, 1943, meeting was a culmination of a number of prior preliminary group meetings. During the autumn and winter of 1942-43, Serbian, Slovenian, and Croatian groups held their respective congresses and formed the Serbian Vidovdan Council, the Slovenian American Council, and the Council of Americans of Croatian Descent. On June 19, 1943, the leaders of these groups met in Pittsburgh and formed the United Committee of Croatian, Serbian, and Slovenian Americans. The Bulgarians and Macedonians met in Detroit on July 17-18. They were invited to send representatives to the meeting of the United Committee of Croatian, Serbian, and Slovenian Americans called for August 7, in Cleveland. These representatives accepted the suggestion and the name of the organization was changed to the United Committee of South Slavic Americans. Mr. Adamic, as president, was authorized to explore the possibilities of establishing contact with Greek, Albanian, and other Balkan American organizations, groups and individuals. It should be noted at this point that this procedure parallels the practice now in force in Europe of establishing Communist-dominated and inspired national liberation committees among the nations mentioned above.

"Another meeting of the United Committee of South Slavic Americans was held at the Fort Pitt Hotel in Pittsburgh on November 13, 1943. The organization published a bulletin under the personal editorship of Louis Adamic, issues of which have been devoted largely to reprints from his pro-Soviet book, *My Native Land.*

"The United Committee has received unstinting support from Mirko Markovich, Moscow-trained past editor of the Communist *Slobodna Rech* (Free Expression) of Pittsburgh. This paper featured a speech of Earl Browder in its issue of December 5, 1939, page 6. In its December 26, 1939, issue, it acclaimed the Communist slogan 'The Yanks are not coming' and displayed the Soviet star above the American flag in place of the eagle on its front page.

"The Fort Pitt meeting featured in the *Daily Worker* of November 19, 1943, demanded lend-lease aid to the Communist-supported Yugoslav People's Army headed by Tito and deplored American aid to Mikhailovich. It urged a reversal of our support of the Yugoslav Government-in-exile.

"Mr. Adamic later addressed a rally of the Cleveland Slovenian-American National Council praising the 'partisan tradition,' denying that it was a Russian invention.

"The extent to which pro-Communist groups operating in the orbit of the American Slav Congress were given official recognition is indicated by a short-wave broadcast to Yugoslavia on September 28, 1943, with the approval of the Office of War Information and participated in by the Croatian American Council, the Serbian American Vidovdan Congress, the Slovenian American National Council, and the Bulgarian Macedonian Victory Congress, all combined in the United Committee of South Slavic Americans . . . .

"*Adamic and the Communist Party, U.S.A.:* On August 2, 1948, Louis F. Budenz, former managing editor of the (Communist) *Daily Worker*, testified before a Senate investigating committee regarding his relations as a Communist Party official with Louis Adamic. Denying that Adamic was actually a member of the party, Mr. Budenz said that Communist officials had succeeded in 'poisoning the mind' of Adamic to the point of carrying out some Communist objectives. Budenz had been assigned by the party to the job of corrupting Adamic. To further this purpose, he introduced Adamic to Avrum Landy, who was in charge of directing the party's work among foreign-language groups. In denying Budenz' charges, Mr. Adamic admitted that 'Budenz was one of my numerous sources of information' in writing his book *My Native Land*. In the *Daily Worker* of November 3, 1943, and also of January 9, 1944, we find highly laudatory reviews of this book by Budenz. The reviewer declared that 'Louis Adamic . . . granted the palm to the *Daily Worker* for its dispatches on the actualities in the South Slav country.'

"In his pamphlet *Teheran, Our Path in War and Peace*, Earl Browder, then general secretary of the Communist Party, U.S.A., declares, 'Only Louis Adamic's sensational book *My Native Land*, issued toward the end of 1943, with its devastating and unanswerable record of facts, finally broke the newspaper blockage on the truth about Yugoslavia.' According to the testimony of Budenz before the Committee on Un-American Activities on November 22, 1946, the manuscript of this work was shown to Browder before its publication. The work was subsequently selected as the monthly choice of the Book Find Club, a Communist front.

"As early as September 22, 1943, an article by Louis Adamic appeared in the *Daily Worker*, concerning the influence of the Russian revolution. In 1943, he signed a statement which appeared in the *New York Times* on December 22, eulogizing George Dimitrov, former general secretary of the Communist International. On January 4 of the next year, the *Daily Worker* carried an article by Adamic, lauding the same individual. The *New York World-Telegram* of September 21, 1944, described a dinner in honor of Ferdinand Smith, a Communist now the subject of deportation proceedings. Adamic was a sponsor of this affair.

On April 7, 1948, the *Daily Worker* carried the name of Louis Adamic as a signer of a protest against the arrest of Pablo Neruda, a Chilean Communist poet.

"*Adamic and American foreign policy*: With the exception of the period when Russia was our ally during World War II, the Communists and their front organizations have been consistently hostile to American foreign policy.

"Adamic has signed statements attacking American foreign policy in Germany (*Daily Worker*, January 28, April 15, 1948), Yugoslavia (*Bulletin* of the United Committee of South Slavic Americans, April 1946), and Panama (on March 16, 1949). The standard Communist work attacking 'American imperialism' is *Bases and Empire*, by George Marion, a member of the *Daily Worker* staff. This book has been publicly approved by Louis Adamic.

"The leading spokesman of the movement organized by the Communists against the foreign policy of the United States is, of course, Henry A. Wallace, presidential candidate supported by the Progressive Party and the Communist Party, U.S.A. Adamic was a member of the platform committee of the Progressive Party at its Philadelphia convention in July 1948. He contributed financially toward the campaign and actively wrote and spoke in its support. As part of his contribution toward the Wallace campaign, Adamic changed the name of his publication from *Trends and Tides* to *Resist*. In his first 'resistance number' for January-March 1948, he explains its purpose in language which counsels resistance to the policies of our Government: 'It spearheads a movement which must get under way in the U.S. during 1948 . . . a movement which must begin to *resist* by every moral, legal, and political means the artificially created hysteria now whirling toward World War III . . . *resist* the lie now astride the White House, the State Department, the press and radio . . . *resist* the enormous distortion of facts and ideas involved in our relations with Russia, Yugoslavia, etc. . . . *resist* the un-American, fascist developments evident all over the U.S. . . . *resist* the militarization of America.'

"Mr. Adamic's reactions to the Freedom Train express his hostility toward the exhibit and that for which it stands. In the same issue of *Resist*, he asks pointedly whether the purpose of the exhibit was 'to implant in the people's subconscious minds a concern for the paper and the cloth in the showcases and thus replace any passion for the meaning in such documents as the Declaration of Independence, the Constitution, the Bill of Rights?' How many Government employees, he asks, 'were doing anything to resist the present attacks on civil rights in Washington and almost throughout the country?' And again, he inquires, 'How many had felt an impulse to resist the so-called loyalty tests . . .?'

"When American fliers were shot down over Yugoslavia, Adamic charged that the United States was out to 'provoke the Yugoslavs to unwise action.'

"As a manifestation of his pro-Soviet sympathies, Mr. Adamic has been a supporter of a number of organizations and activities devoted to promoting the cause of the Soviet Union. From 1943 to 1946, he has been a sponsor of the National Council of American-Soviet Friendship, cited as subversive by Attorney General Tom C. Clark on December 4, 1947, and September 21, 1948. In May 1948, he signed its statement in support of Henry A. Wallace's open letter to Joseph Stalin. The magazine *Soviet Russia Today* for July 1948 carried a laudatory article by Adamic. In 1943, he sponsored a dinner celebration in honor of the twenty-fifth anniversary of the Red Army, under the auspices of *Soviet Russia Today*.

"Mr. Adamic's antagonistic views of the United States, his hopes for a Communist revolution, and his completely pro-Russian bias are summarized in his article entitled 'Conspiracy Against Peace,' appearing in the *Slavic American* for the winter of 1947, and from which we quote: 'I believe that we Americans are . . . dangerous . . . to ourselves and the rest of the world. We are in a dangerous state of mind intricately involved in the vast distortion of Soviet-American relations. That distortion is mostly the work of our American lords, our conscious and unconscious counter-revolutionaries, who control the press and radio, who boss much of our educational system and, less firmly, many of our churches; who are afraid of today's widespread revolutionary developments . . . . And their immediate purpose, already dangerously realized, is to get control of our national soul in order to have us where they want us when the next depression comes about, and in order to have a chance to kill off the Revolution . . . .

" 'They (the counterrevolutionaries) and the Baruchs fiddle, and fellows like Truman, Byrnes, Vandenberg, Dewey, and Pegler dance . . . . We have, at best, very little time to frustrate this conspiracy disguised as patriotism . . . . Many of these peoples (the now backward peoples of the world) right now have no other inspiration than communism and the Russian . . . . It so happens that it was our press . . . [that] began the present propaganda war between the U.S. and the U.S.S.R. . . . What is more, it is we who began the present "cold war." . . . The world is going left. I believe we should go along . . . .'."

Adamic's dual affection for Stalin's Soviet Union and Tito's Yugoslavia was severely strained over the so-called rift when Tito allegedly declared his independence from Soviet control. Until that time, Adamic had considered Yugoslavia to be leading the fight on behalf of world Communism against the western nations. He was most reluctant to turn against the Soviet Union. He even hoped that he personally could serve as a mediator between Tito and Stalin, but in the last analysis, his sympathies rested with Tito. Writing in the *New York Star* of July 11, 1948, he explained that Tito had turned against the Soviet Union over "a question of manners." He certainly did not think that there had been an irrevocable break. He said that "in a Two-World situation, there is no doubt what side Yugoslavia is now on or what side she will remain on . . . . Essentially, the crisis between the Cominform and the Yugoslavs is not political, but one in human relations . . . . Both sides are more or less at fault . . . [and] from the angle of the Soviet orbit, it may be all to the good in the long run."

From January until August 1949, Adamic visited in Yugoslavia, where his commitment to Tito was sealed. Much of Adamic's posthumous *The Eagle and the Roots* is a laudatory biography of Tito.

On September 4, 1951, Adamic died under mysterious circumstances at his New Jersey home. A bullet had penetrated his brain and a .22 calibre rifle was found lying across his knees. He was found in his second-floor bedroom-study. The lower floor of his house and his garage across the road had been set afire with rags soaked in fuel oil. Many observers acquainted with Adamic's background suspected that he had been slain by American Communists who were unhappy over Adamic's persistent pro-Titoism. He had been the object of threats for about two years. He had suffered at least one brutal beating earlier in 1951. However, New Jersey police authorities accepted his widow's explanation that he was a suicide, induced by overwork and anxiety over world conditions. His old acquaintance Bogdan Raditsa held a contrary view: "People who knew Adamic well – and I was one of them – have reacted with almost unanimous skepticism to the suggestion that he killed himself. If there is such a thing as the 'non-suicide' type, Adamic belonged to it. He was ambitious, money-loving, fame-obsessed. He was selfish and egotistic; he had worked out an informal, everyday technique for using people to promote his books and ideas that was most impressive. Moreover, he had plans – and plans always mean the future.

"He was writing a book. It was a large, detailed book, the book of a man who again has a Cause. It was ready to be published by a well-known house, and seemed certain to hit the bestseller lists. It would increase his fame, it would make him money, it would advance his Cause. It is most unlikely that such a man would kill himself at such a time – not before the reviews, so to speak. So those who knew Adamic well will continue to doubt that he took his life."

COMFORT A. ADAMS was born on November 1, 1868 in Cleveland, Ohio, son of Katherine Peticolas and Comfort Adams. He married Elizabeth Parsons. He was an alumnus of Case School of Applied Science (B.S., 1890). From 1891 until 1893, he studied mathematics and physics at Harvard University. In 1891, Adams began a lifelong association with Harvard University. He was on the faculty as an instructor of electrical engineering (1891-1895); assistant professor (1896-1905); and professor (1906-1916). From 1914 until 1936, he was the Lawrence Professor of Engineering. In 1919, he was the dean of the Harvard Engineering School. In 1935 and 1936, he was the Gordon McKay Professor of Electrical Engineering, and after 1936, he was professor emeritus. From 1919 until 1921, he was chairman of the division of engineering for the National Research Council. He was a consulting engineer for the American Tool and Machine Company (1905-1930); the Okonite Company (1915-1958); Okonite Callender Cable Company (1925-1958); Babcock and Wilcox Company (1926-1958); General Electric (1927-1932); and the Budd Company (1934-1947).

Adams was affiliated with the American Committee for Democracy and Intellectual Freedom ("a Communist-front organization operating among college teachers and professors" – "subversive and un-American"); the American Committee for Protection of Foreign Born ("founded by the Communist Party in order to exploit racial divisions in the United States for its own revolutionary purposes"); the American Committee to Save Refugees ("subversive and Communist" – "perform[ing] a most valuable function for the international Communist movement"); the Citizens Committee To Free Earl Browder ("a strictly Communist Party Affair"); the Committee of One Thousand ("Communist created and controlled"); the Council for Pan-American Democracy ("subversive and Communist"); the Greater New York Emergency Conference on Inalien-able Rights ("Communist front"); the Joint Anti-Fascist Refugee Committee ("subversive and Communist"); the National Emergency Conference ("Communist front"); the National Emergency Conference for Democratic Rights ("Communist front" – "subversive"); the National Federation for Constitutional Liberties ("under Communist Party domination and headed by responsible Party functionaries" – "one of the viciously subversive organizations of the Communist Party"); and Open Letter in Defense of Harry Bridges ("Communist front"). He died in February 1958.

JANE ADDAMS was born on September 6, 1860 in Cedarville, Illinois, daughter of Sarah Weber and John Addams. She was an alumna of Rockford College (A.B., 1882). She attended Woman's Medical College of Pennsylvania for less than a year. She was the author of *Democracy and Social Ethics* (1902); *Newer Ideals of Peace* (1907); *The Spirit of Youth and the City Streets* (1909); *Twenty Years at Hull House* (1910); *A New Conscience and an Ancient Evil* (1912); *The Long Road of Woman's Memory* (1916); *Peace and Bread in Time of War* (1922); *The Second Twenty Years at Hull House* (1930); *The Excellent Becomes the Permanent* (1932); and *My Friend, Julia Lathrop* (1935). She was co-author of *Women at The Hague: The International Congress of Women and Its Results* (1915). Among the publications she contributed to were *Atlantic*, *International Journal of Ethics*, *New Republic*, and *North American Review*.

From 1883 until 1889, Addams was preoccupied with her own ill health and what her future vocation might be. During that period, she traveled extensively in Europe. She spent a brief time in Baltimore, where she attended lectures at Johns Hopkins University and did some charity work. In the course of her travels, she visited Toynbee Hall in London's East End. This was a settlement house operated by a group of Oxonians who were seeking a socialist solution to what they considered the evils and problems of the industrial revolution.

In her travels, Addams was accompanied by Ellen Gates Starr, a Socialist who had spent some time at Brook Farm, a Socialist colony. She had studied under George Ripley, a Fourierist leader. Addams, for her part, had studied under Bronson Alcott, another Fourierist socialist, when she was at Rockford College. At Toynbee Hall, Addams and Starr encountered pioneer Fabian Socialists, including Sidney and Beatrice Webb and Samuel Barnett. Barnett encouraged Addams and Starr to create a settlement house in America modelled along the lines of Toynbee Hall. The Webbs became such close friends of Addams that they stayed with her on their several trips to America.

In 1889, Addams and Starr opened Hull House in Chicago as one of the first settlement houses in the United States. Until her death in 1935, Addams directed the settlement, which over the years acquired a conglomeration of buildings. She made Hull House one of the most influential centers of socialist activity in the United States. It was in reality America's Fabian center. The workers, residents, and guests at Hull House came from all walks of life. They were representative of every profession, but there was a heavy emphasis on academicians and the relatively new breed of social workers. Under the guidance of Addams, their interests included local politics, working hours and wages and conditions for women, welfare procedures, child labor, housing conditions — especially in tenement districts, recognition of labor unions, industrial safety, compulsory school attendance, the protection of immigrants, sweat shops, garbage collections, prostitution, woman's suffrage, and just about any other area of social and economic stress encountered by Americans living in an urban environment during the latter part of the Nineteenth Century and the early part of the Twentieth Century.

The Hull House group, depending on the perspective of the observer, were regarded as social workers or charity workers or do-gooders or busybodies. No matter how they were characterized, they were all reformers and they all proved to be ideologically on the left. Most of them had strong ties either with formal Socialist and Communist parties, or at least with socialist or communist movements.

On the scene at Hull House, the reformers developed a boarding house for working girls, cooking and sewing and other houskeeping classes, a playground, a dispensary, a day nursery, a music school, a book bindery, an art gallery, a little theater, a boys' club, a labor museum, a community kitchen, and a gymnasium. Hull House was also a meeting center for radical groups and the scene of lectures given by radical leaders from the United States and abroad. Many of the reformers made Hull House their full-time or part-time residence. Others visited there with a regularity and a devotion comparable to that of religionists visiting a shrine.

Among those who cooperated with Addams in making Hull House an internationally famous center of Fabianism were Alice Hamilton, Grace Abbott, Sophonisba Breckinridge, Florence Kelley, Julia Lathrop, Harriet Monroe, Vida Scudder, Mary McDowell, Robert Morss Lovett, George D. Herron, Victor Berger, William L. Chenery, Henry Demarest Lloyd, Lyman Gage, Francis Hackett, and George Swope. Many of these individuals had a strong influence on the development of Addams' socialist philosophy. She also owed much to the pragmatism of John Dewey and William James, to the revolutionary socialism of the Italian Mazzini, to the socialism and pacifism of Ruskin and Tolstoi, and to the positivism of Comte.

As was the wont of so many of America's Socialists in the early part of the Twentieth Century, Addams gravitated toward the ranks of pacifists who labored, for one reason or another, under the principle that socialism could be achieved on a national and even an international scale if pacifism became a way of national-international life.

Some time in the immediate years prior to World War I, Addams expanded her reformer's horizons beyond Chicago. The first indication that she sought wider fields to conquer came in 1912 when she attended Theodore Roosevelt's Bull Moose Convention and seconded his nomination for the presidency of the United States on the third-party ticket. She campaigned for Roosevelt throughout the country — an understandable gesture since the Bull Moose platform could reasonably be interpreted as a Socialist manifesto.

By the time of the 1912 election, Addams had achieved a considerable measure of fame. Her several books, especially *Twenty Years at Hull House*, had been well received and noticed in reformist circles. In 1909, she had become the first woman president of the National Conference of Charities and Correction (later called the National Conference of Social Work). In 1910, she became the first woman to receive an honorary degree from Yale University. In 1911, she became the head of the National Federation of Settlements, a position she held until her death. In 1911, she began a three-year term as first vice-president of the National American Woman Suffrage Association.

At the outbreak of World War I in 1914, Addams plunged deeply into the radical movements that directed their energies against war in general and America's participation in particular. Addams talked in terms of outlawing war and discovering moral substitutes for war. These were themes that had become commonplace in the utterances and writings of the era's social reformers, who were indignant that the distractions and inconveniences of war would retard their progress toward a socialist society. They were not concerned with the justness of war. They were not concerned about the guilt of aggressors. They were not concerned about the imposition of unwanted political structures upon suffering peoples. Their concern was a socialist utopia transcending national boundaries and governed by the standards of their own elite group of know-it-all reformers.

In 1914, Addams became a leader of the Anti-Preparedness Committee, designed to oppose any preparation for war, offensive or defensive, by the United States government. When Addams joined this group, which later was called the American Union Against Militarism, she fell in with many of the nation's leading leftwing radicals, including Allan Benson, Max and Crystal Eastman, Zona Gale, Charles T. Hallinan, John Haynes Holmes, Florence Kelley, Paul Kellogg, Alice Lewisohn, Louis P.

Lochner, Lillian Wald, James P. Warbasse, and Stephen S. Wise. This group of radicals was at first concerned with preaching the necessity of American neutrality and non-preparedness for war. When America did become involved in the war, the American Union Against Militarism expanded its activities by creating a Civil Liberties Bureau. The Bureau, under the guise of protecting free speech and civil liberties, worked to encourage and to protect conscientious objectors and draft dodgers and to protect the "civil liberties" of alleged seditionists. Addams was a member of the Civil Liberties Bureau, and again found herself in company with some of America's most inflammatory radicals. In late 1917, the group enlarged its name to National Civil Liberties Bureau, and in 1920, it became the American Civil Liberties Union. Addams was a charter member of the ACLU's national committee, along with individuals who would become leaders of the various Communist and Socialist parties over the next several decades. They included Louis Budenz, Elizabeth Gurley Flynn, William Z. Foster, Morris Hillquit, Abraham Johannes Muste, Norman Thomas, and Harry F. Ward.

In 1914 and 1915, Addams joined Rosika Schwimmer and Louis Lochner in establishing the American Peace Federation. Lochner and Schwimmer would later be exposed by various government agencies as two dangerous Reds working against the interests of the United States. At the same time, Addams was president of the Women's Peace Party, which was in cahoots with the Socialist Party, the Emergency Peace Federation, the American Union Against Militarism, and the Civil Liberties Bureau. The two Bolsheviks, Schwimmer and Lochner, although not members, were indirectly but strongly connected with the group through their association with Addams.

In 1915, Addams went to The Hague as a representative of the Women's Peace Party. She was accompanied by Lochner and by Sophonisba Breckinridge from Hull House. At The Hague, they were joined by Schwimmer. Delegates from 18 countries met at the international Congress of Women at The Hague, and Addams was the presiding officer. From that Congress, there was created the Women's International Committee for Permanent Peace which, in 1919, became known as the Women's International League for Peace and Freedom. From 1915 until her death, Addams was president of the WILPF. She presided over meetings of the WILPF at The Hague (1915 and 1922), Zurich (1919), Vienna (1921), Washington (1924), Dublin (1926), and Prague (1929). Under Addams' direction, the WILPF grew until it had branches in more than twenty-five countries and a membership which it claimed was in excess of 50,000. In the 1920's, it became an affiliate of the War Resisters International, which had as its objectives the overthrow of capitalism and imperialism and the establishment of a new social and international order – an order in keeping with the lines laid down by Marx and Lenin.

As the head of WILPF, Addams was generally recognized as the leading feminine pacifist in the United States and certainly one of the most prominent in the world. Perhaps the highlight of her career came in 1931 when she shared the Nobel Peace Prize with Nicholas Murray Butler. The money (approximately $16,000) which accompanied the prize was donated by her to the WILPF. In the same year, she received the $5,000 M. Carey Thomas Prize from Bryn Mawr College.

The major peace organizations which Addams joined during the World War I period were only a minor portion of her leftist affiliations. She was not merely a letterhead name, but rather an activist, in most of the radical groups extant in her time. (It was not until 1972 that her most extreme affiliation became known. At that time, Maurice Malkin, a charter member and long-time official of the CPUSA, wrote in his book, *Return To My Father's House*, that Jane Addams became a secret Communist Party member in 1928 under the auspices of Arne Swaback, a Party organizer in Chicago.)

Addams' affiliations included the American Association for Labor Legislation (socialist); the American Association for Old Age Security (socialist); the American Committee on Information About Russia (pro-Soviet propaganda group); the American Society for Cultural Relations with Russia ("Communist front"); the Berger National Foundation (socialist organization); the Chicago Scottsboro Committee of Action ("Communist front"); the Committee on Militarism in Education (a supporting organization of the U.S. Congress against War, "completely under the control of the Communist Party"); the Debs Memorial Radio Station Committee (socialist); the Foreign Policy Association (a highly influential and highly effective pro-Communist vehicle); the Hands Off China Committee (pro-Communist); the Immigrants' Protective League (radical-leftist); the Intercollegiate Socialist Society and the League for Industrial Democracy (socialist); the International Committee for Political Prisoners (an ultra-leftist fund-raising enterprise for seditionists); the League of Women Voters (leftist); the National Association for the Advancement of Colored People (ultra-radical); the National Consumers League (socialist); the National Council for Prevention of War ("a group which harbored anarchists, pacifists, Communists, and anti-anti-Communists"); the National Religion and Labor Foundation ("Communist front"); the National Save Our Schools Committee (anti-American pressure group); the People's Legislative Service (a Socialist lobby); the Public Ownership League of America (socialist); the Russian-American Industrial Corporation (pro-Soviet); Russian Reconstruction Farms ("Communist enterprise"); the Sacco-Vanzetti National League (part of a Communist propaganda campaign); the Student Congress Against War ("Communist-controlled"); and Survey Associates (socialist). She died in May 1935.

THOMAS ADDIS was born on July 27, 1881 in Edinburgh, Scotland, son of Cornelia Campbell and Thomas Addis. He came to the United States in 1911. In 1917 he was naturalized as an American citizen. He married Elesa Partridge. He was an alumnus of the University of Edinburgh (M.B. and Ch.B., 1905; M.D., 1908). He was the author of *Glomerular Nephritis* (1948).

From 1911 until 1949, Addis was a professor of medicine at Stanford University's Medical School.

Addis has been affiliated with the American Committee for the Protection of Foreign Born ("founded by the Communist Party in order to exploit racial divisions in the United States for its own revolutionary purposes"); the American Committee for Yugoslav Relief ("subversive and Communist"); the American Council on Soviet Relations ("established by the Communist Party ... directed and controlled by the Party, and operated to aid and support Party objectives concerning the defense and support of the Soviet Union"); American Friends of Spanish Democracy ("Communist front"); American Friends of the Chinese People ("Communist front"); the American League for Peace and Democracy ("established . . . in an effort to create public sentiment on behalf of a foreign policy adapted to the interests of the Soviet Union . . . [and] designed to conceal Communist control, in accordance with the new tactics of the Communist International"); the American Peace Mobilization ("formed . . . under the auspices of the Communist Party and the Young Communist League" – "one of the most seditious organizations which ever operated in the United States"); American Youth for Democracy ("subversive and Communist" – "part of Soviet psychological warfare against the United States"); the California Labor School ("a subversive and Communist organization"); the China Aid Council ("Communist controlled"); the Citizens Committee for Harry Bridges ("Communist"); the Citizens Committee To Free Earl Browder ("a strictly Communist Party affair"); the Civil Rights Congress ("created and established by the Communist Party as an organization which would utilize defense of civil rights for Party purposes and raise and maintain mass defense and bail funds for Party use . . . ."); the Committee for a Democratic Far Eastern Policy ("Communist"); the Committee for Citizenship Rights ("to protect Communist subversion from any penalties under the law"); the Committee for Free Political Advocacy ("Communist front"); the Committee of One Thousand ("Communist-created and controlled"); the Committee of Welcome for the Red Dean of Canterbury (a Communist Party enterprise); the Conference for Democratic Action ("Communist

front"); Consumers Union (in the "solar system of organizations around the [Communist] Party"); the Coordinating Committee To Lift the [Spanish] Embargo ("one of the numerous Communist-front enterprises which were organized around the Communists' agitation over the Spanish Civil War"); the Council for Pan-American Democracy ("subversive and Communist"); the Cultural and Scientific Conference for World Peace ("a propaganda front for Soviet foreign policy and Soviet culture"); the Golden Book of American Friendship with the Soviet Union ("pro-Soviet propaganda enterprise"); In Defense of the Bill of Rights (a Communist Party enterprise); the International Workers Order ("from its very inception demonstrated by its pronouncements, its activities, and the authoritative statements of the Communist Party that it is a subservient instrument of the Communist Party of the United States"); the Jefferson School of Social Science ("a Communist Institution modeled along the lines of the new Communist policy which led to the decision to change the Communist Party into some kind of an educational institution"); the Joint Anti-Fascist Refugee Committee ("subversive and Communist"); the Medical Bureau and North American Committee To Aid Spanish Democracy ("subversive and un-American"); the National Conference on American Policy in China and the Far East ("Communist"); the National Council of American-Soviet Friendship ("subversive and Communist" – "specializing in pro-Soviet propaganda"); the National Committee of the Arts, Sciences, and Professions ("Communist front used to appeal to special occupational groups"); the National Emergency Conference ("Communist front"); the National Federation for Constitutional Liberties ("under Communist Party domination and headed by responsible Party functionaries" – "one of the viciously subversive organizations of the Communist Party"); Open Letter for Closer Cooperation with the Soviet Union (issued by "a group of Communist Party stooges"); the Reichstag Fire Trial Anniversary Committee ("Communist front . . . formed . . . by prominent Communists and Communist sympathizers"); [Morris U.] Schappes Defense Committee ("a front organization with a strictly Communist objective, namely, the defense of a self-admitted Communist who was convicted of perjury in the courts of New York"); the [William] Schneiderman- [Sam] Darcy Defense Committee ("Communist"); *Science and Society* ("a Communist publication"); the United American Spanish Aid Committee ("Communist enterprise"); and Veterans of the Abraham Lincoln Brigade ("directed, dominated and controlled by the Communist Party").

Addis signed a statement defending the Communist Party. He was a close associate of leading West Coast Communists. He was an especial friend of J. Robert Oppenheimer, the physicist who was found to be a security risk. He was often identified in sworn testimony as a member of the Communist Party. He died in June 1949.

DEVERE ALLEN was born on June 24, 1891 in Providence, Rhode Island, son of Sarah Champlin and Henry Allen. He married Marie Hollister. He was an alumnus of Oberlin College (A.B., 1917). (He was president of Oberlin's ultra-leftist Intercollegiate Socialist Society.) He was the author of *The Fight for Peace* (1930); *Will Socialism End the Evil of War?* (1913); *The Caribbean*; *Laboratory of World Cooperation*

(1943); *Some Prudence Island Aliens* (1946); and *What Europe Thinks About America* (1948). He was co-author of *Peace Is the Victory* (1944). He was editor of *Pacifism in the Modern World* (1929); *Adventurous Americans* (1932); and *Above All Nations* (1948).

In 1917 and 1918, Allen was editor of *The Rational Patriot*. From 1918 until 1921, he was editor of *Young Democracy*. From 1921 until 1933, he was with *The World Tomorrow* (Socialist publication) as managing editor (1921-1925) and editor (1925-1933). In 1930 and 1931, he was in Europe as a special correspondent for American newspapers and magazines. In 1931 and 1932, he was an associate editor of *The Nation*. From 1933 until 1944, he was with the Worldover Press (formerly Nofrontier News Service) as founder, editor, and director. He also served as the European bureau director for Worldover Press in Brussels (1939-1940), the Latin American bureau in Havana (1942) and Mexico City (1942-1944). He lectured at Harvard summer school and the Williamstown Institute of Politics. He was a faculty member of the Institute of International Relations, conducted jointly by Haverford College, Wellesley College, Duke University, Cornell University, Northwestern University, and the ultra-leftist-pacifist American Friends Service Committee. He was a member of the advisory committee for Swarthmore College's Peace Collection.

Allen was a member of the national executive committee of the Socialist Party. He was state chairman of the Labor Party of Connecticut. He was a candidate for the United States Senate for Connecticut on the Socialist ticket in 1932 and 1934. He was a gubernatorial candidate in Connecticut on the Labor Party ticket. He was a member of the

ALLPORT

executive committee of the Labor and Socialist International. He was an American member of the ultra-leftist World Council of the War Resisters' International. He was a member of the national committee and vice-chairman of the War Resisters' League in America. He was a member of the world honorary committee of the ultra-leftist International Campaign Against War and Militarism. He was a member of the editorial board of the *American Socialist Review*. He was a member of the national council of the Workers' Defense League ("defending political undesirables who are subject to deportation"). He was a member of the international policy committee of the ultra-leftist-pacifist Fellowship of Reconciliation and an editor of that organization's publication, *Fellowship*. He was a director and lecturer for the socialistic League for Industrial Democracy. He was a member of the ultra-radical American Civil Liberties Union and the ultra-radical Americans for Democratic Action. He was on the advisory committee for the defense of Leon Trotsky. He was a member of the national advisory committee of the ultra-leftist Sacco-Vanzetti National League. He was on the American advisory board for the Organization of Progress, which advocated giving Soviet Russia hundreds of thousands of dollars to use in purchasing goods from the United States before the recognition of Russia. He was also affiliated with such leftist one-world groups as the World Constitutional Convention, Students for Federal World Government, and Action for World Federation. He was also affiliated with American Friends of Spanish Democracy ("Communist front"); the American League Against War and Fascism ("subversive and Communist" – "established in the United States in an effort to create

public sentiment on behalf of a foreign policy adapted to the interests of the Soviet Union"); the American League for Peace and Democracy ("subversive and Communist" – "established in an effort to create public sentiment on behalf of a foreign policy adapted to the interests of the Soviet Union . . . [and] designed to conceal Communist control in accordance with the new tactics of the Communist International"); the American Student Union ("without exception . . . supported defensive teachers and students charged with Communist activity" – "pliable instrument in the hands of the Communist Party"); Brookwood Labor College ("Communistic"); the League for Independent Political Action (ultra-leftist); the League for Mutual Aid ("Communist enterprise"); the Medical Bureau To Aid Spanish Democracy ("Communist enterprise"); the National Student League ("the Communists' front organization for students"); the North American Committee To Aid Spanish Democracy ("Communist"); the United States Congress Against War ("completely under the control of the Communist Party"); and the Red-laden World Congress Against War. He died in August 1955.

GORDON W. ALLPORT was born on November 11, 1897 in Montezuma, Indiana, son of Nellie Wise and John Allport. He married Ada Gould. He was an alumnus of Harvard University (A.B., 1919; A.M., 1921; Ph.D., 1922). In 1922 and 1923, he pursued graduate studies at the University of Berlin and the University of Hamburg, and in 1923 and 1924, at Cambridge University. From 1922 until 1924, he held a Sheldon Traveling Fellowship. He was the author of *Personality: A Psychological Interpretation* (1937); *The Use of Personal Documents in Psychological Science* (1942); *The*

Individual and His Religion (1950); *The Nature of Personality: Selected Papers* (1950); *The Nature of Prejudice* (1954); *Becoming: Basic Considerations for a Psychology of Personality* (1955); *Personality and the Social Encounter: Selected Papers* (1960); *Pattern and Growth in Personality* (1961); and *Letters from Jenny* (1965). He was the co-author of *Studies in Expressive Movement* (1933); *The Psychology of Radio* (1935); *Trait-Names: A Psycho-lexical Study* (1936); and *The Psychology of Rumor* (1947). He was the editor of *Journal of Abnormal and Social Psychology* (1937-1949).

In 1919 and 1920, Allport was an instructor in English at Robert College in Istanbul, Turkey. From 1924 until 1926, he was an instructor in social ethics at Harvard University. From 1926 until 1930, he was an assistant professor in psychology at Dartmouth College. From 1930 until 1967, he was at Harvard University as an assistant professor of psychology (1930-1936); associate professor (1937-1941); professor (1942-1967); and chairman of the psychology department (1937-1946). In 1956, he was visiting overseas consultant of the Institute for Social Research at the University of Natal in Durban, South Africa. During World War II, he was a member of the emergency committee on psychology of the National Research Council. From 1945 until 1955, he was a director of the National Opinion Research Center in Chicago.

Allport was affiliated with the American Committee for Democracy and Intellectual Freedom ("subversive and un-American" – "a Communist front organization operating among college teachers and professors"); the American Committee for Protection of Foreign Born ("founded by the Communist Party in order to exploit racial divisions in the United States for its own revolutionary purposes"); the American League for Peace and Democracy ("subversive and Communist" – "established . . . in an effort to create public sentiment on behalf of a foreign policy adapted to the interests of the Soviet Union . . . [and] designed to conceal Communist control, in accordance with the new tactics of the Communist International"); the American Student Union ("without exception . . . supported defense of teachers and students charged with Communist activity" – "pliable instrument in the hands of the Communist Party"); the Civil Defense Letter Committee (leftist-pacifist); the Committee of Welcome for the Red Dean of Canterbury (a Communist Party enterprise); the Coordinating Committee To Lift the [Spanish] Embargo ("one of the numerous Communist-front enterprises which were organized around the Communists' agitation over the Spanish Civil War"); Defenders of Three Against HUAC (three fellow-travelers in contempt of Congress; the Fellowship of Reconciliation (ultra-leftist-pacifist); Freedom House Bookshelf Committee (composed of the most brazen leftists in the literary and academic world, promoting books by notable leftists); the Medical Bureau and North American Committee To Aid Spanish Democracy ("subversive and un-American"); the National Commission for UNESCO (leftist-oriented); the National Committee To Repeal the McCarran Act ("Communist front" – "subversive"); the National Committee for a Sane Nuclear Policy (ultra-leftist-pacifist); the National Council of the Arts, Sciences, and Professions ("a Communist front used to appeal to special occupational groups"); the National Emergency Conference ("Communist front"); the National Emergency Conference for Democratic Rights ("Communist front" – "subversive"); the National Federation for Constitutional Liberties ("under Communist Party domination and headed by responsible Party functionaries" – "one of the viciously subversive organizations of the Communist Party"); *New Masses* ("weekly journal of the Communist Party"); the Social Science Research Council ("leftist-oriented"); and the Spanish Refugee Relief Campaign ("Communist front"). He signed clemency petitions for Communists Frank Wilkinson and Carl Braden. He signed an open letter to President John F. Kennedy, urging him to arrange a "diplomatic detente" with Cuba's Communist dictator, Fidel Castro. He died in October 1967.

SHERWOOD ANDERSON was born on September 13, 1876 in Camden, Ohio, son of Emma Smith and Irwin Anderson. He was married to and divorced from Cornelia Lane, Tennessee Mitchell, and Elizabeth Prall. His fourth wife was Eleanor Copenhaver. He was educated in public schools. For a brief time he attended Wittenburg College. He was the author of *Windy McPherson's Son* (1916); *Marching Men* (1917); *Mid-American Chants*, poems (1918); *Winesburg, Ohio* (1919); *Poor White* (1920); *The Triumph of the Egg* (1921); *Many Marriages* (1922); *Horses and Men* (1923); *A Story Teller's Story* (1924); *Dark Laughter* (1925); *The Modern Writer* (1925); *Sherwood Anderson's Notebook* (1926); *Tar: Middle West Childhood* (1927); *New Testament* (1927); *Hello Towns* (1929); *Perhaps Women* (1931); *Beyond Desire* (1932); *Death in the Woods* (1933); *No Swank* (1934); *Puzzled America* (1935); *Kit Brandon* (1936); *Plays* (1937); *Home Town*, Face of America Series (1940);

and *Memoirs,* posthumously (1942).

Anderson held a variety of jobs. He sold newspapers, worked as a farm hand, labored in factories, worked in a cold storage plant, served briefly in Cuba as a soldier after the hostilities were over in the Spanish-American War, and worked for an advertising concern in Chicago and for a mail order house in Cleveland. From 1897 until 1899, he manufactured house paints in Elyria, Ohio. From 1900 until about 1916, when his first book was published, he worked as an advertising copy writer. While he was writing his first novel, he composed semi-autobiographical pieces and published them in pamphlet form. He was aided in his search for a publisher by a group of famous writers in Chicago, including Floyd Dell, Theodore Dreiser, Ben Hecht, and Carl Sandburg. From 1927 until 1929, he was owner and editor of two newspapers in Marion, Virginia – the *Smyth County News*, a Republican paper, and the *Marion Democrat*. For the rest of his life, he devoted most of his working time to his writings.

Anderson was affiliated with the ultra-radical American Civil Liberties Union, and especially its National Council on Freedom from Censorship and its Committee on Labor Injunctions; the American Committee for Protection of Foreign Born ("founded by the Communist Party in order to exploit racial divisions in the United States for its own revolutionary purposes"); the American Committee for Struggle Against War ("Communist front"); the American Committee of Liberals for the Freedom of [Tom] Mooney and [Warren K.] Billings ("formed by the International Labor Defense [the legal arm of the Communist Party]"); the American League Against War and Fascism ("subversive and Communist" – "established in the United States in an effort to create public sentiment on behalf of a foreign policy adapted to the best interests of the Soviet Union"); the American League for Peace and Democracy ("established . . . in an effort to create public sentiment in behalf of a foreign policy adapted to the interests of the Soviet Union . . . [and] designed to conceal Communist control, in accordance with the new tactics of the Communist International"); the American Pushkin Committee ("Communist front"); the American Relief Ship for Spain ("Communist Party front enterprise"); Artists Union ("a group primarily interested in Communist agitation and activity among artists"); the China Aid Council ("Communist-controlled"); the Coordinating Committee To Lift the [Spanish] Embargo ("one of the numerous Communist-front enterprises which were organized around the Communists' agitation over the Spanish Civil War"); the Emergency Committee for Southern Political Prisoners ("Communist front"); Film Audiences for Democracy ("Communist front"); Films for Democracy ("Communist front"); the John Reed Clubs ("out-and-out Communist organizations which preceded the contemporary Communist front organizations which cater to so-called liberals"); the League of Professional Groups for [William Z.] Foster and [James W.] Ford ("the members of this organization were committed to the objectives of the Communist Party"); the Medical Bureau and North American Committee To Aid Spanish Democracy ("subversive and un-American"); Motion Picture Artists Committee ("Communist front"); the National Committee for People's Rights ("composed primarily of openly-avowed members of the Communist Party and veteran fellow-travelers of the Communist Party"); the National

Committee for the Defense of Political Prisoners ("subversive and Communist"); the Non-Partisan Committee for the Reelection of Congressman Vito Marcantonio ("Communist front"); Open Letter for Closer Cooperation with the Soviet Union (issued by "a group of Communist Party stooges"); Public Use of Arts Committee ("Communist front"); the Student Congress Against War ("Communist controlled"); *Student Review* (a publication of the National Student League, "the Communist front organization for students"); Theater Union ("Communist front"); the Washington Committee To Lift [the] Spanish Embargo ("Communist front"); and the Workers Theater Council of Chicago ("Communist Party cultural activity"). He died in March 1941.

NEWTON ARVIN was born on August 23, 1900 in Valparaiso, Indiana, son of Jessie Hawkins and Frederic Arvin. He was an alumnus of Harvard University (A.B., 1921). He was the author of *Hawthorne* (1929); *Whitman* (1938); and *Herman Melville* (1950). He was the compiler of *The Heart of Hawthorne's Journals* (1929); *Hawthorne's Short Stories* (1946); *The Selected Letters of Henry Adams* (1952); and *Longfellow* (1963). In 1951, he received the National Book Award.

From 1922 until 1960, Arvin was at Smith College as an instructor in English (1922-1928); assistant professor (1928-1933); associate professor (1933-1940); and professor (1940-1960). In 1951, he was a visiting lecturer at Ohio State University. In 1952 and 1953, he was a visiting lecturer at Harvard University. In 1935 and 1936, he held a Guggenheim fellowship. From 1939 until 1963, he was with the Corporation of Yaddo as director

(1939-1954) and member of the corporation (1954-1963).

Arvin was affiliated with the American Committee for Struggle Against War ("Communist front"); the American Friends of Spanish Democracy ("Communist front"); the Golden Book of American Friendship with the Soviet Union ("pro-Soviet propaganda enterprise"); the League of American Writers ("subversive and Communist" – "began openly to follow the Communist Party line as dictated by the foreign policy of the Soviet Union"); the League of Professional Groups for [William Z.] Foster and [James W.] Ford ("the members of this organization were committed to the objectives of the Communist Party"); the Marcus Graham Defense Committee (Communist front); the Marcus Graham Freedom of the Press Committee (Communist front); the National Student League ("the Communists' front organization for students"); the National Writers' Congress ("Communist front"); *New Masses* ("weekly journal of the Communist Party"); Open Letter to American Liberals ("project of well-known Communists and Communist collaborators" – "in defense of the progressive movement undertaken by the Soviet Union"); the Open Letter for Closer Cooperation with the Soviet Union (issued by "a group of Communist Party stooges"); *Partisan Review* ("a Communist publication"); and Veterans of the Abraham Lincoln Brigade ("directed, dominated and controlled by the Communist Party"). He died in March 1963.

HENRY A. ATKINSON was born on August 26, 1877 in Merced, California, son of Sarah Yeargin and Thomas Atkinson. He was married to the late Grace Olin. His second wife was Marjorie Jefferson Weber. He was an alumnus of Pacific Methodist College (A.B., 1897). He also studied at the Garrett Bible Institute of Northwestern University. In 1902, he was ordained a Congregational minister. He was the author of *The Church and Industrial Warfare* (1914); *The Church and the People's Play* (1915); *Men and Things* (1918); and *Prelude to Peace* (1937). He was co-author of *Causes of War* (1932).

Atkinson held Congregational pastorates in Albion, Illinois (1902-1904); Springfield, Ohio (1904-1908); and Atlanta, Georgia (1908-1911). From 1908 until 1911, he was a professor of sociology at the Atlanta Theological Seminary. From 1911 until 1918, he was secretary of the Social Service Commission of Congregational Churches in the United States. In 1918, he was extension secretary of the leftist-pacifist League To Enforce Peace. From 1918 until 1955, he was general secretary of the World Alliance and the Church Peace Union, both of which were leftist-oriented. From 1944 until 1956, he was chairman of the leftist-oriented Non-sectarian Anti-Nazi League. From 1940 until 1956, he was co-chairman of the leftist-oriented Council Against Intolerance in America. In 1945, he received an appointment from the U.S. Department of State to serve as an unofficial consultant at the founding conference of the United Nations.

Atkinson was a member of the leftist-oriented American Association for the United Nations. He was also affiliated with the American Association for a Democratic Germany (leftist-oriented); the American Committee for Non-Participation in Japanese Aggression ("Communist front"); the American Committee To Save Refugees ("subversive and Communist" – "perform[ing] a most valuable function for the international Communist movement"); American Friends of Czecho-Slovakia (leftist-oriented); the American League Against War and Fascism ("subversive and Communist" – "established in the United States in an effort to create public sentiment on behalf of a foreign policy adapted to the interests of the Soviet Union"); the American Round Table on India ("Communist front"); the American-Russian Institute ("subversive" – "Communist" – "specializing in pro-Soviet propaganda"); the American Youth Congress ("subversive" – "one of the most influential front organizations ever set up by the Communists in this country" – "the Communists were in complete control"); the China Aid Council ("Communist-controlled"); the Committee for Peace Through World Cooperation ("it is significant that the Committee . . . received its chief publicity in the Communist press"); the Committee To Welcome the Red Dean of Canterbury ("Communist enterprise"); the League of American Writers ("subversive and Communist" – "began openly to follow the Communist Party line as dictated by the foreign policy of the Soviet Union"); the National Committee To Combat Anti-Semitism ("Communist front"); the *Protestant Digest* ("a magazine which has faithfully propagated the Communist Party line under the guise of being a religious journal"); the Union of Concerted Peace Efforts ("Communist front"); the World Citizenship Movement (leftist-oriented); and World Youth Congress ("Communist conference"). He died in January 1960.

EMILY GREENE BALCH was born on January 8, 1867 in Jamaica Plain, Massachusetts, daughter of Ellen Noyes and Francis Balch. She was an alumna of Bryn Mawr College (A.B., 1889). In

1889 and 1890, she had a year of private study with Franklin H. Giddings, a sociologist. In 1890 and 1891, on a fellowship from Bryn Mawr, she was in Paris studying political economy with Pierre Emile Lavasseur. In 1895, she pursued graduate studies at Radcliffe College and the University of Chicago. In 1896, at the University of Berlin, she studied under the German economists Gustav Schmoller and Adolf Wagner. She was the author of *Public Assistance of the Poor in France* (1893); *Outline of Economics* (1899); *A Study of Conditions of City Life* (1903); *Our Slavic Fellow-Citizens* (1910); *Approaches to the Great Settlement* (1918); *Refugees As Assets* (1939); *The Miracle of Living*, poems (1941); *One Europe* (1947); *Vignettes In Prose* (1952); and *Toward Human Unity, or Beyond Nationalism* (1952). She was co-author of *Women at The Hague* (1915). She was co-author and editor of *Occupied Haiti* (1927).

From 1897 until 1918, Balch was at Wellesley College as an instructor in economics (1897-1903); associate professor (1903-1913); and professor of political economy and social science (1913-1918). From 1904 until 1906, on leave of absence from Wellesley, she studied Slavic immigration in Austria-Hungary and in Slavic settlements within the United States. In 1908 and 1909, she was a member of the Massachusetts State Commission on Industrial Education. In 1913 and 1914, she was a member of the Massachusetts State Commission on Immigration. From 1914 until 1917, she was a member of the City Planning Board of Boston. In 1891, she became interested in social work, and was on the staff of the Children's Aid Society in Boston. In 1892, with Vida Scudder, she helped to found the Denison House Settlement, where she was the head social worker for two years. In this same period, she joined the American Federation of Labor. She was a founder of the Women's Trade Union League. She helped draft the first minimum wage bill ever presented to an American legislative body.

During World War I, Balch became deeply involved in pacifist activities. In 1915, with members of the Women's Peace Party, she went to the international Congress of Women at The Hague. As a delegate of the Congress, she traveled to Russia and the Scandinavian countries to discuss peace terms with government leaders. In 1916, she spent some time in Stockholm as a member of the Neutral Conference for Continuous Mediation, established by Henry Ford, the automobile manufacturer. In 1916 and 1917, she was in New York City agitating for peace, and she took a leading role in pacifist circles in opposition to United States entry into World War I. In 1918, the trustees of Wellesley College dismissed her from the faculty because "of her outspoken views on pacifism and economics." In 1919, she was on the editorial staff of the radical *Nation* magazine. In 1919, she went to Zurich, Switzerland, to attend the second meeting of the international Congress of Women. At that time, the group changed its name to Women's International League for Peace and Freedom. She was elected the first international secretary of WILPF, a post she held for three years. She remained an active member of WILPF for the rest of her life. She served the organization as a member of its international executive committee, as vice-chairman of its United States section, and from 1936 until 1961, she was its honorary president.

In her pacifism, Balch agitated for international control of defense bases, of the polar regions, of the Mediterranean Sea, and of the Panama and Suez Canals. In the course of her career, one of her most important proposals was for a women's international political party. In 1946, she was a co-winner of the Nobel Peace Prize. In 1947, she petitioned President Harry S. Truman to grant amnesty to World War II conscientious objectors. In 1955, she supported the Red-operated Asian-African Conference.

Balch was affiliated with the American Committee for Protection of Foreign Born ("founded by the Communist Party in order to exploit racial divisions in the United States for its own revolutionary purposes"); the American League Against War and Fascism ("subversive and Communist" – "established in the United States in an effort to create public sentiment on behalf of a foreign policy adapted to the interests of the Soviet Union"); the [Victor] Berger National Foundation (Socialist); the Bill of Rights Conference (subversive); Brief [*amicus curiae*] for the Communist Party ("Communist Party enterprise"); the Citizens' Committee to Free Earl Browder ("a strictly Communist Party affair"); the Civil Liberties Bureau (ultra-leftist-pacifist); the Committee for a Democratic Far Eastern Policy ("Communist"); the Committee for Peaceful Alternatives to the Atlantic Pact ("a Communist front organization . . . as part of Soviet psychological warfare against the United States"); the Emergency Peace Federation (dominated by socialists); the Fellowship of Reconciliation (ultra-leftist-pacifist); the Hiroshima Commemorative Committee (ultra-leftist); the Inter-Collegiate Socialist Society (radical Socialist); the International Workers Order ("from its very inception demonstrated by its pronouncements, its activities, and the authoritative statements of the Communist Party that it is a subservient instrument of the Communist Party of the United States"); the League for Industrial Democracy (Socialist); the Mid-Century Conference for Peace ("aimed at assembling as many gullible persons possible under Communist direction and turning them into a vast sounding board for Communist propaganda"); the National Committee To Repeal the McCarran Act ("Communist front" – "subversive"); the National Committee To Secure Justice for Morton Sobell ("Communist front [in] the Communist campaign for [atomic spy] Morton Sobell"); the People's Councils (Socialist); and the Stockholm Peace Appeal ("Communist 'peace' campaign"). She died in January 1961.

RUTH BENEDICT was born on June 5, 1887 in New York City, daughter of Beatrice Shattuck and Frederick Fulton. She was married to and separated from the late Stanley Benedict. She was an alumnus of Vassar College (A.B., 1909) and Columbia University (Ph.D., 1923). She attended the New School for Social Research. She was the author of *The Concept of the Guardian Spirit in North America* (1923); *Tales of the Cochiti Indians* (1931); *Patterns of Culture* (1934); *Zuni Mythology*, 2 volumes (1935); *Race, Science and Politics* (1940); and *The Chrysanthemum and the Sword: Patterns of Japanese Culture* (1946). She was editor of the *Journal of American Folklore* (1923-1939). She was a contributor to *The Making of Man* (1929). She contributed articles to the *Journal of American Psychology, Atlantic Monthly, Annals* of the American Academy of Political and Social Science, the *American Anthropologist*, the *American Journal of Orthopsychiatry, Pro-*

ceedings of the International Congress of Americanists, and *Memoirs* of the American Anthropological Association. From 1928 until 1933, she contributed poetry, under the pseudonym of Anne Singleton, to *Nation* and *Poetry*.

In 1910, Benedict engaged in social work in Buffalo, New York. From 1911 until 1914, she taught in a girls' school in California. Between 1914 and 1919, she was a housewife, leaving her housewife status for only a brief time in 1917 for social work. In 1919, she enrolled in the New School for Social Research. (On April 24, 1920, the Joint Legislative Committee Investigating Seditious Activities for the Senate of the State of New York said that the New School "has been established by men who belong to the ranks of near Bolshevik intelligentsia.") At the New School, Benedict studied under Alexander Goldenweiser, an anthropologist. Goldenweiser was a member of the American Socialist Society and on the faculty of its training school, the Rand School of Social Science. After a year with Goldenweiser, Benedict was sent by him to study under his anthropological colleague and Socialist comrade, Franz Boas, at Columbia University.

After only three semesters of study under Boas, Benedict received her Ph.D. from Columbia. This unusual situation was created because Boas managed to get her full credit for her year's study at the New School applied to her Ph.D. work at Columbia, even though the New School was unaccredited. By the time Benedict arrived at Columbia, Boas had established a highly influential center for Socialist-oriented anthropologists.

In 1922 and 1923, Benedict assisted Boas in teaching a course at Barnard College. (At Barnard, Benedict exerted considerable influence on Margaret Mead, an undergraduate, who became an internationally famous anthropologist and equally famous leftist.)

From 1923 until 1948, Benedict was on the faculty of Columbia University as a lecturer in anthropology (1923-1930); assistant professor (1930-1936); associate professor (1936-1948); acting head of the anthropology department (1936-1939); and professor (1948). As an anthropologist she made field trips to the Serrano Indians in Southern California (1922); the Pueblo Indians of Zuni and Cochiti in the Southwest (1924 and 1925); the Pima Indians in the Southwest (1926); the Mescalero Apache Indians of the Southwest (1931); and the Blackfoot Indians of Montana (1939). From 1943 until 1946, she was on a leave of absence from Columbia while serving with the Bureau of Overseas Intelligence of the Red-laden Office of War Information. In 1947, as a result of the reception accorded Benedict's *The Chrysanthemum and the Sword: Patterns of Japanese Culture*, Columbia University received a substantial grant of money from Naval Research to establish under her direction a program of research in contemporary cultures. In 1948, as director of the Naval Research Project, she gave seminars on education for Red-ridden UNESCO in Czecho-Slovakia.

Benedict's first major work was *Patterns of Culture*, published in 1934. The idea for the book was propounded by Franz Boas, Margaret Mead, and some of their leftist colleagues who wanted to promote Socialism through the medium of a popularized anthropological study. For two years, Benedict worked at amalgamating into a single manuscript the various works of more than twenty Socialist-oriented anthropologists and the relatively new breed of so-called social scientists. The book, which came out under Benedict's name, was eventu-

ally translated into at least 14 languages, and more than a million copies have been sold. It became one of the most widely-used required studies in the social science curricula of American colleges.

In simple terms, *Patterns of Culture* was a successful attempt by Benedict to promote socialism rather than individualism as a desirable guide for American society. In Benedict's methodology, she considered all of the world's cultures to be an integrated whole. She ascribed to individual cultures psychiatric and psychological concepts which would be normally applied to individual people. This approach made of her *Patterns of Culture* a study in generalities. Her special target in the book was the American capitalist society, especially its industrial and business leaders. By design she selected two obscure tribes as prototypes for American capitalists and one similar tribe as a prototype to represent the Socialists whom she admired and who, she felt, should be leading and dominating American society.

For the capitalist side of her analogy, she presented a study of the Dobuan tribe of New Guinea and the Kwakiutl tribe of Vancouver Island. For her Socialist prototype, she chose Zuni Indians. The Dobuans, who were handicapped by a harsh environment and an inherent low mental capacity, had a primitive civilization. She said of the tribe: "The Dobuan, therefore, is dour, prudish, and passionate, consumed with jealousy and resentment. Every moment of prosperity he conceives himself to have wrung from a malicious world by a conflict in which he has worsted his opponent." The Dobuans, in her opinion, were similar to the 18th century American Puritans, who were, again in her opinion, the lineal ancestors of America's 20th century capitalist leaders. She wrote: "In our own generation extreme forms of ego gratification are culturally supported in a similar fashion. Arrogant and unbridled egoists as family men, as officers of the law and in business, have been again and again portrayed by novelists and dramatists, and they are familiar in every community. Like the behavior of Puritan divines, their courses of action are often more asocial than those of the inmates of penitentiaries. In terms of the suffering and frustration that they spread about them there is probably no comparison. There is very possibly at least as great a degree of mental warping. Yet they are entrusted with positions of great influence and importance and are as a rule fathers of families. Their impress both upon their own children and upon the structure of our society is indelible. They are not described in our manuals of psychiatry because they are supported by every tenet of our civilization."

Later she added to this thesis when she wrote: "There is a further corollary. From the point of view of absolute categories of abnormal psychology, we must expect in any culture to find a large proportion of the most extreme abnormal types among those who from the local point of view are farthest from belonging to this category. The culture, according to its major preoccupations, will increase and intensify hysterical, epileptic, or paranoid symptoms, at the same time relying socially in a greater and greater degree upon these very individuals. Western civilization allows and culturally honors gratifications of the ego which according to any absolute category would be regarded as abnormal. The portrayal of unbridled and arrogant egotists as family men, as officers of the law, and in business has been a favorite topic of novelists, and they are familiar

in every community. Such individuals are probably mentally warped to a greater degree than many inmates of our institutions who are nevertheless socially unavailable. They are extreme types of those personality configurations which our civilization fosters." ("Anthropology and the Abnormal," *Journal of General Psychology*, No. 2, 1934.)

For her other invidious comparison with American capitalists, Benedict chose the Kwakiutl, notorious for their pathological gambling, of whom she wrote: "The megalomaniac paranoid trend is a definite danger in our society. The chief motive that the institutions of the Kwakiutl rely upon and which they share in great measure with modern society is the motive of rivalry. Rivalry is a struggle that is not centered upon the real objects of the activity but upon outdoing a competitor . . . . Rivalry is notoriously wasteful. It ranks low in the scale of human values. It is a tyranny from which, once it is encouraged in any culture, no man may free himself. The wish for superiority is gargantuan; it can never be satisfied. The contest goes on forever. The more goods the community accumulates, the greater the counters with which men play, but the game is as far from being won as it was when the stakes were small. The social waste is obvious. It is just as obvious in the obsessive rivalry of Middletown where houses are built and clothing bought and entertainments attended that each family may prove that it has not been left out of the game.

"It is an unattractive picture. In Kwakiutl life the rivalry is carried out in such a way that all success must be built upon the ruin of rivals; in Middletown in such a way that individual choices and direct satisfactions are reduced to a minimum and conformity is sought beyond all other human gratifications. In both cases it is clear that wealth is not sought and valued for its direct satisfaction of human needs but as a series of counters in the game of rivalry. If the will to victory were eliminated from the economic life, distribution and consumption of wealth would follow quite different 'laws.' "

For a heroic example of Socialism in action, Benedict selected the Zuni Indians, because of their dependence upon collectivist practices and their antagonism toward individual efforts. She ignored the fact that the Zunis were in a steady cultural decline and that their earlier reliance upon collectivism was necessitated by generations of threats by their enemies, to the extent that the Zunis were in a permanent state of military preparation.

The scholarly format of *Patterns of Culture* with its superficial psychiatric, psychological, and sociological concepts served Benedict's objective of promoting Socialism through anthropology, for she succeeded in hoodwinking budding anthropologists and even veteran social science practitioners.

In 1943, Benedict struck another major blow for the cause of Socialism when she collaborated with her ultra-leftist colleague Gene Weltfish in writing the booklet *Races of Mankind*. It was issued by the Public Affairs Committee led by old-time Socialists such as Harry Laidler and George Soule. Somehow, in 1944, fifty-five thousand copies of the booklet were purchased by the War Department for distribution through the Army's Information and Education program. The distribution came to a halt when the House Military Affairs Committee decided that the booklet was nothing but a Red tract. The Communists were incensed at the ban on the Benedict-Weltfish item and said, in their *Daily Worker*, that it was "difficult to reconcile such an act with the cause for which we are fighting." But the furore only served to increase interest in *Races of Mankind*, and more than 750,000 copies were distributed by private organizations, including the leftist-dominated CIO's War Relief Committee.

Benedict was affiliated with *Amerasia* ("Communist-controlled"); the American Association of Scientific Workers ("Communist front"); the American Committee for Democracy and Intellectual Freedom ("subversive and un-American" – "a Communist front organization operating among college teachers and professors"); the American Committee for Protection of Foreign Born ("founded by the Communist Party in order to exploit racial divisions in the United States for its own revolutionary purposes"); the American Committee To Save Refugees ("perform[ing] a most valuable function for the international Communist movement"); the Citizens' Emergency Conference for Inter-Racial Unity ("Communist front"); the Committee for Equal Justice for Mrs. Recy Taylor ("Communist front"); the Council for Pan-American Democracy ("subversive and Communist"); the Greater New York Emergency Conference on Inalienable Rights ("Communist front"); the Institute of Pacific Relations ("an instrument of Communist policy, propaganda and military intelligence"); the League of American Writers ("subversive and Communist" – "began openly to follow the Communist Party line as dictated by the foreign policy of the Soviet Union"); the National Emergency Conference ("Communist front"); the National Federation for Constitutional Liberties ("under Communist Party domination and headed by responsible

Party functionaries" – "one of the viciously subversive organizations of the Communist Party"); the National Wartime Conference of the Professions, the Sciences, the Arts, the White-Collar Fields ("Communist front"); the School for Democracy ("established by Communist teachers ousted by the public school system of New York City"); and the United American Spanish Aid Committee ("Communist"). Benedict died in September 1948. She was eulogized in the Communists' *Daily Worker* of October 13, 1948.

WILLIAM ROSE BENÉT was born on February 2, 1886 in Fort Hamilton, New York, son of Frances Rose and James Benét. He was married to the late Teresa Thompson and the late Elinor Wylie. He was married to and divorced from Lora Baxter. His fourth wife was Marjorie Flack. He was an alumnus of Sheffield Scientific School of Yale University (Ph. B., 1907). He was the author of *Merchants from Cathay* (1913); *The Falconer of God* (1914); *The Great White Wall* (1916); *The Burglar of the Zodiac* (1918); *Perpetual Light* (1919); *Moons of Grandeur* (1920); *The First Person Singular* (1922); *The Flying King of Kurio* (1926); *Wild Goslings* (1927); *Man Possessed* (1927); *Rip Tide* (1932); *Starry Harness* (1933); *Golden Fleece* (1935); *With Wings As Eagles: Air Ballads* (1940); *The Dust Which Is God* (1941); *Day of Deliverance: A Book of Poems in Wartime* (1944); *Timothy's Angels* (1947); and *The Stairway of Surprise* (1947). He was co-author of *Adolphus, the Adopted Dophin* (1941). He was co-translator of Paul Claudel's *The East I Know* (1914). He was editor of *Poems for Youth* (1923); *Fifty Poets; An Auto-Anthology* (1933); and *Reader's Encyclopedia* (1948). He was co-

editor of *Twentieth Century Poetry* (1930); *The Oxford Anthology of American Literature* (1938); *The Poetry of Freedom: An Anthology* (1945); and *Crowell Handbook for Readers and Writers* (1947). He won the National Playwriting Award for his *Day's End: A Fantasia in One Act*, produced in 1939. In 1942, he was awarded the Pulitzer Prize for poetry.

From 1907 until 1911, Benét was a free-lance writer (mostly poetry). From 1911 until 1918, he was with *Century Magazine* as a reader (1911-1914) and assistant editor (1914-1918). In 1918, he spent eleven months as a non-flying officer in the U.S. Air Service. In 1919, he was with Corman Company, an advertising agency. In 1919 and 1920, he was an assistant editor of *The Nation's Business*. From 1920 until 1924, he was an associate editor of the Literary Review of the *New York Evening Post*. From 1924 until 1929, he was an associate editor of *Saturday Review of Literature*, and from 1929 until 1950, he continued to be a contributing editor. In 1929 and 1930, he was an editor for Brewer and Warren, Inc. In the summers in 1936 and 1937, he taught and lectured at Mills College.

On one occasion, Benét wrote: "I am not a Communist and I do not always agree with *New Masses* ["weekly journal of the Communist Party"], but I think anyone is unintelligent who does not read it." In earlier years, Benét had contributed poetry to that publication's predecessor, *Masses*. Communist or not, Benét accumulated an impressive list of affiliations with far-left groups, including the American Committee for Protection of Foreign Born ("founded by the Communist Party in order to exploit racial divisions in the United States for its own revolutionary purposes"); the American

Committee for Spanish Freedom ("Communist"); the American Committee for Yugoslav Relief ("subversive and Communist"); the American Council for a Democratic Greece ("subversive and Communist"); the Artists' Front To Win the War ("Communist front" – "included representatives of the theater, of literature, music, art, science, and education, with long and active records of support for Communist-front organizations and for the variegated turns of the Communist Party line"); the Celebration of the 25th Anniversary of the Red Army ("Communist enterprise"); the Civil Rights Congress ("created and established by the Communist Party as an organization which would utilize defense of civil rights for Party purposes and raise and maintain mass defense and bail funds for Party use"); the Committee for a Democratic Far Eastern Policy ("Communist"); the Committee for Equal Justice for Mrs. Recy Taylor ("Communist front"); the Committee of One Thousand ("Communist-created and controlled"); the Committee To Defend Don West ("Communist front"); the Congress of American-Soviet Friendship ("Communist front"); Contemporary Writers ("subversive and Communist"); the Coordinating Committee To Lift the [Spanish] Embargo ("one of the numerous Communist front enterprises which were organized around the Communists' agitation over the Spanish Civil War"); the Council for Pan American Democracy ("subversive and Communist"); Films for Democracy ("Communist front"); the Freedom From Fear Committee ("Communist front"); Friends of Italian Democracy ("Communist front"); Friends of the Abraham Lincoln Brigade ("completely controlled by the Communist Party"); the Independent Citizens Committee of the Arts, Sciences, and Professions ("Communist front"); the Jefferson School of Social Science ("a Communist institution modeled along the lines of the new Communist policy which led to the decision to change the Communist Party into some kind of an educational institution"); the Joint Anti-Fascist Refugee Committee ("subversive and Communist"); the League of American Writers ("subversive and Communist" – "began openly to follow the Communist Party line as dictated by the foreign policy of the Soviet Union"); the National Citizens' Political Action Committee ("Communist front"); the National Committee for Defense of Political Prisoners ("subversive and Communist"); the National Committee for People's Rights ("composed primarily of openly avowed members of the Communist Party and veteran fellow-travelers of the Communist Party"); the National Committee To Abolish the Poll Tax ("Communist front"); the National Council of American-Soviet Friendship ("subversive and Communist" – "specializing in pro-Soviet propaganda"); the National Federation for Constitutional Liberties ("under Communist Party domination and headed by responsible Party functionaries" – "one of the viciously subversive organizations of the Communist Party"); the National Institute of Arts and Letters ("Communist front"); Progressive Citizens of America ("political Communist front" – "subversive"); the Reichstag Fire Trial Anniversary Committee ("Communist front . . . formed . . . by prominent Communists and Communist sympathizers"); the [Morris U.] Schappes Defense Committee ("front organization with a strictly Communist objective, namely, the defense of a self-admitted Communist who was convicted of perjury in the courts of New York"); *Soviet Russia Today*

("Communist-controlled publication"); the Spanish Refugee Appeal ("subversive" – "Communist front"); Testimonial Dinner for Ferdinand C. Smith, a Communist official; the ultra-leftist United World Federalists; Veterans of the Abraham Lincoln Brigade ("directed, dominated and controlled by the Communist Party"); the Washington Committee To Lift [the] Spanish Embargo ("Communist front"); and the Win-the-Peace Conference ("Communist front"). Benet died in May 1950.

VICTOR LOUIS BERGER was born on February 28, 1860 in Nieder-Rehbach, Austria-Hungary, son of Julia and Ignatz Berger. He married Meta Schlichting. He studied at the Gymnasium at Leutschau, Austria, the University of Vienna, and the University of Budapest. He came to the United States in 1878.

From 1880 until 1890, Berger was a teacher of German in the Milwaukee, Wisconsin public schools. From 1892 until 1898, he was the founder-editor of the *Wisconsin Vorwärts*, a Milwaukee daily. From 1901 until 1911, he was editor of the *Social Democratic Herald,* known as the *Milwaukee Leader* after 1911; and from 1911 until 1929, he was publisher of the *Leader.*

During his school-teaching years, Berger joined the Socialist Labor Party, but left it in 1889 because he was dissatisfied with its rigid adherence to Marxism. In 1896, as a Socialist, he attended the People's Party (Populists) Convention as a delegate. When the People's Party nominated William Jennings Bryan as their presidential candidate, Berger and other Socialists decided to withdraw their support from the Populists. In 1897, Berger joined with other dissident Socialists and formed the short-lived Social Democracy of America. In 1898, after the dissidents quarrelled amongst themselves, Berger left the Social Democracy of America and helped to found the Social Democratic Party, known as the Socialist Party after 1900. From 1898 until 1927, Berger was on the new party's national executive board, and from 1927 until 1929, he was national chairman of the Socialist Party.

From 1892 until his death in 1929, Berger was the unquestioned leader of the very strong Socialist movement in Milwaukee and throughout Wisconsin. As a member and representative of Milwaukee's local in the International Typographical Union, as a delegate to many American Federation of Labor Conventions, as an editor and writer in his newspapers and pamphlets, and as a political candidate and office holder, he established Socialism as a durable force in Wisconsin. In 1904, on the Socialist Party ticket, he was an unsuccessful candidate for Mayor of Milwaukee, for the U.S. Senate, and for the U.S. House of Representatives. In 1907, as a Socialist, he was elected as a member of Milwaukee's charter convention. In 1910, as a Socialist, he was elected Alderman-at-Large in Milwaukee. In 1910, he was elected as the first Socialist in the Congress of the United States, representing a district that compromised fourteen wards in Milwaukee, the city of North Milwaukee, and four towns and villages. He served in the House of Representatives from March 4, 1911, until March 3, 1913. In 1912 and 1914, he was unsuccessful in his attempts to win reelection to the Congress.

At the outbreak of World War I, Berger adopted as his own the Socialist Party's adamant opposition to America's involvement. Through his editorials and other writings and in his public utterances, Berger was so vehement that his opposition to the war brought him into serious confrontation with the federal government. In October 1917, his *Milwaukee Leader* was denied second-class mail rights by the Postmaster-General of the United States under terms of the Espionage Act. (The Postmaster-General's action was reviewed and affirmed by the Supreme Court of the United States in 1921.) Berger's views on World War I were the standard Socialist ones. He saw that particular war as a conflict between imperialist and capitalist nations, in which someone's imperialism and capitalism would gain at the expense of labor and Socialism.

In February 1918, Berger was indicted, along with four other Socialists, under the Espionage Act. In December 1918, the trial of Berger and the other Socialists began in the United States District Court for the Northern District of Illinois, with Kenesaw Mountain Landis as presiding judge. In January 1919, Judge Landis issued a verdict of guilty in Berger's case; a motion for a new trial was denied, but an appeal by Berger was granted, and he was released on bail.

In the meantime, in 1918, Berger was elected for the second time to Congress. On November 10, 1919, the members of the House of Representatives, by a vote of 309 to 1, denied Berger his seat in the House on grounds that he had been disloyal to the United States by giving aid and comfort to the enemy in time of war. In December 1919, a special Congressional election was held, by order of the Governor or Wisconsin, to fill the seat which had been denied to Berger. Berger was an overwhelming winner in the special election. On January 10, 1920, and on February 25, 1921, the House of Representatives for the second and third times voted to deny Berger his seat.

On January 31, 1921, the Landis decision against Berger was reversed by the Supreme Court of the United States. In 1922, the federal government withdrew all charges against Berger. On December 3, 1923, the House of Representatives, without a dissenting vote, allowed Berger to take his seat. He served three successive terms in the Congress but was unsuccessful in a bid for reelection in 1928.

Since his death, Berger has been represented in Socialist and other literature as having been content to see the Socialist utopia evolve by gradual and peaceful processes. On one occasion, the *Saturday Evening Post* described Berger as merely a nominal socialist who was in reality a mild and gentle civic and social reformer. Such a description was contradicted in no uncertain terms by Berger himself. At the Socialist Party's 1908 Convention, Berger said: "Comrade Chairman and Comrades: There is a growing tendency, not only in this country but in other countries, to deprecate political action. That tendency you can see in Italy and France, even in Germany to some extent, although less there than anywhere else, and in this country. The Syndicalists in Italy fight political action. They call themselves Socialists and are members of the Socialist Party. There is a strong element or was at least in this country doing the same thing, and I have heard it pleaded many a time right in our own meetings by speakers that come to our meetings, that the only salvation for the proletariat of America is direct action; that the ballot box is simply a humbug. Now I don't doubt that in the last analysis we must shoot, and when it comes to shooting Wisconsin will be there. We always make good."

In the *Social Democratic Herald* of Milwaukee of July 31, 1909, Berger was just as inflammatory when he wrote: "No one will claim that I am given to the reciting of 'revolutionary' phrases. On the contrary, I am known to be a 'constructive' Socialist. However, in view of the plutocratic lawmaking of the present day, it is easy to predict that the safety and hope of this country will finally lie in one direction only – that of a violent and bloody revolution. Therefore, I say, each of the 500,000 Socialist voters and of the 2,000,000 workingmen who instinctively incline our way, should, besides doing much reading and still more thinking, also have a good rifle and the necessary rounds of ammunition in his home and be prepared to back up his ballot with his bullets if necessary."

In the curious presidential election of 1912, when Woodrow Wilson's Democratic Party and Theodore Roosevelt's Bull Moose Party were stealing planks of Eugene Debs' Socialist Party in a wholesale manner, Berger made a hasty retreat from an inflammatory posture to one of calm and dignity. In the course of the campaign, he presented his own scholarly political position paper to forestall defections by Socialists to the upstart and pseudo-Socialist parties of Wilson and Roosevelt. He was painstaking in his efforts to portray himself as a patient gradualist. He wrote: "Why am I going to vote for Debs? As good a man as Eugene V. Debs is, I am not going to vote for him in the sense one is voting for Wilson, Taft, or Roosevelt – I simply vote the ticket of the Socialist Party. I have no hope that the Socialist Party will elect its candidate for President in this election. With us, the Socialist movement and its principles are paramount – not the candidate.

"The Socialist Party stands for the collective ownership of all the social means of production and distribution in the interest of the whole people. Socialists say that this step is the necessary and natural outcome of the concentration of wealth and of the development of capitalism.

"Antagonists of Socialism in the past claimed that collective ownership of an industry was impossible because the personal supervision and control of the owner was absolutely necessary to the success of any enterprise. Today we see that the greatest undertakings are those in which the stockholders and owners have nothing to do with the management of affairs and are only drawing dividends.

"In all of our large industrial concerns – stock companies, railroads, and trusts – business is managed and carried on by a few paid officials. These men might just as well be paid by the state, or the nation (as the case may be), to carry on the enterprise in the interest of the people, as paid by a few wealthy men to carry it on for their individual profit.

"Moreover, we find that whenever the nation, state or community has undertaken to own and manage any large industry, railroad, mine, factory, telegraph, telephone, mill, or canal, etc., this invariably redounded to the benefit of the commonwealth – the inherent weakness of our political spoils system notwithstanding. This idea, carried out gradually and logically, involves a complete change of our economic and political system.

"Political equality under the present system is a snare and delusion. The wage worker who depends upon a master or upon the master class for an opportunity to make a living is not on terms of equality with his master. Political liberty and economic despotism are incompatible. The Socialist Party proposed to supplement our political democracy by industrial democracy.

"No one dreams of abolishing private property. On the contrary, we propose to secure private property to every citizen, to the many million men and women who under the present system have no chance of ever having any. Productive capital only is to be owned in common, by the nation, the state, or the municipality as the exigencies of the case may require. Business will be carried on for use and not for profit. This is the case now in the post office, waterworks, public schools, etc., wherever owned and managed by the people. Such is the aim of the Socialist Party.

"The usual argument in defense of the present vicious system is not that it is right or good but that it is here and must stay. We Socialists think this a foolish assertion. We believe the American people great and strong enough to get rid of anything that is not good or harmful.

"The Capitalist system did not always exist. It followed the Feudal system, which replaced a system based upon ancient chattel slavery. The Capitalist system has undoubtedly done some good in this world. The Capitalist system was useful. It has concentrated economic forces and has made possible the production of wealth on a very large scale. The Capitalist system was a step in the evolution to freedom, but only a step. It has now outlived its usefulness. It has become oppressive to the great majority of the people. Therefore it must pass away.

"The growing restiveness of the people generally – the willingness of the trusts and other great industrial undertakings to accept governmental control – the crumbling of the two great Capi-

talist parties – the fact that the most intelligent of their politicians are trying to steal Socialistic planks and adopt them for their own platforms are so many signs of the change that is upon us.

"The Socialist Party has not a majority as yet. But Socialistic ideas have permeated the great majority. The trusts and economic evolution, on the one hand, and the natural discontent of the people with the lowering of their standard of living, on the other hand, are working for Socialism. Therefore, we laugh at the contention that the Socialist Party is still comparatively small. Every great party has had a small beginning – and the Socialist Party is growing exceedingly fast.

"The phrase of 'getting on the bandwagon' is a stupid phrase. Who is on the 'bandwagon'? Not the common citizen, not the average voter. The scheming financiers, and the sleek office seekers are on the 'bandwagon.'

"To the common citizen, the workingman, the underpaid clerk, the disappointed professional man – to the disinherited of every description – we Socialists say: 'Better vote for what you want, even if you do not get it, than vote for what you do not want and get it!'

"Why should we wait with our work until the majority of the votes is with us? The majority is always indolent and often ignorant. We cannot expect them to be anything else with their present social surroundings. The majority have never brought about consciously and deliberately any great social change. They have always permitted an energetic minority to prepare the way. But the majority was always there when the fact itself was to be accomplished. Therefore, our sole object in state and nation for the next few years is to elect a respectable minority of Socialists.

"We want a Socialist minority respected on account of its numbers — respected because it represents the most advanced economic and political intelligence of the day — respected because it contains the most sincere representatives of the proletariat, the class that has the most to gain and nothing to lose.

"Given such a respectable minority in Congress and in the legislature of every state of the Union within the next few years, the future of our people, the future of this country will be safe."

During Berger's four terms in the Congress, what radicalism he displayed in his legislative speeches and proposals was, for the most part, merely a few years ahead of time. Virtually everything he sponsored would be statutory reality to some degree in the next few decades. He stumped for child labor laws, federal farm subsidies, public works programs of the federal government to relieve unemployment, self-government for the District of Columbia, an eight-hour working day, woman suffrage, government ownership of the radio industry, old age pensions, and government ownership of the railroads. His most extreme domestic proposal was to abolish the United States Senate. As for foreign policy, he concerned himself mainly with international disarmament.

In 1928, when he made his last and unsuccessful bid for re-election to the Congress, he supported the presidential candidacy of Democrat Alfred E. Smith, whose opposition to the prohibition amendment appealed to Berger.

On July 16, 1929, Berger suffered serious injuries when struck by a streetcar in Milwaukee. He died on August 7, 1929.

MARY McLEOD BETHUNE was born on July 10, 1875 in Mayesville, South Carolina, daughter of Patsy McIntosh and Samuel McLeod. She married Albert Bethune. She attended Scotia Seminary in Concord, North Carolina, and the Moody Bible Institute in Chicago, Illinois.

In 1897 and 1898, Bethune was an instructor at the Haines Institute in Augusta, Georgia. From 1899 until 1903, she taught at the Mission School in Palatka, Florida. In 1904, she founded the Daytona (Florida) Normal and Industrial Institute. In 1923, her school merged with the Cookman Institute of Jacksonville and became the Daytona Collegiate Institute. In 1928, the school was renamed the Bethune-Cookman College, and she served as president of the institution until her retirement as president emeritus in 1947. From 1947 until 1955, she was a trustee of Bethune-Cookman and, in 1954 and 1955, was president of the college's advisory board.

From 1936 until 1944, Bethune was director of Negro affairs in the National Youth Administration and a special advisor to President Franklin D. Roosevelt on Minority affairs. In 1942, she was a special assistant to the Secretary of War, helping to select candidates for the first officer's training school for the Women's Auxiliary Army Corps (later called the Women's Army Corps). In 1945, she was a special emissary of the U.S. Department of State to the founding conference of the United Nations in San Francisco. She was on the executive board of the National Committee on Atomic Information. For sixteen years (1937-1953), she was president of the National Council of Negro Women, which she founded. She was president of the United States branch of the United Peoples of Africa. She was a vice-president of the National Association for the Advancement of Colored People and the National Urban League. She was on the board of counsellors of the women's division of the Democratic National Committee. She was president of the Central Life Insurance Company of Tampa and a director of the Afro-American Life Insurance Company of Jacksonville. She was decorated with the Spingarn Award of the NAACP, the Brotherhood Award of the National Conference of Christians and Jews, the Francis A. Drexel Award, the Youth's City Award, the Thomas Jefferson Award, the Haitian Medal of Honor, the Order of the Star of Africa from Liberia, the Robert S. Abbott Memorial Award, the Elijah P. Lovejoy Medal, and the Dorie Miller Gold Cup.

Bethune's affiliations included the American Committee for Protection of Foreign Born ("founded by the Communist Party in order to exploit racial divisions in the United States for its own revolutionary purposes"); the American Committee for Yugoslav Relief ("subversive and Communist"); the American League for Peace and Democracy ("subversive and Communist" – "established . . . in an effort to create public sentiment on behalf of a foreign policy adapted to the interests of the Soviet Union . . . [and] designed to conceal Communist control, in accordance with the new tactics of the Communist International"); the American Round Table on India ("Communist front"); the American Slav Congress ("Moscow-inspired and directed federation of Communist-dominated organizations seeking by methods of propaganda and pressure to subvert the 10,000,000 people in this country of Slavic descent"); the American Youth Congress ("subversive" – "one of the most influential front organizations ever set up by the Communists in this country" – "the Communists were in complete control"); American Youth for a Free World (an American affiliate of the "World Federation of Democratic Youth . . . the Communist clearing house for international student and youth information"); American Youth for Democracy ("subversive and Communist" – "formed . . . for the purpose of exploiting to the advantage of a foreign power the idealism, inexperience, and craving to join which is characteristic of American college youth" – "part of Soviet psychological warfare against the United States"); the Civil Rights Congress ("created and established by the Communist Party as an organization which would utilize defense of civil rights for Party purposes and raise and maintain mass defense and bail funds for Party use"); the Congress of American-Soviet Friendship ("Communist front"); the Coordinating Committee To Lift the [Spanish] Embargo ("one of the numerous Communist-front enterprises which were organized around the Communists' agitation over the Spanish civil war"); the Council Against Intolerance in America (leftist); the Council of Young Southerners ("Communist front" – "has important interlocking personnel with the important Communist front organizations which attempt to attract youth"); the Council on African Affairs ("subversive and Communist"); Daughters of the American Depression ("Communist front"); *Fight* ("official organ of the American League Against War and Fascism, subversive and Communist"); Independent Citizens Committee of the Arts, Sciences, and Professions ("Communist front"); the League of Young Southerners ("Communist front"); the Methodist Federation for Social Action ("the organization's influence has been consistently wielded on behalf of Communist causes and the Communist line as expressed through the party and its innumerable subsidiaries"); Nation Associates (pro-Soviet); the National Citizens' Political Action Committee ("Communist front"); the National Committee To Abolish the Poll Tax ("Communist front"); the National Committee To Win the Peace ("subversive and Communist"); the National Council of American-Soviet Friendship ("subversive and Communist" – "specializing in pro-Soviet propaganda"); the National Emergency Conference ("Communist front"); the National Emergency Conference for Democratic Rights ("Communist front" – "subversive"); the National Federation for Constitutional Liberties ("under Communist Party domination and headed by responsible Party functionaries" – "one of the viciously subversive organizations of the Communist Party"); the National Negro Congress ("subversive and Communist" – "characterized as an organization operating in the field of civil rights under Communist Party domination and headed by responsible Party functionaries"); the National Negro Women's Council ("Communist front"); the National Sharecroppers' Fund ("Communist front"); the Negro People's Committee To Aid Spanish Democracy ("set up by the Communists for propaganda purposes in support of the Spanish loyalists"); People's Peace ("Communist front"); Russian Reconstruction Farms ("Communist enterprise"); *Social Questions Bulletin* (Communist-line publication of the Methodist Federation for Social Action); the Southern Conference Educational Fund (financial backbone of racial agitators including the black power revolutionaries); the Southern Conference for Human Welfare ("a Communist-front organization which seeks to attract southern liberals on the basis of its seeming interest in the problems of the South"); the Southern Negro Youth Congress ("subversive and among the affiliates and committees of the Communist Party, U.S.A., which seeks to alter the form of government of the United States by unconstitutional means"); Testimonial Dinner for Ferdinand C. Smith ("Communist Party affair"); United Front for [Angelo] Herndon ("an adjunct to the International Labor Defense, the legal arm of the Communist Party"); the Washington Committee for Democratic Action ("subversive and Communist"); and the Women's International League for Peace and Freedom (ultra-leftist-pacifist).

In 1946, Bethune received the *New Masses* award for greater inter-racial understanding at a dinner held in her honor. In 1947, *New Masses* gave her an award "for contributions made to promote democracy and inter-racial unity." (The *New Masses* was a weekly journal of the Communist Party.) In 1949, she signed a call for the Communists' Fifth Congress of Youth. She died in May 1955.

In 1960, the Congress of the United States, in a Joint Resolution, authorized the erection in the District of Columbia of a memorial to Mary McLeod Bethune. The project for the monument belongs to the National Council of Negro Women, and the Congressional authorization for its construction date was extended for two years in 1971.

ALICE STONE BLACKWELL was born on September 14, 1857 in East Orange, New Jersey, daughter of Lucy Stone and Henry Blackwell. She was an alumna of Boston University (A.B., 1881). She was the author of *Lucy Stone, Pioneer of Woman's Rights*

(1930). She was the editor of *The Little Grandmother of the Russian Revolution – Catherine Breshkovsky's Own Story* (1917). She was the translator and compiler of *Armenian Poems* (1896 and 1916); *Songs of Russia* (1906); *Songs of Grief and Gladness* (1908); *A Hungarian Poet* (1929); and *Some Spanish-American Poets* (1929). She was co-compiler of *The Yellow Ribbon Speaker* (1911).

In 1883, Blackwell joined the editorial staff of *Woman's Journal*, a magazine owned and operated by her parents. (Her mother, Lucy Stone, was the founder and head of the American Woman Suffrage Association, and the *Woman's Journal* was the mouthpiece for the suffragettes.) In 1909, when her father died, she became editor-in-chief of the *Woman's Journal*, a post she held until 1917, when the *Journal* merged with the *Woman Voter* and the *Headquarters News-Letter* to become the *Woman Citizen,* of which she was a contributing editor. During her long career with the *Journal*, she did the major share of the work involved in the publication; she gathered copy, read proof, and wrote book reviews and columns. And, in the same era (1886-1905), she edited the *Woman's Column*, which was devoted to suffragette items that were distributed free to newspapers throughout the country. In 1890, she effected a merger of two rival suffragette groups, the American Woman Suffrage Association and the National Woman Suffrage Association, into the National American Woman Suffrage Association, which she served as recording secretary for about twenty years. As one of the nation's leading suffragettes, she was in great demand as a lecturer, and she made frequent appearances before legislative committees on behalf of women's suffrage.

Aside from suffrage, Blackwell had a variety of interests that ranged from innocuous do-goodism to extreme radicalism. She took an interest in the suffering Armenians, became secretary of Friends of Armenia, helped find employment for Armenian refugees, and was eventually decorated with the Order of Melusine by Armenian Prince Guy de Lusignan. She was a member of the American League for India's Freedom, the Women's Christian Temperance Union, the ultra-radical American Civil Liberties Union, and the ultra-radical National Association for the Advancement of Colored People, the Women's Trade Union League, and the Anti-Vivisection League. She was a founder of the Friends of Russian Freedom, an anti-Czarist group, and she became a close friend and active supporter of Catherine Breshkovsky, the "little grandmother of the Russian [Bolshevik] Revolution."

When the Nineteenth Amendment to the Constitution of the United States was ratified and women's suffrage became a reality, Blackwell scattered her radical energies in all directions. She was instrumental in founding the League of Women Voters in Massachusetts, a branch that has been historically in the vanguard of the leftist wing of that national organization. She was a staunch supporter of the short-lived Non-Partisan League, a purely Socialist political enterprise. In 1924, she was a presidential elector for the radical Progressive Party ticket of Robert La Follette and Burton K. Wheeler. In the early 1920's she became a dedicated advocate of Sacco and Vanzetti, the murderous anarchists, whose plight as convicted murderers under the death penalty became a *cause célebre* for Communists and other radicals throughout the world. While Vanzetti awaited his execution in Massachusetts State Prison, Blackwell was his most prolific correspondent.

Throughout the 1920's, Blackwell was a visible rabble-rouser at demonstrations and protest meetings in Boston. She bombarded newspaper editors with letters, pleading her different radical causes. She made no secret of either her Socialist ideology or her sympathy for the leftwing radicals who were being uncovered by national and state law enforcement agencies.

Blackwell's affiliations included the American Committee for Protection of Foreign Born ("founded by the Communist Party in order to exploit racial division in the United States for its own revolutionary purposes"); the American Peace Society (ultra-leftist-pacifist); the Citizens' Committee To Free Earl Browder ("a strictly Communist Party affair"); Commonwealth College ("Communist"); the Committee on Indian Civil Rights ("Communist front"); International Labor Defense ("subversive and Communist" – "legal arm of the Communist Party" – "part of an international network of organizations for the defense of Communist lawbreakers"); the Marcus Graham Freedom of the Press Committee (an ultra-radical group in support of an anarchist); the Mary Ware Dennett Defense Committee (ultra-leftist); the Massachusetts Council of American-Soviet Friendship ("subversive and Communist" – "specializing in pro-Soviet propaganda"); the Mother Bloor Celebration Committee ("Communist front"); the National Council of American-Soviet Friendship ("subversive and Communist" – "specializing in pro-Soviet propaganda"); the National Federation for Constitutional Liberties ("under Communist Party domination and headed by responsible Party functionaries" – "one of the viciously sub-

versive organizations of the Communist Party"); the National Mooney-Billings Committee (dominated by Socialists); the National Popular Government League (Socialist); an Open Letter for Closer Cooperation With the Soviet Union (issued by "a group of Communist Party stooges"); Rally To Honor the Eighth Year of United States-Soviet Ties (Communist Party project); Russian Reconstruction Farms ("Communist enterprise"); Russian War Relief ("Communist enterprise"); and United Front for [Angelo] Herndon ("an adjunct to the International Labor Defense, the legal arm of the Communist Party"). She died in March 1950.

MARC BLITZSTEIN was born on March 2, 1905 in Philadelphia, Pennsylvania, son of Anna Levitt and Samuel Blitzstein. He married Eva Goldbeck. He was a student at the University of Pennsylvania (1921-1923), Curtis Institute (1924-1926), and *Akademie der Kuenste* in Berlin (1927). At Curtis, he studied composition under Rosario Scalero, and at the same time studied piano in New York City with Alexander Siloti. In 1926 and 1927, he studied composition with Nadia Boulanger in Paris, and with Arnold Schönberg. He held Guggenheim fellowships in 1940-1941 and 1941-1942. In 1962 and 1963, he held a John Golden fellowship at Bennington College. In 1963 and 1964, he held a Yaddo fellowship and a Chapelbrook Foundation fellowship.

Blitzstein was a musical prodigy. At the age of six, he made his public debut as a pianist. At the age of fifteen, he was a soloist with the Philadelphia Orchestra. In 1927, some of his compositions were performed for the first time in the United States. In 1929, his one-act opera, *Triple Sec*, was presented by the

BLITZSTEIN

Society for Contemporary Music in Philadelphia. In 1930, *Triple Sec* was performed by the Theatre Guild in New York City. In that period, other works by Blitzstein included the one-act operas *Parabola and Circula* (1929) and *The Harpies* (1931), and the choral opera, *The Condemned* (1933). He composed the *Children's Cantata* (1935). In the early 1930's he joined a composers' collective which included two German Communists – Hanns Eisler and Bertoldt Brecht. Brecht encouraged Blitzstein to compose what became one of the most controversial operettas of that era – *The Cradle Will Rock*. He had decided by that time that his music should carry a social message, which, in the lexicon of his environment, meant anti-fascist, anti-capitalist, pro-Communist propaganda. The operetta was sponsored by the Works Progress Administration's Federal Theatre Project, which had become a haven for Red artists. Its producers were Orson Welles and John Houseman. The first performance of *The Cradle Will Rock* was to have taken place in the Maxine Elliott Theatre, but the federal government barred its performance. In order to avoid union difficulties over an unauthorized presentation, *The Cradle Will Rock* was performed in the Venice Theatre. Blitzstein played the score on an upright piano from a stage completely devoid of scenery. The actors performed their roles from seats in the audience. The spectacle became a highlight in Red art circles. The stark nature of the performance (*sans* orchestra, *sans* scenery, *sans* costumes) was a feature of revivals of *The Cradle Will Rock* by the New York City Opera Company in 1947 and 1960.

In 1937, Blitzstein composed *I've Got the Tune*, a radio song-play which was commissioned and produced by the Columbia Broadcasting System. It had a "social message." In 1939, he composed *No For An Answer*, another propaganda piece. It was produced for the first time in 1941 and was revived in 1960, by the New York Opera Company. His symphonic poem, *Freedom Morning*, was performed in 1944 by the Philadelphia Orchestra, and later by the London Symphony, Royal Air Force Symphony, and New York Philharmonic. In 1945 and 1946, his *Airborne Symphony* was performed by the New York City Symphony Orchestra and the Shaw Chorale. It was conducted by fellow-traveler Leonard Bernstein. In 1948, his ballet, *The Guests*, was performed in New York City and in London. In 1949, his *Regina*, an opera based upon fellow-traveler Lillian Hellman's play, *The Little Foxes*, was introduced in New York City.

In the early 1950's, Blitzstein adapted and translated the Kurt Weill-Bertholdt Brecht *Threepenny Opera*. It was first performed at the 1952 Brandeis University music festival. In 1958 and later, it became a highly successful presentation in off-Broadway and other theaters. In 1955, his *Reuben, Reuben*, an opera, was produced in Boston. In 1957, his *This Is the Garden*, a cantata, was performed in Carnegie Hall. In 1958, his symphonic study, *Lear*, was performed by the New York Philharmonic. In 1959, he wrote the music and the lyrics for *Juno and the Paycock*, a musical produced in New York City. In 1960, the Ford Foundation and the Metropolitan Opera Association collaborated in commissioning Blitzstein to compose an opera based upon the Sacco-Vanzetti case of the 1920's, when the plight of the two murderous anarchists became a *cause célèbre* for Communists and fellow-travelers throughout the world.

Among Blitzstein's other works were scores and incidental music for motion pictures, including *Surf and Seaweed* (1931), *Spanish Earth* (1940), *Native Land* (1941), and *Night Shift* (1942); and for plays, including *Julius Caesar* (1937), *Danton* (1939), *Another Part of the Forest* (1946), *Androcles and the Lion* (1946), *A Midsummer Night's Dream* (1958), *A Winter's Tale* (1958), and *Toys in the Attic* (1960). He contributed articles to *Modern Music, Musical Quarterly, Theatre Arts, New York Times, New York Herald Tribune, Boston Transcript, London Listener, Der Querschnitt,* and *La Revue Musicale.* He lectured at the Downtown Music School of New York City, the New School for Social Research, Columbia University, Brandeis University, Bennington College, Dartmouth College, Vassar College, the Brooklyn Institute for Arts and Sciences, the Philadelphia Art Alliance, and the Tanglewood Festival. He was a founder and vice-president of the Arrow Music Press. He received awards for composition from the Newspaper Guild and the National Institute of Arts and Letters — tributes generally accorded to leftists.

Blitzstein was affiliated with the American Council on Soviet Relations ("subversive" — "established by the Communist Party, directed and controlled by the Party, and operated to aid and support Party objectives concerning the defense and support of the Soviet Union"); the American Friends of Spanish Democracy ("Communist front"); the American Friends of the Chinese People ("Communist front"); the American Labor Party ("Communist dissimulation extends into the fields of political parties forming political front organizations such as the . . . American Labor Party"); the American Peace Mobilization ("formed . . . under the auspices of the Communist Party and the Young Communist League" — "one of the most seditious organizations which ever operated in the United States"); the American-Soviet Music Society (leftist); the American Writers Congress ("subversive"); the American Youth for Democracy ("subversive and Communist" — "part of Soviet psychological warfare against the United States"); the Banquet in Honor of Mother Bloor's 85th Birthday ("Communist Party festivity"); the Citizens' Committee to Free Earl Browder ("a strictly Communist Party affair"); the Civil Rights Congress ("created and established by the Communist Party as an organization which would utilize defense of civil rights for Party purposes and raise and maintain mass defense and bail funds for Party use"); the Committee for the Re-election of Benjamin J. Davis (Communist Party candidate for political office); the Committee of Professional Groups for [Earl] Browder and [James W.] Ford ("Communist candidates for president and vice-president of the United States in 1936"); the Conference on Constitutional Liberties in America ("an important part of the solar system of the Communist Party's front organizations"); the Coordinating Committee To Lift the [Spanish] Embargo ("one of the numerous Communist-front enterprises which were organized around the Communists' agitation over the Spanish Civil War"); the Cultural and Scientific Conference for World Peace ("Communist front" — "a propaganda front for Soviet foreign policy and Soviet culture"); *Friday* (Communist-controlled); Friends of the Abraham Lincoln Brigade ("completely controlled by the Communist Party"); the Golden Book of American Friendship with the Soviet Union ("pro-Soviet propaganda enterprise"); the International Labor Defense ("subversive and Communist" – "legal arm of the Communist Party" – "part of an international network of organizations for the defense of Communist lawbreakers"); the Jewish People's Committee ("subversive and Communist" – "an organization which has been nothing more or less than an adjunct of the Communist Party"); the League of American Writers ("subversive and Communist" – "began openly to follow the Communist Party line as dictated by the foreign policy of the Soviet Union"); *Masses and Mainstream* ("a Communist magazine"); May Day Parades in 1946 and 1947 ("Communist demonstrations"); the Musicians Committee To Aid Spanish Democracy ("Communist front"); the National Council of the Arts, Sciences, and Professions ("a Communist front used to appeal to special occupational groups"); the National Federation for Constitutional Liberties ("under Communist Party domination and headed by responsible Party functionaries" – "one of the viciously subversive organizations of the Communist Party"); *New Masses* ("weekly journal of the Communist Party"); the New Theatre League ("Communist front"); Open Letter for Closer Cooperation with the Soviet Union (issued by "a group of Communist Party stooges"); Open Letter in Defense of Harry Bridges ("Communist front"); People's Radio Foundation ("subversive and Communist organization"); People's Songs, Inc. ("subversive"); Progressive Citizens of America ("political Communist front" – "subversive"); Rally To Honor the Eighth Year of United States-Soviet Ties (Communist Party project); the [Morris U.] Schappes Defense Committee ("a front organization with a strictly Communist objective, namely, the defense of a self-admitted

Communist who was convicted of perjury in the courts of New York"); Stage for Action ("subversive"); Statement by American Progressives on the Moscow Trials ("obviously a document concocted in defense of the line of the Communist Party and undoubtedly originated in the headquarters of the Communist Party"); Theatre Arts Committee ("Communist front"); Veterans of the Abraham Lincoln Brigade ("directed, dominated, and controlled by the Communist Party"); and the Washington Committee To Lift [the] Spanish Embargo ("Communist front"). He died in January 1964.

ERNST BOAS was born on February 4, 1891 in Worcester, Massachusetts, son of Marie Krackowizer and Franz Boas. He married the late Helen Sisson. He was an alumnus of Columbia University (B.S., 1910; M.A., 1912; and M.D., 1914). He was the author of *The Heart Rate* (1932); *The Unseen Plague: Chronic Diseases* (1940); *Treatment of the Patient Past Fifty* (1941, 1944, and 1947); and *Coronary Artery Disease* (1949). He was co-author of *The Challenge of Chronic Diseases* (1929).

Intermittently, from 1917 until 1955, Boas was at Columbia University's College of Physicians and Surgeons, as instructor in pathology (1917); instructor in physiology (1920-1921); post-graduate teacher of courses on diseases of the heart (1926-1955); and assistant clinical professor of medicine (1938-1951). From 1917 until 1919, he was an associate physician at Mt. Sinai Hospital, as a Captain in the Medical Reserve Corps of the U.S. Army. In 1929 and 1930, he was an attending physician at Montefiore Hospital. From 1923 until 1929, he was associate editor of *Modern Hospital.*

Boas was affiliated with the American Committee To Save Refugees ("perform[ing] a most valuable function for the international Communist movement"); the American Friends of Spanish Democracy ("Communist front"); the American League for Peace and Democracy ("subversive and Communist" – "established . . . in an effort to create public sentiment on behalf of a foreign policy adapted to the interests of the Soviet Union . . . [and] designed to conceal Communist control, in accordance with the new tactics of the Communist International"); the Citizens' Emergency Conference for Interracial Unity ("Communist front"); the Committee of One Thousand ("Communist created and controlled"); *Consumer Reports* (publication of Consumers Union, a "Communist front"); the Coordinating Committee on Civil Liberties (leftist); the Coordinating Committee To Lift the [Spanish] Embargo ("one of the numerous Communist-front enterprises which were organized around the Communists' agitation over the Spanish Civil War"); the Council for Pan-American Democracy ("subversive and Communist"); the Cultural and Scientific Conference for World Peace ("Communist front" – "a propaganda front for Soviet foreign policy and Soviet culture"); Friends of the Abraham Lincoln Brigade ("completely controlled by the Communist Party"); the Independent Citizens Committee for the Arts, Sciences and Professions ("Communist front"); the Jefferson School of Social Science ("a Communist institution modeled along the lines of the new Communist policy which led to the decision to change the Communist Party into some kind of an educational institution"); the Medical Bureau To Aid Spanish Democracy ("Communist enterprise"); the National Citizens Political Action Committee ("Communist

front"); the National Council of the Arts, Sciences, and Professions ("a Communist front used to appeal to special occupational groups"); the National Emergency Conference ("Communist front"); the National Federation for Constitutional Liberties ("under Communist Party domination and headed by responsible Party functionaries" – "one of the viciously subversive organizations of the Communist Party"); the National Wartime Conference of the Professions, the Sciences, the Arts, the White-Collar Fields ("Communist front"); *New Masses* ("weekly journal of the Communist Party"); Physicians Forum ("Communist front"); Progressive Citizens of America ("political Communist front" – "subversive"); Veterans of the Abraham Lincoln Brigade ("directed, dominated and controlled by the Communist Party"); and the Wartime Budget Conference ("Communist front"). He died in March 1955.

FRANZ BOAS was born on July 9, 1858 in Minden, Westphalia (Germany), son of Sophie Meyer and M. Boas. He married Marie Krackowizer. From 1877 until 1881, he attended the Universities of Heidelberg, Bonn, and Kiel. In 1881, he received his Ph.D. from Kiel. He was the author of *The Growth of Children* (1896 and 1904); *Changes in Form of Body of Descendants of Immigrants* (1911); *The Mind of Primitive Man* (1911 and 1938); *Kultur und Rasse* (1913); *Primitive Art* (1927); *Anthropology and Modern Life* (1928 and 1938); and *Race, Language and Culture* (1940). He was co-author of *General Anthropology* (1938) and *Dakota Grammar* (1941). He was a contributor to *The Making of Man* (1929).

In 1883 and 1884, Boas went on an Arctic expedition as a geographer and spent an entire year living in an Eskimo settlement in Baffin Land. His experiences with the Eskimos led him to decide on a career as an anthropologist. In 1885, upon his return from Baffin Land, he was appointed an assistant at the Royal Ethnological Museum in Berlin, and also docent of geography at the University of Berlin. In 1886, he left Germany to make ethnological investigations of the Indians of British Columbia. He was commissioned for this task by the British Association for the Advancement of Science. From 1888 until 1892, he was docent of anthropology at Clark University. (The appointment at Clark started Boas out on a career wherein he became internationally famous as the founder of the American School of Anthropology. The unusual aspect was that he had not formally studied anthropology and his degrees were taken in geography.) From 1892 until 1895, he was the chief assistant of the Department of Anthropology at the Chicago Exposition. In 1896, he joined the faculty of Columbia University as a lecturer in physical anthropology. Three years later, he became Columbia's first professor of anthropology, and held that position until he retired in 1936. From 1936 until 1938, he was professor emeritus-in-residence at Columbia, and after 1938, professor emeritus. From 1896 until 1905, he was with the department of anthropology in the American Museum of Natural History as assistant curator (1896-1901) and curator (1901-1905). Between 1886 and 1931, he made anthropological investigations in North America, Mexico, and Puerto Rico. At various times, he was president of the American Folklore Society, the New York Academy of Sciences, the American Academy of Arts and Sciences, and the American Anthropological Society.

At Columbia, Boas developed what became widely known as the Boas School of Anthropology. The predominant themes of the Boas School were that (1) environment determined the nature of man; (2) cultural rather than physical characteristics should be the anthropologist's main concern; and (3) the conclusions garnered by the anthropologist in his cultural studies should be presented selectively so as to promote collectivism as the most desirable way of life. His protégés included Gene Weltfish, Ruth Benedict, Margaret Mead, Clyde Kluckhohn, Otto Klineberg, and M.F. Ashley-Montague. The Boas School of anthropologists were committed to promoting Socialism through their teachings and writings on anthropology and through their collaboration with collectivists from the other so-called social sciences. For example, Boas and two of his fellow faculty members, Ruth Benedict and Communist Bernhard J. Stern, helped to produce *The Making of Man*, an anthology which became a basic text in social science classrooms in colleges and universities throughout the United States. Similar studies which emanated from the Boas School gave Boas and his adherents a virtual monopoly on the teaching of anthropology in this country.

Boas was not content to promote collectivism from his university post. He was a political activist during his teaching career and after his retirement. He was a member of the Socialist Party. (As a young man in Germany, Boas had known a radically socialist family environment. His parents were both radical and had been active supporters of the Reds during the 1848 upheaval in Germany.) He was the national chairman of the American Committee for Democracy and Intellectual Freedom ("subversive and un-American" – "a Communist-front organization operation among college teachers and professors"). His other affiliations included the ultra-radical American Civil Liberties Union; the American Committee for Anti-Nazi Literature ("individuals and organizations connected with it identify this committee as a Communist-front organization"); the American League for Peace and Democracy ("subversive and Communist" – "established . . . in an effort to create public sentiment on behalf of a foreign policy adapted to the interests of the Soviet Union . . . [and] designed to conceal Communist control, in accordance with the new tactics of the Communist International"); the American Committee for Protection of Foreign Born ("founded by the Communist Party in order to exploit racial divisions in the United States for its own revolutionary purposes"); the American Committee for Struggle Against War ("Communist front"); the American Committee To Save Refugees ("perform[ing] a most valuable function for the international Communist movement"); the American Council on Soviet Relations ("subversive" – "established by the Communist Party . . . directed and controlled by the Party, and operated to aid and support Party objectives concerning the defense and support of the Soviet Union"); the American Council To Combat Nazi Invasion ("Communist front"); the American Labor Party ("Communist dissimulation extends into the field of political parties forming political front organizations such as the . . . American Labor Party"); American Peace Mobilization ("formed . . . under the auspices of the Communist Party and the Young Communist League" – "one of the most seditious organizations which ever operated in the United States"); the Ameri-

can Society for Cultural Relations with Russia ("Communist front"); the Anti-Nazi Federation of New York ("Communist front"); the Citizens' Committee To Free Earl Browder ("a strictly Communist Party affair"); the Committee on Election Rights ("a Communist front whose function was to agitate for placing the Communist Party on the ballot throughout the United States"); the Committee on Indian Civil Rights ("Communist front"); the Committee To Defend America by Keeping Out of War ("Communist front"); the Conference on Pan American Democracy ("Communist front"); the Council for Pan American Democracy ("subversive and Communist"); Descendants of the American Revolution ("a Communist-front organization set up as a radical imitation of the Daughters of the American Revolution. The Descendants have uniformly adhered to the line of the Communist Party"); the Emergency Peace Mobilization ("Communist front"); *Equality* magazine ("a Communist organ assuming the guise of champion against anti-Semitism"); Films for Democracy ("Communist front"); *Friday* magazine ("Communist-controlled" – "never-failing support of Communist-initiated front organizations, unions, and campaigns"); the German-American Emergency Conference ("Communist front"); the Greater New York Emergency Conference on Inalienable Rights ("Communist front"); International Labor Defense ("subversive and Communist" – "legal arm of the Communist Party" – "part of an international network of organizations for the defense of Communist lawbreakers"); the John Reed Clubs ("out-and-out Communist organizations which preceded the contemporary Communist-front organizations which cater to so-called liberals");

the League of American Writers ("subversive and Communist" – "began openly to follow the Communist Party line as dictated by the foreign policy of the Soviet Union"); the Medical Aid Division of the Spanish Refugee Relief Campaign ("Communist front"); the Medical Bureau and North American Committee To Aid Spanish Democracy ("subversive and un-American"); the National Committee for the Defense of Political Prisoners ("subversive and Communist"); the National Committee To Aid Victims of German Fascism ("an auxiliary of the Communist Party"); the National Conference on Constitutional Liberties in America ("Communist front"); the National Emergency Conference for Democratic Rights ("Communist front" – "subversive"); the National Council To Aid Agricultural Workers ("Communist front"); the National Federation for Constitutional Liberties ("under Communist Party domination and headed by responsible Party functionaries" – "one of the viciously subversive organizations of the Communist Party"); *New Masses* ("weekly journal of the Communist Party"); the New York Conference for Inalienable Rights ("Communist front"); the New York State Conference on National Unity ("Communist front"); the Non-Sectarian Committee for Political Refugees ("affiliate of the International Labor Defense, the legal arm of the Communist Party"); the North American Spanish Aid Committee ("Communist"); People's Front for Peace ("a project . . . in which Communist organizations predominated"); Refugee Scholarship and Peace Campaign ("Communist front"); Russian War Relief ("Communist enterprise"); the [Morris U.] Schappes Defense Committee ("a front organization with a strictly Communist objective, namely, the defense of

a self-admitted Communist who was convicted of perjury in the courts of New York"); *U.S. Week* ("Communist-front publication"); and the Washington Committee To Lift [the] Spanish Embargo ("Communist front"). He died in December 1942.

LOUIS B. BOUDIN was born on February 15, 1874 in Russia, son of Frome Feld and Peter Boudin. He came to the United States in 1891 and was naturalized as an American citizen in 1897. He was married to the late Leah Kanefsky and Anna Pavitt. He was an alumnus of New York University (LL.B., 1896 and LL.M., 1897). He was the author of *The Theoretical System of Karl Marx* (1907); *Socialism and War* (1915); and *Government by Judiciary*, 2 volumes (1932).

Boudin was admitted to the bars of New York State (1898) and the United States (1919). From 1938 until 1952, he was a member of Boudin, Cohn & Glickstein in New York City. He was an unsuccessful candidate for the offices of Chief Justice and Associate Justice of the New York State Court of Appeals and Justice of the Supreme Court of New York State. He was a member of the national committee and the New York executive committee of the Socialist Party. He was on the national board of the Socialist Trade and Labor Alliance. He was a delegate to the International Socialist Congress at Stuttgart (1907) and Copenhagen (1910). He was a co-editor of the radical *American Labor Monthly;* also of *Class Struggle*, an organ of the Communist League of Struggle, a leftist splinter group of Trotskyites, devoted to Leninism and his Bolshevik principles; and also of *New Review*, published from 1913 until 1916 to educate Socialists in the United

States on the theories, principles, methods, and history of the International Socialist Movement.

Boudin spent much of his legal career as an attorney for Communist-controlled unions. He served as a national officer of the Socialists' Intercollegiate Socialist Society and its successor, the League for Industrial Democracy. He was also affiliated with the American Committee for Protection of Foreign Born ("founded by the Communist Party in order to exploit racial divisions in the United States for its own revolutionary purposes"); the American Labor Party ("Communist dissimulation extends into the field of political parties forming political front organizations such as the ... American Labor Party"); the American League for Peace and Democracy ("subversive and Communist" — "established ... in an effort to create public sentiment on behalf of a foreign policy adapted to the interests of the Soviet Union ... [and] designed to conceal Communist control, in accordance with the new tactics of the Communist International"); the American Relief Ship for Spain ("Communist Party front enterprise"); the American-Russian Institute ("subversive" — "Communist" — "specializing in pro-Soviet propaganda"); Celebration of 15 Years of Biro Bidjan ("Communist project"); Consumers Union (in the "solar system of organizations around the [Communist] Party"); the Coordinating Committee To Lift the [Spanish] Embargo ("one of the numerous Communist-front enterprises which were organized around the Communists' agitation over the Spanish civil war"); Friends of the Abraham Lincoln Brigade ("completely controlled by the Communist Party"); Friends of the Soviet Union ("created, directed, and controlled by the Communist Party ... and

operated to aid and support Party objectives concerning the defense and support of the Soviet Union"); the International Committee for Political Prisoners (fundraising enterprise for seditionists); the International Labor Defense ("subversive and Communist" — "legal arm of the Communist Party" — "part of an international network of organizations for the defense of Communist lawbreakers"); the Lawyers' Committee on American Relations with Spain ("during the Spanish Civil War, the Communist Party organized ... [the Lawyers' Committee] as a part of one of its major propaganda campaigns in the Party's entire history in this country"); the National Emergency Conference ("Communist front"); the National Federation for Constitutional Liberties ("under Communist Party domination and headed by responsible Party functionaries" — "one of the viciously subversive organizations of the Communist Party"); the National Lawyers Guild ("the foremost legal bulwark of the Communist Party, its front organizations, and controlled unions"); *New Masses* ("weekly journal of the Communist Party"); the Non-Partisan Committee for the Re-election of Congressman Vito Marcantonio ("Communist front"); the School for Democracy ("established by Communist teachers ousted from the public school system of New York City"); *Science and Society* ("a Communist publication"); and Veterans of the Abraham Lincoln Brigade ("directed, dominated and controlled by the Communist Party"). He died in May 1952.

WALTER RUSSELL BOWIE was born on October 8, 1882 in Richmond, Virginia, son of Elizabeth Branch and Walter Bowie. He married Jean Laverack. He was an alumnus of Harvard University (B.A., 1904 and M.A., 1905) and Virginia Theological Seminary (B.D., 1908). He was ordained a deacon of the Protestant Episcopal Church in 1908, and a priest in 1909. He was the author of *The Master of the Hill: A Biography of John Meigs* (1917); *The Road of the Star* (1922); *Some Open Ways to God* (1924); *The Inescapable Christ* (1925); *The Master: A Life of Jesus Christ* (1928 and 1958); *On Being Alive* (1931); *The Heroism of the Unheroic* (1933); *The Story of the Bible* (1934); *The Renewing Gospel* (1935); *Great Men of the Bible* (1937); *Lift Up Your Hearts* (1939 and 1956); *Remembering Christ* (1940); *The Bible* (1940); *Sunrise in the South, The Life of Mary-Cooke Branch Munford* (1942); *Which Way Ahead?* (1943); *Preaching* (1954); *The Story of the Church* (1955); *Lift Up Your Hearts* (1955); *Finding God Through Saint Paul* (1956); *Christ Be With Me* (1958); *I Believe in Jesus Christ* (1959); *The Living Story of the New Testament* (1959); *Jesus and the Trinity* (1960); *Men of Fire: Torchbearers of the Gospel* (1961); *Women of Light* (1963); *The Living Story of the Old Testament* (1964); *The Compassionate Christ* (1965); *What is Protestantism?* (1965); and *Where You Find God* (1967). He was the author of numerous children's books: *The Children's Year* (1916); *Sunny Windows and Other Sermons for Children* (1921); *The Armour of Youth* (1923); *Chimes and the Children* (1926); *When Jesus Was Born: The Story of Christmas for Little Children* (1928); *The Story of Jesus for Young People* (1937); and *Bible Story for Boys and Girls,* two volumes (1951 and 1952). He was the editor of Henry Sloane Coffin's *Joy in Believing* (1956). He was associate editor of *The Interpreter's Bible.*

From 1908 until 1911, Bowie was rector of Emmanuel Church in Greenwood, Virginia. From 1911 until 1923, he was rector of St. Paul's Church in Richmond, Virginia. From 1923 until 1939, he was rector of Grace Church in New York City. From 1939 until 1950, he was at Union Theological Seminary in New York City as professor of practical theology (1939-1950) and dean of students (1945-1950). From 1950 until 1955, he was professor of homiletics at the Virginia Theological Seminary in Alexandria. In 1935, he was the Lyman Beecher lecturer at Yale Divinity School. In 1939, he was the Hale lecturer at Seabury-Western Theological Seminary. In 1955, he lectured at the Philadelphia Divinity School.

Bowie was affiliated with the American Committee for Non-Participation in Japanese Aggression ("Communist front"); the American Committee for Protection of Foreign Born ("founded by the Communist Party in order to exploit racial divisions in the United States for its own revolutionary purposes"); the American Committee To Save Refugees ("perform[ing] a most valuable function for the international Communist movement"); the American League for Peace and Democracy ("subversive and Communist" — "established . . . in an effort to create public sentiment on behalf of a foreign policy adapted to the interests of the Soviet Union . . . [and] designed to conceal Communist control, in accordance with the new tactics of the Communist International"); the American Society for Cultural Relations with Russia ("Communist front"); Church League for Industrial Democracy (socialist); the Citizens' Committee for Harry Bridges ("Communist"); the Citizens Committee To Free Earl Browder ("a strictly Communist Party affair"); the Citizens'

Emergency Conference for Interracial Unity ("Communist front"); the Civil Rights Congress ("created and established by the Communist Party as an organization which would utilize defense of civil rights for Party purposes and raise and maintain mass defense and bail funds for Party use"); the Committee on Militarism and Education ("supporting organization of the U.S. Congress Against War, completely under the control of the Communist Party"); the Coordinating Committee To Lift the [Spanish] Embargo ("one of the numerous Communist-front enterprises which were organized around the Communists' agitation over the Spanish Civil War"); the Council Against Intolerance in America (leftist); the Emergency Committee for Strikers' Relief (socialist); the Exiled Writers Committee ("Communist enterprise"); the Federal Council of Churches (Red-laden); the Friends of Italian Democracy ("Communist front"); the Greater New York Emergency Conference on Inalienable Rights ("Communist front"); the International Labor Defense ("subversive and Communist" – "legal arm of the Communist Party" – "part of an international network of organizations for the defense of Communist lawbreakers"); the Joint Anti-Fascist Refugee Committee ("subversive and Communist"); the League of American Writers ("subversive and Communist" – "began openly to follow the Communist Party line as dictated by the foreign policy of the Soviet Union"); the National Citizens Committee on Relations with Latin America (dominated by socialists); the National Citizens Political Action Committee ("Communist front"); the National Committee To Abolish the Un-American Activities Committee ("to lead and direct the Communist Party's 'Operation Aboli-

tion' campaign"); the National Committee To Repeal the McCarran Act ("Communist front and subversive"); the National Council of the Arts, Sciences, and Professions ("a Communist front used to appeal to special occupational groups"); the National Emergency Conference for Democratic Rights ("Communist front" – "subversive"); the National Federation for Constitutional Liberties ("under Communist Party domination and headed by responsible Party functionaries" – "one of the viciously subversive organizations of the Communist Party"); the Non-Intervention Citizens Committee (dominated by Socialists and Communists); the North American Committee To Aid Spanish Democracy ("Communist"); Open Letter in Defense of Harry Bridges ("Communist front"); *Protestant* ("with an eye to religious groups, the Communists have formed religious fronts such as the Protestant"); *Protestant Digest* ("a magazine which has faithfully propagated the Communist Party line under the guise of being a religious journal"); the [Morris U.] Schappes Defense Committee ("a front organization with a strictly Communist objective, namely, the defense of a self-admitted Communist who was convicted of perjury in the courts of New York"); the United American-Spanish Aid Committee ("Communist"); Veterans of the Abraham Lincoln Brigade ("directed, dominated and controlled by the Communist Party"); War Resisters League (leftist-pacifist); and the Washington Committee to Lift [the] Spanish Embargo ("Communist front"). He died in April 1969.

DWIGHT J. BRADLEY was born on December 16, 1889 in Yankton, South Dakota, son of Lillian Jaques and Dan Bradley. He married Kathryn Culver and Elizabeth Whiting. He was an alumnus of

Oberlin College (A.B., 1912) and Pacific School of Religion (B.D., 1915). He was a student at Rollins College (1909-1910); Western Reserve University (1910-1911); and Oberlin Theological Seminary (1912-1913). He was ordained a minister of the Congregational Church in 1915. He was the author of *The Recovery of Religion*, (1929); *Creative Worship* (1930); *Fellowship of Prayer* (1932); *The Secret Stair* (1937); *Highways of the Spirit* (1937); *By Faith* (1938); *Our Times – What Has The Bible to Say?* (1940); *Freedom of the Soul* (1943); and *Your Problem – Can It be Solved?* (1945). He was co-author of *Adventure Eternal* (1937).

In 1914 and 1915, Bradley was an assistant at Plymouth Church in Oakland, California. He was minister of Highland Church in Cleveland, Ohio (1915-1917); First Church in El Paso, Texas (1917-1920); First Church in Webster Groves, Missouri (1920-1930); First Church in Newton Centre, Massachusetts (1930-1934); and the Union Church in Boston (1934-1938). From 1933 until 1938, he was at Andover-Newton Theological School as associate professor of worship (1933-1934) and professor of social ethics (1934-1938). From 1938 until 1943, he was director of the Council for Social Action of the Congregational Christian Churches in the United States. From 1944 until 1946, he was director of the Religious Associates of the National Citizens Political Action Committee. From 1946 until 1957, he was a consultant on personal and group adjustment and a lecturer.

Bradley was active in the Red-laden Federal Council of Churches. His affiliations included the American Committee for Protection of Foreign Born ("founded by the Communist Party in order to exploit racial divisions in the United States for its own revolutionary purposes"); the American Committee in Aid of Chinese Industrial Cooperatives ("Communist-controlled"); the American Council for a Democratic Greece ("subversive and Communist"); the American Friends of Spanish Democracy ("Communist front"); the American League for Peace and Democracy ("subversive and Communist" – "established . . . in an effort to create public sentiment on behalf of a foreign policy adapted to to the interests of the Soviet Union . . . [and] designed to conceal Communist control, in accordance with the new tactics of the Communist International"); the Citizens Emergency Conference for Interracial Unity (leftist); the Committee for a Boycott Against Japanese Aggression ("the Committee was featured in the *Daily Worker*, official organ of the Communist Party, and in that paper alone"); the Committee for a Democratic Far Eastern Policy ("Communist"); the Coordinating Committee To Lift the [Spanish] Embargo ("one of the numerous Communist-front enterprises which were organized around the Communists' agitation over the Spanish Civil War"); the Joint Anti-Fascist Refugee Committee ("subversive and Communist"); the Medical Bureau and North American Committee to Aid Spanish Democracy ("subversive and un-American"); the National Citizens' Political Action Committee ("Communist front"); the National Federation for Constitutional Liberties ("under Communist Party domination and headed by responsible Party functionaries" – "one of the viciously subversive organizations of the Communist Party"); the National Religion and Labor Foundation ("Communist front"); an Open Letter in Defense of Harry Bridges ("Communist front"); *Protestant* ("with an eye to religious groups, the Communists have formed religious fronts such as the *Protestant*"); the *Protestant Digest* ("a magazine which has faithfully propagated the Communist Party line under the guise of being a religious journal"); Russian War Relief ("Communist enterprise"); Spanish Refugee Appeal ("subversive" – "Communist front"); Southern Conference for Human Welfare ("a Communist front organization which seeks to attract Southern liberals on the basis of its seeming interest in the problems of the South"); the Union of Concerted Peace Efforts ("Communist front"); and the Win-the-Peace Conference ("Communist front"). He died in December 1957.

SOPHONISBA PRESTON BRECK-INRIDGE was born on April 1, 1866 in Lexington, Kentucky, daughter of Issa Desha and William Breckinridge. She was an alumnus of Wellesley College (S.B., 1888) and the University of Chicago (Ph.M., 1897; Ph.D., 1901; and J.D., 1904). From 1897 until 1901, she studied political science on a fellowship. In 1895, she was admitted to the Kentucky bar. She was the author of *Legal Tender, A Study in American Monetary History* (1901); *New Homes for Old* (1921); *Madeline McDowell Breckinridge, a Leader in the New South* (1921); *Family Welfare Work in a Metropolitan Community: Selected Case Records* (1924); *Public Welfare Administration: Select Documents* (1927 and 1938); *Marriage and the Civic Rights of Women: Separate Domicile and Independent Citizenship* (1931); *Women in the Twentieth Century: A Study of Their Political, Social and Economic Activities* (1933); *The Family and the State: Select Documents* (1934); *Social Work and the Courts: Select Statutes and Judicial Decisions* (1934); and *The Illinois Poor*

Law and Its Administration (1939). She was co-author of *The Delinquent Child and the Home* (1912); *The Modern Household* (1912); and *Truancy and Non-Attendance in the Chicago Schools* (1917). She was co-founder (1927) and editor (1927-1948) of *Social Service Review*. She contributed articles to *Journal of Political Economy*.

For a few years, until 1894, Breckinridge taught high school mathematics in Washington, D.C. In 1894 and 1895, she studied law in her father's office. From 1901 until 1933, she was at the University of Chicago as docent in political science (1901-1903); assistant dean of women (1902); instructor (1903-1909); assistant professor of social economy (1909-1920); associate professor (1920-1925); professor (1925-1929); dean of pre-professional social service students and Samuel Deutsch professor of public welfare administration (1929-1933); and dean of the College of Arts, Literature and Science (1923-1929). Although she retired in 1933 as professor emeritus, she continued teaching courses in public welfare for the next nine years. From 1907 until 1920, she was a teacher in and dean of the Chicago School of Civics and Philanthropy, which, in 1920, was incorporated into the University of Chicago as the Graduate School of Social Service Administration.

From 1907 until 1920, Breckinridge spent a part of each year as a resident of Hull House, which Jane Addams had made a center of Fabian Socialism and other forms of leftist-radicalism. Breckinridge was one of the Chicago area's busiest social workers. She interested herself in housing problems, juvenile courts, child labor laws, immigrants, women's trade unions, women's wages and hours, and public health. She was an early and active member of the radical-led National Association for the Advancement of Colored People. She was a vice president of the National American Woman Suffrage Association. She was a member of the Women's Peace Party and a delegate from that leftist group to the Women's Peace Congress at The Hague in 1915. From that Congress, she was an instrumental founder of the ultra-leftist-pacifist Women's International League for Peace and Freedom. Along the way, she was active in other leftist-oriented groups, such as the League of Women Voters, the Women's Trade Union League, the American Association of University Women, the Urban League, the American Association of Social Workers, and the Illinois Citizens Political Action Committee.

Breckinridge's other affiliations included the Abraham Lincoln School ("an adjunct of the Communist Party"); the American Association for a Democratic Germany (leftist); the ultra-radical American Civil Liberties Union; the American Committee for Democracy and Intellectual Freedom ("subversive and un-American" – "a Communist-front organization operating among college teachers and professors"); the American Committee for the Protection of Foreign Born ("founded by the Communist Party in order to exploit racial divisions in the United States for its own revolutionary purposes"); the American Council on Soviet Relations ("subversive" – "established by the Communist Party . . . directed and controlled by the Party, and operated to aid and support Party objectives concerning the defense and support of the Soviet Union"); the American League for Peace and Democracy ("subversive and Communist" – "established . . . in an effort to create public sentiment on behalf of a foreign policy adapted to the interests of the Soviet Union . . . [and] designed to conceal Communist control, in accordance with the new tactics of the Communist International"); the Chicago Committee for the Struggle Against War ("Communist front"); the Chicago Repertory Group ("Communist front"); the Chicago Workers Committee on Unemployment (pro-Socialist); the China Aid Council ("Communist-controlled"); the Citizens Committee To Free Earl Browder ("a strictly Communist Party affair"); the Civil Liberties Bureau (Red-controlled pacifist group); the Civil Rights Congress ("created and established by the Communist Party as an organization which would utilize defense of civil rights for Party purposes and raise and maintain mass defense and bail funds for Party use"); the Committee for Citizenship Rights ("to protect Communist subversion from any penalties under the law"); the Committee on Militarism in Education (a supporting organization of the U.S. Congress Against War, "completely under the control of the Communist Party"); the Coordinating Committee To Lift the [Spanish] Embargo ("one of the numerous Communist-front enterprises which were organized around the Communists' agitation over the Spanish Civil War"); the Greater New York Emergency Conference on Inalienable Rights ("Communist front"); the Mary Ware Dennett Defense Committee (ultra-leftist); the Medical Bureau and North American Committee To Aid Spanish Democracy ("subversive and un-American"); the Mother Bloor Celebration Committee ("Communist Party festivity"); the National Consumers League (Socialist-controlled); the National Council of American-Soviet Friendship ("subversive and Communist" – "specializing in pro-Soviet propaganda"); the National Emergency Conference ("Communist front"); the National Federation for Constitutional Liberties ("under Communist Party domination and headed by responsible Party functionaries" – "one of the viciously subversive organizations of the Communist Party"); the National Negro Congress ("subversive and Communist" – "characterized as an organization operating in the field of civil rights under Communist Party domination and headed by responsible Party functionaries"); Russian Reconstruction Farms ("Communist enterprise"); the Spanish Refugee Appeal ("subversive" – "Communist front"); and Workers Defense League (defending political undesirables who are subject to deportation). She died in July 1948.

LOUIS BROMFIELD was born on December 27, 1896 in Mansfield, Ohio, son of Annette Coulter and Charles Bromfield. He married Mary Wood. He was a student at Cornell University, Ohio Northern University, and Columbia University. He was the author of *The Green Bay Tree* (1924); *Possession* (1925); *Early Autumn* (1926); *A Good Woman* (1927); *The House of Women*, play (1927 and 1929); *The Strange Case of Miss Annie Spragg* (1928); *Awake and Rehearse; Twenty-four Hours; A Modern Hero; The Farm* (1933); *Here Today*, four novelettes (1934); *De Luxe*, play (1935); *Times Have Changed*, play (1935); *The Man Who Had Everything; The Rains Came* (1937); *It Takes All Kinds*, novelettes and stories (1938); *England, A Dying Oligarchy*, pamphlet (1938); *Night in Bombay* (1939); *Wild Is the River* (1941); *Until the Day Break* (1942); *Mrs. Parkington* (1943); *What Became of Anna Bolton* (1944); *The World We Live In*, stories (1944); *Pleasant Valley* (1945); *A Few Brass Tacks* (1946); *Agricultural Economics; The*

World We Live In, stories (1946); *Kenny,* stories (1947); *Colorado* (1947); *Malabar Farm* (1948); *The Wild Country* (1948); *Out of the Earth* (1950); *Mr. Smith* (1951); *A New Pattern for a Tired World* (1954); *From My Experience: The Pleasures and Miseries of Life on a Farm* (1955); and *Animals and Other People* (1955). He was a contributor to *Bobbed Hair.* He was awarded a Pulitzer Prize in 1926 for *Early Autumn.*

During World War I, Bromfield served in the French Army as an ambulance driver and as liaison between French and British forces. Between 1919 and 1923, he held a variety of jobs. He worked for the New York City News Association and the Associated Press. He was a private tutor; a foreign editor and critic for *Musical America*; a theater, music, and art critic for *Bookman;* assistant to a theatrical producer; advertising manager for the publishing house of G.P. Putnam's Sons; and an original staff member of *Time* magazine.

From 1923 until 1939, Bromfield pursued his writing career while living in France, with the exception of a few years he spent living in India. In 1939, he returned to the United States and he established a cooperative farm near Mansfield, Ohio. His interest in farming caused him to become politically active as a Democrat, but he was a severe critic of the New Deal's farm program. Because of his dissatisfaction with the manner in which the Roosevelt Administration handled the food production program during World War II, he left the Democratic Party in 1944 and joined the Republicans.

Although Bromfield was an expatriate until 1939, he accumulated an impressive number of leftist affiliations in the following few years. He was affiliated with Allied Voters Against Coudert ("example of the Communist apparatus for character assassination in operation against one who opposed the efforts of the Communist Party to undermine and destroy American democracy"); the American Committee for Protection of Foreign Born ("founded by the Communist Party in order to exploit racial divisions in the United States for its own revolutionary purposes"); the American Committee To Save Refugees ("subversive and Communist" – "perform[ing] a most valuable function for the international Communist movement"); the American Council on Soviet Relations ("subversive" – "established by the Communist Party . . . directed and controlled by the Party, and operated to aid and support Party objectives concerning the defense and support of the Soviet Union"); the American League for Peace and Democracy ("subversive and Communist" – "established . . . in an effort to create public sentiment on behalf of a foreign policy adapted to the interests of the Soviet Union . . . [and] designed to conceal Communist control, in accordance with the new tactics of the Communist International"); the American Rescue Ship Mission ("Communist Party project"); the American Round Table on India ("Communist front"); the Celebration of the 25th Anniversary of the Red Army ("Communist enterprise"); the Conference for the Release of International Volunteers in Spanish and French Prison Camps ("Communist enterprise"); the Congress of American-Soviet Friendship ("Communist front"); the Coordinating Committee To Lift the [Spanish] Embargo ("one of the numerous Communist front enterprises which were organized around the Communists' agitation over the Spanish Civil War"); Federal Union (leftist-globalist); Film Audiences for Democracy ("Communist front"); Films for Democracy ("Communist front"); Friends of the Abraham Lincoln Brigade ("completely controlled by the Communist Party"); the German-American Emergency Conference ("Communist front"); the Joint Anti-Fascist Refugee Committee ("subversive and Communist"); the League of American Writers ("subversive and Communist" – "began openly to follow the Communist Party line as dictated by the foreign policy of the Soviet Union"); the National Council of American-Soviet Friendship ("subversive and Communist" – "specializing in pro-Soviet propaganda"); the National Wartime Conference of the Professions, the Sciences, the Arts, the White-Collar Fields ("Communist front"); the North American Spanish Aid Committee ("Communist"); Russian War Relief ("Communist enterprise"); [Morris U.] Schappes Committee ("a front organization with a strictly Communist objective, namely, the defense of a self-admitted Communist who was convicted of perjury in the courts of New York"); *Soviet Russia Today* ("Communist-controlled publication"); the ultra-radical Union for Democratic Action; the United American Spanish Aid Committee ("Communist"); the United States-Soviet Friendship Congress ("Communist front"); the ultra-leftist United World Federalists; and Veterans of the Abraham Lincoln Brigade ("directed, dominated and controlled by the Communist Party"). He died in March 1956.

VAN WYCK BROOKS was born on February 16, 1886 in Plainfield, New Jersey, son of Sarah Ames and Charles Brooks. He was married to the late Eleanor Stimson. His second wife was Gladys Billings. He was an alumnus of Harvard University (A.B., 1907). He was

BROOKS

the author of *The Wine of the Puritans: A Study of Present-Day America* (1909); *The Malady of the Ideal* (1913); *John Addington Symonds* (1914); *The World of H.G. Wells* (1915); *America's Coming-of-Age* (1915); *Letters and Leadership* (1918); *The Ordeal of Mark Twain* (1920 and 1933); *The Pilgrimage of Henry James* (1925); *Emerson and Others* (1927); *The Life of Emerson* (1932); *Sketches in Criticism* (1932); *Three Essays on America* (1934); *On Literature Today* (1941); *Opinions of Oliver Allston* (1941); *A Chilmark Miscellany* (1948); *The Writer in America* (1953); *Scenes and Portraits, Memories of Childhood and Youth* (1954); *John Sloan, A Painter's Life* (1955); *Helen Keller, A Sketch for a Portrait* (1956); *Days of the Phoenix: The Nineteen-Twenties I Remember* (1957); *From a Writer's Notebook* (1958); *The Dream of Arcadia: American Writers and Artists in Italy, 1760-1915* (1958); *Howells: His Life and World* (1959); *From the Shadow of the Mountain: My Post-Meridian Years* (1961); *Fenollosa and His Circle, With Other Essays in Biography* (1962); and *An Autobiography*, published posthumously (1965). He was also author of a five-volume series, "Makers and Finders: A History of the Writer in America, 1800-1915," including *The Flowering of New England, 1815-1865* (1936 and 1946); *New England Indian Summer, 1865-1915* (1940); *The World of Washington Irving* (1944); *The Times of Melville and Whitman* (1947); and *The Confident Years, 1885-1915* (1952 and 1955).

In 1907 and 1908, Brooks worked as a journalist in England. He also worked as a literary agent for Curtis-Brown and Company, literary agents. From 1908 until 1911, he worked for the *Standard Dictionary, Collier's Encyclopedia,* and *World's Work.* From 1911 until 1913, he was at Stanford University as an instructor in English. In 1913 and 1914, he was a teacher for the Workers' Educational Association of South Norwood in England. From 1914 until 1918, he was a translator of French books for the publishing house of Century Company. In 1917 and 1918, he was associate editor of *The Seven Arts.* From 1920 until 1924, he was literary editor of *The Freeman.* From 1926 until 1931, he suffered a period of mental illness, but during this time he wrote two articles for *Encyclopaedia Britannica*, one for the *Dictionary of American Biography*, and for about a year, a weekly paper for the *Independent.* In 1923, he won the Dial prize for distinguished critical work. In 1937, for his *The Flowering of New England*, he won the Pulitzer Prize for history and the National Book Award. In 1946, he received the Gold Medal of the National Institute of Arts and Letters. In 1954, he received the Theodore Roosevelt Medal.

Throughout a great part of his life, Brooks was a member of the Socialist Party. He was affiliated with the ultra-radical American Civil Liberties Union; the American Committee for Democracy and Intellectual Freedom ("subversive and un-American" – "a Communist front organization operating among college teachers and professors"); the American Committee for Non-Participation in Japanese Aggression ("Communist front"); the American Committee for Protection of Foreign Born ("founded by the Communist Party in order to exploit racial divisions in the United States for its own revolutionary purposes"); the American Committee for Spanish Freedom ("Communist"); the American Committee for Yugoslav Relief ("subversive and Communist"); the American Committee To Save Refugees

271

("perform[ing] a most valuable function for the international Communist movement"); the American Friends of Spanish Democracy ("Communist front"); the American Friends of the Soviet Union ("Communist front" – "primarily concerned with the carrying on of propaganda in behalf of the Soviet Union and its system of government"); the American League for Peace and Democracy ("subversive and Communist" – "established in an effort to create public sentiment on behalf of a foreign policy adapted to the interests of the Soviet Union ... [and] designed to conceal Communist control, in accordance with the new tactics of the Communist International"); the American Relief for Greek Democracy (leftist); the American Society for Technical Aid to Spanish Democracy ("Communist front"); the American Student Union ("without exception ... supported defense of teachers and students charged with Communist activity" – "pliable instrument in the hands of the Communist Party"); the Committee for a Boycott Against Japanese Aggression ("the committee was featured in the *Daily Worker*, official organ of the Communist Party, and in that paper alone"); the Committee for a Democratic Far Eastern Policy ("Communist"); the Committee of One Thousand ("Communist-created and controlled"); the Committee To Save Spain and China ("Communist front"); the Congress of American Revolutionary Writers ("subversive and Communist"); the Congress of American-Soviet Friendship ("Communist front"); the Coordinating Committee To Lift the [Spanish] Embargo ("one of the numerous Communist front enterprises which were organized around the Communist agitation over the Spanish Civil War"); the Council for Pan-American Democracy ("subver-

sive and Communist"); Freedom House ("highly influential center for anti-anti-Communism"); Friends of Italian Democracy ("Communist front"); the Golden Book of American Friendship with the Soviet Union ("pro-Soviet propaganda enterprise"); the Greater New York Emergency Conference on Inalienable Rights ("Communist front"); the Hiroshima Commemorative Committee (ultra-leftist); the Independent Citizens Committee of the Arts, Sciences and Professions ("Communist front"); Jewish Black Book Committee ("Communist front"); the League of American Writers ("subversive and Communist" – "began openly to follow the Communist Party line as dictated by the foreign policy of the Soviet Union"); the Medical Bureau and North American Committee To Aid Spanish Democracy ("subversive and un-American"); the ultra-radical National Association for the Advancement of Colored People; the National Committee To Abolish the Un-American Activities Committee ("to lead and direct the Communist Party's 'operation abolition' campaign"); the National Committee To Combat Anti-Semitism ("Communist front"); the National Council of American-Soviet Friendship ("subversive and Communist" – "specializing in pro-Soviet propaganda"); the National Emergency Conference ("Communist front"); the National Emergency Conference for Democratic Rights ("Communist front" – "subversive"); the National Federation for Constitutional Liberties ("under Communist Party domination and headed by responsible Party functionaries" – "one of the viciously subversive organizations of the Communist Party"); the National Writers Congress ("Communist front"); the Nation Associates (pro-Soviet); *New Masses* ("weekly journal of the Communist Party"); the Non-

Partisan Committee for the Re-election of Congressman Vito Marcantonio ("Communist front"); the Pablo Neruda [Chilean Communist] Defense Committee (Communist Party project); the Progressive Citizens of America ("political Communist front" – "subversive"); Rally To Honor the 8th Year of United States-Soviet Ties ("Communist Party enterprise"); the [Morris U.] Schappes Defense Committee ("a front organization with a strictly Communist objective, namely, the defense of a self-admitted Communist who was convicted of perjury in the courts of New York"); *Soviet Russia Today* ("Communist-controlled publication"); the United American Spanish Aid Committee ("Communist"); the United World Federalists ("the most prestigious group of fellow-travelers and dupes working for world government at the expense of United States sovereignty"); Veterans of the Abraham Lincoln Brigade ("directed, dominated, and controlled by the Communist Party"); the Washington Committee To Lift [the] Spanish Embargo ("Communist front"); the Western Writers' Congress ("Communist front"); and the Writers' and Artists' Committee for Medical Aid to Spain ("a Communist front set up for the purpose of agitation and propaganda"). He died in May 1963.

HEYWOOD CAMPBELL BROUN was born on December 7, 1888 in Brooklyn, New York, son of Henriette Brose' and Heywood Broun. He was married to and divorced from Ruth Hale. His second wife was Connie Madison, *neé* Constantina Maria Incoronata Fruscella. He attended Harvard University (1906-1910). He was the author of *A.E.F. – With General Pershing and American Forces* (1918); *Seeing Things at Night* (1921); *Pieces of Hate and Other Enthusiasms* (1922); *The Boy Grew Older* (1922); *The Sun Field* (1923); *Sitting on the World* (1924); *Gandle Follows His Nose* (1926); and *It Seems to Me* (1935). He was co-author of *Noncensorship* (1922); *Anthony Comstock, Roundsman of the Lord* (1927); and *Christians Only: A Study in Prejudice* (1931).

From 1910 until 1912, Broun was a reporter for the *New York Morning Telegraph*. In 1912, he traveled to China and Japan with a threatrical company. From 1912 until 1921, he was with the *New York Tribune* as sportswriter (1912-1915), drama critic (1915-1917), war correspondent (1917-1919), and literary editor and drama critic (1919-1921). From 1921 until 1928, he wrote a daily column, "It Seems to Me," for the *New York World*. From 1928 until 1939, his column appeared in the *New York Telegram* (later the *World-Telegram*) and was syndicated by the Scripps-Howard newspaper chain. In 1939, he was publisher of *Broun's Nutmeg*, a literary and humorous weekly. Between 1925 and 1931, on an irregular basis, he wrote columns for *The Nation, New Republic*, and the *C.I.O. News*. He lectured on drama at Columbia University and at the extremely radical Rand School.

As a columnist, Broun was one of the most widely read journalists in America. He championed the cause of Eugene V. Debs, Sacco and Vanzetti, and other projects favored by the Communist Party and the rest of the far left in America. He was a steady apologist for the Communist Party in the United States, and for the Stalinist regime in the Soviet Union. He was a member of the Socialist Party and in 1930 was an unsuccessful candidate for Congress on the Socialist Party ticket. In 1933, he was the major force behind the founding of the American Newspaper Guild, and served as the Guild's president from 1933 until 1939.

In 1938, not under oath, Broun denied present or past membership in the Communist Party. At least three former officials of the Communist Party, all of whom testified under oath, remembered Broun as either a member of the Party or a highly trustworthy collaborator. In 1939, Joseph Zack Kornfedder testified that in his opinion, the Communist Party's influence in the American Newspaper Guild was due in great part to the presence of Heywood Broun. As for Broun's membership in the Communist Party, Kornfedder testified before the Dies Committee: "I think the first time he was a party member was back in 1928, if I remember rightly. He was a member for, I think, about two years and dropped out. Later on he worked along with them and probably was a member, but now he is at odds with them again, it seems. He broke with them on account of the new [Stalin-Hitler] pact."

Benjamin Gitlow, another former Communist Party official, also testified in September 1939. He was asked: "Do you know that up until August 24, 1939, Mr. Broun was, let us say, universally known in trade-union circles to be carrying out Communist Party policies?" Gitlow replied: "It is generally stated he was carrying out Communist Party policies in the trade-unions." In October 1939, Maurice Malkan, also before the Dies Committee, stated he did not believe Kornfedder was accurate in his recollection of Broun's Communist Party membership. Malkan said: "He did not join in 1928; he joined in 1933 . . . . " Malkan told the Committee that he helped to organize the American Newspaper Guild. He stated definitely that Broun was a Communist in 1933, but he also described Broun as: "One of those Party members who never came to Party headquarters, because he did not want it known that he was a member of the Communist Party." It was Malkan's estimate that Broun left the Party sometime in 1939. (In his *Return to My Father's House*, published in 1972, Malkan again referred to Broun as a Communist. Malkan wrote: "I first knew Broun as an old-time Socialist, who was then working on the *New York World*. According to communist records that I handled, Broun had been a dues-paying Party member since April 1933.")

There is some evidence of an extrinsic nature that Broun, if he had been a member, left the Communist Party as did others on the issue of the Hitler-Stalin Pact. In any case, in the last year of his life, Broun was converted to Catholicism.

Broun's affiliations included the ultra-radical American Civil Liberties Union; the American Committee for Protection of Foreign Born ("founded by the Communist Party in order to exploit racial divisions in the United States for its own revolutionary purposes"); the American Friends of Spanish Democracy ("Communist front"); the American League Against War and Fascism ("subversive and Communist" – "established in the United States in an effort to create public sentiment on behalf of a foreign policy adapted to the interests of the Soviet Union"); the American League for Peace and Democracy ("subversive and Communist" – "established . . . in an effort to create public sentiment on behalf of a foreign policy adapted to the interests of the Soviet Union . . . [and] designed to conceal Communist control, in accordance with the new tactics of the Communist International"); the American Youth

Congress ("subversive" – "one of the most influential front organizations ever set up by the Communists in this country" – "the Communists were in complete control"); the Anti-Nazi Federation of New York ("Communist front"); the Ben Leider Memorial Fund ("Communist front, honoring the first American Communist to die in the Spanish Civil War"); the Berger National Foundation (socialist organization); Book Union ("distributors of Communist literature" – "Communist [Party] book club"); Call for the 5th Congress of Youth in 1939 (a Communist Party enterprise); the Citizens Committee for Striking Seamen ("the composition of the citizens committee clearly indicates its Communist nature"); the Committee for Support of *Il Nuovo Mondo* (pro-Communist paper published for Italians in the United States); the Conference for Progressive Political Action (socialist-dominated); Consumers Union (in the "solar system of organizations around the [Communist] Party"); the Coordinating Committee To Lift the [Spanish] Embargo ("one of the numerous Communist-front enterprises which were organized around the Communists' agitation over the Spanish Civil War"); the Council for Pan-American Democracy ("subversive and Communist"); Descendants of the American Revolution ("a Communist-front organization set up as a radical imitation of the Daughters of the American Revolution. The Descendants have uniformly adhered to the line of the Communist Party"); the Emergency Committee for Strikers Relief (socialist); the Federation of Unemployed Workers Leagues of America (Communist-controlled); Film Audiences for Democracy ("Communist front"); Films for Democracy ("Communist front"); Friends of the Abraham Lincoln Brigade ("completely controlled by the Communist Party"); the Friends of the Soviet Union ("created, directed, and controlled by the Communist Party . . . and operated to aid and support Party objectives concerning the defense and support of the Soviet Union"); the League for Industrial Democracy (socialist); the Medical Bureau and North American Committee To Aid Spanish Democracy ("subversive and un-American"); the *Mid-Western Record* (Communist Party publication); the Mother Ella Reeve Bloor Banquet ("Communist Party festivity"); the National Committee for the Defense of Political Prisoners ("subversive and Communist"); the National Committee to Aid Victims of German Fascism ("an auxiliary of the Communist Party"); the National Congress for Unemployment and Social Insurance ("Communist front"); the National Scottsboro Action Committee ("Communist Party was in complete control"); the National Student League (the Communists' front organization for students"); the National [Tom] Mooney Council of Action (Communist-controlled); *New Masses* ("weekly journal of the Communist Party"); New York Tom Mooney Committee ("Communist front"); the Non-Partisan Committee for the Re-election of Congressman Vito Marcantonio ("Communist front"); the Political Prisoners Bail Fund Committee ("the personnel and the objectives . . . make it obvious . . . that the organization was a Communist Party front"); the War Resisters League (leftist-pacifist); Workers International Relief ("Communist front"); and Young Pioneers ("Communist"). He died in December 1939.

EUGENE L[EONARD] BURDICK was born on December 12, 1918, in

Sheldon, Iowa, son of Marie Ellerbrook and Jack Burdick. He married Carol Warren. He was an alumnus of Stanford University (B.A., 1942) and Oxford University in England, where he was a Rhodes Scholar (Ph.D., 1950). He was the author of *The Ninth Wave* (1956); *The Blue of Capricorn* (1961); *The 480* (1964); and *Nina's Book* (1965). He was co-author of *The Ugly American* (1958); *Fail-Safe* (1962); and *Sarkhan* (1964). He was co-editor of *American Voting Behavior* (1959).

From 1948 until 1950, while at Oxford, Burdick was a correspondent for the *New York Times* and *New Yorker* magazine. From 1950 until 1965, he was successively an assistant professor, associate professor, and professor of political theory at the University of California at Berkeley. In 1950 and 1951, he was a staff member of the Naval War College at Newport, Rhode Island. In 1946, he held a Houghton-Mifflin Literary Fellowship. He was a fellow of the leftist-oriented Center for the Advancement of the Study of Behavioral Sciences. From 1957 until 1965, he was a consultant to the ultra-leftist Center for the Study of Democratic Institutions. He served as a consultant on foreign policy to the U.S. Department of State. He was a member of the ultra-radical Americans for Democratic Action. He was on the national advisory board of United World Federalists (the most prestigious group of fellow-travelers and dupes working for world government at the expense of United States sovereignty).

When the Book-of-the-Month Club promoted *The Ugly American* — the collaborative work of Burdick and William J. Lederer — Burdick achieved instant fame. The book, although a clumsy literary effort, was a successful leftist propaganda tract. In its essentials, the book called for a highly-disciplined American diplomatic corps modeled upon the totalitarian disciplined emissaries of the Soviet Union. Burdick and his co-author wanted an elitist group representing the United States in foreign lands rather than representative Americans. The book was so poorly written and its propaganda touches so subtle that it confused critics of both the left and the right and its very title — *The Ugly American* — was almost universally misconstrued and misapplied.

In 1962, when Burdick collaborated with Harvey Wheeler on *Fail-Safe*, the Book-of-the-Month Club again selected Burdick for its promotional efforts. *Fail-Safe*, another propaganda tract, was remarkably similar to a book published four years earlier — Peter Bryant's *Red Alert*. The Burdick-Wheeler book achieved sales in the millions in hardcover and paperback format, and it later became a highly profitable motion picture. The book had as its basic theme the inevitability of accidental nuclear warfare and the danger, as of 1962, that such warfare would be critical. Even after the book was published, Burdick preached this theme. He said on one occasion: "I don't know of a scientist who has a direct knowledge of 'fail-safe' who isn't worried. This is something people ought to know."

The most perceptive criticism of *Fail-Safe* was presented by Sidney Hook in a *New Leader* book review (December 10, 1962), and in his own book, *The Fail-Safe Fallacy*, published in 1963. Wheeler and Burdick presented a situation wherein the United States' retaliatory bombing system became totally disorganized, causing six United States bombers to make a nuclear attack which destroyed Moscow. In atonement, the President of the United States ordered American bombers to demolish New York City.

The full context of *Fail-Safe* was a scaremongering plea for disarmament and appeasement with the Soviet Union, along with an intellectually dishonest representation of the safeguards prepared by the American military to prevent accidental nuclear warfare. A few of Dr. Hook's observations are pertinent: (1) "It [*Fail-Safe*] is an emotionally surcharged political tract designed to prove that the greatest danger to the survival of free institutions in the world today is our defense system." (2) "To the extent that this [the inevitability of accidental nuclear warfare] is believed, it is certain to encourage the appeasement of Nikita Khrushchev, portrayed by the authors as a man of noble character and profound thought." (3) "The authors present Khrushchev as a man of tragic dimensions, more sinned against than sinning, reluctant to demand a cruel and gratuitous price for an accident which he agrees is no one's fault, a humanist and a reflective critic of Bolshevik Leninism .... He leaves the stage a philosopher pledged to reasonable compromise." (4) "*Fail-Safe* is also morally objectionable because of the colors in which it portrays the civilian experts on how to survive war if it is forced on us ... by describing them as money-hungry monsters, their entire intellectual activity in behalf of a free society is called into question." Burdick died in July 1965.

HENRY SEIDEL CANBY was born on September 6, 1878 in Wilmington, Delaware, son of Ella Seidel and Edward Canby. He married Marion Gause. He was an alumnus of Yale University (Ph. B., 1899 and Ph.D., 1905). He was the author of *The Short Story* (1902); *The Short Story in English* (1909); *A Study of the Short Story* (1913); *College Sons and College Fathers* (1915); *Education*

by Violence (1919); *Our House* (1919); *Everyday Americans* (1920); *Definitions* (1922); *Definitions,* second series (1924); *Better Writing* (1926); *American Estimates* (1929); *Classic Americans* (1931); *The Age of Confidence* (1934); *Alma-Mater – The Gothic Age of the American College* (1936); *Seven Years' Harvest* (1936); *Thoreau: A Biography* (1939); *The Brandywine* (1941); *Handbook of English Usage* (1942); *Walt Whitman, An American* (1943); *Family History* (1945); *American Memoir* (1947); and *Turn West, Turn East: Mark Twain and Henry James* (1951). He was co-author of *English Composition in Theory and Practice* (1909); *Elements of Composition* (1913); *Facts, Thought and Imagination* (1917); *Good English* (1918); *Saturday Papers* (1921); and *Designed for Reading* (1934). He was editor of *The Works of Henry D. Thoreau* (1937). He was co-editor of *The Book of the Short Story* (1903); *Selections from Robert Louis Stevenson* (1911); *Selections from Masefield* (1917); *War Aims and Peace Ideals* (1919); and *Anthony and Cleopatra* (1921). He was a contributor to the *Literary History of the United States* (1948). He has contributed articles to the *Encyclopaedia Britannica.*

From 1900 until 1961, Canby was at Yale University as an assistant in literary composition (1900-1903); an instructor (1903-1908); assistant professor (1908-1916); advisor in literary composition (1916-1922); and lecturer with professorial rank (1922-1961). In 1910 and 1911, he lectured in English at Dartmouth College. In 1918, he lectured at Cambridge University in England. In 1923, he lectured in English at the University of California. In 1945, he was a visiting lecturer at Australian and New Zealand universities. He was an associate fellow at Silliman College of Yale University. From 1911 until 1920, he was assistant editor of *Yale Review*. From 1920 until 1924, he was editor of the Literary Review of the *New York Evening Post*. From 1924 until 1936, he was editor of the *Saturday Review of Literature*, and from 1936 until 1958, he was chairman of the board of editors of that publication. From 1926 until 1958, he was chairman of the board of judges of the Book-of-the-Month Club, which persistently promoted the literary outpourings of leftists. In 1918, he was employed by the British Ministry of Information as a liaison man in Great Britain, Ireland, and France. During World War II, he was employed as a consultant to the Bureau of Publications of the Red-laden Office of War Information.

Canby was affiliated with the ultra-radical American Civil Liberties Union; the American Committee for Protection of Foreign Born ("founded by the Communist Party in order to exploit racial divisions in the United States for its own revolutionary purposes"); the American Friends of Spanish Democracy ("Communist front"); the American Pushkin Committee ("Communist front"); the Bill of Rights Conference ("subversive"); Brief [*amicus curiae*] for the Communist Party ("Communist Party enterprise"); the Committee of One Thousand ("Communist-created and controlled"); the Committee of Welcome for the Red Dean of Canterbury (England's most notorious pro-Soviet apologist among the clergy); the Coordinating Committee To Lift the [Spanish] Embargo ("one of the numerous Communist front enterprises which were organized around the Communists' agitation over the Spanish Civil War"); the Council on Foreign Relations (the unofficial but operative directorate of all facets of United States foreign policy); the Hiroshima Commemorative Committee (ultra-leftist); the Independent Citizens Committee of the Arts, Sciences, and Professions ("Communist front"); the Joint Anti-Fascist Refugee Committee ("subversive and Communist"); the League of American Writers ("subversive and Communist" – "began openly to follow the Communist Party line as dictated by the foreign policy of the Soviet Union"); the National Committee for an Effective Congress ("well-financed ultra-leftist political pressure group"); the National Committee for a Sane Nuclear Policy (ultra-leftist-pacifist); the National Committee To Abolish the Un-American Activities Committee ("to lead and direct the Communist Party's 'operation abolition' campaign"); the National Council on Freedom from Censorship (ultra-leftist); the National Institute of Arts and Letters ("Communist front"); the National Wartime Conference of the Professions, the Sciences, the Arts, the White-Collar Fields ("Communist front"); *New Masses* ("weekly journal of the Communist Party"); the Reichstag Fire Trial Anniversary Committee ("Communist front . . . formed . . . by prominent Communists and Communist sympathizers"); and the Washington Committee To Lift [the] Spanish Embargo ("Communist front"). He died in April 1961.

ANTON J. CARLSON was born on January 29, 1875 in Bohuslan, Sweden, son of Hedwig Anderson and Carl Jacobson. He came to the United States in 1891. He was married to Esther Sheagren. He was an alumnus of Augustana College and Theological Seminary in Illinois (A.B., 1898; M.A., 1899) and Stanford University (Ph.D., 1902). He was the author of *Control of Hunger in Health and Disease* (1916) and co-author of *The Machinery of the Body* (1937). In 1899, Carlson was an assistant pastor of the Lutheran Church in Anaconda, Montana. In 1900, he left the ministry to devote himself full-time to science. From 1901 until 1903, he was an assistant in physiology at Stanford University. In 1903 and 1904, he was a research associate at Carnegie Institution in Washington, D.C. From 1904 until 1956, he was at the University of Chicago as an associate in physiology (1904-1905); assistant professor (1906-1909); associate professor (1909-1914); professor (1914-1929); chairman of the physiology department (1916-1940); the Frank P. Hixon Distinguished Service Professor (1929-1940); and professor emeritus (1940-1956). From 1905 until 1907, he was an instructor at the Marine Biological Laboratory in Woods Hole, Massachusetts. In 1935, he lectured in China under the auspices of the Rockefeller Foundation. He was a consultant to the U.S. Food and Drug Administration, the U.S. Public Health Service, the Federal Trade Commission, the Office of War Information, and the Office of Price Administration. At various times, he was president of the American Association for the Advancement of Science, the American Physiological Society, the Union of American Biological Societies, the Institute of Medicine, the American Biological Society, the Federation of American Societies for Experimental Biology, the National Society for Medical Research, the Gerontological Society, and the American Association of University Professors.

At the 1950 national convention of the Communist Party, Carlson was one of six American scientists hailed for their service to the cause of peace. Carlson was affiliated with the Abraham Lincoln School ("an adjunct of the Communist Party"); the American Association of Scientific Workers ("Communist front"); the ultra-radical American Civil Liberties Union; the American Committee for Democracy and Intellectual Freedom ("subversive and un-American" – "Communist-front organization operating among college teachers and professors"); the American Committee for Protection of Foreign Born ("founded by the Communist Party in order to exploit racial divisions in the United States for its own revolutionary purposes"); the American Committee To Save Refugees ("perform[ing] a most valuable function for the international Communist movement"); the American Continental Congress for Peace ("another phase in the Communist 'peace' campaign, aimed at consolidating anti-American forces throughout the Western Hemisphere"); the American Friends of Spanish Democracy ("Communist front"); the American League Against War and Fascism ("subversive and Communist" – "established in the United States in an effort to create public sentiment on behalf of a foreign policy adapted to the interests of the Soviet Union"); the American League for Peace and Democracy ("subversive and Communist" – "established . . . in an effort to create public sentiment on behalf of a foreign policy adapted to the interests of the Soviet Union . . . [and] designed to conceal Communist control, in accordance with the new tactics of the Communist International"); the American Peace Crusade ("Communist front"); the American Peace Mobilization ("formed under the auspices of the Communist Party and the Young Communist League" – "one of the most seditious organizations which ever operated in the United States"); the American People's Congress and Exposition for Peace ("Communist front"); Brief [*amicus curiae*] for the Communist Party ("Communist enterprise"); the Chicago Committee To Secure Justice in the Rosenberg Case ("Communist front"); the Chicago Council of American-Soviet Friendship ("subversive and Communist" – "specializing in pro-Soviet propaganda"); the Claude Lightfoot Defense Committee ("Communist enterprise"); the Committee for a Democratic Far Eastern Policy ("Communist"); the Committee for Medical Freedom (leftist); the Committee for Peaceful Alternatives to the Atlantic Pact ("a Communist front organization . . . as part of Soviet psychological warfare against the United States"); the Conference for World Peace Through Negotiation (pro-Communist); Consumers Union (in the "solar system of organizations around the [Communist] Party"); the Coordinating Committee To Lift the [Spanish] Embargo ("one of the numerous Communist-front enterprises which were organized around the Communists' agitation over the Spanish Civil War"); the Cultural and Scientific Conference for World Peace ("Communist front"); the Hiroshima Commemorative Committee (ultra-leftist); the Institute of Pacific Relations ("an instrument of Communist policy, propaganda, and military intelligence"); the Jefferson School of Social Science ("Communist institution modeled along the lines of the new Communist policy which led to the decision to change the Communist Party into some kind of an educational institution"); the Medical Bureau and North Atlantic Committee To Aid Spanish Democracy ("subversive and un-American"); the Mid-Century Conference for Peace ("aimed at assembling as many gullible persons possible under Communist direction and turning them into a vast sounding board for Communist propaganda"); the National Committee To Defeat the Mundt Bill ("a

Communist lobby . . . which has carried out the objectives of the Communist Party in its fight against anti-subversive legislation"); the National Committee To Repeal the McCarran Act ("a Communist front" – "subversive"); the National Committee To Secure Justice for Morton Sobell ("Communist front [in] the Communist campaign for [atomic spy] Morton Sobell"); the National Conference To Win Amnesty for Smith Act Victims ("subversive" – "Communist"); the National Council Against Conscription ("Communist front"); the National Council of the Arts, Sciences, and Professions ("a Communist front used to appeal to special occupational groups"); the National Emergency Conference ("Communist front"); the National Federation for Constitutional Liberties ("under Communist Party domination and headed by responsible Party functionaries" – "one of the viciously subversive organizations of the Communist Party"); the Non-Partisan Committee for Lillian Herstein (Farmer-Labor [Socialist] ticket, 1932); the Rescue Ship Mission ("Communist front"); the Stockholm Peace Appeal ("Communist 'peace' campaign"); and the World Peace Congress ("organized under Communist initiative in various countries throughout the world"). He died in September 1956.

EVANS CARLSON was born on February 26, 1896 in Sidney, New York, son of Joetta Evans and Thomas Carlson. He was married to Dorothy Secomb, Etelle Sawyer, and Peggy Tatum. He attended George Washington University. He was the author of *Twin Stars of China* (1940) and *The Chinese Army – Its Origin and Military Efficiency* (1940).

As a youngster, Carlson was a dropout from Vergennes High School in Vermont. At the age of sixteen, in 1912, he enlisted in the U.S. Army. In 1915, after serving in the Philippines and Hawaii, he was discharged with the rank of top sergeant. After a year's work with an artesian well-digging company and a surveying crew, he was recalled to army serice during the Mexican Border Incident. During World War I, he served in the United States and France and achieved the rank of captain. From 1920 until 1922, he worked for a canning company.

In 1922, Carlson enlisted in the U.S. Marine Corps as a private and a year later was commissioned a second lieutenant. From 1923 until 1927, he was stationed at various Marine posts in the United States and in Cuba. From 1927 until 1929, he was an operations and intelligence officer in Shanghai, China. From 1930 until 1933, he was in Nicaragua, where U.S. Marines were helping to organize Nicaragua's National Guard. From 1933 until 1935, he was back in Shanghai as an intelligence officer. From 1935 until 1937, he had stateside duty at Quantico, Virginia; as the commanding officer at President Franklin D. Roosevelt's camp in Warm Springs, Georgia; as commanding officer of a U.S. Marine detachment at the Texas Centennial Exposition; and as a student at Marine Corps Schools.

In 1937, Carlson went to Peiping to study Chinese and to serve as acting Naval attaché. Shortly after he reached China, he joined the Communist Chinese army of Mao Tse-tung, who was then in battle against Japanese forces. Carlson remained with the Communists for two years and became well-versed in their theories and practices of guerrilla warfare. He also became so pro-Communist in his public utterances, as he heaped praises upon the Chinese Communists, that his superiors reprimanded him. Con-

sequently, angered by the reaction to his remarks, he resigned from the Marines as captain in 1939 and returned to America.

After leaving the Marines, Carlson lectured and wrote about his experiences with the Chinese Communists, whom he praised while belittling the Chinese forces of Chiang Kai-shek. He also became a very vocal anti-Japanese propagandist. His two books, published in 1940, were most favorably received by leftist critics.

In 1940 and 1941, as a private citizen, Carlson returned to China and made a tour of eight provinces in which the Communists had developed industrial cooperatives, modeled along the lines of those to be found in the Soviet Union. To Carlson, the cooperative was the democratic method of survival in a crisis.

In 1941, after returning from China, Carlson applied for recommissioning in the Marine Corps. In May 1941, he was commissioned a major, and at his own suggestion was assigned the task of assembling and training a Marine guerrilla unit. With the aid of his executive officer, Major James Roosevelt, son of the President, he put together a battalion that became known as Carlson's Raiders. The Raiders had two successful engagements at Makin Island and Guadalcanal before they were consolidated into a regular Marine Raider Regiment.

Carlson's Raiders, which he called the Kung-ho or Gung-ho Battalion, were organized and commanded in the fashion of the Communist army units Carlson had spent two years observing. He had decided that American armed forces were organized and governed by inconsistent and incongruous aristocratic methods rather than by the "democratic" methods of the Chinese Communists that he preferred. In his battalion, officers' privileges and the officers' mess were abolished. All personnel wore the same clothing and carried the same equipment. There were self-criticism sessions such as are common in the armies of Red China and the Soviet Union. Indoctrination sessions (cooperation meetings) were frequent, and the men were lectured on "democracy," religion, and freedom. And, over all, there was Carlson in the role of a patriarch, serving as counsellor, confessor, and big brother to all other officers and men. Everyone but Carlson was equal.

Carlson continued to serve in the Marines until in 1946 he retired with the rank of colonel because of wounds received in action. By 1946, he had attained the temporary rank of brigadier general, and had acquired an impressive list of decorations, including three Navy Crosses, the Legion of Merit, two Purple Hearts, three Presidential Unit Citations, the Italian War Cross, the Nicaraguan Presidential Order of Merit, and the Nicaraguan Medal of Distinction.

Freda Utley, a former Communist who was an experienced hand in China, wrote in her *The China Story:* "If one seeks for an explanation why Communist sympathizers were able to exert so strong an influence on the American press and public, one must take into account the mixed motives which determine attitudes and actions. In many cases the primary impulse which impelled newspapermen, authors, and Foreign Service officers to espouse the Chinese Communist cause may have been sympathy for the Chinese people, and a romantic faith in Communist professions and promises. Few Americans understood that the miserable condition of the Chinese people was due to technological backwardness and ancient traditions, aggravated by war. Nor did most of them realize that Communism could not cure the ills of China, but would inevitably lead to even worse poverty and the extinction of liberty. Such a man, for instance, was Evans Carlson, the simple soldier who had been beguiled into believing that the Communists were 'true Christians.' "

Utley described Carlson as having "embraced the cause of the Chinese people with childlike fervor." She said that his enthusiastic praise for the Chinese Communists astounded even the most rabidly pro-Communist elements among America's China hands. (Utley undoubtedly underestimated Carlson's attachment to the Chinese Communists by attributing it to the fact that he found them to be "true Christians." He had been thoroughly indoctrinated, as attested by a reply Carlson sent to U.S. Ambassador Nelson T. Johnson when the latter asked him to evaluate the nature of the Chinese Communists. Wrote Carlson to Johnson: "Their political doctrines are representative democracy; their economic doctrines are the cooperative theory, and only in their social application are they Communists, for they place a great deal of emphasis on social equality. . . . They want democracy in China, free speech, free press, and the rest.")

As early as 1939, Carlson was deeply involved with the Institute of Pacific Relations. He was closely associated with Frederick Vanderbilt Field and Owen Lattimore, who were later identified under oath as Communists, and with Edward C. Carter, the Secretary General of the Institute.

In 1951, after five months of preliminary investigation, the Senate Internal Security Subcommittee held hearings on the AIPR. Between July 25, 1951 and

June 20, 1952, the SISS heard sixty-six witnesses in one of the most extensive Congressional hearings ever held. The SISS sought to determine: "(a) Whether or to what extent the Institute of Pacific Relations was infiltrated and influenced or controlled by agents of the communist world conspiracy; (b) Whether or to what extent these agents and their dupes worked through the Institute into the United States Government to the point where they exerted an influence on United States far eastern policy; and if so, whether and to what extent they still exert such influence; (c) Whether or to what extent these agents and their dupes led or misled American public opinion, particularly with respect to far eastern policy."

When the SISS completed its hearings, it concluded: "The Institute of Pacific Relations has not maintained the character of an objective, scholarly, and research organization. The IPR has been considered by the American Communist Party and by Soviet officials as an instrument of Communist policy, propaganda and military intelligence. The IPR disseminated and sought to popularize false information including information originating from Soviet and Communist sources . . . . The effective leadership of the IPR used IPR prestige to promote the interests of the Soviet Union in the United States. A group of persons operating within and about the Institute of Pacific Relations exerted a substantial influence on United States far eastern policy. The IPR was a vehicle used by the Communists to orientate American far eastern policies toward Communist objectives."

In the course of the 1952 SISS hearings, former Communist Louis Budenz identified Carlson as a Communist Party member. He said that Carlson was widely discussed in Communist Party cirles as the man "who would lead the movement for a Red China in the United States." Budenz also said that Michael Blankfort, the author of Carlson's authorized biography, *The Big Yankee*, was a Communist. Blankfort later denied being a Communist, but *The Big Yankee* was distributed by Liberty Book Club, which was organized in New York for the distribution of Communist books.

Carlson's own 1940 book, *The Chinese Army*, was published by the Institute of Pacific Relations. He wrote for two IPR publications, *Far Eastern Survey* and *Pacific Affairs,* and he was affiliated with *Amerasia. Amerasia* was organized under Communist auspices, and it became the center of a *cause célèbre* in 1945, when hundreds of classified U.S. government documents were discovered in the *Amerasia* offices. According to the Senate Internal Security Subcommittee, the "IPR family ordinarily treated it [*Amerasia*] as simply another of their own publications . . . [and] articles and writers were readily shunted back and forth among [IPR's] *Pacific Affairs*, [IPR's] *Far Eastern Survey* and *Amerasia.*" (Besides writing for IPR, Carlson lectured under the auspices of the organization.)

The IPR maintained a vast interlock with Communist-controlled organizations and publications. Of these, Carlson was a contributor to *China Today*, the official organ of the American Friends of the Chinese People ("Communist front"). He was a member of the China Aid Council ("Communist-controlled"). He was chairman of the Committee for a Democratic Far Eastern Policy ("Communist"). He was on the advisory committee of INDUSCO [American Committee in Aid of Chinese Industrial Cooperatives] ("Communist-controlled").

Among Carlson's other affiliations

were the American Committee for Non-Participation in Japanese Aggression ("Communist front"); American Youth for Democracy ("subversive and Communist" – "part of Soviet psychological warfare against the United States"); the China Conference Arrangements Committee ("Communist front"); the Civil Rights Congress ("created and established by the Communist Party as an organization which would utilize defense of civil rights for Party purposes and raise and maintain mass defense and bail funds for Party use"); the Hollywood Writers Mobilization for Defense ("subversive and Communist"); the First State-Wide Legislative Conference in California ("complete subservience to the twists and turns of the Communist Party line"); the Los Angeles Emergency Committee To Aid the Strikers ("Communist front"); the National Committee To Win the Peace ("subversive and Communist"); the Progressive Citizens of America ("subversive" – "political Communist front"); and the Writers' Congress ("subversive and Communist.").

Carlson died in May 1947. In California, the Communists memorialized him by naming their Party's club the Evans Carlson Club.

RUDOLF CARNAP was born on May 18, 1891 in Ronsdorf-Wuppertal, Germany, son of Anna Dorpfeld and Johannes Carnap. He came to the United States in 1935 and became a naturalized citizen in 1941. He married the late Elizabeth Ina von Stöger. He was a student at the University of Freiberg and the University of Jena, receiving his Ph.D. from the latter in 1921. He was the author of *Der Raum* (1922); *Psysikalische Begriffsbildung* (1926); *Der logische Aufbau der Welt* (1928 and 1960); *Scheinprobleme in der Philos-*

ophie (1928 and 1964); *Albriss der Logistik* (1929); *The Unity of Science* (1934); *Logische Syntax der Sprache* (1934 and 1937); *Die Aufgabe der Wissenschaftslogik* (1934); *Philosophy and Logical Syntax* (1935); *Foundations of Logic and Mathematics* (1939); *Introduction to Semantics* (1942); *Formalization of Logic* (1943); *Meaning and Necessity: A Study in Semantics and Modal Logic* (1947 and 1956); *Logical Foundations of Probability* (1950 and 1962); *The Nature and Application of Inductive Logic* (1951); *The Continuum of Inductive Methods* (1952); *Einfuehrung in die symbolische Logik* (1954 and 1960); *Introduction to Symbolic Logic and its Applications* (1958); *Philosophical Foundations of Physics* (1966); and *The Logical Structure of the World* (1967). He was co-author of *Induktire Logik und Wahrscheinlichkeit* (1958). He was a contributor to *Factors Determining Human Behavior* (1937); *The International Encyclopedia of Unified Science*, Volumes I and III (1938 and 1939); *An Outline of the Theory of Semantic Information* (1952); *Communication Theory* (1953); *Readings in the Philosophy of Science* (1953); *The Foundations of Science and the Concepts of Psychology and Psychoanalysis* (1956); *Logical Positivism* (1959); *Logic, Methodology and Philosophy of Science* (1961); and *Essays on the Foundation of Mathematics* (1961). His writings are collected in *The Philosophy of Rudolf Carnap* (1964), edited by Paul A. Schlipp.

From 1926 until 1930, Carnap was a lecturer in philosophy at the University of Vienna. From 1931 until 1935, he was a professor of natural philosophy at the German University in Prague, Czecho-Slovakia. From 1936 until 1952, he was a professor of philosophy at the

University of Chicago. From 1952 until 1954, he was a fellow of the Institute for Advanced Study in Princeton, New Jersey. From 1954 until 1970, he was at the University of California at Los Angeles as professor of philosophy (1954-1962) and research philosopher (1962-1970).

Carnap was affiliated with the American Committee for Protection of Foreign Born ("founded by the Communist Party in order to exploit racial divisions in the United States for its own revolutionary purposes"); Brief [amicus curiae] for the Communist Party ("Communist Party enterprise"); the Committee for Medical Freedom (leftist); the Committee for Peaceful Alternatives to the Atlantic Pact ("Communist front organization . . . a part of Soviet psychological warfare against the United States"); the Cultural and Scientific Conference for World Peace ("Communist front"); the International Workers Order ("from its very inception, demonstrated by its pronouncements, its activities, and the authoritative statements of the Communist Party that it is a subservient instrument of the Communist Party in the United States"); the Mid-Century Conference for Peace ("aimed at assembling as many gullible persons possible under Communist direction and turning them into a vast sounding board for Communist propaganda"); the National Assembly for Democratic Rights ("created, dominated and controlled by members and officials of the Communist Party"); the National Committee To Abolish the Un-American Activities Committee ("to lead and direct the Communist Party's 'operation abolition' campaign"); the National Committee To Repeal the McCarran Act ("a Communist front" – "subversive"); the National Committee To Secure Justice in the Rosenberg Case

("Communist front organized . . . to conduct the United States phase of a mammoth propaganda campaign designed to obliterate the crime of and exploit the Rosenbergs and their codefendant, Morton Sobell, for the purposes of international Communism"); the National Council of the Arts, Sciences and Professions ("a Communist front used to appeal to special occupational groups"); and the World Peace Appeal ("Communist Party campaign"). He died in September 1970.

CARRIE CHAPMAN CATT was born on January 9, 1859 in Ripon, Wisconsin, daughter of Maria Clinton and Lucius Lane. She was married first to Leo Chapman and second to George Catt. She was an alumna of Iowa State College (B.S., 1880).

From 1881 until 1885, Catt was at Mason City (Iowa) High School as principal (1881-1883) and superintendent (1883-1885). In 1885, she was co-owner and editor of the *Mason City Republican*. In 1886, she was a newspaper reporter in San Francisco. In 1887, she joined the Iowa Woman Suffrage Association and began a long career as a suffragette. From 1890 until 1892, she was state organizer and lecturer for the Iowa State Woman Suffrage Association. From 1892 until 1919, intermittently, she was with the National American Woman Suffrage Association as organizer and lecturer (1892-1900) and president (1900-1904 and 1915-1919). In 1902, she organized the International Woman Suffrage Alliance, and she was president of the organization from 1904 until 1923. In 1919, she founded the League of Women Voters and was honorary president of the organization from 1919 until 1947.

Catt worked throughout her entire

life for socialist, internationalist, and pacifist objectives. Her ideological leftism became a continuing inspiration for the League of Women Voters. She cooperated with the nation's most radical pacifists prior to World War I, between the World Wars and immediately prior to World War II. She concentrated her energies on disarmament, proposals for United States membership in the League of Nations, and non-intervention by the United States in World War II — at a time when non-intervention was the liberal-leftist line. Catt's affiliations included the American Association for the United Nations (leftist group); the Coordinating Committee To Lift the [Spanish] Embargo ("one of the numerous Communist-front enterprises which were organized around the Communists' agitation over the Spanish Civil War"); the Council for National Defense (leftist-pacifist); the Institute of Pacific Relations ("an instrument of Communist policy, propaganda, and military intelligence"); the National Committee on the Cause and Cure of War (leftist-pacifist); the National Council of American-Soviet Friendship ("subversive and Communist" — "specializing in pro-Soviet propaganda"); Open Letter in Defense of Harry Bridges ("Communist front"); and. the Women's Peace Party (dominated by America's leading female Reds). She died in March 1947.

BENNETT CERF was born on May 25, 1898 in New York City, son of Fredericka Wise and Gustave Cerf. He was married to and divorced from Sylvia Sidney. His second wife was Phyllis Fraser (*née* Helen Nichols). He was an alumnus of Columbia University (A.B., 1919 and Litt. B., 1920). He was editor of *Great German Short Novels and Stories* (1933); *Pocket Book of War Humor* (1942); *The Pocket Book of Modern American Plays* (1942); *Try And Stop Me* (1944); *Famous Ghost Stories* (1944); *Laughing Stock* (1945); *Anything for a Laugh* (1946); *The Unexpected* (1948); *Shake Well Before Using; A New Collection of Impressions and Anecdotes, Mostly Humorous* (1948); *Laughter, Incorporated: The Cream of the Recent Crop of Stories and Anecdotes, Harvested, Assorted and Prepared for Market* (1950); *Good for a Laugh: A New Collection of Humorous Tidbits and Anecdotes From Aardvark to Zythum* (1952); *An Encyclopedia of Modern American Humor* (1954); *The Life of the Party* (1956); *Vest Pocket Book For All Occasions* (1956); *Reading for Pleasure* (1957); *Jokes of the Year* (1957); *Twenty-Four Favorite One-Act Plays* (1958); *New Book of Jokes*, (1958); *The Laugh's on Me* (1959); *Bennett Cerf's Bumper Crop of Anecdotes and Stories, Mostly Humorous, About the Famous and Near Famous* (1959); *Book of Laughs* (1959); *Out on a Limerick: A Collection of Over 300 of the World's Best Printable Limericks, Assembled, Revised, Dry-Cleaned, and Annotated by Mr. Cerf* (1960); *Book of Riddles* (1960); *More Riddles* (1961); *Four Contemporary American Plays* (1961); *Six American Plays for Today* (1961); *Riddle-De-Dee: 458, Count Them, 458 Riddles Old and New For Children from 12 to 112* (1962); *Houseful of Laughter* (1963); *Book of Animal Riddles* (1964); *Bennett Cerf's Little Riddle Book* (1964); *Laugh Day* (1965); and *Treasury of Atrocious Puns* (1968). He was co-editor of *The Bedside Book of Famous British Stories* (1940); *Sixteen Famous American Plays* (1941); *Sixteen Famous British Plays* (1942); *Thirty Famous One-Act Plays* (1943); *Famous Plays of Crime and Detection, From*

Sherlock Holmes to Angel Street (1946); *An Anthology of Famous American Stories* (1953); and *Bennett Cerf's Take Along Treasury* (1963).

From 1920 until 1923, Cerf was employed by a Wall Street brokerage house. In 1922 and 1923, he was a financial reporter for the *New York Herald Tribune.* In 1923 and 1924, he was a vice-president of Boni and Liveright, a publishing firm. In 1925, with Donald Klopfer, he bought from Boni and Liveright the Modern Library book series. From 1925 until 1971, he was president of Modern Library. In 1927, Klopfer and Cerf founded the publishing firm of Random House. The partners purchased the output of the Nonesuch Press, a British firm that specialized in beautiful limited editions. Random House printed the Nonesuch books and its own. From 1927 until 1966, when he became chairman of the board, Cerf was president of Random House. In 1966, Random House was purchased by the Radio Corporation of America. From 1945 until 1971, Cerf was director of Bantam Books. In 1960, Cerf's Random House purchased the publishing firm of Alfred A. Knopf, Inc. From 1952 until 1966, Cerf was a panelist on "What's My Line," a Columbia Broadcasting System television program. He was a director of the Radio Corporation of America, Inc. and Metro-Goldwyn-Mayer, Inc. From 1942 until 1957, he wrote a column, "Trade Winds," for *Saturday Review of Literature* (later *Saturday Review*). For many years, he wrote a daily feature, "Try and Stop Me," for King Features Syndicate, and a column, "Cerfboard," for *This Week* magazine.

As a publisher, Cerf heavily favored Communist, fellow-traveling and avant-garde authors, including André Malraux, Vincent Sheean, Sinclair Lewis, Robert Penn Warren, Quentin Reynolds, Havelock Ellis, James Michener, Edgar Snow, Gertrude Stein, W.H. Auden, Marcel Proust, John Strachey, Philip Roth, and William Styron.

During the mid-1930's, Cerf was a vocal defender of the Red side of the Spanish Civil War. His sympathies for the "Republicans" were so strong that he visited Spain during the course of the conflict. His affiliations included the American Committee for Spanish Freedom ("Communist"); the American Pushkin Committee ("Communist front"); the Conference on Pan-American Democracy ("Communist front"); *Equality* (Communist Party enterprise); Freedom House Bookshelf Committee (comprised of the most brazen leftists in the literary and academic world, promoting books by notable leftists); the Joint Anti-Fascist Refugee Committee ("subversive and Communist"); the Julius Rosenthal Memorial Committee ("a Communist front organization which belonged to the large group of Spanish aid committees which the Communist Party so successfully exploited"); the Lawyers' Committee on American Relations with Spain ("During the Spanish Civil War, the Communist Party organized . . . [the Lawyers' Committee] as a part of one of its major propaganda campaigns in the Party's entire history in this country"); the National Committee Against Censorship of the Theatre Arts ("Communist front"); the National Committee for People's Rights ("composed primarily of openly avowed members of the Communist Party and veteran fellow-travelers of the Communist Party"); and Veterans of the Abraham Lincoln Brigade ("directed, dominated and controlled by the Communist Party"). He died in August 1971.

ZECHARIAH CHAFEE JR. was born

on on December 7, 1885 in Providence, Rhode Island, son of Mary Sharpe and Zechariah Chafee. He married Bess Searle. He was an alumnus of Brown University (A.B., 1907) and Harvard Law School (LL.B., 1913). He was the author of *Freedom of Speech* (1920); *Cases on Equitable Relief Against Torts* (1924); *The Inquiring Mind* (1928); *State House vs. Pent House – Legal Problems of the Rhode Island Race Track Row* (1937); *America Now* (1938); *The Constitutional Convention That Never Met*, two parts (1938 and 1939); *Cases on Equitable Remedies* (1939); *Free Speech in the United States* (1941); *Weathering the Panic of '73* (1942); *Reissued Notes on Bills and Notes* (1943); *Government and Mass Communications* (1947); *Some Problems of Equity* (1950); *Documents on Fundamental Human Rights* (1951); *How Human Rights Got Into the Constitution* (1952); *Freedom of Speech and Press* (1955); and *The Blessings of Liberty* (1956). He was co-author of *The Next War* (1925); *Freedom and the Modern World* (1928); *Harvard Legal Essays* (1934); *Cases on Equity* (1934 and 1946); and *Return to Freedom* (1944). He was editor of *Brannon's Negotiable Instruments Law* (1926) and *Pound's Cases on Equitable Relief Against Defamation* (1930). He was a contributor to *Civilization in the United States* (1922). He contributed articles to publications, including the *New York Evening Post*, the *New Republic*, and *The Nation*.

From 1907 until 1957, with the exception of four years, Chafee was associated with the Builders Iron Foundry of Providence, Rhode Island, as secretary and assistant treasurer (1907-1910); member of the board of directors (1914-1944); and chairman of the board (1944-1957). From 1913 until 1916, he practiced law with the firm of Tillinghast and Collins in Providence. From 1916 until 1957, he was on the faculty of Harvard University's Law School as assistant professor of law (1916-1919); professor (1919-1938); Langdell Professor of Law (1938-1950); University Professor (1950-1956); and Lowell Institute Lecturer (1956-1957). From 1936 until 1942, he was syndic of Harvard University Press. He lectured on law in summer sessions at Columbia University (1923, 1925, and 1932) and the University of Chicago (1936). In 1923, he was chairman of the Committee on Coal and Civil Liberties reporting to the United States Coal Commission. From 1929 until 1931, he was a consultant to the National Commission on Law Observance and Enforcement. From 1943 until 1947, he was a member of the Freedom of Press Commission. In 1947 and 1948, he was a member of the United Nations' Subcommittee on Freedom of Information and the Press.

For more than three decades, Chafee was one of the legal profession's most articulate opponents of espionage and sedition statutes, anti-subversive congressional and state legislative investigating committees, loyalty oaths, and any and all anti-Communist measures adopted in the interest of security in either the government or private sectors.

Chafee concentrated his critical fire on three eras of unusual anti-subversive activity on the part of government authorities. The anti-espionage and anti-sedition laws attendant on World War I and World War II, and the anti-Communist investigative activities of the late 1940's and early 1950's, were particularly obnoxious to Chafee. If he were to be believed, the United States underwent reigns of terror in those three eras. If he were to be taken literally, the United

States in these three particular eras was nothing less than a police state under the firm control of thoroughly intolerant flag-waving super-patriots who imposed their brand of conformity by using legislative, executive, and judicial powers in the suppression of the Bill of Rights.

In the full context of his writings, Chafee went far beyond the bounds of libertarian concern in regard to the Bill of Rights, especially those features of the Bill of Rights most germane to the Communist threat: freedom of speech, freedom of the press, and the Fifth Amendment. By his refusal to acknowledge the conspiratorial nature of Communism, the international control of America's Communist Party, and the subversive accomplishments of Communists, he was an advocate of license – far beyond rights – to Communists in government service or in the private sector to promote their cause without hindrance. He held to the opinion that the Constitution of the United States afforded protection to Communists no matter how anti-American their behavior. To complete his logic, the Constitution carried within itself the means of its own destruction. He would never acknowledge that advocacy – no matter how effective – to overthrow the government of the United States was a crime against the United States and liable to punishment by the United States. He refused, of course, to acknowledge that Communists were committed to an allegiance above and beyond their allegiance, by birth or naturalization, to the United States. He refused to acknowledge that for a Communist the promotion of the Communist cause was a full-time duty no matter his profession or occupation, no matter his employer, no matter any oathbound or contractual obligation.

In his strenuous efforts to defend what he considered "free speech," Chafee confused advocacy with discussion, propaganda with truth, and proselytizing with teaching. In his *Free Speech in the United States*, these confusions were evident along with his heavy reliance upon generalities and/or exceptions to prove his point of view or to disparage an opposing point of view. In that portion of his book which defended free speech against the antisedition statutes of the World War I and World War II eras, he wrote: "Speech should be fruitful as well as free. Our experience introduces this qualification into the classical argument of Milton and John Stuart Mill, that only through open discussion is truth discovered and spread. In their simpler times, they thought it enough to remove legal obstacles like the censorship and sedition prosecutions. Mill assumed that if men were only left alone, their reasoning powers would eventually impel them to choose the best ideas and the wisest course of action."

Chafee never did explain why he considered the times of Mill and Milton "simpler," nor did he offer proof that their methods were effective. He continued: "To us this policy is too exclusively negative. For example, what is the use of telling an unpopular speaker that he will incur no criminal penalties by his proposed address, so long as every hall owner in the city declines to rent him space for his meeting and there are no vacant lots available? There should be municipal auditoriums, schoolhouses out of school hours, church forums, parks in summer, all open to thresh out every question of public importance, with just as few restrictions as possible; for otherwise the subjects that most need to be discussed will be the very subjects that will be ruled out as unsuitable for discussion."

To carry Chafee's argument beyond his weasel words, a Communist or any avowed enemy of the government should be granted facilities supported by taxpayers to advocate the overthrow of the very government the taxpayer supports.

In a return to his original analogy, Chafee presented a conglomeration of hyperbole, half-truths, non-sequiturs, and extraneous and gratuitous judgments and opinions. He wrote: "Of late years the argument of Milton and Mill has been questioned, because truth does not seem to emerge from a controversy in the automatic way their logic would lead us to expect. For one thing, reason is less praised nowadays than a century ago; instead, emotions conscious and unconscious are commonly said to dominate the conduct of men. Is it any longer possible to discover truth amid the clashing blares of advertisements, loud speakers, gigantic billboards, party programs, propaganda of a hundred kinds? To sift the truth from all these half-truths seems to demand a statistical investigation beyond the limits of anybody's time and money.

"So some modern thinkers despairingly conclude that the great mass of voters cannot be trusted to detect the fallacies in emotional arguments by Communists and so on, and hence must be prevented from hearing them. Even the intellectuals do not seem to do much better in reaching Truth by conflicting arguments.

"Nevertheless, the main argument of Milton and Mill still holds good. All that this disappointment means is that friction is a much bigger drag on the progress of Truth than they supposed. Efforts to lessen that friction are essential to the success of freedom of speech. It is a problem, not for law but for education in the wide sense that includes more than schools and youngsters. The conflict of oral evidence and arguments can be made increasingly profitable by wise improvements in technique. Anybody who has attended a forum knows how much depends on an able chairman and on sensible rules enforced by him. Journalists and other writers value accuracy of facts far more than formerly – we can expect even more from them in the future. None of us can get rid of our emotions, but we can learn to drive them in harness. As for blazing propaganda on both sides, young Americans can be trained to keep alive the gumption which comes down to us from Colonial farmers; this will make them distrust all men who conceal greed or a lust for power behind any flag, whether red or red-white-and-blue.

"Reason is more imperfect than we used to believe. Yet it still remains the best guide we have, better than our emotions, better even than patriotism, better than any single human guide, however exalted his position.

"A second point deserves renewed emphasis. The effect of suppression extends far beyond the agitators actually put in jail, far beyond the pamphlets physically destroyed. A favorite argument against free speech is that the men who are thus conspicuously silenced had little to say that was worth hearing. Concede for the moment that the public would suffer no serious loss if every communist leaflet were burned or if some prominent pacifist were imprisoned, as perhaps he might be under the loose language of the unprecedented federal sedition law passed last year, for discouraging drafted men by talk about plowing every fourth boy under. Even so, my contention is that the pertinacious orators and writers who get hauled up are merely extremist spokesmen for a mass of more thoughtful and more retiring men and women, who share in varying degrees the same critical attitude toward prevailing policies and institutions. When you put the hotheads in jail, these cooler people do not get arrested — they just keep quiet. And so we lose things they could tell us, which would be very advantageous for the future course of the nation. Once the prosecutions begin, then the hush-hush begins too. Discussion becomes one-sided and artificial. Questions that need to be threshed out do not get threshed out.

"The Supreme Court, though much more anxious to support liberty of speech than it was twenty years ago, can do nothing to keep discussion open during an emergency. Cases of suppression will get to Washington long after the emergency is over. What counts is what the local United States judges do. Still more important is the attitude of the prosecutors and police, because they can stifle free speech by breaking up meetings by arrests and confiscating pamphlets, and then not bothering to bring many persons to trial.

"Above all, the maintenance of open discussion depends on all the great body of unofficial citizens. If a community does not respect liberty for unpopular ideas, it can easily drive such ideas underground by persistent discouragement and sneers, by social ostracism, by boycotts of newspapers and magazines, by refusal to rent halls, by objections to the use of municipal auditoriums and schoolhouses, by discharging teachers and professors and journalists, by mobs and threats of lynching. On the other hand, an atmosphere of open and unimpeded controversy may be made as fully a part of the life of a community as any other American tradition. The law plays only a small part in either suppression or freedom. In the long run the public gets just as much freedom of speech as it really wants . . . . "

But perhaps no passage on free speech better demonstrated Chafee's warped view of the American scene than when he wrote of the pre-World War II sedition bills: "Behind the dozens of sedition bills in Congress last session, behind teachers' oaths and compulsory flag salutes, is a desire to make our citizens loyal to their government. Loyalty is a beautiful idea, but you cannot create it by compulsion and force. A government is at bottom the officials who carry it on: legislators and prosecutors, school superintendents and police. If it is composed of legislators who pass shortsighted sedition laws by overwhelming majorities, of narrow-minded school superintendents who oust thoughtful teachers of American history and eight-year-old children whose rooted religious convictions prevent them from sharing in a brief ceremony — a government of snoopers and spies and secret police — how can you expect love and loyalty? You make men love their government and their country by giving them the kind of government and the kind of country that inspire respect and love: a country that is free and unafraid, that lets the discontented talk in order to learn the causes for their discontent and end those causes, that refuses to impel men to spy on their neighbors, that protects its citizens vigorously from harmful acts while it leaves the remedies for objectionable ideas to counter-argument and time."

To the unthinking or uninformed, what Chafee described could only be interpreted as an America akin to the worst of all totalitarian regimes. He offered no proof that any thoughtful teacher was ever ousted for merely teaching American history, or that any man had ever been impelled to spy on his neighbor, or that any reasonable person believed that loyalty could be created by compulsion and force. He made no mention of the fact that the courts, where confronted with a clash between a flag salute and a religious conviction, favored the latter.

One of Chafee's pet peeves was the use of informants in the anti-Communist investigating committees and courts. To Chafee, the informants were spies, and through some perverse sort of reasoning, he discovered that "the very nature of a spy's work requires lying." Which merely proved that Chafee knew little about spies or spying. He wrote: "I want to make absolutely clear my position about spies as witnesses against men accused of political crimes. I am not saying that such spies will tell nothing in court except lies. Undoubtedly, some of them will do their best to tell the truth during their whole testimony while many others will mix a good deal of truth with falsehoods. What I do say is that there is a much greater risk of false testimony from spies than from ordinary men. Every witness, no matter how honest, is naturally inclined to make a good showing for his side. I know this from my own experience in will cases. But, in the case of most witnesses, any risks from this inclination are offset by several checks. Truthfulness is a requisite of most normal occupations from bookkeeping to the practice of medicine. An ingrained habit of telling the truth is carried onto the witness stand. And the ordinary witness knows that any lack of veracity may be detected when he testifies, as he usually does, about matters which are capable of objective proof or on which he can be contradicted by disinterested eye-witnesses of the facts.

"But when spies appear in court, such checks operate in a much weaker way. The very nature of a spy's work requires lying. He has to deceive his associates into thinking him one of themselves. The longer he does spying, the greater the tendency for the boundary between truth and falsehood to be blurred . . . . And the subject-matter of a spy's testimony in political cases is often incapable of neutral verification. He has enormous power to imagine words which were never said. The only other possible eyewitnesses of the transaction he narrates are usually the suspected person he is helping to punish and other members of the alleged conspiracy. It is impossible to let in the light of day upon these dusky happenings. The trouble is not that you cannot be sure a spy is lying. The trouble is you cannot be sure he is telling the truth. The risk of false testimony is tremendously increased."

On the same theme, he said on another occasion: "I am disturbed by the growing inclination to turn spies into heroes. One of the earliest lessons learned by children is, as I have already said, that tale-bearing on one's comrades is a dirty business . . . . Spies sometimes become agents provocateurs, who incite the very crimes they are hired to report . . . . A still more pervasive evil of spies is the breakdown of confidence in social and family life. Intercourse is poisoned when one never knows if his fellow-guest at dinner is going to report his casual statements to the secret police . . . .

"The worst spy of all is the renegade. He has already doublecrossed the community by engaging in wrongdoing and then doublecrossed his associates by deserting them and helping to punish them. After such an experience, truthtelling does not come naturally. The renegade has to make a good story in order to obtain immunity for his own admitted misconduct. Hence there is a great temptation to exaggerate or falsify the behavior of his former associates . . . .

"The political spy can send human beings to prison or deprive them of a job, and he may have strong motives to warp his story for personal reasons or to shield himself . . . . The very nature of a spy's work requires lying. He has to deceive his associates into thinking him one of themselves . . . . The fact that it is hard to obtain convictions for political crimes without the use of spies is not an argument for using spies. It is an argument against having political crimes."

Chafee saw the terrifying collusion between the three branches of government on the state and national level to suppress freedom indiscriminately in that bane of all anti-anti-Communists, the Age of McCarthyism. He wrote: "Determination of guilt in a criminal prosecution is made by a jury and reviewed by judges; and the test of guilt is defined in a statute with considerable clearness. All these safeguards are conspicuously lacking in the novel methods of suppression which have recently sprung up . . . . There is ever so much more suppression today through proceedings which have no juries, no substantial supervision by judges, and vague definitions of wrong-doing . . . .

"Run rapidly over some of the current methods of suppression and see what persons do the deciding and penalizing instead of jurymen. In legislative investigations, the denouncing and ousting from jobs is done by legislators with an eye on reelections and party axes to grind. Loyalty programs in federal and state governments are run by administrative officials, who can drive men out of their chosen careers and often make it hard for them to get any private work. If loyalty programs are extended to industry, the decision is made by businessmen who are often afraid of losing government contracts. In public schools and universities, the loss of a career is inflicted by educational officials, who are sometimes threatened by a statute with being severely punished themselves if they decide the teacher is innocent and are afterwards ruled to have been mistaken. Many efforts are made to extend the same system to private schools and colleges. Books are weeded out from schools and colleges by officials. The extensive outlawing of organizations contemplated by the McCarran Act will be done by a board of five men specially selected as watch-dogs of sedition. Administrators can also stifle organizations by choking off the financial contributions which are essential to their existence; they can deprive potential givers of exemptions from income taxes and sometimes threaten them with prosecution if they give money to a red-listed group. The denial of passports is chiefly left to the uncontrolled discretion of one official whose name is unknown to the public. If a war or declared emergency exists, administrators will decide who shall be sent to concentration camps under the McCarran Act. And over and above all these penalties imposed on American citizens by officials is the constant smearing of them by single speakers on the floor of the legislature and single columnists, who now exercise the power to take away any man's good name and blackmail his customers and sponsors with threats of boycott and very likely ruin his chances of supporting himself, his wife and his children. Not only do jurymen have almost nothing to do with the suppressions just listed, but judges too are pretty much out of the picture."

Chafee offered a dismal and unwarranted conclusion: " . . . There is as yet no evidence that a majority of the Supreme Court Justices will give any protection to freedom of thought and expression from legislative investigations, loyalty programs, purges of teachers, and test oaths . . . . If judges cannot or will not review suppressions, then legislators and officials are left free to penalize speech and even thoughts as much as they may desire, and they desire a great deal."

When Chafee argued in behalf of Communist teachers, he ignored the fact that it was common rather than exceptional for responsible educators to present scholarly expositions of Communism and other major "isms" just as they presented similar expositions of various religions, economic theories, and philosophies. This one-sided approach was evident when he wrote: "The difficulty about speech is that what is poison in one country seems to be the chief and favorite dish in another country. The poison here is Communism and I have to spend a great deal of time trying to persuade people that they ought to allow Communism to be put in print and to be put in oral discussions and even to be discussed in educational institutions.

"We have a bill, I regret to say, pending in our state legislature that no person who is a member of the Communist Party or who advocates its doctrines shall be permitted to teach in any school or college in Massachusetts, including the institution in which I am a teacher. And if such a person is permitted, not only can the teacher be put in jail but also the college can be heavily fined and the president of the college can be put in jail.

"Now the arguments that are used in behalf of this bill are that Communism is poison and therefore the tender little children who attend my classes should not be permitted to imbibe any of its poison.

"We cannot tell what is poison and what is not poison in advance. But our faith is that human beings themselves, given time and given discussion, will be able to separate the wheat from the tares. Whether Communism will turn out to be the wheat or the tare, I don't know, but I want to give people an ample chance to find out."

Chafee had written as though any responsible academic institution lacked a voluminous supply of Communist material available to its faculty and student body and as though Communism had been seriously neglected in classroom and seminar discussions. He wrote as if only a Communist could explain Communism, though he certainly would not have argued that only a criminal could explain crime. And most revealing – in the prime of his life, as a professor at one of the world's leading universities and as one of America's better-known civil libertarians, he confessed that he was not sure whether Communism was or was not a poisonous ideology.

Chafee's special pleadings for Communists were certainly not made from the impartiality of an ivory tower. He had more than a nodding acquaintance with the Communist movement in the United States. He had been affiliated with the American Committee for Democracy and Intellectual Freedom ("subversive and un-American" – "a Communist-front organization operating among college teachers and professors"); the Citizens' Committee To Free Earl Browder ("a strictly Communist Party affair"); the Fellowship of Reconciliation (ultra-leftist-pacifist); the National Committee To Defeat the Mundt Bill ("a Communist lobby . . . which has carried out the objectives of the Communist Party in its fight against anti-subversive legislation"); the National Committee To Repeal the McCarran Act ("Communist front" – "subversive"); the National Committee To Secure Justice in the Rosenberg Case ("Communist front organized . . . to conduct the United States phase of a mammoth propaganda campaign designed to obliterate the crime of and exploit the Rosenbergs and their codefendant Morton Sobell for the purposes of international Communism"); the National Council Against Conscription ("Communist front"); the National Council of the Arts, Sciences, and Professions ("a Communist front used to appeal to special occupational groups"); the National Federation for Constitutional Liberties ("under Communist Party domination and headed by responsible Party functionaries" – "one of the viciously subversive organizations of the Communist Party"); Statement Defending the Communist Party (Communist enterprise); and Veterans of the Abraham Lincoln Brigade ("directed, dominated and controlled by the Communist Party"). He died in February 1957.

RUFUS E. CLEMENT was born on June 26, 1900 in Salisbury, North Carolina, son of Emma Williams and George Clement. He married Pearl Johnson. He was an alumnus of Livingston College (A.B., 1919); Garrett Biblical Institute (B.D., 1922); Northwestern University (A.M., 1922, and Ph.D., 1930). He has contributed articles to the *Journal of Negro Education*, the *Dictionary of American Biography*, the *Southern Frontier*, the *Journal of Higher Education, Negro Digest*, and the *Journal of Educa-*

tional Sociology. He was a member of the editorial board of *Phylon*, Atlanta University's journal on race and culture.

From 1922 until 1931, Clement was at Livingston College as instructor in history (1922-1925) and professor of history and dean of the college (1925-1931). From 1931 until 1937, he was the dean of the Louisville Municipal College for Negroes of the University of Louisville. From 1937 until 1967, he was president of Atlanta University.

Clement was affiliated with the leftist American Association for the United Nations; the ultra-radical American Civil Liberties Union; the American Committee for Democracy and Intellectual Freedom ("subversive and un-American" – "a Communist front organization operating among college teachers and professors" – "defended Communist teachers"); the American Committee for Protection of Foreign Born ("founded by the Communist Party in order to exploit racial divisions in the United States for its own revolutionary purposes"); the American Committee To Save Refugees ("perform[ing] a most valuable function for the international Communist movement" – "subversive and Communist"); the American Council on Soviet Relations ("subversive" – "established by the Communist Party . . . directed and controlled by the Party, and operated to aid and support Party objectives concerning the defense and support of the Soviet Union"); Citizens United To Abolish the Wood-Rankin Committee [HCUA] (leftist); the Civil Rights Congress ("created and established by the Communist Party as an organization which would utilize defense of civil rights for Party purposes and raise and maintain mass defense and bail funds for Party use"); the Committee for a Democratic Far Eastern Policy ("Communist"); the Committee of Welcome for the Red Dean of Canterbury (England's most notorious pro-Soviet apologist among the clergy); the Cultural and Scientific Congress for World Peace ("Communist front" – "a propaganda front for Soviet foreign policy and Soviet culture"); the Independent Citizens' Committee of the Arts, Sciences and Professions ("Communist front"); the Joint Anti-Fascist Refugee Committee ("subversive and Communist"); the Mid-Century Conference for Peace ("aimed at assembling as many gullible persons possible under Communist direction and turning them into a vast sounding board for Communist propaganda"); the ultra-radical National Association for the Advancement of Colored People; the National Committee To Abolish the Poll Tax ("Communist front"); the National Conference on American Policy in China and the Far East ("Communist"); the National Council of the Arts, Sciences and Professions ("Communist front used to appeal to special occupational groups"); the National Federation for Constitutional Liberties ("under Communist Party domination and headed by responsible Party functionaries" – "one of the viciously subversive organizations of the Communist Party"); the National Sharecroppers' Fund ("Communist front"); Promoting Enduring Peace Inc. (ultra-leftist-pacifist); Progressive Citizens of America ("political Communist front" – "subversive"); *Protestant* ("with an eye to religious groups, the Communists have formed religious fronts such as the *Protestant*"); *Protestant Digest* ("a magazine which has faithfully propagated the Communist Party line under the guise of being a religious journal"); the Southern Conference Educational Fund (financial backbone of racial agitators, including the black power revolutionaries); the Southern Conference for Human Welfare ("a Communist-front organization which seeks to attract southern liberals on the basis of its seeming interest in the problems of the South"); the Southern Negro Youth Congress ("subversive and among the affiliates and committees of the Communist Party, USA, which seeks to alter the form of government of the United States by unconstitutional means"); the United World Federalists (the most prestigious group of fellow-travelers and dupes working for world government at the expense of United States sovereignty); the Win-the-Peace Conference ("Communist front"); and the World Peace Congress ("organized under Communist initiative in various countries throughout the world.") He died in November 1967.

ALBERT BUCKNER COE was born on April 16, 1888 in Henderson, North Carolina, son of Laura Buckner and Samuel Coe. He married Katharine Chalmers. He was an alumnus of Western Maryland College in Westminster (A.B., 1909) and Yale Divinity School (B.D., 1922). He was a summer student at Johns Hopkins University and Cambridge University in England. He was the author of *Born For Victory* (1936) and *Let Us Pray* (1952).

Coe was a Congregational pastor in Somerville, Massachusetts (1922-1925), Waterbury, Connecticut (1925-1930), and Oak Park, Illinois (1930-1949). From 1949 until 1958, he was president of the Massachusetts Congregational Conference and Missionary Society. From 1936 until 1942, he was a member of the executive committee of the General Council of Congregational Christian Churches. From 1931 until 1949, he was director of the Chicago Congregational Union. He was a member of the Federal Council of

Churches' ultra-leftist Commission on Bases for a Just and Durable Peace. His Oak Park Church welcomed Communist and Socialist speakers.

Coe was affiliated with American Peace Mobilization ("formed . . . under the auspices of the Communist Party and the Young Communist League" – "one of the most seditious organizations which ever operated in the United States"); the American-Russian Institute ("subversive" – "Communist" – "specializing in pro-Soviet propaganda"); Appeal for Amnesty for Communist Party Leaders Imprisoned Under the Smith Act (Communist Party project); the Atlantic Union Committee (leftist-internationalist); the Church Peace Mission (calling for peaceful resistance to Communism and unilateral disarmament by the United States); the Citizens' Committee To Free Earl Browder ("a strictly Communist Party affair"); the Committee for Peaceful Alternatives to the Atlantic Pact ("a Communist front organization . . . as part of Soviet psychological warfare against the United States"); the Committee of One Thousand ("Communist created and controlled"); the Federal Council of Churches (Red-laden); the Fellowship of Reconciliation (ultra-leftist-pacifist); the Mid-Century Conference for Peace ("aimed at assembling as many gullible persons as possible under Communist direction and turning them into a vast sounding board for Communist propaganda"); the National Council of the Arts, Sciences and Professions ("a Communist front used to appeal to special occupational groups"); the National Committee To Win Amnesty for Smith Act Victims ("subversive" – "Communist"); the Testimonial Dinner in Honor of W.E.B. Du-Bois (pro-Communist enterprise); and Union for Concerted Peace Efforts (leftist-pacifist). He died in February 1970.

HENRY SLOANE COFFIN was born on January 5, 1877 in New York City, son of Euphemia Sloane and Edmund Coffin. He married Dorothy Eells. He was an alumnus of Yale University (B.A., 1897 and M.A., 1900) and Union Theological Seminary (B.D., 1900). He also studied at New College in Edinburgh, Scotland (1897-1899) and the University of Marburg in Germany (1899). He was ordained a Presbyterian minister in 1900. He was the author of *The Creed of Jesus* (1907); *Social Aspects of the Cross* (1911); *The Christian and the Church* (1912); *University Sermons* (1914); *The Ten Commandments* (1915); *Some Christian Convictions* (1915); *In a Day of Social Rebuilding* (1918); *A More Christian Industrial Order* (1920); *What Is There in Religion?* (1922); *Portraits of Jesus Christ in the New Testament* (1926); *What to Preach* (1926); *The Meaning of the Cross* (1931); *What Men Are Asking – Some Current Questions in Religion* (1933); *God's Turn* (1934); *Religion Yesterday and Today* (1940); *The Public Worship of God* (1946); *God Confronts Man in History* (1947); and *A Half Century of Union Theological Seminary* (1954). He was co-author of *Some Social Aspects of the Gospel* (1912); *Church and State in the Modern World* (1937); *The Ministry* (1949); and *Isaiah in Interpreter's Bible* (c. 1950). He is co-editor of *Hymns of the Kingdom* (1910).

In New York City, Coffin held pastorates at the Bedford Park Church (1900-1905) and the Madison Avenue Church (1905-1926). From 1904 until 1945, he was at the Red-laden Union Theological Seminary as professor of practical theology (1904-1926) and president (1926-1945). In 1943 and 1944, he was Moderator of the Presbyterian Church in the United States. In 1946 and 1947, he was the Joseph Cook lecturer in China and India. He lectured at Yale University, Princeton University, Emory University, New York University, Harvard University, Columbia University, Williams College, Amherst College, Smith College, Mt. Holyoke College, Wellesley College, the United Free Church Colleges in Glasgow and Aberdeen, and New College in Edinburgh.

Coffin was affiliated with the American Association for the United Nations (leftist group); the American Committee for Protection of Foreign Born ("founded by the Communist Party in order to exploit racial divisions in the United States for its own revolutionary purposes"); the American Committee for Yugoslav Relief ("subversive and Communist"); the American Committee To Save Refugees ("perform[ing] a most valuable function for the international Communist movement"); the American Crusade To End Lynching (leftist-racist agitators); the American Relief Ship for Spain ("Communist Party front enterprise"); the American Society for Cultural Relations with Russia ("Communist front"); the Committee for Norman Thomas ("perennial Socialist Party candidate for the presidency of the United States"); the Federal Council of Churches (Red-laden); Fellowship of Reconciliation (ultra-leftist-pacifist); the League of American Writers ("subversive and Communist" – "began openly to follow the Communist Party line as dictated by the foreign policy of the Soviet Union"); the Mary Ware Dennett Defense Committee (ultra-leftist); the Medical Aid to the Soviet Union ("Communist front"); the National Council of American-Soviet Friendship ("subversive and Communist" – "specializing in pro-Soviet propaganda"); the Non-Intervention Citizens Committee (leftist group); *Protestant* ("with an eye to religious groups, the Communists have formed religious fronts such as the *Protestant*"); *Protestant Digest* ("a magazine which has faithfully propagated the Communist Party line under the guise of being a religious journal"); Russian War Relief ("Communist enterprise"); *Soviet Russia Today* ("Communist-controlled publication"); the Student Congress Against War ("Communist-controlled"); the Union of Concerted Peace Efforts ("Communist front"); and the United States-Soviet Friendship Congress ("Communist front"). He died in November 1954.

FELIX S. COHEN was born on July 3, 1907 in New York City, son of Mary Ryshpan and Morris Cohen. He married Lucy Kramer. He was an alumnus of Harvard University (A.M., 1927 and Ph.D., 1929) and Columbia University (LL.B., 1931). He was the author of *Ethical Systems and Legal Ideals* (1933); *Handbook of Federal Indian Law* (1941); and *Combatting Totalitarian Propaganda: A Legal Appraisal* (1944). He was the co-author of *Readings in Jurisprudence and Legal Philosophy* (1951). In 1932, he was admitted to the New York bar.

In 1932 and 1933, Cohen practiced law in New York City and was a lecturer at the ultra-radical New School for Social Research. From 1933 until 1943, he was an assistant solicitor with the United States Department of the Interior. From 1936 until 1948, he was a member of the board of appeals of the Department of the Interior. In 1939, he was a special assistant to the Attorney General of the United States. In 1939 and 1940, he was chief of the Indian Law Survey for the United States Department of Justice. From

1943 until 1948, he was an associate solicitor with the Department of the Interior. He was a visiting lecturer at Yale University's Law School (1946-1953) and at City College of New York (1948-1953).

One of the most perceptive evaluations of Cohen appears in Rose Martin's *Fabian Freeway*: "Felix Cohen was schooled in the subtleties of socialist manipulations from early childhood. He received counsel and training not only from his socialist father [Morris R. Cohen], but also from Felix Frankfurter, Norman Thomas, John Dewey, Sidney Hook and scores of other key figures in the socialist and communist movements in America. In his college years, Felix Cohen came under the tutelage of Harry A. Overstreet, who had been a colleague of his father in both the socialist movement and in the Department of Philosophy at City College of New York.

"Felix Cohen was completely devoted to the socialist cause and also thoroughly schooled in the devious art of leftwing duplicity. He was recognized as an authority on sociological jurisprudence by the entire leftist underworld — communist, socialist and Fabian. With his father's aid he further managed to sell himself as a 'liberal' to Holmes, Cardozo and Brandeis.

"He was chosen as a contributor to the *Encyclopedia of Social Sciences*, which was edited by his comrades in both the communist and socialist movements. He wrote articles on sociological jurisprudence for the law journals of Harvard, Yale, Columbia and many other universities and colleges throughout the United States.

"Some of the publications and institutions Felix Cohen wrote for were: *The Legal Conscience; American Bar Association Journal*, 1931; *Harvard Law Review*, 1940; *Yale Law Journal*, 1950; Ohio State University College of Law; *The Journal of the History of Ideas; Southwestern Social Science Quarterly*, 1937; Publications of the United States Department of Interior, 1939; *Minnesota Law Review*, 1947; *Modern Law Review* (London), 1937; *American Scholar*, 1952; *Journal of Philosophy,* 1939; N.Y.U. School of Law, 1936; American Association for the Advancement of Science, 1946; *Journal of Social Issues*, 1947; Yale Philosophy Club, 1951; Catholic University in Washington, D.C. (Roman Law), 1949; Anti-Defamation League, 1954; *Columbia Law Review*, 1935; *Congress Weekly*, 1953; *Brooklyn Law Review*, 1934; *National Lawyers Guild Quarterly*, 1938 (communistic); *University of Pittsburgh Law Review*, 1952; *The Monist*, 1929; *Social Science*, 1946; *Illinois Law Review*, 1937; *Encyclopedia of Social Sciences*; League for Industrial Democracy, 1940; *Contemporary Jewish Record*, 1940; American Jewish Committee, 1949; American Philosophical Association, 1953; *Georgetown Law Journal*, 1942."

In the *American Socialist Quarterly,* in 1935, while an employee of the federal government, Cohen tutored his Socialist comrades: "It is impossible to attempt the overthrow of capitalism as an economic system without at the same time attacking the substance of capitalist law .... [But] it is possible for a revolutionary party, with perfect consistency, to proclaim loyalty to the idea of law and order, to the principles of the constitution, and even, in large measure, to the language of statutes and the announced principles of the judge-made law, while at the same time waging a relentless struggle against the substance of the capitalist legal order. Indeed, the attack upon the substance of capitalist law may be very greatly strengthened by an appeal to the professed principles and ideals of the law and the constitution. The ideals of equality, liberty, and democracy which capitalist courts and legislators have proclaimed will offer a perfect base for socialist attack upon the legal foundations of capitalism . . . Socialists can learn from their adversaries that it is always possible to attack existing law, and, if the power is available, to destroy existing law, in the name of democracy, justice, and liberty, in the name of the great ideals of the American Constitution, and in the name of law itself."

There was no question about Cohen's desire for a Socialist overthrow of American capitalism. He wrote, as an advocate rather than as an expositor: "It would be instructive to consider what transformations a Socialist Supreme Court could work in American law by utilizing the tactics of capitalist judges. . . . There is probably no part of the law or the constitution which the Supreme Court could not demolish, if the need arose, in the name of the constitution itself."

Cohen made certain, as he instructed his fellow Socialists, that they understood they were in a class war and that they should profit from historical examples wherein the law was utilized by one class to defeat another: "At no point in the Nazi march to power did the German masses as a whole feel that any procedure of constitutional government was being violated. The Weimar Constitution was destroyed according to its own recipes. The death of political democracy was celebrated by plebiscites carried through within the forms of political democracy . . . . What is more important about these examples of capitalist use of the myth of legality is that they show conclusively the disparity between the form of the law, impartial, classless, and eternal, and the changing class content of the law, and thus indicate that a revolutionary interpretation of existing legal forms is possible.

"Accepting the forms and symbols of the law and the Constitution but substituting a socialist for a capitalist class content, a revolutionary party can attack the whole substance of capitalist oppression, in terms of these very symbols, as illegal and unconstitutional, and defend as legal and constitutional every act which circumstances make it expedient for the revolutionary forces to undertake . . . .

"If, then, even in the Russia of November 1917, practical revolutionaries found it necessary to appeal to the forms of legality and constitutionality in order to lead a successful insurrection, how much more obvious is the possibility of appealing to the forms and ideals of American law and American constitutional principles in leading the masses to the Second American Revolution. For in the masses of the American public, even more than in the Russian populace of 1917, are imprinted faith and pride in the established symbols of democracy, hallowed by the blood of American workers in revolution and civil war, faith and pride in the established forms of popular government, in the traditional political ideals of liberty and equality. About such symbols, forms and ideals there cluster human loyalties so powerful that neither the judges of the United States Supreme Court nor the leaders of the Russian Bolshevik Party can lead a successful assault upon established legal institutions without appealing to these loyalties by making out a plausible claim of legality for the attack on law . . . .·

"A second basis of socialist attack upon the realities of capitalist law is offered by the guarantees of freedom and civil liberties which the Bills of Rights of our federal and state constitutions contain. I am not suggesting, of course, that the forces of social revolution can rely upon these paper promises, which are flagrantly violated even in minor industrial conflicts and are even more flagrantly perverted by capitalist courts to serve as barriers against social control of industry. What I do believe is that the language of our Bills of Rights offers excellent battle-cries for American socialism . . . .

"There is . . . [another] feature of the American constitutional scene which a revolutionary party must be prepared to utilize for its own purposes. That is the fact of federalism, i.e., the division of sovereignty between the nation and the states. Most of the essential functions of government in this country are still administered by the states and their local subdivisions, rather than by the nation as a whole. It seems to me to be the height of romanticism to picture the future growth of socialism in America in terms of the sudden attainment of national power. Long before the forces of socialism are able to secure such power, they must have attained power in the more advanced states of the union, as they have already attained some degree of power in a few towns and cities . . . .

"The appeal to legality can serve a revolutionary purpose only if it is linked with a clear recognition that the legal and constitutional ideals invoked are opposed to the actual substance of capitalist law, that every moral principle which the law purports to defend is violated, again and again, in the name of the law itself. The revolutionary claim of legality can be substantiated only by exposing the hypocrisy of capitalist legality. Revolution can assume a defensive posture only by convicting the forces of capitalism of offensive measures against the law and the Constitution . . . .

"There is no choice between legal means to power and illegal means to power. All effective means to power will be denounced as illegal by those whose vested interests are threatened, and defended as legal by the revolutionary forces, if these forces are led by practical revolutionaries and not by incurable romantics. The question of legality will be decided not in party conferences before the revolution, but after the fact. If the revolution is successful, the revolution's claim of legality turns out to be correct."

Cohen was hopeful that through collusion of lawyers and judges who were committed to Socialism, constitutional law could be so manipulated and so interpreted as to produce a legal framework for a Socialist state. If all went well for the Socialists, judges would make decisions from a Socialist bias and lawyers would accept as definitive and irrevocable such warped decisions. He wrote: "In form, such law must derive from the language of the written constitution; in substance, such law must be based upon the revolutionary will and the power of the masses. The theoretical claim of constitutionality is relevant only insofar as it is itself a potent factor in organizing this will and this power and disorganizing the opposing class forces . . . . In this period, it is the task of a revolutionary party to substitute, within the legal framework of society, a socialist content for a capitalist content. Until the existing weapons of class oppression can be utterly destroyed, they must be pointed in a new direction."

After Cohen's death, many of his

essays were published in a book entitled *The Legal Conscience*. The book was hailed by Socialists from the legal profession and from many areas of the academic field. Although Cohen had been dedicated to the prostitution of American constitutional law as a means of deceiving the American people into an acceptance of Socialism, he was virtually canonized as a humanitarian, philosopher, scholar, and teacher. Yet in his *The Legal Conscience*, he made no secret of the fact that what he wanted for America was Socialism in the atheistic mold of the Soviet Union. He wrote: "Socialism, as the fulfillment of democracy, offers all men the power out of which moral responsibility is born .... Redefining the moral virtues and vices, it replaces the heroes, saints, and gods of the past with new exemplars of the good life, as in Russia ....

"The task of laughing down the provincialities of contemporary class culture, of breaking the control of art by monopolistic groups, of liberating taste and enjoyment from the slavery of pecuniary and competitive canons, of exposing the provincial ethical assumptions that bar the road to useful thought in the fields of economics, jurisprudence, and sociology, of liberating human imaginations so that men may see through complex economic and political structures to the joy or suffering they create, of dramatizing the institutions of society so that they evoke the forces of love and hate which have been traditionally directed towards personalities, of widening human loyalties to the point where one may look to his own future impersonally and find in a social ideal inspiring patterns of life, these are not tasks for the Sunday School moralists of the individualist tradition. In these tasks every realm of human culture must make its revolutionary contribution.

"Politicians, artists, and steel workers may have little of importance to say to each other in the nations of the west. That is not true in Soviet Russia .... A socialist society makes universal the material security which the flowering of the human spirit requires as the condition of existence."

Cohen's commitment to revolutionary Socialism and his contempt for traditional American mores was perhaps best revealed when he explained with his personal approval the way in which Socialists would create a revolutionary morality. By "redefining the moral virtues and vices," he said, "it replaces the heroes, saints, and gods of the past with new exemplars of the good life, as in Russia, for instance, the figure of Christ, who deals with all things in an intimate and personal way, has been replaced by the figure of Lenin, the exponent of statistical morality."

Cohen died in October 1953.

KYLE S. CRICHTON was born on November 5, 1896 in Peale, Pennsylvania, son of Margaret Nelson and William Crichton. He married Mary Collier. He was an alumnus of Lehigh University (A.B., 1917). He was the author of *Law and Order, Ltd.* (1928); *Redder Than the Rose* (1935); *Reading From Left to Right* (1936); *The Proud People* (1944); *The Marx Brothers* (1950); *George Whigham* (1951); *The Happiest Millionaire*, a play (1956); and *Total Recoil* (1960). He was co-author of *My Philadelphia Father* (1955) and *My Partner-in-Law: The Life of George Morton Levy* (1957).

Prior to 1922, Crichton worked as a coal miner, turret-lathe operator, open-hearth puddler, and newspaper reporter. From 1922 until 1929, he operated an advertising agency in Albuquerque, New Mexico. From 1929 until 1933, he was an associate editor of Charles Scribner's Sons, a publishing firm. From 1933 until 1949, he was an associate editor and writer for *Collier's Weekly*.

Crichton wrote *Redder Than the Rose* and *Reading From Left to Right* under the pseudonym of Robert Forsythe. He also used this same pseudonym while writing a weekly column for the Communist publication *New Masses*. Eugene Lyons, in his *The Red Decade*, offered a portrait of the *Collier's-New Masses*, Crichton-Forsythe split personality: "His prosaic workaday identity is Kyle Crichton, long the theatre and movie writer for *Collier's*. He is a tall, stooped, spectacled, rather professorial or clerical gentleman. The last thing you would guess him to be from his looks and talk is the author of a weekly chunk of creampuffery for the masses – press-agent gurglings about Hollywood starlets, vaudeville comics, theatre hopefuls, skating queens and the like. The man and his work are so ludicrously at odds that it is a safe guess he despises his hacking and hates himself for it. The first time I looked at this dignified person I felt I could understand the bitter and uninhibited name-calling in his romantic communist incarnation as Robert Forsythe. The *New Masses* Forsythe, I felt, was trying to prove in issue after issue that under the surface of *Collier's* Kyle Crichton there was really an audacious fellow with a mind and a soul and, above all, literary guts. Precisely because his *Collier's* stuff was so sickly saccharine, his defense of the Kremlin's tortuous line had to be written in gall and bile. The sardonic Burton Rascoe hit the nail on the head when he disposed of Crichton-Forsythe with the phrase, 'So red the pose.' " (Lyons also told of how "Crichton reviewed a book by 'Forsythe' for the old *Life* and found it exceedingly good!")

Crichton-Forsythe was affiliated with the American Committee for Protection of Foreign Born ("founded by the Communist Party in order to exploit racial divisions in the United States for its own revolutionary purposes"); the American Committee To Save Refugees ("perform[ing] a most valuable function for the international Communist movement"); the American League Against War and Fascism ("subversive and Communist – "established in the United States in an effort to create public sentiment on behalf of a foreign policy adapted to the interests of the Soviet Union"); the American League for Peace and Democracy ("subversive and Communist" – "established . . . in an effort to create public sentiment on behalf of a foreign policy adapted to the interests of the Soviet Union . . . [and] designed to conceal Communist control, in accordance with the new tactics of the Communist International"); American Friends of Spanish Democracy ("Communist front"); American Friends of the Chinese People ("Communist front"); the American Society for Technical Aid to Spanish Democracy ("Communist front"); Appeal for Pardon for Robert Stamm (German Communist); the Artists' Front To Win the War ("Communist front" – "included representatives of the theater, of literature, music, art, science, and education, with long and active records of support for Communist-front organizations and for the variegated turns of the Communist Party line"); the Cultural and Scientific Conference for World Peace ("Communist front" – "a propaganda front for Soviet foreign policy and Soviet culture"); Friends of the Abraham Lincoln Brigade ("completely controlled by the Communist Party"); Frontier Films ("Communist front"); the Golden Book of American Friendship with the Soviet Union ("pro-Soviet propaganda enterprise"); the Joint Anti-Fascist Refugee Committee ("subversive and Communist"); the Julius Rosenwald Memorial Committee ("a Communist front organization which belonged to the large group of Spanish aid committees which the Communist Party so successfully exploited"); the League of American Writers ("subversive and Communist" – "began openly to follow the Communist line as dictated by the foreign policy of the Soviet Union"); the League of Professional Groups for [William Z.] Foster and [James W.] Ford ("the members of this organization were committed to the objectives of the Communist Party"); the Medical Bureau To Aid Spanish Democracy ("Communist enterprise"); the Motion Picture Artists' Committee ("Communist front"); the National Committee for People's Rights ("composed primarily of openly avowed members of the Communist Party and veteran fellow travelers of the Communist Party"); the National Committee for the Defense of Political Prisoners ("subversive and Communist"); the North American Spanish Aid Committee ("Communist"); Open Letter for Closer Cooperation with the Soviet Union (issued by "a group of Communist Party stooges"); the United American Spanish Aid Committee ("Communist"); the Veterans of the Abraham Lincoln Brigade ("directed, dominated and controlled by the Communist Party"); and the Writers' and Artists' Committee for Medical Aid to Spain ("a Communist front set up for the purpose of agitation and propaganda").

Crichton died in November 1960.

ABRAHAM CRONBACH was born on February 16, 1882 in Indianapolis, Indiana, son of Hannah Itzig and Marcus Cronbach. He married Rose Hentel. He was an alumnus of the University of Cincinnati (B.A., 1902) and Hebrew Union College (D.D., 1915). He was ordained a rabbi in 1906. He pursued graduate studies at Cambridge University in England (1911-1912) and the University of Berlin (1912). He was the author of *Prayers of the Jewish Advance* (1924); *Jewish Peace Book* (1932); *Religion and Its Social Setting* (1933); *The Quest for Peace* (1934); *The Bible and Our Social Outlook* (1941); *Judaism for Today* (1954); *Realities of Religion* (1957); *Autobiography* (1959); *Stories Made of Bible Stories* (1961); and *Reform Movements in Judaism* (1963). He contributed to *Approaches to World Peace: Fourth Symposium of the Conference on Science, Philosophy and Religion* (1944). He also contributed to publications, including the Hebrew Union College *Monthly* and *Annual*, the *Journal of Religion*, the *American Israelite*, the *B'nai B'rith Magazine*, and *Psychology Bulletin*.

From 1906 until 1915, Cronbach was rabbi of Temple Beth El in South Bend, Indiana. From 1915 until 1917, he was assistant rabbi at New York City's Free Synagogue. From 1917 until 1919, he was rabbi of Temple Israel in Akron, Ohio. From 1919 until 1922, he was chaplain for the Chicago Federation of Synagogues. From 1922 until 1965, he was at Hebrew Union College in Cincinnati as professor of social studies (1922-1950) and professor emeritus (1950-1965). From 1939 until 1965, he was secretary and managing editor of the Hebrew Union College *Annual*. From 1939 until 1965, he was a traveling lecturer in institutes on Judaism, sponsored by the Union of American Hebrew Congregations.

Cronbach was affiliated with the American Biro Bidjan Committee ("Communist front"); the American Committee for Protection of Foreign Born ("founded by the Communist Party in order to exploit racial divisions in the United States for its own revolutionary purposes"); the American Continental Congress for World Peace ("another phase in the Communist 'peace' campaign, aimed at consolidating anti-American forces throughout the Western Hemisphere"); the American Peace Crusade ("Communist front"); the American Peace Mobilization ("formed . . . under the auspices of the Communist Party and the Young Communist League" — "one of the most seditious organizations which ever operated in the United States"); an Appeal for Amnesty for Communist Party Leaders Imprisoned Under the Smith Act (Communist Party project); the Bill of Rights Conference ("subversive"); Brief [amicus curiae] for the Communist Party ("Communist Party enterprise"); the Civil Rights Congress ("created and established by the Communist Party as an organization which would utilize defense of civil rights for Party purposes and raise and maintain mass defense and bail funds for Party use"); the Committee for Citizenship Rights ("to protect Communist subversion from any penalties under the law"); the Committee for a Democratic Far Eastern Policy ("Communist"); the Committee for Medical Freedom (leftist); the Committee for Peaceful Alternatives to the Atlantic Pact ("Communist front organization . . . as part of Soviet psychological warfare against the United States"); the Committee To Defend America by Keeping Out of War ("Communist front"); the Committee

To Defend the Victims of the Committee on Un-American Activities (a petition by ultra-leftists to the United Nations in 1950); the Committee To End Sedition Laws ("under complete domination by the Communist Party"); the Emergency Civil Liberties Committee ("Communist front" — "subversive"); the Emergency Peace Mobilization ("Communist front"); the Fellowship of Reconciliation (ultra-leftist-pacifist); the Hiroshima Commemorative Committee (ultra-leftist); International Labor Defense ("subversive and Communist" — "legal arm of the Communist Party" — "part of an international network of organizations for the defense of Communist lawbreakers"); the International Workers Order ("from its very inception demonstrated by its pronouncements, its activities, and the authoritative statements of the Communist Party that it is a subservient instrument of the Communist Party of the United States"); the Jefferson School of Social Science ("a Communist institution modeled along the lines of the new Communist policy which led to the decision to change the Communist Party into some kind of an educational institution"); the Jewish Peace Fellowship (leftist-pacifist); the Mid-Century Conference for Peace ("aimed at assembling as many gullible persons possible under Communist direction and turning them into a vast sounding board for Communist propaganda"); the National Assembly for Peace ("Communist front"); the National Committee To Repeal the McCarran Act ("Communist front" — "subversive"); the National Committee To Secure Justice in the Rosenberg Case ("Communist front organized . . . to conduct the United States phase of a mammoth propaganda campaign designed to obliterate the crime of and exploit the Rosenbergs and their co-defendant Morton Sobell for the purposes of international Communism"); the National Committee To Win Amnesty for Smith Act Victims ("subversive" – "Communist"); the National Council Against Conscription ("Communist front"); the National Council of the Arts, Sciences and Professions ("a Communist front used to appeal to special occupational groups"); the National Federation for Constitutional Liberties ("under Communist Party domination and headed by responsible Party functionaries" – one of the viciously subversive organizations of the Communist Party"); the National Religion and Labor Foundation ("Communist front"); Peace Information Center ("Communist front"); Promoting Enduring Peace, Inc. (ultra-leftist-pacifist); Religious Freedom Committee (an ultra-leftist group working for the abolition of the House Committee on Un-American Activities); the [Morris U.] Schappes Defense Committee ("a front organization with a strictly Communist objective, namely, the defense of a self-admitted Communist who was convicted of perjury in the courts of New York"); the School of Jewish Studies ("adjunct of the Communist Party"); the Scientific and Cultural Conference for World Peace ("Communist front" – "a propaganda front for Soviet foreign policy and Soviet culture");and the World Peace Congress ("organized under Communist initiative in various countries throughout the world"). Cronbach died in April 1965.

BARTLEY C[AVANAUGH] CRUM was born on November 28, 1900 in Sacramento, California, son of Emma Cavanaugh and James Crum. He married Gertrude Bosworth. He was an alumnus of the University of California (A.B.,

1922 and J.D., 1924). He was the author of *Behind the Silken Curtain* (1947).

In 1924, Crum was admitted to the California bar and began his practice in San Francisco. From 1924 until 1928, he was associated in law with John Francis Neylan. From 1938 until 1949, he was associated with Philip S. Ehrlich. In 1949, he was admitted to the New York bar and became a partner in the firm of Hays, Podell, Algase, Crum and Feuer. In 1942, he was special counsel to the President's Committee on Fair Employment Practices. In 1945, he was a consultant to the United States delegation to the United Nations founding conference in San Francisco. In 1946, he became president of radio stations KYA in San Francisco and KLAC in Los Angeles.

In 1940, Crum was the western campaign manager for the Republican presidential candidate, Wendell Willkie. In 1944, Crum was national chairman of Independent Republicans for Roosevelt, but retained his membership in the Republican Party. By 1946, he had joined and become the vice president of the Progressive Citizens of America, which was a political Communist front. However, when the PCA named Henry Wallace to be its presidential candidate in 1948, Crum resigned his membership.

Crum's defection from the Progressive Citizens of America was not characteristic of his attitude toward the left. Prior to and after 1947, he compiled an impressive history of leftist activities and affiliations. He had belonged to the predecessor organizations of the Progressive Citizens of America – the Independent Citizens Committee of the Arts, Sciences, and Professions ("Communist front") and the National

Citizens Political Action Committee ("Communist front"). While he still professed to be a Republican, he left little doubt that he wanted the Republican Party to assume a leftist posture in order to promote a welfare state. On matters of foreign policy, he also followed the leftist line. He was bitterly opposed, in 1945, to participation in the World Court by the anti-Communist regime of Spain, and to its membership in the United Nations. In 1945, he volunteered his services to an international panel of lawyers who were preparing the defense of two Spanish Communists. In 1947, he opposed the Truman Administration's program for military and financial aid to Greece and Turkey, which were threatened by Communist "liberation." He insisted that the United States should not aid such "reactionary" powers and that the problems of Greece and Turkey should be assigned to the United Nations.

In 1946, Crum was one of six American members of an Anglo-American Committee of Inquiry in Palestine. His experiences on that Committee were the subject of his book, *Behind the Silken Curtain*, published in 1947. It was promoted by the Communists through such means as their *New Masses* ("weekly journal of the Communist Party"); the American Youth for Democracy ("subversive and Communist" – "part of Soviet psychological warfare against the United States"); and the Book Find Club, which consistently promoted pro-Communist literature. In 1947, Crum was one of the attorneys representing the Hollywood Ten in their appearance before the House Committee on Un-American Activities, when all of them refused to answer questions regarding membership in the Communist Party or affiliations with Communists or Communist organizations. In 1947, Crum preached the standard leftist line against proposals in Congress to outlaw the Communist Party. He completely misrepresented the legislation at hand when he wrote: "It is unconstitutional and utterly stupid for government to attempt to prevent people from thinking or believing as they wish." He followed this with a standard inanity: "As a non-Communist, I think the most effective answer to the Marxist is to make our democracy work by providing equality and job opportunities for all, strengthening the trade unions, and raising the standard of living."

Crum's affiliations included the Action Committee To Free Spain Now ("Communist"); the American Association for the United Nations (leftist group); the American Committee for Spanish Freedom ("Communist"); the American Committee for Jewish Writers, Artists and Scientists ("Communist front"); the American-Russian Institute ("subversive" – "Communist" – "specializing in pro-Soviet propaganda"); the American Slav Congress ("Moscow-inspired and directed federation of Communist-dominated organizations seeking by methods of propaganda and pressure to subvert the 10,000,000 people in this country of Slavic birth or descent"); the American Youth for Democracy ("subversive and Communist" – "part of Soviet psychological warfare against the United States"); the California Labor School ("a subversive and Communist organization"); the Committee for a Democratic Far Eastern Policy ("Communist"); Fight for Freedom, Inc. (a leftist pressure group advocating United States intervention in World War II); Friends of the Spanish Republican Committee (leftist); the Hollywood Democratic Committee ("Communist front"); the Joint Anti-Fascist Refugee Committee ("subversive and Communist"); the ultra-radical National Association for the Advancement of Colored People; the National Committee To Win the Peace ("subversive and Communist"); the National Conference on the German Problem (dominated by leftists); the National Federation for Constitutional Liberties ("under Communist Party domination and headed by responsible Party functionaries" – "one of the viciously subversive organizations of the Communist Party"); the National Lawyers Guild ("the foremost legal bulwark of the Communist Party, its front organizations, and controlled unions"); Russian War Relief ("Communist enterprise"); the Society for the Prevention of World War III (loaded with notorious veteran fellow-travelers); the Spanish Refugee Appeal ("subversive" – "Communist front"); the Tom Mooney Labor School ("Communist Party school"); Veterans of the Abraham Lincoln Brigade ("directed, dominated and controlled by the Communist Party"); and the Win-the-Peace Conference ("Communist front"). He died in December 1959.

HENRY W. L. DANA was born on January 26, 1881 in Boston, Massachusetts, son of Edith Longfellow and Richard Dana. He was an alumnus of Harvard University (A.B., 1903; A.M., 1904; and Ph.D., 1910). He was the author of *The Six Centuries Since Dante* (1926); *Opinions and Attitudes in the Twentieth Century; Shaw in Moscow* (1934); *The Theatre in a Changing Europe: Development of Soviet Drama* (1937); *Handbook on Soviet Drama* (1938); *The Craigie House: The Coming of Longfel-*

low (1939); *The Dana Saga* (1911); *Longfellow and Dickens: The Story of a Trans-Atlantic Friendship* (1943); *Drama in Wartime Russia* (1943); *History of the Modern Drama: Russia* (1947); *The Origin and Development of Longfellow's "Evangeline"* (1947); and *The Longfellow House: History and Guide* (1948). He was editor of *Seven Soviet Plays* (1946) and *Two Years Before the Mast* (1946).

In 1903 and 1904, Dana was a teacher in St. Paul's School in Concord, New Hampshire. From 1904 until 1906, he was a teacher in the Thacher School in Ojai, California. From 1908 until 1910, he was an assistant in comparative literature at Harvard University. From 1910 until 1912, he was a lecturer in English at the Sorbonne of the University of Paris. From 1912 until 1917, he was at Columbia University as an instructor in comparative literature (1912-1916) and assistant professor (1917). From 1921 until 1932, he was a lecturer at the New School for Social Research, which was "established by men who belonged to the ranks of near-Bolshevik Intelligentsia, some of them being too radical in their views to remain on the faculty of Columbia University."

Dana lived in the Soviet Union in 1927-1928, in 1931-1932, and in 1934-1935. An avowed Communist, he was banned from England in 1932. He was affiliated with the American Committee for Struggle Against War ("Communist front"); the American Council on Soviet Relations ("subversive" – "established by the Communist Party . . . directed and controlled by the Party, and operated to aid and support Party objectives concerning the defense and support of the Soviet Union"); the American League Against War and Fascism ("subversive and Communist" – "established in the United States in an effort to create public sentiment on behalf of a foreign policy adapted to the interests of the Soviet Union"); the American League for Peace and Democracy ("subversive and Communist" – "established in an effort to create public sentiment on behalf of a foreign policy adapted to the interests of the Soviet Union [and] designed to conceal Communist control, in accordance with the new tactics of the Communist International"); American Peace Mobilization ("formed . . . under the auspices of the Communist Party and the Young Communist League" – "one of the most seditious organizations which ever operated in the United States"); the American Pushkin Committee ("Communist front"); the American Russian Institute ("subversive" – "Communist" – "specializing in pro-Soviet propaganda"); the American Writers Congress ("subversive"); the Artists' Front To Win the War ("Communist front" – "included representatives of the threatre, of literature, music, art, science, and education, with long and active records of support for Communist-front organizations and for the variegated turns of the Communist Party line"); Book Union, Inc. ("distributors of Communist literature" – "Communist [Party] book club"); Brookwood Labor College ("Communistic"); the Celebration for the Adoption of a New Constitution for the Soviet Union in 1937 (Communist enterprise); the Committee for Citizenship Rights ("to protect Communist subversion from any penalties under the law"); the Committee of Professional Groups for [Earl W.] Browder and [James W.] Ford (Communist Party candidates for president and vice-president of the United States in 1936); the Committee To Defend America by Keeping Out of War ("Communist front"); the Fellowship of Reconciliation (ultra-leftist-pacifist); the Friends of the Soviet Union ("created, directed, and controlled by the Communist Party . . . and operated to aid and support Party objectives concerning the defense and support of the Soviet Union"); the Golden Book of American Friendship with the Soviet Union ("pro-Soviet propaganda enterprise"); the International Labor Defense ("subversive and Communist" – "legal arm of the Communist Party" – "part of an international network of organizations for the defense of Communist lawbreakers"); the John Reed Clubs ("out-and-out Communist organizations which preceded the contemporary Communist front organizations which cater to so-called liberals"); the League for Industrial Democracy (Socialist); the League of Professional Groups for [William Z.] Foster and [James W.] Ford ("the members of this organization were committed to the objectives of the Communist Party"); the Liberty Defense League (Socialist); the Massachusetts Council of American-Soviet Friendship ("subversive and Communist" – "specializing in pro-Soviet propaganda"); the National Committee for People's Rights ("composed primarily of openly-avowed members of the Communist Party and veteran fellow-travelers of the Communist Party"); the National Committee for the Defense of Political Prisoners ("subversive and Communist"); the National Committee for the Student Congress Against War ("Communist-controlled"); the National Committee To Aid Striking Miners Fighting Starvation ("Communist front"); the National Federation for Constitutional Liberties ("under Communist Party domination and headed by responsible Party functionaries" – "one of the viciously subversive organizations of the Communist Party"); the National Reception Committee to the Russian Delegation, 1943 ("Communist Party enterprise"); the National Student League ("the Communists' front organization for students"); *New Masses* ("weekly journal of the Communist Party"); *New Theatre* ("a Communist Party publication"); New Theatre League ("Communist front"); People's Council ("modeled after the Council of Workmen's and Soldiers' Councils, the Sovereign power of Russia today [1920]"); School for Democracy ("established by Communist teachers ousted from the public school system of New York City"); *Soviet Russia* ("official organ of the Friends of Soviet Russia, which was created by the Communist Party"); a Statement by American Progressives on the Moscow Trials ("obviously a document concocted in defense of the line of the Communist Party and undoubtedly originated in the headquarters of the Communist Party"); a Statement Defending the Communist Party (Communist Party enterprise); the Student Congress Against War ("Communist controlled"); *Theatre Arts* ("pro-Communist monthly"); the United American Spanish Aid Committee ("Communist"); and the World Congress Against War ("sponsored by the Communist International"). He died in April 1950.

NED H[ARLAND] DEARBORN was born on June 2, 1893 in Conneautville, Pennsylvania, son of Katharine Rogers and John Dearborn. He married Enid Williams and Glennie Grant. He was an alumnus of Columbia University's Teachers College (B.S., 1921; M.A., 1924; and Ph.D., 1925). Prior to his years at Columbia, he graduated (1912) from the State Normal School at Edinboro, Pennsylvania, and began a teaching career. He was a student at Grove City College in the summer of 1916. He was the author of *Introduction to Teaching* (1925); *The Oswego Movement in American Education* (1925); and *Once in a Lifetime* (1936). He was co-author of *Social Studies in Teachers Colleges* (1928). He wrote articles for *Current History*.

In 1912, Dearborn was assistant supervising principal of the public school in Harmonsburg, Pennsylvania. From 1913 until 1920, he was supervising principal in the public schools at Harmonsburg (1913-1914), at West Springfield (1914-1918), and at Conneautville (1918-1920) – all in Pennsylvania. From 1921 until 1923, he was director of training at the State Normal School in Oswego, New York, and directed that institution's summer sessions in 1922, 1923, and 1925. From 1923 until 1925, he was assistant to the director of the Commonwealth Fund's division of educational research. From 1925 until 1929, he was director of the teacher training division of New York State's Department of Education. From 1929 until 1959, he was on the faculty of New York University as professor of education (1929-1959) and dean of the division of general education (1934-1942). From 1942 until 1959, he was with the National Safety Council as executive vice-president (1942-1944) and president (1944-1959).

In 1939, when Dearborn was dean at New York University, he was a leader in the New York College Teachers Union, American Federation of Teachers, and the newly formed American Committee for Democracy and Intellectual Freedom. The latter group was composed of scientists, educators, and persons in related professions who alleged that their purpose was "to promote education for democracy and to publicize scientific facts which would counteract prejudice and undemocratic movements." The occasion for the founding of the American Committee was the investigation being conducted into Communist, Nazi, and Fascist activities in the New York public schools by the Rapp-Coudert Committee of the New York Legislature. Under New York law, individuals were barred from teaching and civil service jobs if they advocated the overthrow of government by force and violence, or disseminated printed materials advocating such action.

The American Committee received favorable publicity in the Communists' *Daily Worker*, and its membership included college and university deans and some of the nation's better known scientists and educators. Dearborn was instrumental in issuing "An Appeal for Unity Behind Democracy," which was the American Committee's position paper against the Rapp-Coudert investigation. Said the appeal, "The basic test of his [a teacher's] professional ability and integrity lies within the school. There the teacher must not be an advocate or a propagandist . . . . As a responsible citizen, on the other hand, a teacher shares the rights and prerogatives of all citizens of the United States . . . . Punitive action because of personal beliefs or legal political activity is inconsistent with the very principles of democracy . . . . Propaganda must not be confused, as it often is, with an honest presentation of two conflicting views with frank discussion and analysis." New York State Senator Frederick R. Coudert Jr., chairman of the investigating committee, was not intimidated by the American Committee's pretentious position paper, which had no relevance to the issues at stake. Coudert knew that the American Committee was led by

Dearborn and veteran fellow-traveler Franz Boas, both of whom were major figures in the New York College Teachers Union, which had as its executive secretary a Communist, Moses I. Finkelstein. As a result of the Rapp-Coudert Committee's work, a great number of Communist teachers were expelled from the city's educational system, including Finkelstein, a teacher at the New York City College, who was serving also as executive secretary of the American Committee for Democracy and Intellectual Freedom.

Dearborn remained with the American Committee as it cooperated with major Communist fronts in the promotion of Communist enterprises such as the fight to abolish the Special Committee on Un-American Activities of the Congress of the United States, in the promotion of a Communist-line foreign policy for the United States, and in the continuing battle to defend Communist educators from exposure.

Dearborn's other affiliations included the American Committee To Save Refugees ("perform[ing] a most valuable function in the international Communist movement"); the American Investors Union ("Communist front" – "the principal tactic employed by the American Investors Union has been to send representatives, first obtaining proxies for them, to stockholders' meetings of various business corporations, for the purpose of harassing the management of those corporations"); *Equality* (Communist Party enterprise); Film Audiences for Democracy ("Communist front"); the Greater New York Emergency Conference on Inalienable Rights ("Communist front"); the National Federation for Constitutional Liberties ("under Communist Party domination and headed by responsible Party functionaries" – "one of the viciously subversive organizations of the Communist Party"); the New York State Conference on National Unity ("Communist front"); and the Washington Committee for Democratic Action ("subversive and Communist"). He died in August 1962.

EUGENE VICTOR DEBS was born on November 5, 1855 in Terre Haute, Indiana, son of Marguerite Bettrich and Jean Debs. He was married to Katherine Metzel. He was the author of *Walls and Bars* (1927).

In 1870, Debs worked in the Vandalia paint shop of the Terre Haute and Indianapolis Railway. From 1871 until 1874, he was a locomotive fireman. From 1874 until 1879, he worked in a wholesale grocery firm. In 1875, he helped to organize a local in Terre Haute of the Brotherhood of Locomotive Firemen, and became secretary of the local. In 1878, he became associate editor of the *Firemen's Magazine*, the official organ of the Brotherhood. In 1880, he became general secretary and treasurer of the Brotherhood, and editor and manager of the *Firemen's Magazine.* He held those positions for twelve years. In the meantime, he served as city clerk of Terre Haute for two two-year terms, and for one two-year term in the lower house of the Indiana Legislature. In 1892, he resigned his offices in the Brotherhood but was immediately re-elected by unanimous vote. In the 1880's, aside from his duties with the Brotherhood of Locomotive Firemen, he was instrumental in organizing the Brotherhood of Railway Brakemen, the Brotherhood of Railway Carmen, and the Switchmen's Mutual Aid Association.

In 1893, Debs helped to organize and became the first president of the American Railway Union. In less than a year,

he led a successful strike against the Great Northern Railroad. Less than two months after the Great Northern strike was settled, employees of the Pullman Company went out on strike in South Chicago. Debs' American Railway Union supported the strikers by instituting a boycott against the movement of Pullman cars. For his part, Debs became the virtual leader of the strike. The President of the United States, Grover Cleveland, ordered federal troops to the scene of the strike on grounds that the United States mails were being obstructed. An injunction was issued against the strikers and a federal grand jury indicted Debs and three others for conspiracy to obstruct the mails. They were arrested and shortly thereafter were arrested again and held in contempt of court for violating the injunction. Eventually, Debs received a six-month sentence on the contempt charge; he spent the time in the McHenry County Jail at Woodstock, Illinois. When Debs completed his jail sentence, he announced that he was now a Socialist. He had spent the greater part of six months in jail studying the writings of Marx, Engels, and other Socialists.

In 1896, Debs campaigned for William Jennings Bryan. In 1897, most of those who remained in the American Railway Union after losing the Pullman strike followed Debs into the Social Democratic Party of America. In 1900, the Social Democratic Party and the Socialist Labor Party supported Debs as their fusion candidate for the presidency of the United States. He received 96,116 votes. (In 1904, 1908, 1912, and 1920, he was the Socialist Party's candidate for the presidency.)

In 1904, when Debs was a presidential candidate for the second time, he received 402, 321 votes. By that time, he had become associate editor of the Socialist weekly, *Appeal To Reason*, published in Girard, Kansas. From 1900 until 1906, he devoted all of his energies to his editorial work and to lecture tours to promote the *Appeal* and the Socialist Party. In 1905, he was a major factor in the founding of the Industrial Workers of the World, the Wobblies. Debs did not remain as a member of the Wobblies for very long, but he did remain friendly with its leaders and on many occasions defended the Wobblies against their critics. He did of course remain the leader of the Socialist Party. In 1908 and 1912, as the Socialist Party's candidate for the presidency, he received 420,973 votes and 901,062 votes, respectively. In 1916, he decided not to be a candidate. In 1917, at an annual national convention of the Socialist Party, the delegates denounced United States entry into World War I and advised the members of the Party to oppose the war by all the means in their power. Debs approved the delegates' stand.

In 1908, when Debs accepted the Socialist Party's presidential nomination, he spoke as a relatively orthodox Socialist. Within a dozen years from that time he would be a flaming Red revolutionary, ready to to use America's labor force to upset the nation's entire economic, political, and social structure. In 1908, however, his Socialist appeal was the standard fare of the era: the laborer and farmer were the oppressed victims of capitalism with its trusts, its industrial tycoons, its utilities magnates, its large property owners, its controlled Congress, and its ranks of unemployed. To remedy all these ills, Debs offered the ballot box as a solution. He reasoned that with the Socialists in political power, the great industries and utilities would be owned and operated by the people, all industry would be completely organized, and society would have a scientific foundation.

Debs made no call to man the barricades in 1908. But there could be no doubt that behind his political, economic, and even religious arguments, the gospel according to Marx was the essence of his brand of Socialism. He said, in part: "I am in revolt against capitalism (and that doesn't mean to say, my friends, that I am hating you – not the slightest). I am opposed to capitalism because I love my fellowmen; and if I am opposing you I am opposing you for what I believe to be your good; and though you spat upon me with contempt, I should still oppose you to the extent of my power.

"I don't hate the workingman because he has turned against me. I know the poor fellow is too ignorant to understand his self-interest, and I know that as a rule the workingman is the friend of his enemy and the enemy of his friend. He votes for men who represent a system in which labor is simply merchandise; in which the man who works the hardest and longest has the least to show for it.

"If there is a man on this earth who is entitled to all the comforts and luxuries of this life in abundance, it is the man whose labor produces them . . . . I am opposing the system under which we live today because I believe it is subversive of the best interests of the people. I am not satisfied with things as they are, and I know that no matter what administration is in power, even were it a Socialist administration, there will be no material change in the condition of the people until we have a new social system based upon the mutual economic interests of the whole people; until you and I and all of us collectively own those things that we collectively need and use.

"That is a basic economic proposition. As long as a relatively few men own the railroads, the telegraph, the telephone, own the oilfields and the gasfields and the steel mills and the sugar refineries and the leather tanneries — own, in short, the sources and means of life — they will corrupt our politics, they will enslave the working class, they will impoverish and debase society, they will do all things that are needful to perpetuate their power as the economic masters and the political rulers of the people. Not until these great agencies are owned and operated by the people can the people hope for any material improvement in their social condition. Is the condition fair today, and satisfactory to the thinking man?

"According to the most reliable reports at our command, as I speak here this afternoon, there are at least four million working men vainly searching for employment. . . . Nothing is more humiliating than to have to beg for work, and a system in which any man has to beg for work stands condemned. No man can defend it. Now the rights of one are as sacred as the rights of a million. Suppose you happen to be the one who has no work. This republic is a failure so far as you are concerned. Every man has the inalienable right to work . . . .

"Nature's storehouse is full to the surface of the earth. All of the raw materials are deposited here in abundance. We have the most marvelous machinery the world has ever known. Man has long since become master of the natural forces and made them work for him. Now he has but to touch a button and the wheels begin to spin and the machinery to whir, and wealth is produced on every hand in increasing abundance.

"Why should any man, woman, or child suffer for food, clothing, or shelter? Why? The question cannot be answered. Don't tell me that some men are too lazy to work. Suppose they are too lazy to work, what do you think of a social system that produces men too lazy to work? If a man is too lazy to work, don't treat him with contempt. Don't look down upon him with scorn as if you were a superior being. If there is a man who is too lazy to work, there is something the matter with him. He wasn't born right or he was perverted in this system. You could not, if you tried, keep a normal man inactive, and if you did he would go stark mad. Go to any penitentiary and you will find the men there begging for the privilege of doing work.

"I know by close study of the question exactly how men become idle. I don't repel them when I meet them. I have never yet seen the tramp I was not able to receive with open arms . . . .

"Your material interest and mine in the society of the future will be the same. Instead of having to fight each other like animals, as we do today, and seeking to glorify the brute struggle for existence — of which every civilized human being ought to be ashamed — instead of this, our material interests are going to be mutual. We are going to jointly own these mammoth machines, and we are going to operate them as joint partners, and we are going to divide all the products among ourselves . . . .

"When you know enough to know what your interest is, you will support the great party that is organized upon the principle of collective ownership of the means of life. This party will sweep into power upon the issue of emancipation just as republicanism swept into power upon the Abolition question half a century ago . . . .

"What do I propose to do for [the] farmer? Nothing. I only want him to know that he is robbed every day in the week; and, if I can awaken him to the fact that he is robbed under the capitalist system, he will fall into line with the Socialist movement, and will march to the polls on election day, and instead of casting his vote to fasten the shackles upon his limbs more firmly, he will vote for his emancipation. All I have to do is to show that farmer, that day laborer, that tramp that they are victims of this system, that their interests are identical, that they constitute the millions, and that the millions have the votes. The Rockefellers have the dollars, but we have the votes; and when we have sense enough to know how to use the votes, we will have not only the votes but the dollars for all the children of men.

"This seems quite visionary to some of you and especially to those of you who know nothing about economics. I could not begin to tell you the story of social evolution this afternoon; of how these things are doing day by day, of how the world is being pushed into socialism, and how it is bound to arrive, no matter whether you are for it or against it. It is the next inevitable phase of civilization. It isn't a scheme, it isn't a contrivance. It isn't anything that is made to order. The day is coming when you will be pushed into it by unseen hands whether you will or not. Nothing can be introduced until the people want it, and when the majority want it they will know how to get it.

"I venture the prophecy that within the next five years you will be completely dispossessed. You are howling against the trusts, and the trusts are laughing at you. You keep on voting in the same old way, and the trusts keep on getting what you produce. You say Congress will give you some relief. Good heavens! Who will save us from Congress? Don't you know that Congress is made up almost wholly of trust lawyers and corporation attorneys? . . .

"The world is just beginning to awaken and is soon to sing its first anthem of freedom. All the signs of the times are cheering. Twenty-five years ago there was but a handful of socialists; today there are a half million. When the polls are closed next fall you will be astounded. The Socialist movement is in alliance with the forces of progress . . . . The Socialist Party stands today where the Republican Party stood fifty years ago. It is in alliance with the forces of evolution, the one party that has a clear-cut, overmastering, overshadowing issue; the party that stands for the people, and the only party that stands for all the people. In this system we have one set who are called capitalists and another set who are called workers; and they are at war with each other.

"Now, we Socialists propose that society in its collective capacity shall produce not for profit but in abundance to satisfy human wants; that every man shall have the inalienable right to work and receive the full equivalent of all he produces; that every man may stand fearlessly erect in the pride and majesty of his own manhood.

"Every man and every woman will then be economically free. They can, without let or hindrance, apply their labor, with the best machinery that can be devised, to all the natural resources, do the work of society and produce for all; and then receive in exchange a certificate of value equivalent to that of their production. Then society will improve its institutions in proportion to the progress of invention. Whether in the city or on the farm, all things productive will be carried forward on a gigantic scale. All industry will be completely organized. Society for the first time will have a scientific foundation. Every man, by being economically free, will have some time for himself. He can then take a full and perfect breath. He can enjoy life with his wife and children because then he will have a home.

"We are not going to destroy private property. We are going to establish private property — all the private property necessary to house man, keep him in comfort, and satisfy his wants. Eighty percent of the people of the United States have no property today. A few have got it all. They have dispossessed the people, and when we get into power we will dispossess them. We will reduce the workday and give every man a chance. We will go to the parks, and we will have music, because we will have time to play music and desire to hear it . . . .

"Our conduct is determined by our economic relations. If you and I must fight each other to exist, we will not love each other very hard. We can go to the same church and hear the same minister tell us in good conscience that we ought to love each other, and the next day we approach some business transaction. Do we remember what the minister told us? No; it is gone until next Sunday. Six days in the week we are following the Golden Rule reversed. Now, when we approach a business transaction in competition, what is more natural than that we should try to get the better of it? — get the better of our fellowman? — cheat him if we can? . . .

"I am not a prophet. I can no more penetrate the future than you can. I do study the forces that underlie society and the trend of evolution. I can tell by what we have passed through about what we will have in the future; and I know that capitalism can be abolished and the people put in possession. Now, when we have taken possession and we jointly own the means of production, we will no longer have to fight each other to live; our interests, instead of being competitive, will be cooperative. We will work side by side. Your interest will be mine and mine will be yours. That is the economic condition from which will spring the humane social relation of the future.

"When we are in partnership and have stopped clutching each other's throats, when we have stopped enslaving each other, we will stand together, hands clasped, and be friends. We will be comrades, we will be brothers, and we will begin the march to the grandest civilization the human race has ever known."

In June 1918, Debs spoke at a Socialist Party state convention in Canton, Ohio. He was bitterly critical of the Wilson Administration's prosecution of alleged seditionists. He pronounced himself to be as guilty as some of those in jail. He attacked America's involvement in the war, using the common Red line against war in general. He said: "The master class has always declared the war; the subject class has always fought the battles. The master class has had all to gain and nothing to lose, while the subject class has had nothing to gain and all to lose — especially their lives." On the scene in Canton, the United States Attorney for the Northern District of Ohio, E.S. Wertz, had stenographers make a transcript of Debs' speech. Wertz sent a copy of the transcript to the Attorney General of the United States. He indicated what portions of Debs' speech he thought might be in violation of the Espionage Act. The Attorney General did not believe as strongly as

316

Wertz that Debs had committed sedition, but he did not tell Wertz to refrain from prosecution. The Attorney General wrote to Wertz: "Coming then to the question of whether Debs' speech does violate that law, the case is not without serious doubts. In the opinion of the Department, most of the passages marked by you, in and of themselves, do not violate the law. For instance, criticism of the courts, of their administration of the war laws, can hardly be called an attack on the 'form of government of the United States . . . .' Abuse of the actions of plutocrats of this country, real or imaginary, can hardly be brought within any of the express provisions of the Espionage Act. There are certain passages, however, some of which you have marked, which, taken in connection with the context, might be held to have crossed the line between lawful and unlawful utterances . . . . These parts of the speech, taken in connection with the context, bring the speech close to, if not over, the line, though the case is by no means a clear one. All in all the Department does not feel strongly convinced that a prosecution is advisable."

Four days after Debs made his Canton speech, he was indicted by a federal grand jury in Cleveland for violation of the Espionage Act. After a four-day trial in September 1918, Debs was found guilty and sentenced to ten years imprisonment on each of two counts with the sentences to run concurrently. Debs had told his jury: "I have been accused of having obstructed the war. I admit it. Gentlemen, I abhor war. I would oppose the war if I stood alone . . . . I wish to admit everything that has been said respecting me from this witness chair. I wish to admit everything that has been charged against me except what is embraced in the indictment . . . . I cannot take back a word. I can't repudiate a sentence. I stand before you guilty of having made this speech . . . prepared to take the consequences of what there is embraced."

In the course of the trial, Debs also uttered a passage which has become famous in leftist circles: "While there is a lower class, I am in it; while there is a criminal element, I am of it; while there is a soul in prison, I am not free."

In March 1919, the Supreme Court of the United States rejected an appeal by Debs against the Cleveland verdict. In April, Debs entered the penitentiary at Moundsville, West Virginia. In June, he was transferred to the penitentiary in Atlanta, Georgia. Two days after his appeal was turned down, Debs spoke at a Socialist Party rally in Cleveland, where he said: "With every drop of blood in my veins, I despise their laws and I will defy them . . . . I am going to speak to you as a Socialist, as a Revolutionist, and as a Bolshevist, if you please." In the *Socialist Call* of August 6, 1919, he said: "The Socialist Party stands fearlessly and uncompromisingly for the overthrow of the labor-robbing, war-breeding and crime-inciting capitalist system." While in Atlanta, he was quoted in the *Socialist Call* of October 18, 1919, as saying: "My attitude has not changed one whit since I came to prison. I will make no promises of any kind or nature to obtain my freedom. I want to come out as [German Communist Karl] Liebknecht came out. The proletariat of Germany shook the empire of Germany to its foundations, and the beasts of Berlin readily found it convenient to unlock the barred doors."

When the Supreme Court rejected Debs' appeal and he entered prison, President Woodrow Wilson and Attorney General Mitchell Palmer were besieged with requests to grant clemency to Debs.

Wilson was adamant — and remained so throughout his administration — in his refusal to release Debs. In the summer of 1920, most of Wilson's cabinet, including the Attorney General, recommended Debs' release. Labor leaders and political activists of the left and the center had previously petitioned in vain. But Wilson ignored the pressures and Debs remained in prison until President Warren G. Harding ordered his release on Christmas Eve, 1921.

In the meantime, at the Socialist Party's 1920 convention in New York City, Debs was nominated for the fifth time as the Party's presidential candidate. On June 1, 1920, the official bulletin of the Socialist Party carried Debs' acceptance of the nomination. He made it clear that he was then on the extreme left when he said: "Before serving time here, I made a series of addresses supporting the Russian Revolution, which I consider the greatest single achievement in all history. I still am a Bolshevik. I am fighting for the same thing here they are fighting for there. I regret that the Convention did not see its way clear to affiliate with the 3rd International without qualification . . . . I must be perfectly frank with you. I have read the platform adopted by the convention, and I wish I might say that it has my unqualified approval. It is a masterly piece of writing, and it states the essential principles of the Socialist movement, but I believe that it could have been made more effective if it had stressed the class struggle more prominently and if more emphasis had been laid on the industrial organization.

"I do not believe in captious criticism, but I want to be frank with you and state my position. I must do this if I am to prove worthy of the high confidence reposed in me. However, a plat-

form is not so very important after all. We can breathe the breath of revolution in any platform. A platform is not altogether unlike a musical instrument. You can play the particular tune you want on it."

From his prison cell, Debs campaigned in 1920 mostly through press releases and statements printed in Socialist Party publications. He did poll 915,302 votes but it was only about 3.5 per cent of the total vote cast in contrast to the nearly 6 per cent he received in 1912.

After Debs was released from prison in 1921, he continued to be a leader of the Socialist Party although he never again ran for political office. In 1924, he and his fellow Socialists supported the presidential candidacy of Robert M. La-Follette Sr. and his Progressive Party. In 1925, Debs became editor of a new Socialist weekly, *The American Appeal*, published in Chicago. In October 1926, he died after a year-long siege of ill health.

ADOLF DEHN was born on November 22, 1895 in Waterville, Minnesota, son of Emilie Haase and Arthur C. Dehn. He married Virginia Engleman. He was a student at the Minneapolis Art School in Minnesota (1914-1917) and at New York's Art Students League (1917-1918). He was the author of *Water Color Painting* (1945); *How to Print and Draw Lithographs* (1950); and *Water Color, Gouache and Casein Painting* (1955). He contributed articles to *Art Digest, Art News, Arts, Coronet,* and *Time.* He contributed illustrations to *Dial, Fortune, Harper's Bazaar, Jugend, The Liberator, New Masses* ("weekly journal of the Communist Party"), *New Yorker,* and *Vogue.*

Between 1921 and 1929, Dehn traveled through France, Germany, and England, and settled in Vienna. After 1929, he lived in New York City. His art works were black and white drawings, lithographs, and water colors. At various times, he was represented in the Metropolitan Museum of Art, the Whitney Museum of American Art, the Brooklyn Museum, the Minneapolis Institute of Fine Arts, the British Museum, the Honolulu Museum, the Boston Museum of Fine Arts, the Albertina Museum of Vienna, the Library of Congress, the New York City Public Library, and the Museum of Modern Art. He was awarded first prizes by the Philadelphia Art Alliance (1936), the Philadelphia Print Club (1939), and Chicago International Water Color Exhibition (1943).

Dehn was affiliated with the American Artists' Congress ("Communist front"); the American Committee To Save Refugees ("perform[ing] a most valuable function for the international Communist movement"); American Group, Inc. ("Communist front"); the American League for Peace and Democracy ("subversive and Communist" − "established . . . in an effort to create public sentiment on behalf of a foreign policy adapted to the interests of the Soviet Union . . . [and] designed to conceal Communist control, in accordance with the new tactics of the Communist International"); American Peace Mobilization ("formed . . . under the auspices of the Communist Party and the Young Communist League" − "one of the most seditious organizations which ever operated in the United States"); *Art Front* (Communist Party-line magazine); Artists' League of America ("Communist front"); the China Aid Council ("Communist-controlled"); the Civil Rights Congress ("created and established by the Communist Party as an organization which would utilize defense of civil rights for Party purposes and raise and maintain mass defense and bail funds for Party use"); the Committee for the Re-election of Benjamin J. Davis (Communist Party candidate for political office); the Cultural and Scientific Conference for World Peace ("Communist front" − "a propaganda front for Soviet foreign policy and Soviet culture"); the Dance Congress and Festival ("Communist front"); the Golden Book of American Friendship with the Soviet Union ("pro-Soviet propaganda enterprise"); International Workers Order ("from its very inception demonstrated by its pronouncements, its activities, and the authoritative statements of the Communist Party that it is a subservient instrument of the Communist Party of the United States"); the John Reed Clubs ("out-and-out Communist organizations which preceded the contemporary Communist front organizations which cater to so-called liberals"); the Joint Anti-Fascist Refugee Committee ("subversive and Communist"); the League of Professional Groups for [William Z.] Foster and [James W.] Ford ("the members of this organization were committed to the objectives of the Communist Party"); *Masses and Mainstream* ("Communist publication"); the National Committee for Defense of Political Prisoners ("subversive and Communist"); the National Institute of Arts and Letters ("Communist front"); New Theatre League ("Communist front"); Russian War Relief ("Communist enterprise"); and *Workers Monthly* ("Communist Party publication"). He died in May 1968.

PAUL de KRUIF was born on March 2, 1890 in Zeeland, Michigan, son of Hendrika Kremer and Hendrik de Kruif. His first marriage ended in divorce. His second wife was the late Rhea Barbarin. His third wife was Eleanor Lappage. He was an alumnus of the University of Michigan (B.S., 1912 and Ph.D., 1916). He was the author of *Our Medicine Men* (1922); *Microbe Hunters* (1926); *Hunger Fighters* (1928); *Seven Iron Men* (1929); *Men Against Death* (1932); *The Fight for Life* (1938); *Toward a Healthy America* (1939); *Activities of the National Foundation for Infantile Paralysis in the Field of Virus Research* (1939); *Dr. Ehrlich's Magic Bullet* (1940); *Health Is Wealth* (1940); *Kaiser Wakes the Doctors* (1943); *The Male Hormone* (1945); *A Man Against Insanity* (1957); and *The Sweeping Wind, a Memoir* (1962). He was a collaborator in the writing of Sinclair Lewis' *Arrowsmith* (1925). He was co-author of *Yellow Jack* (1934); *Why Keep Them Alive?* (1936); and *Life Among the Doctors* (1949). He was a contributor to *Civilization in the United States: An Inquiry by Thirty Americans* (1922) and *America Organizes to Win the War* (1922). He also wrote articles for numerous magazines, including *Century, Country Gentleman, Forum, Hearst's International, Ladies' Home Journal,* and *Reader's Digest.*

In 1916 and 1917, and from 1918 until 1920, de Kruif was an assistant professor of bacteriology at the University of Michigan. From 1920 until 1922, he was an associate in pathology at the Rockefeller Institute for Medical Research. From 1922 until 1971, he was a free-lance writer. He was a consultant to the Chicago Board of Health and the Michigan State Health Department. He was secretary of the general scientific committee of the National Foundation for Infantile Paralysis. He was a co-founder and the long-time secretary of the President's Birthday Ball Commis-

sion for Infantile Paralysis Research.

De Kruif was affiliated with the American Congress for Peace and Democracy and the American League for Peace and Democracy ("subversive and Communist" – "established . . . in an effort to create public sentiment on behalf of a foreign policy adapted to the interests of the Soviet Union . . . [and] designed to conceal Communist control, in accordance with the new tactics of the Communist International"); the Coordinating Committee To Lift the [Spanish] Embargo ("one of the numerous Communist-front enterprises which were organized around the Communists' agitation over the Spanish Civil War"); the Federation of Architects, Engineers, Chemists, and Technicians, and its publication, *Technical America* ("its leaders . . . cooperate fully with the Communist Party and controlled organizations"); Friends of the Soviet Union ("created, directed, and controlled by the Communist Party . . . and operated to aid and support Party objectives concerning the defense and support of the Soviet Union"); Frontier Films ("Communist front"); the Golden Book of American Friendship with the Soviet Union ("pro-Soviet propaganda enterprise"); *Health and Hygiene* (magazine of the Daily Worker's Medical Advisory Board); the International Workers Order ("from its very inception demonstrated by its pronouncements, its activities, and the authoritative statements of the Communist Party that it is a subservient instrument of the Communist Party of the United States"); the League of American Writers ("subversive and Communist" – "began openly to follow the Communist Party line as dictated by the foreign policy of the Soviet Union"); the Medical Bureau and North American Committee To Aid Spanish Democracy ("subversive and un-American"); the National Writers' Congress ("Communist front"); *New Masses* ("weekly journal of the Communist Party"); an Open Letter for Closer Cooperation with the Soviet Union (issued by "a group of Communist Party stooges"); and a Statement by American Progressives on the Moscow Trials ("obviously a document concocted in defense of the line of the Communist Party and undoubtedly originated in the headquarters of the Communist Party"). He died in March 1971.

DANIEL DE LEON was born on December 14, 1852 on the Island of Curaçao off the coast of Venezuela, son of Sara Jesurun and Salomon De Leon. He was married first to Saro Lobo, and second to Bertha Canary. He studied at gymnasia in Hildesheim, Germany, and in Amsterdam, Holland. He was an alumnus of Columbia College (LL.B., 1878). He came to the United States in 1874. His most important pamphlets were *Two Pages from Roman History* (1903); *What Means This Strike?* (1898); and *Socialist Reconstruction of Society* (1905). He was the translator of Karl Marx's *The Eighteenth Brumaire of Louis Napoleon*, and of seventeen of the nineteen historical romances in Eugene Sue's series, *The Mysteries of the People, or The History of a Proletarian Family Across the Ages.*

When De Leon first came to America, he settled in New York City. For a brief time, he was associate editor of a Spanish language newspaper which advocated Cuban independence. He taught school in Westchester County and simultaneously attended Columbia College. After receiving his law degree, he practiced in Texas for about four years. In 1883, he won a prize lectureship at Columbia College and for the next six years he taught Latin-American diplomacy there. In 1886, he became active in politics, supporting the mayoralty candidacy of Henry George, the single-tax advocate. In 1888, he began a lifetime of activity in the labor movement when he joined the Knights of Labor. In 1890, he joined the Socialist Labor Party. A year later, he was named national lecturer for the SLP and the party's gubernatorial candidate in New York. In 1892, he became editor of SLP's *The People*, a weekly which became a daily in 1900 and went out of print in 1914.

By 1892, De Leon was the major leader of the Socialist Labor Party. Not only was he its spokesman, but he was also the leading policy-maker of that portion of the SLP's membership which was bitterly opposed to existing trade unions. De Leon and his followers insisted that the structure and management of America's trade unions violated the basic principles of Socialism. In 1895, De Leon's opposition to the trade union system caused him to lead a secession movement which caused a major break in the Knights of Labor. He organized his followers into the Socialist Trade and Labor Alliance. The Alliance became in effect an adjunct of the Socialist Labor Party, but De Leon was able to attract only a minority of the Knights of Labor to his side.

In 1896, in one of his most famous addresses, De Leon explained the difference between his views of socialism and those of his opponents. He criticized his opponents as nothing more than reformers. He considered himself and his followers to be revolutionists. He said: "Whenever a change leaves the internal mechanism untouched, we have Reform; whenever the internal mechanism is changed we have Revolution."

"Of course, no internal change is possible without external manifestations. The internal changes denoted by the revolution or evolution of the lizard into the eagle go accompanied with external marks. So with society. And therein lies one of the pitfalls into which dilettantism or 'Reforms' invariably tumble. They have noticed that externals change with internals; and they rest satisfied with mere external changes without looking behind the curtain. But of this more presently.

"We Socialists are not Reformers; we are Revolutionists. We Socialists do not propose to change forms. We care nothing for forms. We want a change of the inside of the mechanism of society, let the form take care of itself. We see in England a crowned monarch; we see in Germany a sceptered emperor; we see in this country an uncrowned President, and we fail to see the essential difference between Germany, England, and America. That being the case, we are skeptics as to forms. We are like grown children in the sense we like to look at the inside of things and find out what is there.

"One more preliminary explanation. Socialism is lauded by some as an angelic movement; by others it is decried as a devilish scheme . . . . Socialism is neither an aspiration of angels nor a plot of devils. Socialism moves with its feet firmly planted on the ground and its head not lost in the clouds; it takes Science by the hand, asks her to lead, and goes whithersoever she points. It does not take Science by the hand, saying: 'I shall follow you if the end of the road please me.' No! it takes her by the hand and says: 'Whithersoever thou leadest, thither am I bound to go.' The Socialists, consequently, move as intelligent men; they do not mutiny because, instead of having wings, we have arms and cannot fly as we would wish.

"What, then, with an eye single upon the difference between Reform and Revolution, does Socialism mean? To point out that, I shall take up two or three of what I may style the principal nerve centers of the movement.

"One of these principal nerve centers is the question of 'government' or the question of 'state.' . . . Not until we reach the great works of the American Morgan, of Marx and Engels, and of other Socialist philosophers, is the matter handled with that scientific lucidity that proceeds from facts, leads to sound conclusions, and breaks the way to practical work. Not until you know and understand the history of the 'state' and 'government' will you understand one of the cardinal principles upon which Socialist organization rests, and will you be in a condition to organize successfully.

"We are told that 'government' has always been as it is today, and always will be. This is the first fundamental error of what Karl Marx justly calls capitalist vulgarity of thought.

"When man started on his career, after having got beyond the state of the savage, he realized that cooperation was a necessity to him. He understood that together with others he could face his enemies in a better way than alone; he could hunt, fish, fight more successfully. Following the instructions of the great writer Morgan — the only great and original American writer upon this question — we look to the Indian communities, the Indian settlements as a type of the social system that our ancestors, all of them, without exception, went through at some time.

"The Indian lived in the community condition. The Indian lived under a system of common property. As Franklin described it in a sketch of the history and alleged sacredness of private property, there was no such thing as private property among the Indians. They cooperated, worked together, and they had a Central Directing Authority among them . . . . Its function was to direct the cooperative or collective efforts of the communities, and, in so doing, it shared actively in the productive work of the communities. Without it, its work, the work of the communities, would not have been done.

"When, in the further development of society, the tools of production grew and developed; . . . when the art of smelting iron ore was discovered; when thereby that leading social cataclysm, wrapped in the mists of ages, yet discernible, took place that rent former communal society in twain along the line of sex, the males being able, the females unable to wield the tool of production – then society was cast into a new mold; the former community with its democratic equality of rights and duties vanishes, and a new social system turns up, divided into two sections – the one able, the other unable to work at production. The line that separated these two sections, being at first the line of sex, could, in the very nature of things, not yet be sharp or deep. Yet, notwithstanding, in the very shaping of these two sections – one able, the other unable to feed itself – we have the first premonition of the classes, of class distinctions, of the division of society into the independent and the dependent, into master and slaves, ruler and ruled.

"Simultaneously with this revolution, we find the first changes in the nature of the Central Directing Authority, of that body whose original function was to share in, by directing, production. Just as soon as economic equality is destroyed and the economic classes crop up in society, the functions of the Central Directing Authority gradually begin to change, until, finally, when, after a long range of years, moving slowly at first and then with the present hurricane velocity under capitalism proper, the tool has developed further and further and still further, and has reached its present fabulous perfection and magnitude; when, through its private ownership the tool has wrought a revolution within a revolution by dividing society no longer along the line of sex but strictly along the line of ownership or nonownership of the land on and the tool with which to work; when the privately owned, mammoth tool of today has reduced more than 52 percent of our population to the state of being utterly unable to feed without first selling themselves into wage slavery, while it, at the same time, saps the ground from under about 39 percent of our people, the middle class, whose puny tools, small capital, render them certain victims of competition with the large capitalists and makes them desperate; when the economic law that asserts itself upon the system of private ownership of the tool has concentrated these private owners into about 8 percent of the nation's inhabitants, has thereby enabled this small capitalist class to live without toil, and to compel the majority, the class of the proletariat, to toil without living; when, finally, it has come to the pass in which our country now finds itself, that, as was stated in Congress, 94 percent of the taxes are spent in 'protecting property' – the property of the trivially small capitalist class – and not in protecting life; when, in short, the privately owned tool has wrought this work, and the classes – the idle rich and the working poor – are in full bloom – then the Central Directing Authority of old stands transformed; its pristine functions of aiding in, by directing, production have been supplanted by the functions of holding down the dependent, the slave, the ruled, i.e., the working class. Then, and not before, lo, the state, the modern state, the capitalist state! Then, lo, the government, the modern government, the capitalist government – equipped mainly, if not solely, with the means of suppression, of oppression, of tyranny!

" . . . Socialism is not anarchy. Socialism does not, like the chicken in the fable just out of the shell, start with the knowledge of that day. Socialism rejects the premises and the conclusions of anarchy upon the state and upon government. What Socialism says is: 'Away with the economic system that alters the beneficent functions of the Central Directing Authority from an aid to production into a means of oppression.' And it proceeds to show that, when the instruments of production shall be owned no longer by the minority, but shall be restored to the commonwealth; that when, as the result of this, no longer the minority or any portion of the people shall be in poverty, and classes, class distinctions, and class rule shall, as they necessarily must, have vanished, that then the Central Directing Authority will lose all its repressive functions and is bound to reassume the functions it had in the old communities of our ancestors, become again a necessary aid and assist in production.

"The Socialist, in the brilliant simile of Karl Marx, sees that a lone fiddler in his room needs no director; he can rap himself to order, with his fiddle to his shoulder, and start his dancing tune and stop whenever he likes. But just as soon as you have an orchestra, you must also have an orchestra director – a Central Directing Authority. If you don't, you may have a Salvation Army powwow; you may have a Louisiana Negro breakdown; you may have an Orthodox Jewish synagogue where every man sings in whatever key he likes; but you won't have harmony – impossible . . . .

"Our system of production is in the nature of an orchestra. No one man, no one town, no one state can be said any longer to be independent of the other; the whole people of the United States, every individual therein, is dependent and interdependent upon all the others. The nature of the machinery of production; the subdivision of labor which aids cooperation and which cooperation fosters, and which is necessary to the plentifulness of production that civilization requires, compel a harmonious working together of all departments of labor, and thence compel the establishment of a Central Directing Authority, of an orchestra director, so to speak, of the orchestra of the Cooperative Commonwealth.

"Such is the state or government that the Socialist revolution carries in its womb. Today, production is left to anarchy, and only tyranny, the twin sister of anarchy, is organized.

"Socialism, accordingly, implies organization; organization implies directing authority; and the one and the other are strict reflections of the revolutions undergone by the tool of production. Reform, on the other hand, skims the surface, and with 'Referendums' and similar devices limits itself to external tinkerings.

"The second nerve center of Socialism that will serve to illustrate the difference between Reform and Revolution is its materialistic groundwork . . . .

"Watch the process of 'moral development' in this country – the classic ground in many ways to study history in, for the reason that the whole development of mankind can be seen here, portrayed in a few years, so to speak. You know how, today, the Northern people put on airs of morality on the score of having 'abolished chattel slavery,' the 'traffic in human flesh,' 'gone down South and fought, and bled, to free the Negro,' etc., etc. Yet we know that just as soon as manufacturing was introduced in the North, the North found that it was too expensive to own the Negro and take care of him; that it was much cheaper not to own the worker; and, consequently, that they 'religiously,' 'humanely' and 'morally' sold their slaves to the South, while they transformed the white people of the North, who had no means of production in their hands, into wage slaves, and mercilessly ground them down. In the North, chattel slavery disappeared just as soon as the development of machinery rendered the institution unprofitable. The immorality of chattel slavery became clear to the North just as soon as, standing upon that higher plane that its higher material development raised it to, it acquired a better vision. The benighted South, on the contrary, that had no machinery, remained with eyes shut, and she stuck to slavery till the slave was knocked out of her fists.

"Guided by the light of this and many similar lessons of history, Socialism builds upon the principle that the 'moral sentiment,' as illustrated by the fate of the slave, is not the cause but a powerful aid to revolutions. The moral sentiment is to a movement as important as the sails are to a ship. Nevertheless, important though sails are, unless a ship is well laden, unless she is soundly, properly, and scientifically constructed, the more sails you pile up and spread

out, the surer she is to capsize. So with the organizations that are to carry out a revolution. Unless your Socialist organizations are as sound as a bell; unless they are as intolerant as science; unless they will plant themselves squarely on the principle that two and two make four, and under no circumstances allow that they make five, the more feeling you put into them, the surer they are to capsize and go down. On the contrary, load your revolutionary ship with the proper lading of science; hold her strictly to the lodestar; try no monkeyshines and no dillyings and dallyings with anything that is not strictly scientific, or with any man who does not stand on our uncompromisingly scientific platform; do that, and then unfurl freely the sails of morality; then the more your sails, the better off your ship; but not unless you do that, will you be safe, or can you prevail.

"Socialism knows that revolutionary upheavals and transformations proceed from the rockbed of material needs. With a full appreciation of and veneration for moral impulses that are balanced with scientific knowledge, it eschews, looks with just suspicion upon, and gives a wide berth to balloon morality, or be it those malarial fevers that reformers love to dignify with the name of 'moral feelings.'

"A third nerve center of Socialism by which to distinguish Reform from Revolution is its manly, aggressive posture. The laws that rule sociology run upon lines parallel with and are the exact counterparts of those that natural science has established prevail in sociology.

"In the first place, the central figure in biology is the species, not the individual specimen. Consequently, that is the central figure on the field of sociology that corresponds to and represents the species on the field of biology. In sociol-

325

ogy, the economic classes take the place of the species in biology.

"In the second place, struggle, and not piping peace; assimilation by the ruthless process of the expulsion of all elements that are not fit for assimilation, and not external coalition – such are the laws of growth in biology, and such they are and needs must be in sociology.

"Hence, Socialism recognizes in modern society the existence of a struggle of classes, and the line that divides the combatants to be the economic line that separates the interests of the property-holding capitalist class from the interests of the propertyless class of the proletariat. As a final result of this, Socialism, with the Nazarene, spurns as futile, if not wicked, the method of cajolery and seduction, or the crying of 'Peace, peace, where there is no peace,' and cuts a clean swath, while Reform is eternally entangled in its course of charming, luring, decoying."

Within the Socialist Trade and Labor Alliance, De Leon's advocacy of Marxism proved to be too extreme a position for most of the members. The dissidents withdrew the Alliance and formed the Socialist Party of America, which became a viable political party. The clash within the Alliance seriously weakened the Socialist Labor Party, but De Leon maintained leadership of the group as long as he lived.

In 1905, De Leon was instrumental in forming the Industrial Workers of the World, the Wobblies. He merged what was left of his Socialist Trade and Labor Alliance with the Wobblies.

In his early association with the Wobblies, De Leon became a spokesman for the group. He considered the Wobblies to be the ideal political and economic combination in the labor movement to promote and to accomplish

Socialism. In what was called "The Preamble of I.W.W.," he said: "Inestimable is the value, dignified the posture of the political movement. It affords the labor movement the opportunity to ventilate its purposes, its aspirations, and its methods, free, over and aboveboard, in the noonday light of the sun, whereas otherwise, its agitation would be consigned to the circumscribed sphere of the rat hole. The political movement renders the masses accessible to the propaganda of labor; it raises the labor movement above the category of a 'conspiracy'; it places the movement in line with the spirit of the age, which, on the one hand, denies the power of 'conspiracy' in matters that not only affect the masses but in which the masses must themselves be intelligent actors, and, on the other hand, demands the freest of utterance.

"In short and in fine, the political movement bows to the methods of civilized discussion: It gives a chance to the peaceful solution of the great question at issue. By proclaiming the urgency of political as well as of industrial unity, the preamble amply and sufficiently proclaims the affinity of the economic with the political movement. At the same time, by expressly proclaiming that the 'taking and holding' is an act that falls wholly within the province of the economic organization, the preamble has locked a dangerous switch, a switch running into which would bring grave danger, the danger of rendering the Socialist, which means the labor movement, illusory, and a roosting place for the 'intellectual' riff-raff of bourgeois society.

"The ballot is a weapon of civilization; the ballot is a weapon that no revolutionary movement of our times may ignore except at its own peril; the Socialist ballot is the emblem of right.

For that very reason the Socialist ballot is 'weaker than a woman's tears, / Tamer than sleep, fonder than ignorance,/ Less valiant than the virgin in the night,/ and skilless as unpractised infancy,' unless it is backed by the might to enforce it. That requisite might is summed up in the industrial organization of the working class.

"Now, mind you, that might the labor movement needs, as much, I would almost say, against the political movements its own breath heats into being as against the capitalist tyrant himself. It needs that might against the capitalist tyrant to put the quietus upon him; it also needs that might to prevent the evil consequences to which, in this corrupt atmosphere of bourgeois society, the political movement is inevitably exposed. The two points are vital. Much, infinitely more than appears at first sight, hangs thereby.

"Despite the sharply marked economic feature of the labor movement, the principle that it is bound to take on a political form also is founded on no fine-spun theory. Even discounting the force of the sociologic arguments . . . which point to the inevitableness of the political manifestation of the labor movement, there is a consideration . . . which, when properly weighed, places the matter beyond the peradventure of a doubt. That consideration is the existence of universal suffrage in the land.

"The institution is so bred in the bones of the people that, although it has become a gravel in the shoe of the capitalist, he, powerful though he is, dares not abolish it outright. Among such a people, chimerical is the idea of expecting to conduct a great movement, whose palpable aim is a Socialist Revolution, to the slogan of 'Abstinence from the ballot box!' The proposition cannot choose but brand its supporters as freaks. Whether the economic movement wills it or not, its political phase will assert itself on the political field. Men from its own ranks and men from outside its ranks will raise the standard of labor politics.

"Nor will the capitalist be slow in endeavoring, while humoring the thing, to draw the sting from it. Watchfully though he guards his political burg, he will, from time to time, carefully select some 'promising' candidate from the labor ticket, and allow him admission or, maybe, he is sometimes taken napping and some labor candidate slips through the fingers of his outposts at the ballot box. Subjected to the lures and wiles at the disposal of the capitalist, these successful labor candidates in the parliaments of capitalism, ten to one, succumb. They succumb either because of their own inherently corrupt souls or their muddle-headedness. In either case they betray the working class; the effect is harmfully felt by the economic movement.

"Against this danger there is but one protection – the Industrial, that is, the class-conscious economic organization to keep that ballot straight. Nothing short of such an economic organization will prevent the evil, because nothing short of such an economic organization can keep sharp the edge of the special sword wielded by the political movement of labor . . . . It is purely destructive. The economic movement may take a little at a time. It may do so because its function is ultimately to 'take and hold' the full plants of production and save them for the human race. The political movement, on the contrary, has an entirely different function: Its function is wholly to tear down the political burg of capitalist tyranny.

"It follows herefrom that the political movement of labor may not even remotely partake even of the appearance of compromise. It exemplified the revolutionary aim of the labor movement; it must be uncompromisingly revolutionary. This fact dictates the conduct of the successful political candidates of labor in the parliaments of capitalism. . . .

"Without the might of the class-conscious economic movement back of the political, the political movements that the labor movement inevitably promotes in America will not only be divided but, as a further result, will promote that confusion of thought that runs into corruption and that, reacting back upon the economic movement itself, helps to scuttle its efficiency. It surely is no accident that, without exception, all the labor candidates so far allowed by the capitalist class to filter through their garrisons at their election defiles, whenever the office to which they were allowed to be returned elected was of any importance, have uniformly 'parliamentarized,' that is, 'log-rolled,' in short, sold out the revolution.

"It is a matter of self-protection with the economic organization to watch and control the political.

"There now remains only one point to consider, and I am through. It is the point with regard to the necessity of the industrial organization in order to supplement the right of the ballot with the might requisite to put the quietus upon the capitalist class itself. The point implies what is generally but wrongly meant by 'the general strike,' a term that, through misuse by its own advocates, who have hitherto placed the cart before the horse, is greatly misunderstood and should be replaced by the more appropriate term of 'the general lockout of the capitalist class.'

"Political power is reached through the ballot box. But the ballot box is not an open field; it is a veritable defile. That defile is held by the agents of the capitalist class. The election inspectors and returning boards are capitalist appointees; they are veritable garrisons with which the capitalist class holds the defile. To imagine that these capitalist garrisons of the election defiles will complacently allow the candidates of the revolution, whose program is the dismantling of the political burg of capitalism, peacefully to file through is to indulge in a mooncalf's vision. The revolutionary ballot of labor is counted out now; it has been counted out from the first day of its appearance; it will be counted out even more extensively in the future . . . .

" . . . But let the capitalist attempt, under the pressure of the political temperature raised by the ballot of labor — let him attempt to strike. In possession of the might conferred and implied by the industrial organization of their class, the working class would forthwith lock out the capitalist class. Without political organization, the labor movement cannot triumph; without economic organization, the day of its political triumph would be the day of its defeat.

"Industrialism means might. Craft unionism means impotence. All the plants of production, aye, even the vast wealth for consumption, is today in the keeping of the working class. It is workingmen who are in charge of the factories, the railroads, the mines, in short, all the land and machinery of production; and it is they, also, who sit as watchdogs before the pantries, the cellars, and the safe-deposit vaults of the capitalist class; aye, it is they who carry the guns in the armies.

"But this place of vantage is of no

avail to them under craft unionism. Under craft unionism, only one craft marches into the battlefield at a time. By idly looking on, the other crafts scab it upon the combatant. What with that and the likewise idle onlooking of those divisions of the workers who man the commissary department, so to speak, of the capitalist class, the class struggle presents, under craft unionism, the aspect of petty riots in which the empty stomachs and empty hands of the working class are pitted against the full ones of the employing class.

"The impotence wherewith the right of the working class has hitherto been smitten is now to be transformed into a might without which that right is but mockery. The signal for that transformation was struck last week at the convention of the Industrial Workers of the World; and the word has gone out, as it could go out from no other country but America, in language that fits our full-grown capitalist development: 'Unite! Unite on the economic field upon the only basis on which economic unity is possible − the basis of the solidarity of the working class, the only solid fact from which political unity can be reflected! Unite! Unite upon the only economic principle capable of backing up the right of the labor ballot with the might to enforce it! Unite for the general strike at the ballot box, to overthrow the political robber burg of capitalism, backed by the general strike against, or, rather, the general lockout of, the capitalist class from the industrial fields that it has usurped. Unite for the emancipation of the working class, and to save civilization from a catastrophe!' "

In 1908, De Leon, who had been too extreme for the Knights of Labor and too extreme for most members of the Socialist Trade and Labor Alliance, found that he was not extreme enough for the Wobblies. In 1908, the Wobblies, who were determined to accomplish their objectives by violence if necessary, refused De Leon participation in their national convention. He and a small band of followers organized what became known as the Workers' International Industrial Union. In the last six years of his life, De Leon had to be content with the promotion of his Marxian Socialism through the relatively small units of the Socialist Labor Party and the W.I.I.U. He made very little headway toward his dream of creating a revolutionary workers' organization on industry-wide bases. He had perhaps more than any other man in his era impressed upon the American Socialist movement that the goal of controlling production and distribution was attainable through the dual forces of economics and politics. Even Nicolai Lenin, the archdisciple of Marx, when he learned of De Leon's teachings, expressed his appreciation of them by describing them as compatible in their essentials to what he believed to be the necessary Soviet system.

In an interview with Robert Minor, as reported in the *New York World* of February 4, 1919, Lenin said: "The American Daniel De Leon first formulated the idea of a Soviet government, which grew up on his idea. Future society will be organized along Soviet lines. There will be Soviet rather than geographical boundaries for nations. Industrial unionism is the basic thing. That is what we are building.

"The idea of constructive Industrial Unionism, the conception that such a union is the germ of the future Industrial Government, the discovery and amplification of the idea belongs to the American Daniel De Leon, a member and the acknowledged leader of the Socialist Labor Party from the time he became connected with the Labor Movement in the late eighties until his death in 1914. This is S.L.P.-ism or what all our opponents in the Labor Movement have scoffingly designated, 'De Leonism.' "

Although De Leon's Marxism was appreciated by neither the Socialist Party nor the Wobblies, he had made a lasting impression upon the Socialist movement in this country. He died in May 1914.

WILLIAM EDWARD DODD was born on October 21, 1869 in Clayton, North Carolina. He married Martha Johns. He was an alumnus of Virginia Polytechnic Institute (B.S., 1895, and M.S., 1897) and the University of Leipzig (Ph.D., 1900). He was the author of *Jefferson's Ruckkehr zur Politik, 1796* (1900); *A Life of Nathaniel Macon* (1903); *Life of Jefferson Davis* (1907); *Statesmen of the Old South; or, From Radicalism to Conservative Revolt* (1911); *Expansion and Conflict* (1915); *The Cotton Kingdom* in the *Chronicles of America* Series (1919); *Woodrow Wilson and His Work* (1920); *Lincoln or Lee: Comparison and Contrast of the Two Greatest Leaders in the War Between the States* (1928); and *The Old South: Struggle for Democracy* (1937). He was co-author and editor of *Riverside History of the United States* (1928). He was co-editor of *The Public Papers of Woodrow Wilson,* six volumes (1925-1927). He was also a contributor to numerous periodicals, including *Century,* the *American Mercury,* the *Contemporary Review,* and the *Virginia Quarterly Review.*

From 1900 until 1908, Dodd was a professor of history at Randolph-Macon College. From 1908 until 1933, he was a professor of history at the University of Chicago. From 1933 until 1937, he was the United States Ambassador to Germany. He was a book reviewer for *Saturday Review of Literature, Nation, South Atlantic Quarterly,* and the *New York Times.*

As a diplomat, Dodd was a total failure — so much so that he was recalled from Berlin by the Department of State, to the relief of the German government and the foreign diplomatic corps in Berlin. He retired to a farm in Virginia where he spent the last three years of his life. (His two children, William Jr. and Martha [Mrs. Alfred K. Stern] became infamous in their own right. William traveled in Communist circles in the United States and Europe. Martha and her husband went into self-imposed exile to avoid prosecution on charges of espionage.)

Dodd's affiliations included the American Committee for Democracy and Intellectual Freedom ("subversive and un-American" — "a Communist-front organization operating among college teachers and professors"); the American Committee for Non-Participation in Japanese Aggression ("Communist front"); the American Friends of Spanish Democracy ("Communist front"); the American Friends of the Chinese People ("Communist front"); the American League Against War and Fascism ("subversive and Communist" — "established in the United States in an effort to create public sentiment on behalf of a foreign policy adapted to the interests of the Soviet Union"); the American Relief Ship for Spain ("Communist Party front enterprise"); the Chicago Forum Council (outlet for Communist and Socialist propagandists); the China Aid Council ("Communist-controlled"); the Civil Rights Congress ("created and established by the Communist Party as an organization which would utilize defense of civil rights for Party purposes and raise and maintain mass defense and bail funds for Party use"); the Committee for a Boycott Against Japanese Aggression ("the committee was featured in the *Daily Worker*, official organ of the Communist Party, and in that paper alone"); the Conference on Pan American Democracy ("Communist front"); Films for Democracy ("Communist front"); Film Audiences for Democracy ("Communist front"); the Lawyers Committee on American Relations with Spain ("during the Spanish Civil War, the Communist Party organized . . . [the Lawyers Committee] as a part of one of its major propaganda campaigns in the Party's entire history in this country"); the National Citizens Committee on Relations with Latin America (dominated by Socialists); and the Washington Committee To Lift [the] Spanish Embargo ("Communist front"). He died in February 1940.

THEODORE DREISER was born on August 27, 1871 in Terre Haute, Indiana, son of Sarah Schanab and John Dreiser. He was married to and divorced from Sarah Osborne and Helen Richardson. He was a student at Indiana University for one year. He was the author of *Sister Carrie* (1900); *Jennie Gerhardt* (1911); *The Financier* (1912); *A Traveller at Forty* (1913); *The Titan* (1914); *The Genius* (1915); *Plays of the Natural and the Supernatural* (1916); *A Hoosier Holiday* (1916); *Life, Art and America* (1917); *Free and Other Stories* (1918); *Twelve Men* (1919); *The Hand of the Potter*, play (1919); *Hey Rub-a-Dub-Dub – A Book of Essays and Philosophy* (1920); *Newspaper Days: A Book About Myself* (1922); *The Color of a Great City*

(1923); *An American Tragedy* (1925); *Moods, Cadenced and Declaimed* (1926 and 1935); *Chains: Lesser Novels and Stories* (1927); *Dreiser Looks at Russia* (1928); *A Gallery of Women* (1929); *My City* (1929); *Epitaph* (1930); *Fine Furniture* (1930); *Dawn* (1931); *Tragic America* (1932); and *America Is Worth Saving* (1941). Two of his books, *The Bulwark* (1946) and *The Stoic* (1947), were published posthumously. He was the editor of *The Living Thoughts of Thoreau* (1939). His book *An American Tragedy* was later made into a film under the title, *A Place In the Sun*.

In 1892, Dreiser was on the staff of the *Chicago Daily Globe*. In 1892 and 1893, he was dramatic critic and traveling correspondent for the *St. Louis Globe-Democrat*. In 1893 and 1894, he was a traveling correspondent for the *St. Louis Republic*. From 1895 until 1898, he was editor of *Every Month*, a literary and musical magazine. From 1898 until 1905, he was a free-lance contributor to such publications as *Harper's, Scribner's, McClure's, Cosmopolitan, Munsey's,* and *Ainsley's*. In 1905 and 1906, he was editor of *Smith's* magazine. In 1906 and 1907, he was managing editor of *Broadway* magazine. From 1907 until 1910, he was editor-in-chief of the Butterick publications, including *Designer, Delineator, New Idea,* and *English Delineator*. From 1932 until 1934, he was associate editor of *American Spectator*. In 1941, he received the Randolph Bourne Medal from the League of American Writers. In 1944, he received the Merit Award from the American Academy of Arts and Letters.

Few, if any, of Dreiser's literary contemporaries acquired as much fame or attracted as much criticism as he. Dreiser was lionized and imitated by the literary set – the same set that called him banal, verbose, ungrammatical, prolix, clumsy, heavy-handed, plodding, formless, asymmetrical. His forte was realism or naturalism, especially in his novels. Official and unofficial censors, as well as hostile and friendly critics, took notice of the extraordinary range of his intellectual facets. He revealed himself at various times to be amoral, agnostic, atheistic, sensual, fatalistic, anti-capitalistic, anti-religious, anti-Jewish, anti-Negro, anti-Christian, antisocial and anarchistic. On one occasion, he wrote a passage that indicated his highly eccentric and idiosyncratic intellectual make-up: "I have lived now to my fortieth year and have seen a good deal of life. . . . But I am one of those curious persons who cannot make up their minds about anything. I read and read . . . . But I find that one history contradicts another, one philosopher drives out another. Essayists, in the main, point out flaws and paradoxes in the current conception of things, novelists, dramatists and biographers spread tales of endless disasters, or silly illusions concerning life, duty, opportunity and the like. And I sit here and read and read, when I have time, wondering."

To Dreiser, man was merely a power-seeking, pleasure-seeking animal who had no reason to respect social convention, absolute truths, or moral codes. Man lived in a "stony universe," a world without meaning or reason, a "damnable scheme of things," a "grim, bitter world." In his strange intellectual peregrinations, Dreiser found little but imperfection in his native America, yet he became rapturous over the Soviet Union after he visited the Communist hell-land.

During his lifetime, Dreiser represented himself as a non-Communist, but after his death, the Communists' *Daily Worker* said that he had been "a member in good standing of the Communist Party." The Communists' weekly journal *New Masses*, described the reaction to Dreiser's death in the Soviet Union: "It was with deep sorrow that Soviet intellectuals and the Soviet reading public learned of Theodore Dreiser's death. . . . The Soviet people were aware that in Dreiser they had an earnest and high-principled friend . . . . On the occasion of his death commemorative meetings and lectures were held in Moscow, Leningrad and other Soviet cities . . . . The State Publishing House is to issue a new edition of his collected works."

Dreiser's public affiliations included the ultra-radical American Civil Liberties Union; the American Committee for Struggle Against War ("Communist front"); the American Committee for Protection of Foreign Born ("founded by the Communist Party in order to exploit racial divisions in the United States for its own revolutionary purposes"); the American Council on Soviet Relations ("subversive" – "established by the Communist Party . . . directed and controlled by the Party, and operated to aid and support Party objectives concerning the defense and support of the Soviet Union"); the American League Against War and Fascism ("subversive and Communist" – "established in the United States in an effort to create public sentiment on behalf of a foreign policy adapted to the interests of the Soviet Union"); the American League for Peace and Democracy ("subversive and Communist" – "established . . . in an effort to create public sentiment on behalf of a foreign policy adapted to the interests of the Soviet Union . . . [and] designed to conceal Communist control, in accordance with the new tactics of the Communist International"); the American Peace Crusade ("Communist front"); the American

Peace Mobilization ("formed . . . under the auspices of the Communist Party and the Young Communist League" – "one of the most seditious organizations which ever operated in the United States"); the American Pushkin Committee ("Communist front"); American Revolutionary Writers ("subversive and Communist"); the American Writers' Congress ("subversive"); *China Today* (official organ of the Communist-controlled American Friends of the Chinese People); the Citizens Committee To Free Earl Browder ("a strictly Communist Party affair"); the Committee for the Defense of Paul and Gertrude Rugg ("Communist front"); the Committee To Defend America by Keeping Out of War ("Communist front"); the Congress of American Revolutionary Writers ("subversive and Communist"); the Co-ordinating Committee To Lift the [Spanish] Embargo ("one of the numerous Communist-front enterprises which were organized around the Communists' agitation over the Spanish Civil War"); the Emergency Committee for Southern Political Prisoners ("Communist front"); the Emergency Peace Mobilization ("Communist front"); the Dreiser Committee on Coal (Communist-controlled); Film Audiences for Democracy ("Communist front"); Films for Democracy ("Communist front"); *Friday* ("Communist-controlled" – "never-failing support of Communist-initiated front organizations, unions, and campaigns"); Hollywood Writers Mobilization ("subversive and Communist" – "the record discloses that the present all-out patriotism of the leading spirits of the Communist front organization is primarily conditioned upon their loyalty to the Soviet Union"); the International Committee for Political Prisoners (fund-raising enterprise for seditionists); the International

Committee for Struggle Against War (organized and controlled by Moscow's International League Against Imperialism); *International Literature* ("official organ of the International Union of Revolutionary Writers, a Communist front"); the International Union of Revolutionary Writers ("Communist front"); the John Reed Clubs ("out-and-out Communist organizations which preceded the contemporary Communist front organizations which cater to so-called liberals"); the Lawyers Committee on American Relations with Spain ("during the Spanish Civil War, the Communist Party organized . . . [the Lawyers Committee] as a part of one of its major propaganda campaigns in the Party's entire history in this country"); the League of American Writers ("subversive and Communist" – "began openly to follow the Communist Party line as dictated by the foreign policy of the Soviet Union"); the League of Professional Groups for [William Z.] Foster and [James W.] Ford ("the members of this organization were committed to the objectives of the Communist Party"); the Medical Bureau and North American Committee To Aid Spanish Democracy ("subversive and un-American"); the Motion Picture Artists' [Spanish Aid] Committee ("Communist front"); the National Committee for Peoples' Rights ("Communist front"); the National Committee for the Defense of Political Prisoners ("subversive and Communist"); the National Federation for Constitutional Liberties ("under Communist Party domination and headed by responsible Party functionaries" – "one of the viciously subversive organizations of the Communist Party"); the National Right To Work Congress ("out-and-out Communist Party affair"); the National Student League ("the Communists' front organization for students"); *New Masses* ("weekly journal of the Communist Party"); the North American Committee To Aid Spanish Democracy ("Communist"); *Partisan Review* ("a Communist publication"); the [Luiz Carlos] Prestes Defense Committee (Prestes was a member of the Brazilian Communist Party); the Revolutionary Writers Federation ("American section of Moscow's International Union of Revolutionary Writers"); Russian War Relief ("Communist enterprise"); the [Morris U.] Schappes Defense Committee ("a front organization with a strictly Communist objective, namely, the defense of a self-admitted Communist who was convicted of perjury in the courts of New York"); the [William] Schneiderman- [Sam] Darcy Defense Committee (two Communist Party leaders); *Soviet Russia Today* ("official organ of Friends of Soviet Russia, which was created by the Communist Party"); Veterans of the Abraham Lincoln Brigade ("directed, dominated, and controlled by the Communist Party"); the Workers' Cultural Federation (a collection of Communist revolutionary groups); Workers International Relief ("Communist front"); the World Congress Against War ("sponsored by the Communist International"); and the Youth Anti-War Congress (Communist Party operation). He died in December 1945.

WILLIAM E. B. DuBOIS was born on February 23, 1868 in Great Barrington, Massachusetts, son of Mary Burghardt and Alfred DuBois. He was married first to Nina Gomer; his second wife was Shirley Graham. He was an alumnus of Fisk University (A.B., 1888) and Harvard University (A.B., 1890; A.M., 1891; and Ph.D. 1895). He also pursued graduate studies at the University of Berlin (Germany). He was the author of *The Suppression of the Slave Trade*

(1896); *The Philadelphia Negro* (1899); *The Souls of Black Folk* (1903); *John Brown* (1909); *Quest of the Silver Fleece* (1911); *The Negro* (1915); *Darkwater* (1920); *The Gift of Black Folk* (1924); *Dark Princess* (1928); *Black Reconstruction* (1935); *Black Folk: Then and Now* (1939); *Dusk of Dawn* (1940); *Color and Democracy* (1945); *The World and Africa* (1947); *In Battle for Peace* (1952); *The Black Flame, A Trilogy: The Ordeal of Mansart* (1957) – *Mansart Builds a School* (1959) – *Worlds of Color* (1961); and *Autobiography* (1968). He contributed articles to many publications, including *Atlantic Monthly, World's Work*, and *Independent.*

From 1894 until 1896, DuBois was professor of Greek and Latin at Wilberforce University. In 1896 and 1897, he was an assistant instructor at the University of Pennsylvania. From 1897 until 1910, he was professor of economics at Atlanta University and editor of the University's annual *Studies of the Negro Problems.* From 1910 until 1932, he was director of publications for the National Association for the Advancement of Colored People and editor of that organization's periodical, *Crisis.* From 1940 until 1944, he was editor of *Phylon.* From 1933 until 1945, he was editor-in-chief of the *Encyclopaedia of the Negro.* In 1943 and 1944, he was head of the sociology department at Atlanta University. From 1944 until 1948, he was director of the NAACP's department of special research. From 1949 until 1954, he was vice chairman of the Council on African Affairs. From 1961 until 1963, he was the head of preliminary planning for *Encyclopaedia Africana.*

In the course of his autobiographical writings, DuBois indicated that he first encountered racial discrimination and became racially conscious when he went to

Fisk University. In his days at Harvard, he became a rigid segregationist and decided that he would ask "no fellowship of my fellow students," and as for his own part, he would "disdain and forget as far as . . . possible that outer, whiter world." The depths of his racism in that era could be appreciated as he wrote of his feelings when his first-born died. In his grief, he talked of the "awful gladness in my heart." He wrote: "No bitter meanness shall sicken his baby heart 'til it die a living death, no taunt shall madden his happy boyhood . . . . Well sped, my boy, before the world had dubbed your ambition insolence, had held your ideals unattainable, and taught you to cringe and bow. Better this nameless void . . . than a sea of sorrow for you." At that same time, he said that "the problem of the twentieth century is the problem of the color line." The fact that he held three degrees from Harvard University and that he had already experienced success as an author and educator seemed to have been forgotten as he portrayed himself as oppressed – at least symbolically – because he had African ancestors. Although he had been born and brought up in an environment free of racial discrimination, his real or imagined slights at Fisk University left him scarred and apparently without hope for healing. Fifteen years after leaving Fisk, he wrote: "I saw the race-hatred of the whites as I had never dreamed of it before – naked and unashamed! The faint discrimination of my hopes and desires paled into nothing before this great, red monster of cruel oppression . . . . I am urged into full manhood, with the ruins of some ideals about me, but with others planted above the stars . . . determined, even unto stubbornness, to fight the good fight."

The good fight came for DuBois vis-à-vis Booker T. Washington, a Negro educator, a native Virginian born in slavery, and the celebrated founder of Tuskegee Institute. Washington had said: "The wisest among my race understand that the agitation of questions of social equality is the extremest folly, and that progress in the enjoyment of all the privileges that will come to us must be the result of severe and constant struggle rather than of artificial forcing. No race that has anything to contribute to the markets of the world is long in any degree ostracized. It is important and right that all privileges of the law be ours, but it is vastly more important that we be prepared for the exercise of these privileges. The opportunity to earn a dollar in a factory just now is worth infinitely more than the opportunity to spend a dollar in an opera-house."

Throughout his adult life, Washington labored to impress upon Negroes that they would have a rewarding role in America's progress only if they developed industrial and agricultural skills through vocational training in a massive "self-help" program among Negroes. From the whites Washington asked for cooperation and understanding which would result in "interlacing our industrial, commercial, civil, and religious life with yours in a way that shall make the interests of both races one. In all things that are purely social we can be as separate as the fingers, yet one as the hand in all things essential to mutual progress." There were Negro intellectuals who disagreed sharply with Washington. They alleged that Washington was leading his fellow Negroes into a surrender of political rights and a permanent system of social segregation.

The most prominent among the anti-Washington Negroes was DuBois. In a total misrepresentation of Washington's views, DuBois said: "Mr. Washington apologizes for injustice, North and South, does not rightly value the privilege and duty of voting, belittles the emasculating effects of caste distinctions, and opposes the higher training and ambition of our brighter minds. . . . [therefore] we must unceasingly and firmly oppose him."

Eric F. Goldman, in his *Rendezvous with Destiny*, remarked that "the clash between Washington and DuBois was not simply a question of temperament. Washington, the older man, accepted industrialism uncritically. DuBois, coming to maturity in the progressive era, approached all problems with an assumption that the big businessman had to be watched. He noted that Washington emphasized the training of Negroes for manual labor, concerned himself little with opening college opportunities, and was ardently supported by a number of powerful industrialists. Putting these facts together, DuBois saw the whole Washington program as a mechanism by which a cheap, submissive supply of labor would be provided for a rapidly industrializing South. 'Unconsciously or not,' DuBois believed, Washington was providing 'a voteless herd to run the machines and wash the dishes for the new aristocracy. Negroes would be educated enough to be useful but not enough, or not in the right way, to be able to assert self-respect.' " (Goldman offered these reflections after having interviewed DuBois.)

As part of his opposition to Washington, DuBois led a series of meetings which culminated in a grandstand play at Harper's Ferry where the maniacal John Brown had led his murderous raid to free Negro slaves almost a half century earlier. At the dawn's early light, a small group of barefooted Negroes, all of whom were professional men, stood on the site made famous by John Brown and adopted resolutions that had been drafted by DuBois. The resolutions declared: "We want full mankind suffrage, and we want it now, henceforth and forever. Second. We want discrimination in public accommodations to cease. Separation in railway and street cars, based simply on race and color, is un-American, undemocratic, and silly . . . . Third. We claim the right of free men to walk, talk, and be with them that wish to be with us. No man has a right to choose another man's friends, and to attempt to do so is an impudent interference with the most fundamental human privilege.

"Fourth. We want the laws enforced against rich as well as poor; against Capitalist as well as Laborer; against white as well as black. We are not more lawless than the white race, we are more often arrested, convicted and mobbed. . . . We want the Constitution of the country enforced. We want Congress to take charge of the Congressional elections. We want the Fourteenth Amendment carried out to the letter and every State disfranchised in Congress which attempts to disfranchise its rightful voters . . . . Fifth. We want our children educated . . . . And when we call for education, we mean real education. We believe in work. We ourselves are workers, but work is not necessarily education. Education is the development of power and ideal. We want our children trained as intelligent human beings should be, and we will fight for all time against any proposal to educate black boys and girls simply as servants and underlings, or simply for the use of other people. They have a right to know, to think, to aspire.

"These are some of the chief things

which we want. How shall we get them? By voting where we may vote; by persistent, unceasing agitation; by hammering at the truth; by sacrifice and work . . . . "

DuBois' strongest thrust at Washington's "self-help" program came in 1905 when DuBois and a group of collectivists founded the Niagara Movement. DuBois planned, as an immediate goal, to train a Negro elite – "the Talented Tenth" – which could lead the Negro masses in a militant program to agitate for unconditional political and social equality. Out of the Niagara Movement, there emerged – in 1909 – the National Association for the Advancement of Colored People with its announced purposes: "To promote equality of rights and eradicate caste or race prejudice among the citizens of the United States; to advance the interest of colored citizens; to secure for them impartial suffrage; and to increase their opportunities for securing justice in the courts, education for their children, employment according to their ability, and complete equality before the law."

The formation of the NAACP was urged by the leading radicals of the era, including Jane Addams, John Dewey, William Lloyd Garrison, John Haynes Holmes, Lincoln Steffens, Brand Whitlock, Lillian Wald, Rabbi Stephen Wise, and Ray Stannard Baker. Among the first officials of the NAACP were more radicals, including: Frances Blascoer, John Milholland, Mary White Ovington, Walter E. Sachs, Oswald Garrison Villard, and William English Walling. Other radicals were among the first NAACP members: James W. Johnson, Florence Kelly, William Pickens, Charles E. Russell, and E.R.A. Seligman. (Many of these individuals were already or would soon become enrolled in the newly formed Intercollegiate Socialist Society

[which later became the League for Industrial Democracy], and within a few years they were prominent in various pacifist groups, including the Fellowship of Reconciliation and the American Civil Liberties Union. The NAACP gave them one more vantage point – agitation for Negroes' equality – from which they could promote Socialism and other facets of radicalism.)

Moorfield Storey, a white attorney from Boston, was the first president of the NAACP. DuBois became the organization's first director of publicity and research and the editor of its monthly magazine, *Crisis*. For twenty-four years, *Crisis* served as DuBois' regular outlet for unbridled racism. In one of his editorials, he set the tone for the magazine when he wrote: "The most ordinary Negro is a distinct gentleman, but it takes extraordinary training and opportunity to make the average white man anything but a hog." From 1909 until 1934, DuBois – in this country and abroad – was the most prominent spokesman for the NAACP.

In its early history, the NAACP proved to be a natural attraction for Communists. DuBois, the real leader of the organization, "hailed the Russian Revolution of 1917," and he traveled to the Soviet Union in 1926 and 1936. He especially liked "the racial attitudes of the Communists."

In 1920, the question of the Negro in America had been discussed at the second world congress of the Communist International. At that time, the Negro in America was described as a "national" minority rather than a "racial" minority.

By 1922, the Communists in America had received their orders from the Communist International to exploit Negroes in the Communist program against the peace and security of the United

States. In 1923, the NAACP began to receive grants from the Garland Fund, which was a major resource for the financing of Communist Party enterprises. (Officials of the Fund included Communists Robert W. Dunn, Elizabeth Gurley Flynn, William Z. Foster, Benjamin Gitlow, and Scott Nearing, along with prominent leftwingers Roger Baldwin, Emanuel Celler, Paul H. Douglas, Morris Ernst, Ernest Gruening, Sidney Hillman, Freda Kirchwey, Judah L. Magnes, Mary E. McDowell, Moorfield Storey, Oswald Garrison Villard, and Harry F. Ward.) The grants continued until at least 1934.

There could be no doubt that the NAACP was of particular interest to the Communist Party. At the fourth national convention of the Workers (Communist) Party in 1925, the comrades were told that it was "permissible and necessary for selected Communists (not the party membership as a whole) to enter its [NAACP's] conventions and to make proposals calculated to enlighten the Negro masses under its influence as to the nature and necessity of the class struggle, the identity of their exploiters. . . . "

In 1928, the Communist International instructed American Negro Communists to work for a Negro-controlled State composed of all contiguous Southern countries having majority black populations — the so-called Black Belt. In 1930, the Communist International instructed the entire Communist Party, U.S.A., to organize the Negroes of the South for the purpose of setting up a separate state and government in the South.

The noted Negro journalist George Schuyler, who was familiar with the personnel and operations of the NAACP, has written of this era: "This was the time the veteran Socialist, Dr. W.E.B. DuBois (then the acknowledged intellectual leader of Aframerica, and editor of the *Crisis* since 1910), wrote an editorial in January 1934 to plug *for* segregation. He declared that 'the thinking colored people of the United States must stop being stampeded by the word segregation.' With considerable exaggeration, he held that segregation was 'more insistent, more prevalent and more unassailable by appeal and argument' than ever before; that Negroes must 'fight segregation with segregation,' and he told them to 'voluntarily and insistently organize our economic and social power no matter how much segregation is involved.' This shocked the NAACP directors. But, DuBois continued to urge that Negroes 'cut intercourse with white Americans to the minimum demanded by decent living.' " (Mr. Schuyler's observations appeared in *The Review of the News*, December 18, 1968.)

DuBois' views, so overtly compatible with the Communists' plans for a segregated Negro America, were an embarrassment to the NAACP which, of necessity, had to depend upon financial and other support from white America. And in 1934, DuBois separated from the NAACP. (He returned ten years later, but within four more years he left the NAACP permanently and devoted his energies full-time to working for Communist projects.)

On November 26, 1961, the Communist Party's *Worker* announced that the ninety-three-year-old DuBois had joined the Communist Party, USA. The *Worker* reproduced a letter from DuBois to the Party's General Secretary, Gus Hall. DuBois wrote: "On this first day of October, 1961, I am applying for admission to membership in the Communist Party of the United States. I have been long and slow in coming to this conclusion, but at last my mind is settled.

"In college I heard the name of Karl Marx, but read none of his works, nor heard them explained. At the University of Berlin, I heard much of those thinkers who had definitely answered the theories of Marx, but again we did not study what Marx himself had said. Nevertheless, I attended meetings of the Socialist Party and considered myself a Socialist.

"On my return to America, I taught and studied for sixteen years. I explored the theory of Socialism and studied the organized social life of American Negroes; but still I neither read nor heard much of Marxism. Then I came to New York as an official of the new NAACP and editor of the *Crisis* magazine. The NAACP was capitalist oriented and expected support from rich philanthropists.

"But it had a strong Socialist element in its leadership in persons like Mary Ovington, William English Walling and Charles Edward Russell. Following their advice, I joined the Socialist Party in 1911. I knew then nothing of practical socialist politics and in the campaign of 1912, I found myself unwilling to vote the Socialist ticket, but advised Negroes to vote for Wilson. This was contrary to Socialist Party rules and consequently I resigned from the Socialist Party.

"For the next twenty years I tried to develop a political way of life for myself and my people. I attacked the Democrats and Republicans for monopoly and disfranchisement of Negroes; I attacked the Socialists for trying to segregate Southern Negro members; I praised the racial attitudes of the Communists, but opposed their tactics in the case of the Scottsboro boys and their advocacy of a Negro state. At the same time I began to study Karl Marx and the Communists; I read *Das Kapital* and other Communist literature; I hailed the Russian Revolution of 1917, but was puzzled at the contradictory news from Russia.

"Finally in 1926, I began a new effort: I visited Communist lands. I went to the Soviet Union in 1926, 1936, 1949 and 1959; I saw the nation develop. I visited East Germany, Czechoslovakia and Poland. I spent ten weeks in China traveling all over the land. Then, this summer, I rested a month in Rumania.

"I was early convinced that Socialism was an excellent way of life, but I thought it might be reached by various methods. For Russia I was convinced she had chosen the only way open to her at the time. I saw Scandinanivia choosing a different method, half-way between Socialism and Capitalism. In the United States I saw Consumers Cooperation as a path from Capitalism to Socialism, while England, France and Germany developed in the same direction in their own way. After the depression and the Second World War, I was disillusioned. The Progressive movement in the United States failed. The Cold War started. Capitalism called Communism a crime.

"Today I have reached a firm conclusion: Capitalism cannot reform itself; it is doomed to self-destruction. No universal selfishness can bring social good to all.

"Communism — the effort to give all men what they need and to ask of each the best they can contribute — this is the only way of human life. It is a difficult and hard end to reach — it has and will make mistakes, but today it marches triumphantly on in education and science, in home and food, with increased freedom of thought and deliverance from dogma. In the end Communism will triumph. I want to help to bring that day.

"The path of the American Communist Party is clear: It will provide the United States with a real Third Party and thus restore democracy to this land. It will call for: (1) Public ownership of natural resources and of all capital. (2) Public control of transportation and communications. (3) Abolition of poverty and limitation of personal income. (4) No exploitation of labor. (5) Social medicine, with hospitalization and care of the old. (6) Free education for all (7) Training for jobs and jobs for all. (8) Discipline for growth and reform. (9) Freedom under law. (10) No dogmatic religion.

"These aims are not crimes. They are practiced increasingly over the world. No nation can call itself free which does not allow its citizens to work for these ends."

In his answer to DuBois, Hall wrote: "In reply to your letter of October 1st in which you made application for membership in the Communist Party of the United States allow me to relate the following: I read it before our National Board on October 13th, where it was greeted with the highest enthusiasm and responded to with many heartfelt testimonials to the titanic labors which you have performed over a glorious span of 60 years of dedicated services and leadership in the cause of human progress, peace, science and culture.

"Already in 1906 in your historic 'Address to the Country of the Niagara Movement,' you had perceived the main line of development of our century, and wrote these prophetic words: 'The morning breaks over the hills. Courage, brothers! The battle for humanity is not lost or losing. The Slav is rising in his might, the yellow minions are testing liberty, the black Africans are writhing toward the light, and everywhere the laborer is opening the gates of Opportunity and Peace.'

"And so it has come, and is coming to pass. And knowledgeable people every where are mindful of the fact that your selfless labors and mighty works have been a powerful contribution to the dawn of our new epoch, the epoch of the final triumph of man over all manner of oppression, discrimination and exploitation.

"You (the first Negro to receive the Doctor of Philosophy degree from Harvard University, in 1895) are the acknowledged Dean of American letters and most eminent living American scholar. As editor, sociologist, historian, novelist, poet, publicist, lecturer, and organizer, you have made enduring contributions. Your life is a monumental example of achievement for all Americans.

"For 50 years you have been a tireless champion of the national liberation of the African peoples and new Africa's wise counselor and 'elder statesman.' For more than 60 years you have been the foremost philosopher, theoretician and practical organizer of the glorious Negro people's freedom struggle.

"You have authored numerous books, each of which is a weapon against colonialism, racism, and imperialism, and for the victory of the cause of peace, freedom and the brotherhood of peoples. You have raised your voice powerfully and incessantly against war machinations, for world peace and disarmament, for friendship with the socialist countries and co-existence between the two world social systems.

"Your act of joining the Communist Party at this time not only expresses that recognition of the new world reality, of the great turn of the people of the world toward socialism for the solution of

340

mankind's need for peace, brotherhood and well-being, but it constitutes an invitation and a challenge to men and women of science and culture, to creative thinkers of all countries, to the Negro masses and their outstanding leaders both here and abroad, to avail themselves of the social science of Marxism-Leninism and the fraternity of the Communist Parties to give new wings to their cause and their works.

"You have chosen to join our Party precisely at the time when with brazen effrontery to the trends of the times, the most backward ultra-reactionary forces in our country's national life have temporarily dragooned the Supreme Court's majority into upholding the most flagrantly un-Constitutional thought-control laws – the McCarran Act and Smith Act, designed to muzzle free speech, ban freedom of association, persecute Communists and suppress our Party.

"This is symbolic of the personal courage and heroic exercise of social responsibility which have characterized your service and leadership to the people's cause throughout your long life. In joining the Communist Party, you have made that association which was clearly indicated by the very logic of your life.

"Dear Dr. DuBois, welcome into the membership of our Party! The title of Party Member is an honorable and worthy title worn with pride by the most dedicated and farseeing, the best sons and daughters of the workers and peoples of all lands in the first ranks of struggle for mankind's happy future."

The DuBois-Hall exchange was a well-contrived bit of theatre. Certainly by 1961, the Communist Party, USA, owed a debt of gratitude to DuBois that spanned its history from the very beginning. Few individuals had made greater contributions to Communism in this country and abroad than DuBois. He had left his imprint in Europe, Africa, and Asia. His affiliations with Communist Party and other ultra-leftist projects in this country were legion.

DuBois was affiliated with the All-America Anti-Imperialist League ("the [Communist] Party was wholly responsible for the establishment and subsequent control of the league"); the American Committee for Protection of Foreign Born ("founded by the Communist Party in order to exploit racial divisions in the United States for its own revolutionary purposes"); the American Committee for Struggle Against War ("Communist front"); the American Council for a Democratic Greece ("subversive and Communist"); the American International Peace Congress (Communist enterprise); the American Labor Party ("Communist dissimulation extends into the field of political parties forming political front organizations such as the . . . American Labor Party"); the American Peace Crusade ("Communist front"); the American Pushkin Committee ("Communist front"); the *American Socialist* (ultra-leftist publication); the American Society for Cultural Relations with Russia ("Communist front"); American Youth for Democracy ("subversive and Communist" – "part of Soviet psychological warfare against the United States"); the Berger National Foundation (Socialist organization); the California Labor School ("a subversive and Communist organization"); the China Welfare Appeal, Inc. ("subversive"); the Citizens' Committee To Free Earl Browder ("a strictly Communist Party affair"); the Citizens' Committee To Secure Bail for Martin Young ("Communist"); the Citizens' Emergency Defense Committee ("subversive"); the Civil Rights Congress ("created and established by the Communist Party as an organization which would utilize defense of civil rights for Party purposes and raise and maintain mass defense and bail funds for Party use"); the Committee for a Democratic Far Eastern Policy ("Communist"); the Committee for Free Political Advocacy ("Communist front"); the Conference for Legislation in the National Interest ("under complete domination by the Communist Party"); the Conference for World Peace Through Negotiations (pro-Communist); the Council on African Affairs ("subversive and Communist"); the *Daily Worker* (official organ of the Communist Party); Friends of the Soviet Union ("created, directed, and controlled by the Communist Party . . . and operated to aid and support Party objectives concerning the defense and support of the Soviet Union"); the Golden Book of American Friendship with the Soviet Union ("pro-Soviet propaganda enterprise"); the Independent Progressive Party (Socialist-dominated); the International Committee for Political Prisoners (to raise funds for jailed seditionists); the Jefferson School of Social Science ("a Communist institution modeled along the lines of the new Communist policy which led to the decision to change the Communist Party into some kind of an educational institution"); the Joint Anti-Fascist Refugee Committee ("subversive and Communist"); the League for Independent Political Action (Socialist); *Mainstream* (monthly cultural and literary organ of the Communist Party); *Masses and Mainstream* (a Communist magazine); the National Assembly for Peace ("Communist front"); the National Committee To Repeal the McCarran Act ("Communist front" – "subversive"); the National Committee To Secure Justice in the Rosenberg Case ("Communist front organized . . . to

conduct the United States phase of a mammoth propaganda campaign designed to obliterate the crime of and exploit the Rosenbergs and their co-defendant Morton Sobell for the purposes of international Communism"); the National Committee To Win Amnesty for Smith Act Victims ("subversive" – "Communist"); the National Conference on American Policy in China and the Far East ("Communist"); the National Council for Protection of Foreign Born Workers ("Communist subsidiary"); the National Council of American-Soviet Friendship ("subversive and Communist" – "specializing in pro-Soviet propaganda"); the National Council of the Arts, Sciences, and Professions ("Communist front used to appeal to special occupational groups"); the National Free Browder Congress ("Communist front"); the National Institute of Arts and Letters ("Communist front"); the National Non-Partisan Committee To Defend the Rights of the Twelve Communist Leaders (pro-Communist); *New Masses* ("weekly journal of the Communist Party"); *New World Review* ("monthly propaganda organ on the Soviet Union, Red China, and the Communist satellites"); the New York Conference To Repeal the Walter McCarran Law and Defend Its Victims (subversive); the Peace Information Center ("Communist front"); Progressive Citizens of America ("political Communist front" – "subversive"); *Science and Society* ("a Communist publication"); the Scientific and Cultural Conference for World Peace ("a propaganda front for Soviet foreign policy and Soviet culture"); the Socialist Unity Forum (ultraleftist); the Southern Negro Youth Congress ("subversive and among the affiliates and committees of the Communist Party, USA, which seeks to alter the form of government of the United States by unconstitutional means"); *Soviet Russia Today* ("Communist-controlled publication"); the Voice of Freedom Committee ("subversive" – to defend pro-Communist radio commentators); the Washington Book Shop ("Communist Party enterprise"); the Win-the-Peace Conference ("Communist front"); the World Peace Appeal ("Communist Party campaign"); the World Congress Against War ("sponsored by the Communist International"); and the World Peace Congress ("organized under Communist initiative in various countries throughout the world"). DuBois' books were advertised and sold by Communist bookshops. His writings were published by Communist publishing houses. He was a candidate for political office on the Communist-controlled American Labor Party ticket. He endorsed Communist candidates for political office. He was always the recipient of generous and favorable notice in the Communist press.

DuBois was personally involved in the defense of such notorious Communists as Eugene Dennis, Gerhardt Eisler, Philip Foner, Simon Gerson, Ben Gold, V.J. Jerome, Pablo Neruda of Chile, Harry Sacher, and Alexander Trachtenberg. In 1948, when the Communist Party's twelve leaders were arrested, DuBois began his involvement in the case by first sponsoring a general statement attacking the arrest. He then sponsored a "Statement by Negro Americans" on behalf of the Communist Party leaders. In 1949, he filed a brief in the Supreme Court of the United States on behalf of the leaders. In 1952 and 1954 respectively, he signed appeals to Presidents Truman and Eisenhower requesting amnesty for the twelve.

In 1947, when a move was underway to outlaw the Communist Party, the *Daily Worker* reported: " . . . Almost 100 Negro leaders, headed by W.E.B. DuBois . . . called upon President Truman to repudiate decisively steps to illegalize the Communist Party . . . . As Negro Americans . . . we cannot be unmindful that this proposal to outlaw the Communist Party comes precisely when our Federal Government professes grave concern over the democratic rights of peoples in far distant parts of the world."

DuBois was a special pleader for the atomic spys Julius and Ethel Rosenberg and Morton Sobell. To the American people and their government he offered a couplet: "We are the murderers hurling mud./ We are the witchhunters drinking blood." While the Rosenbergs were awaiting execution, he said: "[It is] America [that] should be asking a pardon from the Rosenbergs, and not the Rosenbergs who should be asking clemency." DuBois' ultimate gesture was to officiate at the funeral of the Rosenbergs.

In 1950 a permanent committee of the World Peace Congress, headed by international Communists, met to launch the boldest and most far-reaching maneuver of the then current Communist "peace" movement – the world-wide circulation of "peace petitions." The drive for signatures for what became known as the Stockholm Appeal was the most extensive piece of psychological warfare ever conducted by any organization on a world scale. The maneuver took place just three months before the outbreak of Communist aggression against South Korea, and the Stockholm Appeal was intended as a smoke screen for such aggression. In the United States, it was the hope of Communist Party leaders to obtain five million signatures to the Stockholm Appeal. DuBois was chairman of the Peace Information Center, which had charge of the petition campaign. While in that capacity, he was asked to register as a foreign agent by the Department of Justice. He refused to do so, and was subsequently indicted for his refusal by a federal grand jury. The case against DuBois was eventually dismissed, but not before he had accomplished the Communist Party's purposes. The government was unable to prove a contractual relationship between DuBois and the Soviet Union. (DuBois' personal view of the Korean War was the straight Communist line. He described it as "a civil dispute for which the United States and especially South Korea were principally responsible.")

DuBois' contributions to the Communists' "peace" campaign did not go unrewarded. In 1952, he received the International Peace Prize of the World Peace Congress. In 1958, he received the Lenin International Peace Prize, a tribute reserved for those who make heroic efforts on behalf of the International Communist movement.

Beginning with the 1917 Bolshevik revolution, DuBois was obsessed with Communism as practiced in the Soviet Union. He took full advantage of opportunities to sing the praises of the Leninist and Stalinist regimes. As a complete apologist he neglected mention of forced labor, slave labor camps, or the total suppression of political, religious, and civil rights in the Soviet Union. As early as 1920, through the Pan-African Congresses which he instituted, he urged Africans to look toward the Soviet Union and its Communism for inspiration. Advising peoples to adopt Communism was a life-time habit of DuBois. In 1958, as he celebrated his 90th birthday at Howard University, he said: "Today the United States is fighting world progress; progress which must be toward socialism and against colonialism and war. Socialism is inevitable, and Communism is one way to achieve it. But, whether it is achieved by Communist dictatorship or by Democracy, its aim of giving to each what he needs and demanding what best he can give, is the inevitable aim of civilization and sooner or later will triumph."

In January 1959, DuBois visited the Soviet Union at the invitation of the Soviet Committee for the Defense of "Peace." The Communists made the most of the visit. They conferred on DuBois an honorary degree in history from the Moscow State University for his "outstanding service to science and for his prominent role in the world progressive public movement." The Communists also made capital of an interview between DuBois and Khrushchev during which the two comrades allegedly discussed "vital questions concerning the struggle for peace against the threat of atomic war." From the Soviet Union DuBois went to Red China.

The Red Chinese accorded DuBois a reception that would have been appropriate to a friendly head of state. DuBois responded to the treatment in the manner of a highly disciplined international Communist propagandist. He and his Chinese comrades proved to be fully aware of their opportunity to make anti-American, pro-Communist publicity that would reach a world-wide audience. On February 23, 1959, the Red Chinese news service carried a dispatch from Peiping which read: "Dr. W.E.B. DuBois this afternoon addressed 1,000 cheering professors and students who gathered at a meeting in Peiping University held in honor of his 91st birthday. Girl students presented the famous Negro scholar and Mrs. DuBois with flowers and pinned their university badges on the visitors. Many faculty members and students from the institute of foreign languages and the college of international relations also attended the function.

"Speaking of his impressions on China, Dr. DuBois said that China after long centuries had risen to her feet and leapt forward. He added that since liberation 'China can take the insults of the United States and still hold her head high. She can make machines or go without machines when America refuses to sell her American manufactures, even when it hurts American industry and throws her workers out of jobs.

" 'China had been in hell too long not to believe in a heaven of her own making; this she is doing,' Dr. DuBois added. He asked more African people to visit China, and said that understanding came from direct knowledge. He warned against U.S. promises of freedom to the African people. Dr. DuBois said: 'Beware, Africa, America bargains for your soul; America would have you believe that they freed your grandchildren; that Afro-Americans are full Americans, treated like equals, paid fair wages as workers, promoted for merit, and free to learn and earn and travel across the world.

" 'This is not true. Some are near freedom, some approach equality with whites, some have achieved education, but the price for this has too often been slavery of mind, distortion of truth, and oppression of our own people. Of 18 million Afro-Americans, 12 million are still second-class citizens of the United States, serfs in farming, low-paid laborers in industry, and repressed members of union labor. Most American Negroes do not vote. Even the rising 6 million are liable to insult and discrimination at any time,' Dr. DuBois noted.

"Dr. DuBois warned the African people: 'Don't let the West invest when you can avoid it. This is not politics; it is common sense; it is learning from experience; it is trusting your friends and watching your enemies,' he added.

"Before Dr. DuBois' speech, Vice President Chon Pei-yuan, of Peiping University, spoke and greeted the guests from America. He said that . . . Dr. and Mrs. DuBois had always taken a most sympathetic interest in the struggle of the Chinese people. 'Dr. DuBois has justly condemned the flagrant occupation by the U.S. Government of our territory Taiwan.' "

Later on the same day, the news service carried further accounts of the reception given to DuBois: "A colorful Chinese-style banquet was given in honor of Dr. W.E.B. DuBois' 91st birthday in Peiping this evening. It was attended by Vice Premier Chen I and his wife, Kuo Mo-jo, chairman of the China Peace Committee, and many other well-known people. The birthday party was sponsored by the China Peace Committee and the Chinese People's Association for Cultural Relations with Foreign Countries.

"In offering congratulations to Dr. DuBois on his birthday, Kuo Mo-jo said . . . that U.S. imperialism is at present the No. 1 enemy of the peace-loving people of the world. 'In such an inclement political atmosphere, marked with deceit and tyranny, Dr. DuBois has struggled relentlessly for several decades. This is a brilliant demonstration of the desire of the American people for peace and righteousness,' Kuo Mo-jo noted. Paying tribute to Dr. DuBois for his life of militancy, Kuo Mo-jo said that 'countless American and African working people groaning under the yoke of monopoly capital and race prejudice take Dr. DuBois as the standard bearer of their struggle.'

"Kuo Mo-jo also expressed gratitude

to Dr. DuBois and his wife, Shirley Graham, for their support to the Chinese people in their struggles and for their efforts to safeguard world peace . . . .

"Telegrams of greetings to Dr. DuBois from Soong Ching-ling and from American friends and Soviet friends were read out . . . .

"Reports of Premier Chou En-lai's reception of the renowned U.S. Negro scholar, Dr. W.E.B. DuBois, and his wife, and his dinner for them yesterday evening are carried in the major Peiping papers today. The *People's Daily* front-pages the report of the reception and a picture showing Premier Chou En-lai warmly shaking hands with Dr. DuBois. It also carries a feature article on a visit to Dr. DuBois and his wife by its correspondent. The paper carries in its literature columns a short poem by Kuo Mo-jo praising Dr. DuBois' efforts for the emancipation of the Negro people and for world peace.

"It also carries an article by the writer Mao Tun greeting Dr. DuBois' 91st birthday. The writer quotes an old Chinese saying, 'The moon is full and life is long.' He writes: 'In Dr. DuBois we see the Negro people's wisdom and bravery and the American people's tradition of peace, freedom, and universal love. His just struggle has given energetic support to the progressive movement in the United States and Latin America, exercised tremendous influence on the independence movement of the Negro people in Africa, and provided great inspiration to the just struggle of the fairminded people the world over.' . . . . "

Before DuBois left Red China, he composed a poem, "I Sing to China," which read, in part: "Down then, religion and church, temple and pagoda;/ Away, myth and miracle, creed and dogma./ Rejoice, honesty, God lives again!/ But not your God, Europe and America!/ Not that, not that;/ No Christ to kill, no faith to fan;/ What China worships is a man./ A workingman./ Commune, Communes, with the elect of Heaven,/ With Mother Earth, daughter of Sky and Sun;/ Born of democracy, fertilized by communism,/ Parents of revolution, makers of the world."

Less than two years after DuBois had accomplished his major propaganda coups in the Soviet Union and Red China, he wrote his famous letter to Gus Hall applying for membership in the Communist Party, U.S.A. At about the same time he was making this absolutely meaningless gesture, he travelled to Ghana, where the eccentric but dedicated Communist, Kwame Nkrumah, was holding sway. DuBois not only made a home for himself there, but became a Ghanaian citizen and began to work on his *Encyclopedia Africana*. One of Du-Bois' last major efforts for the Communist cause was in the form of an article that was published in the *Accra Evening News* of November 27, 1962. In the article, "Ghanaians Need Discipline and Faith in Their Future," he wrote: "Science is a stern unyielding master. It brooks no rival, neither in church nor state, neither in wish nor dream. It seeks eternal and immutable truth attained slowly and painfully with infinite toil and endless sacrifice. Either it guides civilisation or civilisation dies. You must master science. You must obey its laws. You and the world must admit that in exact science today, the Soviet Union leads mankind: not in war but in search for truth.

"What can man do today to make a decent and happy world? He cannot rely on chance, guessing and gambling. Life is not a lottery. He cannot follow the well-meant fairytales of dogmatic religion. He must know, he must work, he must earn and sacrifice.

"Year before last, in 1958, I took a marvellous journey. Already before that I had travelled widely. Beginning as a young man I had traversed the United States, North, East, West, and South. I had seen Canada and Mexico. Then I made in the next sixty-six years, fifteen trips to Europe.

"I also saw something of China and Japan and a bit of Africa. In these years, I saw mostly what I already knew by reading and listening. I was European-cultured. I believed in the unfortunate necessity of wealth and poverty, in the inevitability of disease, in the natural backwardness of Asia and Africa. Of course, this belief was not complete. My faith in Europe was not absolute. But on the whole I thought I was living in a world about as good as was humanly possible.

"Then I spent a sudden year abroad mostly in a new world of Socialism: in the Soviet Union, in China, in Czechoslovakia and East Germany, in Sweden. And then back to a new view of France, Holland and England. I returned to America a man renewed in faith and spirit, reborn in vision, revived in strength. I had not visited Paradise. I had not seen perfect human beings or people universally happy, without fear or apprehension. But I did see a thousand million people who were trying a new way of life. Life in which progress and poverty did not live side by side, without starvation and luxury, cheek by jowl; without men holding millions which they never earned, with children in school and schools for all, with no barriers of caste and color, birth and heritage, with pensions for the sick, with no man unemployed.

"What struck me in these socialist and Communist countries, was the discipline under which the people were working. It was not slavery. It was discipline born out of the conception of right and wrong, of respect for the manners of former days; of obedience to law, willingness to sacrifice and a belief in justice for all.

"When we, in America, and you, in Africa, think of freedom we think often of the right of a man to do anything he pleases to do. But manifestly this kind of freedom leads nowhere. There must be for the individual and for the Nation a plan of life based on law. No matter what your opinion may be, the law of gravity holds. If you lean too far out of the window, you fall and are hurt. If you do not obey the laws of health you die before your time. Effect has a cause and wrongdoing brings unfailing retribution.

"These are laws of nature, we cannot change them. If we disobey them, we suffer accordingly. In addition to this there is customary law – that which is called the culture of a tribe or a nation or a continent. It is the ancient way in which people for generations have been carrying on life, and while it is never complete and perfect it is at any particular time a digest of the wisdom of men who have lived and thought. As such it must be followed until it is proven unfit for the present. It must change from time to time, it can never be complete and done away with. The culture of a land is its life.

"In all civilized countries there is statutory law which limits the freedom of every man. His attitude toward law is the mark of a civilized man. All laws are not just, some laws are manifestly unjust; but nevertheless, law is the only way in which life can be planned for the benefit of all. If laws are wrong they must be changed but not by individual

347

whim, rather by the decision of the mass of men who live under them. The mass of men are the last appeal.

"Thus with a knowledge of history and science life must be planned individually and nationally according to what we think best and bowing towards right and with manners that make human contact, decent and reasonable; with obedience and sacrifice and a sense of justice, we earn the freedom for which all men strive. But this freedom must be earned, it does not come easily. It is not the free gift of nature. It is the orderly result of knowledge, of planning and discipline.

"When, however, once it is gained it shows itself in self-respect, in realization of our power in self-expression. It becomes the basis of literature and art and here in West Africa, your chance to develop a great expression of art and the great literature is unlimited. As I saw the opening of Parliament with its ceremony, with its riot of color and sound, with its dignity and humour, I realised again what a rich heritage Africa has and how necessary it is for us to look towards socialism and communism for that planning and discipline which will lead towards greater freedom.

"There is a widely held belief that citizens of Socialist and Communist lands are prisoners and that prisoners of the state are slaves. On the contrary, I have nowhere in the world seen such satisfied workers as in the Soviet Union or such happy workers and healthy children as in China. While the prisoners [sic] of the United States are filled with discontent and despair, the prisons of Russia are schools which lead criminals to citizenship and train them in trades with happiness in family life.

"I do not say that all the world will follow Russia or China, Czechoslovakia and East Germany, Hungary, Rumania, and Bulgaria; but I am absolutely certain that the overwhelming trend of humanity today, is towards socialism. India is a socialist country. In Scandinavia are socialist states; Britain resists socialism in vain. West Germany has intended socialist institutions. Italy and France are owning and controlling capital. Even the United States is continually taking steps towards state control of capital and ownership of natural resources; and all socialist countries are gradually envisioning a complete communism of equal men, each doing what he can do best, and receiving what he needs for health and comfort and as free as the welfare of all men allows men to be free. To this great end I want Africa to march.

"Then Ghana will show the world not the old 19th century pattern of a group of the rich following the luxury of a decadent Europe and the waste of a ruthless America, surrounded by a writhing mass of poverty-stricken people, but the nation will be represented by seven million hard and happy workers doing what the nation needs done for the welfare of all and with the workers living in simple sanitary homes amid the flowers and foliage of this beautiful land. With no tired babies strapped to weary backs, but nurseries for all children, with scientific care and thoughtful training; with children in kindergartens and youth in school and the nation taught to read and think, and sing and dance and grow in power and accomplishment.

"There are people who will tell you that this dream is impossible. That always most men must be poor, sick and ignorant and that only the lucky few can hope for a decent life. This is a lie. The vast majority of men in the 21st century will be happier than the aristocracy of this war-torn twentieth, if only you will lead the way. Will loose the genius now prisoned by poverty and emancipate the ability now enslaved by ignorance. In peace and plenty let Ghana join the Soviet Union and China and usher in the new world."

DuBois died in August 1963 in Ghana. The Communists in the United States have perpetuated his name through the creation of their DuBois Clubs and in other ways. His books remain as standard fare in Communist and pro-Communist circles.

WALTER DURANTY was born on May 25, 1884 in Liverpool, England. He married Mrs. Anna Enwright. He graduated from Emmanuel College, Cambridge, with a degree in Classics (*c.* 1906). He was the author of *Moscow Trials* (1929); *The Curious Lottery and Other Tales of Russian Justice* (1929); *Duranty Reports Russia* (1934); *I Write As I Please* (1935); *One Life, One Kopeck* (1937); *The Gold Train* (1938); *The Kremlin and the People* (1941); *Search for a Key*, autobiographical novel (1943); *U.S.S.R., The Story of Soviet Russia* (1944); and *Stalin & Co.: The Politburo — the Men Who Run Russia* (1949). He was co-author of *Return to the Vineyard* (1945).

From 1913 until 1939, Duranty was a foreign correspondent for the *New York Times*. In 1929, he received the O. Henry Memorial Award for a short story. From 1921 until 1939, he was stationed in Moscow. In 1932, he was awarded the Pulitzer Prize for his dispatches from Moscow. From 1939 until 1941, he was a correspondent for the North American Newspaper Alliance (NANA). After 1941, he was a free-lance writer but did carry out assignments for NANA. In the last years of his life, he was more or less in retirement in California.

In all the history of American journalism, no correspondent for a major newspaper was more irresponsible than Duranty during the years he spent in Moscow. It is difficult to imagine the most dedicated Communist in the Soviet Union ever presuming to tell the American people through the pages of the *New York Times* the ludicrous stories about the Soviet Union and its leaders that Duranty wrote for twenty years. In his dispatches and books, there was strong evidence that he never did understand Communism. He either did not understand what he saw in Russia or, if he did, he refused to believe or to report what he did see.

Eugene Lyons, who was on the Moscow scene contemporaneously with Duranty, offered in his *The Red Decade* a somewhat charitable but revealing explanation of Duranty's behavior: "The case of Walter Duranty of the *New York Times* is too complex for treatment in brief. I can no more than touch it. ... Mr. Duranty had that peculiarly disdainful attitude toward the masses that one finds among some middle-class Britishers — a kind of colonial distaste for 'natives.' ... The perpetual marvel, for him, seemed to be that certain Russians in power were fairly intelligent and almost human — despite the fact that they were natives. His readers overseas could not understand that his refusal to be perturbed by mounting horrors in Russia was at least in part an expression of his low opinion of the victims. At moments when the rest of us might be shaken by some calamity involving vast suffering, Duranty remained urbanely calm. He thus got himself a world-wide reputation as 'a friend of the Soviets' based largely on his superior attitude toward the Soviet people and disinterest in the whole Bolshevik business.

"His role as the understanding friend of the Bolsheviks had brought him fame, and he stuck to it. He was pretty candid on that score . . . . The identification was purely professional. His own explanation for his failure to react to Russian horrors is that his war experiences had left him immune to such things. Curiously, though, he grew downright maudlin when those who suffered were people closer to his own kind.

". . . He took a crack at reporters who indulged in 'moral judgments' — those who 'prate of ruthless methods and the iron age and lament the brutality which drove through to its goal regardless of sacrifice and suffering.' Duranty is too clever not to realize that ignoring ruthless methods or their consequences in human blood also implies moral judgments, though on another plane. If being moved by mass suffering is bad reporting, pretending to look upon it in terms of the vivisection of animals (as he did on page 304 of *I Write As I Please*) seems to some of us even worse reporting.

" 'I'm a reporter, not a humanitarian,' he boasted. 'I had no intention of being an apologist for the Stalin administration,' he added farther on. All the same, he admitted in relation to the iron age: 'I allowed my critical faculty to lapse and failed to pay proper attention to the cost and immediate consequences of the policies that I had foreseen . . . . I had tried to make myself think like a true-blue Stalinist in order to find out what true-blue Stalinists were thinking, and had succeeded too well.' In plainer English, his dispatches were written from the true-blue Stalinist angle. And the humor of it is that the most capitalist paper in America paid the cable tolls, and that the true-blue Stalinist version won a capitalistic Pulitzer Prize for foreign correspondence . . . .

"In *I Write As I Please*, a book of over 300 pages, only about 30 pages are devoted to the crucial Russian years between 1928 and 1934, when it was written. Those were the most cruel, heartbreaking years; they compromised about half of Duranty's total Soviet experience at the time; yet he gave about 10 per cent of the space to it and the rest to the relatively pleasanter previous period. This lack of proportion too, implies a moral judgment, if only negatively — a slurring over horror, whereby the true-blue ones are not too sharply discomfited.

"Of all his elliptical writing, perhaps his handling of the famine was most celebrated. It was the logical extreme of his oft-repeated assertion that 'you can't make an omelet without breaking eggs.' Now he made his omelet by referring to the famine as 'undernourishment' and to its consequences as deaths due to 'the diseases of malnutrition.'

" . . . He went all-out in hailing the advent of 'democracy' under the Stalin Constitution. That document, he wrote in the Sunday *Times* of July 19, 1936, 'is an outward and visible sign of an inward and spiritual change in the Russian people and its leaders . . . . In this nineteenth year of the Soviet State, there is introduced a new Constitution, under which the Russian masses emerge from their tutelage and are called upon to receive their rights and undertake their duties as a free and democratic people.' This on the very eve of the bloodiest period in Russia's history and the final confirmation of Russia's emergence as a totalitarian state! 'External enemies are no longer feared and internal enemies have been defeated and scotched, if not totally eliminated,' he concluded. The 'confessions' were being extorted in G.P.U.

cellars while Duranty indited these words.

"The *Times* paid the bill for this strange reporting. The mischief of it was that Duranty's dispatches, in all these years of the building of the great Russian myth, had a resonance and authority which they would have lacked in the *Daily Worker*. The liberals had in his true-blue reports clinching corroboration of their self-deceptions."

Duranty's upside-down view was perhaps best expressed in his own words, written in the concluding chapter of his *I Write As I Please:* "Looking backward over the fourteen years I have spent in Russia, I cannot escape the conclusion that this period has been a heroic chapter in the life of Humanity. During these years the first true Socialist State, with all that that implies in planned economy, in the ownership of production and means of production, in communal effort as opposed to individual effort and in communal pride and interest in everything that the community rather than the individual accomplished, was constructed and set moving despite incredible difficulties. I am profoundly convinced that the U.S.S.R. is only just beginning to exercise its tremendous potentialities. According to Soviet law a man 'comes of age' at eighteen, and this is the eighteenth year of New Russia's existence. The fourteen years which I have seen have been a time of growth and construction, a sort of larval period from which the adult creature is only just emerging. The U.S.S.R. is now economically and financially independent; it has the largest and perhaps the most powerful army in Europe; it has vast territory and resources, which it is learning to develop and use. In short, the U.S.S.R. has recovered the position lost by the Tsarist Empire in 1917 of one of

the great world powers. This progress at home and abroad has been paralleled by a remarkable advance of the Soviet leaders in knowledge and wisdom; am I wrong in believing that Stalin is the greatest living statesman and that Litvinov is the ablest foreign minister? Not only these two but other Soviet leaders have grown with the growth of their country and gained in mental capacity to meet the growing magnitude of the problems which they have had to solve. More important still, Stalin and his associates have carried with them the strongest and most intelligent elements of the Russian people, and have created a national unity and enthusiasm which the Tsarist Empire never knew. They have learned by their own errors and pulled themsleves up by their own bootstraps, and the nation has followed them. Nothing that may be said abroad about the tyranny and high-handedness of the Bolshevik regime can alter the fact that the Russian masses think and speak of 'our' *Rodina* [homeland], 'our' technicians, 'our' successes and 'our' failures."

A year after Duranty's *I Write As I Please* was published, his "greatest living statesman," Stalin, was purging his "associates" in a series of trials wherein lifelong Bolsheviks — Stalin's comrades-in-arms — confessed to the worst crimes possible against Stalin, the Communist Party, and the Soviet Union. The spectacle of the purge trials caused consternation to Communists throughout the world, who couldn't believe that their revolutionary heroes, with few exceptions, were traitors of long standing. But Duranty reassured his readers and Communists everywhere that the purge trials were legitimate. The confessions, he insisted, were sincerely and voluntarily given. Stalin was blameless.

Duranty's years as a slavish apologist for the barbarous Stalin regime had their reward when Stalin told him: "You have done a good job in your reporting of the U.S.S.R., although you are not a Marxist, because you tried to tell the truth about our country, and to understand and explain it to your readers."

By 1949, when Duranty's *Stalin & Co.* was published, the American public — to some extent — could realize that Stalin had raped Poland, Latvia, Lithuania, and Estonia, and that eastern Europe and eastern Germany and Czechoslovakia had been ruthlessly enslaved by "good old Joe." Stalin's post-war conduct, however, did not dismay Duranty, who peddled his book on television and radio, telling his audiences to read *Stalin & Co.* and discover that Stalin was not responsible for what everyone thought were his diabolical deeds. No, according to Duranty, Stalin was a prisoner of the bad men in the Kremlin — the Politburo.

Duranty died in October 1957.

KERMIT EBY was born on September 21, 1903 in St. Joseph County, Indiana, son of Lizzie Schwalm and Elmer Eby. He married Retha Fish. He was an alumnus of Manchester College (A.B., 1927). He pursued graduate studies at the University of Chicago (1929-1931). He was the author of *The God in You; Paradoxes of Democracy; For Brethren Only*; and *Protests of an Ex-organization Man*. He also authored several pamphlets: *Letters to Dad* (1945); *Political Primer* (1944); *Labor and Education* (1944); and *Labor and Religion* (1944).

From 1927 until 1937, Eby was a high-school principal at Clinton, Indiana (1927-1929) and Ann Arbor, Michigan (1931-1937). From 1937 until 1942, he was executive secretary of the Chicago Teachers Union. From 1942 until 1948, he was with the CIO in Washington as assistant director of education (1942-1945) and director of education and research (1945-1948). From 1948 until 1962, he was at the University of Chicago as associate professor of social sciences (1948-1952) and professor (1952-1962).

Eby was affiliated with Action for World Federation (anti-American sovereignty group); the American Committee for Protection of Foreign Born ("founded by the Communist Party in order to exploit racial divisions in the United States for its own revolutionary purposes"); the American Forum for Socialist Education ("subversive and under Communist domination"); the Bill of Rights Conference ("subversive"); a Brief [*amicus curiae*] for the Communist Party ("Communist Party enterprise"); the Chicago Committee To Secure Justice in the Rosenberg Case (local auxiliary of the National Committee, "Communist front organized ... to conduct the United States phase of a mammoth propaganda campaign designed to obliterate the crime of and exploit the Rosenbergs and their co-defendant, Morton Sobell, for the purposes of international Communism"); the Church Peace Mission ("calling for peaceful resistance to Communism and unilateral disarmament by the United States"); the Committee for Peaceful Alternatives to the Atlantic Pact ("Communist front organization ... as part of Soviet psychological warfare against the United States"); the Highlander Folk School (leftist); the League for Industrial Democracy (socialist); the Methodist Federation for Social Action ("the organization's influence has been consistently wielded on behalf of Communist causes and the Communist line as expressed through the party and its innumerable subsidiaries"); the Mid-Century Conference for Peace ("aimed at assembling as many gullible persons possible under Communist direction and turning them into a vast sounding board for Communist propaganda"); the National Commission for UNESCO (leftist); the National Committee for a Sane Nuclear Policy (ultra-leftist-pacifist); the National Committee To Abolish the Un-American Activities Committee ("to lead and direct the Communist Party's 'Operation Abolition' campaign"); the National Committee To Repeal the McCarran Act ("Communist front" — "subversive"); the National Lawyers Guild ("the foremost legal bulwark of the Communist Party, its front organizations, and controlled unions"); the *Protestant* ("with an eye to religious groups, the Communists have formed religious fronts such as the *Protestant*"); the Religious Freedom Committee (an ultra-leftist group working for the abolition of the HCUA); the Southern Conference Educational Fund (financial backbone of racial agitators, including the Black Power revolutionaries); and Students for Federal World Government (anti-United States sovereignty group).

Eby died in August 1962.

SHERWOOD EDDY was born on January 19, 1871 in Leavenworth, Kansas, son of Margaret Norton and George Eddy. He was married first to Maud Arden and second to Louise Gates. He was an alumnus of Yale University (Ph.B., 1891). He also studied at Union Theological Seminary (1891-1893) and Princeton University (1894-1896). He was the author of *India Awakening* (1911); *The New Era in Asia* (1913); *The Students of Asia* (1915); *Suffering and the War* (1916); *With Our Soldiers in France* (1917); *Everybody's World*

(1920); *Facing the Crisis* (1922); *The New World of Labor* (1923); *New Challenges to Faith* (1926); *Religion and Social Justice* (1927); *Sex and Youth* (1928); *The Challenge of Russia* (1930); *The Challenge of the East* (1931); *The World's Danger Zone: Manchuria* (1932); *The Challenge of Europe* (1933); *Russia Today: What We Can Learn About It* (1934); *A Pilgrimage of Ideas: The Reeducation of Sherwood Eddy* (1934); *Europe Today* (1937); *Revolutionary Christianity* (1939); *I Have Seen God Do It* (1939); *The Kingdom of God and the American Dream* (1941); *Man Discovers God* (1943); *A Portrait of Jesus: A Twentieth Century Life of Christ* (1943); *A Century With Youth: A History of the Y.M.C.A.* (1944); *I Have Seen God Work in China* (1944); *Pathfinders of the World Missionary Crusade* (1945); *Is God in History?* (1947); *You Will Survive After Death* (1950); *Eighty Adventurous Years, an Autobiography* (1955); and *Why I Believe* (1957). He was co-author of *The Abolition of War* (1924); *Makers of Freedom* (1926); and *Creative Pioneers* (1937).

From 1896 until 1911, Eddy was a national secretary of the YMCA, working in India. From 1911 until 1930, he was the YMCA secretary for Asia, and worked among students in China, India, Japan, Korea, the Soviet Union, and the Near East. Between World War I and World War II, he conducted the American Seminar, which was an annual tour and survey for American educators, who accompanied him to European countries and the Soviet Union. During World War II, he conducted tours in North Africa; after the war the European tours were resumed.

In 1930, Eddy retired from his official YMCA activities to become an active campaigner for the Socialist Party in the

United States. During the course of his work with the YMCA, Eddy became a steadfast apologist for the Stalinist regime in the Soviet Union. In 1930, he told several audiences in the United States that in the Soviet Union "there is a healthy trade-union democracy among the workers" and "there is very little convict labor in Russia." Eight years later, when Stalin was conducting his infamous purge trials of Leon Trotsky and other old-time Bolshevik comrades, Eddy told the Communists' *Daily Worker*: "In my own mind, after reading the reports of these two trials, the guilt of treason on the part of those who were sentenced, and the double guilt of Trotsky as the archconspirator, is now thoroughly established." While Eddy clung to his defense of Stalin's integrity, hordes of America's most Red-tinted liberals were expressing their first disillusionment with the barbarous regime of Stalin as evidenced by the phony trials.

In the mid-1930's, Eddy was the operator of a Socialist cooperative farm venture in Hillhouse, Mississippi. Associated with him were John and Mark Rust, two brothers who had perfected a cotton-picking machine. Eddy reported on the venture in the Communists' *People's Press* of April 18, 1936: "After negotiations, several of us formed the Rust Foundation, which will utilize nine-tenths of the profit of the invention of the machine, and when it reaches the stage of mass production, will found a series of cooperative farms, cooperative stores and educational projects . . . . The whole situation is full of dynamite and of possibilities for good or evil — peonage, serfdom, poverty, disease, robbery, lynching and violence on the one hand, or a cooperative commonwealth on the other."

Aside from his continuing efforts on behalf of the Socialist Party, Eddy accumulated an impressive list of radical affiliations, including the ultra-radical American Civil Liberties Union; the American Committee To Save Refugees ("perform[ing] a most valuable function for the international Communist movement"); American Friends of Spanish Democracy ("Communist front"); the American League for Peace and Democracy ("subversive and Communist" — "established . . . in an effort to create public sentiment . . . on behalf of a foreign policy adapted to the interests of the Soviet Union . . . [and] designed to conceal Communist control, in accordance with the new tactics of the Communist International"); the Berger National Foundation (Socialist organization); the Brookwood Labor College ("Communistic"); the Celebration for the Adoption of a New Constitution for the Soviet Union in 1937 (Communist enterprise); the China Aid Council ("Communist-controlled"); the Civil Rights Congress ("created and established by the Communist Party as an organization which would utilize defense of civil rights for Party purposes and raise and maintain mass defense and bail funds for Party use"); the Committee on Militarism in Education (the supporting organization of the U.S. Congress Against War, "completely under the control of the Communist Party"); the Committee To Save Spain and China ("Communist front"); the Conference for Progressive Political Action (pro-Socialist); the Coordinating Committee To Lift the [Spanish] Embargo ("one of the numerous Communist-front enterprises which were organized around the Communists' agitation over the Spanish Civil War"); the *Daily Worker* ("official organ of the Communist Party"); Descendants of the

American Revolution ("a Communist-front organization set up as a radical imitation of the Daughters of the American Revolution. The Descendants have uniformly adhered to the line of the Communist Party"); the Emergency Committee for Strikers Relief (Socialist); the Fellowship of Reconciliation (ultra-leftist-pacifist); the International Rescue Committee (Socialist-lined); the League for Industrial Democracy (Socialist); the Mary Ware Dennett Defense Committee (ultra-leftist); the Medical Bureau and North American Committee To Aid Spanish Democracy ("subversive and un-American"); the National Citizens Committee on Relations with Latin America (dominated by Socialists); the National Federation for Constitutional Liberties ("under Communist Party domination and headed by responsible Party functionaries" – "one of the viciously subversive organizations of the Communist Party"); the National Religion and Labor Foundation ("Communist front"); *Protestant Digest* ("a magazine which has faithfully propagated the Communist Party line under the guise of being a religious journal"); Russian Reconstruction Farms ("Communist enterprise"); the [Morris U.] Schappes Defense Committee ("a front organization with a strictly Communist objective, namely, the defense of a self-admitted Communist who was convicted of perjury in the courts of New York"); the Southern Negro Youth Congress ("subversive and among the affiliates and committees of the Communist Party, U.S.A., which seeks to alter the form of government of the United States by unconstitutional means"); *Soviet Russia Today* ("Communist controlled publication"); the Spanish Refugee Appeal ("subversive" – "Communist front"); the Washington Committee To Lift [the] Spanish Embargo ("Communist front"); the Workers Defense League (defending political undesirables who are subject to deportation); and *World Tomorrow* (Socialist publication). He died in March 1963.

RICHARD THEODORE ELY was born on April 13, 1854 in Ripley, New York, son of Harriet Mason and Ezra Ely. He married, first, Anna Anderson, His second wife was Margaret Hahn. He was an alumnus of Columbia University (A.B., 1876, and A.M., 1879); the University of Heidelberg (Ph.D., 1879); and Hobart College (LL.D., 1892). He also studied for one year at Dartmouth College. He was a fellow in Letters at Columbia University (1876-1879). He was a student at the University of Halle, at the University of Geneva, and at the Royal Statistical Bureau in Berlin (1877-1880). He was the author of *French and German Socialism in Modern Times* (1883); *Past and Present of Political Economy* (1884); *Recent American Socialism* (1885); *The Labor Movement in America* (1886); *Taxation in American States and Cities* (1888); *Problems of Today* (1888), *Social Aspects of Christianity* (1889); *Introduction to Political Economy* (1889); *Socialism and Social Reform* (1894); *The Social Law of Service* (1896); *Monopolies and Trusts* (1900); *Studies in the Evolution of Industrial Society* (1903); *Property and Contract in Their Relation to the Distribution of Wealth*, two volumes (1914); *Hard Times – The Way In and the Way Out* (1931); and *Ground Under Our Feet* (1938). He was the co-author of *Outlines of Economics*, sixth edition (1937); *Elementary Economics* (1904, 1917, and 1923); *Elements of Land Economics* (1926); *The Great Change* (1935); and *Land Economics* (1940). He was a collaborator in the writing of

Foundations of National Prosperity (1917). He was the editor of Macmillan's *Citizen's Library of Economics, Politics, and Sociology*, Macmillan's *Social Science Textbook Series*, Macmillan's *Land Economics Series*, and Crowell's *Library of Economics and Politics*. He was the founder and editor of *The Journal of Land and Public Utility Economics*. He contributed articles to publications, including *North American Review, The Forum, Harper's*, and *Century* magazine.

From 1881 until 1882, Ely was the head of the department of political economy at The Johns Hopkins University. From 1892 until 1925, he was at the University of Wisconsin as professor of political economy and director of the school of economics, political science, and history. From 1925 until 1943, he was honorary professor of economics. From 1925 until 1933, he was professor of economics at Northwestern University. In 1913, he lectured on political economy at the University of Wisconsin. He was a founder, a director, and the president of the Institute for Economic Research, Inc. With the American Economic Association, he was a founder, secretary (1885-1892), and president (1899-1901). He was a founder and secretary of the Christian Social Union.

Ely was one of the first American economists in the academic field to consider that economics could and should be used in a political fashion to develop socialism. Eric Goldman, in his *Rendezvous with Destiny,* offered a summary – based upon Ely's own writings – of how Ely adapted Reform Darwinism to economics: "When Ely won a fellowship for study abroad in 1876 and made the usual choice of Germany, he assumed that he was going merely to learn more about the 'absolute' truths of life.

"Ely was not in Germany a year before the absolute truths were melting into a wondrously fluid world. At Heidelberg he came under the influence of Karl Knies, a professor with a passionate sympathy for the German workingman, who taught a 'Historical,' evolutionary economics which argued the possibility and wisdom of social reform. After three years of Germany, indignation seemed anything but pointless to Ely. He returned to the United States vowing to work for a different America through a different economics. 'If this world was to be a better world,' Ely was sure, '. . . we must have a new economics.'

"Teaching at Johns Hopkins until 1892 and then at the University of Wisconsin, Ely helped make those universities centers of dissidence by his pioneer work in developing a Reform Darwinian economics. Ely's economics was the Historical system of Professor Knies, with a still heavier emphasis on evolution and on environment. The prevalent 'natural laws' of economics, Ely maintained, were actually products of an environment of extremes of wealth and were 'used as a tool in the hands of the greedy and the avaricious for keeping down and oppressing the laboring classes.' Since the alleged laws were merely man-made rationalizations, they could and should evolve into a new economics. The sensible kind of new economics would be based on the assumption that 'to upbuild human character in men you must establish for them right social relations'; that right social relations come from a healthy economic environment; and that environments can be quickly made more healthy by state action and by permitting the underprivileged to act in their own behalf through trade-unions or similar organizations."

While in Germany, Ely received inspiration to organize what became the American Economic Association. He wrote: "I remember very distinctly Conrad's [Johannes Conrad, professor of political economy at the University of Halle] speaking to us Americans in his seminary one evening, urging us to organize a similar association in the United States upon our return, emphasizing the fact that times were changing. The old order was passing away, and if economic students were to have any influence whatever upon the course of practical politics, it would be necessary to take a new attitude towards the whole subject of social legislation; and if the United States were to have any particular influence in the great social legislation and the great readjustment of society on its legal side which seemed to be coming, an association of this sort would have very real value. I decided then that, as soon as I could, I would begin the agitation for such an association."

In 1885, Ely and other socialists organized the American Economic Association. They enumerated four objectives for their AEA: "(1) The encouragement of economic research; (2) The publication of economic monographs; (3) The encouragement of perfect freedom in all economic discussion; (4) The establishment of a bureau of information designed to aid all members with friendly counsel in their economic studies."

To like-minded academicians interested in political economy, they offered a four-point platform: "(1) We regard the state as an educational and ethical agency whose positive aid is an indispensable condition of human progress. While we recognize the necessity of individual initiative in industrial life, we hold that the doctrine of *laissez faire* is unsafe in politics and unsound in morals; and that it suggests an inadequate ex-

planation of the relations between the state and the citizens. (2) We do not accept the final statements which characterized the political economy of a past generation; for we believe that political economy is still in the first stages of its scientific development, and we look not so much to speculation as to an impartial study of actual conditions of economic life for the satisfactory accomplishment of that development. We seek the aid of statistics in the present and of history in the past. (3) We hold that the conflict of labor and capital has brought to the front a vast number of social problems whose solution is impossible without the united efforts of church, state, and science. (4) In the study of the policy of government, especially with respect to restrictions on trade and to protection of domestic manufactures, we take no partisan attitude. We are convinced that one of the chief reasons why greater harmony has not been attained is because economists have been too ready to assert themselves as advocates. We believe in a progressive development of economic conditions which must be met by corresponding changes of policy."

At the founding conference of the AEA, Ely expanded on the objectives and platform of his creation. He was anxious that the AEA's members begin the publication of monographs as soon as possible. He was hopeful that in a very short time, the AEA would be able to circulate a substantial list of books as suggested readings that could encourage individuals to join him and his colleagues in their socialist crusade. He made no secret of the fact that he expected the AEA's leaders to go far beyond the ivory tower. He said: "One aim of our association should be the education of public opinion in regard to economic questions and economic literature. In no other science is there so much quackery, and it must be our province to expose it and bring it into merited contempt. A review at each of our meetings of the economic works of the past year, if published in our proceedings, might help in the formation of enlightened judgment."

Ely made no secret of the fact that he was aiming to achieve socialism, but he stopped short of what he termed "pure" socialism, although he never provided a clear-cut distinction. He said: "Coming to the platform, a position is first of all taken in regard to the state, because it is thought necessary precisely at this time to emphasize its proper province. No one invited to join this association, certainly no one who has been active in calling this meeting, contemplates a form of pure socialism. 'We recognize the necessity of individual initiative.' We would do nothing to weaken individual activity, but we hold that there are certain spheres of activity which do not belong to the individual, certain functions which the great cooperative society – called the state – must perform to keep the avenues open for those who would gain a livelihood by their own exertions. The avenues to wealth and preferment are continually blocked by a greed of combinations of men and by monopolists, and individual effort and initiative are thus discouraged. Two examples will suffice.

"You know that in the Western grazing regions water is often scarce, and those who control the streams virtually own the country. Now it is a notorious fact that unlawful combinations seize upon these streams and, keeping others from them, retain exclusive privileges which shut off effectually individual exertions on the part of those not in the ring. A second example is found in unjust discriminations in freight charges which have built up the fortunes of the favored, and ruined competitors. In looking over the field of economic life, it is evident that there is a wide feeling of discouragement, repressing the activities of the individual, because the avenues to material well-being are so often blocked. Then there are things which individuals ought not to perform because the functions concerned are public; and in certain places the wastes of private competition are too enormous. There are, likewise, important things which individual effort is powerless to effect, e.g., the education of the masses."

In common with so many socialists and populists of his era, Ely raised the spectre of *laissez-faire* as the cause of America's sociological and economic problems. He would fight the spectre with a system of "social ethics." He said: "We hold that the doctrine of *laissez faire* is unsafe in politics and unsound in morals, and that it suggests an inadequate explanation of the relations between the state and the citizens. In other words, we believe in the existence of a system of social ethics; we do not believe that any man lives for himself alone, nor yet do we believe social classes are devoid of mutual obligations corresponding to their infinitely varied interrelations. All have duties as well as rights, and, as Emerson said several years ago, it is time we heard more about duties and less about rights. We who have resolved to form an American Economic Association hope to do something toward the development of a system of social ethics.

"It is asked: What is meant by *laissez faire*? It is difficult to define *laissez faire* categorically, because it is so absurd that its defenders can never be induced to say precisely what they mean. Yet it stands for a well-known, though rather vague, set of ideas, to which appeal is made every day in the year by the bench, the bar, the newspapers, and our legislative bodies. It means that government, the state, the people in their collective capacity, ought not to interfere in industrial life; that, on the contrary, free contract should regulate all the economic relations of life and public authority should simply enforce this, punish crime, and preserve peace. It means that the laws of economic life are natural laws like those of physics and chemistry, and that this life must be left to the free play of natural forces. One adherent used these words: 'This industrial world is governed by natural laws . . . . These laws are superior to man. Respect this providential order – let alone the work of God.'

"The platform then emphasizes the mission of the state and the mission of the individual in that state. *To distinguish between the proper functions of the two must be one of the purposes of our association.*"

In April 1891, Ely was instrumental in the founding of the Christian Social Union and he was elected secretary of the Union. It was his hope that the Church would take a more active part in the struggle against America's sociological woes. In effect, when Ely brought about the formation of the Christian Social Union, he was organizing the "social gospel" practitioners along formal lines. Ely was optimistic that Christian principles could be confused with socialist principles, the end result being socialism – but something short of "pure" socialism. At the 1885 organizing meeting of the AEA, he had offered a preview of what he hoped to accomplish with the Christian Social Union: "The mission of the church is likewise emphasized, and for this there is good reason which cannot, perhaps, be better stated than in the words of Professor Macy of Iowa College. I quote from a letter recently received from him: 'The preacher, in an important sense, is to be the originator of true social science; his work is to render possible such a science. The physical scientist needs no preacher. There is an external material thing which compels belief. For the most part, men have no selfish interest in believing other than the truth in regard to the material world. Those who devote themselves to the study of matter are led naturally into a truth-loving and truth-telling spirit, and they can laugh at the preacher. But those who devote themselves to the study of the conflicting interests of men have on their hands altogether a different task. There is no external material thing to solve their doubts, and men prefer to believe that which is not true; and when they believe the truth, they often think it best to pretend to believe the false. Falsehood, deception, lying, and above all an honest and dogged belief in error – these are athwart the path which might lead to a real social science. And who can tackle these better than the preacher?'

"In addition to these words of Professor Macy, it may be said that we wish to accomplish certain practical results in the social and financial world, and believing that our work lies in the direction of practical Christianity, we appeal to the church, the chief of the social forces in this country, to help us, to support us, and to make our work a complete success, which it can by no possibility be without her assistance. The religious press of the country can aid us greatly in our task, and it will not, I believe, refuse its co-operation. Its influence is enormous, and notwithstanding all that has been said against it to the contrary, I believe that today it is the fairest, purest, and most liberal press in the country."

Ely made it quite plain that the AEA was going to be virtually monolithic and that there would be many in the economic field who would be unwelcome. It was obvious that Ely did not want his crusade for socialism distracted by differences of opinion over methodology or theory. He explained: "It may be asked: Why have any platform at all? Why not simply invite all interested in political economy to come together and aid in reconomic research? The reply is not a difficult one. This association intends to combine two ends. It proposes to influence public opinion; also to investigate and study. Now, if there has ever been found in any place an economic society without the advocacy, either open or concealed, of certain tendencies, at least, it has not come to my knowledge. I do not believe it would be wise to attempt such a thing. The fundamental differences between economists are so radical that they cannot all work profitably together.

"Our platform is very broad and will include nearly all those who can cooperate advantageously with us. It advocates simply certain methods of study and the accomplishment of reforms by certain means which alone seem to us to promise valuable results. We believe in historical and statistical inquiries and examinations into actual conditions, and should we include those who do not, there would be division at the start. If two people are journeying together to a certain goal and come to a fork in the road, it is evident that they must part company if each insists on believing that their common destination lies in a different direction. That is our case. We have little faith that the methods advocated by certain economists will ever lead to any valuable results. They may take their own way, and far be it from us to hinder them, but we must part company.

"Again, it is not easy to arouse interest in an association which professes nothing. This proposed economic association has been greeted with enthusiasm precisely because it is not colorless, precisely because it stands for something.

"Finally, it is of the utmost importance to us to emphasize certain fundamental views in order to bring them prominently before the public. It is essential that intelligent men and women should distinguish between us and certain economists in whom there is little faith. The respect for political economy as it has been hitherto taught is very slight. I think it has been kept alive largely by ignorance, on the one hand; on the other, by the cloak it affords to wrong-doing and the balm it offers to still the voice of outraged conscience.

"On every side we find intelligent people dissatisfied with it, throwing all political economy to the winds, while John Stuart Mill repudiated his own economic system, and one of the most careful students of economic facts, Thorold Rogers, finds its conclusions so at variance with the results of his investigations that he rejects it with scorn and believes it necessary to build up a new political economy by a long and careful process, piecemeal, as he himself expresses it. We of this association must come before the public with the unequivocal assertion that we, also, refuse to accept as final 'the statements which characterize the political economy of a past generation, and that we believe our science is in the first stages of its scientific development.'

"Our attitude is a modest one and must, I think, appeal to the best intelligence of the country. We acknowledge our ignorance and if we claim superiority to others, it is largely on the very humble ground that we know better what we do not know. We confess our ignorance but are determined to do our best to remedy it, and we call upon those who are willing to go to work in the spirit to come forward and help us."

More than any other individual in the AEA, Ely was able to put into effect the ambitious monograph program mentioned at the initial meeting. As editor of the Macmillan *Citizen's Library* and the *Social Science Textbook Series* and the Crowell *Library of Economics and Politics*, he was able to amass a vast literature written by socialists to proselytize high-school and college students and faculty members for his socialist crusade. Within a generation, American students had become virtually a captive audience for Ely and his disciples. He had been able to put into print, under the aegis of respectable publishing houses, many prominent American and British Socialists, including Jane Addams, Franklin H. Giddings, John Hobson, Robert Hunter, Thomas Kirkup, Edward Allsworth Ross, John Spargo, Lester F. Ward, and Charles Zueblin.

The influence of Ely down to the present time is impossible to measure. What can be seen, however, is that his socialist ideas in political economy saturated the literature of the field and that the proponents of his ideas dominated the political economy departments of scores of major state and private colleges and universities. To the present time, the Ely-inspired monographs are still compulsory or suggested readings in high schools, colleges, and universities, or else they are conspicuous as "documentary" evidence cited by the modern-day Elyites. He died in October 1943.

HAVEN EMERSON was born on October 19, 1874 in New York City, son of Susan Tompkins and John Haven Emerson. He married Grace Parrish. He was an alumnus of Harvard University (A.B., 1896) and Columbia University (A.M. and M.D., 1899). He was the author of *Alcohol, Its Effects on Man* (1934). He was the reviser of *Flint's Manual of Auscultation and Percussion* (1916). He was the editor of *Alcohol and Man* (1932); *The Baker Memorial, 1930-1939* (1941); *Administrative Medicine* (1942); and *Local Health Units for the Nation* (1946).

From 1899 until 1915, Emerson had a private medical practice in New York City and was an assistant attending physician at Seton Hospital for Tuberculosis, St. Mary's Hospital for Children, and Roosevelt Hospital. From 1902 until 1914, he was an associate in physiology and medicine at Columbia University's College of Physicians and Surgeons. From 1914 until 1917, he was with New York City's Department of Health as sanitary superintendent and deputy commissioner (1914), and president of the Board of Health and commissioner of the department (1915-1917). From 1917 until 1919, he served in the U.S. Army Medical Corps. In 1919, he was at Cornell University as a professor of preventive medicine, and established a department of hygiene and preventive medicine there. In 1919 and 1920, he was director of the Cleveland Hospital and Health Survey and a lecturer at the Teachers College of Columbia University and the New York School of Social Work. In 1920 and 1921, he was a medical adviser to the U.S. Veterans Bureau. From 1922 until 1940, at Columbia University's College of Physicians and Surgeons, he was professor of public health, and was first executive officer of the Delamar Institute of Public Health.

In 1940, he retired as professor emeritus. In 1943, he was a professorial lecturer at the University of Minnesota. From 1942 until 1956, he was a visiting lecturer at the University of Michigan's School of Public Health. From 1937 until 1957, he was a member of New York City's Board of Health. He directed health and hospital surveys in Philadelphia (1925), Boston (1934), Detroit (1934), Trenton and Mercer counties in New Jersey (1944), Minneapolis (1945), and Athens, Greece (1929). From 1920 until 1940, he did work for the Health Organization of the League of Nations. He held high offices in numerous groups, including the Association on American Indian Affairs, the National Committee on Indian Health, the National Medical Council of the Planned Parenthood Federation, and the National Committee on Maternal Health. He received the U.S. Distinguished Service Medal (1926), the Sedgwick Medal of the American Public Health Association (1935), the Lasker Award of the American Public Health Association (1949), the Gold Heart Award of the American Heart Association (1953), the Distinguished Service Award of the Columbia-Presbyterian Medical Center (1953), and the New York Academy of Medicine's Plaque (1955).

Emerson was affiliated with the American Committee for Indonesian Independence ("Communist front"); the American Committee for Protection of Foreign Born ("founded by the Communist Party in order to exploit racial divisions in the United States for its own revolutionary purposes"); the American Committee To Save Refugees ("perform[ing] a most valuable function for the international Communist movement"); American Friends of Spanish Democracy ("Communist front"); the American League for Peace and Democ- racy ("subversive and Communist" – "established in an effort to create public sentiment on behalf of a foreign policy adapted to the interests of the Soviet Union . . . [and] designed to conceal Communist control, in accordance with the new tactics of the Communist International"); the American Society for Cultural Relations with Russia ("Communist front"); the China Aid Council ("Communist-controlled"); the Citizens' Committee To Defend Representative Government ("Communist front"); the Committee on Indian Civil Rights ("Communist front"); the Coordinating Committee To Lift the [Spanish] Embargo ("one of the numerous Communist-front enterprises which were organized around the Communists' agitation over the Spanish Civil War"); the Cultural and Scientific Conference for World Peace ("Communist front" – "a propaganda front for Soviet foreign policy and Soviet culture"); the Greater New York Emergency Conference on Inalienable Rights ("Communist front"); the Medical Bureau and North American Committee To Aid Spanish Democracy ("subversive and un-American"); the National Council of the Arts, Sciences, and Professions ("a Communist front used to appeal to special occupational groups"); the National Emergency Conference ("Communist front"); the National Emergency Conference for Democratic Rights ("Communist front" – "subversive"); Russian War Relief ("Communist enterprise"); the Spanish Refugee Relief Campaign ("Communist front"); *Survey,* later *Survey Graphic* (Socialistic); and Veterans of the Abraham Lincoln Brigade ("directed, dominated and controlled by the Communist Party"). He died in May 1957.

HENRY PRATT FAIRCHILD was

born on August 18, 1880 in Dundee, Illinois, son of Isabel Pratt and Arthur Fairchild. He was married to the late Mary Townsend. He was an alumnus of Doane College of Nebraska (A.B., 1900) and Yale University (Ph.D., 1909). He was the author of *Greek Immigration to the United States* (1911); *Immigration: A World Movement and Its American Significance* (1913); *Outline of Applied Sociology* (1916); *Elements of Social Science* (1924); *The Melting-Pot Mistake* (1926); *The Foundations of Social Life* (1927); *Profits or Prosperity?* (1932); *General Sociology* (1934); *This Way Out* (1936); *People: The Quantity and Quality of Population* (1939); *Economics for the Millions* (1940); *Main Street: The American Town, Past and Present* (1941); *Race and Nationality as Factors in American Life* (1947); *The Prodigal Century* (1950); and *Versus: Reflections of a Sociologist* (1950). He was the editor of *Immigrant Backgrounds* (1927); *The Obligation of Universities to the Social Order* (1933); *Survey of Contemporary Sociology* (1934); *Dictionary of Sociology* (1944); and, posthumously, *Anatomy of Freedom* (1957). He was general editor of the Wiley *Social Science Series.*

From 1900 until 1903, Fairchild was an instructor at International College in Smyrna, Turkey. From 1903 until 1906, he was state secretary of Doane College. In 1909 and 1910, he was professor of economics and sociology at Bowdoin College. From 1910 until 1918, he was at Yale University as assistant professor of economics (1910-1912) and assistant professor of the science of society (1912-1918). In 1918 and 1919, he was an associate director of the personnel department of War Camp Community Service. From 1919 until 1956, he was at New York University as professor of social economy and director of the Bureau of Community Service and Research (1919-1924), professor of sociology (1924-1945), chairman of the department of sociology in the University's Graduate School of Arts and Sciences (1938-1945), and professor emeritus (1945-1956). He lectured at the University of California's summer school (1923) and the University of Southern California's summer school (1940). He was a round table leader at the Institute of Politics at Williams College (1924). From 1919 until 1921, he was executive secretary of the Connecticut State Commission on Child Welfare. In 1919 and 1920, he was educational director of the University Settlement in New York City. In 1923, he was an investigator for the National Research Council and a special immigration agent in Europe for the U.S. Department of Labor.

Fairchild was president of the Population Association of America (1931-1935); the People's League for Economic Security (1934-1938); the Town Hall Club (1934-1940); the American Sociological Society (1936); and the American Eugenics Society (1929-1931). He was vice president of the Planned Parenthood Federation (1939-1948).

In 1939 and 1940, Fairchild was president of Film Audiences for Democracy ("Communist front"). In 1942, he was presiding officer at the Congress of American-Soviet Friendship ("Communist front"). From 1934 until 1937, he was chairman of the Commonwealth Federation, a Socialist organization.

Fairchild was identified in sworn testimony as a member of the Communist Party. In 1941 and 1947, he signed statements in defense of the Communist Party. In 1949, he signed a statement on behalf of convicted Communist Party leaders. His affiliations included Allied Voters Against Coudert ("an example of the Communist apparatus for character assassination in operation against one who opposed the efforts of the Communist Party to undermine and destroy American democracy"); the ultra-radical American Civil Liberties Union; the American Committee for Democracy and Intellectual Freedom ("subversive and un-American" – "a Communist front organization operating among college teachers and professors"); the American Committee for Indonesian Independence ("Communist front"); the American Committee for Protection of Foreign Born ("founded by the Communist Party in order to exploit racial divisions in the United States for its own revolutionary purposes"); the American Committee To Save Refugees ("perform[ing] a most valuable function for the international Communist movement" – "subversive and Communist"); the American Continental Congress for World Peace ("another phase in the Communist 'peace' campaign, aimed at consolidating anti-American forces throughout the Western Hemisphere"); the American Council on Soviet Relations ("subversive" – "established by the Communist Party . . . directed and controlled by the Party and operated to aid and support Party objectives concerning the defense and support of the Soviet Union"); the American Friends of Spanish Democracy ("Communist front"); the American League Against War and Fascism ("subversive and Communist" – "established in the United States in an effort to create public sentiment on behalf of a foreign policy adapted to the interests of the Soviet Union"); the American League for Peace and Democracy ("subversive and Communist" – "established . . . in an effort to create public

sentiment on behalf of a foreign policy adapted to the interests of the Soviet Union . . . [and] designed to conceal Communist control, in accordance with the new tactics of the Communist International"); the American Peace Crusdade ("Communist front"); the American-Russian Institute for Cultural Relations with the Soviet Union ("subversive" – "Communist" – "specializing in pro-Soviet propaganda"); the American Slav Congress ("Moscow-inspired and directed federation of Communist-dominated organizations seeking by methods of propaganda and pressure to subvert the 10,000,000 people in this country of Slavic birth or descent"); American Youth for Democracy ("subversive and Communist" – "part of Soviet psychological warfare against the United States"); the Artists' Front To Win the War ("Communist front" – "included representatives of the theater, of literature, music, art, science, and education, with long and active records of support for Communist-front organizations and for the variegated turns of the Communist Party line"); the Celebration of the 25th Anniversary of the Red Army (Communist enterprise); the Citizens' Committee for Harry Bridges ("Communist"); the Citizens Committee To Defend Representative Government ("Communist front"); the Citizens' Committee To Free Earl Browder ("a strictly Communist Party affair"); the Civil Rights Congress ("created and established by the Communist Party as an organization which would utilize defense of civil rights for Party purposes and raise and maintain mass defense and bail funds for Party use"); the Committee for a Boycott Against Japanese Aggression ("the committee was featured in the *Daily Worker*, official organ of the Communist Party, and in that paper alone"); the

Committee for a Democratic Far Eastern Policy ("Communist"); the Committee for Free Political Advocacy ("Communist front"); the Conference for Legislation in the National Interest ("under complete domination by the Communist Party"); the Consumers National Federation ("transmission belt" for the Communist Party's influence and ideology − "Communist front"); the Coordinating Committee To Lift the [Spanish] Embargo ("one of the numerous Communist-front enterprises which were organized around the Communists' agitation over the Spanish Civil War"); the Council for Pan American Democracy ("subversive and Communist"); the Council for the Advancement of the Americas (ultraleftist); the Cultural and Scientific Conference for World Peace ("Communist front" − "a propaganda front for Soviet foreign policy and Soviet culture"); the Emergency Civil Liberties Committee ("Communist front" − "subversive"); the Greater New York Emergency Conference on Inalienable Rights ("Communist front"); the Independent Citizens Committee of the Arts, Sciences and Professions ("Communist front"); the International Labor Defense ("subversive and Communist" − "legal arm of the Communist Party" − "part of an international network of organizations for the defense of Communist lawbreakers"); the Jefferson School of Social Science ("a Communist institution modeled along the lines of the new Communist policy which led to the decision to change the Communist Party into some kind of an educational institution"); the Joint Anti-Fascist Refugee Committee ("subversive and Communist"); the League for Independent Political Action (Socialist); the League of American Writers ("subversive and Communist" − "began openly to follow the

Communist Party line as dictated by the foreign policy of the Soviet Union"); *Masses and Mainstream* ("a Communist magazine"); the Medical Bureau and North American Committee to Aid Spanish Democracy ("subversive and un-American"); the National Committee To Defeat the Mundt Bill ("a Communist lobby . . . which has carried out the objectives of the Communist Party in its fight against anti-subversive legislation"); the National Committee To Repeal the McCarran Act ("a Communist front" − "subversive"); the National Committee To Secure Justice for the Rosenbergs and Morton Sobell ("Communist front organized . . . to conduct the United States phase of a mammoth propaganda campaign designed to obliterate the crime of and exploit the Rosenbergs and their co-defendant Morton Sobell for the purposes of international Communism"); the National Committee To Win Amnesty for Smith Act Victims ("subversive" − "Communist"); the National Council of American-Soviet Friendship ("subversive and Communist" − "specializing in pro-Soviet propaganda"); the National Council of the Arts, Sciences and Professions ("a Communist front used to appeal to special occupational groups"); the National Emergency Conference ("Communist front"); the National Emergency Conference for Democratic Rights ("Communist front" − "subversive"); the National Federation for Constitutional Liberties ("under Communist Party domination and headed by responsible Party functionaries" − "one of the viciously subversive organizations of the Communist Party"); the National People's Committee Against Hearst ("subversive and Communist"); the National Wartime Conference of the Professions, the Sciences, the Arts, the White-Collar Fields ("Communist front"); *New*

Masses ("weekly journal of the Communist Party"); an Open Letter for Closer Cooperation with the Soviet Union (issued by "a group of Communist Party stooges"); the People's Radio Foundation ("subversive and Communist organization"); Progressive Citizens of America ("political Communist front" – "subversive"); the Provisional Committee for Democratic Rights (leftist); the Reichstag Fire Trial Anniversary Committee ("Communist front . . . formed . . . by prominent Communists and Communist sympathizers"); Russian War Relief ("Communist enterprise"); the [Morris U.] Schappes Defense Committee ("a front organization with a strictly Communist objective, namely, the defense of a self-admitted Communist who was convicted of perjury in the courts of New York"); *Science and Society* ("Communist publication"); *Soviet Russia Today* ("Communist-controlled publication"); the Stockholm Appeal ("Communist 'peace' campaign"); Veterans of the Abraham Lincoln Brigade ("directed, dominated and controlled by the Communist Party"); the Washington Committee To Lift [the] Spanish Embargo ("Communist front"); and the World Congress for Peace in Paris ("organized under Communist initiative").

Fairchild died in October 1956.

LION FEUCHTWANGER was born on July 7, 1884 in Munich, Germany. He married Marthe Löffler. From 1903 until 1907, he studied at the University of Berlin and the University of Munich. He was an alumnus of the University of Munich (Ph.D., 1918).

From 1908 until 1911, Feuchtwanger worked on *Die Schaubühne (The Stage)*, a literary critical paper. He wrote *Der Tönerne Gott (God of Thunder)* in 1911. During World War II, while travelling in French North Africa, he was taken prisoner in Tunis, but escaped after seventeen days. He returned to Germany, where he spent five and a half months in army service. During the war, he wrote four plays which were either suppressed or delayed in production by the government. They were *Vasantasena, Warren Hastings, Peace,* and *Kriegsgefangenen (Prisoners of War)*. In Munich, he produced plays, including Gorky's *Lower Depths*. He wrote a drama, *1918*, which caused public demonstrations of such a nature that its production was suppressed after one performance. In 1921, he wrote *Jud Süss (Power)*, a novel. In 1922, he wrote *Die Hässliche Herzogin (The Ugly Duchess)*. In 1928, he wrote *The Oil Islands*, a play. In 1929, he wrote *Pep: J.L. Wetcheek's American Song Book*. In 1930, he wrote *Erfolg (Success)*. In 1931, he began work on a trilogy: *Josephus,* published in 1932; *The Jew of Rome,* published in 1935; and *Josephus and the Emperor,* published in 1942.

In 1932 and 1933, Feuchtwanger travelled in America. In 1933, as a politically undesirable Red, he had his house and money confiscated by the German government, and went as an exile to France. In 1934 he wrote a novel, *The Oppermanns,* and three plays. In 1936 and 1937, he lived in Moscow, and while there, he wrote *Marianne in India; Moscow 1937; The Pretender;* and *Exile*.

After the fall of France, Feuchtwanger and his wife escaped across Spain and Portugal and arrived in the United States in late 1940. After arriving in America, he wrote *The Devil in France* (1941); *Paris Gazette* (1942); *Double, Double, Toil, and Trouble* (1943); *Simone* (1944); *Stories from Far and Near* (1945); *Proud Destiny* (1947); *The Devil in Boston,* play (1948); *This is the Hour:*

A Novel About Goya (1951); *'Tis Folly To Be Wise: A Novel About Jean-Jacques Rousseau* (1953); *Raquel, The Jewess of Toledo,* novel; *The Widow Capet,* play (1956); *Centum Opuscula,* essays (1956); and *Jephthah and His Daughter* (1958). In 1953, he received the National Art and Literary Prize of Berlin. In 1957, he received the Literary Prize of Munich.

Feuchtwanger was affiliated with the American Committee for Yugoslav Relief ("subversive and Communist"); the American Committee To Save Refugees ("perform[ing] a most valuable function for the international Communist movement"); the American Continental Congress for World Peace ("another phase in the Communist 'peace' campaign, aimed at consolidating anti-American forces throughout the Western Hemisphere"); the American Rescue Ship Mission ("Communist Party project"); the Bill of Rights Conference ("subversive"); the Civil Rights Congress ("created and established by the Communist Party as an organization which would utilize defense of civil rights for Party purposes and raise and maintain mass defense and bail funds for Party use"); the Committee for the Defense of Paul and Gertrude Rugg (pro-Communist); the Committee of Welcome for the Red Dean of Canterbury (Communist Party enterprise); the Cultural and Scientific Conference for World Peace ("Communist front" – "a propaganda front for Soviet foreign policy and Soviet culture"); the German-American Emergency Conference ("Communist front"); the Jewish People's Committee ("subversive and Communist" – "an organization which has been nothing more nor less than an adjunct of the Communist Party"); the Joint Anti-Fascist Refugee Committee ("subversive and Communist"); the

League of American Writers ("subversive and Communist" – "began openly to follow the Communist Party line as dictated by the foreign policy of the Soviet Union"); the Mid-Century Conference for Peace ("aimed at assembling as many gullible persons as possible under Communist direction and turning them into a vast sounding board for Communist propaganda"); the Motion Picture Artists Committee ("Communist front"); the National Committee To Combat Anti-Semitism ("Communist front"); the National Council of American-Soviet Friendship ("subversive and Communist" – "specializing in pro-Soviet propaganda"); *New Currents* (published by the American Committee of Jewish Writers, Artists, and Scientists, a "Communist front"); *New Masses* ("weekly journal of the Communist Party"); Russian War Relief ("Communist enterprise"); *Soviet Russia Today* ("Communist-controlled publication"); the Stockholm Peace Appeal ("Communist 'peace' campaign"); World Peace Congress ("organized under Communist initiative in various countries throughout the world"); and the Writers' Congress ("subversive and Communist"). He died in December 1958.

DOROTHY CANFIELD FISHER was born [as Dorothea] on February 17, 1879 in Lawrence, Kansas, daughter of Flavia Camp and James Canfield. She married John Fisher. She was an alumna of Ohio State University (Ph.B., 1899) and Columbia University (Ph.D., 1904). She also studied at the Sorbonne in Paris. Either as Dorothy Canfield or as Dorothy Canfield Fisher, she was the author of *Corneille and Racine in England* (1904); *Gunhild* (1907); *The Squirrel-Cage* (1912); *The Montessori Mother* (1913); *Mothers and Children* (1914);

Hillsboro People (1915); *The Bent Twig* (1915); *The Real Motive* (1916); *Understood Betsy* (1917); *Home-Fires in France* (1918); *The Day of Glory* (1919); *The Brimming Cup* (1921); *Rough-Hewn* (1922); *Raw Material* (1923); *The Home-Maker* (1924); *Made-to-Order Stories* (1925); *Her Son's Wife* (1926); *Why Stop Learning?* (1927); *The Deepening Stream* (1930); *Basque People* (1931); *Bonfire* (1933); *Fables for Parents* (1937); *Seasoned Timber* (1939); *Tell Me a Story* (1940); *Nothing Ever Happens* (1940); *Our Young Folks* (1943); *American Portraits* (1946); *Four Square* (1949); *Something Old, Something New* (1949); *Paul Revere and the Minute Men* (1950); *Independence and the Constitution* (1950); *A Fair World For All* (1952); *Vermont Tradition: The Biography of an Outlook on Life* (1953); *A Harvest of Stories* (1956); *Memories of Arlington, Vermont* (1957); and *Long Remember*, posthumously (1959). She was co-author of *English Rhetoric and Composition* (1906); *What Shall We Do Now?* (1906); and *Fellow-Captains* (1916). She was translator of Giovanni Papini's *Life of Christ* (1921) and Adriano Tilgher's *Work* (1930). In 1943, she won the O'Henry award for her short story, *The Knothole,* published in *Yale Review.*

From 1902 until 1905, Fisher was secretary of the Horace Mann School in New York City. From 1921 until 1923, she was a member of the State Board of Education in Vermont. From 1926 until 1951, she was on the selection committee of the Book-of-the-Month Club, which habitually promoted the works of Communists and fellow-travelers. Aside from her literary work, she interested herself in promoting woman suffrage, adult education, and internationalism.

Fisher was affiliated with the American Association for the United Nations (leftist group); the ultra-radical American Civil Liberties Union; the American Committee for Protection of Foreign Born ("founded by the Communist Party in order to exploit racial divisions in the United States for its own revolutionary purposes"); the American Committee To Save Refugees ("perform[ing] a most valuable function for the international Communist movement"); American Friends of Spanish Democracy ("Communist front"); the American League for Peace and Democracy ("subversive and Communist" – "established . . . in an effort to create public sentiment on behalf of a foreign policy adapted to the interests of the Soviet Union . . . [and] designed to conceal Communist control, in accordance with the new tactics of the Communist International"); the American Round Table on India ("Communist front"); the American Society for Cultural Relations with Russia ("Communist front"); American Youth Congress ("subversive" – "one of the most influential front organizations ever set up by the Communists in this country" – "the Communists are in complete control"); the Citizens' Committee for Better Education ("Communist front"); Citizens United To Abolish the Wood-Rankin Committee (pro-Communist project); the Committee for a Far Eastern Policy ("Communist"); the Committee of One Thousand ("Communist-created and controlled"); the Coordinating Committee To Lift the [Spanish] Embargo ("one of the numerous Communist-front enterprises which were organized around the Communists' agitation over the Spanish Civil War"); the Council Against Intolerance in America (leftist); the Cultural and Scientific Conference for World Peace ("Communist front" – "a propaganda front for Soviet foreign policy and Soviet culture"); *Equality* ("Communist Party enterprise"); Federal Union (leftist-globalist); Film Audiences for Democracy ("Communist front"); Films for Democracy ("Communist front"); the Joint Anti-Fascist Refugee Committee ("subversive and Communist"); the League of Women Shoppers ("Communist controlled front"); the League of American Writers ("subversive and Communist" – " began openly to follow the Communist Party line as dictated by the foreign policy of the Soviet Union"); the Medical Bureau and North American Committee To Aid Spanish Democracy ("subversive and un-American"); the ultra-radical National Association for the Advancement of Colored People; the National Committee To Repeal the McCarran Act ("Communist front" – "subversive"); the National Council of American-Soviet Friendship ("subversive and Communist" – "specializing in pro-Soviet propaganda"); the National Council of the Arts, Sciences, and Professions ("a Communist front used to appeal to special occupational groups"); the National Institute of Arts and Letters ("Communist front"); the Reichstag Fire Trial Anniversary Committee ("Communist front . . . formed . . . by prominent Communists and Communist sympathizers"); Russian War Relief ("Communist enterprise"); the [Morris U.] Schappes Defense Committee ("a front organization with a strictly Communist objective, namely, the defense of a self-admitted Communist who was convicted of perjury in the courts of New York"); the United American Spanish Aid Committee ("Communist"); the United States-Soviet Friendship Congress ("Communist front"); the United World Federalists (the most prestigious group of fellow-travelers and dupes working for world government at the expense of United States sovereignty); the Washington Committee To Lift [the] Spanish Embargo ("Communist front"); and the Writers' and Artists' Committee for Medical Aid to Spain ("a Communist front set up for the purpose of agitation and propaganda"). She died in November 1958.

ROYAL WILBUR FRANCE was born on July 27, 1883 in Lowville, New York, son of Hannah James and Joseph France. He married the late Ethel Camp. His second wife was Ruth Crawford. He was an alumnus of George Washington University (A.B., 1904) and Hamilton College (A.M., 1908). In 1906, he was admitted to the New York bar. He was a student at Albany Law School. He was the author of *Compromise* (1936) and *My Native Grounds* (1957).

From 1906 until 1908, France was a member of Knapp and France, a legal firm in New York City. From 1908 until 1929, he continued his law practice with Duell, Warfield, and Duell (1908-1916); Konta, Kirchwey, France, and Michael (1918-1921); and Barber and France (1928-1929). In 1916 and 1917, he was vice-president and general manager of the Triangle Film Company. From 1921 until 1928, he was with Salt's Textile Company as vice president (1921-1924) and president (1925-1928). In 1928 and 1929, he was a vocational advisor at Columbia University. From 1929 until 1952, he was a professor of economics at Rollins College. He was a guest professor at *Centro de Estudio de Mexico* (1937); Hamilton College (1947); and the University of Massachusetts (1948-1949). From 1943 until 1945, he was on the public panel of the National War Labor Board. He served as an arbitrator in labor disputes for the National Wage Stabiliza-

FRANCE

tion Board and the National Conciliation Service. When he left Rollins College, he resumed his law practice. A great many of his clients were Fifth Amendment pleaders before Congressional investigating committees.

From 1956 until 1961, France was executive secretary of the National Lawyers Guild ("the foremost legal bulwark of the Communist Party, its front organizations and controlled unions"). He was on the executive board of the Emergency Civil Liberties Committee ("Communist front" – "subversive"). He was on the executive board of the American Committee for Protection of Foreign Born ("founded by the Communist Party in order to exploit racial divisions in the United States for its own revolutionary purposes"). France's other affiliations included the ultra-radical American Civil Liberties Union; the American Peace Crusade ("Communist front"); the Citizens Emergency Defense Conference ("subversive"); the Citizens Victory Committee for Harry Bridges ("Communist front"); the Civil Rights Congress ("created and established by the Communist Party as an organization which would utilize defense of civil rights for Party purposes and raise and maintain mass defense and bail funds for Party use"); the Committee for Equal Justice for Mrs. Recy Taylor ("Communist front"); the Council for Pan American Democracy ("subversive and Communist"); the Council on African Affairs ("subversive and Communist"); the Fellowship of Reconciliation (ultra-leftist-pacifist); the Hiroshima Commemorative Committee (ultra-leftist); the Independent Voters for Corliss Lamont (pro-Communist); the International Workers Order ("from its very inception demonstrated by its pronouncements, its activities, and the authoritative statements of

the Communist Party that it is a subservient instrument of the Communist Party in the United States"); the Jefferson School of Social Science ("a Communist institution modeled along the lines of the new Communist policy which led to the decision to change the Communist Party into some kind of an educational institution"); the Methodist Federation for Social Action ("the organization's influence has been consistently wielded on behalf of Communist causes and the Communist line as expressed through the party and its innumerable subsidiaries"); the National Assembly for Democratic Rights ("created, dominated and controlled by members and officials of the Communist Party"); the National Committee To Abolish the Un-American Activities Committee ("to lead and direct the Communist Party's 'Operation Abolition' campaign"); the National Committee To Repeal the McCarran Act ("Communist front" – "subversive"); the National Committee To Secure Justice in the Rosenberg Case ("Communist front organized . . . to conduct the United States phase of a mammoth propaganda campaign designed to obliterate the crime of and exploit the Rosenbergs and their codefendant Morton Sobell for the purposes of international Communism"); the National Committee To Win Amnesty for Smith Act Victims ("subversive" – "Communist"); the National Council of American-Soviet Friendship ("subversive and Communist" – "specializing in pro-Soviet propaganda"); the National Council of the Arts, Sciences, and Professions ("a Communist front used to appeal to special occupational groups"); the National Federation for Constitutional Liberties ("under Communist Party domination and headed by responsible Party functionaries" – "one of the viciously subversive organizations of the Communist Party "); a Petition in Defense of Communist School (Communist Party enterprise); the Religious Freedom Committee (an ultra-leftist group working for the abolition of the HCUA); the Southern Conference Educational Fund (financial backbone of racial agitators, including the black power revolutionaries); the Workers Defense League (defending political undesirables who are subject to deportation); and World Fellowship, Inc. (ultra-leftist-pacifist). He died in July 1962.

WALDO FRANK was born on August 25, 1889 in Long Branch, New Jersey, son of Helene Rosenberg and Julius Frank. He was married to and divorced from Margaret Naumburg and Alma Magoon. His third wife was Jean Klempner. He was an alumnus of Yale University (B.A. and M.A., 1911). He was the author of *The Unwelcome Man* (1917); *The Art of Vieux Colombier* (1918); *Our America* (1919); *The Dark Mother* (1920); *Rahab* (1922); *City Block* (1922); *Holiday* (1923); *Salvos* (1924); *Chalk Face* (1924); *Virgin Spain* (1926); *Time-Exposures* (1926); *The Rediscovery of America* (1928); *New Year's Eve* (1929); *Primer Mensaje a la American Hispaña* (1930); *American Hispaña – A Portrait and A Prospect* (1931); *Dawn in Russia* (1932); *The Death and Birth of David Markand* (1934); *In the American Jungle* (1927); *The Bridegroom Cometh* (1938); *Chart for Rough Water: Our Role in a New World* (1940); *Summer Never Ends* (1941); *Ustedes y Nosotros* (1942); *South American Journey* (1943); *The Jew in Our Day* (1944); *Island in the Atlantic* (1946); *Birth of a World: Bolivar in Terms of His Peoples* (1951); *Not Heaven* (1953); *Bridgehead: The Drama of Israel* (1957); *The Rediscovery of Man* (1958); and *The Prophetic Island: A Portrait of Cuba* (1961). He was co-author of *The Novel of Tomorrow* (1922); *The American Caravan* (1928); *Man and His World* (1929); and *Sex in Civilization* (1929). He was co-author and editor of *America and Arthur Steiglits* (1934). He edited and wrote the introduction to Marsden Hartley's *Adventures in the Arts* (1921); Jean Toomer's *Cane* (1923); the Modern Library edition of *Plays of Molière* (1924); *Tales from the Argentine* (1930); Mariano Azuela's *Marcela* (1932); *Collected Poems of Hart Crane* (1933); Ricardo Gulraldes' *Don Segundo Sombra* (1934); and André Malraux' *Days of Wrath* (1936). He was the translator of Jules Romans' *Lucienne* (1925). He contributed to *La Revista de Occidente* (Madrid), and *The Menorah Journal*.

In 1911, Frank was a drama critic for the *New Haven Courier-Journal*. In 1911 and 1912, he wrote for the *New York Times* and the *New York Post*. In 1913, he traveled in Europe. In 1914 and 1915, he was a free-lance writer. In 1916, he was a co-founder and co-editor of *Seven Arts* magazine which in its one-year history published Sherwood Anderson, Randolph Bourne, Padraic Colum, Floyd Dell, John Dewey, John Dos Passos, Theodore Dreiser, Max Eastman, Robert Frost, D.H. Lawrence, Walter Lippmann, Amy Lowell, Eugene O'Neill, Romain Rolland, and Carl Sandburg.

From 1917 until 1919, Frank was a correspondent for *La Nouvelle Revue Française* and *Europe* (Paris) and a contributing editor for *New Republic* and *Masses* (Communist publication). He also lectured on modern art and literature at the radical New School for Social Research.

After 1917, most of Frank's energies were devoted to his published books. In 1929, he lectured on American Civilization and Culture at the National Universities of Mexico, Argentina, Bolivia, and Peru. In the 1940's and 1950's, he made extensive lecture tours in Latin America.

Frank's *Birth of a World: Bolivar in Terms of His Peoples* was written on a commission from the Venezuelan regime of Romulo Betancourt. His *The Prophetic Island: A Portrait of Cuba* was commissioned by the Castro regime of Communist Cuba. Frank was paid $25,000 and the book was published by Marzani & Munsell, a Communist publishing house.

In the 1950's Frank was invited to lecture in Peking by the Red Chinese government. When the Department of State refused to grant him a visa, he was defended in his suit against the State Department by Leonard B. Boudin of the Emergency Civil Liberties Committee ("Communist front" – "subversive"). The suit was financed by the Bill of Rights Fund, which was initiated by a $50,000 donation from veteran fellow traveler Corliss Lamont. (Frank was an old friend of the Chinese Communists. As early as 1934, he had written: "If the people of the United States know what is happening in China, if they know the glorious history of the Chinese Communists . . . there will rise a storm of protest against American and European aid for Chiang Kai-shek.")

Frank was one of the earliest American supporters and propagandists for the Castro regime. He was the founding chairman of the Fair Play for Cuba Committee, which was a propaganda outlet in the United States for Communist Cuba and financed by Castro.

In 1936, Frank hit the campaign trail with Earl Browder, Communist Party candidate for president of the United States. Frank was at that time a correspondent for the *Daily Worker*. He testified under oath that he had never been a member of the Communist Party. He never denied that he was at least a non-card-carrying Communist and that he faithfully followed the Communist line, with rare exceptions, during his adult life. From time to time, he did quarrel with certain tactics of the Communist Party, but in general he was a devoted fellow traveler.

Frank was affiliated with the ultraradical American Civil Liberties Union; the American Committee for Protection of Foreign Born ("founded by the Communist Party in order to exploit racial divisions in the United States for its own revolutionary purposes"); the American Committee of Jewish Writers, Artists and Scientists ("Communist front"); the American Continental Congress for World Peace ("another phase in the Communist 'peace' campaign, aimed at consolidating anti-American forces throughout the Western Hemisphere"); the American Forum for Socialist Education ("subversive and under Communist domination"); American Friends of Spanish Democracy ("Communist front"); the American Pushkin Committee ("Communist front"); American Revolutionary Writers ("subversive and Communist"); the American Society for Technical Aid to Spanish Democracy ("Communist front"); the American Student Union ("without exception . . . supported defense of teachers and students charged with Communist activity" – "pliable instrument in the hands of the Communist Party"); the American Writers Congress ("subversive"); the Book Union ("distributors of Communist literature"); a Brief [*amicus curiae*] for the Communist Party ("Communist Party enterprise"); Brookwood Labor College ("Communistic"); the Chicago Workers Theatre ("Communist front"); *China Today* (official organ of the Communist-controlled American Friends of the Chinese People); the Civil Rights Congress ("created and established by the Communist Party as an organization which would utilize defense of civil rights for Party purposes and raise and maintain mass defense and bail funds for Party use"); the Committee for Equal Justice for Mrs. Recy Taylor ("Communist front"); the Committee of Professional Groups for [Earl] Browder and [James W.] Ford ("Communist candidates for President and Vice President" of the United States in 1936); the Committee To End Sedition Laws ("under complete domination by the Communist Party"); the Congress of American Revolutionary Writers ("subversive and Communist"); the Congress of American-Soviet Friendship ("Communist front"); the Coordinating Committee To Lift the [Spanish] Embargo ("one of the numerous Communist-front enterprises which were organized around the Communists' agitation over the Spanish Civil War"); *Daily Worker* ("official organ of the Communist Party"); the Emergency Committee for Southern Political Prisoners ("Communist front"); the First Congress of the Mexican and Spanish American Peoples of the United States ("Congress was planned at a secret gathering of Communist Party leaders from the South and Southwest"); Friends of the Cuban Revolution (pro-Communist); Friends of the Soviet Union ("created, directed, and controlled by the Communist Party . . . and operated to aid and support Party objectives concerning the defense and support of the Soviet Union"); Frontier Films ("Communist front"); the International Labor Defense ("subversive and Communist" – "legal arm of the Communist Party" – "part of an international network of organizations for the defense of Communist lawbreakers"); the Inter-

national Union of Revolutionary Writers ("Communist front"); the John Reed Clubs ("out-and-out Communist organizations which preceded the contemporary Communist front organizations which cater to so-called liberals"); *Labor Defender* ("Communist magazine"); the League of American Writers ("subversive and Communist" – "began openly to follow the Communist Party line as dictated by the foreign policy of the Soviet Union"); the League of Professional Groups for [William Z.] Foster and [James W.] Ford ("the members of this organization were committed to the objectives of the Communist Party"); *Liberation* (pro-Communist publication); the Medical Aid to [Castro's] Cuba Committee (ultra-leftist); the National Committee To Abolish the Un-American Activities Committee ("to lead and direct the Communist Party's 'Operation Abolition' campaign"); the National Committee for People's Rights ("composed primarily of openly avowed members of the Communist Party and veteran fellow-travelers of the Communist Party"); the National Committee for the Defense of Political Prisoners ("subversive and Communist"); the National Committee To Aid Striking Miners Fighting Starvation ("Communist front"); the National Committee To Repeal the McCarran Act ("Communist front" – "subversive"); the National Committee To Secure Justice for Morton Sobell ("Communist front [in] the Communist campaign for [atomic spy] Morton Sobell"); the National Committee To Secure Justice in the Rosenberg Case ("Communist front organized . . . to conduct the United States phase of a mammoth propaganda campaign designed to obliterate the crime of and exploit the Rosenbergs and their codefendant Morton Sobell for the purposes of international Communism"); the National Committee To Win Amnesty for Smith Act Victims ("subversive" — "Communist"); the National Council of American-Soviet Friendship ("subversive and Communist" — "specializing in pro-Soviet propaganda"); the National Federation for Constitutional Liberties ("under Communist Party domination and headed by responsible Party functionaries" — "one of the viciously subversive organizations of the Communist Party"); the National Institute of Arts and Letters ("Communist front"); the National Student League ("the Communists' front organization for students"); the National Writers Congress ("Communist front"); *New Currents* (published by the American Committee of Jewish Writers, Artists, and Scientists, a "Communist front"); *New Masses* ("weekly journal of the Communist Party"); New York Committee for a Sane Nuclear Policy (ultra-leftist-pacifist); the Non-Partisan Committee for the Re-election of Congressman Vito Marcantonio ("Communist front"); an Open Letter for Closer Cooperation with the Soviet Union ("issued by a group of Communist Party stooges"); an Open Letter in Defense of Harry Bridges ("Communist front"); *Partisan Review* semi-monthly publication of the John Reed Clubs, "out-and-out Communist organizations"); the Political Prisoners Bail Fund Committee ("Communist front"); the Prisoners Relief Fund ("Communist front"); Luiz [Carlos] Prestes Defense Committee (on behalf of a leader of the Communist Party of Brazil — "a Communist organization"); the [Morris U.] Schappes Defense Committee ("a front organization with a strictly Communist objective, namely, the defense of a self-admitted Communist who was convicted of perjury in the courts of New York"); *Soviet Russia Today* ("Communist-controlled publication");

the *Sunday Worker* ("Communist Party newspaper"); the Union for Democratic Action (Red-lined outfit whose guiding genius was Louis Fraina, one of America's first Communists); United World Federalists (the most prestigious group of fellow travelers and dupes working for world government at the expense of United States sovereignty); World Youth Festival (Communist operation); and Youth and Students for Peace and Friendship (pro-Communist). He died in January 1967.

EDWARD FRANKLIN FRAZIER was born on September 24, 1894 in Baltimore, Maryland, son of Mary Clark and James Frazier. He married Marie Brown. He was an alumnus of Howard University (A.B., 1916); Clark University (A.M., 1920); and the University of Chicago (Ph.D., 1931). He was a research fellow at the New York School of Social Work (1920-1921) and a fellow of the American-Scandinavian Foundation in Denmark (1921-1922). He was the author of *The Negro Family in Chicago* (1932); *The Free Negro Family* (1932); *The Negro Family in the United States* (1939); *Negro Youth at the Crossways* (1940); *The Negro in the United States* (1949); and *Black Bourgeoisie* (1957). He received the Anisfield award for the best book in the field of race relations for his *The Negro Family in the United States*. The book received very favorable reviews in the Communists' *Daily Worker* and *People's World* and was sold in the Communists' Workers Book Shop in New York City.

From 1922 until 1927, Frazier was director of the Atlanta School of Social Work. From 1929 until 1934, he was professor and head of the department of sociology at Fisk University. From 1934 until 1962, he was professor and head of the department of sociology at Howard University. He lectured at the New York School of Social Work and Columbia University. In 1940 and 1941, he held a Guggenheim fellowship for study in Brazil and the West Indies. In 1949, he was chairman of a committee of experts on race for the Red-laden UNESCO. In 1956, he received the McIver Lectureship Award of the American Sociological Society.

Frazier was affiliated with the American Youth Congress ("subversive" – "one of the most influential front organizations ever set up by the Communists in this country" – "the Communists were in complete control"); the Citizens Committee To Free Earl Browder ("a strictly Communist Party affair"); the Civil Rights Congress ("created and established by the Communist Party as an organization which would utilize defense of civil rights for Party purposes and raise and maintain mass defense and bail funds for Party use"); the Committee for a Democratic Far Eastern Policy ("Communist"); the Coordinating Committee To Lift the [Spanish] Embargo ("one of the numerous Communist-front enterprises which were organized around the Communists' agitation over the Spanish Civil War"); the Council on African Affairs ("subversive and Communist"); *Daily Worker* ("official organ of the Communist Party"); the Emergency Civil Liberties Committee ("Communist front" – "subversive"); the George Washington Carver School ("adjunct of the Communist Party"); the Mid-Century Conference for Peace ("aimed at assembling as many gullible persons as possible under Communist direction and turning them into a vast sounding board for Communist propaganda"); the National Citizens' Political Action Committee ("Communist front"); the National

Committee To Repeal the McCarran Act ("Communist front" – "subversive"); the National Council of American-Soviet Friendship ("subversive and Communist" – "specializing in pro-Soviet propaganda"); the National Council of the Arts, Sciences, and Professions ("a Communist front used to appeal to special occupational groups"); the National Federation for Constitutional Liberties ("under Communist Party domination and headed by responsible Party functionaries" – "one of the viciously subversive organizations of the Communist Party"); the National Non-Partisan Committee To Defend the Rights of the Twelve Communist Leaders (pro-Communist); the Negro People's Committee To Aid Spanish Democracy ("set up by the Communists for propaganda purposes in support of the Spanish Loyalists"); *New Masses* ("weekly journal of the Communist Party"); *Science and Society* ("Communist publication"); *Social Work Today* ("Communist magazine"); the Southern Conference Educational Fund (financial backbone of racial agitators, including the black power revolutionaries); the Southern Conference for Human Welfare ("a Communist-front organization which seeks to attract southern liberals on the basis of its seeming interest in the problems of the South"); the Southern Negro Youth Congress ("subversive and among the affiliates and committees of the Communist Party, U.S.A., which seeks to alter the form of government of the United States by unconstitutional means"); the Stockholm Peace Appeal ("Communist 'peace' campaign"); the Washington Committee for Democratic Action ("Communist front"); the Win-the-Peace Conference ("Communist front"); and the World Peace Congress ("organized under Communist initiative in various countries throughout the world"). He died in May 1962.

JOSEPH FREEMAN was born on October 7, 1897 in Piratin, Poltawa, Ukraine, son of Stella Lvovitch and Isaac Freeman. He came to the United States in 1904 and became a naturalized citizen in 1920. He was an alumnus of Columbia University (A.B., 1919). He was the author of *The Soviet Worker: An Account of the Economic, Social, and Cultural Status of Labor in the U.S.S.R.* (1932); *An American Testament: A Narrative of Rebels and Romantics* (1936); *Never Call Retreat* (1943); and *The Long Pursuit* (1947). He was the co-author of *Dollar Diplomacy: A Study in American Imperialism* (1925); *Voices of October: Art and Literature in Soviet Russia* (1930); and *Dreams That Money Can Buy*, film script (1947).

In 1919, Freeman was on the editorial staff of Harper's *Illustrated History of the World War*. In 1920, he was a correspondent in Paris for the *Chicago Tribune*. In 1921, he was a correspondent in London for the *New York Daily News* and the *Chicago Tribune*. From 1921 until 1923, he was an assistant editor of the *Liberator*, a short-lived paper owned by the Communist Party. In 1924, he was publicity director for the American Civil Liberties Union, which at the time was virtually an adjunct of the Communist Party. From 1925 until 1931, intermittently, he was with the TASS news agency of the Soviet Union as New York correspondent. From 1926 until 1937, intermittently, he was with *New Masses* as co-founder and editor (1926), Moscow correspondent (1926-1927), Mexico correspondent (1929), and editor (1931-1933 and 1936-1937). *New Masses* was successor to *The Masses*, which began publishing in 1910. *New Masses*, a weekly publication, was an officially controlled organ of the Communist Party, which dealt principally with problems in the arts and sciences from the Party point of view. The publication was financed by the Garland Fund, a major source of financing for Communist Party enterprises.

While Freeman was editor of *New Masses*, the contributors to the publication, and the editorial board, included some of America's most famous Communists and other radicals: Whittaker Chambers, John Dos Passos, Robert Dunn, Hugo Gellert, Michael Gold, William Gropper, Charles Yale Harrison, Langston Hughes, Louis Lozowick, Scott Nearing, James Rorty, Upton Sinclair, Agnes Smedley, and Mary Heaton Vorse.

From 1934 until 1936, Freeman was co-founder and co-editor of *Partisan Review*. During Freeman's tenure, the *Partisan Review* was under complete control of Communists, and most of its contributors were publicly known to be associated with the Communist movement. On the masthead of its first edition, the *Partisan Review* carried the following description: "A Bi-Monthly of Revolutionary Literature Published by the John Reed Club of New York." The John Reed Clubs were out-and-out Communist Party groups named after one of the original American Communists, John Reed, who died in Moscow and was buried in the Kremlin. From 1937 until 1940, Freeman appeared to have left the Communist scene. He was a free-lance writer, contributing articles and stories to such publications as *Reader's Digest, Nation, Fortune*, and *Harper's*. (Later he contributed articles to *New Republic, Tomorrow*, and *Life*.) From 1940 until 1942, he was publicity director of the ultra-radical American Civil Liberties Union – a position he had also held in 1924. In 1943, he joined the editorial staff of "Information Please," a radio program. He helped to draft radio programs and worked on the preliminary plans for the *Information Please Almanac*, which was first published in 1947. In 1945, he toured France, Germany, and Austria, under USO and Special Services auspices, with the radio program. In 1948, he was publicity director for the Poet's Theatre. From 1948 until 1952, he was on the staff of Edward L. Bernays, a public relations firm. From 1953 until 1961, he was on the staff of Executive Research, Inc., a public relations firm. From 1952 until 1959, he was the public relations director for the annual conventions of the American Pulp and Paper Association. Among various jobs held by Freeman were those of editor of the *Young Judaean*, staff member of *Women's Wear Daily,* staff member of *Garment News,* staff member of *American Hebrew*, and teacher for the Amalgamated Clothing Workers Union. In 1952, he was a fellow of the Newberry Library in Chicago. In 1939, he lectured at Harvard University as a guest of the Nieman Fellows.

At the age of 17, Freeman joined the Socialist Party. His later affiliations included the All-America Anti-Imperialist League ("the [Communist] Party was wholly responsible for the establishment and subsequent control of the League"); the American Committee for Protection of Foreign Born ("founded by the Communist Party in order to exploit racial divisions in the United States for its own revolutionary purposes"); the American Committee for Struggle Against War ("Communist front"); the American Pushkin Committee ("Communist

front"); the American Relief Ship for Spain ("Communist Party front enterprise"); the American Society for Cultural Relations With Russia ("Communist front"); the American Society for Technical Aid to Spanish Democracy ("Communist front"); the Anti-Nazi Federation of New York ("Communist front"); the Appeal for Pardon for Robert Stamm (German Communist); the Ben Leider Memorial Fund ("Communist front" honoring the first American Communist to die in the Spanish Civil War); the Book Union ("distributors of Communist literature" – "Communist [Party] book club"); *China Today* (official organ of the Communist-controlled American Friends of the Chinese People); the Committee of Professional Groups for [Earl] Browder and [James W.] Ford (Communist candidates for President and Vice-President of the United States in 1936); the Congress of American Revolutionary Writers ("subversive and Communist"); *Dynamo* ("a journal of revolutionary poetry published by Communists"); Friends of the Soviet Union ("created, directed and controlled by the Communist Party . . . and operated to aid and support Party objectives concerning the defense and support of the Soviet Union"); the Harry Alan Potamkin Film School ("Communist front"); *International Literature* ("official organ of the International Union of Revolutionary Writers"); the International Union of Revolutionary Writers ("Communist front"); the Jewish People's Committee ("subversive and Communist" – "an organization which has been nothing more nor less than an adjunct of the Communist Party"); the John Reed Clubs ("out-and-out Communist organizations which preceded the contemporary Communist front organizations which cater to so-called liberals"); the Joint Committee for the Defense of the Brazilian People ("Communist front"); *Labor Defender* ("official organ of the International Labor Defense, legal arm of the Communist Party"); the League of American Writers ("subversive and Communist" – "began openly to follow the Communist Party line as dictated by the foreign policy of the Soviet Union"); the Mother Bloor Celebration Committee ("Communist Party festivity"); the National Council for the Protection of Foreign Born Workers ("Communist subsidiary"); the National Committee To Aid the Victims of German Fascism ("an auxiliary of the Communist Party"); the National People's Committee Against Hearst ("subversive and Communist"); the National Student League ("the Communists front organization for students"); *New Theatre* ("a Communist Party publication"); the Revolutionary Writers Federation ("American section of Moscow's International Union of Revolutionary Writers"); Student Congress Against War ("Communist-controlled"); *Student Review* ("published by the National Student League, a Communist front"); *Theatre Arts* ("a pro-Communist monthly"); the Workers' Film and Photo League ("Communist front"); Workers' International Relief ("Communist front"); Workers' Theatre ("Communist front"); the World Congress Against War ("sponsored by the Communist International"); the Writers' and Artists' Committee for Medical Aid to Spain ("a Communist front set up for the purpose of agitation and propaganda"); and the Young Pioneers Camp (Communist enterprise). He died in August 1965.

LEWIS STILES GANNETT was born on October 3, 1891 in Rochester, New York, son of Mary Lewis and William Gannett. He was married to and divorced from Mary Ross. His second wife was Ruth Arens. He was an alumnus of Harvard University (A.B., 1913 and A.M., 1915). He studied at the Universities of Berlin and Freiburg (1913-1914). He was the author of *Young China* (1926); *Sweet Land* (1934); and *Cream Hill* (1949). He was the translator of *The Reconstruction of Europe* (1916) and *The End of Reparations* (1931). He was the editor of *A Liberal in Wartime: The Education of Albert De Silver* (1940); *I Saw It Happen* (1942); and the multi-volume *Mainstream of America* series (1953-1966).

In 1916 and 1917, Gannett was a reporter for the *New York World*. From 1917 until 1919, he was in France working for the pacifist American Friends Service Committee. In 1919, he was a correspondent at the Paris Peace Conference for *Survey,* a Socialist publication. From 1919 until 1928, he was on the staff of the ultra-radical *Nation* magazine. In 1922 and 1923, he was an American correspondent for the *Manchester Guardian.* From 1928 until 1956, he was a member of the editorial staff of the *New York Herald-Tribune*, and from 1930 until 1956, he wrote a daily column, "Books and Things," for that journal.

In his years with the *New York Herald-Tribune* as its chief literary critic, Gannett consistently praised books written by leftists. He was especially forceful in promoting the output of the pro-Soviet, pro-Red China, Institute of Pacific Relations coterie. He was a member of the Socialist Party. His other affiliations included the All-America Anti-Imperialist League ("the [Communist] Party was wholly responsible for the establishment and subsequent control of the League"); the American Committee for Anti-Nazi

German Seamen ("Communist front" – "the objective of the organization was to propagandize for a Communist Germany to take the place of Nazi Germany"); the American Committee for Democracy and Intellectual Freedom ("subversive and un-American" – "a Communist-front organization operating among college teachers and professors"); the American Friends of Spanish Democracy ("Communist front"); the American Fund for Public Service ("a major source for the financing of Communist Party enterprises such as the *Daily Worker* and *New Masses*, official Communist publications, Federated Press, Russian Reconstruction Farms, and International Labor Defense"); the American League for Peace and Democracy ("subversive and Communist" – "established . . . in an effort to create public sentiment on behalf of a foreign policy adapted to the interests of the Soviet Union . . . [and] designed to conceal Communist control, in accordance with the new tactics of the Communist International"); the American-Russian Institute for Cultural Relations with the Soviet Union ("subversive" – "Communist" – "specializing in pro-Soviet propaganda"); the American Student Union ("without exception . . . supported defense of teachers and students charged with Communist activity" – "pliable instrument in the hands of the Communist Party"); the Book Find Club (promoting pro-Communist literature); Friends of the Soviet Union ("created, directed, and controlled by the Communist Party . . . and operated to aid and support Party objectives concerning the defense and support of the Soviet Union"); the Golden Book of American Friendship with the Soviet Union ("pro-Soviet propaganda enterprise"); the International Committee for Political Prisoners (an ultra-leftist fund-raising enterprise for seditionists); the League for Industrial Democracy (socialist); the League of American Writers ("subversive and Communist" – "began openly to follow the Communist Party line as dictated by the foreign policy of the Soviet Union"); *Liberator* ("Communist magazine"); the Medical Bureau and North American Committee To Aid Spanish Democracy ("subversive and un-American"); the ultra-radical National Association for the Advancement of Colored People; *New Masses* ("weekly journal of the Communist Party"); People's Lobby (socialist); a Reception in Honor of the 10th Anniversary of International Publishers ("Communist Party publishing house"); Russian War Relief ("Communist enterprise"); *Soviet Russia* ("official organ of the Friends of Soviet Russia which was created by the Communist Party"); Veterans of the Abraham Lincoln Brigade ("directed, dominated, and controlled by the Communist Party"); Writers' and Artists' Committee for Medical Aid to Spain ("a Communist front set up for the purpose of agitation and propaganda"); and the Writers' Board (pro-Communist). He died in February 1966.

RUDOLPH GANZ was born on February 24, 1877 in Zürich, Switzerland, son of Sophia Bartenfield and Rudolph Ganz. He married the late Mary Forrest. His second wife was Esther La Berge. He studied in Conservatories of Music in Zürich, Lausanne, and Strassburg, and with Busoni in Berlin. He studied composition with Blanchet in Lausanne and with Urban in Berlin.

At the age of ten, Ganz made his debut in Lausanne as a cellist, and at the age of twelve, as a pianist. Between 1889 and 1899, he made extended concert tours in Europe. In 1900, he made his debut as a composer with the Berlin Philharmonic Orchestra. From 1901 until 1905, he was head of the piano department at the Chicago Musical College. From 1905 until 1921, he was a concert artist playing with various musical organizations in the United States and Canada. From 1921 until 1927, he was conductor of the St. Louis Symphony Orchestra. From 1927 until 1954, he was at the Chicago Musical College, which became a part of Roosevelt University, as vice president (1927-1933) and president (1933-1954). In 1954, he retired as president emeritus. From 1939 until 1949, he was conductor of the New York Philharmonic and San Francisco Young People's Concerts. He also conducted children's concerts of the Chicago Symphony Orchestra. He was a composer of symphonies, concertos for piano and orchestra, and symphonic sketches.

Ganz was affiliated with the American Committee for Indonesian Independence ("Communist front"); the American Committee for Protection of Foreign Born ("founded by the Communist Party in order to exploit racial divisions in the United States for its own revolutionary purposes"); the American Council on Soviet Relations ("subversive" – "established by the Communist Party ... directed and controlled by the Party, and operated to aid and support Party objectives concerning the defense and support of the Soviet Union"); the American Rescue Ship Mission ("Communist Party project"); American Youth for Democracy ("subversive and Communist" – "part of Soviet psychological warfare against the United States"); the Coordinating Committee To Lift the [Spanish] Embargo ("one of the numerous Communist-front enterprises which were organized around the Communists'

agitation over the Spanish Civil War"); the Council for Pan-American Democracy ("subversive and Communist"); the Independent Citizens Committee of the Arts, Sciences, and Professions ("Communist front"); the National Council of American-Soviet Friendship ("subversive and Communist" – "specializing in pro-Soviet propaganda"); the National Federation for Constitutional Liberties ("under Communist Party domination and headed by responsible Party functionaries" – "one of the viciously subversive organizations of the Communist Party"); and the Spanish Refugee Appeal ("subversive" – "Communist front"). He died in August 1972.

CHRISTIAN GAUSS was born on February 2, 1878 in Ann Arbor, Michigan, son of Katherine Bischoff and Christian Gauss. He married Alice Hussey. He was an alumnus of the University of Michigan (A.B., 1898 and A.M., 1899). He was the author of *The German Emperor As Shown in His Public Utterances* (1915); *Through College on Nothing a Year* (1915); *Why We Went to War* (1918); *Life in College* (1930); and *A Primer for Tomorrow* (1934). He was the translator of Ferrero's *The Women of the Caesars*, and co-translator of Bainville's *History of France* (1925). He was editor of *Selections From Jean Jacques Rousseau* (1914); *Democracy Today, An American Interpretation* (1917); and Flaubert's *Madame Bovary* (1930).

From 1899 until 1901, Gauss was instructor of Romance languages at the University of Michigan. From 1901 until 1905, he was at Lehigh University as instructor of modern languages (1901-1903) and assistant professor (1903-1905). From 1905 until 1951, he was at Princeton University as assistant professor of Romance languages

(1905-1907); professor of modern languages (1907-1951); chairman of the department of modern languages (1913-1936 and 1943-1951); dean of the college (1925-1945); dean of the alumni (1946-1951); literary editor of Princeton's *Alumni Weekly* (1914-1920); and dean emeritus (1946-1951). In 1913, he was the non-resident lecturer of the Ropes Foundation for Comparative Literature at the University of Cincinnati. In 1915 and 1916, he was a graduate lecturer at New York University and a lecturer at Columbia University's Institute of Arts and Science. He was an associate editor of the *Journal of Education*. He was on the editorial board of *The American Scholar*.

Gauss was affiliated with the American Association for a Democratic Germany (leftist-oriented); the ultra-radical American Civil Liberties Union; the American Committee for Democracy and Intellectual Freedom ("subversive and un-American" — "a Communist-front organization operating among college teachers and professors"); the American Committee To Save Refugees ("perform[ing] a most valuable function for the international Communist movement"); the American Rescue Ship Mission ("Communist Party project"); the Celebration of the 25th Anniversary of the Red Army ("Communist enterprise); the Committee of One Thousand ("Communist-created and controlled"); the Committee of Welcome for the Red Dean of Canterbury ("England's most notorious pro-Soviet apologist among the clergy"); the Coordinating Committee To Lift the [Spanish] Embargo ("one of the numerous Communist-front enterprises which were organized around the Communists' agitation over the Spanish Civil War"); Friends of Italian Democracy ("Communist front"); the Joint Anti-Fascist Refugee Committee ("subversive and Communist"); the Lawyers Committee on American Relations with Spain ("during the Spanish Civil War, the Communist Party organized . . . [the Lawyers Committee] as a part of one of its major propaganda campaigns in the Party's entire history in this country"); the National Council of American-Soviet Friendship ("subversive and Communist" — "specializing in pro-Soviet propaganda"); the National Council of the Arts, Sciences, and Professions ("a Communist front used to appeal to special occupational groups"); the National Emergency Conference for Democratic Rights ("Communist front" — "subversive"); the Reichstag Fire Trial Anniversary Committee ("Communist front . . . formed . . . by prominent Communists and Communist sympathizers"); *Soviet Russia Today* ("Communist-controlled publication"); the Spanish Refugee Relief Campaign ("Communist front"); the United World Federalists (the most prestigious group of fellow-travelers and dupes working for world government at the expense of United States sovereignty); and the Washington Committee To Lift [the] Spanish Embargo ("Communist front"). He died in November 1951.

HELEN HALL was born on January 4, 1892 in Kansas City, Missouri, daughter of Beatrice Dakin and Wilford Hall. She married Paul Kellogg. She was educated at Columbia University (1912-1914) and the New York School of Social Work (1914-1915). She was the author of *Case Studies of Unemployment* (1931).

In 1916, Hall organized the Neighborhood House in Eastchester, New York. In 1917, she was a case worker for the Department of Child Welfare in Westchester County, New York. In 1918 and 1919, she was a director of American Red Cross activities in France. In 1919, she organized and directed the YWCA in Alsace. From 1920 until 1922, she organized and directed recreational activities in China and the Philippines for the U.S. War Department. From 1922 until 1933, she was the director of University House in Philadelphia. From 1933 until 1951, she was the head worker at the Henry Street Settlement House in New York, a Socialist center in the mold of Jane Addams' Hull House in Chicago. From 1928 until 1951, she was chairman of the unemployment commission of the National Federation of Settlements. In 1932 and 1933, she was a member of the federal action committee of the American Association of Social Workers. From 1934 until 1940, she was president of the National Federation of Settlements. In 1934, she was second vice-president of the National Conference of Social Work. In 1934 and 1935, she was a member of the national advisory council of the President's Commission on Economic Security.

Hall was affiliated with the American Friends of the Chinese People ("Communist front"); the American League Against War and Fascism ("subversive and Communist" – "established in the United States in an effort to create public sentiment on behalf of the foreign policy adapted to the interests of the Soviet Union"); the American Committee for Peace and Democracy ("subversive and Communist" – "established . . . in an effort to create public sentiment on behalf of a foreign policy adapted to the interests of the Soviet Union . . . [and] designed to conceal Communist control, in accordance with the new tactics of the Communist International"); the American Youth Congress ("subversive" – "one of the most influential front organizations ever set up by the Communists in this country" – "the Communists were in complete control"); the Committee for a Boycott Against Japanese Aggression ("the committee was featured in the *Daily Worker*, official organ of the Communist Party, and in that paper alone"); the Consumer-Farmer Milk Cooperative, Inc. ("Communist front"); the Consumers National Federation ("transmission belt for the Communist Party's influence and ideology" – "Communist front"); the Coordinating Committee To Lift the [Spanish] Embargo ("one of the numerous Communist-front enterprises which were organized around the Communists' agitation over the Spanish Civil War"); the East Side Committee of American-Soviet Friendship ("Communist front"); Film Audiences for Democracy ("Communist front"); the Foreign Policy Association (a highly influential and highly effective pro-Communist vehicle); Gerson Supporters ("the Communist Party organized a campaign in defense of the appointment of Simon W. Gerson as confidential assistant to the borough president of Manhattan"); the Greater New York Emergency Conference on Inalienable Rights ("Communist front"); the Medical Bureau and North American Committee To Aid Spanish Democracy ("subversive and un-American"); the Milk Consumers Protective Committee ("Communist front"); the New York League of Women Shoppers ("Communist-controlled front"); a Testimonial Dinner for Ferdinand C. Smith ("Communist Party affair"); the Wartime Budget Conference ("Communist front"); and the Washington Committee To Lift [the] Spanish Embargo ("Communist front"). She died in October 1951.

ALICE HAMILTON was born on

February 27, 1869 in New York City, daughter of Gertrude Pond and Montgomery Hamilton. She was an alumna of the University of Michigan (M.D., 1893). She served internships at the Women's and Children's Hospital in Minneapolis and the New England Hospital for Women and Children in Boston, Massachusetts. She furthered her medical studies and research at the University of Leipzig and the University of Munich (1895-1896), the Johns Hopkins University (1896-1897), the University of Chicago (1898-1900), and the Pasteur Institute in Paris (1903). Between 1912 and 1924, she made on-the-scene studies of dangerous trades and safety measures for workers in those trades in Austria, Belgium, England, France, Germany, Italy, Japan, The Netherlands, and the Soviet Union. She was the author of *Industrial Poisons in the United States* (1925); *Industrial Toxicology* (1934); and *Exploring the Dangerous Trades* (1943). She contributed articles to *Atlantic, Harper's, American Journal of Public Health, American Journal of Medical Science, Journal of Infectious Diseases, American Scholar, Journal of the American Medical Association, New England Journal of Medicine, Bulletin of the New York Academy of Medicine, Johns Hopkins Hospital Bulletin, Survey Graphic, Nation, New Republic, Ladies' Home Journal,* and *Living Age.*

From 1897 until 1902, Hamilton was a professor of pathology at the Woman's Medical School of Northwestern University. From 1902 until 1910, she was a researcher at the John McCormick Memorial Institute in Chicago, where she was concerned primarily with the bacteriology of infectious diseases. In 1910, she was the medical investigator for the Occupational Diseases Commission of Illinois. From 1911 until 1921, she investigated industrial poisons and occupational diseases for the United States Department of Labor. From 1913 until 1935, she was assistant professor of industrial medicine in the School of Public Health of Harvard University. In 1935, she retired as professor emeritus from Harvard. From 1924 until 1930, she was an American representative on the health committee of the League of Nations. In 1937 and 1938, and in 1940, she conducted investigations for the U.S. Department of Labor.

From 1897 until 1919, Hamilton was a resident of Jane Addams' Hull House, a famous center of Fabian Socialism. At Hull House, Hamilton became closely associated with many of the era's most famous radicals, including Eugene V. Debs, Emma Goldman, Florence Kelley, Peter Kropotkin, Julia Lathrop, Sidney and Beatrice Webb, and H.G. Wells. From 1919 until 1935, she generally spent several months a year at Hull House.

Amid the circle of the Hull House socialists, Hamilton began a lifetime career of promoting socialized medicine and socialist political reforms of all sorts. She became involved in some of Jane Addams' most celebrated radical political activities. She joined Addams in her Red-inspired pacifist crusade during World War I. She accompanied Addams to The Hague in 1915 and was instrumental in founding the ultra-leftist Women's International League for Peace and Freedom. The association with the W.I.L.P.F. began a lifetime of affiliations that included the American Association for Labor Legislation (Socialist); the ultra-radical American Civil Liberties Union; the American Association for Anti-Nazi Literature ("individuals and organizations connected with it identify this Committee as a Communist front organization"); the American Committee for Democracy and Intellectual Freedom ("subversive and un-American" – "a Communist-front organization operating among college teachers and professors"); the American Committee for Protection of Foreign Born ("founded by the Communist Party in order to exploit racial divisions in the United States for its own revolutionary purposes"); the American Committee to Save Refugees ("perform [ing] a most valuable function for the international Communist movement"); American Friends of Spanish Democracy ("Communist front"); the American Peace Crusade ("Communist front"); the American-Russian Institute for Cultural Relations with the Soviet Union ("subversive" – "Communist" – "specializing in pro-Soviet propaganda"); the American-Soviet Science Society ("subversive"); Brief [amicus curiae] for the Communist Party (Communist Party enterprise); Brief [amicus curiae] in the Case of Morton Sobell (Communist Party enterprise); the Citizens Committee To Free Earl Browder ("a strictly Communist Party affair"); the Civil Rights Congress ("created and established by the Communist Party as an organization which would utilize defense of civil rights for Party purposes and raise and maintain mass defense and bail funds for Party use"); the Committee for Citizenship Rights ("to protect Communist subversion from any penalties under the law"); the Committee for Free Political Advocacy ("Communist front"); the Committee for Peaceful Alternatives to the Atlantic Pact ("a Communist front organization . . . as part of Soviet psychological warfare against the United States"); the Committee of Welcome for the Red Dean of Canterbury (England's most notorious pro-Soviet apologist among the clergy); the Committee To End Sedition Laws ("under complete domination by the Communist Party"); the Consumers National Federation ("transmission belt" for the Communist Party's influence and ideology – "Communist front"); Friends of Italian Democracy ("Communist front"); Friends of the Soviet Union ("created, directed, and controlled by the Communist Party . . . and operated to aid and support Party objectives concerning the defense and support of the Soviet Union"); the Greater New York Emergency Conference on Inalienable Rights ("Communist front"); the Hiroshima Commemorative Committee (ultra-leftist); the International Committee for Political Prisoners (an ultra-leftist fund-raising enterprise for seditionists); the International Workers Order ("from its very inception demonstrated by its pronouncements, its activities, and the authoritative statements of the Communist Party that it is a subservient instrument of the Communist Party of the United States"); the Mid-Century Conference for Peace ("aimed at assembling as many gullible persons as possible under Communist direction and turning them into a vast sounding board for Communist propaganda"); the National Assembly for Democratic Rights ("created, dominated, and controlled by members and officials of the Communist Party"); the National Council of American-Soviet Friendship ("subversive and Communist" – "specializing in pro-Soviet propaganda"); the National Council of the Arts, Sciences and Professions ("a Communist front used to appeal to special occupational groups"); the National Committee To Abolish the Un-American Activities Committee ("to lead and direct the Communist Party's 'Operation Abolition' campaign"); the National Committee To Repeal the McCarran Act

("Communist front" – "subversive"); the National Committee To Secure Justice for Morton Sobell ("Communist front [in] the Communist campaign for the [atomic spy]"); the National Consumers League (socialist); the National Emergency Conference ("Communist front"); the National Emergency Conference for Democratic Rights ("Communist front" – "subversive"); the National Federation for Constitutional Liberties ("under Communist Party domination and headed by responsible Party functonaries" – "one of the viciously subversive organizations of the Communist Party"); the National Free Browder Congress ("Communist front"); the Physicians Forum ("Communist front"); the Russian Reconstruction Farms ("Communist enterprise"); *Science and Society* ("Communist publication"); the Southern Conference Educational Fund ("financial backbone of racial agitators, including the black power revolutionaries"); *Soviet Russia Today* ("Communist-controlled publication"); and World Peace Appeal ("Communist Party campaign"). She died in September 1970.

OSCAR HAMMERSTEIN II was born on July 12, 1895 in New York City, son of Alice Nimmo and William Hammerstein. He was married to and divorced from Myra Finn. His second wife was Dorothy Blanchard. He was an alumnus of Columbia University (A.B., 1916). He attended Columbia's School of Law for two years.

In 1918, Hammerstein began a lifelong career in the theatrical business. He achieved considerable fame as a writer, alone or in collaboration, of the books and lyrics of musical plays, produced for the stage and motion pictures. His stage work included *Wildflower* (1923); *Rose Marie* (1924); *Sunny* (1925); *The Desert Song* (1926); *Show Boat* (1927); *New Moon* (1928); *Sweet Adeline* (1929); *Music in the Air* (1932); *May Wine* (1935); *Oklahoma* (1943); *Carmen Jones* (1943); *Carousel* (1945); *Allegro* (1947); *South Pacific* (1949); *The King and I* (1951); *Me and Juliet* (1953); *Pipe Dream* (1955); and *Flower Drum Song* (1958). His motion picture work included *Show Boat; The King and I; Swing High, Swing Low; High, Wide and Handsome; The Story of Vernon and Irene Castle; The Great Waltz*; and *State Fair*. Among the honors he received were a Special Pulitzer Award (1944); the Donaldson Award (1944, 1945, and 1946); the Critics Award (1946 and 1949); the Motion Picture Academy Award (1945 and 1946); the Pulitzer Prize Drama Award (1949); and the Antoinette Perry Awards on three separate occasions.

Away from his theatrical work, Hammerstein was affiliated with a number of leftist enterprises, including the American Committee for Protection of Foreign Born ("founded by the Communist Party in order to exploit racial divisions in the United States for its own revolutionary purposes"); the Committee for Equal Justice for Mrs. Recy Taylor ("Communist front"); the Committee for the First Amendment ("Communist front"); the Freedom from Fear Committee ("Communist front"); the Hollywood Anti-Nazi League ("Communist front"); the Hollywood Democratic Committee ("Communist front"); the Hollywood League for Democratic Action ("Communist front"); the Hollywood Writers Mobilization ("subversive and Communist" – "the record discloses that the present all-out patriotism of the leading spirits of this Communist front organization is primarily conditioned upon their loyalty to the Soviet Union"); the Independent Citizens Committee of the Arts, Sciences and Professions ("Communist front"); the National Committee for a Sane Nuclear Policy (ultra-leftist-pacifist); the National Institute of Arts and Letters ("Communist front"); People's Songs ("subversive"); Russian War Relief ("Communist enterprise"); Southern Negro Youth Congress ("subversive and among the affiliates and committees of the Communist Party, USA, which seeks to alter the form of government of the United States by unconstitutional means"); the United World Federalists (the most prestigious group of fellow-travelers and dupes working for world government at the expense of United States sovereignty); the Win-the-Peace Conference ("Communist front"); and the Writers Board for Government (leftist). He died in August 1960.

SAMUEL DASHIELL HAMMETT was born on May 27, 1894 in St. Mary's County, Maryland, son of Annie Bond and Richard Hammett. He was married to and divorced from Josephine Dolan. He was educated at Baltimore Polytechnical Institute. He was the author of *Red Harvest* (1929); *The Dain Curse* (1929); *The Maltese Falcon* (1930); *The Glass Key* (1931); *Creeps by the Night* (1931); *The Thin Man* (1934); *Continental Operator* (1945); *Return of the Continental Operator* (1945); *Blood Money* (1942); *Adventures of Sam Spade* (1944); and *Hammett Homicides* (1946). He wrote scripts for three radio series: "The Thin Man," "The Fat Man," and "The Adventures of Sam Spade." Several of his books became motion picture films and he worked in Hollywood on the film scripts.

Before 1922, when his writing career began, Hammett worked at a variety of odd jobs. His longest stay in any one position was eight years as a Pinkerton detective, and his experiences in that position were the basis for many of his novels. He served as an enlisted man in the U.S. Army in World War I and World War II.

In 1953, the Permanent Subcommittee on Government Operations, under the chairmanship of U.S. Senator Joseph R. McCarthy, investigated the operations of the State Department's overseas libraries. The Subcommittee discovered that many of the books on display in the libraries were written by Communists. Hammett's books were among those about which the Subcommittee expressed concern. In the course of the Subcommittee's hearings, Hammett was called upon to testify, and under oath, he invoked the Fifth Amendment when asked about his affiliations with the Communist Party. In 1951, Hammett, as a trustee of the Civil Rights Congress, had supplied bail for eleven Communists who were on trial for conspiracy. When four of the Communists jumped bail, Hammett refused to tell authorities the names of those who had contributed to the bail fund. He refused to produce the records of the Civil Rights Congress and was subsequently cited for contempt of court and was sentenced to a six-month jail sentence. The Civil Rights Congress, which he headed, was created and established by the Communist Party "as an organization which would utilize defense of civil rights for Party purposes and raise and maintain mass defense and bail funds for Party use." In 1946 and 1947, Hammett had been an instructor at the Jefferson School of Social Science, an "adjunct of the Communist Party" and "a Communist institution modelled along the lines of the [then] new Communist policy, which led to the decision to change the Communist Party into some kind of an educational institution."

Hammett was a member of the national board of the Independent Citizens Committee of the Arts, Sciences and Professions, a "Communist front." He was a member of the advisory board of *Soviet Russia Today,* a "Communist-controlled publication." He had been president of the League of American Writers, which was "subversive and Communist" and which "began openly to follow the Communist Party line as dictated by the foreign policy of the Soviet Union."

Hammett's other affiliations included Allied Voters Against Coudert ("an example of the Communist apparatus for character assassination in operation against one who opposed the efforts of the Communist Party to undermine and destroy American democracy"); the American Committee for Democracy and Intellectual Freedom ("subversive and un-American" – "a Communist-front organization operating among college teachers and professors"); the American Committee for Protection of Foreign Born ("founded by the Communist Party in order to exploit racial divisions in the United States for its own revolutionary purposes"); the American Committee To Save Refugees ("perform[ing] a most valuable function for the international Communist movement"); the American Continental Congress for World Peace ("another phase in the Communist 'peace' campaign, aimed at consolidating anti-American forces throughout the Western Hemisphere"); the American Council on Soviet Relations ("subversive" – "established by the Communist Party . . . directed and controlled by the Party, and operated to aid and support Party objectives concerning the defense and support of the Soviet Union"); the American Labor Party ("Communist dissimulation extends into the field of political parties forming political front organizations such as the . . . American Labor Party"); the American Peace Crusade ("Communist front"); the American Peace Mobilization ("formed under the auspices of the Communist Party and the Young Communist League" – "one of the most seditious organizations which ever operated in the United States"); the American Relief Ship for Spain ("Communist Party front enterprise"); the American Writers Congress ("subversive"); the Citizens' Committee for Harry Bridges ("Communist"); the Citizens' Committee To Free Earl Browder ("a strictly Communist Party affair"); the Committee for a Boycott Against Japanese Aggression ("the committee was featured in the *Daily Worker,* official organ of the Communist Party, and in that paper alone"); the Conference for Legislation in the National Interest ("under complete domination by the Communist Party"); the Conference on Constitutional Liberties in America ("an important part of the solar system of the Communist Party's front organizations"); the Congress of American Revolutionary Writers ("subversive and Communist"); Consumers Union (in the "solar system of organizations around the [Communist] Party"); the Coordinating Committee To Lift the [Spanish] Embargo ("one of the numerous Communist-front enterprises which were organized around the Communists' agitation over the Spanish Civil War"); the Council for the Advancement of the Americas (ultra-leftist); the Cultural and Scientific Conference for World Peace ("Communist front" – "a propaganda front for Soviet foreign policy and Soviet culture"); *Equality* ("Communist Party enterprise"); Film Audiences for Democracy ("Communist front"); Films for Democracy ("Communist front");

Friends of the Abraham Lincoln Brigade ("completely controlled by the Communist Party"); the Golden Book of American Friendship with the Soviet Union ("pro-Soviet propaganda enterprise"); In Defense of the Bill of Rights ("Communist Party enterprise"); the Joint Anti-Fascist Refugee Committee ("subversive and Communist"); *Masses and Mainstream* ("Communist magazine"); Motion Picture Artists [Spanish Aid] Committee ("Communist front"); the National Committee To Repeal the McCarran Act ("Communist front" – "subversive"); the National Committee To Secure Justice in the Rosenberg Case ("Communist front organized . . . to conduct the United States phase of a mammoth propaganda campaign designed to obliterate the crime of and exploit the Rosenbergs and their codefendant Morton Sobell for the purposes of international Communism"); the National Committee To Win Amnesty for Smith Act Victims ("subversive" – "Communist"); the National Council of the Arts, Sciences and Professions ("a Communist front used to appeal to special occupational groups"); the National Emergency Conference for Democratic Rights ("Communist front" – "subversive"); the National Federation for Constitutional Liberties ("under Communist Party domination and headed by responsible Party functionaries" – "one of the viciously subversive organizations of the Communist Party"); *New Masses* ("weekly journal of the Communist Party"); the New York Tom Mooney Committee ("Communist front"); the North American Spanish Aid Committee ("Communist"); an Open Letter for Closer Cooperation with the Soviet Union (issued by "a group of Communist Party stooges"); the [Morris U.] Schappes Defense Committee ("a front organization with a strictly Communist objective, namely, the defense of a self-admitted Communist who was convicted of perjury in the courts of New York"); a Statement by American Progressives on the Moscow Trials ("obviously a document concocted in defense of the line of the Communist Party and undoubtedly originated in the headquarters of the Communist Party"); the Stockholm Peace Appeal ("Communist 'peace' campaign"); United Labor and Citizens' Committee for Jobs and Recovery ("set up by Communists"); Veterans of the Abraham Lincoln Brigade ("directed, dominated and controlled by Communist Party"); and the Washington Committee To Lift [the] Spanish Embargo ("Communist front").

Hammett died in January 1961.

S[AMUEL] RALPH HARLOW was born on July 20, 1885 in Boston, Massachusetts, son of Caroline Usher and Samuel Harlow. He was married to the late Marion Stafford. His second wife was Elizabeth Grigorakis. He was an alumnus of Harvard University (A.B., 1908); Columbia University (M.A., 1915); and Hartford Theological Seminary (Ph.D., 1929). He also studied at Union Theological Seminary. He was the author of *The Life of H. Roswell Bates* (1914); *Student Witness for Christ* (1918); *The Church on a War Basis* (1918); *Through Foreign Window Panes* (1922); *Prayer for Times Like These* (1941); *Honest Answers to Honest Questions* (1941); *Thoughts for Times Like These* (1957); and *A Life After Death* (1961). He was co-author of *The Life and Teachings of Jesus* (1930) and *Social and Religious Problems of Young People* (1926).

From 1909 until 1911, Harlow was an assistant minister at the Spring Street Presbyterian Church in New York City. In 1912, he was ordained to the ministry of the Congregational Church. From

1912 until 1922, he was chaplain and head of the department of sociology at International College in Smyrna, Turkey. From 1923 until 1953, he was professor of religion and social ethics at Smith College. From 1951 until 1960, he was a visiting professor at Springfield College. In 1953 and 1954, he was a visiting professor at Pierce College in Athens, Greece. In 1954 and 1955, he was a visiting professor at Fisk University. In 1938 and 1939, under the auspices of the leftist-pacifist Carnegie Endowment for International Peace, he was a visiting professor in Asia and the Near East. From 1916 until 1922, he was general secretary of the Student Voluntary Movement in the Near East. In 1918, he was regional director of the Y.M.C.A. with the American Expeditionary Force in France.

Harlow, like many of his clerical contemporaries, was a pacifist and a promoter of the leftist-oriented "social gospel" that was such a strong theme among those who had studied at the Union Theological Seminary. He was a member of the Socialist Party and ran for Congress in Massachusetts on that Party's ticket. He was active in the Red-dominated Federal Council of Churches. He received a citation from the ultra-leftist American Veterans Committee. He was on the national board of the ultra-radical National Association for the Advancement of Colored People. His other affiliations included the ultra-radical American Civil Liberties Union; the American Committee for Protection of Foreign Born ("founded by the Communist Party in order to exploit racial divisions in the United States for its own revolutionary purposes"); the American Federation of Teachers (leftist-oriented); the American League Against War and Fascism ("subversive and Communist" – "established in the United States in an effort to create public sentiment on behalf of a foreign policy adapted to the interests of the Soviet Union"); the American League for Peace and Democracy ("subversive and Communist" – "established . . . in an effort to create public sentiment on behalf of a foreign policy adapted to the interests of the Soviet Union . . . [and] designed to conceal Communist control, in accordance with the new tactics of the Communist International"); the American-Russian Institute ("subversive" – "Communist" – "specializing in pro-Soviet propaganda"); the American Student Union ("without exception . . . supported defense of teachers and students charged with Communist activity" – "pliable instrument in the hands of the Communist Party"); the Committee for a Democratic Far Eastern Policy ("Communist"); the Committee for Peaceful Alternatives to the Atlantic Pact ("a Communist-front organization . . . as part of Soviet psychological warfare against the United States"); the Fellowship of Reconciliation (ultra-leftist-pacifist); the Golden Book of American Friendship with the Soviet Union ("pro-Soviet propaganda enterprise"); the Greater New York Emergency Conference on Inalienable Rights ("Communist front"); the John Reed Clubs ("out-and-out Communist organizations which preceded the contemporary Communist front organizations which cater to so-called liberals"); the League for Industrial Democracy (Socialist); the National Committee To Repeal the McCarran Act ("Communist front" – "subversive"); the National Conference on American Policy in China and the Far East ("Communist"); the National Federation for Constitutional Liberties ("under Communist Party domination and headed by responsible Party functionaries" – "one of the viciously subversive organizations of the

Communist Party"); the National Religion and Labor Foundation ("Communist front"); the National Sharecroppers Fund ("Communist front"); the *Protestant* ("with an eye to religious groups, the Communists have formed religious fronts such as the *Protestant*"); the *Protestant Digest* ("a magazine which has faithfully propagated the Communist Party line under the guise of being a religious journal"); the [Morris U.] Schappes Defense Committee ("a front organization with a strictly Communist objective, namely, the defense of a self-admitted Communist who was convicted of perjury in the courts of New York"); the [William] Schneiderman-[Sam] Darcy Defense Committee ("Communist"); the War Resisters League (leftist-pacifist); the World Peace Appeal ("Communist Party campaign"); and World Peaceways (Socialist). He died in August 1972.

FOWLER VINCENT HARPER was born on July 21, 1897 in Germantown, Ohio, son of Cora Rudy and Ellahue Harper. He was married to and divorced from Grace Gill. His second wife was Miriam Cohen. He was an alumnus of Ohio Northern University (A.B., 1921 and LL.B., 1923); State University of Iowa (A.M., 1925); and the University of Michigan (S.J.D., 1927). He was also a student at Denison University (1915-1917). He was a fellow at the University of Pennsylvania (1933). He was the author of *Treatise on the Law of Torts* (1933); *Give Me Liberty* (1942); *Law and Democratic Society* (1945); *Problems of the Family* (1952); *The Law of Torts* (1956); and *Justice Rutledge and the Bright Constellation* (1964). He was editor of *Bohlen's Cases on Torts,* fourth edition (1941) and *Readings in Torts* (1941). He was co-editor of *Cases on Torts* (1933) and *Cases and Material on Judicial Technique in Conflict of Laws* (1937). He was a reporter for special chapters in *Restatement of Torts* (1934). He was a contributor to *Les Sources du Droit* (1935).

In 1921 and 1922, Harper was an English instructor and football coach at Wilmington College in Ohio. From 1926 until 1928, he was an assistant professor of law at the University of North Dakota. In 1928 and 1929, he was an associate professor of law at the University of Oregon. From 1929 until 1935, he was successively an associate professor and professor of law at Indiana University. In 1935 and 1936, he was a professor of law at the University of Texas. In 1936 and 1937, he was a professor of law at Louisiana State University. From 1937 until 1946, he was again a professor of law at Indiana University. From 1947 until 1965, he was at Yale University as visiting professor (1947), professor (1948-1957), and the Simeon E. Baldwin Professor of Law (1957-1965). He was a visiting lecturer at the University of Puerto Rico (1944-1945, 1955-1956, and 1964). In 1939 and 1940, he was general counsel of the Federal Security Agency. From 1941 until 1943, he was deputy chairman of the War Manpower Commission. In 1943, he served on the Board of Economic Welfare. From 1943 until 1945, he was solicitor for the Department of the Interior. From 1936 until 1965, he was an editorial advisor for the Bobbs-Merrill Publishing Company. In 1956 and 1957, he was a Fulbright lecturer in law at the University of Lucknow and the University of Delhi. At the same time, he lectured throughout India under the auspices of the United States Information Agency. In 1960 and 1961, under the auspices of the United

States Department of State, he lectured in Kenya, Ethiopia, Ghana, and Nigeria. He was an active Democrat and participated in the 1940 and 1944 Democratic National Conventions.

In 1954, Harper, who claimed to be opposed to the teachings and policies of the Communist Party, filed an *amicus curiae* brief on behalf of 14 California Communists who had been convicted of violating the Smith Act. Harper claimed that the conviction of the Communists violated their constitutional rights to free speech. Harper had more than a casual acquaintance with the Communist movement. His affiliations included the American Committee for Protection of Foreign Born ("founded by the Communist Party in order to exploit racial divisions in the United States for its own revolutionary purposes"); the Bill of Rights Conference ("subversive"); the Emergency Civil Liberties Committee ("Communist front" – "subversive"); the Jefferson School of Social Science ("a Communist institution modeled along the lines of the new Communist policy which led to the decision to change the Communist Party into some kind of an educational institution"); *Jewish Life* ("Communist front publication"); the Lawyers Committee on American Relations With Spain ("during the Spanish Civil War, the Communist Party organized ... [the Lawyers Committee] as a part of one of its major propaganda campaigns in the Party's entire history in this country"); the National Committee To Abolish the Un-American Activities Committee ("to lead and direct the Communist Party's 'Operation Abolition' campaign"); the National Committee for a Sane Nuclear Policy (ultra-leftist-pacifist); the National Committee To Defeat the Mundt Bill ("a Communist lobby ... which has carried out the objectives of the Communist Party in its fight against anti-subversive legislation"); the National Committee To Repeal the McCarran Act ("Communist front" – "subversive"); the National Council of the Arts, Sciences, and Professions ("a Communist front used to appeal to special occupational groups"); the National Emergency Conference ("Communist front"); the National Lawyers Guild ("the foremost legal bulwark of the Communist Party, its front organizations, and controlled unions"); the National Negro Congress ("subversive and Communist" – "characterized as an organization operating in the field of civil rights under Communist Party domination and headed by responsible Party functionaries"); the Progressive Citizens of America ("political Communist front" – "subversive"); and Promoting Enduring Peace, Inc. (ultra-leftist-pacifist). He died in January 1965.

MARION HATHWAY was born on July 31, 1895 in North Tonawanda, New York, daughter of Alice Shelley and William Hathway. She married Theodore Parker. She was an alumna of Radcliffe College (A.B., 1916) and the University of Chicago (A.M., 1927 and Ph.D., 1933). She was the author of *The Young Cripple and His Job* (1928) and *The Migratory Worker and Family Life* (1937). She was co-author of *Public Relief in Washington, 1853-1933* (1934). She was co-author and editor of *Education for the Public Social Services* (1941). She was the editor of the Social Service Series, published by Houghton-Mifflin Company.

In 1920 and 1921, Hathway worked for Y.W.C.A.'s Central Committee in Denver. From 1921 until 1926, she was assistant director of the bureau of attendance for Denver's public schools.

From 1927 until 1931, she was on the faculty of the University of Washington. From 1932 until 1938, and from 1941 until 1951, she was at the University of Pittsburgh as a member of the faculty in the school of social work and as an assistant director in the division of social work. From 1938 until 1941, she was executive secretary for the American Association of Schools for Social Work. From 1951 until 1955, she was professor of social economy and director of the graduate department at Bryn Mawr College. In 1949 and 1950, she was secretary of the National Conference of Social Work.

Hathway was affiliated with the American Committee for Protection of Foreign Born ("founded by the Communist Party in order to exploit racial divisions in the United States for its own revolutionary purposes"); the American Committee for Yugoslav Relief ("subversive and Communist"); the American Committee To Save Refugees ("perform[ing] a most valuable function for the international Communist movement"); the American League for Peace and Democracy ("subversive and Communist" – "established . . . in an effort to create public sentiment on behalf of a foreign policy adapted to the interests of the Soviet Union . . . [and] designed to conceal Communist control, in accordance with the new tactics of the Communist International"); the American Rescue Ship Mission ("Communist Party project"); the Civil Rights Congress ("created and established by the Communist Party as an organization which would utilize defense of civil rights for Party purposes and raise and maintain mass defense and bail funds for Party use"); the Committee for a Democratic Far Eastern Policy ("Communist"); the Committee for Citizenship Rights ("to protect Communist subversion from any penalties under the law"); the Commit-

tee To Defend America by Keeping Out of War ("Communist front"); the Council for Pan-American Democracy ("subversive and Communist"); the Cultural and Scientific Conference for World Peace ("Communist front" – "a propaganda front for Soviet foreign policy and Soviet culture"); the Emergency Peace Mobilization ("Communist front"); the Joint Anti-Fascist Refugee Committee ("subversive and Communist"); the League of Women Shoppers ("Communist-controlled front"); the National Committee To Repeal the McCarran Act ("Communist front" – "subversive"); the National Council of the Arts, Sciences, and Professions ("a Communist front used to appeal to special occupational groups"); the National Federation for Constitutional Liberties ("under Communist Party domination and headed by responsible Party functionaries" – "one of the viciously subversive organizations of the Communist Party"); an Open Letter in Defense of Harry Bridges ("Communist front"); the Physicians Forum ("Communist front"); the Progressive Party ("one of the largest and most successful fronts ever created by the Communists"); *Science and Society* ("Communist publication"); Social Workers Committee To Aid Spanish Democracy ("Communist front"); *Social Work Today* ("Communist magazine"); and the Spanish Refugee Appeal ("subversive" – "Communist front"). She died in November 1955.

ARTHUR GARFIELD HAYS was born on December 12, 1881 in Rochester, New York, son of Laura Garson and Isaac Hays. He was married to and divorced from Blanche Marks. His second wife was Aline Fleisher. He was an alumnus of Columbia University (B.A., 1902; M.A., 1905; and LL.B., 1905). He was admitted to the New York bar in 1905. He was the author of *Enemy Property in America* (1923); *Let Freedom Ring* (1928; revised 1937); *Trial by Prejudice* (1933); *Democracy Works* (1939); and *City Lawyer*, autobiography (1942). He was co-author of *Don't Tread on Me* (1928). He was a contributor to publications, including *Nation* magazine.

In his early years of practicing law, Hays was with several New York City legal firms: Bowers and Sands; Hays, Kaufman, and Lindheim; Hays and Wadhams; and Hays, St. John, and Moore. He finally settled with Hays, St. John, Abramson, and Schulman. He practiced most branches of law, including corporate and criminal. His greatest fame, however, came through his activities for more than three decades as counsel for the ultra-radical National Association for the Advancement of Colored People and the ultra-radical American Civil Liberties Union. He defended leftwing labor leaders and unions, anarchists, Communists, and Socialists. In his professional work and in his private activities, he fought against censorship laws. He took part in many cases involving freedom of the press, freedom of speech, and freedom of assembly. Invariably, he was on the side of license vis-à-vis regulation.

In politics, Hays was a gadfly. Prior to 1912 he was a Republican, but he bolted the Party to join Theodore Roosevelt's Bull Moose Progressives. In 1916, he campaigned for the Republicans. In 1919, he was with the short-lived Farmer-Labor Party. In 1924, he worked for La Follette's Progressive Party. In 1932, he was a member of the National Progressive League, working for the election of Franklin D. Roosevelt. After 1932, he remained in the Democratic Party, but on the extreme left.

In 1948, Hays testified before the House Committee on Un-American Activities. He denied under oath present or past membership in the Communist Party. He also testified: "I personally have never belonged to a front organization." Hays was affiliated with the All-America Anti-Imperialist League ("the [Communist] Party was wholly responsible for the establishment and subsequent control of the league"); the American Committee for Protection of Foreign Born ("founded by the Communist Party in order to exploit racial divisions in the United States for its own revolutionary purposes"); the American League Against War and Fascism ("subversive and Communist" – "established in the United States in an effort to create public sentiment on behalf of a foreign policy adapted to the interests of the Soviet Union"); the American League for Peace and Democracy ("subversive and Communist" – "established . . . in an effort to create public sentiment on behalf of a foreign policy adapted to the interests of the Soviet Union . . . [and] designed to conceal Communist control, in accordance with the new tactics of the Communist International"); the American Society for Cultural Relations with Russia ("Communist front"); the Berger National Foundation (Socialist organization); Brookwood Labor College ("Communistic"); the Citizens Committee for Harry Bridges ("Communist"); the Citizens' Committee To Free Earl Browder ("strictly a Communist Party affair"); the Committee for a Boycott Against Japanese Aggression ("the committee was featured in the *Daily Worker*, official organ of the Communist Party, and in that paper alone"); the Committee for Free Political Advocacy ("Communist front"); the Committee on Coal and Great Power (Socialist); Consumers Union (in the "solar system of organizations around the [Communist] Party"); the Coordinating Committee To Lift the [Spanish] Embargo ("one of the numerous Communist-front enterprises which were organized around the Communists' agitation over the Spanish Civil War"); the Emergency Committee for Strikers Relief (Socialist); the Federated Unemployed Workers Leagues (Socialist); the International Committee for Political Prisoners (to raise funds for jailed seditionists); the International Labor Defense ("subversive and Communist" – "legal arm of the Communist Party" – "part of an international network of organizations for the defense of Communist lawbreakers"); the John Reed Clubs ("out-and-out Communist organizations which preceded the contemporary Communist front organizations which cater to so-called liberals"); the Lawyers Committee on American Relations With Spain ("during the Spanish Civil War, the Communist Party organized . . . [the Lawyers Committee] as a part of one of its major propaganda campaigns in the Party's entire history in this country"); the League of American Writers ("subversive and Communist" – "began openly to follow the Communist Party line as dictated by the foreign policy of the Soviet Union"); the Methodist Federation for Social Action ("the organization's influence has been consistently wielded on behalf of Communist causes and the Communist line as expressed through the party and its innumerable subsidiaries"); the National Citizens Committee on Relations with Latin America (dominated by Socialists); the National Committee To Secure Justice in the Rosenberg Case ("Communist front organized . . . to conduct the United States phase of a mammoth propaganda campaign designed to obliterate the crime of and exploit the Rosenbergs and

their codefendant Morton Sobell for the purposes of international Communism"); the National Council for Protection of Foreign Born Workers ("Communist subsidiary"); the National Council on Freedom From Censorship (ultra-leftist); the National Council To Aid Agricultural Labor ("Communist front"); the National Lawyers Guild ("the foremost legal bulwark of the Communist Party, its front organizations, and controlled unions"); the National Mooney-Billings Committee (dominated by Socialists); the National People's Committee Against Hearst ("subversive and Communist"); the National Wartime Conference of the Professions, the Sciences, the Arts, the White-Collar Fields ("Communist front"); the Non-Partisan Committee for the Re-election of Congressman Vito Marcantonio ("Communist front"); the Public Use of Arts Committee ("Communist front"); Russian Reconstruction Farms ("Communist enterprise"); and the Washington Committee To Lift [the] Spanish Embargo ("Communist front"). He died in December 1954.

DONALD HENDERSON was born on February 4, 1902 in New York City, son of Jean Crawford and Daniel Henderson. He was married to the late Elinor Curtis. His second wife was Florence McGee. He was an alumnus of Columbia University (A.B., 1925 and A.M. 1926). He also studied at the School of International Studies in Geneva, Switzerland. In 1925, he held a Garth Fellowship at Columbia University.

Before Henderson attended college, he was employed as a farm laborer and railroad telegrapher. From 1926 until 1928, he was an instructor of economics at Rutgers University. From 1928 until 1933, he was an instructor of economics at Columbia University. From 1934 until

1937, he was an organizer for agricultural labor, employed by the American Federation of Labor. From 1937 until 1949, he was international president of the Feed, Tobacco, Agricultural and Allied Workers Union. From 1949 until 1953, he was secretary-treasurer of Food, Tobacco, Agricultural and Allied Workers of the United States. For many years he was a member of the national executive board of the CIO. In the late 1930's and early 1940's, he was president of the United Cannery, Agricultural, Packing, and Allied Workers.

In 1953, Henderson testified before the Senate Permanent Subcommittee on Government Operations. When asked about his Communist Party membership, he invoked the Fifth Amendment. He had previously invoked the Fifth Amendment when he testified before the Senate Internal Security Subcommittee on February 14, 1952. On July 8, 1953, under oath, Manning Johnson, an ex-Communist Party official, identified Henderson as a Communist at hearings of the House Committee on Un-American Activities.

In 1944, the House Special Committee on Un-American Activities reported: "Donald Henderson, general president of the United Cannery, Agricultural, Packing, and Allied Workers (C.I.O. affiliate), is prominent in the C.I.O. Political Action Committee. On January 14, 1944, Henderson addressed a national conference of the Political Action Committee which was held at the Park Central Hotel in New York City.

"There is no secrecy about Donald Henderson's membership in the Communist Party. He has been a publicly avowed card-holding member for more than 10 years. In that period of time, he has subserviently followed all the ideological zig-zagging of the party line, including the patently seditious activities of the American Peace Mobilization (to which the Department of Justice was totally blind) and the current pretended superpatriotism of all the Muscovite stool pigeons. In some cases, the C.I.O. Political Action Committee might seek the shelter of ignorance concerning the communist connections of its active leaders, but emphatically not in the case of Henderson. No German-American Bundist ever worked more assiduously than Donald Henderson for the destruction of American free institutions. When the C.I.O. Political Action Committee includes among its leaders such men as Henderson, it demonstrates beyond dispute the un-American nature of its objectives. Who is Henderson that he should be welcomed to a place of leadership in an organization which sets out to spend $2,000,000 to influence the 1944 elections to the end that the Congress of the United States should be brought under the complete domination of a sinister minority pressure group? Let his public record answer the question!

"In the September 1935 issue of *The Communist*, Donald Henderson appeared as the author of an article entitled 'The Rural Masses and the Work Of Our Party.' The article opened with the following statement: 'On the basis of the Open Letter, during the past 2 years our party has been successful in developing policies and organization which are rapidly achieving a successful turn to mass revolutionary work and influence in the cities and among the industrial urban proletariat.' Note that Henderson used the phrase 'our party.' Later, in his article, Henderson wrote of the necessity for the Communist Party to 'carry through' its idea of 'Soviet power . . . in the small cities, towns, and villages, and on the farms.'

"Donald Henderson has not only functioned as a leader in the Communist Party and in the top ranks of the C.I.O. He has also been extraordinarily energetic in the leadership of the numberless front organizations of the Communist Party. In the spring of 1933, Henderson was dropped from the teaching staff of Columbia University. For a number of weeks, the Communists carried on a noisy agitation for his reinstatement, but to no avail. The clamor of the Communists against Columbia University for its action in the case of Henderson was expressed chiefly through its front organization for students, the National Student League. Henderson was secretary of the National Student League, about which Earl Browder wrote as follows: 'From the beginning, it has been clearly revolutionary in its program and activities' (*Communism in the United States*, by Earl Browder, p. 43) . . . .

"In August 1932 the Communist International sponsored an international gathering at Amsterdam which was known as the World Congress Against War. That gathering called upon the proletariat of the world to prepare to 'turn imperialist war into civil war.' The delegates to the Amsterdam congress were instructed to organize in their respective countries national branches to be affiliated with the world organization. In the United States, in the fall of 1932, the American Committee for Struggle Against War was organized in response to these instructions of the Amsterdam congress. Donald Henderson became executive director of the American branch.

"During the Christmas holidays of 1932, the Student Congress Against War was convened at the University of Chicago. This gathering was held at the direct instigation of the (Amsterdam) World Congress Against War. The Chicago Congress was completely controlled by the Communists of the National Student League. Donald Henderson was the principal organizer of the gathering. He was also the floor leader who voiced the Communist Party line on every issue which arose. On the program of the Student Congress Against War, Henderson was listed as a speaker and as a member of its national committee. The gathering ended its sessions by adopting the program of the (Amsterdam) World Congress Against War, which, as has been pointed out, called for 'the turning of imperialist war into civil war.' For many years, the latter slogan represented one of the chief objectives of the Communist movement throughout the world.

"In the spring of 1933 the Arrangements Committee for the United States Congress Against War was organized at a meeting held in the New School for Social Research in New York City. Donald Henderson was made secretary of the committee. The United States Congress Against War convened in St. Nicholas Arena, New York City, on September 29, 1933. Donald Henderson was executive secretary of the gathering, which was completely under the control of the Communist Party. Earl Browder was a leading figure in all its deliberations. In his report to the Communist International, Browder stated: 'The Congress from the beginning was led by our Party quite openly' (*Communism in the United States* by Earl Browder, p. 184).

"The United States Congress Against War adopted a 10-point program which became the platform of the American League Against War and Fascism. That platform included the following: 'To work toward the stopping of the manufacture and transport of munitions and all other materials essential to the conduct of war, through mass demonstrations, picketing, and strikes.' Years later, this was translated into overt acts when the Communist-led C.I.O. unions did everything possible, especially through strikes, to stop the manufacture of 'munitions and all other materials essential to the conduct of war.' Donald Henderson was a leading figure not only in the adoption of this seditious platform at the United States Congress Against War in 1933 but also in its treasonable translation into action under the auspices of the Communist Party and the American Peace Mobilization in 1940-41.

"The American League Against War and Fascism was launched at the United States Congress Against War. Donald Henderson was made executive secretary of the American League, a post which he held until the Communist Party transferred him to work in the agricultural field. When the American League Against War and Fascism changed its name to the American League for Peace and Democracy, Donald Henderson remained a member of the organization's national committee. The American League was eventually disbanded after Hitler and Stalin signed their pact, and a few months later the American Peace Mobilization took its place as the principal Communist Party front dealing with international questions.

"The American Peace Mobilization was launched in Chicago in September 1940. Donald Henderson was elected a member of the organization's national council. The treasonable character of the American Peace Mobilization is now generally conceded. The organization aided and abetted strikes in many of the country's most important defense industries. These strikes were political in nature and aimed at leaving the United States in a position of unpreparedness.

The organization conducted a picket line in front of the White House in the spring of 1941, withdrawing its pickets within a few hours of Hitler's march against Russia . . . .

"The . . . record of Henderson's Communist positions and activities is clear proof that he is one of the leaders in whom the Communist Party places extraordinary confidence. Despite the utterly un-American character of Donald Henderson's activities and affiliations over the past twelve years, and despite his publicly acknowledged membership in the Communist Party, Sidney Hillman permits him to take a place of leadership in the C.I.O. Political Action Committee. There is no possibility of disputing the charge which has been levelled at Hillman by the right-wing leaders of the American Labor Party, namely that he has entered into a conspiracy with the Communist Party. That conspiracy has as its main objective the subordination of the Congress of the United States to an un-American minority pressure group."

Henderson's other affiliations included the African Aid Committee (leftist-racist agitators); the All-American Anti-Imperialist League ("the [Communist] Party was wholly responsible for the establishment and subsequent control of the League"); the American Committee for Protection of Foreign Born ("founded by the Communist Party in order to exploit racial divisions in the United States for its own revolutionary purposes"); the American Continental Congress for World Peace ("another phase in the Communist 'peace' campaign, aimed at consolidating anti-American forces throughout the Western Hemisphere"); the American Council for a Democratic Greece ("subversive and Communist"); the Amercan Slav Congress ("Moscow-inspired and directed federation of Communist-dominated organizations seeking by methods of propaganda and pressure to subvert the 10,000,000 people in this country of Slavic birth or descent"); the American Student Union ("without exception . . . supported defense of teachers and students charged with Communist activity" – "pliable instrument in the hands of the Communist Party"); American Youth for Democracy ("subversive and Communist" – "part of Soviet psychological warfare against the United States"); the Bill of Rights Conference ("subversive"); the Citizens' Committee To Free Earl Browder ("strictly a Communist Party affair"); the Civil Rights Congress ("created and established by the Communist Party as an organization which would utilize defense of civil rights for Party purposes and raise and maintain mass defense and bail funds for Party use"); the Committee for a Democratic Far Eastern Policy ("Communist"); the Committee for Free Political Advocacy ("Communist front"); the Committee for Peaceful Alternatives to the Atlantic Pact ("a Communist front organization . . . as part of Soviet psychological warfare against the United States"); Commonwealth College ("Communist"); the Coordinating Committee To Lift the [Spanish] Embargo ("one of the numerous Communist-front enterprises which were organized around the Communists' agitation over the Spanish Civil War"); the *Daily Worker* ("official organ of the Communist Party"); *Fight* ("official organ of the American League Against War and Fascism [American League for Peace and Democracy], subversive and Communist"); First Congress of the Mexican and Spanish-American Peoples of the United States ("Congress was planned at a secret gathering of Communist Party leaders from the South and Southwest"); Friends of the Soviet Union ("created, directed, and controlled by the Communist Party . . . and operated to aid and support Party objectives concerning the defense and support of the Soviet Union"); the Golden Book of American Friendship with the Soviet Union ("pro-Soviet propaganda enterprise"); the International Labor Defense ("subversive and Communist" – "legal arm of the Communist Party" – "part of an international network of organizations for the defense of Communist lawbreakers"); the International Workers Order ("from its very inception demonstrated by its pronouncements, its activities, and the authoritative statements of the Communist Party that it is a subservient instrument of the Communist Party of the United States"); the Joint Committee for Trade Union Rights ("jointly with the International Labor Defense supported and defended Communist Party leaders . . . when they were serving prison terms"); the *March of Labor* (an instrument of the Communist Party); the Mid-Century Conference for Peace ("aimed at assembling as many gullible persons as possible under Communist direction and turning them into a vast sounding board for Communist propaganda"); the National Committee To Defeat the Mundt Bill ("a Communist lobby . . . which has carried out the objectives of the Communist Party in its fight against anti-subversive legislation"); the National Council of American-Soviet Friendship ("subversive and Communist" – "specializing in pro-Soviet propaganda"); the National Federation for Constitutional Liberties ("under Communist Party domination and headed by responsible Party functionaries" – "one of the viciously subversive organizations of the

Communist Party"); the National Negro Congress ("subversive and Communist" − "characterized as an organization operating in the field of civil rights under Communist Party domination and headed by responsible Party functionaries"); the National Non-Partisan Committee To Defend the Rights of Twelve Communist Leaders (pro-Communist); *New Masses* ("weekly journal of the Communist Party"); the New Theatre League ("Communist front"); the Progressive Party ("one of the largest and most successful fronts ever created by the Communists"); the [Morris U.] Schappes Defense Committee ("a front organization with a strictly Communist objective, namely, the defense of a self-admitted Communist who was convicted of perjury in the courts of New York"); the Stockholm Peace Appeal ("Communist 'peace' campaign"); the *Student Review* (published by the National Student League, a Communist front); Veterans of the Abraham Lincoln Brigade ("directed, dominated and controlled by the Communist Party"); and the World Peace Congress ("organized under Communist initiative in various countries throughout the world"). He died in September 1953.

JOSEPHINE FREY HERBST was born on March 5, 1897 in Sioux City, Iowa, daughter of Mary Frey and William Herbst. She married John Herrmann. She was an alumna of the University of California at Berkeley (A.B.,1918). She was a student at Morningside College, the University of Iowa, and the University of Washington. She was the author of *Nothing Is Sacred* (1928); *Money for Love* (1929); *Pity Is Not Enough* (1933); *The Executioner Waits* (1934); *Rope of Gold* (1939); *Satan's Sergeants* (1941); *Somewhere the Tempest Fell* (1948); *The Watcher*

with the Horn (1955); *New Green World* (1956); and *A View of the Nation* (1960). She was the author of the introduction to Ring Lardner's *Gullible's Travels* (1965). Her works are included in O'Brien's *Best Short Stories of 1931*. She was a contributor to publications including *American Mercury, Arts, Commentary, Kenyon Review, Nation, New Republic, Noble Savage, Partisan Review, Scribner's*, and *Smart Set*. Her awards included a Guggenheim fellowship in fiction (1936); a Longview Foundation award (1960); a Rockefeller Foundation grant (1965); and a National Institute of Arts and Letters grant (1966).

Between 1918 and 1922, Herbst worked in a print shop, in a department store, as a case-worker for a charitable organization, as a publicity writer, and as an editorial reader for *Smart Set* magazine. Between 1922 and 1925, she lived in Germany, Italy, and France. She visited the Soviet Union in 1930. In 1935, she was a special correspondent in Germany for the *New York Post* and *Nation* magazine. In 1935, she also served as a special correspondent in Cuba. In 1937, she was a special correspondent in Spain, reporting on the Civil War there. In 1939, she was a special correspondent in South America. In 1941 and 1942, she was a writer, at the German desk, for the Office of the Coordinator of Information (later known as the Office of Strategic Services). She was discharged without warning from that position. She did not return to government employment. Throughout most of her life, she was a free-lance writer.

Herbst was affiliated with the Abraham Lincoln School ("an adjunct of the Communist Party"); *Anvil* ("distinctly a Communist publication"); the Book

Union ("distributors of Communist literature" – "Communist [Party] book club"); the Committee of Professional Groups for [Earl] Browder and [James W.] Ford ("Communist candidates for president and vice-president of the United States in 1936"); the Congress of American Revolutionary Writers ("subversive and Communist"); *Daily Worker* ("official organ of the Communist Party"); *Daily World* ("official organ of the Communist Party"); the Emergency Committee for Southern Political Prisoners ("Communist front"); *Fight* ("official organ of the American League Against War and Fascism [American League for Peace and Democracy], subversive and Communist"); *Friday* (Communist-controlled); Frontier Films ("Communist front"); the Golden Book of American Friendship With the Soviet Union ("pro-Soviet propaganda enterprise"); *International Literature* ("official organ of the International Union of Revolutionary Writers"); the International Union of Revolutionary Writers ("Communist front"); the John Reed Clubs ("out-and-out Communist organizations which preceded the contemporary Communist front organizations which cater to so-called liberals"); *Labor Defender* ("Communist magazine"); the League of American Writers ("subversive and Communist" – "began openly to follow the Communist Party line as dictated by the foreign policy of the Soviet Union"); the Mother Ella Reeve Bloor Banquet (Communist Party affair); the National Committee for People's Rights ("composed primarily of openly avowed members of the Communist Party and veteran fellow travelers of the Communist Party"); the National Committee for the Defense of Political Prisoners ("subversive and Communist"); *New Masses* ("weekly journal of the Communist Party"); the Non-partisan Committee for the Re-election of Congressman Vito Marcantonio ("Communist front"); *Partisan Review* ("semi-monthly publication of the John Reed Clubs"); the [Luiz Carlos] Prestes Defense Committee ("on behalf of a leader of the Communist Party of Brazil"); Prisoners' Relief Fund ("Communist front"); the Revolutionary Writers Federation ("American section of Moscow's International Union of Revolutionary Writers"); *Sunday Worker* ("Communist Party newspaper"); the United Committee To Aid Vermont Marble Workers ("Communist front"); and *Woman Today* ("Communist magazine"). She died in January 1969.

GEORGE DAVIS HERRON was born on January 21, 1862 in Montezuma, Indiana, son of Isabella Davis and William Herron. He was married to and divorced from Mary Everhard. His second wife was Carrie Rand. His third wife was Friede Schoeberle. He studied at Ripon College in Wisconsin and in England, Germany, and Italy. In 1883, he entered the Congregational ministry. He was the author of *The Larger Christ* (1891); *The Call of the Cross* (1892); *A Plea for the Gospel* (1892); *The Christian State* (1895); *Social Meanings of Religious Experiences* (1896); *Between Caesar and Jesus* (1899); *Why I Am a Socialist* (1900); *The Day of Judgment* (1904); *From Revolution to Revolution* (1907); *The Menace of Peace* (1917); *Woodrow Wilson and the World's Peace* (1917); *Germanism and the American Crusade* (1918); and *The Defeat in the Victory* (1921).

In 1890 and 1891, Herron was pastor of the First Congregational Church in Lake City, Minnesota. In 1891, he became pastor of the First Congregational

Church in Burlington, Iowa. At Burlington, he organized the Institute of Christian Sociology which was merely a Socialist adult education class, where he denounced the capitalist system with its competition and profit motivation. He interpreted the Bible to mean that true Christianity was the same as Socialism.

About seventeen months after Herron assumed his pastorate at Burlington, a wealthy parishioner, Mrs. E.D. Rand, established him in a newly-created chair at Iowa College (later Grinnell), where he was a professor of applied Christianity. For the next six years, he taught on and off campus his confusion of Christianity and Socialism, and in so doing he attracted a great deal of national attention. He was, however, so extreme and so radical in his denunciation of traditional social, political, and economic values that he became *persona non grata* at Iowa College. In 1899, he resigned his teaching chair and joined the Socialist Party.

By 1899, Herron had become enamored of Carrie Rand, daughter of Mrs. E.D. Rand, his benefactor. With the encouragement of the two women he began a crusade to reform the Socialist Party from within, and tried to impose his admixture of Socialist principles and his personal interpretation of Christianity upon his colleagues in the Socialist Party, who were in the midst of severe factional struggles that centered upon strategy and tactics in the very mundane political arena. At that time, Herron's teachings were what became widely known in the leftist church circles as the social gospel. In a series of lectures delivered by him during that period, he expressed the essence of his Socialism *cum* Christianity: "The common ownership of natural resources follows a clear line of Christian teaching from the be-

ginning of that teaching with Jesus Christ. Nearly all His statements of religious principles are in terms of human relations; and His idea was altogether more communistic than we care to discover. Reduced to economic terms, the realization of His ideal of the kingdom of Heaven could mean nothing less than an all-inclusive, non-exclusive communism of opportunity, use, and service. It may be a debatable matter whether any form of communism is practicable; but it is not open to question that Jesus never contemplated anything else than an organization of human life in which all men should work together for the common good, and each have according to his needs or power to use . . . .

"The undeviating hostility of Christ and His witnesses to individual wealth cannot be evaded by following John Wesley's immoral advice to make all one can and then give all one can. The philanthropy of economic extortion is the greatest immediate menace to religion and social progress. The gifts that come not from willful extortion but from as clean hands as the system of things will suffer any man to have are apt to be even more misleading than the benevolence of avarice, because they seem to justify and make Christian what is really anti-Christ. Let us honor such contributions as they deserve to be honored, or concede the economic and historical necessity of individual wealth in the social evolution; but let us not deceive ourselves and become false teachers to the people by speaking of such wealth as Christian.

"Wealth is a power in the world, and often a power for good, while a rich man may be very useful and generous, and his motives noble; but, however religious and philanthropic he be, the rich man stands in the antithesis of the Christian attitude toward the world. We cannot honestly imagine one in Christ's state of mind, one feeling as Christ felt, one coming at the world from His point of view, giving himself to acquiring individual wealth. Strictly speaking, a rich Christian is a contradiction of terms. This is a hard saying, and it places every one of us in positions of dreadful inconsistency and difficulty; but it is the bald, naked reality of Jesus' teaching.

"Let us confess that we are all alike guilty; that none of us are really Christian, if it comes to this; but let us be men enough to look the truth straight in the face . . . .

"Of course, one should not throw away nor destroy nor desecrate any property that is in his hands. He ought not and cannot individually extricate himself from the system that now exists. But the very least that a Christian can do in the existing order is to administer what he possesses for the common good, in the most literal sense of the term. A man cannot be Christian without being practically communistic; as a possessor of property, he is simply a steward having in trust what belongs to others. With this, he must exhaust his possibilities in changing the system from one of private ownership and competition into the common ownership and cooperative service of the kingdom of Heaven. Sometimes I think that a single man of great economic power, accepting such a stewardship, with the heart of Christ in him, could change the world.

"The question as to whether economic brotherhood is practicable is a question of whether Christianity is practicable. If Jesus dwelt at the heart of God, and knew the law and secret of the universe, it is not worthwhile trying to establish society on any other basis than that of the universal communism of the

Father who maketh His sun to rise on the evil and the good, and sendeth rain on the just and unjust; the Father who, when His children had wasted the abundant resources of life which He had already given them, redeemed them by giving them more resources. Before we dismiss such a social basis as a dream, let us well consider our free schools, the free street railways in the Australian city, the free highways unto the ends of the earth, and many other initiatives in the common life of today, which indicate that we are in the beginnings of a tremendous change upward into communism which Jesus disclosed as universal life and order.

"In the fullness of its times, we shall have a new Christian synthesis upon which to base the religious movement which the social spirit seeks, and it will guide society through storm and change. The details of that synthesis do not yet appear; but in the outline emerging from the confusion of our faith, we may behold an economic of the kingdom of Heaven. It will so state the facts and forces which are the sum of Jesus' idea, in such clear terms of present social need, as to afford a definite, tangible, working program of social faith.

"It comes, after the long winter of apostolic faith, as a new religion springing up from the seed of Christ in the human soil. It promises a faith for which men will once more be ready to live or die with equal joy."

In 1901, Herron's wife, Mary Everhard, divorced him on grounds of desertion. The court awarded her and her five children Carrie Rand's personal fortune of $60,000. Two months after the divorce, Herron attracted widespread notoriety when he married Carrie Rand in a Socialist rite wherein each chose the other as companion against all coercive institutions. In her *Fabian Freeway*, Rose Martin provided a description of the ceremony: "One Saturday evening in May, with the scent of flowers filling the room, George Herron and Carrie Rand announced to a small circle of Socialist comrades and to the world at large the accomplished fact of their 'spiritual union' – the long-standing 'marriage of our souls.' Next, the host of the evening, Dr. Charles Brodie Patterson, editor of *The Arena* and *Mind*, made a brief address. He was followed by the Reverend William Thurston Brown of Plymouth Church, Rochester, whose Annunciation Service was described by one listener as a 'poem in prose.' Each of the fourteen guests present, among them the romantic poet, Richard Le Gallienne, was invited to make a brief verbal offering to the consummation of this love union. William Mailly, national secretary of the young Social Democratic Party (soon to be merged into the Socialist Party), declared that the marriage meant, above all, a more complete consecration to Socialism!

"Uplifting as the event may have seemed to sentimental Socialists of the period, Dr. Herron's colleagues and neighbors back in Iowa found it both bizarre and shocking. Just ten days later the council of the First Congregational Church in Grinnell recommended that Dr. Herron be dropped from church membership rolls, deposed from the Christian ministry, and removed from the teaching staff at Grinnell College, a church-sponsored institution. While the Socialist press attempted to depict Dr. Herron as a martyr to his political beliefs, the circumstances of his divorce from a loyal wife, and his remarriage without benefit of clergy, were the actual reasons for his ouster."

With his wife Herron went to Italy where he lived on the Rand estate near Fiesole. While abroad, Herron continued to be an influence in the Socialist Party, especially in international affairs. Before the Herrons went to Italy they were instrumental in the founding of the Rand School. Mrs. Rand, Herron's patroness, died in 1905 and in her will left a trust fund of $200,000 to "carry on and further the work to which I have devoted the later years of my life" – Socialism. Mrs. Rand named Carrie and George Herron trustees of the fund. With a supplemental gift of money from Carrie Herron, Mrs. Rand's legacy was used to establish "an intellectual center for the Socialist movement in the United States" – the Rand School. Within a short time the Rand School was a thriving Marxian-Socialist training center for labor agitators.

Meanwhile, in Italy, Herron was busy writing books and spreading his own brand of Socialism. Along the way, he decided that Christianity was an inadequate basis or medium for the Socialist revolution that he envisioned as necessary to overthrow the existing capitalist system. By 1910, Biblical allusions and Christian terminology disappeared from his writings.

During the course of World War I, Herron broke with the Socialist Party. He developed a hatred of Germany and could not countenance the pacifism of his Socialist colleagues, who, for the most part, were adamantly opposed to United States intervention in the European conflict. They insisted that the war was waged between capitalistic, imperialistic powers and that United States participation would retard the growth of Socialism; therefore, it behooved Socialists to stand by and watch the anti-Socialist powers destroy themselves as speedily as possible.

Herron viewed World War I as the collapse of capitalism predicted by Karl Marx. Herron wanted the United States to hasten the collapse by entering the sacred crusade in which, "for the first time in the earth's annals, a great and powerful people has gone to war for humanity." This was the theme of Herron's *Germanism and the American Crusade*. Herron thought that President Woodrow Wilson was the ideal crusader who would lead the United States to destroy Germany and bring the world closer to a Socialist utopia. All of this was spelled out in Herron's maudlin *Woodrow Wilson and the World's Peace*.

During the course of World War I, Herron somehow gained the confidence of President Wilson and the Germans who were involved in the peace negotiations. He was instrumental in persuading the Germans to place their confidence in Wilson, who, he told them, would offer them a just and fair peace settlement if they would only acknowledge Germany's war guilt. They followed Herron's advice; they acknowledged guilt; and then had a monstrous "peace" imposed on them by the vindictive allies at Versailles. The terms of the settlement would later play a major role in the rise of Hitler.

Herron's break with the Socialist Party in the United States during the course of World War I was also prompted by the Party's sympathetic attitude toward the Bolshevik revolution in Russia and the diversion of funds from the Rand School toward Communist enterprises. Herron was originally somewhat favorably inclined toward the Bolsheviks, but after direct personal experience with them he reversed himself. President Wilson sent Herron and journalist William Allen White as his personal emissaries to the Prinkipo Conference, where they met with Bolshevik leaders. The Conference became a total fiasco when the Bolsheviks refused to listen to any American suggestions that the discordant Russian elements settle their differences so as to present an orderly representation at the peace negotiations.

Herron's role in the entire period of the negotiations was that of a total failure. He remained in his self-imposed exile in Italy. He continued to propagate his Socialist views through European and American periodicals. He finally despaired of the United States and other nations as the hope of Socialism. Italy, he felt, was the best hope for the anti-capitalist, Socialist utopia he envisioned. He died in October 1925.

MORRIS HILLQUIT was born Misca Hillkowitz on August 1, 1869 in Riga, Latvia, Russia, son of Rebecca Levene and Benjamin Hillkowitz. He married Vera Levene. He attended Alexander Gymnasium in Riga (1881-1886). He came to the United States in 1886. He attended high school in New York City for a brief time. He was an alumnus of the University of the City of New York (LL.B., 1893). In 1893, he was admitted to the New York bar. He was the author of *History of Socialism in the United States* (1903); *Socialism in Theory and Practice* (1909); *Socialism Summed Up* (1912); *From Marx to Lenin* (1921); and *Loose Leaves from a Busy Life,* autobiography published posthumously (1934). He was the co-author of *Socialism, Promise or Menace* (1914).

Between his high-school days in New York City and his entrance into law school, Hillquit worked briefly in a shirt factory and for a picture frame company. He also worked as a promoter, business manager, and associate editor for the *Arbeiter Zeitung*, the first American-Yiddish paper in New York City. In that period, he also helped to organize the United Hebrew Trades, a pioneer union activity of garment workers in New York City. In 1887, he took a job as a clerk in the Socialist Labor Party's office in New York City and became a member of the Party.

Hillquit's association with the garment industry, with the Socialist Labor Party, and with labor organizations served as a basis for his entire career. From 1893 until 1933, he was a practicing lawyer. In those forty years, he proved to be one of the most durable and successful leftwing lawyers on the American scene. He defended anarchists, Socialists, and assorted other leftists in what were unpopular causes of the era. On the other hand, he was not averse to taking on major corporations as clients, and in 1918 and 1919 he worked for his most unusual and controversial client − the Soviet Government Bureau, which had located in New York City, although it was not recognized as an official entity by the United States government.

Hillquit was active to some extent in attempts − some unsuccessful − to organize unions in the garment industry. From 1913 until 1933, he was general counsel for one of the largest and most successful garment unions, the International Ladies' Garment Workers Union.

Hillquit's fame on the American scene would not rest in the long run upon his legal or union activities. He earned his niche in American history as one of the most important leaders of Socialism and the Socialist Party.

Between 1887 and 1899, Hillquit acquired the status of a leader in the Socialist Labor Party, which was firmly under the control of Daniel De Leon. De Leon was an implacable foe of unions as they had developed in the United States.

He did not like any form of organized labor except on an industry-wide basis. Hillquit, on the other hand, believed that the cause of Socialism could be best served if the Socialist Labor Party cooperated with the American Federation of Labor and the Knights of Labor, the two major established labor bodies. In 1899, the differences between Hillquit and De Leon became so irreconcilable that Hillquit led a group of his followers out of the Socialist Labor Party. They joined Eugene V. Debs and Victor Berger, who had formed the Social Democratic Party. Hillquit and his faction supported the presidential candidacy of Eugene Debs in 1900, and a year later, mainly through Hillquit's efforts, a merger was affected between the Debs and Hillquit groups, forming the Socialist Party of America.

From 1901 until his death in 1933, Hillquit was one of the most active and prominent leaders of the Socialist Party. From 1901 until 1906, he was a national committeeman from New York. From 1906 until 1933, he was chairman of the national committee. From 1907 until 1912, and from 1916 until 1933, he was a member of the national executive committee. In 1921, he was national chairman. In 1926, he was keynote speaker at the Party's national convention. He was the American delegate to the International Socialist Congresses at Amsterdam (1904), Stuttgart (1907), and Copenhagen (1910). He attended the Vienna International Union of Socialist Societies convention at Hamburg (1923), Marseilles (1925), Brussels (1926), and Vienna (1931). From 1904 until 1933, he was a member of the International Socialist Bureau. He was the Socialist candidate for the House of Representatives (1906-1908, 1916, 1918, and 1920) and the mayoralty of

New York City (1917, 1921, and 1932).

Aside from his formal Socialist Party activities, Hillquit joined Socialists, Communists, and other fellow-traveling leftists in a variety of organizations, including the American Civil Liberties Union, the American League To Limit Armaments, the Berger National Foundation, the Conference for Progressive Political Action, the Emergency Peace Federation, the Federation of Unemployed Workers' Leagues, the Fellowship of Reconciliation, the National Citizens Committee on Relations with Latin America, the National Mooney-Billings Committee, the Non-Intervention Committee, and the People's Councils. He was a teacher and trustee of the Rand School of Social Science, a training ground for Socialist agitators in the labor movement. For ten years, he was a director of the Intercollegiate Socialist Society (later named the League for Industrial Democracy), the major Socialist effort in this century to bring Socialism to college and university campuses.

At the outbreak of World War I, Hillquit, like most American Socialists, adopted a strong pacifist posture. Pacifism became the Socialist Party line. In 1915, Hillquit prepared a peace program for the Socialist Party that was offered as a guide to the belligerents and to the United States government. In general, the Socialists demanded that no annexations or indemnities result from the war, that the peace negotiators recognize and guarantee the right of political self-determination, and that they also agree to effect disarmament and to support a play for international government.

In 1915, in a debate with Republican Congressman Augustus P. Gardner of Massachusetts, Hillquit presented his anti-war and anti-militarism views — views which were the basic arguments of the Socialist Party in its attempt to forestall intervention by the United States in the European conflict.

Hillquit said, during the course of that debate with Gardner: "I maintain that the argument of modern American militarism is based on a colossal fallacy. The United States is not in danger of war. It has never been safer from hostile attack than it is at this period. I maintain that wars are man-made; that the civilized nations of today have it within their power to abolish them, and that, as far as the United States is concerned, we shall never face another war, unless we deliberately choose to make war.

"What was the cause of the appalling slaughter which is now shaking the foundations of Europe? Let us analyze it carefully, for the fate of unfortunate Europe holds a solemn warning for us, on the happier side of the Atlantic. The total area of Europe is 3,570,000 square miles, or just as large as the continental United States, including Alaska. That area is peopled by more than four hundred million human beings, and is divided into twenty-two separate political sovereignties, many of which are in turn composed of several distinct countries, more or less loosely connected by the ties of a common political government. The boundaries of these numerous countries have been formed arbitrarily and capriciously by the unreasoning process of historical development. They split ethnological units and combine incongruous national groups; they cut off large sections of the continent from necessary maritime outlets, and often impede free commerce and intercourse between the nations. The political history of Europe is a chronicle of succeeding changes of its map and of international intrigues and wars which have caused or accompanied such changes.

And every war between two or more countries has created deep international grudges, has laid the foundation for new wars.

"The everlasting strife between the nations of crowded and divided Europe has become more acute in recent times through the growth of international trade. Although a warship has never helped to sell a can of sardines or a bale of cotton, the nations of Europe have conceived the superstitious notion that a country's oversea trade must be protected by a strong navy. Although no colony has ever been of financial or material advantage to the mother-country, the trading classes of Europe have come to believe that their prosperity depends on the 'ownership' of large oversea colonies. The leading countries of Europe thus entered into a ruinous rivalry in naval construction and in the acquisition of colonial possessions. Within the last thirty years England and France have acquired whole empires in Africa, and Germany has secured a colonial territory five times the size of the fatherland. The imperialistic policy of expansion has become the keynote of European international politics. The territory available for colonies was soon preempted, and the further expansion of colonial possessions of each European country had mainly to be accomplished at the expense of other European powers. Every country suspected the other of a design to expand and to steal colonies; every country was eager to expand and ready to steal colonies. Each mistrusted the peaceful intentions of its neighbor, and began to increase its armies and navies. It was all done for the 'national security,' not in preparation for war but in 'preparation against war,' ... just as a sort of 'peace insurance,' but each nation wanted to be a little more secure than the other, and so the European rivalry of armament started on its mad career. The world has never been afflicted with such an insane spirit of militarism as it has within the last forty years.

"Long before the outbreak of the war Europe was divided into hostile camps, and was in full battle array. Its countries had an abundance of battleships, torpedo boat destroyers, submarines, aeroplanes, Zeppelins, forts, guns, rifles, ammunition and big armies. They were ready for war – and they got their war. Their anti-war insurance turned out to be a bad case of over-insurance.

"For all the human lives that have been ruthlessly destroyed in this war, for the homes that have been wrecked, for the towns and villages that have been devastated, for the fiendish atrocities that have been perpetrated and the sufferings that have been inflicted on mankind, the 'patriots' of Europe who have been urging on their gullible countrymen the need of ever greater military preparedness, bear an awful share of responsibility. To sum up then, the main causes of the great European war were artificial political boundaries, historical grudges, commercial rivalry, imperialism and militarism.

"Turning now from this analysis to an examination of the conditions in the United States we find a complete absence of all factors that naturally make for war, and a happy combination of conditions calculated to ensure lasting peace. Our country is so vast in territory, so varied and abundant in natural wealth and resources, that we are as a nation economically self-sufficient. The United States is more self-sufficient than any country in the world. If we were today cut off from the world market; if we could not import or export a dollar's worth of goods, our population could still live in comfort and abundance. But there is no need for abandoning our foreign trade. No country will make war on us just because we sell to it our wheat or corn or buy from it its cloth or dyestuffs. We need no seaports for our trade that we do not have, for we own the whole coastline on both sides of our continent. We are not hampered by vexatious boundaries and customs duties in moving our goods from inland points to harbors, for we own every inch of the solid territory between the two oceans, from the Canadian to the Mexican border. If national boundaries were obliterated in Europe, if England, France, Italy, Germany, Austria and all other European countries would unite into one great federation of nations with a common government and administration, if the ideal of the United States of Europe would become a reality, that would clearly mean the end of wars in Europe. Well, in the United States we have actually accomplished what to Europe is still an iridescent dream of the remote future – we have established a thoroughly harmonious and indissoluble federation of states.

"We need no colonies . . . . We have no national grudges to settle . . . . And finally we have no neighbors who may involve us in war . . . . Remains the question whether we are or ever can be in danger of invasion by a great non-American power. I maintain that to any mind not clouded by hysteria such a danger can only appear in the nature of a huge joke.

"The trouble with our apostles of militarism is that they still think in the terms of the early middle ages, when nations were wandering across the scantily inhabited globe in nomadic hordes seeking settlements, or making war on each other for pillage or booty. They do not realize that the great civilized nations of modern times cannot be conquered, destroyed, or subjugated, particularly a nation so situated as the United States.

"The gospel of our awakening military 'patriotism' would be amusing, if it were not so serious and dangerous. The appeal to national vanity and aggressive combativeness, the appeal to the animal instincts in men is always dangerous, but it is particularly so in these times of universal war-madness. The propaganda for increased armaments at this time is pregnant with gravest menace to the well-being and security of the nation, particularly because it is likely to be promoted and intensified by sordid economic interests. I refer to the so-called 'armor ring,' which has reaped the prime and only benefit from the billions this nation has expended for armaments, and whose business interests are best served by war scares, war preparations and actual wars.

"Strenuous preparation 'against war' means not only invitation of war, it means the brutalization of the country. A military power is a despotic power and training for war has a most demoralizing effect on the youth of the country. You may say all you want about the ennobling influences of military discipline and the 'martial spirit,' but it is a matter of common and notorious knowledge that the barracks of professional soldiers reek with brutality, vice and degeneracy.

"But this is not all. There is another side to military preparedness . . . . In the last twenty years we have expended upward of $3,191,000,000 on our army and navy, exclusive of pensions. And still we are ludicrously unprepared, and are urged to increase our military and naval forces. And these monstrous annual of-ferings at the altar of the military mo-loch must be taken from the vitally necessary works of social progress and civilization. With a fraction of the mil-lions expended for military purposes we could provide for a sufficient and effi-cient corps of mine, railroad and factory inspectors and for the maintenance of proper safeguards, which would reduce these frightful industrial casualties to a minimum.

"Tens of thousands of our people annually succumb to the ravages of tuberculosis, the typical disease of pover-ty. We could practically stamp out the dread white plague by applying a portion of the senseless military expenditures to the building of numerous sanitaria, offer-ing plenty of fresh air and nourishing food to the unfortunate victims of the disease.

"There are hundreds of thousands of aged workers in all parts of the country succumbing in helpless and pathetic des-titution. They have spent their man-hood, their strength and lives in useful service to their fellow men . . . . We owe a duty to these aged public servants, the soldiers and heroes of our industries. Less than half of the military budget would provide old-age pensions for them and enable them to close their lives in moderate comfort and decent self-respect.

"Just at this time the United States is undergoing one of the severest economic trials in its history. The wheels of its industrial process have become hope-lessly clogged. Millions of American workers are without jobs and without bread. With an expenditure of a hundred million dollars, taken from the war budget, the government could organize numerous industrial enterprises, set the destitute jobless toilers to the work of making things they need for the sus-tenance of their lives, revive business and break the vicious circle of busi-ness depression, unemployment and poverty.

"With the millions and billions of dollars called for by unproductive mili-tary expenses we could improve our system of education, raise the condition of our workers, and introduce measures of civic and social justice, which would make this country vastly stronger, more irresistible and unconquerable than all the dreadnaughts and aeroplanes in cre-ation.

"Some day the orgy of murder and blood which is now devouring Europe will cease. The unfortunate nations at war will pause, bleeding, exhausted, ashamed . . . . They will look to us for comfort, for hope. What shall be our answer? Shall it be the same vicious rat-tling of sabres, or shall it be a message of peace, a promise of a saner, better, hu-maner world for the future? Let it be peace. The United States can never be-come a first-class military power. Let us center our ambition, our hope and as-piration on making our country the first great peace power of the world."

After the United States government made its formal declaration of war in 1917, the Socialist Party met in conven-tion at St. Louis, and Hillquit was its most prominent spokesman. He led the Socialist Party to condemn the war, which in his simplistic terms was a result of economic rivalries between imperial-istic nations. According to Hillquit, the prosecution of the war was anathema to Socialists because it hurt the cause of labor and retarded the advance of Social-ism in the United States and throughout the world.

During the course of the war, when the Bolshevik Revolution took place in

Russia, Hillquit was highly enthusiastic, as were most Socialists in America. His attitude was: "The basis of our sympathy with Soviet Russia is, in the first place, that we recognize Soviet Russia as a government of the working classes of Russia – of the underdog, if you want it." In 1920, however, at the Socialist Party convention in New York, the delegates voted against affiliation with the Communist International, though the Socialist Party continued to endorse the International and the Soviet Government. The Socialist Party had decided to concentrate on increasing its strength in the United States. There were hopes that the Socialist Party would be the backbone of a strong labor party that could become a real political force on the American national scene. At the 1921 Socialist Party national convention, Hillquit offered a resolution which the convention adopted. The resolution spelled out plans for what amounted to a united political labor front. Said Hillquit's resolution: "The task of reconquering and maintaining our civil rights and liberties and securing substantial measures of economic relief can be accomplished only through the united and concerted action of all progressive, militant and class-conscious workers, industrial and agricultural, in the United States . . . . Be it therefore Resolved, that the Incoming National Executive Committee be instructed to make a careful survey of all radical and labor organizations in the country, with a view of ascertaining their strength, disposition and readiness to cooperate with the socialist movement upon a platform not inconsistent with that of the party and on a plan which will preserve the integrity and economy of the Socialist party. Resolved, that the National Executive Committee report its findings with recommendations to the next annual convention of the Socialist party."

To implement the Hillquit resolution, the Socialist Party joined other leftist groups in supporting the presidential candidacy of Robert M. La Follette Sr. and his third party in 1924. After 1924, the Socialist Party, disappointed in La Follette's campaign, in which Hillquit took a major part, decided that a labor party was not feasible and that the Socialist Party should maintain itself as an independent political entity. Hillquit supported this position as long as he lived.

While Hillquit was alive, and even since his death, descriptions of his political convictions have been widely at variance. His followers and his critics have never seemed able to agree as to what part of the Socialist spectrum he belonged – left, center, or right. In the full context of his career, there are some clearly defined positions which make his Socialism more understandable. He did believe that Socialists should work to make their program as attractive as possible to Americans. This meant that the Socialists should use American terminology and discard the European terminology as much as possible in their literature. He believed that Socialism could best advance through the American labor movement and that Socialists could infiltrate and take over organized labor unions. He believed that militancy and violence on the part of Socialists would antagonize Americans who were likely converts to the Socialist cause. He believed, throughout most of his career as a Socialist Party leader, that open alliances with Communists were detrimental to the Socialist cause. In other words, Hillquit, imitative of the British Fabian Socialists, wanted his party to follow a policy of gradualism while wearing a cloak of respectability.

Under close analysis, Hillquit in his Socialist preachings did not differ markedly from the Marxist-Leninist line. He was simply able to present the line in something less than inflammatory language.

In 1920, Hillquit wrote *Present-Day Socialism*, a pamphlet published by the Rand School of Social Science. Extracts from that pamphlet, written after Hillquit had spent 33 years in the Socialist movement, probably portray his brand of Socialism as well as anything written by him before or after. In the pamphlet he wrote: "Socialism is distinctly a modern movement . . . . The Socialist movement was called into life by economic conditions which have developed within very recent times . . . . Its program is an attempted solution of the problems inherent in these conditions. The cardinal demand of Socialism is the abolition of private ownership in the vital sources and instruments of wealth production, and there was practically no physical basis and no rational justification for such a demand before about the beginning of the nineteenth century . . . .

"Modern society is split into two principal economic groups or classes: the users of the machinery of production, who do not own it, and the owners, who do not use it; the employers and the employees, the capitalists and the workers, those who derive their income from 'profits' and those who depend for their living on 'wages.' The classes are not fixed by law, but they are determined just as effectively by economic position, and as the modern industrial system is unfolding, they tend to become permanent and even hereditary.

"And there is war between and among the classes. War, sometimes overt and violent, sometimes concealed and even unconscious, but war nevertheless. The war is all the more intense and irrepressible because it springs not from personal hostility or accidental misunderstandings, but from ever-present basic economic antagonism.

"There is war between employer and employee . . . . There is war between employer and employer . . . . There is war between worker and worker . . . . There is war between producer and user . . . . Class divisions have always existed in the recorded history of the human race. But advancing civilization has gradually abolished all privileges based on birth and caste, and it has been left to the capitalist system of production to evolve a new form of economic classes based on the relation to the ownership of the tools and production.

"The Socialists do not exult in the existence of classes and class struggles, and do not 'preach' class hatred. They merely point out the obvious fact of economic classes and class antagonism. It is no more reasonable to charge the 'Socialist agitator' with fomenting class wars than it would be to hold the meteorologist responsible for storms. As a matter of fact, the Socialist movement is the only organized force in modern society which consciously seeks to abolish all class divisions and class struggles.

"The dominant Socialist party of Russia (now known as the Communist Party) has established a political regime based upon the absolute and exclusive rule of the working classes. This system, styled the Dictatorship of the Proletariat, has for a time been followed by the Communists of Hungary, and is advocated by some 'extreme' groups of Socialists of the different countries of Europe and in America. Within the ranks of the Socialist movement at large opinion is sharply divided upon the issue of the Dictatorship of the Proletariat. But whether the principle is sound or unsound, or whether it is of general or special applicability, it is not incompatible with the Socialist ideal of a classless society. For neither the Russian Communists nor any other adherents of the 'dictatorship,' profess to see in it any more than a transitory and passing form of political organization, a sort of war measure in the Socialist struggle to abolish the capitalist system and to combat counter-revolutionary movements. With the disappearance of the idle exploiting classes and transformation of the whole able-bodied and sound-minded population into useful workers, the rule of the workers will automatically become synonymous with the rule of the people; the 'dictatorship' of the working class will yield to the democratic government of an equal and classless nation of productive men and women . . . .

"The Socialists demand that the basic industries of the nation, the business of providing the necessaries of life, be conducted by the community for the benefit of its members . . . . Socialism would substitute the prevailing method of private enterprise for individual profit by a system of social production for collective use.

"Stated in more concrete terms, the Socialist program calls for the public or collective ownership and operation of the principal instruments and agencies for the production and distribution of wealth — the land, mines, railroads, steamboats, telegraph and telephone lines, mills, banks, factories and modern machinery. This is the main program of the whole Socialist movement and the political creed of all Socialists. It is the unfailing test of Socialist conformity, and admits of no limitation or variation.

Whoever accepts this program is a Socialist, whoever does not, is not . . . .

"The Socialist program is primarily one of economic reform. It is not directly concerned with religious or domestic institutions, moral conceptions or intellectual problems. It does not 'threaten the home' or 'attack religion,' and is not hostile to true modern culture. It advocates a definite plan of industrial reorganization and is chargeable with all that is fairly inferrable from that plan, but no more.

"Socialism has for that reason sometimes been characterized as a grossly materialistic movement. It is anything but that. The Socialists appreciate very keenly all efficient political, social and moral reforms. But they expect such reforms to follow economic improvements as the effect follows the cause. The common ownership of the sources and instruments of wealth production would necessarily mean a more equitable distribution of wealth among people and greater economic security for all human beings. It would do away with the mad competitive struggle for individual gain, and would remove the principal cause of civic and political corruption, crime, vice, brutality and ignorance. Just because the Socialist movement is based on a solid and sound economic foundation, it holds out a true social ideal . . . .

"Under normal conditions the introduction of a Socialist regime depends on two main conditions: First, the economic situation of the country must be ripe for the change. Second, the people of the country must be ready for it.

"Whether the Socialist order be ushered in by a revolutionary coup d'état, or by a series of legislative enactments or executive orders, it can be maintained only by the people in control of the country. In other words, Socialism, like any other national political program, can be realized only when its adherents, sympathizers and supporters, are numerous enough to wrest the machinery of government from their opponents, and to use it for the realization of their program.

"Socialism is primarily a movement of education and propaganda. The Socialist propaganda does not originate from a mere desire to spread the truth – for the benefit of the unconverted, as the Christian propaganda is said to be inspired by a general ethical zeal to save souls. The Socialist propaganda is the very life-nerve of the movement. Upon its success or failure depends the fate of Socialism. The educational and propagandist activities dominate all other forms of organized Socialist work, and none but the closest observers can appreciate the gigantic accomplishments of the movement in this field.

"Socialism necessarily involves an immediate material loss to the capitalist classes – and a corresponding gain to the working classes. The Socialists, therefore, make their appeal primarily to the workers . . . .

"The deeper objects of Socialist politics are: (1) To make propaganda for the cause of Socialism, for which political campaigns always offer favorable opportunities. (2) To acquaint the workers with the concrete political problems of the country and to educate them in practical politics. (3) To gain representation in the legislatures and in executive offices in order to secure true reforms for the workers, to train them in the art of statesmanship and to afford them larger opportunities for propaganda. (4) To wean the workers from the influence of the old parties, to develop their political independence and class consciousness and to organize them

for the final practical task of the Socialist movement – the winning of the government for the workers.

"In the Socialist conception, politics is only a means to an end . . . . The Socialist aim in politics is to better the lot of the workers, to curb the power of the capitalist classes, to extend the social and industrial functions of the government and to place the latter more directly in the hands of the people – all with the ultimate object of transforming the present industrial and political system into a social democracy . . . . All Socialist reform measures are formulated with the distinct object of improving tne position of the workers in their struggle for the ultimate overthrow of the entire system of capitalism."

Hillquit died in October 1933.

WILLIAM ERNEST HOCKING was born on August 10, 1873 in Cleveland, Ohio, son of Julia Pratt and William Hocking. He married Agnes O'Reilly. He was an alumnus of Harvard University (A.B., 1901; A.M., 1902; and Ph.D., 1904). In 1902 and 1903, he was a Harvard fellow at the University of Gottingen, the University of Berlin, and the University of Heidelberg. He was the author of *Two Extensions of the Use of Graphs in Elementary Logic* (1909); *On the Law of History* (1909); *The Meaning of God in Human Experience* (1912); *Human Nature and Its Remaking* (1918 and 1929); *Morale and Its Enemies* (1918); *Immanuel Kant and International Policies* (1924); *Man and the State* (1926); *Present Status of the Philosophy of Law and of Rights* (1926); *The Self, Its Body and Freedom* (1928); *Types of Philosophy* (1929 and 1939); *Spirit of World Politics: With Special Studies of the Near East* (1932); *Memorial Addresses* (1935); *Lasting Elements of In-*

dividualism (1937); *Thoughts on Death and Life* (1937); *Living Religions and a World Faith* (1940); *Recent Trends in American Philosophy* (1941); *Science, Value, and Religion* (1942); *What Man Can Make of Man* (1942); *Science and the Idea of God* (1944); *Freedom of the Press* (1947); *Experiment in Education: What We Can Learn From Teaching Germany* (1954); *The Coming World Civilization* (1956); *Meaning of Immortality in Human Experience* (1957); and *Strength of Men and Nations: A Message to USA vis-à-vis USSR* (1959). He was co-author of *Preface to Philosophy* (1945) and *George Herbert Palmer*, and co-author and editor of *Rethinking Missions: A Layman's Inquiry After One Hundred Years* (1932). He was the editor of *Dilemma of Religious Knowledge* (1931). He was on the advisory board of the *Journal of Social Philosophy*.

From 1904 until 1906, Hocking was an instructor in the history and philosophy of religion at Andover Theological Seminary. In 1905 and 1906, he was an instructor in the history and philosophy of religion at Harvard University. From 1906 until 1908, he was at the University of California as an instructor (1906-1907) and assistant professor (1907-1908). From 1908 until 1914, he was at Yale University as an assistant professor of philosophy (1908-1913) and professor (1913-1914). From 1914 until 1966, he was on the faculty of Harvard University as professor of philosophy (1914-1920); Alford Professor (1920-1943); chairman of the division of philosophy and psychology (1935-1937); chairman of the department of philosophy (1937-1943); and professor emeritus (1943-1966). In 1913 and 1914, he lectured in philosophy at Princeton University. In 1918 and 1919, he was Mills Professor at the University of California. From 1937 until 1939, he was

the Gifford Lecturer at Glasgow University. In 1938, he was the Hibbert Lecturer at Oxford University and Cambridge University. In 1946, he was the Flint lecturer at the University of California at Los Angeles. In 1947, he was the William James Lecturer at Harvard University. In 1947 and 1948, he was a guest professor at the University of Leiden.

Hocking was affiliated with the Committee for Free Political Advocacy ("Communist front"); the Committee of One Thousand ("Communist-created and controlled"); the Committee of Welcome for the Red Dean of Canterbury (England's most notorious pro-Soviet apologist among the clergy); the Cultural and Scientific Conference for World Peace ("Communist front" – "a propaganda front for Soviet foreign policy and Soviet culture"); the Hiroshima Commemorative Committee (ultra-leftist); the Institute of Pacific Relations ("an instrument of Communist policy, propaganda, and military intelligence"); the Medical Aid to [Castro's] Cuba Committee (ultra-leftist); the National Committee To Abolish the Un-American Activities Committee ("to lead and direct the Communist Party's 'Operation Abolition' campaign"); the National Committee To Repeal the McCarran Act ("Communist front" – "subversive"); the National Committee To Win Amnesty for Smith Act Victims ("subversive and Communist"); the National Council of American-Soviet Friendship ("subversive and Communist" – "specializing in pro-Soviet propaganda"); the National Council of the Arts, Sciences, and Professions ("a Communist front used to appeal to special occupational groups"); the National Non-partisan Committee To Defend the Rights of 12 Communist Leaders (pro-Communist); the *Protestant* ("with an eye to religious groups, the

Communists have formed religious fronts such as *Protestant*"); and the *Protestant Digest* ("a magazine which has faithfully propagated the Communist Party line under the guise of being a religious journal"). Hocking died in June 1966.

JOHN HAYNES HOLMES was born on November 29, 1879 in Philadelphia, Pennsylvania, son of Alice Haynes and Marcus Holmes. He married Madeleine Baker. He was an alumnus of Harvard University (A.B., 1902; and S.T.B., 1904). In 1904, he was ordained to the Unitarian ministry. He was the author of *The Revolutionary Function of the Modern Church* (1912); *Marriage and Divorce* (1913); *Is Death the End?* (1915); *New Wars for Old* (1916); *Religion for Today* (1917); *The Life and Letters of Robert Collyer* (1917); *Readings From Great Authors* (1918); *The Grail of Life* (1919); *Is Violence the Way Out?* (1920); *New Churches for Old* (1922); *Patriotism Is Not Enough* (1925); *Palestine Today and Tomorrow* (1929); *The Heart of Scott's Poetry* (1932); *The Sensible Man's View of Religion* (1933); *Through Gentile Eyes* (1938); *Rethinking Religion* (1938); *Out of Darkness* (1942); *The Second Christmas, and Other Stories* (1943); *The Affirmation of Immortality* (1947); *My Gandhi* (1953); and *I Speak for Myself* (1959). He was co-author of the play *If This Be Treason* (1935). He was editor of Robert Collyer's *Clear Grit* (1914). He was editor of the Unitarian periodicals *Unity* (1921-1946) and *The Unitarian Advance*. He was a contributor to periodicals, including the *New York Herald-Tribune* and the *American Dictionary of National Biography*. He was the recipient of the Ainsfield-Wolf award in 1960 for his *I Speak for Myself*.

From 1904 until 1907, Holmes was minister of the Third Religious Society (Unitarian) of Dorchester, Massachusetts. From 1907 until 1919, he was minister of the Unitarians' Church of the Messiah in New York City. In 1919, he resigned from the Unitarian ministry. He had decided to work as an independent and to reorganize his church as a free society rather than a sectarian church. He changed its name to The Community Church, and he remained as its minister until 1949 when he retired, becoming minister emeritus.

From 1914 until 1938, Holmes traveled frequently and extensively abroad. He visited England, Europe, the Soviet Union, and the Near East. In 1929, he went to Palestine on a special mission for the Zionists, and for his work he received the Annual Gottheil Medal. From 1929 until 1964, he was president of the All-World Gandhi Fellowship. In 1947 and 1948, under the auspices of the Watumull Foundation, he went to India as the Rabindranath Tagore Memorial Professor at Benares University.

Shortly after Holmes assumed his ministry in New York City at the Church of the Messiah, he plunged into what became a lifetime of radicalism. In 1909, he was a founder of the ultra-radical National Association for the Advancement of Colored People; he served as vice president of that organization for fifty-five years. During World War I, he joined America's most prominent Red-oriented pacifists in their protests against war in general, United States preparation for and involvement in World War I, conscription, and prosecution of conscientious objectors and draft evaders. This work involved him in such organizations as the American Union Against Militarism, the Civil Liberties Bureau, and eventually the American Civil Liberties Union, which he served in the highest official capacities from its founding until his death in 1964. He was a long-time top official of the Socialists' League for Industrial Democracy and a member of the Socialist Party. His other affiliations included the All-America Anti-Imperialist League ("the [Communist] Party was wholly responsible for the establishment and subsequent control of the League"); the American Committee for Protection of Foreign Born ("founded by the Communist Party in order to exploit racial divisions in the United States for its own revolutionary purposes"); the American Committee To Save Refugees ("perform[ing] a most valuable function for the international Communist movement"); the American Friends of Spanish Democracy ("Communist front"); the American League Against War and Fascism ("subversive and Communist" – "established in the United States in an effort to create public sentiment on behalf of a foreign policy adapted to the interests of the Soviet Union"); the American League To Limit Armaments (ultra-leftist-pacifist); the American Pushkin Committee ("Communist front"); the Berger National Foundation (Socialist); the Brookwood Labor College ("Communistic"); the Celebration for the Adoption of a New Constitution for the Soviet Union in 1937 (a Communist enterprise); the Church Peace Mission (leftist-oriented); the Citizens Committee To Defend Representative Government ("Communist front"); the Citizens Committee To Free Earl Browder ("a strictly Communist Party affair"); the Committee of Welcome for the Red Dean of Canterbury (England's most notorious pro-Soviet apologist among the clergy); Commonwealth College ("Communist"); the Conference on Peaceful Alternatives to the Atlantic Pact ("initiated by Communists"); the Consumer-Farmer Milk Co-

operative ("Communist front"); the Council Against Intolerance in America (leftist); the Descendants of the American Revolution ("a Communist-front organization set up as a radical imitation of the Daughters of the American Revolution. The Descendants have uniformly adhered to the line of the Communist Party"); the Emergency Committee for Strikers Relief (Socialist); the Emergency Peace Federation (dominated by Socialists); the Federated Unemployed Workers Leagues of New York (pro-Communist); the Fellowship of Reconciliation (ultra-leftist-pacifist); *Fight* ("official organ of the American League Against War and Fascism [American League for Peace and Democracy], subversive and Communist"); Friends of the Soviet Union ("created, directed, and controlled by the Communist Party . . . and operated to aid and support Party objectives concerning the defense and support of the Soviet Union"); the Greater New York Emergency Conference on Inalienable Rights ("Communist front"); Icor ("the aims of Icor have been primarily propagandistic in behalf of the Soviet Union"); *Il Nuovo Mondo* (pro-Communist paper published for Italians in the United States); the International Committee for Political Prisoners (to raise funds for jailed seditionists); the Jewish People's Committee ("subversive and Communist" – "an organization which has been nothing more nor less than an adjunct of the Communist Party"); the Joint Committee on Unemployment (dominated by Socialists); *Labor Age* (militant Socialist publication put out by Abraham J. Muste and Louis Budenz); the Labor Defense Council ("organized for the primary purpose of aiding the Communist defendants in the Michigan criminal syndicalist case in the early days of the

Communist movement in this country"); the League for Amnesty of Political Prisoners (on behalf of Reds and anarchists); the League for Mutual Aid ("Communist enterprise"); the League for the Organization of Progress ("dominated by Communists and Socialists"); the League of American Writers ("subversive and Communist" – "began openly to follow the Communist Party line as dictated by the foreign policy of the Soviet Union"); the Marcus Graham Defense Committee (an ultra-radical group in support of an anarchist); *Messenger* (pro-Soviet publication); the Mid-Century Conference for Peace ("aimed at assembling as many gullible persons possible under Communist direction and turning them into a vast sounding board for Communist propaganda"); the National Committee To Win Amnesty for Smith Act Victims ("subversive" – "Communist"); the National Committee for a Sane Nuclear Policy (ultra-leftist-pacifist); the National Committee To Abolish the Un-American Activities Committee ("to lead and direct the Communist Party's 'Operation Abolition' campaign"); the National Committee To Repeal the McCarran Act ("Communist front" – "subversive"); the National Consumers League (Socialist); the National Council of American-Soviet Friendship ("subversive and Communist" – "specializing in pro-Soviet propaganda"); the National Emergency Conference for Democratic Rights ("Communist front" – "subversive"); the National People's Committee Against Hearst ("subversive and Communist"); the National Religion and Labor Foundation ("Communist front"); the National Student League ("the Communist front organization for students"); *New Masses* ("weekly journal of the Communist Party"); the New York Conference Against War ("Communist front"); the New York Tom Mooney Committee ("Communist front"); the Non-Intervention Citizens Committee (pro-Soviet); a Petition on Behalf of Communist Party Leaders (Communist Party enterprise); Pioneer Youth of American (Socialist); [Luiz Carlos] Prestes Defense Committee (on behalf of a leader of the Communist Party of Brazil – "a Communist front"); Promoting Enduring Peace, Inc. (ultra-leftist-pacifist); Rand School ("a Marxian-Socialist training school for labor agitators"); the Rosenberg Clemency Appeal ("Communist front"); Russian Reconstruction Farms ("Communist enterprise"); the Sacco-Vanzetti National League (part of a Communist propaganda campaign); *Socialist Review* ("official theoretical organ of the Socialist Party"); the Spanish Refugee Relief Campaign ("Communist front"); United World Federalists (the most prestigious group of fellow-travelers and dupes working for world government at the expense of United States sovereignty); the War Resisters League (leftist-pacifist); the Women's International League for Peace and Freedom (ultra-leftist-pacifist); and *World Tomorrow* (Socialist publication).

In 1939, at the time of the Hitler-Stalin Pact, it appeared that after three decades of pro-Soviet – or at least pro-Communist – sympathetic activities and affiliations, Holmes was undergoing a change of heart. In common with so many fellow-travelers, he was utterly confused by the alliance of Stalin with the arch-villain Hitler. Said Holmes: "I am sick over this business as though I saw my father drunk and my daughter on the street. And all the more, since I feel that I have deceived myself as well as been deceived.

"If we liberals were right on certain single aspects of the Russian Revolution, we were wrong, disgracefully wrong, on the question as a whole. We were wrong because, in our enthusiasm over Russia's liberation from the Czar, our hope for the further liberation of the Russian people from economic as well as political serfdom and our vision of a new world springing from the womb of this Russian experiment, we permitted ourselves to condone wrongs that we knew must be wrongs. We consented to violations of principle that we knew to be fatal to the moral integrity of mankind. We defended, or at least apologized for, evils in the case of Russia which horrified us wherever else they appeared, and by whomsoever else they were done. We accepted covertly, if not openly, the most dangerous and ultimately disastrous idea that can lodge within the human mind, namely, that the end justifies the means."

In 1939, many Communists, fellow travelers, and duped liberals deserted the Red cause once and for all. However, Holmes recovered from his shock after a brief spell and resumed his pro-Communist radicalism, which continued until his death in April 1964.

CHARLES HAMILTON HOUSTON was born on September 3, 1895 in Washington, D.C., son of Mary Hamilton and William Houston. His first wife was Margaret Moran. His second wife was Henrietta Williams. He was an alumnus of Amherst College (A.B., 1915) and Harvard University (LL.B., 1922, and S.J.D., 1923). He pursued graduate studies at the University of Madrid as a Sheldon Traveling Fellow. In 1924, he was admitted to the bar of Washington, D.C.

From 1915 until 1917, he taught English at Howard University. From 1924 until 1950, he practiced law in the District of Columbia with Houston and

Houston (1924-1939) and Houston, Houston, Hastie and Waddy (1939-1950). From 1924 until 1935, he was at Howard University's Law School as an instructor in law (1924-1929) and associate professor and vice-dean (1929-1935). From 1933 until 1935, he was a member of the District of Columbia Board of Education. From 1935 until 1950, he was with the ultra-radical National Association for the Advancement of Colored People as special counsel (1935-1940) and member of the national legal aid committee (1940-1950).

Houston's affiliations included the Abolish Peonage Committee ("Communist front"); the African Aid Committee (leftist-racist agitators); the American Committee for Protection of Foreign Born ("founded by the Communist Party in order to exploit racial divisions in the United States for its own revolutionary purposes"); the American Continental Congress for World Peace ("another phase in the Communist 'peace' campaign, aimed at consolidating anti-American forces throughout the Western Hemisphere"); American Friends of Spanish Democracy ("Communist front"); the American Peace Mobilization ("formed . . . under the auspices of the Communist Party and the Young Communist League" – "one of the most seditious organizations which ever operated in the United States"); the Civil Rights Congress ("created and established by the Communist Party as an organization which would utilize defense of civil rights for Party purposes and raise and maintain mass defense and bail funds for Party use"); the Committee for Equal Justice for Mrs. Recy Taylor ("Communist front"); the Committee for Free Political Advocacy ("Communist front"); the Conference on Constitutional Liberties in America

("Communist front"); the Council on African Affairs ("subversive and Communist"): the International Juridical Association ("Communist front" – "an organization which actively defended Communists and consistently followed the Communist Party line"); International Labor Defense ("subversive and Communist" – "legal arm of the Communist Party"); the Lawyers Committee on American Relations with Spain ("during the Spanish Civil War, the Communist Party organized . . . [the Lawyers Committee] as a part of one of its major propaganda campaigns in the Party's entire history in this country"); the National Committee To Abolish the Poll Tax ("Communist front"); the National Committee To Defeat the Mundt Bill ("a Communist lobby . . . which has carried out the objectives of the Communist Party in its fight against anti-subversive legislation"); the National Council of American-Soviet Friendship ("subversive and Communist" – "specializing in pro-Soviet propaganda"); the National Federation for Constitutional Liberties ("under Communist Party domination and headed by responsible Party functionaries" – "one of the viciously subversive organizations of the Communist Party"); the National Lawyers Guild ("the foremost legal bulwark of the Communist Party, its front organizations, and controlled unions"); the National Negro Congress ("subversive and Communist" – "characterized as an organization operating in the field of civil rights under Communist Party domination and headed by responsible Party functionaries"); the National Non-Partisan Committee To Defend the Rights of the 12 Communist Party Leaders (pro-Communist); *New Masses* ("weekly journal of the Communist Party"); the Non-Partisan Committee for the Re-election

of Congressman Vito Marcantonio ("Communist front"); the [Morris U.] Schappes Defense Committee ("a front organization with a strictly Communist objective, namely, the defense of a self-admitted Communist who was convicted of perjury in the Courts of New York"); the United Front for [Angelo] Herndon ("an adjunct to the International Labor Defense, the legal arm of the Communist Party"); Veterans of the Abraham Lincoln Brigade ("directed, controlled, and dominated by the Communist Party"); and the Washington Committee for Democratic Action ("subversive and Communist"). He died in April 1950.

[JAMES] LANGSTON HUGHES was born on February 1, 1902 in Joplin, Missouri, son of Carrie Langston and James Hughes. He was an alumnus of Lincoln University (A.B., 1929). He also attended Columbia University. He was the author of *The Weary Blues* (1926); *Fine Clothes to the Jew* (1927); *Not Without Laughter* (1930); *Dear Lovely Death* (1931); *The Negro Mother* (1931); *The Dream Keeper* (1932); *Scottsboro Limited* (1932); *The Ways of White Folks* (1934); *A New Song* (1938); *The Big Sea* (1940); *Shakespeare in Harlem* (1942); *Freedom's Plow* (1943); *Jim Crow's Last Stand* (1943); *Lament for Dark People and Other Poems* (1944); *Fields of Wonder* (1947); *One-Way Ticket* (1949); *The First Book of Africa* (1950); *Simple Speaks His Mind* (1950); *Montage of a Dream Deferred* (1951); *Laughing to Keep From Crying* (1951); *The First Book of Negroes* (1952); *The First Book of Rhythms* (1954); *Famous American Negroes* (1954); *The First Book of Jazz* (1955); *Famous Negro Music Makers* (1955); *The First Book of the West Indies* (1956); *I Wonder As I Wander*

(1956); *Simple Stakes a Claim* (1957); *Langston Hughes Reader* (1958); *Famous Negro Heroes of America* (1958); *Selected Poems* (1959); *Ask Your Mama* (1961); *The Best of Simple* (1961); *Fight for Freedom: The Story of the NAACP* (1962); *Something in Common, and Other Stories* (1963); *Five Plays* (1963); and *Simple's Uncle Sam* (1965). He was translator of Garcia Lorca's *Gyspy Ballads* (1951) and *Selected Poems of Gabriel Mistral* (1957). He was co-translator of Jacques Roumain's *Masters of Dew* (1957) and Nicolas Guillen's *Cuba Libre* (1957). He was co-author of *Popo and Fifina* (1941); *The Sweet Flypaper of Life* (1955); and *A Pictorial History of the Negro in America* (1956). He was librettist for *The Barrier* (1950) and *Troubled Island* (1959). He was lyricist for *Just Around the Corner* and *Street Scene*. He was editor of *Four Lincoln University Poets* (1930); *An African Treasury* (1960); *Poems From Black Africa* (1963); *New Negro Poets U.S.A.* (1964); *The Book of Negro Humor* (1965); and *The Best Short Stories by Negro Writers* (1967). He was co-editor of *The Poetry of the Negro, 1746-1749* (1949); *Lincoln University Poets* (1954); and *The Book of Negro Folklore* (1958).

Between his studies at Columbia University and his graduation from Lincoln University, Hughes travelled to Europe and Africa as a seaman and worked at odd jobs in Paris, in Italy, and in New York City. From 1926 until his death in 1967, he devoted most of his life to writing poems, plays, novels, short stories, translations, anthologies, motion picture and television scripts, lyrics, and librettoes. A portion of his output was directed toward a juvenile market and a large portion was obviously designed to be pro-Communist propaganda.

One of Hughes' critics wrote: "We acknowledge perforce, that the current mode of fiction, poetry, and plays call for loading the text . . . with depravities, obscenities, and miscellaneous, malodorous barnyard dirt. Hughes goes far beyond the call of duty in piling filth on filth . . . . He is master of the sly and wily innuendo – the remark that is either innocent or guilty, depending on the reader's 'wised up' reaction. This, in the judgment of some mature yet not hidebound guardians of developing intellects, makes the most unworthy, most unrewarding type of reading matter which can be placed in the hands of inquiring youth . . . . The part-time joy and jollity of Hughes, as exemplified particularly in his short stories, are thinly spread over bitter, thrice bitter, bedrock sarcasm and hatred."

One of Hughes' most celebrated poems was the blasphemous *Goodbye, Christ*: "Listen, Christ,/ You did alright in your day, I reckon –/ But that day's gone now./ They ghosted you up a swell story, too,/ Called it Bible – /But it's dead now/ The popes and the preachers've/ Made too much money from it./ Kings, generals, robbers, and killers –/ Even to the Tzar and the Cossacks./ Even to Rockefeller's church./ Even to the Saturday Evening Post./ You ain't no good no more;/ They've pawned you/ Till you've done wore out./ Goodbye,/ Christ Jesus, Lord God Jehovah,/ Beat it on away from here now./ Make way for a new guy with no religion at all –/ A real guy named/ Marx Communist, Lenin Peasant, Stalin Worker, ME – / I said, Me!/ Go ahead on now,/ You're getting in the way of things, Lord./ And please take Saint Gandhi with you when you go/ And Saint Pope Pius/ And Saint Aimee McPherson,/ And big black Saint Becton of the Consecrated Dime./ And step on the gas, Christ!/ Move! /Don't be so slow 'bout movin'!/ The world is mine from now on –/ And nobody's gonna sell ME/ To a king, or a general,/ Or a millionaire."

In his *Ballad of Lenin*, Hughes was effusive in his praise: "Comrade Lenin of Russia/ High in a marble tomb,/ Move over, Comrade Lenin,/ And give me room./ I am Ivan, the peasant,/ Boots all muddy with soil./ I fought with you, Comrade Lenin,/ Now I have finished my toil./ I am Chico, the Negro,/ Cutting cane in the sun./ I lived for you, Comrade Lenin,/ Now my work is done./ I am Chang from the foundries/ On strike in the streets of Shanghai/ For the sake of the Revolution/ I fight, I starve, I die./ Comrade Lenin of Russia/ Rises in the Marble tomb/ On guard with the fighters forever – / The world is our room!"

His admiration for the Soviet Union expressed in *Worker's Song* knew no bounds: "Now across the water in Russia/ They have a big U.S.S.R./ The Fatherland of the Soviets/ But that is mighty far/ From New York or Texas or California too/ So listen fellow-workers/ This is what we have to do./ Put one more S in the U.S.A./ To make it Soviet./ One more S in the U.S.A./ Oh, we'll live to see it yet/ When the land belongs to the farmers/ And the factories belong to the workingmen –/ The U.S.A. when we take control/ Will be the U.S.S.A. then."

In 1932 and 1933, Hughes was in the Soviet Union. He claimed that he was there to aid in the writing of a scenario on Negro life for a film being made in Moscow. It was at that very time that Communist leaders in the Soviet Union were playing host to many American Negroes who were trained to be leaders for the Communist Party in the United States. In 1936 and 1937, Hughes' sympathies for the Reds in the Spanish Civil War caused him to be a correspondent in Madrid for the *Baltimore Afro-American*. In 1931 and 1932, he lectured at Negro schools and colleges in the southern states. In 1947, he was a visiting professor in creative writing at Atlanta University. In 1949, he was a poet-in-residence at the University of Chicago. He was a contributing editor to Atlanta University's *Phylon* journal.

Hughes accumulated many awards and honors, including the Palms Intercollegiate Poetry Award; the *Opportunity* magazine Poetry Prize; the Harmon Prize and Gold Medal; a Guggenheim Fellowship for creative work; a Rosenwald Fellowship; a grant-in-aid from the American Academy of Arts and Letters; and the National Association for the Advancement of Colored People's Spingarn Medal.

While Hughes was alive, he went no further in admissions than to say that for a period of time he had pro-Communist sympathies. He testified before the Permanent Subcommittee on Government Operations in 1953 when it was under the chairmanship of U.S. Senator Joseph R. McCarthy. Hughes was asked whether or not there was ever a period of time in his life when he believed in the Soviet form of government. He said that there had been a period when he was sympathetic with Soviet ideology. He said the period began coincidental with the Scottsboro case and the American depression. It continued for some 10 or 12 years or more – "certainly up to the Nazi-Soviet Pact, and perhaps, in relation to some aspects of the Soviet ideology, further, because we were allies, as you know, with the Soviet Union during the war. So some aspects of my writing would reflect that relationship, that war relationship." Hughes estimated that his complete break with the Soviet ideology occurred in approximately 1948 or 1949.

Hughes never would admit membership in the Communist Party and after his death his apologists would never go further than to indicate that he had undergone a period of sympathy toward some Communist-line positions. However, two former officials, Louis Budenz and Manning Johnson, testified under oath that they knew Hughes to be a member of the Communist Party. As early as 1944, the House Special Committee on Un-American Activities described Hughes as a card-holding member of the Communist Party.

Hughes' affiliations included the All-America Anti-Imperialist League ("the [Communist] Party was wholly responsible for the establishment and subsequent control of the League"); the American Labor Party ("Communist dissimulation extends into the field of political parties forming political front organizations such as the . . . American Labor Party"); the American League Against War and Fascism ("subversive and Communist" − "established in the United States in an effort to create public sentiment on behalf of a foreign policy adapted to the interests of the Soviet Union"); the American League for Peace and Democracy ("subversive and Communist" − "established . . . in an effort to create public sentiment on behalf of a foreign policy adapted to the interests of the Soviet Union . . . [and] designed to conceal Communist control, in accordance with the new tactics of the Communist International"); the American Peace Mobilization ("formed . . . under the auspices of the Communist Party and the Young Communist League" − "one of the most seditious organizations which ever operated in the United States"); the American Pushkin Committee ("Communist front"); the American Revolutionary Writers ("subversive and Communist"); the American-Russian Institute ("subversive" − "Communist" − "specializing in pro-Soviet propaganda"); the American Student Union ("without exception . . . supported defense of teachers and students charged with Communist activity" − "pliable instrument in the hands of the Communist Party"); American Youth for Democracy ("subversive and Communist" − "part of Soviet psychological warfare against the United States"); the Anti-Nazi Federation of New York ("Communist front"); *Anvil* ("distinctly a Communist publication" − "managed and edited by Communists, and most of its contributors were publicly attached to the Communist movement"); the Artists' League of America ("Communist front"); Arts, Sciences and Professions for May Day (Communist enterprise); the Book Union ("distributors of Communist literature" − "Communist [Party] book club"); the Celebration for the Adoption of a New Constitution for the Soviet Union in 1937 (Communist enterprise); *Champion* ("official organ of the Young Communist League and the International Workers Order"); the Civil Rights Congress ("created and established by the Communist Party as an organization which would utilize defense of civil rights for Party purposes and raise and maintain mass defense and bail funds for Party use"); the Committee for a Democratic Far Eastern Policy ("Communist"); the Committee for Peaceful Alternatives to the Atlantic Pact ("a Communist front organization . . . as part of Soviet psychological warfare against the United States"); the Committee for the Re-election of Benjamin J. Davis (a Communist Party candidate for political office); the Committee of Professional Groups for [Earl] Browder and [James W.] Ford ("Communist candidates for president and vice president" of the United States); the Committee To Defend Don West ("Communist front"); the Coordinating Committee To Lift the [Spanish] Embargo ("one of the numerous Communist-front enterprises which were organized around the Communists' agitation over the Spanish Civil War"); the Council for the Advancement of the Americas (ultra-leftist); the Council for Pan-American Democracy ("subversive and Communist"); the Cultural and Scientific Conference for World Peace ("Communist front" — "a propaganda front for Soviet foreign policy and Soviet culture"); *Daily Worker* ("official organ of the Communist Party"); *Dynamo* ("a journal of revolutionary poetry published by Communists"); Friends of the Abraham Lincoln Brigade ("completely controlled by the Communist Party"); Friends of the Soviet Union ("created, directed, and controlled by the Communist Party . . . and operated to aid and support Party objectives concerning the defense and support of the Soviet Union"); the Golden Book of American Friendship with the Soviet Union ("pro-Soviet propaganda enterprise"); the Independent Citizens Committee of the Arts, Sciences and Professions ("Communist front"); the International Labor Defense ("subversive and Communist" — "legal arm of the Communist Party" — "part of an international network of organizations for the defense of Communist lawbreakers"); *International Literature* ("official organ of the International Union of Revolutionary Writers, a Communist front"); the International Work-

ers Order ("from its very inception demonstrated by its pronouncements, its activities, and the authoritative statements of the Communist Party that it is a subservient instrument of the Communist Party of the United States"); the John Reed Clubs ("out-and-out Communist organizations which preceded the contemporary Communist front organizations which cater to so-called liberals"); the Joint Anti-Fascist Refugee Committee ("subversive and Communist"); *Labor Defender* ("Communist magazine"); the League of American Writers ("subversive and Communist" — "began openly to follow the Communist Party line as dictated by the foreign policy of the Soviet Union"); the League of Professional Groups for [William Z.] Foster and [James W.] Ford ("the members of this organization were committed to the objectives of the Communist Party"); the League of Struggle for Negro Rights ("Communist Negro organization"); *Masses and Mainstream* ("a Communist magazine"); the Medical Bureau and North American Committee to Aid Spanish Democracy ("subversive and un-American"); *Midwest Daily Record* ("Communist publication"); the National Citizens Political Action Committee ("Communist front"); the National Committee for the Defense of Political Prisoners ("subversive and Communist"); the National Committee for People's Rights ("composed primarily of openly avowed members of the Communist Party and veteran fellow travelers of the Communist Party"); the National Committee To Aid the Victims of German Fascism ("an auxiliary of the Communist Party"); the National Council of American-Soviet Friendship ("subversive and Communist" — "specializing in pro-Soviet propaganda"); the National Emergency Conference for Democratic Rights

("Communist front" – "subversive"); the National Federation for Constitutional Liberties ("under Communist Party domination and headed by responsible Party functionaries" – "one of the viciously subversive organizations of the Communist Party"); the National Institute of Arts and Letters ("Communist front"); the National Negro Congress ("subversive and Communist" – "characterized as an organization operating in the field of civil rights under Communist Party domination and headed by responsible Party functionaries"); the National Writers Congress ("Communist front"); the Negro Cultural Committee ("Communist front"); the Negro Playwrights Co., Inc. ("Communist front"); *Negro Quarterly* ("Communist publication"); *New Order* ("official organ of the International Workers Order, subversive and Communist"); *New Masses* ("weekly journal of the Communist Party"); *New Theatre* ("Communist Party publication"); the New Theatre League ("Communist front"); the Non-Partisan Committee for the Re-election of Congressman Vito Marcantonio ("Communist front"); the Non-Sectarian Committee for Political Refugees ("affiliate of the International Labor Defense, the legal arm of the Communist Party"); an Open Letter for Closer Cooperation with the Soviet Union (issued by "a group of Communist Party stooges"); *Partisan* ("semi-monthly publication of the John Reed Clubs"); People's Radio Foundation ("subversive and Communist organization"); People's Songs ("subversive"); the Reichstag Fire Trial Anniversary Committee ("Communist front . . . formed . . . by prominent Communists and Communist sympathizers"); the San Francisco Labor School ("Communist"); the [Morris U.] Schappes Defense Committee ("a front organization with a

strictly Communist objective, namely, the defense of a self-admitted Communist who was convicted of perjury in the courts of New York"); the School for Democracy ("established by Communist teachers ousted from the public school system of New York City"); the Southern Conference for Human Welfare ("a Communist-front organization which seeks to attract southern liberals on the basis of its seeming interest in the problems of the South"); the Southern Negro Youth Congress ("subversive and among the affiliates and committees of the Communist Party, USA, which seeks to alter the form of government of the United States by unconstitutional means"); *Soviet Russia Today* ("the leading propaganda journal for the Soviet Union in the United States"); Statement by American Progressives on the Moscow Trials ("obviously a document concocted in defense of the line of the Communist Party and undoubtedly originated in the headquarters of the Communist Party"); *Sunday Worker* ("Communist Party newspaper"); the United States Congress Against War and Fascism ("completely under the control of the Communist Party"); Veterans of the Abraham Lincoln Brigade ("directed, dominated and controlled by the Communist Party"); Voice of Freedom Committee ("subversive" – to defend pro-Communist radio commentators); the Workers Cultural Federation (Communist revolutionary cultural groups); *Workers Monthly* ("official organ of the Workers Party" – "Communist"); and the Writers and Artists Committee for Medical Aid to Spain ("a Communist front set up for the purpose of agitation and propaganda").

One of Hughes' last major works for the far left was his book *Fight for Freedom: The Story of the NAACP,* published in 1962. Hughes wrote: "Attempts to label the NAACP subversive, Communist-influenced, or out-and-out Communist have continued for a long time. The late Negro professional witness, ex-Communist Manning Johnson, since discredited, testified before two southern legislative committees to the effect that the NAACP was 'a vehicle of the Communist Party designed to overthrow the government of the United States.' " (Johnson was not a professional witness but a genuinely repentant American who, from his years as a top Negro Communist, testified accurately before, and cooperated fully with, federal and state investigating committees and agencies. He was discredited only by the Communist Party, its fellow travelers, and its dupes. He did identify Hughes as a Communist. He did testify as to the Communist character of the NAACP, since he was assigned the job of bringing Negro organizations into the Communist orbit.) Hughes, however, in his whitewash of the NAACP (which had conferred its highest award – the Spingarn Medal – upon him in 1960), wrote: "Utterly disregarding the truth, these malicious and irresponsible accusations ignore evidence, so clearly on the record, that the NAACP is not and was not Communist and has never even remotely been under Communist influence. Since its earliest years, its top officials from Joel Spingarn and James Weldon Johnson to Walter White and Roy Wilkins have attacked communism in no uncertain terms in both speaking and writing . . . [and] until recently, the official Communist program for Negroes called for the establishment of a separate Negro nation, an idea that was directly opposite to the NAACP's philosophy of integration." (Spingarn and Johnson were officials when the NAACP was receiving grants from the Garland Fund, the outfit which was created to finance Communist enterprises. White, as George Schuyler noted, worked hand-in-hand with the Communists. Wilkins, on the NAACP's staff since 1931, went out of his way to praise the Communist Party for the help it gave to the Negroes. And, from 1937 until 1949, Wilkins was affiliated with a number of Communist fronts and enterprises. He did become somewhat discreet after 1949 [in 1949 and 1950, he was acting executive secretary and, since 1955, he has been the executive secretary of the NAACP], but in 1965 he joined with notorious Communist leaders to memorialize the deceased Communist W.E.B. DuBois. And, Hughes conveniently forgot that the Communists and the NAACP set aside temporarily the idea of a separate Negro nation only because American Negro masses simply showed no interest in such a separation.)

Hughes died in May 1967. He was eulogized in the liberal and Communist press with just about equal sentimentality. The Communists, even after his death and long after he had allegedly severed all of his connections with the Communist movement, continued to promote his writings in their publications and their bookshops.

ELLSWORTH HUNTINGTON was born on September 16, 1876 in Galesburg, Illinois, son of Mary Herbert and Henry Huntington. He married Rachel Brewer. He was an alumnus of Beloit College (A.B., 1897); Harvard University (A.M., 1902); and Yale University (Ph.D., 1909). He was the author of *Explorations in Turkestan*, two volumes (1905); *The Pulse of Asia* (1907); *Asia – A Geography Reader* (1912); *Palestine and Its Transformation* (1911); *The Cli-*

matic Factor, As Illustrated in Arid America (1914); *Civilization and Climate* (1915 and 1924); *World Power and Evolution* (1919); *Red Man's Continent* (1919); *Earth and Sun* (1923); *The Character of Races* (1924); *West of the Pacific* (1925); *Quaternary Climates* (1925); *The Pulse of Progress* (1926); *The Human Habitat* (1927); *Tomorrow's Children – The Goal of Eugenics* (1935); *Season of Birth* (1938); *Principles of Economic Geography* (1940); and *Mainsprings of Civilization* (1945). He was co-author of *Principles of Human Geography* (1920); *Business Geography* (1922); *Climatic Changes* (1922); *Modern Business Geography* (1924); *The Builders of America* (1927); *Living Geography* (1932); *Economic and Social Geography* (1933); *After Three Centuries* (1934); *Europe* (1935); and *Geography in Human Affairs* (1947).

From 1897 until 1901, Huntington was an instructor and the president's assistant at Euphrates College in Harput, Turkey. In 1901, he explored the canyons of the Euphrates River, and for this work received the Gill Memorial from the Royal Geographical Society of London. In 1903 and 1904, he was a member of the Pumpelly Expedition to Russian Turkestan. In 1905 and 1906, he was a member of the Barrett Expedition to Chinese Turkestan, and for this work was awarded the Maunoir Medel of the Geographical Society of Paris and the Club Medal of the Harvard Travelers Club. In 1906 and 1907, he was a non-resident Hooper Fellow of Harvard University. From 1907 until 1947, he was on the faculty of Yale University as instructor in geography (1907-1910); assistant professor (1910-1915); research associate in geography with the rank of professor (1917-1947); and professor emeritus (1945-1947). In 1909, he made

an expedition to Asia Minor, Palestine, and the Syrian Desert as a representative of Yale University and a special correspondent for *Harper's* magazine. From 1910 until 1914, he was a research associate for the Carnegie Institution and made climatic investigations in the United States, Mexico, and Central America. He was an associate editor of *Geographical Review, Economic Geography*, and *Ecology and Social Philosophy*. He was president of the Association of American Geographers (1923), the Ecological Society of America (1917), and the American Eugenics Society.

Huntington was affiliated with the American Committee for Democracy and Intellectual Freedom ("subversive and un-American" – "a Communist-front organization operating among college teachers and professors"); the American Committee To Save Refugees ("perform[ing] a most valuable function for the international Communist movement"); the American Rescue Ship Mission ("Communist Party project"); the Citizens Committee To Free Earl Browder ("a strictly Communist Party affair"); the Citizens Victory Committee for Harry Bridges ("Communist front"); the Civil Rights Congress ("created and established by the Communist Party as an organization which would utilize defense of civil rights for Party purposes and raise and maintain mass defense and bail funds for Party use"); the Council for Pan-American Democracy ("subversive and Communist"); the Independent Citizens Committee of the Arts, Sciences and Professions ("Communist front"); the International Labor Defense ("subversive and Communist" – "legal arm of the Communist Party" – "part of an international network of organizations for the defense of Communist lawbreakers"); the National Emergency Conference for Democratic Rights ("Communist front" – "subversive"); the National Federation for Constitutional Liberties ("under Communist Party domination and headed by responsible Party functionaries" – "one of the viciously subversive organizations of the Communist Party"); *New Masses* ("weekly journal of the Communist Party"); and Veterans of the Abraham Lincoln Brigade ("directed, dominated and controlled by the Communist Party"). He died in October 1947.

DAVID DALLAS JONES was born on November 19, 1887 in Greensboro, North Carolina, son of Mary Jane Holley and Sidney Jones. He married Susie Williams. He was an alumnus of Wesleyan University (B.A., 1911) and Columbia University (M.A., 1930). He was a student at the University of Chicago in the summers of 1912 and 1913.

From 1911 until 1914, Jones was a secretary with the International Committee of the YMCA in New York City. From 1914 until 1923, he was executive secretary of the YMCA in St. Louis. From 1923 until 1925, he was a general field agent for the Commission on Interracial Cooperation. In 1926, the Methodist Church asked Jones to re-organize Bennett College, a Negro co-educational institution, into a women's college. From 1926 until his retirement in 1955, he was president of Bennett College. He was a member of the school board in Greensboro, North Carolina. He was president of the National Association of Schools and Colleges of the Methodist Church. He was active in the leftist-oriented National Council of Churches.

Jones was affiliated with the Civil Rights Congress ("created and established by the Communist Party as an organization which would utilize defense of civil rights for Party purposes and raise and maintain mass defense and bail funds for Party use"); the Council on African Affairs ("subversive and Communist"); the Cultural and Scientific Conference for World Peace ("Communist front" – "a propaganda front for Soviet foreign policy and Soviet culture"); the Methodist Federation for Social Action ("the organization's influence has been consistently wielded on behalf of Communist causes and the Communist line as expressed through the party and its innumerable subsidiaries"); the National Committee To Repeal the McCarran Act ("Communist front" – "subversive"); the National Council of the Arts, Sciences, and Professions ("a Communinist front used to appeal to special occupational groups"); the National Federation for Constitutional Liberties ("under Communist Party domination and headed by responsible Party functionaries" – "one of the viciously subversive organizations of the Communist Party"); the National Negro Congress ("subversive and Communist" – "characterized as an organization operating in the field of civil rights under Communist Party domination and headed by responsible Party functionaries"); the [Morris U.] Schappes Defense Committee ("a front organization with a strictly Communist objective, namely, the defense of a self-admitted Communist who was convicted of perjury in the courts of New York"); the Southern Conference for Human Welfare ("a Communist-front organization which seeks to attract Southern liberals on the basis of its seeming interest in the problems of the South"); and the Southern Negro Youth Congress ("subversive and among the affiliates and committees of the Communist Party, USA, which seeks to alter the form of government of the

United States by unconstitutional means"). He died in January 1956.

ARTHUR KALLET was born on December 15, 1902 in Syracuse, New York, son of Etta Kaplan and Barnett Kallet. He was married to the late Opal Boston. His second wife was Mary Fitzpatrick. He was an alumnus of Massachusetts Institute of Technology (B.S., 1924). He was the author of *Counterfeit: Not Your Money but What It Buys* (1935). He was co-author of *100,000,000 Guinea Pigs* (1933).

From 1924 to 1927, Kallet did editorial work for the New York Edison Company. From 1927 until 1934, he was editor of *Industrial Standardization* for the American Standards Association. From 1929 until 1932, he was in the publicity department of the New York Regional Plan Association. From 1932 until 1935, he was secretary of Consumers Research, Inc. From 1936 until 1957, he was founder and director of Consumers Union. From 1958 to 1972, he was executive director of *The Medical Letter*. From 1958 until 1972, he was president of Drug and Therapeutics Information, Inc. From 1961 until 1972, he was president of Buyers Laboratory, Inc.

In "Where Are They Now?" in *Newsweek* (January 22, 1968), Kallet was described as a "muckraker" of the thirties. *Newsweek* said: "He [Kallet] has not spoken to co-author [Frederick J.] Schlink since 1935 when they were both on the staff at Consumer Research. The magazine was in the midst of a bitter strike, and Kallet sided with the strikers, Schlink with management." In an obituary of Kallet on February 26, 1972, the *New York Times* said: "In the early nineteen-thirties, he [Kallet] worked as secretary of Consumers Research, Inc.,

where Mr. Schlink was technical director. In a strike there in 1935, however, he sided with the strikers and broke with Mr. Schlink." In *Odyssey of a Fellow Traveler*, J.B. Matthews, who would serve for many years as director of research for the House Special Committee on Un-American Activities, wrote about the breaches which occurred between him, as a fellow-traveler, and the Communists. One breach of which he wrote "was based primarily on the ethical grounds [and] occurred in the summer and fall of 1935 in connection with a so-called strike at Consumers Research.

"For a number of years, I had been a member of the board of directors of Consumers' Research and also its vice-president. Early in the history of that organization, I became acquainted with its founder and present president, F.J. Schlink. Consumers' Research as conceived and administered by Schlink is an organization engaged in making comparative ratings of consumers' goods and in publishing these ratings as a confidential service to ultimate consumers. Whatever may have been the political viewpoints of some of us who were connected with Consumers' Research, the only political view which could possibly be implicit in the organization's own nature and functioning is one which presupposes an economic system of free, private, and competitive enterprise. Under a totalitarian or collectivist state in which politicians assume all control over the production and distribution of goods, there could not and would not be tolerated any independent agency for testing and rating consumers' goods. Under a communist state, there are no competing brands whose relative merits may be considered. All the evils long associated with monopoly are present in the highest possible degree in a society where the state becomes the absolute monopolist — the lone capitalist, if you please — in production and distribution.

"For many years, the communists took the position that consumers as such could not be organized for revolutionary purposes. It neglected, therefore, to set up any united fronts whose purpose was to exploit consumers' interests, on behalf of Moscow. In 1935, this position was reversed and the communists decided to launch a whole new series of united front organizations for consumers . . . . Arthur Kallet and Susan Jenkins were the Party's advisors-extraordinary in this enterprise of gulling consumers into the peripheral movements of communism.

"In a prospectus of the *People's Press*, a radical paper of which he is one of the editors, Arthur Kallet was described as the 'leader' of the strike at Consumers' Research. Kallet, in turn, described Susan Jenkins as the leader of the same strike, in an article which he wrote for the *New Masses* of September 17, 1935. The fact was that the two of them were co-leaders of the strike.

"Kallet denies publicly that he is a member of the Communist Party; and he told me under circumstances which would lead me to place complete credence in his statement that he did not carry a Party card. At the same time, he assured me that he took his 'political directives' from the Party. In connection with launching the Communist Party into the field of consumer agitation, Kallet informed me that he had been in frequent touch with a certain Mr. Siskind whom he described as the Communist Party organizer for New York City. I had not heard at the time (July 7, 1935), of any one by the name of Siskind who was among the high functionaries of the Communist Party, but I have since learned from the *Daily Worker* (January 3, 1935), that a George Siskind was known officially as 'agit-prop director of the New York District of the Communist Party.'

"Whether Kallet holds a Party membership card or not is of no special significance. The cumulative evidence of his public statements and activities leaves no doubt about his being a communist in his views or about his closeness to the Communist Party. In a statement on consumer cooperatives which he wrote for publication, he said: 'Cooperation does provide a splendid escape from participation in the day to day struggles against the capitalist system; it permits a great many people to express their resentment by "playing store." But the emphasis is not on "tomorrow a new society" but "tomorrow maybe we'll be able to begin paying dividends." As consumer cooperatives are generally run they are a business, not a revolution.'

"The foregoing view of Kallet's was the orthodox Communist Party position on consumer cooperatives at the time it was written. Since that time, however, the Party has changed its 'line' on the subject, and Kallet has altered his view accordingly. Both have been busily engaged in recent years in an effort to bring consumer cooperatives within the Party's united front movement. In some instances, they have had notable success. Nevertheless, the statement which I have quoted from Kallet is a clear exposition of communist ideology and should leave no doubt concerning its author's political allegiances.

"One of the Communist Party's numerous united front publications is a magazine called *Health & Hygiene*. Kallet is currently listed in this magazine as a member of its editorial board.

"In the November, 1937, issue of

Scribner's magazine, Don Wharton wrote an article on Kallet, in which he said: 'He [Kallet] will tell anyone that he dislikes our economic system, that he feels it is doomed, and that he hopes the Russian experiment works out so well that we shall be compelled to adopt it. He denies that he is a member of the Communist Party and so does many a man whose name is right there on the party rolls.'

"In the February, 1938, issue of *Scribner's*, Kallet published a reply to Wharton's article, but nowhere in his reply did he repudiate, directly or indirectly, this description of his communist views and hopes.

"In the December, 1937, issue of *Sales Management*, Kallet was quoted as saying that he was a 'New Dealer 'way over on the left.' That is as good a description of present-day communists as one can find. It fits Earl Browder as well as it does Kallet.

"The first strike-office which Kallet opened in New York at the time of his attempt to capture Consumers' Research was at the headquarters of the *New Masses*, known to all as a Communist Party weekly publication.

"Shortly after the calling of the strike at Consumers' Research, Kallet held what was called a 'public trial' of F.J. Schlink and me in Town Hall in New York. Heywood Broun was named as 'presiding judge' and Vito Marcantonio as 'prosecuting attorney.' It is a matter of public knowledge that Broun and Marcantonio are fellow travelers of the Communist Party.

"When Kallet proposed a list of names of persons to act as investigators or arbitrators of the strike at Consumers' Research, he included, along with those of well-known fellow travelers, the name of Clarence Hathaway, editor of the *Daily Worker*. Norman Thomas was irate at my refusal to accept any of the names which Kallet had presented.

"Among the sponsors whom Kallet chose to adorn the letterhead of the western branch of his present communist united front, Consumers Union, was Harry Bridges.

"I have gone into the documentary evidence of Kallet's relation to the Communist Party at some length, because it is not possible otherwise to indicate clearly that I had my final break with the Communist Party over the issue of the strike at Consumers' Research.

"Susan Jenkins, Kallet's co-leader in the strike, admitted under cross-examination in the Chancery Court of New Jersey that she had worked for the *Daily Worker*, and further that she had omitted to state this fact in her application for employment at Consumers' Research.

"Among other ends which Kallet and Susan Jenkins had in view in furthering the work of the Communist Party in the field of consumer agitation, was the capture of Consumers' Research as an auxiliary for the Party. Kallet maintained, however, that it would be necessary to eliminate F.J. Schlink from the organization in order to do this, or at least to deprive him of his dominant control over it. Kallet alleged that Schlink was a fascist.

"Occupying the influential position which was mine in the many united fronts of the Communist Party, as well as my position in Consumers' Research, I was naturally called into the deliberations to lay plans for eliminating Schlink. I refused, and refused with emphasis, to go along in the scheme. ... At no time in my numerous left-wing political activities did I consciously engage in any of the conspiratorial moves to wreck or seize control of other organizations. I believed in a genuine united front of all radical groups and persons, not in united front ruses such as characterize the history of the Communist Party from its beginnings.

"I was duly warned by Kallet and others that a campaign of character assassination would follow my refusal to serve the Communist Party in the manner proposed. Sheer decency, even revolutionary decency as I conceived it, left me no course but to fight Kallet's move to capture Consumers' Research. I continued up until the moment that the strike was called to hope that my high standing with Communist Party leaders would cause Kallet to hesitate in carrying out his plan.

"Nevertheless, the strike was called on the pretext that three employees at Consumers' Research who had written contracts for temporary jobs with the organization had received notice of the termination of their employment on account of their union activities. Two of them had contracts which expired at the end of the summer and the usual routine notices, three weeks in advance of the date of expiration of these contracts, were sent them. The third man was employed on a six months' trial basis, and, having been found unsatisfactory, he, too, received the usual advance notice of the termination of his contract. The union under the leadership of Kallet and Susan Jenkins demanded the reinstatement of these three men on the ground, as Miss Jenkins herself stated on the stand at the hearings of the NLRB, that 'human rights' took precedence over 'the fact that under the terms of their contract, Consumers' Research had a right to dismiss them when they did.' Despite this frank and unqualified admission on the part of Susan Jenkins, the

National Labor Relations Board eventually ordered the reinstatement of these three men (as well as all those who had gone on strike) and the payment to them of $3,106.75 as back salary . . . .

"At least two of these contracts for temporary employment were signed before the law which set up the National Labor Relations Board was enacted. The NLRB, therefore, assumed the power to alter a contractual relationship which existed prior to its own being. It is clear enough that the NLBR brushed aside all questions of the legality of these contracts and entered the business of falsely imputing motives for whose existence there was not the slightest evidence.

"As a matter of fact, not one of the three men or any of the strikers was ever reinstated. Furthermore, the sum of $3,106.75 which the NLRB ordered paid as back salary to the three men was never paid. In an eventual settlement of the case out of court, there were discussions – no written evidence – to the effect that two of the three men should receive $50 each. According to the letter of settlement, it was stated that this claim of $3,106.75 'has been amicably adjusted by the payment of $1,500, which also covers other matters.' The clause, 'which also covers other matters,' meant that the three men were to receive a sum whose lower and upper limits were one cent and $1,499.99. How much of the $1,500 was for the 'other matters,' and what were the 'other matters'? The answer to these two questions is left, so far as the letter of settlement is concerned, in Stygian darkness. Naturally, the question now arises as to why a government agency spent thousands of dollars in 'defense of workers' rights' and ultimately agreed to a settlement which left the amount of the material compensation to the allegedly wronged workers in complete darkness somewhere below the level of $1,500. That question, too, is easy to answer. The Communists set out to take over a consumers' organization or, failing in that, to organize one of their own united front maneuvres to draw consumers, as such, into the sphere of the Communist Party's influence. By the time the above settlement was made, the communists had already failed completely in their first alternative and had succeeded in the other. Their own united front for consumers was functioning, and there was, therefore, no longer any useful service which the NLRB could perform for them by attempting to enforce its preposterous order. Such are the ways of the Communist Party, and such the ways of government in this new age of the abundant life!

"Rarely have I derived more satisfaction from a job than that which I experienced in helping to defeat the communist conspiracy to capture effective control of Consumers' Research. I had not at any time considered myself a permanent member of the organization's staff, but when Kallet and Susan Jenkins cooked up their little plot to take over the organization I remained on the staff long enough to see the matter through to its final conclusion. When the settlement was finally made, I offered my resignation immediately, and on June 30, 1938, I severed my staff connections."

In 1944, the House Special Committee on Un-American Activities reported: "Consumers Union was founded in the winter of 1935-36. Arthur Kallet was the real founder of the organization and has remained its active head from the beginning until the present time. Kallet's Communist Party alias was 'Edward Adams.' Under that alias, he appeared as editor of the magazine *Health and Hygiene*. Oddly enough, while using the

alias 'Edward Adams,' one of Kallet's professed passions was the correct labeling of goods. He has appeared many times before congressional committees to attack manufacturers and advertisers for misleading labels on their wares. When *Health and Hygiene* was first published, it carried on its masthead the line 'Magazine of the Daily Worker Medical Advisory Board.' The *Daily Worker* was the official newspaper of the Communist Party.

"The history of Consumers Union is largely the story of Arthur Kallet. After his collaboration on the famous best seller, *100,000,000 Guinea Pigs*, the Communist Party looked upon Kallet as its chief representative in the party's effort to exploit the grievances of consumers. As an author, Kallet was invited to participate in the founding of the Congress of American Revolutionary Writers, which later became the League of American Writers. In issuing the call to the Congress of American Revolutionary Writers, Kallet signed his name to the following declaration: 'The capitalist system crumbles so rapidly before our eyes that, whereas ten years ago scarcely more than a handful of writers were sufficiently far-sighted and courageous to take a stand for proletarian revolution, today hundreds of poets, novelists, dramatists, critics, short story writers and journalists recognize the necessity of personally helping to accelerate the destruction of capitalism and the establishment of a workers' government.' (*Daily Worker*, January 18, 1935, p. 5.) Earl Browder himself was one of Kallet's cosigners of the foregoing statement. It is obvious, of course, that everyone who signed the statement was, in every proper sense of the word, a Communist.

"Aside from the use of the alias 'Edward Adams,' Kallet made little or no effort to conceal his closeness to the Communist Party. The *Daily Worker* (December 21, 1935, p. 3) carried a two-column spread entitled 'Introducing the Staff.' The staff referred to was the staff of the *Sunday Worker*, which was the Sunday edition of the Communist Party's *Daily Worker*. Arthur Kallet's name appeared on the staff of the *Sunday Worker*.

"In 1935, Kallet published his book entitled *Counterfeit*. In this book, he openly advertised his political philosophy as one which aimed at the abolition of the American system of privately owned industry, and hinted rather directly that Soviet Russia was his pattern for a new American system. *Counterfeit* dealt chiefly with private competitive brands of goods and, of course, advocated their abolition. A system of grade labeling was offered as a substitute.

"In recent years there has been considerable agitation for the introduction of a system of grade labeling. On May 8, 1943, the Office of Price Administration promulgated order MPR-339 which required the extensive use of grade labeling. Immediately (May 10 to June 8, 1943, and June 14-30, 1943), the Interstate Commerce Committee of the House of Representatives held open hearings on the Office of Price Administration's order. As a result of these hearings, a provision was included in the House appropriations bill which prohibited the Office of Price Administration's carrying out its order for grade labeling. More than from any other individual, the agitation which had led the Office of Price Administration to require grade labeling stemmed from Arthur Kallet and his little group of Communist-controlled 'consumer' organizations. In assessing the real purposes of these organizations, it is well to place quotation marks around the word 'consumer.' The Attorney General, Mr. Francis Biddle, has called attention in his order for the deportation of Harry Bridges to the fact that Communist-front organizations have on the one hand an ostensible aim which is used to deceive the unwary and on the other hand an ultimate aim which is the Communist aim of revolution.

"Kallet has been directly and personally involved in the setting up of what Lenin called 'a solar system of organizations around the party'; only in Kallet's case these organizations have for the most part been allegedly devoted in one way or another to the interests of the consumer. Among the 'solar system' of 'consumer' organizations in which Kallet has had a hand as founder, official, or adviser are the following: Consumers Union; *Health and Hygiene*; League of Women Shoppers; Milk Consumers Protective Committee; Consumer-Farmer Milk Cooperative; Coordinating Committee Against the High Cost of Living; Amerian Investors Union; Consumers National Federation; and New York State Conference on National Unity.

"Consumers Union grew directly out of a strike at Consumers Research in 1935. The organizer of the strike was one Susan Jenkins who had formerly been an employee of the *Daily Worker*, and so testified before the chancery court in the State of New Jersey. Negotiations prior to the strike were carried on with the management of Consumers Research by Susan Jenkins and Walter Trumbull, the latter having obtained credentials as a union organizer. Trumbull was the Communist who was court-martialed while in the United States Army and sentenced to 40 years for carrying on Communist propaganda among the armed forces (sentence later reduced).

"Consumers Union has a small labor advisory board which includes among its members the following: Ben Gold, publicly avowed Communist Party member and president of the International Fur and Leather Workers Union; Louis Weinstock, member of the national committee of the Communist Political Association; and Michael Quill, president of the Transport Workers Union, who has been identified by numerous witnesses as a member of the Communist Party.

"Much of the advertising of Consumers Union in its campaign for members has been run in the Communist press. It has run numerous ads in the *Daily Worker*, the *New Masses, Soviet Russia Today*, and *Fight* (official magazine of the American League for Peace and Democracy).

"Harry Bridges was one of the sponsors of the west coast branch of Consumers Union. Helen Gahagan Douglas and Donald Ogden Stewart, also on the west coast, have been active in Consumers Union. Robert A. Brady and Goodwin Watson, both removed from high Government positions recently on charges of Communist activity, have been members of the board of directors of Consumers Union. A check of the sponsors of Consumers Union will show an extensive interlocking directorate with Communist-front organizations.

"Kallet's objectives for Consumers Union may be judged by his own words published in his book *Counterfeit* in the same year he founded Consumers Union. In that volume, he wrote as follows: 'Goods counterfeiting cannot be ended so long as it pays; that is, so long as industry is privately owned and profits are the motivating force behind production, and to suggest any easy remedy would be to offer only one more counterfeit to consumers . . . . The reader may ask the pertinent question as to how completely goods counterfeiting has been eliminated along with private industry in Soviet Russia.'

"In January 1942 the Pennsylvania Commonwealth counsel cited Consumers Union as a Communist-front organization before the reviewing board of the Philadelphia County Board of Assistance.

"In 1943 the joint fact-finding committee in its report to the Fifty-Fifth California Legislature (p. 102) stated that Consumers Union was 'created by the Communist Party and used for the purpose of spreading propaganda in schools and through women's clubs.'

"On April 21, 1943, the special committee of the Appropriations Committee of the House of Representatives found Consumers Union to be 'subversive and un-American.'

"In April 1940, the Committee for Cultural Freedom, headed by John Dewey, found that Consumers Union was a Communist-front organization."

Kallet's other affiliations included the American Committee for Democracy and Intellectual Freedom ("subversive and un-American" – "a Communist front organization operating among college teachers and professors"); the American Friends of the Chinese People ("Communist front"); the American League for Peace and Democracy ("subversive and Communist" – "established . . . in an effort to create public sentiment on behalf of a foreign policy adapted to the interests of the Soviet Union . . . [and] designed to conceal Communist control, in accordance with the new tactics of the Communist International"); the American Youth Congress ("subversive" – "one of the most influential front organizations ever set up by the Communists in this country" – "the Communists were in complete control"); the Coordinating Committee Against Profiteering ("Communist front"); the International Workers Order ("from its very inception demonstrated by its pronouncements, its activities, and the authoritative statements of the Communist Party that it is a subservient instrument of the Communist Party of the United States"); the Jewish People's Committee ("subversive and Communist" – "an organization which has been nothing more nor less than an adjunct of the Communist Party"); the League for Mutual Aid ("Communist enterprise"); the National Council To Aid Agricultural Labor ("Communist front"); the National Federation for Constitutional Liberties ("under Communist Party domination and headed by responsible Party functionaries" – "one of the viciously subversive organizations of the Communist Party"); the National Wartime Conference of the Professions, the Sciences, the Arts, the White-Collar Fields ("Communist front"); *New Masses* ("weekly journal of the Communist Party"); the New York Peace Association ("Communist front"); the New York Professional Workers Conference on Social Insurance ("Communist front"); the Open Letter to American Liberals ("project of well-known Communists and Communist collaborators" – "in defense of the progressive movement undertaken by the Soviet Union"); United Action Against Fascism and Anti-Semitism ("Communist front"); United American Artists ("Communist front"); and *U.S. Week* ("Communist front publication"). He died in February 1972.

FLORENCE KELLEY was born on September 12, 1859 in Philadelphia,

Pennsylvania, daughter of Caroline Bonsall and William Kelley. She was married to and divorced from Lazare Wischnewtzky. She was an alumna of Cornell University (B. Litt., 1892) and Northwestern University (LL.B., 1894). She was the author of *Some Ethical Gains Through Legislation* (1905) and *Modern Industry* (1913). She was editor of Edmond Kelly's *Twentieth Century Socialism* (1910). She translated Friedrich Engels' *The Condition of the Working Class in England in 1844* (1887). She compiled *The Supreme Court and Minimum Wage Legislation* (1925) and *Comment of the Legal Profession on the District of Columbia Minimum Wage* (1925). She contributed articles to the *American Journal of Sociology*; the *Annals* of the American Academy of Political and Social Science; *Arena; Century; Charities; Independent; International Review*; the *Journal of Political Economy; Outlook*; and *Survey*.

After receiving a degree from Cornell, Kelley applied for admission to the University of Pennsylvania where she hoped to study law. Her application was rejected because the University was not admitting women. In 1883, while touring Europe, she enrolled at the University of Zürich where she studied for about three years. During her stay at Zürich she became a Marxian Socialist. It was at that period that she translated Friedrich Engels' book and thus became a close friend of Marx's collaborator. (Her correspondence with Engels was collected by Friedrich Sorge, director of the Communist Party's First International, and deposited in the New York Public Library.) She also translated and published an address by Karl Marx on free trade.

In 1886, Kelley departed from Switzerland for the United States with her

435

husband, a Russian-born Socialist, who hoped to establish a medical practice in New York City. In New York City, Kelley and her husband joined the Marxist Socialist Labor Party, but although she became immediately active in Party affairs, the couple was expelled about a year later.

By 1891, Kelley's husband had failed to prosper, and she went to Illinois, where she divorced him, resuming her maiden name. In Chicago, she took up residence at Jane Addams' Hull House, where she remained for eight years. Hull House, a settlement house, was − although only three years old when she arrived − already an internationally famous center of Fabian Socialists who, in the guise of social workers, were promoting Socialism through a variety of occupations and through political activism.

Before her arrival at Hull House, Kelley's main interests were Socialism and woman's suffrage. However, she became interested in child labor and other real or imaginary problems attendant on industry. In 1892, the Illinois Bureau of Labor Statistics hired her to investigate working conditions in the garment industry. In 1893, the Federal Commissioner of Labor, Carroll D. Wright, hired her to survey slum areas of Chicago. She became an instant expert on child labor, sweatshops, and factory working conditions for women. Through her lobbying efforts, the Illinois legislature passed a factory act, regulating work-hours for women, controlling tenement sweatshops, and outlawing child labor. From 1893 until 1897, she was a factory inspector, helping to enforce the legislation.

In 1899, Kelley moved to New York and took up residence at Lillian Wald's Henry Street Settlement, another Fabian Socialist center frequented by many of those who had been encountered by Kelley at Hull House. She lived there for twenty-five years.

In 1899, Kelley became general secretary of the new National Consumers League, organized by Josephine Shaw Lowell. Until her death in 1932, she was the guiding force behind the NCL. She edited its publications, organized sixty branches in twenty states, and served as spokesman at international conferences, at legislative hearings, and before audiences of clubwomen and others. Under her direction, the NCL became a major factor in the Socialists' drive to monopolize social reform. The progressive and dynamic growth of American industry was a convenient target for the "reformers" who concentrated on child labor, sweatshops, women's working conditions, industrial safety, and compulsory education for children. It was Kelley's contention that industry and industrial workers should come under the complete control of government, and in order to achieve that control, socialist legislation should be enacted and enforced. To make the NCL effective, she recruited many prominent individuals to its executive board, including Newton D. Baker, Secretary of War during the Wilson Administration; Eleanor Roosevelt; Jane Addams, Julia Lathrop, and Alice Hamilton of Hull House; John Haynes Holmes; Mrs. J. Borden Harriman; Dean Roscoe Pound; and Frances Perkins, Secretary of Labor throughout all of President Franklin D. Roosevelt's administrations. The NCL was aided financially by the Garland Fund, which was a generous benefactor of a myriad of Communist enterprises.

In 1907, an Oregon ten-hour working day law for women was the subject of an appeal to the Supreme Court of the

United States. To defend the law, Kelley and an aide, Josephine Goldmark, persuaded Goldmark's uncle, Louis Brandeis, to join the defense. For two weeks, Kelley and Goldmark with the aid of other Socialists amassed a collection of reports, statistics, and precedents from foreign courts which with a short legal argument composed what became known as the Brandeis Brief. Using the device of overkill, Brandeis smothered the legal facts in the case with mountains of extraneous economic and sociological arguments, while completely ignoring pertinent American judicial precedents. The "Brief" resulted in a victory for the Brandeis-Kelley-Goldmark combine in *Muller v. Oregon* (1908). (In 1915, Brandeis was appointed Associate Justice of the Supreme Court, and the Kelley-Goldmark team, with the help of Felix Frankfurter, collaborated on many decisions rendered by Brandeis in the ensuing years.)

After she led the successful defense of the Oregon Ten-Hour Law, Kelley lobbied around the country and was successful in getting similar legislation passed in many states. She was also instrumental in the passage of state-level minimum wage legislation, and in 1912, she was influential through her lobbying efforts in the establishment by Congress of the Children's Bureau.

Kelley's energies were not completely devoted to the National Consumers League. She joined other Socialists in organizing the National Association for the Advancement of Colored People. She joined the Socialists' Intercollegiate Socialist Society (later renamed the League for Industrial Democracy) and served the organization as vice-president (1912-1918 and 1921-1923) and president (1918-1920). (In 1912, Kelley joined the Socialist Party of Eugene V. Debs.) She was a founding member of the leftist-pacifist Women's International League for Peace and Freedom, which was headed by her old friend Jane Addams of Hull House.

Along with Anna Louise Strong, one of America's all-time best-known women Communists, Kelley was responsible for drafting the proposed Child Labor Amendment to the Constitution of the United States – a measure which was fully supported by the Communist Party, but which failed to gain ratification by the necessary number of states.

Among Kelley's affiliations were the ultra-leftist American Union Against Militarism, the Communist-dominated Liberty Defense League, the Socialist-dominated Women's Trade Union League, the Socialist-dominated Public Ownership League, and the Socialist-dominated People's Legislative Service.

She died in February 1932.

ROCKWELL KENT was born on June 21, 1882 in Tarrytown Heights, New York, son of Sara Holgate and Rockwell Kent. He was married to and divorced from Kathleen Whiting and Frances Lee. His third wife was Sally Johnstone. He studied at the Horace Mann School of New York and the Columbia School of Architecture. He studied art under William M. Chase, Robert Henri, Hayes Miller, and Abbott H. Thayer. He was the author and/or illustrator of *The Seven Ages of Man* (1918); *Alaska Drawings* (1919); *Wilderness, A Journal of Quiet Adventure in Alaska* (1920 and 1930); *Voyaging Southward From the Strait of Magellan* (1924; revised 1968); *The Bookplates and Marks of Rockwell Kent* (1929); *N by E* (1930 and 1933); *A Birthday Book* (1931); *Rockwellkentiana* (1933); *How I Make a Wood Cut* (1934); *Salamina* (1935);

Later Bookplates and Marks of Rockwell Kent (1937); *Forty Drawings Done by Rockwell Kent to Illustrate the Works of William Shakespeare* (1937); *This Is My Own*, autobiography (1940); *A Northern Christmas* (1941); *On Earth Peace* (1942); *Rockwell Kent* (1945); *The Mad Hermit* (1955); *It's Me O Lord*, autobiography (1955); *Of Men and Mountains* (1959); *Greenland Journal* (1962); and *Voyaging* (1968). He illustrated special editions of *Moby Dick, Candide, Beowulf, The Canterbury Tales*, and *Leaves of Grass.* He was editor of *World-Famous Paintings* (1939 and 1947). He was editor of the publication, *Creative Art*, and contributing editor of *Colophon.* His illustrations have appeared in publications, including *Vanity Fair* and *Harper's Monthly.*

From 1902 until 1914, Kent worked as an architect and carpenter in New England and Minnesota. In that same period, he began a serious career as an artist, and in 1904 the National Academy of Art displayed two of his paintings. In 1914, he traveled to Newfoundland to continue his painting and from that experience he produced "The Seiners," the first modern American painting to be hung in the Frick Collection in New York. In subsequent years, he traveled, lived, and painted in Alaska, Tierra del Fuego, Greenland, France, and Ireland. Along the way, he worked as a xylographer, lithographer, cartoonist, advertising artist, muralist, trade union leader, and dairy farmer. His works hang or have been shown in the Cleveland Museum, the Metropolitan Museum, the Chicago Art Institute, the Phillips Memorial Gallery, the Brooklyn Museum, The Hermitage in Leningrad, and the Pushkin Museum in Moscow. (In 1960, Kent presented eighty of his landscape paintings and eight hundred of his drawings to the Soviet Union.)

On July 1, 1953, Kent testified before the U.S. Senate Permanent Subcommittee on Government Operations. When asked if he were a member of the Communist Party, he pleaded the protection of the Fifth Amendment. In the course of his testimony, he said: "I know very little about communism. I have come to a judgment about communism. I remember reading the Martin Dies book, listing what seemed to me practically every organization in America that was in my opinion doing good work, working for the Negroes, for freedom, for the poor, for good legislation. My conclusion on finishing that book was what would America be without these so-called Communist fronts. What would it be without the Communists."

On January 19, 1941, the International Workers Order held a celebration in honor of Kent's election as vice president of the Order. Kent provided biographical notes for a souvenir program in which he said: "When I was a young fellow I was very much disturbed by there being some people with lots of money and lots of people with no money. I thought a lot about it and I read a lot about it, so that when I voted for the first time, I voted socialist. I'm still disturbed by the fact that there are some people with a lot of money and a lot of people with no money and a few millions with no jobs, and that the world is rich in resources and that people are starving to death, and that all of the people in the world want to live and yet a good part of the time they're busy killing each other. I take these phenomena of life very seriously. Consequently I rate even my being an artist and a writer by being heart and soul a revisionist."

In 1939, Benjamin Gitlow, a charter executive of the Communist Party, USA, testified under oath at hearings of the House Special Committee on Un-American Activities that Kent was a member of the Communist Party. Former Communist official Louis Budenz made the same sort of identification in 1948 at hearings of the Washington State Joint Legislative Fact-Finding Committee.

In April 1967, Kent was awarded the Lenin "Peace" Prize and a cash award of about $10,000 by the Soviet Union. The "Peace" Committee hailed Kent as an artist whose works "are permeated with warmth and respect for man – the toiler and fighter." The Committee also said: "Kent's speeches against the dirty war of the United States in Vietnam, in defense of the heroic people of Vietnam who are fighting for honor and independence of their homeland, are known throughout the world."

On July 6, 1967, Kent announced that he was donating his Lenin "Peace" Prize cash award of $10,000 to North Vietnam. He presented the gift to North Vietnam's Ambassador to Moscow, Nguyen Phe Chan, to whom he also presented a letter which read: "I am deeply outraged at the unprovoked and the utterly illegal invasion of the territories of the people of Viet Nam by my country's armed forces; and as a citizen, conscience stricken at my own *de facto* involvement in my country's shameful act." He then transmitted "to the suffering women and children of Viet Nam's Liberation Front the sum of $10,000, it being but a token of my shame and sorrow."

Kent was made an honorary member of the Soviet Academy of Arts. He was constantly extolled in the official Communist Party press in the United States, the Soviet Union, and elsewhere. In 1956, the Senate Internal Security Subcommittee included Kent's name in its list of the eighty-two most active and typical sponsors of Communist front organizations. Kent's affiliations included the American Committee for Anti-Nazi Literature ("Communist front"); the American Committee for Democracy and Intellectual Freedom ("subversive and un-American" – "a Communist-front organization operating among college teachers and professors"); the American Committee for Spanish Freedom ("Communist"); the American Committee for Yugoslav Relief ("subversive and Communist"); the American Committee To Save Refugees ("perform[ing] a most valuable function for the international Communist movement"); the American Continental Congress for World Peace ("another phase in the Communist 'peace' campaign, aimed at consolidating anti-American forces throughout the Western Hemisphere"); the American Council on Soviet Relations ("subversive" – "established by the Communist Party . . . directed and controlled by the Party, and operated to aid and support Party objectives concerning the defense and support of the Soviet Union"); American Friends of Spanish Democracy ("Communist front"); the American Labor Party ("Communist dissimulation extends into the field of political parties forming political front organizations such as the . . . American Labor Party"); the American League for Peace and Democracy ("subversive and Communist" – "established . . . in an effort to create public sentiment on behalf of a foreign policy adapted to the interests of the Soviet Union . . . [and] designed to conceal Communist control, in accordance with the new tactics of the Communist International"); the American Peace Crusade ("Communist front"); the American Peace Mobilization ("formed . . . under the auspices of the Communist Party and the Young Communist League" — "one of the most seditious organizations which ever operated in the United States"); the American Pushkin Committee ("Communist front"); the American Russian Institute ("subversive" — "Communist" — "specializing in pro-Soviet propaganda"); the American Slav Congress ("Moscow-inspired and directed federation of Communist-dominated organizations seeking by methods of propaganda and pressure to subvert the 10 million people in this country of Slavic birth or descent"); the American Youth Congress ("subversive" — "one of the most influential front organizations ever set up by the Communists in this country" — "the Communists were in complete control"); American Youth for Democracy ("subversive and Communist" — "part of Soviet psychological warfare against the United States"); Appeal for Pardon of German Communist [Robert Stamm]; the Artists Front To Win the War ("Communist front" — "included representatives of the theater, of literature, music, art, science, and education with long and active records of support for Communist-front organizations and for the variegated turns of the Communist Party line"); the Artists League of America ("Communist front"); Arts, Sciences, and Professions for May Day (Communist enterprise); the Bill of Rights Conference ("subversive"); Brief [amicus curiae] on Behalf of the Communist Party vs. the Subversive Activities Control Board (Communist Party enterprise); Celebration of 15 Years of Biro Bidjan ("Communist project"); the *Chicago Star* (Communist Party publication); the China Aid Council ("Communist-controlled"); the Citizens Committee for Constitutional Liberties ("created, dominated, and controlled by members and officials of the Communist Party"); the Citizens Committee for [Israel] Amter ("Communist candidate for public office"); the Citizens Committee for Harry Bridges ("Communist front"); the Citizens' Committee To Free Earl Browder ("a strictly Communist Party affair"); the Citizens' Emergency Defense Conference ("subversive"); the Civil Rights Congress ("created and established by the Communist Party as an organization which would utilize defense of civil rights for Party purposes and raise and maintain mass defense and bail funds for Party use"); the Committee for a Democratic Far Eastern Policy ("Communist"); the Committee for Citizenship Rights ("to protect Communist subversion from any penalties under the law"); the Committee for Free Political Advocacy ("Communist front"); the Committee for the Freedom of Sam Milgrom ("Communist front"); the Committee for the Re-election of Benjamin J. Davis (Communist Party candidate for political office); the Committee of Professional Groups for [Earl] Browder and [James W.] Ford (Communist candidates for president and vice-president of the United States in 1936); the Committee To Defend Alexander Trachtenberg, Communist Party official; the Committee to Defend America by Keeping Out of War ("Communist front"); the Committee To End Sedition Laws (Communist Party project); the *Communist International* (official publication of the Comintern); the Conference for Legislation in the National Interest ("under complete domination by the Communist Party"); the Coordinating Committee To Lift the [Spanish] Embargo ("one of the numerous Communist-front enterprises which were organized around the Communists' agitation over the Spanish Civil War"); the Council for Pan-American

Democracy ("subversive and Communist"); the Cultural and Scientific Conference for World Peace ("Communist front" – "a propaganda front for Soviet foreign policy and Soviet culture"); the *Daily Worker* ("official organ of the Communist Party"); the Emergency Civil Liberties Committee ("Communist front" – "subversive"); the Federal Arts Council of the Workers Alliance ("Communist front"); the First Congress of the Mexican and Spanish-American Peoples of the United States ("Congress was planned at a secret gathering of Communist Party leaders from the South and Southwest"); the Friends of the Soviet Union ("created, directed, and controlled by the Communist Party . . . and operated to aid and support Party objectives concerning the defense and support of the Soviet Union"); *Friday* (Communist-controlled publication); the International Labor Defense ("subversive and Communist" – "legal arm of the Communist Party" – "part of an international network of organizations for the defense of Communist lawbreakers"); the International Workers Order ("from its very inception demonstrated by its pronouncements, its activities, and the authoritative statements of the Communist Party that it is a subservient instrument of the Communist Party of the United States"); the John Reed Clubs ("out-and-out Communist organizations which preceded the contemporary Communist front organizations which cater to so-called liberals"); the Joint Anti-Fascist Refugee Committee ("subversive and Communist"); the League of American Writers ("subversive and Communist" – "began openly to follow the Communist Party line as dictated by the foreign policy of the Soviet Union"); *Mainstream* ("monthly cultural and literary organ of the Communist Party");

Masses and Mainstream ("a Communist magazine"); the Medical Bureau and North American Committee To Aid Spanish Democracy ("subversive and un-American"); Mother Ella Reeve Bloor Birthday Celebrations (Communist Party enterprises); the Motion Picture Artists Committee ("Communist front"); the National Assembly for Democratic Rights ("created, dominated, and controlled by members and officials of the Communist Party"); the National Committee for Peoples Rights ("composed primarily of openly avowed members of the Communist Party and veteran fellow-travelers of the Communist Party"); the National Committee for the Defense of Political Prisoners ("subversive and Communist"); the National Committee To Abolish the Un-American Activities Committee ("to lead and direct the Communist Party's 'Operation Abolition' campaign"); the National Committee To Secure Justice for the Rosenbergs and Morton Sobell ("Communist front organized . . . to conduct the United States phase of a mammoth propaganda campaign designed to obliterate the crime of and exploit the Rosenbergs and their codefendant Morton Sobell for the purposes of international Communism"); the National Council of American-Soviet Friendship ("subversive and Communist" – "specializing in pro-Soviet propaganda"); the National Federation for Constitutional Liberties ("under Communist Party domination and headed by responsible Party functionaries" – "one of the viciously subversive organizations of the Communist Party"); the National Institute of Arts and Letters ("Communist front"); the National Non-Partisan Committee To Defend the Rights of the 12 Communist Leaders (pro-Communist); the National Wartime Conference of the Professions, the Sciences, the

Arts, the White-Collar Fields ("Communist front"); *New Horizons for Youth* (Communist front publication); *New Masses* ("weekly journal of the Communist Party"); the New York Peace Association ("Communist front"); the Non-Partisan Committee for the Re-election of Congressman Vito Marcantonio ("Communist front"); the North American Spanish Aid Committee ("Communist"); an Open Letter for Closer Co-operation with the Soviet Union (issued by "a group of Communist Party stooges"); An Open Letter in Defense of Harry Bridges ("Communist front"); the Peiping Peace Conference (international Communist project); the People's Radio Foundation ("subversive and Communist organization); People's Songs, Inc. ("subversive"); *People's World* ("Communist Party newspaper"); the [Luiz Carlos] Prestes Defense Committee (on behalf of a leader of the Communist Party of Brazil − "a Communist organization"); the Progressive Citizens of America ("political Communist front" − "subversive"); the Progressive Committee To Rebuild the American Labor Party ("Communist front"); the Provisional United Labor and Peoples Committee for May Day (Communist Party enterprise); the Public Use of Arts Committee ("Communist front"); the Reichstag Fire Trial Anniversary Committee ("Communist front" . . . formed . . . by prominent Communists and Communist sympathizers"); Russian War Relief ("Communist enterprise"); the Saturday Forum Luncheon Group ("Communist front"); the [Morris U.] Schappes Defense Committee ("a front organization with a strictly Communist objective, namely, the defense of a self-admitted Communist who was convicted of perjury in the courts of New York"); *Social Work Today* (a Communist magazine); *Soviet Russia Today* (Communist-controlled publication); the Stockholm Peace Appeal ("Communist 'peace' campaign"); the Tallentire Jubilee Committee ("Communist front"); a Testimonial Dinner for Ferdinand C. Smith ("Communist Party affair"); the United American Artists Union ("Communist front"); the United American Spanish Aid Committee ("Communist"); the United Committee To Aid Vermont Marble Workers ("Communist front"); Veterans of the Abraham Lincoln Brigade ("directed, dominated and controlled by the Communist Party"); Voice of Freedom Committee ("subversive" − to defend pro-Communist radio commentators); the Washington Committee for Democratic Action ("subversive and Communist"); the Washington Committee To Lift [the] Spanish Embargo ("Communist front"); the Win-the-Peace Conference ("Communist front"); the World Peace Congress in Paris (international Communist project); the Writers' and Artists' Committee for Medical Aid to Spain ("a Communist front set up for the purpose of agitation and propaganda"); and *Youth* (publication of American Youth for Democracy, "subversive and Communist").

Kent died in March 1971.

DOROTHY KENYON was born on February 17, 1888 in New York City, daughter of Maria Stanwood and William Kenyon. She was an alumna of Smith College (A.B., 1908) and New York University (J.D., 1917). In 1917, she was admitted to the New York bar.

In 1917 and 1918, Kenyon served as a research specialist for a group of lawyers whose clients needed briefings for work at the Paris Peace Conference. She also worked in that period with Colonel Edward M. House and his curious Committee of Inquiry, which was

President Woodrow Wilson's alleged brain trust to assist him in the peace negotiations in Paris. In 1919, she joined the legal firm of Pitkin, Rosenson, and Henderson in New York City. From 1925 until 1930, she had her own law firm. From 1930 until 1939, she was a partner in the firm of Straus and Kenyon. In 1934, she was on the advisory council on taxes for the New York City's Comptroller's office. In 1935, she was chairman of the New York Minimum Wage Board. In 1936, she was a member of the New York State Committee on Minimum Wage Legislation; chairman of a committeee to study procedures in women's courts; and First Deputy Commissioner of Licenses for New York City. In 1937, she was vice-chairman of the New York Commisssion on the National Public Housing Conference. In 1939, she was appointed by New York City's Mayor Fiorello La Guardia to fill a vacancy on the Municipal Court. She served on the bench for less than a year. In 1940, she resumed her practice of law. From 1938 until 1943, she was a member of the League of Nations Committee on the Legal Status of Women. From 1946 until 1949, she was a United States delegate to the United Nations Commission on the Status of Women. She was active in the Socialistic Cooperative League of America. She was on the advisory council of the Euthanasia Educational Fund. As early as 1965, she lobbied for a liberalized abortion law in New York.

Kenyon was a prominent leader in the ultra-radical American Civil Liberties Union, the leftist League of Women Voters, the ultra-radical Americans for Democratic Action, and the Union for Democratic Action, a Red-lined outfit whose guiding genius was Louis Fraina, one of America's first Communists. She was at one time a member of the Socialist Party. She was a founder of the American Labor Party ("Communist dissimulation extends into the field of political parties forming political front organizations such as the . . . American Labor Party"). She was a staunch opponent of anti-Communist, anti-subversive investigating committees. On at least two occasions before such committees, she denied vehemently that she had had affiliations with Communist Party enterprises. However, her affiliations included the American Committee for Anti-Nazi Literature ("individuals and organizations connected with it identify this committee as a Communist front organization"); the American Committee for Democracy and Intellectual Freedom ("subversive and un-American" – "a Communist-front organization operating among college teachers and professors"); the American Youth Congress ("subversive" – "one of the most influential front organizations ever set up by the Communists in this country" – "the Communists were in complete control"); the Associated Blind, Inc. ("Communist front"); the Committee for the Election of John T. McManus ("Communist front"); Consumers League of New York (Socialist-dominated); Consumers National Federation ("transmission belt" for the Communist Party's influence and ideology – "Communist front"); the Coordinating Committee To Lift the [Spanish] Embargo ("one of the numerous Communist-front enterprises which were organized around the Communists' agitation over the Spanish Civil War"); the Council for Pan-American Democracy ("subversive and Communist"); Descendants of the American Revolution ("Communist front organization set up as a radical imitation of the Daughters of the American Revolution. The Descendants adhered to the line of the Communist Party"); Film Audiences for

Democracy ("Communist front"); [Simon W.] Gerson Supporters ("Communist front"); the Greater New York Emergency Conference on Inalienable Rights ("Communist front"); the International Labor Defense ("subversive and Communist" – "legal arm of the Communist Party" – "part of an international network of organizations for the defense of Communist lawbreakers"); the Lawyers Committee on American Relations with Spain ("during the Spanish Civil War, the Communist Party organized . . . [the Lawyers Committee] as a part of one of its major propaganda campaigns in the Party's entire history in this country"); the League for Mutual Aid ("Communist enterprise"); the League of Women Shoppers ("Communist-controlled front"); the Mary Ware Dennett Defense Committee (ultra-leftist); the Milk Consumers Protective Committee ("Communist front"); the National Citizens Political Action Committee ("Communist front"); the National Council on Freedom from Censorship (pro-Communist); the National Council of American-Soviet Friendship ("subversive and Communist – "specializing in pro-Soviet propaganda"); the New York Tom Mooney Committee ("Communist front"); Pioneer Youth of America (Socialist); the Political Prisoners Bail Fund Committee ("the personnel and the objectives . . . make it obvious that the organization was a Communist Party front"); the [Morris U.] Schappes Defense Committee ("a front organization with a strictly Communist objective, namely, the defense of a self-admitted Communist who was convicted of perjury in the courts of New York"); the Testimonial Dinner for Ferdinand C. Smith ("Communist Party affair"); the Urban League of New York (leftist); Veterans of the Abraham Lincoln Brigade ("directed, dominated and controlled by the Communist Party");,the Washington Committee To Lift [the] Spanish Embargo ("Communist front"); and the Westchester Conference for Democratic Rights ("Communist front"). She died in February 1972.

FRANK KINGDON was born on February 27, 1894 in London, England, son of Matilda Caunt and John Kingdon. He was married to and divorced from Gertrude Littlefield and Marcella Markham. He came to the United States in 1912 and was naturalized in 1918. He was an alumnus of Boston University (A.B., 1920) and Albion College (D.D., 1927). He pursued graduate studies, on a Jacob Sleeper Fellowship, at Harvard University (1920-1921) and Michigan State College (1921). He was the author of *Religious Implications of Modern Science* (1926); *Humane Religion* (1930); *When Half-Gods Go* (1933); *Life of John Cotton Dana* (1940); *1776, and Today* (1941); *Our Second War of Independence* (1942); *Jacob's Ladder: The Days of My Youth* (1943); *The Man in the White House* (1944); *The Inside Story of the Coming Election* (1944); and *An Uncommon Man: or, Henry Wallace and 60 Million Jobs* (1945). He was a contributor to *Freedom* (1940) and *Architects of the Republic, As FDR Said* (1950).

In 1912, Kingdon arrived in Portland, Maine, where he was ordained as a minister in the Methodist Church. In 1912 and 1913, he did parish work in North Palermo and China, Maine. From 1913 until 1915, he was a pastor in Harmony, Maine. From 1916 until 1921, he was a pastor in Hull, Massachusetts. From 1921 until 1928, he was a pastor in Lansing, Michigan. From 1928 until 1934, he was a pastor in East Orange, New Jersey. From 1934 until 1936, he was president of Dana College. In 1936, when Dana merged with four other colleges to form the University of Newark, Kingdon became president of the new institution, and remained in that position for four years. In 1940, he resigned his presidency to study movements in the United States that he said were "designed to break down the nation's democratic ideals." As part of his study, he became educational director of the Citizenship Educational Service, which described itself as "engaged in coordinating democratic education among social welfare, civic, and labor organizations." In the same period, he became chairman of the New York chapter of the interventionist Committee To Defend America by Aiding the Allies. He was also chairman of the Emergency Rescue Committee and an executive committeeman of the Committee for Refugee Education and the United States Committee for the Care of European Children. He had become one of the country's most active interventionists. He was evangelistic in a crusade to have the United States fight in the "people's war" to bring about a new world order in which there would be "modification of *laissez-faire* capitalism in the interests of economic justice; the establishment of recognized international law; and the repudiation of war." He was hopeful that at the end of the war there would be established an international congress, an international court, and an international army.

During World War II, Kingdon served briefly as a special assistant to the chairman of the War Manpower Commission and to the chairman of the War Production Board. He was a political commentator on radio stations WMCA, WOR, and WINS. He became extremely active in promoting a fourth term for President Franklin D. Roosevelt. In 1944, he be-

came a leading figure in Sidney Hillman's National Citizens Political Action Committee, one of the most impressive Communist front organizations ever assembled. The cream of America's fellow-travelers had joined Hillman's group with one major purpose in mind – the re-election of Franklin D. Roosevelt.

In the post-war period, Kingdon continued to promote his leftist views through his radio broadcasts and a daily column which he wrote for the leftist *New York Post*. In 1946, he became a leader of the Progressive Citizens of America. The organization was formed by a merger of ten groups, all of which were loaded down with fellow-travelers. The most important of the ten groups were the National Citizens Political Action Committee and the Independent Citizens Committee of the Arts, Sciences and Professions, both of which would eventually be cited as Communist fronts.

Kingdon was for a brief time co-chairman of the Progressive Citizens of America, but he resigned his position when the real powers within the PCA decided to form the Progressive Party as a vehicle for the presidential candidacy of Henry A. Wallace. Kingdon, for reasons which have never been fully revealed, left the PCA even though he had been one of Wallace's strongest boosters. It is reasonable to suppose that Kingdon had little faith in the prospects of a third party and that he hoped the PCA would work within the structure of the Democratic Party. At any rate, when he did resign, he offered an explanation that revealed more about the inner workings of the PCA than it did of Kingdon's reasons for his resignation. He wrote: "Who asked Henry Wallace to run? The answer is in the record. The Communist Party, through William Z. Foster and Eugene Dennis, were the first. I am no red-hater. I believed it possible for American liberals to cooperate with Communists for social ends immediately desirable. The saddest lesson I learned in 1947 was that this is impossible. All citizens, including Communists, have a right to put forward a candidate. All I am saying is that their candidate is theirs. They are his sponsors. He is named by them to serve their ends."

After the Wallace fiasco, Kingdon's political activities dwindled. For a few more years, he continued his political commentaries on radio and his daily column in the *New York Post*. Then, in the 1950's, he became co-founder of *American Salesman*, an educational-type publication devoted to ideas and techniques on selling, advertising, promotion, marketing, and merchandising. In the 1960's, he lectured at the ultra-radical New School for Social Research.

Aside from his leadership in the National Citizens' Political Action Committee and the Progressive Citizens of America, Kingdon had such an impressive list of hard-core affiliations that he could not reasonably be considered an "innocent" or a "dupe." He was affiliated with the American Committee for Democracy and Intellectual Freedom ("subversive and un-American" – "a Communist-front organization operating among college teachers and professors"); the American Committee for Yugoslav Relief ("subversive and Communist"); the American Council for a Democratic Greece ("subversive and Communist"); the American Slav Congress ("Moscow-inspired and directed federation of Communist-dominated organizations seeking by methods of propaganda and pressure to subvert the 10,000,000 people in this country of Slavic birth or descent"); the American Student Union ("without exception . . . supported defense of teach-ers and students charged with Communist activity" – "pliable instrument in the hands of the Communist Party"); the American Youth Congress ("subversive" – "one of the most influential front organizations ever set up by the Communists in this country" – "the Communists were in complete control"); the Citizens United To Abolish the Wood-Rankin Committee (pro-Communist project); the Greater New York Emergency Conference on Inalienable Rights ("Communist front"); the Independent Citizens Committee of the Arts, Sciences and Professions ("Communist front"); the John Reed Clubs ("out-and-out Communist organizations which preceded the contemporary Communist front organizations which cater to so-called liberals"); the Methodist Federation for Social Action ("the organization's influence has been consistently wielded on behalf of Communist causes and the Communist line as expressed through the party and its innumerable subsidiaries"); the ultra-radical National Association for the Advancement of Colored People; the National Emergency Conference ("Communist front"); the National Wartime Conference for the Professions, the Sciences, the Arts, the White-Collar Fields ("Communist front"); Russian War Relief ("Communist enterprise"); the Union for Democratic Action (Red-lined outfit whose guiding genius was Louis Fraina, one of America's first Communists); the United Student Peace Committee ("Communist front"); Veterans of the Abraham Lincoln Brigade ("directed, dominated and controlled by the Communist Party"); the Voice of Freedom Committee ("subversive" – to defend pro-Communist radio commentators); and the Win-the-Peace Conference ("Communist front").

Kingdon died in February 1972.

ALFRED KREYMBORG was born on December 10, 1883 in New York City, son of Louise Nasher and Hermann Kreymborg. He was married to and divorced from Gertrude Lord. His second wife was Dorothy Bloom. He was the author of *Love and Life and Other Studies* (1910); *Apostrophes* (1912); *Erna Vitek* (1914); *Troubadour: An Autobiography* (1925); *Our Singing Strength* (1929); and *I Am No Hero* (1933). His volumes of poetry include *Mushrooms* (1916); *Blood of Things* (1920); *Less Lonely* (1923); *Scarlet and Mellow* (1926); *Funnybone Alley* (1927); *The Lost Sail* (1928); *Manhattan Men* (1929); *The Little World* (1914); and *After* (1932). His plays include *Plays for Merry Andrews* (1920); *Puppet Plays* (1923); *Rocking Chairs and Other Comedies* (1925); *Lima Beans* (1925); *There's A Moon Tonight* (1926); *How Do You Do, Sir, and Other Short Plays* (1934); and *The Four Apes and Other Fables of Our Day* (1939). He is the editor of *Anthology of American Poetry, Lyric America, 1630-1930* (revised edition, 1935) and *Poetic Drama: An Anthology of Plays in Verse* (1941).

For most of his career, Kreymborg was a free-lance poet, critic, playwright, and lecturer. For a few years, he supported himself as a professional chess-player. Briefly, he was a founder and editor of three literary publications, *The Glebe, Others,* and *Broom.* From 1927 until 1936, he was co-editor of *American Caravan,* an anthology of experimental writing. He taught for two years at Briarcliff Junior College. During the depression, he was director of a Poets' Theatre for the Works Progress Administration.

From the nature of his hard-core affiliations, it is reasonable to assume that Kreymborg was a Communist. The affiliations included the American Committee for Democracy and Intellectual Freedom ("subversive and un-American" – "a Communist-front organization operating among college teachers and professors"); the American Writers Union ("Communist front"); the Arts, Sciences, and Professions for May Day (Communist Party enterprise); the Artists Front To Win the War ("Communist front" – "included representatives of the theater, of literature, music, art, science, and education, with long and active records of support for Communist front organizations and for the variegated turns of the Communist Party line"); Book Union ("distributors of Communist literature" – "Communist [Party] book club"); the Citizens Committee for Harry Bridges ("Communist"); the Citizens Committee To Free Earl Browder ("a strictly Communist Party affair"); the Committee for Free Political Advocacy ("Communist front"); the Committee for the Re-election of Benjamin J. Davis (Communist Party candidate for political office); Contemporary Writers ("subversive and Communist"); the Cultural and Scientific Conference for World Peace ("Communist front" – "a propaganda front for Soviet foreign policy and Soviet culture"); the Dance Congress and Festival ("Communist front"); the Emergency Committee for Southern Political Prisoners ("Communist front"); Friends of the Abraham Lincoln Brigade ("completely controlled by the Communist Party"); Friends of the Soviet Union ("created, directed, and controlled by the Communist Party . . . and operated to aid and support Party objectives concerning the defense and support of the Soviet Union"); the Jefferson School of Social Science ("a Communist institution modeled along the lines of the new

Communist policy which led to the decision to change the Communist Party into some kind of an educational institution"); the John Reed Clubs ("out-and-out Communist organizations which preceded the contemporary Communist front organizations which cater to so-called liberals"); the Joint Anti-Fascist Refugee Committee ("subversive and Communist"); the League of American Writers ("subversive and Communist" – "began openly to follow the Communist Party line as dictated by the foreign policy of the Soviet Union"); the League of Professional Groups for [William Z.] Foster and [James W.] Ford ("the members of this organization were committed to the objectives of the Communist Party"); *Masses and Mainstream* ("Communist magazine"); May Day Parades in 1946 and 1947 (Communist projects); the Mother Ella Reeve Bloor Birthday Celebration ("Communist Party festivity"); the National Committee Against Censorship of the Theatre Arts ("Communist front"); the National Committee for Peoples Rights ("composed primarily of openly avowed members of the Communist Party and veteran fellow travelers of the Communist Party"); the National Committee for the Defense of Political Prisoners ("subversive and Communist"); the National Federation for Constitutional Liberties ("under Communist Party domination and headed by responsible Party functionaries" – "one of the viciously subversive organizations of the Communist Party"); *New Masses* ("weekly journal of the Communist Party"); the ultra-radical New School for Social Research; *New Theatre* ("Communist Party publication); an Open Letter for Closer Cooperation with the Soviet Union (issued by "a group of Communist Party stooges"); an Open Letter in Defense of Harry Bridges ("Communist

front"); the Political Prisoners Bail Fund Committee ("the personnel and the objectives . . . make it obvious . . . that the organization was a Communist Party front"); the School for Democracy ("established by Communist teachers ousted from the public school system of New York City"); *Soviet Russia Today* ("Communist-controlled publication"); the Stockholm Peace Appeal ("Communist 'peace' campaign"); *Sunday Worker* ("Communist Party newspaper"); Veterans of the Abraham Lincoln Brigade ("directed, dominated and controlled by the Communist Party"); the Voice of Freedom Committee ("subversive" – to defend pro-Communist radio commentators); the Washington Committee To Lift [the] Spanish Embargo ("Communist front"); and the World Peace Congress ("organized under Communist initiative in various countries throughout the world"). He died in August 1966.

HARRY W. LAIDLER was born on February 18, 1884 in Brooklyn, son of Julia Heary and William Laidler. He married Agnes Armington. He was an alumnus of Wesleyan University (A.B., 1907), Brooklyn Law School (L.B., 1910), and Columbia University (Ph.D., 1914). He was the author of *Boycotts and the Labor Struggle* (1914); *Socialism in Thought and Action* (1920); *A History of Socialist Thought* (1927); *Concentration of Control in American Industry* (1931); *The Road Ahead: A Primer of Capitalism and Socialism* (1932); *Socializing Our Democracy* (1935); *A Program for Modern America* (1936); *American Socialism* (1937); and *Social-Economic Movements* (1944). He was co-author of *Power Control* (1928) and *What Do You Know About Labor?* (1956). He was editor of *Social Anticipations* (1927) and *Socialist Planning and a Socialist

Program (1932). He was co-editor of *The Socialism of Today* (1916); *State Socialism: Pro and Con* (1917); *New Tactics in Social Conflict* (1926); *Prosperity?* (1927); and *The Socialism of Our Times* (1929). Much of Laidler's work was in the form of brochures. He was the author of *The British Cooperative Movement* (1917); *Public Ownership Here and Abroad* (1923); *How America Lives* (1924); *Roads to Freedom* (1924); *Unemployment and Its Remedies* (1930); *Incentives Under Capitalism and Socialism* (1933); *America in the Depression* (1935); *Putting the Constitution to Work* (1936); *Consumers' Cooperation* (1937); *Toward a Farmer-Labor Party* (1938); *The Federal Government and Functional Democracy* (1940); *British Labor's Rise to Power* (1945); and *Socialism in the United States: Brief History* (1952). He was editor of *Thirty-five Years of Educational Pioneering* (1941); *Economics of Defense and Reconstruction* (1941); *Maximum Production: Warfare and Welfare* (1942); *The Role of the Races in Our Future Civilization* (1942); *British Labor on Reconstruction in War and Peace* (1943); *The Third Freedom: Freedom From Want* (1943); *Postwar Planning for Peace and Full Employment* (1944); *The League for Industrial Democracy: Forty Years of Education* (1945); *A Program for Labor and Progressives* (1948); *John Dewey at Ninety* (1950); *Needed: A Moral Awakening in America* (1952); and *How Free Is Free Enterprise* (1954). He contributed articles to *New Republic, New Leader, Current History, North American Review, Annals* of the American Academy of Political Science, *Survey Graphic, Encyclopaedia Britannica, Encyclopedia Americana,* and *American People's Encyclopedia Yearbook.*

From 1907 until 1910, Laidler was a reporter for the *Brooklyn Eagle.* In 1911, he was admitted to the New York Bar. Meanwhile, he had taken a strong interest in Socialism. After high school, he attended the Socialists' Ruskin College for Workingmen in Missouri and the American Socialist College in Kansas. In 1904, he travelled about Kansas and Oklahoma lecturing as a Socialist missionary. In 1905, he was one of the founders (with Upton Sinclair, Jack London, Clarence Darrow, Thomas Higginson, and others) of the Intercollegiate Socialist Society. Laidler founded the ISS's first chapter at Wesleyan. From 1910 until 1921, he was the executive secretary of the ISS. From 1913 until 1919, he was editor of the *Intercollegiate Socialist.* From 1919 until 1921, he was editor of the *Socialist Review.* In 1921, when the ISS changed its name to League for Industrial Democracy, Laidler became executive director, and held the post until 1957, when he became director emeritus. From 1920 until 1970, he was with the National Bureau of Economic Research as director (1920-1970), vice-president (1928), president (1930-1932 and 1948-1949), and chairman of the board of directors (1932-1934). From 1924 until 1951, he was a member of the industrial division of the Red-laden Federal Council of Churches. From 1951 until 1953, he was in the social welfare department of the ultra-leftist National Council of Churches. From 1942 until 1945, he was a lecturer in economics at the College of the City of New York. In 1942 and 1943, he was a lecturer in economics at New York University. In 1943 and 1944, he was a lecturer in economics at Brooklyn College. As the spokesman for the League for Industrial Democracy, he was a guest lecturer at more than two hundred colleges. From 1962 until 1970, he was a consultant to *Information Please Almanac*. From 1931 until 1965, he was a director of the National Housing Conference. From 1943 until 1970, he was a member of the Public Affairs Committee. As a political candidate and as a campaigner, Laidler was connected at various times with the Socialist Party, the American Labor Party, and the Liberal Party. Among the offices he sought were governor of New York, borough president, U.S. Senator, and city councilman. His only success was election as city councilman in New York City for one term (1941-1942). He was a frequent traveler to Europe, where he studied Socialism in action, and on at least two occasions he visited the Soviet Union to observe the first of Stalin's Five-Year Plans. He also attended international Socialist congresses.

Laidler always insisted that the League for Industrial Democracy "never promoted the Marxian cult. We conceived of the Socialist society as one with a mixed economy, an economy with public, cooperative and private ownership, the ultimate objective of which was real equality of opportunity for every man and woman so he or she could achieve the fulfillment of his or her potentialities."

In Laidler's most important work, *Socialism in Thought and Action*, first published in 1920, his exegesis of Socialist thought was so close to Marxian thought that only nit-picking would find any differences. Over the years, his prolific output of Socialist writings merely repeated and/or embellished the opening passages of his 1920 work. In his first major book, he wrote: "The belief that socialism is destined to constitute the next step in industrial evolution has sustained the modern socialist in his struggle against present conditions. The passionate devotion of millions of men and women to the socialist cause, however, can be accounted for primarily by the profound conviction that socialism would eradicate the burning evils of modern civilization and usher in an era of equality of opportunity and of genuine brotherhood. No group of social thinkers has done more telling work than have the socialists in analyzing and exposing present-day evils.

"The indictment of the socialists has differed widely from that of numerous other critics. Socialists have never sought to call again into being 'the good old days of the past.' To the extent that they have consistently followed their philosophy, they have refused to attribute fundamental social ills to the activities of 'malefactors of great wealth' or to 'the innate wickedness of human nature.'

"They have endeavored to evaluate capitalism rather than to indulge in wholesale condemnation, and have freely contended that the present economic order is a distinct advance over former industrial systems. Few more impressive testimonials to the achievements of capitalism have, in fact, been written than that of Marx and Engels in *The Communist Manifesto*, published in 1848. The capitalist class, they held in part, 'during its rule of scarce one hundred years has created more massive and more colossal productive forces than have all preceding generations together. Subjection of nature's forces to man, machinery, application of chemistry to industry and agriculture, steam-navigation, railways, electric telegraphs, clearing of whole continents for cultivation, canalization of rivers, whole populations conjured out of the ground — what earlier century had even a presentiment that such productive forces slumbered in the lap of social labor?'

"Socialists do not necessarily base

their advocacy of a new social order on the ground that the lot of the workers is becoming absolutely worse. They do believe, however, that capitalism is failing properly to utilize the marvelous productive forces at its command; that the hand and brain workers are sharing but inadequately in the increased productivity of modern industry; that capitalism retards the development of individuality among the masses of mankind and that, having largely performed its social function and outgrown its usefulness, it should yield to a more scientific and equitable industrial order than at present exists.

"There are many counts in the socialist indictment. One of the chief of these is that capitalism involves enormous wastes in material and in men, both in the realm of production and in that of distribution. Under capitalism, a lamentably small percentage of workers engaged in gainful occupations are actually employed as direct producers of essential commodities.

"Many of the goods produced for profit, furthermore, have but little merit . . . . A large amount of labor also goes into the production of expensive luxuries and personal services which afford comparatively little additional happiness to their recipients, while diverting the energies of thousands from the production of the necessities of life for the many. Witness, for instance, the vast army of menial servants, lackeys, chauffeurs, caterers, governesses, private tutors, grooms, makers of expensive dresses, furniture and houses, and shopkeepers who cater solely to the peculiar tastes of the rich.

"Even when labor is expended in producing actual necessities of life, many wastes are in evidence that could be eliminated under a cooperative sys-tem . . . . The wastes arising from duplication in competitive manufacture are repeated on an even larger scale in agriculture . . . . Nor are social losses evidenced only in private manufacture and farming. They are seen as well in the exploitation of natural resources for private gain.

"The chief wastes dealt with by socialists, however, are generally those connected with the distribution of commodities. Competition demands the expenditure of enormous sums in securing a market, in 'drumming up trade.' First come the voluminous correspondence with prospective customers, and the compilation and mailing of countless circulars, calendars, samples and prizes to induce the customer to buy. The one item of newspaper advertising is enormous and is growing by leaps and bounds.

"The cost of brilliantly displayed 'ads' in magazines is also becoming increasingly great. And besides all this, there are the ever present miscellaneous 'ads' that besmirch the city and countryside. 'The greater portion of down-town illumination, the multiplicity of electric signs, on side-walk and housetop . . . the desecration of cliff and field with thousands of hideous emblazonments; the sandwich man and the fake orientals who perambulate the streets; the inharmonious confusion of streets signs,' all figure in the merry game of advertising as well as in the price of the article to the consumer.

"Latterly the business of advertising is being regarded to an increasing extent as a highly paid profession. Special schools are established to teach this new art; colleges are giving extensive courses therein. Periodicals are vying with each other in the elucidation of its intricacies, and long volumes are describing the psychological methods whereby an unsophisticated public may be induced to purchase goods of plus and minus merit with joyful exaltation.

"These advertising campaigns involve the labor not only of those professionally engaged in the advertising business, but of a host of workers in a large variety of trades. In the printing trades a considerable portion of workers ranking in the census as engaged in production are busy at printing 'not books or newspapers, or magazines, but advertising matter, competitive price lists, wrappers, trade labels, bill-heads, account books, posters, etc., which are merely called into existence by the struggle of various competitive sellers to reach the consumer,' and which could largely be eliminated under a cooperative system of industry. Much of this matter is misleading; some of it, issued for the purpose of deceiving. The reader must pay the price.

"Another source of economic waste under competitive conditions is the system of commercial travelers .... Millions of hours are wasted in the endeavor to persuade weary merchants of the eternal virtues of particular lines of goods, and of the huge demand awaiting their purchase. Under a cooperative system, one salesman in the industry could exhibit the complete line of samples, while most of the staple articles could be ordered by mail. That the work of many of these travelers is superfluous from the standpoint of social production is indicated by the ability of combinations largely to dispense with their services.

"Nor does the waste of distribution end here. After the order for goods has been secured, and the commodity prepared in the factory, considerable loss is incurred in transferring the commodity to the consumer. Eastern factories, in supplying orders, ship bulky commodities to the west, while competing firms send freights from that section thousands of miles to eastern customers .... When finally the commodity arrives at the city of its destination, it is frequently handled by hosts of middlemen — jobbers, wholesalers, speculators, retailers — before reaching the consumer.

"The losses involved in keeping up thousands of insignificant retail establishments, each with its separate clerical force, its inadequate stock and its individual accounts and delivery service, constitute a big social waste. The anarchy of competitive delivery also involves much social loss. That which holds true of the distribution of food pertains to practically every other necessity of life.

"The evils of unemployment, of industrial accidents and preventable diseases, resulting from untoward industrial conditions, are but further indications of the manner in which modern industry fails properly to utilize its wealth of human resources.

"We have thus seen that socialists criticize the capitalist system on the ground of its inefficiency. A further count in the socialist indictment is that the present system of private ownership leads to an inequitable distribution of wealth; that it means untold wealth for the few and poverty for the many; and that this inequality runs directly counter to the welfare and happiness of mankind.

"Socialists condemn the present system, however, not only on account of its effect on the physical well-being of the community, but also because of its reactions on the intellectual and ethical life of society. Indeed most socialists contend that, even though poverty were entirely eliminated, under capitalism, even though each man and woman willing to work were assured of safe employment, of reasonable hours, of healthful surroundings, and of wage which would permit him to supply his family with decent food, decent clothing and decent shelter; even though all employers were enlightened and adequate labor legislation passed and enforced; in fact, even though the workers no longer suffered any of the physical ills which capitalism now brings in its wake, nevertheless the present system would be condemned because of its disastrous reactions on the intellectual, the aesthetic and the ethical life of the masses.

"Through workingmen's compensation laws, social insurance against sickness, accident, old age and unemployment, employment agencies, minimum wage legislation, eight hour laws, stricter factory and tenement laws, the extension of public education and public health activities, the increase of taxation of incomes and inheritances, the regulation of prices and profits, the public ownership of the more important public utilities, etc. — the criminally low wages, the long hours, the high prices, the insecurity of employment, the ignorance of the masses may conceivably be, in large part, eliminated, and a well fed, fairly well educated working class living above the starvation line, may envolve.

"However, so long as the profit system, the wage system, lasts, so long will those in control of industry receive an unearned increment, so long will the workers be dependent on economic masters, so long will the vitiating spirit of arrogant lordship on the one hand and dependence on the other prevent that highest moral development which only a free and economically democratic society can bring about."

Laidler's affiliations included the American Student Union ("without exception . . . supported defense of teachers and students charged with Communist activity" — "pliable instrument in the hands of the Communist Party"); the Berger National Foundation (Socialist); the Brookwood Labor College ("Communistic"); the Committee on Coal and Giant Power (Socialist); the Consumers National Federation ("transmission belt for the Communist Party's influence and ideology" — "Communist front"); the Fellowship of Reconciliation (ultra-leftist-pacifist); the Golden Book of American Friendship with the Soviet Union ("pro-Soviet propaganda enterprise"); the *Il Nuovo Mondo* National Committee (pro-Communist); the Milk Consumers Protective Committee ("Communist front"); the League for the Organization of Progress (Socialist and pro-Communist); the National Advisory Council on Radio in Education (Socialist enterprise); *New Frontier* (pro-Soviet publication); Open Road, Inc. (affiliate of the Soviet Union's Intourist travel agency, a major Communist propaganda center); People's Freedom Union (pro-Soviet); People's Lobby (Socialist); Rand School (training school for Socialists and other Red agitators); the Sacco-Vanzetti National League (part of a pro-Communist propaganda campaign); the United States Congress Against War ("completely under the control of the Communist Party"); and the Workers' Defense League (to defend political undesirables who are subject to deportation.) Laidler died in July 1970.

OLIVER WATERMAN LARKIN was born on August 17, 1896 in Medford, Massachusetts, son of Kate Waterman and Charles Larkin. He married Ruth McIntire. He was an alumnus of Harvard University (A.B., 1918, and A.M., 1919).

He was the author of *Art and Life in America* (1949) and *Samuel F.B. Morse and American Democratic Art* (1954). He has contributed articles to publications including *Antiques, College Art Journal, Magazine of Art, Saturday Review of Literature, School and Society, Stage,* and the *William and Mary Quarterly.*

From 1921 until 1924, Larkin was an assistant in fine arts at Harvard University. From 1924 until 1970, he was at Smith College as assistant professor of art (1924-1926), associate professor (1926-1931), professor (1931-1961), and the Jessie Wells Post Professor of Art (1961-1970). In 1925 and 1926, he was an instructor in art at Iowa State University. In 1950 and 1955, he lectured at the Harvard Student Council's American Seminar Studies for European Students in Salzburg, Austria. In 1950, he received the Pulitzer Prize in American history for his *Art and Life in America.*

Larkin was affiliated with the American Committee for Protection of Foreign Born ("founded by the Communist Party in order to exploit racial divisions in the United States for its own revolutionary purposes"); the American Committee To Save Refugees ("perform[ing] a most valuable function for the international Communist movement"); the American League for Peace and Democracy ("subversive and Communist" – "established . . . in an effort to create public sentiment on behalf of a foreign policy adapted to the interests of the Soviet Union . . . [and] designed to conceal Communist control, in accordance with the new tactics of the Communist International"); the American League Against War and Fascism ("subversive and Communist" – "established in the United States in an effort to create public sentiment on behalf of a foreign policy adapted to the interests of the Soviet Union"); the Artists' Front To Win the War ("Communist front" – "included representatives of the theater, of literature, music, art, science, and education, with long and active records of support for Communist-front organizations and for the variegated turns of the Communist Party line"); the Committee To Defend America by Keeping Out of War ("Communist front"); the Conference on Constitutional Liberties in America ("an important part of the solar system of the Communist Party's front organizations"); the Cultural and Scientific Conference for World Peace ("Communist front" – "a propaganda front for Soviet foreign policy and Soviet culture"); the Descendants of the American Revolution ("a Communist-front organization set up as a radical imitation of the Daughters of the American Revolution. The Descendants have uniformly adhered to the line of the Communist Party"); the Independent Citizens Committee of the Arts, Sciences, and Professions ("Communist front"); the National Council of the Arts, Sciences and Professions ("a Communist front used to appeal to special occupational groups"); the National Federation for Constitutional Liberties ("under Communist Party domination and headed by responsible Party functionaries" – "one of the viciously subversive organizations of the Communist Party"); *New Masses* ("weekly journal of the Communist Party"); Progressive Citizens of America ("political Communist front" – "subversive"); *Science and Society* ("Communist publication"); and *Theatre Arts* (pro-Communist monthly).

Larkin died in December 1970.

JOHN HOWLAND LATHROP was born on June 6, 1880 in Jackson, Michigan, son of Alice Osborne and Arthur Lathrop. He was married to Lita Schlesinger. He was an alumnus of Harvard University (A.B., 1905) and Meadville Theological School (B.D., 1903, and D.D., 1923). He also studied at the University of Jena (Germany), the University of Chicago, New York University, and the New School for Social Research. In 1905, he was ordained to the ministry of the Unitarian Church. He was the author of *The Living Faith of a Unitarian* and *Toward Discovering a Religion.* He was co-editor of and a contributor to *Rumania: Ten Years After 1928.* He contributed articles to the *Christian Register*, the *Syrian Register*, and the *Encyclopaedia Britannica.*

From 1905 until 1911, Lathrop was minister of the First Unitarian Church in Berkeley, California. From 1911 until 1957, he was minister of the First Unitarian Congregational Church (Church of the Savior) in Brooklyn, New York. In 1957, he became minister emeritus. He was president of the International Association for Liberal Christianity and Religious Freedom. He was president of the Euthanasia Society of America. He was a director of the leftist-oriented Urban League of Greater New York.

Lathrop was active in the Red-laden Federal Council of Churches. He was a leader in the Socialist Party. He was vice-chairman of the American Labor Party ("Communist dissimulation extends into the field of political parties forming political front organizations such as the . . . American Labor Party"). His other affiliations included the Ambijan Committee for Emergency Aid to the Soviet Union ("Communist front"); the American Committee for Democracy and Intellectual Freedom ("subversive and un-American" – "a Communist-

front organization operating among college teachers and professors"); the American Committee for Protection of Foreign Born ("founded by the Communist Party in order to exploit racial divisions in the United States for its own revolutionary purposes"); the American Council for a Democratic Greece ("subversive and Communist"); the American Peace Mobilization ("formed . . . under the auspices of the Communist Party and the Young Communist League" – "one of the most seditious organizations which ever operated in the United States"); the American Youth Congress ("subversive" – "one of the most influential front organizations ever set up by the Communists in this country" – "the Communists were in complete control"); an Appeal for Amnesty for 11 Communist Leaders (Communist Party project); the Brooklyn Citizens Committee To Defeat the Mundt Bill ("a Communist lobby . . . which has carried out the objectives of the Communist Party in its fight against anti-subversive legislation"); the Brooklyn Committee for Repeal of the Smith Act (Communist Party project); the China Welfare Appeal ("subversive"); the Citizens' Committee To Defend Representative Government ("Communist front"); the Committee for a Democratic Far Eastern Policy ("Communist"); the Committee for Equal Justice for Mrs. Recy Taylor ("Communist front"); the Committee for Peaceful Alternatives to the Atlantic Pact ("a Communist front organization . . . part of Soviet psychological warfare against the United States"); the Committee To Defend America by Keeping Out of War ("Communist front"); the Committee To Secure Justice for Morton Sobell ("Communist front [in] the Communist campaign for the [atomic spy]"); the Committee of Welcome for the Red Dean of

Canterbury, England's most notorious pro-Soviet apologist among the clergy; Consumers National Federation ("transmission belt" for the Communist Party's influence and ideology – "Communist front"); the Cultural and Scientific Conference for World Peace ("Communist front" – "a propaganda front for Soviet foreign policy and Soviet culture"); the Emergency Peace Mobilization ("Communist front"); [Simon W.] Gerson Supporters ("Communist front"); the Greater New York Committee for a Sane Nuclear Policy (ultra-leftist-pacifist); the Greater New York Emergency Conference on Inalienable Rights ("Communist front"); the Hiroshima Commemorative Committee (ultra-leftist); the Interfaith Committee for Peace Action (leftist-pacifist); the Mid-Century Conference for Peace ("aimed at assembling as many gullible persons as possible under Communist direction and turning them into a vast sounding board for Communist propaganda"); the ultra-radical National Association for the Advancement of Colored People; the National Committee To Abolish the Un-American Activities Committee ("to lead and direct the Communist Party's 'Operation Abolition' campaign"); the National Committee To Secure Justice in the Rosenberg Case ("Communist front organized . . . to conduct the United States phase of a mammoth propaganda campaign designed to obliterate the crime of and exploit the Rosenbergs and their co-defendant Morton Sobell for the purposes of international Communism"); the National Committee To Win Amnesty for Smith Act Victims ("subversive" – "Communist"); the National Conference on American Policy in China and the Far East ("Communist"); the National Consumers League (Socialist-dominated); the National Council of American-Soviet Friendship ("subversive and Communist" – "specializing in pro-Soviet propaganda"); the National Council of the Arts, Sciences and Professions ("a Communist front used to appeal to special occupational groups"); the National Federation for Constitutional Liberties ("under Communist Party domination and headed by responsible Party functionaries" – "one of the viciously subversive organizations of the Communist Party"); an Open Letter in Defense of Harry Bridges ("Communist front"); the Peoples Institute of Applied Religion ("subversive and Communist"); Promoting Enduring Peace, Inc. (ultra-leftist-pacifist); the Religious Freedom Committee (an ultra-leftist group working for the aboliton of the HCUA); the [Morris U.] Schappes Defense Committee ("a front organization with a strictly Communist objective, namely, the defense of a self-admitted Communist who was convicted of perjury in the courts of New York"); and the War Resisters League (leftist-pacifist).

Lathrop died in August 1967.

SINCLAIR LEWIS was born on February 7, 1885 in Sauk Centre, Minnesota, son of Emma Kermott and Edwin Lewis. He was married to and divorced from Grace Hegger and Dorothy Thompson. He is an alumnus of Yale University (A.B., 1907). He was the author of *Hike and the Aeroplane*, under the pen-name of Tom Graham (1912); *Our Mr. Wrenn* (1914); *The Trail of the Hawk* (1915); *The Job* (1917); *The Innocents* (1917); *Free Air* (1919); *Main Street* (1920); *Babbitt* (1922); *Arrowsmith* (1925); *Mantrap* (1926); *Elmer Gantry* (1927); *The Man Who Knew Coolidge* (1928); *Dodsworth* (1929); *Ann Vickers* (1933); *Work of Art* (1934); *It Can't Happen Here* (1935); *Prodigal Parents* (1938);

Bethel Merriday (1940); Gideon Planish (1943); Cass Timberlane (1945); Kingsblood Royal (1947); and World So Wide (1951). He is the author of the play Hobohemia (1919). He is co-author of the plays Jayhawker (1934); It Can't Happen Here (1936); and Angela Is Twenty-Two (1938-1939). His plays in book form are Jayhawker (1935); Dodsworth, with Sidney Howard (1935); and It Can't Happen Here (1938).

During his college days, Lewis was a reporter for the New Haven Journal and Courier. In college vacations, he made two trips abroad. He became a Socialist and spent some time at Upton Sinclair's Socialist colony in New Jersey. In 1907 and 1908, he was a telegraph editor for the Waterloo (Iowa) Courier. In 1908, he worked briefly for the Charity Organization Society as an investigator. In 1908 and 1909, he joined a colony of artists and writers at Carmel-by-the-Sea and then became a reporter for the San Francisco Bulletin and a desk editor for the Associated Press. Between 1910 and 1916, he did editorial work for Volta Review, the Frederick A. Stokes Company (a publishing firm), Adventure magazine, Transatlantic Tales, the Publishers' Newspaper Syndicate, and the George H. Doran Company (a publishing firm). In the late 1930's and early 1940's, he was a book editor for Newsweek, but otherwise, from 1916 until 1951, he was a free-lance writer.

Lewis achieved his early fame with the publication of Main Street, an unbridled attack upon the mores of middle-class, small town America. The book was one of the best-selling novels of its time. In later books, his targets were evangelists, medical foundations, social workers, Rotarians, Kiwanians, and always middle class America. In writing Arrowsmith, he was assisted with tech-nical advice by fellow-traveler Paul de Kruif. In writing Elmer Gantry, he was aided by a leftist clergyman, Leon M. Birkhead. In 1926, he was awarded the Pulitzer Prize for Arrowsmith, but he rejected it on grounds that he did not deserve it, because the prize was originally designed "for the American novel ... which shall best present the wholesome atmosphere of American life and the highest standard of American manners and manhood." In 1930, he received the Nobel Prize in literature. He accepted it. In 1935, his It Can't Happen Here was a forecast in fiction form of a fascist takeover in America. His Red sympathies were quite evident throughout the story. The book proved to be most attractive to Communists, who promoted it in their press and sold it in their bookstores. The Red-laden Federal Theatre Project performed a drama based on the book on stages throughout the country.

In 1935, at a Communist-operated Writers' Congress, Lewis was named to the world presidium of the International Writers Association in Defense of Culture. On the presidium with Lewis were some of the world's best-known Communists and Socialists in the literary field, including George Bernard Shaw, André Gide, Henri Barbusse, Romain Rolland, Maxim Gorki, Aldous Huxley, Selma Lagerlöf, and Thomas Mann.

On New Year's Day, 1936, at the height of Stalin's barbarism, Lewis wired his greetings to the Soviet Union: "Allow me on New Year's to express the hope that progressive America and progressive Russia will continue to defend the interests of world peace."

As a writer, Lewis enjoyed the professional acclaim and the personal friendship of America's large and growing Socialist literary society. He was not a perennial joiner, but the affiliations he did have were enough to indicate that his sympathies were definitely leftist. He was affiliated with the American Society for Cultural Relations with Russia ("Communist front"); the Brookwood Labor College ("Communistic"); the Motion Picture Artists Spanish Aid Committee ("Communist front"); the Medical Bureau and North American Committee To Aid Spanish Democracy ("subversive and un-American"); the National Institute of Arts and Letters ("Communist front"); and the National Mooney-Billings Committee (dominated by Socialists and Communists). He died in January 1951.

MURRAY D. LINCOLN was born on April 18, 1892 in Raynham, Massachusetts, son of Helen Andrews and Minot Jackson. He married Anne Hurst. He was an alumnus of Massachusetts Agricultural College (B.S., 1914). He was the author of *Vice President in Charge of Revolution* (1960).

In 1914, Lincoln was a county agricultural agent in Connecticut. From 1915 until 1917, he was the agricultural agent for the Plymouth County Trust in Brockton, Massachusetts. While in that position he organized one of the first cooperative milk distributing plants in New England. From 1917 until 1919, he was the agricultural agent for the Society for Savings Bank in Cleveland, Ohio. In 1919, he was very instrumental in the formation of the Ohio Farm Bureau Federation, and from 1920 until 1948, he served as executive secretary of the Federation. As the Federation's executive secretary, he organized the Farm Bureau Mutual Automobile Insurance Company (1926), the Farm Bureau Mutual Fire Insurance Company (1934), and the Farm Bureau Mutual Life Insur-

ance Company (1936). From 1926 until 1955, he served as president and general manager of these three insurance companies. In 1955, the farm bureau insurance companies underwent a change of name to the Nationwide Insurance Companies, including the fire, automobile, and life companies and a general insurance company. From 1955 until he retired in 1964, Lincoln was president of Nationwide.

In the late 1930's, Lincoln was instrumental in the founding of the Cooperative League of the United States, and he served the League as president from 1941 until 1965. In the same period, he was vice-president and on the executive committee of the International Cooperative Alliance. He expanded the activities of the Ohio Farm Bureau Federation by investing in the Farm Bureau Cooperative Association and the Farm Bureau Agricultural Credit Corporation.

In 1945, Lincoln was a founder of the Cooperative for American Remittances to Europe, later known as the Cooperative for American Relief Everywhere, but better known by the acronym CARE. From 1945 until 1957, Lincoln served as president of CARE.

Through his work as head of the Ohio Farm Bureau Federation, as head of the Cooperative League of America, and as head of CARE, Lincoln became the most prominent leader and certainly the most powerful individual in the cooperative movement in the United States. And, of course, his influence and power were present in all those foreign countries where CARE operated. For more than forty years, Lincoln waged relentless war against capitalism, especially in America. He detested the profit motive and the free enterprise features of American business. It was long his desire that the pressures of a labor-farm bloc, working through cooperatives, should destroy capitalism. As early as 1931, the Cooperative League's manual said: "In the course of time the capitalistic savages who now people this fair continent will go the way of the mound-builders and American Indians. A new race, representing a cooperative civilization, will take their place." In his long career as a cooperative leader, Lincoln echoed the sentiments expressed in the manual. He frequently told his audiences over the years that when the "revolution" became a reality, the cooperatives would control and manage business and agriculture. It was not unusual for Lincoln to promote his anti-capitalist revolution in legislative hearings, where he proved to be a strong endorser of the welfare state in all its collectivist facets. He of course did not consider the welfare state to be the ultimate answer; rather, the cooperative commonwealth was Lincoln's panacea for farmers and the labor force.

During his presidency of CARE, Lincoln cleverly concealed the "cooperative" nature of the organization. It solicited funds only under its initials – CARE. Americans who, out of a sense of charity, contributed to the support of CARE generally did not recognize that they were helping to promote good will for the cooperative system in nations throughout the world. Through Lincoln's efforts, the money made in a capitalist system was being used to promote its destruction. To the members of his Cooperative League, Lincoln admitted what he was doing with CARE. In the League's literature in 1950, it was stated: "[CARE is] a cooperative which has become a household word not only in America, but in twenty countries overseas, is best known by its initials and very seldom thought of as a cooperative by America's millions . . . . CARE has resulted in the aid for the needy and has built up a reservoir of good-will for cooperatives the world over. It has laid the groundwork for a strong and enduring relationship between co-ops here and abroad."

In the area of politics, Lincoln was ostensibly a Republican for most of his life. During the several administrations of Franklin Delano Roosevelt, Lincoln was for the most part a critic of the New Deal because many of its revolutionary reforms detracted from the drive for power on the part of cooperatives. However, sometime during the course of World War II, Lincoln made his peace with the New Deal, and he was able to get along with the Truman Administration's Fair Deal. As a matter of fact, Lincoln became a founder and a director of the ultra-radical Americans for Democratic Action, and in 1950, after briefly flirting with the idea of trying to gain the Republican nomination for the U.S. Senate in Ohio, he became a Democrat. In the 1950's, he had more than a nodding acquaintance with leftwing radicals. He joined the hue and cry against nuclear testing. He joined with the disarmament buffs and appeasement fanatics in the ultra-leftist National Committee for a Sane Nuclear Policy. He became very vocal in his support for expanded East-West trade between the United States and Socialist and Communist countries. In 1962, he achieved his greatest notoriety by his personal responsibility for the sponsorship by the Nationwide Insurance Companies of a television program featuring Alger Hiss. At the time, Hiss, who had served time in the penitentiary for perjury relating to his espionage activities, was in one of his periodic rehabilitation phases. He made the most

459

of the opportunity to castigate those government officials who had managed to bring him to his much-belated fate for having betrayed this nation. Despite mountains of criticism against the American Broadcasting Company and the Nationwide Insurance Companies for providing Hiss a one-sided forum, Lincoln was not a bit repentant, but rather proud of his part in the pro-Communist fiasco. He died in November 1966.

EDUARD CHRISTIAN LINDEMAN

was born on May 9, 1885 in St. Clair, Michigan, son of Frederika von Piper and Frederick Lindeman. He married Hazel Taft. He was an alumnus of Michigan Agricultural College (B.S., 1911). He was the author of *College Characters* (1912); *The Community* (1921); *Social Discovery* (1924); *The Meaning of Adult Education* (1926); *Urban Sociology* (1928); *Dynamic Social Research* (1933); *Social Education* (1933); *Wealth and Culture* (1935); and *Leisure: A National Issue* (1939). He was the editor of *Emerson, the Basic Writings of America's Sage* (1947). He was a contributing editor to *Youth Service Digest* and advertising editor of *Rural America*. He was on the editorial staff of Penguin Books, Inc.

In 1911 and 1912, Lindeman was editor of *The Gleaner* in Detroit. From 1912 until 1914, he was a social worker in Lansing. From 1915 until 1917, he was a teacher and extension worker at Michigan Agricultural College. In 1918 and 1919, he was a teacher at the YMCA College in Chicago. From 1919 until 1921, he was a teacher at the North Carolina College for Women. In 1924, he was a teacher at the New York School of Social Work at Columbia University. Between 1925 and 1943, he lectured at the ultra-radical New School for Social Research (1925-1927), Pendle Hill (1933-1934), Temple University (1934-1935), the University of California (1936 and 1938), Columbia University (1941-1942), Stanford University (1941); the University of Wisconsin (1943); and, as the Walter Rauschenbush Lecturer, the Colgate-Rochester Divinity School (1943).

Lindeman was an official, member, consultant, or advisor of a wide variety of leftist-oriented educational and social work organizations and agencies, including the American Association for Adult Education, the Public Education Association, the Progressive Education Association, the National Council of Parent Education, the World Association for Adult Education, the Educational Bureau of America, the American Labor Educational Service, the New Jersey State Conference of Social Work, the New Jersey Social Planning Commission, the National Housing Association, the New York Council on Housing, the New York Council on Adult Education, and the National Urban League. From 1935 until 1938, he was director of the Department of Community Organization for Leisure in the Works Progress Administration. In 1939, he was on the advisory committee of the White House Conference on Children in Democracy. He was an advisor to the Institute for Propaganda Analysis, founded and directed by a veteran fellow-traveler, Clyde Miller. He was on the committee on research and education of the Red-laden Federal Council of Churches.

Eugene Lyons in his *The Red Decade* revealed a striking example of Lindeman's commitment to leftism: "In the March 8, 1933, number, the . . . [*New Republic*] presented an extraordinary article under the title 'Is Human Nature Changing in Russia?' The author, a social worker named Eduard C. Lindeman, had just sojourned in Utopia. The date is significant – it was the hardest and bloodiest moment in Soviet Russia's existence up to that time, a moment of wholesale starvation, intensified terror, inner tensions in the ranks of the ruling party itself which would have frightful consequences in the gigantic blood purges of a few years later.

"It was a period, I can attest, when even the most optimistic friends of Stalin who knew the facts whispered in private about the sharpening dangers. The professional press agents of the regime among foreign writers, indeed, had to admit the horrors of the crisis, if only to explain them away. But this American tourist somehow missed it all. Had he set out to compose a satire to kid his fellow-liberals, he could have done no better than in this lightheartedly earnest article.

"Lindeman reported that 'in the first place, there is stability in contemporary Russia and there is solidarity.' It must have shocked the G.P.U. under the pathologically bloodthirsty Henry Yagoda, then engaged on his most ambitious mass production of corpses, to learn from the American weekly that 'revolutionary vigilance tends to relax in all spheres because there is no longer any real danger of counter-revolutionary movements from within.' Of course, 'the primary hungers are not satisfied,' but the Russians, being a peculiar breed of animal, enjoy that: 'There are other goals which have thus far served to release energies and to promote faith.'

"The investigator also reported that 'prostitution, homosexuality and suicide' were 'disappearing.' Homosexuality was so rampant in Moscow and Leningrad at the time that the government soon thereafter exiled hundreds of the afflicted men and women, among them certain high officials, from those cities. The preceding year, in connection with the domestic passport edict, there had been a terrifying wave of suicides in the larger cities; I knew personally of several families which had killed themselves en masse. Little girls below the age of puberty were offering themselves for a little bread on the streets of Kiev and other cities in the famine area at the very moment Lindeman was making his report.

"On and on his report went, making one 'deduction' from non-existing but gratifying facts after another. 'Is it possible for human nature to change with sufficient rapidity and depth to attain those revolutionary goals which constitute the essence of the communist program?' he asked, and answered with a resounding YES. The Russians, he proved to the satisfaction of American liberals, 'are teaching the world . . . the latent capacity of human nature to adapt itself to changing circumstances.' They were indeed – adapting themselves to life by decree, chronic undernourishment, mass executions. But that, of course, is not what he referred to. He actually detected a revision of human character exactly in the period when the Kremlin leaders, to meet the clamoring insistence of the old character, were restoring piecework, bonuses and a thousand other devices, along with increased police pressure.

"The temper of such imaginative 'studies' of Russia on the spot may be judged from one episode elaborated by Lindeman. He saw a crowd of Muscovites assisting an officer in disentangling a traffic snarl resulting from an accident. Such gregariousness and helpfulness has always been common in Russia. But the American tourist eagerly read a socialist moral into it. He 'medi-

461

tated' on the 'event,' and decided that 'Here, then was an illustration of voluntary collectivism. No, it was more than that; it was a demonstration of unity between the citizen and his government.' This meditated proof, of course, outweighed for him the involuntary collectivism and the tragic disunity between state and citizens at that very moment being demonstrated in the South Russian famine."

Lindeman's affiliations included the ultra-radical American Civil Liberties Union; the American Committee for Anti-Nazi Literature ("individuals and organizations connected with it identify this committee as a Communist front organization"); the American Committee for Non-participation in Japanese Aggression ("Communist front"); the American Committee for Protection of Foreign Born ("founded by the Communist Party in order to exploit racial divisions in the United States for its own revolutionary purposes"); the American Committee for Struggle against War ("Communist front"); the American Council on Soviet Relations ("subversive" – "established by the Communist Party . . . directed and controlled by the Party, and operated to aid and support Party objectives concerning the defense and support of the Soviet Union"); the American Investors Union, Inc. ("Communist front" – "the principal tactic employed by the American Investors Union has been to send representatives, first obtaining proxies for them, to stockholders' meetings of various business corporations for the purpose of harassing the management of those corporations"); the American League Against War and Fascism ("subversive and Communist" – "established in the United States in an effort to create public sentiment on behalf of a foreign

policy adapted to the interests of the Soviet Union"); the American League for Peace and Democracy ("subversive and Communist" – "established . . . in an effort to create public sentiment on behalf of a foreign policy adapted to the interests of the Soviet Union . . . [and] designed to conceal Communist control, in accordance with the new tactics of the Communist International"), the American Society for Cultural Relations with Russia ("Communist front"); the American Youth Congress ("subversive" – "one of the most influential front organizations ever set up by the Communists in this country" – "the Communists were in complete control"); the ultra-radical Americans for Democratic Action; Brookwood Labor College ("Communistic"); *Champion* (official organ of the Young Communist League and the International Workers Order, "subversive and Communist"); China Aid Council ("Communist-controlled"); the Citizens' Committee To Free Earl Browder ("strictly a Communist Party affair"); the Committee on Militarism in Education (supporting organization of the U.S. Congress Against War, "completely under the control of the Communist Party"); Commonwealth College ("Communist"); the Conference for Progressive Political Action (Socialist-dominated); the Coordinating Committee To Lift the [Spanish] Embargo ("one of the numerous Communist-front enterprises which were organized around the Communists' agitation over the Spanish Civil War"); the Council Against Intolerance in America (leftist); the Council for Pan-American Democracy ("subversive and Communist"); the Emergency Committee for Strikers Relief (Socialist); the Fellowship of Reconciliation (ultra-leftist-pacifist); the Greater New York Emergency Conference on Inalienable Rights ("Communist front"); the Institute of Pacific Relations ("an instrument of Communist policy, propaganda and military intelligence"); the International Committee for Political Prisoners (to raise funds for jailed seditionists); the Interprofessional Association for Social Insurance ("Communist front"); the Joint Anti-Fascist Refugee Committee ("subversive and Communist"); the Labor Temple School (pro-Communist); the League Against Fascism (Socialist); the League for Mutual Aid ("Communist enterprise"); the League of American Writers ("subversive and Communist" – "began openly to follow the Communist Party line as dictated by the foreign policy of the Soviet Union"); the Medical Bureau and North American Committee To Aid Spanish Democracy ("subversive and un-American"); the National Child Labor Committee (Socialist-dominated); the National Council of American-Soviet Friendship ("subversive and Communist" – "specializing in pro-Soviet propaganda"); the National Emergency Conference for Democratic Rights ("Communist front" – "subversive"); the National Sharecroppers Fund ("Communist front"); the New York State Conference on National Unity ("Communist front"); the People's Congress for Democracy and Peace ("Communist front"); People's Lobby (Socialist); Pioneer Youth of America (Socialist); Social Workers Committee To Aid Spanish Democracy ("Communist front"); the Southern Conference for Human Welfare ("a Communist-front organization which seeks to attract southern liberals on the basis of its seeming interest in the problems of the South"); the Union for Democratic Action (Red-lined outfit whose guiding genius was Louis Fraina, one of America's first Communists); and the World Congress Against War ("sponsored by the Communist International").

Lindeman died in April 1953.

ALAIN LeROY LOCKE was born on September 13, 1886 in Philadelphia, Pennsylvania, son of Mary Hawkins and Pliny Locke. He was an alumnus of Harvard University (A.B., 1907 and Ph.D., 1918). From 1907 until 1910, he studied at Oxford University as a Rhodes scholar. In 1910 and 1911, he studied at the University of Berlin. Before going to Harvard, he graduated from the two-year Philadelphia School of Pedagogy. He was the author of *Race Contacts and Inter-Racial Relations* (1916); *The Problem of Classification in Theory of Value* (1918); *The New Negro* (1925); *The Negro in America* (1933); *Frederick Douglass: A Biography of Anti-Slavery* (1935); *Negro Art: Past and Present* (1936); and *The Negro and His Music* (1937). He was editor of *The Negro in Art* (1940). He was co-editor of *Plays of Negro Life* (1927) and *When Peoples Meet: A Study in Race and Culture* (1942).

From 1912 until 1916, Locke was assistant professor of philosophy and education at Howard University. From 1918 until his retirement in 1951, he was a professor and head of the department of philosophy at Howard. In 1927 and 1928, he was an exchange professor at Fisk University. In 1943, he was in Haiti as an Inter-American Exchange Professor. He was a visiting professor at the University of Wisconsin (1945-1946), the New School for Social Research (1947), and the College of the City of New York (1948).

Locke was affiliated with the American Committee for Protection of Foreign Born ("founded by the Communist Party in order to exploit racial divisions in the United States for its own revolutionary purposes"); the American League for

Peace and Democracy ("subversive and Communist" – "established . . . in an effort to create public sentiment on behalf of a foreign policy adapted to the interests of the Soviet Union . . . [and] designed to conceal Communist control, in accordance with the new tactics of the Communist International"); the American Society for Cultural Relations With Russia ("Communist front"); the China Conference Arrangements Committee ("Communist front"); the Committee for a Democratic Far Eastern Policy ("Communist"); the Committee of Welcome for the Red Dean of Canterbury (England's most notorious pro-Soviet apologist among the clergy); the Conference on Constitutional Liberties in America ("an important part of the solar system of the Communist Party's front organizations"); the Council for Pan-American Democracy ("subversive and Communist"); the Council on African Affairs ("subversive and Communist"); the George Washington Carver School ("adjunct of the Communist Party"); the Golden Book of American Friendship with the Soviet Union ("pro-Soviet propaganda technique"); the Jefferson School of Social Science ("a Communist institution modeled along the lines of the new Communist policy which led to the decision to change the Communist Party into some kind of an educational institution"); the League of American Writers ("subversive and Communist" – "began openly to follow the Communist Party line as dictated by the foreign policy of the Soviet Union"); the Metropolitan Music School ("controlled by Communists"); the ultra-radical National Association for the Advancement of Colored People; the National Emergency Conference ("Communist front"); the National Federation for Constitutional Liberties ("under Communist Party

domination and headed by responsible Party functionaries" – "one of the viciously subversive organizations of the Communist Party"); the National Negro Congress ("subversive and Communist" – "characterized as an organization operating in the field of civil rights under Communist Party domination and headed by responsible Party functionaries"); the National Student League ("the Communists' front organization for students"); the National Wartime Conference of the Professions, the Sciences, the Arts, the White-Collar Fields ("Communist front"); Negro Playwrights, Inc. ("Communist front"); *New Masses* ("weekly journal of the Communist Party"); People's Songs, Inc. ("subversive"); the School for Democracy ("established by Communist teachers ousted from the public school system of New York City"); the Southern Negro Youth Congress ("subversive and among the affiliates and committees of the Communist Party, U.S.A., which seeks to alter the form of government of the United States by unconstitutional means"); *Survey Graphic* (Socialist); Veterans of the Abraham Lincoln Brigade ("directed, dominated and controlled by the Communist Party"); the Washington Committee for Democratic Action ("subversive and Communist"); and the Win-the-Peace Conference ("Communist front").

Locke died in June 1954.

JACK LONDON was born on January 12, 1876 in San Francisco, California, son of Flora Wellman and W.H. Chaney. His stepfather was John London. He was married to and divorced from Bessie Maddern. His second wife was Charmian Kittredge. For a brief time he attended the University of California. He was the author of *The Son of the*

Wolf (1900); *Tales of the Far North* (1900); *The God of His Fathers and Other Stories* (1901); *A Daughter of the Snows* (1902); *The Children of the Frost* (1902); *The Cruise of the Dazzler* (1902); *The People of the Abyss* (1903); *Kempton-Wace Letters* (1903); *The Call of the Wild* (1903); *The Faith of Men* (1904); *The Sea Wolf* (1904); *The Game* (1905); *War of the Classes* (1905); *Tales of the Fish Patrol* (1905); *Moon-Face* (1906); *Scorn of Women*, play (1906); *White Fang* (1907); *Before Adam* (1907); *Love of Life* (1907); *The Iron Heel* (1907); *The Road* (1907); *Martin Eden* (1909); *Lost Face* (1909); *Revolution* (1910); *Burning Daylight* (1910); *Theft* (1910); *When God Laughs* (1910); *Adventure* (1911); *The Cruise of the Snark* (1911); *South Sea Tales* (1911); *Smoke Bellow Tales* (1912); *The House of Pride* (1912); *A Son of the Sun* (1912); *The Night-Born* (1913); *The Abysmal Brute* (1913); *John Barleycorn* (1913); *The Valley of the Moon* (1913); *The Strength of the Strong* and *The Mutiny of the Elsinore* (1914); *The Scarlet Plague* (1915); *The Star Rover* (1915); and *The Little Lady of the Big House* (1916).

Separating truth from fiction in London's career is made difficult by the mass of contradictions which exist both in his own writings and in those of his biographers and critics. In some manner, even the name of London's real father and London's birth out of wedlock have been misrepresented in what would usually be considered reliable sources. Somehow, London's stepfather acquired the status of an outdoorsman and adventurer rather than his real occupation as a grocer, boarding house owner, and chicken farmer.

At the age of fifteen, London left Oakland, California, where his mother and stepfather had settled, and traveled for some months as a hobo. When he returned home, he became an oyster pirate in the San Francisco area. In 1893 and 1894, he sailed on a seal-hunting vessel to the coasts of Japan and Siberia. When he returned to the United States, he resumed his career as a hobo, but his travels were cut short when he was jailed as a vagrant in Niagara Falls, New York. In 1895, he spent some time in Oakland High School and even enrolled at the University of California, but his college days were few in number. At about that time, as a result of his assiduous reading, he decided that he was a Socialist. In and around Oakland, he became a soapbox orator, preaching Socialism. In 1896, he joined the gold rush to the Klondike; after about one year, he returned home without gold but with a background of experiences that would serve him well as a writer. In 1898 and 1899, he experienced his first literary success by selling short stories to the *Overland Monthly* and the *Black Cat*. In 1899, the *Atlantic Monthly* bought his "An Odyssey of the North," a story which led to the publication of his first book in 1900. Over the next sixteen years, he became the best-paid and most widely read novelist in the world. He continued traveling to acquire material for his books. In 1904, he traveled to the Far East, where for a period of about five months he reported to the *New York Journal* on the Russo-Japanese War. From 1907 until 1909, he traveled to the South Seas aboard his luxurious fifty-five-foot yacht, *Snark*. He acquired a large ranch in California on which he built an extravagant castle, where he lived in capitalistic splendour.

In 1905, London took his first and only fling in politics by running on the Socialist Party ticket for the mayoralty of Oakland. In that same year, he joined with other famous Socialists in the founding of the Intercollegiate Socialist

Society, which, under both that name and its later name, the League for Industrial Democracy, became the Socialists' most important educational and proselytizing effort on college and university campuses throughout the United States. To launch the ISS, London went on a nation-wide tour of campuses, lecturing on Socialism. He traveled with a Korean valet, who dressed London carefully in what could only be described as a foppish mode. As London travelled about the country, he appended to his signature on hotel registers the phrase, "Yours for the Revolution!" The lecture tour proved to be a success, and chapters of the ISS sprang up on campuses across the nation.

In 1905, in his *War of the Classes*, London — unmistakably *nouveau riche* — wrote of how he became a Socialist. It was a fanciful account, but it does give an indication of its author's talent for confusing truth and fiction. He wrote: "It is quite fair to say that I became a Socialist in a fashion somewhat similar to the way in which the Teutonic pagans became Christians — it was hammered into me. Not only was I not looking for Socialism at the time of my conversion but I was fighting it. I was very young and callow, did not know much of anything, and though I had never even heard of a school called 'Individualism,' I sang the paean of the strong with all my heart.

"This was because I was strong myself. By strong I mean that I had good health and hard muscles, both of which possessions are easily accounted for. I had lived my childhood on California ranches, my boyhood hustling newspapers on the streets of a healthy Western city, and my youth on the ozone-laden waters of San Francisco Bay and the Pacific Ocean. I loved life in the open, and I toiled in the open, at the hardest kinds of work. Learning no trade, but drifting along from job to job, I looked on the world and called it good, every bit of it. Let me repeat, this optimism was because I was healthy and strong, bothered with neither aches nor weaknesses, never turned down by the boss because I did not look fit, able always to get a job at shoveling coal, sailorizing, or manual labor of some sort.

"And because of all this, exulting in my young life, able to hold my own at work or fight, I was a rampant individualist. It was very natural. I was a winner. Wherefore I called the game, as I saw it played, or thought I saw it played, a very proper game for MEN. To be a MAN was to write man in large capitals on my heart. To adventure like a man, and fight like a man, and do a man's work (even for a boy's pay) — these were things that reached right in and gripped hold of me as no other thing could. And I looked ahead into long vistas of a hazy and interminable future, into which, playing what I conceived to be a MAN'S game, I should continue to travel with unfailing health, without accidents, and with muscles ever vigorous. As I say, this future was interminable. I could see myself only raging through life without end like one of Nietzsche's *blond beasts*, lustfully roving and conquering by sheer superiority and strength.

"As for the unfortunates, the sick and ailing and old and maimed, I must confess I hardly thought of them at all, save that I vaguely felt that they, barring accidents, could be as good as I if they wanted to real hard, and could work just as well. Accidents? Well, they represented FATE, also spelled out in capitals, and there was no getting around FATE. Napoleon had had an accident at Waterloo, but that did not dampen my desire to be another and later Napoleon. Further, the optimism bred of a stomach which could digest scrap iron and a body which flourished on hardships did not permit me to consider accidents as even remotely related to my glorious personality.

"I hope I have made it clear that I was proud to be one of nature's strong-armed noblemen. The dignity of labor was to me the most impressive thing in the world. Without having read Carlyle or Kipling, I formulated a gospel of work which put theirs in the shade. Work was everything. It was sanctification and salvation. The pride I took in a hard day's work well done would be inconceivable to you. It is almost inconceivable to me as I look back upon it. I was as faithful a wage slave as ever capitalist exploited. To shirk or malinger on the man who paid me my wages was a sin, first, against myself, and second, against him. I considered it a crime second only to treason, and just about as bad.

"In short, my joyous individualism was dominated by the orthodox bourgeois ethics. I read the bourgeois papers, listened to the bourgeois preachers, and shouted at the sonorous platitudes of the bourgeois politicians. And I doubt not, if other events had not changed my career, that I should have evolved into a professional strikebreaker . . . and had my head and my earning power irrevocably smashed by a club in the hands of some militant trades unionist.

"Just about this time, returning from a seven months' voyage before the mast, and just turned eighteen, I took it into my head to go tramping. On rods and blind baggages I fought my way from the open West, where men bulked big and the job hunted the man, to the congested labor centers of the East, where men were small potatoes and hunted the job for all they were worth. And on this new *blond-beast* adventure I found myself looking upon life from a new and totally different angle. I had dropped down from the proletariat into what sociologists love to call the 'submerged tenth,' and I was startled to discover the way in which that submerged tenth was recruited.

"I found there all sorts of men, many of whom had once been as good as myself and just as *blond-beastly*; sailormen, soldiermen, labormen, all wrenched and distorted and twisted out of shape by toil and hardship and accident, and cast adrift by their masters like so many old horses. I battered on the drag and slammmed backgates with them, or shivered with them in boxcars and city parks, listening the while to life histories which began under auspices as fair as mine, with digestions and bodies equal to and better than mine, and which ended there before my eyes in the shambles at the bottom of the Social Pit.

"And as I listened my brain began to work. The woman of the streets and the man of the gutter drew very close to me. I saw the picture of the Social Pit as vividly as though it were a concrete thing, and at the bottom of the Pit I saw them, myself above them, not far, and hanging on to the slippery wall by main strength and sweat. And I confess a terror seized me. What when my strength failed, when I should be unable to work shoulder to shoulder with the strong men who were as yet babes unborn?

"And there and then I swore a great oath. It ran something like this: 'All my days I have worked hard with my body, and according to the number of days I have worked, by just that much am I nearer the bottom of the Pit. I shall climb out of the Pit, but not by the muscles of my body shall I climb out. I shall do no more hard work, and may God strike me dead if I do another day's hard work with my body more than I absolutely have to do.' And I have been busy ever since running away from hard work.

"Incidentally, while tramping some 10,000 miles through the United States and Canada, I strayed into Niagara Falls, was nabbed by a fee-hunting constable, denied the right to plead guilty or not guilty, sentenced out of hand to thirty days' imprisonment for having no fixed abode and no visible means of support, handcuffed and chained to a bunch of men similarly circumstanced, carted down country to Buffalo, registered at the Erie County Penitentiary, had my head clipped and my budding mustache shaved, was dressed in convict stripes, compulsorily vaccinated by a medical student who practised on such as we, made to march the lockstep, and put to work under the eyes of guards armed with Winchester rifles — all for adventuring in *blond-beastly* fashion. Concerning further details deponent sayeth not, though he may hint that some of his plethoric national patriotism simmered down and leaked out the bottom of his soul somewhere — at least, since that experience he finds that he cares more for men and women and little children than for imaginary geographical lines.

"To return to my conversion. I think it is apparent that my rampant individualism was pretty effectively hammered out of me, and something else as effectively hammered in. But, just as I had been an individualist without knowing it, I was now a Socialist without knowing it, withal an unscientific one. I had been reborn, but not renamed, and I was running around to find out what manner of thing I was. I ran back to California and opened the books. I do not remember which ones I opened first. It is an unimportant detail anyway. I was already It, whatever It was, and by aid of the books I discovered that It was a Socialist. Since that day I have opened many books, but no economic argument, no lucid demonstration of the logic and inevitableness of Socialism affects me as profoundly and convincingly as I was affected on the day when I first saw the walls of the Social Pit rise around me and felt myself slipping down, down, into the shambles at the bottom."

London died — an apparent suicide — in November 1916. Since his death, he has become one of the few American authors whose works have been widely published and read in Communist countries.

ROBERT MORSS LOVETT was born on December 25, 1870 in Boston, Massachusetts, son of Elizabeth Russell and Augustus Lovett. He married Ida Mott-Smith. He was an alumnus of Harvard University (A.B., 1892). He was the author of *Richard Gresham* (1904); *A Winged Victory* (1907); *Cowards*, a play (1914); *Edith Wharton* (1925); *Preface to Fiction* (1930); and *All Our Years* (1948). He was co-author of *A History of English Literature* (1902); *A First View of English Literature* (1905); and *History of the Novel in England* (1932). He was compiler of *Selected Poems of William Vaughn Moody* (1930). He was co-compiler of *British Poetry and Prose* (1928) and *A College Reader* (1937).

In 1892 and 1893, Lovett was at Harvard University as an assistant in English (1892) and an instructor (1893). From 1893 until 1936, he was at the University of Chicago, as instructor in English (1893-1896), assistant professor (1896-1904), associate professor (1904-1909), professor (1909-1936), and dean of junior colleges (1907-1920).

In 1939, he was a lecturer at Northwestern University. From 1939 until 1943, in the employ of the Department of the Interior, he was Governor Secretary of the Virgin Islands. In 1944, he was a visiting professor of English at the University of Puerto Rico. In 1945, he was a visiting professor of English at Fisk University. In 1919, he was editor of *The Dial.* From 1921 until 1940, he was literary editor of the *New Republic.* In 1944 he was executive assistant to the Governor of the Virgin Islands.

When Lovett settled in Chicago, he joined Jane Addams' Hull House circle of pacifists, American Socialists, Communists, and British Fabian Socialists. When Lovett became a resident of Hull House, he began a career of radicalism that has not been surpassed by anyone in this century. Of course, he did not go unnoticed. In 1935, an Illinois Senate investigating committee recommended his dismissal from the University of Chicago. In 1943, two congressional investigating committees recommended his dismissal from government employment, but his continuance in the Virgin Islands position was vigorously defended by President Franklin D. Roosevelt and Secretary of the Interior Harold L. Ickes.

In the course of testimony before the Special Committee on Un-American Activities in 1943, Lovett made statements that indicate to some extent the nature of his ideology: "I do not [consider the Communist Party to be a subversive organization] . . . . So far as my knowledge of the Communist Party goes, it is not committed to the policy of destroying this government by force or violence . . . . I have been a friend of the Soviet Union since 1917 and have watched that experiment with the greatest interest and sympathy . . . . The Communist Party is a political party. Nothing more than that, in its public character. The Communists may have other interests in politics, but the Communist Party certainly is a political organization." A few years earlier, Lovett said that though "the Communist Party stands in general for the same type of change in social order as that represented by Norman Thomas . . . personally I feel that the Socialist Party is nearer to American ideology." And, although Lovett has denied that he ever joined the Socialist Party, he admitted voting for that Party's presidential candidate, Thomas, in 1936.

In one period of his career, Lovett held high executive positions in four organizations simultaneously: The ultra-radical American Civil Liberties Union; the Socialists' League for Industrial Democracy, of which he was president for twenty years; the Garland Fund, of which he was a founder and trustee dispensing funds to a myriad of Communist enterprises; and the Federated Press, run by Communists for purely Communist purposes.

Lovett's other affiliations included the All-America Anti-Imperialist League ("the [Communist] Party was wholly responsible for the establishment and subsequent control of the league"); the American Committee for Democracy and Intellectual Freedom ("subversive and un-American" — "a Communist-front organization operating among college teachers and professors"); the American Committee for Protection of Foreign Born ("founded by the Communist Party in order to exploit racial divisions in the United States for its own revolutionary purposes"); the American Committee for Struggle Against War ("Communist front"); the American Council on Soviet Relations ("subversive" — "established by the Communist Party . . . directed and controlled by the Party, and operated to aid and support Party objec-

469

tives concerning the defense and support of the Soviet Union"); the American Friends of Spanish Democracy ("Communist front"); the American Friends of the Chinese People ("Communist front"); the American Fund for Public Service ("a major source for the financing of Communist Party enterprises, such as the *Daily Worker* and *New Masses*, official Communist publications, Federated Press, Russian Reconstruction Farms, and International Labor Defense"); the American League Against War and Fascism ("subversive and Communist" – "established in the United States in an effort to create public sentiment on behalf of a foreign policy adapted to the interests of the Soviet Union"); the American League for Peace and Democracy ("subversive and Communist" – "established . . . in an effort to create public sentiment on behalf of a foreign policy adapted to the interests of the Soviet Union . . . [and] designed to conceal Communist control, in accordance with the new tactics of the Communist International"); the American Peace Crusade ("Communist front"); the American Peace Mobilization ("formed . . . under the auspices of the Communist Party and the Young Communist League" – "one of the most seditious organizations which ever operated in the United States"); the American Pushkin Committee ("Communist front"); the American Russian Institute ("subversive" – "Communist" – "specializing in pro-Soviet propaganda"); the American Student Union ("without exception . . . supported defensive teachers and students charged with Communist activity" – "pliable instrument in the hands of the Communist Party"); the American Youth Congress ("subversive" – "one of the most influential front organizations ever set up by the Communists in this country" – "the Communists were in complete control"); the Berger National Foundation (socialist); the Bill of Rights Conference ("subversive"); the Book Union ("distributors of Communist literature" – "Communist [Party] book club"); the Brookwood Labor College ("Communistic"); the California Labor School ("a subversive and Communist organization"); *Champion of Youth* ("official organ of the Young Communist League and International Workers Order"); the Chicago Emergency Committee for Strikers Relief (socialist); the Chicago Forum Council (pro-Communist); the Chicago Workers Theatre ("Communist front"); the China Aid Council ("Communist-controlled"); *China Today* ("Communist Party-controlled publication"); the Citizens Committee for Harry Bridges ("Communist"); the Civil Rights Congress ("created and established by the Communist Party as an organization which would utilize defense of civil rights for Party purposes and raise and maintain mass defense and bail funds for Party use"); the Committee for a Boycott Against Japanese Aggression ("the Committee was featured in the *Daily Worker*, official organ of the Communist Party, and in that paper alone"); the Committee for the Defense of Marion Bachrach ("Communist front"); the Committee on Militarism in Education (a supporting organization of the U.S. Congress Against War, "completely under the control of the Communist Party"); the Committee To Defend Alexander Trachtenberg ("Communist front"); the Committee To Defend America by Keeping Out of War ("Communist front"); the Committee to End Sedition Laws ("under complete domination by the Communist Party"); the Committee To Save Spain and China ("Communist front"); the Committee

To Secure Justice in the Rosenberg Case ("Communist front organized . . . to conduct the United States phase of a mammoth propaganda campaign designed to obliterate the crime of and exploit the Rosenbergs and their co-defendant Morton Sobell for the purposes of international Communism"); the Conference for Progressive Political Action (Socialist-dominated); the Conference for World Peace Through Negotiation (pro-Communist); the Conference on Constitutional Liberties ("Communist front"); the Congress of American Revolutionary Writers ("subversive and Communist"); the Council Against Intolerance in America (leftist); the Cultural and Scientific Conference for World Peace ("Communist front" – "a propaganda front for Soviet foreign policy and Soviet culture"); the Farmer-Labor Political Federation (Socialist); the Federation for Repeal of the Levering Act (strongly supported by Communists and apologists for the Communist Party); *Fight* ("official organ of the American League Against War and Fascism [American League for Peace and Democracy], subversive and Communist"); the Fellowship of Reconciliation (ultra-leftist-pacifist); Film Audiences for Democracy ("Communist front"); Films for Democracy ("Communist front"); the Free Tom Mooney Congress ("Communist front"); Friends of the Abraham Lincoln Brigade ("completely controlled by the Communist Party"); the Friends of the Soviet Union ("created, directed, and controlled by the Communist Party . . . and operated to aid and support Party objectives concerning the defense and support of the Soviet Union"); the Golden Book of American Friendship with the Soviet Union ("pro-Soviet propaganda enterprise"); the Greater Boston Peace Strike Committee ("Com-munist front"); the Hiroshima Commemorative Committee (ultra-leftist); In Defense of Culture (Communist project); the International Committee for Political Prisoners ("an ultra-leftist fund-raising enterprise for seditionists"); the International Labor Defense ("subversive and Communist" – "legal arm of the Communist Party" – "part of an international network of organizations for the defense of Communist lawbreakers"); the International Workers Order ("from its very inception demonstrated by its pronouncements, its activities, and the authoritative statements of the Communist Party that it is a subservient instrument of the Communist Party of the United States"); the International Workers of the World ("subversive"); the Jefferson School of Social Science ("a Communist institution modeled along the lines of the new Communist policy which led to the decision to change the Communist Party into some kind of an educational institution"); the John Reed Clubs ("out-and-out Communist organizations which preceded the contemporary Communist front organizations which cater to so-called liberals"); the Joint Anti-Fascist Refugee Committee ("subversive and Communist"); the League for Independent Political Action (Socialist); the League for the Organization of Progress (pro-Communist); the League of American Writers ("subversive and Communist" – "began openly to follow the Communist Party line as dictated by the foreign policy of the Soviet Union"); the League for Mutual Aid ("Communist enterprise"); the Marcus Graham Defense Committee ("Communist front"); the Medical Bureau and North American Committee To Aid Spanish Democracy ("subversive and un-American"); the Mother Ella Reeve Bloor Banquet ("Communist Party festivity"); the National Assembly for Peace ("Communist front"); the National Committee for People's Rights ("composed primarily of openly-avowed members of the Communist Party and veteran fellow-travelers of the Communist Party"); the National Committee for the Defense of Political Prisoners ("subversive and Communist"); the National Committee To Aid Striking Miners Fighting Starvation ("Communist front"); the National Committee To Aid Victims of German Fascism ("an auxiliary of the Communist Party"); the National Committee To Repeal the McCarran Act ("Communist front" – "subversive"); the National Committee To Win Amnesty for Smith Act Victims ("subversive" – "Communist"); the National Council for the Protection of Foreign-Born Workers ("Communist subsidiary"); the National Council of American-Soviet Friendship ("subversive and Communist" – "specializing in pro-Soviet propaganda"); the National Council of the Arts, Sciences, and Professions ("a Communist front used to appeal to special occupational groups"); the National Emergency Conference ("Communist front"); the National Emergency Conference for Democratic Rights ("Communist front" – "subversive"); the National Federation for Constitutional Liberties ("under Communist Party domination and headed by responsible Party fuctionaries" – "one of the viciously subversive organizations of the Communist Party"); the National Institute of Arts and Letters ("Communist front"); the National Mooney-Billings Committee ("part of Communist Party agitation"); the National Mooney Council of Action ("formed by the Communists' International Labor Defense"); the National Peoples Committee Against Hearst ("subversive and Communist");

the National Right-to-Work Congress ("out-and-out Communist Party affair"); the National Save Our Schools Committee (pro-Communist); the National Writers Congress ("Communist front"); *New Masses* ("weekly journal of the Communist Party"); *New World Review* ("monthly propaganda organ on the Soviet Union, Red China, and the Communist satellites"); the Non-Partisan Committee for the Re-election of Congressman Vito Marcantonio ("Communist front"); an Open Letter for Closer Cooperation With the Soviet Union (issued by "a group of Communist Party stooges"); an Open Letter to American Liberals ("project of well-known Communists and Communist-collaborators" – "in defense of the progressive movement undertaken by the Soviet Union"); *Partisan* ("semi-monthly publication of the John Reed Clubs"); People's Congress for Democracy and Peace ("Communist front"); the People's Front for Peace ("a project . . . in which Communist organizations predominated"); the People's Legislative Service (a Socialist lobby); Russian Reconstruction Farms ("Communist enterprise"); Russian War Relief ("Communist enterprise"); the Sacco-Vanzetti National League ("part of a Communist propaganda campaign"); *Science and Society* ("Communist publication"); *Soviet Russia Today* ("Communist-controlled publication"); Student Congress Against War ("Communist-controlled"); the United American Spanish Aid Committee ("Communist"); the U.S. Congress Against War ("completely under the control of the Communist Party"); the Workers Defense League (defending political undesirables who are subject to deportation); the World Congress Against War ("sponsored by the Communist International"); and the World Peace Congress ("organized under

Communist initiative in various countries throughout the world"). Maurice Malkan, in his *Return to My Father's House*, published in 1972, said that as a Communist Party organizer in Chicago, he worked closely with Robert Morss Lovett, "keeping his [Communist] Party book and advising him on current policy." Lovett died in February 1956.

HALFORD E. LUCCOCK was born on March 11, 1885 in Pittsburgh, son of Etta Anderson and Naphtali Luccock. He married Mary Whitehead. He was an alumnus of Northwestern University (B.A., 1906); Union Theological Seminary (B.D., 1909); and Columbia University (M.A. 1909). In 1910, he was ordained to the Methodist Episcopal ministry. He was the author of *Fares Please!* (1916); *Five-Minute Shop Talks* (1916); *Studies in the Parables of Jesus* (1917); *The Christian Crusade for World Democracy* (1918); *The New Map of the World* (1919); *Skylines: The Haunted House and Other Sermons* (1923); *Preaching Values in New Translations of the New Testament* (1928); *Jesus and the American Mind* (1930); *Contemporary American Literature and Religion* (1934); *Christian Faith and Economic Change* (1936); *Christianity and the Individual* (1937); *The Acts of the Apostles in Present Day Preaching* (1938); *American Mirror* (1941); *In the Minister's Workshop* (1944); *Marching Off the Map* (1952); *Like a Mighty Army: Selected Letters of Simeon Stylites* (1954); *Unfinished Business* (1956); *Living Without Gloves: More Letters of Simeon Stylites* (1957); *Preaching Values in the Epistles of Paul: Volume I, Romans and the First Corinthians* (1959); and *365 Windows* (1960). He was co-author of *The Mid-Week Service* (1916) and *The Story of Methodism* (1926).

From 1910 until 1916, Luccock did pastoral work in Brooklyn, New York, and in Windsor and New Haven, Connecticut. In 1916, he retired from the active ministry. From 1916 until 1918, he was an instructor in Greek and registrar at Drew Theological Seminary in New Jersey. From 1918 until 1924, he was editorial secretary of the Methodist Board of Foreign Missions. From 1924 until 1928, he was a contributing editor of the *Christian Advocate*. From 1924 until 1936, he was a member of the Conference of the Methodist Board of Foreign Missions. From 1928 until 1953, he was professor of homiletics at Yale University. In 1953, he became professor emeritus. He was a columnist for *Christendom* ("Through the Novelist's Window"); for the *Christian Herald* ("Daily Meditations"); and for *Christian Century*, under the pseudonym Simeon Stylites.

Luccock was affiliated with the American Committee for Democracy and Intellectual Freedom ("subversive and un-American" – "a Communist-front organization operating among college teachers and professors"); the Committee for Peaceful Alternatives to the Atlantic Pact ("a Communist front organization . . . as part of Soviet psychological warfare against the United States"); the Committee of Welcome for the Red Dean of Canterbury (England's most notorious pro-Soviet apologist among the clergy); the Committee on Militarism in Education (supporting organization of the U.S. Congress Against War, "completely under the control of the Communist Party"); the Conference on Constitutional Liberties in America ("an important part of the solar system of the Communist Party's front organizations"); the Coordinating Committee To Lift the [Spanish] Embargo ("one of the numerous Communist-front enterprises which were organized around the Communists' agitation over the Spanish Civil War"); the Red-laden Federal Council of Churches; the Fellowship of Reconciliation (ultra-leftist-pacifist); the International Labor Defense ("subversive and Communist" – "legal arm of the Communist Party" – "part of an international network of organizations for the defense of Communist lawbreakers"); the Methodist Federation for Social Action ("the organization's influence has been consistently wielded on behalf of Communist causes and the Communist line as expressed through the party and its innumerable subsidiaries"); the Mid-Century Conference for Peace ("aimed at assembling as many gullible persons as possible under Communist direction and turning them into a vast sounding board for Communist propaganda"); the National Religion and Labor Foundation ("Communist front"); the Non-Intervention Citizens Committee (dominated by Socialists and Communists); an Open Letter for Closer Cooperation with the Soviet Union (issued by "a group of Communist Party stooges"); the Peace Information Center ("Communist front"); the *Protestant* ("with an eye to religious groups, the Communists have formed religious fronts such as the *Protestant*"); the *Protestant Digest* ("a magazine which has faithfully propagated the Communist Party line under the guise of being a religious journal"); the Washington Committee To Lift [the] Spanish Embargo ("Communist front"); the *World Peace Appeal* ("Communist Party campaign"); and the *World Tomorrow* (Socialist publication). He died in November 1960.

FRANCIS JOHN McCONNELL was born on August 18, 1871 in Trinway, Ohio, son of Nancy Chalfant and Israel McConnell. He married Eva Thomas. He was an alumnus of Ohio Wesleyan University (A.B., 1894) and Boston University (S.T.B., 1897 and Ph.D., 1899). He entered the Methodist Episcopal ministry in 1894. He was the author of *The Diviner Immanence* (1906); *Christmas Sermons* (1909); *Religious Certainty* (1910); *Christian Focus* (1911); *The Increase of Faith* (1912); *Personal Christianity* (1914); *Understanding the Scriptures* (1917); *Democratic Christianity* (1919); *Public Opinion and Theology* (1920); *The Preacher and the People* (1922); *Is God Limited?* (1924); *The Christlike God* (1927); *Borden Parker Browne* (1929); *The Prophetic Ministry* (1930); *The Christian Ideal and Social Control; Christianity and Coercion* (1933); *John Wesley* (1939); *Evangelicals, Revolutionists and Idealists* (1942); and *By The Way, An Autobiography* (1952).

From 1894 until 1909, McConnell did pastoral work in West Chelmsford (1894-1897), Newton Upper Falls (1897-1899), Ipswich (1899-1902), and Cambridge (1902-1903) – all in Massachusetts. From 1903 until 1909, he was a pastor in Brooklyn. From 1909 until 1912, he was pastor of De Pauw University. In 1912, he was elected bishop of the Methodist Episcopal Church. He was a visiting professor at Columbia University (1932-1933), Drew University (1934), the Garrett Bible Institute (1934), and Yale University (1946). In 1930, he was the Lyman Beecher Lecturer at Yale University. In 1931, he was the Barrows Lecturer in India.

In 1929, McConnell was president of the Red-laden Federal Council of Churches. In 1929, 1932, and 1936, he was on the campaign committees of the Socialist Party. From 1939 until 1949, he was vice-president of the League for Industrial Democracy, the most important social influence on the nation's campuses. His other affiliations include the American Association for Old Age Security (Socialist); the ultra-leftist American Civil Liberties Union; the American Committee for Democracy and Intellectual Freedom ("subversive and un-American" – "a Communist-front organization operating among college teachers and professors"); the American Committee for Protection of Foreign Born ("founded by the Communist Party in order to exploit racial divisions in the United States for its own revolutionary purposes"); the American Committee To Save Refugees ("perform[ing] a most valuable function for the international Communist movement"); the American Friends of Spanish Democracy ("Communist front"); the American Friends of the Chinese People ("Communist front"); the American League Against War and Fascism ("subversive and Communist" – "established in the United States in an effort to create public sentiment on behalf of a foreign policy adapted to the interests of the Soviet Union"); the American League for Peace and Democracy ("subversive and Communist" – "established . . . in an effort to create public sentiment on behalf of a foreign policy adapted to the interests of the Soviet Union . . . [and] designed to conceal Communist control, in accordance with the new tactics of the Communist International"); the American Relief Ship for Spain ("Communist Party front enterprise"); the American Student Union ("without exception . . . supported defense of teachers and students charged with Communist activity" – "pliable instrument in the hands of the Communist Party"); the Appeal for Lawrence Simpson (Communist Party member); the Bill of Rights Congress ("subversive"); the Brookwood Labor College ("Communistic"); the China Aid Council (Communist-controlled); the Citizens Committee To Free Earl Browder ("a strictly Communist Party affair"); the Civil Rights Congress ("created and established by the Communist Party as an organization which would utilize defense of civil rights for Party purposes and raise and maintain mass defense and bail funds for Party use"); the Committee for Peace Through World Cooperation ("it is significant that the Committee . . . received its chief publicity in the Communist press"); the Committee on Militarism in Education (supporting organization of the U.S. Congress Against War, "completely under the control of the Communist Party"); the Committee To Save Spain and China ("Communist front"); the Congress of American-Soviet Friendship ("Communist front"); the Coordinating Committee To Lift the [Spanish] Embargo ("one of the numerous Communist-front enterprises which were organized around the Communists' agitation over the Spanish Civil War"); the Emergency Committee for Strikers Relief (Socialist); Exiled Writers Committee ("Communist enterprise"); Federated Unemployed Workers Leagues of New York (pro-Communist); the Fellowship of Reconciliation (ultra-leftist-pacifist); *Fight* ("official organ of the American League Against War and Fascism [American League for Peace and Democracy], subversive and Communist"); the Foreign Policy Association (a highly influential and highly effective pro-Communist vehicle); the International Labor Defense ("subversive and Communist" – "legal arm of the Communist Party" – "part of an international network of organizations for the defense of Communist lawbreakers"); the Japanese-American Committee for Democracy ("Communist-controlled organization"); the Joint Committee for the Defense of the Brazilian People ("Communist front"); the Joint Committee on Un-Employment (dominated by Socialists); the Labor Research Association (Communist Party subsidiary); the League of American Writers ("subversive and Communist" – "began openly to follow the Communist Party line as dictated by the foreign policy of the Soviet Union"); the Medical Bureau and North American Committee To Aid Spanish Democracy ("subversive and un-American"); the Methodist Federation for Social Service ("the organization's influence has been consistently wielded on behalf of Communist causes and the Communist line as expressed through the party and its innumerable subsidiaries"); the Michigan Civil Rights Federation ("subversive and Communist"); the National Citizens Committee on Relations With Latin America (pro-Soviet); the National Citizens Political Action Committee ("Communist front"); the National Committee To Abolish the Poll Tax ("Communist front"); the National Conference on Civil Liberties ("Communist front"); the National Council for the Prevention of War (a group which harbored anarchists, pacifists, Communists, and anti-anti-Communists); the National Council of American-Soviet Friendship ("subversive and Communist" – "specializing in pro-Soviet propaganda"); the National Emergency Conference for Democratic Rights ("Communist front" – "subversive"); the National Federation for Constitutional Liberties ("under Communist Party domination and headed by responsible Party functionaries" – "one of the viciously subversive organizations of the Communist Party"); the National Re-ligion and Labor Foundation ("Communist front"); the National Right to Work Congress ("out-and-out-Communist Party affair"); the National Save Our Schools Committee ("dominated by Socialists and Communists"); the National Sharecroppers Fund ("Communist front"); the New York Peace Association ("Communist-inspired organization"); the Non-Partisan Committee for the Re-election of Congressman Vito Marcantonio ("Communist front"); the North American Committee To Aid Spanish Democracy ("Communist"); the Peoples Institute of Applied Religion ("subversive and Communist"); the Peoples Lobby (Socialist); the *Protestant* ("with an eye to religious groups, the Communists have formed such religious fronts as the *Protestant*"); *Protestant Digest* ("a magazine which has faithfully propagated the Communist Party line under the guise of being a religious journal"); the Public Ownership League of America (Socialist); the Reichstag Fire Trial Anniversary Committee ("Communist front . . . formed . . . by prominent Communists and Communist sympathizers"); the [Morris U.] Schappes Defense Committee ("a front organization with a strictly Communist objective, namely, the defense of a self-admitted Communist who was convicted of perjury in the courts of New York"); the Social Workers Committee To Aid Spanish Democracy ("Communist front"); the Spanish Refugee Relief Campaign ("Communist front"); the Washington Committee To Lift [the] Spanish Embargo ("Communist front"); Washington Friends of Spanish Democracy ("Communist front"); and *World Tomorrow* (Socialist publication). He died in August 1953.

RUTH McKENNEY was born on

November 18, 1911 in Mishawaka, Indiana, daughter of Marguarite Flynn and John McKenney. She married Richard Bransten. From 1928 until 1931, she attended Ohio State University. She was the author of *My Sister Eileen* (1938); *Industrial Valley* (1939); *The McKenney's Carry On* (1940); *Jake Home* (1943); *Loud Red Patrick* (1947); *Love Story* (1950); *Here's England* (1950); *All About Eileen* (1952); *Far From Home* (1954); and *Mirage* (1956). She was co-author of *Love Reason Courage Hard Work* and *Statements on the Tourist Racket* (1960).

In 1932 and 1933, McKenney was a reporter for the *Akron Beacon-Journal.* From 1933 until 1937, she was a reporter for the *New York Post.* In 1937, she married Richard Bransten, a Communist, who used the pseudonym Bruce Minton. He became an editor of *New Masses*, the "weekly journal of the Communist Party." In 1936, she began writing stories for the *New Yorker* magazine. In 1938, her first book, *My Sister Eileen*, brought her a great deal of fame. Later, the book was made into a stage play and a motion picture film. In later years, it was the basis for a musical, *Wonderful Town.* Although *My Sister Eileen* gave McKenney a reputation as a humorist, her other early writings were not amusing. Her *Industrial Valley* was an alleged documentary account of a strike conducted by the United Rubber Workers of America, under the guidance of Communist agitators. McKenney was on the side of the Reds. Her *Jake Home*, published in 1943, was nothing less than Communist propaganda. From 1937 until 1946, she was an editor and columnist ("Strictly Personal") for *New Masses.* She was, of course, a member of the Communist Party, as was her husband. In 1946, they were both allegedly expelled from the Communist Party for "deviationism." In the late 1940's and in the 1950's, McKenney and her husband lived mostly in Europe. In 1955, Bransten, alias Minton, died, an apparent suicide, in London.

McKenney was affiliated with the American Committee To Save Refugees ("perform[ing] a most valuable function for the international Communist movement"); the American Peace Mobilization ("formed . . . under the auspices of the Communist Party and the Young Communist League" – "one of the most seditious organizations which ever operated in the United States"); the Artists Front To Win the War ("Communist front" – "included representatives of the theater, of literature, music, art, science, and education, with long and active records of support for Communist front organizations and for the variegated turns of the Communist Party line"); the Citizens Committee for Harry Bridges ("Communist"); *Friday* magazine ("Communist-controlled"); the League of American Writers ("subversive and Communist" – "began openly to follow the Communist Party line as dictated by the foreign policy of the Soviet Union"); the Open Letter for Closer Cooperation With the Soviet Union (issued by "a group of Communist Party stooges"); the Tallentire Jubilee Committee ("Communist front"); and the Twentieth Anniversary for the *Daily Worker* ("Communist festivity"). She died in July 1972.

ROBERT MORRISON MacIVER was born on April 17, 1882 in Stornoway, Scotland, son of Christine Morrison and Donald MacIver. He married Ethel Peterkin. He was an alumnus of the University of Edinburgh (M.A., 1903 and D.Ph., 1915) and Oxford University (B.A., 1907). He was the author of *Community*

– *A Sociological Study* (1917); *Labor in the Changing World* (1919); *Elements of Social Science* (1921); *The Modern State* (1926); *Relation of Sociology to Social Work* (1931); *Society – Its Structure and Changes* (1931); *Economic Reconstruction* (1934); *Society – A Textbook of Sociology* (1937); *Leviathan and the People* (1939); *Social Causation* (1942); *Toward an Abiding Peace* (1943); *The Web of Government* (1947); *The More Perfect Union* (1949); *The Ramparts We Guard* (1950); *Democracy and the Economic Challenge* (1952); *Academic Freedom in Our Time* (1955); *The Pursuit of Happiness* (1955); *Life: Its Dimensions and Its Bounds* (1960); *The Challenge of the Passing Years* (1962); *Power Transforms* (1964); and *As A Tale That Is Told* (1968).

From 1907 until 1915, MacIver was a lecturer on political science and sociology at the University of Aberdeen. From 1915 until 1927, he was at the University of Toronto as professor of political science (1915-1922) and head of the political science department (1922-1927). From 1927 until 1936, he was professor of political science at Barnard College. From 1929 until 1950, he was the Lieber Professor of political philosophy and sociology at Columbia University. From 1950 until 1952, although in retirement as professor emeritus, he was a special lecturer at Columbia in the department of public law and government. From 1955 until 1961, he was the director of a Juvenile Delinquency Evaluation Project for the city of New York. From 1963 until 1965, he was president of the ultra-radical New School for Social Research, and in 1965 and 1966, he was chancellor of the institution. He retired in 1966.

MacIver was affiliated with the American Association for a Democratic Germany (pro-Communist); the American Committee for Anti-Nazi Literature ("individuals and organizations connected with it identify this Committee as a Communist-front organization"); the American Committee for Democracy and Intellectual Freedom ("subversive and un-American" – "a Communist-front organization operating among college teachers and professors"); the American Committee To Save Refugees ("perform[ing] a most valuable function for the international Communist movement"); the American Friends of Spanish Democracy ("Communist front"); the Anti-Nazi Federation of New York ("Communist front"); a Brief [*amicus curiae*] in the Case of the Communist Party, U.S.A, *v.* the Subversive Activities Control Board (pro-Communist); the Citizens Committee for Constitutional Liberties ("created, dominated and controlled by members and officials of the Communist Party"); the Civil Defense Letter Committee (leftist-pacifist); the Consumer-Farmer Milk Cooperative ("Communist front"); Encampment for Citizenship (leftist); the Institute for International Order (leftist); the National Committee To Abolish the Un-American Activities Committee ("to lead and direct the Communist Party's 'Operation Abolition' camapaign"); the National Committee To Aid Victims of German Fascism ("an auxiliary of the Communist Party"); the National Council for Civic Responsibility (an anti-anti-Communist group which was so leftist that its formation was hailed by the Communist Party); a Petition on Behalf of Carl Braden and Frank Wilkinson (Communist Party project); and the United World Federalists (the most prestigious group of fellow-travelers and dupes working for world government at the expense of

United States sovereignty). He died in June 1970.

THOMAS MANN was born on June 6, 1875 in Lubeck, Germany, son of Julia da Silva-Bruhns and Johann Mann. He married Katja Pringsheim. He was educated at the Lübeck Gymnasium. For a brief time he studied at the University of Munich. In 1938, he came to the United States, and in 1944, he became a United States citizen. He was the author of *Der Kleine Herr Friedemann* (1898); *Buddenbrooks* (1901; English translation, 1924); *Tristan* (1903); *Fiorenza*, play (1906); *Death in Venice* (1912; new translation, 1930); *Tonio Kröger* (1914); *Royal Highness* (1916; English translation, 1924); *Reflections of a Non-Political Man* (1918); *A Man and His Dog* (1918; English translation, 1930); *Bashan and I* (1923); *The Magic Mountain* (1924; English translation, 1924); *Disorder and Early Sorrow* (1926); *Children and Fools*, nine short stories including *Little Herr* (1928; English translation, 1928); *Essays and Criticism – Three Essays* (1929); *Mario and the Magician* (1929; English translation, 1931); *A Sketch of My Life* (1930); *Past Masters and Other Essays*, thirteen essays (1933; English translation, 1933); *Nocturnes*, three stories (1934); *Joseph and His Brothers* (1934); *Young Joseph* (1935); *Stories of Three Decades*, all Mann's fiction except novels (1936; English translation, 1936); *An Exchange of Letters* (1937); *Freud, Goethe, Wagner* (1937; English translation, 1937); *This Peace* (1938); *Joseph In Egypt* (1938; English translation, 1938); *The Coming Victory of Democracy* (1938; English translation, 1938); *This War* (1940); *The Beloved Returns,* novel (1940; English translation, 1940); *The Transposed Heads*, a legend of India (1941; English translation, 1941); *Joseph the Provider*, novel (1944); *The Tables of Law* (1945); *Essays of Three Decades* (1947); *Doctor Faustus,* novel (1948); *The Holy Sinner* (1951); *The Black Swan* (1954); *Selected Essays* (1941); *Order of the Day: Political Essays and Speeches* (1942); and *Listen, Germany* (1943).

By 1933, Mann was one of the most celebrated writers in Germany's history. In 1929, he had been awarded the Nobel Prize in literature. His fame was international, and he was repeatedly acclaimed as a humanitarian, a liberal, a man of great moral integrity, and a true freedom fighter. He was a legend in his own time, even before his fifty-fifth birthday.

It is difficult to pinpoint how and when the Mann legend began. In his early years he was a complete militarist and nationalist. In 1915, after Germany became engaged in World War I, he wrote: "War! It is purification, liberation, an enormous hope . . . . The victory of Germany will be a paradox, nay, a wonder: a victory of the soul over numbers. The German soul is opposed to the pacifist ideal of civilization, for is not peace the element of civil corruption?"

Mann condemned Tsarist Russia in no uncertain terms. When Lenin took over he expressed his "high respect for the historic event of the Russian revolution," and through the Stalin years Mann was fulsome in his praise of the Soviet Union. On the other hand, when Hitler rose to power in the Germany where Mann was the literary hero, Mann was rather subdued in his "humanitarian" and "liberal" appraisal of the Nazi leader: "Since history has spoken, I have kept silent. This is my decision – to live in complete seclusion devoted to my personal tasks."

In 1933, while Mann was in Holland, the Nazi authorities noticed that his name was associated with an anti-Nazi, pro-Communist publication, *Die Sammlung*. The Nazis threatened to ban Mann's book and he thought it prudent to remain abroad rather than be a "freedom fighter at home." He began a lifetime in self-imposed exile, and from his exile havens during the next decade, he became a vociferous critic of the Nazi regime. His first outburst came in 1936 when he denounced the Nazis as anti-Christian, amoral, and deadly enemies of civilization. Later that year, the Nazis stripped him of his citizenship.

In 1938, Mann arrived in the United States, where he would be lionized during the next fourteen years. For a few years, he lived in New Jersey and lectured at Princeton University. In 1941, he moved to California. He was made a Fellow of the Library of Congress as a consultant in German literature. He was in great demand as a lecturer, and made many nation-wide lecture tours, speaking to audiences that astounded him by their size and enthusiasm.

In America, Mann became a political activist. He found himself surrounded by friends of the far left, including Charlie Chaplin, Hanns Eisler, Eugene and Agnes Meyer of the *Washington Post*, Soviet Ambassador Maxim Litvinov, columnist Drew Pearson, commentator Elmer Davis, Undersecretary of State Sumner Welles, Eleanor Roosevelt, Henry Wallace, Gerhart Eisler, and a large host of Communists and fellow-travelers.

In 1944, Mann and his wife became American citizens. He immediately plunged into the fourth-term campaign for Franklin D. Roosevelt, whom he virtually idolized. Mann wrote at the time of Roosevelt's death: "An epoch ends. The America to which we came ceases to exist." On another occasion,

Mann remarked of Roosevelt's death: "Here at home there was hatred of the Jews, the Russians, the English, but not of the Germans, against whom one was forced to wage war .... That statesman [Roosevelt], however, lord of the White House for the fourth time, the aristocratic friend of the people, the equal of the European dictators in the skillful manipulation of the masses, but their born opponent, the great politician of the good, whom the popular war against Japan had provided with the means to defeat the Fascism saved by 'Munich' in 1938 – that man was marked for death."

Throughout the course of World War II, Mann labored tirelessly with American Communists, fellow travelers, and German émigrés such as himself to extol the virtues of the Soviet Union and to promote a Carthaginian peace for Germany. During the war, he wrote hopefully in his diary: "The proclamation of a national bolshevism and union with Russia are by no means impossibilities. This country [Germany] can never become a decent democratic republic."

Long before Mann became an American citizen, he began a busy career in Communist front and other leftist organizations. His affiliations included Action for World Federation (ultra-leftist); Actors' Laboratory Theatre (pro-Communist); the American Committee for Protection of Foreign Born ("founded by the Communist Party in order to exploit racial divisions in the United States for its own revolutionary purposes"); the American Committee for Yugoslav Relief ("subversive and Communist"); the American Committee To Save Refugees ("perform[ing] a most valuable function for the international Communist movement"); the American Continental Congress for World Peace ("another phase in the Communist 'peace' campaign, aimed at consolidating anti-American forces throughout the Western Hemisphere"); the American Council for a Democratic Greece ("subversive and Communist"); the American League Against War and Fascism ("subversive and Communist" – "established in the United States in an effort to create public sentiment on behalf of a foreign policy adapted to the interests of the Soviet Union"); the American-Russian Institute ("subversive" – "Communist" – "specializing in pro-Soviet propaganda"); the Celebration of the 25th Anniversary of the Red Army (Communist enterprise); Citizens United To Abolish the Wood-Rankin Committee (pro-Communist project); the Civil Rights Congress ("created and established by the Communist Party as an organization which would utilize defense of civil rights for Party purposes and raise and maintain mass defense and bail funds for Party use"); the Committee for a Democratic Far Eastern Policy ("Communist"); the Committee for the First Amendment ("Communist front"); the Committee for Peaceful Alternatives to the Atlantic Pact ("a Communist-front organization . . . as part of Soviet psychological warfare against the United States"); the Committee of One Thousand ("Communist-created and controlled"); the Committee of Welcome for the Red Dean of Canterbury (England's most notorious pro-Soviet apologist among the clergy); the Congress of American-Soviet Friendship ("Communist front"); Consumers Union (in the "solar system of organizations around the [Communist] Party" – "Communist front"); the Cultural and Scientific Conference for World Peace ("Communist front" – "a propaganda front for Soviet foreign policy and Soviet culture"); Federal Union (leftist-pacifist-internationalist); Film Audiences for Democracy ("Communist front"); Films for Democracy ("Communist front"); the Freedom from Fear Committee ("Communist front"); Friends of Democracy ("Communist front"); the Hollywood Independent Citizens Committee of the Arts, Sciences and Professions ("Communist front"); the Hollywood Writers Mobilization ("subversive and Communist" – "the record discloses that the present all-out patriotism of the leading spirits of this Communist front organization is primarily conditioned upon their loyalty to the Soviet Union"); the Independent Citizens Committee of the Arts, Sciences and Professions ("Communist front"); the International Workers Order ("from its very inception demonstrated by its pronouncements, its activities, and the authoritative statements of the Communist Party that it is a subservient instrument of the Communist Party of the United States"); the Joint Anti-Fascist Refugee Committee ("subversive and Communist"); the Lawyers Committee on American Relations With Spain ("during the Spanish Civil War, the Communist Party organized . . . [the Lawyers Committee] as a part of one of its major propaganda campaigns in the party's entire history in this country"); the League of American Writers ("subversive and Communist" – "began openly to follow the Communist Party line as dictated by the foreign policy of the Soviet Union"); the Mid-Century Conference for Peace ("aimed at assembling as many gullible persons as possible under Communist direction and turning them into a vast sounding board for Communist propaganda"); the National Committee to Combat Anti-Semitism ("Communist front"); the National Conference on American Policy in China and the Far East ("Communist"); the Na-

481

tional Council of American-Soviet Friendship ("subversive and Communist" – "specializing in pro-Soviet propaganda"); the National Council of the Arts, Sciences and Professions ("a Communist front used to appeal to special occupational groups"); the National Federation for Constitutional Liberties ("under Communist Party domination and headed by responsible Party functionaries" – "one of the viciously subversive organizations of the Communist Party"); the National Institute of Arts and Letters ("Communist front"); *New Masses* ("weekly journal of the Communist Party"); an Open Letter for Closer Cooperation With the Soviet Union (issued by "a group of Communist Party stooges"); Russian War Relief ("Communist enterprise"); *Soviet Russia Today* ("Communist-controlled publication"); Spanish Refugee Appeal ("subversive" – "Communist front"); the Stockholm Peace Appeal ("Communist 'peace' campaign"); Students for Federal World Government (leftist-internationalist); United World Federalists ("the most prestigious group of fellow-travelers and dupes working for world government at the expense of United States sovereignty"); the Win-the-Peace Conference ("Communist front"); the World Citizenship Movement (leftist-internationalist); the World Federation of Democratic Youth ("a pressure group on behalf of Soviet foreign policy"); and the World Peace Congress ("organized under Communist initiative in various countries throughout the world"). Aside from his front activities, he repeatedly petitioned on behalf of Communists imprisoned or subject to deportation.

In 1948, Mann became an enthusiastic supporter and campaigner for Henry Wallace, the Progressive Party's presidential candidate who had the full support of the Communist Party. Mann said of Wallace that he was "America's most faithful son . . . [who] doesn't let himself be intimidated by those idiots who insult him." The issue in that presidential campaign, from Wallace's viewpoint, was complete appeasement of the Soviet Union. In defense of that policy, Mann said: "Because I am not a capitalist, I don't have enough fear of the Russian threat to the capitalist-bourgeois way of life. But as far as I can see, Russia doesn't threaten the thing that matters most: Peace."

In 1949, for the first time in sixteen years, Mann visited Germany, where he received the Goethe Prize in ceremonies at Frankfurt-am-Main in West Germany. At a press conference, he was asked if he thought that there were any differences between Nazism and Communism. He replied that there were moral differences, and explained further: "Communism has a certain relation to the ideal of humanity and the ideal of a better future for mankind. National Socialism resembled nihilism. It was diabolical." A few days after the ceremonies in Frankfurt, Mann received another Goethe Prize in Weimar, East Germany. When the Communists honored Mann at Weimar, they accompanied the prize with a citation saying: "We thank you, Thomas Mann, that you, the proven fighting humanist, when the time has come, have risen openly against the folly of our era, as you defined anti-Bolshevism, and that you have recognized the need for a just and unbiased evaluation of the historical phenomenon of the great Soviet Union." Mann replied to his Communist hosts on the remarkable differences he had found between West and East Germany. In West Germany he was treated as "the last representative of the bourgeois era." But in East Germany, he was greeted, he said, not as an old fogy, but rather as one who could help to build a new world in East Germany – and such a prospect pleased him very much.

As a result of Mann's visit to Weimar, he was severely criticized by Olberg, a Swedish journalist, who thought that Mann had given the Communists a propaganda boon. Mann replied to Olberg: " . . . The fact that I reserve the right to make a distinction between the attitude of Communism toward the idea of humanity, and the absolute baseness of fascism; that I refuse to participate in the hysteria of persecuting Communists and in warmongering; and that I speak for peace in a world whose future can no longer be imagined without Communist elements – this alone is sufficient to gain for me a certain confidence in the sphere of that social religion, which I have not sought [but] which . . . I will never be able to consider as a bad sign for my intellectual and moral health."

By 1951, there seemed no limit to the lengths to which Mann would go to lavish praise upon Communism and Communists. For example, in May 1951, Johannes R. Becher, a Soviet propaganda leader in East Germany, celebrated his 60th birthday. Mann used the opportunity to extend felicitations to Becher and at the same time to endorse Communism and Becher's commitment to it. Said Mann: " . . . Let me say this: Even more, or almost more than the poet and writer, I love and honor Johannes R. Becher the man – this deeply stirred heart, moved by sincere impulses, that I have felt beating on so many occasions, particularly during our meeting when I visited Weimer in 1949 – a personal experience which has left behind a lasting impression of his nature and his being. The essence of his being I felt to be an unselfishness, pure and absorbing

as a flame; a readiness to serve, fervent to the point of suffering, which totally penetrates his poetry and his writings; an *ethos* of community which predestines him emotionally to be a Communist, and which politically has become a Communist creed.

"His Communism has positively patriotic color; as a matter of fact it fulfills itself in patriotism. One has only to read his poems to know that his impetus toward service to the community, to the people, is first and last the fervent wish to serve his people, the German people, and to be its loving and faithful adviser, to the best of his knowledge and conscience. I think the day will come when the German people in its entirety will thank him for his love."

In 1952, after only eight years of American citizenship, Mann left the United States to take up residence in Switzerland. A few months before his death in August 1955, he revisited East and West Germany, and on the occasion of his 80th birthday, he was made an honorary citizen of his native Lübeck.

VITO MARCANTONIO was born on December 10, 1902 in New York City, son of Angelina De Dobitis and Samuel Marcantonio. He married Miriam Sanders. He was an alumnus of New York University Law School (LL.B., 1925). He was admitted to the New York bar in 1926.

In 1920, Marcantonio organized the Harlem Tenants League and led the group in a successful tenants' strike. Soon after he joined the Fiorello H. LaGuardia Political Club. In 1924, he was campaign manager for LaGuardia's successful race for Congress. He continued to manage successful campaigns for LaGuardia until 1934, when La-

Guardia ran for mayor. From 1926 until 1930, he worked in LaGuardia's office. In 1930, he served as United States Assistant District Attorney. In 1934, as the candidate on the Republican and City Fusion tickets, he won LaGuardia's old seat in Congress. In 1936, he was defeated for re-election as the Republic-All Peoples's Party candidate. In 1938, he was elected as the Republican and American Labor Party candidate. In 1940, he was re-elected. In 1942 and 1944, he was again re-elected, as the Republican, American Labor Party, and Democratic candidate. In 1946, he was defeated in the Republican primary but won re-election. In 1948, he ran on the American Labor Party ticket, with only the *Daily Worker*, of all the New York newspapers, supporting him. In 1948, he was an important leader in Henry A. Wallace's Progressive Party, and he remained in that Party, becoming chairman in 1952. In 1950, although he was state chairman of the American Labor Party, he was defeated for re-election to Congress on the American Labor ticket. In 1953, he resigned his chairmanship of the American Labor Party when he and Communist Party leaders had differences of opinion over political strategy and tactics.

In the Congress, Marcantonio followed the straight Communist line on matters of foreign and domestic policy. So persistent was Marcantonio in his Communist sympathies that even the *New York Times*, in 1948, branded him as un-American. Said the *Times:* "So consistently has Representative Vito Marcantonio accepted, spoken for and voted the Communist line during the last decade that the registered voters may well ask themselves, as they go to the polls on Nov. 2, whether they are going to vote Russian or American."

Marcantonio frequently denied that he was a Communist. His affiliations included the Abolish Peonage Committee ("Communist front"); the American Committee for Protection of Foreign Born ("founded by the Communist Party in order to exploit racial divisions in the United States for its own revolutionary purposes"); the American Continental Congress for World Peace ("another phase in the Communist 'peace' campaign, aimed at consolidating anti-American forces throughout the Western Hemisphere"); the American Council on Soviet Relations ("subversive" – "established by the Communist Party . . . directed and controlled by the Party, and operated to aid and support Party objectives concerning the defense and support of the Soviet Union"); the American Friends of Spanish Democracy ("Communist front"); the American Friends of the Chinese People ("Communist front"); the American League for Peace and Democracy ("subversive and Communist" – "established . . . in an effort to create public sentiment on behalf of a foreign policy adapted to the interests of the Soviet Union . . . [and] designed to conceal Communist control, in accordance with the new tactics of the Communist International"); the American Peace Mobilization ("formed . . . under the auspices of the Communist Party and the Young Communist League" – "one of the most seditious organizations which ever operated in the United States"); the American Slav Congress ("Moscow-inspired and directed federation of Communist-dominated organizations seeking by methods of propaganda and pressure to subvert the 10,000,000 people in this country of Slavic birth or descent"); the American Student Union ("without exception . . . supported defense of teachers and students charged with Communist activity" – "pliable instrument in the hands of the Communist Party"); the American Youth Congress ("subversive" – "one of the most influential front organizations ever set up by the Communists in this country" – "the Communists were in complete control"); the Anti-Nazi Committee of Yorkville ("Communist front"); Associated Blind, Inc. ("Communist front"); the Bill of Rights Conference ("subversive"); the Bronx Anti-Poll Tax Committee ("Communist front"); the Citizens Committee to Aid Striking Seamen ("Communist front"); the Citizens Committee To Free Earl Browder ("a strictly Communist Party affair"); the Civil Rights Congress ("created and established by the Communist Party as an organization which would utilize defense of civil rights for Party purposes and raise and maintain mass defense and bail funds for Party use"); the Claudia Jones Defense Committee ("Communist front"); the Committee for the Support of *Il Nuovo Mondo* (pro-Communist paper published for Italians in the United States); the Committee of Sponsors for the Celebration of 15 Years of Biro Bidjan ("Communist project"); the Committee To Defend America by Keeping Out of War ("Communist front"); the Conference on Constitutional Liberties in America ("an important part of the solar system of the Communist Party's front organizations"); the Conference for Peaceful Alternatives to the Atlantic Pact ("Communist front organization . . . as part of Soviet psychological warfare against the United States"); Consumers Union (in the "solar system of organizations around the [Communist] Party"); the Council for Pan-American Democracy ("subversive and Communist"); the Daughters of the American Depression ("Communist front"); Descendants of the American Revolution ("a Communist-front organization set up as a radical imitation of the Daughters of the American Revolution. The Descendants have uniformly adhered to the line of the Communist Party"); Emergency Peace Mobilization ("Communist front"); *Equality* ("Communist Party enterprise"); Federal Arts Council of the Workers Alliance ("Communist front"); the First Congress of the Mexican and Spanish-American Peoples of the United States ("planned at a secret gathering of Communist Party leaders from the South and Southwest"); Friends of the Abraham Lincoln Brigade "completely controlled by the Communist Party"); the German-American Anti-Nazi Students Committee ("Communist front"); the German-American League for Culture ("Communist front"); the Gerson Supporters ("the Communist Party organized a campaign in defense of the appointment of Simon W. Gerson as confidential assistant to the borough president of Manhattan"); the Golden Book of American Friendship with the Soviet Union ("pro-Soviet propaganda enterprise"); the Greater New York Emergency Conference on Inalienable Rights ("Communist front"); Icor ("the aims of Icor have been primarily propagandistic in behalf of the Soviet Union"); Indusco ("Communist-controlled"); the International Labor Defense ("subversive and Communist" – "legal arm of the Communist Party" – "part of an international network of organizations for the defense of Communist lawbreakers"); the International Red Aid in Moscow ("the parent organization of the various Communist defense organizations"); the International Workers Order ("from its very inception demonstrated by its pronouncements, its activities, and the authoritative statements of the Communist

Party that it is a subservient instrument of the Communist Party of the United States"); the Joint Anti-Fascist Refugee Committee ("subversive and Communist"); the Lawyers Committee on American Relations With Spain ("during the Spanish Civil War, the Communist Party organized . . . [the Lawyers Committee] as a part of one of its major propaganda campaigns in the Party's entire history in this country"); the Medical Bureau and North American Committee To Aid Spanish Democracy ("subversive and un-American"); the Mother Ella Reeve Bloor Celebration Committee ("Communist Party festivity"); the National Committee for the Defense of Political Prisoners ("subversive and Communist"); the National Committee To Abolish the Poll Tax ("Communist front"); the National Committee To Combat Anti-Semitism ("Communist front"); the National Committee To Win Amnesty for Smith Act Victims ("subversive" – "Communist"); the National Emergency Conference for Democratic Rights ("Communist front" – "subversive"); the National Federation for Constitutional Liberties ("under Communist Party domination and headed by responsible Party functionaries" – "one of the viciously subversive organizations of the Communist Party"); the National Labor Conference for Peace (pro-Communist); the National Lawyers Guild ("the foremost legal bulwark of the Communist Party, its front organizations, and controlled unions"); the National Non-Partisan Committee To Defend the Rights of the 12 Communist Leaders (pro-Communist); the National Peoples Committee Against Hearst ("subversive and Communist"); the National Right to Work Congress ("out-and-out Communist Party affair"); *New Masses* ("weekly journal of the Communist Party"); the

New Theatre League ("Communist"); the New York Peace Association ("Communist-inspired organization"); the New York State Conference of Negro Youth ("Communist front"); the New York Tom Mooney Committee ("Communist front"); the Non-Sectarian Committee for Political Refugees ("affiliate of the International Labor Defense, the legal arm of the Communist Party"); the North American Spanish Aid Committee ("Communist"); the Project Workers Council for Joint Action ("Communist front"); the Public Use of Arts Committee ("Communist front"); the [Morris U.] Schappes Defense Committee ("a front organization with a strictly Communist objective, namely, the defense of a self-admitted Communist who was convicted of perjury in the courts of New York"); the School for Democracy ("established by Communist teachers ousted from the public school system of New York City"); the Sleepy Lagoon Defense Committee ("Communist front"); the United Front for [Angelo] Herndon ("an adjunct to the International Labor Defense, the Legal Arm of the Communist Party"); Veterans of the Abraham Lincoln Brigade ("directed, dominated and controlled by the Communist Party"); and the Washington Committee for Democratic Action ("subversive and Communist").

Marcantonio died in August 1954.

ALEXANDER MEIKLEJOHN was born on February 3, 1872 in Rochdale, England, son of Elizabeth France and James Meiklejohn. He married, first, Nannine La Villa; his second wife was Helen Everett. He came to the United States in 1880. He was an alumnus of Brown University (A.B., 1893 and A.M., 1895) and Cornell University (Ph.D., 1897). He was the author of *The Liberal College*

(1920); *Freedom and the College* (1923); *Philosophy* (1926); *The Experimental College* (1933); *What Does America Mean?* (1935); *Education Between Two Worlds* (1942); *Free Speech and Its Relation to Self Government* (1948); and *Political Freedom – The Constitutional Powers of the People* (1960).

From 1897 until 1912, Meiklejohn was at Brown University as instructor in philosophy (1897-1899); assistant professor (1899-1903); associate professor (1903-1906); professor of logic and metaphysics (1906-1912); and dean (1901-1912). From 1912 until 1923, he was president of Amherst College. Because of his Red-oriented radicalism – on and off campus – Meiklejohn's resignation was forced by the trustees of Amherst. From 1925 until 1938, he was at the University of Wisconsin as the Brittingham Professor of philosophy. From 1927 until 1933, he was the head of the Experimental College, which he founded at the University of Wisconsin. He did away with grades, formal examinations, and a disciplined curriculum. As had been the case at Amherst, his radicalism came under severe criticism, leading to the closing of his Experimental College. In 1938, he retired from the University of Wisconsin as professor emeritus. In 1938, he was a visiting professor at Dartmouth College. From 1938 until 1942, he was the head of the San Francisco School for Social Studies, which he founded as an adult education center. After 1942, he devoted most of his time to writing and to leftwing activities. His leftism centered on an extremely broad construction of the First Amendment of the Constitution of the United States. He was a vigorous opponent of any governmental action which directly or indirectly imposed any limits upon freedom of speech. Under the banner of civil liberties, he waged an all-out battle against congressional investigating committees. He was sweeping in his condemnation of loyalty oaths. He was especially solicitous of the civil rights of Communists.

Meiklejohn was a founder of the ultra-leftist American Civil Liberties Union and for many years served on the organization's national committee. He was a long-time vice-chairman of the League for Industrial Democracy, the most important Socialist influence on American campuses. In 1964, he joined the ultra-radical Center for the Study of Democratic Institutions, where he was given an opportunity to promote his liberal interpretation of the Constitution.

Meiklejohn's affiliations included the American Committee for Protection of Foreign Born ("founded by the Communist Party in order to exploit racial divisions in the United States for its own revolutionary purposes"); the American Student Union ("without exception . . . supported defense of teachers and students charged with Communist activity" – "pliable instrument in the hands of the Communist Party"); the Berger National Foundation (Socialist); the Committee on Militarism in Education (a supporting organization of the U.S. Congress Against War, "completely under the control of the Communist Party"); the Conference for Progressive Political Action (Socialist-dominated); the Emergency Civil Liberties Committee ("Communist front and subversive"); the Jefferson School of Social Science ("a Communist institution modeled along the lines of the new Communist policy which led to the decision to change the Communist Party into some kind of an educational institution"); the Marcus

487

Graham Freedom of the Press Committee (an ultra-radical group in support of an anarchist); the National Citizens Committee for Sacco and Vanzetti (pro-Communist"); the National Committee To Abolish the Un-American Activities Committee ("to lead and direct the Communist Party's 'Operation Abolition' campaign"); the National Committee To Repeal the McCarran Act ("Communist front" – "subversive"); the National Committee To Secure Justice in the Rosenberg Case ("Communist front organized ... to conduct the United States phase of a mammoth propaganda campaign designed to obliterate the crime of and exploit the Rosenbergs and their codefendant Morton Sobell for the purposes of international Communism"); the National Committee To Win Amnesty for Smith Act Victims ("subversive" – "Communist"); the National Lawyers Guild ("the foremost legal bulwark of the Communist Party, its front organizations, and controlled unions"); the National Mooney-Billings Committee ("dominated by Socialists); the National Save Our Schools Committee (dominated by Communists and Socialists); the New York Conference against War (leftist); and Promoting Enduring Peace, Inc. (ultra-leftist-pacifist).

Meiklejohn was the recipient of tributes usually reserved for leftists, including the Teachers Union Award for Defense of Constitutional Liberties and the Franklin D. Roosevelt Award of the National Lawyers Guild. In 1963, his lifetime of leftism was rewarded with the Presidential Medal of Freedom, presented by Lyndon B. Johnson. In 1957, alumni and former faculty members of Meiklejohn's ultra-radical Experimental College at the University of Wisconsin established a fund for an annual Alexander Meiklejohn Award to a college or university administrator, trustee, or governing board making an outstanding contribution to academic freedom. The award has invariably been given to a leftist.

Meiklejohn died in December 1964. He was eulogized in the Communists' *National Guardian* as a philosopher, educator, author, and implacable foe of the witch-hunt.

WESLEY CLAIR MITCHELL was born on August 5, 1874 in Rushville, Illinois, son of Lucy McClellan and John Mitchell. He married Lucy Sprague. He is an alumnus of the University of Chicago (A.B., 1896 and Ph.D., 1899). He pursued graduate studies at the Universities of Halle and Vienna (1897-1898). He was the author of *A History of the Greenbacks* (1903); *Gold Prices and Wages Under the Greenback Standard* (1908); *Business Cycles* (1913); *The Making and Using of Index Numbers* (1915); *Business Cycles, The Problem and Its Setting* (1927); and *The Backward Art of Spending Money* (1937). He was co-author of *Income In the United States – Its Amount and Distribution* (1921); *Recent Economic Changes* (1929); *Recent Social Trends* (1933); and *Measuring Business Cycles* (1946). He was editor of *History of Prices During the War: Business Cycles and Unemployment* (1923).

In 1899 and 1900, Mitchell worked in the U.S. Census Bureau. From 1900 until 1902, he was an instructor in economics at the University of Chicago. Between 1902 and 1912, he was at the University of California as an assistant professor of commerce (1902-1907) and professor of political economy (1908-1912). In 1907 and 1908, he lectured on economics at Harvard University. Between 1913 and 1944, he was at Columbia University as a lecturer in economics (1913-1914) and professor of economics (1914-1919 and 1922-1944). In 1918 and 1919, he was chief of the price section of the War Industries Board. From 1919 until 1921, he lectured at the New School for Social Research, and from 1919 until 1931, he was a director of the ultra-radical institution. From 1920 until 1945, he was director of research for the National Bureau of Economic Research. In 1930 and 1931, he was the George Eastman visiting professor at Oxford University. In 1934, he was the Hitchcock Professor at the University of California. In 1935, he was the Messenger lecturer at Cornell University. From 1927 until 1930, he was chairman of the leftist-oriented Social Science Research Council. From 1929 until 1933, he was chairman of the President's Research Commission on National Trends. He was a member of the National Planning Board, the Federal Emergency Administration of Public Works, and the National Resources Board. He was president of the American Statistical Association, and the Academy of Political Science.

Mitchell was a member of the Socialist Party. He was also affiliated with the American Association for Labor Legislation (dominated by Socialists and Communists"); the American Committee for Democracy and Intellectual Freedom ("subversive and un-American" – "a Communist-front organization operating among college teachers and professors"); the American Friends of Spanish Democracy ("Communist front"); the American Society for Cultural Relations with Russia ("Communist front"); the Civil Rights Congress ("created and established by the Communist Party as an organization which would utilize defense of civil rights for Party purposes and

raise and maintain mass defense and bail funds for Party use"); the Council on Foreign Relations (the unofficial but operative directorate of all facets of United States foreign policy); the Emergency Committee for Strikers Relief (Socialist); the Greater New York Conference on Inalienable Rights ("Communist front"); In Defense of the Bill of Rights ("Communist Party enterprise"); *Liberator* ("Communist magazine"); the National Council of American-Soviet Friendship ("subversive and Communist" – "specializing in pro-Soviet propaganda"); the National Emergency Conference ("Communist front"); the National Emergency Conference for Democratic Rights ("Communist front" – "subversive"); the National Mooney-Billings Committee (dominated by Socialists); the National Wartime Conference of the Professions, the Sciences, the Arts, the White-Collar Fields ("Communist front"); the New York State Conference on National Unity ("Communist front"); the Rand School of Social Science (a Marxian-Socialist training school for labor agitators); Russian War Relief ("Communist enterprise"); and Survey Associates (Socialist). He died in October 1948.

PHILIP MURRAY was born on May 25, 1886 in Blantyre, Scotland, son of Rose Ann Layden and William Murray. He married Elizabeth Lavery. He was co-author of *Organized Labor and Production* (1940).

At the age of ten, Murray began six years as a coal miner in his native Scotland. In 1902, he was brought by his family to the United States and went to work as a coal miner in Pennsylvania. In 1904, he instigated a miners' strike in Westmoreland County, becoming involved in what proved to be a lifetime of activity in union affairs. In 1911, he became an American citizen. In 1912, he was elected to the executive board of the United Mine Workers of America. In 1916, he was elected president of District No. 5 (Pittsburgh) of the UMW. In 1919, he began a twenty-year tenure as vice-president of the International Union of Mine Workers. From 1940 until 1952, he was president of the Congress of Industrial Organizations (CIO). From 1942 until 1952, he was president of the United Steelworkers of America. In 1917 and 1918, he was a member of the War Labor Board and the National Bituminous Coal Production Committee. In 1935, he was a member of the National Industrial Recovery Board and the National Recovery Administration's Advisory Council. During World War II, he was a member of the National Defense Mediation Board. In 1950 and 1951, he was co-chairman of the United Labor Policy Committee. From 1941 until 1952, he was a member of the executive board of the International Confederation of Free Trade Unions. From 1918 until 1952, he was a member of Pittsburgh's Board of Education.

As president of the CIO, Murray was prone to denounce Communism and Communists in his public utterances. However, in 1944, the Special Committee on Un-American Activities reported on the extent of Communist influence and control in the CIO and the CIO's Political Action Committee. On Communism in the CIO, the Special Committee said: "Two men, more than any others, were responsible for the split in ranks of organized labor which led to the creation of the C.I.O. Those two men are John L. Lewis and Sidney Hillman. In 1938 and 1939, the Special Committee on Un-American Activities did all that was humanly possible within the scope of its powers to warn John L. Lewis and other leaders of the C.I.O. that the Communists were moving in on their organization *en masse.* Their only response to the committee was silence or abusive language.

"On February 29, 1944, John L. Lewis made a public statement concerning Communists in the C.I.O. (*New York Times*, February 29, 1944, p.1). Belated as this statement may be, it confirms in toto what the Special Committee on Un-American Activities found 5 years ago and what it finds today. Lewis' statement, as quoted in the *New York Times*, reads as follows: 'When I was organizing the C.I.O. we picked up a lot of Communists in one unit after another as we grew – including Harry Bridges. But if I had not resigned the chairmanship and left the C.I.O. in 1940 I can tell you the Communists would have been weeded out of the C.I.O. long before now. Instead, as anyone might expect who has seen them throw their weight around inside labor organizations, the Communists dominate the C.I.O. today. Philip Murray is today the prisoner of the Communists in his own union. They control him and the C.I.O. through their seats on his executive committee. And there isn't a blessed thing he can do about it. Sidney Hillman is just as badly off. Both of them have got to play ball with the Communists now, or die.

" 'As heroic Russia battles against our German enemy in Europe, the Communists in our labor movement naturally hang on to the coattails of the Red Army and try to build an ideological bridge between our loyalty to Russia and their own pet schemes. This is a sheer abuse of our good will toward Russia. And, of course, the Communists in our labor unions are not even good Russians. What good citizen is not for a Russian victory over Germany in this war? Yet the Communists in the unions play hard on the trick idea that America cannot fight side by side with Russia and at the same time fight against American Communists and fellow travelers here. That is an outrageous contention.'

"The Special Committee on Un-American Activities finds that Communist leadership is strongly entrenched in the following unions which are at present affiliated with the C.I.O.: American Communications Association; International Federation of Architects, Engineers, Chemists, and Technicians; International Fur and Leather Workers Union; International Longshoremen's and Warehousemen's Union; International Union of Fishermen and Allied Workers of America; International Union of Mine, Mill, and Smelter Workers; International Woodworkers of America; Marine Cooks and Stewards Association of the Pacific Coast; National Maritime Union of America; State, County, and Municipal Workers of America; and Transport Workers Union of America."

On the CIO's Political Action Committee, the Special Committee on Un-American Activities reported: "The origin of the idea of the C.I.O. Political Action Committee is of real importance. That origin was definitely with the Communist Party and some of its leaders.

"In June 1943, the Workers Library Publishers – official Communist Party publishing agency – brought out a pamphlet by Frank Ryhlick entitled 'Congress and You.' In the July 1943 issue of *The Communist* – official monthly organ of the Communist Party – Earl Browder and Eugene Dennis contributed articles entitled 'Hold the Home Front' and 'Victory and the 1944 Elections,' respectively. These writings by Ryhlick, Browder, and Dennis cut the

pattern for the C.I.O. Political Action Committee. They appeared some weeks before the formation of the Hillman organization. An examination of the views of Ryhlick, Browder, and Dennis shows how they anticipated in every respect the organization and activity of the C.I.O. Political Action Committee. In his article, entitled 'Hold the Home Front,' Browder wrote, as follows: 'We must unite the C.I.O. behind the leadership of Phil Murray and his clear and correct program for the labor movement, and we must work with every honest leading element who goes along with Murray in the fullest collaboration, giving them our confidence and support without any regard to possible past or present ideological differences . . . . We must build the unit of all anti-Axis elements for the war now, and for the 1944 elections, which are already a practical issue today in the course of the conduct of the war.'

"In his article, entitled 'Victory and the 1944 Elections,' Dennis wrote as follows: 'In analyzing the political situation and alignments within the country, special consideration should be given to the approaching 1944 elections. To begin with, we must understand that next year's national elections are not a postwar problem and not a problem to be resolved solely in 1944 . . . . Recent experience has proved that one of the most important channels for developing labor's united action and influencing political developments is in the formation and activity of joint labor legislative committees.'

"Ryhlick wrote in his pamphlet, as follows: 'Political mobilization has become an all-embracing framework, within which lie the solutions to the many related problems confronting the people of America – problems including the opening of a second front, American-Soviet relations, economic planning, aid for the farmers, rationing and price control and taxes, wages and working conditions, abolition of racial discrimination, a Victory Congress. The entire nation could well take to heart the following words of George Addes, who with Richard Frankensteen is helping President Thomas give real leadership to the United Auto Workers: "It is obvious that whatever gains we will make we will have to achieve them through political action."

"Other Communist Party publications such as the *New Masses* and *Daily Worker* bore down heavily upon the need for an organization like the C.I.O. Political Action Committee, in the weeks which preceded the formation of Hillman's committee."

Former Communist official Louis Budenz in his *This Is My Story* identified Murray as a member of the Communist Party. Murray was affiliated with the American Youth Congress ("subversive" – "one of the most influential front organizations ever set up by the Communists in this country" – "the Communists were in complete control"); *Champion* ("official organ of the Young Communist League and the International Workers Order"); the China Aid Council ("Communist-controlled"); the Citizens' Victory Committee for Harry Bridges ("Communist front"); the Congress of American-Soviet Friendship ("Communist front"); *Daily Worker's* 20th Anniversary Celebration ("official organ of the Communist Party"); Indusco ("Communist-controlled"); the International Workers Order ("from its very inception demonstrated by its pronouncements, its activities, and the authoritative statements of the Communist Party that it is a subservient instrument of the Communist Party of the United States"); the Jewish People's Committee ("subversive and Communist" – "an organization which has been nothing more nor less than an adjunct of the Communist Party"); the ultra-radical National Association for the Advancement of Colored People; the National Citizens Political Action Committee ("Communist front"); the National Committee To Combat Anti-Semitism ("Communist front"); the National Committee To Abolish the Poll Tax ("Communist front"); the National Negro Congress ("subversive and Communist" – "characterized as an organization operating in the field of civil rights under Communist Party domination and headed by responsible Party functionaries"); the National Council of American-Soviet Friendship ("subversive and Communist" – "specializing in pro-Soviet propaganda"); the Progressive Citizens of America ("political Communist front" – "subversive"); *Soviet Russia Today* ("Communist-controlled publication"); and a Testimonial Dinner for Ferdinand C. Smith (Communist Party affair").

Murray died in November 1952.

ABRAHAM JOHANNES MUSTE was born on January 8, 1885 in Zierikzee, The Netherlands, son of Adriana Jonker and Martin Muste. He came to the United States in 1891 and acquired derivative United States citizenship in 1896. He was married to the late Anna Huizenga. He was an alumnus of Hope College (A.B., 1905; A.M., 1909) and Union Theological Seminary (B.D., 1913). He attended the Theological Seminary of the Dutch Reformed Church in New Brunswick, New Jersey. He pursued graduate studies at New York University and Columbia University. He was the author of *Non-violence in an Aggressive World* (1940) and *Not By Night* (1947).

In 1905 and 1906, Muste was a teacher of Latin and Greek at Northwestern Classical Academy in Orange City, Iowa. In 1909, he was licensed and ordained to the ministry of the Dutch Reformed Church in America. From 1909 until 1914, he was minister of the Fort Washington Collegiate Church in New York City. From 1914 until 1917, he was minister of the Central Congregational Church in Newtonville, Massachusetts. In 1918, he was enrolled as a minister of the Society of Friends (Quakers) at Providence, Rhode Island. In 1919, he became involved in labor affairs. In 1920 and 1921, he was general secretary of the Amalgamated Textile Workers of America. From 1921 until 1933, he was the educational director, fund raiser, and teacher at Brookwood Labor College in Katonah, New York. From 1937 until 1940, he was director of the Presbyterian Labor Temple in New York City. From 1940 until 1953, he was executive secretary of the Fellowship of Reconciliation, and in 1953, he retired as secretary emeritus.

In February 1957, Muste was the head of a delegation of observers who were invited to attend the sessions of the 16th National Convention of the Communist Party. In a report prepared for the Senate Internal Security Subcommitee in March 1957, FBI Director J. Edgar Hoover said: "The Communists boasted of having 'impartial observers' cover the convention. However, most of these so-called impartial observers were hand-picked before the convention started and were reportedly headed by A.J. Muste, who has long fronted for Communists and who recently circulated an amnesty petition calling for the release of Communist leaders convicted under the Smith Act. Muste's report on the convention was biased, as could be expected."

The report of Muste and his colleagues mentioned by Hoover said in part: "Since reference has been made to these matters in the press and elsewhere, we wish to state that the sessions of the convention were democratically conducted with vigorous discussion of all matters brought to the floor. There were many indications that no individual or group was in a position to control the convention."

The Muste group went to great legths to discount the prevalent reports that the Communist movement in the United States and abroad was wracked with dissension: "However, in view of the upheavals in Poland and Hungary, the open airing in the *Daily Worker* in recent months of wide divergences among CP leaders and members, and the conduct of the recent convention as we observed it, to suppose, as some apparently do, that the ferment in the Communist movement here and abroad is merely an elaborate stage effect and that nothing is really happening seems to us to fly in the face of the evidence."

In reply to Hoover's allegations, Muste wrote: "Not only was I not connected with any Communist fronts ...but I took a leading part as the executive secretary of the F.O.R. [Fellowship of Reconciliation] in analyzing and exposing the dangers and fraudulent character of 'united fronts' and in persuading the F.O.R. groups, both here and in other countries not to take part in such activities as the World Council of Peace and its affiliated groups, the Stockholm Peace Petition, etc. What criticism there has been in pacifist and other peace groups during those years was to the effect that I was too 'rigid' and perhaps 'unreconciling' about such matters. To what pass have we come if a single individual – and he the head of the FBI presumably charged in a special and delicate manner with the protection of citizens against attack and the defense of our liberties – can make charges against an individual in the casual manner that you have used in this case?

"I raise this question not, except in a very minor degree, on my own behalf. I do have some means of publicity and a long public record of being open and above-board in what I do, whatever views people may hold as to my behavior . . . . We are taught in the Scripture . . . that it is the business of those who have influence or power to be specially considerate of the weak and to 'take care not to offend one of these little ones.' There are, alas, a good many people in this country who have little if any means to defend themselves, who have been injured, materially and spiritually, by those who have power and prestige . . . . I hope that I may hear from you. If you should have time to discuss these matters with me on a personal basis, I should appreciate it. I should perhaps make it clear that I am conscientiously opposed to responding to summons to appear before any government official or agency engaged in investigating the political or religious opinions of myself or others."

Two months after Hoover had issued his report on Muste's attendance at the Communist Party Convention, Muste instituted the American Forum for Socialist Education. On May 17, 1957, Senator James O. Eastland, chairman of the Senate Internal Security Subcommittee, wrote to Muste: "The Internal Security Subcommittee has scheduled a hearing next Tuesday on the nature of the American Forum for Socialist Education. This is in connection with the

subcommittee's inquiry into the nature of Communist activities in the United States.

"You are listed as chairman of the forum, and therefore I would appreciate your answering just a few questions about the organization. It would be most helpful if I had your reply by Tuesday, in which event it will be put in the record on that day. In any event I ask you these questions for the record.

"The subcommittee would like to know from you to what extent Mr. Albert E. Blumberg was a moving factor in the formation of the American Forum for Socialist Education. Would you tell us the extent of your dealing with Mr. Blumberg in this and all related matters during the last 18 months? Did you present a memo to Mr. Blumberg outlining an exchange of opinion on the whole subject of a union by the Communist and Socialist-minded groups? If you did present such a memorandum, would you supply the subcommittee with a copy thereof? Will you tell us also of your dealings with other representatives of the Communist Party, U.S.A., with relation to the forum?

"The subcommittee would like to have a full account of the following matters pertaining to the formation of the American Forum for Socialist Education: (1) When and by whom was the formation of this organization first suggested to you? (2) Who handled contacts with prospective members of the AFFSE national committee? To what extent were these contacts personal, and to what extent by mail? (3) What meetings have been held, and where, attended by persons now members of the AFFSE national committee, at which formation of the AFFSE and related matters were discussed? (4) Has each of the 40 members of the AFFSE national committee personally assented to serving as such? To whom, and in what form, were such assents given? Does each of these 40 members have an equal vote in management of the affairs of the AFFSE? (5) Is there any group or body other than the AFFSE national committee which is or will be concerned with AFFSE policy or administration? Who are the members of the administrative and executive staff of the AFFSE?

"I ask you also to inform the subcommittee as fully as your knowledge permits respecting the source or sources of funds used by or available to the American Forum for Socialist Education."

Muste, in a reply to Eastland, was adamant in his refusal to cooperate with the Senate Internal Security Subcommittee. He also took advantage of the opportunity to re-open the matter of J. Edgar Hoover's allegations against him: "I am in receipt of your letter of May 17, 1957, addressing to me a long series of questions relating to American Forum – For Socialist Education. May I call your attention to the fact that this letter was sent to an old address and had to be forwarded from there? Consequently, it did not actually come into my hands until late yesterday, Wednesday afternoon, May 22, 1957.

"It is relevant in this connection to point out also that many weeks ago I sent you and the subcommittee a copy of a letter dated April 2, 1957, and addressed to Mr. J. Edgar Hoover, Chief of the Federal Bureau of Investigation. A communication from Mr. Hoover to your subcommittee dealt with the presence at the Communist Party convention in February of a number of observers, all non-Communists and outspoken critics of Communist totalitarianism. Mr. Norman Thomas, among others, had been associated with me in working out this project.

"Mr. Hoover in his communication to your subcommittee spoke of me as having 'long fronted for Communists' which, as any one who has any acquaintance with these matters knows, was the exact opposite of the truth since I have for over 20 years been an intransigent opponent of united fronts with Communists. A major basis for Mr. Hoover's charge was that I had taken some part a year or so ago in a petition to the President for amnesty for Communists convicted under the Smith Act, a petition in which over 40 well-known citizens such as Mrs. Eleanor Roosevelt, Norman Thomas, and Dr. John C. Bennett, the dean of Union Theological Seminary, New York, joined.

"That there should be in such high quarters a pattern of thinking which can regard the exercise of the right of petition by such citizens as evidence of Communist 'fronting' is truly alarming and exposes the existence of the virus of political inquisition, one of the marks of totalitarianism, in the highest official quarters.

"Turning now to your letter of May 17 to me, I regard it in its context as evidence of the same dangerous tendencies. The American Forum has just come into existence. Its development has been completely open and aboveboard. Its launching was announced to the press together with the list of members of a provisional national committee whose connections were easily identifiable.

"Now, before American Forum can engage in any activity other than announcing formation of a committee, your subcommittee announces that it is investigating the forum in connection with communism. It issues subpoenas to 5 persons, 1 of whom is not on the national committee. Mr. Victor Perlo is someone who has never had the remotest connection with discussions leading to formation of American Forum. I have never known him or had the slightest connection with him. It is impossible to avoid the inference that the purpose of bringing his name into this picture at all is to suggest some devious connection of American Forum, organized purely for purposes of open discussion, with espionage or other such treasonable activities. In any case, you and your staff workers are well aware of the fact that in the atmosphere which has been created in our country such an inference about American Forum is bound to be drawn by many people and because of this many who would like to take part in its work will be forced to shun it or be subjected to persecution.

"There seemed for a time to be a tendency among congressional investigating committees such as yours to exercise some care in a matter of this kind, to investigate first without advance publicity and not to expose loyal citizens to public inquisition and persecution before there was some slight ground for supposing that questionable activities had taken place. In this case not even this minimum of care to observe the old American tradition of not branding citizens as somehow guilty before they have ever been charged with any crime, seems to have been observed.

"I must on grounds of conscience and in line with my conception of my duty as a citizen in a democratic society, decline to answer the questions in your letter, written by you as chairman and on behalf of the Senate Internal Security Subcommittee.

"As I have already stated, American Forum was organized in a completely open and above board fashion. Since you make reference to such matters as united action and 'the whole subject of a union between Communist and Socialist-minded groups' let me observe that there has never been any question of American Forum having anything to do with such matters or anything except discussion between people who differ on many fundamental issues, not people who have an agreed-upon basis for common action. In making this statement, I do not mean to imply that if there had been talks relating to legal activities of a political nature, your committee or any such Government agency would, in my opinion, have a right to conduct an inquisition into them, any more than I think any such agency has a right to conduct such an inquisition into your political activities which, as you must know, are also unpopular in many quarters.

"Your letter makes a reference to memorandums. Any that I have had anything to do with or American Forum as a body have been freely sent around to anyone who might be interested and are in no way secret. In view of the pervasive espionage activities which unfortunately characterize our country in this period, I surmise your subcommittee already has these materials.

"Primarily, my declination of the request to answer the questions presented by you in your official capacity is due to my firm conviction that inquisition into the political – the same would be true of religious – views and activities of citizens is evil, a resort to methods characteristic of totalitarian regimes, unconstitutional and profoundly un-American. In a free society, we have to draw a line between advocacy, discussion, and all such matters on the one hand, and acts which are illegal, subversive, or treasonable on the other hand. The line between the two may not always be easy to draw. This is precisely the basis on which totalitarian regimes seek to justify all their antidemocratic measures. We must not go up that road to perdition.

"Should I be subpoenaed to appear before the Internal Security Subcommittee, it would be impossible for me to do more than appear and state my reasons for declining to answer questions of the nature set forth in your letter of May 17, 1957. I can assure you that if this should come to pass, I shall not appeal to the fifth amendment. This is not meant, however, as a reflection on any individual who may have done so.

"It happens, Mr. Eastland, that I differ profoundly from you on such very fundamental matters as the position citizens should take toward the unanimous Supreme Court decision on integration in the public schools and on the whole question of relations between races. I do not see how your attitude can be squared with democratic concepts or with the central teachings of the Christian faith. I also believe that because of its effect on hundreds of millions of people in all parts of the world, your stand and activities relative to these matters constitute an immense threat to the security and good name of the United States and certainly give a major assist to Communist propaganda.

"Yet I am aware of the complicated character in these problems and of relations between human beings. And I trust you can and will believe me when I say that I have no personal animosity toward you. Both of us, in the final analysis, do not stand before any human tribunal but before the judgment seat of God. May we both humbly seek divine guidance at all times and especially with regard to the situation in which we happen now to be involved."

When Muste announced the establishment of the American Forum for Socialist Education, he issued a statement of purpose: "American Forum is organized in order to stimulate study and serious, untrammeled discussion of the problems of socialism in the United States. There is a growing interest in such discussion among all elements that think of themselves as related to historic Socialist and labor traditions, values and objectives – however deep and bitter their differences may have been. Moreover, there are indications that in the ranks of labor, among farmers, in the colleges and among the American people generally there are many who do not accept the status quo and who are developing an interest in political discussions provided a fresh and undogmatic approach is undertaken.

"Those who organize American Forum do so not on the ground that the problems of building a sound and effective American left have been solved and agreement for action has been reached. Their simple aim is to promote study and especially continuous discussion in a situation where many of the answers are not known and much division, confusion, and consequent frustration exist. They believe that all individuals from all elements should be involved in this, provided they commit themselves to a free exchange of views in a spirit of inquiry.

"American Forum holds that eventual Socialist unity requires clarity on fundamental social issues, along with tolerance of differences on other matters and comradely discussion of them within a common forum. It believes, therefore, that all important problems must be frankly and sharply discussed but equally that the discussion should be oriented to the future and not the past and concentrate on discussion of the program of a democratic Socialist movement in the United States and how such a movement may be brought into being.

"Since it is of the greatest importance that large numbers of people, including youth, be drawn into discussion locally, from labor unions, farm organizations, colleges, churches, etc., American Forum will have as one of its aims the formation, encouragement, and assistance of local groups or committees for this purpose. This may include assistance to local groups in setting up forums, etc., and going beyond mere occasional discussion meetings.

"Other purposes will be: (1) To call attention to the various periodicals and publications of groups whose members are involved in the discussions and encourage people to read them; and to publish bulletins or pamphlets under its own imprint as occasion requires. (2) To organize regional and national conferences, and by these and other means to contribute not only to intellectual clarification but to the building of a new morale and ethic, a spirit of fair play, labor militancy, determination, and hope among the progressive and radical forces in this country."

It was not the American Forum's statement of purpose which aroused the interest of the Senate Internal Security Subcommittee. The Subcommittee was interested in the Forum's officers and national committeemen, who were to work for the Forum's purposes. The Subcommittee recognized in the list issued by Muste some well-known names associated with the Communist Party and Communist causes. They included James Aronson, John T. McManus, Russell Nixon, and Harvey O'Connor, who had pleaded the protection of the Fifth

Amendment when asked to affirm or deny their Communist Party affiliations. Some names on the Forum's roster had been cited under oath as members of the Communist Party; they included Carl Braden, Russell Nixon, Albert E. Blumberg, Joseph Starobin, and Clifford T. McAvoy. Most of the other names on the roster belonged to individuals easily recognizable as inveterate joiners of Communist fronts and participants in Communist Party enterprises.

Muste's protestations against J. Edgar Hoover's allegations and the Senate Internal Security Subcommittee's interest in the American Forum for Socialist Education can best be appreciated by a review of Muste's extraordinary career in American radicalism. His affiliations with radical groups and individuals and his own personal radical activism eventually spanned more than half a century. In 1912, he voted for the Socialist Party's presidential candidate, Eugene V. Debs. He would later admit that he never cast a vote for a Democrat or a Republican for a major national or state office, and by the 1960's, even the Socialist Party was not radical enough for him.

When Muste studied at Columbia University, he met and developed a close and lasting friendship with John Dewey, whose revolutionary educational philosophy was matched by his radical political bent. At Union Theological Seminary, Muste developed an equally close and lasting friendship with Norman Thomas, who, over the years, richly deserved the title of patriarch of the Socialist Party.

When Muste was serving as pastor in Newtonville, just prior to the outbreak of World War I, he assumed the veil of pacifism for the first time. Later in his life, after some fits of public militancy, the veil would be his permanent garb.

When the United States entered World War I, Muste's pacifism became intolerable to many of his parishioners and neighboring clergymen, and he resigned his pastorate in 1917. He then began to work on a voluntary basis for the new-born, Red-saturated American Civil Liberties Union in Boston on behalf of conscientious objectors and draft evaders. It was at that same time that he joined the Quakers. He did not work as a Quaker minister but instead helped to form a Comradeship in Boston of so-called pacifists and very real political radicals — many of them clergymen.

In 1919, Muste and his colleagues of the Comradeship became involved in a rather riotous strike of textile workers in Lawrence, Massachusetts. Muste became a leader of the strike and was jailed for the first time for radical activities. The Lawrence episode served as the inaugural of a long career for Muste in America's radical and militant labor movement. From the Lawrence strike, he moved on to become the general secretary of the Amalgamated Textile Workers, but his complete lack of success caused him to resign the position after less than two years.

Although Muste had been on the labor scene for only a brief time, he was obviously recognized by influential radicals as an important leader. When he organized the Brookwood Labor College in 1921, he received the support of 13 national and international unions as well as the notorious Garland Fund, which habitually financed Communist Party enterprises. Brookwood, with Muste heading a radical socialist faculty, was nothing more nor less than a school for labor agitators. The students at Brookwood were thoroughly imbued with the tenets of Communism, socialism, and other forms of radicalism through the teachings of practitioners of these isms.

Muste's position at Brookwood gave him an entree to the hierarchy of the American labor movement. He was placed on the executive committee of the Workers Education Bureau, the educational branch of the American Federation of Labor. He was removed from that post after six years, in 1929, because of his increasingly obvious Red activism. In the meantime, he had written articles for Labor Age, the official organ of the Labor Publication Society, which he served as a member of its board of directors. The Society was staunchly opposed to the American Federation of Labor, and it eventually caused the formation of the Congress of Industrial Organizations — CIO — to organize mass production industries.

In 1924, Muste, in common with so many radical laborites, campaigned for Robert M. La Follette Sr., the presidential candidate of the Progressive Party. The Progressives had attracted supporters from a broad segment of the right-to-left political spectrum. By this time, however, Muste was at the extreme left of the spectrum as a confirmed Trotskyite Marxist-Leninist.

In 1929, Muste became the founder of the Conference for Progressive Labor Action. He became chairman of the group known as Musteites, a "definitely anti-imperialist, anti-militarist and international labor movement." The Musteites urged the formation of a labor party in America, and the group was among the first to call for full diplomatic recognition by the United States of the Soviet Union. The Musteites were so extreme that they would not tolerate Socialists in their membership. Their principal accomplishment was to instigate violent strikes in North Carolina's textile industry. The Musteites' cadres were known as the Unemployed Leagues. The Musteites also organized the National Unemployed League, which instigated the 1934 Auto-Lite strike in Toledo and the 1936 Goodyear Tire strike in Akron, both of which were extremely violent. The 1936 strike saw the first use of the sit-down, which became a favorite of Communists in France and the United States.

The Musteites, when they were first organized, professed as their intention the reformation of the American Federation of Labor from within, but the AFL's leaders were not receptive. The Marxist-Leninist character of the Conference for Progressive Labor Action was blatantly advertised on the letterhead of the group: "The Conference for Progressive Labor Action is an organization of militants which roots itself in American soil and seeks to face the realities of American life. It helps the workers in their daily struggles for bread and justice, against injunctions, Yellow-Dog contracts and official brutality. It seeks to stimulate in the existing and potential labor organizations a progressive, realistic, militant labor spirit and activity. It aims to inspire the workers to take control of industry and government, abolish the present capitalist system and build a workers' republic, and an economic system operated for the benefit of the masses and not of the few."

Muste had set the tone when he addressed the Brookwood Labor College's seniors in 1929 and said: "Brookwood stands on the basis of the class struggle; a school which does not accept the capitalist system." A colleague of Muste's in the CPLA, Louis Budenz, who would become one of America's most prominent Communists, customarily introduced Muste to audiences as the "American Lenin."

Muste's work with the CPLA eventually caused so much dissension among the members of Brookwood's administration and faculty that he resigned in 1933 – his extreme militancy had proven to be intolerable for some of his queasier colleagues.

With Brookwood behind him, Muste established the American Workers Party, which replaced the Conference of Progressive Labor Action. In 1934, Muste's American Workers Party merged with the Communist League of America, the Trotskyites, under the leadership of James Cannon, who had been encouraged to cooperate with Muste by Leon Trotsky. Out of the merger came the Workers Party of the United States, which had as its avowed purpose "the overthrow of capitalist rule in America and the creation of a workers' state." The merger was understandable, since Muste was not only a professed Trotskyite but was deeply admired and respected by Trotsky himself.

In 1934, when the merger was accomplished, Muste became national chairman of the Workers Party. The Party had a Declaration of Principles which read: "The Workers Party of the U.S. is founded on the great principles of revolutionary theory and practice stated by Marx and Lenin and tested by the experience of the class struggle on an international scale, above all in the Russian Revolution in 1917 (the 'October Revolution'). The Workers Party conceives as its duty the realistic application of these principles to the present historical situation. Since its primary task is the defeat of the enemy at home – the overthrow of the capitalist government of the United States – the Workers Party will seek, first and foremost, to demonstrate to the working class of the U.S. and its allies that the application of the principles of revolutionary Marxism is the sole means for the fulfillment of their historical needs and interests."

The Muste-led Workers Party's program was clearly inspired by Leninism: "The fundamental mass instrument of this struggle for power ... will be the Worker's Councils (Soviets). The Workers' Councils ... are the organs which mobilize the workers for the revolutionary assault as well as the organization form of state power after the victory. It is through them, not through the existing governmental apparatus, which represents the interest only of the capitalist minority, that the workers will overthrow the capitalist class and take power .... The workers will abolish the whole machinery of the capitalist state in order to render it incapable of counter-revolutionary activity and because it cannot serve as the instrumentality for establishing a new social order. Its place will be taken by the workers' state, based on the Workers' Councils. The workers' state, while assuring and continually extending far more genuine and substantial democratic rights to the masses than ever accorded to them under capitalism, will function as a dictatorship of the working class against its enemies."

In 1935, Muste became a victim of an internecine quarrel when the leaders of the old Communist League of America decided on a change of tactics. They prepared a merger with Socialists in order to weaken and eventually destroy the Socialist Party. Muste's extremism would not countenance even the briefest flirtation with the Socialists and his stubbornness led to his loss of control of the Workers Party.

In 1936, Muste went to Europe on a vacation which combined pleasure with business. He attended an international meeting of Trotskyites in Paris, where he encountered the same sort of tacticians who had defeated him in the United States over the question of a temporary alliance with Socialists. He also visited Trotsky in Norway, where the Bolshevik leader was in exile from the wrath of Stalin. During the week that he spent with Trotsky, Muste came to appreciate the man as much as his principles of revolution, and the feeling was apparently mutual even though Trotsky had obviously engineered Muste's fall from power in the United States.

As a result of Muste's trip to Europe and his visit with Trotsky, there developed a curious twist in Muste's career. He retained his admiration for Trotsky but alleged that he had become disillusioned with the Trotskyite Workers Party in America. He further claimed that as a result of his trip to Europe he had been reconverted to Christianity and that he now considered himself a Calvinist Socialist. For almost a decade he had been a minister without portfolio or any visible attachment to any religious practices. Now, however, he advocated a combination of Christian nonviolence and Marxism to change society, and he presented the appearance of having made an irrevocable split with the Trotskyites.

At this stage of his career, Muste resumed a relationship with the Fellowship of Reconciliation. In 1916, he had become a member of FOR, a radical, pacifist group that operated under the halo of religious orientation. From 1926 until 1929, while still at Brookwood, he served as national chairman of FOR. In 1936 and 1937, he served on FOR's national council and as the group's Industrial Secretary. While holding the latter position, he was a leader in the violence-ridden hosiery workers' strike in Reading, Pennsylvania. He left FOR to become director of the Presbyterian Labor Temple for three years, and during that time, he was reinstated in the Presbytery of New York as a minister. (This would be Muste's last ministerial work, and in the last two decades of his life he seldom attended any church services, but there is no evidence that he ever renounced his claim to the title of clergyman.)

In 1940, Muste returned to FOR as executive secretary. After retiring from that position in 1953, he never again held regular employment. For all practical purposes, Muste's 13-year tenure as FOR's executive secretary was probably the most productive period of his life for influencing the radical life of America. It was in that period that he inspired such protégés as Bayard Rustin, James Farmer, and George Houser, all of whom later became leaders among the black racial agitators who have convulsed the United States for more than two decades. As the leader of FOR, Muste became a close and trusted advisor to Martin L. King Jr., the arch agitator of the 1950's and 1960's. It was Muste who inspired the foundation of the Congress of Racial Equality, which was led by his protégés and for which over a period of several years he was the most productive fund raiser.

In 1948, Muste was instrumental in organizing the American Peacemakers Group, and he served as secretary of these radical pacifists during the group's first five years of existence. In 1950, he was the leading organizer of the Church Peace Mission, an offshoot of FOR, which had as its purpose the conversion of churchmen — clergy and laity — to absolute opposition to war. Muste was able to recruit into his Church Peace Mission Quakers and peace fellowships of the Baptist, Episcopalian, Lutheran, Methodist, Presbyterian, and United Universalist Churches. He also received the cooperation of such radical religionists as John Haynes Holmes, Martin Luther King Jr., Walter G. Muelder, and Clarence Pickett.

When Muste ended his regular employment by his retirement from FOR in 1953, he entered a new phase of his career as a gadabout elder statesman of ultra-leftist-pacifism in America and elsewhere. He also became a prominent participant in both obvious and thinly disguised Communist Party enterprises. He was no stranger to front activities. In 1933, he was on the arrangements committee for the United States Congress Against War ("completely under the control of the Communist Party") which produced the American League Against War and Fascism ("subversive and Communist" — "established in the United States in an effort to create public sentiment on behalf of a foreign policy adapted to the interests of the Soviet Union"). In the same year, he was a member of the executive committee of the National Scottsboro Action Committee ("Communist Party was in complete control"). In 1934, he was national chairman of the National Committee To Aid the Victims of German Fascism ("an auxiliary of the Communist Party"). He was vice president of the Pioneer Youth of America, a Socialist organization mainly financed by the Red-controlled Garland Fund. He was chairman of the Manumit Associates in support of a Socialist school for children, also financed by the Garland Fund. As early as 1921, he was on the national committee of the Red-controlled American Civil Liberties Union and on the board of directors of the League for Industrial Democracy, one of the most influential of all Socialist organizations in America. In the 1930's he was a member of the executive committee of the Committee on Militarism in Education, which propagandized against military training in schools and colleges and was supported by the Fellowship of Reconciliation, the League for Industrial Democracy, the Women's International League for Peace and Freedom, the American Civil Liberties Union, and the Federal Council of Churches, organizations in which Muste was very active. He was a leader in the National Tom Mooney Council of Action, which was organized by the International Labor Defense ("the legal arm of the Communist Party"). He was a member of the Committee for the Support of *Il Nuovo Mondo*, a campaign publication issued on behalf of the anarchists Sacco and Vanzetti, whose attempt to escape capital punishment became a *cause célèbre* for Communists throughout the world. He was a vice president of the Red-oriented American Federation of Teachers. He was on the executive committee of the League for Independent Political Action, which was thoroughly Socialist in its personnel and program and of great aid and comfort to the Communist Party. He also contributed to the League's *Common Sense*. He was on the national committee of the War Resisters League and a contributing editor of its *World Tomorrow*. The WRL boasted that its members took an oath saying: "I declare it to be my intention never to take part in war, offensive or defensive, international or civil, whether it be by bearing arms, making or handling munitions, voluntarily subscribing

to war loans, or using my labor for the purpose of setting others free for war service." (Muste received the War Resisters League's Peace Award in 1958.) He was on the national advisory board of the National Religion and Labor Foundation ("a Communist front"). He lectured at Camp Conawapa and the summer institute of the Mohegan Colony House – two Red enterprises. He worked hand-in-hand with the Communists to organize the Progressive Miners of America Union. He was a member of the Continental Congress of Workers and Farmers for Economic Reconstruction, a Socialist Party organization that adhered to the Marxist line for abolition of capitalism by a state takeover of all means of production. He was a member of the National Committee on Labor Injunctions, an ACLU project to protect Red labor agitators from legal recourse taken by employers. He was a contributor to *Fight* ("subversive and Communist"). He was founder and editor of *Liberation*, which was never anything but a pro-Communist publication. He was a member of the pro-Soviet *Nation* Associates. He was a member of the Consumers National Federation ("a transmission belt for the Communist Party's influence and ideology"). He was a member of the Greater New York Emergency Conference on Inalienable Rights ("Communist front").

In later years, Muste joined in an Appeal for Amnesty for Communist Party Leaders Imprisoned Under the Smith Act, a Communist Party project. He was also affiliated with the Citizens Committee for a Just Settlement of the Hospital Strike (led by Leon Davis, a Communist, in 1959); the Committee for Socialist Unity, a coalition of Communists, Communist splinter groups, and other leftists, to whom he gave an address at the United Socialist Rally for May Day; the Medical Aid to [Castro's] Cuba Committee (a pro-Communist project); the Nonviolent Committee for Cuban Independence [under Castro] (a pro-Communist project); the Militant Labor Forum (operated by the Socialist Workers Party); the Monroe Defense Committee (on behalf of the pro-Communist racial agitator, Robert Williams); the National Committee To Abolish the Un-American Activities Committee ("to lead and direct the Communist Party's 'Operation Abolition' campaign"); and the National Committee To Secure Justice in the Rosenberg Case ("Communist front organized . . . to conduct the United States phase of a mammoth propaganda campaign designed to obliterate the crime of and exploit the Rosenbergs and their codefendent Morton Sobell for the purposes of international Communism").

Muste was affiliated with a wide variety of national and international pacifist and disarmament groups. In 1948, he was founder of the Central Committee for Conscientious Objectors. In the 1950's and 1960's, he was prominent in the activities of the ultra-leftist-pacifist National Committee for a Sane Nuclear Policy and the ultra-leftist-pacifist Nonviolent Action Against Nuclear Weapons. He was a chief organizer of the Committees of Correspondence (1960), later known as the Council of Correspondence. This radical organization called for "unilateral steps toward disarmament both on principle and as a practical strategy which represents neither surrender to Communism nor wishful fantasy, since no country courageous and rational enough to thus disarm would be an easy victory for any form of dictatorship. We risk a great deal in reliance on nuclear arms: we must be willing to take risks in pursuit of peace."

One of Muste's most important undertakings was the chairmanship of the Committee for Nonviolent Action. Under his direction, the CNVA carried on well-publicized demonstrations at the Atlas missile base in Mead, Nebraska, during the summer of 1959. Muste, as a result of his participation at Mead, was convicted, fined and sentenced for trespassing on a military reservation. In the summer and fall of 1960, the CNVA demonstrated in New London, Connecticut, against the construction and arming of Polaris submarines.

In 1958, the CNVA sponsored protest cruises by the *Golden Rule* and the *Phoenix* as a demonstration against nuclear bomb testing by the United States in the Pacific. In 1962, similar demonstrations by *Everyman I, II,* and *III* were made against Soviet and United States nuclear testing, and the cruises were planned and financed in great part through the personal efforts of Muste.

Two of the most ambitious projects of Muste's CNVA were peace walks. In 1960 and 1961, Muste helped in the planning and financing of a "San Francisco to Moscow Peace Walk" that attracted the most favorable type of publicity in the international Communist press. In 1964, the venture was repeated with the CNVA's Quebec to Washington to Guantanamo Peace Walk. Although the "peace walks" were pure and simple Communist propaganda stunts, Muste had no difficulty recruiting hordes of dupes to walk a few miles for the benefit of the press media's cameramen.

As a leader of CNVA, Muste also directed demonstrations at the Pentagon, so-called "prayer" vigils, "peace" fasts, and draft-card burnings. He and his followers accepted arrest as a matter of course, and their antics were duly recorded and photographed in a sympathetic manner by the national television networks, which presented the spectacles on a regular basis to the viewing audiences, but with never a hint in the accompanying commentaries that Muste and his crew were simply propaganda tools of the Communist movement.

In November 1959, Muste went to Accra, Ghana, to coordinate an interracial, international demonstration against France's atomic bomb testing in the Sahara. In December 1963, he was in India, where he had been called by disciples of Gandhi, who wanted him to teach them to apply the principles and teachings of Gandhi vis-a-vis Red China.

From India, Muste went to London, where forty-four peace organizations established the International Confederation for Disarmament and Peace and named Muste an international co-chairman of the group.

In 1961, Muste was elected as one of three co-chairmen of a World Council to direct the newly-formed International Peace Brigade. Muste said that the Brigade would need a corps of at least a thousand volunteers who were ready "to give substantial blocs of time and to be on call for emergency service in international projects related to the abolition of war and the use of nonviolent attitudes and methods in the achievement of national independence and basic social change eliminating poverty and exploitation." In its "statement of principles and aims," the Brigade said: "Individuals, governments, peoples are imprisoned in the habits, ideologies and institutions of violence which they themselves have devised and built. Common sense, political wisdom and profound moral imperatives compel us to break out of this condition. Men must find and be ready to experiment with an alternative. That alternative is nonviolence."

In 1962, the Brigade offered a further explanation of its program: "Although it was decided that conciliatory efforts and constructive service would be a definite part of the Brigade's activities, its distinguishing characteristic would be active participation and demonstration as a nonviolent, non-national volunteer force committed in many cases to a particular 'side' or 'cause' judged most consistent with the Brigade's aims. The Brigade will remain, however, uncommitted to any political or national group in general, as well as to any laws, customs or disciplines inconsistent with the Brigade's aims, using civil disobedience as a major positive 'weapon' or method of action where judged necessary. The Brigade is not, therefore, a 'neutral' force so much as one concerned with achieving just ends through peaceful rather than violent and destructive action."

Muste took an active interest in the projects of the Brigade. In 1962, through the cooperation of Julius Nyerere, president of the Tanganyika African National Union, and Kenneth Kaunda, head of the United National Independence Party of Northern Rhodesia, the World Peace Brigade established a training center for nonviolent action in Dar es Salaam, Tanganyika. Muste was very pleased that his group was able to make a beginning for agitation by outsiders in the African pro-Communist "independence" struggle. He could see the need in all other countries for the type of agitation he had instigated in the United States, and he was hopeful that the Brigade would be able to give the agitation a centralized direction: "Of course there must be strong movements within each country, but a series of isolated or tenuously related national organizations and movements simply cannot deal intelligently and seriously with the threat of war and the task of building a sane society. There must be international thinking, planning, action. From another angle, every important action within a nation can now be politically and morally strengthened by the inclusion of World Peace Brigade volunteers . . . . None of our organizations has hitherto had a structure for concentrated and continuous international planning and action . . . .

"It is tremendously important that it is also the Gandhian movement in India which has now been brought into living relationship with the movement in the United States and the United Kingdom, because this immediately gives us a base in Asia and a relationship to Africa of a kind which Western peace movements did not and could not have. Therefore it makes it global in a sense which it would not otherwise be, both actually and potentially . . . . A beginning has been made in realizing Gandhi's concept of a world *Shanti sena* (peace army)."

In the 1960's, Muste devoted a great deal of energy to groups in opposition to United States participation in the Vietnam War. He was a rallying point in such organizations as the Vietnam Day Committee, the Fort Hood Three Defense Committee, the Fifth Avenue Vietnam Peace Parade Committee, the Spring Mobilization Committee to End the War in Vietnam, the Committee for the International Days of Protest, and the National Mobilization Committee to End the War

in Vietnam. In countless meetings, parades, and demonstrations he rubbed elbows with every variety of Communist and Socialist, with racial agitators, with duped do-gooders, with street militants, and with frenetic youths who seemed hypnotized by the octogenarian whose capacity for trouble-making and rabble-rousing appeared limitless.

Muste was especially anxious to work with Communists in his anti-Vietnam War protests. As spokesman for the Spring Mobilization Committee, he welcomed Communists into its ranks. Said he: "We adhere to the policy of 'non-exclusion,' first and most of all, because it is right in principle. . . . People of the Left (Communists with or without quotation marks) should be permitted and expected to function normally in the political life of the country . . . . In practice a non-Communist coalition is in danger of becoming an anti-Communist one . . . . What no doubt clinches the matter is that if we were to abandon the 'non-exclusion' principle we will quickly disintegrate . . . ."

In the last year of his life, Muste made two of his most memorable gestures in the name of "pacifism." In April 1966, he led four of his followers on a trip to Saigon, where they hoped to perform a ritualistic anti-war demonstration. In Saigon, the five agitators were unusually quiet for several days; when they finally began a demonstration the Saigon authorities promptly placed them in custody and they departed from South Vietnam on the first available plane. In December 1966, Muste accompanied three Red-oriented clergymen to Hanoi. They were Pastor Martin Niemöller of Germany, Rabbi Abraham Feinberg of Toronto, and Ambrose Reeves, former Anglican Bishop of Johannesburg, South

Africa. The fours travelers, on their mission of "peace and sympathy," received a warm and cordial welcome from North Vietnam's leading butcher, Ho chi Minh. The North Vietnamese Communists made the most of the opportunity afforded by the visit of the four stooges to reap a propaganda harvest around the world. It was especially gratifying to the Communists that Muste said that his objective on the trip was to protest against the United States role (not that of North Vietnam) in South Vietnam. In Hanoi, Muste also drafted a "peace" message to the American people and an invitation for President Lyndon B. Johnson to visit Hanoi. The message received Ho chi Minh's imprimatur and was broadcast widely in press conferences, publicity releases, and through a CBS-TV interview by Muste.

On February 11, 1967, less than two months after his return from Hanoi, Muste died at the age of eighty-two, a hero to Communists both at home and abroad. From the Soviet Union, the Soviet "Peace" Committee expressed its condolences to the American peace movement and cited Muste's courage and adherence to principles in his fight against aggression and injustice. (He had been singularly silent throughout his entire lifetime about aggression and injustice perpetrated by the Soviet Union or any other Communist power.) From Hanoi, Ho chi Minh wired his condolences: "Am profoundly grieved learn demise AJ Muste, outstanding fighter for peace and democratic movement in USA and world, loyal and valiant friend of Vietnamese people." Arnold Johnson of the Communist Party's hierarchy offered the Party's farewell in a sentimental eulogy in the pages of the *Worker*. He mentioned the Party's "deep sense of loss" at Muste's death, and made due mention of the tremendous cooperation extended to the Party over the years by the "dean of the peace movement." Unmentioned but certainly not forgotten by Johnson was Muste's endorsement, less than a year earlier, of the political candidacy of Herbert Aptheker, the Communist Party's chief theoretician, who sought a seat in Congress from Brooklyn.

One of the most unusual tributes paid to the deceased Muste came from U.S. Senator Robert F. Kennedy, who called Muste "one of those rare men of whom it can be said that our inability to follow his example speaks more to his excellence than to the limitations in ourselves."

GUSTAVUS MYERS was born on March 20, 1872 in Trenton, New Jersey, son of Julia Hillman and Abram Myers. He married Genevieve Whitney. He was educated in various schools in Philadelphia and New York. He was the author of *History of Public Franchises in New York City* (1900); *History of Tammany Hall* (1901 and 1917); *History of the Great American Fortunes* (1910 and 1936); *Beyond the Borderline of Life* (1910); *History of the Supreme Court of the United States* (1912); *History of Canadian Wealth* (1914); *The German Myth* (1918); *Ye Olden Blue Laws* (1921); *History of American Idealism* (1925); *America Strikes Back* (1935); *The Ending of American Hereditary Fortunes* (1939); and *History of Bigotry in the United States* (posthumously, 1943), for which he did the research on a Guggenheim Fellowship awarded in 1941.

In 1891, Myers worked for the *Philadelphia Record*. In 1892, he moved to New York, where he remained the rest of his life. He joined the Populist Party at a time when it was giving way to the newborn Socialist Party. He was not a political activist, but he promoted Socialism through his reportorial and editorial writings in various New York newspapers and through his articles in a host of magazines. He was a severe and biased critic of capitalism and capitalists. The economic and social difficulties to be found in America he ascribed completely to the capitalist system. In his view, government at all levels was in the hands of a relatively few economic royalists. In harmony with his contemporary muckraking literary colleagues – most of whom held strong ties to Socialism – he found a solution to Socialism that merely paraphrased the works of Marx, Engels, Debs, Sinclair, Ely, and others. The nationalization of industry and resources, the redistribution of wealth, revolutionary legislation, and a political upheaval at the polls were some of Myers' solutions for the economic tribulations of an industrial America.

Myers' *History of the Great American Fortunes* was his most durable work. It was the result of eight years of research and writing, accomplished in his narrow Socialist environment, but it was completed at a time when Socialism had become the vogue in many traditional academic areas – history, economics, political science, anthropology, sociology, and philosophy – at major university and college campuses throughout the nation. The work was published by the Charles H. Kerr and Company concern, a Socialist organization. Although produced in three volumes, and written in the plodding language usual with the dedicated Socialist, it became one of the most popular of all reference books mentioned in bibliographies of works representative of many academic areas of interest. In fact, Myers reached a stature comparable to that of Charles A. Beard, Franz Boas, Richard Ely, Morris Hillquit, Harry Laidler, Eugene Debs, and others whose Socialistic writings virtually smothered other required and recommended readings in college classrooms throughout America.

Although Myers severed his formal ties with the Socialist Party during World War I when he disagreed with the Socialist opposition to American involvement in that war, he did not surrender his commitment to Socialism. In his writings, for the rest of his life, he did not deviate from Socialist principles. He did not, however, achieve the acclaim for his later writings that had been accorded *History of the Great American Fortunes*. In 1936, there was a revival of fame for Myers when his major work was reissued in a one-volume format. He died in December 1942.

JOHN SCHOLTE NOLLEN was born on January 15, 1869 in Pella, Iowa, son of Sara Scholte and John Nollen. He married the late Emeline Bartlett. His second wife was Louise Bartlett. He was an alumnus of Central College (A.B., 1885); the State University of Iowa (A.B., 1888); and the University of Leipzig (Ph.D., 1892). He pursued graduate studies at the University of Zurich (1890-1891); the Sorbonne and Collège de France (1893); and the University of Berlin (1900-1901). He was the author of *Goethe's Götz von Berlichingen auf der Buhne* (1893); *Chronology and Practical Bibliography of Modern German Literature* (1903); *Outline History of Modern German Literature*, for the Lake German Series (1903); *Two Addresses* (1907); *What Is That in Thy Hand?* (1911); *The Warfare of Peace* (1913); *God and the Nations* (1914);

and *Think on These Things* (1915). He was the editor of Kleist's *Prinz Friedrich von Homburg* (1899); Schiller's *Poems* (1905); Schiller's *Maria Stuart* (1909); *German Poems, 1800-1850* (1912); *Educational Pioneer: Centennial History of Grinnell College* (1946); and *The Way, The Truth, The Life* (1948). He was a contributor to *The German Classics* (1913).

From 1885 until 1887, Nollen was an instructor at the Central College of Iowa. From 1888 until 1890, he was a tutor in Cham, Switzerland. From 1893 until 1903, he was a professor of modern languages at Iowa (now Grinnell) College. From 1903 until 1907, he was a professor of German at Indiana University. From 1907 until 1918, he was president of Lake Forest University. In 1917 and 1918, he was president of the Association of American Colleges. From 1918 until 1920, he worked for the YMCA in Europe. From 1920 until 1952, he was at Grinnell College as dean (1920-1931); acting president (1931); president (1931-1940); and president emeritus (1940-1952). In 1927 and 1928, he was a visiting professor at Pomona and Scripps Colleges in Claremont, California.

Nollen was affiliated with the American Committee for Protection of Foreign Born ("founded by the Communist Party in order to exploit racial divisions in the United States for its own revolutionary purposes"); the American Peace Society (ultra-leftist-pacifist); the Committee for a Democratic Far Eastern Policy ("Communist"); the Committee for Peaceful Alternatives to the Atlantic Pact ("a Communist-front organization . . . as part of Soviet psychological warfare against the United States"); the Fellowship of Reconciliation (ultra-leftist-pacifist); the International Labor Defense ("subversive and Communist" – "legal arm of the Communist Party" – "part of an international network of organizations for the defense of Communist lawbreakers"); the International Workers Order ("from its very inception demonstrated by its pronouncements, its activities, and the authoritative statements of the Communist Party that it is a subservient instrument of the Communist Party of the United States"); the Joint Anti-Fascist Refugee Committee ("subversive and Communist"); the Mid-Century Conference for Peace ("aimed at assembling as many gullible persons as possible under Communist direction and turning them into a vast sounding board for Communist propaganda"); the National Committee To Repeal the McCarran Act ("Communist front" – "subversive"); the National Conference To Defend the Bill of Rights ("subversive"); and the National Federation for Constitutional Liberties ("under Communist Party domination and headed by responsible Party functionaries" – "one of the viciously subversive organizations of the Communist Party"). He died in March 1952.

CLIFFORD ODETS was born on July 18, 1906 in Philadelphia, son of Pearl Geisinger and Louis Odets. He was married to and divorced from Luise Rainer. His second wife was the late Bette Grayson. He was the author of many plays, including *Waiting for Lefty* (1935); *Awake and Sing* (1935); *Till the Day I Die* (1935); *Paradise Lost* (1935); *I Can't Sleep* (1936); *The General Died at Dawn*, scenario for screen (1936); *Golden Boy* (1937); *Rocket to the Moon* (1938); *Silent Partner* (1939); *Night Music* (1940); *Clash by Night* (1941); *Humoresque* (1942);

None But the Lonely Heart (1943); *Deadline at Dawn* (1944); *The Big Knife* (1948); *The Country Girl* (1950); *The Flowering Peach* (1954); *The Winner* (1954); *Sweet Smell of Success* (1956); *Cue for Passion* (1958); *Story on Page One* (1959); and *Love Among the Ruins* (1963). He wrote *Jacobowsky and the Colonel*, an adaptation of a play by Franz Werfel (1943).

Odets left high school after two years. Between 1923 and 1925, he was an actor with an amateur group, the Drawing Room Players, and with Harry Kemp's Poet's Theatre. From 1925 until 1927, he performed on radio with a group of actors he had organized, and also by himself as the Roving Reciter. From 1928 until 1930, he was an actor with the Theatre Guild. From 1931 until 1934, he worked for the Group Theatre. After 1934, he was a playwright for the Broadway stage and a script writer for Hollywood films.

In 1952, Odets testified before the House Committee on Un-American Activities that for a period of about eight or nine months in 1934 and 1935, he had been a member of the Communist Party. He claimed that he had been recruited by a fellow actor in the Group Theatre, J. Edward Bromberg. He further testified that he had severed his ties with the Communist Party.

Odets' *Waiting for Lefty*, which was written and produced during the period of his admitted Communist Party membership, was hailed by the Communist Party in 1935 and became a regular part of Communist propaganda in the years after. Several of Odets' later plays — *Awake and Sing, Till the Day I Die* and *Paradise Lost* — were also Communist-line productions.

In 1949, fourteen years after Odets' alleged break with the Communist Par-

ty, he proclaimed publicly: "I cannot blame the Soviet Union because an apocalyptic beast is running loose in our world today and its name is Money, Money, Money. As an American, in the tradition of all American artists of the past, the moral values of my world are in question, not Russia's." At the same time, he deplored "one of the greatest frauds ever perpetrated against the American people, the fraud that the Soviet Union is making a war against the United States."

In 1952, when Odets appeared before the House Committee on Un-American Activities, he was confronted with his long post-1935 career of Communist front affiliations. He was asked: "How do you reconcile your statement that your break with the Communist Party was complete and final with this record of affiliation with Communist-front organizations as shown by these exhibits?" Odets replied: "Well, I will say again, as I said before, that the lines of leftism, liberalism, in all of their shades and degrees, are constantly crossing like a jangled chord on a piano. It is almost impossible to pick out which note is which note. I have spoken out on what I thought were certain moral issues of the day, and I found myself apparently in line with your documentation, I have found myself frequently on platforms with Communists that I did not know about then but evidently are now known Communists. I have said before that many of these people have some very good tunes. They have picked up some of our most solemn and sacred American tunes and they sing them. If I as an American liberal must sometimes speak out the same tune, I must sometimes find myself on platforms, so to speak, with strange bedfellows. I have never wittingly, since those early days, have never wittingly joined or spoken on an exclusively Communist program or platform, not to my knowledge. I see that one must do one of two things. One must pick one's way very carefully through the mazes of liberalism and leftism today or one must remain silent. Of the two, I must tell you frankly I would try to pick the first way, because the little that I have to say, the little that I have to contribute to the betterment or welfare of the American people could not permit me to remain silent."

Odets was affiliated with the American Committee for Spanish Freedom ("Communist"); the American Committee To Save Refugees ("perform[ing] a most valuable function for the international Communist movement"); the American Continental Congress for World Peace ("another phase in the Communist 'peace' campaign, aimed at consolidating anti-American forces throughout the Western Hemisphere"); the American League for Peace and Democracy ("subversive and Communist" – "established . . . in an effort to create public sentiment on behalf of a foreign policy adapted to the interests of the Soviet Union . . . [and] designed to conceal Communist control, in accordance with the new tactics of the Communist International"); the American Relief Ship for Spain ("Communist Party front enterprise"); American Writers Union ("subversive"); the American Youth Congress ("subversive" – "one of the most influential front organizations ever set up by the Communists in this country" – "the Communists were in complete control"); Artef ("Communist front" – "one of the oldest Communist Party organizations"); Book Union ("distributors of Communist literature" – "Communist [Party] book club"); California Labor School ("a subversive and Communist organization"); the Celebration of 15 Years of Biro Bidjan ("Communist project"); the China Aid Council ("Communist-controlled"); the Citizens Committee for Harry Bridges ("Communist"); the Civil Rights Congress ("created and established by the Communist Party as an organization which would utilize defense of civil rights for Party purposes and raise and maintain mass defense and bail funds for Party use"); the Committee for a Boycott Against Japanese Aggression ("the committee was featured in the *Daily Worker*, official organ of the Communist Party, and in that paper alone"); the Committee for Free Political Advocacy ("Communist front"); the Committee of One Thousand ("Communist created and controlled"); the Congress of Revolutionary Writers ("subversive and Communist"); the Congress of American-Soviet Friendship ("Communist front"); the Coordinating Committee To Lift the [Spanish] Embargo ("one of the numerous Communist-front enterprises which were organized around the Communists' agitation over the Spanish Civil War"); the Cultural and Scientific Conference for World Peace ("Communist front" – "a propaganda front for Soviet foreign policy and Soviet culture"); the Cultural Workers in Motion Pictures and Other Arts ("Communist front"); *Daily Worker* ("official organ of the Communist Party"); Friends of the Abraham Lincoln Brigade ("completely controlled by the Communist Party"); Frontier Films ("Communist front"); the Golden Book of American Friendship with the Soviet Union ("pro-Soviet propaganda enterprise"); In Defense of the Bill of Rights ("Communist Party enterprise"); the International Labor Defense ("subversive and Communist" – "legal arm of the Communist Party" – "part of an international network of organizations for the defense of Communist lawbreakers"); *International Literature* ("official organ of the International Union of Revolutionary Writers"); International Union of Revolutionary Writers ("Communist front"); the League of American Writers ("subversive and Communist" – "began openly to follow the Communist Party line as dictated by the foreign policy of the Soviet Union"); the May Day Parade of 1948 ("Communist Party enterprise"); the Medical Bureau and North American Committee To Aid Spanish Democracy ("subversive and un-American"); the Mid-Century Conference for Peace ("aimed at assembling as many gullible persons as possible under Communist direction and turning them into a vast sounding board for Communist propaganda"); the Mother Ella Reeve Bloor Birthday Celebration (Communist Party festivity); the National Committee Against Censorship of the Theatre Arts ("Communist front"); the National Council of American-Soviet Friendship ("subversive and Communist" – "specializing in pro-Soviet propaganda"); the National Council of the Arts, Sciences, and Professions ("a Communist front used to appeal to special occupational groups"); the National Non-Partisan Committee To Defend the Rights of the Twelve Communist Leaders (pro-Communist); the National Writers Congress ("Communist front"); *New Masses* ("weekly journal of the Communist Party"); New Theatre ("Communist Party publication"); New Theatre School for Dramatic Art ("Communist front"); an Open Letter for Closer Cooperation with the Soviet Union (issued by "a group of Communist Party stooges"); the Progressive Citizens of America ("political

Communist front" – "subversive"); the Rally To Honor the 8th Year of United States-Soviet Ties (Communist Party festivity); *Soviet Russia Today* ("Communist-controlled publication"); *Sunday Worker* ("official organ of the Communist Party"); Statement in Defense of the Communist Party (pro-Communist); Theatre Arts Committee ("Communist front"); the United Office and Professional Workers of America ("Communist-controlled"); the Win-the-Peace Conference ("Communist front"); the World Peace Congress ("organized under Communist initiative in various countries throughout the world"); and the Writers and Artists Committee for Medical Aid to Spain ("a Communist front up for the purpose of agitation and propaganda").

Odets died in August 1963.

G[EORGE] ASHTON OLDHAM was born on August 15, 1877 in Sunderland, England, son of Annie Banks and Joseph Oldham. He was brought to the United States in 1886. He married Emily Gould. He was an alumnus of Cornell University (A.B., 1902) and General Theological Seminary (B.D., 1905). He pursued his studies at Columbia University, and at Oxford University in England in the summer of 1909. He was ordained a deacon of the Protestant Episcopal Church in 1905, and a priest in 1906. He was the author of *A Fighting Church* (1917); *The Catechism Today* (1929); *Lambeth Through American Eyes*; and *America First*, a poem.

In 1902, Oldham was an instructor in English at Cornell University. In 1905, he was a curate at Grace Church in New York City. From 1906 until 1908, he was a curate at St. Thomas Church in New York City, and chaplain at Columbia University. He was rector of St.

Luke's Church in New York City (1909-1917) and St. Ann's Church in Brooklyn (1917-1922). From 1922 until 1929, he was bishop coadjutor in the Diocese of Albany. From 1929 until 1949, he was bishop of Albany. For twenty-five years, he was president of St. Agnes School in Albany. He was active in the Red-laden Federal Council of Churches. He was a militant anti-militarist and was active in the World Alliance for International Peace and the World Peace Association.

Oldham was affiliated with Action for World Federation (leftist-internationalist); the American Association for the United Nations (leftist-internationalist); the American Committee for Non-Participation in Japanese Aggression ("the committee was featured in the *Daily Worker*, official organ of the Communist Party, and in that paper alone"); the American Committee for Yugoslav Relief ("subversive and Communist"); the American Friends of Spanish Democracy ("Communist front"); American Friends of the Chinese People ("Communist front"); the American League Against War and Fascism ("subversive and Communist" − "established in the United States in an effort to create public sentiment on behalf of a foreign policy adapted to the interests of the Soviet Union"); the Americans of South Slavic Descent (ultra-leftist); Americans United for World Organization (leftist-internationalist); Atlantic Union (leftist-internationalist); Church Peace Union (leftist-oriented); the Council Against Intolerance in America (leftist); the Council on Foreign Relations (the unofficial but operative directorate of all facets of United States foreign policy); the Emergency Civil Liberties Committee ("Communist front" − "subversive"); Federal Union ("leftist-interna-

tionalist"); the Foreign Policy Association (a highly influential and highly effective pro-Communist vehicle); Indusco ("Communist-controlled"); the International Labor Defense ("subversive and Communist" − "legal arm of the Communist Party" − "part of an international network of organizations for the defense of Communist lawbreakers"); the Mid-Century Conference for Peace ("aimed at assembling as many gullible persons as possible under Communist direction and turning them into a vast sounding board for Communist propaganda"); the National Committee To Combat Anti-Semitism ("Communist front"); the National Committee To Repeal the McCarran Act ("Communist front" − "subversive"); the National Council of American-Soviet Friendship ("subversive and Communist" − "specializing in pro-Soviet propaganda"); the National Federation for Constitutional Liberties ("under Communist Party domination and headed by responsible Party functionaries" − "one of the viciously subversive organizations of the Communist Party"); the *Protestant* ("with an eye to religious groups, the Communists have formed religious fronts such as the *Protestant*"); the *Protestant Digest* ("a magazine which has faithfully propagated the Communist Party line under the guise of being a religious journal"); the Stockholm Peace Appeal ("Communist 'peace' campaign"); Students for World Government (leftist-internationalist); the Union for Concerted Peace Efforts (leftist-internationalist); and the World Youth Conference ("Communist conference"). He died in April 1963.

J[ULIUS] ROBERT OPPENHEIMER

was born on April 22, 1904 in New York City, son of Ella Freedman and Julius Oppenheimer. He married Katherine

Puening Harrison. He was an alumnus of Harvard University (B.A., 1926) and the Georgia-Augusta University of Göttingen (Ph.D., 1927). He pursued graduate studies at Christ College of Cambridge University in England. In 1928, he pursued post-doctoral studies, as a National Research Fellow, at Harvard University and the California Institute of Technology. In 1929, he held an International Education Board Fellowship at the University of Leyden and the *Technische Hochschule* in Zurich. He was the author of *Science and the Common Understanding* (1954); *The Open Mind* (1955); and *Some Reflections on Science and Culture* (1960).

From 1929 until 1947, Oppenheimer served concurrently on the faculties of the University of California and the California Institute of Technology. At the University of California, he was an assistant professor of theoretical physics (1929-1930); associate professor (1930-1935); and professor (1935-1947). At the California Institute of Technology, he was an associate professor of physics (1929-1937) and professor (1937-1947).

In 1941, Oppenheimer attended a meeting of a special committee which had been established by the National Academy of Sciences. The committee, under the chairmanship of Dr. Arthur H. Compton, reviewed the prospects and feasibility of the different uses of atomic energy for military purposes. As a result of the Academy meeting, Oppenheimer devoted some time to preliminary calculations about the construction and performance of atomic bombs. As part of his study, he attended staff and policy meetings at the Radiation Laboratory in Berkeley, where a program was already under way for the electromagnetic separation of uranium isotopes. And, in the latter part of 1941, he attended a conference in Chicago at which the Metallurgical Laboratory was established to produce plutonium.

In the spring of 1942, Compton invited Oppenheimer to assume the directorship of various physical studies preliminary to the design and construction of an atomic bomb. Oppenheimer accepted Compton's invitation and became an employee of the Metallurgical Laboratory.

During the summer of 1942, Oppenheimer supervised a study group of scientists at Berkeley. The group explored the physical problems of atomic bombs, atomic explosions, and the possibility of using fission explosions to initiate thermonuclear reactions.

By the late summer of 1942, Oppenheimer decided that scattered experimental projects were not practical if the development of an atomic bomb were to be speedily accomplished. He later explained: "... After a review of the experimental work, I became convinced, as did others, that a major change was called for in the work on the bomb itself. We needed a central laboratory devoted wholly to this purpose, where people could talk freely with each other, where theoretical ideas and experimental findings could affect each other, where the waste and frustration and error of the many compartmentalized experimental studies could be eliminated, where we could begin to come to grips with chemical, metallurgical, engineering, and ordnance problems that had so far received no consideration. We, therefore, sought to establish this laboratory for a direct attack on all the problems inherent in the most rapid possible development and production of atomic bombs."

In the autumn of 1942, Oppenheimer

brought his proposals for a central laboratory to the attention of Major General Leslie R. Groves, who had been placed in charge of the atomic bomb project which was given the code name of Manhattan District. Groves not only agreed on the necessity for a central laboratory but also had it constructed at a site selected by Oppenheimer – Los Alamos, New Mexico. The general plan was that the Manhattan District would be a civilian establishment within a military post. Oppenheimer later explained: "The site of Los Alamos was selected, in part at least, because it enabled those responsible to balance the obvious need for security with the equally important need of free communication among those engaged in the work. Security, it was hoped, would be achieved by removing the laboratory to a remote area, fenced and patrolled, where communication with the outside was extremely limited. Telephone calls were monitored, mail was censored, and personnel who left the area – something permitted only for the clearest of causes – knew that their movements might be under surveillance. On the other hand, for those within the community, fullest exposition and discussion among those competent to use the information was encouraged."

In the meantime, on April 28, 1942, Oppenheimer had filled out a personal security questionnaire upon accepting employment with the Metallurgical Laboratory. In the summer of 1942, Dr. Compton informed Oppenheimer that there was a question with regard to his security clearance, because he had a leftwing background. At the same time Compton assured Oppenheimer that this would not interfere with his work on the atomic bomb program.

In March 1943, although his security clearance had not yet been approved, Oppenheimer was appointed by Compton and Groves to be director of the laboratory at Los Alamos. On July 15, 1943, Groves directed that clearance for Oppenheimer be issued without delay. Groves did this against the advice of his security officers, who had learned from Army Counter-Intelligence that Oppenheimer was a potential security risk. (On March 24, 1947, Groves, in a letter to the Secretary of War, explained his support of Oppenheimer: "When I was first placed in charge of the atomic-bomb development in September, 1942, I found a number of persons working on the project who had not received proper security clearances. One of these was Dr. Oppenheimer, who had been studying certain of the theoretical problems concerning the explosive force of the bomb. The security organization, then not under my control, did not wish to clear Dr. Oppenheimer because of certain of his associations, particularly those of the past. After consideration of the availability and caliber of suitable scientists, I decided that it would be in the best interests of the United States to use Dr. Oppenheimer's services. Prior to this, I reviewed Dr. Oppenheimer's complete record personally. It was apparent to me that he would not be cleared by any agency whose sole responsibility was military security. Nevertheless, my careful study made me feel that, in spite of that record, he was fundamentally a loyal American citizen and that, in view of his potential overall value to the project, he should be employed. I ordered accordingly that he be cleared for the Manhattan Project. Since then, I have learned many things amplifying that record but nothing which, if known to me at that time, would have changed my decision.

"In connection with the above statement, it must be remembered that the provisions of the Atomic Energy Act of 1946 did not control my actions prior to the enactment of that law. My decisions in respect to clearances of personnel were based on what I believed to be the best overall interests of the United States under the then-existing circumstances. As I have long since informed the Atomic Energy Commission, I do not consider that all persons cleared for employment by the Manhattan District, while under my command, should be automatically cleared by the Atomic Energy Commission, but that that Commission should exercise its own independent judgment based on present circumstances.")

Oppenheimer remained as director at Los Alamos until his resignation on October 16, 1945. His tenure included the successful test of the atom bomb on July 16, 1945, and the August 1945 bombings of Hiroshima and Nagasaki in Japan.

Although Oppenheimer was granted a security clearance by Groves, security personnel did not lose their interest in him. They became especially anxious about Oppenheimer when, in the summer of 1943, he paid an overnight visit to a former fiancée who was known to be a member of the Communist Party. As a result of this visit, Oppenheimer was interviewed on August 25, 1943, by Lieut. Lyall Johnson, a security officer. Thus began a long series of similar interviews for Oppenheimer. He met with Lieut. Colonel Boris T. Pash and Lieut. Colonel John R. Landsdale, security officers, and Major General Groves. In later years (1946, 1950, and 1952), Oppenheimer would be interviewed by agents of the Federal Bureau of Investigation.

In March 1947, Oppenheimer's security status was the subject of a letter from FBI Director J. Edgar Hoover to David E. Lilienthal, Chairman of the Atomic Energy Commission. At the time, individuals who had been cleared while working for the Manhattan District were being re-examined by the FBI for clearances in accordance with provisions of the post-war Atomic Energy Act. Mr. Hoover's letter, which contained derogatory information on Oppenheimer, was studied by Chairman Lilienthal and the members of the Atomic Energy Commission. After holding a conference on the matter, Lilienthal and the Commissioners contacted Lieut. General Groves, Dr. James E. Conant, and Dr. Vannevar Bush — all former associates of Oppenheimer — for help in evaluating the information contained in Hoover's letter. The AEC group also contacted the White House through the person of Clark M. Clifford, special counsel to President Truman. For all practical purposes the evaluation proceedings were quite perfunctory. The White House offered no response whatsoever. The investigation was summarily closed in a meeting of the Atomic Energy Commission on August 6, 1947, when a security clearance was authorized for Oppenheimer.

When Oppenheimer resigned from his Los Alamos post in 1945, he returned to his teaching position at the California Institute of Technology, but he did not sever his ties with government service. He had occasion in 1954 to summarize his post-war activities: "From the close of the war, when I returned to the west coast, until finally in the spring of 1947 when I went to Princeton as the director of the Institute for Advanced Study, I was able to spend very little time at home and in teaching in California. In October 1945, at the request of Secretary of War Patterson, I had testified before the House Committee on Military Affairs in support of the May-Johnson bill, which I endorsed as an interim means of bringing about without delay the much needed transition from the wartime administration of the Manhattan District to postwar management of the atomic-energy enterprise. In December 1945, and later, I appeared at Senator McMahon's request in sessions of his Special Committee on Atomic Energy, which was considering legislation on the same subject. Under the chairmanship of Dr. Richard Tolman, I served on a committee set up by General Groves to consider classification policy on matters of atomic energy. For 2 months, early in 1946, I worked steadily as a member of a panel, the Board of Consultants to the Secretary of State's Committee on Atomic Energy, which, with the Secretary of State's Committee, prepared the so-called Acheson-Lilienthal report. After the publication of this report, I spoke publicly in support of it. A little later, when Mr. Baruch was appointed to represent the United States in the United Nations Atomic Energy Committee, I became one of the scientific consultants to Mr. Baruch and his staff in preparation for and in the conduct of our efforts to gain support for the United States' plan. I continued as a consultant to General Osborn when he took over the effort.

"At the end of 1946 I was appointed by the President as a member of the General Advisory Committee to the Atomic Energy Commission. At its first meeting I was elected Chairman, and was reelected until the expiration of my term in 1952. This was my principal assignment during these years as far as the atomic-energy program was concerned, and my preoccupation apart from academic work. A little later I was appointed to the Committee on Atomic Energy of the Research and Development Board, which was to advise the Military Establishment about the technical aspects of the atomic-energy program; I served on it for 7 years; and twice was designated Chairman of special panels set up by the Committee." It was because of these activities that Oppenheimer's clearance was of such moment in 1947.

Until October 30, 1947, there was no public mention that Oppenheimer's background was clouded. However, on that date, his name was mentioned in connection with an instance of alleged espionage during the course of testimony being given by Louis J. Russell, a former FBI agent who appeared before the House Committee on Un-American Activities. In May 1950, Paul Crouch, a former Communist Party official, in testimony before the California Committee on Un-American Activities, said that he had attended a Party meeting in 1941 at Oppenheimer's house. For all practical purposes, the mention of Oppenheimer's name by Russell in 1947 and by Crouch in 1950 created no real problem for Oppenheimer. The trouble came in 1953.

On November 7, 1953, William L. Borden, former executive director of the Joint Committee on Atomic Energy, wrote to FBI Director J. Edgar Hoover. Said Borden: "This letter concerns J. Robert Oppenheimer. As you know, he has for some years enjoyed access to various critical activities of the National Security Council, the Department of State, the Department of Defense, the Army, Navy, and Air Force, the Research and Development Board, the Atomic Energy Commission, the Central Intelligence Agency, the National Security Resources Board, and the National Science Foundation. His access covers most new weapons being developed by the Armed Forces, war plans at least in comprehensive outline, complete details as to atomic and hydrogen weapons and stockpile data, the evidence on which some of the principal CIA intelligence estimates is based, United States participation in the United Nations and NATO, and many other areas of high security sensitivity.

"Because the scope of his access may well be unique, because he has had custody of an immense collection of classified papers covering military, intelligence, and diplomatic as well as atomic-energy matters, and because he also possesses a scientific background enabling him to grasp the significance of classified data of a technical nature, it seems reasonable to estimate that he is and for some years has been in position to compromise more vital and detailed information affecting the national defense and security than any other individual in the United States.

"While J. Robert Oppenheimer has not made major contributions to the advancement of science, he holds a respected professional standing among the second rank of American physicists. In terms of his mastery of Government affairs, his close liaison with ranking officials, and his ability to influence high-level thinking, he surely stands in the first rank, not merely among scientists but among all those who have shaped postwar decisions in the military, atomic energy, intelligence, and diplomatic fields. As chairman or as an official or unofficial member of more than 35 important Government committees, panels, study groups, and projects, he has oriented or dominated key policies involving every principal United States security department and agency except the FBI.

"The purpose of this letter is to state my own exhaustively considered opinion, based upon years of study, of the available classified evidence, that more probably than not J. Robert Oppenheimer is an agent of the Soviet Union.

"This opinion considers the following factors, among others: (1) The evidence indicating that as of April of 1942 − (a) He was contributing substantial monthly sums to the Communist Party; (b) His ties with communism had survived the Nazi-Soviet Pact and the Soviet attack upon Finland; (c) His wife and younger brother were Communists; (d) He had no close friends except Communists; (e) He had at least one Communist mistress; (f) He belonged only to Communist organizations, apart from professional affiliations; (g) The people whom he recruited into the early wartime Berkeley atomic project were exclusively Communists; (h) He had been instrumental in securing recruits for the Communist Party; and (i) He was in frequent contact with Soviet espionage agents. (2) The evidence indicating that − (a) In May 1942, he either stopped contributing funds to the Communist Party or else made his contributions through a new channel not yet discovered; (b) In April 1942 his name was formally submitted for security clearance; (c) He himself was aware at the time that his name had been so submitted; and (d) He thereafter repeatedly gave false information to General Groves, the Manhattan District, and the FBI concerning the 1939-April 1942 period. (3) The evidence indicating that − (a) He was responsible for employing a number of Communists, some of them nontechnical, at wartime Los Alamos; (b) He selected one such individual to write the official Los Alamos history; (c) He was a vigorous supporter of the H-bomb program until August 6, 1945 (Hiroshima), on which day he personally urged each senior individual working in this field to desist; and (d) He was an enthusiastic sponsor of the A-bomb program until the war ended, when he immediately and outspokenly advocated that the Los Alamos Laboratory be disbanded. (4) The evidence indicating that — (a) He was remarkably instrumental in influencing the military authorities and the Atomic Energy Commission essentially to suspend H-bomb development from mid-1946 through January 31, 1950; (b) He has worked tirelessly, from January 31, 1950, onward, to retard the United States H-bomb program; (c) He has used his potent influence against every postwar effort to expand capacity for producing A-bomb material; (d) He has used his potent influence against every postwar effort directed at obtaining larger supplies of uranium raw material; and (e) He has used his potent influence against every major postwar effort toward atomic power development, including the nuclear-powered submarine and aircraft programs as well as industrial power projects.

"From such evidence, considered in detail, the following conclusions are justified: (1) Between 1929 and mid-1942, more probably that not, J. Robert Oppenheimer was a sufficiently hardened Communist that he either volunteered espionage information to the Soviets or complied with a request for such information. (This includes the possibility that when he singled out the weapons aspect of atomic development as his personal specialty, he was acting under Soviet instructions.) (2) More probably than not, he has since been functioning as an espionage agent. (3) More probably than not, he has since acted under a Soviet directive in influencing United States military, atomic

energy, intelligence, and diplomatic policy.

"It is to be noted that these conclusions correlate with information furnished by Klaus Fuchs, indicating that the Soviets had acquired an agent in Berkeley who informed them about electromagnetic separation research during 1942 or earlier.

"Needless to say, I appreciate that probabilities identifiable from existing evidence might, with review of future acquired evidence, be reduced to possibilities; or they might also be increased to certainties. The central problem is not whether J. Robert Oppenheimer was ever a Communist; for the existing evidence makes abundantly clear that he was. Even an Atomic Energy Commission analysis prepared in early 1947 reflects that conclusion, although some of the most significant derogatory data had yet to become available. The central problem is assessing the degree of likelihood that he in fact did what a Communist in his circumstances, at Berkeley, would logically have done during the crucial 1939-1942 period — that is, whether he became an actual espionage and policy instrument of the Soviets. Thus, as to this central problem, my opinion is that, more probably than not, the worst is in fact the truth.

"I am profoundly aware of the grave nature of these comments. The matter is detestable to me. Having lived with the Oppenheimer case for years, having studied and restudied all data concerning him that your agency made available to the Atomic Energy Commission through May 1953, having endeavored to factor in a mass of additional data assembled from numerous other sources, and looking back upon the case from a perspective in private life, I feel a duty simply to state to the responsible head of the security agency most concerned the conclusions which I have painfully crystallized and which I believe any fairminded man thoroughly familiar with the evidence must also be driven to accept. The writing of this letter, to me a solemn step, is exclusively on my own personal initiative and responsibility."

When Mr. Borden sent his letter to J. Edgar Hoover, he also sent a copy to the Joint Commitee on Atomic Energy. Reaction to Borden's letter was not long in coming. On December 23, 1953, Major General K.D. Nichols, General Manager of the Atomic Energy Commission, informed Oppenheimer that "Section 10 of the Atomic Energy Act of 1946 places upon the Atomic Energy Commission the responsibility for assuring that individuals are employed by the Commission only when such employment will not endanger the common defense and security. In addition, Executive Order 10450 of April 27, 1953, requires the suspension of employment of any individual where there exists information indicating that his employment may not be clearly consistent with the interests of the national security. As a result of additional investigation as to your character, associations, and loyalty, and review of your personnel security file in the light of the requirements of the Atomic Energy Act and the requirements of Executive Order 10450, there has developed considerable question whether your continued employment on Atomic Energy Commission work will endanger the common defense and Security and whether such continued employment is clearly consistent with the interests of the national security."

In his letter to Oppenheimer, Nichols presented specific items of derogatory information concerning Oppenheimer's activities before, during, and after his tenure as director of the Los Alamos Manhattan Project. Nichols told Oppenheimer: "In view of your access to highly sensitive classified information, and in view of these allegations which, until disproved, raise questions as to your veracity, conduct and even your loyalty, the Commission has no other recourse, in discharge of its obligations to protect the common defense and security, but to suspend your clearance until the matter has been resolved. Accordingly, your employment on Atomic Energy Commission work and your eligibility for access to restricted data are hereby suspended, effective immediately, pending final determination of this matter."

Oppenheimer was offered the opportunity of appearing before an Atomic Energy Commission personnel security board and was told that the findings of the board and its recommendations regarding his eligibility for employment with the AEC would be transmitted to Nichols. He was informed that in the event of an adverse decision, he could either appeal his case to the personnel security review board or ask for consideration of the case by the five members of the Atomic Energy Commission.

On March 4, 1954, Oppenheimer sent a lengthy reply to Nichols. He offered a rather detailed review of his entire career as well as some refutation of the derogatory items that were contained in the Nichols letter. In the meantime, Oppenheimer had requested a hearing before the AEC's personnel security board. The hearing was held from April 12 through May 6, 1954. The chairman of the board was Dr. Gordon Gray. Its members were Dr. Ward V. Evans and Mr. Thomas A. Morgan. The board heard forty witnesses (including Oppenheimer), all of whom testified under oath. More than 3,000 pages of testimony were compiled, and a comparable number of pages of file material were reviewed by the board. Oppenheimer was represented by counsel, usually four in number. He confronted every witness appearing before the board and he had the privilege of cross-examination.

On May 27, 1954, the personnel security board made known its "specific findings" as to the allegations contained in Nichols' letter of December 23, 1953 to Oppenheimer. Said the board: "1. It was reported that in 1940 you were listed as a sponsor of the Friends of the Chinese People, an organization which was characterized in 1944 by the House Committee on Un-American Acitivities as a Communist-front organization. The Board concludes that this allegation is true . . . .

"2. It was further reported that in 1940 your name was included on a letterhead of the American Committee for Democracy and Intellectual Freedom as a member of its National Executive Committee. The American Committee for Democracy and Intellectual Freedom was characterized in 1942 by the House Committee on Un-American Activities as a Communist-front which defended Communist teachers, and in 1943 it was characterized as subversive and Un-American by a Special Subcommittee of the House Committee on Appropriations. The Board concludes that this allegation is true . . . .

"3. It was further reported that in 1938 you were a member of the Western Council of the Consumers Union. The Consumers Union was cited in 1944 by the House Committee on Un-American Activities as a Communist-front headed by the Communist Arthur Kallet. The Board concludes that this allegation is true.

"4. It was further reported that you stated in 1943 that you were not a Communist, but had probably belonged to every Communist-front organization on the west coast and had signed many petititons in which Communists were interested. The Board concludes that this statement was made by Dr. Oppenheimer, and the Board had before it considerable evidence indicating Dr. Oppenheimer's membership in, and association with, Communist-front organizations and activities on the west coast. However, Dr. Oppenheimer, in his answer, claimed that the quotation was not true and that if he had said anything along the lines quoted, it was a half-jocular overstatement. The Board had before it a memorandum, dated September 14, 1943, prepared by Lt. Col. John Lansdale Jr., who was then head of Security and Intelligence for the Manhattan District, which reported 'Oppenheimer categorically stated (to General Groves) that he himself was not a Communist and never had been, but stated that he had probably belonged to every Communist-front organization on the west coast and signed many petititons concerning matters in which Communists were interested.' The Board also had before it a transcript of an interview between Colonel Lansdale and Dr. Oppenheimer on September 12, 1943, which reflected that Colonel Lansdale had asked Dr. Oppenheimer, 'You've probably belonged to every front organization on the coast,' to which Dr. Oppenheimer replied 'just about.' The transcript further records that Dr. Oppenheimer also stated that he thought he would have been considered at one time a fellow-traveler and that 'my association with these things was very brief and very intense.'

"Dr. Oppenheimer in his testimony

defined 'fellow-traveler' as 'someone who accepted part of the public program of the Communist Party, who was willing to work with and associate with Communists, but who was not a member of the party.' He testified to having been a fellow-traveler from late 1936 or early 1937, with his interest beginning to taper off after 1939, and with very little interest after 1942. He further stated that within the framework of his definition of a fellow-traveler, he would not have considered himself as such after 1942. He further states that with respect to things that the Communists were doing, in which he still had an interest, it was not until 1946 that it was clear to him that he would not collaborate with Communists no matter how much he sympathized with what they pretended to represent.

"5. It was reported that in 1943 and previously you were intimately associated with Dr. Jean Tatlock, a member of the Communist Party in San Francisco, and that Dr. Tatlock was partially responsible for your association with Communist-front groups. The Board concludes that this allegation is true. Dr. Oppenheimer in his testimony before this Board admitted having associated with Jean Tatlock from 1936 until 1943. He stated that he saw her only rarely between 1939 and 1943, but admitted that the association was intimate. He admitted having seen Jean Tatlock under most intimate circumstances in June or July of 1943, during the time when he was Director of the Los Alamos Laboratory, and admitted that he knew she had been a Communist and that there was not any reason for him to believe that she was not at that time still a Communist. He named several Communists, Communist functionaries or Communist sympathizers whom he had met through Jean Tatlock, or as a result of his association with her . . . .

"6. It was reported that your wife, Katherine Puening Oppenheimer, was formerly the wife of Joseph Dallet, a member of the Communist Party, who was killed in Spain in 1937 fighting for the Spanish Republican Army. The Board concludes that this allegation is true . . . .

"7. It was further reported that during the period of her association with Joseph Dallet, your wife became a member of the Communist Party. The Communist Party had been designated by the Attorney General as a subversive organization which seeks to alter the form of government of the United States by unconstitutional means, within the purview of Executive Order 9835 and Executive Order 10450. The Board concludes that this allegation is true . . . .

"8. It was reported that your brother Frank Friedman Oppenheimer became a member of the Communist Party in 1936 and has served as a party organizer and as educational director of the professional section of the Communist Party in Los Angeles County. The Board concludes that this allegation is true . . . .

"9. It was further reported that your brother's wife, Jackie Oppenheimer, was a member of the Communist Party in 1938. The Board concludes that this allegation is true . . . .

"10. And that in August, 1944, Jackie Oppenheimer assisted in the organization of the East Bay branch of the California Labor School. On the basis of information before it, the Board concludes that this allegation is true . . . .

"11. It was further reported that in 1945 Frank and Jackie Oppenheimer were invited to an informal reception at the Russian Consulate, that this invitation was extended by the American-

Russian Institute of San Francisco and was for the purpose of introducing famous American scientists to Russian scientists who were delegates to the United Nations Conference on International Organization being held at San Francisco at that time, and that Frank Oppenheimer accepted this invitation. On the basis of information before it, the Board concludes that this allegation is true . . . .

"12. It was further reported that Frank Oppenheimer agreed to give a 6-week course on The Social Implications of Modern Scientific Development at the California Labor School, beginning May 9, 1946. The American-Russian Institute of San Francisco and the California Labor School have been cited by the Attorney General as Communist organizations within the purview of Executive Order 9835 and Executive Order 10450. On the basis of information before it, the Board concludes that this allegation is true . . . .

"13. It was reported that you have associated with members and officials of the Communist Party, including Isaac Folkoff, Steve Nelson, Rudy Lambert, Kenneth May, Jack Manley, and Thomas Addis. The Board concludes that this allegation is substantially true. Dr. Oppenheimer in his answer and in his testimony admitted having associated with Isaac Folkoff, Steve Nelson, Rudy Lambert, Kenneth May, and Thomas Addis. He testified that he knew at the time of his association with them that Folkoff, Nelson, Lambert, and May were Communist Party functionaries, and that Addis was either a Communist or close to one. He admitted that his associations with these persons continued until 1942. There was no evidence before the Board with respect to an association with Jack Manley . . . .

"14. It was reported that you were a subscriber to the *Daily People's World*, a west coast Communist newspaper, in 1941 and 1942. The Board concludes that this allegation is true . . . .

"15. It was reported in 1950 that you stated to an agent of the Federal Bureau of Investigation that you had in the past made contributions to Communist-front organizations, although at the time you did not know of Communist Party control or extent of infiltration of these groups. You further stated to an agent of the Federal Bureau of Investigation that some of these contributions were made through Isaac Folkoff, whom you knew to be a leading Communist Party functionary, because you had been told that this was the most effective and direct way of helping these groups. The Board finds that Mr. Oppenheimer made the statements attributed to him by the Federal Bureau of Investigation. The Board concludes that Dr. Oppenheimer in the past made contributions to Communist-front organizations and that some of these contributions were made through Isaac Folkoff, a leading Communist Party functionary. Dr. Oppenheimer testified that he contributed to Spanish causes through Communist Party channels from the winter of 1937-38 until early in 1942. He said that he had contributed more than $500 and less than $1,000 each year during this period. He testified that he had made the contributions in cash and, in explaining how these contributions came to an end, he said (in referring to Pearl Harbor) that he 'didn't like to continue a clandestine operation of any kind at a time when I saw myself with the possibility or prospect of getting more deeply involved in the war.' Dr. Oppenheimer in his answer admitted making the contributions through Thomas Addis and Isaac Folkoff. He testified that he knew Addis was a Communist or very close to a Communist. He knew that Folkoff was connected with the Communist Party. In addition, Dr. Oppenheimer admitted having contributed about $100 in cash to the Strike fund of one of the major strikes of 'Bridges' Union' about 1937 or 1938.

"16. It was reported that you attended a house-warming party at the home of Kenneth and Ruth May on September 20, 1941, for which there was an admission charge for the benefit of *The Peoples World*, and that at this party you were in the company of Joseph W. Weinberg and Clarence Hiskey, who were alleged to be members of the Communist Party and to have engaged in espionage on behalf of the Soviet Union. It was further reported that you informed officials of the United States Department of Justice in 1942 that you had no recollection that you had attended such a party, but that since it would have been in character for you to have attended such a party, you would not deny that you were there. The Board concludes on the basis of information before it, that it was probable that Dr. Oppenheimer attended 'the house-warming party' at the home of Kenneth and Ruth May. The Board concludes that Dr. Oppenheimer made the statements to the United States Department of Justice officials attributed to him . . . .

"17. It was reported that you attended a closed meeting of the professional section of the Communist Party of Alameda County, Calif., which was held in the latter part of July or early August 1941, at your residence, 19 Kenilworth Court, Berkeley, Calif., for the purpose of hearing an explanation of a change in Communist Party policy. It was further reported that you denied that you attended such a meeting and that such a meeting was held in your home. The Board is of the opinion that the evidence with respect to this meeting is inconclusive . . . .

"18. It was reported that you stated to an agent of the Federal Bureau of Investigation in 1950 that you attended a meeting in 1940 or 1941, which may have taken place at the home of Haakon Chevalier, which was addressed by William Schneiderman, whom you knew to be a leading functionary of the Communist Party. In testimony in 1950 before the California State Senate Committee on Un-American Activities, Haakon Chevalier was identified as a member of the Communist Party in the San Francisco area in the early 1940's. The Board finds that Dr. Oppenheimer made the statements attributed to him by the Federal Bureau of Investigation . . . .

"19. It was reported that you have consistently denied that you have ever been a member of the Communist Party. It was further reported that you stated to a representative of the Federal Bureau of Investigation in 1946 that you had a change of mind regarding the policies and politics of the Soviet Union about the time of the signing of the Soviet-German Pact in 1939. It was further reported that during 1950 you stated to a representative of the Federal Bureau of Investigation that you had never attended a closed meeting of the Communist Party; and that at the time of the Russo-Finnish War and the subsequent break between Germany and Russia in 1941, you realized the Communist Party infiltration tactics into the alleged anti-fascist groups and became fed up with the whole thing and lost what little interest you had. Dr. Oppenheimer testified that he had never been a member of the Communist Party. The Board finds that Dr. Oppenheimer made the statements attributed to him by the Federal Bureau of Investigation.

"19a. Prior to April 1942 you had contributed $150 per month to the Communist Party in the San Francisco area, and that the last such payment was apparently made in April 1942 immediately before your entry into the atomic bomb project. The Board concludes on the basis of testimony and other information before it that Dr. Oppenheimer made periodic contributions through Communist Party functionaries to the Communist Party in the San Francisco area in amounts aggregating not less than $500 nor more than $1,000 a year during a period of approximately 4 years ending in April 1942. As of April 1942, Dr. Oppenheimer had been for several months participating in Government atomic energy research activities. He executed a questionnaire for Government clearance on April 28, 1942, and subsequently assumed full-time duties with the atomic energy project.

"19b. During the period 1942-45 various officials of the Communist Party, including Dr. Hannah Peters, organizer of the Professional Section of the Communist Party, Alemeda County, Calif., Bernadette Doyle, secretary of the Alameda County Communist Party, Steve Nelson, David Adelson, Paul Pinsky, Jack Manley, and Katrina Sandow, are reported to have made statements indicating that you were then a member of the Communist Party; that you could not be active in the party at that time; that your name should be removed from the Party mailing list and not mentioned in any way; that you had talked the atomic bomb question over with Party members during this period; and that several years prior to 1945 you had told Steve Nelson that the Army was working on an atomic bomb. The Board finds that during the period 1942-45, Dr. Hannah Peters, Bernadette Doyle, Steve Nelson, Jack Manley, and Katrina Sandow made statements indicating that Dr. Oppenheimer was then a member of the Communist Party; and that the other statements attributed to officials of the Communist Party in the allegation were made by one or more of them. The Board does not find on the basis of information available to it that such statements were made by David Adelson and Paul Pinsky.

"19c. You stated in August of 1943 that you did not want anybody working for you on the project who was a member of the Communist Party, since 'one always had a question of divided loyalty' and the discipline of the Communist Party was very severe and not compatible with complete loyalty to the project. You further stated at that time that you were referring only to present membership in the Communist Party and not to people who had been members of the party. You stated further that you knew several individuals then at Los Alamos who had been members of the Communist Party. You did not, however, identify such former members of the Communist Party to the appropriate authorities. It was also reported that during the period 1942-45 you were responsible for the employment on the atomic bomb project of individuals who were members of the Communist Party or closely associated with activities of the Communist Party, including Giovanni Rossi Lomanitz, Joseph W. Weinberg, David Bohm, Max Bernard Friedman, and David Hawkins. In the case of Giovanni Rossi Lomanitz, you urged him to work on the project, although you stated that you knew he had been very much of a 'Red' when he first came to the University of California and that you emphasized to him that he must forego all political activity if he came on to the project. In August 1943 you protested against the termination of his deferment and requested that he be returned to the project after his entry into the military service.

"The Board concludes that Dr. Oppenheimer did state in 1943 that he did not want anybody working for him on the project who was a member of the Communist Party, since 'one always had a question of divided loyalty' and the discipline of the Communist Party was very severe and not compatible with complete loyalty to the project. He further stated at that time he was referring only to present membership in the Communist Party and not to people who had been members of the Party. He stated further that he knew several individuals then at Los Alamos who had been members of the Communist Party. He did not, however, identify such former members of the Communist Party to the appropriate authorities. The Board concludes that Dr. Oppenheimer was responsible for the employment on the atom bomb project of Giovanni Rossi Lomanitz at Berkeley and David Hawkins at Los Alamos. The Board concludes that Dr. Oppenheimer asked for the transfer of David Bohm to Los Alamos, although Bohm was closely associated with the Communist Party.

"Dr. Oppenheimer testified that he understood that Hawkins had left-wing associations; and that Hawkins 'talked about philosophy in a way that indicated an interest and understanding and limited approval anyway of Engels.'

"The Board does not conclude that Dr. Oppenheimer was responsible for the employment of Friedmann or Weinberg

on the atomic energy program. Dr. Oppenheimer testified that Joseph W. Weinberg was a graduate student of his; that he had heard that Weinberg had been a member of the Young Communist League before coming to Berkeley, and the Board had before it a transcript of a conversation with Dr. Oppenheimer indicating that at least by August 1943, he knew Weinberg to be a member of the Communist Party and that he 'suspected that before but was not sure.' Weinberg gave Oppenheimer as a reference at the time he (Weinberg) obtained employment at the Radiation Laboratory on April 22, 1943.

"Dr. Oppenheimer testified that he asked General Groves for the transfer of David Bohm to Los Alamos in 1943 . . . . Dr. Oppenheimer testified that he thought that in 1946 or 1947 he helped Bohm get a job as Assistant Professor of Physics at Princeton. The Board finds that Dr. Oppenheimer did urge Lomanitz to work on the project although he knew he had been very much a 'Red' when he first came to the University of California and, in fact, during his attendance at the University, and that Dr. Oppenheimer later stated to a Manhattan District official that he had warned Lomanitz that he must forego all political activity if he came to the project . . . .

"20. It was reported that you stated to representatives of the Federal Bureau of Investigation on September 5, 1946, that you had attended a meeting in the East Bay and a meeting in San Francisco at which there were present persons definitely identified with the Communist Party. When asked the purpose of the East Bay meeting and the identity of those in attendance, you declined to answer on the ground that this had no bearing on the matter of interest being discussed. The Board concludes that this allegation is true . . . .

"21. It was reported that you attended a meeting at the home of Frank Oppenheimer on January 1, 1946, with David Adelson and Paul Pinsky, both of whom were members of the Communist Party. It was further reported that you analyzed some material which Pinsky hoped to take up with the Legislative Convention in Sacramento, California. The Board concludes that this allegation is true.

"22. It was reported in 1946 that you were listed as vice chairman on the letterhead of the Independent Citizens Committee of the Arts, Sciences, and Professions, Inc., which has been cited as a Communist-front by the House Committee on Un-American Activities. The Board concludes that this allegation is true, although the Board finds that Dr. Oppenheimer advised the organizations in a letter on October 11, 1946, that he was not in accord with its policy and wished to resign.

"23. It was reported that prior to March 1, 1943, possibly 3 months prior, Peter Ivanov, secretary at the Soviet Consulate, San Francisco, approached George Charles Eltenton for the purpose of obtaining information regarding work being done at the Radiation Laboratory for the use of Soviet scientists; that George Charles Eltenton subsequently requested Haakon Chevalier to approach you concerning this matter; that Haakon Chevalier thereupon approached you, either directly or through your brother, Frank Friedman Oppenheimer, in connection with this matter; and that Haakon Chevalier finally advised George Charles Eltenton that there was no chance whatsoever of obtaining the information. It was further reported that you did not report this episode to the appropriate authorities until several months after its occurrence; that when you initially discussed this matter with the appropriate authorities on August 26, 1943, you did not identify yourself as the person who had been approached, and you refused to identify Haakon Chevalier as the individual who had made the approach on behalf of George Charles Eltenton; and that it was not until several months later, when you were ordered by a superior to do so, that you so identified Haakon Chevalier. It was further reported that upon your return to Berkeley following your separation from the Los Alamos project, you were visited by the Chevaliers on several occasions; and that your wife was in contact with Haakon and Barbara Chevalier in 1946 and 1947. The Board concludes that this allegation is substantially true.

"24. It was reported that in 1945 you expressed the view that 'there is a reasonable possibility that it (the hydrogen bomb) can be made,' but that the feasibility of the hydrogen bomb did not appear, on theoretical grounds, as certain as the fission bomb appeared certain, on theoretical grounds, when the Los Alamos Laboratory was started; and that in the autumn of 1949 the General Advisory Committee expressed the view that 'an imaginative and concerted attack on the problem has a better than even chance of producing the weapon within 5 years.' It was further reported that in the autumn of 1949 and subsequently, you strongly opposed the development of the hydrogen bomb: (1) on moral grounds, (2) by claiming that it was not feasible, (3) by claiming that there were insufficient facilities and scientific personnel to carry on the development, and (4) that it was not politically desirable. It was further reported that even after it was determined, as a matter of national policy, to proceed with development of a hydrogen bomb, you continued to oppose the project and declined to cooperate fully in the project. It was further reported you departed from your proper role as an adviser to the Commission by causing the distribution, separately and in private, to top personnel at Los Alamos of the majority and minority reports of the General Advisory Committee on development of the hydrogen bomb for the purpose of trying to turn such top personnel against the development of the hydrogen bomb. It was further reported that you were instrumental in persuading other outstanding scientists not to work on the hydrogen bomb project, and that the opposition to the hydrogen bomb, of which you are the most experienced, most powerful, and most effective member, has definitely slowed its development.

"The Board confirms that in 1945 Mr. Oppenheimer expressed the view, that 'there is reasonable possibility that it (the hydrogen bomb) can be made,' but that the feasibility of the hydrogen bomb did not appear, on theoretical grounds, as certain as the fission bomb appeared certain on theoretical grounds, when the Los Alamos Laboratory was started; and that in August of 1949, the General Advisory Committee expressed the view that 'an imaginative and concerted attack on the problem has a better than even chance of producing the weapon within 5 years.'

"With respect to Dr. Oppenheimer's attitude and activities in relation to the hydrogen bomb in World War II, the evidence shows that Dr. Oppenheimer during this period had no misgivings about a program looking to thermonuclear development and, indeed, during

the latter part of the war, he recorded his support of prompt and vigorous action in this connection. When asked under cross-examination whether he would have opposed dropping an H-bomb on Hiroshima, he replied that 'It would make no sense,' and when asked 'Why?' replied, 'The target is too small.' He testified further under cross-examination that he believed he would have opposed the dropping of an H-bomb on Japan because of moral scruples although he did not oppose the dropping of an A-bomb on the same grounds. During the postwar period, Dr. Oppenheimer favored, and in fact urged, continued research in the thermonuclear field and seemed to express considerable interest in results that were from time to time discussed with him. However, he was aware that the efforts being put forth in this endeavor were relatively meager and he knew that if research were continued at the same pace, there would be little likelihood of success for many years. Testimony in this connection indicated that there was a feeling on his part that it was more important to go forward with a program for the production of a wider range of atomic bombs.

"The Board finds further that in the autumn of 1949, and subsequently, Dr. Oppenheimer strongly opposed the development of the hydrogen bomb on moral grounds; on grounds that it was not politically desirable; he expressed the view that there were insufficient facilities and scientific personnel to carry on the development without seriously interfering with the orderly development of the program for fission bombs; and until the late spring of 1951, he questioned the feasibility of the hydrogen bomb efforts then in progress.

"Dr. Oppenheimer testified that what

he was opposing in the fall of 1949 was only a 'crash program' in the development and production of thermonuclear weapons. In this connection, Dr. Oppenheimer contended that the main question relating to thermonuclear weapons presented to the GAC at its meeting of October 29, 1949, was whether or not the United States should undertake such a crash program. The Board does not believe that Dr. Oppenheimer was entirely candid with the Board in attempting to establish this impression. The record reflects that Dr. Oppenheimer expressed the opinion in writing that the 'super bomb should never be produced,' and that the commitment to this effect should be unqualified. Moreover, the alternatives available to the GAC were not a choice between an 'all-out effort' and no effort at all; there was a middle course which might have been considered.

"The Board further concludes that after it was determined, as a matter of national policy (January 31, 1950) to proceed with development of a hydrogen bomb, Dr. Oppenheimer did not oppose the project in a positive or open manner, nor did he decline to cooperate in the project. However, Dr. Oppenheimer is recognized in scientific circles as one of the foremost leaders in the atomic energy field and he has considerable influence on the 'policy direction' of the atomic program. The Board finds that his views in opposition to the development of the H-bomb as expressed in 1949 became widely known among scientists, and since he did not make it known that he had abandoned these views, his attitude undoubtedly had an adverse effect on recruitment of scientists and the progress of the scientific effort in this field. In other words, the Board finds, that if Dr. Oppenheimer

had enthusiastically supported the thermonuclear program either before or after the determination of national policy, the H-bomb project would have been pursued with considerably more vigor, thus increasing the possibility of earlier success in this field.

"The Board finds that Dr. Oppenheimer was not responsible for the distribution, separately and in private, to top personnel at Los Alamos of the majority and minority reports of the General Advisory Committee on development of the hydrogen bomb, but that such distribution was made on the direction of the then general manager of the Atomic Energy Commission, Carroll L. Wilson, apparently in order to prepare the personnel at Los Alamos to discuss the matter with the Chairman of the Joint Committee on Atomic Energy of the Congress.

"The Board does not find that Dr. Oppenheimer urged other scientists not to work on the program. However, enthusiastic support on his part would perhaps have encouraged other leading scientists to work on the program. Because of technical questions involved, the Board is unable to make a categorical finding as to whether the opposition to the hydrogen bomb 'has definitely slowed down its development.' The Board concludes that the opposition to the H-bomb by many persons connected with the atomic energy program, of which Dr. Oppenheimer was the 'most experienced, most powerful, and most effective member,' did delay the initiation of concerted effort which led to the development of a thermonuclear weapon."

The personnel security board, in addition to its "specific findings," presented "general considerations." As part of its general considerations the board said: "On the one hand, we find no evidence of disloyalty. Indeed, we have before us much responsible and positive evidence of the loyalty and love of country of the individual concerned. On the other hand, we do not believe that it has been demonstrated that Dr. Oppenheimer has been blameless in the matter of conduct, character, and association. We could in good conscience, we believe, conclude our difficult undertaking by a brief, clear, and conclusive recommendation to the general manager of the Commission in the following terms: There can be no tampering with the national security, which in times of peril must be absolute, and without concessions for reasons of admiration, gratitude, reward, sympathy, or charity. Any doubts whatsoever must be resolved in favor of the national security. The material and evidence presented to this Board leave reasonable doubts with respect to the individual concerned. We, therefore, do not recommend reinstatement of clearance."

In its decision not to reinstate Oppenheimer's security clearance, the board said that the controlling considerations were: "(1) We find that Dr. Oppenheimer's continuing conduct and associations have reflected a serious disregard for the requirement of the security system. (2) We have found a susceptibility to influence which could have serious implications for the security interests of the country. (3) We find his conduct in the hydrogen-bomb program sufficiently disturbing to raise a doubt as to whether his future participation, if characterized by the same attitudes in a Government program relating to the national defense, would be clearly consistent with the best interests of security. (4) We have regretfully concluded that Dr. Oppenheimer has been less than candid in several instances in his testimony before this Board."

The board's decision was made by Chairman Gray and Mr. Morgan. Dr. Evans disagreed with his colleagues and thought that Oppenheimer's clearance should be reinstated. Evans was in agreement with Gray and Morgan in their evaluation of Oppenheimer's leftist associations, activities and policies. He insisted, however, that Oppenheimer had been cleared in 1947 by the AEC when most of the same derogatory information was known. He further insisted that Oppenheimer did not hinder the development of the H-bomb and there is absolutely nothing in the testimony to show that he did.

On June 12, 1954, the AEC's general manager, K.D. Nichols, transmitted the recommendations of the personnel security board and his own recommendations to the Atomic Energy Commissioners. Nichols recommended that Oppenheimer's clearance should not be reinstated. He laid special stress on Oppenheimer's Communist activities by saying: "The record contains no direct evidence that Dr. Oppenheimer gave secrets to a foreign nation or that he is disloyal to the United States. However, the record does contain substantial evidence of Dr. Oppenheimer's association with Communists, Communist functionaries, and Communists who did engage in espionage. He was not a mere 'parlor pink' or student of Communism as a result of immaturity and intellectual curiosity, but was deeply and consciously involved with hardened and militant Communists at a time when he was a man of mature judgment.

"His relations with these hardened Communists were such that they considered him to be one of their number. He admits that he was a fellow traveler, and that he made substantial cash contributions direct to the Communist Party over a period of 4 years ending in 1942. The record indicates that Dr. Oppenheimer was a Communist in every respect except for the fact that he did not carry a party card. These facts raise serious questions as to Dr. Oppenheimer's eligibility for clearance reinstatement.

"It is suggested that Dr. Oppenheimer has admitted many of the facts concerning his past association with Communists and the Communist Party. Whether this be true or not, it appears to me that Dr. Oppenheimer's admissions in too many cases have followed, rather than preceded, investigation which developed the facts. It appears that he is not inclined to disclose the facts spontaneously, but merely to confirm those already known. I find no great virtue in such a plea of guilt; certainly it does not cause me to dismiss Dr. Oppenheimer's past associations as matters of no consequence simply on the ground that he has admitted them."

The Atomic Energy Commissioners were five in number: Chairman Lewis L. Strauss, and members Eugene M. Zuckert, Joseph Campbell, Thomas E. Murray, and Henry D. Smyth. Messrs. Strauss, Zuckert, and Campbell signed the majority opinion, directing that Oppenheimer's security clearance not be reinstated. Mr. Murray concurred in the majority decision with a separate opinion, and Zuckert and Campbell issued additional statements in support of their conclusions. Dr. Smyth dissented from the majority and voted to reinstate Oppenheimer's clearance.

In the aftermath of Oppenheimer's encounter with the personnel security board of the Atomic Energy Commission, he was given an overwhelming vote of confidence by the Institute for Advanced Study's board of directors, who agreed unanimously that Oppenheimer should be retained as the Institute's director — a position he held until his retirement in 1966.

Even before the AEC rejected Oppenheimer's reinstatement for security clearance, he had become a martyr in the eyes of the liberal-leftist establishment. He was portrayed in novels and the press media as a victim of McCarthyism, a victim of the Red-baiters, a victim of a national mania for security, and a persecuted repentant sinner. The Alsop brothers, Stewart and Joseph, pleaded his case in *We Accuse: The Story of the Miscarriage of American Justice in the Case of J. Robert Oppenheimer.* Charles P. Curtis did the same in his *The Oppenheimer Case: The Trial of a Security System.* In Europe, theater audiences were treated to a completely dishonest presentation in a drama by a West German playwright titled *In The Matter of J. Robert Oppenheimer.* Arthur Schlesinger Jr. wrote an article proving that Oppenheimer had to be forgiven because the Soviet Union had any information Oppenheimer could have given the Reds before he could have given it to them.

In 1955, the Ford Foundation's Fund for the Republic financed an hour-long interview between the Columbia Broadcasting System's Edward R. Murrow and Oppenheimer. Hundreds of reproductions of the interview were made for free distribution to collegiate and civic groups. The interview was a deliberately contrived whitewash of Oppenheimer, who emerged from the propaganda effort as a much-maligned and abused innocent victim of vicious and narrow-minded reactionaries. From his alma mater, Harvard, Oppenheimer received a year's appointment as the James professor – to lecture on ethics and philosophy.

In 1961, the ultra-leftist Federation of American Scientists petitioned the Atomic Energy Commission to review Oppenheimer's security revocation. The Federation argued that Oppenheimer was a victim of his times and that the AEC would not have suspended his security clearance had his case been considered some years later.

The pressure applied by the Federation of American Scientists produced the intended effect, evidenced when President John F. Kennedy invited Oppenheimer to an April 29, 1962 White House dinner held in honor of forty-nine Nobel Prize winners. The invitation was an obvious trial balloon to test public reaction to Oppenheimer eight years after his appearance before the AEC's personnel security board.

In March 1963, the ten-member General Advisory Committee to the Atomic Energy Commission unanimously recommended that the AEC present its $50,000 Fermi Award for 1963 to Oppenheimer. The five Atomic Energy Commissioners unanimously accepted the advisory committee's recommendation and, in turn, they submitted the nomination to the White House. Through discreet inquiries the AEC group had learned that President Kennedy was very much in favor of the gesture toward Oppenheimer. On the day of his death, President Kennedy announced his plans to make a personal presentation of the award.

On December 2, 1963, at a White House ceremony, President Lyndon B. Johnson presented to Oppenheimer a citation, a gold medal, and a $50,000 check. Said Johnson, "One of President Kennedy's most important acts was to sign the award" to Oppenheimer. In his turn, Oppenheimer said: "In his later years, Jefferson often wrote of the 'brotherly spirit of science, which unites into one family all its votaries of whatever grade, and however widely dispersed throughout the different quarters of the globe.'."... We have not, I know, always given evidence of that brotherly spirit of science. This is not because we lack vital common or intersecting scientific interests.

"It is in part because, with countless other men and women, we are engaged in this great enterprise of our time, testing whether men can both preserve and enlarge life, liberty and the pursuit of happiness, and live without war as the great arbiter of history. In this enterprise, no one bears a greater responsibility than the President of the United States. I think it just possible, Mr. President, that it has taken some charity and some courage for you to make this award today. That would seem to be a good augury for all our futures. These words I wrote down almost a fortnight ago. In a somber time I gratefully and gladly speak them to you."

The Fermi Award was widely regarded in the press and in scientific circles as a not-too-subtle effort by the liberal Kennedy Administration to rehabilitate Oppenheimer and to encourage the disarmament and appeasement advocates both in and out of government. The award certainly emboldened Oppenheimer, who in May 1964, in an address at California Institute of Technology, expressed his regret that a suggestion by Niels Bohr had not been adopted. Bohr had proposed that all atomic bomb secrets be handed over to the Soviet Union as a gesture of trust in order that heads of state could calmly discuss the uses of nuclear energy for peaceful purposes.

In June 1966, Oppenheimer received an honorary degree from Princeton University. He was hailed for his contribution to the atomic energy program. The doctoral citation said: "[As a] physicist and sailor, philosopher and horseman, linguist and cook, lover of fine wine and better poetry, he has added distinction to an already great institute and strengthened the Princeton community of learning." Nothing was said about Oppenheimer's fame as America's most celebrated security risk. He died in February 1967.

G[ARFIELD] BROMLEY OXNAM was born on August 14, 1891 in Sonora, California, son of Mamie Job and Thomas Oxnam. He married Ruth Fisher. He was an alumnus of the University of Southern California (A.B., 1913) and Boston University (S.T.B., 1915). He pursued graduate studies at Harvard University and the Massachusetts Institute of Technology. He also studied in China, Japan, and India. He was ordained to the Methodist ministry in 1916. He was the author of *The Mexican in Los Angeles* (1920); *Social Principles of Jesus* (1923); *Russian Impressions* (1927); *Youth and the New America* (1928); *The Ethical Ideals of Jesus in a Changing World* (1941); *By This Sign, Conquer* (1942); *Behold Thy Mother* (1944); *Facing the Future Unafraid* (1944); *Preaching in a Revolutionary Age* (1944); *Labor and Tomorrow's World* (1945); *Stimulus of Christ* (1948); *Personalities in Social Reform* (1950); *The Christian's Vocation* (1950); *The Church and Contemporary Change* (1950); *On This Rock* (1951); *I Protest* (1954); and *A Testament of Faith* (1958). He was editor of *Effective Preaching* (1929); *Creative Preaching* (1930); *Contemporary Preaching* (1931); *Varieties of Present Day Preaching* (1932); and *Preaching and the Social Crisis* (1933).

In 1916 and 1917, Oxnam was pastor of the Methodist Church of Poplar, California. From 1917 until 1927, he was pastor of the Church of All Nations, head of the All Nations Foundation in Los Angeles, and executive secretary of the Los Angeles Missionary and Church Extension Society. From 1919 until 1923, he was professor of social ethics at the University of Southern California. In 1927 and 1928, he was professor of practical theology at Boston University. From 1928 until 1936, he was president of De Pauw University. In 1936, he was elected as bishop of the Methodist Church. He served as resident bishop of Omaha (1936-1939), Boston (1939-1944), New York (1944-1952), and Washington, D.C. (1952-1960). He delivered the Enoch Pound lectures at Bangor Seminary (1940), the Merrick lectures at Ohio Wesleyan University (1941), the Fondren lectures at Southern Methodist University (1944), the Lyman Beecher lectures at Yale University (1944), the Earl lectures at the Pacific School of Religion (1945), the Alden-Tuthill lectures and the Hoover lectures at the University of Chicago (1948-1949), and the Ezra Squire Tipple lectures at Drew University (1949). From 1944 until 1946, he was president of the Red-laden Federal Council of Churches. He was a presiding officer of the organizing conference of the leftist-oriented National Council of Churches in 1950. From 1948 until 1954, he was president of the leftist-oriented World Council of Churches.

Oxnam had a long career of association with pacifists and Socialists. His sympathies toward the Soviet Union, which he visited at least three times, were unmistakable. He was an advocate of United States diplomatic recognition of Russia long before such recognition was extended. Later, he was an advocate of United States diplomatic recognition of Red China when such action was a primary concern of a newly gathered Red China lobby. Although he was a pacifist, his ideology was set aside when the United States became involved in the war against Nazi Germany. He was a bitter critic of the Franco regime in Spain, but that was a typical posture of anti-anti-Communists in the 1930's and 1940's. He was a long-time promoter of world government and followed the usual line that world government meant world peace, or world peace meant world government. But he offered no practical means to achieve either condition.

In July 1953, Oxnam appeared before the House Committee on Un-American Activities at his own request. He had insisted that some information in the Committee's files relating to him was in error. In a ten-hour session, Oxnam was given every opportunity to explain his long-time association with leftist groups. He was treated, in the course of the hearings, with patient understanding by the committeemen and the counsel, despite his rather argumentative and hostile demeanor. Out of the experience, Oxnam wrote a book, *I Protest*. What he said of his "ten-hour ordeal" bore little resemblance to the printed record of the hearing. Oxnam had asked for the hearing, and under such conditions it would be expected that he would be content to clear the record wherever he felt that it was erroneous or maligned him in any way. Oxnam, however, portrayed himself as a victim of a conspiracy engineered by informants and the congressman on the Committee. As a clergyman, he seemed somehow to think that his endorsement of and participation in enterprises far beyond the scope of his religious duties and responsibilities enjoyed some sort of immunity. He was like a small boy caught with his hand in the cookie jar, seeking exoneration by blaming his mother for making the cookies. Oxnam, on the basis of the public record and his own testimony, was a fellow traveler. In his hysterical book, however, he is angry that the Committee, through its investigations, through friendly witnesses, and through Oxnam's own testimony, was able to discover the simple fact that he was one. No question was raised concerning his right to be a fellow traveler, or to continue being a fellow traveler. If his story was to be taken as truth, however, Oxnam had undergone an inquisition so terrifying as to make plausible to the American people the belief that a climate of fear had been created by anti-Communists to suppress freedoms of speech, religion, and assembly. He was especially critical of former Communists who had emerged from their mistaken past willing to impart information about the very organizations Oxnam had supported and which the Communist Party controlled.

Oxnam was affiliated with the Action Committee To Free Spain Now ("Communist"); the American Association for the United Nations (leftist-internationalist); the ultra-radical American Civil Liberties Union; the American Committee for Spanish Freedom ("Communist"); the American Committee for Yugoslav Relief ("subversive and Communist"); the American Roundtable on India ("Communist front"); the American-Russian Institute ("subversive" – "Communist" – "specializing in pro-Soviet propaganda"); the American Slav Congress ("Moscow inspired and directed federation of Communist-dominated organizations seeking by methods of propaganda and pressure to subvert the 10,000,000 people in this country of Slavic birth or descent"); the ultra-radical Americans for Democratic Action; the Committee on Militarism in Education (a supporting organization of the U.S. Congress Against War, "completely under the control of the Communist Party"); the Council Against Intolerance in America (leftist); the Fellowship of Reconciliation (ultra-leftist-pacifist); the Friends of Italian Democracy ("Communist front"); the League for the Organization of Progress (dominated by Socialists and Communists); the Massachusetts Council of American-Soviet Friendship ("subversive and Communist" – "specializing in pro-Soviet propaganda"); the Medical Bureau and North American Committee To Aid Spanish Democracy ("subversive and un-American"); the Methodist Federation for Social Action ("the organization's influence has been consistently wielded on behalf of Communist causes and the Communist line as expressed through the party and its innumerable subsidiaries"); the ultra-radical National Association for the Advancement of Colored People; the National Committee To Abolish the Poll Tax ("Communist front"); the National Council of American-Soviet Friendship ("subversive and Communist" – "specializing in pro-Soviet propaganda"); the National Federation for Constitutional Liberties ("under Communist Party domination and headed by responsible Party functionaries" – "one of the viciously subversive organizations of the Communist Party"); the Progressive Citizens of America ("political Communist front" – "subversive"); the *Protestant Digest* ("a magazine which has faithfully propagated the Communist Party line under the guise of being a religious journal"); the leftist-oriented Protestants and Other Americans United; *Soviet Russia Today* ("Communist-controlled publication"); Spanish Refugee Appeal ("subversive" – "Communist front"); and Veterans of the Abraham Lincoln Brigade ("directed, dominated and controlled by the Communist Party"). Oxnam died in March 1963.

ALBERT WENTWORTH PALMER was born on May 18, 1879 in Kansas City, Missouri, son of Deborah Brininstool and Albert Palmer. He married Sara Wedd. He was an alumnus of the University of California (B.L., 1901) and Yale University (B.D., 1904). He was ordained a minister of the Congregational Church in 1904. He was the author of *Drift Toward Religion* (1914); *The Human Side of Hawaii* (1924); *The New Christian Epic* (1927); *Paths to the Presence of God* (1931); *Orientals in American Life* (1934); *The Minister's Job* (1937); *The Art of Conducting Public Worship* (1939); *Come, Let Us Worship* (1941); *Aids to Worship* (1944); *The Light of Faith* (1945); and *How Religion Helps* (1948).

From 1904 until 1907, Palmer was an assistant pastor in Redlands, California. He was a pastor in Oakland, California (1907-1917); Honolulu (1917-1924); and Oak Park, Illinois (1924-1930). From 1911 until 1917, he was an instructor in pastoral and social problems at Pacific Theological Seminary. During World War I, he was a YMCA secretary in the United States and Siberia. From 1930 until 1946, he was at Chicago Theological Seminary as professor of theology and president. In 1946, he retired as president emeritus. From 1946 until 1948, he was moderator of the General Conference of Congregational Christian Churches. From 1946 until 1949, he was minister of radio for the First Congregational Church in Los Angeles. From 1949 until 1954, he was a lecturer in religion at the University of Southern California.

Palmer frequently made appeals on behalf of the Communist Party and Communist leaders. He was affiliated with the American Peace Mobilization ("formed . . . under the auspices of the Communist Party and the Young Communist League" – "one of the most seditious organizations which ever operated in the United States"); the Committee for a Democratic Far Eastern Policy ("Communist"); the Committee for Peaceful Alternatives to the Atlantic Pact ("a Communist front organization . . . as part of Soviet psychological warfare against the United States"); the Committee on Militarism in Education (a supporting organization of the U.S. Congress Against War, "completely under the control of the Communist Party"); the Committee to Prevent Compulsory Military Training (leftist-pacifist); the Council for Pan-American Democracy ("subversive and Communist"); the Red-laden Federal Council of Churches; the Fellowship of Reconciliation (ultra-leftist-pacifist); the Mid-Century Conference for Peace ("aimed at assembling as many gullible persons as possible under Communist direction and turning them into a vast sounding board for Communist propaganda"); the National Committee To Repeal the McCarran Act ("Communist front" – "subversive"); the National Committee To Secure Justice in the Rosenberg Case ("Communist front organized . . . to conduct the United States phase of a mammoth propaganda campaign designed to obliterate the crime of and exploit the Rosenbergs and their codefendant Morton Sobell for the purposes of international Communism"); the National Committee To Win Amnesty for Smith Act Victims ("subversive" – "Communist"); and the National Federation for Constitutional Liberties ("under Communist Party domination and headed by responsible Party functionaries" – "one of the viciously subversive organizations of the Communist Party"). He died in December 1954.

DOROTHY ROTHSCHILD PARKER was born on August 22, 1893 in West End, New Jersey, daughter of Eliza Marston and J. Henry Rothschild. She was married to and divorced from Edwin Parker II and Alan Campbell. She remarried Alan Campbell. She was the author of *Men I'm Not Married To; Women I'm Not Married To* (1922); *Enough Rope*, poems (1926 and 1934); *Sunset Gun*, poems (1928 and 1934); *Laments for the Living*, stories (1930); *Death and Taxes*, poems (1931); *After Such Pleasures*, stories (1932); *Collected Poems – Not So Deep As a Well*, poems (1936); and *Here Lies*, stories (1939). She was co-author of *High Society* (1920). She collaborated in writing plays: *Close Harmony* (1924); *The Coast of Illyria* (1949); and *Ladies of the Corridor* (1953). Her omnibus volumes include *Collected Stories* (1942); *Collected Poetry* (1944); *Dorothy Parker* (1944); and *The Best of Dorothy Parker* (1952). She was the editor of *The Portable F. Scott Fitzgerald* (1945) and *Lee Chronicle: Studies of the Early Generations of the Lees of Virginia* (1957). She was co-editor of *Short Story: A Thematic Anthology* (1965). She was co-author of screenplays, including *Here Is My Heart* (1934); *One Hour Late* (1935); *Big Broadcast of*

1936 (1935); *Mary Burns, Fugitive* (1935); *Paris in Spring* (1935); *Three Married Men* (1936); *Lady Be Careful* (1936); *The Moon's Our Home* (1936); *Suzy* (1936); *A Star is Born* (1937); *Sweethearts* (1938); *Crime Takes a Holiday* (1938); *Trade Winds* (1938); *Flight Into Nowhere* (1938); *Five Little Peppers and How They Grew* (1939); *Weekend for Three* (1941); *Saboteur* (1942); *A Gentle Gangster* (1943); *Mrs. Skeffington* (1944); *Smash-up: The Story of a Woman* (1947); and *The Fan* (1949).

In 1916 and 1917, Parker was on the staff of *Vogue* magazine. From 1917 until 1920, she was a drama critic for *Vanity Fair*. From 1925 until 1957, she was a contributor to *New Yorker*. She was a sometime lecturer at Los Angeles State College. For a few years, she was a book reviewer for *Esquire* magazine.

Parker claimed that she was a Communist, although she was never identified as one by any Communist or former Communist. She did, however, have a long career of radicalism. In 1927, she was arrested in Massachusetts for demonstrating against the execution of two Reds, Nicola Sacco and Bartolomeo Vanzetti. During the Spanish Civil War she visited Spain to express her sympathy for the Reds, and when she returned to the United States, she was an activist in fronts which supported the Spanish Red cause. In 1944, a friend of Parker's, Edmund Wilson, offered a feeble apology for her Red activities which certainly had not ceased by 1944. Wilson wrote: "A decade or more ago she went out to Hollywood and more or less steadily stayed there, and, once away from her natural habitat, New York, she succumbed to the expiatory mania that has become epidemic with film-writers and was presently making

earnest appeals on behalf of those organizations which talked about being 'progressive' and succeeded in convincing their followers that they were working for the social revolution, though they had really no other purpose than to promote the foreign policy of the Soviet Union."

Parker was affiliated with the American Committee for Protection of Foreign Born ("founded by the Communist Party in order to exploit racial divisions in the United States for its own revolutionary purposes"); the American Committee for Yugoslav Relief ("subversive and Communist"); the American Continental Congress for World Peace ("another phase in the Communist 'peace' campaign, aimed at consolidating anti-American forces throughout the Western Hemisphere"); the American Council for a Democratic Greece ("subversive and Communist"); the American Labor Party ("Communist dissimulation extends into the field of political parties forming political front organizations such as the . . . American Labor Party"); the American League for Peace and Democracy ("subversive and Communist" — "established . . . in an effort to create public sentiment on behalf of a foreign policy adapted to the interests of the Soviet Union . . . [and] designed to conceal Communist control, in accordance with the new tactics of the Communist International"); the American Relief Ship for Spain ("Communist Party front enterprise"); the Artists' Front To Win the War ("Communist front" — "included representatives of the theater, of literature, music, art, science, and education, with long and active records of support for Communist front organizations and for the variegated turns of the Communist Party line"); the Citizens Committee for Harry Bridges ("Communist"); the Civil Rights Congress ("created and established by the Communist Party as an organization which would utilize defense of civil rights for Party purposes and raise and maintain mass defense and bail funds for Party use"); Consumers Union (in the "solar system of organizations around the [Communist] Party"); Contemporary Writers ("subversive and Communist"); the Coordinating Committee To Lift the [Spanish] Embargo ("one of the numerous Communist-front enterprises which were organized around the Communists' agitation over the Spanish Civil War"); the Cultural and Scientific Conference for World Peace ("Communist front" – "a propaganda front for Soviet foreign policy and Soviet culture"); Friends of the Abraham Lincoln Brigade ("completely controlled by the Communist Party"); the Golden Book of American Friendship With the Soviet Union ("pro-Soviet propaganda enterprise"); History Today, Inc. ("controlled by the Communist Party"); the Hollywood Anti-Nazi League ("Communist front"); the Hollywood League for Democratic Action ("Communist front"); the International Workers Order ("from its very inception demonstrated by its pronouncements, its activities, and the authoritative statements of the Communist Party that it is a subservient instrument of the Communist Party of the United States"); the Joint Anti-Fascist Refugee Committee ("subversive and Communist"); the Lawyers Committee on American Relations With Spain ("during the Spanish Civil War, the Communist Party organized . . . [the Lawyers Committee] as a part of one of its major propaganda campaigns of the Party's entire history in this country"); the League of American Writers ("subversive and Communist" – "began openly to follow the Communist

Party line as dictated by the foreign policy of the Soviet Union"); the League of Women Shoppers ("Communist-controlled front"); *Mainstream* ("monthly cultural and literary organ of the Communist Party"); the Marcus Graham Freedom of the Press Committee (an ultra-radical group in support of an anarchist"); the Medical Bureau and North American Committee To Aid Spanish Democracy ("subversive and un-American"); the New York League of Women Shoppers ("Communist-controlled front"); the New York Tom Mooney Committee ("Communist front"); an Open Letter to American Liberals ("project of well known Communists and Communist collaborators" – "in defense of the progressive movement undertaken by the Soviet Union"); People's Songs, Inc. ("subversive"); Progressive Citizens of America ("political Communist front" – "subversive"); the Southern Conference for Human Welfare ("a Communist front organization which seeks to attract Southern Liberals on the basis of its seeming interest in the problems of the South"); the Southern Negro Youth Congress ("subversive and among the affiliates and committees of the Communist Party, USA, which seeks to alter the form of government of the United States by unconstitutional means"); Stage for Action ("subversive"); a Statement by American Progressives on the Moscow Trials ("obviously a document concocted in defense of the line of the Communist Party and undoubtedly originated in the headquarters of the Communist Party"); the United American Spanish Aid Committee ("Communist"); the United Labor and Citizens Committee for Jobs and Recovery ("set up by Communists"); the Voice of Freedom Committee ("subversive" – to defend pro-

Communist radio commentators); the Washington Committee for Spanish Refugee Aid ("Communist front"); the Washington Committee To Lift [the] Spanish Embargo ("Communist front"); and the Win-the-Peace Conference ("Communist front"). She died in June 1967. She left the bulk of her estate to the arch racial agitator, Martin Luther King Jr. In the event of his death, the estate was to go to the ultra-radical National Association for the Advancement of Colored People.

EDWARD LAMBE PARSONS was born on May 18, 1868 in New York City, son of Helen White and Arthur Parsons. He married Bertha Brush. He was an alumnus of Yale University (B.A., 1889). He was a graduate of Union Theological Seminary (1892) and Episcopal Theological School in Cambridge, Massachusetts (1894). He was ordained a deacon of the Protestant Episcopal Church in 1894, and a priest in 1895. From 1892 until 1894, he was a fellow at the University of Berlin. He was the author of *What Is the Christian Religion?* (1927); *Victory With Christ* (1942); and *The Diocese of California, 1915-1940* (1958). He was co-author of *The American Prayer Book* (1937).

In 1894 and 1895, Parsons was an assistant pastor at Grace Church in New York City. He was rector of Trinity Church in Menlo Park, California (1896-1900), St. Matthews Church in San Mateo, California (1900-1904), and St. Mark's Church in Berkeley, California (1904-1919). In 1919, he was consecrated bishop coadjutor of California. From 1924 until his retirement in 1941, he was bishop of California. From 1897 until 1902, he was an instructor in philosophy at Stanford University. Over a twenty-five-year period, he frequently lectured on the philosophy of religion and liturgics at the Church Divinity School of the Pacific at Berkeley. From 1928 until 1943, he was chairman of the Protestant Episcopal Church Committee on Approaches to Unity and chairman of the Standing Liturgical Committee (1903-1946). From 1923 until 1950, he was president of the Episcopal League for Social Action. He was president of the Church League for Industrial Democracy (Socialist). From 1921 until 1929, he was president of the board of trustees of Mills College. From 1941 until 1956, he was chairman of the board of the ultra-leftist American Civil Liberties Union of Nothern California.

Parsons was affiliated with the American Committee for Protection of Foreign Born ("founded by the Communist Party in order to exploit racial divisions in the United States for its own revolutionary purposes"); the American Committee for Spanish Freedom ("Communist"); the American Committee To Save Refugees ("perform[ing] a most valuable function for the international Communist movement"); the American Friends of Spanish Democracy ("Communist front"); the American Round Table on India ("Communist front"); an Appeal for Amnesty for Eleven Communist Leaders (pro-Communist project); the California Labor School ("a subversive and Communist organization"); the Citizens' Committee To Free Earl Browder ("a strictly Communist Party affair"); Citizens United To Abolish the Wood-Rankin Committee (pro-Communist project); the Citizens Victory Committee for Harry Bridges ("Communist front"); the Civil Rights Congress ("created and established by the Communist Party as an organization which would utilize defense of civil rights for Party purposes and raise and maintain mass defense and bail funds for Party use"); the Committee for a Democratic Far Eastern Policy ("Communist"); the Committee for Citizenship Rights ("to protect Communist subversion from any penalties under the law"); the Committee for Free Political Advocacy ("Communist front"); the Committee for Peaceful Alternatives to the Atlantic Pact ("initiated by Communists"); the Committee of Welcome for the Red Dean of Canterbury (England's most notorious pro-Soviet apologist among the clergy); the Committee on Militarism in Education (supporting organization of U.S. Congress Against War, "completely under the control of the Communist Party"); the Coordinating Committee To Lift the [Spanish] Embargo ("one of the numerous Communist-front enterprises which were organized around the Communists' agitation over the Spanish Civil War"); the Council for Pan-American Democracy ("subversive and Communist"); the Federation for the Repeal of the Levering Act (strongly supported by Communists and apologists for the Communist Party"); the Joint Anti-Fascist Refugee Committee ("subversive and Communist"); the Medical Bureau To Aid Spanish Democracy ("Communist enterprise"); the Mid-Century Conference for Peace ("aimed at assembling as many gullible persons as possible under Communist direction and turning them into a vast sounding board for Communist propaganda"); the ultra-radical National Association for the Advancement of Colored People; the National Committee To Abolish the Poll Tax ("Communist front"); the National Committee To Repeal the McCarran Act ("Communist front" – "subversive"); the National Committee To Win Amnesty for Smith Act Victims ("subversive" – "Communist"); the National Conference To Defend the Bill of Rights ("subversive");

the National Council of American-Soviet Friendship ("subversive and Communist" – "specializing in pro-Soviet propaganda"); the National Council of the Arts, Sciences, and Professions ("a Communist front used to appeal to special occupational groups"); the National Emergency Conference ("Communist front"); the National Emergency Conference for Democratic Rights ("Communist front" – "subversive"); the National Federation for Constitutional Liberties ("under Communist Party domination and headed by responsible Party functionaries" – "one of the viciously subversive organizations of the Communist Party"); the National Free Browder Congress ("Communist Party affair"); the North American Committee To Aid Spanish Democracy ("Communist"); the *Protestant* ("with an eye to religious groups, the Communists have formed religious fronts such as the *Protestant*"); the Rosenberg Clemency Appeal ("Communist front organized . . . to conduct the United States phase of a mammoth propaganda campaign designed to obliterate the crime of and exploit the Rosenbergs and their codefendant Morton Sobell for the purposes of international Communism"); Russian War Relief ("Communist enterprise"); *Soviet Russia Today* ("Communist-controlled publication"); the Spanish Refugee Appeal ("subversive" – "Communist front"); the Spanish Refugee Relief Campaign ("Communist front"); the Veterans of the Abraham Lincoln Brigade ("directed, dominated and controlled by the Communist Party"); the Washington Committee To Lift [the] Spanish Embargo ("Communist front"); and the Win-the-Peace Conference ("Communist front"). Parsons died in July 1960.

CLARENCE EVAN PICKETT was

born on October 19, 1884 in Cissna Park, Illinois, son of Huldah Macy and Evan Pickett. He married Lilly Peckham. He was an alumnus of Penn College in Iowa (B.A., 1910) and Hartford Theological Seminary (B.B., 1913). He was ordained in 1913 to the ministry of the Society of Friends. He pursued graduate studies at Harvard Divinity School (1922-1923). He was the author of *For More Than Bread* (1953).

Pickett was minister of the Friends Meeting in Toronto, Canada (1913-1917) and the Friends Meeting in Oskaloosa, Iowa (1917-1919). From 1919 until 1922, he was secretary of Young Friends in America. From 1923 until 1929, he was professor of Biblical literature at Earlham College. From 1929 until 1965, he was with the American Friends Service Committee (AFSC) as executive secretary (1929-1950), honorary executive secretary (1950-1955), and executive secretary emeritus (1955-1965). In 1952, he was a member of the Presidential Commission on Naturalization and Immigration. From 1950 until 1955, he was a member of the international Quaker delegation at the United Nations General Assembly. From 1961 until 1965, he was a member of the National Advisory Council of the Peace Corps.

Pickett as its executive secretary was a major factor in the AFSC's feverish leftwing activities that began simultaneously with his assumption of the position. Since 1929, the AFSC has been for all practical purposes a pro-Soviet front in its activities at home and abroad. It has cooperated with the Communists in countless projects and enterprises. In its own projects, it has willingly and deliberately provided hospitable forums for Communists and fellow travellers. It has gone far beyond the bounds of religious-oriented pacifism by counseling and lobbying for non-Quaker conscientious objectors and draft evaders. It has been a source of pro-Soviet propaganda and it has worked for a pro-Soviet United States foreign policy. The AFSC's leaders, including Pickett, condemned the anti-Communist forces of Spain and the Nazi regime in Germany but refrained from the slightest criticism of the Soviet Union or Communist Cuba. The AFSC joined the ultra-left in the United States and abroad in every major front agitating for disarmament and the cessation of nuclear testing. In 1947, while Pickett was executive secretary, it was a co-recipient of the Nobel Peace Prize.

Few Americans other than Communist Party members have enjoyed more frequent and more favorable notices in the official Communist press than Pickett. The Communists recognized him as a valiant and durable ally in their campaign to abolish anti-Communist, anti-subversive Congressional investigating committees. He was vigorous in his opposition to anti-Communist and anti-subversive legislation. He could always be relied upon to sign appeals and petitions on behalf of indicted, convicted, and imprisoned Communists. He publicly denounced any United States policy that appeared to him to be anti-Communist. He was an early promoter of United States diplomatic recognition of Red China and Communist Cuba. He was a participant in countless Communist-inspired "peace" meetings. He joined the Communists in their agitation for civilian review boards of police departments, and he served as chairman of the Philadelphia Police Advisory Board, the first such group in a major city. He joined militant racists in their demonstrations carried on in the name of "civil rights." In 1962, he walked in a picket line outside the White

House with the ultra-leftist Women for Peace, carrying a poster denouncing United States nuclear testing. After he had demonstrated, he entered the White House to attend a dinner honoring Nobel Prize winners.

Pickett was affiliated with the American Committee for Yugoslav Relief ("subversive and Communist"); the American Committee on Africa (leftist); the American-Russian Institute ("subversive" – "Communist" – "specializing in pro-Soviet propaganda"); the Church Peace Mission (calling for peaceful resistance to Communism and for unilateral disarmament by the United States); the Committee for a Democratic Spain (dominated by Communists and fellow travelers); the Committee for Medical Freedom (ultra-leftist); the Committee for Nonviolent Action (ultra-leftist-pacifist); the Committees of Correspondence (ultra-leftist); the Emergency Civil Liberties Committee ("Communist front" – "subversive"); the Federation for the Repeal of the Levering Act (strongly supported by Communists and apologists for the Communist Party); the Fellowship of Reconciliation (ultra-leftist-pacifist); the Highlander Folk School (leftist agitators); the National Committee for a Sane Nuclear Policy (ultra-leftist-pacifist); the National Committee To Abolish the Un-American Activities Committee ("to lead and direct the Communist Party's 'Operation Abolition' campaign"); the ultra-radical New School for Social Research; Promoting Enduring Peace, Inc. (ultra-leftist-pacifist); and *Soviet Russia Today* ("Communist-controlled publication). He died in March 1965. He was eulogized in the Communists' *National Guardian.*

DAVID de SOLA POOL was born on May 16, 1885 in London, England, son of Abigail Davis and Eleazar Pool. He married Tamar Hirschenson. He was an alumnus of the University of London (B.A., 1903) and the University of Heidelberg (Ph. D., 1906). He completed his rabbinical studies at the University of Berlin. He was the author of *The Kaddish* (1909); *Learning Among the Puritans of New England* (1911); *Capital Punishment in Jewish Literature* (1916); and *Portraits Etched in Stone* (1952). He was co-author of *An Old Faith in the New World* (1955).

From 1907 until 1955, when he retired, Pool was rabbi of the Spanish and Portuguese Synagogue (Shearith Israel) in New York City. In 1919, Pool was one of the three American representatives on the Zionist Commission to Palestine. He was president of Young Judea of America (1915-1919 and 1924-1925); the New York Board of Jewish Ministers (1916-1917); the Union of Sephardic Congregations (1928-1970); and the Synagogue Council of America (1938-1940). In 1959, he was on the United States delegation to the NATO congress.

Pool was affiliated with the American Biro Bidjan ("Communist front"); the American Committee for Protection of Foreign Born ("founded by the Communist Party in order to exploit racial divisions in the United States for its own revolutionary purposes"); the American Committee for Yugoslav Relief ("subversive and Communist"); American Relief for Greek Democracy (pro-Communist); Americans of South Slavic Descent (ultra-leftist); the Atlantic Union Committee (leftist-internationalist); the Council on Foreign Relations (the unofficial but operative directorate of all facets of United States foreign policy); Federal Union (leftist-internationalist); the Greater New York Emergency Conference on Inalienable Rights ("Communist front"); the International Labor Defense ("subversive and Communist" – "legal arm of the Communist Party" – "part of an international network of organizations for the defense of Communist lawbreakers"); the Joint Anti-Fascist Refugee Committee ("subversive and Communist"); the Mid-Century Conference for Peace ("aimed at assembling as many gullible persons as possible under Communist direction and turning them into a vast sounding board for Communist propaganda"); the National Federation for Constitutional Liberties ("under Communist Party domination and headed by responsible Party functionaries" – "one of the viciously subversive organizations of the Communist Party"); the New York Council of American-Soviet Friendship ("subversive and Communist" – "specializing in pro-Soviet propaganda"); the Spanish Refugee Appeal ("subversive" – "Communist front"); and the United World Federalists (the most prestigious group of fellow-travelers and dupes working for world government at the expense of United States sovereignty).

Pool died in December 1970.

ARTHUR UPHAM POPE was born on February 7, 1881 in Phoenix, Rhode Island, son of Imogene Titus and Louis Pope. He was married to and divorced from Bertha Clark. His second wife was Phyllis Ackerman. He was an alumnus of Brown University (B.A., 1904 and M.A., 1905). He is the author of *Persian Art* (1925); *Early Oriental Carpets* (1926); *Persian Art and Culture* (1928); *An Introduction to Persian Art* (1930); *The Revival of the Art of Carpet Weaving* (1931); *Lincoln and an Urgent World Problem* (1943); *Maxim Litvinoff* (1943); and *Masterpieces of Persian Art*

(1945). He was co-editor, co-annotator, co-translator, and a contributor to *A Survey of Persian Art, from Prehistoric Times to the Present* (1931-1938).

From 1904 until 1906, and from 1908 until 1910, Pope was an instructor of philosophy at Brown University. From 1914 until 1917, he was an assistant professor of philosophy at the University of California. In 1917 and 1918, he was an associate professor of philosophy at Amherst College. In 1923 and 1924, he was director of the California Art Museum in San Francisco. From 1925 until 1935, he was advisory curator of Muhammedan art at Chicago's Art Institute. From 1925 until 1969, he was an adviser to the Iranian (Persian) government. From 1928 until 1969, he was an adviser on Persian art to the Pennsylvania Museum. From 1930 until 1969, he was director of the American Institute of Persian Art and Archeology. He was director of the Iranian Institute's Architectural Survey of Iran and the Asia Institute's School for Asiatic Studies. In 1935, he was the associate director of the International Exhibition of Iranian Art and the co-director of the International Congress for Iranian Art and Archeology in Leningrad, U.S.S.R. From 1947 until 1953, he was chancellor of the Asia Institute. In 1953, he retired as chancellor emeritus. In 1960, he was the organizer and director of the International Congress of Iranian Art in New York City and Washington, D.C. He was president of the Institute of Archeological Studies in Teheran and the International Association of Iranian Art and Archeology. Between 1929 and 1969, he made nineteen research expeditions to Iran.

In 1945, Pope was one of fourteen American scientists and scholars who attended the celebration of the 220th anniversary of the Russian Academy of Sciences. They were guests of the Soviet government. In his report of the trip, Pope's pro-Soviet bias was overwhelming as he said: "One of the most important aspects of the Soviet Union today – one that we had felt at the beginning and all through our visit, was the robust intellectual interest throughout the country. There is intense intellectual fervor. There is a zest for ideas such as we hardly know now, which marked the great tide of the Renaissance and of Elizabethan England; for serious books on different subjects. An edition of 100,000 sets of the collected works of Emanuel Kant was exhausted in 92 days. In the United States we would not contemplate the risk in publishing such an edition of such a difficult work. At the time of the World Series, our papers are crammed full of sports events. But not even the World Series, nor any murder trial, ever took such a place in the American papers as the 220th anniversary of the Academy of Sciences took in the Soviet papers. Science means a great deal to the whole Russian people. The last 25 years have seen the development of first-class intelligence, of mass contributions, not merely in art and literature, but in all the sciences. The Soviet Union consciously and deliberately has made science the basis of the life that is to come. And they said, when the news came of the end of the war with Germany, 'Now we can live again.' Although there was grief in every heart, suffering throughout the land and serious damage to the economy of the country, nevertheless, with zest, enthusiasm, and joy they turned to building a new world – a world based upon knowledge. Both Lenin and Stalin had seen that in this new country without experience, without training, lacking

competent personnel in administration or teaching, sorely beset by enemies within and without, and backward, only through the application of discipline and trained knowledge would the Soviet Union be able to survive and progress. Hence, science was made the cornerstone of the policy of the new government. Now, every elevator man or chauffeur knows who Komarov is, knows who founded the academy, and knows about the great academy with its 1 million volume library, with its 4,500 highly trained experts working in 78 institutions (more than all the other countries put together). They know that that is one of the great sources of strength of the Soviet Union.

"At one important meeting, the Russian professor, Peter Kapitsa, made a noble and moving address, 'Science knows no boundaries; it knows no discriminations of creed or race. Science is a universal need of all mankind and it is something that reaches across all kinds of prejudices. It unites men into noble and idealistic enterprise. Science requires the intelligence and skillful cooperation of the leading thinkers of all nations. It is not the work of 1 country, or 1 university, or 1 man. It is a human enterprise and it requires the best that is in it. It requires also generous and intelligent help on the part of the government.' The Soviet Union looks forward to a world in which science will assure the welfare for all."

Away from art, archeology, and architecture, Pope was a long-time fulsome apologist for the Soviet Union and a pro-Communist activist in the United States. By his maudlin treatment of Stalin's henchman in *Maxim Litvinoff,* he was recognized as the "official" American biographer of Litvinov, whose diplomatic duplicity played such an important role in President Franklin D. Roosevelt's decision to extend diplomatic recognition to the Soviet Union in 1933.

Pope was affiliated with the American Committee for Chinese War Orphans ("Communist front"); the American Committee for Protection of Foreign Born ("founded by the Communist Party in order to exploit racial divisions in the United States for its own revolutionary purposes"); the American Committee To Save Refugees ("perform[ing] a most valuable function for the international Communist movement"); the American Council on Soviet Relations ("subversive" – "established by the Communist Party ... directed and controlled by the Party, and operated to aid and support Party objectives concerning the defense and support of the Soviet Union"); the American Russian Institute ("subversive" – "Communist" – "specializing in pro-Soviet propaganda"); the American Slav Congress ("Moscow-inspired and directed federation of Communist-dominated organizations seeking by methods of propaganda and pressure to subvert the 10,000,000 people in this country of Slavic birth or descent"); American Youth for Democracy ("formed ... for the purpose of exploiting to the advantage of a foreign power the idealism, inexperience, and craving to join which is characteristic of American college youth" – "part of Soviet psychological warfare against the United States"); the Artists League of America ("Communist front"); the Celebration of the 25th Anniversary of the Red Army (Communist enterprise); the China Aid Council ("Communist-controlled"); the Citizens Committee To Free Earl Browder ("a strictly Communist Party affair"); the Committee for a Democratic Far Eastern Policy ("Communist"); Friends of Chinese Democracy

("Communist-controlled"); Indusco ("Communist-controlled"); the Institute of Pacific Relations ("an instrument of Communist policy, propaganda and military intelligence"); the Joint Anti-Fascist Refugee Committee ("subversive and Communist"); the National Assembly for Democratic Rights ("created, dominated and controlled by members and officials of the Communist Party"); the National Committee To Combat Anti-Semitism ("Communist front"); the National Council for Public Morale ("Communist front"); the National Council of American-Soviet Friendship ("subversive and Communist" – "specializing in pro-Soviet propaganda"); the National Federation for Constitutional Liberties ("under Communist Party domination and headed by responsible Party functionaries" – "one of the viciously subversive organizations of the Communist Party"); *New Masses* ("weekly journal of the Communist Party"); People's Radio Foundation, Inc. ("subversive and Communist organization"); the Reichstag Fire Trial Anniversary Committee ("Communist front ... formed ... by prominent Communists and Communist sympathizers"); the Scientific and Cultural Conference for World Peace ("Communist front" – "a propaganda front for Soviet foreign policy and Soviet culture"); and *Soviet Russia Today* ("Communist-controlled publication"). He died in September 1969.

EDWIN McNEILL POTEAT was born on November 20, 1892 in New Haven, Connecticut, son of Harriet Gordon and Edwin Poteat. He married Wilda Hardman. He was an alumnus of Furman University (A.B., 1912 and A.M., 1913) and Southern Baptist Theological Seminary (Th.M., 1916). He was the author of

POTEAT

Coming to Terms with the Universe (1931); *Jesus and the Liberal Mind* (1933); *The Reverend John Doe, D.D.* (1934); *Thunder Over Sinai* (1936); *The Social Manifesto of Jesus* (1937); *Centurion*, poem (1938); *These Shared His Passion* (1938); *These Shared His Cross* (1939); *These Shared His Power* (1941); *Four Freedoms and God* (1943); *Over the Sea, the Sky*, poetry (1945); *Last Reprieve?* (1945); *Parables of Crisis* (1950); *God Makes the Difference* (1951); and *Mandate to Humanity* (1953).

From 1917 until 1925, Poteat was a missionary for the Southern Baptist Convention, working in the Province of Honan in China. From 1926 until 1929, he was an associate professor of philosophy and ethics at the University of Shanghai. In 1929, he was ordained to the Baptist ministry. He was a minister in Raleigh, North Carolina (1929-1937), and Cleveland, Ohio (1937-1944). From 1944 until 1948, he was president of Colgate-Rochester Divinity School. From 1948 until 1955, he was a minister in Raleigh, North Carolina. He was national president of the leftist-oriented Protestants and Other Americans United for Separation of Church and State. He was active in the Red-laden Federal Council of Churches.

Poteat's affiliations included the Citizens Committee To Secure Bail for Martin Young (an affiliate of the American Committee for Protection of Foreign Born, "founded by the Communist Party in order to exploit racial divisions in the United States for its own revolutionary purposes"); the Civil Rights Congress ("created and established by the Communist Party as an organization which would utilize defense of civil rights for Party purposes and raise and maintain mass defense and bail funds for Party use"); the Committee for a Democratic Far Eastern Policy ("Communist"); the Committee for Peaceful Alternatives to the Atlantic Pact ("a Communist-front organization . . . as part of the Soviet psychological warfare against the United States"); the Council for Pan-American Democracy ("subversive and Communist"); the Emergency Civil Liberties Committee ("Communist front" – "subversive"); the Fellowship of Reconciliation (ultra-leftist pacifist); the International Labor Defense ("subversive and Communist" – "legal arm of the Communist Party" – "part of an international network of organizations for the defense of Communist lawbreakers"); the National Association for the Advancement of Colored People (ultra-radical); the National Committee To Combat Anti-Semitism ("Communist front"); the National Committee To Repeal the McCarran Act ("Communist front" – "subversive"); the National Committee To Win the Peace ("subversive and Communist"); the National Council of American-Soviet Friendship ("subversive and Communist" – "specializing in pro-Soviet propaganda"); the National Federation for Constitutional Liberties ("under Communist Party domination and headed by responsible Party functionaries" – "one of the viciously subversive organizations of the Communist Party"); the National Religion and Labor Foundation ("Communist front"); the People's Institute of Applied Religion ("subversive and Communist"); the *Protestant* ("with an eye to religious groups, the Communists have formed religious fronts such as the *Protestant*"); the *Protestant Digest* ("a magazine which has faithfully propagated the Communist Party line under the guise of being a religious journal"); and the [Morris U.] Schappes Defense Committee ("a front organization with a strictly Communist objective, namely, the defense of a self-admitted Communist who was convicted of perjury in the courts of New York"). Poteat died in December 1955.

WALTER RAUTENSTRAUCH was born on September 7, 1880 in Sedalia, Missouri, son of Anna Nichter and Julius Rautenstrauch. He married Minerva Babb. He is an alumnus of the University of Missouri (B.S., 1902) and the University of Maine (M.S., 1903). He pursued graduate studies at Cornell University (1903-1904). He was the author of *Syllabus of Lectures on Machine Design* (1906); *Machine Drafting* (1908); *The Economics of Business Enterprise* (1939); and *Who Gets the Money?* (1939). He was co-author of *Mechanical Engineers Handbook* (1916); *The Successful Control of Profits* (1930); *Tomorrow in the Making* (1939); *Industrial Surveys and Reports* (1940); *The Design of Manufacturing Enterprises* (1941); *Principles of Modern Industrial Organization* (1944); and *Economics of Industrial Management* (1949).

From 1902 until 1903, Rautenstrauch was an instructor in engineering at the University of Maine. From 1904 until 1906, he was an assistant professor at Cornell University. From 1906 until 1946, he was a professor of industrial engineering at Columbia University. He retired in 1946 as professor emeritus. He was a consultant engineer to various manufacturing industries.

Rautenstrauch was affiliated with the American Association of Scientific Workers ("Communist front"); the American Council for Democratic Greece ("subversive and Communist"); the American Committee for Democracy and Intellectual Freedom ("subversive and un-American" – "a Communist-front organization operating among college teachers and professors"); the American Committee for Indonesian Independence ("Communist front"); the American Committee for Protection of Foreign Born ("founded by the Communist Party in order to exploit racial divisions in the United States for its own revolutionary purposes"); the American Committee To Save Refugees ("perform[ing] a most valuable function for the international Communist movement"); the American League for Peace and Democracy ("subversive and Communist" – "established . . . in an effort to create public sentiment on behalf of a foreign policy adapted to the interests of the Soviet Union . . . [and] designed to conceal Communist control, in accordance with the new tactics of the Communist International"); the American Peace Mobilization ("formed . . . under the auspices of the Communist Party and the Young Communist League" – "one of the most seditious organizations which ever operated in the United States"); American Relief for Greek Democracy ("Communist front"); the American Youth Congress ("subversive" – "one of the most influential front organizations ever set up by the Communists in this country" – "the Communists were in complete control"); American Youth for Democracy ("subversive and Communist" – "formed . . . for the purpose of exploiting to the advantage of a foreign power the idealism, inexperience, and craving to join which is characteristic of American college youth" – "part of Soviet psychological warfare against the United States"); the Bill of Rights Conference ("subversive"); the Citizens Committee for Harry Bridges ("Communist"); the Citizens Committee To Free Earl Browder ("a strictly Communist Party affair"); the Citizens Emergency

Committee for Interracial Unity ("Communist front"); the Civil Rights Congress ("created and established by the Communist Party as an organization which would utilize defense of civil rights for Party purposes and raise and maintain mass defense and bail funds for Party use"); the Committee for a Boycott Against Japanese Aggression ("the committee was featured in the *Daily Worker*, official organ of the Communist Party, and in that paper alone"); the Committee for Citizenship Rights ("to protect Communist subversion from any penalties under the law"); the Committee for Equal Justice for Mrs. Recy Taylor ("Communist front"); the Committee for Free Political Advocacy ("Communist front"); the Committee on Election Rights ("a Communist front whose function was to agitate for placing the Communist Party on the ballot throughout the United States"); the Committee To Defend America by Keeping Out of War ("Communist front"); the Conference on Constitutional Liberties in America ("an important part of the solar system of the Communist Party's front organizations"); Consumers Union (in the "solar system of organizations around the [Communist] Party"); the Council for Pan American Democracy ("subversive and Communist"); the Council on African Affairs ("subversive and Communist"); the Cultural and Scientific Conference for World Peace ("Communist front" — "a propaganda front for Soviet foreign policy and Soviet culture"); the Emergency Peace Mobilization ("Communist front"); the Federation of Architects, Engineers, Chemists and Technicians ("its leaders . . . cooperate fully with the Communist Party and controlled organizations"); *Friday* ("Communist-controlled"); the German-American Emergency Conference ("Communist front"); the Greater New York Emergency Conference on Inalienable Rights ("Communist front"); the Independent Citizens Committee of the Arts, Sciences and Professions ("Communist front"); Indusco ("Communist-controlled"); the International Labor Defense ("subversive and Communist" — "legal arm of the Communist Party" — "part of an international network of organizations for the defense of Communist lawbreakers"); the International Workers Order ("from its very inception demonstrated by its pronouncements, its activities, and the authoritative statements of the Communist Party that it is a subservient instrument of the Communist Party of the United States"); the Jefferson School of Social Science ("a Communist institution modeled along the lines of the new Communist policy which led to the decision to change the Communist Party into some kind of an educational institution"); the Joint Anti-Fascist Refugee Committee ("subversive and Communist"); the Joint Committee for Trade Union Rights ("jointly with the International Labor Defense supported and defended Communist Party leaders . . . when they were serving prison terms"); the League for Industrial Democracy (Socialist); the League of American Writers ("subversive and Communist" — "began openly to follow the Communist Party line as dictated by the foreign policy of the Soviet Union"); the Methodist Federation for Social Action ("the organization's influence has been consistently wielded on behalf of Communist causes and the Communist line as expressed through the party and its innumerable subsidiaries"); the National Conference on American Policy in China and the Far East ("Communist"); the National Council on American-Soviet Friendship ("subversive and Communist" – "specializing in pro-Soviet propaganda"); the National Council of the Arts, Sciences, and Professions ("a Communist front used to appeal to special occupational groups"); the National Emergency Conference for Democratic Rights ("Communist front" – "subversive"); the National Federation for Constitutional Liberties ("under Communist Party domination and headed by responsible Party functionaries" – "one of the viciously subversive organizations of the Communist Party"); *New Masses* ("weekly journal of the Communist Party"); an Open Letter for Closer Cooperation with the Soviet Union (issued by "a group of Communist Party stooges"); an Open Letter in Defense of Harry Bridges ("Communist front"); Progressive Citizens of America ("political Communist front" – "subversive"); the Reichstag Fire Trial Anniversary Committee ("Communist front . . . formed by prominent Communists and Communist sympathizers"); the Saturday Forum Luncheon Group ("Communist front"); the [Morris U.] Schappes Defense Committee ("a front organization with a strictly Communist objective, namely, the defense of a self-admitted Communist who was convicted of perjury in the courts of New York"); the School for Democracy ("established by Communist teachers ousted from the public school system of New York City"); *Science and Society* ("Communist publication"); the Stockholm Peace Appeal ("Communist 'peace' campaign"); the United American Spanish Aid Committee ("Communist"); Veterans of the Abraham Lincoln Brigade ("directed, dominated and controlled by the Communist Party"); the Washington Peace Mobilization ("Communist-controlled organization"); the West Side

Citizens Committee To Free Earl Browder ("Communist front"); and the World Peace Congress ("organized under Communist initiative in various countries throughout the world").

Rautenstrauch died in January 1951.

JOHN REED was born on October 22, 1887 in Portland, Oregon, son of Margaret Green and Charles Reed. He married Anne Mohan. He was an alumnus of Harvard University (A.B. 1910). He was the author of *Diana's Debut* (1910); *Sanger* (1913); *The Day in Bohemia: or, Life Among the Artists* (1913); *Everymagazine: An Immorality Play* (1913); *Insurgent Mexico* (1914); *The War in Eastern Europe* (1916); *Tamburlaine, and Other Poems* (1917); *Red Russia* (1919); *Ten Days That Shook the World* (1919); and *Daughter of the Revolution* (posthumously, 1927). Among the plays he wrote were *Moondown, Enter Dibble, Constancy, Freedom, The Eternal Quadrangle,* and *The Peace That Passeth Understanding.* In 1913, he produced the play *The Pageant of the Paterson Strike* in New York City.

In the four years after his graduation from Harvard, Reed led the life of a literary and journalistic gadabout. He came under the influence of two muckrakers, Lincoln Steffens and Ida Tarbell. He joined the staff of *American* magazine and wrote articles for *Saturday Evening Post, Collier's,* and *Smart Set.* In 1913, as a reporter for *Metropolitan* magazine and the *New York World*, he spent four months with Pancho Villa's army in Mexico. The reporting by Reed and his subsequent book, *Insurgent Mexico*, were sophomoric efforts at best. From his Mexican experiences, Reed went to Colorado, where he became an admirer of the militantly radical Wobblies, the International Workers of the World. From Colorado, he went to New Jersey, where he was arrested for his participation in a silk-workers' strike at Paterson. Meanwhile, he had joined the staff of *Masses*, a flaming Red publication run by a leading contemporary radical, Max Eastman.

In 1914 and 1915, Reed was in Europe as a war correspondent for the *New York World* and *Metropolitan* magazine. He traveled on both the Eastern and Western fronts with the German, Serbian, Bulgarian, Rumanian, and Russian armies. As a war correspondent, he was a conspicuous failure.

In 1917, Reed went to Russia with credentials from *Masses, Socialist Call*, and *Seven Arts*. He was accompanied by his bride, Louise Bryant. In Russia, Reed was a witness to the Bolshevik Revolution, and his experiences and reflections on the event were recorded in his *Ten Days That Shook the World*. He became a close associate of Nikolai Lenin and wrote propaganda for the Bolsheviks that was directed at soldiers in the trenches and people throughout the world.

When Reed decided to return to the United States, Lenin and Leon Trotsky decided that he should travel as a diplomat, and they appointed him consul of the Bolshevik regime to New York. The appointment was not appreciated by United States authorities, and it was withdrawn by Lenin before Reed reached New York. Nevertheless, Reed arrived safely in New York with an enormous amount of revolutionary propaganda and source material for the book he would soon write, *Ten Days That Shook the World*.

After Reed returned to America, he joined the Socialist Party and became prominent in what was called its leftwing faction. Reed was expelled from the Party's convention in 1919, and with Benjamin Gitlow he organized the Communist Labor Party. The CLP was opposed by the newly-formed Communist Party, led by Louis Fraina, Jay Lovestone, and Charles Ruthenberg. While in the United States, Reed was tried on charges of sedition associated with his editorship of *Masses*. It was his second trial on these charges, the first having been conducted *in absentia*. Both trials ended with hung juries.

Reed was not only leader of the CLP but also the editor of its organ, *Voice of Labor*. He was anxious that the Bolsheviks in Russia recognize the Communist Labor Party, rather than the Russian-Slav-controlled Communist Party, as their American counterpart. In 1919, he journeyed back to Russia, using a forged passport, as the CLP's representative to the Congress of the Communist International. He arrived in Moscow during the winter of 1919. To his surprise, the Comintern refused his request that they recognize his CLP as the legitimate Communist group in America. The Comintern desired that the opposing factions in the United States be unified.

While Reed was in Moscow, he learned that he was under indictment in Chicago on sedition charges. He decided to return to the United States but had difficulty getting out of Russia. After two unsuccessful attempts, he managed to reach Finland. He carried with him revolutionary contraband, confidential instructions, letters, and one million Finnish marks, to be converted into American currency and used to finance Communist activities in the United States. Reed was apprehended by Finnish authorities and held in jail for more than two months. He tried in vain to obtain an American passport, but when he learned that the Finns had given

American authorities access to his contraband, he withdrew his request for a passport and asked the Finns to let him return to Russia. He went back to Moscow, where he attended the second Congress of the Comintern and was elected to the Comintern's executive committee.

At the Comintern's Congress, despite his continuing friendship with Lenin, Reed found that his plans for Communist strategy were overruled by Comintern leaders. Reed, however, remained loyal to the Comintern, and when he was ordered to make an arduous trip to a Comintern Congress in Baku, as a representative of the American proletariat, he obeyed. The trip was taken while Reed was in ill health, caused by his confinement in Finland. Shortly after his return from Baku, Reed died in Moscow in October 1920. Reed was so highly regarded by Lenin as a propaganda tool that he became the first (and is still the only) American to be buried in the Kremlin walls. His name was perpetuated in the United States when the Communists formed John Reed Clubs. In 1926, his *Ten Days That Shook the World* was reprinted with an introduction written by Lenin. The book is invariably described by leftists as an accurate historical account of the Bolshevik revolution. In fact, the book was written by one who knew little or nothing of Russian history, and who spoke little or no Russian. From his college days and throughout the ten remaining years of his life, he led an extremely narrow existence in an environment that was totally Red-oriented. At best, he was an idealistic adventurer who had failed in his two major attempts at reporting: Villa's revolution in Mexico and the war in Europe. When he became involved in the factional squabbles of the Communists in the United States and when he clashed with the Comintern personnel in Russia, he was a rank amateur among professionals. He was a dupe who died for a cause he didn't understand and whose leaders held his life cheap. But he was a worthwhile symbol for the Communist revolutionaries as an early American martyr. Former Communist Bertram D. Wolfe once wrote: "John Reed was as American as apple pie and store cheese. Yet he was one of the founders of the Communist International, and his ashes lie under the Kremlin wall. From a mansion in Portland, Oregon, through respectable Harvard College to the heart of Moscow – such was the trajectory of his life."

ELMER L. RICE was born Elmer L. Reizenstein on September 28, 1892 in New York City, son of Fanny Lion and Jacob Reizenstein. He was married to and divorced from Hazel Levy and Betty Field. His third wife was Barbara Marshall. He was an alumnus of New York Law School (LL.B., 1912). He studied dramatic composition at Columbia University. He was the author of many plays, including *On Trial* (1914); *Iron Cross* (1917); *Home of the Free* (1917); *For the Defense* (1919); *It Is the Law* (1922); *The Adding Machine* (1923); *Street Scene* (1929); *The Subway* (1929); *See Naples and Die* (1929); *The Left Bank* (1931); *Counsellor-at-Law* (1931); *Black Sheep* (1932); *We, The People* (1933); *Judgment Day* (1934); *Between Two Worlds* (1934); *Not For Children* (1936); *American Landscape* (1938); *Two on an Island* (1940); *Flight to the West* (1941); *A New Life* (1943); *Dream Girl* (1945); *The Grand Tour* (1951); *The Winner* (1954); *Cue for Passion* (1958); and *Love Among the Ruins* (1963). He was co-author of the plays *Wake up, Jona-*

than (1921); *Close Harmony* (1924); and *Cock Robin* (1927). He wrote *The Mongrel*, an adaptation of the German play by Hermann Bahr (1924), and *Is He Guilty?*, an adaptation of *The Blue Hawaii* by German Rudolph Lothar (1927). One of his plays, *A Diadem of Snow*, was serialized in *The Liberator* (1918). He was the author of several books, including *A Voyage to Purilia* (1930); *Imperial City* (1937); *The Show Must Go On* (1949); *The Living Theatre* (1959); and *Minority Report: An Autobiography* (1963). His omnibus volumes are *Plays* (1933); *Three Plays Without Words* (1934); *Two Plays* (1935); *Other Plays* (1935); *Seven Plays* (1950); and *Three Plays* (1965). He was the editor of *One Act Plays for Stage and Studies*, fifth series (French, 1929). He was a contributor to periodicals, including *Collier's* and *New Yorker*. In 1929, he received the Pulitzer Prize for his *Street Scene*.

From 1908 until 1912, Rice worked as a law clerk. In 1913, he was admitted to the New York bar, but he never practiced law. He experienced instant success as a playwright with his *On Trial*, produced in 1914. As a young man, he was dramatic director for the University Settlement and chairman of the Inter-Settlement Dramatic Society. From 1918 until 1920, he was a scenarist with Samuel Goldwyn Pictures Corporation. He was also a writer for Famous Players-Lasky Corporation and Real Art Films. He organized the Morningside Players in New York City. He was the owner and operator of the David Belasco Theatre. In 1935 and 1936, he was regional director for the Works Progress Administration's Federal Theatre Project, which proved to be a haven for leftwing theatrical personnel. From 1937 until 1959, he was director and co-founder of the Playwrights' Producing Company, and his associates

were Maxwell Anderson, S.N. Behrman, Sidney Howard, and Robert E. Sherwood. In 1954, he was a lecturer in English at the University of Michigan. In 1957 and 1958, he was an adjunct professor at New York University. He was president of the Dramatists' Guild and the Authors' League of America. He was a long-time national official of the ultra-leftist American Civil Liberties Union. He made frequent appeals and petitions on behalf of Communists. He was a confirmed Socialist but he insisted that he did not adhere to Marxism-Leninism and that his ideology did not embrace "any historical or economic dogma, but the development of a society in which the implements of production are employed primarily for the satisfaction of human needs, rather than for the enrichment and aggrandizement of a few individuals. There is no greater fallacy than the identification of the imperialism and totalitarianism of the Soviet Union with true socialism." He was never a member of the Socialist or any other party, and claimed his socialism was of the "utopian variety." In 1932, however, Rice campaigned for William Z. Foster and James W. Ford, the Communist Party candidates for president and vice president of the United States.

Rice was affiliated with the American Association of the United Nations (a leftist group); the American Committee for Democracy and Intellectual Freedom ("subversive and un-American" − "a Communist-front organization operating among college teachers and professors"); the American Committee for Protection of Foreign Born ("founded by the Communist Party in order to exploit racial divisions in the United States for its own revolutionary purposes"); the American League Against War and Fascism ("subversive and Communist" − "established in the United States in an effort to create public sentiment on behalf of a foreign policy adapted to the interests of the Soviet Union"); the American League for Peace and Democracy ("subversive and Communist" – "established . . . in an effort to create public sentiment on behalf of a foreign policy adapted to the interests of the Soviet Union . . . [and] designed to conceal Communist control, in accordance with the new tactics of the Communist International"); the American Committee for Spanish Freedom ("Communist"); the American Pushkin Committee ("Communist front"); American Relief for Greek Democracy (leftist); the American Round Table on India ("Communist front"); Artef ("Communist front" – "one of the oldest Communist Party organizations"); Citizens United To Abolish the Wood-Rankin Committee (pro-Communist project); the Committee Against Theatre Censorship ("Communist front"); the Committee of Welcome for the Red Dean of Canterbury (England's most notorious pro-Soviet apologist among the clergy); the Congress of American-Soviet Friendship ("Communist front"); the Coordinating Committee To Lift the [Spanish] Embargo ("one of the numerous Communist-front enterprises which were organized around the Communists' agitation over the Spanish Civil War"); the Council for Pan American Democracy ("subversive and Communist"); the Film and Photo League ("Communist front"); the Freedom House Bookshelf Committee (comprised of the most brazen leftists in the literary and academic world, promoting books by notable leftists); Friends of the Abraham Lincoln Brigade ("completely controlled by the Communist Party"); Friends of the Soviet Union ("created, directed, and controlled by the Communist Party . . . and operated

to aid and support Party objectives concerning the defense and support of the Soviet Union"); the Golden Book of American Friendship with the Soviet Union ("pro-Soviet propaganda enterprise"); *International Literature* ("official organ of the International Union of Revolutionary Writers, a Communist front"); the Interprofessional Association for Social Insurance ("Communist front"); the League of American Writers ("subversive and Communist" – "began openly to follow the Communist Party line as dictated by the foreign policy of the Soviet Union"); *Liberator* ("Communist magazine"); the Medical Bureau To Aid Spanish Democracy ("Communist enterprise"); Nation Associates (pro-Soviet); the National Citizens Emergency Relief Committee To Aid Strikers' Families (Socialist); the National Committee Against Censorship of Theatre Arts ("Communist Party cultural activity"); the National Council for a Fair Employment Practices Committee (ultraleftist); the National Committee for a Sane Nuclear Policy (ultra-leftist-pacifist); the National Committee To Win Amnesty for Smith Act Victims ("subversive" – "Communist"); the National Council for Civic Responsibility (an anti-anti-Communist group which was so leftist that its formation was hailed by the Communist Party); the National Council of American-Soviet Friendship ("subversive and Communist" – "specializing in pro-Soviet propaganda"); the National Council on Freedom from Censorship (ultra-leftist); the National Institute of Arts and Letters ("Communist front"); *New Masses* ("weekly journal of the Communist Party"); *New Theatre* ("Communist Party publication"); the Non-Partisan Committee for the Re-election of Congressman Vito Marcantonio ("Communist front"); Open Road ("Communist front"); the Rand School of Social Science (a Marxian-Socialist training school for labor agitators); Russian War Relief ("Communist enterprise"); *Soviet Russia Today* ("Communist-controlled publication"); the United World Federalists (the most prestigious group of fellow-travelers and dupes working for world government at the expense of United States sovereignty"); and the Writers and Artists Committee for Medical Aid to Spain ("a Communist front set up for the purpose of agitation and propaganda"). Rice died in May 1967.

EDWARD ALSWORTH ROSS was born on December 12, 1866 in Virden, Illinois, son of Rachel Alsworth and William Ross. He married Rosamond Simons. He was an alumnus of Coe College (A.B., 1886) and the Johns Hopkins University (Ph.D., 1891). He pursued graduate studies at the Univeristy of Berlin (1888-1889). He was the author of *Honest Dollars* (1896); *Social Control* (1901); *The Foundations of Sociology* (1905); *Sin and Society* (1907); *Social Psychology* (1908); *Latter Day Sinners and Saints* (1910); *The Changing Chinese* (1911); *Changing America* (1912); *The Old World in the New* (1914); *South of Panama* (1915); *Russia in Upheaval* (1918); *What Is America?* (1919); *The Principles of Sociology* (1920, 1930, and 1938); *The Russian Bolshevik Revolution* (1921); *The Social Trend* (1922); *The Social Revolution in Mexico* (1923); *The Outlines of Sociology* (1923); *The Russian Soviet Republic* (1923); *Roads to Social Peace* (1924); *Reports on the Employment of Native Labor in Portuguese Africa* (1925); *Civic Sociology* (1925 and 1933); *Standing Room Only?* (1927); *World Drift* (1928); *Seventy*

Years of It (1936); and *New Age Sociology* (1940). He was co-author of *Changes in the Size of American Families in One Generation* (1924) and *Readings in Civil Sociology* (1926).

In 1891 and 1892, Ross was a professor of economics at the University of Indiana. In 1892 and 1893, he was an associate professor of political economy and finance at Cornell University. From 1893 until 1900, he was professor of sociology at Stanford University. From 1901 until 1906, he was a professor of sociology at the University of Nebraska. From 1906 until 1937, he was a professor of sociology at the University of Wisconsin. He lectured in sociology at Harvard University (1902), the University of Chicago (1896 and 1905), and Northwestern University (1939). In 1892 and 1893, he was secretary of the American Economics Association. In 1914 and 1915, he was president of the American Sociological Society.

Through his studies at Berlin and Johns Hopkins, Ross was thoroughly imbued with Socialism with a distinctly European flavor. His closest academic associates were among the leading Socialists of the day. They included Richard T. Ely, Franklin H. Giddings, George Elliot Howard, Albion W. Small, and Lester F. Ward. He was a prominent member of the nation's most important Socialist groups: the American Fabian Society, the American Socialist Society, and the Socialist Party. He was a pioneer in the teaching and writing of sociology that was totally oriented to a Socialist, and even a Marxist, philosophy. He was dismissed from his teaching post at Stanford University in 1900 because of his radicalism.

Ross's affiliations included the ultra-leftist American Civil Liberties Union; the American Committee for Democracy and Intellectual Freedom ("subversive and un-American" – "a Communist-front organization operating among college teachers and professors"); the American Committee for Protection of Foreign Born ("founded by the Communist Party in order to exploit racial divisions in the United States for its own revolutionary purposes"); the American Committee To Save Refugees ("perform[ing] a most valuable function for the international Communist movement"); the American Council on Soviet Relations ("subversive" – "established by the Communist Party . . . directed and controlled by the Party, and operated to aid and support Party objectives concerning the defense and support of the Soviet Union"); the American Friends of the Chinese People ("Communist front"); the American Society for Cultural Relations with Russia ("Communist front"); the Berger National Foundation (Socialist); Brookwood Labor College ("Communistic"); the Friends of the Soviet Union ("created, directed, and controlled by the Communist Party . . . and operated to aid and support Party objectives concerning the defense and support of the Soviet Union"); the Golden Book of American Friendship with the Soviet Union ("pro-Soviet propaganda enterprise"); the Greater New York Emergency Conference on Inalienable Rights ("Communist front"); *International Literature* ("official organ of the International Union of Revolutionary Writers, a Communist front"); the Joint Committee on Unemployment (dominated by Socialists); the League for the Organization of Progress (dominated by Communists and Socialists); the National Emergency Conference ("Communist front"); the National Federation for Constitutional Liberties ("under Communist Party domination and headed by responsible Party functionaries" – "one of the

viciously subversive organizations of the Communist Party"); the National Popular Government League (dominated by Socialists); the National Save Our Schools Committee (pro-Communist); Peoples Legislative Service (Socialist); the Rand School of Social Science (a Marxian-Socialist training school for labor agitators); and Veterans of the Abraham Lincoln Brigade ("directed, dominated and controlled by the Communist Party"). Ross died in July 1951.

ISADORE RUBIN was born on June 5, 1912 in Wilmington, Delaware, son of Anna Salkind and Morris Rubin. He married Phyllis Cooper. He was an alumnus of the City College of New York (B.A., 1932, and M.S., 1933). He was the author of *150 Sex Questions and Answers* (1961) and *Sexual Life After Sixty* (1965). He was co-author of *Sex in the Adolescent Years: New Directions in Guiding and Teaching Youth*. He was the editor of *Homosexuals Today* (1965). He was a contributor to the *Journal of Marriage and the Family*, the *Medical Times*, and the *Journal of the Association of Women College Deans and Counselors.*

Prior to May 1950, Rubin was a high school teacher of English in the New York City school system. In 1950 and 1951, he was one of eight teachers who underwent a series of trials conducted by the New York City Board of Education. The teachers, including Rubin, were dismissed from the school system on the ground that they had refused to answer questions concerning their membership in the Communist Party. The dismissal was effective in February 1951. In October 1951, Rubin entered the employ of the New York City's Teachers Union (United Public Workers of America). He became a member of the Union's executive committee and co-chairman of its political committee. He was also editor of the Union's newspaper, *Teachers News*. Since at least 1938, the Teachers Union had been completely under the control of Communists, and in 1950, it was expelled from the CIO on grounds that the policies and activities were "consistently directed toward the achievement of the program and the purposes of the Communist Party rather than the objectives and policies set forth in the CIO constitution." As for *Teachers News*, it had a long history of publishing the Communist line and serving as a propaganda outlet and publicity medium for Communist fronts and Communist Party enterprises.

In 1952, Rubin testified before the Senate Internal Security Subcommittee. He proved to be an obstreperous, argumentative, and thoroughly uncooperative witness. When asked about his membership in the Communist Party, he pleaded the Fifth Amendment, and — most unusual — also pleaded the Fifth Amendment when asked if he had been a member of the Communist Party while serving in the U.S. Army during World War II. Rubin remained with the Teachers Union and *Teachers News* until 1956. In 1956, he became managing editor of *Sexology* magazine. Later, he became editor of *Lux* magazine. From 1964 until 1970, he was the treasurer and director of the Sex Information and Education Council of the United States (SIECUS), and was editor of the Council's newsletter. Under his supervision, SIECUS, with the cooperation of federal, state, and municipal agencies, promoted a successful nationwide campaign to saturate public and private schools with sex education programs. In various guises, the programs were foisted upon high school and elementary school children. The literature promoted by and provided by SIECUS was often the product of fellow-travelers and aroused a great deal of controversy.

Rubin was a member of the American Association of Marriage Counsellors and the National Council on Family Relations. He was a member of the Communist Party as early as 1944. He was also associated with the American Committee for Protection of Foreign Born ("founded by the Communist Party in order to exploit racial divisions in the United States for its own revolutionary purposes") and the Conference for Legislation in the National Interest ("under complete domination by the Communist Party"). He died in August 1970.

HAROLD ORDWAY RUGG was born on January 17, 1886 in Fitchburg, Massachusetts, son of Merion Davidson and Edward Rugg. He was married to and divorced from Bertha Miller and Louise Krueger. His third wife was Elizabeth Page. He was an alumnus of Dartmouth College (B.S., 1908, and B.S.C.E., 1909) and the University of Illinois (Ph.D., 1915). He was the author of *Experimental Determination of Mental Discipline in School Studies* (1916); *Statistical Methods Applied to Education* (1917); *The Reconstruction of Mathematics* (1918); *Home Economics in American Schools* (1921); *The Social Science Pamphlets*, 12 volumes (1921-1928); *A Primer of Graphics and Statistics* (1925); *Syllabus of the Course in the Psychology of the Elementary School Subjects* (1926); *The Child Centered School* (1928); *Introduction to American Civilization* (1929), revised edition, *Our Country and Our People* (1938); *Changing Civilizations in the Modern World* (1930), revised edition, *Changing Countries and Changing Peoples* (1938); *Introduction to Problems of*

American Culture (1931); revised edition, *Community and National Life* (1940); *Culture and Education in America* (1931); *A History of American Civilization − Economic and Social* (1931); *A History of American Government and Culture* (1931); *Changing Governments and Changing Cultures* (1932); *The Great Technology* (1933); *American Life and the School Curriculum* (1936); *The First Book of the Earth* (1936); *Nature Peoples* (1936); *Communities of Men* (1936); *Peoples and Countries* (1936); *The Building of America* (1936); *Man at Work: His Industries* (1936); *Man at Work: His Arts and Crafts* (1937); *America's March Toward Democracy* (1937); *The Conquest of America* (1937); *Mankind Throughout the Ages* (1938); *Citizenship and Civic Affairs* (1940); *That Men May Understand: An American in the Long Armistice* (1941); *Now Is the Moment* (1943); *Foundations for American Education* (1947); *The Teacher of Teachers* (1952); and *Imagination*, posthumously (1963). He was co-author of *Fundamentals of High School Mathematics* (1918) and *The Teacher in School and Society* (1950). He was the founder and editor of the New World Education Series (from 1950). He was the editor of *Readings in the Foundation of Education,* two volumes (1940). He was editor of the *Journal of Educational Psychology* (1920-1931) and *Frontiers of Democracy* (1939-1943). He was social studies editor of *Scholastic Magazine* (1930-1940). He was on the editorial board of *Social Frontier* (1934-1939).

From 1909 until 1911, Rugg was an assistant professor in civil engineering at Millikin University in Decatur, Illinois. From 1911 until 1915, he was an instructor of engineering drawing at the University of Illinois. From 1915 until 1920, he was, successively, an instructor, assistant professor, and associate professor of education at the University of Chicago. From 1920 until 1951, he was a professor of education at Columbia University's Teachers College. In 1951, he became professor emeritus. In 1952 and 1953, he was a Fulbright Lecturer in Egypt. In 1953 and 1954, he was a visiting professor at the University of Puerto Rico. From 1921 until 1923, he was president of the Educational Research Association. In 1925, he was a member of the Philippine Educational Commission and the Puerto Rico Education Commission.

At Teachers College, and in his writing, Rugg was one of the all-time great promoters of social science. He participated in the revolutionary educational reforms promoted by progressive educators John Dewey and William H. Kilpatrick and a host of their colleagues and disciples.

Rugg, as an educationist, was throughly dissatisfied with the traditional methods of teaching individual subjects, such as geography, economics, history, and political science in American schools. He believed that such studies should be amalgamated into one subject: social science. It was his belief that the best way of life for America was "democracy." To him, democracy was a religion, and democratic education was the catechism and creed of that religion. He believed that if enough Americans were given a democratic education, the United States would be a democracy and, he hoped, a leader in a world of democracies. He further believed that if the United States handed out enough bribes in the form of "foreign aid," the nations of the world would become democratic.

Throughout most of his writings, when Rugg talked about democracy, he was not talking about a form of government, but rather a type of society. His ultimate dream was that there would be one international government protecting one democratic society. But first, of course, he was interested in creating a democratic society in America. The creation, he believed, could be accomplished through education by professional teachers with the full cooperation of the government. In simple terms, he wanted a planned society. He vehemently denied that he was sympathetic toward Communism, Socialism, fascism, or any other totalitarian system. Yet at the same time, the government he wanted to see protecting the American democratic society would have as its objective the providing of total cradle-to-grave security for every American. The government would provide "work, a place on the land, and credit or monetary means . . . health and enjoyment of life, social security, education, rest, recreation, and adventure."

Rugg was not happy with the way in which American society had developed through the contributions of unregimented, undisciplined individuals. He did not like the concept that society was the product of man; he wanted man to be the product of society. He did not like the concept of the family as a spiritually oriented group. He would have preferred to have the family serve as an educational training center, promoting democracy, promoting the ideal of social order, and promoting conformity. In simple terms, he placed society above family in the order of importance, just as he placed it above the individual.

Until the family could be imbued with a crusading fervor for democracy, the burden of indoctrination would fall upon professional educators. The edu-

cator, in his opinion, was the "chosen change agent, the clear guide for the culture-molding process." The school in which such a teacher worked was nothing more nor less than an "enterprise in guided living." The guided living would require the professional educator to be highly selective in what he imparted to students, in order that the students should become democratic-minded. Eventually such students, as family leaders, would be able to supplement the work of professional teachers. Such brainwashed family leaders were provided with mandates by Rugg: "(1) The family should help its members to understand the great world problem of organization for peace. (2) It should also help its members to understand, as well as possible, the problem of full employment and full production and the political and economic issues involved in it. (3) It should help children and youth to become aware of the great forces that have been, and are now, changing American life. The family should resist cultural change. It must assist youth to understand change, to adjust to change, and to begin to assess what is good and bad in the new and old. (4) The family also should make youth realize the great influence of science and free thought in promoting American social progress, the importance of facts and reason, and thegreat and cherished American heritage of intellectual and personal freedom. (5) The family must finally play its part in creating an awareness of the need for greater social control in a society that is becoming interdependent, of the need for cooperation as well as individual freedom, and of group objectives and behavior as well as purely individualistic goals and behavior."

In the midst of World War II, Rugg viewed President Franklin Delano Roosevelt as the ideal instrument through which world-wide democracy could be promoted. He asked the President to create an Office of Education for Peace. He was hopeful that the President would authorize a massive and incessant propaganda campaign to convince Americans of the desirability of democracy. The propaganda would consist of eight points that, if taken completely to heart by the American people, would unite them in a crusade for world government and a universal democratic society. Rugg's eight points were: "The idea that every nation on earth must be disarmed . . . that all armaments be pooled and administered by a central world 'police force.' — The idea that in worth and dignity, in sovereignty and personality, all individuals and peoples of the earth are equal and there shall be no more imperial exploitation of the weak by the strong. — The idea of the fragile interdependence of our people with the other industrialized peoples of the earth . . . so that most of the human race now stand or fall together. — The idea that now we have on this continent the makings of a great civilization — the abundant life . . . that things are plentiful, not scarce, as our fathers said. — The idea that a people as rich as ours, need not fear a debt, even as large and growing as is ours. — The idea that the farms and factories can safely be run at full employment in peace-time as well as in war. — The idea that the government can take vigorous steps to prevent a depression at the close of Today's War Abroad. — The idea that a people can afford whatever it can produce."

Throughout his entire career at Teachers College and through all his prolific writings, Rugg taught the very same ideas that were promulgated by individuals who were bent on creating social democracy — their polite euphemism for Socialism. They controlled the major departments at Columbia University and they had their imitators in other universities and teachers' colleges throughout the nation. Some proudly proclaimed their adherence to Socialism. Some flaunted their ties with Communism. Some, like Rugg, denied vehemently their adherence to anything but democracy, which in their strange lexicon acquired an aura of sanctity. At least Rugg did admit in the full context of his work that he was striving for conformity in a materialistic society. He preferred conformity and order to individualism because he felt that individualism in most instances was passé. He expressed that view in these terms: "We can see now that in the modern complex world no individual is really 'free.' Hour after hour, year after year, he is poured into the mold of existing family, neighborhood, and national culture. He becomes essentially what his psychological environment makes him . . . . This is not to deny the large role of inherited capacities for original invention. Because of them a few individuals of unusual initiative do break through the molding influences of the family, the neighborhood, and the other groups in which they live, reacting against certain aspects of the culture and perhaps succeeding in making some of them over. But the ingrained idea of the 'free' individual, certainly as freedom was conceived of in the simple frontier world of earlier days, must be given up. The social structure today impinges heavily and inescapably on each individual life. Individual and society form a single integral organic structure from which no separate individual can escape to lead a 'free,' uninfluenced life."

In the 1920's and 1930's, textbooks written by or under the direction of Rugg literally saturated hundreds of school systems in the United States. The teaching of social science had become commonplace and this development was due in great part to Rugg. In the late 1930's and early 1940's, however, the content of Rugg's books came under fire from individuals who at long last realized what Rugg was trying to do. It was not that his critics were alarmed at the corruption he had perpetrated by promoting the integration of various studies into social science. They were alarmed at what they suspected to be un-American, pro-Communist, or pro-Socialist ideas. Few realized that Rugg was not wedded to anything but a materialistic conformity that could be imposed more easily than the better-known isms of Communism and Socialism. In substance, however, his "democracy" did not differ essentially from any totalitarianism. He died in May 1960.

CHARLES EDWARD RUSSELL was born on September 25, 1860 in Davenport, Iowa, son of Lydia Rutledge and Edward Russell. He was married to the late Abby Rust. His second wife was Theresa Hirschl. He graduated from St. Johnsbury (Vermont) Academy in 1881. He was the author of *Such Stuff As Dreams* (1902); *The Twin Immortalities* (1904); *The Greatest Trust in the World* (1905); *The Uprising of the Many* (1907); *Lawless Wealth* (1908); *Thomas Chatterton, the Marvelous Boy* (1908); *Songs of Democracy* (1909); *Why I Am a Socialist* (1910); *Business, the Heart of the Nation* (1911); *The Passing Show* (1912); *Stories of the Great Railroads* (1912); *These Shifting Scenes* (1914); *The Story of Wendell Phillips* (1915); *Unchained Russia* (1918); *After the Whirlwind* (1919); *Bolshevism and the*

United States (1919); *The Story of the Non-Partisan League* (1920); *The Outlook for the Philippines* (1922); *Railroads, Melons, Rates and Wages* (1922); *The Hero of the Filipinos – José Rizal* (1923); *Julia Marlowe – Her Life and Art* (1926); *The American Orchestra and Theodore Thomas* (1927); *A-Rafting on the Mississipp'* (1928); *An Hour of American Poetry* (1929); *From Sandy Hook to 62°* (1929); *Haym Salomon and the Revolution* (1930); *Blaine of Maine* (1931); and *Bare Hands and Stone Walls* (1933).

Between 1877 and 1884, Russell was with his father's newspaper, the *Davenport* (Iowa) *Gazette*, as typesetter, telegraph editor, and managing editor. In 1884, he was night editor of the *Minneapolis Tribune*. In 1885, he was managing editor of the *Minneapolis Journal*. In 1886, he was managing editor of the *Detroit Tribune*. Between 1886 and 1892, he was a reporter for the *New York Commercial Advertiser, New York Times, New York World*, and *New York Herald*. From 1892 until 1894, he was assistant city editor of the *New York Herald*. From 1894 until 1897, he was city editor of the *New York World*. From 1897 until 1900, he was a managing editor of the *New York American*. From 1900 until 1902, he was publisher of the *Chicago American and Examiner*. After 1902, he was a free-lance writer and lecturer. In 1928, he received the Pulitzer Prize in biography for his *The American Orchestra and Theodore Thomas*.

In 1917, President Woodrow Wilson sent Russell to Russia, with the rank of envoy extraordinary, on a special diplomatic mission. In 1918, Russell lectured throughout the United States on behalf of the U.S. Committee of Public Information. In 1919, he was the Committee's commissioner to Great Britain and Ireland, and toured Europe, speaking under the auspices of the Committee. In 1919, he was a member of the President's Industrial Commission.

Russell was a very active member of the Socialist Party. He received the Party's nomination for governor of New York (1910 and 1912), United States Senator (1914), and mayor of New York City (1913), and was an unsuccessful candidate for the Party's nomination for President (1912 and 1916). During the course of World War I, he was one of the very few Socialist leaders who did not march under the banner of pacifism to oppose the United States involvement in the war. Although he differed in this matter from most Socialists, he pleaded on their behalf when they were imprisoned for their wartime conduct.

Russell was a founder of the ultra-radical National Association for the Advancement of Colored People. His other affiliations included the American Friends of Spanish Democracy ("Communist front"); the Berger National Foundation (Socialist); the Coordinating Committee To Lift the [Spanish] Embargo ("one of the numerous Communist-front enterprises which were organized around the Communists' agitation over the Spanish Civil War"); the League for Industrial Democracy ("the most influential Socialist educational and proselytizing group on American university and college campuses"); the League of American Writers ("subversive and Communist" – "began openly to follow the Communist Party line as dictated by the foreign policy of the Soviet Union"); the Marcus Graham Freedom of the Press Committee (an ultra-radical group in support of an anarchist); the National Emergency Conference ("Communist front"); the Na-

tional Federation for Constitutional Liberties ("under Communist Party domination and headed by responsible Party functionaries" – "one of the viciously subversive organizations of the Communist Party"); the Non-Partisan League (Socialist); the Public Ownership League of America (Socialist); the Washington Committee for Aid to China ("Communist-controlled"); and the Washington Committee To Lift [the] Spanish Embargo ("Communist front"). He died in April 1941.

CARL SANDBURG was born on January 6, 1878 in Galesburg, Illinois, son of Clara Anderson and August Sandburg. He married Lillian Steichen. He attended Lombard College (1898-1902). He was the author of *In Reckless Ecstasy* (1904); *The Plaint of a Rose* (1905); *Incidentals* (1905); *You and Your Job* (1906); *Chicago Poems* (1916); *Cornhuskers* (1918); *The Chicago Race Riots, July, 1919* (1919); *Smoke and Steel* (1920); *Rootabaga Stories* (1922); *Slabs of the Sunburnt West* (1922); *Rootabaga Pigeons* (1923); *Selected Poems of Carl Sandburg* (1926); *Songs of America* (1926); *Abraham Lincoln: The Prairie Years*, two volumes (1927); *Abe Lincoln Grows Up*, children's version (1928); *Good Morning, America* (1928); *Rootabaga Country: Selections from Rootabaga Stories and Rootabaga Pigeons* (1929); *Steichen, The Photographer* (1929); *Early Moon* (1930); *Potato Face* (1930); *The People, Yes* (1936); *Smoke and Steel* [and] *Slabs of the Sunburnt West*, reprint (1938); *A Lincoln and Whitman Miscellany* (1938); *Abraham Lincoln: The War Years*, four volumes (1939); *Abraham Lincoln: The Sangamon Edition*, six volumes (1940); *Bronze Wood* (1941); *Storm Over the Land* (1942); *Smoke and Steel, Slabs of* the *Sunburnt West* [and] *Good Morning America*, omnibus volume (1942); *Home Front Memo* (1943), *Poems of the Midwest*, two volumes (1946); *The Lincoln Reader: An Appreciation* (1947); *Remembrance Rock*, novel (1948); *Lincoln Collector, the Story of Oliver R. Barrett's Great Private Collection* (1949); *Complete Poems* (1950); *Always the Young Strangers*, autobiography (1952); *A Lincoln Preface* (1953); *Abraham Lincoln: The Prairie Years and the War Years*, one-volume condensation of previous six volumes (1954); *Prairie-Town Boy* (1955); *The Sandburg Range* (1957); *The Fiery Trail* (1959); *Address Before a Joint Session of Congress, February 12, 1959* (1959), or, *Carl Sandburg on Abraham Lincoln* (1959), or, *Abraham Lincoln, 1809-1859* (1959); *Abraham Lincoln*, three-volume condensation of earlier work (1959); *Harvest Poems, 1910-1960* (1960); *Wind Song* (1960); *Six New Poems and a Parable* (1960); *Address Upon the Occasion of Abraham Lincoln's One Hundredth Inaugural Anniversary* (1961); *Honey and Salt* (1963); *The Wedding Procession of the Rag Doll and the Broom Handle and Who Was in It* (1967); and *The Letters of Carl Sandburg* (1968). He compiled and edited material for *The American Songbag* (1927) and *Carl Sandburg's New American Songbag* (1950). He was co-author of *Mary Lincoln, Wife and Widow* (1932) and *Photographs of Abraham Lincoln* (1944). He wrote the commentary for the government film *Bomber*. He wrote the captions for Edward Steichen's mural photography, *Road to Victory*, and he wrote the prologue for Steichen's photographic exhibit, *The Family of Man*. He was a contributor to *Tomorrow, Poetry, Saturday Evening Post, Little Review,* *New Leader, Nation,* and *Playboy.*

Among the prizes and awards Sandburg received were the Helen Haire Levinson prize ($200) for "Chicago," published in *Poetry* for March 1914; Poetry Society of America Prize (co-winner, 1919 and 1920); Royal Order of the North Star, conferred on him by the Swedish government (1938); Commander of the Royal Order of the North Star, conferred on him by the Swedish government (1953); a special gold medal presented to him by the King of Sweden for his accomplishments in fine arts (1959); election to membership in the Amerian Academy of Arts and Letters (1940); the American Academy of Arts and Letters' gold medal for historical and biographical poetry (1952); Poetry Society of America medal (1953); Tamiment Institute Award (1953); silver medal of the Civil War Round Table (1954); Award of Merit from the University of Lousville (1955); the Albert Einstein Award of Yeshiva College (1956); and the Presidential Medal of Freedom (1964).

In 1904, after a few years of wandering and doing odd jobs and a brief fling at collegiate studies, Sandburg began his lifetime writing career. In 1907, he began a lifetime career in Socialism. From 1907 until 1910, he was district organizer in Milwaukee for the Social Democratic Party of Wisconsin. At the same time, he found an outlet for his Socialist writings in the *International Socialist Review* and *La Follette's Weekly*. From 1910 until 1912, he was secretary to Milwaukee's Socialist mayor, Emil Seidel. From 1912 until 1917, in Chicago, Sandburg's Socialist writings appeared in the *Daily Socialist*, for which he was a feature writer; *System* magazine, of which he was an associate editor; and *Day Book* and the

American Federation of Labor's literature, for which he was a reporter.

In 1917, Sandburg was for a brief period an editorial writer for the *Chicago American*. From 1917 until 1928, he was a reporter and motion-picture editor for the *Chicago Daily News*. In 1918, he went to Norway and Sweden, ostensibly to report on the Finnish revolution as a correspondent for the Newspaper Enterprise Association. From 1941 until 1945, he wrote a weekly syndicated column for the *Chicago Times*, and during the same period he made radio broadcasts for the Red-lined Office of War Information.

Probably no literary figure in American history enjoyed more adulation than Sandburg. No matter what he wrote – history, biography, fiction, poetry, or folksongs – he reaped kudos from the liberal critics. He became a legend in his own time despite his pedestrian histories, his romanticized biographies, and his indecipherable poetry, which was laced with a highly affected pseudo-patriotism. He and his idolizing fellow ideologues worked overtime to portray him as a homespun philosopher and spokesman for the "common" man. Sandburg made his own contribution to the contrived image when he wrote: "I am the people – the mob – the crowd – the mass. Did you know that all the work of the world is done through me?" On another occasion he said: "I am a Christian, a Quaker, a Moslem, a Buddhist, a Shintoist, a Confucian, and maybe a Catholic pantheist or a Joan of Arc who hears voices – I am all of these and more."

On February 12, 1959, Sandburg was the first private citizen ever to address a joint session of the Congress of the United States. His appearance came about because of his writings on Lincoln, whose birthday was being memorialized.

No other Lincoln scholar, whatever his level of scholarly competence, has ever received such notice from the Congress.

More than thirty colleges gave Sandburg honorary degrees. Many schools throughout the United States were named in his honor. High school reading lists for history, poetry, and literature classes are saturated with Sandburg's works.

Sandburg was affiliated with the American Committee for Protection of Foreign Born ("founded by the Communist Party in order to exploit racial divisions in the United States for its own revolutionary purposes"); the American Peace Mobilization ("formed . . . under the auspices of the Communist Party and the Young Communist League" – "one of the most seditious organizations which ever operated in the United States"); the American Rescue Ship Mission ("Communist Party project"); the American Writers Congress ("subversive"); the Federated Press ("certain Communist fronts are organized for the purpose of promulgating Communist ideas and misinformation into the bloodstream of public opinion. Examples of such organizations are the . . . Federated Press"); Friends of the Abraham Lincoln Brigade ("completely controlled by the Communist Party"); the Friends of the Soviet Union ("created, directed, and controlled by the Communist Party . . . and operated to aid and support Party objectives concerning the defense and support of the Soviet Union"); the Joint Anti-Fascist Refugee Committee ("subversive and Communist"); *Masses* ("Communist publication"); the Musicians' Congress Committee ("Communist front"); the National Committee To Abolish the Un-American Committee ("to lead and direct the Communist Party's 'Operation Abolition' campaign"); the National Council of American-Soviet Friendship ("subversive and Communist" — "specializing in pro-Soviet propaganda"); and the United American Spanish Aid Committee ("subversive and Communist"). He died in July 1967.

Maurice Malkan — a former Communist Party official — in his *Return to My Father's House*, published in 1972, wrote of an occasion in 1919 when he and some of his fellow Communists were "shocked to learn that the poet, Carl Sandburg, had been detained by U.S. Customs officials in New York. He was one of our mainstays among American intellectuals, and had gone to the Scandinavian countries and Finland as a correspondent — and as a Soviet courier. We had eagerly awaited his return with an important message from Lenin and a large quantity of money and literature. News that he had been detained on his arrival caused great concern .... After a while, we received a call from the Customs House. A $10,000 check to [Santeri] Nuorteva [Communist leader of the Finnish Socialist Federation], drawn on a New York bank, had been taken away from Sandburg, and he was being held for questioning. A week later the poet appeared at our office, accompanied by Charles Recht, legal representative of the Soviet government from 1917 until his death nearly a half-century later. Sandburg had been permitted to retain the messages from Lenin, which were later translated as *A Letter to American Working Men*, and published in *The Revolutionary Age* and *The Liberator*. Carl Sandburg remained a loyal friend to the Soviet Union — a friendship that continued for decades .... "

ARTHUR MEIER SCHLESINGER was born on February 27, 1888 in Xenia, Ohio, son of Katharine Feurle and Bernhard Schlesinger. He married Elizabeth Bancroft. He was an alumnus of Ohio State University (A.B., 1910) and Columbia University (Ph.D., 1918). He was the author of *The Colonial Merchants and the American Revolution* (1918); *Salmon Portland Chase* (1919); *New Viewpoints in American History* (1922); *Political and Social History of the United States* (1925); *Historical Scholarship in America* (1932); *Political and Social Growth of the United States* (1933), reissued as *Political and Social Growth of the American People* (1941), abridged edition published as *The Rise of Modern America* (1951); *The Rise of the City, 1878-1898*, a part of "A History of American Life" (1933); *The New Deal in Action* (1938); *Learning How to Behave, Historical Study of American Etiquette Books* (1946); *Paths to the Present* (1949 and 1963); *The American as Reformer* (1950); *Prelude to Independence: The Newspaper War on Britain, 1764-1776* (1957); *In Retrospect: The History of a Historian* (1963); and *The Birth of the Nation* (1968). He was co-author of *A Syllabus of United States History* (1915); *A New Syllabus of American Political History* (1925 and 1928); *The Reinterpretation of American Literature* (1928); *Research in the Social Sciences* (1929); *Essays on Research in the Social Sciences* (1931); *Historical Scholarship in America* (1932); *Approaches to American Social History* (1937); *Land of the Free* (1944); and *Harvard Guide to American History* (1954). He was the editor of *The Atlantic Migration* (1940); *Immigration in American History* (1940); and *The Cotton Kingdom* (1953). He was co-editor of *A History of American Life*, thirteen volumes (1927-1948). He was on the editorial board of *New England*

Quarterly (1928-1965). He received the Justin Winsor prize from the American Historical Association for his *The Colonial Merchants and the American Revolution*.

From 1912 until 1919, Schlesinger was successively an instructor, assistant professor, and professor of American history at Ohio State University. From 1919 until 1924, he was a professor of American history and head of the department of history at the University of Iowa. From 1924 until 1965, he was at Harvard University as professor of history (1924-1939), Francis Lee Higginson Professor (1939-1954), and professor emeritus (1954-1965). In 1934, he was a visiting professor at the University of London and the University of Edinburgh. In 1948 and 1949, he was a visiting lecturer at the University of Leyden. From 1942 until 1946, he was a member of the U.S. Government Committee on Records of War Administration. From 1951 until 1955, and from 1961 until 1965, he was a member of the National Historical Publications Committee. From 1943 until 1946, he was a member of the Commission on Freedom of the Press, an ultra-leftist project. From 1948 until 1954, he was chairman of the United Labor Committee of Massachusetts. He was president of the American Historical Association (1942); and the New England History Teachers Association (1938-1939). He was a member (1924-1941) and chairman (1930-1933) of the leftist-oriented Social Science Research Council.

Schlesinger was one of the most widely read and praised historians of his era. He belonged to the liberal socialistic school of historians that came out of Columbia University's progressive milieu of social scientists who believed that highly selective teachings and writings would produce social democrats for a social democracy.

Schlesinger was affiliated with the ultra-leftist American Civil Liberties Union; the American Committee for Democracy and Intellectual Freedom ("subversive and un-American" – "a Communist-front organization operating among college teachers and professors"); the American Friends of Spanish Democracy ("Communist front"); the American Student Union ("without exception . . . supported defense of teachers and students charged with Communist activity" – "pliable instrument of the Communist Party"); the ultra-radical Americans for Democratic Action; the Civil Rights Congress ("created and established by the Communist Party as an organization which would utilize defense of civil rights for Party purposes and raise and maintain mass defense and bail funds for Party use"); the National Citizens' Political Action Committee ("Communist front"); the National Emergency Conference ("Communist front"); the National Emergency Conference for Democratic Rights ("Communist front" – "subversive"); and the National Federation for Constitutional Liberties ("under Communist Party domination and headed by responsible Party functionaries" – "one of the viciously subversive organizations of the Communist Party"). He died in October 1965.

VIDA D. SCUDDER was born on December 15, 1861 in Madura, India, daughter of Harriet Dutton and David Scudder, American citizens. She was an alumna of Smith College (A.B., 1884 and A.M., 1889). She also pursued graduate studies in England, France, and Italy. She was the author of *The Life of the Spirit in the Modern Poets* (1895);

The Witness of Denial (1896); *Social Ideals in English Letters* (1898); *Introduction to the Study of English Literature* (1901); *A Listener in Babel* (1903); *The Disciple of a Saint* (1907); *Socialism and Character* (1912); *The Church and the Hour* (1917); *The Morte d'Arthur of Sir Thomas Malory, Introduction to Arthurian Romance* (1917); *Social Teachings of the Christian Year* (1921); *Brother John — A Tale of the First Franciscans* (1927); *The Franciscan Adventure* (1931); *On Journey* (1937); *The Privilege of Age: Essays, Secular and Spiritual* (1939); *Father Huntington* (1940); and *My Quest for Reality* (1952). She was the editor of Macaulay's *Lord Clive* (1889); *Introduction to the Writings of John Ruskin* (1890); Shelley's *Prometheus Unbound* (1892); *Works of John Woolman* (1910); Bede's *History of England* (1911); and *English Poems* (1915). She was translator and editor of *Selected Letters of St. Catherine of Siena* (1905).

From 1892 until 1927, Scudder served successively as instructor, assistant professor, associate professor, and professor of English literature at Wellesley College. In 1927, she retired as professor emeritus.

As a young woman, Scudder began a lifetime career as a Socialist. She was a member of the Society of Christian Socialists. She was a charter member of the Christian Social Union (Socialist). She was an organizer of the Socialist-oriented College Settlement Association. She was on the executive committee of the Intercollegiate Socialist Society (1912-1916) and vice president of its successor organization, the League for Industrial Democracy (1921-1954) — the most important educational and proselytizing Socialist organization on American university and college campuses. She was a member of the Church Socialist League and the Church League for Industrial Democracy — both completely Socialist in their principles and activities. She was a teacher at the Rand School of Social Science — a Marxian-Socialist training school for labor agitators. She was an early and long-time official of the ultra-leftist American Civil Liberties Union.

Scudder was also affiliated with the American Committee for Democracy and Intellectual Freedom ("subversive and un-American" — "a Communist-front organization operating among college teachers and professors"); the American Committee for Protection of Foreign Born ("founded by the Communist Party in order to exploit racial divisions in the United States for its own revolutionary purposes"); the American Committee To Save Refugees ("perform[ing] a most valuable function for the international Communist movement"); the American Friends of Spanish Democracy ("Communist front"); the American League for Peace and Democracy ("subversive and Communist" — "established . . . in an effort to create public sentiment on behalf of a foreign policy adapted to the interests of the Soviet Union . . . [and] designed to conceal Communist control, in accordance with the new tactics of the Communist International"); the American Student Union ("without exception . . . supported defense of teachers and students charged with Communist activity" — "pliable instrument in the hands of the Communist Party"); the American Writers Congress ("subversive"); the Berger National Foundation (Socialist); Brookwood Labor College ("Communistic"); the Civil Rights Congress ("created and established by the Communist Party as an organization which would utilize defense of civil rights for Party purposes and raise and maintain mass defense and bail funds for Party use"); the Committee for Free Political Advocacy ("Communist front"); the Committee To Aid Families of Smith Act Victims (pro-Communist); the Committee To Defend Alexander Trachtenberg ("pro-Communist"); Commonwealth College ("Communist"); the Coordinating Committee To Lift the [Spanish] Embargo ("one of the numerous Communist-front enterprises which were organized around the Communists' agitation over the Spanish Civil War"); the Greater New York Emergency Conference on Inalienable Rights ("Communist front"); *Il Nuovo Mondo* National Committee ("pro-Communist"); the National Federation for Constitutional Liberties ("under Communist Party domination and headed by responsible Party functionaries" − "one of the viciously subversive organizations of the Communist Party"); an Open Letter for Closer Cooperation with the Soviet Union (issued by "a group of Communist Party stooges"); the *Protestant* ("with an eye to religious groups, the Communists have formed religious fronts such as the *Protestant*"); the *Protestant Digest* ("a magazine which has faithfully propagated the Communist Party line under the guise of being a religious journal"); the Reichstag Fire Trial Anniversary Committee ("Communist front . . . formed . . . by prominent Communists and Communist sympathizers"); Russian War Relief ("Communist enterprise"); the Sacco-Vanzetti National League (part of a Communist propaganda campaign); the Stockholm Peace Appeal ("Communist 'peace' campaign"); Veterans of the Abraham Lincoln Brigade ("directed, dominated and controlled by the Com-

munist Party"); the Washington Committee To Lift [the] Spanish Embargo ("Communist front"); and the World Peace Congress ("organized under Communist initiative in various countries throughout the world").

Scudder died in October 1954.

GEORGE H. SELDES was born on November 16, 1890 in Alliance, New Jersey, son of Anna Saphro and George Seldes. He married Helen Wiesman. In 1912 and 1913, he attended Harvard University. He was the author of *You Can't Print That* (1929); *Can These Things Be* (1931); *World Panorama* (1933); *The Vatican Yesterday − Today From America* (1934); *Sawdust Caesar* (1935); *Freedom of the Press* (1935); *Lords of the Press* (1938); *You Can't Do That* (1938); *The Catholic Crisis* (1940); *Witch Hunt* (1940); *The Facts Are* (1942); *Facts and Fascism* (1943); *One Thousand Americans* (1947); *The People Don't Know* (1949); *Tell the Truth and Run* (1952); *The Great Quotations* (1961); and *Never Tire of Protesting* (1968).

In 1909 and 1910, Seldes was a reporter for the *Pittsburgh Leader*. Between 1910 and 1916, he was a copy desk editor and night editor of the *Pittsburgh Post*. In 1916, he was managing editor of *Pulitzer's Review*. In 1916 and 1917, he worked for the United Press in London. In 1917 and 1918, he was a reporter for the Army edition in Paris of the *Chicago Tribune* and a correspondent with the American Expeditionary Forces in France. From 1919 until 1927, he worked for the *Chicago Tribune* as an assistant to the *Tribune's* London correspondent, as acting head of the *Tribune's* Berlin bureau, as a Moscow correspondent, and as head of the *Tribune's* Rome bureau. From 1928 until 1970, he was a free-lance writer, except for a stint in 1936 and 1937 as a war correspondent in Spain for the *New York Post*. He contributed articles to *Saturday Evening Post, Harper's, Scribner's, McCall's, Nation,* and *New Republic*.

In 1940, Seldes began a ten-year career of publishing *In Fact*, a newsletter. He said when he first began publishing that he would print "the real inside news, the kind newspapers frequently get but dare not print." He was going to "fight Fascism." He explained: "The viewpoint of *In Fact* is simple: it is in favor of every idea, movement and organization that is for what we carelessly call liberalism, democracy, progress, but it intends to show up the frauds which hide behind these words; it is pro-labor, and especially pro-progressive labor. It believes in the 'general welfare' as written in the Constitution and challenges any publication feeding out of the hand of Big Business to prove by acts that its policy is the same."

After *In Fact* had been published for only four years, the Special Committee on Un-American Activities cited it as a Communist front. Seldes claimed that *In Fact's* circulation had reached a high of 176,000, but it fell to 55,000 by 1950, and Seldes stopped publishing it.

Seldes was affiliated with the American Committee for Democracy and Intellectual Freedom ("subversive and un-American" – "a Communist-front organization operating among college teachers and professors"); the American Committee for Protection of Foreign Born ("founded by the Communist Party in order to exploit racial divisions in the United States for its own revolutionary purposes"); the American Committee to Save Refugees ("perform [ing] a most valuable function for the international Communist movement"); the American League for Peace and Democracy ("subversive and Communist" – "established ... in an effort to create public sentiment on behalf of a foreign policy adapted to the interests of the Soviet Union ... [and] designed to conceal Communist control, in accordance with the new tactics of the Communist International"); American Peace Mobilization ("formed ... under the auspices of the Communist Party and the Young Communist League" – "one of the most seditious organizations which ever operated in the United States"); the Artists' Front To Win the War ("Communist front" – "included representatives of the theater, of literature, music, art, science, and education, with long and active records of support for Communist-front organizations and for the variegated turns of the Communist Party line"); the Committee To Defend America by Keeping Out of War ("Communist front"); Friends of the Abraham Lincoln Brigade ("completely controlled by the Communist Party"); Frontier Films ("Communist front"); the Golden Book of American Friendship with the Soviet Union ("pro-Soviet propaganda enterprise"); the Harry Bridges Defense Committee ("Communist front"); the Joint Anti-Fascist Refugee Committee ("subversive and Communist"); the League of American Writers ("subversive and Communist" – "began openly to follow the Communist Party line as dictated by the foreign policy of the Soviet Union"); the Marcus Graham Freedom of the Press Committee (ultra-radical group in support of an anarchist); the National Citizens Political Action Committee ("Communist front"); the National Emergency Conference for Democratic Rights ("Communist front" – "subversive"); the National Federation for Constitutional Liberties ("under Communist Party domination and headed by responsible Party functionaries" – "one of the viciously subversive organizations of the Communist Party"); *New Masses* ("weekly journal of the Communist Party"); and a Statement by American Progressives on the Moscow Trials ("obviously a document concocted in defense of the line of the Communist Party and undoubtedly originated in the headquarters of the Communist Party"). Seldes died in September 1970.

BEN[JAMIN] SHAHN was born on September 12, 1898 in Kovno, Russia, son of Gittel Lieberman and Hessel Shahn. He was married to and divorced from the late Tillie Goldstein. His second wife was Bernarda Bryson. He attended New York University (1919-1920), the College of the City of New York (1920-1921), and the National Academy of Design (1921-1923). He studied art in Paris between 1925 and 1928.

In the 1920's Shahn joined the Communist Party's propaganda campaign on behalf of Nicola Sacco and Bartolomeo Vanzetti, two Reds who were executed for murder in Massachusetts. In 1932, Shahn completed twenty-three paintings on the Sacco-Vanzetti affair. In 1933, he joined another Communist Party propaganda campaign on behalf of the imprisoned Red, Tom Mooney. In 1933, Shahn assisted Mexican Communist Diego Rivera on the latter's murals for the RCA building in Rockefeller Center in New York City. One of these murals was so obviously a Communist propaganda piece that it was destroyed by those who paid for it.

In 1934 and 1935, Shahn worked for the New York City Public Works Art Project. In 1934, he worked briefly for the Federal Relief Administration. From 1935 until 1938, he was an artist and designer for the Farm Security Admin-istration. In 1940, the federal government paid him $19,980 to paint murals in the Social Security building in Washington, D.C. In 1942 and 1943, he worked for the Red-lined Office of War Information. In 1956 and 1957, he was the Charles Eliot Norton Professor at Harvard University.

Shahn's works were exhibited at the Art Institute of Chicago, the Detroit Institute of Arts, the Newark Museum Association, the Metropolitan Museum of Art, the Museum of Modern Art, the Phillips Gallery in Washington, D.C., and the Museum of the City of New York. He had exhibitions in various European cities and he was a guest lecturer at many American universities and colleges. His works invariably were devoted to Communist-line themes.

In July 1959, Shahn testified before the House Committee on Un-American Activities. His works had been selected for display at a United States National Exhibition in Moscow. Under oath, Shahn pleaded the Fifth Amendment when asked about his Communist Party membership, especially during the period when he was employed by the federal government. He also refused to testify as to whether he had contributed his works to raise money for Communist Party enterprises.

Shahn was affiliated with the American Artists' Congress ("Communist front"); the American Continental Congress for World Peace ("another phase in the Communist 'peace' campaign, aimed at consolidating anti-American forces throughout the Western Hemisphere"); the American Writers' Congress ("subversive"); the Appeal for Amnesty for Communist Leaders Convicted Under the Smith Act (Communist Party project); *Art Front* ("Communist front"); Artists Union ("a group primarily interested in Communist agitation and activity among artists"); the Bill of Rights Conference ("subversive"); the Cultural and Scientific Conference for World Peace ("Communist front" – "a propaganda front for Soviet foreign policy and Soviet culture"); the John Reed Clubs ("out-and-out Communist organizations which preceded the contemporary Communist front organizations which cater to so-called liberals"); *Masses and Mainstream* ("Communist magazine"); *Morning Freiheit* ("Communist Yiddish daily subsidized by the Comintern"); the National Citizens' Political Action Committee ("Communist front"); the National Committee To Abolish the Un-American Activities Committee ("to lead and direct the Communist Party's 'Operation Abolition' campaign'); the National Council of American-Soviet Friendship ("subversive and Communist" – "specializing in pro-Soviet propaganda"); the National Council of the Arts, Sciences, and Professions ("a Communist front used to appeal to special occupational groups"); the National Institute of Arts and Letters ("Communist front"); *New Masses* ("weekly journal of the Communist Party"); Progressive Citizens of America ("political Communist front" – "subversive"); the Spanish Refugee Appeal ("subversive" – "Communist front"); and the Women's International League for Peace and Freedom (ultra-leftist-pacifist). Shahn died in March 1969.

GUY EMERY SHIPLER was born on July 31, 1884 in Warsaw, New York, son of Mary Danley and John Shipler. He married Rebekah Schultze. He attended Hobart College (1902-1905) and graduated from the General Theological Seminary (1910). In 1910 he was ordained a deacon, and in 1911 a priest, of the Protestant Episcopal Church.

In 1900, Shipler was a reporter for the *Rochester Evening Times*. In 1906 and 1907, he was a reporter for the *Boston Traveler*. In 1910 and 1911, he was assistant rector of St. Peter's Church in St. Louis. From 1911 until 1917, he was rector of the Church of the Epiphany in Cincinnati. In 1918 and 1919, he was chaplain of the New Jersey State Militia. From 1917 until 1968, he was with *The Churchman*, a monthly magazine allied with the Episcopal Church, as managing editor (1917-1922) and editor-in-chief (1922-1968). In 1916 and 1917, he was editor of *Social Service News* in Cincinnati. He was chairman of the board of directors of the Save the Children Federation. He was a member of the League of Nations Association. He served as secretary and president of the Associated Church Press.

In 1947, Shipler and six other Protestant clergymen visited Communist Yugoslavia. Flying in the face of facts, he said at a press conference in Belgrade: "In the light of what we have seen and the inquiries we have made, we wish to state without reservation of any kind that there is today in Yugoslavia complete freedom of worship and respect for religious beliefs and institutions." He explained that "Catholic priests and monks who were killed by Tito's regime were punished not because of their religion but because they had committed crimes against the people." Shipler was rabid in his anti-Catholicism because, he charged, Catholic clergy intruded upon political affairs. At the same time, Shipler – a clergyman – was constantly agitating for more liberal divorce laws and laws that would permit voluntary euthanasia. His *Churchman* adhered so closely to the Communist line that it was scarcely distinguishable from an official publication of the Communist Party.

Shipler was affiliated with the American Association for the United Nations (leftist-internationalist); the American Committee for Democracy and Intellectual Freedom ("subversive and un-American" – "a Communist-front organization operating among college teachers and professors"); the American Committee for Protection of Foreign Born ("founded by the Communist Party in order to exploit racial divisions in the United States for its own revolutionary purposes"); the American Committee for Spanish Freedom ("Communist"); the American Committee To Save Refugees ("perform[ing] a most valuable function for the international Communist movement"); the American Friends of Spanish Democracy ("Communist front"); the American League for Peace and Democracy ("subversive and Communist" – "established . . . in an effort to create public sentiment on behalf of a foreign policy adapted to the interests of the Soviet Union . . . [and] designed to conceal Communist control, in accordance with the new tactics of the Communist International"); the American Relief for Spain ("Communist Party front enterprise"); the American Round Table on India ("Communist front"); the American Society for Cultural Relations with Italy (pro-Communist); the American Youth Congress ("subversive" – "one of the most influential front organizations ever set up by the Communists in this country" – "the Communists were in complete control"); American Youth for Democracy ("subversive and Communist" – "part of Soviet psychological warfare against the United States"); an Appeal for Amnesty for Communist Party Leaders Imprisoned Under the Smith Act ("Communist Party project"); the China Aid Council ("Communist-controlled"); the Church League for Industrial Democracy (Socialist); Citizens United To Abolish the Wood-Rankin Committee (pro-Communist project); the Civil Rights Congress ("created and established by the Communist Party as an organization which would utilize defense of civil rights for Party purposes and raise and maintain mass defense and bail funds for Party use"); the Committee for a Democratic Far Eastern Policy ("Communist"); the Committee of Welcome for the Red Dean of Canterbury (England's most notorious pro-Soviet apologist among the clergy); the Committee To Save Spain and China ("Communist front"); the Coordinating Committee To Lift the [Spanish] Embargo ("one of the numerous Communist-front enterprises which were organized around the Communists' agitation over the Spanish Civil War"); the Council for Pan American Democracy ("subversive and Communist"); the Cultural and Scientific Conference for World Peace ("Communist front" – "a propaganda front for Soviet foreign policy and Soviet culture"); the Emergency Civil Liberties Committee ("Communist front" – "subversive"); *Equality* ("Communist Party enterprise"); the Red-laden Federal Council of Churches; Federal Union (leftist-internationalist); Friends of the Abraham Lincoln Brigade ("completely controlled by the Communist Party"); the Greater New York Emergency Conference on Inalienable Rights ("Communist front"); the Hiroshima Commemorative Committee (ultra-leftist); *Jewish Life* ("published by the New York Buro of the Communist Party"); the Joint Anti-Fascist Refugee Committee ("subversive and Communist"); the Medical Aid to [Castro's] Cuba Committee (ultra-leftist); the Medical Bureau and North American Committee To Aid Spanish Democracy ("subversive and un-

American"); the Mid-Century Conference for Peace ("aimed at assembling as many gullible persons as possible under Communist direction and turning them into a vast sounding board for Communist propaganda"); the ultra-radical National Association for the Advancement of Colored People; the National Committee To Abolish the Un-American Activities Committee ("to lead and direct the Communist Party's 'Operation Abolition' campaign"); the National Committee To Abolish the McCarran Act ("Communist front" — "subversive"); the National Committee To Win Amnesty for Smith Act Victims ("subversive" — "Communist"); the National Committee To Win the Peace ("subversive and Communist"); the National Council of American-Soviet Friendship ("subversive and Communist — specializing in pro-Soviet propaganda"); the National Council of the Arts, Sciences, and Professions ("a Communist front used to appeal to special occupational groups"); the National Emergency Conference for Democratic Rights ("Communist front" — "subversive"); the National Federation for Constitutional Liberties ("under Communist Party domination and headed by responsible Party functionaries" — "one of the viciously subversive organizations of the Communist Party"); the National Religion and Labor Foundation ("Communist front"); the North American Committee To Aid Spanish Democracy ("Communist"); the Progressive Citizens of America ("political Communist front" — "subversive"); the *Protestant* ("with an eye to religious groups, the Communists have formed religious fronts such as the *Protestant*"); the *Protestant Digest* ("a magazine which has faithfully propagated the Communist Party line under the guise of being a religious journal");

the Reichstag Fire Trial Anniversary Committee ("Communist front . . . formed . . . by prominent Communists and Communist sympathizers"); the Religious Freedom Committee (an ultra-leftist group working for the abolition of the House Committee on Un-American Activities); the Rosenberg Clemency Appeal ("Communist front organized . . . to conduct the United States phase of a mammoth propaganda campaign designed to obliterate the crime of and exploit the Rosenbergs and their codefendant Morton Sobell for the purposes of international Communism"); Russian War Relief ("Communist enterprise"); the [Morris U.] Schappes Defense Committee ("a front organization with a strictly Communist objective, namely, the defense of a self-admitted Communist who was convicted of perjury in the courts of New York"); *The Slavic American* ("official organ of the American Slav Congress, subversive and Communist"); the Society for the Prevention of World War III (leftist-pacifist); the Spanish Refugee Relief Campaign ("Communist front"); the Veterans of the Abraham Lincoln Brigade ("directed, dominated and controlled by the Communist Party"); the Voice of Freedom Committee ("subversive" — to defend pro-Communist radio commentators); the Win-the-Peace Conference ("Communist front"); the World Citizenship Movement (leftist-internationalist); and the World Peace Congress ("organized under Communist initiative in various countries throughout the world").

Shipler died in April 1968.

ABBA HILLEL SILVER was born on January 28, 1893 in Neinstadt, Schirwindt, Lithuania, son of Diana Seaman and Moses Silver. He came to the United States in 1902. He married Virginia

Horkheimer. He was an alumnus of the University of Cincinnati (A.B., 1915) and Hebrew Union College, where he was ordained a rabbi in 1915 (D.D., 1925). He was the author of *History of Messianic Speculations in Israel* (1927); *Democratic Impulse in Jewish History* (1928); *What Is Happening to the American Home Today?* (1928); *Religion in a Changing World* (1930); *World Crisis and Jewish Survival* (1941); *Vision and Victory* (1949); *Where Judaism Differed: An Inquiry Into the Distinctiveness of Judaism* (1956); *Moses and the Original Torah* (1961); *Servant of the Lord* (1966); and *Therefore Choose Life* (1967).

From 1915 until 1917, Silver was a rabbi of Congregation L'Shem Shamayin in Wheeling, West Virginia. From 1917 until 1963, he was rabbi of Temple Tifereth Israel in Cleveland, Ohio, one of the largest Reform congregations in America. He served as a visiting minister at the University of Chicago, Harvard University, Cornell University, Syracuse University, Purdue University, and New York University. In 1940, he gave the Dudleian lectures at Harvard University.

Silver was one of America's most active Zionists and a major architect of the program which achieved a Jewish homeland in Israel. He was a founder and president of the Theodor Herzl Zion Club in New York City, the first boys' group in the American Zionist movement. From 1938 until 1943, he was chairman of the United Palestine Appeal. From 1938 until 1944, he was co-chairman of the United Jewish Appeal. In 1943, along with Stephen M. Wise, he founded the American Zionist Emergency Council. From 1945 until 1947, he was president of the Central Conference of American Rabbis. In 1945 and 1946, he was president of the

SILVER

Zionist Organization of America. In 1947, he was chairman of the American section of the Jewish Agency for Palestine. He presented the Zionist case to United Nations and to the United States States Congress.

Zionism was not Silver's only interest beyond his rabbinical duties. He was an active opponent of anti-Communist and anti-subversive investigations by government agencies. He was a pro-labor activist and proponent of socialistic and statist legislation. He was a member of the National World Court Committee and the American League for India's Freedom. When Hitler came to power, Silver joined Samuel Untermeyer in instigating an American boycott of German trade – to the consternation of many Jewish leaders and the United States diplomatic corps.

Silver's affiliations included the American Association for the United Nations (leftist-internationalist); the ultra-leftist American Civil Liberties Union; the American Committee for Anti-Nazi Literature ("individuals and organizations connected with it identify this committee as a Communist front organization"); the American Committee for Yugoslav Relief ("subversive and Communist"); the American League for Peace and Democracy ("subversive and Communist" – "established . . . in an effort to create public sentiment on behalf of a foreign policy adapted to the interests of the Soviet Union . . . [and] designed to conceal Communist control, in accordance with the new tactics of the Communist International"); the American Rescue Ship Mission ("Communist Party project"); the American Round Table on India ("Communist front"); the Berger National Foundation (Socialist); the Committee of Welcome for the

Red Dean of Canterbury (England's most notorious pro-Soviet apologist among the clergy); the Committee on Militarism in Education (a supporting organization of the U.S. Congress Against War, "completely under the control of the Communist Party"); Film Audiences for Democracy ("Communist front"); Films for Democracy ("Communist front"); the Medical Bureau and North American Committee To Aid Spanish Democracy ("subversive and un-American"); the National Committee To Abolish the Poll Tax ("Communist front"); the National Committee to Secure Justice in the Rosenberg Case ("Communist front organized . . . to conduct the United States phase of a mammoth propaganda campaign designed to obliterate the crime of and exploit the Rosenbergs and their co-defendant Morton Sobell for the purposes of international Communism"); the National Council of American-Soviet Friendship ("subversive and Communist" – "specializing in pro-Soviet propaganda"); and Russian War Relief ("Communist enterprise"). He died in November 1963.

MARY MELINDA SIMKHOVITCH was born on September 8, 1867 in Chestnut Hill, Massachusetts, daughter of Laura Holms and Isaac Kingsbury. She married Vladimir Simkhovitch. She was an alumna of Boston University (A.B., 1890). She pursued graduate studies at Radcliffe College in 1892. She studied at the University of Berlin, on a Women's Educational and Industrial Union scholarship, in 1893 and 1894. She was the author of *The City Worker's World In America* (1917); *Neighborhood*, autobiography (1938); and *Group Life* (1942). She was co-author of *Quicksand: The Way of Life in the Slums*

(1942) and *Here Is God's Plenty* (1949).

From 1890 until 1892, Simkhovitch was a Latin teacher in Somerville (Mass.) High School. In 1898, she was a settlement worker at the College Settlement in New York City. From 1899 until 1901, she held a similar position at the Friendly Aid House in New York City. In 1902, she founded the Cooperative Social Settlement Society, the parent organization of Greenwich House, a settlement house which she directed until her retirement as director emeritus in 1946. From 1907 until 1910, she was adjunct professor of social economy at Barnard College. From 1910 until 1913, she was an associate in social economy at Columbia University's Teachers College. From 1912 until 1915, she was a lecturer at the New York School of Social Work.

Although Greenwich House was a center of Socialism and a force behind socialist reforms on a municipal and state level, it never achieved the fame of Jane Addams' Hull House or the Henry Street Settlement of Lillian Wald in New York City. However, Simkhovich was a close friend and associate of such Socialist luminaries as Eleanor Roosevelt, Frances Perkins, Carl Schurz, Felix Adler, and Jacob Riis. She was a Socialist though evidently not a party member. She described herself as a liberal, and put her definition of liberalism in writing: "Liberalism, the middle of the road, is supposed to be fast disappearing. And in its place are the forces of Fascism and Communism, the dogma of intolerance, propagandist in spirit, suppressing inquiring criticism or the experience of opposition in any form. Liberalism is now pictured as a weak, uncertain course, incapable of decision and with no chance of a future. But if the spirit of liberalism is the attempt to understand the complexity of our times and step by step to effect change, rebuilding on the basis of factual knowledge and in the light of new desires, then liberalism, notwithstanding the prophets of today, is the only road possible for adult men and women who see the destruction that necessarily takes place in the train of revolution and want to avoid that waste. But this liberal road is not possible unless education, social legislation, and labor organization can overtake social need."

Simkhovitch was affiliated with the American Committee for Protection of Foreign Born ("founded by the Communist Party in order to exploit racial divisions in the United States for its own revolutionary purposes"); the American Group, Inc. ("Communist front"); the American Youth Congress ("subversive" – "one of the most influential front organizations ever set up by the Communists in this country" – "the Communists were in complete control"); the Committee of One Thousand ("Communist created and controlled"); the Congress of American-Soviet Friendship ("Communist front"); the Congress of American Women ("subversive and Communist"); the Consumer-Farmer Milk Cooperative, Inc. ("Communist front"); the Consumers National Federation ("transmission belt for the Communist Party's influence and ideology" – "Communist front"); the Coordinating Committee To Lift the [Spanish] Embargo ("one of the numerous Communist-front enterprises which were organized around the Communists' agitation over the Spanish Civil War"); Descendants of the American Revolution ("a Communist-front organization set up as a radical imitation of the Daughters of the American Revolution. The Descendants have uniformly adhered to the line of the

Communist Party"); the Greater New York Emergency Conference on Inalienable Rights ("Communist front"); the Milk Consumers Protective Committee ("Communist front"); the National Council of American-Soviet Friendship ("subversive and Communist" – "specializing in pro-Soviet propaganda"); the National Wartime Conference of the Professions, the Sciences, the Arts, the White-Collar Fields ("Communist front"); Russian War Relief ("Communist enterprise"); the Social Workers Committee To Aid Spanish Democracy ("Communist front"); *Social Work Today* ("Communist magazine"); and the Washington Committee to Lift [the] Spanish Embargo ("Communist front").

Simkhovich died in November 1951.

UPTON BEALL SINCLAIR was born on September 20, 1878 in Baltimore, Maryland, son of Priscilla Harden and Upton Sinclair. He was married to and divorced from Meta Fuller. His second wife was the late Mary Kimbrough. His third wife was Mary Willis. He was an alumnus of the College of the City of New York (A.B., 1897). He pursued graduate studies at Columbia University (1897-1901). He was the author of *Saved by the Enemy* (1898); *Wolves of the Navy; or, Clif Faraday's Search for a Traitor* (1899); *A Soldier Monk* (1899); *A Soldier's Pledge* (1899); *Springtime and Harvest* (1901), later published as *King Midas* (1901); *The Journal of Arthur Stirling* (1903); *Prince Hagen: A Phantasy* (1903); *Manassas: A Novel of the War* (1904), revised edition published as *Theirs Be the Guilt: A Novel of War Between the States* (1959); *A Captain of Industry* (1906); *The Jungle*, which first appeared as a serial in *The Appeal to Reason,* a Socialist journal (1906); *The Industrial Republic: A*

Study of the America of Ten Years Hence (1907); *The Overman* (1907); *The Moneychangers* (1908); *The Metropolis* (1908); *Samuel the Seeker* (1910); *The Fasting Cure* (1911); *Love's Pilgrimage*, autobiography (1911); *The Millennium: A Comedy of the Year 2000* (1912); *Plays of Protest* (1912); *Damaged Goods*, a novelization of Brieux's play *Les Avaries* (1913); *Sylvia* (1913); *Sylvia's Marriage* (1914); *King Coal, a Novel of the Colorado Strike* (1917); *The Profits of Religion: An Essay in Economic Interpretation* (1918 and 1927); *Jimmie Higgins*, a war novel (1919); *The Brass Check: A Study of American Journalism* (1919; eighth edition, 1920); *100%: The Story of a Patriot* (1920); *The Book of Life: Mind and Body* (1921); *They Call Me Carpenter: A Tale of the Second Coming* (1922); *The Goose-Step: A Study of American Education* (1923); *Hell: A Verse Drama and Photo-Play* (1923); *The Goslings: A Study of the American Schools* (1924); *Singing Jailbirds: A Drama in Four Acts* (1924); *Bill Porter: A Drama of O. Henry in Prison* (1925); *Mammonart: An Essay in Economic Interpretation* (1925); *Spokesman's Secretary* (1926); *Letters to Judd, An American Workingman* (1926); *Oil!*, novel (1927), adapted as a four-act play with the same title (1929); *Money Writes!* (1927); *Boston* (1928); *Mental Radio* (1930, revised 1962); *Mountain City* (1930); *Peter Grudge Becomes a Secret Agent*, from *100%* (1930); *Roman Holiday*, novel (1931); *The Wet Parade* (1931); *American Outpost: A Book of Reminiscences*, autobiography (1932), published in England as *Candid Reminiscences: My First Thirty Years* (1932); *Spy* (1932); *Upton Sinclair Presents William Fox* (1933); *I, Governor of California: and How I Ended Poverty. A*

True Story of the Future (1933); *The EPIC Plan for California* (1934); *EPIC Answers: How to End Poverty in California* (1934); *An Upton Sinclair Antheology*, compiled by I.O. Evans (1934, revised 1947); *I, Candidate for Governor: and How I Got Licked* (1935); *Depression Island* (1935); *We, People of America, and How We Ended Poverty: A True Story of The Future* (1935); *What God Means to Me: An Attempt at a Working Religion* (1935 and 1936); *Co-op: A Novel of Living Together* (1936); *The Gnomobile: A Gnice Gnew Gnarrative with Gnonsense, but Gnothing Gnaughty*, a children's story (1936), released as a motion picture by Walt Disney (1965); *Wally for Queen: The Private Life of Royalty* (1936); *The Flivver King: A Story of Ford-America* (1937); *No Parasan!: A Story of the Battle of Madrid* (1937); *Little Steel* (1938); *Our Lady* (1938); *Your Million Dollars* (1939), published also as *Letters to a Millionaire* (1939); *Marie Antoinette*, play (1939); *Expect No Peace!* 1939; *What Can Be Done About America's Economic Troubles* (1939); *Telling the World* (1940); *Peace or War in America: A Debate Between Upton Sinclair and the Honorable Philip F. La Follette* (1941); *A Giant's Strength*, play (1948); *Another Pamela; or, Virtue Still Rewarded* (1950); *The Enemy Had It Too*, play (1950); *A Personal Jesus: Portrait and Interpretation* (1952); *What Didymus Did* (1954); *The Cup of Fury* (1956); *It Happened to Didymus*, moral fable (1958); *My Lifetime in Letters* (1960); *Cicero: A Drama of Ancient Rome* (1960; produced, 1961); *Affectionately, Eve*, satirical novel (1961); and *Autobiography of Upton Sinclair* (1962).

Under the pseudonym of Clarke Fitch, Sinclair wrote *Clif, the Naval Cadet; or, Exciting Days at Annapolis*

(1902); *From Port to Port; or, Clif Faraday in Many Waters* (1903); *The Cruise of the Training Ship; or, Clif Faraday's Pluck* (1903); and *A Strange Cruise; or, Clif Faraday's Yacht Chase* (1903). Under the pseudonym of Frederick Garrison, he wrote *Off for West Point; or Mark Mallory's Struggle* (1903) and *On Guard; or, Mark Mallory's Celebration* (1903). He was the author of the "Lanny Budd" series, including *World's End* (1940); *Between Two Worlds* (1941); *Dragon's Teeth* (1942); *Wide Is the Gate* (1943); *Presidential Agent* (1944); *Dragon Harvest* (1945); *A World to Win* (1946); *Presidential Mission* (1947); *One Clear Call* (1948); *O Shepherd, Speak!* (1949); and *The Return of Lanny Budd* (1953). His *World's End* was the Literary Guild Selection in 1940. He received a Pulitzer Prize in 1943 for *Dragon's Teeth.* He was co-author of *Good Health and How We Won It, with an Account of the New Hygiene* (1909) and *Terror in Russia: Two Views* (1938). He was a collaborator in *League for Industrial Democracy: Forty Years of Education* (1945). He was the editor of *The Cry for Justice* (1915, revised edition 1963).

Sinclair was a Socialist by the time he was twenty years of age. In 1902, he joined the Socialist Party. In 1905, he was a founder of the Intercollegiate Socialist Society (later the League for Industrial Democracy), which became the most influential Socialist organization on American university and colleges campuses. In 1906, with the publication of *The Jungle*, he became one of the leading muckrakers of his era. (Rose Martin in her *Fabian Freeway* provided a revealing account of the circumstances surrounding the writing of *The Jungle*, which was Sinclair's first lucrative work. Wrote Miss Martin: "At the moment, Sinclair was engaged in completing still another novel, *The Jungle*, a subsidized exposé of conditions in the Chicago stockyards, which he wrote without ever having been in Chicago. His source was an early American Marxist, A.M. Simons, who had written a pamphlet, called *Packingtown*, six years before. Simons did the 'research' for Sinclair and served as a model for the election-night orator in the final pages of *The Jungle*. Because muckraking was just coming into style, and because President Theodore Roosevelt had a legitimate bone to pick with the meat packers dating from the beef scandals of the Spanish-American War, Sinclair's sixth novel proved a sensation, catapulting him into a long and profitable career as a Socialist muckraker. When President Theodore Roosevelt invited Upton Sinclair to come to Chicago as one of a commission to investigate the stockyards, the latter prudently declined. In his place, he sent Ella Reeve Bloor, 'the little nutbrown woman' later known to Communists as Mother Bloor, whose son, Hal Ware, was to found a Communist espionage cell within the United States Department of Agriculture in 1934.")

With the money he made from sales of *The Jungle*, Sinclair opened the Helicon Home Colony, a Socialist commune, in Englewood, New Jersey. The experiment lasted about a year and came to an end when a fire destroyed the building. With the fame he had acquired, Sinclair made his first attempt at politics when he ran, unsuccessfully, on the Socialist Party ticket in the New Jersey Congressional elections of 1906. Later, in California, Sinclair was a Socialist Party candidate for Congress (1920), for the U.S. Senate (1922), and for governor (1926 and 1930).

In 1917, Sinclair resigned from the

Socialist Party because he disagreed with those Socialist leaders who were advocating pacifism and opposing intervention in the world war by the United States. (Later, he said that he regretted his action and by hindsight discovered that the Socialist dissidents were correct.) In 1918 and 1919, he published *Upton Sinclair's*, a journal in which he expressed all-out support for President Woodrow Wilson's policies.

Sinclair rejoined the Socialist Party and remained in it until 1934, when he decided to seek the governorship of California on the Democratic ticket. He won the primary but lost the election to his Republican opponent. It was his last political contest. But Sinclair attracted national attention in the gubernatorial campaign which he waged on his EPIC (End Poverty in California) program. He called for Socialist measures that would provide full employment, generous pension plans, government ownership of production facilities, and a general program of "production for use."

After 1934, Sinclair did not return to the Socialist Party; he remained a Democrat. He continued his voluminous output of writings, and became a special favorite in Communist and Socialist countries. His books were translated into more than forty languages. (Sinclair's fame abroad was indicated in 1932 when he was nominated for the Nobel Peace Prize.)

In 1938, Sinclair went to great lengths to deny that he was a Communist, but confirmed that he was a Socialist. In an affidavit submitted to the Special Committee on Un-American Activities, he said: "It has been widely reported in the press that at least two of the witnesses before the Dies Committee have said that I was a Communist; that I had held positions in the Communist Party, and had taken part in consultations for the determining of Communist policies.

"The fact is that I have never been a member of the Communist Party and have never been a Communist. I have never advocated Communism, but on the contrary, in every book, pamphlet, and magazine article in which I have discussed the subject I have explained that I am not a Communist and why. I have been for more than thirty-five years a Socialist, and for the greater part of that time have been a member of the Socialist party. In 1904, I founded the Intercollegiate Socialist Society, which is now the League for Industrial Democracy; in 1906, I was candidate of the Socialist party for Congress from New Jersey; in 1917, I resigned from the Socialist party in a public statement declaring my support of the United States government in the World War. After the war I rejoined the Socialist party and ran for Congress in California in 1920; for the United States in 1922; for governor of California in 1926, and again in 1930. In 1933 I joined the Democratic party and won its nomination for the governorship of California in 1934. Just recently I joined the National Progressive party.

"For more than thirty-five years past I have used the following definition of Socialism as the doctrine and procedure which I advocate: the social ownership and democratic control of the instruments and means of production. I believe and teach that the change from private competititve or monopoly ownership to public and cooperative ownership can be brought about peaceably and gradually under our present Constitution. I have written many books and pamphlets in the effort to prove this, and I have never, in my writings or any other way, advocated the bringing about of the change by any other method.

"Bolshevism, which is the doctrine now known as Communism, or Leninism, advocates the overthrow of capitalist governments by the workers and the establishment of a dictatorship of the proletariat. This was the method used in Russia, and from the time that it occurred I have defended the right of the Russian workers to settle their own affairs. I opposed the armed intervention of the United States government to put down the Russian revolution. I have always and everywhere defended the right of the Russians, the Spanish, the Chinese, and all other peoples, to determine their own form of government, without military intervention such as we ourselves took part in against the Russian people. I have denounced the attacks of Germany and Italy upon the people of Spain, and the policy of our government in denying the duly elected people's government of Spain the right to purchase arms for its own defense. But in discussing the domestic affairs of the American people, I have invariably argued that, since they enjoy democratic institutions and have the ability to change their government and their business affairs at any time they please, they should make the necessary changes by democratic and orderly processes, and under the Constitution.

"In my book, *The Brass Check*, published in 1920, appears a chapter entitled 'The Case of Russia.' I wrote on page 385: 'Let me make clear at the outset my point of view, oft repeated. I am not a Bolshevik, and have never been a Bolshevik.' I then went on to define the word Bolshevik and explain my belief in the democratic method of procedure, adding: 'I am well aware that this method will be slower, but I believe it will be quicker in the long run, because it will avoid the waste incidental to civil war, and the possibilities of failure and temporary reaction.' On page 386 I added: 'But such a program, of course, can be effective only in a country where political rights are recognized.'

"This is a perfectly obvious distinction which any honest person can understand at once. Where people have political rights they should use them to get such economic changes as they need and desire. Where they have no political rights they have to win them, by the same method that our forefathers won them in 1776, and as the British and French and other people won them through a long series of struggles.

"In *The Book of Life*, published in 1922, I give a detailed study of all these problems, occupying more than one hundred pages. There is a chapter beginning on page 179, entitled 'Confiscation or Compensation,' in which I defined the method of compensation of the owners of industry. The following chapter demonstrates the futility of efforts to bring about a proletarian revolution in the United States. The entire work defends the cooperative method and advocates peaceable, orderly, cooperative change.

"In the pamphlet, *Letters to Judd*, first published in 1925 and reprinted in 1932 and 1933, are several chapters endeavoring to maintain this same thesis. I presented an edition of 100 thousand copies of this book to the Socialist party, and it was used in the presidential campaign of 1932.

"The pamphlet, *The Way Out*, first published in 1933, presents long arguments to the same effect. Near the end of 1933, I launched the so-called 'Epic Plan' to End Poverty in California. This plan proposed to put the unemployed at productive labor to produce the goods which they themselves were going to consume. In the first pamphlet, *I, Governor of California: And How I Ended Poverty*, of which nearly a quarter of a million copies were circulated during the campaign in California, I took the utmost pains to make clear the democratic procedure proposed for this plan. The book was from beginning to end an account of an imaginary democratic procedure by which I, as elected governor of California, would bring about the end of poverty in California by peaceable and orderly methods.

"I told what the opposition of the Communists to this plan would be, and the opposition of the Communists to the plan was in actual fact exactly as I had foretold in the pamphlet. The evidence of this is given in detail in the history of the Epic campaign which I published immediately after the campaign, under the title of *I, Candidate for Governor: And How I Got Licked*. The fact that I was called a Communist during the campaign meant nothing except that the opponents of the plan were afraid of its success, and in order to defeat it they told lies about Upton Sinclair and his ideas. They even went so far as to print a fake circular, attributed to the Communists, endorsing our Epic campaign. This trick was first tried during the primary campaign and was fully exposed, but nevertheless the same fraudulent circular was used during the general election campaign.

"The Communists fought the Epic campaign as hard as they knew how. They printed circulars denouncing Epic and threw handfuls of these circulars from the balconies at mass meetings where I spoke. The Communist organ of San Francisco referred to the Epic Plan as 'one more addled egg from the blue buzzard's nest.' They printed cartoons ridiculing me and my idea.

"Every Communist in the United States knows that I am not a Communist. So does every reactionary know it. The reactionaries desire to have no economic change in the United States, but to continue the present system of exploiting labor for the benefit of a small class. They find it a cheap and easy method to discredit all advocates of economic reform by calling them Communists. This saves the need of argument and is supposed to keep the people from finding out the truths which scientific Socialism has to offer to the world.

"The hired agents of big business who traveled from California, provided with elaborate typewritten copies of fraudulent material to be laid before the Dies Committee, knew that Upton Sinclair is not and never has been a Communist, and does not advocate and never has advocated Communism.

"One of these witnesses stated that I had taken part in a conference in Senator Olson's office in November 1935, in which plans had been made to advance Communism in California. I have not been in Senator Olson's office since the 1934 election, and in November 1935, I was on an automobile tour with my wife in which we covered some 12 thousand miles and I lectured about the Epic Plan in a score of cities in the middle west and on the Atlantic coast from Albany to Boston and on down to Florida. I have a mass of newspaper clippings and other evidence concerning this tour."

Sinclair's disavowal of Communism must be weighed against the host of associations he had with the left before and after he submitted his affidavit. His affiliations included the leftist-international Action for World Federation, Students for Federal World Government, and the World Constitutional Convention; the All-American Anti-Imperialist

League ("the [Communist] Party was wholly responsible for the establishment and subsequent control of the league"); the ultra-leftist American Civil Liberties Union; the American Committee for Protection of Foreign Born ("founded by the Communist Party in order to exploit racial divisions in the United States for its own revolutionary purposes"); the American Committee for Struggle Against War ("Communist front"); the American Committee of Liberals for the Freedom of [Tom] Mooney and [Warren K.] Billings ("formed by the International Labor Defense [the legal arm of the Communist Party]"); the American Friends of Spanish Democracy ("Communist front"); the American Friends of the Soviet Union ("Communist front" – "primarily concerned with the carrying on of propaganda in behalf of the Soviet Union and its system of government"); the American Fund for Public Service [Garland Fund] ("a major source for the financing of Communist Party enterprises such as the *Daily Worker* and *New Masses*, official Communist publications, Federated Press, Russian Reconstruction Farms and International Labor Defense"); the American League Against War and Fascism ("subversive and Communist" – "established in the United States in an effort to create public sentiment on behalf of a foreign policy adapted to the interests of the Soviet Union"); the American League for Peace and Democracy ("subversive and Communist" – "established . . . in an effort to create public sentiment on behalf of a foreign policy adapted to the interests of the Soviet Union . . . [and] designed to conceal Communist control, in accordance with the new tactics of the Communist International"); the American Relief Ship for Spain ("Communist Party front

enterprise"); the American Student Union ("without exception . . . supported defense of teachers and students charged with Communist activity" – "pliable instrument in the hands of the Communist Party"); the Berger National Foundation (Socialist); Brookwood Labor College ("Communist"); the Committee for a Boycott Against Japanese Aggression ("the committee was featured in the *Daily Worker*, official organ of the Communist Party, and in that paper alone"); Commonwealth College ("Communist"); the Conference for Progressive Political Action (ultra-leftist coalition); the Congress of American Soviet Friendship ("Communist front"); the Coordinating Committee To Lift the [Spanish] Embargo ("one of the numerous Communist-front enterprises which were organized around the Communists' agitation over the Spanish Civil War"); the Council for Pan American Democracy ("subversive and Communist"); Emergency Committee for Southern Political Prisoners ("Communist front"); First Congress of the Mexican and Spanish American Peoples of the United States ("Congress was planned at a secret gathering of Communist Party leaders from the South and Southwest"); Friends of the Abraham Lincoln Brigade ("dominated, directed and controlled by the Communist Party"); the Golden Book of American Friendship with the Soviet Union ("pro-Soviet propaganda enterprise"); Icor ("the aims of Icor have been primarily propagandistic in behalf of the Soviet Union"); the International Committee for Political Prisoners (to raise funds for jailed seditionists); the International Committee for the World Congress Against War ("organized and controlled by Moscow's International League against Imperialism"); the International Labor Defense ("subversive and

Communist" – "legal arm of the Communist Party" – "part of an international network of organizations for the defense of Communist law-breakers"); *International Literature* of Moscow ("Communist"); International Workers Aid (Communist propaganda organization); the John Reed Clubs ("out-and-out Communist organizations which preceded the contemporary Communist front organizations which cater to so-called liberals"); the Joint Anti-Fascist Refugee Committee ("subversive and Communist"); *Liberator* ("Communist magazine"); the League of American Writers ("subversive and Communist" – "began openly to follow the Communist Party line as dictated by the foreign policy of the Soviet Union"); the Medical Bureau and North American Committee To Aid Spanish Democracy ("subversive and un-American"); the Mother Ella Reeve Bloor Birthday Committee ("Communist Party festivity"); the National Committee for People's Rights ("composed primarily of openly avowed members of the Communist Party and veteran fellow travelers of the Communist Party"); the National Committee for the Defense of Political Prisoners ("subversive and Communist"); the National Committee To Aid Striking Miners Fighting Starvation ("Communist front"); the National Council of American-Soviet Friendship ("subversive" – "Communist" – "specializing in pro-Soviet propaganda"); the National Emergency Conference for Democratic Rights ("Communist front" – "subversive"); the National Federation for Constitutional Liberties ("under Communist Party domination and headed by responsible Party functionaries" – "one of the viciously subversive organizations of the Communist Party"); the National Institute of Arts and Letters ("Communist front"); the National Right-to-Work Congress ("out-and-out Communist Party affair"); the National Writers Congress ("Communist front"); *New Masses* ("weekly journal of the Communist Party"); the North American Committee To Aid Spanish Democracy ("Communist"); North American Spanish Aid Committee ("Communist"); *People's Daily World* ("official organ of the Communist Party"); [Luiz Carlos] Prestes Defense Committee (in behalf of a leader of the Communist Party of Brazil – "a Communist organization"); the Rand School of Social Science (a Marxian-Socialist training school for labor agitators); the Revolutionary Writers Federation ("American section of Moscow's International Union of Revolutionary Writers"); Sacco-Vanzetti National League (part of a Communist Party propaganda campaign); the United States Congress Against War ("completely under the control of the Communist Party"); Veterans of the Abraham Lincoln Brigade ("directed, dominated and controlled by the Communist Party"); the Washington Committee To Lift [the] Spanish Embargo ("Communist front"); the Western Writers Conference ("Communist front"); the Workers International Relief (Communist propaganda organization); Workers' Cultural Federation (coalition of Communist revolutionary groups); Workers Party ("seeks to alter the form of government of the United States by unconstitutional means"); World Congress Against War and Fascism ("sponsored by the Communist International"); and Writers and Artists Committee for Medical Aid to Spain ("a Communist front set up for the purpose of agitation and propaganda"). Sinclair died in November 1968.

AGNES SMEDLEY was born in 1894 in rural northwest Missouri, daughter of Sarah Rolls and Charles Smedley. She was married to and divorced from Ernest W. Brundlin. She attended the Normal School at Tempe, Arizona (1911), the University of California (summer of 1915), New York University (1916-1917), and the University of Berlin (1927-1928). She was the author of *Daughter of Earth* (1929); *Chinese Destinies* (1933); *China's Red Army Marches* (1934); *China Fights Back: An American Woman With the Eighth Route Army* (1938); *Battle Hymn of China* (1943); and *The Great Road: The Life and Times of Chu Teh* (posthumously, 1956).

Many of the details of Smedley's early years are obscure. It is known that she was taken to southern Colorado by her parents when she was about ten years of age. She never completed elementary school and she never attended high school. After a series of briefly held jobs, she attended the Normal School at Tempe while supporting herself working as a waitress. She was married in 1912 and spent the next several years in California.

In California, Smedley was a part-time student at the University of California. She did some teaching in a normal school. She was introduced to and accepted Socialism as an ideology (the well-known Socialist Upton Sinclair was a strong and personal influence upon her). Her husband sought and obtained a divorce.

In 1916, Smedley went to New York City. She went to night school at New York University and in the daytime she worked for a magazine. She increased her commitment to Socialism and joined the Socialists in their protests against intervention by the United States in World War I. She met and studied with Lala Laipat Rai, an exiled Indian, who introduced her to a subversive Indian nationalist group, Friends of Freedom for India. Smedley worked for the group by keeping their correspondence, their codes, and other secret materials.

In March 1918, Smedley and Salindranath Ghose, an Indian nationalist, were arrested, and she was charged with violating the Espionage Act and the U.S. Criminal Code by failure to register as an agent of a foreign government. She was released on bail, and her case never came to trial. In June 1918, a federal grand jury in San Francisco indicted Smedley, Ghose, and others on charges of fraud perpetrated against the United States government by representing themselves as part of an accredited diplomatic mission from the Nationalist Party of India. But Smedley was never brought to trial on this charge.

In 1919, Smedley sailed for Europe from New York as a stewardess on a Polish-American freighter. She jumped ship in Danzig and made her way to Berlin, where she met Virendranath Chattopadhyaha. Although he was married, Smedley lived with him as his common-law wife for a period of about eight years. In Berlin, Smedley was a sometime student at the University of Berlin, where she also taught an English seminar.

In 1921, Smedley went to Moscow as a member of a delegation from Germany to attend a meeting of Indian revolutionaries. A few months later, she was in Switzerland with her travel expenses paid by the Soviet Government. After Switzerland she attended the Congress of German Syndicalists at Düsseldorf. (She used several aliases at Düsseldorf, including Mrs. Petroikos.)

During her Berlin residence, Smedley

experienced domestic quarrels with Chattopadhyaha. As a result, she contemplated suicide on at least one occasion, and for two years she underwent psychoanalytic treatment. Also, during her Berlin years, she joined a group of Republican, Socialist, and Communist physicians in opening the first German birth-control clinic. (Smedley had been friendly in New York with Margaret Sanger, the famous birth-control advocate.)

In the 1923-1926 period, Smedley wrote two studies on Indian history, which were published in German historical journals. In 1927, while spending time in Denmark and Czecho-Slovakia, she wrote her first book, *Daughter of Earth*, a semi-autobiographical novel – a work which she described as "a desperate attempt to reorient my life."

In 1928, Smedley broke away from Chattopadhyaha. (He had become a member of the Communist Party, and after Hitler came to power he fled Germany and went to Moscow.) Smedley negotiated a contract with the *Frankfurter Zeitung* to be correspondent for the journal in the Far East. (*The Zeitung* was the official organ of the German Social Democratic Party.)

In May 1929, Smedley arrived in Shanghai with an American passport. She had travelled from Berlin to Moscow, where she attended meetings of the Sixth Communist International Congress. From Moscow, she travelled across Siberia to Harbin, Mukden, Tientsin, and Peiping, and along the way she used her own name and the aliases Mrs. Petroikos and Alice Bird.

From 1929 until 1933, Smedley remained in China, making Shanghai her base of operations. The Shanghai police determined that she was in the direct service of the Far Eastern Bureau of the Central Committee of the Comintern. She received her orders directly from the Comintern in Moscow, and did not contact Soviet Communists in the Shanghai area. The Shanghai police kept Smedley under surveillance, and further determined that she had been assigned by the Comintern to establish Communist organizations among workers. The police considered her to be a member of the All-China Labor Federation, which was supported by the Comintern's Far Eastern and Pan Pacific Bureaus. She was also a member of the Noulens Defense Committee, a Communist front established by International Red Aid to work for the freedom of two convicted Red Spies, Paul and Gertrude Ruegg, known as the Noulens, who were leaders of the Far Eastern Bureau in Shanghai.

Smedley was a member of the Communist fronts, China League for Civil Rights; Friends of the Soviet Union; and League Against Imperialism. She also kept in contact with Indian revolutionaries, some of whom were in Shanghai, and she edited propaganda for the Shanghai branch of the Indian Youth League and contributed money to other Indian revolutionary organizations. (In Berlin she had belonged to the Hindustan Association of Berlin and the Berlin Indian Revolutionary Society.)

Smedley had first attracted the attention of the Shanghai police when an article she wrote about preparations of the Shanghai authorities to suppress anticipated Communist disturbances appeared in the *Frankfurter Zeitung* and then in *Izvestia* of Moscow. In addition to her work for the *Zeitung*, she wrote articles for the leftist *China Weekly Review* of Shanghai. In 1930, she wrote for *New Masses*, the weekly journal of the Communist Party, USA. Anonymously, she contributed an article to the *Rote Fähne*, official organ of the Communist Party in Germany. In 1933, she wrote for *International Literature* of Moscow, the official organ of the Comintern's International Union of Revolutionary Writers.

In 1930, Smedley visited Canton, China, where she was arrested by Chinese officials at the request of British secret police, who claimed she was a Comintern agent traveling on a false passport. She was under house arrest for several weeks and was released only because the German Consul intervened on her behalf. When she returned to Shanghai she became involved with Richard Sorge, head of a Soviet spy ring. Through Smedley, Sorge recruited the services of Ozaki Hozumi, a Japanese news correspondent. Smedley met Ozaki Hozumi through Irene Wiedemeyer, owner of the Zeitgeist Bookshop, a Communist front and mail drop for Communist spies.

Smedley became Sorge's most able assistant, and he relied upon her to supply Chinese recruits for his ring. For her part, with the help of Ozaki Hozumi, she set up spy rings in Peiping and Tientsin.

In 1933, Smedley — suffering from ill health — went to the Soviet Union. While there she wrote her *China's Red Army Marches*, a maudlin tribute and a highly biased history of the Communist campaign from 1927 to 1931 against the Kuomintang armies of Chiang Kai-shek. Also, while in the Soviet Union, she was on the staff of the International Union of Revolutionary Writers.

In 1934, Smedley left the Soviet Union, travelled through central Europe and France, and then sailed to the United States. She made an unsuccessful search for work in New York City, and by 1935 she was back in Shanghai, and again under strict police surveillance.

From 1936 until 1941, Smedley spent considerable time with the Chinese Communist army and its leaders. She became friendly with Chou En-lai, Chu Teh, Peng Teh-livei, and Mao Tse-tung. She travelled with the army. She did publicity work for the Chinese Red Cross. She lectured and wrote as a virtual publicity agent for the Red Army. She became a correspondent for the *Manchester Guardian*, which was an outlet for her pro-Communist dispatches. In 1941, ill health forced her to leave China and she returned to the United States. (A few months after her departure Richard Sorge and Ozaki Hozumi were arrested as spies by the Japanese. They were executed in 1944.)

In the United States, from 1941 until 1950, Smedley became affiliated with a number of organizations, including *Amerasia* ("Communist-controlled publication"); the American Continental Congress for World Peace ("another phase in the Communist 'peace' campaign, aimed at consolidating anti-American forces throughout the Western Hemisphere"); Book Union ("distributors of Communist literature" — "Communist [Party] book club"); the Civil Rights Congress ("created and established by the Communist Party as an organization which would utilize defense of civil rights for Party purposes and raise and maintain mass defense and bail funds for Party use"); the Committee for a Democratic Far Eastern Policy ("Communist"); the Congress of American Revolutionary Writers ("subversive and Communist"); the Cultural and Scientific Conference for World Peace ("Communist front" — "a propaganda front for Soviet foreign policy and Soviet culture"); the Institute of Pacific Relations ("an instrument of Communist policy, propaganda and military intelligence");

the Joint Anti-Fascist Refugee Committee ("subversive and Communist"); the League of American Writers ("subversive and Communist" – "began openly to follow the Communist Party line as dictated by the foreign policy of the Soviet Union"); the Mother Ella Reeve Bloor Banquet (Communist Party festivity); *Partisan Review* ("Communist"); the *Protestant* ("with an eye to religious groups, the Communists have formed religious fronts such as the *Protestant'*); and the World Peace Congress ("organized under Communist initiative in various countries throughout the world"). She became a familiar figure on lecture platforms and radio broadcasts as she continued her role as a propagandist for the Chinese Communists. She lectured for a time at Skidmore College. She wrote articles for the pro-Communist publications, *PM* and the *New York Star*. She took an active part in the 1948 Wallace-for-President campaign – that year's favorite Communist Party project. In 1943, her *Battle Hymn of China* was published by Alfred A. Knopf, Inc., and selected by the Book Find Club, which regularly promoted pro-Communist literature. She also contributed articles to the ultra-radical *New Republic, Asia,* and *Nation.*

During the American occupation of Japan in the immediate post-World War II years, General Douglas MacArthur's intelligence staff, under the leadership of Major General Charles A. Willoughby, uncovered the story of the Sorge spy ring and the relationship of Smedley to the ring. In 1948, against the wishes of Willoughby and his staff, the Secretary of the Army insisted that the report of the Sorge ring be released – which it was. Then, in February 1949, the Pentagon virtually repudiated the report. The International News Service reported:

"The Army's Public Information Division said flatly . . . that it was wrong and in error in charging that Agnes Smedley, an American writer, was a Russian spy. [Colonel] Eyster said 'the Division has no proof to back up the spy charges. The report was based on information from the Japanese police and the report should have said so. While there may be evidence in existence to substantiate the allegations, it is not in our hands. It was a mistake within the Division. The staff failed to handle the release properly. No names should have been used and no charges made.' "

The United Press quoted Eyster further, and also Smedley: "In New York, Miss Smedley promptly called the charges 'despicable lies' and there were others who criticized the Army's method of bringing out this report. Colonel Eyster . . . said the report certainly 'should not have been given out with the philosophy it contained that Americans might well look askance at their neighbors . . . . It is not the Army Department policy to issue papers stating facts as it did about Miss Smedley when the proof is not in our hands. It is not the government policy to tar and feather people unless it has proof. It is stated policy of American justice that a person is innocent until proven guilty.' Eyster said that the report was prepared by intelligence officers in Tokyo and that the 'young fellows that did it proceeded to philosophize and to add their opinion of its effect . . . . The report had been reviewed for its security implications and some parts had been removed. But it has not been properly edited from a public relations standpoint.' "

Smedley, once Eyster had repudiated Willoughby's report, hired long-time Red attorney O. John Rogge, and threatened General MacArthur with a libel suit.

Rogge issued a public statement: "...First we want to know if MacArthur will accept responsibility for reports coming from his office, and if he will, I suggest he get a New York lawyer because we are going to sue. After we get an answer from MacArthur, then we will decide whether to sue Willoughby. MacArthur is the one Miss Smedley wants to sue...."

In reply to the Smedley-Rogge threat, General Willoughby moved to have the attacks directed at him rather than at General MacArthur and he issued a statement: "...The Sorge Spy Report, collating and evaluating certain judicial and other official records found in Japan at the start of the Occupation, was made under my sole direction and, as Chief of Military Intelligence Section, Tokyo, I am responsible for its preparation and direct transmission to the Military Intelligence Division in Washington. It was a 'secret' document developed solely for military intelligence purposes and was not written or intended for public release. The scope of its contents embraced all information procurable here with the comments and deductions therefrom, normal to a security investigative agency. This section would have failed in its duty had it done less....

"I accept fully any responsibility involved and waive any immunities I may possess, to legal or any other action that may be taken or desired. I would in fact welcome, not only as an Intelligence Officer but even more fundamentally as an American citizen, an opportunity thus to emphasize the lurking dangers which threaten American Civilization in subversive systems hiding behind and protected by our free institutions..."

Smedley was the object of great sympathy from the left who considered her as a sort of maligned heroine whose innocence had been besmirched by ambitious witchhunters. Among those who rushed to her defense were former Secretary of the Interior Harold Ickes and former Secretary of War Kenneth C. Royall, who had departed from the government in 1947. The Communist press in the United States and abroad rallied to Smedley's defense. When Willoughby, however, offered himself as defendant in a libel suit, Smedley quieted down − after making the most of her martyrdom − and nothing more was heard from either her or Rogge about a libel suit.

If Smedley had pressed her libel suit, General Willoughby had more than enough proof, including Sorge's own confession, to satisfy any impartial jury that she had been a spy for the Comintern and − almost as a sideline − worked within the Sorge spy ring.

In 1950, at the very time Smedley was being summoned to appear before the House Committee on Un-American Activities, she sailed for England and announced that she intended to complete writing a biography of Chu Teh, the leader of the Chinese Communist armies, whom she had first met in 1937. Shortly after her arrival in England, in May 1950, she died at the Radcliffe Infirmary in Oxford.

In her will, Smedley named General Chu Teh as heir to her U.S. government bonds, royalties due from her published books, and "anything else of value included in her estate." She requested cremation and directed that her ashes "be shipped to China for General Chu Teh, Commander in Chief of the People's Liberation Army, and there be laid to rest at any place designated by General Chu Teh or his heirs." Her request was granted when her ashes were placed in the National Memorial Cemetery of Revolutionary Martyrs in Peking. Her grave was marked with a marble cenotaph and the inscription: "To Agnes Smedley, friend of the Chinese Revolution."

Harold Ickes wrote a tender tribute to Smedley in *New Republic.* In the *Peking People's Daily,* she was recognized for her contributions to the rise of Red China: "It was Agnes Smedley who first made known to the world the truth about Red China, at a time when the world was still deceived by the stories told by the reactionaries. Peace-loving people the world over will also deem the death of Agnes Smedley a great loss at a time when the international reactionary bloc, headed by American imperialists, is attempting to provoke a new antipopular war . . . . "

LILLIAN EUGENIA SMITH was born on December 12, 1897 in Jasper, Florida, daughter of Anne Simpson and Calvin Smith. She attended Piedmont College, Peabody Conservatory, and Columbia University. She was the author of *Strange Fruit* (1944); *Killers of the Dream* (1949; revised, 1963); *The Journey* (1954); *Now Is the Time* (1955); *One Hour* (1959); *Memory of a Large Christmas* (1962); and *Our Faces, Our Worlds* (1964). She contributed articles to *Saturday Review, Redbook, Life, New Republic, Nation,* and the *New York Times.*

From 1921 until 1924, Smith was a music teacher at a Methodist Mission house in Huchow, China. From 1925 until 1949, she was a founder and director in Georgia of the Laurel Falls Girls' Camp, for white girls age six to sixteen. From 1936 until 1946, she was founder, editor and publisher of a literary quarterly titled successively *Pseudopodia, North Georgia Review,*

and *South Today.* She lectured at Indiana University, Vassar College, and the University of Colorado. She appeared frequently on radio and television programs, and as a lecturer before all sorts of literary and service groups. Among her awards were the Page One Award (1944), the Constance Skinner Lindsay Award (1945), the Southern Award (1949), a citation from the National Book Award Committee (1950), the Sidney Hillman Award (1962), the Queen Esther Award of the American Jewish Congress (1965), and the Charles Spurgeon Johnson Award (1966). She was the recipient of a two-year fellowship from the Rosenwald Foundation.

Smith's fame as a novelist rested mainly on her first book, *Strange Fruit,* the love story of a Negro girl and a white man. The setting was the South. The language was earthy and vulgar. The plot involved murder and lynching. And it was a severe indictment of small-town mores in the South. The book attracted extravagant praise from liberal-leftist critics, and predictably — because of its sensationalism — it became a runaway best seller, with almost half a million copies sold within a year. Although Smith continued throughout her life to write and talk against racial segregation (except with regard to her white girls' camp), she never again reached the heights of fame that were hers in the furor over *Strange Fruit.*

Smith was a long-time national official of the ultra-radical National Association for the Advancement of Colored People and the ultra-leftist American Civil Liberties Union. For twenty years she worked with the Congress of Racial Equality (CORE). Through many of those years she seemed blind to the fact that CORE with its sit-ins, freedom rides, and other demonstrations, which disrupted cities and towns across the nation as its leaders goaded law enforcement authorities with cries of "police brutality," was a disruptive force. CORE's leaders, behind slogans of "nonviolence," acted violently, until finally they threw aside all semblance of peacefulness by rallying under the violent banner of "black power." Finally, in 1966, after years of violent behavior under the leadership of trained and accomplished agitators, CORE lost the support of Smith. She sent a telegram of resignation to CORE's director Floyd McKissick. At the same time, she blamed whites as much as blacks for the violent nature of CORE, which she had discovered belatedly. She wrote: "I strongly protest the dangerous and unwise position CORE has taken on the use of violence in effecting racial change. I am therefore resigning from your advisory committee.

"For many years, CORE was firm in its belief in the use of nonviolence and refused tactics dictated by anger and hate. Its leaders believed that only love and compassion, reason, and a vigilant search for truth could bring about creative human relationships. Unfortunately the stubbornness and dishonest methods of segregationists, the violence of the Klan, and the blind complacency of many white church people have made it easy for the haters to take over from the more wise and patient leadership.

"Now we have new killers of the dream. CORE has been infiltrated by adventurers and nihilists, black nationalists and plain old-fashioned haters who have finally taken over. But the whites must carry much of the moral burden for this having occurred. White Americans have not met the creative Negro leadership half-way. They demand that Negroes show more wisdom and patience than they themselves show.

"CORE was pushed hard by the inertia and violence of many white Americans before its wise leadership succumbed. But I do not believe in the use of violence, however great the temptation. We are working for something bigger than civil rights; we are working for better human beings, we are working for excellence in our cultural life. How can we achieve these goals unless all of us meet this challenge with honesty and intelligence and good will and speed?"

Smith was affiliated with the American Peace Mobilization ("formed . . . under the auspices of the Communist Party and the Young Communist League" – "one of the most seditious organizations which ever operated in the United States"); the Committee for Equal Justice for Mrs. Recy Taylor ("Communist front"); the Emergency Peace Mobilization ("Communist front"); the International Labor Defense ("subversive and Communist" – "legal arm of the Communist Party" – "part of an international network of organizations for the defense of Communist lawbreakers"); the National Citizens' Political Action Committee ("Communist front"); the ultra-leftist-pacifist National Committee for a Sane Nuclear Policy; the National Council of American Soviet Friendship ("subversive and Communist" – "specializing in pro-Soviet propaganda"); and the Southern Conference for Human Welfare ("a Communist-front organization which seeks to attract southern liberals on the basis of its seeming interest of the problems of the South"). She died in September 1966.

PITIRIM ALEXANDROVICH SOROKIN was born on January 21,

1889 in Touria, Russia, son of Pelageia Rymskikh and Alexander Sorokin. He married Elena Baratynskaia. He came to the United States in 1923 and became a United States citizen in 1930. He was an alumnus of the University of St. Petersburg (LL.B., 1914; Magistrant of Criminal Law, 1916; and Doctor of Sociology, 1922). He studied at the Teachers College in Kostroma Province, Russia (1903-1906) and at the Psycho-Neurological Institute in St. Petersburg (1909-1910). He was the author of *Crime and Punishment, Service and Reward* (1913); *Leo Tolstoi as a Philosopher* (1915); *Elements of Sociology* (1919); *System of Sociology*, two volumes (1920-1921); *General Theory of Law* (1920); *Today's Russia* (1923); *Essays in Social Politics* (1923); *Leaves From a Russian Diary* (1924; enlarged edition, 1950); *The Sociology of Revolution* (1925); *Social Mobility* (1927); *Contemporary Sociological Theories* (1928); *Social and Cultural Dynamics*, four volumes (1937-1941); *Time-Budgets of Human Behavior* (1939); *The Crisis of Our Age* (1941); *Man and Society in Calamity* (1942); *Sociocultural Causality, Space, Time* (1943); *Russia and the United States* (1944); *Society, Culture and Personality: Their Structure and Dynamics* (1947); *Reconstruction of Humanity* (1948); *Altruistic Love: A Study of American Good Neighbors and Christian Saints* (1950); *Social Philosophies of an Age in Crisis* (1950); *S.O.S.: The Meaning of Our Crisis* (1951); *The Ways and Power of Love* (1954); *Fads and Foibles in Modern Sociology and Related Sciences* (1956); *American Sex Revolution* (1957); *Power and Morality* (1958); *A Long Journey*, autobiography (1963); *The Basic Trends of Our Time* (1963); and *Sociological Theories of Today* (1966). He was co-author of *Principles*

of Rural-Urban Sociology (1929). He was editor of *Explorations in Altruistic Love and Behavior: Symposium* (1950) and *Forms and Techniques of Altruistic and Spiritual Growth: Symposium* (1954). He was co-editor of *A Systematic Source Book in Rural Sociology*, three volumes (1930-1931). He was a contributor to *Twentieth Century Sociology* (1945); *Ideological Differences and World Order* (1949); and *This Is My Philosophy* (1957). He was co-editor of *New Ideas in Sociology* (1913-1915).

In 1917, Sorokin resigned a teaching position which he had held for two years at the University of St. Petersburg – the Russian Revolution had erupted. He became a founder of the Russian Peasant Soviet, editor-in-chief of *The Will of the People*, a member of the Council of the Russian People, a member of the Russian Constituent Assembly, and secretary to Prime Minister Alexander Kerensky of the Provisional Russian Government. When the Bolsheviks overthrew the Kerensky government, Sorokin was arrested and spent three months in prison. When he was released from prison, he helped to organize the League for the Regeneration of Russia in Moscow and he took part in counter-revolutionary activities in Archangel. Again he was arrested and imprisoned, but he was saved from execution and freed through the intercession of Nikolai Lenin.

From 1919 until 1922, Sorokin was at the University of St. Petersburg as founder, first professor, and chairman of the department of sociology. In 1922, Sorokin became involved in difficulties with Soviet authorities. He was arrested, condemned to death, and, finally, banished from the Soviet Union. From Russia he went to Berlin, where he lectured for a short time. Then, upon the invitation of Czecho-Slovakia's President T.G. Masaryk, he went to Prague, where he helped to establish two magazines: *The Farm* and *The Peasants' Russia*. He also served in an advisory capacity to the cooperative schools in Czecho-Slovakia which were "for the training of peasant leaders of the future Russia."

From 1924 until 1930, Sorokin was a professor of sociology at the University of Minnesota. From 1930 until 1968, he was at Harvard University as first professor of sociology (1930-1959), chairman of the sociology department (1930-1942), and director and founder of the Research Center in Creative Altruism (1949-1968). He was president of the International Society for the Comparative Study of Civilizations and the American Sociological Association.

If Sorokin had been completely disillusioned after his unusual hairbreadth escape from the Communist butchers in his native land, he evidently found forgiveness along the way. In the United States, he had enough time away from his academic duties to become involved with leftist projects. Among his affiliations were the American Committee for Protection of Foreign Born ("founded by the Communist Party in order to exploit racial divisions in the United States for its own revolutionary purposes"); the American Peace Crusade ("Communist front"); the American People's Congress and Exposition for Peace ("Communist front"); the American Russian Institute ("subversive" – "Communist" – "specializing in pro-Soviet propaganda"); the American Slav Congress ("Moscow-inspired and directed federation of Communist-dominated organizations seeking by methods of propaganda and pressure to subvert the 10,000,000 people in this country of Slavic birth or descent"); the Committee for Peaceful Alternatives to the Atlantic Pact ("a Communist front organization . . . as part of Soviet psychological warfare against the United States"); the Committee of Welcome for the Red Dean of Canterbury ("England's most notorious pro-Soviet apologist among the clergy"); Educators for [Henry A.] Wallace (a pro-Communist enterprise); the Fellowship of Reconciliation (ultra-leftist-pacifist); the Freedom House Bookshelf Committee (composed of the most brazen leftists in the literary and academic world, promoting books by notable leftists); the International Workers Order ("from its very inception demonstrated by its pronouncements, its activities, and the authoritative statements of the Communist Party that it is a subservient instrument of the Communist Party of the United States"); the Mid-Century Conference for Peace ("aimed at assembling as many gullible persons as possible under Communist direction and turning them into a vast sounding board for Communist propaganda"); the National Committee for a Sane Nuclear Policy (ultra-leftist-pacifist); the National Committee to Abolish the Un-American Activities Committee ("to lead and direct the Communist Party's 'Operation Abolition' campaign"); the National Council of American-Soviet Friendship ("subversive and Communist" – "specializing in pro-Soviet propaganda"); the *Protestant* ("with an eye to religious groups, the Communists have formed religious fronts such as the *Protestant*"); *The Slavic American* ("official organ of the American Slav Congress" – "Communist-dominated"); and the Stockholm Peace Appeal ("Communist 'peace' campaign"). He died in February 1968.

GEORGE HENRY SOULE JR. was born on June 11, 1887 in Stamford, Connecticut, son of Ellen Smyth and George Soule. His second wife was Isobel

Walker. His third wife was the late Flanders Dunbar. He was an alumnus of Yale University (A.B., 1908). He was the author of *The Intellectual and the Labor Movement* (1923); *The Accumulation of Capital* (1924); *Wage Arbitration* (1928); *The Useful Art of Economics* (1929); *A Planned Society* (1932); *The Coming American Revolution* (1934); *The Future of Liberty* (1936); *An Economic Constitution for Democracy* (1939); *Sidney Hillman, Labor Statesman* (1939); *The Strength of Nations: A Study in Social Theory* (1942); *America's Stake in Britain's Future* (1945); *Prosperity Decade; From War to Depression: 1917-1929* (1947); *Introduction to Economic Science* (1948, revised as *The New Science of Economics,* 1964); *The Costs of Health Insurance* (1949); *Compilation Showing Progress and Status of the Defense Minerals Production Program* (1952); *Ideas of the Great Economists* (1952); *Gypsum* (1952); *Economic Forces in American History* (1952; revised with Vincent P. Carosso, as *American Economic History,* 1957); *Men, Wages, and Employment in the Modern U.S. Economy* (1954); *Economics for Living* (1954 and 1961); *Time for Living* (1954); *What Automation Does to Human Beings* (1956); *U.S.A. in New Dimension: The Measure and Promise of America's Resources* (1957); *The Shape of the Future* (1958); *Longer Life* (1958); *Economics: Measurement, Theories, Case Studies* (1961); and *Planning: U.S.A.* (1967). He was co-author of *The New Unionism in the Clothing Industry* (1920) and *Latin America in the Future World* (1945). He contributed articles to periodicals, including *Atlantic Monthly, Independent Woman, Nation, Virginia Quarterly Review, Current History, Dial, Saturday Evening Post, American Economic Review, Foreign Affairs, Harper's,* and *Annals* of the American Academy of Political and Social Science.

From 1908 until 1914, Soule was advertising manager for Frederick A. Stokes Company, a book-publishing firm. Between 1914 and 1947, he was with the ultra-radical *New Republic* magazine as assistant editor (1914-1918) and editor (1924-1947). In 1919, he was on the editorial staff of the *New York Evening Post.* In 1920, along with Stuart Chase, he was a founder of Labor Bureau, Inc., a Socialist organization, and he was director of that Bureau for more than twenty-five years. From 1922 until 1970, he was director-at-large of the National Bureau of Economic Research. From 1948 until 1957, he was a consultant to the Twentieth Century Fund, which has supported numerous leftist causes. He was a founder of the leftist National Planning Association. From 1949 until 1957, he was a professor of economics at Bennington College. He was a visiting professor of economics at Colgate University (1958), Washington College in Maryland (1958-1959), and the University of Tennessee (1961-1962). He was a teacher in summer sessions at Columbia University (1948-1952). He was an associate fellow at Yale University's Trumbull College.

Soule was affiliated with the American Association for Labor Legislation (Socialist); the American Committee for Democracy and Intellectual Freedom ("subversive and un-American" – "a Communist-front organization operating among college teachers and professors"); the American Friends of Spanish Democracy ("Communist front"); the American Friends of the Soviet Union ("Communist front" – "primarily concerned with the carrying on of propaganda in behalf of the Soviet Union and its system of government"); the American Pushkin Committee ("Communist front"); the American Youth Congress ("subversive" – "one of the most influential front organizations ever set up by the Communists in this country" – "the Communists were in complete control"); the Anti-Nazi Federation of New York ("Communist front"); an Appeal for Pardon of Robert Stamm (a German Communist); the Berger National Foundation (Socialist); Brookwood Labor College ("Communistic"); the Committee on Coal and Giant Power (Socialist); the Conference on Pan American Democracy ("Communist front"); the Consumers National Federation ("transmission belt" for the Communist Party's influence and ideology – "Communist front"); the Coordinating Committee To Lift the [Spanish] Embargo ("one of the numerous Communist-front enterprises which were organized around the Communists' agitation over the Spanish Civil War"); the Descendants of the American Revolution ("a Communist-front organization set up as a radical imitation of the Daughters of the American Revolution. The Descendants have uniformly adhered to the line of the Communist Party"); First Congress of the Mexican and Spanish American Peoples of the United States ("Congress was planned at a secret gathering of Communist Party leaders from the South and Southwest); the Fifth Congress of Youth, 1939 ("Communist"); Frontier Films ("Communist front"); Gerson Supporters ("the Communist Party organized a campaign in defense of the appointment of Simon W. Gerson as confidential assistant to the borough president of Manhattan"); In Defense of the Bill of Rights ("Communist front"); the Institute of Pacific Relations ("an instrument of Communist policy, propaganda and military intelligence"); the International Juridical Association ("Communist front" – "an organization which actively defended Communists and consistently followed the Communist line"); International Publishers ("Communist Party's publishing house"); the League for Industrial Democracy (Socialist); the League of American Writers ("subversive and Communist" – "began openly to follow the Communist Party line as dictated by the foreign policy of the Soviet Union"); the Marcus Graham Freedom of the Press Committee (leftist group in defense of an anarchist); the Medical Bureau To Aid Spanish Democracy ("Communist front"); the National Citizens' Action Committee ("Communist front"); the National Committee for People's Rights ("composed primarily of openly avowed members of the Communist Party and veteran fellow travelers of the Communist Party"); the National Committee To Aid the Victims of German Fascism ("an auxiliary of the Communist Party"); the National Emergency Conference ("Communist front"); the National Emergency Conference for Democratic Rights ("Communist front" – "subversive"); the National Religion and Labor Foundation ("Communist front"); the National Writers Congress ("Communist front"); *New Masses* ("weekly journal of the Communist Party"); the North American Committee To Aid Spanish Democracy ("Communist"); the Rand School of Social Science (a Marxian-Socialist training school for labor agitators); and *Soviet Russia Today* ("Communist-controlled"). Soule died in April 1970.

ROBERT KENNETH SPEER was born on August 11, 1898 in Peterboro, Ontario, Canada, son of Mary Stryker and William Speer. He came to the United States in 1914 and became a

United States citizen in 1924. He married Margaret Harrison. His second wife was Alice Hopkins. He was an alumnus of Michigan State Normal College (B.S., 1921) and Columbia University's Teachers College (M.A., 1922, and Ph.D., 1928). He was the author of *Measurement of Appreciation in Poetry, Prose and Art* (1928); *Science in the New Education* (1936); *Supervision in the Elementary School* (1938); *Education and Society* (1942); *Living in Ancient Times* (1946); *Backgrounds of American Living* (1947); and *How We Became Americans* (1947). He was co-author and editor of *National Achievement Tests* (1940). He is the editor of *Life Around Us* (1948); *Better Spelling Series*, four books (1947-1948); and *City and Country Arithmetic Series*, three books (1947-1948).

From 1915 until 1918, Speer was a principal of rural schools in Michigan. In 1922 and 1923, he was a research assistant for the Cleveland Board of Education. In 1923 and 1924, he was principal of an elementary and a high school in Montclair, New Jersey. From 1924 until 1928, he was an assistant director for educational service at Columbia University's Teachers' College. From 1929 until 1959, he was at New York University's School of Education as assistant professor (1928-1929), associate professor (1929-1930), professor (1930-1952), member of the division of advanced studies (1952-1957), and staff member in the department of administration and supervision (1957-1959). In 1944 and 1945, he was supervisor of training for the Sperry Gyroscope Company.

Speer was affiliated with the American Committee for Democracy and Intellectual Freedom ("subversive and un-American" – "a Communist-front organization operating among college teachers and professors"); the American Committee To Save Refugees ("perform-[ing] a most valuable function for the international Communist movement"); the American Friends of Spanish Democracy ("Communist front"); the American Labor Party ("Communist dissimulation extends into the field of political parties forming political front organizations such as the . . . American Labor Party"); the American League for Peace and Democracy ("subversive and Communist" – "established . . . in an effort to create public sentiment on behalf of a foreign policy adapted to the interests of the Soviet Union . . . [and] designed to conceal Communist control, in accordance with the new tactics of the Communist International"); the American Peace Mobilization ("formed . . . under the auspices of the Communist Party and the Young Communist League" – "one of the most seditious organizations which ever operated in the United States"); the American Youth Congress ("subversive" – "one of the most influential front organizations ever set up by the Communists in this country" – "the Communists were in complete control"); the Citizens' Committee for Striking Seamen ("the composition of the Citizens Committee clearly indicates its Communist nature"); the Conference on Constitutional Liberties in America ("an important part of the solar system of the Communist Party's front organizations"); *Equality* ("Communist Party enterprise"); Federation of Children's Organizations (leftist); *Fight* ("official organ of the American League Against War and Fascism [American League for Peace and Democracy], subversive and Communist"); Film Audiences for Democracy ("Communist front"); Gerson Supporters ("the Communist Party organized a campaign in defense of the appointment of Simon W. Gerson as confidential assistant to the borough president of Manhattan"); the Greater New York Emergency Conference on Inalienable Rights ("Communist front"); the Joint Committee for Trade Union Rights ("jointly with the International Labor Defense supported and defended Communist Party leaders . . . when they were serving prison terms"); the National Emergency Conference ("Communist front"); the National Federation for Constitutional Liberties ("under Communist Party domination and headed by responsible Party functionaries" – "one of the viciously subversive organizations of the Communist Party"); the National People's Committee Against Hearst ("subversive and Communist"); an Open Letter to American Liberals ("project of well-known Communists and Communist collaborators" – "in defense of the progressive movement undertaken by the Soviet Union"); the [Morris U.] Schappes Defense Committee ("a front organization with a strictly Communist objective, namely, the defense of a self-admitted Communist who was convicted of perjury in the courts of New York"); and the Washington Committee for Democratic Action ("subversive and Communist"). He died in August 1959.

WILLIAM BENJAMIN SPOFFORD was born on April 5, 1892 in Claremont, New Hampshire, son of Marcia Nourse and Charles Spofford. He married Dorothy Ibbotson. He was an alumnus of Trinity College in Connecticut (B.S., 1914). In 1917, he graduated from Berkeley Divinity School. In 1917, he studied at the New York School of Social Work.

Spofford was ordained a deacon of the Protestant Episcopal Church in 1917 and a priest in 1918. From 1917 until 1919, he was a master at St. Paul's School in Concord, New Hampshire. From 1919 until 1922, he was rector of St. George's Church in Chicago. From 1919 until 1923, he was labor manager for B. Kuppenheimer & Company, clothing manufacturers. From 1919 until 1972, he was editor of *Witness*, the national weekly of the Protestant Episcopal Church. In the mid-1920's, he was rector of St. Paul's Episcopal Church in Chicago. From 1935 until 1948, he was rector of Christ Church in Middletown, New Jersey. He retired from pastoral work in 1948. He was executive secretary of the Church League for Industrial Democracy for several decades.

Throughout the entire history of the Communist Party, USA, Spofford could be relied upon to take his place in the forefront of those clergymen who were willing collaborators in Communist Party projects and enterprises. It is difficult to avoid the conclusion that Spofford was under the discipline of the Communist Party, but he denied this. He did, however, admit that he was willing to work with the Communists in certain matters for certain objectives. In *Witness* (December 1938), he wrote: "The Church League for Industrial Democracy is an organization of the Episcopal Church, composed of approximately 3,000 members, who have pledged themselves to seek to understand the teachings of Christ and to apply them in their own vocations and activities in relation to the present problems of industrial society. There is no connection whatever between the American League for Peace and Democracy and the CLID, or between the Communist Party and the CLID. Some of our members are also members of the American League and accept the program above stated. Others approve of parts and disapprove of other parts. CLID members are, of course, free to join the American League or not as they see fit − or to oppose it if that is their conviction. The proposal was made at the last national meeting of the CLID that we affiliate with the American League. The proposal was overwhelmingly defeated, and as executive secretary I opposed affiliation. I did state, however, that I personally accepted the program of the American League and asked that I be allowed as an individual to cooperate with the organization. This was voted and I have since been active in the American League and am at present proud to be vice chairman.

"In regard to the Communist Party, it is, of course, a secular organization, based upon a materialistic philosophy, and for this reason is quite properly opposed by Christians. Their ultimate purpose is so to order society throughout the world that communism will be universal. However, because of the present world situation, with wars in Spain and China and with the Fascist powers threatening other democratic nations, they have set aside their ultimate objectives in order to join forces in a United Front to maintain peace and democracy. Just as a United Front, including the Communists, was necessary in China if Japanese aggression was to be resisted (a United Front that has received the blessing of Bishop Roots and I think I am safe in saying all our missionaries); just as Hitlerism might have been avoided in Germany and democracy maintained if the people had created a United Front (as Martin Niemöller told a group of us in Berlin last summer just three days before his arrest; so I believe a United Front must be built in the United States if democracy is to be maintained and war avoided. And an effective United Front is built not by various groups stressing their differences but rather by setting aside their differences and uniting wholeheartedly in a minimum program. The Communists, as far as my experience means anything, are sincere in their desire for a United Front and are effective workers for it. Therefore, I am happy to join forces with them, and others, on this minimum program for peace and democracy. When and if they change their 'line' (and I do not believe I shall be so innocent as not to know) it is probable that I shall part company with them."

In the midst of the furor over the Stalin-Hitler Pact of 1939, Spofford demonstrated his unwavering allegiance to Communism by defending the Communist Party, USA, and the Communist regime of the Soviet Union. He consistently praised Communism as an ideology and as a system of government. He was firmly opposed to any governmental activities designed to hinder Communists in America. Among his affiliations were the ultra-leftist American Civil Liberties Union; the American Committee for Protection of Foreign Born ("founded by the Communist Party in order to exploit racial divisions in the United States for its own revolutionary purposes"); the American Continental Congress for World Peace ("another phase in the Communist 'peace' campaign, aimed at consolidating anti-American Forces throughout the Western Hemisphere"); the American Friends of Spanish Democracy ("Communist front"); the American Friends of the Chinese People ("Communist front"); the American League Against War and Fascism ("subversive and Communist" − "established in the United States in an effort to create public sentiment on behalf of a foreign policy adapted to the interests of the Soviet Union"); American Youth for

Democracy ("subversive and Communist" – "part of Soviet psychological warfare against the United States"); Arts, Sciences and Professions for May Day ("Communist Party project"); the Bill of Rights Conference ("subversive"); Brookwood Labor College ("Communistic"); the China Aid Council ("Communist-controlled"); the Citizens' Committee for Harry Bridges ("Communist"); the Citizens' Committee To Free Earl Browder ("a strictly Communist Party affair"); the Civil Rights Congress ("created and established by the Communist Party as an organization which would utilize defense of civil rights for Party purposes and raise and maintain mass defense and bail funds for Party use"); the Committee for a Boycott Against Japanese Aggression ("the committee was featured in the *Daily Worker*, official organ of the Communist Party, and in that paper alone"); the Committee for Peaceful Alternatives to the Atlantic Pact ("a Communist front organization . . . as part of Soviet psychological warfare against the United States"); the Committee for Peace Through World Cooperation ("it is significant that the Committee . . . received its chief publicity in the Communist press"); the Committee To Defend America by Keeping Out of War ("Communist front"); the Conference on Constitutional Liberties in America ("an important part of the solar system of the Communist Party's front organization"); the Coordinating Committee To Lift the [Spanish] Embargo ("one of the numerous Communist-front enterprises which were organized around the Communists' agitation over the Spanish Civil War"); the Emergency Peace Mobilization ("Communist front"); the Red-laden Federal Council of Churches; the Fellowship of Reconciliation (ultra-leftist-

pacifist); *Fight* ("official organ of the American League Against War and Fascism [American League for Peace and Democracy], subversive and Communist"); the Greater New York Emergency Conference on Inalienable Rights ("Communist front"); the Joint Committee for Trade Union Rights ("jointly with the International Labor Defense supported and defended Communist Party leaders . . . when they were serving prison terms"); the Joint Committee on Unemployment ("dominated by Socialists); the National Assembly for Peace ("Communist front"); the National Committee To Abolish the Un-American Activities Committee ("to lead and direct the Communist Party's 'Operation Abolition' campaign"); the National Congress for Unemployment and Social Insurance ("Communist front"); the National Council of American-Soviet Friendship ("subversive and Communist" – "specializing in pro-Soviet propaganda"); the National Council To Aid Agricultural Labor ("Communist front"); the National Federation for Constitutional Liberties ("under Communist Party domination and headed by responsible Party functionaries" – "one of the viciously subversive organizations of the Communist Party"); the Non-Partisan Committee for the Re-election of Congressman Vito Marcantonio ("Communist front"); the North American Committee To Aid Spanish Democracy ("Communist"); an Open Letter in Defense of Harry Bridges ("Communist front"); an Open Letter to American Liberals ("project of well-known Communists and Communist collaborators" – "in defense of the progressive movement undertaken by the Soviet Union"); the People's Institute of Applied Religion ("subversive and Communist"); the Reichstag Fire Trial Anniversary Committee ("Communist front . . . formed . . . by prominent Communists and Communist collaborators"); and the World Youth Festival ("Communist"). Spofford died in October 1972.

VILHJALMUR STEFANSSON was born on November 3, 1879 in Arnes, Manitoba, Canada, son of Ingibjorg Johannesdottir and Johann Stefansson. He married Evelyn Baird. He was an alumnus of the University of Iowa (B.A., 1903). He attended the University of North Dakota (1899-1902), Harvard University Divinity School (1903-1904), and Harvard University Graduate School (1904-1906). He was the author of *My Life with the Eskimo* (1913); *The Friendly Arctic* (1921); *Hunters of the Great North* (1922); *The Northward Course of Empire* (1922); *The Adventure of Wrangel Island* (1925); *The Standardization of Error* (1927); *Adventure in Error* (1936); *The Three Voyages of Martin Frobisher* (1938); *Unsolved Mysteries of the Arctic* (1938); *Iceland: the First American Republic* (1939); *Ultima Thule: Further Mysteries of the Arctic* (1940); *Arctic Manual* (1941); *Greenland* (1942); *Northwest to Fortune* (1958); *Cancer: Disease of Civilization* (1960); and *Discovery*, autobiography (1960). He was the editor of *Compass of the World* (1944); *The Arctic in Fact and Fiction* (1945); *Not by Bread Alone* (1946); *Great Adventures and Explorations* (1947); *New Compass of the World* (1949); and *The Fat of the Land* (1956). In 1905, Stefansson went on an archeological expedition to Iceland under the auspices of Harvard University's Peabody Museum. In 1906 and 1907, he led an ethnological expedition to the Eskimos of the Mackenzie River delta under the auspices of Harvard University and Toronto University. From 1908 until 1912, he led an expedition to the Arctic under the auspices of the American Museum of Natural History and the Canadian Government. He visited and explored the Colville delta, Cape Parry, Coronation Gulf, and Victoria Island. From 1913 until 1918, he led the Canadian Arctic Expedition, which explored the lands and seas of the Alaskan and Canadian Arctic regions.

After 1918, Stefansson generally confined himself to free-lance writing and lecturing. He did some medical experiments with diets. He was a consultant to Pan American Airways (1932-1945), and to the U.S. Navy during World War II. He was president of the History of Science Society (1945) and vice president of the Association of American Geographers (1945). From 1947 until 1962, he was Arctic consultant to Dartmouth College and Curator of Dartmouth's Stefansson Collection of Polar Literature.

Stefansson was affiliated with the Ambijan Committee for Emergency Aid to the Soviet Union ("Communist front"); the American Committee for Democracy and Intellectual Freedom ("subversive and un-American" – "a Communist-front organization operating among college teachers and professors"); the American Committee for Protection of Foreign Born ("founded by the Communist Party in order to exploit racial divisions in the United States for its own revolutionary purposes"); the American Committee for the Settlement of Jews in Biro Bidjan ("Communist front"); the American Committee To Save Refugees ("perform[ing] a most valuable function for the international Communist movement"); the American Council on Soviet Relations ("subversive" – "established by the Communist Party . . . directed and controlled by the Party, and operated to aid and support Party objectives concerning the defense and support of the Soviet Union"); the American Labor Party ("Communist dissimulation extends into the field of political parties forming political front organizations such as the . . . American Labor Party"); the American Rescue Ship Mission ("Communist Party project"); the American-Russian Institute for Cultural Relations with the Soviet Union ("subversive" – "Communist" – "specializing in pro-Soviet propaganda"); the American-Soviet Science Society ("subversive"); the Artists' League of America ("Communist front"); the Celebration of the 25th Anniversary of the Red Army (Communist project); Citizens' Committee To Free Earl Browder ("a strictly Communist Party affair"); the Civil Rights Congress ("created and established by the Communist Party as an organization which would utilize defense of civil rights for Party purposes and raise and maintain mass defense and bail funds for Party use"); the Committee for Citizenship Rights ("to protect Communist subversion from any penalties under the law"); the Golden Book of American Friendship with the Soviet Union ("pro-Soviet propaganda enterprise"); the Greater New York Emergency Conference on Inalienable Rights ("Communist front"); the Institute of Pacific Relations ("an instrument of Communist policy, propaganda and military intelligence"); the National Council of American-Soviet Friendship ("subversive and Communist" – "specializing in pro-Soviet propaganda"); the National Emergency Conference on Inalienable Rights ("Communist front" – "subversive"); the *Protestant Digest* ("a magazine which has faithfully propagated the Communist Party line under the guise of being a religious journal"); a Rally To Honor Eight Years of United States-Soviet Ties (Communist project); the Reichstag Fire Trial Anniversary Committee ("Communist front . . . formed . . . by prominent Communists and Communist sympathizers"); Russian War Relief ("Communist enterprise"); School for Democracy ("established by Communist teachers ousted from the public school system of New York City"); *Soviet Russia Today* ("Communist-controlled"); Tallentire Jubilee Committee ("Communist front"); United American Artists ("Communist front"); and the United States-Soviet Friendship Congress ("Communist front"). He died in August 1962.

[JOSEPH] LINCOLN STEFFENS was born on April 6, 1866 in San Francisco, son of Elizabeth Symes and Joseph Steffens. He was married to Josephine Bontecou. His second wife was Ella Winter. He was an alumnus of the University of California (Ph.B., 1889). Between 1889 and 1892, he studied at the Universities of Berlin, Heidelberg, Leipzig, and at the Sorbonne in Paris. He was the author of *The Shame of the Cities* (1904); *The Struggle for Self-Government* (1906); *Upbuilders* (1909); *The Least of These* (1910); *Moses in Red: The Revolt of Israel As a Typical Revolution* (1926); *The Autobiography of Lincoln Steffens* (1931); *A Boy on Horseback* (1935); *Lincoln Steffens Speaking* (1936); and *Letters of Lincoln Steffens* (1938).

In 1892 and 1893, Steffens was a reporter and assistant city editor for the *New York Evening Post*. From 1892 until 1898, he was city editor of the *New York Commercial Advertiser*. From 1902 until 1906, he was managing editor of *McClure's* magazine. In 1906, Steffens joined with other members of *McClure's* staff in leaving that periodical and buying *Frank Leslie's Monthly*, which was re-named *American* magazine. Others in the group included Ray Stannard Baker, Finley Peter Dunne, John S. Phillips, Ida M. Tarbell, and William Allen White. The group, including Steffens, comprised the better-known muckrakers in American journalism. They were not the first muckrakers, but they were by far the most influential ever to appear simultaneously on the American scene. Their work in *McClure's* and *American* brought on a rash of muckraking articles in all the other contemporary mass-circulation magazines.

After leaving *McClure's*, Steffens spent his life mostly as a free-lance writer. By 1909, his reputation as a muckraker was rather widespread, and consequently, a Boston department store executive, Edward A. Filene, invited him to undertake a muckraking expedition to expose whatever political and social evils Filene imagined to exist in Boston. Once in Boston, however, Steffens was side-tracked by Filene, whose main interest appeared to be the spreading of Socialist cooperatives. Steffens, during his stay in Boston, adopted Socialism as an ideology. He also found time to befriend two young radicals from Harvard University and help them get their start in journalism. They were John Reed, who would be the first American buried in the Kremlin walls, and Walter Lippmann.

In 1914, Steffens went to Mexico and traveled with Venustiano Carranza, a revolutionary leader. In 1917, Steffens traveled to Russia in the company of Charles R. Crane, an industrialist and diplomat who went to see the effects of the war and the internal upheaval on the Russian scene. Steffens returned from Russia favorably impressed with the overthrow of the Tsarist regime. He wrote a laudatory introduction to Leon Trotsky's *The Bolsheviki and World Peace*, published in 1918. In April 1919, Steffens accompanied William C. Bullitt, an emissary of President Woodrow Wilson, to Russia. While there, Steffens interviewed Nikolai Lenin, who so captivated Steffens that when he returned to the United States, he declared: "I have seen the future, and it works." Steffens, who once more visited Russia, never lost his enthusiasm for that Communist State. As late as 1932, Steffens wrote: "It is, I admit, heart and head-breaking to see the job begun and carried on over there by a dictator and a small minority using force when they don't know how otherwise to govern . . . . [But we] can rejoice that the deed was done and a path blazed for us." He also reflected: "My (own) victory in Russia did take some of the fight out of me. The growing success over there made all progressive movements and liberal programs seem superficial, long and rather hopeless. And to start out again at the bottom to plan to search deeper toward the roots for a revolution – that looks like a long, hard course to take for an old, habituated Menshevik with only a thick skin of Bolshevism on his hardened arteries. It is pleasanter, easier, to sit on a fence and contemplate our progress in Russia, watch it work over there, and listen to the Wall Street sentries appraising it right – as they do and as the liberals don't – at its true significance for us; while I encourage younger men like Edmund Wilson and his readers to pick up and bear on the burden here in this our backward country."

In the course of his travels as a reporter, Steffens had occasion to interview the Italian dictator, Benito Mussolini. Steffens was as captivated by Mussolini as he had been by Lenin, and Trotsky, and Stalin. In his *Autobiography*, Steffens wrote: "It was as if the Author of all things had looked down upon this little planet of His, and seeing the physical, mental, moral confusion here, said to Himself, 'How can I, in a flash, clear up these poor humans? I haven't much time for so small a ball of mud, but I must somehow help them to change their minds and catch up with the changes I am making.' And 'I know,' He said: 'I will have a political thunderstorm big enough for all men to notice and not too big for them to comprehend, and through it I will shoot a blazing thunderbolt that will strike down all their foolish old principles, burn up their dead ideas, and separate the new light I am creating from the darkness men have made.' And so He formed Mussolini out of the rib of Italy." In Steffens' topsy-turvy judgment: "Mussolini took the method, the spirit, the stuff of Bolshevism and used it to go — right."

In 1927, Steffens settled in Carmel, California. From 1928 until his death in 1936, he traveled about the United States lecturing and engaging in pro-Communist enterprises. On an irregular basis, he contributed a weekly column to local papers, including *The Carmelite, Controversy*, and *Pacific Weekly*. In his column, his infatuation with the Soviet Union and Communism was most evident, as witness some excerpts: "I have been three times to Soviet Russia since their revolution and I am so sure that they have found the way that I use that observation in our politics, our American politics. I say that Communism fits us like an old hat." — "I am for a United Front over here if the Communists will lead it." — "To me, Lenin is not only the greatest revolutionary, he is also the greatest liberal." — "Even Reds dread the force and violence that the Conservatives make inevitable." — "So, to a poet, to a spirit like Jack Reed, the Communist, death in Moscow must have been the most wonderful thing in the world: a vision of the resurrection and the life of man."

Steffens was affiliated with the American Committee for Struggle Against War ("Communist front"); the American League Against War and Fascism ("subversive and Communist" — "established in the United States in an effort to create public sentiment on behalf of a foreign policy adapted to the interests of the Soviet Union"); the American League for Peace and Democracy ("subversive and Communist" — "established . . . in an effort to create public sentiment on behalf of a foreign policy adapted to the interests of the Soviet Union . . . [and] designed to conceal Communist control, in accordance with the new tactics of the Communist International"); the Anti-Nazi Federation of New York ("Communist front"); Book Union ("distributors of Communist literature" — "Communist [Party] book club"); the Congress of American Revolutionary Writers ("subversive and Communist"); the *Daily Worker* ("official organ of the Communist Party"); the International Student Congress Against War ("Communist controlled"); the International Labor Defense ("subversive and Communist" — "legal arm of the Communist Party" — "part of an international network of organizations for the defense of Communist lawbreakers"); the John Reed Clubs ("out-and-out Communist organizations which preceded the contemporary Communist front organizations which cater to so-called liberals"); the *Labor Defender* ("Communist magazine"); the League for Industrial Democracy (Socialist); the

League of American Writers ("subversive and Communist" – "began openly to follow the Communist Party line as dictated by the foreign policy of the Soviet Union"); the League of Professional Groups for [William Z.] Foster and [James W.] Ford ("the members of this organization were committed to the objectives of the Communist Party"); the National Committee for the Defense of Political Prisoners ("subversive and Communist"); the National Committee To Aid Striking Miners Fighting Starvation ("Communist front"); the National Committee To Aid Victims of German Fascism ("an auxiliary of the Communist Party"); the National Mooney-Billings Committee (dominated by Socialists); *Partisan* (semi-monthly publication of the John Reed Clubs); the San Francisco Workers School ("a school of instruction in Communism"); the Scottsboro Unity Defense Committee (Communist); and the *Sunday Worker* ("official organ of the Communist Party").

Steffens died in August 1936.

JOHN [ERNST] STEINBECK was born on February 27, 1902 in Salinas, California, son of Olive Hamilton and John Steinbeck. He was married to and divorced from Carol Henning and Gwyndolen Conger. His third wife was Elaine Scott. He attended Stanford University, intermittently, from 1919 until 1925. He was the author of *Cup of Gold: A Life of Henry Morgan, Buccaneer* (1929); *Pastures of Heaven* (1932); *To a God Unknown* (1933); *Tortilla Flat* (1935); *In Dubious Battle* (1936); *St. Katy the Virgin*, short story (1936); *Nothing So Monstrous* short story (1936); *Of Mice and Men*, book and play (1937); *The Red Pony* (1937); *The Long Valley* (1936); *The Grapes of Wrath* (1939); *The Forgotten Village* (1941);

Bombs Away: The Story of a Bomber Team (1942); *The Moon Is Down* (1942); *How Edith McGillcuddy Met R.L.S.*, short story (1943); *Cannery Row* (1945); *The Wayward Bus* (1947); *The Pearl* (1947); *A Russian Journal* (1948); *Burning Bright*, a play in story form (1950); *East of Eden* (1952); *Sweet Thursday* (1954); *The Short Reign of Pippin IV: A Fabrication* (1957); *Once There Was a War* (1958); *The Winter of Our Discontent* (1961); *Travels with Charley in Search of America* (1962); *The Short Novels of John Steinbeck* (1963); and *America and Americans* (1966). Steinbeck's scripts include *Of Mice and Men: A Play in Three Acts* (1937); *The Forgotten Village*, film (1941); *The Moon Is Down: A Play in Two Parts* (1943); "A Medal for Benny" in *Best Film Plays – 1945* (1946); *Burning Bright* (1951); *Viva Zapata*, film abriged in *Argosy* (1952); and *Pipe Dream*, musical (1955). He was co-author of *Sea of Cortez* (1941), reissued as *The Log from the Sea of Cortez* (1951). For his *Tortilla Flat, In Dubious Battle*, and *The Grapes of Wrath*, the Commonwealth Club of California awarded him gold medals in general literature for work by a California author. For his play *Of Mice and Men*, he won a silver plaque from the New York Drama Critics Circle. For his novel *Grapes of Wrath*, he received a Pulitzer Prize. And in 1962, he was awarded the Nobel Prize for Literature.

Steinbeck had his first book published in 1929, when he was 27. Prior to that time, he had held a variety of odd jobs, only one of which was related to writing – a short stint as a reporter for the *New York American*. After 1929, except for a year's work as a war correspondent for the *New York Herald Tribune* in World War II and another year's work during the Vietnam War as a correspondent for *Long Island Newsday*, he was a free-lance writer.

In 1947, Steinbeck was invited by the Communists to visit the Soviet Union because he was "a leading proletarian writer." Before that time and since, Steinbeck has been one of the few American writers whose works are allowed to circulate freely in the Soviet Union. Since the appearance of his *Tortilla Flat* in 1935, he has been a favorite of the far left in America. Many of his works, especially *The Grapes of Wrath*, presented a seamy side of American life. Class-consciousness permeated much of his writings. The setting for many of his books was California and his plots centered upon the lives of migrant farm workers and the fishing industry. If Steinbeck was to be believed, the economic woes of lower and middle-class America in and beyond the depression era were deliberately imposed by big businessmen with malice aforethought. Even in America, Steinbeck's friendliest critics regarded him in the same light as did the Soviet Union's literati: he was a proletarian writer. (When Steinbeck received the Nobel Prize in 1962, he more or less admitted his proletarian instincts when he said in his acceptance speech: "The ancient commission of the writer has not changed. He is charged with exposing our many grievous faults and failures, with dredging up to the light our dark and dangerous dreams for the purpose of improvement. Furthermore, the writer is delegated to declare and to celebrate man's proven capacity for greatness of heart and spirit – for gallantry in defeat – for courage, compassion and love.")

Steinbeck was not a chronic joiner of Communist fronts; he was, however, affiliated with the American Writers Congress ("subversive"); the Washington Committee To Lift [the] Spanish Embargo ("Communist front"); and the Western Writers Congress ("Communist front"). He was a severe critic of anti-Communist investigations. He was especially critical of witnesses who cooperated with such committees. But his main contribution to the left was through his writings.

In 1966, Steinbeck became involved in a rather curious propaganda coup for the Communists. A Soviet poet, Yevgeny Yevtushenko, wrote a poem titled "Letter to John Steinbeck," which appeared in *Literaturnaya Gazeta*. The poem called on Steinbeck to speak out against the Vietnam War. A few days later, Steinbeck replied to Yevtushenko with an open letter device published originally in *Long Island Newsday* and later reprinted in newspapers and magazines throughout the country. Steinbeck wrote: "My dear friend Genya: I have just now read those parts of your poem printed in the *New York Times*. I have no way of knowing how good the translation is, but I am pleased and flattered by your devotion.

"In your poem, you ask me to speak out against the war in Vietnam. You know well how I detest all war, but for this one I have a particular and personal hatred. I am against the Chinese-inspired war. I don't know a single American who is for it. But, my beloved friend, you asked me to denounce half a war, our half. I appeal to you to join me in denouncing the whole war.

"Surely you don't believe that our 'pilots fly to bomb children,' that we send bombs and heavy equipment against innocent civilians? This is not East Berlin in 1953, Budapest in 1956, nor Tibet in 1959. You know as well as I do, Genya, that we are bombing oil storage, transport, and the heavy and sophisticated weapons they carry to kill our sons. And where that oil and those weapons come from, you probably know better than I. They are marked in pictograph and in Cyrillic characters. I hope you also know that if those weapons were not being sent, we would not be in Vietnam at all. If this were a disagreement between Vietnamese people, we surely would not be there, but it is not, and since I have never found you to be naive you must be aware that it is not.

"This war is the work of Chairman Mao, designed and generated by him in absentia, advised by Peking and cynically supplied with brutal weapons by foreigners who set it up. Let us denounce this also, my friend, but even more, let us together undertake a program more effective than denunciation.

"I beg you to use your very considerable influence on your people, your government, and on those who look to the Soviet Union for direction, to stop sending the murderous merchandise through North Vietnam to be used against the South. For my part, I will devote every resource I have to persuade my government to withdraw troops and weapons from the South, leaving only money and help for rebuilding. And, do you know, Genya, if you could accomplish your part, my part would follow immediately and automatically.

"But even this is not necessary to stop the war. If you could persuade North Vietnam to agree in good faith to negotiate, the bombing would stop instantly. The guns would fall silent and our dear sons could come home. It is as simple as that, my friend, as simple as that, I promise you. I hope to see you and your lovely wife Galya soon. With all respect and affection, John Steinbeck."

For the benefit of his American readers, Steinbeck managed to place the entire onus for aggression upon Red China's Mao Tse-tung. Somehow Steinbeck managed to write his entire letter without mention of North Vietnam's Ho chi Minh, a Communist for almost half a century, whose indebtedness to the Soviet Union was immeasurable. He also managed to omit any mention of the Viet Cong and their wanton savagery against civilians in South Vietnam. He presented the impression that Yevtushenko was free not only to criticize and influence the military and political strategy of Soviet authorities but would also be allowed to speak freely to the Soviet people and "those who look to the Soviet Union for direction" about ceasing to supply North Vietnam with military hardware. And, most important, Steinbeck — and all who published his open letter in this country — gave Americans the impression that his criticism of Red China and the Soviet Union would be made known to the Soviet people through their press.

After a delay of a week, the *Literaturnaya Gazeta* printed its own version of Steinbeck's reply by offering a summary which omitted anything and everything critical of the Communist regimes of Red China, North Vietnam, and the Soviet Union. The summary said: "John Steinbeck answered this letter a few days ago in the American Newspaper *Newsday*. He not only rejected the plea in Yevtushenko's poem that he condemn United States aggression but also justified the actions of the White House and the Pentagon. Steinbeck sought to deny facts that are obvious to the entire world — the bombing of peaceful cities and villages, the murder of peaceful inhabitants, including women and children. He repeated the hackneyed official American propaganda, distorting the truth about the war in Vietnam and its perpetrators."

The Soviet-written "summary" was accompanied by three articles, critical of Steinbeck, from the Communists' *Daily Worker* of the United States, the French Communists' *L'Humanite*, and *Le Monde* of Paris, a leftist journal. The *Worker* said: "Steinbeck claims the war continues only because the Soviet Union and China are aiding the Vietnamese patriots, but he knows very well that this aid came only after Johnson sent in his massive military forces in an illegal and immoral invasion of South Vietnam." The article in *L'Humanite* insisted that total guilt for aggression belonged to the Americans. It continued: "John Steinbeck approves American aggression. His talent obligated him to defend peace, but he supports the escalation, the generals, the financiers and the business trusts who are delighted by this war." The article in the *Le Monde* called Steinbeck's reply to Yevtushenko a disappointment and said: "But in the final analysis, it is the Americans who are in South Vietnam, not the Russians, and not even the Chinese or the North Vietnamese."

Before the end of 1966, Yevtushenko came to the United States where he was lionized by the radical chic crowd. Steinbeck, in a widely circulated column, came to the defense of his "dear friend Genya." He wrote: "You must have seen a crowd of bloodthirsty but cowardly people urging two others to fight. It's been a little like that in a small way since my friend, the Russian poet Yevtushenko, has been visiting in this country.

"You remember the recent non-lethal thing we had. He wrote a public letter to me setting forth his views based on what information he had. And I answered him using what information I had. I would not have answered him if he had not been my friend and had I not known him to be a good and an honorable man, as well as a good poet. I had no quarrel with him or he with me. It was a discussion — two views based on different information.

"And now, too often during his visit here, he has been badgered and prodded and taunted by those people who thought it was a fight and wanted nothing more than to see it go on. I must say Genya has fielded their wild pitches with skill and adroitness. His message is peace and he is not about to be drawn to battle as an argument. On the other hand, he has never backed down. He believes just as he did when he wrote his first poem, and so do I. And both our stands are based on information not entirely pure. I suspect some of my information and all of his — and perhaps, although I do not know this, he has the same problem.

"And because I feel half informed, I am going to South Vietnam to see with my own eyes and to hear with my own ears. And if it were permitted I would go to the north and to China to look and to listen. And wouldn't it be a good thing if Yevtushenko could come with me to South Vietnam, could meet and talk with our soldiers. And wouldn't it be good if we could go north together. That would be wonderful because both of us would be looking not for arguments but for truth. And this is one man I would trust to know a truth when he saw one. We still might not agree, but at least our point of reference would be what is rather than what we have been told."

Again Steinbeck was aiding the Communists' propaganda machine. He failed to mention that his "dear friend Genya" was here in America as a propagandist for his Soviet bosses, who were anxious that he spread the news that the Soviet Union was on the side of peace. And of course there was no mention by Steinbeck of what propagandistic capital had been made of the Steinbeck-Yevtushenko exchange of "open" letters in the Soviet press earlier in the year.

Ironically, in 1967, when Steinbeck did visit South Vietnam and sent back a flurry of innocuous columns to *Newsday*, the Communists – here and abroad – and the peaceniks in this country branded him a traitor to his principles. And in an obituary at his death in December 1968, the *New York Times* recalled "his hawkish views."

BERNHARD JOSEPH STERN was born on June 19, 1894 in Chicago, son of Hatti Frank and Herman Stern. He married Charlotte Todes. He was an alumnus of the University of Cincinnati (A.B., 1916, and A.M., 1917). He was the author of *Social Factors in Medical Progress* (1927); *Lewis Henry Morgan: Social Evolutionist* (1931); *The Lummi Indians of Northwest Washington* (1934); *Society and Medical Progress* (1941); *American Medical Practice* (1945); and *Historical Sociology and Other Selected Papers* (1959). He was co-author of *Technological Trends and National Policy* (1937); *When Peoples Meet* (1937); *Philosophy of the Future* (1949); and *General Anthropology* (1952). He was editor of *Young Ward's Diary* (1935); and *The Family, Past and Present* (1938). He was assistant editor, beginning with Volume III, of the *Encyclopedia of the Social Sciences* (1930-1934). He was chairman of the board of editors of *Science and Society*. He was a contributor to the *American Sociological Review*, the *American Anthropologist*, *Annals* of the Academy of Polit-

ical and Social Science, and *Social Forces*.

In 1925 and 1926, Stern was a tutor at the College of the City of New York. From 1927 until 1930, he was an assistant professor of sociology at the University of Washington. From 1931 until 1956, he was a lecturer in sociology at Columbia University. From 1932 until 1943, and from 1948 until 1956, he was a lecturer in anthropology at the ultraradical New School for Social Research. In 1944 and 1945, he was a visiting professor of sociology at Yale University. In 1937 and 1938, he collaborated with the Commission on Human Relations of the ultra-leftist Progressive Education Association. In 1939, he participated in the Red-dominated Carnegie Study of the Negro in America.

In 1939, in hearings before the Special Committee on Un-American Activities, Alexander Trachtenberg, the head of International Publishers, the Communist Party's printing house, testified that he had published pamphlets written by Stern under the pseudonym of Bennett Stevens. Trachtenberg estimated that the pamphlets were written about 1929.

In 1952, Stern testified before the Senate Internal Security Subcommittee. He pleaded the Fifth Amendment when asked about the use of a pseudonym. He denied being a Communist as of 1952 or during the previous five years. He pleaded the Fifth Amendment when asked about his Communist Party membership in or prior to 1947.

In 1953, Granville Hicks of Harvard University appeared before the House Committee on Un-American Activities. Hicks testified that he had been recruited into the Communist Party by Stern in the winter of 1934-1935.

Former Communist Party official Louis Budenz, in his *The Techniques of Communism,* discussed the case of Bernhard Stern. Budenz said, in reference to Stern's pleading the Fifth Amendment: "Stern denied that he was a Communist on the day of his appearance before the Sub-Committee. He also denied that he was a Communist the year before. But he refused to answer, on the grounds that it would tend to incriminate him, the question whether he had been a member of the Party several years before. There is only one explanation for such a stand, namely, that in the period about which he refuses to answer, the Party had not yet gone underground. Ex-Communists like Bella Dodd might be available to prove his membership then, and also some record of his affiliation might have been produced. A perjury conviction would have followed, and it was clearly to avoid this that Stern took his peculiar position."

Budenz further explained: "It is important to note, as a sample of Communist tactics, that Stern swore he was not a member of the Communist Party in 1952 or a year before, but refused to answer as to whether he was a member in 1947 or before. This makes plain one of the chief purposes of the refusal to answer on the grounds that it would tend to incriminate the witness. In 1947 and before, Stern knew very well, a number of persons had met with him in cell or branch meetings who had later left the Communists and could testify against him. But after 1947, the situation was different, either because those with whom he had been associated in Communist work had not left or because all vestiges of membership had been removed from him by the Party. We are aware that since 1949, at least, no Communist has had any vestige of membership, and even the rank and file members are only associated in units of five or six members. For many years,

those in key and delicate positions were obliged under Party discipline not to attend branch meetings and no cards were issued to them. In Stern's refusal to tell whether or not he was a Communist in 1947, we get a key to the tactic whereby some persons who are asked the question refuse to answer and some others with a long pro-Communist record answer in the negative. The former group includes those who attended branches and had cards when they were in an obscure position; the latter group has among it those who were in key or delicate positions when they became Communists. These latter people can easily swear that they are not affiliated, since charges of perjury cannot successfully be placed against them. It is the *records* of pro-Communists in education, government, or other agencies which should be primarily considered, therefore, and not whether technically they can be proved to be Communists. If those records reveal a consistent aid to Soviet Russia, its fifth column here, and its fronts, then these individuals are enemies of the United States and should be recognized as such. This is underscored by the record of front affiliations piled up by Stern since 1947, during the period when he swears he was not a Communist."

Stern was affiliated with the African Aid Committee (ultra-leftist-racist agitators); the American Association of Scientific Workers ("Communist front"); the American Committee for Democracy and Intellectual Freedom ("subversive and un-American" – "a Communist-front organization operating among college teachers and professors"); the American Committee for Protection of Foreign Born ("founded by the Communist Party in order to exploit racial divisions in the United States for its own revolutionary purposes"); the American Committee for Struggle Against War ("Communist front"); the American Labor Party ("Communist dissimulation extends into the field of political parties forming political front organizations such as the ... American Labor Party"); the American League Against War and Fascism ("subversive and Communist" – "established in the United States in an effort to create public sentiment on behalf of a foreign policy adapted to the interests of the Soviet Union"); the American League for Peace and Democracy ("subversive and Communist" – "established ... in an effort to create public sentiment on behalf of a foreign policy adapted to the interests of the Soviet Union ... [and] designed to conceal Communist control, in accordance with the new tactics of the Communist International"); the American-Russian Institute ("subversive" – "Communist" – "specializing in pro-Soviet propaganda"); the American Slav Congress ("Moscow inspired and directed federation of Communist-dominated organizations seeking by methods of propaganda and pressure to subvert the 10,000,000 people in this country of Slavic birth or descent"); the American-Soviet Science Society ("subversive"); the Bill of Rights Conference ("subversive"); Book Union ("distributors of Communist literature" – "Communist [Party] book club"); the Citizens Committee of the Upper West Side ("affiliate of the Communist Party"); the Citizens Committee To Free Earl Browder ("a strictly Communist Party affair"); the Civil Rights Congress ("created and established by the Communist Party as an organization which would utilize defense of civil rights for Party purposes and raise and maintain mass defense and bail funds for Party use"); the Committee for Citizenship

Rights ("to protect Communist subversion from any penalties under the law"); the Committee for a Democratic Far Eastern Policy ("Communist"); *Communist International* ("official organ of the Comintern"); the Congress of American Revolutionary Writers ("subversive and Communist"); the Council for Pan American Democracy ("subversive and Communist"); the Cultural and Scientific Conference for World Peace ("Communist front" – "a propaganda front for Soviet foreign policy and Soviet culture"); *Daily Worker* ("official organ of the Communist Party"); the Federation of Architects, Engineers, Chemists, and Technicians ("its leaders ... cooperate fully with the Communist Party and controlled organizations"); *Fight* ("official organ of the American League Against War and Fascism [American League for Peace and Democracy], subversive and Communist"); the Golden Book of American Friendship with the Soviet Union ("pro-Soviet propaganda enterprise"); the International Labor Defense ("subversive and Communist" – "legal arm of the Communist Party" – "part of an international network of organizations for the defense of Communist lawbreakers"); the Jefferson School of Social Science ("a Communist institution modeled along the lines of the new Communist policy which led to the decision to change the Communist Party into some kind of an educational institution"); the John Reed Clubs ("out-and-out Communist organizations which preceded the contemporary Communist front organizations which cater to so-called liberals"); the Joint Anti-Fascist Refugee Committee ("subversive and Communist"); the League for Fair Play ("Communist front"); the League of American Writers ("subversive and Communist" – "began openly to follow the

Communist Party line as dictated by the foreign policy of the Soviet Union"); the Medical Bureau and North American Committee To Aid Spanish Democracy ("subversive and un-American"); the Mother Ella Reeve Bloor Banquet ("Communist Party festivity"); the National Committtee for Defense of Political Prisoners ("subversive and Communist"); the National Committee for Peoples Rights ("composed primarily of openly avowed members of the Communist Party and veteran fellow-travelers of the Communist Party"); the National Committee To Aid Striking Miners Fighting Starvation ("Communist front"); the National Committee To Aid Victims of German Fascism ("an auxiliary of the Communist Party"); the National Committee To Win the Peace ("subversive and Communist"); the National Conference on American Policy in China and the Far East ("Communist"); the National Council of American-Soviet Friendship ("subversive and Communist" – "specializing in pro-Soviet propaganda"); the National Council of the Arts, Sciences, and Professions ("a Communist front used to appeal to special occupational groups"); the National Federation for Constitutional Liberties ("under Communist Party domination and headed by responsible Party functionaries" – "one of the viciously subversive organizations of the Communist Party"); the National Non-Partisan Committee To Defend the Rights of the 12 Communist Leaders ("pro-Communist"); the National Resources Commission (Communist enterprise); the National Wartime Conference of the Professions, the Sciences, the Arts, the White-Collar Fields ("Communist front"); *New Masses* ("weekly journal of the Communist Party"); Physicians Forum ("Communist front"); the Prisoners Relief Fund ("Communist front"); Progressive Citizens of America ("political Communist front" – "subversive"); Saturday Forum Luncheon Group ("Communist front"); the [Morris U.] Schappes Defense Committee ("a front organization with a strictly Communist objective, namely, the defense of a self-admitted Communist who was convicted of perjury in the courts of New York"); the [William] Schneiderman-[Sam] Darcy Defense Committee ("Communist"); the School for Democracy ("established by Communist teachers ousted from the public school system of New York City"); the School of Jewish Studies (branch of the California Labor School, "a subversive and Communist organization"); *Science and Society* ("Communist publication"); *Soviet Russia Today* ("Communist-controlled publication"); Statement of American Progressives on the Moscow Trials ("obviously a document concocted in defense of the line of the Communist Party and undoubtedly originated in the headquarters of the Communist Party"); the Stockholm Peace Appeal ("Communist 'peace' campaign"); Veterans of the Abraham Lincoln Brigade ("directed, dominated and controlled by the Communist Party"); Voice of Freedom Committee ("subversive" – to defend pro-Communist radio commentators); Workers Schools (Communist); World Congress Against War ("sponsored by the Communist International"); World Peace Congress ("organized under Communist initiative in varous countries throughout the world"); and Writers and Artists Committee for Medical Aid to Spain ("a Communist front set up for the purpose of agitation and propaganda").

Stern died in November 1956.

ANNA LOUISE STRONG was born

on November 24, 1885 in Friend, Nebraska, daughter of Ruth Tracy and Sydney Strong. She an alumnus of Oberlin College (B.A., 1905) and the University of Chicago (Ph.D., 1908). In 1902 and 1903, she studied languages in Germany and Switzerland. She was the author of *Songs of the City* (1906); *The King's Palace* (1908); *The Psychology of Prayer* (1909); *On the Eve of Home Rule* (1914); *Ragged Verse by Anise* (1918); *History of the Seattle General Strike* (1919); *The First Time in History* (1924); *Children of Revolution* (1925); *China's Millions* (1928), updated and published as *China's Millions: the Revolutionary Struggles from 1927 to 1935* (1935); *Red Star in Samarkand* (1928); *The Road to the Gray Pamir* (1930); *The Soviets Conquer Wheat* (1931); *I Change Worlds: The Remaking of an American,* autobiography (1935); *This Soviet World* (1936); *The Soviet Constitution* (1937); *Spain in Arms* (1937); *One Fifth of Mankind* (1938); *My Native Land* (1940); *The Soviets Expected It* (1941); *The Russians Are People* (1943); *Wild River* (1944); *The Peoples of the U.S.S.R.* (1944); *The New Lithuania*; *Inside Liberated Poland* (c. 1945); *I Saw the New Poland* (1946); *Tomorrow's China* (1948); *The Chinese Conquer China* (1949); and *Cash and Violence in Laos and Vietnam* (c. 1968). She contributed numerous articles to publications, including *New Statesman and Nation, Nation, Asia, Harper's, Atlantic Monthly,* the *New York Times* and the *Herald Tribune.*

In 1909 and 1910, Strong organized "Know Your City" institutes in Seattle, Portland, Walla Walla, and Spokane. From 1910 until 1914, she directed "Child Welfare" exhibits in New York, Chicago, Kansas City, St. Louis, Rochester, Louisville, Montreal, North Haning-ton (England), Providence, and Dublin (Ireland). From 1914 until 1916, she worked as an exhibit expert for the United States Children's Bureau. From 1916 until 1918, she served in an elective position on the Seattle School Board. She was recalled from the position by petition through the efforts of the Parent-Teachers Association, the Federation of Women's Clubs, and the University Women's Club, because of her leftwing activities. From 1918 until 1921, she was editor of a leftwing labor paper, the *Union Record* of Seattle. In 1921 and 1922, she worked for the American Friends Service Committee on a relief mission which took her to Russia and Poland. From 1922 until 1925, she was the Moscow correspondent for Hearst's International News Service, and her assignment was to cover Central and Eastern Europe. In 1925, she was a correspondent in Russia for the North American Newspaper Alliance. In 1926, she was in the United States on a lecture tour which included Columbia University, Smith College, Stanford University, and Wellesley College. In 1930, she became a founder and managing editor of the *Moscow Daily News*, an English-language newspaper published by the Soviet government. After a year as managing editor, she became a feature writer for the journal. In 1936, she left the Soviet Union and returned to the United States, where she lived on the West Coast. In 1944 and 1945, she was in the Soviet Union and then in Poland. From 1946 until 1949, she spent most of her time travelling throughout North China and Manchuria. In 1949, she was arrested in Moscow and deported on charges of espionage. She returned to the United States, where she faced a federal grand jury and denied that she was a member of the Communist Party. In

1955, the espionage charges against her were withdrawn by the Soviet Union. The authorities said that she had been framed by the former head of the Soviet secret police, Lavrentia Beria, who had been discredited and executed. From 1958 until 1970, she was a resident of Peking, Red China.

Sometime in the 1920's, Strong became a member of the Communist Party. She was later identified as a Communist by former Communist officials Benjamin Gitlow, Igor Bogolepov, and Louis Budenz. She was a widely traveled spy in the pay of the Soviet Union. She traveled extensively in the Soviet Union, in Red China, North Vietnam, and Communist satellites in Europe. She visited with the Reds during the Spanish Civil War. She was one of the most widely read Soviet propagandists in America. She had no difficulty in gaining access to lecture platforms at American colleges and universities and at various service clubs and church forums throughout the country. For almost forty years, through her writings and speeches, she propagandized on behalf of Red China. She was the virtual matriarch of the Red China lobby and during the last twelve years of her life, the Communist Chinese used her as a prize exhibit in Peking. She was the first American member of the Red Guards, and the oldest. From Peking, for almost seven years, she sent a monthly "Letter from China" to the United States extolling the virtues of Mao Tse-tung's regime. Her birthday was generally well-publicized, as Red Chinese officials, including Mao Tse-tung and Chou En-lai, attended her birthday celebrations, and photographs of Strong and her Red Chinese hosts were circulated throughout the world.

Strong did not neglect the opportunity to help the Communists during the Vietnam War. At her advanced age, she was still an accomplished propagandist. For example, in 1964, she was in contact with leftwing anti-war groups in the United States and gave them instructions on how they could best cooperate with North Vietnam. She wrote: "I call attention of my Western friends to the fact that a slogan we have nearly all been using, and that I myself used two weeks ago, namely to call for 'negotiation,' usually in a Geneva-type conference, is NOT the demand of Vietnam. Laos and Cambodia want such a conference and should have it. Vietnam does not ask for it. Her demands given in full in the Vietnam resolution, and given briefly in the Appeal: '(1) The U.S. Government must respect the Geneva Agreements of 1954; (2) Must withdraw its troops, weapons and bases from South Vietnam; and let the Vietnamese people settle their own affairs; (3) Stop its acts of provocation and war against the Democratic Republic of Vietnam (North Vietnam).'

"I asked Vietnamese if they opposed the demand for a reconvened Geneva Conference, as made by their Western friends. They said they did not oppose it if their friends found it a useful talking-point, but they thought their own formulation clearer, simpler, more likely to appeal to the world's people. Every nation in the world wants independence without foreign troops on its soil. Americans also want this; how can they then refuse it to the Vietnamese? People everywhere can understand that a nation that has fought 20 years for independence wants it. To demand 'negotiation' raises complexities. With whom? For what? This can even confuse.

"After much thought, I decide the Vietnamese are right. It is simpler, better to state clear aims than methods that are not clear. 'Take the U.S. troops out; let us settle our own affairs' is a clear, honest demand. 'Negotiate' raises questions. The 1954 Geneva Conference cannot be reconstituted, if only because in 1954 the Vietminh came as victor and now it is not even a participant. The U.S. broke the Agreements and split Vietnam, and now it is the South Vietnam National Front for Liberation that is victor. Will the U.S. negotiate with the NFL? Neither Hanoi nor Peking can speak for the NFL and certainly not those two co-chairmen of Geneva who in ten years never could make the U.S. behave. Too many alleged friends are dreaming up new strait-jackets for South Vietnam; 'Neutralization without Liberation.' The Vietnamese are through with that. They want national sovereignty, not to be wards of any other nation or group of nations. So better just say: 'The U.S. must respect the Geneva Agreements of 1954.' That means: 'Get out.' When the U.S. is ready to get out, a technical method is readily found, Geneva or another. But be clear that no Geneva nations brought it about, but the long hard fight of the Vietnamese."

In 1965, Strong travelled from Peking to Hanoi as leader of an "American" delegation to an anti-American "solidarity" conference. With her were about a dozen other Americans, including three turncoat soldiers who had been brainwashed during the Korean War. In Hanoi, she broadcast over the Communist radio facilities to American servicemen serving in South Vietnam. Her broadcast was the standard Communist line − denouncing United States imperialism and aggression.

In the 1920's and 1930's, Strong, while living in the Soviet Union, portrayed the conditions there as absolutely utopian. She of course was not the only American to do so. American journalists and fellow-travelers were as guilty as she was in propagating a totally false picture of conditions under Stalin. Few Americans, however, reached the heights of ludicrousness and hypocrisy she achieved in her propaganda. Eugene Lyons in his *The Red Decade* presented a pathetic portrait of Strong as he knew her in the Soviet Union. Her father, a minister, had visited her in Moscow. Lyons talked to him, and he wrote: "Anna Louise Strong arrived at my office in Moscow one afternoon in a state of agitation. What had I done to her poor father? Well, I had merely talked to him, frankly but with considerable restraint, about subjects on which he asked for information. Being a sensitive and frail person, it had apparently been too much for the man's constitution, and he had taken to bed. Miss Strong therefore wanted a favor and a promise, to which I agreed gladly and rather contritely. I would not tell her father any more disturbing truths while he remained in Moscow . . . .

"Miss Strong, like her father, is sensitive on these matters. She is not one-tenth part as cocksure and ruthless about the sad Soviet business as she seems to be in books and on the platform. Under her social worker's zeal burns a Puritan conscience. Again and again the impact of Soviet life has been hard on her nerves. I recall days when she sat in my office, on returning from a trip outside Moscow, in a condition of spiritual near-collapse. The mountainous confusions, sorrows, and brutalities were too much for her. Her Junoesque person quivered with honest emotion.

"But always her sense of duty triumphed over these sensibilities. The poor blundering revolution needed her mothering and understanding. Bravely she strode to a typewriter and indited another paean of joy for 'the achievements' of Stalin. Her whole emotional life was invested in this Russia. She could not go back on it. At all costs she must rationalize the facts themselves and rationalize the need for withholding these facts from those with too little understanding in her native America.

"In *This Soviet World* she came dangerously near to confessing that she was concealing things from the readers: 'I tell not the "whole truth," for truth is never "whole"; there are always at least two truths, the truth that is dying and the truth'that is coming into existence.'

"In a pious concern for the unborn truths, she helped the dying ones to their appointed graves. In handling the same famine, for instance, she avoided even the inept denials and evasions of other apologists. A hint so remote that only a perspicacious insider could know what she meant was quite sufficient for her purposes. Indeed, in *This Soviet World*, much of it given over to the peasant problem, the famine was reduced to a mere footnote, in tiny type, in the course of a discussion of censorship: 'The most striking recent example was the suppression of information during the difficult year 1932, a suppression which turned several American journalists permanently against the Soviets. The Soviets believed with some reason that detailed knowledge of their difficulties would provoke the threatened Japanese invasion.'

"And not another word about the famine in the entire volume! In the quoted footnote Miss Strong's implication is that the suppression of the facts rather than the facts themselves turned the journalists. I am one of the journalists involved and had discussed the matter with her repeatedly. She therefore knew full well that it was the horror of the millions of corpses in a human slaughterhouse that went against my grain, not the fact that we were confined to Moscow for the duration of the great killing. A further implication is that while she, these journalists, and a hundred million Soviet citizens knew all about the famine, the simple-minded and trusting Japanese embassy people, correspondents and spies were being fooled! And to cap it all, Miss Strong, having hinted at a story, fails to tell what precisely dangerous information was suppressed, and why she was continuing to ignore it in her book now that the Japanese Ambassador had found it out."

Thirty years later in Red China, Strong was still dealing in hypocrisy. In a radio broadcast, she attempted to convince her audience that the Red Chinese officials and subject peoples were concerned about the condition of Negroes in America. She said: "We .... Americans, living, working, and traveling extensively in China, have seen for ourselves how widely the Chinese people .... give (the American Negroes' struggle for freedom) their full support .... we wish to inform the American Negroes that China herself is an example that shows that racial discrimination and inequality can be abolished ....
The experiences of the Chinese people suggests that the American Negroes will not gain the full benefits under the present social system in America .... We think and hope you also realize that final victory cannot be won until you overthrow the monopoly capitalism of America, your final enemy, and also the enemy of the American people and of the people of the world ....
This Negro struggle is not yet the American Revolution but may spark it. As more and more of the American working class and progressives join to support the Negro movement for 'Freedom Now,' this may win a new birth of freedom for all exploited

Americans and reinforce the anti-imperialist struggles of the world."

Although Strong spent almost half of her life outside of the United States, she nevertheless found time to engage in a myriad of activities promoting the Communist cause. She was affiliated with the Allied Labor News Service ("Communist front"); the All-Union Society for Cultural Relations with Foreigners ("Communist front") *Amerasia* ("Communist-controlled"); the American Committee for Friendship with the Soviet Union ("Communist front"); the American Council on Soviet Relations ("subversive" – "established by the Communist Party . . . directed and controlled by the Party, and operated to aid and support Party objectives concerning the defense and support of the Soviet Union"); the American Peace Mobilization ("formed . . . under the auspices of the Communist Party and the Young Communist League" – "one of the most seditious organizations which ever operated in the United States"); the American-Russian Institute ("subversive" – "Communist" – "specializing in pro-Soviet propaganda"); the American Student Union ("without exception . . . supported defense of teachers and students charged with Communist activity" – "pliable instrument in the hands of the Communist Party"); the American Writers Congress ("subversive"); the American Writers Union ("Communist front"); the California Labor School ("a subversive and Communist organization"); the China Aid Council ("Communist-controlled"); the Committee for a Democratic Far Eastern Policy ("Communist"); the Congress of American Women ("subversive and Communist"); Consumers Union (In the "solar system of organizations around the [Communist] Party"); the Cultural and Scientific Conference for World

Peace ("Communist front" – "a propaganda front for Soviet foreign policy and Soviet culture"); the *Daily People's World* ("official Communist Party organ"); the *Daily Worker* ("official organ of the Communist Party"); Federated Press ("Communist front"); *Friday* ("Communist-controlled"); Friends of the Soviet Union ("created, directed, and controlled by the Communist Party . . . and operated to aid and support Party objectives concerning the defense and support of the Soviet Union"); Icor ("the aims of Icor have been primarily propagandistic in behalf of the Soviet Union"); the Institute of Pacific Relations ("an instrument of Communist policy, propaganda, and military intelligence"); Intourist, Inc. ("Soviet travel agency"); International Publishers ("Communist Party publishing house"); the International Workers Order ("from its inception demonstrated by its pronouncements, its activities, and the authoritative statements of the Communist Party that it is a subservient instrument of the Communist Party of the United States"); the Joint Anti-Fascist Refugee Committee ("subversive and Communist"); *Labor Herald* (official organ of the Trade Union Educational League, "Communist"); the League of American Writers ("subversive and Communist" – "began openly to follow the Communist Party line as dictated by the foreign policy of the Soviet Union"); the *Liberator* ("Communist magazine"); *Masses and Mainstream* ("Communist magazine"); the Mother Ella Reeve Bloor Birthday Celebration ("Communist Party festivity"); the National Council of American-Soviet Friendship ("subversive and Communist" – "specializing in pro-Soviet propaganda"); the National Federation for Constitutional Liberties ("under Communist Party domination and headed by responsible Party functionaries" – "one of the viciously subversive organizations of the Communist Party"); *National Guardian* ("virtual official propaganda arm of Soviet Russia"); *New Masses* ("weekly journal of the Communist Party"); New Theatre League ("Communist front"); an Open Letter to American Liberals ("project of well-known Communists and Communist collaborators" – "in defense of the progressive movement undertaken by the Soviet Union"); Open Road ("Communist front"); *Pacific Affairs* ("international quarterly of the IPR"); the Philadelphia Workers School ("Communist"); *Slavic American* (official organ of the American Slav Congress, "subversive and Communist"); *Soviet Russia Today* ("Communist-controlled publication"); *Soviet Women* ("Communist"); *Spotlight on the Far East* (official organ of the Committee for a Democratic Far Eastern Policy, ("Communist"); a Statement by American Progressives on the Moscow Trials ("obviously a document concocted in defense of the line of the Communist Party and undoubtedly originated in the headquarters of the Communist Party"); *Sunday Worker* ("official organ of the Communist Party"); Tallentier Jubilee Committee ("Communist front"); Unitarian Fellowship for Social Justice (ultraleftist); Veterans of the Abraham Lincoln Brigade ("directed, dominated and controlled by the Communist Party"); the Washington Bookshop ("Communist Party enterprise"); the Washington Committee To Aid Agricultural Workers ("Communist front"); the Washington Commonwealth Federation ("controlled by a Communist Party faction"); Workers International Relief ("Communist front"); and *Workers Monthly* ("Communist Party publication").

Strong died in March 1970.

GENEVIEVE TAGGARD was born on November 28, 1894 in Waitsburg, Washington, daughter of Alta Arnold and James Taggard. She was married to and divorced from Robert Wolf. Her second husband was Kenneth Durant. She was an alumna of the University of California (A.B., 1919). She attended Oahu College in Honolulu. She was the author of *For Eager Lovers* (1922); *Hawaiian Hilltop* (1923); *Words for the Chisel* (1926); *Traveling Standing Still* (1928); *Monologue for Mothers* (1929); *The Life and Mind of Emily Dickinson*, biography (1930); *Remembering Vaughan in New England* (1933); *Not Mine To Finish* (1934); *Calling Western Union* (1936); *Collected Poems: 1918-1938* (1938); *Long View* (1942); *Falcon* (1942); *A Part of Vermont* (1945); *Slow Music* (1946); and *Origin: Hawaii* (1947). She was the editor of *May Days,* an anthology of verse from *Masses* and *Liberator* (1925); *The Unspoken and Other Poems by Anne Bremer* (1927); and *Circumference – Varieties of Metaphysical Verse, 1459-1928,* an anthology (1929). She was co-editor of *Continent's End*, an anthology of contemporary California poets (1925), and *Ten Introductions* (1934). She wrote the lyrics for William Schuman's *Prologue*, first performed in 1939; *Secular Cantata No. 1, This Is Our Time*, by William Schuman; *Holiday Song*; and *Lark*, four-part chorus by Aaron Copland. She was a contributor to periodicals, including *Harper's, Liberator,* and Max Eastman's *Freeman.*

From 1920 until 1926, Taggard was founder and editor of *The Measure: A Journal of Verse.* From 1929 until 1931, she was an instructor in English literature at Mt. Holyoke College. From 1932 until 1935, she was a teacher at Bennington College in Vermont. From 1935 until 1946, she was a teacher at Sarah Lawrence College. In 1931 and 1932, she held a Guggenheim Fellowship and used it to travel to Italy and Majorca. For one summer in the 1930's, she lived in the Soviet Union. Her second husband, Durant, worked in the United States for Tass, the Soviet news agency. She retired from teaching in 1946.

Taggard was a Socialist from her collegiate days. Her affiliations included the American Committee for Protection of Foreign Born ("founded by the Communist Party in order to exploit racial divisions in the United States for its own revolutionary purposes"); the American Committee for Spanish Freedom ("Communist"); the American Friends of the Chinese People ("Communist front"); the American Pushkin Committee ("Communist front"); American Revolutionary Writers ("subversive and Communist"); the American Student Union ("without exception . . . supported defense of teachers and students charged with Communist activity" – "pliable instrument in the hands of the Communist Party"); Book Union ("distributors of Communist literature" – "Communist [Party] book club"); the Committee of Professional Groups for [Earl] Browder and [James W.] Ford (Communist Party candidates for the presidency and vice presidency of the United States in 1936); the Congress of American Revolutionary Writers ("subversive and Communist"); Friends of the Soviet Union ("created, directed, and controlled by the Communist Party . . . and operated to aid and support Party objectives concerning the defense and support of the Soviet Union"); the Golden Book of American Friendship with the Soviet Union ("pro-Soviet propaganda enterprise"); the International Women's Day Celebration (Communist Party proj-

ect): the John Reed Clubs ("out-and-out Communist organizations which preceded the contemporary Communist front organizations which cater to so-called liberals"); the League of American Writers ("subversive and Communist" – "began openly to follow the Communist Party line as dictated by the foreign policy of the Soviet Union"); the League of Women Shoppers ("Communist-controlled front"); *Liberator* ("Communist magazine"); Mother Ella Reeve Bloor Birthday Committee (Communist Party festivity); the National Council of American-Soviet Friendship ("subversive and Communist" – "specializing in pro-Soviet propaganda"); the National Writers Congress ("Communist front"); *New Masses* ("weekly journal of the Communist Party"); Non-Sectarian Committee for Political Prisoners ("affiliate of the International Labor Defense, the legal arm of the Communist Party"); *Partisan Review* ("Communist"); Saturday Forum Luncheon Group ("Communist front"); *Science and Society* ("Communist publication"); a Statement by American Progressives on the Moscow Trials ("obviously a document concocted in defense of the line of the Communist Party and undoubtedly originated in the headquarters of the Communist Party"); the United Committee To Aid Vermont Marble Workers ("Communist front"); and *Women Today* ("Communist front magazine"). She died in March 1948.

ROLLAND JAY THOMAS was born on June 9, 1900 in East Palestine, Ohio, son of Mary Jackson and Jacob Thomas. He married Mildred Wettergren. He was a student at Wooster (Ohio) College (1919-1921).

From 1921 until 1923, Thomas worked for the Bell Telephone Company. From 1923 until 1934, he was an electric welder in the automobile industry. In 1934, he became a union organizer. In 1937, he played an important role in the strikes against Briggs Motor Products, General Motors, and Chrysler Corporation. In his career as a union man, he was president of Chrysler Local No. 7 of the United Auto Workers, president of the United Auto Workers, vice president and president of the International Union of United Auto Workers, and vice president of the Congress of Industrial Workers (CIO). He was a member of the National War Labor Board and of President Franklin Roosevelt's Labor Advisory Commission.

Thomas was affiliated with the Civil Rights Congress ("created and established by the Communist Party as an organization which would utilize defense of civil rights for Party purposes and raise and maintain mass defense and bail funds for Party use"); the Council on African Affairs ("subversive and Communist"); the Joint Anti-Fascist Refugee Committee ("subversive and Communist"); the Joint Committee for Trade Union Rights ("jointly with the International Labor Defense supported and defended Communist Party leaders . . . when they were serving prison terms"); the Michigan Civil Rights Federation ("Communist front"); the National Committee To Abolish the Poll Tax ("Communist front"); the National Committee To Combat Anti-Semitism ("Communist front"); the National Council of American-Soviet Friendship ("subversive and Communist" — "specializing in pro-Soviet propaganda"); the ultra-leftist-pacifist Society for the Prevention of World War III; *Soviet Russia Today* ("Communist-controlled publication"); and the Win-the-Peace Conference ("Communist front"). He was

treasurer of Sidney Hillman's National Citizens' Political Action Committee, one of the largest Communist fronts ever assembled in the United States. He died in April 1967.

CHANNING HEGGIE TOBIAS was born on February 1, 1882 in Augusta, Georgia, son of Clara Robinson and Fair Tobias. He was married to the late Mary Prichard. His second wife was Eva Arnold. He was an alumnus of Paine College (A.B., 1902) and Drew Theological Seminary (B.D., 1905). He was ordained a minister of the Colored Methodist Episcopal Church in 1900.

From 1905 until 1911, Tobias was a professor of biblical literature at Paine College. From 1911 until 1946, he was with the YMCA as secretary of the Student Department (1911-1923) and senior secretary of the Colored Men's Department (1923-1946). He was a long-time official of the Red-laden Federal Council of Churches. In the course of his YMCA work, he traveled to France, Finland, India, Latvia, Denmark, Liberia, Sierra Leone, Gold Coast, Nigeria, Belgian Congo, Ceylon, Estonia, Poland, Czecho-Slovakia, China, and Egypt. In 1951 and 1952, he was an alternate United States delegate to the United Nations General Assembly. He was active in the National Urban League. In the middle 1950's, he was chairman of the board of directors for the ultra-radical National Association for the Advancement of Colored People. He was a long-time director of the Marshall Field Foundation, a generous supporter of leftist causes. He was a trustee of the ultra-radical New School for Social Research. He was active in the leftist Liberal Party of New York.

Tobias was affiliated with the All-Harlem Youth Conference ("supported the policies and measures . . . advocated by the Communist Party and all its front organizations"); the American Committee for Protection of Foreign Born ("founded by the Communist Party in order to exploit racial divisions in the United States for its own revolutionary purposes"); the American Committee for Yugoslav Relief ("subversive and Communist"); the American Committee To Save Refugees ("perform[ing] a most valuable function for the international Communist movement"); the American League for Peace and Democracy ("subversive and Communist" – "established . . . in an effort to create public sentiment on behalf of a foreign policy adapted to the interests of the Soviet Union . . . [and] designed to conceal Communist control, in accordance with the new tactics of the Communist International"); the American Round Table on India ("Communist front"); the American Slav Congress ("Moscow-inspired and directed federation of Communist-dominated organizations seeking by methods of propaganda and pressure to subvert the 10,000,000 people in this country of Slavic birth or descent"); the Citizens Emergency Conference for Interracial Unity ("Communist front"); the Committee for Equal Justice for Mrs. Recy Taylor ("Communist front"); the Council for Pan American Democracy ("subversive and Communist"); the Council on African Affairs ("subversive and Communist"); the Independent Citizens' Committee of the Arts, Sciences and Professions ("Communist front"); the National Citizens' Political Action Committee ("Communist front"); the National Committee To Abolish the Poll Tax ("Communist front"); the National Council of American-Soviet Friendship ("subversive and Communist" – "specializing in pro-Soviet propaganda"); the

National Federation for Constitutional Liberties ("under Communist Party domination and headed by responsible Party functionaries" – "one of the viciously subversive organizations of the Communist Party"); the National Scottsboro Committee of Action ("Communist front"); the New York State Conference on National Unity ("Communist front"); the People's Institute of Applied Religion ("subversive and Communist"); the *Protestant* ("with an eye to religious groups, the Communists have formed religious fronts such as the *Protestant*"); the *Protestant Digest* ("a magazine which has faithfully propagated the Communist Party line under the guise of being a religious journal"); the Reichstag Fire Trial Anniversary Committee ("Communist front . . . formed by prominent Communists and Communist sympathizers"); the Southern Conference for Human Welfare ("a Communist-front organization which seeks to attract southern liberals on the basis of its seeming interest in the problems of the South"); a Testimonial Dinner in Honor of Ferdinand C. Smith ("Communist Party affair"); the Union for Democratic Action (Red-lined outfit whose guiding genius was Louis Fraina, one of America's first Communists); Veterans of the Abraham Lincoln Brigade ("directed, dominated and controlled by the Communist Party"); and the Win-the-Peace Conference ("Communist front").

Tobias died in November 1961.

EDWARD CHACE TOLMAN was born on April 14, 1886 in West Newton, Massachusetts, son of Mary Chace and James Tolman. He married Kathleen Drew. He is an alumnus of Massachusetts Institute of Technology (S.B., 1911) and Harvard University (A.M., 1912, and Ph.D., 1915). He was the author of

Purposive Behavior in Animals and Men (1932). He was co-author of *Comparative Psychology* (1934) and *Drives Toward War* (1942).

From 1915 until 1918, Tolman was an instructor of psychology at Northwestern University. From 1918 until 1959, he was at the University of California in Berkeley as instructor of psychology (1918-1920), assistant professor (1920-1923), associate professor (1923-1928), professor (1928-1954), and professor emeritus (1954-1959). He was president of the American Psychological Association.

Tolman was affiliated with the American Association of Scientific Workers ("Communist front"); the ultra-leftist American Civil Liberties Union; the American Committee for Democracy and Intellectual Freedom ("subversive and un-American" – "a Communist front organization operating among college teachers and professors"); the American Committee for Protection of Foreign Born ("founded by the Communist Party in order to exploit racial divisions in the United States for its own revolutionary purposes"); the American Committee To Save Refugees ("perform[ing] a most valuable function for the international Communist movement"); the American League for Peace and Democracy ("subversive and Communist" – "established . . . in an effort to create public sentiment on behalf of a foreign policy adapted to the interests of the Soviet Union . . . [and] designed to conceal Communist control, in accordance with the new tactics of the Communist International"); the Coordinating Committee To Lift the [Spanish] Embargo ("one of the numerous Communist-front enterprises which were organized around the Communists' agitation over the Spanish Civil War"); the National Emergency Conference ("Communist front"); the National Federation for Constitutional Liberties ("under Communist Party domination and headed by responsible Party functionaries" – "one of the viciously subversive organizations of the Communist Party"); and *New Masses* ("weekly journal of the Communist Party"). He died in November 1959.

CARL [CLINTON] VAN DOREN was born on September 10, 1885 in Vermilion County, Illinois, son of Dora Butz and Charles Van Doren. He was married to and divorced from Irita Bradford and Jean Wright. He was an alumnus of the University of Illinois (B.A., 1907) and Columbia University (Ph.D., 1911). He was the author of *The Life of Thomas Love Peacock* (1911); *The American Novel* (1921 and 1940); *Contemporary American Novelists* (1922); *The Roving Critic* (1923); *Many Minds* (1924); *James Branch Cabell* (1925 and 1932); *Other Provinces* (1925); *The Ninth Wave* (1926); *Swift* (1930); *Sinclair Lewis* (1933); *American Literature – An Introduction* (1933), reissued as *What is American Literature?* (1935); *Three Worlds* (1936); *Benjamin Franklin* (1938); *Secret History of the American Revolution* (1941); *Mutiny in January* (1943); *The Great Rehearsal* (1948); and *Jane Mecom, the Favorite Sister of Benjamin Franklin* (1950). He was co-author of *American Scriptures* (1946) and *American and British Literature Since 1890* (1925 and 1939). He was editor of *Modern American Prose* (1934); *An Anthology of World Prose* (1935); *The Borzoi Reader* (1936); *Benjamin Franklin's Autobiographical Writings* (1945); *Portable Library of Carl Van Doren* (1945); *Letters and Papers of Benjamin Franklin and Richard Jackson* (1947); *The Portable Swift* (1948); and

The Letters of Benjamin Franklin and Jane Mecom (1950). He was translator of Friedrich Hebbel's *Judith* (1914). In 1939, he received the Pulitzer prize for biography for his *Benjamin Franklin.* In 1943, he received the Franklin medal from the American Philosophical Society.

In 1907 and 1908, Van Doren was an assistant in rhetoric at the University of Illinois. From 1911 until 1930, he was at Columbia University as an instructor in English (1911-1914); assistant professor (1914-1916); and associate professor (1916-1930). From 1916 until 1919, he was headmaster of the Brearley School. From 1919 until 1922, he was literary editor of the radical *Nation* magazine. From 1922 until 1925, he was literary editor of *Century* magazine. From 1926 until 1934, he was a founder and editor of *The Literary Guild.* From 1941 until 1944, he was chairman of the Readers' Club. From 1946 until 1950, he was editor of *The Living Library.* From 1926 until 1936, he was on the committee of management for the *Dictionary of American Biography.* From 1917 until 1921, he was managing editor of the *Cambridge History of American Literature.* In 1922, he was managing editor of the *Short History of American Literature.*

Van Doren was a long-time advocate of world government. In 1948, when *The Great Rehearsal* was published, a separate notice was included with every copy of the book. It read: "To the Reader: Often, when I write or speak about the federal structure of our national government, interested people ask me if there is not some way in which they can join in a movement directed to the achievement of a federal system of government on a world scale – at least in a limited form adequate to prevent war . . . . To such interested readers of *The Great Rehearsal,* may I suggest there are several groups in the United States working in this direction – all of them seeking world federal government as the goal and differing mostly in their approaches. That with the policy and program to which I subscribe is United World Federalists, 31 East 74 Street, New York 21, New York. Carl Van Doren." The United World Federalists, then and later, was the most prestigious group of fellow-travelers and dupes working for world government at the expense of United States sovereignty.

Van Doren was affiliated with the American Committee for Anti-Nazi Literature ("individuals and organizations connected with it identify this Committee as a Communist front organization"); the American Pushkin Committee ("Communist front"); the American Society for Cultural Relations with Russia ("Communist front"); Artists' Front To Win the War ("Communist front" – "included representatives of the theatre, of literature, music, art, science, and education, with long and active records of support for Communist front organizations and for the variegated turns of the Communist Party line"); Book Union ("distributors of Communist literature" – "Communist [Party] book club"); the Coordinating Committee To Lift the [Spanish] Embargo ("one of the numerous Communist-front enterprises which were organized around the Communists' agitation over the Spanish Civil War"); the Emergency Committee for Southern Political Prisoners ("Communist front"); the Independent Citizens Committee of the Arts, Sciences and Professions ("Communist front"); the John Reed Clubs ("out-and-out Communist organizations which preceded the contemporary Communist front organizations which cater to so-called liberals"); the Joint Anti-Fascist Refugee Committee ("subversive and Communist"); the National Committee To Combat Anti-Semitism ("Communist front"); the National Council of American-Soviet Friendship ("subversive and Communist" – "specializing in pro-Soviet propaganda"); the National Institute of Arts and Letters ("Communist front"); the National Writers Congress ("Communist front"); and *Partisan Review* ("successor to *Partisan*, the semi-monthly publication of the John Reed Clubs"). He died in July 1950.

MARY van KLEECK was born on June 26, 1883 in Glenham, Dutchess County, New York, daughter of Eliza Mayer and Robert van Kleeck. She was an alumna of Smith College (A.B., 1904). She was the author of *Miners and Management* (1934) and *Creative America* (1936). She was co-author of *Employes' Representation in Coal Mines* (1924); *Technology and Livelihood* (1944); *Technological Basis for National Development* (1948); and *International Trade and Peace* (1961 and 1964). She was the author of books on women in industry published by the Russell Sage Foundation, including *Women in the Bookbinding Trade* (1913); *Artificial Flower Makers* (1913); and *Working Girls in Evening Schools* (1914). She was joint author of studies of social adjustment of atomic energy – efforts to abolish nuclear weapons (1943-1956). She was joint editor of *On Economic Planning* (1935).

From 1909 until she retired in 1948, van Kleeck was director of industrial studies for the Russell Sage Foundation. From 1914 until 1917, she was a teacher of labor problems at the New York School of Social Work. In 1918 and 1919, she was director of Woman in Industry Service for the U.S. Department of Labor, and a member of the War Labor Policies Board. From 1928 until 1948, she was associate director of the International Industrial Relations Institute. In 1931, she was the chairman of the program committee for the World Social Economic Congress. In 1932, she was president of the International Conference of Social Work. She was a member of the board of directors of the Encyclopedia of Social Sciences.

Van Kleeck was identified under oath as a member of the Communist Party by Louis Budenz and Arthur McDowell. She helped to draft legislation on behalf of the Communist Party, USA. She was co-author with Earl Browder, Secretary of the Communist Party, of a Communist Party pamphlet. On July 23, 1938, the *Daily Worker* reported: "The formation of an American Council on Soviet Relations was announced Thursday night at a dinner conference of 275 friends of the Soviet Union . . . . Miss Mary Van Kleeck, Associate Director of the International Industrial Relations Institute, who acted as chairman of the dinner conference, summed up the purposes of the American Council on Soviet Relations as follows: (1) To promote a wider understanding of the fact that the effects of the Soviet Union in the international field are wholly on the side of the forces of peace and democracy. (2) To clear the air of the confusion caused by hostile propaganda against the Soviet Union and place upon the record the facts regarding the real situation in that country and its achievements in the building of a socialist society.

"Explaining the origin of the American Council on Soviet Relations, Miss Van Kleeck said: 'The Council results from the drawing together of a number of people from different professions who are familiar with conditions in the U.S.S.R., and anxious to do their part to increase understanding of Soviet affairs in this country. This group has acted together on a number of occasions during the past year when no existing organization was in a position to undertake the type of meetings and issue the information we felt necessary on specific occasions. For this reason we decided to unite our efforts on a more permanent basis. In the international struggle of democracy against fascism, the interests of the United States and the Soviet Union coincide. Progressive forces in our country believe that the fascist offensive can be blocked only through the fullest cooperation of all forces working in the same direction. It is thus more than ever necessary at this time that the people of the United States and the Soviet Union understand each other.'

"The Council, said Miss Van Kleeck, does not intend to set up any new organizational machinery but will work through existing organizations and act as a medium for the wider dissemination of accurate information about the Soviet Union and its foreign relations, and will undertake only such activities as can be made self-supporting."

Van Kleeck was associated with the American Association for Labor Legislation (Socialist); the ultra-leftist American Civil Liberties Union; the American Committee for Democracy and Intellectual Freedom ("subversive and un-American" – "a Communist front organization operating among college teachers and professors"); the American Committee for Yugoslav Relief ("subversive and Communist"); the American Council for a Democratic Greece ("subversive and Communist"); the American Friends of Spanish Democracy ("Communist front"); the American Labor Party ("Communist dissimulation extends into the field of political parties forming political front organizations such as the ... American Labor Party"); the American League Against War and Fascism ("subversive and Communist" – "established in the United States in an effort to create public sentiment on behalf of a foreign policy adapted to the interests of the Soviet Union"); the American League for Peace and Democracy ("subversive and Communist" – "established ... in an effort to create public sentiment on behalf of a foreign policy adapted to the interests of the Soviet Union ...[and] designed to conceal Communist control, in accordance with the new tactics of the Communist International"); the American Pushkin Committee ("Communist front"); the American-Russian Institute ("subversive" – "Communist" – "specializing in pro-Soviet propaganda"); the American Slav Congress ("Moscow-inspired and directed federation of Communist-dominated organizations seeking by methods of propaganda and pressure to subvert the 10,000,000 people in this country of Slavic birth or descent"); the American Youth Congress ("subversive" – "one of the most influential front organizations ever set up by the Communists in this country" – "the Communists were in complete control"); the Anti-Fascist Congress of Women in Moscow, 1941 (Communist-dominated); Book Union ("distributors of Communist literature" – "Communist [Party] book club"); a Brief [amicus curiae] in the Case of the Communist Party, USA, v. the Subversive Activities Control Board (Communist enterprise); the Citizens Committee To Free Earl Browder ("a strictly Communist Party affair"); the Civil Rights Congress ("created and established by the Communist Party as an organization which would utilize defense of civil rights for Party purposes and raise and maintain mass defense and bail funds for Party use"); the Committee for a Democratic Far Eastern Policy ("Communist"); the Committee for Free Political Advocacy ("Communist front"); the Conference for Peaceful Alternatives to the Atlantic Pact ("initiated by Communists"); the Congress of American Women ("subversive and Communist"); the Coordinating Commitee To Lift the [Spanish] Embargo ("one of the numerous Communist-front enterprises which were organized around the Communists' agitation over the Spanish Civil War"); the Council on African Affairs ("subversive and Communist"); the Cultural and Scientific Conference for World Peace ("Communist front"); the Federation of American Scientists (leftist-pacifist); the Fraternal Federation of Social Insurance ("Communist front"); the Friends of the Soviet Union ("created, directed, and controlled by the Communist Party . . . and operated to aid and support Party objectives concerning the defense and support of the Soviet Union"); Gerson Supporters ("the Communist Party organized a campaign in defense of the appointment of Simon W. Gerson as confidential assistant to the borough president of Manhattan"); the Institute of Pacific Relations ("an instrument of Communist policy, propaganda, and military intelligence"); the Institute of Race Relations ("Communist-dominated"); the International Committee on African Affairs ("Communist-dominated"); the International Women's Congress Against War and Fascism ("Communist front"); the Inter-Professional Association for Social Insurance ("Communist front"); the John Reed Clubs ("out-and-out Com-

munist organizations which preceded the contemporary Communist front organizations which cater to the so-called liberals"); the Joint Anti-Fascist Refugee Committee ("subversive and Communist"); the League of Women Shoppers ("Communist-controlled front"); the National Assembly for Democratic Rights ("created, dominated, and controlled by members and officials of the Communist Party"); the National Citizens Political Action Committee ("Communist front"); the National Committee To Abolish the Un-American Activities Committee ("to lead and direct the Communist Party's 'Operation Abolition' campaign"); the National Committee to Defeat the Mundt Bill ("a Communist lobby . . . which has carried out the objectives of the Communist Party in its fight against anti-subversive legislation"); the National Committee To Secure Justice in the Rosenberg Case ("Communist front organized . . . to conduct the United States phase of a mammoth propaganda campaign designed to obliterate the crime of and exploit the Rosenbergs and their codefendant Morton Sobell for the purposes of international Communism"); the National Congress for Unemployment and Social Insurance ("Communist front"); the National Conference on American Policy in China and the Far East ("Communist"); the National Council of American-Soviet Friendship ("subversive and Communist" – "specializing in pro-Soviet propaganda"); the National Council of the Arts, Sciences, and Professions ("a Communist front used to appeal to special occupational groups"); the *National Guardian* ("virtual official propaganda arm of Soviet Russia"); the National Joint Action Committee for Genuine Social Insurance ("Communist front"); the National Non-Partisan Committee To Defend the Rights of the 12 Communist Leaders (pro-Communist); the National Wartime Conference of the Professions, the Sciences, the Arts, the White-Collar Fields ("Communist front"); *New Masses* ("weekly journal of the Communist Party"); the New York Professional Workers Conference on Social Insurance ("Communist front"); the Non-Partisan Committee for the Reelection of Congressman Vito Marcantonio ("Communist front"); the North American Committee To Aid Spanish Democracy ("Communist"); an Open Letter for Closer Cooperation With the Soviet Union (issued by "a group of Communist Party stooges"); an Open Letter to American Liberals ("project of well-known Communists and Communist collaborators" – "in defense of the progressive movement undertaken by the Soviet Union"); the Political Prisoners Bail Fund Committee ("the personnel and the objectives . . . make it obvious . . . that the organization was a Communist Party front"); the Provisional Committee for a National Congress for Social Security ("Communist front"); Russian War Relief ("Communist enterprise"); the Social Workers Committee To Aid Spanish Democracy ("Communist front"); *Social Work Today* ("Communist magazine"); *Soviet Russia Today* ("Communist-controlled publication"); Spanish Refugee Relief Campaign ("Communist front"); *Survey* (Socialist); the Unemployed Local City Projects Council ("Communist-dominated"); the United Aid for Peoples of African Descent ("Communist-dominated"); the Washington Committee for Democratic Action ("subversive and Communist"); the Washington Committee To Lift [the] Spanish Embargo ("Communist front"); *Women Today* (Communist-front publication); Women's Internation-

al Democratic Federation (leftist); Workers Library Publishers ("Communist"); World Federation of Democratic Youth ("a pressure group on behalf of Soviet foreign policy"); World Labor Congress Against War and Fascism, 1938 (Communist-dominated); World Peace Congress ("organized under Communist initiative in various countries throughout the world"); and World Youth Festival ("Communist operation").

Van Kleeck died in June 1972.

PIERRE VAN PAASSEN was born Pieter Antonie Laurusse van Paassen on February 7, 1895 in Gorcum, Holland, son of Antonia Sizoo and Adriaan van Paassen. His second wife was Cornelia Sizoo. He came to the United States in 1923 and became a naturalized American citizen. He was an alumnus of the University of Paris (B. Th., 1934). He attended Victoria College in Toronto, Canada (1914-1916). He was the author of *Israel and the Vision of Humanity* (1932); *Évolution de la Conception de la Cité de Dieu* (1934); *The Deep Red Banner of the Cross* (1937); *Days of Our Years* (1939); *The Time Is Now!* (1941); *That Day Alone* (1941); *Who's On the Lord's Side? Who?* (1942); *The Forgotten Ally* (1943); *Earth Could Be Fair* (1946); *Why Jesus Died* (1949); *Jerusalem Calling; Visions Rise and Change* (1955); *A Pilgrim's Vow* (1956); *A Crown of Fire* (1960); and *To Number Our Days* (1964). He was co-editor of *Nazism: An Assault on Civilization* (1934).

During World War I, Van Paassen served with the Canadian Army. In 1919 and 1920, he was a reporter for the *Toronto Globe*. From 1921 until 1924, he was a columnist ("The World's Window"); for the *Atlanta Constitution*. From 1924 until 1931, he was a columnist and a roving correspondent for the *New York World* and the North American Newspaper Alliance. In his work, he traveled to Ethiopia, Palestine, Turkey, Rumania, Morocco, Egypt, Nigeria, Spain, Italy, Russia, Poland, and Germany. From 1932 until 1935, he was a roving correspondent for the *Toronto Star*. He interviewed Adolf Hitler and Benito Mussolini. He spent three years in Russia. After 1935, he was a free-lance writer. In 1946, he was ordained to the ministry of the Unitarian Church but he never became attached to any particular church.

Van Paassen was a tireless worker for Zionism. He was active in several Zionist organizations, and as early as 1934 he was made an honorary citizen of Tel Aviv. His newspaper reports and columns, his feature stories and books were consistently written along pro-Communist lines. His affiliations included Allied Voters Against Coudert ("an example of the Communist apparatus for character assassination in operation against one who opposed the efforts of the Communist Party to undermine and destroy American democracy"); the American Committee for Spanish Freedom ("Communist"); the American Committee for Yugoslav Relief ("subversive and Communist"); the American Committee To Save Refugees ("perform-[ing] a most valuable function for the international Communist movement"); the American League Against War and Fascism ("subversive and Communist" – "established in the United States in an effort to create public sentiment on behalf of a foreign policy adapted to the interests of the Soviet Union"); American Relief for Greek Democracy (leftist); the American Rescue Ship Mission ("Communist Party project"); the American-Russian Institute ("subversive" –

"Communist" – "specializing in pro-Soviet propaganda"); the American Society for Cultural Relations with Italy ("Communist front"); the Book Find Club (leftist); the Committee for Peaceful Alternatives to the Atlantic Pact ("a Communist front organization . . . as part of Soviet psychological warfare against the United States"); the Independent Citizens Committee of the Arts, Sciences and Professions ("Communist front"); the International Workers Order ("from its very inception demonstrated by pronouncements, its activities, and the authoritative statements of the Communist Party that it is a subservient instrument of the Communist Party in the United States"); the League of American Writers ("subversive and Communist" – "began openly to follow the Communist Party line as dictated by the foreign policy of the Soviet Union"); the Mid-Century Conference for Peace ("aimed at assembling as many gullible persons as possible under Communist direction and turning them into a vast sounding board for Communist propaganda"); the National Committee To Abolish the Un-American Activities Committee ("to lead and direct the Communist Party's 'Operation Abolition' campaign"); the National Committee To Combat Anti-Semitism ("Communist front"); the National Committee To Repeal the McCarran Act ("Communist front" – "subversive"); the National Council of the Arts, Sciences, and Professions ("a Communist front used to appeal to special occupational groups"); People's Peace ("Communist front"); the *Protestant* ("with an eye to religious groups, the Communists have formed religious fronts such as the *Protestant*"); the *Protestant Digest* ("a magazine which has faithfully propagated the Communist Party line under the guise of a religious journal"); the [Morris U.] Schappes Defense Committee ("a front organization with a strictly Communist objective, namely, the defense of a self-admitted Communist who was convicted of perjury in the courts of New York"); a Testimonial Dinner in Honor of Ferdinand C. Smith ("Communist Party affair"); the United American Spanish Aid Committee ("Communist"); and the Veterans of the Abraham Lincoln Brigade ("directed, dominated and controlled by the Communist Party").

Van Paassen died in January 1968.

OSWALD GARRISON VILLARD was born on March 13, 1872 in Wiesbaden, Germany, son of Fanny Garrison and Henry Villard, American citizens. He married Julia Sandford. He was an alumnus of Harvard University (A.B., 1893, and A.M., 1896). He was the author of *Early History of Wall Street* (1897); *John Brown, 1800-1859 – A Biography Fifty Years After* (1910); *Germany Embattled* (1915); *Some Newspapers and Newspaper Men* (1923); *Prophets True and False* (1928); *The German Phoenix* (1933); *Fighting Years: Memoirs of a Liberal Editor* (1939); *Our Military Chaos* (1939); *Within Germany* (1940); and *The Disappearing Daily* (1944). He was the founder of *Yachting* magazine in 1907.

From 1894 until 1896, Villard was an assistant in history at Harvard University. In 1896 and 1897, he was a reporter for the *Philadelphia Press*. From 1897 until 1918, he was with the *New York Evening Post*, owned by his family. He worked for the *Post* as an editorial writer and managing editor, and in 1917 he became the majority stockholder. He sold the journal in 1918. From 1918 until 1940, he was with the *Nation*,

owned by his family since 1881. He was editor and owner of the *Nation* (1918-1932), publisher and contributing editor (1932-1935), and contributing editor and columnist (1935-1940). In the meantime, he owned *The Nautical Gazette*, which he sold in 1935. He was president of the Fort Montgomery Iron Corporation, the Garrison Realty Company, and the City Club Realty Company.

Throughout his journalistic career, Villard was a radical and one of the nation's most determined and vociferous pacifists. He waged journalistic crusades against United States involvement in the Spanish-American War, World War I, and World War II. He was strongly sympathetic toward conscientious objectors. He was a disarmament buff. He joined Socialists and other radicals in pushing for woman's suffrage. He was a staunch opponent of government interference with radical – even Red – activities. In the early 1920's, his *Nation* was described by the *New York Times* as, "if not actually Bolshevik, so near it that the distinction is not visible to the naked eye."

Villard belonged to the Socialist Party. He was a founder of the ultra-radical National Association for the Advancement of Colored People. He was a founder and long-time official of the ultra-leftist American Civil Liberties Union and its predecessor Civil Liberties Bureau. He was a national officer of the Socialists' League for Industrial Democracy. In 1939, he joined in a call for the Communists' Fifth Youth Congress. Villard's other affiliations included the American Committee for Protection of Foreign Born ("founded by the Communist Party in order to exploit racial divisions in the United States for its own revolutionary purposes"); the American

Committee for Struggle Against War ("Communist front"); the American Friends of Spanish Democracy ("Communist front"); the American Fund for Public Service ("a major source for the financing of Communist Party enterprises such as the *Daily Worker* and *New Masses*, official Communist publications, Federated Press, Russian Reconstruction Farms, and International Labor Defense"); the American League Against War and Fascism ("subversive and Communist" – "established in the United States in an effort to create public sentiment on behalf of a foreign policy adapted to the interests of the Soviet Union"); the American Pushkin Committee ("Communist front"); the American Union Against Militarism (dominated by Socialists and other leftist radicals); the American Youth Congress ("subversive" – "one of the most influential front organizations ever set up by the Communists in this country" – "the Communists were in complete control"); the Berger National Foundation (Socialist); Brookwood Labor College ("Communist"); *Champion* and *Champion of Youth* ("official organs of the Young Communist League and the International Workers Order, subversive and Communist"); the Citizens' Committee To Free Earl Browder ("a strictly Communist Party affair"); the Committee for a Boycott Against Japanese Aggression ("the committee was featured in the *Daily Worker*, official organ of the Communist Party, and in that paper alone"); the Committee on Militarism in Education (a supporting organization of the U.S. Congress Against War, "completely under the control of the Communist Party"); the Committee To Defend America by Keeping Out of War ("Communist front"); the Conference for Progressive Political Action (dominated by Socialists); the Consumers National Federation ("transmission belt" for the Communist Party's influence and ideology – "Communist front"); the Emergency Committee for Strikers Relief (Socialist); the Emergency Peace Federation (dominated by Socialists and Communists); the Fellowship of Reconciliation (ultra-leftist-pacifist); the First Congress of the Mexican and Spanish American Peoples of the United States ("Congress was planned at a secret gathering of Communist Party leaders from the South and Southwest"); Gerson Supporters ("the Communist Party organized a campaign in defense of the appointment of Simon W. Gerson as confidential assistant to the borough president of Manhattan"); the International Committee for Political Prisoners (to raise funds for jailed seditionists); the League Against Fascism (Socialist); the League for Independent Political Action (Socialist); the National Committee To Abolish the Poll Tax ("Communist front"); the National Emergency Conference ("Communist front"); the National Emergency Conference for Democratic Rights ("Communist front" – "subversive"); the National Federation for Constitutional Liberties ("under Communist Party domination and headed by responsible Party functionaries" – "one of the viciously subversive organizations of the Communist Party"); the National People's Committee Against Hearst ("Communist front"); the National Save Our Schools Committee (anti-American pressure group); the Non-Intervention Citizens Committee (dominated by Socialists and Communists); the Non-Partisan Committee for the Re-election of Congressman Vito Marcantonio ("Communist front"); the People's Legislative Service (Socialist lobby); the Rand School of Social Science (a Marxian-

Socialist training school for labor agitators); the Sacco-Vanzetti National League (part of a Communist propaganda campaign); the [Morris U.] Schappes Defense Committee ("a front organization with a strictly Communist objective, namely, the defense of a self-admitted Communist who was convicted of perjury in the courts of New York"); and *World Tomorrow* (Socialist). Villard died in October 1949.

MARY MARVIN HEATON VORSE

was born *c.* 1870 in New York City, daughter of Ellen Blackman and Hiram Heaton. She was married to the late Albert Vorse, the late Joseph O'Brien, and the late Robert Minor, from whom she was divorced. She was educated abroad. She was the author of *The Breaking In of a Yachtsman's Wife* (1908); *The Very Little Person* (1911); *The Autobiography of an Elderly Woman* (1911); *The Heart's Country* (1913); *The Ninth Man* (1918); *The Prestons* (1918); *I've Come to Stay* (1919); *Growing Up* (1920); *Men, and Steel* (1921); *Fraycar's Fist* (1923); *Passaic* (1926); *Second Cabin* (1928); *Strike — A Novel of Gastonia* (1930); *A Footnote to Folly* autobiography (1935); *Labor's New Millions* (1938); *Time and the Town* (1942); and *Here Are the People* (1943).

During World War I, Vorse was a war correspondent for several magazines. In 1918 and 1919, she was an American Red Cross Worker in Europe. In 1921 and 1922, she was a European correspondent for the Hearst newspapers. Throughout most of the 1920's and 1930's she was a free-lance writer for magazines and newspapers. In the mid-1930's she was the publicity director for the Indian Bureau in the Department of the Interior. In the 1930's, she settled in Provincetown, Massachusetts, where she was a founder of the Provincetown Players and where she directed a Montessori School.

In her autobiographical *Footnote to Folly*, Vorse gave an account of twenty years of working for Reds, including William Haywood, leader of the International Workers of the World (Wobblies), and William Z. Foster, chairman of the Communist Party. Her third husband, Robert Minor, was a top-ranking Communist who led the Communist Abraham Lincoln Brigade during the Spanish Civil War. She had a long career as a Communist agitator in the labor field.

Vorse was affiliated with the Citizens' Committee for Harry Bridges ("Communist"); the *Daily Worker* ("official organ of the Communist Party"); the Friends of the Soviet Union ("created, directed, and controlled by the Communist Party . . . and operated to aid and support Party objectives concerning the defense and support of the Soviet Union"); the John Reed Clubs ("out-and-out Communist organizations which preceded the contemporary Communist front organizations which cater to so-called liberals"); the International Union of Revolutionary Writers and its *International Literature* of Moscow ("Communist front"); the Labor Defense Council ("organized for the primary purpose of aiding the Communist defendants in the Michigan criminal syndicalist case in the early days of the Communist movement in this country"); the League of American Writers ("subversive and Communist" — "began openly to follow the Communist Party line as dictated by the foreign policy of the Soviet Union"); the League for Mutual Aid ("Communist enterprise"); *Liberator* ("Communist"); the National Committee for People's Rights ("composed primarily of openly avowed members of the Communist Party and veteran fellow-travelers of the Communist Party"); the National Committee for the Defense of Political Prisoners ("subversive and Communist"); *Soviet Russia* ("Communist-controlled publication"); the *Sunday Worker* ("official organ of the Communist Party"); *The Toiler* ("one of the first Communist publications to appear in the United States"); and Veterans of the Abraham Lincoln Brigade ("directed, dominated and controlled by the Communist Party").

Vorse died in June 1966.

LILLIAN D. WALD was born on March 10, 1867 in Cincinnati, Ohio, daughter of Minnie Schwarz and Max Wald. She graduated from the New York Hospital Training School for Nurses in 1891. She attended Woman's Medical College in 1893. She was the author of *The House on Henry Street* (1915) and *Windows on Henry Street* (1934).

In 1893, Wald began a career in public health nursing in New York City. In 1895, a banker, Jacob Schiff – who a few years later financed the Communist revolutionaries in Russia – bought a house for her to use as a center for her work. After first being called the Nurses' Settlement, it was renamed the Henry Street Settlement. (By 1913, the Settlement consisted of seven houses and two uptown branches in New York City. In 1923, the headquarters for the Henry Street Settlement was a building on Park Avenue.)

Wald was the head worker at the Settlement until 1933 and president until her retirement in 1937. She began the first city school of nursing in the world in New York City. She planned what in 1908, by an Act of Congress, became the Federal Children's Bureau. She devised the American Red Cross program for town and country nursing. She helped to found the department of health and nursing at Columbia University's Teachers College, where she was a lecturer. She was also a lecturer at the New York School of Social Work.

Wald made the Henry Street Settlement far more than a nursing center. It became a Socialist center very similar to Jane Addams' Hull House in Chicago. Wald's Settlement became a gathering place for Socialists to the extent that it was a regular stopover for Socialists, American and foreign, travelling to New York City. Wald formed close friendships with the British Fabian Socialists, including Beatrice and Sidney Webb, Prime Minister Ramsay MacDonald, and Graham Wallas; fellow settlement workers, such as Jane Addams, Florence Kelley, Alice Hamilton, and Alice Stone Blackwell; publicists Oswald Garrison Villard and Ida Tarbell; political figures Eleanor Roosevelt, Henry Morgenthau Jr., Amos Pinchot, Adolf A. Berle Jr., and Frances Perkins; and other well-known individuals such as Theodore Dreiser, Paul Warburg, Van Wyck Brooks, Jacob Riis, and Anna Louise Strong, the Soviet spy. She was a devotee of Tolstoi's pacifism. She was greatly influenced by the single-tax advocate Henry George and Italian revolutionary Mazzini.

As was the case with most settlement workers in her era, Wald was active in the leftist-pacifist crusade. She was the prime organizer of the American Union Against Militarism in 1914 to forestall preparedness for war by the United States. She was joined in her efforts by leading radicals of the day, including Jane Addams, Paul Kellogg, Max and Crystal Eastman, Allan Benson, Zona Gale, John Haynes Holmes, Louis Lochner, James Warbasse, and

Stephen S. Wise. When the cause of the American Union was lost, Wald and her followers went successively into the League for Free Nations Association and the Foreign Policy Association. Most of them were also involved in the formation and early operations of the ultra-leftist American Civil Liberties Union.

Wald's affiliations included the American Association for Labor Legislation (Socialist); the American Committee for Anti-Nazi Literature ("individuals and organizations connected with it identify this committee as a Communist front organization"); the American Friends of Spanish Democracy ("Communist front"); the American-Russian Institute ("subversive" — "Communist" — "specializing in pro-Soviet propaganda"); the American Society for Cultural Relations With Russia ("Communist front"); the American Youth Congress ("subversive" — "one of the most influential front organizations ever set up by the Communists in this country" — "the Communists were in complete control"); the Coordinating Committee To Lift the [Spanish] Embargo ("one of the numerous Communist-front enterprises which were organized around the Communists' agitation over the Spanish Civil War"); the Emergency Committee for Strikers Relief (Socialist); the Emergency Peace Federation (dominated by Socialists); Film Audiences for Democracy ("Communist front"); the Friends of the Soviet Union ("created, directed, and controlled by the Communist Party . . . and operated to aid and support Party objectives concerning the defense and support of the Soviet Union"); the Golden Book of American Friendship With the Soviet Union ("pro-Soviet propaganda"); the Institute of International Education (leftist-oriented); the League of Women Voters (leftist); the *Liberator* ("Communist"); the Liberty Defense League (in support of the Red International Workers of the World — the Wobblies); the Medical Bureau and North American Committee To Aid Spanish Democracy ("subversive and un-American"); the Non-Intervention Citizens Committee (dominated by Socialists and Communists); an Open Letter to American Liberals ("project of well-known Communists and Communist collaborators" — "in defense of the progressive movement undertaken by the Soviet Union"); Russian-American Industrial Corporation ("a political as well as a business interest in the Bolshevik revolution"); the Social Workers Committee To Aid Spanish Democracy ("Communist front"); *Soviet Russia Today* ("Communist-controlled publication"); Survey Associates (Socialist); the Women's International League for Peace and Freedom (ultra-leftist-pacifist); the Women's Peace Party (Socialist); the Women's Trade Union League (dominated by Socialists); and the World Congress Against War ("sponsored by the Communist International"). She died in September 1940.

HARRY FREDERICK WARD was born on October 15, 1873 in London, England, son of Fanny Jeffery and Harry Ward. He married Daisy Kendall. He was an alumnus of Northwestern University (A.B., 1897) and Harvard University (A.M., 1898). He also attended the University of Southern California. He was ordained to the ministry of the Methodist Episcopal Church in 1899. He was the author of *Social Creed of the Churches* (1913); *Social Evangelism* (1915); *Poverty and Wealth* (1915); *The Bible and Social Living* (1916); *The Labor Movement* (1917); *The Gospel for a Working World* (1918); *The Opportunity for Religion*

(1919); *The New Social Order – Principles and Programs* (1919); *The Profit Motive* (1924); *Our Economic Morality* (1929); *Which Way Religion?* (1931); *In Place of Profit* (1933); *Democracy and Social Change* (1940); and *The Soviet Spirit* (1944). He was co-author of *Christianizing Community Life* (1917).

From 1898 until 1900, Ward was head resident at the Northwestern University Settlement. In 1899, he was ordained as a Methodist minister. From 1899 until 1912, he held pastorates in Chicago and Oak Park, Illinois. From 1913 until 1918, he was a professor of social service at Boston University. From 1918 until 1941, he was professor of Christian ethics at Union Theological Seminary, and in 1941 he retired as professor emeritus.

In 1907, Ward was a founder of the Methodist Federation for Social Service [MFSS]. From 1907 until 1911, he was editorial secretary of the Federation, and from 1911 until 1944, he was its general secretary and editor of its *Social Questions Bulletin.*

While Ward made the direction of the MFSS a one-man operation, he was also a guiding genius in the Federal Council of Churches and its two important subsidiary groups: the Commission on the Church and Social Service and the Commission on Peace and Arbitration. His work with the latter Commission ultimately led to the formation of the Church Peace Union and the World Council of Churches.

Through his teaching positions at Boston University and Union Theological Seminary and his work in the Methodist Federation for Social Service and the Federal Council of Churches, Ward was the most important American Protestant clergyman to engage in the promotion of Marxian-oriented Social-

ism under the apparently innocent banners of social action or social service or social gospel. It was his design to educate ministers to relegate their religious ministry to a role inferior to their activities in the secular world. They were to work as social service evangelists for reforms in materialistic matters. Among their proper concerns, according to Ward, were regulatory laws (and enforcement at the various levels of government) governing pure water supplies; food inspections; housing conditions; sanitary and building codes for mission houses, municipal shelter, workhouses, state farms; government financed and maintained playgrounds, comfort stations, social centers, and public schools; women's working conditions; wages and working hours, workmen's compensation; minimum wage standards; industrial education in schools; and anything and everything else in the routine of daily living and working that could be subject to government control. In brief, Ward aimed at a totalitarian system – political, economic, and social – to be imposed upon the American people through the agency of the clergy.

In a manifesto, drafted by Ward, which was accepted by the General Conference of the Methodist Church, he said: "This statement pledges the church to cooperate in a general campaign for church welfare, public health, social purity, organized recreation, industrial safety, a living wage, and international peace; also, in the movements against poverty, overwork, and crime, through civic action to effect all these purposes. It also binds the church unceasingly to labor for the realization of social action, and the Methodist Federation for Social Service is declared to be the executive agency to rally the forces of the church in support of the measures thus approved." Since Ward was the major personality in the MFSS, acceptance of his manifesto meant that the entire Methodist Church was acquiescing in his leadership away from spiritual and toward material concerns. He lost no time in saturating Sunday schools and Methodist missions, in the United States and abroad, with a curriculum centered on his brand of Socialism.

In hearings of the House Committee on Un-American Activities in 1953, several former Communist Party officials testified under oath as to what they knew about Ward. Manning Johnson, in the course of his remarks, said: "Dr. Harry F. Ward, for many years, has been the chief architect for Communist infiltration and subversion in the religious field . . . . He was a member of the Communist Party while I was a member . . . . I would say that he is the Red Dean of the Communist Party in the religious field."

Leonard Patterson, who had been on the Central Committee of the Negro Commission of the Communist Party, recalled his associations with Ward: "In New York City, I believe, in 1933 or early 1934 — I believe it was 1933 — Dr. Ward, Earl Browder, myself, Victor Jerome, Manning Johnson, and other top leading members of the Communist Party were assigned to a top fraction. In other words, a top policymaking body of the Communist Party — by the Central Committee of the Communist Party to prepare . . . for a conference to sponsor a broader conference against war and fascism to be held later on in the year 1933 . . . . This top policy body met at 799 Broadway. where many of the Party front organizations met at that time, and again there was a conference held in Chicago. I believe that was the Second Congress Against War and Fascism . . . . I believe that was in 1935, I might be a little wrong in the date, but research will show, and there we also had a meeting of the fraction while the Congress was there and I was together with Dr. Ward in the top fraction meeting in Chicago also . . . a meeting where only top leading Communist Party members could attend. It was a policymaking body . . . . He [Ward] was present and an active member of that body."

Joseph Zack Kornfeder, who was a graduate of the Lenin School of Political Warfare in Moscow, told the HCUA that while he attended the Lenin School he learned that the Communists wanted to destroy religion in the United States from both within and outside the churches. He said that in the United States the two major organizations utilized to carry out the Communist program of destruction were the Methodist Federation for Social Action and the People's Institute of Applied Religion. Kornfeder testified that Ward was "the theoretical and political leader of this method of operation."

Benjamin Gitlow, a founder and long-time top official of the Communists, was very well acquainted with Ward's career. Gitlow told the HCUA: "The Russian Communists were the first to exploit ministers of the United States and, through them, the church organizations, for the purpose of spreading propaganda in favor of Communist Russia, and for the building up of a pro-Soviet sentiment among church people in America and among Americans generally. I will, if I may, make mention of a few of the prominent American religious leaders who were used for that purpose in the early 1920's: Dr. Kirby Page, Dr. Sherwood Eddy, Jerome Davis, Dr. Harry F. Ward . . . ." Gitlow was asked if in the early 1920's the Communist Party, USA, enlisted the support of church people for its American campaigns and in support of the Communist Party and its activities in the Soviet Union. Gitlow replied: "It certainly did, for the number of ministers that actively supported the Communist Party in those days, though not as large as it is today, was, nevertheless, impressive. [One of] the outstanding clergymen among them [was] Dr. Harry F. Ward . . . . To be specific: before the creation of the front organizations, the ministers who carried out the instructions of the Communist Party or collaborated with it were limited in numbers. [One of] the outstanding ones among them [was] . . . Dr. Harry Ward . . . ." Gitlow brought out the fact that in 1925, Ward delivered a series of lectures at the National University in Peking, China. Gitlow said: "All the lectures delivered in China by Dr. Ward had for their main purpose the bolstering up of the position of the Communist movement in China and winning support of the Chinese intellectuals and Christians in China for the Chinese Communist Movement and for Soviet Russia . . . . I only presented Ward's lectures delivered in China in 1925 because they were discussed at length in Moscow and at the Comintern. The Comintern leaders were of the opinion that clergymen with Dr. Ward's point of view, using the cloak of religion, could render service of inestimable value to the Communist cause in China and to Soviet interests. Besides, the missions and church institutions of China could be used, in the opinion of the Comintern, to cover up Communist espionage activity in China. Clergymen who served in various capacities in China, and who deliberately followed the Communist Party line or who were duped into following it, formed an important branch of the conspiracy to turn China over to the Communists. They not only gave assistance to the Commu-

nists in China but they also carried on effective propaganda in the United States to influence public opinion for their point of view."

Gitlow testified at length about Ward's Methodist Federation for Social Action, formerly for Social Service, and the role it played in the Communist movement: "The Methodist Federation for Social Action . . . was first organized by a group of Socialist, Marxist clergymen of the Methodist Church headed by Dr. Harry F. Ward. Dr. Ward was the organizer, for almost a lifetime its secretary and actual leader. He at all times set its ideological and political pattern. Its objective was to transform the Methodist Church and Christianity into an instrument for the achievement of socialism. It was established in 1907, twelve years before the organization of the Communist Party in the United States in 1919. The outbreak of the Bolshevik Revolution in Russia in November 1917 had a tremendous effect upon the Socialist ministers of this organization and especially upon Dr. Ward. When the Communist Party was organized in 1919, Dr. Ward was already a convinced Communist with a few insignificant minor reservations. By 1920 he was already, though not yet a member of the Communist Party, cooperating and collaborating with the Communist Party. This collaboration of Dr. Ward with the Communist Party was reflected in the expressions and activities of the Methodist Federation for Social Action. The inner hard core of the Methodist Federation consisted . . . of a Communist cell headed by Ward, which functioned under the direction of the Communist Party . . . . In the first place the Methodist Federation was affiliated with and collaborated more closely with the American League Against War and Fascism and the American League for Peace and Democracy .... It was no accident that Dr. Ward, the organizer and leader of the Methodist Federation, became the chairman and served in that capacity for many years, of both the American League Against War and Fascism and the American League for Peace and Democracy .... In the infiltration of the Methodist Church, the Communists were highly successful. To detail the extent of the Communist infiltration of the Methodist Church, the people who served the Communists in the church consciously, and those who were its stooges, would take several hundred pages of testimony .... The principal individuals involved in the Communist conspiracy to subvert the Methodist Church for Communist purposes are: Dr. Harry F. Ward ...."

Gitlow was asked about the rank in importance of the Methodist Federation in the Communist infiltration of religion. He said: "In my opinion the Methodist Federation for Social Action ... set the pattern for setting up similar organizations in the other Protestant denominations. It, in fact, assumed the leadership of the so-called social action movement in the Christian churches, and greatly influenced their ideas and programs they adopted and their activities. It maintained the closest relations with all of them and often collaborated with them. In addition, the Methodist Federation for Social Action officially affiliated with some of the most important Communist-front organizations. Those with which the Methodist Federation did not officially affiliate, the organization usually endorsed, sponsored or supported through its *Social Questions Bulletin* [edited by Ward] or through the recognized leaders of the federation."

Manning Johnson confirmed Gitlow's high estimate of Ward's importance as a Communist functionary leading the Federation and the Communist fronts with which he was affiliated: "The major organizational form of the united front in which the churches were involved was the American League Against War and Fascism, which has been headed by the Reverend Harry F. Ward. That organization was the key Communist Party front. There was no other Communist Party front in all of the solar system of organizations of the Communist Party that involved so many ministers, churches, and religious organizations. In fact, this organization was the key to the infiltration of the church, and as a result of the successful infiltration and penetration they were able to involve these ministers in every other Communist front through the years, even down to the present time .... The majority of the ministers in the American League Against War and Fascism were involved by Harry F. Ward, and ... the Methodist Federation for Social Action ... [which] was invaluable to the Communist Party in its united-front organizations campaign. It was invaluable because through it the Party was able to get contacts with thousands of ministers all over the country .... I might add that quite a few ministers, for example, participated in the united front known as the American League Against War and Fascism, and later called the American League for Peace and Democracy, in which many ministers were involved. In fact, they were so deeply involved through Harry F. Ward that they became the spokesmen, the advocates, the builders, and the leaders of this most important Communist front that engaged in everything from simple assault on a government to espionage, sabotage and the overthrow of the Government of the United States."

Although Ward was the leader of the Methodist Federation, the American League Against War and Fascism, and the American League for Peace and Democracy, he did not neglect his contributions to the Federal Council of Churches and the Church Peace Union. Union Theological Seminary was his base of operations, but he also served as a director of the Garland Fund, which poured its treasures into the very Communist projects that were also served by Ward. For more than twenty years, he served as a founder and the president of the American Civil Liberties Union, which proved to be one of the most influential and successful organizations in the promotion of Communist enterprises and its success was largely attributable to Ward's talent for recruiting prestigious individuals willing to serve the left under the innocuous-appearing banner of "civil liberties."

Ward's other affiliations included the American Committee for Protection of Foreign Born ("founded by the Communist Party in order to exploit racial divisions in the United States for its own revolutionary purposes"); the American Friends of Spanish Democracy ("Communist front"); the American Peace Mobilization ("formed . . . under the auspices of the Communist Party and the Young Communist League" – "one of the most seditious organizations which ever operated in the United States"); the American Society for Cultural Relations with Russia ("Communist front"); the American Youth Congress ("subversive" – "one of the most influential front organizations ever set up by the Communists in this country" – "the Communists were in complete control"); Brookwood Labor College ("Communistic");

the California Labor School ("a subversive and Communist organization"); *China Today* ("official organ of the Communist-controlled American Friends of the Chinese People"); the Citizens' Committee To Free Earl Browder ("a strictly Communist Party affair"); the Committee for Peace Through World Cooperation ("it is significant that the Committee . . . received its chief publicity through the Communist press"); the Committee To Save Spain and China ("Communist front"); the Coordinating Committee To Lift the [Spanish] Embargo ("one of the numerous Communist-front enterprises which were organized around the Communists' agitation over the Spanish Civil War"); the Emergency Peace Federation (dominated by Socialists and Communists); the Emergency Peace Mobilization ("Communist front"); the Fellowship of Reconciliation (ultra-leftist-pacifist); the Friends of the Soviet Union ("created, directed, and controlled by the Communist Party . . . and operated to aid and support Party objectives concerning the defense and support of the Soviet Union"); the Gerson Supporters ("the Communist Party organized a campaign in defense of the appointment of Simon W. Gerson as confidential assistant to the borough president of Manhattan"); Icor ("the aims of Icor have been primarily propagandistic in behalf of the Soviet Union"); the Industrial Workers of the World [Wobblies] ("subversive and un-American"); the International Student Congress Against War and Fascism ("Communist"); the Jefferson School of Social Science ("a Communist institution modeled along the lines of the new Communist policy which led to the decision to change the Communist Party into some kind of an educational institution"); the Jewish People's Committee ("subversive and Communist" – "an organization which has been nothing more nor less than an adjunct of the Communist Party"); the League of American Writers ("subversive and Communist" – "began openly to follow the Communist Party line as dictated by the foreign policy of the Soviet Union"); the Marcus Graham Freedom of the Press Committee (a leftist group in defense of an anarchist); the Mother Ella Reeve Bloor Birthday Committee (Communist Party festivity); the National Emergency Conference ("Communist front"); the National Emergency Conference for Democratic Rights ("Communist front" – "subversive"); the National Federation for Constitutional Liberties ("under Communist Party domination and headed by responsible Party functionaries" – "one of the viciously subversive organizations of the Communist Party"); the National Negro Congress ("subversive and Communist" – "characterized as an organization operating in the field of civil rights under Communist Party domination and headed by responsible Party functionaries"); the National People's Committee Against Hearst ("subversive and Communist"); the National Right-to-Work Congress ("out-and-out Communist Party affair"); the National Wartime Conference of the Professions, the Sciences, the Arts, the White-Collar Fields ("Communist front"); *New Masses* ("weekly journal of the Communist Party"); an Open Letter for Closer Cooperation with the Soviet Union (issued by "a group of Communist Party stooges"); People's Councils ("modeled after the Council of Workmen's and Soldiers' Councils, the sovereign power of Russia today [1920]"); the People's Institute of Applied Religion ("subversive and Communist"); the [Luiz Carlos] Prestes Defense Committee (on behalf of a leader of the Communist Party of Brazil – "Communist front"); the *Protestant* ("with an eye to religious groups, the Communists have formed religious fronts such as the *Protestant*"); the Religious Freedom Committee (ultra-leftists working to abolish the House Committee on Un-American Activities); the Saturday Forum Luncheon Group ("Communist front"); the [Morris U.] Schappes Defense Committee ("a front organization with a strictly Communist objective, namely, the defense of a self-admitted Communist who was convicted of perjury in the courts of New York"); *Soviet Russia Today* ("Communist-controlled publication"); the Veterans of the Abraham Lincoln Brigade ("directed, dominated and controlled by the Communist Party"); *World Tomorrow* (Socialist publication); and the Washington Committee to Lift [the] Spanish Embargo ("Communist front").

Ward died in December 1966. In the Communist press he was eulogized as a "champion of democracy" (*Worker*) and a "crusader for civil liberties" (*National Guardian*). *New World Review* called him a "crusader for democracy" – "concerned with the deeper moral principles undergirding the new Soviet society" – "concerned about peace" – "a prophet whose foundation for action rested on the Judeo-Christian teaching." The *New York Times* characterized him as "a social crusader."

MAX WEBER was born on April 18, 1881 in Byelostok, Russia, son of Julia Getz and Morris Weber. He was brought to the United States in 1891. He married Frances Abrams. He graduated from Pratt Institute (1900). He was the author of *Cubist Poems* (1914); *Essays on Art* (1916); *Primitives* (1927); and *Woodcuts* (1957).

Between 1900 and 1905, Weber was an art teacher in the Lynchb g, Virginia public schools and the S   Normal School in Duluth, Minnesota. From 1905 until 1909, he studied art in France, Italy, Spain, Belgium, and Holland. In 1909, he began exhibiting his paintings in the United States. In 1913, he had his first major one-man exhibition in the Newark Museum. From 1915 until 1923, he virtually retired from exhibitions. In 1920 and 1921, and in 1926 and 1927, he was an art teacher at the Art Students League in New York. The first purchase of his work by a museum was made in 1926. Eventually, his paintings were in the Los Angeles Museum, the Newark Museum, the Metropolitan Museum of Art, the Whitney Museum, the Phillips Memorial Gallery of Washington, D.C., the Carnegie Art Institute, the Museum of Modern Art, the Brooklyn Museum, and the Santa Barbara Museum of Art.

Weber was affiliated with the American Artists Congress ("Communist front"); the American Committee for Protection of Foreign Born ("founded by the Communist Party in order to exploit racial divisions in the United States for its own revolutionary purposes"); the American Committee To Save Refugees ("perform[ing] a most valuable function for the international Communist movement"); the American Continental Congress for World Peace ("another phase in the Communist 'peace' campaign, aimed at consolidating anti-American forces throughout the Western Hemisphere"); the American Friends of Spanish Democracy ("Communist front"); the American Youth for Democracy ("subversive and Communist" – "part of Soviet psychological warfare against the United States"); the Artists' Front To Win the War ("Communist front" – "included representatives of the theater, of literature, music, art, science, and education, with long and active records of support for Communist-front organizations and for the variegated turns of the Communist Party line"); Arts, Sciences and Professions for May Day (Communist enterprise); Celebration of 15 Years of Biro Bidjan ("Communist project"); the China Aid Council ("Communist-controlled"); the Citizens' Committee To Free Earl Browder ("a strictly Communist Party affair"); the Civil Rights Congress ("created and established by the Communist Party as an organization which would utilize defense of civil rights for Party purposes and raise and maintain mass defense and bail funds for Party use"); the Committee for Free Political Advocacy ("Communist front"); the Committee of Professional Groups for [William Z.] Foster and [James W.] Ford (Communist Party candidates for the presidency and vice presidency of the United States in 1936); the Conference for Peaceful Alternatives to the Atlantic Pact ("initiated by Communists"); the Cultural and Scientific Conference for World Peace ("Communist front" – "a propaganda front for Soviet foreign policy and Soviet culture"); the Golden Book of American Friendship with the Soviet Union ("pro-Soviet propaganda enterprise"); the Independent Citizens Comitee of the Arts, Sciences and Professions ("Communist front"); the International Labor Defense ("subversive and Communist" – "legal arm of the Communist Party" – "part of an international network of organizations for the defense of Communist lawbreakers"); the Jewish Peoples Committee ("Communist front"); *Jewish Survey* (pro-Communist); the John Reed Clubs ("out-and-out Communist organizations which preceded the contemporary Communist front organizations which cater to so-called liberals"); the Joint Anti-Fascist Refugee Committee ("subversive and Communist"); *Literary Gazette* of Moscow ("Communist"); *Masses and Mainstream* ("Communist magazine"); the Mother Ella Reeve Bloor Birthday Celebration ("Communist Party festivity"); the National Council of American-Soviet Friendship ("subversive and Communist" – "specializing in pro-Soviet propaganda"); the National Council of the Arts, Sciences, and Professions ("a Communist front used to appeal to special occupational groups"); the National Federation for Constitutional Liberties ("under Communist Party domination and headed by responsible Party functionaries" – "one of the viciously subversive organizations of the Communist Party"); the National Institute of Arts and Letters ("Communist front"); *New Masses* ("weekly journal of the Communist Party"); an Open Letter for Closer Cooperation with the Soviet Union (issued by "a group of Communist Party stooges"); an Open Letter in Defense of Harry Bridges ("Communist front"); an Open Letter to American Liberals ("project of well-known Communists and Communist collaborators" – "in defense of the progressive movement undertaken by the Soviet Union"); Progressive Citizens of America ("political Communist front" – "subversive"); the Public Use of Arts Commitee ("Communist front"); the Reichstag Fire Trial Anniversary Committee ("Communist front . . . formed . . . by prominent Communists and Communist sympathizers"); a Statement by American Progressives on the Moscow Trials ("obviously a document concocted in defense of the line of the Communist Party and undoubtedly originated in the headquarters of the Communist Party"); United American Artists ("Communist front"); and the World Peace Congress ("organized under the Communist initiative in various countries throughout the world").

Weber died in October 1961.

ALEXANDER FELL WHITNEY was born on April 12, 1873 in Cedar Falls, Iowa, son of Martha Batcheller and Joseph Whitney. He married the late Grace Marshman. His second wife was Dorothy Rowley. He was the author of *Main Street – Not Wall Street* (1938).

Between 1888 and 1901, Whitney was a railroad worker, mostly as a brakeman for several railroad companies. From 1901 until 1949, he was with the Brotherhood of Railroad Trainmen as chairman of the general grievance committee (1901-1907), member of the board of the grand trustees (1905-1907), vice president (1907-1928), general secretary and treasurer (1928), and president (1928-1949). From 1932 until 1934, he was chairman of the Railway Labor Executives Association.

Whitney was affiliated with the ultra-leftist American Civil Liberties Union; the American Friends of Spanish Democracy ("Communist front"); the American League for Peace and Democracy ("subversive and Communist" – "established in the United States in an effort to create public sentiment on behalf of a foreign policy adapted to the interests of the Soviet Union . . . [and] designed to conceal Communist control, in accordance with the new tactics of the Communist International"); the American Youth Congress ("subversive" – "one of the most influential front organizations ever set up by the Communists in this country" – "the Communists were in complete control"); *Champion* (official organ of the Young Communist League and the International Workers Order); the Committee To Save Spain and China ("Communist front"); the Coordinating Committee to Lift the [Spanish] Embargo ("one of the numerous Communist-front enterprises which were organized around the Communists' agitation over the Spanish Civil War"); *Fight* ("official organ of the American League Against War and Fascism [American League for Peace and Democracy], subversive and Communist"); Friends of the Abraham Lincoln Brigade ("completely controlled by the Communist Party"); the International Labor Defense ("subversive and Communist" – "legal arm of the Communist Party" – "part of an international network of organizations for the defense of Communist lawbreakers"); the Joint Committee for Trade Union Rights ("jointly with the International Labor Defense supported and defended Communist Party leaders . . . when they were serving prison terms"); the League of American Writers ("subversive and Communist" – "began openly to follow the Communist Party line as dictated by the foreign policy of the Soviet Union"); the National Citizens' Political Action Committee ("Communist front"); the National Committee To Abolish the Poll Tax ("Communist front"); the National Conference on Civil Liberties ("Communist front"); the National Council of American-Soviet Friendship ("subversive and Communist" – "specializing in pro-Soviet propaganda"); the National Federation for Constitutional Liberties ("under Communist Party domination and headed by responsible Party functionaries" – "one of the viciously subversive organizations of the Communist Party"); *New Masses* ("weekly journal of the Communist Party"); the People's Congress for Peace and Democracy ("Communist front"); the

People's World ("official organ of the Communist Party"); the Progressive Citizens of America ("political Communist front" – "subversive"); *Soviet Russia Today* ("Communist-controlled publication"); the United States-Soviet Friendship Congress ("Communist front"); the United World Federalists ("the most prestigious group of fellow travelers and dupes working for world government at the expense of United States sovereignty"); and the Washington Committee To Lift [the] Spanish Embargo ("Communist front"). He died in July 1949.

STEPHEN SAMUEL WISE was born on March 17, 1874 in Budapest, Hungary, son of Sabine Farkashasy and Aaron Wise. He married Louise Waterman. He was an alumnus of Columbia University (A.B., 1892, and Ph.D., 1901). From 1887 until 1891, he studied at the College of the City of New York. He was the author of *The Ethics of Solomon Ibn Gabirol* (1901); *Gabirol's Improvement on the Moral Qualities* (1901); *How To Face Life* (1917); *Child Versus Parent* (1922); *As I See It* (1944); and *Challenging Years*, autobiography (1949). His monthly sermons have been collected and published in *Beth Israel Pulpit*, three volumes; and *Free Synagogue Pulpit*, ten volumes. He was co-author of *The Great Betrayal* (1930). He was the editor of *Opinion, A Magazine of Jewish Life and Letters*.

From 1893 until 1896, he was assistant rabbi of the B'nai Jeshuran Synagogue in New York City, and from 1896 until 1900, he served as rabbi. From 1900 until 1907, he was rabbi of Beth Israel Synagogue in Portland, Oregon. From 1907 until 1949, he was founder and rabbi of the Free Synagogue in New York City. Both in Oregon and in New York, while serving as rabbi, he was an activist in promoting social and political reforms. In 1918, along with Felix Frankfurter and Louis Brandeis, he was a founder of the leftist-oriented American Jewish Congress, and he served the Congress as president from 1924 until 1949. After World War I he was a delegate from the Congress to the Paris Peace Conference, where he was an ardent promoter for the League of Nations. From 1936 until 1949, he was president of the World Jewish Congress.

Until World War I, Wise professed himself to be a pacifist, but he deserted his pacifism when he saw the opportunity for the institution of a Jewish homeland in Palestine arising out of the conflict. Wise had been an ardent Zionist as early as 1898, when he founded the Federation of American Zionists. He had served as editor of the Zionist department of *The American Hebrew* and as the American correspondent for *Die Welt* of Vienna, the official organ of world Zionism. In 1898, he was the American delegate to the second Zionist Congress in Basle, and at the Congress, he was correspondent for the *New York Journal* and *Harper's Weekly*. From 1936 until 1938, he was president of the Zionist organization of America. In 1938, he gave what was probably the best insight into his strong attachment to Zionism when he said: "In 1933, we offered German-Jewish groups an opportunity to unite . . . . They said they were Germans first, Germans who happened to be Jews. I am a Jew who is an American. I was a Jew before I was an American. I have been an American all my life, but I've been a Jew for 4,000 years." During the course of World War II, he was one of the Americans most active in applying pressure on the British to sponsor a homeland for the Jews.

Wise was a long-time active official of the ultra-leftist American Civil Liberties Union and its predecessor, the Civil Liberties Bureau. He was an active member of the Socialist Party. His other affiliations included the Allied Voters Against Coudert ("an example of the Communist apparatus for character assassination in operation against one who opposed the efforts of the Communist Party to undermine and destroy American democracy"); the American Association for Old Age Security (Socialist); the American Association of Labor Legislation (Socialist); the American Biro Bidjan Committee ("Communist front"); the American Committee for Non-Participation in Japanese Aggression ("Communist front"); the American Committee of Jewish Writers, Artists, and Scientists ("Communist front"); the American Friends of Spanish Democracy ("Communist front"); the American Friends of the Chinese People ("Communist front"); the American League Against War and Fascism ("subversive and Communist" – "established in the United States in an effort to create public sentiment on behalf of a foreign policy adapted to the interests of the Soviet Union"); the American League for Peace and Democracy ("subversive and Communist" – "established . . . in an effort to create public sentiment on behalf of a foreign policy adapted to the interests of the Soviet Union . . . [and] designed to conceal Communist control, in accordance with the new tactics of the Communist International"); the American League To Enforce Peace (ultra-leftist); the American Society for Russian Relief (pro-Communist); Brookwood Labor College ("Communistic"); the China Aid Council ("Communist-controlled"); the Citizens Emergency Conference for Interracial Unity ("Communist front"); the Committee for a

Boycott Against Japanese Aggression ("the committee was featured in the *Daily Worker*, official organ of the Communist Party, and in that paper alone"); the Committee of Welcome for the Red Dean of Canterbury (England's most notorious pro-Soviet apologist among the clergy); the Committee on Militarism in Education (a supporting organization of the U.S. Congress against War, "completely under the control of the Communist Party"); the Committee To Save Spain and China ("Communist front"); the Conference on Pan-American Democracy ("Communist front"); the Coordinating Committee To Lift the [Spanish] Embargo ("one of the numerous Communist-front enterprises which were organized around the Communists' agitation over the Spanish Civil War"); the Emergency Peace Federation (dominated by Socialists); the Federation of Unemployed Workers Leagues (Communist-controlled); the *Il Nuovo Mondo* National Committee (pro-Communist); the International Labor Defense ("subversive and Communist" – "legal arm of the Communist Party" – "part of an international network of organizations for the defense of Communist lawbreakers"); the Jewish Black Book Committee ("Communist front"); the Joint Anti-Fascist Refugee Committee ("subversive and Communist"); the Joint Committee on Unemployment (dominated by Socialists); the Mary Ware Dennett Defense Committee (ultra-leftist); the Medical Bureau To Aid Spanish Democracy ("subversive and un-American"); the National Citizens Committee on Relations With Latin America (dominated by Socialists); the National Committee To Abolish the Poll Tax ("Communist front"); the National Federation for Constitutional Liberties ("under Communist Party domination and headed by responsible Party functionaries" – "one of the viciously subversive organizations of the Communist Party"); the National Mooney-Billings Committee (dominated by Socialists); the National Religion and Labor Foundation ("Communist front"); the New York Tom Mooney Committee ("Communist front"); the Non-Intervention Citizens Committee (dominated by Socialists and Communists); Pioneer Youth of America (Socialist); Russian War Relief ("Communist enterprise"); *Soviet Russia Today* ("Communist-controlled publication"); and the Washington Committee To Lift [the] Spanish Embargo ("Communist front"). Wise died in April 1949.

MARY EMMA WOOLLEY was born on July 13, 1863 in Norwalk, Connecticut, daughter of Mary Ferris and Joseph Woolley. She was an alumna of Brown University (A.B., 1894; A.M., 1895). She was the first of only two women ever to receive a B.A. degree, and the first to receive an M.A. degree, from Brown University. She was the author of *History of the Passover Scandal* (1892); *Early History of the Colonial Post Office* (1893); *Development of the Love of Romantic Scenery in America* (1895); *Lida Shaw King: An Appreciation* (1923); and *Internationalism and Disarmament* (1935). She contributed chapters to *Why Wars Must Cease* and *What I Owe to My Father*. She contributed "Women's Colleges in America" to *Encyclopaedia Britannica*.

From 1886 until 1891, Woolley was an instructor at Wheaton Seminary in Massachusetts. From 1895 until 1900, she was at Wellesley College as an instructor in Biblical history (1895-1896); associate professor (1896-1899); and professor and head of the department of Biblical history and literature

(1899-1900). From 1900 until 1937, she was president of Mt. Holyoke College.

In 1921 and 1922, Woolley was in China with the Commission on Christian Education, under the auspices of the Rockefeller Foundation. In 1932, she became the first American woman ever to attend a major diplomatic conference when President Herbert Hoover appointed her to the American delegation to the Conference on Reduction and Limitation of Armaments, held at Geneva. In 1933, President Franklin D. Roosevelt reappointed her to the same conference. From 1927 until 1933, she was president of the leftist-oriented American Association of University Women, and from 1933 until 1939, she served as chairman of the Association's Commission on International Relations.

Wooley had a long career of radicalism. She took part in the pro-Communist activities surrounding the Sacco-Vanzetti affair. She was a long-time opponent of any legislation requiring loyalty oaths for teachers. She was an activist in association with some of the nation's outstanding leftist-pacifists. She was a long-time advocate of world government and a staunch supporter of the League of Nations as a means of achieving world government. She was such a fervent proponent of women's rights that when the time came for her retirement from the presidency of Mt. Holyoke she insisted that her successor be a woman. When the trustees appointed a man, she was so indignant that she never returned to the campus.

Woolley was affiliated with the American Association for Labor Legislation (Socialist); the ultra-leftist American Civil Liberties Union; the American Committee for Democracy and Intellectual Freedom ("subversive and un-American" — "a Communist-front organization operating among college teachers and professors"); the American Committee for Protection of Foreign Born ("founded by the Communist Party in order to exploit racial divisions in the United States for its own revolutionary purposes"); the American Committee To Save Refugees ("perform[ing] a most valuable function for the international Communist movement"); the American Friends of the Chinese People ("Communist front"); the American Peace Society (ultra-leftist-pacifist); the American Pushkin Committee ("Communist front"); the American Relief Ship for Spain ("Communist Party front enterprise"); the American Roundtable on India ("Communist front"); the American Youth Congress ("subversive" — "one of the most influential front organizations ever set up by the Communists in this country" — "the Communists were in complete control"); American Youth for Democracy ("subversive and Communist" — "part of Soviet psychological warfare against the United States"); the Artists Front To Win the War ("Communist front" — "included representatives of the theatre, of literature, music, art, science, and education, with long and active records of support for Communist-front organizations and for the variegated turns of the Communist Party line"); the Committee for Citizenship Rights ("to protect Communist subversion from any penalties under the law"); the Committee on a Just and Durable Peace of the Red-laden Federal Council of Churches; the Committee on Militarism in Education (a supporting organization of the U.S. Congress Against War, "completely under the control of the Communist Party"); the Coordinating Committee To Lift the [Spanish] Embargo ("one of the numerous Communist-front enterprises which were organized around the Communists' agitation over the Spanish Civil War"); the Fellowship of Reconciliation (ultra-leftist-pacifist); Films for Democracy ("Communist front"); Friends of the Abraham Lincoln Brigade ("Completely controlled by the Communist Party"); the Greater New York Emergency Conference on Inalienable Rights ("Communist front"); the Institute of International Education (leftist-oriented); the Institute of Pacific Relations ("an instrument of Communist policy, propaganda and military intelligence"); the Joint Anti-Fascist Refugee Committee ("subversive and Communist"); the Lawyers Committee on American Relations with Spain ("during the Spanish Civil War, the Communist Party organized . . . [the Lawyers Committee] as a part of one of its major propaganda campaigns in the Party's entire history in this country"); the League of American Writers ("subversive and Communist" – began openly to follow the Communist Party line as dictated by the foreign policy of the Soviet Union"); the League of Women Shoppers ("Communist-controlled front"); the National Citizens Committee on Relations with Latin America (dominated by Socialists); the National Committee To Combat Anti-Semitism ("Communist front"); the National Consumers League (Socialist); the National Council for a Permanent Fair Employment Practices Act (Socialist); the National Council of American-Soviet Friendship ("subversive and Communist" – "specializing in pro-Soviet propaganda"); the National Emergency Conference for Democratic Rights ("Communist front" – "subversive"); the National Federation for Constitutional Liberties ("under Communist Party domination and headed by responsible Party functionaries" – "one of the viciously subversive organizations of the Commu-

nist Party"); the National Save Our Schools Committee (pro-Communist); the New York State Conference on National Unity ("Communist front"); the North American Spanish Aid Committee ("Communist"); Open Road ("Communist front"); *Protestant Digest* ("a magazine which has faithfully propagated the Communist Party line under the guise of being a religious journal"); the Reichstag Fire Trial Anniversary Committee ("Communist front . . . formed . . . by prominent Communists and Communist sympathizers"); Russian Reconstruction Farms ("Communist enterprise"); Russian War Relief ("Communist enterprise"); the Sacco-Vanzetti National League (part of Communist propaganda campaign); the [Morris U.] Schappes Defense Committee ("a front organization with a strictly Communist objective, namely, the defense of a self-admitted Communist who was convicted of perjury in the courts of New York"); the [William] Schneiderman-[Sam] Darcy Defense Committee ("Communist"); the Veterans of the Abraham Lincoln Brigade ("directed, dominated and controlled by the Communist Party"); the Washington Committee To Lift [the] Spanish Embargo ("Communist front"); the Win-the-Peace Conference ("Communist front"); the Women's International League for Peace and Freedom (ultra-leftist-pacifist); the World Government Association (ultra-leftist-pacifist); World Peaceways (a supporting organization of the U.S. Congress Against War, "completely under the control of the Communist Party"); and the World Youth Congress (Communist conference). She died in September 1947.

RICHARD WRIGHT was born on September 4, 1908 in Natchez, Mississippi, son of Ellen and Nathan Wright.

He was the author of *Uncle Tom's Children* (1938); *Native Son* (1940); *12 Million Black Voices* (1941); *Black Boy* (1945); *The Outsider* (1953); *Black Power* (1954); *Savage Holiday* (1955); *The Color Curtain* (1956); *Pagan Spain* (1957); *White Man, Listen* (1957); *The Long Dream* (1959); *Eight Men* (1961); and *Lawd Today* (1963.

From 1923 until 1935, Wright worked at odd jobs in Tennessee and Chicago. In that period he began writing, and sold a few poems, articles, and short stories to small publications. From 1935 to 1937, in Chicago, he worked with the Federal Writers' Project of the Works Progress Administration. In 1937, he went to New York, where he also worked in the Federal Writers' Project and did some writing for the *Daily Worker*, the official organ of the Communist Party. He also became a contributing editor to the *New Masses*, the weekly journal of the Communist Party. In 1939, he left the Federal Writers' Project when he was awarded a Guggenheim Fellowship that allowed him the financial resources to complete his first major work, *Native Son*, which was the March 1940 selection of the Book-of-the-Month Club. *Native Son* also gained for him the Spingarn Medal of the ultra-radical National Association for the Advancement of Colored People. In his acceptance speech, Wright said: "It is with a deep sense of responsibility that I accept the Spingarn Medal. I accept in the name of the stalwart, enduring millions of Negroes whose fate and destiny I have sought to depict in terms of scene and narrative in imaginative fiction. It cannot be otherwise, for they are my people, and my writing – which is my life and which carries my convictions – attempts to mirror their struggles for freedom during those troubled days."

In a symposium edited by Richard Crossman, *The God That Failed*, Wright admitted that he was a card-carrying member of the Communist Party from 1934 until 1944. He admitted that his writings were based upon Marxist assumptions. It is worth remarking that while Wright was on the federal payroll, when he received his Guggenheim Fellowship, while he was being praised and lionized by the critics (*American Mercury, Atlantic Monthly, Saturday Review of Literature, Time* magazine), and when his *Native Son* reached the financially lucrative best-seller lists, he was doing nothing less than writing the Communist Party line.

In his contribution to *The God That Failed* and in his autobiographical *Black Boy*, Wright never made clear why he allegedly broke with the Communist Party in 1944. Communism certainly remained on his mind, since a Negro Communist was the protagonist of his book *The Outsider*, published in 1953, seven years after Wright moved to France, where he was to live for the rest of his life. In 1952, in a letter to his publisher, he implied that he left the Communist Party either because it did not need him any longer, or because he felt that he had nothing more to gain from his membership: "In 1944, when Communism in America was at the apogee of its popularity, I felt personally impelled to terminate my Communist membership which I held for ten active years. Under my own steam, with no warning from Hollywood or the Un-American Activities Committee, I broke publicly with Communism and have remained politically inactive since." He certainly never renounced *Native Son*. In 1951, seven years after his alleged break with the Party, he appeared as the leading actor in a motion picture version of the book, made in Argentina. At any rate, after Wright announced that he had left the Party, critics' praise for his work was negligible and awards and fellowships were a thing of the past.

Wright was affiliated with the American Committee for Protection of Foreign Born ("founded by the Communist Party in order to exploit racial divisions in the United States for its own revolutionary purposes"); the American Committee To Save Refugees ("perform[ing] a most valuable function for the international Communist movement"); the American Council on Soviet Relations ("subversive" – "established by the Communist Party . . . directed and controlled by the Party, and operated to aid and support Party objectives concerning the defense and support of the Soviet Union"); the American Peace Mobilization ("formed . . . under the auspices of the Communist Party and the Young Communist League" – "one of the most seditious organizations which ever operated in the United States"); Book Union ("distributors of Communist literature" – "Communist [Party] book club"); the Citizens' Committee for Harry Bridges ("Communist"); the Citizens' Committee To Free Earl Browder ("a strictly Communist Party affair"); the Conference on Constitutional Liberties in America ("an important part of the solar system of the Communist Party's front organizations"); the Congress of American Revolutionary Writers ("subversive and Communist"); *Friday* ("Communist-controlled"); Frontier Films ("Communist front"); the Golden Book of American Friendship with the Soviet Union ("pro-Soviet propaganda enterprise"); the Greater New York Emergency Conference on Inalienable Rights ("Communist front"); the International Labor Defense ("subversive and Communist" – "legal arm of the Com-

munist Party" – "part of an international network of organizations for the defense of Communist lawbreakers"); the International Union of Revolutionary Writers ("Communist front"); the John Reed Clubs ("out-and-out Communist organizations which preceded the contemporary Communist front organizations which cater to so-called liberals"); the League of American Writers ("subversive and Communist" – "began openly to follow the Communist Party line as dictated by the foreign policy of the Soviet Union"); the National Negro Congress ("subversive and Communist" – "characterized as an organization operating in the field of civil rights under Communist Party domination and headed by responsible Party functionaries"); Negro Playwrights, Inc. ("Communist front"); the Non-Sectarian Committee for Political Refugees ("affiliate of the International Labor Defense, the legal arm of the Communist Party"); an Open Letter for Closer Cooperation with the Soviet Union (issued by "a group of Communist Party stooges"); *Partisan Review* (Communist publication); the [Morris U.] Schappes Defense Committee ("a front organization with a strictly Communist objective, namely, the defense of a self-admitted Communist who was convicted of perjury in the courts of New York"); a Statement by American Progressives on the Moscow Trials ("obviously a document concocted in defense of the line of the Communist Party and undoubtedly originated in the headquarters of the Communist Party"); and the Workers Alliance ("subversive and Communist"). He died in November 1960.

RICHARD ROBERT WRIGHT JR. was born on April 16, 1878 in Cuthbert, Georgia, son of Lydia Howard and Richard Wright. He married Charlotte Cragman. He was an alumnus of Georgia State Industrial College (A.B., 1898), the University of Chicago Theological Seminary (B.D., 1901), and the University of Chicago (A.M., 1904). He also studied at the University of Berlin (1903) and the University of Leipzig (1904). He was the author of *The Teaching of Jesus* (1903, 1911, 1917, 1940, and 1943); *The Negro in Pennsylvania* (1911); *Church Financiering* (1919); *Social Service* (1922); and *My Church, Handbook of A.M.E. Church* (1944, 1945, and 1956). He was editor of *Poems of Phillis Wheatley* (1929); *Encyclopedia of African Methodism* (1916 and 1944); *The Mission Study Course* (1943); and *Sermons and Addresses* (1943).

In 1901, Wright was ordained to the ministry of the African Methodist Episcopal Church. In 1900 and 1901, he was an assistant pastor at the Institutional Church in Chicago. From 1901 until 1903, he was an instructor in Hebrew at Payne Theological Seminary in Wilberforce, Ohio. In 1904, he was a pastor in Elgin, Illinois. In 1905, he was a pastor at Trinity Mission in Chicago. From 1905 until 1907, he was a resident worker at a settlement house in Philadelphia and a research fellow in sociology at the University of Pennsylvania. In 1908 and 1909, he was field secretary for the Armstrong Association. From 1909 until 1936, he was editor of the *Christian Recorder* in Philadelphia. From 1909 until 1912 and from 1916 until 1920, he was manager of the Methodist Church's Book Concern. From 1928 until 1930, he was pastor of the Ward African Methodist Episcopal Church in Philadelphia. From 1930 until 1932, he was pastor of the Morris Brown Church and organizer of the Jones Tabernacle in Philadelphia. Meanwhile, he founded the Citizens and Southern Building and Loan Association and the Spring Street Social Settlement House. He was also president of the Citizens and Southern Bank and Trust Company.

Between 1932 and 1942, Wright was at Wilberforce University as president (1932-1936) and acting president (1941-1942). In 1936, he was elected bishop of the African Methodist Episcopal Church and, from 1936 until 1940, he was assigned to South Africa. He was presiding bishop in Kentucky and Tennessee (1940-1946), New York, New England, New Jersey, and Bermuda (1946-1948), Georgia (1948-1951), Arkansas and Oklahoma (1951-1952), West Indies and South America (1952-1956), Mississippi and Louisiana (1956-1957), and the West Indies (1957-1960). From 1960 until 1967, he was the historiographer of the African Methodist Episcopal Church.

Wright was affiliated with the African Aid Committee (ultra-leftist-racist agitators); the American Committee for Protection of Foreign Born ("founded by the Communist Party in order to exploit racial divisions in the United States for its own revolutionary purposes"); the Bill of Rights Conference ("subversive"); the Citizens United To Abolish the Wood-Rankin Committee (pro-Communist project); the Civil Rights Congress ("created and established by the Communist Party as an organization which would utilize defense of civil rights for Party purposes and raise and maintain mass defense and bail funds for Party use"); the Committee for Equal Justice for Mrs. Recy Taylor ("Communist front"); the Committee of One Thousand ("Communist created and controlled"); the Council for Pan American Democracy ("Communist front"); the Council on African Affairs ("subversive and Communist"); the Mid-Century Conference for Peace ("aimed at assembling as many gullible persons as possible under-Communist direction and turning them into a vast sounding board for Communist propaganda"); the National Citizens' Political Action Committee ("Communist front"); the National Committee To Repeal the McCarran Act ("Communist front" – "subversive"); the National Council of the Arts, Sciences, and Professions ("a Communist front used to appeal to special occupational groups"); the Progressive Citizens of America ("political Communist front" – "subversive"); a Testimonial Dinner for Ferdinand C. Smith ("Communist Party affair"); and the Win-the-Peace Conference ("Communist front").

Wright died in November 1967.

INDEX OF ORGANIZATIONS

Abraham Lincoln Brigade IV-1
Advance (precursor of W.E.B. Dubois Clubs) II-181
Advance (publication of Republican Advance) II-159
Advertising Council II-1
African Blood Brotherhood IV-62
All-America Anti-Imperialist League IV-24
American Association For The United Nations I-190
American Association Of University Professors II-11
American Civil Liberties Union I-1
American Committee For Protection Of Foreign Born II-38
American Committee For Struggle Against War IV-30
American Committee To Save Refugees IV-1
American Continental Congress For Peace IV-84
American Friends Of Spanish Democracy IV-1
American Friends Service Committee II-45
American Fund For Public Service IV-26
American Institute Of Pacific Relations I-116
American League Against War And Fascism IV-30
American League For Peace And Democracy IV-30
American Negro Labor Congress IV-62
American Peace Crusade IV-84
American Peace Mobilization IV-30
American People's Meeting IV-30
Americans For Democratic Action I-17
Atlantic Council Of The United States I-63
Atlantic Institute I-63
Atlantic Treaty Organization I-63
Atlantic Union Committee I-63
Black Panthers II-56
Business Executives Move For Vietnam Peace III-1
Businessmen's Education Fund III-1
Californians For Liberal Representation III-12
Carnegie Corporation I-26
Carnegie Endowment For International Peace I-26
Carnegie Foundation For The Advancement Of Teaching I-26

Center For The Study Of Democratic Institutions I-85
Church Peace Mission I-74
Civil Rights Congress IV-62
Clergy And Laymen Concerned About Vietnam II-78
Collegiate Council For The United States I-190
Cominform's Mid-Century Peace Campaign IV-84
Commission To Study The Organization of Peace I-190
Committee For Independent Political Action III-12
Committee For Peaceful Alternatives To The Atlantic Pact IV-84
Committee Of Liaison With Families Of Servicemen
   Detained In North Vietnam III-52
Committee Of Responsibility III-59
Committee On Atlantic Studies I-63
Committee On Political Education I-40
Committee To Defend The Conspiracy III-60
Community For New Politics III-12
Conference Group of U.S. National Organizations Of
   The United States I-191
Congress Of American Women IV-84
Congress Of Industrial Organizations Political Action
   Committee IV-30
Congress Of Racial Equality I-42
Coordinating Committee To Lift The Spanish Embargo IV-1
Council For A Livable World I-46
Council On Foreign Relations I-53
Council For Protection Of Foreign Born II-38
Declaration Of Conscience III-63
Emergency Conference Committee III-67
Emergency Committee For Southern Political Prisoners IV-145
Emergency Peace Mobilization IV-30
Federal Union I-63
Fellowship Of Reconciliation I-74
First United States Congress Against War IV-30
Ford Foundation I-85
Foreign Affairs I-53
Foreign Policy Association I-106

Foreign Policy Bulletin I-106
Freedom and Union I-63
Freedom House I-112
Friends Of The Abraham Lincoln Brigade IV-1
Fund For Education In World Order II-97
Fund For Peace II-97
Fund For The Republic I-85
GI Civil Liberties Defense Committee III-68
Great Decisions Programs I-106
Group Research, Inc. I-172
"Headline Series" I-106
Individuals Against The Crime Of Silence III-69
Institute For American Democracy I-172
Institute Of Pacific Relations I-116
Intercollegiate Socialist Society I-124
Inter-Democracy Federal Unionists I-63
International Association Of Democratic Lawyers IV-193
International Association Of War Veterans IV-30
International Committee For Struggle Against War IV-30
International Juridical Association IV-193
International Labor Defense II-38, IV-193
International Movement For Atlantic Union I-63
International Red Aid II-38, IV-193
International Relations Clubs I-106
International Union Of Revolutionary Writers IV-132
Inter-University Committee For Debate On Foreign Policy III-72
Inter-University Committee For A Public Hearing
    On Vietnam III-72
John Reed Clubs IV-132
Joint Anti-Fascist Refugee Committee IV-1
Labor Youth League IV-84
Lawyer's Committee On American Relations With Spain IV-1
League For Industrial Democracy I-124
League Of American Writers IV-132
League Of Political Education (AFL) I-40
League Of Struggle For Negro Rights IV-62

League Of Women Voters III-88
Medical Bureau And North American Committee To
   Aid Spanish Democracy IV-1
Methodist Federation For Social Action II-105
Methodist Federation For Social Service II-105
Mid-Century Conference For Peace IV-84
Military Industrial Research Survey III-1
National Association For The Advancement Of Colored
   People I-140
National Citizens For UN Day I-190
National Citizens Political Action Committee IV-30
National Coalition Against War, Racism And
   Repression III-112
National Committee For A Sane Nuclear Policy I-153
National Committee For An Effective Congress I-159
National Committee For People's Rights IV-145
National Committee For The Defense Of Political Prisoners IV-145
National Committee To Abolish The House Un-American
   Activities Committee I-167
National Committee To Secure Justice For Morton
   Sobell In The Rosenberg Case IV-147
National Committee To Secure Justice In Rosenberg Case IV-147
National Conference For New Politics III-12
National Convocation On The Challenge Of Building The
   Peace II-97
National Coordinating Committee To End The War In
   Vietnam III-112
National Council Against Conscription I-74
National Council For Civic Responsibility I-172
National Education Association II-115
National Federation For Constitutional Liberties IV-62
National Lawyers Guild IV-193
National Mobilization Committee To End The War
   In Vietnam III-112
National Negro Congress IV-62
National Peace Action Committee III-112

National Religion And Labor Foundation I-74
National Student Association II-145
Negro People's Committee To Aid Spanish Democracy IV-1
New Mobilization Committee To End The War In
   Vietnam III-112
November 8 Mobilization Committee III-112
Open Letter For Closer Cooperation With The
   Soviet Union IV-201
Peace And Freedom Party III-12
Peace Information Center IV-84
Peoples Coalition For Peace And Justice III-112
People's Peace Treaty III-112
Peirce Butler Jr. Foundation For Education In World Law II-97
Political Action Committee (CIO) I-40
Progressive Youth Organizing Committee II-181
Rand School Of Social Science IV-205
Republic Of New Africa III-185
Republican Advance II-159
Republicans For Progress II-159
Ripon Society II-159
Roger Baldwin Foundation I-1
Scientific And Cultural Conference For World Peace IV-84
Sing-In For Peace Committee III-208
Social Questions Bulletin II-105
Social Service Bulletin II-105
Spring Mobilization Committee To End The War In
   Vietnam III-112
Stockholm Peace Appeal IV-84
Student League For Industrial Democracy I-124
Student Mobilization Committee To End The War In
   Vietnam III-112
Student Nonviolent Coordinating Committee I-185
Student League For Industrial Democracy I-124
Student Mobilization Committee To End The War In
   Vietnam III-112
Student Nonviolent Coordinating Committee I-185

Students For A Democratic Society I-124
Turn Toward Peace I-74
United States National Student Association I-190
Union For Democratic Action I-17
United Nations Association Of The United States I-190
United State Committee For The United Nations I-190
United States Veterans Council IV-30
United World Federalists I-195
UN We Believe I-190
Veterans Of The Abraham Lincoln Brigade IV-1
VISTA I-191
W.E.B. Dubois Clubs II-181
Washington Committee For Democratic Action IV-62
Washington Watch, The III-1
Women's International Democratic Federation IV-84
Women's International Strike For Peace II-190
Women Strike For Peace II-190
Workers Defense League I-74
World Affairs Center I-106
World Affairs Councils I-106
World Association Of World Federalists I-195
World Congress Against War IV-30
World Congress Of Intellectuals IV-84
World Peace Congress (Paris) IV-84
World Peace Congress (Sheffield, England-Warsaw, Poland) IV-85
World Peace Council IV-85
Workers Ex-Servicemen's League IV-30
Young Communist Liberation League II-181
Young Workers Liberation League II-181

INDEX OF BIOGRAPHIES

Abel, Iorwith Wilbur I-203
Abernathy, Ralph D. I-204
Abram, Morris II-203
Abt, John J. II-205
Abzug, Bella III-211
Acheson, Dean I-206
Achilles, Theodore II-207
Ackley, Gardner I-207
Adamic, Louis IV-215
Adams, Comfort A. IV-226
Addams, Jane IV-227
Addis, Thomas IV-231
Aiken, George D. II-208
Akers, Anthony B. II-208
Alexander, Robert J. III-213
Alexander, Sadie T.M. II-209
Alinsky, Saul I-207
Allen, Devere IV-233
Allen, Donna I-208
Allen, George V. I-210
Allen, James E. Jr. II-209
Allen, William Sheridan III-214
Allport, Gordon W. IV-234
Alperovitz, Gar III-214
Alsop, Joseph I-210
Alsop, Stewart I-211
Altschul, Frank I-211
Anderson, Clinton P. I-212
Anderson, Dillon II-211
Anderson, Hurst II-211
Anderson, Jack I-213
Anderson, Sherwood IV-236
Anthony, Joseph G. III-215
Aptheker, Herbert III-215
Archer, Glenn L. I-213
Armstrong, Hamilton Fish I-214
Arnold, Thurman I-215
Arnoni, Manachem S. I-216
Arvin, Newton IV-237
Ascoli, Max I-216
Asher, Robert E. III-219

Ashmore, Harry I-217
Atkinson, Henry A. IV-238
Attwood, William II-212
Aurthur, Robert A. III-219
Avakian, Robert B. III-220
Badillo, Herman III-221
Baez, Joan II-214
Bailey, John M. I-218
Baird, William III-222
Balch, Emily Greene IV-239
Baldwin, James I-219
Baldwin, Roger I-220
Ball, George W. I-222
Ball, Lee III-223
Bancroft, Harding II-216
Barber, Bernard III-225
Barber, Joseph III-226
Barghoorn, Frederick I-223
Barish, Jonas A. III-226
Barnard, Harry III-226
Barnes, Joseph I-223
Barnet, Richard J. III-227
Barnett, Doak I-224
Barnett, Robert I-225
Barr, Stringfellow I-226
Barth, Alan I-227
Barton, Allen H. III-238
Barzun, Jacques II-219
Battle, Lucius I-228
Bayh, Birch I-228
Beam, Jacob I-229
Becker, James F. III-238
Beebe, Frederick S. II-220
Beer, Samuel I-229
Beirne, Joseph I-230
Belafonte, Harry II-220
Belfrage, Cedric I-230
Belkin, Samuel III-238
Bell, Daniel II-222
Bell, David I-232
Bendiner, (Marvin) Robert . . . III-239

Benedict, Ruth IV-241
Benét, William Rose IV-245
Benjamin, Robert S. III-239
Bennett, John C. I-232
Bennett, Lerone Jr. III-240
Benoit, Emile III-241
Benson, Lucy III-241
Bentley, Eric III-242
Benton, William I-234
Berelson, Bernard R. II-224
Berger, Victor Louis IV-247
Berle, Adolf A. Jr. I-236
Berman, Daniel M. II-224
Bernstein, Leonard III-243
Berrigan, Daniel II-225
Berrigan, Philip F. II-230
Bessie, Alvah I-237
Bessie, Daniel III-244
Bethe, Hans A. I-238
Bethune, Mary McLeod IV-251
Bevel, James I-240
Biberman, Herbert J. II-234
Bierstedt, Robert III-245
Bingham, Barry II-236
Bingham, Jonathan I-242
Bisson, Thomas A. I-243
Black, Algernon I-244
Black, Eugene I-245
Black, Hugo L. I-246
Blackwell, Alice Stone IV-253
Blake, Eugene I-246
Blanding, Sarah Gibson II-237
Blanshard, Paul I-247
Blaustein, Arthur I. III-246
Blitzstein, Marc IV-225
Block, Herbert I-248
Bloomfield, Lincoln P. III-246
Bloomgarden, Kermit III-247
Boas, Ernst IV-258
Boas, Franz IV-259
Bodde, Derk I-249
Boggs, (Thomas) Hale II-237
Bohlen, Charles I-249
Bolinger, Dwight L. III-247
Bolles, (Edmund) Blair III-247
Bolte, Charles G. II-238

Bond, Julian II-239
Borg, Dorothy III-248
Bosley, Harold A. II-242
Boudin, Kathy II-243
Boudin, Leonard B. II-245
Boudin, Louis B. IV-262
Boulding, Kenneth E. II-248
Bowie, Robert R. II-250
Bowie, Walter Russell IV-263
Bowles, Chester I-250
Bowles, Frank H. III-250
Boyd, Malcolm III-250
Boyle, Kay III-252
Braden, Anne III-253
Bradley, Dwight J. IV-265
Brameld, Theodore II-252
Braybrooke, David III-254
Breckinridge, Sophonisba P. . . IV-267
Bridges, Harry I-251
Brinkley, David I-252
Bromfield, Louis IV-269
Bronk, Detlev I-252
Brooke, Edward W. I-254
Brooks, Van Wyck IV-270
Bross, John A. III-254
Broun, Heywood Campbell . . . IV-273
Brown, Edmund G. (Pat) I-257
Brown, Harrison II-254
Brown, John A. Jr. II-255
Brown, John Mason II-256
Brown, Samuel W. Jr. III-255
Bruce, David I-258
Brzezinski, Zbigniew I-259
Buchenholz, Jane J. III-257
Buchler, Justus III-258
Bullough, Vern L. III-259
Bunche, Ralph I-260
Bundy, McGeorge I-262
Bundy, William I-263
Bunker, Ellsworth I-264
Burden, William A.M. III-259
Burdick, Eugene L(eonard) . . . IV-275
Burdick, Quentin II-256
Burgess, W. Randolph III-260
Burkhardt, Frederick H. II-257
Burns, Arthur F. II-258

Burns, James MacGregor	I-265	Cleveland, Harlan	I-281
Burtt, Edwin A.	II-260	Clinchy, Everett R.	II-277
Butler, Allan M.	II-260	Clubb, Oliver Edmund	I-282
Butler, William F.	III-260	Cochrane, Pat	III-280
Buttenwieser, Benjamin J.	II-262	Coe, Albert Buckner	IV-296
Byers, Nina	III-261	Coffin, Henry Sloane	IV-297
Cabot, Henry B.	II-263	Coffin, Tristram	III-281
Cabot, Thomas D.	II-263	Coffin, William S. Jr.	I-286
Cameron, (Donald) Angus	I-265	Cogen, Charles	II-278
Cammett, John M.	III-261	Cogley, John	II-279
Campbell, John Coert	III-261	Cohelan, Jeffrey	II-280
Canby, Henry Seidel	IV-277	Cohen, Felix S.	IV-298
Canfield, Cass	II-263	Cohen, Robert S.	III-282
Canham, Erwin	I-267	Cohen, Wilbur	I-289
Carey, James B.	I-268	Cole, Charles W.	II-282
Carlson, Anton J.	IV-278	Coles, James S.	III-283
Carlson, Evans	IV-280	Collins, Judy	III-284
Carmichael, Stokely	I-269	Colodny, Robert G.	III-284
Carnap, Rudolf	IV-284	Commager, Henry S.	I-290
Carr, William George	I-272	Conant, James B.	II-282
Carsten, Arlene D.	III-262	Condit, Carl W.	III-286
Carter, Hodding	I-272	Condon, Edward U.	I-291
Case, Clifford	I-273	Converse, Philip E.	III-287
Catt, Carrie Chapman	IV-285	Conyers, John Jr.	I-292
Celler, Emanuel	I-275	Cook, Fred	I-293
Cerf, Bennett	IV-286	Cook, Howard A.	III-287
Cerf, Jay Henry	II-264	Coombs, Philip H.	III-288
Chafee, Zechariah, Jr.	IV-287	Cooper, John Sherman	I-294
Chamberlin, Mark A.	III-262	Cooper, Peter P.	III-288
Charlesworth, James C.	II-265	Copland, Aaron	I-295
Chayes, Abram	II-266	Cordier, Andrew	I-296
Chavez, Cesar	III-263	Coryell, Charles	II-286
Childs, Marquis	I-276	Costigan, Giovanni	III-289
Chisholm, Shirley	II-266	Countryman, Verne	II-286
Chomsky, (Avram) Noam	II-268	Counts, George S.	II-288
Church, Frank	I-276	Cousins, Norman	I-297
Ciardi, John	III-272	Cowan, Louis G.	III-289
Cisler, Walter L.	II-268	Cowles, John	II-293
Clark, Bronson P.	III-274	Cowley, Malcolm	II-294
Clark, Evans	II-269	Cox, Harvey	II-295
Clark, Joseph S.	I-277	Cranston, Allan	II-297
Clark, Ramsey	I-280	Creel, Dana S.	III-290
Clay, William L.	III-274	Crichton, Kyle S.	IV-302
Cleage, Albert L. Jr.	III-275	Criley, Richard	III-290
Cleaver, Eldridge	II-270	Crittenden, William	III-294
Clement, Rufus E.	IV-295	Crockett, George W. Jr.	III-295

Crockett, William J. I-298
Cronbach, Abraham IV-304
Cross, Ephraim III-298
Cross, James E. III-299
Crum, Bartley C(avanaugh) . . . IV-306
Currie, Lauchlin I-298
Dahlberg, Edwin I-301
Dain, Norman III-299
Dana, Henry W.L. IV-308
Dangerfield, George B. III-300
Darrell, Norris II-301
Darrow, Peter P. III-300
Da Silva, Howard II-301
Dassin, Jules II-302
Davenport, Marcia III-301
David, Donald K. III-301
Davidon, William C. II-304
Davidson, William III-301
Davies, John Patton Jr. I-302
Davis, Angela III-302
Davis, Horace Bancroft III-320
Davis, Jerome I-304
Davis, Ossie II-305
Davis, Rennard C. II-306
Day, Gardiner M. II-310
Dean, Arthur I-305
Dean, Vera Micheles I-306
Dearborn, Ned H(arland) IV-310
Debs, Eugene Victor IV-312
Dee, Ruby II-310
Dehn, Adolf IV-318
de Kruif, Paul IV-319
DeLeon, Daniel IV-321
De Lima, Oscar II-311
Dellinger, David II-312
Dellums, Ronald V. III-321
Delson, Robert III-325
Dennis, Donald P. II-318
DeWitt, Robert L. Jr. III-326
DeWolf, L. Harold III-326
DiCesare, Mario A. III-327
Dick, Jane III-327
Dickey, John Sloan III-328
Dilliard, Irving III-328
Dillon, (Clarence) Douglas . . . I-306
Dobbs, Ben III-329

Dodd, William Edward IV-330
Dodge, M. Eugene III-330
Doering, William Von Eggers . . III-330
Donner, Frank I-307
Donohue, F. Joseph II-319
Donovan, Hedley III-330
Dorsen, Norman III-331
Douglas, Helen Gahagan II-319
Douglas, Lewis W. II-323
Douglas, Melvin III-331
Douglas, Paul H. II-323
Douglas, William O. I-307
Dowd, Douglas II-324
Dowling, Walter II-325
Draper, William H. Jr. III-331
Dreiser, Theodore IV-331
Drekmeier, Charles II-325
Dreyfus, Benjamin B. II-326
Drinan, Robert F. II-328
Drummond, Roscoe I-308
Dubinsky, David I-309
Dubofsky, Melvyn III-332
Du Bois, William E. B. IV-334
Dudley, Tilford IV-334
Duffey, Joseph D. III-332
Dugger, Ronnie III-334
Duke, Angier Biddle I-310
Duranty, Walter IV-349
Eaton, Cyrus I-310
Eberle, William D. III-335
Eby, Kermit , ... IV-353
Eddy, Sherwood IV-353
Edel, Abraham II-335
Edelman, Marian III-335
Edsall, John T. III-336
Edwards, Don I-311
Eichelberger, Clark M. II-336
Eisendrath, Maurice N. II-338
Eisenhower, Milton I-313
Elegant, Robert I-314
Elliott, (Albert) Randle III-336
Elliott, Osborn III-337
Ellsberg, Daniel III-337
Ely, Richard Theodore IV-355
Emeny, Brooks II-339
Emerson, Haven IV-361

Emerson, Rupert III-361
Emerson, Thomas I. I-315
Emmerson, John K. I-316
Engberg, Edward III-362
Engel, Irving M. II-340
Engelhard, Charles W. III-362
Engler, Robert III-363
Erlich, Alexander III-363
Ethridge, Mark I-317
Etzioni, Amitai III-364
Evans, Luther II-340
Everett, Ronald (Ron Karenga) . III-364
Evers, Myrlie III-366
Fadiman, Clifton II-341
Fagley, Richard M. III-367
Fairbank, John K. I-317
Fairchild, Henry Pratt IV-362
Falk, Richard A. III-367
Farmer, James I-321
Faulk, John Henry III-370
Feiffer, Jules I-322
Feld, Bernard T. II-342
Ferkiss, Victor C. III-378
Ferry, Wilbur H. (Ping) II-342
Fetter, Elizabeth III-378
Feuchtwanger, Lion IV-366
Field, George II-346
Field, Ruth Pruyn II-350
Finch, Robert H. II-350
Finkelstein, Lawrence S. II-352
Finletter, Thomas I-323
Fischer, Louis I-324
Fisher, Adrian I-325
Fisher, Dorothy Canfield . . . IV-367
Fisher, Roger D. III-379
Fleeson, Doris I-326
Fleischman, Harry F. III-379
Fleming, Denna F. I-326
Flemming, Arthur I-327
Fletcher, Joseph F. I-329
Flexner, Stuart B. III-380
Folsom, Marion I-330
Ford, Henry II I-330
Foreman, Clark H. II-353
Forman, Charles W. III-380
Forman, James III-381

Fortas, Abe I-331
Foster, William C. I-332
Fowler, Henry I-333
Fox, William T.R. III-404
France, Royal Wilbur IV-369
Frank, Isaiah III-405
Frank, Jerome D. I-333
Frank, Waldo IV-371
Frankel, Charles II-357
Franklin, George S. II-358
Franklin, H. Bruce II-359
Fraser, Donald II-360
Frazier, Edward Franklin IV-374
Fredericks, J. Wayne III-405
Freeman, Harrop II-362
Freeman, Joseph IV-376
Freeman, Orville I-334
French, Eleanor III-405
Freund, Gerald III-406
Friendly, Alfred W. I-335
Friendly, Fred W. II-363
Fritchey, Clayton I-336
Fromm, Erich I-336
Frye, William R. III-406
Fuchs, Lawrence H. II-364
Fulbright, J. William I-337
Fuller, C. Dale III-407
Galamison, Milton III-407
Galbraith, John Kenneth I-339
Gallagher, Buell I-340
Gannett, Lewis Stiles IV-378
Ganz, Rudolph IV-379
Gardner, John W. I-342
Gardner, Richard N. II-365
Garrison, Lloyd K. II-366
Garry, Charles R. II-367
Garthoff, Raymond L. III-408
Garwood, Wilmer St. John . . . II-370
Gauss, Christian IV-380
Gavin, James M. I-343
Geismar, Maxwell II-370
Gellhorn, Walter I-344
Genovese, Eugene II-371
Gerassi, John III-409
Gibson, Kenneth III-410
Gideonse, Harry D. II-373

659

Gilder, George	I-345	Halstead, Fred W.	III-434
Gilpatric, Roswell	I-346	Hamer, Lois	III-434
Gittelsohn, Roland B.	II-374	Hamill, Pete	III-435
Glazer, Nathan	II-376	Hamilton, Alice	IV-382
Goheen, Robert	I-347	Hamilton, Charles V.	III-436
Goldberg, Arthur	I-348	Hamilton, Fowler	III-437
Goldman, Eric	II-377	Hammerstein, Oscar II	IV-385
Gonzalez, Henry B.	II-379	Hammett, Samuel Dashiell	IV-386
Goode, William J.	III-411	Hammond, John	II-400
Goodell, Charles E.	II-380	Hammond, Paul Y.	III-438
Goodlett, Carlton B.	III-411	Handlin, Oscar	II-401
Goodman, Paul	II-383	Harburg, Edgar Y.	III-438
Goodrich, Leland	III-416	Harding, Ralph	I-357
Goodwin, Richard	I-349	Hare, Nathan	III-439
Gordon, Kermit	III-417	Harkness, Georgia	II-402
Gore, Albert	II-385	Harlow, S(amuel) Ralph	IV-388
Gorlin, Marilyn	III-417	Harper, Fowler Vincent	IV-390
Gottfried, Alex	III-418	Harriman, Averell	I-358
Gottlieb, Sanford	III-418	Harrington, Donald	I-359
Gould, Laurence M.	II-388	Harrington, Fred H.	III-441
Graham, Frank	II-388	Harrington, Michael	I-360
Gray, Jesse	III-420	Harris, Fred R.	II-403
Greeley, Dana McLean	II-390	Harris, Louis	III-442
Greene, Felix	I-350	Harris, M(arquis) Lafayette	II-404
Gregory, Dick	III-422	Harris, Patricia Roberts	III-443
Grier, Eunice	III-424	Hartke, Vance	I-361
Griswold, Erwin	I-352	Haskins, Caryl P.	III-443
Groppi, James E.	II-391	Hathway, Marion	IV-391
Gross, Chaim	II-395	Hatfield, Mark	I-361
Gross, Ernest	I-353	Hauge, Gabriel	I-363
Gruber, Helmut	III-424	Haughton, Eleanor Leacock	III-444
Gruening, Ernest	I-354	Havighurst, Robert J.	I-364
Gruliow, Leo	III-425	Hawkins, Augustus	III-445
Guinier, Ewart G.	II-395	Hawkins, Edler	II-404
Gullion, Edmund A.	III-425	Hayden, Sterling	II-405
Gundlach, Ralph H.	III-426	Hayden, Thomas E.	II-410
Gupta, Brijen	III-427	Hayes, Samuel P.	II-415
Guttmann, Allen	III-428	Hays, Arthur Garfield	IV-392
Guyer, David L.	III-428	Heald, Henry T.	II-416
Haber, William	II-397	Heckscher, August	I-365
Haddad, William F.	III-429	Heinz, Henry II	II-417
Halaby, Najeeb E.	II-398	Hellman, Lillian	II-417
Hall, Helen	IV-381	Henderson, Donald	IV-394
Hall, Jack W.	I-355	Henderson, William	III-446
Hall, Martin	III-429	Hentoff, Nathan	II-419
Halperin, Morton H.	III-432	Herbst, Josephine Frey	IV-399

Herod, William Rogers III-446
Herron, George Davis IV-400
Hersey, John II-421
Herter, Christian Jr. II-421
Hess, Stephen III-447
Hester, Hugh I-366
Hillquit, Morris IV-404
Hilsman, Roger I-367
Hinton, William H. III-448
Hoagland, Hudson II-422
Hoagland, Mahlon B. III-453
Hobson, Julius W. III-454
Hocking, William Ernest . . . IV-413
Hodges, Donald C. III-455
Hoffman, Abbott (Abbie) . . . II-423
Hoffman, Hallock II-425
Hoffman, Paul I-368
Holland, William L. III-456
Holman, Halsted Reid II-425
Holmes, John Haynes IV-415
Hoopes, Roy III-458
Horn, Francis H. II-427
Houghton, Amory I-370
Houston, Charles Hamilton . . . IV-418
Howe, Harold II I-371
Howe, Irving III-459
Howe, Quincy I-372
Hoyt, Palmer I-372
Hughes, Emmet I-372
Hughes, Harold E. II-427
Hughes, H. Stuart I-373
Hughes, (James) Langston . . . IV-419
Hughes, Thomas L. II-428
Humes, Dollena III-459
Humphrey, Hubert I-374
Hunter, David R. III-460
Huntington, Ellsworth IV-425
Huntington, Samuel P. III-461
Huntley, Chet I-375
Hurley, Ruby II-429
Hurok, Sol I-375
Hutchins, Robert M. I-376
Hutchinson, Dorothy III-462
Innis, Roy III-462
Isaacs, Harold D. III-464
Jack, Homer A. II-430

Jackson, Elmore III-465
Jackson, Jesse II-430
Jacobs, Paul II-432
Javits, Jacob I-378
Jessup, Philip C. I-379
Johnson, Glenna III-465
Johnson, Joseph E. I-380
Johnson, Lyndon B. I-381
Johnson, U. Alexis I-383
Johnson, William A. III-466
Johnston, Winifred III-466
Jones, David Dallas IV-425
Jones, (Everett) LeRoi II-433
Jones, Howard Mumford I-384
Josephson, Matthew I-385
Josephson, William H. III-467
Julian, Percy II-435
Kalb, Marvin L. II-435
Kalish, Donald III-467
Kallet, Arthur IV-428
Kampelman, Max M. II-437
Kastenmeier, Robert W. I-386
Katz, Milton II-438
Katzenbach, Nicholas I-387
Kaysen, Carl II-438
Keating, Edward I-388
Kelley, Florence IV-435
Kempton, (James) Murray . . . II-439
Kennan, George F. I-390
Kennedy, Edward M. I-392
Kennedy, Gerald II-441
Kennedy, Richard S. III-468
Kennedy, Robert F. I-393
Kennedy, Stetson III-469
Kenny, Robert W. I-395
Kent, Rockwell IV-437
Kenyon, Dorothy IV-442
Kerr, Clark I-397
Kerry, John F. III-469
Keyserling, Leon II-442
Killian, James R. Jr. I-399
King, Coretta II-443
King, Martin Luther I-400
Kingdon, Frank IV-444
Kinoy, Arthur II-445
Kintner, Robert I-401

Kirchwey, Freda I-402
Kirk, Grayson I-403
Kirkpatrick, Evron II-446
Kissinger, Henry I-403
Kistiakowsky, George B. II-447
Klein, Charlotte III-474
Klein, Edward E. III-474
Klutznick, Philip M. II-453
Knight, Harold V. III-475
Knight, O.A. II-454
Kohler, Foy I-404
Kohn, Hans II-454
Kolko, Gabriel III-475
Komer, Robert W. I-406
Konvitz, Milton R. II-455
Kraditor, Aileen III-476
Kraft, Joseph I-407
Kreymborg, Alfred IV-447
Kristol, Irving III-476
Krueger, Maynard C. III-477
Kuchel, Thomas I-408
Kunstler, William II-456
Kurzweil, Bettina Aptheker . . . III-477
Laidler, Harry W. IV-448
Lakey, George III-480
Lally, Francis J. II-458
Lamb, Beatrice III-480
Lamont, Corliss I-409
Lampell, Millard I-410
Langer, William L. II-459
Larkin, Oliver Waterman . . . IV-453
Larson, A. William III-481
Larson, Arthur I-412
Lasch, Christopher III-481
Lash, Joseph P. I-414
Lasswell, Harold D. II-460
Lathrop, John Howland IV-454
Lattimore, Owen I-415
Lefever, Ernest W. III-481
Lehmann, Paul L. II-462
Leimas, Carol III-482
Lelyveld, Arthur J. III-482
Lengyel, Emil I-417
Lens, Sidney I-418
Lerner, Max I-419
LeRoy, Gaylord C. III-483

Lester, Julius III-483
Leuchtenberg, William E. III-484
Levertov, Denise III-485
Levin, David III-486
Lewis, Alfred Baker II-462
Lewis, Sinclair IV-456
Lifton, Robert Jay III-486
Lilienthal, David E. II-463
Lincoln, Murray D. IV-458
Lindbeck, John M. III-488
Lindeman, Eduard Christian . . IV-460
Lindsay, George N. Jr. III-488
Lindsay, John V. II-464
Linowitz, Sol M. I-421
Lippmann, Walter I-422
Lipset, Seymour III-489
Littell, Franklin I-423
Livingston, M. Stanley II-470
Locke, Alain LeRoy IV-463
Lockwood, William W. III-490
Lodge, George Cabot II-470
Lodge, Henry Cabot I-425
Loeb, James I-426
London, Jack IV-464
Loos, A(mandus) William II-472
Lord, John Wesley II-472
Lounsbury, Robert H. III-492
Lovett, Robert Morss IV-468
Lowenstein, Allard K. II-475
Lubin, Isador II-478
Luccock, Halford E. IV-473
Luce, David R. III-493
Lunt, Richard D. III-493
Luria, Salvador E. III-493
Lyford, Joseph P. II-480
Lynd, Helen Merrell I-427
Lynd, Robert S. I-428
Lynd, Staughton C. I-429
Lynn, Conrad J. II-483
MacDougall, Curtis D. II-484
MacIver, Robert Morrison . . . IV-477
MacLeish, Archibald I-431
Magnuson, Warren I-432
Mankiewicz, Don M. III-494
Mankiewicz, Frank F. III-494
Mann, Thomas IV-479

Mann, Thomas C. I-433
Mansfield, Michael J. I-433
Marcantonio, Vito IV-483
Marcus, Stanley II-485
Marcuse, Herbert I-435
Mark, Julius III-496
Markovitz, Irving L. III-496
Marks, Leonard I-436
Marshall, Charles B. III-496
Marshall, Lenore G. II-486
Marshall, Thurgood I-437
Mather, Kirtley F. I-440
Mathias, Charles Jr. II-486
Matthews, Herbert I-441
May, Ernest R. III-497
Mayer, Jean III-498
Mays, Benjamin I-442
McCarthy, Eugene I-442
McCarthy, John G. III-498
McCarthy, Mary III-499
McCloskey, Paul N. Jr. III-499
McCloy, John I-445
McConnell, Francis John . . . IV-474
McDaniel, Joseph M. Jr. . . . III-501
McGee, Gale I-447
McGill, Ralph I-448
McGirt, William A. III-501
McGovern, George I-449
McKay, Vernon III-502
McKeever, Porter II-488
McKenney, Ruth IV-476
McKissick, Floyd B. I-450
McNamara, Robert S. I-451
McWilliams, Carey I-452
Meacham, Stewart III-502
Mead, Margaret I-454
Mechanic, David III-510
Meier, August III-510
Meiklejohn, Alexander IV-486
Melman, Seymour I-454
Mendelsohn, Jack III-511
Mendenhall, Thomas C. II . . . III-511
Merchant, Livingston T. II-488
Meselson, Matthew S. III-512
Metcalf, Lee I-455
Meyner, Robert B. II-489

Miller, Arthur I-456
Miller, Clyde I-457
Miller, J. Irwin II-489
Miller, Loren II-491
Miller, Uri II-492
Miller, William R. III-512
Millett, Katherine Murray III-512
Millikan, Max I-458
Millis, Walter I-459
Mink, Patsy III-513
Minot, Stephen III-514
Minow, Newton III-514
Mitchell, Wesley Clair IV-488
Mitford, Jessica I-460
Mondale, Walter F. II-493
Montague, Richard M. III-516
Montgomery, Lucile III-516
Moore, Paul Jr. III-516
Moos, Malcolm II-496
Moran, William E. III-518
Morgan, Edward P. III-519
Morgenthau, Hans I-462
Morray, Joseph P. III-519
Morrisett, Lloyd N. III-520
Morse, Arthur D. III-521
Morse, Bradford II-497
Morse, Wayne L. I-463
Moscoso, Teodoro I-464
Mosely, Philip E. II-498
Mosk, (Morris) Stanley I-465
Mosley, J(ohn) Brooke III-521
Moss, Frank I-465
Mott, Stewart III-522
Moyers, Bill D. III-522
Moynihan, Daniel I-466
Muelder, Walter G. II-499
Mueller, Reuben H. II-500
Mumford, Lewis I-467
Munk, Arthur W. II-501
Murden, Forrest D. Jr. III-524
Murray, Philip IV-489
Muskie, Edmund I-468
Muste, Abraham Johannes . . . IV-492
Myers, Gustavus IV-507
Nader, Ralph III-524
Nason, John W. II-501

Nathan, Robert R. II-502
Neal, Alfred C. III-529
Neal, Fred Warner I-469
Nearing, Scott I-471
Neier, Aryeh III-529
Neumann, William L. III-529
Newfield, Jack II-503
Newman, Robert P. III-530
Niebuhr, Reinhold I-472
Nieburg, Harold L. III-530
Niebyl, Karl H. III-531
Nielsen, Waldemar A. II-504
Niles, Henry E. III-532
Nitze, Paul I-473
Nollen, John Scholte IV-508
Nuchow, Ann Lane III-532
Obenhaus, Victor II-505
O'Connor, Harvey III-533
Odets, Clifford IV-509
Ohmann, Richard M. III-534
O'Laughlin, Alida III-534
Oldham, G(eorge) Ashton . . . IV-512
Olson, William C. III-535
Oppenheimer, J(ulius) Robert . IV-513
O'Neil, Wayne A. III-535
Orlans, Harold III-536
Oser, Jacob III-536
Osgood, Charles I-473
Osgood, Robert E. III-537
Overstreet, Harry I-475
Oxnam, G(arfield) Bromley . . . IV-533
Pace, Frank Jr. III-538
Paffrath, Leslie III-538
Palmer, Albert Wentworth . . . IV-535
Palmer, Norman D. III-539
Parker, Dorothy Rothschild . . IV-536
Parsons, Edward Lambe IV-539
Parsons, Howard L. III-540
Pastore, John O. II-506
Pate, Martha III-540
Patterson, Hugh B. III-541
Patton, James G. I-477
Paulu, Burton III-541
Pearson, Drew I-478
Peck, Sidney M. II-507
Peerman, Dean G. III-542

Pell, Claiborne II-508
Pentony, De Vere E. III-542
Pepper, Claude I-479
Pepper, William F. III-542
Percy, Charles H. I-483
Perkins, James A. II-512
Perlin, Morton J. III-547
Perlmutter, Nathan III-547
Peterson, Esther II-513
Phillips, Channing E. III-548
Phillips, Christopher H. III-549
Pickett, Clarence Evan IV-540
Piel, Gerard III-550
Pifer, Alan J. III-550
Plank, John N. III-551
Platig, E(mil) Raymond III-551
Plimpton, Calvin H. II-515
Plimpton, Francis T.P. II-516
Pond, T(homas) Alexander . . . III-552
Pool, David de Sola IV-542
Pope, Arthur Upham IV-543
Porter, Charles O. III-552
Porter, Keith R. III-554
Porter, Kenneth W. III-555
Porter, Paul A. II-516
Poteat, Edwin McNeill IV-545
Potofsky, Jacob S. I-484
Powell, Adam Clayton Jr. II-517
Preyer, Robert O. III-555
Price, Charles C. II-522
Price, Don K. III-556
Prinz, Joachim II-522
Proxmire, William I-484
Pucciani, Oreste III-557
Pye, Lucian W. III-557
Quigg, Philip W. III-558
Rabi, Isidor I. I-485
Rabinowitch, Eugene I-486
Rabinowitz, Victor III-558
Randall, Francis B. III-559
Randolph, Asa Philip I-487
Raner, Guy H. Jr. III-560
Rapoport, Anatol III-560
Rauh, Joseph L. Jr. I-488
Rautenstrauch, Walter IV-547
Redlich, Norman I-490

Reed, John IV-549
Refregier, Anton III-561
Reid, Whitelaw II-523
Reischauer, Edwin I-491
Reston, James I-492
Reuss, Henry I-493
Reuther, Victor I-494
Reuther, Walter I-494
Rhyne, Charles I-495
Ribicoff, Abraham II-523
Rice, Elmer L. IV-551
Rice, Oscar K. III-562
Richardson, John Jr. II-525
Riesman, David I-497
Robbins, Mildred III-562
Roberts, Chalmers I-498
Robeson, Paul II-525
Robinson, Joseph W. III-563
Roche, John P. I-498
Rockefeller, Nelson I-499
Rogge, Oetje John II-529
Rogow, Arnold A. III-563
Romney, George I-504
Roosa, Robert V. II-531
Roosevelt, James I-506
Roper, Elmo I-507
Rose, Alex I-507
Rosebury, Theodor III-566
Rosen, Sumner M. III-567
Ross, Edward Alsworth IV-554
Rostow, Eugene V. I-507
Rostow, Walt W. I-508
Roth, William M. II-531
Rovere, Richard I-511
Rowan, Carl I-513
Rubin, Isadore IV-555
Rubin, Morris H. III-568
Ruder, William III-568
Rugg, Harold Ordway IV-556
Ruina, Jack P. II-532
Rush, Kenneth III-569
Rusk, Dean I-515
Rustin, Bayard I-517
Russell, Charles Edward . . . IV-560
Rustow, Dankwart A. III-569
Ryan, Robert II-533

Ryan, William Fitts I-520
Salisbury, Harrison I-521
Saloman, Irving II-534
Sampson, Edward E. III-570
Samuelson, Paul I-524
Sandburg, Carl IV-561
Santoni, Ronald III-571
Sarnoff, Irving III-571
Sayre, Francis B. Jr. II-534
Scalpino, Robert A. I-526
Schary, Dore II-535
Scheer, Robert III-572
Scheier, Ivan H. III-574
Schelling, Thomas C. I-528
Schlesinger, Arthur M. Jr. I-529
Schlesinger, Arthur Meier IV-564
Schmidt, Adolph W. II-536
Schoenbrun, David I-530
Schoenman, Ralph III-574
Schomer, Howard III-575
Schuman, Frederick L. I-531
Schurmann, Franz H. II-536
Schwartz, Abba P. I-533
Schwartz, Robert Jay III-575
Schwebel, Stephen M. III-576
Scott, Hugh I-534
Scoville, Mary III-577
Scudder, Vida D. IV-565
Seabury, Paul III-577
Seale, Bobby II-537
Seeger, Pete I-535
Seldes, George H. IV-567
Seligman, Eustace II-543
Senior, Clarence II-544
Sevareid, Eric III-578
Seymour, Whitney North I-537
Shahn, Ben(jamin) IV-569
Shapley, Harlow I-539
Shinn, Roger L. III-583
Shipler, Guy Emery IV-570
Shirer, William L. I-540
Shriver, Sargent I-540
Shulman, Marshall II-545
Shuster, George II-546
Sibley, Mulford Q. III-583
Silver, Abba Hillel IV-572

665

Simkhovitch, Mary Melinda . . . IV-574
Sinclair, Upton Beall IV-575
Smale, Stephen I-543
Smedley, Agnes IV-583
Smith, Gerard C. II-547
Smith, Lella III-585
Smith, Lillian Eugenia IV-588
Smythe, Hugh H. III-585
Snow, Edgar I-544
Sockman, Ralph I-545
Socolar, Sidney J. III-586
Sontag, Susan II-548
Sorenson, Theodore I-546
Sorokin, Pitirim Alexandrovich . IV-589
Soubry, Emile E. III-587
Soule, George Henry Jr. IV-591
Spaeth, Carl B. III-587
Sparling, Edward J. II-553
Speer, Robert Kenneth IV-593
Spock, Benjamin I-547
Spofford, William Benjamin . IV-595
Sproul, Robert G. II-554
Stefansson, Vilhjalmur IV-598
Staley, (Alvah) Eugene II-555
Stampp, Kenneth M. III-587
Steffens, (Joseph) Lincoln . . . IV-599
Steinbeck, John (Ernst) IV-602
Stern, Bernhard Joseph IV-606
Stewart, Maxwell S. I-549
Stewart, Robert B. III-588
Stone, Isidore F. I-551
Stone, Jeremy J. II-558
Stout, Rex I-553
Straus, Donald B. III-589
Strauss, Anna Lord II-559
Streit, Clarence I-554
Strong, Anna Louise IV-609
Struik, Dirk II-560
Stuart, Lyle I-554
Stuber, Stanley I. II-563
Sweezy, Paul M. II-564
Swomley, John M. Jr. III-589
Sylvester, Arthur I-555
Symington, Stuart I-558
Szent-Györgyi, Albert I-560
Taggard, Genevieve IV-615

Tate, Velma III-590
Tatum, Arlo III-590
Taylor, George E. III-591
Taylor, Harold II-566
Taylor, Telford I-561
Thomas, Norman I-562
Thomas, Rolland Jay IV-616
Thompson, Kenneth W. III-592
Thompson, Llewellyn I-564
Thurman, Howard II-570
Tinker, Lorena III-592
Tippett, Donald Harvey II-570
Tobias, Channing Heggie . . . IV-617
Tolman, Edward Chace IV-618
Tracy, Beverlee III-593
Trager, Frank N. II-571
Trask, David F. III-593
Trowbridge, Alexander B. I-564
Truman, David B. III-594
Tuchman, Barbara W. III-594
Tugwell, Rexford Guy I-565
Tunney, John V. III-595
Turgeon, Lynn III-596
Tydings, Joseph I-567
Udall, Morris II-572
Udall, Stewart I-568
Untermeyer, Louis I-569
Urey, Harold C. I-570
Van Doren, Carl (Clinton) . . . IV-619
Van Doren, Mark II-574
Van Dusen, Henry II-575
Van Kleeck, Mary IV-621
Van Paassen, Pierre IV-624
Vaughn, Robert II-576
Villard, Oswald Garrison . . . IV-626
Visscher, Maurice B. III-596
Vorse, Mary Marvin Heaton . . . IV-628
Wadsworth, James J. II-577
Wagner, O(scar) Walter II-578
Wald, George III-597
Wald, Lillian D. IV-629
Waldman, Eric III-598
Walker, Brooks R. III-599
Walls, William J. II-579
Warburg, Frederick M. II-579
Ward, Frederick Champion . . . III-599

Ward, Harry Frederick IV-630
Warren, Earl I-571
Warren, Robert Penn III-599
Washburn, Abbott II-580
Waskow, Arthur I-575
Watson, Arthur K. II-580
Watson, Thomas J. Jr. I-577
Weaver, Robert I-580
Weber, Max IV-636
Wechsler, James II-581
Weigel, Stanley A. III-600
Weinstein, Jacob J. III-601
Welcome, Verda Freeman III-602
Wells, Donald A. III-602
Wells, Herman B. II-582
Westin, Alan F. III-603
Wheeler, Harvey I-583
Wheeler, Walter H. Jr. II-583
Whitaker, Urban Jr. III-603
White, Gilbert F. II-583
Whitney, Alexander Fell IV-638
Wicke, Lloyd II-584
Wieland, William A. I-584
Wiesner, Jerome B. I-588
Wilcox, Francis O. III-604
Wilkins, Roy I-592
Willens, Harold III-605
Williams, G. Mennen I-595
Williams, Haydn III-605
Williams, Robert F. II-585
Williams, William A. I-596
Wilson, Dagmar I-597

Wilson, Harper H. III-606
Windmiller, Marshall III-606
Wingate, Henry S. III-607
Wirtz, Willard I-601
Wise, Stephen Samuel IV-639
Withers, William III-607
Woetzel, Robert K. III-608
Wofsy, Leon III-608
Wolff, Robert P. III-615
Woodward, Donald B. III-615
Woolley, Mary Emma IV-641
Worthy, William I-603
Wright, Quincy I-604
Wright, Richard IV-643
Wright, Richard Robert Jr. . . . IV-645
Wright, Stephen J. III-616
Wriston, Henry I-605
Wulf, Melvin L. III-616
Wyckoff, (Gregory) Jerome . . . III-616
Wyzanski, Charles E. Jr. II-591
Yarmolinsky, Adam I-607
Yntema, Theodore O. III-617
Yost, Charles W. II-592
Yost, Henry T. Jr. III-617
Young, Quentin D. III-617
Young, Stephen I-609
Young, Whitney Jr. I-611
Youngman, William S. III-621
Zahn, Gordon C. III-622
Zalles, Reginald H. III-623
Zander, Arnold S. III-623
Zinn, Howard I-613